Quality In Everything We Do

APPLYING
International
Financial
Reporting
Standards

3RD EDITION

RUTH **PICKER**
Ernst & Young

KEN **LEO**
Consultant

JANICE **LOFTUS**
University of Adelaide

VICTORIA **WISE**
Deakin University

KERRY **CLARK**
Ernst & Young

KEITH **ALFREDSON**
Consultant

WILEY

Third edition published in 2013 by
John Wiley & Sons Australia, Ltd
42 McDougall Street, Milton Qld 4064

Typeset in 9.5/11 pt ITC Giovanni Std Book

The moral rights of the authors have been asserted.

National Library of Australia
Cataloguing-in-Publication entry

Title:	Applying international financial reporting standards / Ruth Picker . . . [et al.].
Edition:	3rd ed.
ISBN:	9780730302124 (pbk.)
Subjects:	Accounting–Standards
Other Authors/ Contributors:	Picker, Ruth
Dewey Number:	657.0218

Cover and internal design images: © Ernst & Young,
© iStockphoto.com / TommL

Typeset in India by Aptara

Printed in China by
Printplus Limited

10 9 8 7 6 5 4 3

FROM THE PROFESSION

Ernst & Young is delighted to support *Applying International Financial Reporting Standards*, 3rd edition — a definitive guide to International Financial Reporting Standards (IFRSs). The year 2005 was a significant milestone in the accounting profession's history — almost 100 countries adopted one set of international standards for the first time. Now, 7 years later, more countries have adopted or have made the decision to adopt IFRS. The challenge for these countries is to achieve global consistency in applying these standards. For example, a French company must account for a business combination in the same way as an Australian or New Zealand company. By contrast, in the past each of these countries had its own national accounting standards, and interpretations were determined at the country level.

This text is an important contribution to the goal of global consistency. It is an invaluable guide to applying IFRSs, written by a distinctive combination of authoritative academics and experienced accounting practitioners.

This text is abundant in practical examples and is ground-breaking in providing such examples in many areas where the standards have changed significantly, such as business combinations and financial instruments. I am sure that the book will be instructive not only to those learning about accounting standards for the first time but also to qualified accountants grappling with the new world of applying IFRSs.

In recent years the role of relevant and reliable financial reporting has been elevated, unfortunately as a result of the global financial crisis. Never in my experience has financial reporting been in the media headlines as much as in the past few years. The opportunity for the accounting profession now is to ensure that our financial reporting standards are appropriate, well understood and consistently applied. The International Accounting Standards Board (IASB) has played its part in implementing a stable platform of IFRSs. The rest is up to us.

I commend the book to you, as you play your part in understanding and applying IFRSs.

Ruth Picker
Global Leader — IFRS Services, Global Professional Practice
Ernst & Young
London

September 2012

BRIEF CONTENTS

CONTENTS

With the completion of the stable platform of international accounting standards in 2004, the International Accounting Standards Board (IASB) established itself as a world leader in the preparation of accounting standards. The financial reporting standards issued by the IASB have now been adopted by an ever increasing number of countries throughout the world. Further, in recent years, we have seen acceptance of these standards by the regulators in the United States.

As evidenced by the current financial crisis, in business, a global perspective is required. For universities, educating students to become a part of a global business environment requires placing more emphasis on understanding accounting principles rather than applying specific local jurisdictional regulations.

Applying International Financial Reporting Standards, 3rd edition, has been written to meet the needs of accounting students and practitioners in understanding the complexities of International Financial Reporting Standards.

This is the third edition of the book. That there is a third edition is due to the acceptance of the book by academics and practitioners throughout the world since its initial publication in 2005. We have welcomed the comments and suggestions received from various people and have tried to ensure that these are reflected in this edition.

The third edition addresses the major changes to a number of accounting standards and the release of new international accounting standards, in particular:
- the IASB's *Conceptual Framework for Financial Reporting*
- IFRS 9 *Financial Instruments*
- IFRS 11 *Joint Arrangements*
- IFRS 13 *Fair Value Measurement*.

The chapters covering these accounting standards now reflect these changes.

The new edition recognises that users of the book have asked for chapters to be added dealing with accounting standards not covered in the first editions. Five new chapters have been added to the book. Accounting standards for which new chapters have been added are:
- IFRS 9 *Financial Instruments*
- IFRS 11 *Joint Arrangements*
- IFRS 13 *Fair Value Measurement*
- IAS 21 *The Effects of Changes in Foreign Exchange Rates*
- IAS 24 *Related Party Disclosures*.

In writing this book, we have endeavoured to ensure that the following common themes flow throughout the text:
- *Accounting standards are underpinned by a conceptual framework.* Accounting standards are not simply a rulebook to be learned by rote. An understanding of the conceptual basis of accounting, and the rationale behind the principles espoused in particular standards, is crucial to their consistent application in a variety of practical applications.
- *The IASB financial reporting standards are principles-based.* Although a specific standard is a stand-alone document, the principles in any standard relate to and are interpreted in conjunction with other standards. To appreciate the application of a specific standard, an understanding of the reasoning within other standards is required. We have endeavoured where applicable to refer to other accounting standards that are connected in principle and application. In particular, extensive references are made to the Basis for Conclusions documents accompanying each standard issued by the IASB. This material, although not integral to the standards, explains the reasoning process used by the IASB and provides indicators of changes in direction being proposed by the IASB.
- *Accounting standards have a practical application.* The end product of the standard-setting process must be applied by accounting practitioners in a variety of organisational structures and practical settings. While a theoretical understanding of a standard is important, practitioners should be able to apply the relevant standard. The author of each chapter has demonstrated the practical application of the accounting standards by providing case studies, examples and journal entries (where relevant). The references to practical situations require the reader to pay close attention to the detailed information discussed, but such a detailed examination is essential to an understanding of the standards. Having only a broad overview of the basic principles is insufficient.

Many people have been directly and indirectly involved in the writing of this book. Our task was made possible by the discussions and debates we have had with many colleagues and with staff associated with the standard-setting bodies, particularly at the IASB. We thank them for their patience and tolerance, as well as the impartation of their knowledge. Writing a book takes time, and this has left less time for family and friends. We thank them also for their support and understanding. We also extend a special thank you to Kent Wilson, University of South Australia, and John Sweeting for preparing the PowerPoint, Test Bank and student practice questions that accompany this textbook. Finally, in a time when the world, with its increasing sophistication, seems to produce situations and pronouncements that have added complexity, we hope that this book assists in the lifelong learning process that ourselves and the readers of this book are continuously engaged in.

Ruth Picker
Ken Leo
Janice Loftus
Victoria Wise
Kerry Clark

September 2012

Ruth Picker

Ruth Picker BA, FCA, FSIA, FCPA, is Global Leader, Global IFRS Services, Global Professional Practice, with Ernst & Young. Ruth has 29 years' experience with Ernst & Young and has held various leadership roles during this time. Up until June 2009, Ruth was Managing Partner — Melbourne and the Oceania Team Leader of Climate Change and Sustainability Services. Prior to this role, Ruth was a senior partner in the Technical Consulting Group, Global IFRS and the firm's Professional Practice Director (PPD) responsible for directing the firm's accounting and auditing policies with the ultimate authority on accounting and auditing issues. She is a member of Ernst & Young's Global IFRS Policy Committee.

Ruth's authoritative insight and understanding of accounting policy and regulation was acknowledged through her appointment to the International Financial Reporting Interpretations Committee (IFRIC), the official interpretative arm of the International Accounting Standards Board. She is currently a member of the IFRIC and the only Australian on that body.

Ruth was responsible for the preparation of Ernst & Young's Corporate Governance Series (which includes guidance for directors and results of numerous corporate governance surveys) and subsequent advice to a number of entities in both the private and public sectors on the application of corporate governance.

Ruth has conducted numerous 'Directors' Schools' for listed company boards. These schools were designed by Ruth and are aimed at enhancing the financial literacy of listed company board members.

She is a frequent speaker and author on accounting issues and has been actively involved in the Australian accounting standard-setting process, being a past member and former deputy chair of the Australian Accounting Standards Board (AASB) and having served on the Urgent Issues Group for 3 years. She has been a long-standing lecturer and Task Force member for the Securities Institute of Australia, serving that organisation for 17 years.

Her written articles have been published in a number of publications, and she is frequently quoted in the media on accounting and governance issues.

In November 2000, Ruth was awarded the inaugural 'Lynne Sutherland Award' — an Ernst & Young award created to recognise those people at Ernst & Young who contribute to the development and retention of women and who support and enhance the ability of Ernst & Young to attract and retain talented people.

Ken Leo

Ken Leo BCom (Hons), MBA, has been an academic for over 40 years, including 20 years as Professor of Accounting at a University in Western Australia. During this time he has taught company accounting to undergraduate and postgraduate students. He has been involved in writing books published by John Wiley & Sons since 1981, and has also written books and monographs for other organisations, including CPA Australia, Group of 100 and the Australian Accounting Research Foundation. As a founding member of the Urgent Issues Group in 1995, he served on this body until 2001. He subsequently served on the Australian Accounting Standards Board from 2002 to 2007, and was deputy chairman for some of that time.

Janice Loftus

Janice Loftus BBus, MCom (Hons), is a senior lecturer in accounting at the University of Adelaide, South Australia. Her teaching interests are in the area of financial accounting and she has written several study guides for distance learning programs. Janice's research interests are in the area of financial reporting. She co-authored Accounting Theory Monograph 11 on solvency and cash condition with Professor M.C. Miller. She has numerous publications on international financial reporting standards, risk reporting, solvency, earnings management, social and environmental reporting, and developments in standard setting in Australian and international journals. Janice co-authored *Accounting: Building Business Skills* published by John Wiley & Sons. She is the editor of *Financial Reporting, Regulation and Governance*. Prior to embarking on an academic career, Janice held several senior accounting positions in Australian and multinational corporations.

Victoria Wise

Victoria Wise BCom, MEcon, PhD, FCPA, FPNA, is a Professor in the School of Accounting, Economics and Finance at Deakin University, Australia. During her 20 years as an academic she has taught financial accounting and auditing to undergraduate, honours and postgraduate students. Victoria has more than 130 publications including books and book chapters, refereed and professional journal articles and conference proceedings. Her journal articles focus on international financial reporting standards, corporate governance and regulatory issues, and public sector and small business financial reporting. Her current research interests include corporate regulation and governance.

Kerry Clark

Kerry Clark BCom, CA, Executive Director — Technical Consulting Group, Global IFRS. Kerry has 17 years' experience with Ernst & Young and is currently on secondment to the Ernst & Young Calgary office in Canada, assisting many of Canada's largest oil and gas companies in their conversion to IFRS. Prior to this she was a key member of the Technical Consulting Group, Global IFRS in the Ernst & Young Melbourne office in Australia where she was responsible for advising clients on the application of IFRS to complex transactions. Kerry has been involved in the authoring of many Ernst & Young publications and *Charter* magazine articles and assisted Ruth Picker in conducting 'Directors' Schools' for listed company boards. She has also spoken on accounting issues in many different forums.

ACKNOWLEDGEMENTS

The author and publisher would like to thank the following copyright holders, organisations and individuals for their permission to reproduce copyright material in *Applying International Financial Reporting Standards*, 3rd edition.

Images

IFRS Foundation: **5** © 2012 IFRS Foundation. All rights reserved. No permission granted to reproduce or distribute. • ASX: **37** From ASX Information Paper 'Capital raising in Australia: Experiences and lessons from the global financial crisis', 29 January 2010, p. 8; created with data sourced from the World Federation of Exchanges © ASX Limited ABN 98 008 624 691 (ASX) 2012. All rights reserved. This material is reproduced with the permission of ASX. This material should not be reproduced, stored in a retrieval system or transmitted in any form whether in whole or in part without the prior written permission of ASX; **40** From ASX Information Paper 'Capital raising in Australia: Experiences and lessons from the global financial crisis', 29 January 2010, p. 19 © ASX Limited ABN 98 008 624 691 (ASX) 2012. All rights reserved. This material is reproduced with the permission of ASX. This material should not be reproduced, stored in a retrieval system or transmitted in any form whether in whole or in part without the prior written permission of ASX. • Ernst & Young — Accounting and Ernst & Young — Sydney: **144** © Ernst & Young. • CPA Australia: **188** From 'IAS 12 *Income Taxes* FACT SHEET', p. 2 © February 2010. Reproduced with the permission of CPA Australia Ltd. • Ernst & Young Global: **255** From 'Implementing phase 1 of IFRS', (second edition), pp. 3–4. Reproduced by permission of Ernst & Young © 2012 EYGM Limited. All Rights Reserved; **256** From 'Implementing phase 1 of IFRS 9', (second edition), pp. 37–8. Reproduced by permission of Ernst & Young © 2012 EYGM Limited. All Rights Reserved; **772** From 'IFRS 8 *Operating Segments:* Implementation Guidance', 2007, p. 4. Reproduced by permission of Ernst & Young © 2012 EYGM Limited. All Rights Reserved; **776** From 'IFRS 8 *Operating Segments:* Implementation Guidance', 2007, p. 8. Reproduced by permission of Ernst & Young © 2012 EYGM Limited. All Rights Reserved. • © American Economic Association: **470** From 'How do you measure a "technological revolution"?' by Corrado and Hulten, *American Economic Review*, vol. 100, no. 2, May 2010, pp. 99–104. Reproduced with permission from The American Economic Association and Carol Corrado. • © Brookings Institution Press: **471** From 'Intangibles: Management, measurement and reporting' by Baruch Lev, Brookings Institution Press, Washington DC, 2001, p. 18. • © Bernard Marr: **490** Adapted from 'Management accounting guideline — impacting future value: How to manage your intellectual capital' by Bernard Marr, published by CMA Canada, AICPA and CIMA, 2005, p. 6. • © Peter Gerhardy: **951** Reproduced with permission from Peter Gerhardy.

Text

Extracts of International Financial Reporting Standards and International Accounting Standards reproduced in this book © 2012 IFRS Foundation. All rights reserved. No permission granted to reproduce or distribute. • Nokia Group: **24, 30, 289, 521, 575–6, 1095** © Nokia. • ICRC — International Committee: **25–6** © International Committee of the Red Cross. • World Federation of Exchanges: **27–8** © World Federation of Exchanges, reproduced with permission. • Phosphagenics Limited: **34–5** Phosphagenics Limited. • Copyright Agency Limited: **39–40** 'The right story on Rio's rights' by John Wasiliev, *Sydney Morning Herald*, 19 July 2009 © News Limited; **809–10** Extracts from 'Hegarty moving again' by Felicity Williams, *The Australian*, 20 March 2009 © News Limited. • Qantas: **47, 127–31, 426–7, 681, 682, 1112–13** © Qantas Airways Limited. • ANZ Bank: **51–3** © Australia and New Zealand Banking Group Limited (ANZ). • Ernst & Young Global: **70, 93** From Ernst & Young Global comment letter — 'Invitation to comment — Fair Value Measurement', dated 28 September 2009. Reproduced by permission of Ernst & Young © 2012 EYGM Limited. All rights reserved; **616–17** Reproduced by permission of Ernst & Young © 2012 EYGM Limited. All Rights Reserved. • Telstra: **120, 121–2** © Telstra. Reproduced with permission from Telstra. • Deutsche Telekom: **123–4** © Deutsche Telekom AG. • AstraZeneca: **124** © AstraZeneca PLC. • Bayer: **125, 159–61, 1095–6** © Bayer AG. • Esprit: **126, 782–4** © Esprit International. • Woolworths Limited: **126, 264, 268, 785–7** © Woolworths Limited. • Ernst & Young — Accounting: **142** © Ernst & Young. • Fisher & Paykel Australia: **197–9, 486–7** © Fisher & Paykel Appliances Holdings Limited. • IFRS Foundation: **216–17, 678, 679, 1155, 1157, 1158, 1159** © 2012 IFRS Foundation. All rights reserved. No permission granted to reproduce or distribute. • Billabong: **274, 281–2, 327, 356–7, 538–42, 668–9, 669, 672, 672–3, 684, 709, 710, 723, 724, 734, 734–5, 747–8, 752, 753, 758, 763, 802–3, 805, 806** © Billabong. Used with permission. • Christian Dior: **463–4** © Christian Dior. • Copyright Clearance Center: **462** From 'Internally generated intangible assets: Framing the discussion" by E Jenkins & W Upton, *Australian Accounting Review*, vol. 11, no. 2 © 2001, John Wiley & Sons; **467** Reprinted from *Journal of Accounting & Public Policy*, vol. 21, iss. 2, Baruch Lev, 'Where have all of Enron's intangibles gone?', pp. 131–35, copyright 2002, with permission from Elsevier http://www.sciencedirect.com/science/journal/02784254; **92** Reprinted from *Accounting Forum*, vol. 30, iss. 1, Hermann et al. 'The quality of fair value measures for property, plant, and equipment', pp. 43–59, © 2006, with permission from Elsevier http://www.sciencedirect.com/science/journal/01559982; **96** Reprinted from *Journal of Accounting & Public Policy*, vol. 27, iss. 2, Benston, 'The shortcomings of fair-value accounting described in SFAS 157', pp. 101–14 © 2008, with permission from Elsevier http://www.sciencedirect.com/science/journal/02784254. • FASB: **466**, **511**, **1087** The FASB material is copyrighted by the Financial Accounting Foundation (FAF), 401 Merritt 7, PO Box 5116, Norwalk, CT 06856-5116, U.S.A., and is reproduced with permission. Complete copies of these documents are available from the FAF. • Rosalind Whiting: **496–8** 'Sporting glory — the great intangible' by Rosalind Whiting & Kyla Chapman, *Australian CPA*, Feb 2003, pp. 24–7. • South China Morning Post: **508** 'Minnow of dairy industry may take over giant' by Jasmine Wang © *South China Morning Post*, 27 September 2008, p. A7. • Wesfarmers Limited: **513–14**, **578** © Wesfarmers Limited. • Amcor: **573–4**, **589** © Amcor Ltd. • Pacific Brands: **594–5** © Pacific Brands Limited. • Xstrata (Corporate HQ UK): **617** © Xstrata plc. • Rio Tinto: **619–20** © Rio Tinto. • BP International: **621–2**, **626** © BP p.l.c. • © BHP Billiton: **625** BHP Billiton. Reproduced with permission from BHP Billiton. • ESMA: **645–6** From 'Extract from the EECS's database of enforcement decisions', April 2007, pp. 11–12 © CESR. Reproduced with permission from ESMA (CESR was replaced by ESMA on 1 January 2011). • Scottish Salmon Company: **646–7** © The Scottish Salmon Company. • Foster's Group Limited: **648–9**, **649–51**, **1140**, **1140–1**, **1146–7**/ © Foster's Group Limited. • HSBC (UK): **670–1**, **787–93** © HSBC Holdings plc. • American Accounting: **1070** From 'The rationale underlying the functional currency choice' by Lawrence Revsine, *The Accounting Review*, vol. LIX, no. 3, July 1984, pp. 504–514 © American Accounting Association. • John Wiley & Sons, Inc: **1074** *Advanced accounting*, second edition by Jeter & Chaney, © 2004 John Wiley & Sons Inc. Reprinted with the permission of John Wiley & Sons, Inc.

Every effort has been made to trace the ownership of copyright material. Information that will enable the publisher to rectify any error or omission in subsequent editions will be welcome. In such cases, please contact the Permissions Section of John Wiley & Sons Australia, Ltd who will arrange for the payment of the usual fee.

1

The IASB and its *Conceptual Framework*

LEARNING OBJECTIVES

After studying this chapter, you should be able to:

1 describe the organisational structure of the key players in setting International Financial Reporting Standards (IFRSs)

2 describe the purpose of a conceptual framework — who uses it and why

3 explain the qualitative characteristics that make information in financial statements useful

4 discuss the going concern assumption underlying the preparation of financial statements

5 define the basic elements in financial statements — assets, liabilities, equity, income and expenses

6 explain the principles for recognising the elements of financial statements

7 distinguish between alternative bases for measuring the elements of financial statements

8 outline concepts of capital.

INTRODUCTION

The purpose of this book is to identify and explain the major concepts and principles of International Financial Reporting Standards (IFRSs) and to help you develop skills in applying them in business contexts. You may be familiar with the accounting treatment for various transactions, such as the purchase of inventory. The text will build on that knowledge and consider the principles and techniques required or permitted by IFRSs in accounting for a range of transactions, events and circumstances.

This chapter begins with an outline of the International Accounting Standards Board (IASB) and its role in setting international accounting standards, which are generally referred to as IFRSs. While IFRSs take precedence, the concepts and principles expounded in the *Conceptual Framework for Financial Reporting* (the *Conceptual Framework*) are generally reflected in the requirements of IFRSs. IFRSs are principles-based standards, not rules-based standards. This means that professional judgement is needed in applying IFRSs as they rely more on concepts and principles, such as a requirement that a value be measured reliably, rather than on objective prescriptions, such as quantitative tests for classification of leases. The *Conceptual Framework* establishes the qualitative characteristics financial information needs to have in order to be useful, as well as definitions and recognition criteria for the elements of financial statements. These principles underlie the exercise of professional judgement in applying IFRSs. The *Conceptual Framework* is also an important source of guidance to standard setters in the development of new standards and to preparers of financial statements in the absence of an applicable accounting standard. Accordingly, study of the *Conceptual Framework* provides a useful foundation to understanding and applying IFRSs.

1.1 THE INTERNATIONAL ACCOUNTING STANDARDS BOARD (IASB)

The purpose of this section is to provide an understanding of the structure of the IASB and its role in the determination of IFRSs. Much of this information has been obtained from the website of the IASB, www.ifrs.org. To keep up to date with what the IASB is doing, this website should be regularly visited. Other useful websites include Ernst & Young, www.ey.com, and the Deloitte IAS Plus website, www.iasplus.com.

1.1.1 Formation of the IASB

In 1972, at the 10th World Congress of Accountants in Sydney, Australia, a proposal was put forward for the establishment of an International Accounting Standards Committee (IASC). In 1973, the IASC was formed, with nine countries — Canada, the United Kingdom, the United States, Australia, France, Germany, Japan, the Netherlands and Mexico — sponsoring the committee. By December 1998, the membership of the IASC had expanded and the committee had completed its core set of accounting standards.

However, the IASC was seen as having a number of shortcomings:
- It had weak relationships with national standard setters; this was due in part to the fact that the representatives on the IASC were not representative of the national standard setters but rather of national professional accounting bodies.
- There was a lack of convergence between the IASC standards and those adopted in major countries, even after 25 years of trying.
- The board was only part time.
- The board lacked resources and technical support.

In 1998, the committee responsible for overseeing the operations of the IASC began a review of the IASC's operations. The results of the review were recommendations that the IASC be replaced with a smaller, full-time International Accounting Standards Board (IASB). In 1999, the IASC board approved the constitutional changes necessary for the restructuring of the IASC. A new International Accounting Standards Committee Foundation was established and its trustees appointed. By early 2001, the members of the IASB and the Standards Advisory Council (SAC) were appointed, as were technical staff to assist the IASB.

The IASB initially adopted the International Accounting Standards (IASs), with some modifications, as issued by the IASC (e.g. IAS 2 *Inventories*). As standards were revised or newly issued by the IASB, they were called International Financial Reporting Standards (e.g. IFRS 8 *Operating Segments*). Hence, the term 'IFRSs' includes both IFRSs and IASs.

1.1.2 The standard-setting structure of the IASB

Available on the IASB website is a document entitled *IASB and the IASC Foundation: Who we are and what we do*. This document is available in nine languages. The IASB is an independent standard-setting board. The IFRS Interpretations Committee (formerly IFRIC) issues interpretations and guidance of the requirements of IFRSs in relation to accounting for specific transactions or events. Compliance with IFRSs includes compliance with IFRIC Interpretations.

The IASB and IFRS Interpretations Committee are appointed and overseen by a geographically and professionally diverse group of Trustees (IFRS Foundation Trustees) who are publicly accountable to a Monitoring Board comprising public capital market authorities. The IFRS Foundation Trustees appoint an IFRS Advisory Council, which provides strategic advice to the IASB and informs the IFRS Foundation Trustees. This structure can be seen diagrammatically in figure 1.1.

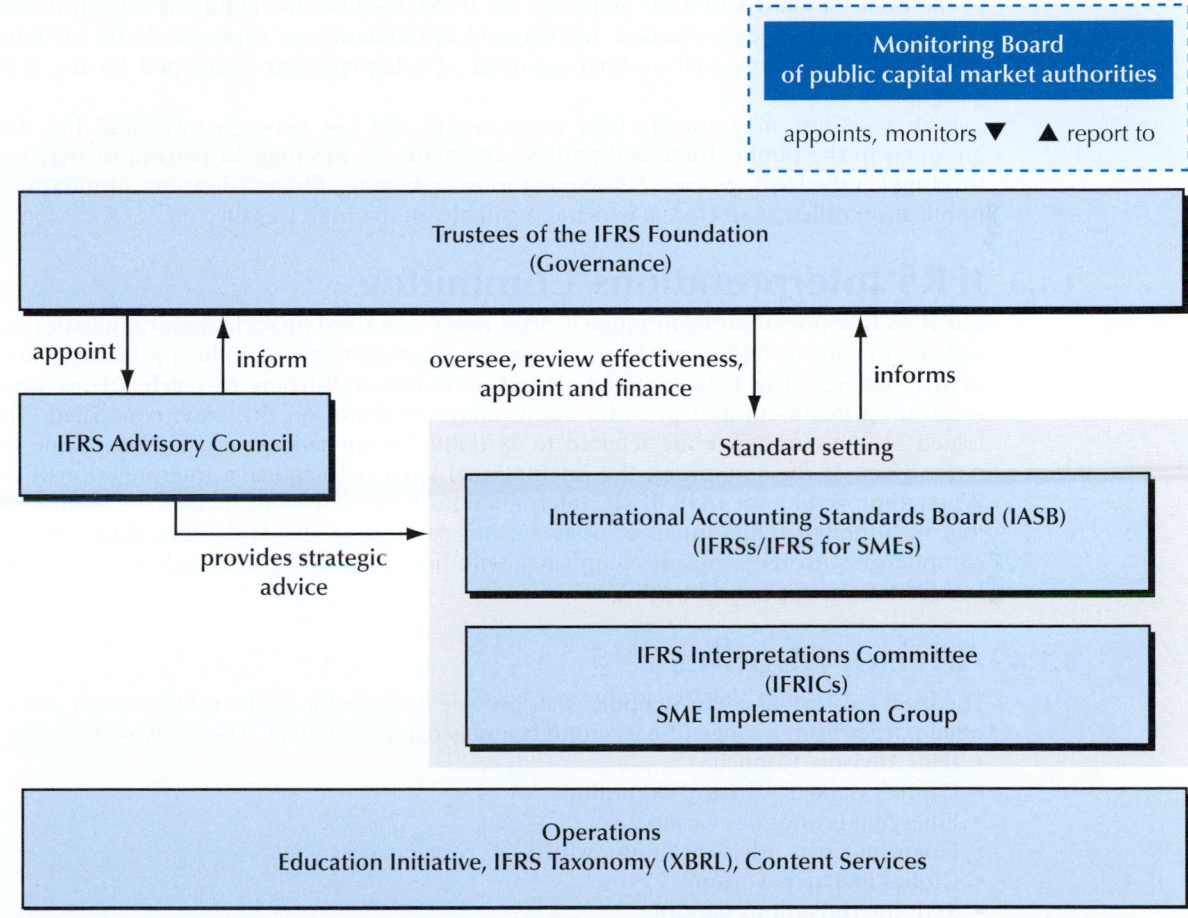

FIGURE 1.1 Institutional structure of international standard setting
Source: IASB (2012)

As of July 2012, the IASB comprises 16 members after the trustees voted to increase the membership from 14 members. The members are experts with a mix of recent practical experience in setting accounting standards, auditing, using financial statements and accounting education. While the mix of members is not based on geographical criteria, the trustees endeavour to ensure that the IASB is not dominated by any particular constituency or geographical interest.

The trustees approved the publication of the booklet *Due Process Handbook for the IASB*. It was updated in 2012 and is available on the IASB's website. The due process for issuing IFRSs comprises the following six stages:

1. *Setting the agenda*. The IASB considers the relevance and reliability of the information that could be provided, the existing guidance (if any), the potential for enhanced convergence of accounting practice, the quality of the standard to be developed and any resource constraints.

2. *Planning the project.* The IASB decides whether it should undertake the project by itself or jointly with another standard setter such as the Financial Accounting Standards Board (FASB).
3. *Developing and publishing the discussion paper.* The IASB may issue a discussion paper; however, this is not mandatory.
4. *Developing and publishing the exposure draft (ED).* The IASB must issue an ED. This is a mandatory step.
5. *Developing and publishing the standard.* The IASB may re-expose an ED, particularly where there are major changes since the ED was first released in stage 4.
6. *Procedures involving consultation and evaluation after an IFRS has been issued.* The IASB may hold regular meetings with interested parties, including other standard-setting bodies, to help understand unanticipated issues related to the practical implementation and potential impact of the IFRS. They also carry out post-implementation reviews of each new IFRS.

The IASB has full discretion over its technical agenda and over the assignment of projects, potentially to national standard setters. In preparing the IFRSs, the IASB has complete responsibility for all technical matters including the preparation and issuance of standards and exposure drafts, including any dissenting opinions on these, as well as final approval of interpretations developed by the IFRS Interpretations Committee.

IASB meetings are normally held every month and last between three and five days. The meetings are open to the public. Interested parties can attend the meetings in person, or may listen and view the meeting via the IASB webcast. Subsequent to each meeting, the decisions are summarised in the form of a publication called *IASB Update* which is available on the IASB website.

1.1.3 IFRS Interpretations Committee

The IFRS Interpretations Committee reviews newly identified financial reporting issues that are not specifically dealt with in IFRSs, and issues for which unsatisfactory or conflicting interpretations have emerged or may emerge. The IFRS Interpretations Committee endeavours to reach a consensus on appropriate accounting treatment and provides authoritative guidance on the issue concerned. The interpretations issued by the committee are referred to as IFRIC Interpretations, taking their name from the previous name given to the committee, the International Financial Reporting Interpretations Committee (IFRIC). When approved by the IASB, IFRIC Interpretations have equivalent status to standards issued by the IASB; that is, although IFRIC Interpretations are not accounting standards, they form part of IFRSs such that compliance with IFRSs means compliance with both accounting standards issued by the IASB and IFRIC Interpretations approved by the IASB.

1.1.4 Advisory bodies

The IASB has formal advisory bodies that provide a means for the board to consult and engage with interested parties from a range of backgrounds and geographical areas. These advisory bodies include the:
- IFRS Advisory Council
- Capital Markets Advisory Committee
- Emerging Economies Group
- Financial Crisis Advisory Group, which has concluded its work
- Global Preparers Forum
- SME Interpretations Group.

Working groups may be established for major projects to provide the IASB with access to additional expertise as required; for example, the Employee Benefits Working Group and the Insurance Working Group. Further information about advisory bodies, including reports and summaries of discussions, can be obtained from the IASB's website.

1.2 THE PURPOSE OF A CONCEPTUAL FRAMEWORK

In 1989, the IASC, the predecessor to the IASB, adopted the *Framework for the Preparation and Presentation of Financial Statements* (the *Framework*). This document was superseded by the *Conceptual Framework for Financial Reporting* (the *Conceptual Framework*) in 2010.

The purpose of a conceptual framework is to provide a coherent set of principles:
- to assist standard setters to develop a consistent set of accounting standards for the preparation of financial statements

- to assist preparers of financial statements in the application of accounting standards and in dealing with topics that are not the subject of an existing applicable accounting standard
- to assist auditors in forming an opinion about compliance with accounting standards
- to assist users in the interpretation of information in financial statements.

The *Conceptual Framework* issued by the IASB provides guidance to preparers in the application of IFRSs. The role of the *Conceptual Framework* in providing guidance for dealing with accounting issues that are not addressed by an IFRS is explicitly reinforced in IFRSs. IAS 8 *Accounting Policies, Changes in Accounting Estimates and Errors* requires preparers to consider the definitions, recognition criteria and measurement concepts in the *Conceptual Framework* when developing accounting policies for transactions, events or conditions in the absence of an IFRS that specifically applies or that applies to similar circumstances. The requirements of IAS 8 are considered in more detail in chapter 18 of this book.

The IASB continues to be involved in a joint project with the FASB in the United States to revise the conceptual framework. The issue of the *Conceptual Framework for Financial Reporting* represents completion of several stages of this project, namely the objectives of financial reporting and the qualitative characteristics. The project is incomplete, with further development continuing on other stages of the project, including the reporting entity concept, definitions of elements of financial statements, and measurement.

The IASB's *Conceptual Framework* comprises four chapters:
- Chapter 1: The objective of general purpose financial reporting
- Chapter 2: The reporting entity (to be added by the IASB)
- Chapter 3: The qualitative characteristics of useful financial reporting
- Chapter 4: The *Framework* (1989): the remaining text (comprising underlying assumption, definition and recognition of elements of financial statements, measurement and concepts of capital).

1.2.1 The objective of financial reporting

The IASB's *Conceptual Framework* deals only with the objective of general purpose financial statements; that is, financial statements intended to meet the information needs common to a range of users who are unable to command the preparation of reports tailored to satisfy their own particular needs.

Paragraph OB2 of the IASB *Conceptual Framework* states the objective of general purpose financial reporting:

> The objective of general purpose financial reporting is to provide financial information about the reporting entity that is useful to present and potential equity investors, lenders and other creditors in making decisions about providing resources to the entity. Those decisions involve buying, selling or holding equity and debt instruments, and providing or settling loans and other forms of credit.

This objective reflects several value judgements made by the IASB and the FASB about the role of financial statements, which are described in the *Basis for Conclusions on Chapter 1: The objective of general purpose financial reporting*. The Basis for Conclusions includes the following arguments:
- Financial statements should reflect the perspective of the entity rather than the perspective of the entity's equity investors. The focus is then on the entity's resources and the changes in them rather than on the shareholders as owners of the entity. Shareholders are providers of resources as are those who provide credit resources to the entity. Under the entity perspective, the reporting entity is deemed to have substance of its own, separate from that of its owners (paragraph BC1.8).
- The key users of financial statements are capital providers — existing and potential investors and lenders. An entity obtains economic resources from capital providers in exchange for claims on those resources. Because of these claims, capital providers have the most critical and immediate need for economic information about the entity. These parties also have common information needs. The focus on these users of information, as opposed to other potential users such as government, regulatory bodies, employees and customers is a narrowing of the user groups in comparison to the groups considered in the former version of the IASB *Conceptual Framework* (paragraphs BC1.9–1.12).

Before the objective of general purpose financial reporting can be implemented in practice, the basic qualitative characteristics of financial reporting information need to be specified. Further, it is necessary to define the basic elements — assets, liabilities, equity, income and expenses — used in financial statements.

1.2.2 The reporting entity

Chapter 2 of the *Conceptual Framework* is reserved for the reporting entity. The IASB and FASB are undertaking a joint project to determine what constitutes a reporting entity for the purposes of general purpose financial reporting. In March 2010, the IASB released an exposure draft titled *Exposure Draft ED/2010/2 Conceptual Framework for Financial Reporting — The Reporting Entity*, with comments due to be received by 16 July 2010. At the time of writing, this phase of the conceptual framework project was on hold until such time as the IASB made its agenda decisions regarding its future work plans. Further information about the developments on this phase of the conceptual framework project can be found on the project web page at www.fasb.org/project/cf_phase-d.shtml.

 ## 1.3 QUALITATIVE CHARACTERISTICS OF USEFUL FINANCIAL INFORMATION

What characteristics should financial information have in order to be included in general purpose financial statements? The following section discusses both the qualitative characteristics of useful information and the constraint on providing useful information. The qualitative characteristics are divided into fundamental qualitative characteristics and enhancing qualitative characteristics.

1.3.1 Fundamental qualitative characteristics

For financial information to be decision useful, it must possess two fundamental qualitative characteristics:
- relevance
- faithful representation.

Relevance

Paragraphs QC6 to QC11 of the IASB's *Conceptual Framework* elaborate on the qualitative characteristic of *relevance*. Information is relevant if:
- it is capable of making a difference in the decisions made by the capital providers as users of financial information
- it has predictive value, confirmatory value or both. Predictive value occurs where the information is useful as an input into the users' decision models and affects their expectations about the future. Confirmatory value arises where the information provides feedback that confirms or changes past or present expectations based on previous evaluations.
- it is capable of making a difference whether the users use it or not. It is not necessary that the information has actually made a difference in the past or will make a difference in the future.

Information about the financial position and past performance is often used as the basis for predicting future financial position and performance and other matters in which users are directly interested, such as future dividends and wage payments, future share prices, and the ability of the reporting entity to pay its debts when they fall due. The predictive ability of information may be improved if unusual or infrequent transactions and events are reported separately in the statement of profit or loss and other comprehensive income.

Materiality is an entity-specific aspect of the relevance of information. Information is *material* if its omission or misstatement could influence the decisions that users make about a specific reporting entity (paragraph QC11).

Small expenditures for non-current assets (e.g. tools) are often expensed immediately rather than depreciated over their useful lives to save the clerical costs of recording depreciation and because the effects on performance and financial position measures over their useful lives are not large enough to affect decisions. Another example of the application of materiality is the common practice by large companies of rounding amounts to the nearest thousand dollars in their financial statements.

Materiality is a relative matter — what is material for one entity may be immaterial for another. A $10 000 error may not be important in the financial statements of a multimillion-dollar company, but it may be critical to a small business. The materiality of an item may depend not only on its relative size but also on its nature. For example, the discovery of a $10 000 bribe is a material event even for a large company. Judgements as to the materiality of an item or event are often difficult. Accountants make judgements based on their knowledge of the company and on past experience, and users of financial statements must generally rely on the accountants' judgements.

Faithful representation

Paragraphs QC12 to QC16 of the IASB's *Conceptual Framework* elaborate on the concept of faithful representation. Faithful representation is attained when the depiction of an economic phenomenon is complete, neutral, and free from material error. This results in the depiction of the economic substance of the underlying transaction. Note the following in relation to these characteristics:

- A depiction is *complete* if it includes all information necessary for faithful representation.
- *Neutrality* is the absence of bias intended to attain a predetermined result. Providers of information should not influence the making of a decision or judgement to achieve a predetermined result.
- As information is provided under conditions of uncertainty and judgements must be made, there is not necessarily certainty about the information provided. It may be necessary to disclose information about the degree of uncertainty in the information in order that the disclosure attains faithful representation.

As explained in paragraph BC3.23 of the *Basis for Conclusions on Chapter 3: Qualitative characteristics of useful financial information*, the boards noted that there are various notions as to what is meant by reliability. The boards believe that the term faithful representation provides a better understanding of the quality of information required (paragraph BC3.24).

The two fundamental qualitative characteristics of financial information may give rise to conflicting guidance on how to account for phenomena. For example, the measurement base that provides the most relevant information about an asset will not always provide the most faithful representation. The *Conceptual Framework* (paragraphs QC17–QC18) explains how to apply the fundamental qualitative characteristics. Once the criterion of relevance is applied to information to determine which economic information should be contained in the financial statements, the criterion of faithful representation is applied to determine how to depict those phenomena in the financial statements. The two characteristics work together. Either irrelevance (the economic phenomenon is not connected to the decision to be made) or unfaithful representation (the depiction is incomplete, biased or contains error) results in information that is not decision useful.

1.3.2 Enhancing qualitative characteristics

The *Conceptual Framework* (paragraph QC19) identifies four enhancing qualitative characteristics:

- comparability
- verifiability
- timeliness
- understandability.

These characteristics are *complementary* to the fundamental characteristics. The enhancing characteristics distinguish *more useful* information from *less useful* information. In relation to these enhancing qualities, note:

- *Comparability* is the quality of information that enables users to identify similarities in and differences between two sets of economic phenomena. Making decisions about one entity may be enhanced if comparable information is available about similar entities; for example, if profit per share is calculated using the same accounting policies.
- *Verifiability* is a quality of information that helps assure users that information faithfully represents the economic phenomena that it purports to represent. Verifiability is achieved if different independent observers could reach the same general conclusions that the information represents the economic phenomena or that a particular recognition or measurement model has been appropriately applied.
- *Timeliness* means having information available to decision makers before it loses its capacity to influence decisions. If such capacity is lost, then the information loses its relevance. Information may continue to be timely after it has been initially provided, for example, in trend analysis.
- *Understandability* is the quality of information that enables users to comprehend its meaning. Information may be more understandable if it is classified, characterised and presented clearly and concisely. Users of financial statements are assumed to have a reasonable knowledge of business and economic activities and to be able to read a financial report.

Alternative accounting policies exist in the treatment of many items, such as inventories and cost of sales, non-current assets and depreciation, intangible assets such as patents, copyrights and goodwill, and leasing transactions. The standard setters have expressed their position regarding the consistency of accounting methods in accounting standard IAS 8 *Accounting Policies, Changes in Accounting Estimates and Errors*, which states that an entity must select and apply its accounting policies in a consistent manner from one period to another. Consistency of practices between entities is also desired. Any change made in an accounting policy by an entity must be disclosed by stating the nature of the change, the reasons the change provides reliable and more relevant information, and the effect of the change in monetary terms on each financial statement item affected. For example, a change in policies may be disclosed in a note such as this:

> During the year, the company changed from the first-in first-out to the weighted average cost method of accounting for inventory because the weighted average cost method provides a more relevant measure of the entity's financial performance. The effect of this change was to increase cost of sales by $460 000 for the current financial year.

Note that the need for consistency does not require a given accounting method to be applied throughout the entity. An entity may very well use different inventory methods for different types of inventory and different depreciation methods for different kinds of non-current assets. (Different inventory costing and depreciation methods are discussed in chapters 9 and 11, respectively.) Furthermore, the need for consistency should not be allowed to hinder the introduction of better accounting methods. Consistency from year to year or entity to entity is not an end in itself, but a means for achieving greater comparability in the presentation of information in general purpose financial statements. The need for comparability should not be confused with mere uniformity or consistency. It is not appropriate for an entity to continue to apply an accounting policy if the policy is not in keeping with the qualitative characteristics of relevance and faithful representation.

1.3.3 Cost constraint on useful financial reporting

Paragraphs QC35 to QC37 of the *Conceptual Framework* note that cost is the constraint that limits the information provided by financial reporting. The provision of information incurs *costs*. The benefits of supplying information should always be greater than the costs. Costs include costs of collecting and processing information, costs of verifying information, and costs of disseminating information. The non-provision of information also imposes costs on the users of financial information as they seek alternative sources of information.

1.4 GOING CONCERN ASSUMPTION

The *Conceptual Framework* retains the going concern assumption. Financial statements are prepared under the assumption that the entity will continue to operate for the foreseeable future. Past experience indicates that the continuation of operations in the future is highly probable for most entities. Thus, it is assumed that an entity will continue to operate at least long enough to carry out its existing commitments. This assumption is called the *going concern assumption* or sometimes the *continuity assumption*.

Adoption of the going concern assumption has important implications in accounting. For example, it is an assumption used by some to justify the use of historical costs in accounting for non-current assets and for the systematic allocation of their costs to depreciation expense over their useful lives. Because it is assumed that the assets will not be sold in the near future but will continue to be used in operating activities, current market values of the assets are sometimes assumed to be of little importance. If the entity continues to use the assets, fluctuations in their market values cause no gain or loss; nor do they increase or decrease the usefulness of the assets. The going concern assumption also supports the inclusion of some assets, such as prepaid expenses and acquired goodwill, in the statement of financial position (balance sheet) even though they may have little, if any, sales value.

If management intends to liquidate the entity's operations, the going concern assumption is set aside and financial statements are prepared on a different basis, such as expected liquidation values. Thus, assets are reported at their expected sales values and liabilities at the amount needed to settle them immediately. Paragraph 25 of IAS 1 *Presentation of Financial Statements* prescribes disclosures when an entity does not prepare financial statements on a going concern basis (see chapter 18 of this book).

1.5 DEFINITION OF ELEMENTS IN FINANCIAL STATEMENTS

The *Conceptual Framework* identifies and defines the elements of financial statements; namely assets, liabilities, equity, income and expenses.

1.5.1 Assets

An *asset* is defined in paragraph 4.4(a) of the *Conceptual Framework* as:

> a resource controlled by the entity as a result of past events and from which future economic benefits are expected to flow to the entity.

This definition identifies three essential characteristics of an asset:
1. The resource must contain *future economic benefits*; that is, it must have the potential to contribute, directly or indirectly, to the flow of cash and cash equivalents to the entity. An asset can cause future economic benefits to flow to the entity in a number of ways:
   - it can be exchanged for another asset

- it can be used to settle a liability
- it can be used singly or in combination with other assets to produce goods or services to be sold by the entity.

2. The entity must have *control* over the future economic benefits in such a way that the entity has the capacity to benefit from the asset in the pursuit of the entity's objectives, and can deny or regulate the access of others to those benefits.

3. There must have been a *past event*; that is, an event or events giving rise to the entity's control over the future economic benefits must have occurred.

An asset may have other characteristics, but the *Conceptual Framework* does not consider them essential for an asset to exist. For instance, assets are normally acquired at a cost incurred by the entity, but it is not essential that a cost is incurred in order to determine the existence of an asset. Similarly, it is not essential that an asset is tangible, that is, has a physical form (see paragraph 4.11 of the *Conceptual Framework*). Assets such as brands, copyrights and patents represent future economic benefits without the existence of any physical substance. Such assets may be classified as intangible assets. Furthermore, assets can be exchanged normally for other assets, but this does not make exchangeability an essential characteristic of an asset. Finally, it is not essential that an asset is legally owned by the reporting entity. Control by the entity often results from legal ownership, but the absence of legal rights or ownership does not preclude the existence of control; for example, a lease (see paragraph 4.12 of the *Conceptual Framework*).

1.5.2 Liabilities

A *liability* is defined in paragraph 4.4(b) of the *Conceptual Framework* as:

> a present obligation of the entity arising from past events, the settlement of which is expected to result in an outflow from the entity of resources embodying economic benefits.

There are a number of important aspects concerning this definition:

- A legal debt constitutes a liability, but a liability is not restricted to being a legal debt. Its essential characteristic is the existence of a *present obligation*, being a duty or responsibility of the entity to act or perform in a certain way. A present obligation may arise as an obligation imposed by notions of equity or fairness (referred to as an 'equitable' obligation), and by custom or normal business practices (referred to as a 'constructive' obligation), as well as those resulting from legally enforceable contracts. For example, an entity may decide as a matter of policy to rectify faults in its products even after the warranty period has expired. Hence, the amounts that are expected to be spent in respect of goods already sold are liabilities.

  It is not sufficient for an entity merely to have an intention to sacrifice economic benefits in the future. A present obligation needs to be distinguished from a future commitment. A decision by management to buy an asset in the future does not give rise to a present obligation. An obligation normally arises when the asset is delivered, or the entity has entered into an irrevocable agreement to buy the asset, with a substantial penalty if the agreement is revoked.

- A liability must result in the *giving up of resources* embodying economic benefits that require settlement in the future. The entity must have little, if any, discretion in avoiding this sacrifice. This settlement in the future may be required on demand, at a specified date, or when a specified event occurs. Thus, a guarantee under a loan agreement is regarded as giving rise to a liability in that a sacrifice is required when a specified event occurs, for example, default under the loan.

  Settlement of a present obligation may occur in a number of ways:
  - by paying cash
  - by transferring other assets
  - by providing services
  - by replacing that obligation with another obligation
  - by converting that obligation to equity
  - by a creditor waiving or forfeiting his or her rights.

- A final characteristic of a liability is that it must have resulted from a *past transaction* or event. For example, the acquisition of goods and the work done by staff give rise to accounts payable and wages payable respectively. Wages to be paid to staff for work they will do in the future is not a liability as there is no past transaction or event and no present obligation.

1.5.3 Equity

Paragraph 4.4(c) of the *Conceptual Framework* defines *equity* as:

> the residual interest in the assets of the entity after deducting all its liabilities.

Defining equity in this manner shows clearly that it cannot be defined independently of the other elements in the statement of financial position. The characteristics of equity are as follows:

- Equity is a residual, that is, something left over. In other words:

$$\text{Equity} = \text{Assets} - \text{Liabilities}$$

- Equity increases as a result of profitable operations, that is, the excesses of income over expenses, and by contributions by owners. Similarly, equity is diminished by unprofitable operations and by distributions to owners (drawings and dividends).
- Equity is influenced by the measurement system adopted for assets and liabilities and by the concepts of capital and capital maintenance adopted in the preparation of general purpose financial statements. (These aspects are discussed later in the chapter.)
- Equity may be subclassified in the statement of financial position, for example, into contributed funds from owners, retained earnings, other reserves representing appropriations of retained earnings, and reserves representing capital maintenance adjustments.

1.5.4 Income

The *Conceptual Framework* defines *income* in paragraph 4.25(a) as:

> Increases in economic benefits during the accounting period in the form of inflows or enhancements of assets or decreases of liabilities that result in increases in equity, other than those relating to contributions from equity participants.

Note that this definition of income is linked to the definitions of assets and liabilities. The definition of income is wide in its scope, in that income in the form of inflows or enhancements of assets can arise from providing goods or services, investing in or lending to another entity, holding and disposing of assets, and receiving contributions such as grants and donations. To qualify as income, the inflows or enhancements of assets must have the effect of increasing equity, excluding capital contributions by owners. Also excluded are certain increases in equity under various inflation accounting models that require the recognition of capital maintenance adjustments.

Another important aspect of the definition is that, if income arises as a result of an increase in economic benefits, it is necessary for the entity to *control* that increase in economic benefits. If control does not exist, then no asset exists. Income arises once control over the increase in economic benefits has been achieved and an asset exists, provided there is no equivalent increase in liabilities. For example, in the case of magazine subscriptions received in advance, no income exists on receipt of the cash because an equivalent obligation also has arisen for services to be performed through supply of magazines to subscribers in the future.

Income can also exist through a reduction in liabilities that increases the entity's equity. An example of a liability reduction is if a liability of the entity is 'forgiven'. Income arises as a result of that forgiveness, unless the forgiveness of the debt constitutes a contribution by owners.

Under the *Conceptual Framework*, income encompasses both revenue and gains. A definition of *revenue* is contained in paragraph 7 of IAS 18 *Revenue* as follows:

> [T]he gross inflow of economic benefits during the period arising in the course of the ordinary activities of an entity when those inflows result in increases in equity, other than increases relating to contributions from equity participants.

Thus revenue represents income which has arisen from 'the ordinary activities of an entity'. On the other hand, *gains* represent income that does not necessarily arise from the ordinary activities of the entity; for example, gains on the disposal of non-current assets or on the revaluation of marketable securities. Gains are usually disclosed in the statement of profit or loss and other comprehensive income net of any related expenses, whereas revenues are reported at a gross amount. As revenues and gains are both income, there is no need to regard them as separate elements under the *Conceptual Framework*.

1.5.5 Expenses

Paragraph 4.25(b) of the *Conceptual Framework* contains the following definition of *expenses*:

> Expenses are decreases in economic benefits during the accounting period in the form of outflows or depletions of assets or incurrences of liabilities that result in decreases in equity, other than those relating to distributions to equity participants.

To qualify as an expense, a reduction in an asset or an increase in a liability must have the effect of decreasing the entity's equity. The purchase of an asset does not decrease equity and therefore does not create an expense. An expense arises whenever the economic benefits in the asset are consumed, expire or are lost. Like income, the definition of expenses is expressed in terms of changes in assets, liabilities and equity. This concept of expense is broad enough to encompass items that have typically been reported in financial statements as 'losses', for example, losses on foreign currency transactions, losses from fire, flood, and so on, or losses on the abandonment of a research project. Losses are expenses that may not arise in the ordinary course of the entity's activities.

1.6 RECOGNITION OF ELEMENTS OF FINANCIAL STATEMENTS

There are recognition criteria to be followed in the preparation and presentation of financial statements in practice. These criteria have been set down as part of the *Conceptual Framework*. *Recognition* means the process of incorporating in the statement of financial position or statement of profit or loss and other comprehensive income an item that meets the definition of an element. In other words, it involves the inclusion of dollar amounts in the entity's accounting system. Note that an item must satisfy the definition of an element before it is 'recognised'.

1.6.1 Asset recognition

The *Conceptual Framework* states in paragraph 4.44 that an asset should be recognised in the statement of financial position when it is probable that the future economic benefits will flow to the entity and the asset has a cost or other value that can be measured reliably. Here, emphasis is placed on criteria for determining *when to record* an asset in the entity's accounting records. An asset is to be recognised only when both the probability and the reliable measurement criteria are satisfied. The term 'probability' refers to the degree of certainty that the future economic benefits will flow to the entity. The benefits should be more likely rather than less likely. For example, some development costs are not recognised as an asset because it is not 'probable' that future economic benefits will eventuate.

Even if such probability of future benefits is high, recognition of an asset cannot occur unless some cost or other value is capable of reliable measurement. Without such a measurement, the qualitative characteristic of 'reliability' will not be achieved. In practice, reliable measurement of internally generated goodwill has been difficult, and therefore such goodwill has not been recognised as an asset. Similarly, reliable measurement of an entity's mineral reserves is difficult. It is argued in the *Conceptual Framework* that assets that cannot be measured reliably may nevertheless be disclosed in notes to the financial statements, particularly if knowledge of the item is considered relevant to evaluating the entity's financial position, performance and cash flows.

1.6.2 Liability recognition

Paragraph 4.46 of the *Conceptual Framework* establishes criteria for the recognition of a liability in an entity's accounting records. A liability is recognised in the statement of financial position when it is probable that an outflow of resources embodying economic benefits will result from settling the present obligation and the amount at which the settlement will take place can be measured reliably.

As with the recognition of assets, 'probable' means that the chance of the outflow of economic benefits being required is likely. The additional need for reliable measurement is an attempt to measure, in monetary terms, the amount of economic benefits that will be sacrificed to satisfy the obligation. Any liabilities that are not recognised in the accounting records because they do not satisfy the recognition criteria may be disclosed in notes to the financial statements, if considered relevant. Further discussion of the recognition of liabilities is provided in chapter 5.

1.6.3 Income recognition

In accordance with paragraph 4.47 of the *Conceptual Framework*, income is recognised in the statement of profit or loss and other comprehensive income when an increase in future economic benefits relating to an increase in an asset or a decrease in a liability can be measured reliably. As with the recognition criteria for assets and liabilities, probability of occurrence and reliability of measurement are presented as the two criteria for income recognition in paragraph 4.38. For many entities, the majority of income in the form of revenues results from the provision of goods and services during the reporting period. There is little uncertainty that the income has been earned since the entity has received cash or has an explicit claim against an external party as a result of a past transaction. However, the absence of an exchange transaction often raises doubts as to whether the income has achieved the required degree of certainty. In situations of uncertainty, the *Conceptual Framework* requires the income to be recognised as long as it is 'probable' that it has occurred and the amount can be measured reliably.

As stated previously, income includes both revenues and gains. The standard setters have provided further requirements for the recognition of revenues in accounting standard IAS 18 *Revenue*, which deals with the recognition of different types of revenue that can arise in an entity. The standard requires all revenue recognised in the entity's financial statements to be measured at the fair value of the consideration received or receivable. Separate recognition criteria are then provided for each different category of revenue. See chapter 4 for a detailed discussion of revenue recognition.

1.6.4 Expense recognition

Just as the income recognition criteria have been developed in the *Conceptual Framework* as a guide to the timing of income recognition, the expense recognition criteria have been developed to guide the timing of expense recognition. The *Conceptual Framework* defines expenses in terms of decreases in future economic benefits in the form of reductions in assets or increases in liabilities of the entity (see the definition of expenses in section 1.5.5). In addition to the probability criteria for expense recognition, the *Conceptual Framework* states that expenses are recognised in the statement of profit or loss and other comprehensive income when a decrease in future economic benefits related to a decrease in an asset or an increase in a liability can be measured reliably (paragraph 4.49). This means that an expense is recognised simultaneously with a decrease in an asset or an increase in a liability. An expense is also recognised in the statement of profit or loss and other comprehensive income when the entity incurs a liability without the recognition of any asset, for example, wages payable.

In years past, the process of recognising expenses was referred to as a 'matching process', whereby an attempt was made to associate each cost with the income recognised in the current period. Costs that were 'associated' with the revenue were then said to be 'matched' and written off to expenses. This idea of matching expenses with income has been dropped in the *Conceptual Framework* in favour of assessing the probability of a decrease in economic benefits that can be measured reliably. Matching is no longer the expense recognition criterion under the *Conceptual Framework*.

1.7 MEASUREMENT OF THE ELEMENTS OF FINANCIAL STATEMENTS

Paragraph 4.54 of the *Conceptual Framework* states:

> Measurement is the process of determining the monetary amounts at which the elements of the financial statements are to be recognised and carried in the balance sheet [statement of financial position] and income statement [statement of profit or loss and other comprehensive income].

Because the concepts of equity, income and expenses are highly dependent on the concepts of assets and liabilities, measurement of the former depends on measurement of the latter. In other words, emphasis is placed on measuring assets and liabilities; the measurement of equity, income and expenses then follows. Measurement is very important in accounting in that it is the process by which valuations are placed on all elements reported in financial statements. Measurements can have an important effect on the economic decisions made by users of those financial statements. The *Conceptual Framework* (paragraph 4.55) points out that a number of different measurement bases may be used for assets, liabilities, income and expenses in varying degrees and in varying combinations in financial statements. They include the following, the most common of which, in practice, is the historical cost basis:

- *Historical cost*. Under the *historical cost* measurement basis, an asset is recorded at the amount of cash or cash equivalents paid or the fair value of the consideration given to acquire it at its acquisition date. Liabilities are recorded at the amount of the proceeds received in exchange for an obligation, or at the amount of cash to be paid out in order to satisfy the liability in the normal course of business.
- *Current cost*. For an asset, *current cost* represents the amount of cash or cash equivalents that would be paid if the same or equivalent asset was acquired currently. A liability is recorded at the amount of cash or cash equivalents needed to settle the obligation currently.
- *Realisable or settlement value*. For an asset, the *realisable value* is the amount of cash or cash equivalents that could be obtained currently by selling the asset in an orderly disposal, or in the normal course of

business. The settlement amount of a liability is the amount of cash or cash equivalents expected to be paid to satisfy the obligation in the normal course of business.

- *Present value*. The present value of an asset means the discounted future net cash inflows or net cash savings that are expected to arise in the normal course of business. The *present value* of a liability is the discounted future net cash outflows that are expected to settle the obligation in the normal course of business.

In relation to measurement principles, the *Conceptual Framework* merely describes practice rather than establishing any principles that should be applied in the measurement of elements of financial statements. The measurement basis most commonly adopted by entities is the historical cost basis, although there is a trend towards greater use of fair values. For example, to comply with IAS 2 *Inventories*, inventories are to be measured at the lower of cost and net realisable value. The list is somewhat dated. There is little use of current cost (replacement cost) in financial statements. The omission of fair value reflects the need to revise and update this chapter of the *Conceptual Framework*. The use of *fair value*, which is defined as 'the price that would be received to sell an asset or paid to transfer a liability in an orderly transaction between market participants at the measurement date' (IFRS 13 *Fair Value Measurement* paragraph 9) is also referred to in many accounting standards.

1.8 CONCEPTS OF CAPITAL

Scant attention has been given to the concept of capital in accounting in the last 30 years, but it was a topic that received considerable focus during the current value debates of the 1960s to the early 1980s. It was argued then, and now, that before an entity can determine its income for any period, it must adopt not only a measurement basis for assets and liabilities, but also a concept of capital. Two main concepts of capital are discussed in the *Conceptual Framework*, namely financial capital and physical capital.

Under the *financial capital* concept, capital is synonymous with the net assets or equity of the entity, measured either in terms of the actual amount of dollars by subtracting the total of liabilities from assets, or in terms of the purchasing power of the dollar amount recorded as equity. Profit exists only after the entity has maintained its capital, measured as either the dollar value of equity at the beginning of the period, or the purchasing power of those dollars in the equity at the beginning of the period.

Under the *physical capital* concept, capital is seen not so much as the equity recorded by the entity but as the operating capability of the entity's assets. Profit exists only after the entity has set aside enough capital to maintain the operating capability of its assets.

A number of different accounting systems have been devised in the past to provide alternatives to the conventional historical cost system, which is the system predominantly used in practice. These alternatives, which represent different combinations of the measurement of assets and liabilities and the concept of capital maintenance, include:

- the *general price level accounting system*, which had its origins in Germany after World War I when inflation reached excessive levels — this system modifies the conventional historical cost system for the effects of inflation and therefore follows a financial capital concept
- *current value systems*, which attempt to measure the changes in the current values of assets and liabilities — these systems include measures of the current buying or input prices of net assets, and/or measures of the current selling or realisable values of net assets. Capital may be measured as either financial or physical.

SUMMARY

This chapter has provided an overview of the structure of the IASB and the process of setting IFRSs, including IFRIC Interpretations. The adoption of IFRSs in many parts of the world has increased the importance of developments in international standards setting.

The *Conceptual Framework* describes the basic concepts that underlie financial statements prepared in conformity with IFRSs. It serves as a guide to the standard setters in developing accounting standards and in resolving accounting issues that are not addressed directly in an accounting standard.

The *Conceptual Framework* identifies the principal classes of users of an entity's general purpose financial statements and states that the objective of financial statements is to provide information — about the financial position, performance and changes in financial position of an entity — that is useful to existing and potential investors, lenders and other creditors in making decisions about providing resources to the entity. It specifies the fundamental qualities that make financial information useful, namely relevance and faithful representation. The usefulness of financial information is enhanced by comparability, verifiability, timeliness and understandability, and constrained by cost.

The *Conceptual Framework* also defines the basic elements in financial statements (assets, liabilities, equity, income and expenses) and discusses the criteria for recognising them. The *Conceptual Framework* identifies alternative measurement bases used in practice and describes alternative concepts of capital maintenance.

Discussion questions

1. Describe the standard-setting process of the IASB.
2. Describe the role of the IFRS Interpretations Committee.
3. How does the IASB influence domestic financial reporting of individual countries? Illustrate your answer with reference to a specific country.
4. Identify the potential benefits of a globally accepted set of accounting standards.
5. Specify the objectives of general purpose financial reporting, the nature of users, and the information to be provided to users to achieve the objectives as provided in the *Conceptual Framework*.
6. Describe the qualitative characteristics of financial information according to the *Conceptual Framework*, distinguishing between fundamental and enhancing characteristics.
7. Outline the fundamental qualitative characteristics of financial reporting information to be considered when preparing general purpose financial statements.
8. Discuss the importance of the going concern assumption to the practice of accounting.
9. Discuss the essential characteristics of an asset as described in the *Conceptual Framework*.
10. Discuss the essential characteristics of a liability as described in the *Conceptual Framework*.
11. A government gives a parcel of land to a company at no charge. The company builds a factory on the land and agrees to employ a certain number of people at the factory for a certain period of time. Considering the definition of income in the *Conceptual Framework*, do you think the receipt of the land is income to the company?
12. Discuss the difference, if any, between income, revenue and gains.
13. Define 'equity' and explain why the *Conceptual Framework* does not prescribe any recognition criteria for equity.
14. In relation to the following multiple choice questions, discuss your choice of correct answer:
    (a) Which of the following statements about the *Conceptual Framework* is incorrect?
        (i) The *Conceptual Framework* considers timeliness and materiality to be constraints on relevant and faithfully represented information.
        (ii) The *Conceptual Framework* states that the elements directly related to the measurement of financial position are assets, liabilities and equity.
        (iii) The *Conceptual Framework* applies to the financial statements of all commercial, industrial and business reporting entities.
        (iv) In accordance with the *Conceptual Framework*, income is recognised when an increase in future economic benefits related to an increase in an asset or a decrease in a liability has arisen that can be measured reliably.
    (b) The *Conceptual Framework*'s enhancing qualitative characteristics include:
        (i) Understandability, timeliness, verifiability and comparability.
        (ii) Faithful representation, relevance, understandability and verifiability.
        (iii) Comparability and reliability.
        (iv) Substance over form and relevance.
    (c) Which of the following statements about the *Conceptual Framework*'s definition of expenses is correct?
        (i) Expenses include distributions to owners.
        (ii) Expenses are always in the form of outflows or depletions of assets.
        (iii) Expenses exclude losses.
        (iv) Expenses are always decreases in economic benefits.
    (d) In accordance with the *Conceptual Framework*, a lender should recognise the forgiveness of its $20 000 interest-free loan as:
        (i) An increase in income and a decrease in a liability.
        (ii) An increase in an expense and a decrease in an asset.
        (iii) An increase in an asset and an increase in income.
        (iv) An increase in an expense and a decrease in a liability.
15. Distinguish between the financial and physical concepts of capital and their implications for the measurement of profit.

Exercises

STAR RATING ★ BASIC ★★ MODERATE ★★★ DIFFICULT

| Exercise 1.1 | RELEVANT INFORMATION FOR AN INVESTMENT COMPANY |

★ A year ago you bought shares of stock in an investment company. The investment company in turn buys, holds and sells shares of business enterprises. You want to use the financial statements of the investment company to assess its performance over the past year.

(a) What financial information about the investment company's holdings would be most relevant to you?

(b) The investment company earns profits from appreciation of its investment securities and from dividends received. How would the concepts of recognition in the *Conceptual Framework* apply here?

| Exercise 1.2 | MEASURING INVENTORIES OF GOLD AND SILVER |

★ IAS 2 *Inventories* allows producers of gold and silver to measure inventories of these commodities at selling price even before they have sold them, which means a profit is recognised at production. In nearly all other industries, however, profit is recognised only when the inventories are sold to outside customers. What concepts in the *Conceptual Framework* might the standard setters have considered with regard to accounting for gold and silver production?

| Exercise 1.3 | RECOGNISING A LOSS FROM A LAWSUIT |

★ The law in your community requires store owners to shovel snow and ice from the pavement in front of their shops. You failed to do that, and a pedestrian slipped and fell, resulting in serious and costly injury. The pedestrian has sued you. Your lawyers say that while they will vigorously defend you in the lawsuit, you should expect to lose $25 000 to cover the injured party's costs. A court decision, however, is not expected for at least a year. What aspects of the *Conceptual Framework* might help you in deciding the appropriate accounting for this situation?

| Exercise 1.4 | FINANCIAL STATEMENTS OF A REAL ESTATE INVESTOR |

★ An entity purchases a rental property for $10 000 000 as an investment. The building is fully rented and is in a prosperous area. At the end of the current year, the entity hires an appraiser who reports that the fair value of the building is $15 000 000 plus or minus 10%. Depreciating the building over 50 years would reduce the carrying amount to $9 800 000.

(a) What are the relevance and faithful representation considerations in deciding how to measure the building in the entity's financial statements?

(b) Does the *Conceptual Framework* lead to measuring the building at $15 000 000? Or at $9 800 000? Or at some other amount?

| Exercise 1.5 | NEED FOR THE *CONCEPTUAL FRAMEWORK* VS. INTERPRETATIONS |

★ Applying the *Conceptual Framework* is subjective and requires judgement. Would the IASB be better off to abandon the *Conceptual Framework* entirely and instead rely on a very active interpretations committee that develops detailed guidance in response to requests from constituents?

| Exercise 1.6 | MEANING OF 'DECISION USEFUL' |

★ What is meant by saying that accounting information should be 'decision useful'? Provide examples.

| Exercise 1.7 | PERFORMANCE OF A BUSINESS ENTITY |

★ A financial analyst says: 'I advise my clients to invest for the long term. Buy good stocks and hang onto them. Therefore, I am interested in a company's long-term earning power. Accounting standards that result in earnings volatility obscure long-term earning power. Accounting should report earning power by deferring and amortising costs and revenues.' How does the *Conceptual Framework* relate to this analyst's view of financial statements?

Exercise 1.8	**GOING CONCERN**

★ What measurement principles might be most appropriate for a company that has ceased to be a going concern (e.g. it is unable to renew loans and is planning to sell major assets needed for existing operations in order to repay creditors)?

Exercise 1.9	**ASSESSING PROBABILITIES IN ACCOUNTING RECOGNITION**

★ The *Conceptual Framework* defines an asset as a resource from which future economic benefits are expected to flow. 'Expected' means it is not certain, and involves some degree of probability. At the same time the *Conceptual Framework* establishes, as a criterion for recognising an asset, that 'it is probable that any future economic benefit associated with the item will flow to or from the entity.' Again, an assessment of probability is required. Is there a redundancy, or possibly some type of inconsistency, in including the notion of probability in both the asset definition and recognition criteria?

Exercise 1.10	**PURCHASE ORDERS**

★ An airline places a non-cancellable order for a new aeroplane with one of the major commercial aircraft manufacturers at a fixed price, with delivery in 30 months and payment in full to be made on delivery.
(a) Under the *Conceptual Framework*, do you think the airline should recognise any asset or liability at the time it places the order?
(b) One year later, the price of this aeroplane model has risen by 5%, but the airline had locked in a fixed, lower price. Under the *Conceptual Framework*, do you think the airline should recognise any asset (and gain) at the time when the price of the aeroplane rises? If the price fell by 5% instead of rising, do you think the airline should recognise any liability (and loss) under the *Conceptual Framework*?

Exercise 1.11	**DEFINITIONS OF ELEMENTS AND RECOGNITION CRITERIA**

★ Explain how you would account for the following items/situations, justifying your answer by reference to the *Conceptual Framework*'s definitions and recognition criteria:
(a) A trinket of sentimental value only.
(b) You are guarantor for your friend's bank loan:
   (i) You have no reason to believe your friend will default on the loan.
  (ii) As your friend is in serious financial difficulties, you think it likely that he will default on the loan.
(c) You receive 1000 shares in X Ltd, trading at $4 each, as a gift from a grateful client.
(d) The panoramic view of the coast from your café's windows, which you are convinced attracts customers to your café.
(e) The court has ordered your firm to repair the environmental damage it caused to the local river system. You have no idea how much this repair work will cost.

Exercise 1.12	**DEFINITIONS AND RECOGNITION CRITERIA**

★ Explain how you would account for the following items, justifying your answer by reference to the definitions and recognition criteria in the *Conceptual Framework*. Also state, where appropriate, which ledger accounts should be debited and credited.
(a) (i) Your firm has been sued for negligence — likely you will lose the case.
   (ii) Your firm has been sued for negligence — likely you will win the case.
(b) Obsolete plant now retired from use.
(c) Receipt of a donation of $10 000.

Exercise 1.13	**DEFINITIONS AND RECOGNITION CRITERIA**

★ Glasgow Accounting Services has just invoiced one of its clients $3600 for accounting services provided to the client. Explain how Glasgow Accounting Services should recognise this event, justifying your answer by reference to relevant *Conceptual Framework* definitions and recognition criteria.

Exercise 1.14	**ASSETS**

★ Lampeter Cosmetics has spent $220 000 this year on a project to develop a new range of chemical-free cosmetics. As yet, it is too early for Lampeter Cosmetics' management to be able to predict whether this project will prove to be commercially successful. Explain whether Lampeter Cosmetics should recognise this expenditure as an asset, justifying your answer by reference to the *Conceptual Framework* asset definition and recognition criteria.

Exercise 1.15	**ASSET DEFINITION AND RECOGNITION**

★ On 28 May 2013, $20 000 cash was stolen from Ming Lee Ltd's night safe. Explain how Ming Lee should account for this event, justifying your answer by reference to relevant *Conceptual Framework* definitions and recognition criteria.

References

IFRS Foundation 2012, *Due Process Handbook for the IASB*, www.ifrs.org.

IFRS Foundation & International Accounting Standards Board 2012, *Who we are and what we do*, www.ifrs.org.

International Accounting Standards Board (IASB) 2010, *Exposure Draft ED/2010/2 Conceptual Framework for Financial Reporting — The Reporting Entity*, www.ifrs.org.

—— 2011, *Conceptual Framework for Financial Reporting*, www.ifrs.org.

—— 2012, *How we are structured*, www.ifrs.org.

Part 2

Elements

2 Shareholders' equity: share capital and reserves

After studying this chapter, you should be able to:

1 describe the equity of a sole proprietor, partnership and company
2 identify the different forms of corporate entities
3 outline the key features of the corporate structure
4 discuss the different forms of share capital
5 account for the issue of both no-par and par value shares
6 account for share placements, rights issues, options, and bonus issues
7 discuss the rationale behind and accounting treatment of share buy-backs
8 outline the nature of reserves and account for movements in retained earnings, including dividends
9 prepare note disclosures in relation to equity, as well as a statement of changes in equity.

2.1 EQUITY

The purpose of this chapter is to introduce the components of the equity section of the statement of financial position, namely contributed capital and reserves. The element of capital will differ depending on the nature of the organisation, whether a sole proprietorship, partnership or company. Reserves comprise equity attributable to the owners of the entity other than amounts directly contributed by the owners. An example of the equity section of the statement of financial position of a for-profit entity is shown in figure 2.1. It contains an extract from the consolidated balance sheet of Nokia Corporation as at 31 December 2010. The accounts were prepared in accordance with International Financial Reporting Standards (IFRSs), and the extract relating to the shareholders' equity of the group is shown in figure 2.1. Note that the two key components are share capital and reserves.

December 31	Notes	2010 EURm	2009 EURm
Capital and reserves attributable to equity holders of the parent			
Share capital	23	246	246
Share issue premium		312	279
Treasury shares, at cost		(663)	(681)
Translation differences	22	825	(127)
Fair value and other reserves	21	3	69
Reserve for invested non-restricted equity		3 161	3 170
Retained earnings		10 500	10 132
		14 384	13 088
Non-controlling interests		1 847	1 661
Total equity		16 231	14 749

FIGURE 2.1 Shareholders' equity of Nokia
Source: Nokia Corporation (2010, p. 18).

With a *sole proprietor*, having a single owner means there is little reason for distinguishing between capital (potentially the initial investment in the business) and profits retained in the business for investment purposes.

Traditionally with *partnerships*, the rights and responsibilities of the partners are specified in a partnership agreement. This document details how the profits or losses of the partnership are to be divided between the partners, including rules relating to distributions on dissolution of the partnership. In accounting for partnerships, a distinction is generally made for each partner between a capital account, to which amounts invested by a partner are credited, and a current account or retained earnings account, to which a partner's share of profits are credited and from which any drawings are debited. As with a sole proprietorship, there generally is no real distinction between capital contributed and profits retained (unless there is some other specification in the partnership agreement, which is unlikely). Both amounts represent the ongoing investment by the partners. On dissolution of the partnership, the distribution to partners is unaffected by whether an equity balance is capital or retained earnings.

With *companies*, the situation is different because their formation is generally governed by legislation, and there is normally a clear distinction made between contributed capital and profits retained in the entity. However, it must be understood that, although the laws governing companies in a particular country may require a distinction between capital and other forms of owners' equity, from an accounting point of view there is no real difference between the various classifications of owners' equity. In other words, apart from any legal restrictions such as those applying to the distribution of dividends, whether an entity has $200 000 of capital and $100 000 of retained earnings, or $100 000 of capital and $200 000 of retained earnings, is of no real importance. In essence, the entity has $300 000 of equity.

This chapter concentrates on the company as the organisational form of interest, with the major account reflecting contributed equity being share capital. However, as noted above, there is no reason, apart from legal reasons specific to a particular jurisdiction, for the organisational form to require major differences in accounting for the equity of an entity.

2.2 TYPES OF COMPANIES

Generally, companies can be distinguished by the nature of the ownership, and the rights and responsibilities of the shareholders. Two types of companies are examined in this section: not-for-profit companies and for-profit companies.

2.2.1 Not-for-profit companies

'Not-for-profit' is not defined in IFRSs. In Australia, whose accounting standards are equivalent to international standards, a not-for-profit entity is defined as an 'entity whose principal objective is not the generation of profit'.

An example of the equity section of the statement of financial position of a not-for-profit entity is shown in figure 2.2, which contains the equity section and two explanatory notes relating to this section from the 2010 statement of financial position of the International Committee of the Red Cross (ICRC). These financial statements are prepared in accordance with IFRSs. As noted in section 2 of the notes to the 2010 consolidated financial statements: 'Currently, the IFRS do not contain specific guidelines for non-profit organizations and non-governmental organizations concerning the accounting treatment and the presentation of the consolidated financial statements.'

FIGURE 2.2 Extract from the consolidated statement of financial position and notes to the accounts at 31 December 2010 (in Swiss franc '000) of the International Committee of the Red Cross

	Notes	2010	2009 (restated)
Restricted Reserves			
Total funds and foundations		32 986	30 516
Total funding of field operations	24	(21 167)	35 810
Total Restricted Reserves		**11 819**	**66 326**
Unrestricted Reserves			
Total reserves designated by the Assembly	25	426 070	455 849
Total other unrestricted reserves	26	14 400	14 400
Total Unrestricted Reserves		**440 470**	**470 249**
Total Reserves		**452 289**	**536 575**

Note 25. Reserves designated by the assembly

(in KCHF)	Future operations	Operational risks	Assets replacement	Financial risks	Human resources	Specific projects	Total
Balance as at 31 December 2008	**191 292**	**30 474**	**167 192**	**16 715**	**19 214**	**2 080**	**426 967**
Use/release during 2009	—	(2 486)	(108)	(38 125)	(7 306)	(2 080)	(50 105)
Allocations 2009	11 339	1 715	16 044	45 704	3 945	240	78 987
Balance as at 31 December 2009 (restated)	**202 631**	**29 703**	**183 128**	**24 294**	**15 853**	**240**	**455 849**
Use/release during 2010	(27 044)	(722)	(864)	(37 315)	(1 457)	(240)	(67 642)
Allocations 2010	—	1 453	3 908	31 910	—	592	37 863
Balance as at 31 December 2010	**175 587**	**30 434**	**186 172**	**18 889**	**14 396**	**592**	**426 070**

(continued)

FIGURE 2.2 *(continued)*

The future operations reserve is intended for situations with insufficient operational funding, which is estimated at an average of four months of expenditure in cash, kind and services (including overheads) over the previous four years, including both at headquarters and in the field. The theoretical level is KCHF 370 461 (in 2009: KCHF 357 145).

26. Other unrestricted reserves

(in KCHF)	2010	2009
General reserves	14 400	14 400
Total	**14 400**	**14 400**

Source: International Committee of the Red Cross (2010, pp. 492, 512).

Not-for-profit companies can be divided into government or public sector companies and private not-for-profit sector entities:

- Entities may be established by the government to undertake various activities of the government, such as the supply of water or electricity, the provision of communications and the running of an airline. The government may own all the issued shares of the company, or a controlling interest in the entity. For the government enterprise to be classified as not-for-profit, the primary objective of the entity must be something other than the earning of profit.
- Organisations such as charities may form a company as their preferred organisational structure to limit their liability. The company may be limited by guarantee, whereby members undertake to contribute a guaranteed amount in the event the company goes into liquidation, but have no rights to dividends or distributions on liquidation. Alternatively, the company may be a non-public company, sometimes called a proprietary company or a closed corporation, where the shares are held by a limited number of shareholders and the shares are not available for purchase by the public.

2.2.2 For-profit companies

For-profit companies may take a number of forms:

- *Proprietary or closed corporations* may be established with limited membership and restrictions on obtaining funds from the public. In some countries, a distinction is made between large and small proprietary companies, with the size being measured in relation to accounting numbers such as gross revenue and gross assets as well as other variables such as the number of employees. Where a proprietary company is classified as large, there is an increased responsibility in relation to the disclosure of information.
- *Public companies* or open corporations generally have a large number of issued shares, with the ownership being widespread. These companies rely on the public for subscription to share offers as well as the provision of debt funding via secured loans such as debentures or through unsecured loans. For-profit companies may be:
- listed — their shares are traded on a stock exchange
- unlisted — the shares are traded through brokers and financial institutions
- limited by guarantee — the members undertake to contribute a guaranteed amount in the event of the company going into liquidation
- unlimited — members are liable for all the debts of the company
- no-liability — members are not required to pay any calls on their shares if they do not wish to continue being shareholders in the company.

The exact rights and responsibilities of shareholders in relation to the different forms of companies will differ according to the relevant companies legislation and other laws specific to the country or countries in which the company operates.

As noted by Nobes & Parker (2002, pp. 21–3) the types of organisations and ownership differ substantially across countries:

> In Germany, France and Italy, capital provided by banks is very significant, as are small family-owned businesses. By contrast, in the United States and the United Kingdom there are large numbers of companies that rely on millions of private shareholders for finance . . .

A proposed grouping of countries into types by financial system has been formalized by Zysman (1983) as follows:
1. capital market systems (e.g. United Kingdom, United States)
2. credit-based government systems (e.g. France, Japan)
3. credit-based financial institution systems (e.g. Germany).

A further point of comparison between 'equity' and 'credit' countries is that, in the latter countries, even the relatively few listed companies may be dominated by shareholders who are bankers, governments or founding families. For example, in Germany, the banks in particular are important owners of companies as well as providers of debt finance . . . In such countries as Germany, France or Italy, the banks or the state will, in many cases, nominate directors and thus be able to obtain information and affect decisions.

Table 2.1 shows the distribution of the world's largest 500 companies by country in 2011, measured by revenue. The United States and Japan have the largest number of top companies and China has the largest rate of increase. Table 2.2 shows the major stock exchanges of the world and their domestic market capitalisation.

TABLE 2.1 Share of the world's top 500 companies (distribution by revenue)

Australia	8	Luxembourg	1
Austria	1	Malaysia	1
Belgium	5	Mexico	3
Belgium/Netherlands	1	Netherlands	12
Brazil	7	Norway	1
Britain	30	Poland	1
Britain/Netherlands	1	Russia	7
Canada	11	Saudi Arabia	1
China	61	Singapore	2
Colombia	1	South Korea	14
Denmark	2	Spain	9
Finland	1	Sweden	3
France	35	Switzerland	15
Germany	34	Taiwan	8
India	8	Thailand	1
Ireland	2	Turkey	1
Italy	10	United States of America	133
Japan	68	Venezuela	1
			500

Source: Fortune magazine (2012).

TABLE 2.2 Major stock exchanges in 2009–10

	Domestic market capitalisation (USD millions)		% change 2010/2009
Exchange	End 2010	End 2009	
Americas			
Bermuda SE	1 534.95	1 360.19	12.8
BM&FBOVESPA	1 545 565.66	1 337 247.68	15.6
Buenos Aires SE	63 909.79	45 744.93	39.7
Colombia SE	208 501.74	140 519.92	48.4
Lima SE	103 347.48	71 662.54	44.2
Mexican Exchange	454 345.22	352 045.44	29.1
NASDAQ OMX	3 889 369.88	3 239 492.44	20.1
NYSE Euronext (US)	13 394 081.80	11 837 793.30	13.1
Santiago SE	341 798.88	230 732.39	48.1
TSX Group	2 170 432.73	1 676 814.19	29.4
Total region	**22 172 888.14**	**18 933 413.02**	**17.1**

(continued)

TABLE 2.2 *(continued)*

Exchange	Domestic market capitalisation (USD millions)		% change 2010/2009
	End 2010	**End 2009**	
Asia — Pacific			
Australian Securities Exchange	1 454 490.57	1 261 909.34	15.3
Bombay SE	1 631 829.54	1 306 520.25	24.9
Bursa Malaysia	408 689.12	289 219.39	41.3
Colombo SE	19 923.86	9 546.66	108.7
Hong Kong Exchanges	2 711 316.16	2 305 142.81	17.6
Indonesia SE	360 388.10	214 941.47	67.7
Korea Exchange	1 091 911.46	834 596.86	30.8
National Stock Exchange India	1 596 625.26	1 224 806.44	30.4
Osaka Securities Exchange	271 831.39	227 913.51	19.3
Philippine SE	157 320.50	86 349.43	82.2
Shanghai SE	2 716 470.22	2 704 778.46	0.4
Shenzhen SE	1 311 370.08	868 374.00	51.0
Singapore Exchange	647 226.41	481 246.70	34.5
Taiwan SE	818 490.46	658 991.37	24.2
Thailand SE	277 731.74	176 956.07	56.9
Tokyo SE Group	3 827 774.20	3 306 082.05	15.8
Total region	**17 434 932.41**	**14 504 654.87**	**20.2**
Europe — Africa — Middle East			
Amman SE	30 864.42	31 826.65	(3.0)
Athens Exchange	67 586.42	112 632.40	(40.0)
BME Spanish Exchanges	1 171 624.98	1 434 540.46	(18.3)
Budapest SE	27 708.41	30 036.63	(7.8)
Casablanca SE	69 152.12	64 478.83	7.2
Cyprus SE	6 834.30	10 268.87	(33.4)
Deutsche Börse	1 429 719.05	1 292 355.31	10.6
Egyptian Exchange	84 276.83	91 207.34	(7.6)
Irish SE	60 368.31	61 291.12	(1.5)
Istanbul SE	307 051.98	233 996.66	31.2
Johannesburg SE	925 007.15	799 023.75	15.8
Ljubljana SE	9 383.46	12 140.92	(22.7)
London SE Group	3 613 063.97	3 453 622.12	4.6
Luxembourg SE	101 128.52	105 048.19	(3.7)
Malta SE	4 322.81	4 080.30	5.9
Mauritius SE	7 752.77	6 582.05	17.8
MICEX	949 148.86	736 306.71	28.9
NASDAQ OMX Nordic Exchange	1 042 153.74	817 222.78	27.5
NYSE Euronext (Europe)	2 930 072.44	2 869 393.11	2.1
Oslo Børs	295 288.30	227 233.23	29.9
Saudi Stock Market — Tadawul	353 409.59	318 733.68	10.9
SIX Swiss Exchange	1 229 356.54	1 064 686.54	15.5
Tehran SE	86 641.52	59 183.54	46.4
Tel Aviv SE	227 614.01	188 733.90	20.6
Warsaw SE	190 231.67	150 961.53	26.0
Wiener Börse	126 031.96	114 076.07	10.5
Total region	**15 345 794.13**	**14 289 662.67**	**7.4**
WFE total	**54 953 614.68**	**47 727 730.56**	**15.1**

Source: Based on statistics from the World Federation of Exchanges website www.world-exchanges.org/statistics.

Many global companies list on a number of stock exchanges. Nokia, for example, is quoted on the following stock exchanges:

- HEX, Helsinki (quoted since 1915)
- Stockholmsborsen (quoted since 1983)
- Frankfurter Wertpapierborse (quoted since 1988)
- New York Stock Exchange (quoted since 1994).

Countries with larger capital markets tend to dominate the overall world market, as movements in these markets have immediate effects on other economies. Note, however, that the size of a country's market does not necessarily correlate with the sophistication of the accounting and regulatory regimes of that country.

 ## 2.3 KEY FEATURES OF THE CORPORATE STRUCTURE

The choice of the company as the preferred form of organisational structure brings with it certain advantages, such as limited liability to shareholders. It also comes with certain disadvantages, such as making the entity subject to increasing government regulation including the forced and detailed disclosure of information about the company. Some features of the company structure that affect the subsequent accounting for a company are described below.

2.3.1 The use of share capital

The ownership rights in a company are generally represented by shares; that is, the share capital of a company comprises a number of units or shares. Each share represents a proportional right to the net assets of the company and, within a class of shares, all shares have the same equal rights. These shares are generally transferable between parties. As a result, markets have been established to provide investors with an ability to trade in shares. Where active markets exist such as with organised stock exchanges, the fair value of a company's shares at a point in time may be measured reliably. A further advantage of transferability is that a change in ownership by one shareholder selling shares to a new investor does not have an effect on the continued existence and operation of the company.

Besides the right to share equally in the net assets, and hence the profits or losses of a company, each share has other rights, including:

- *the right to vote for directors of the company.* This establishes the right of shareholders to have a say as owners in the strategic direction of the company. Where there are a large number of owners in a company, there is generally a separation between ownership and management. The shareholders thus employ professional managers (the directors) to manage the organisation, these managers then providing periodic reports to the shareholders on the financial performance and position of the company. Some directors are executive directors, being employed as executives in the company, while others have non-executive roles. The directors are elected at the annual general meeting of the company, and shareholders exercise their voting rights to elect the directors. The shareholders may vote in person, or by proxy. In relation to the latter, a shareholder may authorise another party to vote on his or her behalf at the meeting; the other party could be the chairperson of the company's board.
- *the right to share in assets on the winding-up or liquidation of the company.* The rights and responsibilities of shareholders in the event of liquidation are generally covered in legislation specific to each country, as are the rights of creditors to receive payment in preference to shareholders.
- *the right to share proportionately in any new issues of shares of the same class.* This right is sometimes referred to as the pre-emptive right. It ensures that a shareholder is able to retain the same proportionate ownership in a company, and that this ownership percentage cannot be diluted by the company issuing new shares to other investors, possibly at prices lower than the current fair value. However, the directors may be allowed to make limited placements of shares under certain conditions.

2.3.2 Limited liability

When shares are issued, the maximum amount payable by each shareholder is set. Even if a company incurs losses or goes into liquidation, the company cannot require a shareholder to provide additional capital. In some countries, shares are issued with a specific amount stated on the share certificate, this amount being called the par value of the share. For example, a company may issue one million shares each with a par value of $1, the company then receiving share capital of $1 million.

Par value shares may also be issued at a premium. For example, where a company requires share capital of $2 million, one million $1 shares may be issued at a premium of $1 per share; in this case, each shareholder is required to pay $2 per share. Similarly, par value shares may be issued at a discount. For example, where a company issues $1 shares at a discount of 20c, the company requires each shareholder to pay 80c per share. The only real purpose of the par value is to establish the maximum liability of the shareholder in relation to the company. Legislation in some countries restricts the issue of shares at a discount, and also establishes the subsequent uses of any share premium received on a share.

Note that the par value does not represent a fair or market value of the share. At the issue date, it would be expected that the par value, plus the premium or minus the discount, would represent the market value of the share. In some countries, such as Australia, the use of par value shares has been replaced by the issue of shares at a specified price with no par value. For example, a company may issue 1000 shares in 2010 at $3 per share, and in 2013 it may issue another 1000 shares at $5 per share. In 2013, the company then has 2000 shares and a share capital of $8000. The issue price becomes irrelevant subsequent to the issue, the key variables being the number of shares issued and the amount of share capital in total. The liability of each shareholder is limited to the issue price of the shares at the time of issue.

The feature of limited liability protects shareholders by limiting the contribution required of them, which in turn places limitations on the ability of creditors to access funds for the repayment of company debts. To protect creditors, many countries have enacted legislation that prohibits companies from distributing capital to shareholders in the form of dividends. Dividends are then payable only from profits, not out of capital. Other forms of legislation require that assets exceed liabilities immediately before a dividend is 'declared'.

2.4 DIFFERENT FORMS OF SHARE CAPITAL

Shares are issued with specific rights attached. Shares are then given different names to signify differences in rights.

2.4.1 Ordinary shares

The most common form of share capital is the ordinary share or common stock. These shares have no specific rights to any distributions of profit by the company, and ordinary shareholders are often referred to as 'residual' equity holders in that these shareholders obtain what is left after all other parties' claims have been met. An example of a company that has only one class of share is Nokia. Information on its shares as at 31 December 2010 was provided in its 2010 annual report in the notes to the financial statements of the parent company. Part of this information is shown in figure 2.3.

Shares and share capital

Nokia has one class of shares. Each Nokia share entitles the holder to one vote at General Meetings of Nokia. On December 31, 2010, the share capital of Nokia Corporation was EUR 245 896 461.96 and the total number of shares issued was 3 744 956 052. On December 31, 2010, the total number of shares included 35 826 052 shares owned by Group companies representing approximately 1.0% of the share capital and the total voting rights. Under the Articles of Association of Nokia, Nokia Corporation does not have minimum or maximum share capital or a par value of a share.

Share capital and shares December 31, 2010	2010	2009	2008	2007	2006
Share capital, EURm	246	246	266	246	246
Shares (1000)	3 744 956	3 744 956	3 800 949	3 982 812	4 095 043
Shares owned by the Group (1000)	35 826	36 694	103 076	136 862	129 312
Number of shares excluding shares owned by the Group (1000)	3 709 130	3 708 262	3 697 872	3 845 950	3 965 730
Number of registered shareholders[1]	191 790	156 081	122 713	103 226	119 143

[1] Each account operator is included in the figure as only one registered shareholder.

FIGURE 2.3 Share capital, Nokia Corporation
Source: Nokia Corporation (2010, p. 72).

Returns to shareholders

As already noted, the shareholders of ordinary shares have no specific rights to dividends, being residual equity holders. Whether a dividend is paid depends on the decisions made by the directors. Regulations in some countries may specify from which equity accounts the dividends can be paid, or whether the company has to meet solvency tests before paying dividends. In some cases, the directors may be allowed to propose a dividend at year-end, but this proposal may have to be approved by the shareholders in the annual general meeting.

2.4.2 Preference shares

Another form of share capital is the preference share. As the name implies, holders of preference shares generally have a preferential right to dividends over the ordinary shareholders. Note firstly that the name of the instrument does not necessarily indicate the rights associated with that instrument. As is discussed in chapter 7, some preference shares are in reality not equity but liabilities, or they may be compound instruments being partially debt and partially equity, sometimes referred to as hybrid securities. Secondly, the rights of preference shareholders may be very diverse. Some preference shares have a fixed dividend; for example, a company may issue preference shares at $10 each with a 4% dividend per annum, thus entitling the shareholder to a 40c dividend per annum. Other common features of preference shares are:

- *cumulative versus non-cumulative shares.* Where a preference share is cumulative, if a dividend is not declared in a particular year, the right to the dividend is not lost but carries over to a subsequent year. The dividends are said to be in arrears. With non-cumulative shares, if a dividend is not paid in a particular year, the right to that dividend is lost.
- *participating versus non-participating shares.* A participating share gives the holder the right to share in extra dividends. For example, if a company has issued 8% participating preference shares and it pays a 10% dividend to the ordinary shareholders, the preference shareholders may be entitled to a further 2% dividend.
- *convertible versus non-convertible shares.* Convertible preference shares may give the holder the right to convert the preference shares into ordinary shares. The right to convert may be at the option of the holder of the shares or at the option of the company itself. As explained in chapter 7, convertible preference shares may need to be classified into debt and equity components.
- *converting preference shares.* With convertible preference shares, whether a conversion into ordinary shares ever occurs depends upon the exercise of an option, but with converting preference shares the terms of issue are such that the shares must convert into ordinary shares at a specified point of time. As explained in chapter 7, converting preference shares may need to be classified as debt.
- *redeemable versus non-redeemable shares.* Subsequent to their issue, redeemable preference shares may be bought back from the shareholders by the company at a price generally established in the terms of issue of the shares. The option to redeem is normally held by the company.

2.5 CONTRIBUTED EQUITY: ISSUE OF SHARE CAPITAL

Once a business has decided to form a public company, it will commence the procedures necessary to issue shares to the public. The initial offering of shares to the public to invest in the new company is called an initial public offering (IPO). To arrange the sale of the shares, the business that wishes to float the company usually employs a promoter, such as a stockbroker or a financial institution, with expert knowledge of the legal requirements and experience in this area. Once the promoter and the managers of the business agree on the structure of the new company, a prospectus is drawn up and lodged with the regulating authority. The prospectus contains information about the current status of the business and its future prospects.

In order to ensure that the statements in the prospectus are accurate, a process of due diligence is undertaken by an accounting firm and a report attached. To ensure that the sale of shares is successful, an underwriter may be employed. The role of the underwriter is to advise on such matters as the pricing of the issue, the timing of the issue and how the issue will be marketed. One of the principal reasons for using an underwriter is to ensure that all the shares are sold, as the underwriter agrees to acquire all shares that are not taken up by the public.

The costs of issuing the shares can then be quite substantial and could amount to 10% of the amount raised. The costs include costs associated with preparing and printing the relevant documentation and marketing the share issue, as well as the fees charged by the various experts consulted which could include accountants, lawyers and taxation specialists. Accounting for these costs is covered in paragraph 37 of IAS 32 *Financial Instruments: Presentation*:

> An entity typically incurs various costs in issuing or acquiring its own equity instruments. Those costs might include registration and other regulatory fees, amounts paid to legal, accounting and other professional advisers, printing costs and stamp duties. The transaction costs of an equity transaction are accounted for as a deduction from equity (net of any related income tax benefit) to the extent they are incremental costs directly attributable to the equity transaction that otherwise would have been avoided. The costs of an equity transaction that is abandoned are recognised as an expense.

The costs are then treated as a reduction in share capital such that the amount shown in share capital immediately after the share issue is the net amount available to the company for operations. The accounting for share issue costs is demonstrated in the next section.

Any costs associated with the formation of the company that cannot be directly related to the issue of the shares, such as registration of the company name, are expensed as the cost is incurred. These outlays do not meet the definition of an asset as there are no expected future economic benefits associated with these outlays that can be controlled by the company.

2.5.1 Issue of no-par shares

ILLUSTRATIVE EXAMPLE 2.1 Issue of no-par shares

Qatar Ltd issues 500 no-par shares for cash at $10 each, incurring share issue costs of $450. Qatar Ltd records on its share register the number of shares issued, and makes the following journal entry:

Cash	Dr	5 000	
Share Capital	Cr		5 000
(Issue of 500 $10 shares)			
Share Capital	Dr	450	
Cash	Cr		450
(Share issue costs)			

If cash is collected from applicants for shares before the shares are issued, the company records the cash received in a cash trust account, and raises an application account to record the balance prior to the issue of the shares. For example, if application monies of $5000 were collected during the month of January and the shares were issued at the end of January, the journal entries would be:

January 1–30	Cash Trust	Dr	5 000	
	Application	Cr		5 000
	(Monies received from applicants for shares)			
31	Application	Dr	5 000	
	Share Capital	Cr		5 000
	(Issue of shares applied for)			
	Cash	Dr	5 000	
	Cash Trust	Cr		5 000
	(Transfer from cash trust on issue of shares)			

The reason for raising the cash trust account is that there may be a minimum number of applications that have to be received in order for the share issue to proceed. When the minimum subscription is not received or applicants are allotted fewer shares than they applied for, application monies collected are paid back to the applicants via the cash trust account.

Shares in limited liability companies are generally issued on a fully paid basis, but, in some cases, shares may be issued so that part of the issue price is payable immediately and part is required to be paid later. In this case, at the appropriate date the company has to make a call on the shareholders for the subsequent payment.

Armenia Ltd issues 500 no-par shares at $10, the terms of issue requiring the shareholders to pay $6 immediately and $4 in 1 year's time. The initial journal entry is:

Cash	Dr	3 000	
Share Capital	Cr		3 000
(Issue of shares)			

The following journal entry is made in 1 year's time:

Call	Dr	2 000	
Share Capital	Cr		2 000
(Call of $4 on 500 shares)			

When the call money is received from shareholders, the following journal entry is made:

Cash	Dr	2 000	
Call	Cr		2 000
(Receipt of call money)			

Directors may be given the power under the regulations governing the company's operations to forfeit shares where the call is not paid. For example, assume that in illustrative example 2.2 the holders of 10 shares declined to pay the $4 call. The company then forfeits the shares, and the following journal entry is made:

Share Capital	Dr	100	
Call	Cr		40
Forfeited Shares Account	Cr		60
(Forfeiture of 10 shares called to $10 and paid to $6 per share)			

Depending on the regulations in the country in which the company is incorporated, the balance in the forfeited shares account may be refunded to the shareholders and the shares cancelled; in this case the account is classified as a liability. If the balance in the forfeited shares account is retained by the company, the account could be called 'Forfeited Shares Reserve' and be included in equity. Alternatively, the company could decide to reissue the shares. For example, the shares could be reissued as fully paid to $10 per share on payment of $8 per share, with the forfeited shares account being used to fund the difference as well as any costs of reissue. Assuming all the shares were reissued, incurring costs of $5, and any balance of the reserve being returned to the former shareholders, the journal entries are shown below.

Cash	Dr	80	
Forfeited Shares Account	Dr	20	
Share Capital	Cr		100
(Reissue of shares)			
Forfeited Shares Account	Dr	40	
Share Issue Costs Payable	Cr		5
Payable to Shareholders	Cr		35
(Share issue costs and monies refundable to shareholders)			
Share Issue Costs Payable	Dr	5	
Payable to Shareholders	Dr	35	
Cash	Cr		40
(Payment of amounts owing)			

2.5.2 Issue of par value shares

Shares issued at a premium

Where shares are issued at a premium, the excess over the par value is credited to an equity account which may be called share premium, additional paid-in capital or share capital in excess of par. The share premium is then a component of contributed equity.

ILLUSTRATIVE EXAMPLE 2.3 Issue of par value shares at a premium

Bhutan Ltd issues 5000 shares of $1 par value at a premium of $2 per share. The journal entry is:

Cash	Dr	15 000	
Share Capital	Cr		5 000
Share Premium	Cr		10 000
(Issue of shares at a premium)			

Shares issued at a discount

Where shares are issued at a discount, the account used in relation to the discount can be the same as that used for a premium, or it can be a separate discount account. The accounting treatment will vary depending on the regulations governing discounts in particular jurisdictions.

ILLUSTRATIVE EXAMPLE 2.4 Issue of par value shares at a discount

Iran Ltd issued 5000 shares of $2 par value at a 50c discount. The journal entry is:

Cash	Dr	7 500	
Discount on Shares	Dr	2 500	
Share Capital	Cr		10 000
(Issue of shares at a discount)			

2.5.3 Oversubscriptions

An issue of shares by a company may be so popular that it is oversubscribed; that is, there are more applications for shares than shares to be issued. Some investors may then receive an allotment of fewer shares than they applied for, or may not be allotted any shares at all.

Figure 2.4 provides an example of the oversubscription of shares in relation to Australian drug delivery company Phosphagenics Limited.

FIGURE 2.4 Oversubscription of shares

Phosphagenics: SPP closes heavily oversubscribed
- $3 million raised; more than 4 times oversubscribed
- Funds now in place for lead pharmaceutical product trials

14 November 2011, Melbourne, Australia: Australian drug delivery technology company Phosphagenics Limited (ASX: POH, OTCQX: PPGNY) has closed its share purchase plan (SPP) heavily oversubscribed.

FIGURE 2.4 (continued)

The company has met its target of raising $3 million via the plan. This capital is in addition to the $24.1 million raised via recent placement to institutions and sophisticated investors. Following the scale-back and rounding of the SPP applications the Company has now allotted a total of 21 433 226 new shares at $0.14 a share.

Over $14 million in application monies was received by the 7 November 2011 SPP close date. For shareholders who applied for less than 1000 shares, they will receive their full applications. For all other applicants they will be subject to a minimum of 1000 shares and a maximum of 71 429 shares based on an 18.5 per cent pro rata allocation of the number of shares held by the applicant as at the record date of 20 October 2011.

Phosphagenics CEO, Dr Esra Ogru, said the outstanding response from shareholders meant the company had sufficient capital to accelerate development towards commercialisation of its lead pharmaceutical product — an oxycodone patch for pain management which uses the company's proprietary TPM® platform technology to deliver the powerful opioid transdermally.

Trials, which will continue throughout 2012, are expected to be completed by 2013.

Dr Ogru said the oversubscription was evidence investors had acknowledged the near-term potential of the technology and Phosphagenics' commercial prospects. This follows on from the heavily oversubscribed placement where most of the institutions and sophisticated investors received only a 20–30 per cent allocation of applications.

'As a result of our recent capital raising and this SPP, we now have sufficient funds to steer our lead pharmaceutical program through pivotal trials,' she said.

The number of ordinary shares now on issue is 967 565 957 shares with new SPP shares to begin trading on 16 November 2011. Refunds arising from the scale-back will be dispatched to shareholders later this week.

Source: Phosphagenics Limited (2011).

In most cases, excess application monies are simply refunded to the applicants. When this happens, the appropriate journal entries are:

Application	Dr	xxx	
Share Capital	Cr		xxx
(Issue of shares applied for)			
Application	Dr	xxx	
Cash	Dr	xxx	
Cash Trust	Cr		xxx
(Transfer from cash trust and refund of excess application money)			

Depending on the company's constitution or the terms of the prospectus, an entity may retain the excess application money as an advance on future calls. In this case the journal entry is:

Application	Dr	xxx	
Calls in Advance	Cr		xxx
Share Capital	Cr		xxx
(Issue of shares)			

China Ltd was incorporated on 1 July 2013. The directors offered to the general public 100 000 ordinary shares for subscription at an issue price of $2. The company received applications for 200 000 shares. The directors then decided to issue 150 000 shares, returning the balance of application money to the unsuccessful applicants.

The appropriate journal entries are:

Cash Trust	Dr	400 000	
Application	Cr		400 000
(Money received on application)			
Application	Dr	300 000	
Share Capital	Cr		300 000
(Issue of shares)			
Cash	Dr	300 000	
Application	Dr	100 000	
Cash Trust	Cr		400 000
(Transfer of cash on issue of shares and refund of excess application money)			

2.6 CONTRIBUTED EQUITY: SUBSEQUENT MOVEMENTS IN SHARE CAPITAL

Having floated the company, the directors may at a later stage decide to make changes to the share capital. For example, at its annual general meeting in March 2011, Pöyry plc, a global consulting and engineering company based in Finland, authorised its Board of Directors to issue new shares. This authorisation is shown in figure 2.5.

Authorisation to issue shares

The Annual General Meeting (AGM) on 10 March 2008 authorised the Board of Directors to decide to issue new shares and to convey the company's own shares held by the company in one or more tranches. The share issue can be carried out as a share issue against payment or without consideration on terms to be determined by the Board of Directors and in relation to a share issue against payment at a price to be determined by the Board of Directors.

A maximum of 11 600 000 new shares can be issued. A maximum of 5 800 000 own shares held by the company can be conveyed. The authorisation is in force for three years from the decision of the AGM.

At the end of 2010 totally 226 727 shares have been issued. After these directed share issues, the maximum number of shares that may be conveyed is 5 573 273 shares.

The Board of Directors proposes that the General Meeting on 10 March 2011 authorise to decide to issue new shares and to convey the Company's own shares held by the Company in one or more tranches. The share issue can be carried out as a share issue against payment or without consideration on terms to be determined by the Board of Directors and in relation to a share issue against payment at a price to determined by the Board of Directors. A maximum of 11 800 000 new shares can be issued. A maximum of 5 900 000 own shares held by the company can be conveyed. The authorisation shall be effective for a period of 18 months.

FIGURE 2.5 An authorisation to increase share capital, Pöyry plc
Source: Pöyry plc (2011, p. 65).

The example in figure 2.5 shows an authorisation for an increase in share capital, but share capital may be either increased or decreased. This section of the chapter discusses the methods a company may use to increase its share capital. Section 2.7 examines how a company may decrease its share capital. Figure 2.6 shows the rising trend in aggregate capital raising on the London Stock Exchange between 1995 and 2009.

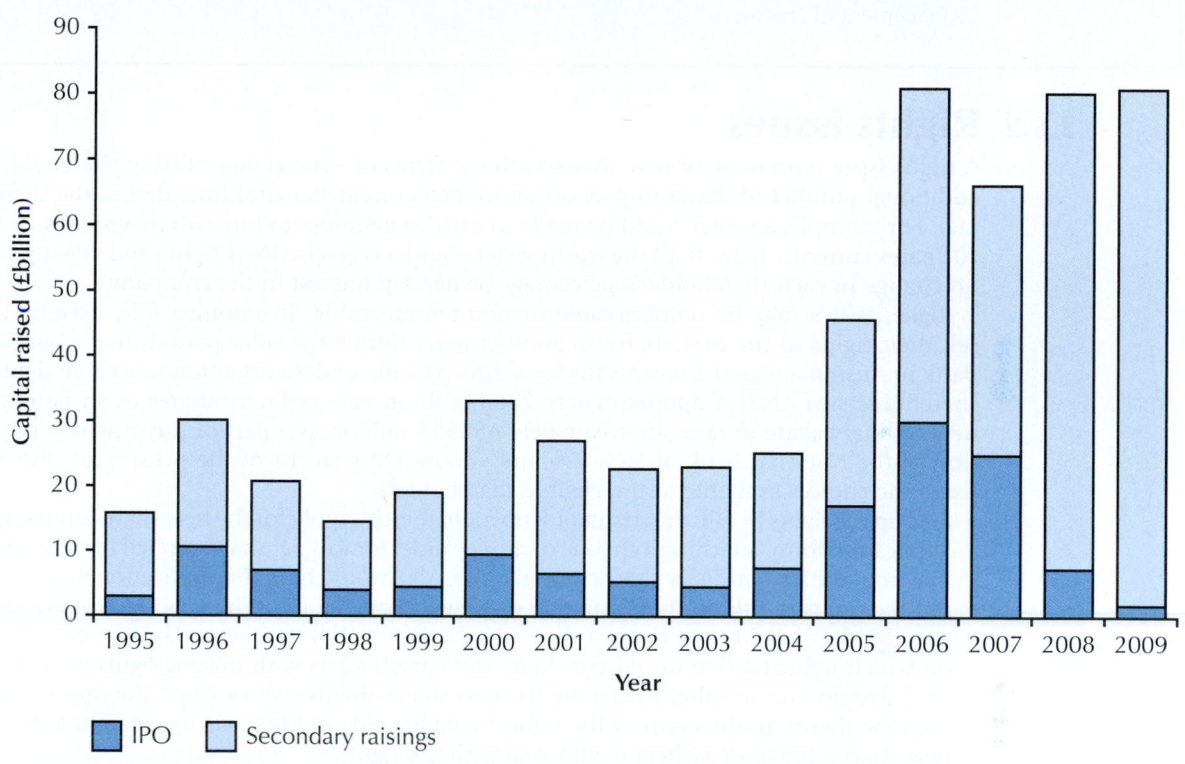

FIGURE 2.6 Capital raised on the London Stock Exchange in the United Kingdom 1995–2009
Source: ASX (2010, p. 8).

2.6.1 Placements of shares

Rather than issue new shares through an issue to the public or current shareholders, the company may decide to place the shares with specific investors such as life insurance companies and superannuation funds. The advantages to the company of a placement of shares are:
- *speed* — a placement can be effected in a short period of time
- *price* — because a placement is made to other than existing shareholders, and to a market that is potentially more informed and better funded, the issue price of the new shares may be closer to the market price at the date of issue
- *direction* — the shares may be placed with investors who approve of the directions of the company, or who will not interfere in the formation of company policies
- *prospectus* — in some cases, a placement can occur without the need for a detailed prospectus to be prepared.

There are potential disadvantages to the existing shareholders from private placements in that the current shareholders will have their interest in the company diluted as a result of the placement. In some countries, the securities regulations place limits on the amounts of placements of shares without the approval of existing shareholders. Further disadvantages to current shareholders can occur if the company places the shares at a large discount. Again, securities laws are generally enacted to ensure that management cannot abuse the placement process and that current shareholders are protected.

Thailand Ltd placed 5000 no-par ordinary shares at $5 each with Turkey Ltd.
The entry in the journals of Thailand Ltd is:

Cash	Dr	25 000	
Share Capital	Cr		25 000
(Placement of shares)			

2.6.2 Rights issues

A rights issue is an issue of new shares with the terms of issue giving existing shareholders the right to an additional number of shares in proportion to their current shareholding; that is, the shares are offered pro rata. For example, an offer could be made to each shareholder to buy two new shares on the basis of every 10 shares currently held. If all the existing shareholders exercise their rights and take up the shares, there is no change in each shareholder's percentage ownership interest in the company.

Rights issues may be renounceable or non-renounceable. If renounceable, existing shareholders may sell their rights to the new shares to another party during the offer period. In November 2003, the ANZ Bank in Australia issued a prospectus for a 2-for-11 fully underwritten renounceable rights issue to existing shareholders of ANZ of approximately 276.7 million new ordinary shares at an issue price of A$13 per new ordinary share to raise approximately A$3597 million as a part of the purchase price for the acquisition of the National Bank of New Zealand Group. On page 14 of the prospectus, the ANZ Bank (2003) listed the choices available to the eligible shareholders:

- take up the rights in full: the shareholders would thereby apply for the new shares on the appropriate application form, attaching a cheque or money order for $13 per share applied for. The bank noted (page 8) that until the new ordinary shares were allotted, ANZ would hold the application monies in a bank account.
- sell the rights in full on the Australian or New Zealand stock exchanges (ASX or NZSX). The shareholders would then instruct their stockbrokers to sell the rights. The prospectus specified the dates on which rights trading would conclude, and shareholders with unsold rights would have to make a final decision on whether to acquire the new shares themselves or forgo the opportunity to take up the new shares. In the event of the rights being unsold, and the existing shareholders not taking up the new shares, the underwriters would deal with the rights.
- sell part of the rights on ASX or NZSX and take up the balance
- transfer all or part of the rights to another person other than via ASX or NZSX. The existing shareholder would then forward to the ANZ a completed renunciation form, the transferee's application form and cheque or money order.
- do nothing. In this case, the underwriters would endeavour to sell the rights to institutional investors at a minimum of $13 per share, with the proceeds less brokerage and other expenses being paid to the existing shareholders.

If the rights issue is non-renounceable, a shareholder is not allowed to sell his or her rights to the new shares and must either accept or reject the offer to acquire new shares in the company.

A major difference between an issue of shares to the public and a rights issue is that with the former, the offer comes from the applicant (the prospective shareholder) and it is for the company to accept or reject the offer. With a rights issue, the prospectus constitutes an offer, which may be accepted or rejected by the existing shareholder.

Investors have to remain aware of events occurring around the time of the rights issue in order to decide whether or not to commit to the investment. Figure 2.7, examining the rights issue offered by the mining giant Rio Tinto, demonstrates this reality.

FIGURE 2.7 Rights issues, Rio Tinto

The right story on Rio's rights

A rights issue is a capital raising exercise that sees companies offer new shares directly to their existing investors. It's a corporate event that holders of CFDs will find themselves participating in if they have positions in the particular companies. This prospect makes it important to be aware of how things can unfold.

FIGURE 2.7 *(continued)*

The rights issue announced in early June by Rio Tinto aimed at raising money to reduce the multi-billion dollar debt it accumulated in 2007 to buy the Alcan aluminium group provides some insights into this. The offer invited share holders to buy 21 new shares for every 40 they owned and pay $28.29 for each new share.

While the offer price came across as a huge discount to the $70-plus Rio share price when it was announced, the first point that traders must appreciate is that this apparent generosity is illusory.

The $28.29 payment is actually like a second instalment amount because when the rights are first allocated to holders they actually have a value. It is a value that can be realised during the trading period that is part of a traditional rights issue exercise.

This trading period which lasts for a week is the time existing holders have to decide whether they will either sell their rights on the market or take up the offer and pay the $28.29 to secure the new shares. When rights trading begins, the illusory aspects of rights offers is highlighted by the value of existing shares falling to reflect the value of the rights that holders now have.

In the case of the Rio offer, when rights trading began in mid June the shares fell from the early $70s region into the mid- and then early $50s as rights changed hands at prices that during the first two days ranged from nearly $32 to just above $24. This trading brought to a head considerable CFD trading activity in Rio Tinto over the fortnight leading up to the rights trading period.

The activity included short holders who were busy trying to get out so they would not have to take further short holdings at the $28.29 rights exercise price.

Then there were the long CFD holders who held positions before the rights announcement and smartly decided to take profits as the Rio share price surged from $66 to $77.

There were also speculators who took long Rio CFDs in the days just before the rights began trading when the share or CFD positions over the shares were still available with the rights attached. They then sold the rights and the stock when Rio went in ex rights trading when positions no longer came with any rights.

An example of this scenario was a trader who acquired 1000 Rio CFDs at $71.80, held the long position overnight, and was allocated 525 Rio rights at a zero cost when the shares went ex-rights and then sold the rights for $30 each and closed out the long position at a price of $59. While there was a loss of $12 800 on the long Rio CFD position, this was more than made up by the $15 750 gain on the rights.

Acquiring CFDs based on a $71.80 Rio share price saw the trader with a position that was worth $71 800 that required a 10 per cent initial margin or $7180. The combined proceeds from the sale were $74 750 and after brokerage and long position interest on the overnight holding, the net profit was $2800.

While this was a smart trade that worked well, it is worth noting that the 10 per cent fall in the Rio share price after rights trading went into the second day would have resulted in a close to $5000 loss on the trade had the position been closed out then. A day later and the rights were down to $24-to-$25 and the shares to $52-to-$54.

A couple of extra points worth noting about CFDs and rights issues:
- The decline in the underlying investment price following the start of rights trading will see long traders facing a margin call on this loss. This will probably require most traders to sell their rights.
- Where a trader is allocated any rights, you need to be aware that this will require some action to realise this value, either selling them over the week long trading period or taking them up by paying the exercise price before a nominated deadline.

Source: Wasiliev, J (2009).

During the 2008–09 global financial crisis (GFC), the largest industry sector raising capital was the financial sector. Figure 2.8 shows the major secondary capital types raised by Australian companies during the GFC period (ASX 2010). The main forms of capital raising were placements, rights offers, dividend reinvestment plans and share purchase plans.

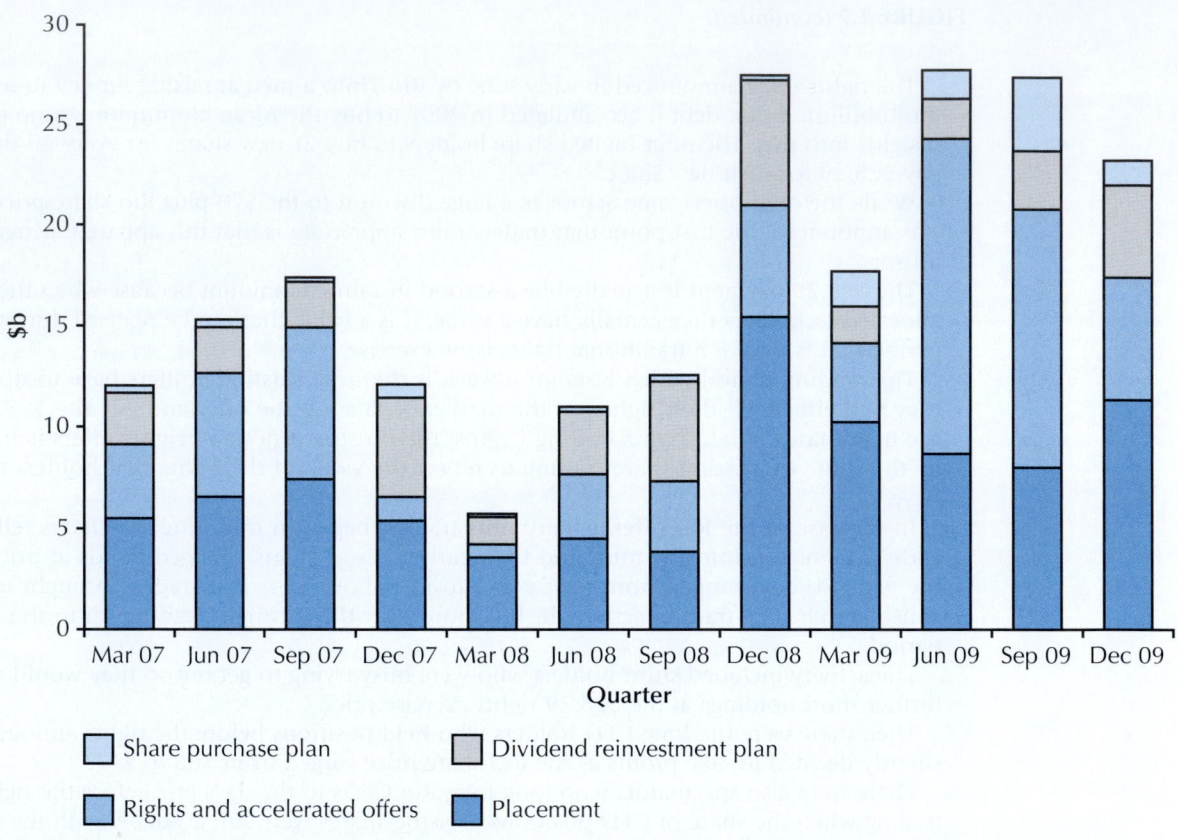

FIGURE 2.8 Secondary issues in Australia during the GFC
Source: ASX (2010, p. 19).

Legend:
- Share purchase plan
- Dividend reinvestment plan
- Rights and accelerated offers
- Placement

ILLUSTRATIVE EXAMPLE 2.7 Rights issue

Pakistan Ltd planned to raise $3.6 million from shareholders through a renounceable one-for-six rights issue. The terms of the issue were 6 million no-par shares to be issued at 60c each, applications to be received by 15 April 2013. The rights issue was fully underwritten. By the due date, the company had received applications for 5 million shares from existing shareholders or parties to whom they had sold their rights. The underwriter acquired the other 1 million shares, and the shares were issued on 20 April 2013.

The journal entries in the company's records are:

April 15	Cash	Dr	3 000 000	
	Application	Cr		3 000 000
	(Application monies)			
	Receivable from Underwriter	Dr	600 000	
	Application	Cr		600 000
	(Amount due from underwriter)			
April 20	Cash	Dr	600 000	
	Receivable from Underwriter	Cr		600 000
	(Receipt from underwriter)			
	Application	Dr	3 600 000	
	Share Capital	Cr		3 600 000
	(Issue of shares)			

2.6.3 Options

A company-issued share option is an instrument that gives the holder the right but not the obligation to buy a certain number of shares in the company by a specified date at a stated price. For example, a company could issue options that gave an investor the right to acquire shares in the company at $2 each, with the options having to be exercised before 31 December 2013. The option holder is taking a risk in that the share price may not reach $2 (the option is 'out of the money') or the share price may exceed $2 (the option is 'in the money').

Where the option holder exercises the option, the company increases its share capital as it issues the shares to the option holder. The company could issue these options to its employees as a part of their remuneration package; or in conjunction with another share issue, rights issue or placement as an incentive to take up the shares offered. The option may be issued free. In the case of options issued to employees, for example, the employees may receive the options as payment for past service. Alternatively, the options may only vest; that is, be exercisable if certain conditions are met, such as the employee remaining with the company for a specified period of time. Accounting for such options is covered in IFRS 2 *Share-based Payment*, the details of which are beyond the scope of this chapter. One of the key features of IFRS 2 is the establishment of the measurement principles in relation to such options. In particular, at the date the options are granted, the fair value of the options is determined and this is used in accounting for the options.

To illustrate: assume a company at 30 June 2013 issues 100 options valued at $1 each to a key executive as a payment for past services. Each option entitles the executive to acquire a share in the company at a price of $3, the current market price of the company shares being $2.90. Assume that on 30 November the share price reaches $3.10 and the executive exercises the option. The journal entries required are shown below.

June 30	Wages Expense	Dr	100	
	Options	Cr		100
	(Options granted to executive)			
Nov. 30	Cash	Dr	300	
	Options	Dr	100	
	Share Capital	Cr		400
	(Exercise of options issued)			

If the share price did not reach $3 within the specified life of the option, then the options would lapse. According to IFRS 2, paragraph 16, the company is then allowed to transfer the balance of the options account to other equity accounts.

Where the options are sold to investors, the company will record an increase in equity. For example, assume A Ltd issued 20 000 options at 50c each to acquire shares in A Ltd at $4 per share. The initial entry recorded by A Ltd is:

Cash	Dr	10 000	
Options*	Cr		10 000
(Issue of options)			

*This account may be called 'Options Reserve' or simply 'Other Equity'.

Options generally have to be exercised by a specific date. Assume that in the case of A Ltd the options had to be exercised by 30 June 2013, and the holders of 18 000 options exercised their rights to acquire A Ltd shares. The journal entries required are:

Cash	Dr	72 000	
Share Capital	Cr		72 000
(Issue of shares on exercise of options)			
Options	Dr	9 000	
Share Capital	Cr		9 000
(Exercise of options)			

Note that the issue price of those options exercised is treated as part of share capital; in essence, these shareholders are paying $4.50 for their shares in A Ltd. However, the journal entries shown may not always be the appropriate ones. The journal entries that need to be made when options are issued may be affected in particular jurisdictions by legal and taxation implications. For example, in Australia it is possible to 'taint' share capital by transferring amounts to that account from retained earnings or other reserves. This affects the subsequent taxation of dividends and returns of capital. The choice of equity accounts used and accounting for movements between these accounts must always be taken after gaining an understanding of legal and taxation effects.

For the options not exercised, the entity could transfer the options balance of $1000 to share capital or a reserve account including retained earnings. Again, legal and taxation implications should be considered in choosing the appropriate accounts to be used. For the example above where the holders of 2000 options did not exercise those options, the journal entry required when the options lapse is:

Options	Dr	1 000	
Options Reserve	Cr		1 000
(Transfer of lapsed options)			

2.6.4 Share warrants

Another form of option is the company-issued warrant. The difference between a warrant and an option is that the warrant is generally attached to another form of financing. For example, the warrant may be attached to an issue of debt, or be given as an incentive to acquire a large parcel of shares in a share issue as an incentive to be involved in the capital raising. The warrants may be detachable or non-detachable. If the latter, then they cannot be traded separately from the shares or debt package to which they were attached. In either case, the warrant has a value and accounting for the issue of warrants is the same as that shown in the previous section for options.

2.6.5 Bonus issues

A bonus issue is an issue of shares to existing shareholders in proportion to their current shareholdings at no cost to the shareholders. The company uses its reserves balances or retained earnings to make the issue. The bonus issue is a transfer from one equity account to another, so it does not increase or decrease the equity of the company. Instead, it increases the share capital and decreases another equity account of the company.

To illustrate: assume a company has a share capital consisting of 500 000 shares. If it makes a 1-for-20 bonus issue from its $100 000 general reserve, it will issue 25 000 shares pro rata to its current shareholders. The journal entry required is:

General Reserve	Dr	100 000	
Share Capital	Cr		100 000
(Bonus issue of 25 000 shares from general reserve)			

Although the bonus issue does not have any effect on the equity of the company, empirical evidence from research into the stockmarket effects of bonus issues shows that share prices tend to increase as a result of bonus issues. The explanation for this effect is that the bonus issue is generally an indicator of future dividend increases. Other reasons for a company making a bonus issue include defending against a takeover bid, particularly following the revaluation of the entity's assets; providing a return to the shareholders; or lowering the current price of the company's shares in the expectation that a lower price per share may make them more tradeable.

2.6.6 Share-based transactions

A company may acquire assets, including other entities, with the consideration for the acquisition being shares in the company itself. Accounting for this form of transaction is covered in chapter 14. Accounting for share-based payments is covered in chapter 8.

2.7 SHARE CAPITAL: SUBSEQUENT DECREASES IN SHARE CAPITAL

A company may decrease the number of shares issued by buying back some of its own shares. The extent to which a company may buy back its own shares and the frequency with which it may do so are generally governed by specific laws within a jurisdiction. A key feature of such regulations is the protection of creditors, as the company is reducing equity by using cash that would have been available to repay debt. Companies may undertake a share buy-back to:

- increase the worth per share of the remaining shares
- manage the capital structure by reducing equity
- most efficiently manage surplus funds held by the company, rather than pay a dividend or reinvest in other ventures.

IFRSs do not prescribe any accounting treatment for share buy-backs. Consider the situation where an entity has issued the following no-par shares over a period of years:

200 000 shares at $1.00	$ 200 000
100 000 shares at $1.50	150 000
200 000 shares at $2.00	400 000
500 000 shares	$ 750 000

Assume the total equity of the entity consists of:

Share capital	$ 750 000
Asset revaluation surplus	20 000
Retained earnings	230 000
	$ 1 000 000

If the company now buys back 50 000 shares for $2.20 per share, a total of $110 000, what accounts should be affected by the buy-back? Is it necessary to determine which shares from past issues have been repurchased?

In essence, the composition of the $1 million equity of the entity is relatively unimportant — it is all equity. The composition is only important if there are tax or dividend distribution issues associated with particular accounts. In the absence of such considerations, whether the equity is share capital or retained earnings is irrelevant. This is demonstrated below:

	Equity composition A	or	Equity composition B
Share capital (500 000 shares)	$ 750 000		$ 550 000
Asset revaluation surplus	20 000		150 000
Retained earnings	230 000		300 000
	$ 1 000 000		$ 1 000 000

The composition of equity here is *per se* irrelevant. Hence, in accounting for the share buy-back, it is immaterial what accounts are affected. The $110 000 write-off could conceivably be taken totally against share capital or retained earnings, or proportionally against all three components of equity. One possible entry is:

Share Capital	Dr	100 000	
Retained Earnings	Dr	10 000	
Cash	Cr		110 000
(Buy-back of 50 000 shares for $110 000)			

If the shares had been issued at a specific par value, then it would be necessary to identify which particular parcel of shares had been repurchased. The share capital would be reduced by the relevant number of shares repurchased times the par value, and the share premium reduced by the appropriate amount relating to that raised on the original issue of shares not identified as being repurchased. However, any remaining balance could be adjusted against any equity account other than the share capital and share premium accounts.

An example of a repurchase of shares is that undertaken by Pöyry plc in 2011. The authorisation for the company to acquire its own shares is shown in figure 2.9.

Authorisation to acquire the company's own shares

The AGM on 11 March 2010 authorised the Board of Directors to decide on acquiring maximum of 5 800 000 own shares with distributable funds. The company's own shares can be acquired in accordance with the decision of the Board of Directors either through public trading or by public offer at their market price at the time of purchase.

The authorisation is effective for a period of 18 months. The Board has not exercised the authorisation during 2010.

The Board of Directors proposes that the General Meeting on 10 March 2011 authorise the Board of Directors to decide on the acquisition of a maximum of 5 900 000 of the Company's own shares by using distributable funds. It is proposed that the authorisation be effective for a period of 18 months. The authorisation granted to the Board of Directors regarding acquisition of the Company's own shares in the previous Annual General Meeting shall expire simultaneously.

FIGURE 2.9 Repurchase of shares, Pöyry plc
Source: Pöyry plc (2011, p. 65).

In some countries, when shares are reacquired, they are held in treasury for reissue instead of being cancelled. Such shares are then referred to as 'treasury shares', and are essentially the same as unissued share capital. For example, if an entity acquires 10 000 of its own shares at $12 per share, it would pass the following entry to record this repurchase:

Treasury Shares	Dr	12 000	
Cash	Cr		12 000
(Repurchase of shares)			

In Nokia's 2010 balance sheet (see figure 2.1), the treasury shares are shown as a reduction in total equity because the share capital of the entity has effectively been reduced by the repurchase of the shares.

2.8 RESERVES

'Reserves' is the generic term for all equity accounts other than contributed equity. A major component is the retained earnings account. This account accumulates the annual profit or loss earned by an entity, and is the primary account from which appropriations are made in the form of dividends. As noted in paragraph 88 of IAS 1 *Presentation of Financial Statements*, this standard requires all items of income and expense recognised in a period to be included in profit or loss unless another standard requires otherwise. Hence, in general, the retained earnings account will accumulate the profit or loss earned over the life of the entity. However, as paragraph 89 also notes, other standards require some gains and losses to be reported directly as changes in equity. Some examples are:

- revaluation of property, plant and equipment (see chapter 11)
- particular foreign exchange differences (see chapter 28)
- remeasurements of available-for-sale financial assets (see chapter 7).

These gains and losses are then recognised as part of reserves. As noted in paragraph 81A of IAS 1, entities are required to disclose movements in these accounts as other comprehensive income for the period.

2.8.1 Retained earnings

'Retained earnings' has the same meaning as 'retained profits' and 'accumulated profit or loss'. The key change in this account is the addition of the profit or loss for the current period. The main other movements in the retained earnings account are:

- dividends paid or declared

- transfers to and from reserves
- changes in accounting policy and errors (see IAS 8 *Accounting Policies, Changes in Accounting Estimates and Errors,* discussed in detail in chapter 18).

Dividends are a distribution from the company to its owners. It is generally the case, under companies legislation, that dividends can be paid only from profits, and not from capital. In some jurisdictions, companies must comply with a solvency test before paying dividends. The purpose in both situations is to protect the creditors, as any money paid to shareholders is money unavailable for paying creditors.

Dividends are sometimes divided into interim and final dividends. Interim dividends are paid during the financial year, while final dividends are declared by the directors at financial year-end for payment sometime after the end of the reporting period. In some companies, the eventual payment of the final dividends is subject to approval of the dividend by the annual general meeting. With the final dividend, there is some debate as to when the company should raise a liability for the dividend, particularly where payment of the dividend is subject to shareholder approval. Some would argue that until approval is received there is only a contingent liability, the entity not having a present obligation to pay the dividend until approval is received. Others argue that there is a constructive obligation existing at year-end and, given customary business practice, the entity has a liability at the end of the reporting period.

In this regard, paragraphs 12 and 13 of IAS 10 *Events after the Reporting Period* state:

12. If an entity declares dividends to holders of equity instruments (as defined in IAS 32 *Financial Instruments: Presentation*) after the reporting period, the entity shall not recognise those dividends as a liability at the end of the reporting period.
13. If dividends are declared after the reporting period but before the financial statements are authorised for issue, the dividends are not recognised as a liability at the end of the reporting period because no obligation exists at that time. Such dividends are disclosed in the notes in accordance with IAS 1 *Presentation of Financial Statements.*

If the dividends are not declared at the end of the reporting period, no liability is recognised at the end of the reporting period. When shareholder approval is required for dividends declared prior to the end of the reporting period, a liability should be recognised only once the annual general meeting approves the dividends, because before that date the entity does not have a present obligation. Until that occurs, the declared dividend is only a contingent liability. (See chapter 5 for further discussion on provisions and contingencies.) It is expected that companies that prefer to raise a liability at year-end will change their regulations or constitution so that dividends can be declared without the need for shareholder approval.

ILLUSTRATIVE EXAMPLE 2.8 Dividends

During the period ending 30 June 2013, the following events occurred in relation to Oman Ltd:

2012	
Sept. 25	Annual general meeting approves the final dividend of $10 000.
Sept. 30	Oman Ltd pays the final dividend to shareholders.

2013	
Jan. 10	Oman Ltd pays an interim dividend of $8 000.
June 30	Oman Ltd declares a final dividend of $12 000, this dividend requiring shareholder approval at the next AGM.

Required

Prepare the journal entries to record the dividend transactions of Oman Ltd.

Solution

2012				
Sept. 25	Dividends Declared	Dr	10 000	
	Dividends Payable	Cr		10 000
	(Dividend of $10 000 authorised by annual meeting)			

Sept. 30	Dividends Payable	Dr	10 000	
	Cash	Cr		10 000
	(Payment of dividend)			
2013				
Jan. 10	Interim Dividend Paid	Dr	8 000	
	Cash	Cr		8 000
	(Payment of interim dividend)			

Notes:
1. No entry is required in relation to the final dividend of $12 000. A contingent liability would be recorded in the notes to the 2013 financial statements.
2. The journal entries contain temporary accounts such as 'Dividends Declared' and 'Interim Dividend Paid'. These accounts are useful in preparing the statement of changes in equity (see section 2.9.2) as well as in the worksheet used in the preparation of consolidated financial statements (see chapter 24). At the end of the reporting period, these temporary accounts are transferred to retained earnings:

	Retained Earnings	Dr	18 000	
	Dividends Declared	Cr		10 000
	Interim Dividend Paid	Cr		8 000
	(Closing entry)			

2.8.2 Other components of equity

Some examples of reserves other than retained earnings are shown below.

Asset revaluation surplus

IAS 16 *Property, Plant and Equipment* allows entities a choice in the measurement of these assets. In particular, entities may choose between measuring the assets at cost (the cost model) or at fair value (the revaluation model). If the fair value basis is chosen, revaluation increases are recognised in other comprehensive income and accumulated in equity via an asset revaluation surplus. (Details of the accounting under a fair value basis for property, plant and equipment is covered in chapter 11.)

The requirement to use the asset revaluation surplus is effectively a measure adopted by the IASB to stop the increase in the fair value of the assets being recognised immediately in profit or loss for the period. It may be argued that this is an application of the prudence concept in that the fair values of the assets may decline in a later period, and to allow the recognition in current period profits of movements in the fair values of assets would introduce volatility into the profit numbers. However, certain movements in the asset revaluation surplus are required by IAS 1 to be disclosed as an item of other comprehensive income in the statement of profit or loss and other comprehensive income.

Having created an asset revaluation surplus, an entity is not restricted in its subsequent disposition. It may be used for payment of dividends or be transferred to other reserve accounts including retained earnings. Amounts recognised directly in the asset revaluation surplus cannot subsequently be recognised in profit or loss for the period even when the revalued asset is disposed of.

Foreign currency translation differences

Foreign currency translation differences arise when foreign operations are translated from one currency into another currency for presentation purposes. (Details of the establishment of this account can be found in chapter 28.) The changes in wealth as a result of the translation process are thereby not taken through profit or loss for the period, and are recognised in profit or loss only if and when the investor disposes of its interest in the foreign operation.

Fair value differences

Under IAS 39 *Financial Instruments: Recognition and Measurement*, paragraph 55, gains and losses on available-for-sale financial assets are recognised directly in equity until the financial asset is derecognised. At this time, the cumulative gain or loss previously recognised in equity is recognised in profit or loss. This is a situation where the IASB allows the recycling of reserves to income, an accounting treatment unavailable with other reserves.

Under IFRS 9 *Financial Instruments* (which will eventually replace IAS 39), at initial recognition, financial assets and liabilities are measured at fair value. Paragraph 5.7.5 of IFRS 9 permits an entity to make an irrevocable election to present in other comprehensive income changes in the fair value of an investment in an equity instrument that is not held for trading. It will not, however, allow recycling of reserves to income.

As an example of the disclosure of reserves, the note disclosure provided by Qantas in its 2011 annual report is shown in figure 2.10.

23. Capital and reserves	Qantas Group	
Reserves	**2011 $m**	**2010 $m**
Employee compensation reserve	65	53
Hedge reserve	80	85
Foreign currency translation reserve	(60)	(29)
	85	109

Nature and purpose of reserves
Employee compensation reserve
The fair value of equity plans granted is recognised in the employee compensation reserve over the vesting period. This reserve will be reversed against treasury shares when the underlying shares vest and transfer to the employee. No gain of loss is recognised in the Consolidated Income Statement on the purchase, sale, issue or cancellation of Qantas' own equity instruments.

Hedge reserve
The hedge reserve comprises the effective portion of the cumulative net change in the fair value of cash flow hedging instruments related to future forecast transactions.

Foreign currency translation reserve
The foreign currency translation reserve comprises all foreign exchange differences arising from the translation of the Financial Statements of foreign controlled entities and associates, as well as from the translation of liabilities that form part of the Qantas Group's net investment in a foreign controlled entity.

FIGURE 2.10 Disclosure of reserves
Source: Qantas (2011, p. 81).

Entities may make transfers between these reserve accounts, or between reserve accounts and other equity accounts such as retained earnings. Where there is a bonus share dividend, a transfer may be made between reserve accounts and share capital. When accounting for retained earnings, as when accounting for dividends, temporary accounts (namely 'Transfer to/from reserve') are used, these being closed at the end of the period to retained earnings. Chapter 11 discusses in detail the application of the revaluation model to property, plant and equipment and the use of that model. IAS 16 *Property, Plant and Equipment* requires the use of an asset revaluation surplus account in accounting for a revaluation increase. Although not specifically stated in IAS 16, increases in an asset revaluation surplus cannot be made via transfers from other reserves or retained earnings because the surplus arises as a result of applying the revaluation model. Paragraph 41 of IAS 16 covers the accounting for an asset revaluation surplus subsequent to its creation. There is no requirement that an asset revaluation surplus must be transferred to retained earnings on derecognition of a revalued asset. IAS 16, however, allows transfers from the surplus account when a revalued asset is derecognised or progressively as the asset is used by the entity.

During the period ending 30 June 2013, the following events occurred in relation to the company Malaysia Ltd:

Jan. 10	$10 000 transferred from retained earnings to general reserve
Feb. 18	$4 000 transferred from asset revaluation surplus to retained earnings
June 15	Bonus share dividend of $50 000, half from general reserve and half from retained earnings

Required

Prepare the journal entries to record these transactions.

Solution

2013				
Jan. 10	Transfer to General Reserve	Dr	10 000	
	General Reserve	Cr		10 000
	(Transfer to general reserve)			
Feb. 18	Asset Revaluation Surplus	Dr	4 000	
	Transfer from Asset Revaluation Surplus	Cr		4 000
	(Transfer from asset revaluation surplus)			
June 15	General Reserve	Dr	25 000	
	Bonus Dividend Paid	Dr	25 000	
	Share Capital	Cr		50 000
	(Bonus issue of shares)			
June 30	Retained Earnings	Dr	31 000	
	Transfer from Asset Revaluation Surplus	Dr	4 000	
	Transfer to General Reserve	Cr		10 000
	Bonus Dividend Paid	Cr		25 000
	(Closing entry)			

2.9 DISCLOSURE

Disclosures in relation to equity are detailed in IAS 1 *Presentation of Financial Statements*. The disclosures relate to specific items of equity as well as the preparation of a statement of changes in equity.

2.9.1 Specific disclosures

The specific disclosures illustrated in figure 2.11 are required by paragraphs 79, 137 and 138 of IAS 1.

FIGURE 2.11 Specific disclosures on equity required by IAS 1

	IAS 1 para.
Note 21: Company information Hong Kong Ltd is a public company registered in Barcelona, Spain. The company's principal activities are the manufacture of woollen goods, ranging from clothing to furnishings for homes and offices. The company is a subsidiary of China Ltd.	*138(a), (b), (c)*
Note 22: Share capital and reserves The company has only one class of share capital, namely ordinary shares. Details in relation to these shares are: • 2 million shares have been authorised for issue by the company	*79(a)* *(i)*

FIGURE 2.11 *(continued)*

	IAS 1 para.
• 500 000 shares have been issued fully paid to €3, and 250 000 shares have been issued at €4, but are paid only to €3 per share	*(ii)*
• the shares issued are no-par shares.	*(iii)*
Number of shares issued at 1 January 2013 500 000	*(iv)*
Issued during 2013 250 000	
Number of shares issued at 31 December 2013 750 000	
There are no restrictions on dividends payable to the shareholders.	*(v)*
There are no shares held by subsidiaries or associates of Hong Kong Ltd, and the company has not repurchased any shares issued.	*(vi)*
The company has issued 50 000 options to current shareholders, each option entitling the holder to buy an ordinary share in Hong Kong Ltd at €2.70, the options having to be exercised by 30 June 2014.	*(vii)*
Reserves	*79(b)*
The plant maintenance reserve of €140 000 was established to inform those with a financial interest in the company that it had a major claim on future funds in relation to the need to maintain the plant in accordance with Spanish government regulations.	
The asset revaluation surplus of €95 000 has arisen as the company uses the revaluation model to measure its landholdings.	
Retained earnings accumulates the annual profit or loss of the entity, other than gains or losses taken directly to equity, and the balance at the end of the reporting period represents the undistributed profits of the entity.	
Note 23: Dividends	*137(a)*
The directors of Hong Kong Ltd in December 2013 proposed dividends of €1 per share for fully paid shares and €0.75 for the partly paid shares, giving a total proposed dividend of €687 500. These dividends have not been recognised in the accounts because their payment is subject to approval by the shareholders at the annual general meeting.	

2.9.2 Statement of changes in equity

Paragraph 106 of IAS 1 requires the preparation of a statement of changes in equity. This paragraph requires the statement to show the following:

(a) total comprehensive income for the period, showing separately the total amounts attributable to owners of the parent and to non-controlling interests;

(b) for each component of equity, the effects of retrospective application or retrospective restatement recognised in accordance with IAS 8; and

(c) [deleted]

(d) for each component of equity, a reconciliation between the carrying amount at the beginning and the end of the period, separately disclosing changes resulting from:
   (i) profit or loss;
   (ii) other comprehensive income; and
   (iii) transactions with owners in their capacity as owners, showing separately contributions by and distributions to owners and changes in ownership interests in subsidiaries that do not result in a loss of control.

These requirements can be met in a number of ways, including using a columnar format. The statement of changes in equity must contain the information in paragraph 106 of IAS 1. The information required by paragraph 107 in relation to dividends may be included in the statement of changes in equity or disclosed in the notes.

Figure 2.12 is a pro forma statement of changes in equity using a non-columnar format. In figure 2.13, the statement of changes in equity disclosed in the 2011 annual report of Australia and New Zealand Banking Group Ltd (ANZ Banking Group Ltd) demonstrates a columnar format for this statement, while its related note displays the non-columnar format.

Statement of changes in equity for the year ended 30 June 2010 millions

	Note	Consolidated		Attributable to shareholders of the parent		The company	
		2010	2009	2010	2009	2010	2009
Comprehensive income Attributable to: Owners of the parent Non-controlling interest							
Share capital Balance at start of year Dividend reinvestment plan Group employee share acquisition scheme Group share option scheme New issues Share buy-back Balance at end of year							
Reserves							
Asset revaluation surplus Balance at start of year Revaluation increase Transfers Balance at end of year							
Foreign currency translation differences Balance at start of year Currency translation adjustments Balance at end of year							
Business combination valuation reserve Balance at start of year Increments — new business combinations Transfers to other reserves Balance at end of year							
Retained earnings Total income and expense for the period Balance of retained earnings at start of year Total available for appropriation Dividends paid or declared Balance of retained earnings at end of year							
Total equity at end of year							

FIGURE 2.12 Pro forma note disclosures relating to the statement of changes in equity in accordance with IAS 1, paragraph 106

FIGURE 2.13 Statement of changes in equity and its related note disclosures for ANZ Banking Group Ltd

Statement of changes in equity for the year ended 30 September

Consolidated	Ordinary share capital $m	Preference shares $m	Reserves¹ $m	Retained earnings $m	Shareholders' equity attributable to equity holders of the Bank $m	Non-controlling interests $m	Total shareholders' equity $m
As at 1 October 2009	**19 151**	**871**	**(1 787)**	**14 129**	**32 364**	**65**	**32 429**
Profit for the period	—	—	—	4 501	4 501	4	4 505
Other comprehensive income	—	—	(795)	(4)	(799)	—	(799)
Total comprehensive income for the period	—	—	(795)	4 497	3 702	4	3 706
Transactions with equity holders in their capacity as equity holders:							
Dividends paid	—	—	—	(2 678)	(2 678)	—	(2 678)
Dividend reinvestment plan	1 007	—	—	—	1 007	—	1 007
Other equity movements:							
Group employee share acquisition scheme	51	—	—	—	51	—	51
Share based payments	—	—	7	—	7	—	7
Group share option scheme	37	—	—	—	37	—	37
Treasury shares OnePath Australia adjustment	(360)	—	—	—	(360)	—	(360)
Adjustment to opening retained earnings on adoption of revised accounting standard AASB 3R	—	—	—	(39)	(39)	—	(39)
Other changes	—	—	(12)	12	—	(5)	(5)
As at 30 September 2010	**19 886**	**871**	**(2 587)**	**15 921**	**34 091**	**64**	**34 155**
Profit for the period	—	—	—	5 355	5 355	8	5 363
Other comprehensive income	—	—	528	(10)	518	—	518
Total comprehensive income for the period	—	—	528	5 345	5 873	8	5 881
Transactions with equity holders in their capacity as equity holders:							
Dividends paid	—	—	—	(3 503)	(3 503)	—	(3 503)
Dividend income on Treasury shares held within the Group's life insurance statutory funds	—	—	—	23	23	—	23
Dividend reinvestment plan	1 367	—	—	—	1 367	—	1 367
Transactions with non-controlling interest	—	—	(22)	—	(22)	(22)	(44)
Other equity movements:							
Group employee share acquisition scheme	45	—	—	—	45	—	45
Share based payments	—	—	(14)	—	(14)	—	(14)
Treasury shares OnePath Australia adjustment	2	—	—	—	2	—	2
Group share option scheme	43	—	—	—	43	—	43
Other changes	—	—	—	1	1	(2)	(1)
As at 30 September 2011	**21 343**	**871**	**(2 095)**	**17 787**	**37 906**	**48**	**37 954**

(continued)

The notes appearing on pages 92 to 208 form an integral part of these financial statements.
1. Further information on other comprehensive income is disclosed in note 29 to the financial statements.

FIGURE 2.13 *(continued)*

29: Reserves and retained earnings

	Consolidated		The Company	
	2011 $m	2010 $m	2011 $m	2010 $m
(a) Foreign currency translation reserve				
Balance at beginning of the year	(2 742)	(1 725)	(773)	(436)
Currency translation adjustments, net of hedges after tax	324	(1 017)	97	(337)
Total foreign currency translation reserve	(2 418)	(2 742)	(676)	(773)
(b) Share option reserve[1]				
Balance at beginning of the year	64	69	64	69
Share-based payments	(13)	7	(13)	7
Transfer of options/rights lapsed to retained earnings[2]	(1)	(12)	(1)	(12)
Total share option translation reserve	50	64	50	64
(c) Available-for-sale revaluation reserve				
Balance at beginning of the year	80	(41)	5	(18)
Valuation gain/(loss) recognised after tax	30	112	(13)	45
Cumulative (gain)/loss transferred to the income statement	16	9	43	(22)
Total available-for-sale revaluation reserve	126	80	35	5
(d) Hedging reserve				
Balance at beginning of the year	11	(90)	(73)	(109)
Gains/(loss) recognised after tax	164	138	128	84
Transfer (to)/from income statement	(6)	(37)	(8)	(48)
Total hedging reserve	169	11	47	(73)
(e) Transactions with non-controlling interests reserve				
Balance at beginning of the year	—	—	—	—
Transactions with non-controlling interests[3]	(22)	—	—	—
Total transactions with non-controlling interests reserve	**(22)**	**—**	**—**	**—**
Total reserves	**(2 095)**	**(2 587)**	**(544)**	**(777)**

1. Further information about share based payments to employees is disclosed in note 46.
2. The transfer of balances form the share option and capital reserves to retained earnings represent items of a distributable nature.
3. The premium in excess of the book value paid to acquire an additional interest in a controlled entity from the non-controlling shareholder.

	Consolidated		The Company	
	2011 $m	2010 $m	2011 $m	2010 $m
Retained earnings				
Balance at beginning of the year	15 921	14 129	11 666	9 950
Profit attributable to shareholders of the Company	5 355	4 501	4 151	4 428
Transfer of options/rights lapsed from share option reserve[1,2]	1	12	1	12
Actuarial gain/(loss) on defined benefit plans after tax[3]	(10)	(4)	24	(18)
Adjustments to opening retained earnings on adoption of revised accounting standard AASB 3R	—	(39)	—	(39)

FIGURE 2.13 *(continued)*

	Consolidated		The Company	
	2011 $m	2010 $m	2011 $m	2010 $m
Dividend income in Treasury shares	23	—	—	—
Ordinary share dividend paid	(3 491)	(2 667)	(3 491)	(2 667)
Preference share dividend paid	(12)	(11)	—	—
Retained earnings at end of year	17 787	15 921	12 351	11 666
Total reserves and retained earnings	**15 692**	**13 334**	**11 807**	**10 889**

1. Further information about share based payments to employees is disclosed in note 46 to the financial statements
2. The transfer of balances from the share option, general and capital reserves to retained earnings represent items of a distributable nature.
3. ANZ has taken the option available under AASB 119 to recognise actuarial gains/losses on defined benefit superannuation plans directly in retained profits (refer note 1 F(vi) and note 45).

(a) Foreign currency translation reserve
The translation reserve comprises exchange differences, net of hedges, arising on translation of the financial statements of foreign operations, as described in note 1 A(viii). When a foreign operation is sold, attributable exchange differences are recognised in the income statement.

(b) Share option reserve
The share option reserve arises on the grant of options, performance rights and deferred share rights to selected employees under the ANZ share option plan. Amounts are transferred out of the reserve and into share capital when the equity investments are exercised. Refer to note 1 C(iii).

(c) Available-for-sale revaluation reserve
Changes in the fair value and exchange differences on the revaluation of available-for-sale financial assets are taken to the available-for-sale revaluation reserve. Where a revalued available-for-sale financial asset is sold, that portion of the reserve which relates to that financial asset, is realised and recognised in the income statement. Where the available-for-sale financial asset is impaired, that portion of the reserve which relates to that asset is recognised in the income statement. Refer to note 1 E(iii).

(d) Hedging reserve
The hedging reserve represents hedging gains and losses recognised on the effective portion of cashflow hedges. The cumulative deferred gain or loss on the hedge is recognised in the income statement when the hedged transaction impacts the income statement. Refer to note 1 E(ii).

Source: ANZ Bank (2011, pp. 90, 136–7).

SUMMARY

The corporate form of organisational structure is a popular one in many countries, particularly because of the limited liability protection that it affords to shareholders. These companies' operations are financed by a mixture of equity and debt. In this chapter the focus is on the equity of a corporate entity. The components of equity recognised generally by companies are share capital, other reserves and retained earnings. Share capital in particular is affected by a variety of financial instruments developed in the financial markets, offering investors instruments with an array of risk–return alternatives. Each of these equity alternatives has its own accounting implications. The existence of reserves is driven by traditional accounting as well as the current restrictions in some accounting standards for some wealth increases to be recognised directly in equity rather than in current income. Even though definite distinctions are made between the various components of equity, it needs to be recognised that they are all equity and differences relate to jurisdictional differences in terms of restrictions on dividend distribution, taxation effects and rights of owners. IAS 1 requires detailed disclosures in relation to each of the components of equity.

Discussion questions

1. Discuss the nature of a reserve. How do reserves differ from the other main components of equity?
2. A company announces a final dividend at the end of the financial year. Discuss whether a dividend payable should be recognised.

3. The telecommunications industry in a particular country has been a part of the public sector. As a part of its privatisation agenda, the government decided to establish a limited liability company called Telecom Plus, with the issue of 10 million $3 shares. These shares were to be offered to the citizens of the country. The terms of issue were such that investors had to pay $2 on application and the other $1 per share would be called at a later time. Discuss:
   (a) the nature of the limited liability company, and in particular the financial obligations of acquirers of shares in the company
   (b) the journal entries that would be required if applications were received for 11 million shares.
4. Why would a company wish to buy back its own shares? Discuss.
5. A company has a share capital consisting of 100 000 shares issued at $2 per share, and 50 000 shares issued at $3 per share. Discuss the effects on the accounts if:
   (a) the company buys back 20 000 shares at $4 per share
   (b) the company buys back 20 000 shares at $2.50 per share.
6. A company has a share capital consisting of 100 000 shares having a par value of $1 per share and issued at a premium of $1 per share, and 50 000 shares issued at $2 par and $1 premium. Discuss the effects on the accounts if:
   (a) the company buys back 20 000 shares at $4 per share
   (b) the company buys back 20 000 shares at $2.50 per share.
7. What is a rights issue? Distinguish between a renounceable and a non-renounceable issue.
8. What is a private placement of shares? Outline its advantages and disadvantages.
9. Discuss whether it is necessary to distinguish between the different components of equity rather than just having a single number for shareholders' equity.
10. For what reasons may a company make an appropriation of its retained earnings?

Exercises
STAR RATING ★ BASIC ★★ MODERATE ★★★ DIFFICULT

| Exercise 2.1 | **RESERVES AND DIVIDENDS** |

★ Prepare journal entries to record the following unrelated transactions of a public company:
(a) payment of interim dividend of $30 000
(b) transfer of $52 000 from the asset revaluation surplus to the general reserve
(c) transfer of $34 000 from the general reserve to retained earnings
(d) issue of 240 000 bonus shares, fully paid, at $2 per share from the general reserve.

| Exercise 2.2 | **DIVIDENDS** |

★ India Ltd's share capital currently consists of 40 000 ordinary shares issued with a par value of $5 per share, and 20 000 10% preference shares issued at $10 each. In relation to the preference shares, dividends have not been paid for the 2 years prior to the current year. The company plans to pay out $100 000 in dividends in the current period, meeting all past obligations (where applicable) to shareholders.
   Determine how much each class of shares should receive under the following situations:
(a) the preference shares are non-cumulative and non-participating
(b) the preference shares are cumulative and non-participating
(c) the preference shares are cumulative and participating. Assume that the participation agreement requires that the ordinary shareholders receive the same percentage of dividend as the preference shareholders, and that any balance of dividends to be paid is shared in proportion to the issued share capital of each class.

| Exercise 2.3 | **RIGHTS ISSUE** |

★ Laos Ltd had share capital of one million $1 shares, fully paid. As it needed finance for certain construction projects, the company's management decided to make a non-renounceable rights issue to existing shareholders of 200 000 new shares at an issue price of $5 per share. The rights issue was to be fully underwritten by Finance Brokers Ltd. The prospectus was issued on 15 February 2013 and applications closed on 15 March 2013. Costs associated with the rights issue and the eventual issue of the shares were $10 000.

(a) If 80% of the rights were exercised by the due date, provide journal entries made by Laos Ltd in relation to the rights issue and the eventual share issue.

(b) If the rights issue was not underwritten and any unexercised rights lapsed, what would be the required journal entries?

Exercise 2.4

SHARE ISSUE, OPTIONS

★ Jordan Ltd has the following shareholders' equity at 1 January 2014:

Share capital — 500 000 shares	$1 240 000
Asset revaluation surplus	350 000
Retained earnings	110 000

On 1 March the company decided to make a public share issue to raise $600 000 for new capital development. The company issued a prospectus inviting applications for 200 000 $3 shares, payable in full on application. Shareholders who acquired more than 10 000 shares were allowed to buy options at 50 cents each. These options enabled the owner to buy shares in Jordan Ltd at $3.50 each, the acquisition having to occur before 31 December 2014.

By 25 March the company had received applications for 250 000 shares and for 20 000 options. The shares and options were allotted on 2 April, and money returned to unsuccessful applicants on the same day. All applicants who acquired options also received shares.

By 31 December 2014, the company's share price had reached $3.75. Holders of 18 000 options exercised their options in December. The remaining options lapsed.

Required

Prepare the journal entries in the records of Jordan Ltd in relation to the equity transactions in 2014.

Exercise 2.5

DIVIDENDS, CALLS ON SHARES AND BONUS ISSUE

★ The equity of Japan Ltd at 1 January 2015 was as follows:

Share capital		
600 000 shares fully paid	$600 000	
400 000 shares issued for $1 and paid to 50c	200 000	$ 800 000
General reserve		200 000
Plant maintenance reserve		50 000
Retained earnings		80 000
Total equity		$1 130 000

The following events occurred during the year:

June 25	Interim dividend of 10c per share paid, with partly paid shares receiving a proportionate dividend.
July 10	Call of 50c per share on the partly paid shares.
July 31	Collection of call money.
Sept. 15	Bonus share issue of one share for each 10 shares held, at $1 per share, allocated from general reserve.
Dec. 31	Directors announce that a dividend of 20c per share will be paid in September, subject to approval at the February annual general meeting. Transfer of plant maintenance reserve to general reserve. The company earned a profit of $60 000.

Required

(a) Prepare the journal entries to give effect to the above events.
(b) Prepare the equity section of the statement of financial position at 31 December 2015.

<table>
<tr><td>**Exercise 2.6**</td><td>**ISSUE OF ORDINARY AND PREFERENCE SHARES**</td></tr>
<tr><td>★★</td><td>Prepare journal entries and ledger accounts to record the following transactions for Kuwait Ltd:</td></tr>
</table>

2015	
April 1	A prospectus was issued inviting applications for 100 000 ordinary shares at an issue price of $1.50, fully payable on application. The prospectus also offered 100 000 10% preference shares at an issue price of $2, fully payable on application. The issue was underwritten at a commission of $4500, being $500 relating to the issue of ordinary shares and the balance for preference shares. All unsuccessful application monies were to be returned to the applicants.
April 10	Applications closed with the ordinary issue oversubscribed by 40 000 shares and the preference shares undersubscribed by 15 000 shares.
April 15	100 000 ordinary shares were allotted and applications for 40 000 shares were rejected and money refunded. 100 000 preference shares were also allotted.
April 20	The underwriter paid for the shares allocated to her, less the commission due.

<table>
<tr><td>**Exercise 2.7**</td><td>**RIGHTS ISSUE, PLACEMENT OF SHARES**</td></tr>
<tr><td>★★</td><td>The shareholders' equity of Iraq Ltd on 1 January 2014 was:</td></tr>
</table>

Share capital — 200 000 shares fully paid	$400 000
General reserve	200 000
Retained earnings	100 000

The following transactions occurred during the year ended 31 December 2014:
1. On 1 February 2014, a renounceable one-for-two rights issue was made to existing shareholders. The issue price was $2 per share, payable in full on application. The issue was underwritten for a commission of $5000. The issue closed fully subscribed on 31 March, the holders of 40 000 shares having transferred their rights. The underwriting commission was paid on 5 March.
2. On 30 June 2014, 10 000 shares were privately placed with Asian Investments Ltd at $2 per share.

Required

Prepare the general journal entries to record the above transactions.

<table>
<tr><td>**Exercise 2.8**</td><td>**SHARE ISSUE, OPTIONS**</td></tr>
<tr><td>★★</td><td>On 30 June 2013, the equity accounts of Brunei Ltd consisted of:</td></tr>
</table>

175 000 'A' ordinary shares, issued at $2.50 each, fully paid	$437 500
50 000 6% cumulative preference shares, issued at $3 and paid to $2	100 000
Options (20 000 at 56c each)	11 200
Accumulated losses	(6 250)

As the company had incurred a loss for the year ended 30 June 2013, no dividends were declared for that year. The options were exercisable between 1 March 2014 and 30 April 2014. Each option allowed the holder to buy one 'A' ordinary share for $4.50.

The following transactions and events occurred during the year ended 30 June 2014:

2013	
July 25	The directors made the final call of $1 on the preference shares.
Aug. 31	All call monies were received except those owing on 7500 preference shares.
Sept. 7	The directors resolved to forfeit 7500 preference shares for non-payment of the call. The constitution of the company directs that forfeited amounts are not to be refunded to shareholders. The shares will not be reissued.
Nov. 1	The company issued a prospectus offering 30 000 'B' ordinary shares payable in two instalments: $3 on application and $2 on 30 November 2015. The offer closed on 30 November.
Nov. 30	Applications for 40 000 'B' ordinary shares were received.
Dec. 1	The directors resolved to allot the 'B' ordinary shares pro rata with all applicants receiving 75% of the shares applied for. Excess application monies were allowed to be held. The shares were duly allotted.
Dec. 5	Share issue costs of $5200 were paid.
2014 April 30	The holders of 15 000 options applied to purchase shares. All monies were sent with the applications. All remaining options lapsed. The shares were duly issued.

Required

(a) Prepare general journal entries to record the above transactions.
(b) If Brunei Ltd buys back 25 000 preference shares for $3.50 per share, what factors would its accountant have to consider in determining how best to record the transaction in the accounts?

Exercise 2.9	ISSUE OF OPTION AND SHARES, FORFEITURE OF SHARES
★★	Prepare ledger accounts to record the following transactions for Nepal Ltd:

2015	
July 1	A prospectus was issued inviting applications for 100 000 ordinary shares at an issue price of $3, with $2 payable on application and the balance payable on 10 June 2016. The prospectus also offered 50 000 10% preference shares at $2, fully payable on application. The issue was underwritten at a commission of $6500, allocated equally between the classes of shares.
July 21	Applications closed with the ordinary share issue oversubscribed by 20 000 and the preference shares undersubscribed by 15 000.
July 31	All shares were allotted, and application money refunded to unsuccessful applicants for ordinary shares.
Aug. 14	The underwriter paid amounts owing less commission.
Dec. 1	The directors resolved to give each ordinary shareholder, free of charge, one option for every two shares held. The options are exercisable prior to 1 June 2016 and allow each holder to acquire one ordinary share at an exercise price of $2.70. Options not exercised prior to that date lapse.
2016 June 1	The holders of 40 000 options elected to exercise those options and 40 000 shares were issued.

June 10	The balance payable on the ordinary shares was received from holders of 95 000 ordinary shares.
June 15	The shares on which call money was not received were forfeited.
June 25	The forfeited shares were placed with a financial institution, paid to $3 on payment of $2.80. The cash was received from the financial institution, and any balance in the forfeited shares account returned to the former shareholders. Reissue costs amounted to $550.

Exercise 2.10   BUY-BACK OF SHARES

★★ Vietnam Ltd decided to repurchase 10% of its ordinary shares under a buy-back scheme for $5.60 per share. At the date of the buy-back, the equity of Vietnam Ltd consisted of:

Share capital — 4 million shares fully paid	$4 000 000
General reserve	600 000
Retained earnings	1 100 000

The costs of the buy-back scheme amounted to $3500.

Required

(a) Prepare the journal entries to account for the buy-back. Explain the reasons for the entries made.
(b) Assume that the buy-back price per share was equal to 70c per share. Prepare journal entries to record the buy-back, and explain your answer.
(c) Assume that, instead of the share capital shown above, Vietnam Ltd had issued 1 million shares at a par value of $1 and a share premium of $3 per share. Rework your answers to (a) and (b) under this new scenario.

Exercise 2.11   RIGHTS ISSUE, CALL ON SHARES, ISSUE OF OPTIONS

★★ The share capital of Syria Ltd on 30 June 2014 was:

120 000 'A' ordinary shares issued at $1.50, paid to 75c	$ 90 000
50 000 'B' ordinary shares issued at $2.00, fully paid	100 000
100 000 9% preference shares issued at $1, paid to 80c	80 000
	$270 000

The following transactions occurred during 2014 and 2015:

2014	
Nov. 1	The company makes a one-for-five rights offer to its 'B' ordinary shareholders. The rights are renounceable, and allow holders to obtain 'B' ordinary shares for $2.25 per share, payable in full on application.
Nov. 30	The holders of 40 000 'B' ordinary shares accept the rights offer by the expiry date. The shares are duly allotted.
2015	
Jan. 16	A call of 75c per share is made on all 'A' ordinary shares. All call money except that owed by the holder of 10 000 shares is received by 31 January.
Feb. 5	Shares on which calls are unpaid are forfeited and cancelled.

Mar. 17	To assist with cash flow difficulties, the company issued a prospectus inviting offers for 50 000 options to acquire 'A' ordinary shares at an issue price of 60c per option, payable in full on application. Each option, exercisable prior to 31 December 2015, allows the holder to acquire one 'A' ordinary share for $1.78.
Mar. 31	Offers had been received for 35 000 options and these were duly allotted.
Dec. 31	The holders of 25 000 options had exercised their options, with money paid on exercise, and 25 000 'A' ordinary shares were issued. The remaining options lapsed. Costs of issuing the shares amounted to $2000.

Required

Prepare journal entries to record the above transactions in the records of Syria Ltd.

Exercise 2.12

★★★

SHARE ISSUE, OPTIONS, STATEMENT OF CHANGES IN EQUITY

On 30 June 2013, the equity accounts of Taiwan Ltd consisted of:

120 000 ordinary shares, issued at $2.50 each, fully paid	$300 000
Options (80 000 at 50c each)*	40 000
General reserve	30 000
Forfeited shares reserve	2 000
Retained earnings	75 000

* The options were exercisable between 1 May 2014 and 31 May 2014. Each option allowed the holder to buy one ordinary share for $3 each.

Additional information

The following transactions and events occurred during the year ended 30 June 2014:

- The final 6c per share dividend for the year ended 30 June 2013 was paid on 27 September 2013. Shareholder approval to pay the dividend had been obtained at the annual general meeting on 20 September.
- On 1 October, the directors issued a prospectus offering 40 000 ordinary shares at an issue price of $2.80, payable $2 on application and 80c as a future call. The closing date for application was 31 October 2013. The share issue was underwritten by Support Stockbrokers for a fee of $2500, payable on 15 November 2013.
- By 31 October 2013, applications for 50 000 shares had been received.
- On 5 November 2013, the directors allotted the shares pro rata, with applicants receiving 80% of their requested shares. The company's constitution allows excess application monies to be retained and used to offset future calls payable.
- On 15 November 2013, the underwriting fee was paid.
- On 31 December 2013, the directors announced an interim dividend of 3c per share payable in cash on 1 February.
- To raise funds for expansion, the directors sold a parcel of 80 000 ordinary shares to Safe Superannuation Fund on 28 April 2014 at an issue price of $2.90 per share.
- By 31 May 2014, the holders of 65 000 options had indicated that they wished to purchase shares. On 2 June 2014, 65 000 ordinary shares were issued with monies being payable by 21 June. Options not exercised duly lapsed.
- All outstanding monies were received with respect to shares issued to option holders.
- Profit for the year was $69 420. On 30 June 2014, the directors decided to:
  - transfer $30 000 to the general reserve
  - declare a final 5c per share dividend. Shareholder approval for this dividend will be sought at the annual general meeting in September 2014.

Required

(a) Prepare general journal entries, including any closing entries required, to record the above transactions. (Narrations are not required, but show all workings.)

(b) Prepare a statement of changes in equity for the year ended 30 June 2014.

(c) Taiwan Ltd has recognised a 'Forfeited shares reserve' as part of equity. Explain how and why such a reserve would be created.

SHARES, OPTIONS, DIVIDENDS AND RESERVE TRANSFERS

★★★ The equity of Maldives Ltd at 30 June 2014 consisted of:

400 000 ordinary 'A' shares issued at $2.00, fully paid	$ 800 000
300 000 ordinary 'B' shares issued at $2.00, called to $1.20	360 000
50 000 6% preference shares issued at $1.50, fully paid	75 000
Share options issued at 60c, fully paid	24 000
Retained earnings	318 000

The options were exercisable before 28 February 2015. Each option entitled the holder to acquire two ordinary 'C' shares at $1.80 per share, the amount payable on notification to exercise the option.

The following transactions occurred during the year ended 30 June 2015:

2014	
Sept. 15	The preference dividend and the final ordinary dividend of 16c per fully paid share, both declared on 30 June 2014, were paid. The directors do not need any other party to authorise the payment of dividends.
Nov. 1	A one-for-five renounceable rights offer was made to ordinary 'A' shareholders at an issue price of $1.90 per share. The expiry date on the offer was 30 November 2014. The issue was underwritten at a commission of $3000.
Nov. 30	Holders of 320 000 shares accepted the rights offer, paying the required price per share, with the renounced rights being taken up by the underwriter. Ordinary 'A' shares were duly issued.
Dec. 10	Money due from the underwriter was received.
2015	
Jan. 10	The directors transferred $35 000 from retained earnings to a general reserve.
Feb. 28	As a result of options being exercised, 70 000 ordinary 'C' shares were issued. Unexercised options lapsed.
April 30	The directors made a call on the ordinary 'B' shares for 80c per share. Call money was payable by 31 May.
May 31	All call money was received except for that due on 15 000 shares.
June 18	Shares on which the final call was unpaid were forfeited.
June 26	Forfeited shares were reissued, credited as paid to $2, for $1.80 per share, the balance of the forfeited shares account being refundable to the former shareholders.
June 27	Refund paid to former holders of forfeited shares.
June 30	The directors declared a 20c per share final dividend to be paid on 15 September 2015.

Required

(a) Prepare general journal entries to record the above transactions.
(b) Prepare the equity section of the statement of financial position as at 30 June 2015.

DIVIDENDS, SHARE ISSUES, SHARE BUY-BACKS, OPTIONS AND MOVEMENTS IN RESERVES

★★★ Singapore Ltd, a company whose principal interests are in the manufacture of fine leather shoes and handbags, was formed on 1 January 2012. Prior to the 2015 period, Singapore Ltd had issued 110 000 ordinary shares:
• 95 000 $30 shares were issued for cash on 1 January 2012

- 5000 shares were exchanged on 1 February 2013 for a patent that had a fair value at date of exchange of $240 000
- 10 000 shares were issued on 13 November 2014 for $50 per share.

At 1 January 2015, Singapore Ltd had a balance in its retained earnings account of $750 000, while the general reserve and the asset revaluation surplus had balances of $240 000 and $180 000 respectively. The purpose of the general reserve is to reflect the need for the company to regularly replace certain of the shoe-making machinery to reflect technological changes.

During the 2015 financial year, the following transactions occurred:

Feb. 15	Singapore Ltd paid a $25 000 dividend that had been declared in December 2014. Liabilities for dividends are recognised when they are declared by the company.
May 10	10 000 shares at $55 per share were offered to the general public. These were fully subscribed and issued on 20 June 2015. On the same date, another 15 000 shares were placed with major investors at $55 per share.
June 25	The company paid a $20 000 interim dividend.
June 30	The company revalued land by $30 000, increasing the asset revaluation surplus by $21 000 and the deferred tax liability by $9000.
July 1	The company early adopted IFRS 4 in relation to insurance. The transitional liability on initial adoption was $55 000 more than the liability recognised under the previous accounting standard. This amount was recognised directly in retained earnings.
July 22	Singapore Ltd repurchased 5000 shares on the open market for $56 per share. The repurchase was accounted for by writing down share capital and retained earnings by an equal amount.
Nov. 16	Singapore Ltd declared a 1-for-10 bonus issue to shareholders on record at 1 October 2015. The whole of the general reserve was used to create this bonus issue.
Dec. 1	The company issued 100 000 options at 20 cents each, each option entitling the holder to acquire an ordinary share in Singapore Ltd at a price of $60 per share, the options to be exercised by 31 December 2016. No options had been exercised by 31 December 2015.
Dec. 31	Singapore Ltd calculated that its profit for the 2015 year was $150 000. It declared a $30 000 final dividend, transferred $40 000 to the general reserve, and transferred $30 000 from the asset revaluation surplus to retained earnings.

Share issue costs amount to 10% of the worth of any share issue.

Required

(a) Prepare the general journal entries to record the above transactions.
(b) Prepare the statement of changes in equity for Singapore Ltd for the year ended 31 December 2015.

Exercise 2.15
★★★

SHARE ISSUES, OPTIONS, RIGHTS ISSUES, DIVIDENDS, RESERVE TRANSFERS

The equity of Yemen Ltd on 30 June 2013 (end of the reporting period) consisted of:

280 000 ordinary shares, issued at $2.40 each and called to $2.40	$672 000
Calls in arrears (24 000 shares × 80c)	(19 200)
General reserve	290 000
Retained earnings	53 780

Additional information
The following transactions and events relating to share issues and options occurred during the year ended 30 June 2014:
- On 15 July 2013, the directors forfeited the shares on which the call was outstanding. Forfeited shares are not to be reissued and the company's constitution requires that any forfeited amounts be refunded to the former shareholders. Refund cheques were sent on 26 July 2013. Any outstanding dividends were still payable to former shareholders.

- On 1 August 2013, a rights offer (offering 5% preference shares at an issue price of $2.80 per share) was made to existing shareholders on the basis of one preference share for every two ordinary shares held. Shares were payable in full on allotment and rights were renounceable. The issue was underwritten for a fee of $5000.
- The rights offer closed undersubscribed on 31 August 2013, and rights in respect of 40 000 shares were transferred to the underwriter. On 1 September 2013, the shares were allotted. The underwriter paid for its allotment of shares, net of its fee, on 10 September 2013. All other monies were received by 21 September 2013.
- On 1 March 2014, the directors offered for sale 100 000 options at 10c each. Each option gave the holder the right to purchase one ordinary share for $2.80 each. Options were exercisable between 1 April 2015 and 30 June 2015. The option offer closed with 80 000 applications being received. Options were duly allotted on 2 April 2014.

The following transactions and events relating to dividends and reserve transfers occurred during the year ended 30 June 2014:

- On 29 September 2013, the final dividend of 10c per share for the year ended 30 June 2013 was paid. The dividend had been declared on 28 June 2013. Shareholder approval is not required for a declaration of dividends.
- On 2 January 2014, the directors declared and paid an ordinary interim share dividend of one ordinary share, valued at $3, for every four ordinary shares held. The dividend was funded from the general reserve.
- On 30 June 2014, the directors transferred $30 000 from the general reserve to retained earnings, declaring the 5% preference dividend as well as a final ordinary dividend of 8c per share. The loss for the year ended 30 June 2014 was $36 000.

Required

(a) Prepare general journal entries to record the transactions relating to share issues and options for the year ending 30 June 2014.
(b) Prepare general journal entries, including any closing entries required, to record the transactions relating to dividends and reserve transfers for the year ended 30 June 2014.
(c) If the company's constitution required all dividends to be approved by the shareholders at the annual general meeting before they could be paid, explain how and why your recording of the dividend payment on 29 September 2013 would change. Assume shareholder approval was granted on 20 September 2013.

Exercise 2.16 **OPTIONS, SHARES, DIVIDENDS, RESERVES**

★★★ The statement of changes in equity for Philippines Ltd for the year ended 30 June 2015 is as follows:

PHILIPPINES LTD Statement of Changes in Equity for the year ended 30 June 2015	
Profit for the year	$ 69 420
Other comprehensive income	0
Total comprehensive income for the year	$ 69 420
Movements in equity during the year ended 30 June 2015 were:	
Share capital	
Balance at 1 July 2014	$300 000
Issue of 40 000 ordinary shares @ $2.00	80 000
Share issue costs: public issue	(2 500)
Issue of 80 000 ordinary shares @ $2.90 to public	232 000
Issue of 50 000 ordinary shares @ $3.00 on exercise of options costing 40c	170 000
Calls in advance on issue of 80 000 shares @ $2.90 to public	20 000
Balance at 30 June 2015	$779 500
Options	
Balance at 1 July 2014	$ 24 000
Transfer to share capital on exercise	(20 000)
Transfer to reserve on lapse	(4 000)
Balance at 30 June 2015	$ 0

General reserve	
Balance at 1 July 2014	$110 000
Bonus issue of shares	(80 000)
Transfer from retained earnings	30 000
Balance at 30 June 2015	$ 60 000
Options reserve	
Balance at 1 July 2014	$ 0
Transfer of lapsed options	$ 4 000
Balance at 30 June 2015	4 000
Retained earnings	
Balance at 1 July 2014	$ 75 000
Dividends declared	(8 000)
Dividends paid	(4 000)
Transfer to general reserve	(30 000)
Profit for the period	69 420
Balance at 30 June 2015	$102 420

Required

Provide journal entries in relation to:
(a) issue of shares on exercise of options, and related transfers to/from reserves
(b) issue of shares to public
(c) dividends
(d) movements in general reserve.

Note: None of the entries should contain the account Retained Earnings.

Exercise 2.17	DIVIDENDS, SHARE-ISSUES, OPTIONS, RESERVE TRANSFERS

★★★ Mongolia Ltd's equity as at 30 June 2012 was as follows:

120 000 ordinary A shares, issued at $1.10, fully paid	$132 000
150 000 ordinary B shares, issued at $1.20, called to 70c	105 000
100 000 8% cumulative preference shares, issued at $1, fully paid	100 000
Calls in advance (30 000 shares)	15 000
Share issue costs	(11 200)
General reserve	160 000
Retained earnings	158 000
Total equity	$658 800

The general journal is used for all entries.
The following events occurred after 30 June 2012:

2012	
Sep. 30	The final 10c per share ordinary dividend and the preference dividend, both declared on 25 June 2012, were paid. Shareholder approval is not required for payment of dividends.
Oct. 31	A prospectus was issued inviting offers to acquire 1 option for every 2 ordinary A shares held at a price of 80c per option, payable by 30 November 2012. Each option entitles the holder to 1 ordinary A share at a price of 70c per share and are exercisable in November 2014. Any options not exercised by 30 November 2014 will lapse.
Nov. 30	Offers and monies were received for 50 000 options, and these were issued.
2013 Jan. 15	The final call on ordinary B shares was made, payable by 15 February 2013.

Feb. 15	All call monies were received.
April 20	50 000 preference shares were repurchased at $1.10 per share. The repurchase was accounted for by writing down Preference Share Capital by $50 000 and Retained Earnings by the balance.
June 30	The profit for the year was $44 000. The directors decided to transfer $20 000 from the general reserve to retained profits and declared a 10c per share dividend and the preference dividend, both payable on 30 September 2013.
Sept. 30	The final ordinary and preference dividends declared on 30 June 2013 were paid.
Dec. 15	A 5c/share interim ordinary dividend was declared and paid.
2014 Jan. 31	The directors made a 1-for-5 renounceable rights offer to ordinary B shareholders at an issue price of $1.50 per share. The offer's expiry date was 28 February 2014.
Feb. 28	Holders of 120 000 shares accepted the rights offer. Shares were issued, with monies payable by 15 March 2014.
Mar. 15	All monies were received.
June 30	Profit for the year was $56 000. The directors, in lieu of declaring a final dividend, made a 1-for-10 bonus issue from the general reserve to all shareholders. Ordinary A shares were valued at $1.20 each, ordinary B shares were valued at $1.60 each and preference shares were valued at $1.15 each.
Nov. 30	Holders of 40 000 options exercised their options, and 40 000 ordinary A shares were issued. Monies were payable by 20 December 2014.
Dec. 20	All monies were received.
2015 Jan. 10	A 5c per share interim ordinary dividend was declared and paid.
June 30	Profit for the year was $48 000. The directors declared a 10c per share final dividend and the preference dividend, both payable on 30 September 2015.

Required

(a) Prepare general journal entries and closing entries to record the above transactions and events.
(b) Prepare the following general ledger accounts (T format) for the period 30 June 2012 to 30 June 2015:
  - Share capital (Ordinary A)
  - Share capital (Ordinary B)
  - Share capital (Preference).

Exercise 2.18

★★★

DIVIDENDS, SHARE ISSUES, FORFEITURE OF SHARES

On 30 June 2012 the equity of Malaysia Ltd was as follows:

50 000 5% cumulative preference shares, issued at $1.20, fully paid	$ 60 000
100 000 ordinary shares, issued at $1.15, fully paid	115 000
Options (15 000 @ 50c)	7 500
Share issue costs	(2 610)
General reserve	123 100
Retained earnings	136 340

Each option entitles the holder to acquire 1 ordinary share at a price of $1.10 per share, exercisable by 31 March 2013. Any options not exercised by this date will lapse. The books are balanced 6-monthly.

The following events occurred during the year ended 30 June 2013:

2012	
Aug. 15	The final 8c per share ordinary dividend and the final preference dividend, both declared on 30 June 2012, were paid in cash. Shareholder approval is required for payment of dividends and was obtained at the annual general meeting of 2 August.
Oct. 1	A prospectus was issued offering 60 000 ordinary shares at an issue price of $1.20 per share, payable 35c on application, 35c on allotment and 50c on a first and final call. The closing date for applications was 31 October 2012. The issue was underwritten at a commission of $1500.
Oct. 31	Applications were received for 75 000 shares by this date.
Nov. 2	The directors allotted 4 shares for every 5 applied for, with allotment monies due by 30 November 2012. In accordance with the constitution, surplus application monies were kept as an advance on future calls and allotment monies. The underwriting commission was paid.
Nov. 30	All allotment monies owing were received by this date.
2013	
Jan. 5	An interim 5c per share ordinary dividend was paid in cash.
Jan. 31	The first and final call was made, with monies due by 28 February 2013.
Feb. 28	$28 500 call monies were received by this date.
Mar. 20	The shares on which the call was unpaid were forfeited. The company is entitled to keep any balance arising from forfeiture of shares.
Mar. 31	12 000 shares were allotted as a result of 12 000 options having been exercised, with allotment monies due by 30 April 2013.
April 30	All allotment monies were received by this date.
May 31	A 1-for-4 bonus issue was made from the general reserve, with the shares valued at $1.20 each.
June 30	A 10c per share final dividend was declared, payable on 15 August 2013. Net profit for the year ended 30 June 2013 was $29 460.

Required

(a) Prepare general journal entries and closing entries to record the above transactions.
(b) Prepare the Options and Retained Earnings ledger accounts for the period 30 June 2012 to 30 June 2013.

References

ANZ Bank 2003, *Prospectus*, Australia and New Zealand Banking Group Limited, Australia, www.anz.com.au.
——2011, *2010 annual report*, Australia and New Zealand Banking Group Limited, Australia, www.anz.com.au.
Australian Securities Exchange (ASX) 2010, *Capital raising in Australia: experiences and lessons from the Global Financial Crisis*, ASX Information Paper, 29 January, www.asx.com.au.
Fortune magazine 2011, 'Fortune global 500', 21 July, available from http://money.cnn.com/-magazines/fortune/global500/2011.
International Committee of the Red Cross 2011, *ICRC annual report 2010*, Switzerland, www.icrc.org.
Nobes, C & Parker, R 2002, *Comparative international accounting*, 7th edn, Pearson Education Limited, England.
Nokia 2011, *Nokia in 2010*, Nokia Corporation, Finland, www.nokia.com.
Phosphagenics Limited 2011, *SPP closes heavily oversubscribed*, Phosphagenics Limited, company announcement, Clayton, Victoria, 14 November.
Pöyry plc 2011, *Annual report 2010*, Pöyry plc, Finland, www.poyry.com.
Qantas 2011, *Annual report 2011*, Qantas Airways Limited, Australia, www.qantas.com.au.
Wasiliev, J 2009, 'The right story on Rio's rights', *The Sydney Morning Herald*, 19 June, www.smh.com.au.

3 Fair value measurement

ACCOUNTING STANDARDS IN FOCUS

IFRS 13 *Fair Value Measurement*

LEARNING OBJECTIVES

After studying this chapter, you should be able to:

1 explain the need for an accounting standard on fair value measurement
2 understand the key characteristics of the term 'fair value'
3 explain the steps in determining the fair value of non-financial assets
4 understand how to measure the fair value of liabilities
5 explain how to measure the fair value of an entity's own equity instruments
6 discuss issues relating to the measurement of the fair value of financial instruments
7 prepare the disclosures required by IFRS 13 *Fair Value Measurement*
8 discuss the issues associated with the measurement and use of fair values.

3.1 THE NEED FOR A STANDARD ON FAIR VALUE MEASUREMENT

Under accounting standards issued by the International Accounting Standards Board (IASB), there are various ways in which assets are required to be measured. Many standards specify how assets are to be initially recognised, and some standards specify or give choices on measurement subsequent to initial recognition. The two main measures used are cost and fair value, for example:

• Paragraph 15 of IAS 16 *Property, Plant and Equipment* requires an item of property, plant and equipment that qualifies for recognition as an asset to be measured initially at its cost.
• Paragraph 24 of IAS 38 *Intangible Assets* requires intangible assets to be measured initially at cost.
• Paragraph 43 of IAS 39 *Financial Instruments: Recognition and Measurement* requires financial assets to be measured at fair value.
• Both IAS 16 and IAS 38 allow entities the choice, subsequent to initial recognition, of measuring assets using the cost model or the revaluation model.

Other measurement methods used in accounting standards are net realisable value, fair value less costs of disposal, recoverable amount and value in use.

In relation to the measurement of liabilities, IAS 39 requires financial liabilities to be measured at fair value, while liabilities in general are measured in accordance with paragraph 36 of IAS 37 *Provisions, Contingent Liabilities and Contingent Assets*, that is, at the best estimate of the expenditure required to settle the present obligation at the end of the reporting period.

Prior to 2011, many accounting standards defined the term 'fair value' as:

> The amount for which an asset could be exchanged, or a liability settled, between knowledgeable, willing parties in an arm's length transaction.

Various accounting standards also provided guidance on the measurement of fair value such as IAS 38 *Intangible Assets* which provided a hierarchy of fair value measurement, while IAS 40 *Investment Property* contained a discussion of the meaning of 'a transaction between knowledgeable, willing parties'. The IASB, however, believed that there was a need to issue a separate International Financial Reporting Standard (IFRS) on fair value measurement. In May 2009, the IASB issued the exposure draft *Fair Value Measurement*.

Three reasons for issuing the exposure draft were given in the Introduction:

(a) to establish a single source of guidance for all fair value measurements required or permitted by IFRSs to reduce complexity and improve consistency in their application;
(b) to clarify the definition of fair value and related guidance in order to communicate the measurement objective more clearly;
(c) to enhance disclosures about fair value to enable users of financial statements to assess the extent to which fair value is used and to inform them about the inputs used to derive those fair values.

The objectives of IFRS 13 *Fair Value Measurement* are succinctly stated in paragraph 1:

• to define fair value
• to set out in a single standard a framework for measuring fair value
• to require disclosures about fair value measurement.

Ernst & Young (2005) noted that if the IASB were to advocate its fair value approach on the grounds of relevance, this position is only tenable if the meaning of fair value is both clear and unambiguous and if the fair value of an asset and liability can be measured with sufficient reliability to justify its use as the primary basis of asset and liability measurement. An accounting standard on fair value measurement would hopefully allay such concerns about the use of fair value to measure assets and liabilities.

In preparing a separate accounting standard on the measurement of fair value, the IASB was *not* proposing to introduce new requirements for the use of fair value as the required measurement method, or to eliminate current practicability exceptions to the measurement of fair value such as that in IAS 41 *Agriculture*.

The IASB took a number of steps prior to issuing an exposure draft to ensure that users of financial statements would understand the reasoning behind the IASB's approach as well as to gain insights from initial feedback. Some of the steps undertaken by the IASB in preparing the 2009 exposure draft were:

• In November 2005, the IASB published a discussion paper *Measurement Bases for Financial Accounting — Measurement on Initial Recognition*.
• In November 2006, the IASB published a discussion paper *Fair Value Measurements* using Statement of Financial Accounting Standards No. 157 *Fair Value Measurements* (SFAS 157), issued by the Financial

Accounting Standards Board (FASB) in the United States, as a basis. IFRS 13 contains much of the content of SFAS 157.

In May 2011, the IASB issued IFRS 13 *Fair Value Measurement*.

There are a number of parts to IFRS 13, the document consisting of:

- the accounting standard
- Appendix A: Defined terms — this Appendix is an integral part of the standard
- Appendix B: Application guidance — this Appendix is an integral part of the standard
- Appendix C: Effective date and transition — this Appendix is an integral part of the standard
- Basis for Conclusions
- Illustrative Examples.

IFRS 13 applies when another accounting standard requires or permits fair value to be used and when information about fair value is to be disclosed. Paragraphs 6 and 7 set out situations where IFRS 13 does not apply, such as to share-based payment transactions within IFRS 2 *Share-based Payment* and leasing transactions within the scope of IAS 17 *Leases*. The standard also does not apply to measurements that have similarities to fair value such as net realisable value in IAS 2 *Inventories* or value in use in IAS 36 *Impairment of Assets*.

 3.2 THE DEFINITION OF FAIR VALUE

As noted in section 3.1, the definition of fair value used in many IFRSs prior to the issue of IFRS 13 was that fair value was 'the amount for which an asset could be exchanged, or a liability settled, between knowledgeable, willing parties in an arm's length transaction'.

Paragraph 1 of IFRS 13 states the need to define fair value. This definition is stated in Appendix A as:

> The price that would be received to sell an asset or paid to transfer a liability in an orderly transaction between market participants at the measurement date.

Why change the definition of fair value?

In paragraph BC30 of the Basis for Conclusions on IFRS 13, it is noted that in both definitions:

- the exchange transaction is hypothetical — that is, the measurement of fair value is not based on an actual transaction but a hypothetical transaction
- the exchange transaction is orderly — that is, it is not a forced transaction or a distress sale.

Paragraph BC30 also provides three reasons for the change in the definition:

1. The previous definition did not specify whether an entity was buying or selling the asset. It was then uncertain whether fair value was an exit (selling) price or an entry (buying) price. The new definition requires the use of an exit price.
2. In the previous definition, it was unclear what was meant by 'settling' a liability. Who are the knowledgeable parties? Does this mean the creditor or other parties? The new definition requires measurement by reference to the transfer of a liability to a party who may not be the creditor.
3. There was no explicit statement in the previous definition whether the exchange or settlement took place at the measurement date or at some other date. The new definition specifies that the fair value is the price at the measurement date.

3.2.1 Current exit price

Exit price is defined in Appendix A as follows:

> The price that would be received to sell an asset or paid to transfer a liability.

An important feature of the definition of fair value is that it is an exit price based on the perspective of the entity that holds the asset or owes the liability. The exit price is based on expectations about the future cash flows that will be generated by the asset subsequent to the sale of the asset or transfer of the liability to an acquiring entity. These cash flows may be generated from use of the asset or from sale of the asset by the acquiring entity. Even where the entity holding the asset intends to use it rather than sell it, the fair value is measured as an exit price by reference to the sale of the asset to a market participant who will use the asset or sell it.

Similarly, with a liability, an entity may continue to hold a liability until settlement or transfer the liability to another entity. The fair value in both cases is based on expected cash outflows by the entity.

In contrast, an entry price is one that would be paid to buy an asset or received to incur a liability. According to paragraph BC44 of the Basis for Conclusions on IFRS 13, the IASB concluded that a current entry price and a current exit price will be equal when they relate to the same asset or liability on the same date in the same form in the same market. However, valuation experts informed the IASB that, in a business combination, an exit price for an asset or liability acquired or assumed might differ from an exchange price — entry or exit — if:

- an entity's intended use for an acquired asset is different from its highest and best use
- a liability is measured on the basis of settling it with the creditor rather than transferring it to a third party.

The equivalence of exit prices and entry prices was questioned by Ernst & Young (2009, p. 5) in their response to the IASB exposure draft:

> The ED seems to minimise any distinction between measurements based on entry prices versus exit prices, based on a belief that a current entry price and a current exit price are equal when they relate to the same asset or liability in the same market. In our view, this conclusion is only true for assets and liabilities that trade in active markets, as it takes competitive market forces to derive a single price. The price in a principal-to-principal transaction that occurs outside of an active market is the result of a unique negotiation between buyer and seller, considering the specific attributes of both parties in the transaction, but not other market participants. As such, an entity may negotiate a different price in a transaction to sell the asset to one party than it would pay to buy the same asset from another party. In practice, we believe many constituents relate an entry price notion as more akin to an entity-specific measurement, whereas exit price is clearly a market-based measurement. The Board should consider such limitations when it evaluates the decision usefulness of fair value measures versus other measurement objectives, such as value in use.[1]

The Group of 100 (G100) is an organisation of chief financial officers from Australia's largest business enterprises with a purpose of advancing Australia's financial competitiveness. In its response to the IASB's exposure draft, the G100 (2009, pp. 1–2) questioned the use of an exit price to measure fair value, stating:

> The G100 does not support the universal application of an exit value approach to determining fair values because it does not give sufficient weight to the intentions of management and directors. The G100 considers that what constitutes an appropriate measure of fair value will depend on the circumstances in which the fair value is being determined. We believe that the financial statements of the reporting entity should reflect the perspective of the entity as a going concern rather than that of a hypothetical market participant...
>
> While such a measure may be appropriate for financial instruments we do not believe that an exit price based measure provides useful information for certain classes of non-financial assets such as property, plant and equipment where an entity-specific measure may be more appropriate.

Similar concerns about decision-usefulness of exit prices were expressed by Ernst & Young (2009, p. 4):

> However, it is unclear to us why fair value based on an exit price would always provide more decision-useful information than a 'value-in-use' measure about the timing, amount and uncertainty of cash flows for assets and liabilities other than those that will be sold, settled or transferred for cash or another financial instrument.

Paragraph 57 of IFRS 13 notes that, when an entity acquires an asset or assumes a liability in an exchange transaction, the transaction price is the amount paid by the entity. This is an entry price. In contrast, the fair value of the asset or liability is the price that would be received to sell the asset or paid to transfer the liability. This is an *exit* price.

3.2.2 Orderly transactions

The definition of fair value requires that an asset be sold or a liability transferred in an orderly transaction. An orderly transaction is defined in Appendix A to IFRS 13 as:

> A transaction that assumes exposure to the market for a period before the measurement date to allow for marketing activities that are usual and customary for transactions involving such assets or liabilities; it is not a forced transaction (e.g. a forced liquidation or distress sale).

As noted earlier, fair value is measured by considering a hypothetical transaction in a market. To determine that fair value, the entity will make observations in current markets. The markets to be observed must be those containing orderly transactions. Prices of goods sold at 'sale price' or in a liquidation or fire sale are not appropriate to the measurement. Similarly, prices between entities which are not at arm's length are not prices from orderly transactions.

---

[1] Note that this quotation is an extract from Ernst & Young's comment letter and readers should refer to the full letter for a detailed understanding of the issues raised. Further, the views expressed may not reflect the current thinking of Ernst & Young firms. Reproduced by permission of Ernst & Young © 2012 EYGM Limited. All Rights Reserved.

Hence, an entity may have acquired an asset as a result of a transaction that was not orderly. In this case, the amount paid — the actual price — is not necessarily equal to the fair value of the asset.

3.2.3 Market participants

The definition of fair value specifies that the transaction be between market participants. A definition of market participants is given in Appendix A to IFRS 13:

> Buyers and sellers in the principal (or most advantageous) market for the asset or liability that have all of the following characteristics:
> (a) They are independent of each other, i.e. they are not related parties as defined in IAS 24, although the price in a related party transaction may be used as an input to a fair value measurement if the entity has evidenced that the transaction was entered into at market terms.
> (b) They are knowledgeable, having a reasonable understanding about the asset or liability and the transaction using all available information, including information that might be obtained through due diligence efforts that are usual and customary.
> (c) They are able to enter into a transaction for the asset or liability.
> (d) They are willing to enter into a transaction for the asset or liability, i.e. they are motivated but not forced or otherwise compelled to do so.

The definition of fair value used prior to the issue of IFRS 13 contained the phrase 'knowledgeable, willing parties in an arm's length transaction'. According to paragraph BC56 of the Basis for Conclusions on IFRS 13, this phrase expresses the same notion as the definition of market participants used in IFRS 13. However, the IASB believes the definition of market participants makes the concept clearer. The definition provides more information about each of the four descriptors of a market participant. The definition also adds the descriptor of the buyer and seller being able to enter the market — that is, not being restricted from entering the market.

As the fair value is measured by reference to a hypothetical transaction, the valuer must determine the potential market participants. The assumptions used in the valuation are those that would be made by these participants — not those made by the entity itself.

In paragraph BC58 of the Basis for Conclusions on IFRS 13, the IASB raised the issue of information symmetry — that is, is it possible for another entity to be as knowledgeable about an asset as the entity that holds the asset? Any transaction will be based on uncertainty as potentially neither party to the transaction is perfectly informed. Both parties undertake risks on entering into a transaction. However, it is assumed that both parties will undertake efforts to obtain the relevant information about an asset prior to committing to the transaction.

Paragraphs 22 and 23 of IFRS 13 state:

> 22 An entity shall measure the fair value of an asset or a liability using the assumptions that market participants would use when pricing the asset or liability, assuming that market participants act in their economic best interest.
> 23 In developing those assumptions, an entity need not identify specific market participants. Rather, the entity shall identify characteristics that distinguish market participants generally, considering factors specific to all the following:
> (a) the asset or liability;
> (b) the principal (or most advantageous) market for the asset or liability; and
> (c) market participants with whom the reporting entity would enter into a transaction in that market.

Note three points from these paragraphs:
1. The assumptions made in measuring fair value are those that would be made by the market participants, not by the reporting entity. The fair value measure is not an entity-specific value.
2. There is no need to identify specific market participants. The concentration is on the characteristics of the participants. For example, it is not necessary to identify, say, BHP Billiton as a potential market participant; rather, the entity just needs to be identified as a large manufacturer of iron and steel that uses certain assets in the manufacturing process.
3. Some factors to be considered are given. Factor (a), asset or liability, is discussed in sections 3.3.1 and 3.4, while factor (b), the principal (or most advantageous) market, is discussed in section 3.3.3.

The proposal that the fair value should not be an entity-specific value was questioned by Nestlé in its response to the IASB on its exposure draft. Nestlé (2009, p. 3) made the following comment:

> Such a market-based measurement method should be driven by the market in which the entity operates. We consequently believe that the entity being a market participant itself must consider assumptions that other market participants would use in pricing the asset or liability in addition to its own entity-specific assumptions.

Ernst & Young (2009, pp. 4–5) in its response to the IASB exposure draft noted that it was important to consider the trade-off between relevance and reliability in assessing the measurement of fair value:

> [W]e believe that choosing a measurement basis for any asset or liability includes evaluating the balance between the relevance of the information provided and its reliability with respect to fair value, such as assessment includes weighing the relevance of market participant assumptions versus entity-specific assumptions in predicting expected future cash inflows and outflows associated with an asset or liability. This evaluation also includes assessing the trade-off between the potential for management bias in entity-specific assumptions versus the subjectivity of market-based assumptions for assets and liabilities without an active market.[2]

3.2.4 Transaction and transport costs

Transaction costs are the incremental direct costs to sell an asset or transfer a liability and are defined in Appendix A of IFRS 13 as:

> The costs to sell an asset or transfer a liability in the principal (or most advantageous) market for the asset or liability that are directly attributable to the disposal of the asset or the transfer of the liability and meet both of the following criteria:
> (a) They result directly from and are essential to that transaction.
> (b) They would not have been incurred by the entity had the decision to sell the asset or transfer the liability not been made (similar to costs to sell, as defined in IFRS 5).

Transport costs are defined in Appendix A of IFRS 13 as:

> The costs that would be incurred to transport an asset from its current location to its principal (or most advantageous) market.

Both transaction and transport costs affect the determination of the fair value of an asset or liability. When determining the principal (or most advantageous) market in which an asset may be sold, the level of transaction costs will be considered. In general, lower transaction costs will indicate a more advantageous market. The determination of the most advantageous market will then affect the measurement of the fair value. However, the price used to measure the fair value of an asset or liability will not be adjusted for these costs. The reason for this is that these costs are not considered to be a characteristic of the asset or liability. Instead they are specific to a transaction and will change from transaction to transaction.

An asset may have to be transported from its present location to the principal (or most advantageous) market. As the location of an asset or a liability is a characteristic of the asset or liability, it will have a different fair value because of associated transport costs. For example, if an entity located in a capital city is considering buying a vehicle, then a vehicle located in a country town has a different fair value compared to one located in the capital city because of the transport costs associated with the vehicle in the country town. In contrast, transaction costs such as registration costs are not a characteristic of the asset. A price in the principal (or most advantageous) market is then adjusted for the transport costs. Illustrative example 3.1 shows the how transport costs and transaction costs are used in the measurement of fair value.

ILLUSTRATIVE EXAMPLE 3.1 Transaction costs and transport costs

An entity sells Asset XYZ in a number of markets including Market B.

In Market B, the price that would be received is $26; transaction costs are $2 and the costs to transport Asset XYZ to Market B are $1.

Both transaction costs and transport costs are used to determine that Market B is the most advantageous market in that both are used to determine the net amount to be received by the entity — in this case, $23. This net amount is compared with that receivable in other markets to determine the most advantageous market.

Having determined that Market B is the principal (or most advantageous) market, the fair value of Asset XYZ is measured at $25, being $26 less transport costs of $1.

The measurement of fair value is then adjusted for transport costs but not for transaction costs.

Source: Adapted from IASB 2011, IFRS 13 *Fair Value Measurement, Illustrative Examples*, Example 6 — Level 1 principal (or most advantageous) market, p. 12.

---

[2] Note that this quotation is an extract from Ernst & Young's comment letter and readers should refer to the full letter for a detailed understanding of the issues raised. Further, the views expressed may not reflect the current thinking of Ernst & Young firms. Reproduced by permission of Ernst & Young © 2012 EYGM Limited. All Rights Reserved.

3.3 APPLICATION TO NON-FINANCIAL ASSETS

IFRS 13 considers its application to:
- non-financial assets
- liabilities and an entity's own equity instruments.

Section 3.3 considers the application of IFRS 13 in measuring the fair value of non-financial assets while sections 3.4 and 3.5 consider liabilities and equity respectively. Whereas financial assets include cash, shares in other entities and rights to receive cash from other entities, non-financial assets include property, plant and equipment and intangibles.

In paragraph B2 of Appendix B *Application guidance* of IFRS 13, the IASB notes that there are four steps that an entity needs to undertake to make a fair value measurement. (Note that Appendix B is an integral part of IFRS 13.) An entity has to determine:

(a) the particular asset or liability that is the subject of the measurement (consistently with its unit of account).
(b) for a non-financial asset, the valuation premise that is appropriate for the measurement (consistently with its highest and best use).
(c) the principal (or most advantageous) market for the asset or liability.
(d) the valuation technique(s) appropriate for the measurement, considering the availability of data with which to develop inputs that represent the assumptions that market participants would use when pricing the asset or liability and the level of the fair value hierarchy within which the inputs are categorised.

Sections 3.3.1 to 3.3.4 consider these four steps.

3.3.1 What is the particular asset that is the subject of the measurement?

Paragraph 11 of IFRS 13 provides the key principle when determining the asset to be measured:

A fair value measurement is for a particular asset or liability. Therefore, when measuring fair value, an entity shall take into account the characteristics of the asset or liability if market participants would take those characteristics into account when pricing the asset or liability at the measurement date. Such characteristics include, for example, the following:
(a) the condition and location of the asset; and
(b) restrictions, if any, on the sale or use of the asset.

Some of the key questions that need to be asked when determining the asset to be measured are then:
- *What is the location of the asset?* The location of the asset may be different from the market, and the asset has to be transported to the market. Transport costs will then be incurred. If there are difficulties in transporting the asset, as well as time constraints, these factors may affect the fair value of the asset.
- *What is the condition of the asset?* Many of the factors that are considered in depreciating an asset will be of relevance here, such as remaining useful life, physical condition, expected usage, and technical or commercial obsolescence.
- *Are there any restrictions on sale or use of the asset?* There may be legal limits on the use of the asset (e.g. patents, licences or expiry dates of related lease contracts).
- *Is the asset a stand-alone asset or is it a group of assets?* Where a fair value is being calculated for impairment purposes, the assets being valued may be a cash generating unit as defined in IAS 36 *Impairment of Assets*. Similarly, if the fair value relates to a business, the definition of a business in IFRS 3 *Business Combinations* would need to be considered. In Appendix A of IFRS 13, unit of account is the term used to describe the level at which an asset is aggregated or disaggregated in an accounting standard for recognition purposes.

Note that, in considering these factors, the premise is that the market participants will be taking these factors into consideration when determining how they would price the asset.

A further consideration relates to whether or not 'blockage factors' should be considered in determining fair value. This relates to the volume of assets being sold — for example, is it a single vehicle or a fleet of vehicles? In general, the price per unit would be expected to fall if a large volume of the units were being sold as a package. Paragraph 69 prohibits the use of a blockage factor, arguing that a blockage factor is not relevant. As noted in paragraph BC42 of the Basis for Conclusions on IFRS 13, the transaction being considered between the market participants is a hypothetical transaction, and as such, the determination of fair value does not consider any entity-specific factors that might influence the transaction. Blockage is an entity-specific factor. Hence, assets should be measured on a per unit basis. However, note paragraph 69 of IFRS 13. If there is a quoted price in an active market, such as for a number of identical assets, an entity must use that quoted price without adjustment when measuring fair value. In this circumstance, the price in the active market is not entity-specific. An active market is defined in Appendix A as follows:

> A market in which transactions for the asset or liability take place with sufficient frequency and volume to provide pricing information on an ongoing basis.

3.3.2 What is the valuation premise appropriate for measurement of fair value?

The fair value of an asset is measured by considering what a market participant would pay to buy the asset. The market participant will determine this by considering the potential cash flows from the asset, whether from sale or use of the asset. The market participant may have a number of alternative ways in which it can sell or use the asset. Fair value is measured by considering the highest and best use of the asset. Highest and best use is defined in Appendix A of IFRS 13 as:

> The use of a non-financial asset by market participants that would maximise the value of the asset or the group of assets and liabilities (e.g. a business) within which the asset would be used.

According to paragraph 28 of IFRS 13, these uses must be:
- physically possible, taking into account the physical characteristics of the asset
- legally permissible, considering any legal restrictions (e.g. zoning regulations on the use of property)
- financially feasible, in that the use of the asset must result in the market participant obtaining an appropriate return from the asset.

The highest and best use is not based on how the reporting entity is currently using the asset. Note the following:
- The highest and best use is based on how the market participants will use the asset — for example, a competing use for land on which a factory currently stands may be use of the land for residential purposes.
- The reporting entity, however, does not have to make an intensive search for other potential uses if there is no evidence to suggest that the current use is not its highest and best use (paragraph 29). On 2 November 2009, at the IASB roundtable held at the FASB offices in Norwalk in the United States, one participant argued that it is rare that the highest and best use of a commodity would be something other than its actual current use in its current form, citing that an entity with crude oil should not have to look to all the different potential uses of that oil such as refined oil, gasoline, and electricity through oil burning plants.
- For competitive reasons, the reporting entity may have decided not to use an acquired asset — for example, the entity may have acquired a trademark that competes with its own trademark. However, the fair value of the acquired trademark is based on its highest and best use by market participants, not on the current use by the reporting entity holding the asset. Disclosure is also required where an asset is not being used in its highest and best use.

In its response to the IASB on its exposure draft, Royal Dutch Shell (2009, p. 4) expressed that it had a problem with the notion of the highest and best use assumption:

> The question nonetheless remains whether the assumptions underlying the revised definition are appropriate for the current values ascribed to all assets and liabilities. In particular, we perceive there will be real issues of practical application of the revised definition to non-financial assets and liabilities. Take, for example, the measurement of assets and liabilities that are taken on as a result of a business combination. The highest and best use assumption as applied to an item of property, plant and equipment disregards the entity's intended use for the asset, ignoring the motivation of the investor for entering into the combination (even though the investor would meet the definition of a market participant immediately prior to finalising the combination). Ignoring the entity's specific circumstances is therefore illogical and results in unrepresentative amounts being recognised for the asset acquired, and for goodwill.

The highest and best use of an asset establishes the valuation premise to be used to measure the fair value of that asset (paragraph 31 of IFRS 13).

In-combination valuation premise

When a fair value is measured under this premise, the highest and best use of the asset is where the market participants obtain maximum value principally through using the asset *in combination with other assets and liabilities as a group.*

Paragraph 31(a) states that if the fair value of an asset is measured under this premise, the fair value is measured on the basis of the price that would be received in a current transaction to sell the asset assuming that the asset would be used with other assets and liabilities as a group and that those assets and liabilities (complementary assets and liabilities) would be available to market participants. For example, as noted in paragraph B3(c) of Appendix B *Application guidance* of IFRS 13, if the asset is work-in-progress which would be converted into finished goods, in determining the fair value of the work-in-progress, it is assumed that the market participants have or would be able to acquire any necessary machinery for that conversion process.

Note that the fair value is based on the asset being sold to other market participants to be used by them. The asset is sold as an individual asset, not as part of a group of assets. However, the asset will then be used by the market participants in conjunction with other assets. The fair value of an asset, even though used in conjunction with other assets, is not determined by an allocation of the fair value of the group of assets. It is based on the sale of an individual asset. The unit of account is effectively dependent on what is specified in other accounting standards (paragraph 32).

The IASB looked at the question of whether a value determination under the in-combination valuation premise should be considered an exit price (paragraph BC77 of the Basis for Conclusions on IFRS 13). As the asset is being sold to market participants to be used in conjunction with other assets, the transfer price is an exit price. Market participants need all the assets in a cash-generating unit to achieve the cash flows necessary for a successful business. These assets must be acquired to form the cash-generating unit. The fair value of the asset being measured is what the market participants would pay for one of the assets as part of the cash-generating unit. It would be difficult, if not impossible, to determine the future cash flows generated by each of the assets in the group, but a replacement cost of each part of the cash-generating unit is potentially determinable. As noted in paragraph BC79 of the Basis for Conclusions on IFRS 13, the IASB recognised that in some cases an entity will need to measure fair value using another valuation technique, such as an income approach, or the cost to replace or recreate the asset.

A further question considered by the IASB was whether the exit price for specialised equipment is equal to its scrap value (paragraph BC78 of the Basis for Conclusions on IFRS 13). An item of specialised equipment would generally be used in conjunction with other assets; hence the valuation premise would be in-use rather than in-exchange. The exit price is then based on the sale of the specialised equipment to market participants who will use the specialised equipment in conjunction with other assets to obtain a return. The in-use valuation premise assumes there are market participants who will use the asset in combination with other assets and that those assets are available to them (paragraph 31 of IFRS 13).

Under IAS 36 *Impairment of Assets*, recoverable amount is determined as the higher of value in use and fair value less costs of disposal. It should be noted that there is a difference between value in use and a fair value measure determined under the in-use valuation premise as the objective of each of those measures is different. Value in use measures the expected cash flows an entity expects to receive from using those assets. This is an entity-specific value. In contrast, fair value measured under the in-use premise is based on the cash flows that market participants would expect to receive from using the asset. However, the two measures may often be the same if determined as a market-based value.

Stand-alone valuation premise

As noted in paragraph 31(b) of IFRS 13, under this premise, the fair value of the asset is the price that would be received in a current transaction to sell the asset to market participants *who would use the asset on a stand-alone basis* — that is, not in combination with other assets or liabilities.

Decisions concerning the highest and best use of an asset and the relevant valuation premise are considered in illustrative examples 3.2 and 3.3.

ILLUSTRATIVE EXAMPLE 3.2 Determining highest and best use and valuation premise

An entity acquires a research and development (R&D) project in a business combination. The entity does not intend to complete the project. If completed, the project would compete with one of its own R&D projects. Instead the entity intends to hold the project to prevent its competitors from obtaining access to the technology. The project is expected to provide defensive value, principally by improving the prospects for the entity's own competing technology.

Under IFRS 3 *Business Combinations*, the acquiring entity is required to measure the R&D asset acquired at fair value. To measure the fair value at initial recognition, it is necessary to determine the highest and best use of the project by the market participants and the valuation premise.

Some possible uses and their related valuation premises are:

(a) The highest and best use of the R&D project may be where the market participants would continue to develop the R&D project to maximise its use within their own operations. The relevant valuation premise is the in-combination valuation premise. The fair value of the R&D project would be determined on the basis of the price that the reporting entity would receive on selling the R&D project to the market participants, assuming that these market participants would use the R&D asset in conjunction with their other assets as a group and that these assets are available to the market participants.

(b) The highest and best use may be for the market participants to cease development of the project. This might occur if the project is not expected to provide a market rate of return if completed. The relevant valuation premise is the stand-alone valuation premise as the asset will exist as a stand-alone asset and not be used in conjunction with other assets. The fair value of the R&D project would be determined on the basis of the price that would be received on sale of the project by itself to market participants. The fair value may be zero.

Source: Adapted from IASB 2011, IFRS 13 *Fair Value Measurement, Illustrative Examples,* Example 3 — Research and development project, pp. 7–8.

ILLUSTRATIVE EXAMPLE 3.3 Determining highest and best use and valuation premise

In a business combination, an entity acquires land on which a factory stands. The land is currently developed for industrial use. Nearby sites have recently been developed for residential use as sites for high-rise apartment buildings. Recent zoning changes have meant that the land could now also be used for residential purposes.

The highest and best use of the land would be determined by comparing the results from the following possible uses:

- The land could continue to be used as currently used, namely as a site for the factory, and the factory would continue to operate. The valuation premise in this scenario is the in-combination valuation premise, as the fair value of both the land and the factory would be based on selling these assets to market participants who would also use these assets for industrial purposes in conjunction with their other assets.
- The land could be made into a vacant site for residential purposes. The valuation premise is then a stand-alone valuation premise as the land is sold as a stand-alone asset. Use of the land for residential purposes would mean that the factory would need to be demolished. The fair value of the land would then be calculated net of the cost of demolition of the factory and other costs of conversion to a vacant site.

In this situation, the fair value of the factory may be linked to the fair value of the land on which it is situated. The fair value of the factory may be zero if the land has an alternative use, such as for residential purposes, and the factory is demolished. According to paragraph BC73 of the Basis for Conclusions on IFRS 13, the standard setters decided that 'when an entity uses a non-financial asset in a way that differs from its highest and best use (and that asset is measured at fair value), the entity must simply disclose that fact and why the asset is being used in a manner that differs from its highest and best use...'

Source: Adapted from IASB 2011, IFRS 13 *Fair Value Measurement, Illustrative Examples,* Example 2 — Land, p. 7.

3.3.3 What is the principal (or most advantageous) market for the asset?

Paragraph 16 of IFRS 13 states:

A fair value measurement assumes that the transaction to sell the asset or transfer the liability takes place either:
(a) in the *principal market* for the asset or liability; or
(b) in the absence of a principal market, in the *most advantageous market* for the asset or liability.

Appendix A contains a definition of principal market, as follows:

The market with the greatest volume and level of activity for the asset or liability.

The principal market is then the largest market for the non-financial asset. According to paragraph 17, an entity need not make an exhaustive search of all markets in order to determine which market is the principal market. In fact, unless evidence to the contrary exists, the market in which the entity usually enters to sell this type of asset is presumed to be the principal market.

Where there is no principal market, the entity needs to determine the most advantageous market. Appendix A contains the following definition:

> The market that maximises the amount that would be received to sell the asset or minimises the amount that would be paid to transfer the liability, after considering transaction costs and transport costs.

The determination of the most advantageous market is then based on a comparison of the amounts receivable from entering a number of markets. The most advantageous market is the one that offers the highest return. Illustrative example 3.4 provides an example of determining the most advantageous market, with a consideration of transport and transaction costs.

ILLUSTRATIVE EXAMPLE 3.4 Most advantageous market

Asset XYZ is sold in two different active markets.

In Market A, the price that would be received is $27; transaction costs are $2 and the costs to transport Asset XYZ to Market A are $3.

In Market B, the price that would be received is $26; transaction costs are $2 and the costs to transport Asset XYZ to Market B are $1.

The fair value of the asset is measured using the price in the most advantageous market. The most advantageous market is the one that maximises the amount that would be received to sell the asset, after considering transaction costs and transport costs.

In Market A, the net amount received by the entity is $22, that is, $27 − $2 − $3.

In Market B, the net amount received by the entity is $23, that is, $26 − $2 − $1.

Market B is then the most advantageous market. The fair value of the asset is $25, being the amount received net of transport costs. Although transaction costs are used to determine the most advantageous market, they are not used in the calculation of fair value.

Source: Adapted from IASB 2011, IFRS 13 *Fair Value Measurement, Illustrative Examples,* Example 6 — Level 1 principal (or most advantageous) market, p. 12.

Paragraph 18 of IFRS 13 raises the situation where, on measurement date, the price receivable in the principal market is less than a more advantageous price receivable in another market. In this case, the price used to measure fair value is that receivable in the principal market.

An entity may be in a situation where it may be able to access different markets at different points of time — that is, not all markets are always accessible to the entity. The principal (or most advantageous) market must be one that the entity can access at the measurement date (paragraph 19).

The IASB reasoned that the principal market was the most liquid market and provided the most representative input for a fair value measurement (paragraph BC52 of the Basis for Conclusions on IFRS 13). The IASB also believed that most entities made operational decisions based upon an objective of maximisation of profits; therefore entities would choose the most advantageous market in which to conduct operations. The most advantageous market would then often be the market that the entity usually enters, or expects to enter.

In paragraph 21 of IFRS 13, the situation where there is no observable market for a specific asset is considered — for example, a patent or a trademark. In such cases, the reporting entity must assume that a transaction takes place at the measurement date, and consider the characteristics of market participants who might be involved in a transaction to acquire the asset under consideration and how that asset would be dealt with by those participants.

3.3.4 What is the valuation technique appropriate for the measurement?

Having determined the nature of the asset being valued, the highest and best use for the item, the valuation premise applicable, and the principal (or most advantageous) market in which the asset can be sold, the next step is to estimate the price at which the asset will be transacted in an orderly transaction between market participants.

Valuation techniques

According to paragraph 61 of IFRS 13, an entity must use valuation techniques to measure fair value. The objective of using a valuation technique is to estimate the price at which an orderly transaction would take place between market participants at the measurement date under current market conditions. Three possible valuation techniques are noted in paragraph 62, namely:

1. the market approach
2. the cost approach
3. the income approach.

The market approach is defined in Appendix A of IFRS 13 as:

> A valuation technique that uses prices and other relevant information generated by market transactions involving identical or comparable (i.e. similar) assets, liabilities or a group of assets and liabilities, such as a business.

The prices are obtained directly from information gathered from the activities in markets.

The cost approach is defined in Appendix A of IFRS 13 as:

> A valuation technique that reflects the amount that would be required currently to replace the service capacity of an asset (often referred to as current replacement cost).

It is the amount a market participant would pay to acquire or construct an asset that has the same qualities as the asset being valued. This may involve consideration of the amount to be paid for a new asset, with this amount then adjusted for both physical deterioration and technological obsolescence.

The income approach is defined in Appendix A of IFRS 13 as:

> Valuation techniques that convert future amounts (e.g. cash flows or income and expenses) to a single current (i.e. discounted) amount. The fair value measurement is determined on the basis of the value indicated by current market expectations about those future amounts.

The approach does not then rely on information generated by observation of prices generated in a market place. The fair value is based upon market expectations about future cash flows, or income and expenses associated with that asset. Present value techniques are an example of techniques used in applying the income approach. The fair value of an asset is then not based on an observed market price but rather is generated by discounting the expected earnings from the use of the asset by a market participant. Paragraphs B13–B30 of Appendix B provide details about present value techniques.

Choice of technique

IFRS 13 does not propose a hierarchy of valuation techniques. Some valuation techniques are better in some circumstances than others. Judgement is required in selecting the appropriate valuation technique for the situation.

However, some guidance in the choice of technique is provided in IFRS 13:

- The technique must be appropriate to the circumstances (paragraph 61).
- There must be sufficient data available to apply the technique (paragraph 61).
- The technique must maximise the use of observable inputs and minimise the use of unobservable inputs (paragraph 61).
- In some cases, multiple techniques are used with the results being weighed and evaluated (paragraph 63).
- Valuation techniques used to measure fair value must be consistently applied. Paragraph 65 provides examples of situations where a change in technique may be appropriate, such as when new markets develop or new information becomes available.

How different valuation techniques may be used is shown in illustrative example 3.5.

ILLUSTRATIVE EXAMPLE 3.5 Valuation techniques

An entity acquires a group of assets which includes an income-producing software asset internally developed for licence to customers.

The highest and best use of the software asset is determined to be in its use in combination with other assets. The valuation premise is then 'in-combination'.

Information about market transactions for comparable software is unavailable. The income and cost approaches could be applied as follows:

- The income approach is applied using a present value technique. The cash flows reflect the income stream expected to result from licence fees obtained from the software asset over its economic life.

- The cost approach is applied by estimating the amount that would be required currently to construct a substitute software asset of comparable utility.

Source: Adapted from IASB 2011, IFRS 13 *Fair Value Measurement, Illustrative Examples*, Example 5 — Software asset, p. 11.

Inputs to valuation techniques

According to Appendix A of IFRS 13, inputs are defined as:

The assumptions that market participants would use when pricing the asset or liability, including assumptions about risk, such as the following:
(a) the risk inherent in a particular valuation technique used to measure fair value (such as a pricing model); and
(b) the risk inherent in the inputs to the valuation technique.
Inputs may be observable or unobservable.

Regardless of which valuation technique is used, assumptions will be made in the application of the technique. A key aspect of the inputs is their classification into observable or unobservable, as the technique applied in the measurement of fair value of an asset must maximise the use of observable inputs.

Observable inputs are defined in Appendix A as:

Inputs that are developed using market data, such as publicly available information about actual events or transactions, and reflect the assumptions that market participants would use when pricing the asset or liability.

Unobservable inputs are defined in Appendix A as:

Inputs for which market data are not available and that are developed using the best information available about the assumptions that market participants would use when pricing the asset or liability.

As noted earlier, in choosing a valuation technique it is necessary to maximise the use of observable inputs and minimise the use of unobservable inputs. Hence, an income approach valuation technique that maximises the use of observable inputs and minimises the use of unobservable inputs may provide a better measure of fair value than a market valuation technique that requires significant adjustment using unobservable inputs.

Fair value hierarchy — prioritising inputs

To achieve consistency and comparability in the measurement of fair values, IFRS 13 provides a hierarchy of inputs showing which inputs are considered to be given higher priority in determining a fair value measurement.

Four important points critical to understanding the uses of these inputs are:
1. The inputs are prioritised into three levels — Level 1, Level 2 and Level 3.
2. The fair value hierarchy gives the highest priority to quoted market prices in active markets for identical assets and liabilities and the lowest priority to unobservable inputs (paragraph 72).
3. Where observable inputs are used, they must be *relevant* observable inputs (paragraph 67). As noted in paragraph BC151 of the Basis for Conclusions on AASB 13, some respondents to the IASB expressed concerns about being required to use observable inputs during the global financial crisis that started in 2007 when the available observable inputs were not representative of the asset or liability being measured at fair value. Observability is then not the only criteria applied when selecting inputs; the inputs must be relevant as well as observable. Market conditions may require adjustments to be made to current observable inputs in measuring fair value.
4. The availability of inputs and their relative subjectivity potentially affects the selection of the valuation technique; however, the fair value hierarchy prioritises the *inputs* to the valuation techniques, not the techniques themselves.

Having selected the inputs and applied a valuation technique(s), a fair value measure is made. The fair value measure is then categorised. It is categorised *in its entirety* at the same level of the fair value hierarchy as the *lowest* level input that is significant to the entire measurement (paragraph 73). Hence a valuation technique that relies solely on Level 1 inputs produces a Level 1 valuation measurement. However, if that measurement also uses some Level 3 inputs that are significant to the fair value measure, then that fair value measure is classified as a Level 3 valuation measure. As is discussed in more detail below, paragraph 93(b) of IFRS 13 requires, for each class of assets and liabilities measured at fair value, the disclosure of the level of the fair value hierarchy within which the fair value measurements are categorised in their entirety (Level 1, 2 or 3).

Level 1 inputs

Level 1 inputs are defined in Appendix A as:

> Quoted prices (unadjusted) in active markets for identical assets or liabilities that the entity can access at the measurement date.

Markets such as for vehicles, property, and equity instruments on a securities exchange would generally be regarded as active markets. It would be expected that active markets would not exist for intangible assets such as patents and trademarks. As noted in paragraph 77, a quoted price in an active market provides the most reliable evidence of fair value and shall be used whenever available. A market would not be considered active if:

* there has been a significant decrease in the volume and level of activity for the asset or liability when compared with normal market activity
* there are few recent transactions
* price quotations are not based on current information
* price quotations vary substantially over time or among market-makers.

However, Level 1 inputs must also be prices for *identical* items. For vehicles and buildings, the items may be similar but are not identical. New vehicles may be identical, but it is unlikely that used vehicles would be identical. Shares and other financial instruments, both financial assets, are examples of assets which are identical and traded in active markets.

Level 2 inputs

Level 2 inputs are defined in Appendix A as:

> Inputs other than quoted prices included within Level 1 that are observable for the asset or liability, either directly or indirectly.

Note firstly that these inputs, like Level 1 inputs, are observable. According to paragraph 82, level 2 inputs include:

* quoted prices for similar assets or liabilities in active markets
* quoted prices for identical or similar assets or liabilities in markets that are not active
* inputs other than quoted prices that are observable for the asset or liability, such as interest rates and yield curves, volatilities, prepayment speeds, and credit risks
* inputs that are derived from or corroborated by observable market data by correlation or other means.

It may be necessary to make adjustments to Level 2 inputs. For example, in relation to quoted prices for similar assets, these may have to be adjusted for the condition of the assets or the location of the assets. Depending where the information for the adjustments is found, making adjustments may lead to the fair value measure being categorised at Level 3 rather than Level 2.

Paragraph B35 in Appendix B contains examples of Level 2 inputs:

* *Finished goods inventory at a retail outlet:* Level 2 inputs include either a price to customers in a retail market or a wholesale price to retailers in a wholesale market, adjusted for differences between the condition and location of the inventory item and the comparable (i.e. similar) inventory items.
* *Building held and used:* A Level 2 input would be the price per square metre for the building derived from observable market data, or derived from prices in observed transactions involving comparable buildings in similar locations.
* *Cash-generating unit:* A Level 2 input may involve obtaining a multiple of earnings or revenue from observable market data by observing transactions of similar businesses.

In all cases, reference is made to market data, and the prices are observable either directly (that is, the price is available) or indirectly (that is, information is derived from prices).

Level 3 inputs

Level 3 inputs are defined in Appendix A as:

> Unobservable inputs for the asset or liability.

Whereas Level 1 and Level 2 inputs are based on observable market data, with Level 3 inputs the inputs are unobservable. The data used may be that of the entity itself, which may be adjusted for factors that market participants may build into the valuation, or to eliminate the effects of variables that are specific to this entity but not relevant to other market participants.

Examples of Level 3 inputs include:

* *Cash-generating unit:* A Level 3 input would include a financial forecast of cash flow or earnings based on the entity's own data.

- *Trademark:* A Level 3 input would be to measure the expected royalty rate that could be obtained by allowing other entities to use the trademark to produce the products covered by the trademark.
- *Accounts receivable:* A Level 3 input would be to measure the asset based upon the amount expected to be recovered based upon the entity's historical record of recoverability of accounts receivable.

In all cases the fair value measure is based upon inputs that are not observable in a market.

In illustrative example 3.6, an example is given where different valuation techniques could be used to measure the fair value of an asset, with a consideration of the level of inputs that might be used.

ILLUSTRATIVE EXAMPLE 3.6 Valuation techniques and inputs used

An entity acquired a machine in a business combination that is held and used in its operations. The machine was initially acquired from a supplier and was then customised by the entity for use in its own operations.

The highest and best use of the machine is its use in combination with other assets as a group. The valuation premise is then 'in-combination'.

Two valuation techniques that could be applied are the market approach and the cost approach. The income approach is not applicable as the machine by itself does not generate cash flows or earnings; the earnings are generated by its use in combination with other assets, within a cash-generating unit.

Market approach

This would be applied by determining quoted prices for similar machines adjusted for differences between the machine, as customised, and other machines and taking into account the effects of location and condition of the asset. The inputs here are Level 2 inputs as they arise from observable market prices, being quoted prices for similar machines.

Cost approach

The entity would estimate the amount that would currently be required to construct a substitute (customised) machine of comparable utility. Again, adjustments would be necessary for the effects of location and condition of the asset acquired. The inputs applied here are Level 2 inputs as they are based on observable market data, namely the cost of construction.

Both prices obtained are effectively current replacements costs. The entity would need to evaluate the results of applying both valuation approaches. It needs to consider the subjectivity of the information used in the valuations, the range of values supplied by the valuation approach, the ability of an approach to be able to adjust for the condition of the machine, for example, there may be a secondhand market for used machines whereas it is impossible to construct a used machine. The level of customisation may also affect the decision as extensive customisation would lend more weight to the use of the cost approach as current market prices would not be available for customised machines.

If the fair value were based on the application of both approaches, then as Level 2 inputs are used under both approaches, the fair value measure would be classified as a Level 2 valuation.

Source: Adapted from IASB 2011, IFRS 13 *Fair Value Measurement, Illustrative Examples*, Example 4 — Machine held and used, pp. 9–10.

 3.4 APPLICATION TO LIABILITIES

This section applies to both financial and non-financial liabilities.

Prior to the issue of IFRS 13, the measurement of a liability was commonly based on the amount required to *settle* the present obligation. As per its definition in IFRS 13, fair value is the amount paid to *transfer* a liability. The fair value measurement thus assumes that the liability is transferred to another market participant at the measurement date. According to paragraph 34(a) of IFRS 13, the transfer of a liability assumes:

> A liability would remain outstanding and the market participant transferee would be required to fulfil the obligation. The liability would not be settled with the counterparty or otherwise extinguished on the measurement date.

The liability then stays in existence and is dealt with by the market participant assuming the liability is transferred at measurement date. However, the IASB argued in paragraph BC82 of the Basis for Conclusions on IFRS 13 that the fair value of a liability from the perspective of market participants who owe the liability is the same regardless of whether it is settled or transferred. This is because both settlement and transfer of a liability reflect all costs incurred, whether direct or indirect, and the entity faces the same risks as a market participant transferee. Similar thought processes are needed to estimate both the amount to settle a liability and the amount to transfer that liability.

Many of the principles established in section 3.3 of this chapter dealing with measurement of fair value of non-financial assets also apply to the measurement of the fair value of liabilities. In section 3.3 it is noted that according to paragraph B2 there are four steps in measuring the fair value of an asset. However, with liabilities there are only three steps in the measurement process — the entity must determine:

1. the particular liability that is the subject of the measurement (consistent with its unit of account)
2. the principal (or most advantageous) market for the asset or liability
3. the valuation technique(s) appropriate for the measurement.

The question of the highest and best use only applies when determining the fair value of an asset. As noted in paragraph BC65 of the Basis for Conclusions on IFRS 13, the IASB concluded that the highest and best use concept does not apply to liabilities. The ability of an entity to discharge a liability in a number of ways, such as immediate settlement or fulfilment of the contact, is not seen as a liability having alternative uses. Also, entity-specific factors are not considered to affect fair value.

In their joint response to the IASB, the three professional accounting bodies in Australia, referred to as the Representatives of the Australian Accounting Profession (2009, pp. 3–4), disagreed that the notions of highest and best use should not be applied to liabilities. They said:

> just as a market participant would seek to maximise profits from an asset, a market participant would seek to maximise gains from a liability (which would also represent the most advantageous market). Therefore where a liability can be settled or extinguished by more than one way, such as payment of a penalty, then the fair value should reflect this lowest price.

For some liabilities, such as financial liabilities, an observable market may exist and a quoted price may be obtained to measure the fair value of the liability. Where this is not available, valuation techniques must be used. The objective of a fair value measurement of a liability, when using a valuation technique, is to estimate the price that would be paid to transfer the liability between market participants at the measurement date under current market conditions. In all cases, an entity must maximise the use of relevant observable inputs and minimise the use of unobservable inputs.

In most circumstances, a liability will be *held as an asset* by another entity — for example, a loan is recognised as a payable by one entity, the recipient of the loan, and a receivable by another entity, the lender. In such cases, paragraph 37 of IFRS 13 requires that the measurement of the fair value of the liability be calculated from the perspective of a market participant that holds the identical item as an asset at measurement date. From the standard setter's perspective, the fair value of a liability equals the fair value of a properly defined corresponding asset.

Paragraph 38 of IFRS 13 states that measurement of the corresponding asset should be in the following descending order of preference:
- the quoted price of the asset in an active market
- the quoted price for the asset in a market that is not active
- a valuation under a technique such as:
  - an income approach: present value techniques could be used based on the expected future cash flows a market participant would expect to receive from holding the liability as an asset.
  - a market approach: the measure would be based on quoted prices for similar liabilities held by other parties as assets.

Illustrative example 3.7 demonstrates a situation where an entity uses a market approach valuation technique for a liability.

ILLUSTRATIVE EXAMPLE 3.7 Liability held as an asset

On 1 January 2015, Kangaroo Ltd issues at par $2 million BBB-rated exchange-traded 5-year fixed rate debt instruments with an annual 10% interest coupon.

On 31 December 2015, the instrument is trading as an asset in an active market at $929 per $1000 of par value after payment of accrued interest. Kangaroo Ltd uses the quoted price of the asset in an active market as its initial input into the fair value measurement of its liability. This measure is $1 858 000, being $929/$1000 × $2 000 000.

In determining whether the price of the asset can be used to measure the liability, Kangaroo Ltd needs to assess whether the price of the assets includes any factors that would not be included in the price of the liability — such as the effect of third-party credit enhancements. If there are none then the liability can be measured at a fair value of $1 858 000.

Source: Adapted from IASB 2011, IFRS 13 *Fair Value Measurement, Illustrative Examples,* Example 12 — Debt obligation: quoted price, pp. 20–1.

Where a corresponding *asset is not held* by another entity, such as in the case of an entity that must decommission an oil platform when drilling ceases, the entity measuring the fair value of a liability must use a valuation technique from the perspective of a market participant that owes the liability (paragraph 40). In such cases a present value technique could be applied.

Paragraphs B13–B30 of Appendix B provide information about using present value techniques to measure fair value. Paragraph B13 notes the following elements that will be captured by using a present value technique:

- an estimate of future cash flows
- expectations about variations in the amount and timing of the cash flows representing the uncertainty inherent in the cash flows
- the time value of money, represented by a risk-free interest rate
- a risk premium, being the price for bearing the uncertainty inherent in the cash flows
- other factors that market participants would take into account
- non-performance risk.

An example of the use of the present value technique for a simple debt obligation is given in illustrative example 3.8

ILLUSTRATIVE EXAMPLE 3.8 Present value technique: debt obligation

On 1 January 2015, Koala Ltd issued at par in a private placement a $2 million BBB-rated 5-year fixed rate debt instrument with an annual 10% interest coupon rate.

At 31 December 2015, Koala Ltd still carried a BBB credit rating. Market conditions, including interest rates and credit spreads for a BBB-quality credit rating and liquidity, remain unchanged from the date of issue of the debt instrument. However, Koala Ltd's credit spread had deteriorated by 50 basis points because of a change in its risk of non-performance. If the instrument were issued at 31 December 2015, the instrument would need to have an interest rate of 10.5%.

Using a present value technique, the fair value of the debt instrument at 31 December 2015 would be calculated as:

$2 000 000 × 0.670735 [Present value of single sum at end of 4 years at 10.5%]	$1 341 470
$200 000 × 3.1359 [Present value of an annuity for 4 years at 10.5%]	627 180
	$1 968 650

The fair value is then $1 968 650.

Source: Adapted from IASB 2009, IFRS 13 *Fair Value Measurement, Illustrative Examples,* Example 13 — Debt obligation: present value technique, pp. 21–2.

The present value technique may also be used for non-financial liabilities as shown in illustrative example 3.9

ILLUSTRATIVE EXAMPLE 3.9 Present value technique: decommissioning liability

On 1 January 2015, Emu Ltd assumed a decommissioning liability in a business combination. The entity is legally required to dismantle and remove an offshore oil platform at the end of its useful life, which is estimated to be 10 years.

If Emu Ltd were contractually allowed to transfer its decommissioning liability to a market participant, Emu Ltd considers that the market participant would need to take into account the following inputs:

- labour costs — these would be developed on the basis of current marketplace wages, adjusted for expected wage increases with the final amount to be determined on a probability-weighted basis
- allocation of overhead costs
- compensation for undertaking the activity including profit and a premium for undertaking the risks involved
- effects of inflation
- time value of money, represented by the risk-free rate
- non-performance risk relating to the risk that Emu Ltd will not fulfil the obligation, including Emu Ltd's own credit risk.

The risk-free rate of interest for a 10-year maturity at 1 January 2015 is 5%. Emu Ltd adjusts that rate by 3.5% to reflect its risk of non-performance including its credit risk. Hence the interest rate used in the present value calculation is 8.5%.

The present value calculation was then determined as follows:

Expected labour costs	$131 250
Allocated overhead and equipment costs	105 000
Contractor's profit margin (20% of total costs of $236 250)	47 250
Expected cash flows before inflation adjustment	$283 500
Inflation factor (4% for 10 years)	1.4802
Expected cash flows adjusted for inflation	$419 637
Market risk premium (0.05 × $419 637)	20 982
Expected cash flows adjusted for market risk	$440 619
Expected present value using a discount rate of 8.5% for 10 years	$194 879

The fair value of the decommissioning liability at 1 January 2015 determined using the present value technique is then $194 879.

Source: Adapted from IASB 2011, IFRS 13 *Fair Value Measurement, Illustrative Examples,* Example 11 — Decommissioning liability, pp. 17–20.

Non-performance risk

The fair value of a liability will reflect the effect of non-performance risk, which is defined in Appendix A as:

> The risk that an entity will not fulfil an obligation. Non-performance risk includes, but may not be limited to, the entity's own credit risk.

Non-performance is discussed in paragraphs 42–44 of IFRS 13. Non-performance risk includes an entity's own credit risk. When measuring the fair value of a liability, it is necessary to consider the effect of an entity's credit risk and any other risk factors that may influence the likelihood that the obligation will not be fulfilled (paragraph 43). Illustrative example 3.10 demonstrates the valuation of liabilities with a consideration of non-performance risk.

ILLUSTRATIVE EXAMPLE 3.10 Valuation of liabilities and non-performance risk

Wallaby Ltd and Dingo Ltd enter into a contractual obligation to pay cash of $500 to Bandicoot Ltd in five years' time. Wallaby Ltd has a AA credit rating and can borrow at 6%, while Dingo Ltd has a BBB credit rating and can borrow at 12%.

Wallaby Ltd would measure its liability at a fair value of $374, being the present value of $500 in 5 years' time at 6% p.a. Dingo Ltd will measure its liability at a fair value of $284, being the present value of $500 in 5 years' time at 12% p.a.

At initial recognition, the fair value of the liability of each entity reflects the credit standing of that entity.

Source: Adapted from IASB 2011, IFRS 13 *Fair Value Measurement, Illustrative Examples,* paragraph IE32, p. 16.

Some respondents to the IASB questioned the decision-usefulness of taking non-performance risk into consideration when valuing a liability (paragraph BC95 of the Basis for Conclusions on IFRS 13). The problem they saw was that a change in an entity's credit standing — whether deterioration or improvement — would affect the fair value of the liability. This would lead to gains and losses being recognised in profit or loss for the period, potentially affecting the usefulness of the reported numbers. The IASB argued that this issue was beyond the scope of the fair value measurement project.

3.5 APPLICATION TO MEASUREMENT OF EQUITY INSTRUMENTS

Measurement of equity instruments may be needed in such circumstances where an entity undertakes a business combination and issues its own equity instruments in exchange for a business. In general the principles set out in section 3.4 in relation to liabilities also apply to equity instruments. The fair value measure assumes that an entity's own equity instruments are transferred to a market participant at measurement date. Paragraph 34(b) of IFRS 13 notes that the transfer assumes the following:

> An entity's own equity instrument would remain outstanding and the market participant transferee would take on the rights and responsibilities associated with the instrument. The instrument would not be cancelled or otherwise extinguished on the measurement date.

In measuring an equity instrument at fair value, as with assets and liabilities, the objective is to estimate an exit price at measurement date from the perspective of a market participant who holds the instrument as an asset. If a company is the issuer of an equity instrument such as an ordinary share, then in order to exit from that instrument, the company must either cancel the share or repurchase the share. The company must then measure the fair value of the equity instrument from the perspective of a market participant who holds the instrument as an asset — for example, the company would need to consider what it would need to pay a shareholder to repurchase the share.

3.6 ISSUES RELATING TO MEASUREMENT OF FAIR VALUE OF FINANCIAL INSTRUMENTS

Financial instruments consist of both financial assets and financial liabilities. IAS 32 *Financial Instruments: Presentation* contains definitions of these terms. This section covers two issues relating to the measurement of fair value of these instruments.

3.6.1 Inputs based on bid and ask prices

Some input measures are based on market prices where there are both bid prices — the price a dealer is willing to pay — and ask prices — the price a dealer is willing to sell. An example is a foreign exchange dealer who is willing to exchange one currency for another, such as exchanging Australian dollars for Japanese yen. In such cases paragraph 70 of IFRS 13 states that the price within a bid–ask spread that is most representative of fair value should be used to measure fair value. Paragraph 72 notes that the use of a mid-market price may be used as a practical expedient.

3.6.2 Offsetting positions

An entity may hold both financial assets and financial liabilities, and as such is exposed to both market risk and credit risk. An entity may hold both assets and liabilities in a particular market and manage these as a group, having a net exposure to risk. In such a situation, IFRS 13 allows an entity to apply an exception in the measurement of fair value. Paragraph 48 of IFRS 13 states that in such circumstances the measurement of the net financial asset may be based on the price that would be received to sell a net long position, while for a net financial liability the measurement would be based on the price to transfer a net short position for a particular risk exposure in an orderly market.

Paragraph 49 provides conditions under which this exception may be applied, including that an entity must manage the group of financial assets and liabilities on a net exposure basis as a part of its documented risk management strategy.

3.7 DISCLOSURE

Paragraphs 91–99 provide the disclosures required under IFRS 13. The key principle is stated in paragraph 91:

An entity shall disclose information that helps users of its financial statements assess both of the following:
(a) for assets and liabilities that are measured at fair value on a recurring or non-recurring basis in the statement of financial position after initial recognition, the valuation techniques and inputs used to develop those measurements.
(b) for recurring fair value measurements using significant unobservable inputs (Level 3), the effect of the measurements on profit or loss or other comprehensive income for the period.

'Recurring' fair value measures are those that other IFRSs require or permit in the statement of financial position at the end of the period. 'Non-recurring' fair value measurements are those that other IFRSs require or permit in particular circumstances — for example, under the application of IFRS 5 *Non-current Assets Held for Sale and Discontinued Operations* in relation to non-current assets held for sale.

In order for users of the financial statements to be able to assess the relevance of the fair value information provided, IFRS 13 requires the disclosure of both the valuation techniques used to measure fair value as well as the inputs used to measure fair value. All fair value methods are considered to be able to provide reliable measures of fair value; however, users need disclosures about the methods used and the inputs in order to be able to assess the extent of subjectivity of the techniques used.

For each class of assets and liabilities measured at fair value, paragraph 93(a) and (b) of IFRS 13 requires the disclosure of:

(a) ... the fair value measurement at the end of the reporting period and for non-recurring measurements, the reasons for the measurement ...
(b) ... the level of the fair value hierarchy within which the fair value measurements are categorised in their entirety (Level 1, 2 or 3).

Figure 3.1 demonstrates the disclosures required by paragraphs 93(a) and (b).

FIGURE 3.1 Disclosure requirements complying with paragraphs 93(a) and (b) of IFRS 13

(CU in millions)		Fair value measurements at the end of the reporting period using			
Description	31/12/X9	Quoted prices in active markets for identical assets (Level 1)	Significant other observable inputs (Level 2)	Significant unobservable inputs (Level 3)	Total gains (losses)
Recurring fair value measurements					
Trading equity securities[a]:					
Real estate industry	93	70	23		
Oil and gas industry	45	45			
Other	15	15			
Total trading equity securities	153	130	23		
Other equity securities[a]:					
Financial services industry	150	150			
Healthcare industry	163	110		53	
Energy industry	32			32	
Private equity fund investments[b]	25			25	
Other	15	15			
Total other equity securities	385	275		110	
Debt securities:					
Residential mortgage-backed securities	149		24	125	

FIGURE 3.1 *(continued)*

Description	31/12/X9	Quoted prices in active markets for identical assets (Level 1)	Significant other observable inputs (Level 2)	Significant unobservable inputs (Level 3)	Total gains (losses)
Commercial mortgage-backed securities	50			50	
Collateralised debt obligations	35			35	
Risk-free government securities	85	85			
Corporate bonds	93	9	84		
Total debt securities	412	94	108	210	
Hedge fund investments:					
Equity long/short	55		55		
Global opportunities	35		35		
High-yield debt securities	90			90	
Total hedge fund investments	180		90	90	
Derivatives:					
Interest rate contracts	57		57		
Foreign exchange contracts	43		43		
Credit contracts	38			38	
Commodity futures contracts	78	78			
Commodity forward contracts	20		20		
Total derivatives	236	78	120	38	
Investment properties:					
Commercial — Asia	31			31	
Commercial — Europe	27			27	
Total investment properties	58			58	
Total recurring fair value measurements	1 424	577	341	506	
Non-recurring fair value measurements					
Assets held for sale[(c)]	26		26		(15)
Total non-recurring fair value measurements	26		26		(15)

(a) On the basis of its analysis of the nature, characteristics and risks of the securities, the entity has determined that presenting them by industry is appropriate.

(b) On the basis of its analysis of the nature, characteristics and risks of the investments, the entity has determined that presenting them as a single class is appropriate.

(c) In accordance with IFRS 5, assets held for sale with a carrying amount of CU35 million were written down to their fair value of CU26 million, less costs to sell of CU6 million (or CU20 million), resulting in a loss of CU15 million, which was included in profit or loss for the period.

(*Note:* A similar table would be presented for liabilities unless another format is deemed more appropriate by the entity.)

Source: IASB 2011, IFRS 13 *Fair Value Measurement, Illustrative Examples,* Example 15 — Assets measured at fair value, pp. 26–7.

Further disclosures are required when there are *changes in the inputs* used to measure fair value. Paragraph 93(c) of IFRS 13 requires disclosure of any transfers between Level 1 and Level 2 of the fair value hierarchy, the reasons for those transfers, and the entity's policy for determining when transfers between levels are deemed to have occurred.

Paragraph 93(d) of IFRS 13 requires disclosures in relation to recurring and non-recurring measurements categorised within Level 2 and Level 3 of the fair value hierarchy. In particular, entities must disclose a description of the valuation techniques used and the inputs used in the fair value measurement. Where there has been a change in the valuation technique used, this fact must be disclosed as well as the reasons for change. Where the inputs are categorised as Level 3, an entity must disclose quantitative information about the significant unobservable inputs used in the fair value measurement. Figure 3.2 provides an example of such disclosures.

FIGURE 3.2 Disclosure requirements complying with paragraph 93(d) of IFRS 13

Quantitative information about fair value measurements using significant unobservable inputs (Level 3)				
(CU in millions)				
Description	**Fair value at 31/12/X9**	**Valuation technique(s)**	**Unobservable input**	**Range (weighted average)**
Other equity securities:				
Healthcare industry	53	Discounted cash flow	weighted average cost of capital long-term revenue growth rate long-term pre-tax operating margin discount for lack of marketability[a] control premium[a]	7%–16% (12.1%) 2%–5% (4.2%) 3%–20% (10.3%) 5%–20% (17%) 10%–30% (20%)
		Market comparable companies	EBITDA multiple[b] revenue multiple[b]t discount for lack of marketability[a] control premium[a]	10–13 (11.3) 1.5–2.0 (1.7) 5%–20% (17%) 10%–30% (20%)
Energy industry	32	Discounted cash flow	weighted average cost of capital long-term revenue growth rate long-term pre-tax operating margin discount for lack of marketability[a] control premium[a]	8%–12% (11.1%) 3%–5.5% (4.2%) 7.5%–13% (9.2%) 5%–20% (10%) 10%–20% (12%)
		Market comparable companies	EBITDA multiple[b] revenue multiple[b] discount for lack of marketability[a] control premium[a]	6.5–12 (9.5) 1.0–3.0 (2.0) 5%–20% (10%) 10%–20% (12%)
Private equity fund investments	25	Net asset value[c]	n/a	n/a
Debt securities:				
Residential mortgage-backed securities	125	Discounted cash flow	constant prepayment rate probability of default loss severity	3.5%–5.5% (4.5%) 5%–50% (10%) 40%–100% (60%)
Commercial mortgage-backed securities	50	Discounted cash flow	constant prepayment rate probability of default loss severity	3%–5% (4.1%) 2%–25% (5%) 10%–50% (20%)
Collateralised debt obligations	35	Consensus pricing	offered quotes comparability adjustments (%)	20–45 −10% − +15% (+5%)

FIGURE 3.2 *(continued)*

Description	Fair value at 31/12/X9	Valuation technique(s)	Unobservable input	Range (weighted average)
Hedge fund investments:				
High-yield debt securities	90	Net asset value[(c)]	n/a	n/a
Derivatives:				
Credit contracts	38	Option model	annualised volatility of credit[(d)] counterparty credit risk[(e)] own credit risk[(e)]	10%–20% 0.5%–3.5% 0.3%–2.0%
Investment properties:				
Commercial — Asia	31	Discounted cash flow	long-term net operating income margin cap rate	18%–32% (20%) 0.08–0.12 (0.10)
		Market comparable approach	price per square metre (USD)	$3 000–$7 000 ($4 500)
Commercial — Europe	27	Discounted cash flow	long-term net operating income margin cap rate	15%–25% (18%) 0.06–0.10 (0.80)
		Market comparable approach	price per square metre (EUR)	€4 000–€12 000 (€8 500)

(a) Represents amounts used when the entity has determined that market participants would take into account these premiums and discounts when pricing the investments.
(b) Represents amounts used when the entity has determined that market participants would use such multiples when pricing the investments.
(c) The entity has determined that the reported net asset value represents fair value at the end of the reporting period.
(d) Represents the range of the volatility curves used in the valuation analysis that the entity has determined market participants would use when the pricing contracts.
(e) Represents the range of the credit default swap spread curves used in the valuation analysis that the entity has determined market participants would use when pricing the contracts.

(*Note:* A similar table would be presented for liabilities unless another format is deemed more appropriate by the entity.)

Source: IASB 2011, IFRS 13 *Fair Value Measurement, Illustrative Examples,* Example 17 — Valuation techniques and inputs, pp. 29–31.

For assets and liabilities measured at fair value in *Level 3* of the fair value hierarchy, paragraph 93(e) of IFRS 13 requires disclosure of a reconciliation from the opening balances to the closing balances and disclosure of specified information about what caused the change. Figure 3.3 demonstrates the disclosures required by paragraph 93(e).

Paragraph 97 of IFRS 13 sets out disclosures required where a class of assets and liabilities is *not* measured at fair value, but for which the fair value is disclosed. In particular, the level of the fair value hierarchy must be disclosed. it could be argued that the requirement to disclose the fair value hierarchy level for assets and liabilities not measured at fair value should not be required as disclosure of the fair values of these items is sufficient.

Where the *current use* of an asset differs from its *highest and best use*, paragraph 93(i) requires disclosure of that fact and the reasons the asset is being used in a manner that differs from its highest and best use.

Fair value measurements using significant unobservable inputs (Level 3)

(CU in millions)	Other equity securities			Debt securities			Hedge fund investments	Derivatives	Investment properties		Total
	Healthcare industry	Energy industry	Private equity fund	Residential mortgage-backed securities	Commercial mortgage-backed securities	Collateralised debt obligations	High-yield debt securities	Credit contracts	Asia	Europe	
Opening balance	49	28	20	105	39	25	145	30	28	26	495
Transfers into Level 3				60(a)/(b)							60
Transfers out of Level 3				(5)(b)(c)							(5)
Total gains or losses for the period											
Included in profit or loss			5	(23)	(5)	(7)	7	5	3	1	(14)
Included in other comprehensive income	3	1									4
Purchases, issues, sales and settlements											
Purchases	1	3			16	17		18			55
Issues											
Sales				(12)			(62)				(74)
Settlements								(15)			(15)
Closing balance	53	32	25	125	50	35	90	38	31	27	506
Change in unrealised gains or losses for the period included in profit or loss for assets held at the end of the reporting period	5		5	(3)	(5)	(7)	(5)	2	3	1	(9)

(a) Transferred from Level 2 to Level 3 because of a lack of observable market data, resulting from a decrease in market activity for the securities.
(b) The entity's policy is to recognise transfers into and transfers out of Level 3 as of the date of the event or change in circumstances that caused the transfer.
(c) Transferred from Level 3 to Level 2 because observable market data became available for the securities.
(*Note:* A similar table would be presented for liabilities unless another format is deemed more appropriate by the entity.)

FIGURE 3.3 Disclosure requirements complying with paragraph 93(e) of IFRS 13
Source: IASB 2011, IFRS 13 *Fair Value Measurement, Illustrative Examples*, Example 16 — Reconciliation of fair value measurements within Level 3 of the fair value hierarchy, p. 28.

3.8 SOME QUESTIONS ABOUT FAIR VALUE MEASUREMENT

The fair value measurement requirements have generally been well accepted by the market. However, the accounting literature contains many questions about the application of fair value measurements in practice. This section raises some of these questions.

3.8.1 How reliable are the fair value numbers?

Because the fair values can be based on unobservable data, the question of whether the fair value numbers can be considered reliable has been raised. Benston (2008) stated:

> Perhaps of greatest importance to independent public accountants, the examples presented show that fair values other than those taken from quoted prices (level 1) could be readily manipulated by opportunistic and over-optimistic managers, would be costly to make, and very difficult for auditors to verify and challenge.

Using the example given in illustrative example 3.2, Benston (2008) argues that given the variety of possible courses open to management action — continue to develop the project, lock up the project or discontinue the project — and the different forms the assumptions might then take, this 'illustrates the costliness of the required determination, its propensity for manipulation, and the difficulty of verification by auditors'.

3.8.2 Does past experience warn us against the extensive use of fair values?

Benston (2006) discussed the use of fair values by Enron, an American energy company which collapsed in 2001 as a result of a number of accounting scandals. The following information and analysis concerning Enron's activities is based on his paper.

Enron extensively used Level 3 inputs and in some cases Level 2 inputs in measuring fair value. Its failure in December 2001 had many causes but there is strong reason to believe that Enron's early and continuing use of Level 3 inputs played an important role in its demise. However, other contributing factors to Enron's demise were basing management compensation on fair value measures as well as the non-recognition and recording of reductions in value under the assumption that such moves were assumed to be temporary.

Some examples of Enron's fair value practices were as follows:

- In 1992, Enron signed a 20-year contract to supply natural gas to the developer of a large electric generating plant under construction, Sithe Energies. Enron immediately recorded the net present value of that contract as current earnings. Additional gains were recognised in later years. A loss was never recorded on this contract until after Enron declared bankruptcy.
- In 2000, Enron sold 7% of Enron Energy Services to institutional investors for $130 million. Based on this sale — which might have qualified as a Level 2 input — Enron valued the company at $1.9 billion, which allowed it to record a $61 million profit.
- Enron signed a contract in 2001 with Eli Lilly to make improvements in energy supply and use over 15 years, discounting these amounts by 8.25–8.50%. Enron valued the contract at $1.3 billion and recorded a $38 million gain. Within two years, this contract was considered to be worthless.
- In 2000, Enron announced a 20-year project (Braveheart) with Blockbuster to broadcast movies on demand to television viewers. Enron did not have the technology to deliver the movies and Blockbuster did not have the rights to the movies to be broadcast. However, Enron assigned a fair value of $125 million to its Braveheart investment. A profit of $53 million was recognised immediately, even though no sales had as yet been made, and a further $53 million profit was recorded in early 2001. In October 2001, Enron had to announce that it reversed the profits made in relation to this project. This contributed to its loss of public trust and subsequent bankruptcy.

It was subsequently revealed by the Examiner in Bankruptcy that the auditors, Arthur Andersen, had assumed the following in the valuation process: the business would be established in 10 major Metropolitan areas within 12 months, eight new areas would be added per year until 2010 and each would grow at 1% p.a., digital subscriber lines would be used by 5% of the households increasing to 32% by 2010, and Braveheart would get 50% of this market. A net cash flow from each of these households was determined, discounted by 31–34%, and a fair value determined.

Does this example provide an illustration of the weakness of using Level 3 inputs? How can one determine whether or not such assumptions about a first-time project are reasonable?

Revaluations of property, plant and equipment in the United States have had a chequered history. Hermann, Saudagaran and Thomas (2006) provided the following history of revaluations in the United States:

> Revaluations have not always been a violation of U.S. GAAP. Prior to about 1940, upward valuations of property, plant and equipment were an acceptable accounting alternative in the United States. Montgomery's 1940 edition of *Auditing* makes reference to write-ups or footnote disclosures of appraisal values for property, plant and equipment as though, from an auditing perspective, these practices were clearly acceptable accounting alternatives. (Montgomery 1940, pp. 238–241). After 1940, accounting academics in the United States continued to express support for either the upward valuation of property, plant and equipment or the footnote disclosures of current market values (Graham & Dodd 1951, p. 180; Paton & Dixon 1958, p. 457; Weston 1953, p. 489).
>
> The demise of fair value measures for property, plant and equipment in the United States can be linked to the early years of the SEC [Securities and Exchange Commission]. Neither the SEC nor the earliest private accounting standard setting bodies in the United States (i.e. the Committee on Accounting Procedures) produced explicit rules addressing the issue of upward asset valuations. Rather the removal of fair value measures and/or fair value disclosures of property, plant and equipment in financial reporting was imposed through progressively more stringent administrative procedures by the SEC (Walker, 1992). The SEC began discouraging fair value accounting for property, plant and equipment in response to unsubstantiated asset revaluations by corporations in the 1920s prior to the establishment of the SEC (Zeff, 1995, p. 59). According to Walter Schuetze, former chief accountant to the SEC, the SEC considered fair value numbers to be too soft (Schuetze, 2001, p. 10). Initially in the mid to late 1930s, the SEC discouraged, but did not restrict, asset write-ups to fair value in the filing of financial information leading to the registration of securities for public offering. By the 1940s, the SEC had essentially removed the option of upward revaluation of property, plant and equipment through the enforcement of financial statement information filed with SEC registration statements. By the 1950s, this ban had been extended to the disclosure of fair values in the footnotes to the financial statements. All of this was accomplished indirectly through internal enforcement procedures within the SEC without ever issuing a formal statement disallowing the practice of fair value accounting for property, plant and equipment. It was many years later that APB Opinion No. 6 (AICPA, 1965) formally stated that '... property, plant and equipment should not be written up by an entity to reflect appraisal, market or current values which are above cost to the entity' (para. 17).

It is then a question of whether the requirements of IFRS 13 will lead to information that is not considered to be too soft.

3.8.3 Are the fair value measures not based on directly observable market prices costly to determine?

Benston (2008) noted that fair values are not restricted to market prices, but may be based on imaginary prices that might be offered by hypothetical independent acquirers of its assets and liabilities who are participants in non-existent markets. In determining a fair value, managers must determine the highest and best use for assets, and how the hypothetical market participants may use the assets in their own operations. In doing this, management might undertake present value analyses or seek to determine current replacement costs. All of this is an expensive exercise for management.

3.8.4 Should measures based upon unobservable inputs be called fair values?

In 2005, Ernst & Young noted the practical reality that a Level 3 subjective assessment will be necessary for many assets and liabilities required to be measured at fair value. This will include intangible assets, assets acquired in a business combination, unquoted equity securities, pension costs, and biological assets during the growth phase. In all these cases, many hypotheses will have to be made in determining a market price for the asset or liability. Ernst & Young argued that it would be inappropriate to refer to such calculated values as 'fair value'. This was not seen as just a matter of semantics but rather that the term 'fair value' implies to a reader active and liquid markets with knowledgeable and willing buyers and sellers and observable arm's length transactions — not values calculated on the basis of hypothetical markets, with hypothetical buyers and sellers. Ernst & Young queried whether these hypothetical amounts are sufficiently understandable, reliable, relevant and comparable to be suitable for financial reporting.

In IFRS 13, the standard setters have attempted to allay some of these concerns by requiring extensive disclosures about the measurement of fair values and the level of inputs used. Whether this will be sufficient to overcome the concerns raised in 2005 by Ernst & Young is a key question.

3.8.5 Can the measurement of fair value be prescribed before the measurement section of the *Conceptual Framework* has been determined?

In this chapter, the focus has been primarily on explaining the proposals in IFRS 13. 'When' to use fair value was not one of the stated objectives of IFRS 13. However, one worry for many people is that the standard-setting boards are moving to a fair value regime whereby all assets and liabilities will be reported at fair value. A point of concern here is that the IASB has not yet completed the measurement section of the *Conceptual Framework*. Note, for example the following statements made by Royal Dutch Shell (2009) and Ernst & Young (2009) in their responses to the IASB exposure draft:

> In our view, a broader review of when fair values should be applied is required. This is because application of the assumptions embodied in the revised definition [of fair value], in particular the exit price and highest-and-best-use assumptions, will in some cases result in measurements of non-financial assets and liabilities that are misleading. We are especially concerned by the use of the revised definition in the context of business combinations. [Royal Dutch Shell]

> [W]e do not believe that fair value, as defined, provides decision-useful information (or the most decision-useful information) in all situations where IFRS currently requires (or permits) fair value as the measurement. That is, our primary concerns relate to the potential consequences of 'when' fair value measures are used, not 'how' the measurement is determined . . .

> [I]t seems premature to require entities to apply the new fair value standard before completing the *Measurement* chapter within the Conceptual Framework. In our view, a Conceptual Framework that establishes the objectives of financial reporting and the measurement alternatives best suited to meet those objectives serves as the foundation for developing consistent and conceptually sound global accounting standards. [Ernst & Young][3]

A difficult task to be faced by the standard setters will be in terms of the measurement philosophy to be adopted in the *Conceptual Framework*. Whittington (2008), a former member of the IASB, argued that there are two broad schools of thought or world views in relation to measurement — the fair value view and the alternative view.

Whittington (2008, pp. 157–8) sees the main features of the fair value view as follows:

- *Usefulness for economic decisions* is the sole objective of financial reporting.
- *Current and prospective investors and creditors* are the reference users for general purpose financial statements.
- *Forecasting future cash flows*, preferably as directly as possible, is the principal need of those users.
- *Relevance* is the primary characteristic required by financial statements.
- *Reliability* is less important and is better replaced by representational faithfulness, which implies a greater concern for capturing economic substance, and less with statistical accuracy.
- Accounting information needs ideally to reflect the *future*, not the past, so past transactions and events are only peripherally relevant.
- Market process should give an informed, *non-entity specific* estimate of cash flow potential, and *markets* are generally sufficiently complete and efficient to provide evidence for representational faithful measurement on this basis.

Under this view, cost is seen as an inappropriate measurement as it relates to a past event while future cash flows will result from future exit prices.

Whittington admits the alternative view is more difficult to articulate (2008, p. 158) than the fair value view, but provides the following as the main features of that view (2008, p. 159):

- *Stewardship*, defined as accountability to present shareholders, is a distinct objective, ranking equally with decision usefulness.
- *Present shareholders* of the holding company have a special status as users of financial statements.
- *Future cash flows* may be *endogenous*: feedback from shareholders and markets in response to accounting reports may influence management decisions.
- Financial reporting relieves *information asymmetry* in an uncertain world, so *reliability* is an essential characteristic.
- *Past transactions and events* are important both for stewardship and as *inputs* to the prediction of future cash flows.
- The economic environment is one of *imperfect and incomplete markets* in which market opportunities are *entity-specific*.

---

[3] Note that this quotation is an extract from Ernst & Young's comment letter and readers should refer to the full letter for a detailed understanding of the issues raised. Further, the views expressed may not reflect the current thinking of Ernst & Young firms. Reproduced by permission of Ernst & Young © 2012 EYGM Limited. All Rights Reserved.

Under this view, cost can be a relevant measurement basis while performance reports may be more important than balance sheets.

Decisions by the standard-setting boards on the qualitative characteristics of information, and the objectives of financial reporting will influence the place of fair value measurement in accounting. This may then affect how fair value is measured, particularly in relation to entity-specific or non-entity-specific measures, and to what assets are measured at fair value. Benston (2008, p. 101) has argued that eventual adoption of fair values for all assets and liabilities accords with the FASB's shift towards a balance sheet rather than an income statement approach to financial reporting.

SUMMARY

The debate over the best measurement method for assets and liabilities is not a new one in the accounting literature. Discussions of the decision-usefulness of various models of current value accounting have occupied many pages in accounting journals and were the focus of the research of many academics. Current accounting standards rely primarily on the use of historical cost but the use of fair values has become increasingly common in recent years, particularly with the focus on financial instruments. The standard setters therefore decided that it was time to produce an accounting standard on fair value measurement, with the focus on how to measure fair value rather than on when to use those fair values. This has resulted in the issue of IFRS 13 *Fair Value Measurement* by the IASB.

IFRS 13 contains a new definition of fair value which seeks to clarify questions raised in the application of the definition in current accounting standards. A key feature of that definition is that fair value is a current exit price rather than an entry price. The concepts of orderly transactions and market participants assist in determining the nature of the market in which the fair value is to be measured.

The determination of fair value requires an entity to undertake four steps in the valuation process. Concepts such as the valuation premise that is appropriate to the measurement and the highest and best use of an asset are critical in the measurement process. IFRS 13 also provides valuation techniques that can be used. Critical to the measurement process are the assumptions that market participants make when using a valuation technique. The assumptions or inputs are classified into three levels; the classification being based on the use of observable and unobservable inputs. In choosing a valuation technique an entity should seek to maximise the number of observable inputs used. A fair value measure is categorised in its entirety in the same level of the fair value hierarchy as the lowest level input that is significant to the entire measurement.

A key element of IFRS 13 is the requirement to disclose sufficient information about the fair value measures used. Users of financial statements should be able to assess the methods and inputs used to develop the fair value measurements, and to see the effects on income.

The standard setters have not yet completed the *Conceptual Framework*, with the chapter on measurement yet to be written. As there is a link between how to measure fair value and when to use fair value measures, there is still a lot of work to be undertaken by the standard setters to convince users of financial statements that disclosed fair values are in fact fair.

Discussion questions

1. Name three current accounting standards that permit or require the use of fair values.
2. What are the main objectives of IFRS 13?
3. What are the key elements of the definition of 'fair value'?
4. How does the proposed definition of fair value differ from that used in current accounting standards?
5. How does entry price differ from exit price?
6. Is the reporting entity a market participant?
7. Does the measurement of fair value take into account transport costs and transaction costs? Explain.
8. What are the key steps in determining a fair value measure?
9. Explain the difference between the current use of an asset and the highest and best use of that asset.
10. Explain the difference between the in-combination valuation premise and the stand-alone valuation premise.
11. What is the difference between an entity's principal market and its most advantageous market?
12. What valuation techniques are available to measure fair value?
13. Explain the fair value hierarchy.
14. Explain the different levels of fair value inputs.
15. How does the measurement of the fair value of a liability differ from that of an asset?

Exercises

| Exercise 3.1 | VALUATION PREMISE FOR MEASUREMENT OF FAIR VALUE |

★ Snapper Ltd conducts a business that makes women's shoes. It operates a factory in an inner suburb of Perth, Australia. The factory contains a large amount of equipment that is used in the manufacture of shoes. Snapper Ltd owns both the factory and the land on which the factory stands. The land was acquired in 2005 for $200 000 and the factory was built in that year at a cost of $520 000. Both assets are recorded at cost, with the factory having a carrying amount at 30 June 2014 of $260 000.

In recent years there has been a property boom in Perth with residential house prices doubling such that the average price of a house is approximately $500 000. A recent valuation of the land on which the factory stands as performed by a property valuation group and based on recent sales of land in the area has the land at a value of $1 000 000. The land is now considered prime residential property given its closeness to the city and, with its superb river views, its suitability for building executive apartments. It would cost $100 000 to demolish the factory to make way for these apartments to be built. It is estimated that to build a new factory on the current site would cost around $780 000.

The directors of Snapper Ltd want to measure both the factory and the land at fair value as at 30 June 2014.

Required

Discuss how you would measure these fair values.

| Exercise 3.2 | HIGHEST AND BEST USE |

★ Bream Ltd is in the business of bottling wine, particularly for small wineries that cannot afford sophisticated technical equipment and want to concentrate on the growing of the grapes themselves. One of the key features of the bottles that are used by Bream Ltd is that, for the bottles used for white wine and champagne, they have an in-built insulation device that is successful in keeping the contents of the bottle cold, with the temperature being unaffected by the bottle being held in the hand.

In January 2014, Solar-Blue, a company experimenting with energy sources useful in combating climate change, produced a device which, when attached to the outside of a container, could display the actual temperature of the liquid inside. The temperature was displayed by the highlighting of certain colours on the device. Exactly how this device could be attached to wine bottles had yet to be specifically determined. However, Bream Ltd believed that its employees had the skills that would enable the company to determine the feasibility of such a project. Whether the costs of attaching the device to wine bottles would be prohibitive was also unknown.

As Bream Ltd was concerned that competing wine bottling companies may acquire the device from Solar-Blue, it paid $100 000 for the exclusive rights to use the device with bottles.

The accountant wants to measure the fair value of the asset acquired.

Required

Discuss the process of determining this fair value.

| Exercise 3.3 | IN-COMBINATION VALUATION PREMISE |

★ Herring Ltd acquired a business that used a large number of assets that worked in combination to produce a product saleable in offshore markets. One feature of the assets of the business is that it includes a computer program that enables the inputs to the manufacturing process to be transferred in a predetermined routine to the assets that work together to produce the output.

In measuring the fair value of the computer program, management of Herring Ltd determined that the valuation premise was 'in-combination' as the program worked together with other assets in the business.

Required

Discuss how the various valuation approaches may be applied in the determination of the fair value of the computer program.

| Exercise 3.4 | CHARACTERISTICS OF AN ASSET |

★ Mr Merman owned a large house on a sizeable piece of land in London. The property had been in his family since around 1889. Mr Merman was 92 years old and was incapable of taking care of the large property. He wanted to move into a retirement village and so sold his property to the MedSea Group which was an association of doctors. The doctors wanted to use the house for their medical practice as it was centrally situated, had many rooms and had an 'old-world' atmosphere that would make patients feel comfortable.

The house was surrounded by a large group of trees that had been planted by the Merman family over the years. The trees covered a large portion of the land. MedSea did not want to make large alterations to the house as it was suitable for a doctors' surgery. Only minor alterations to the inside of the house and some maintenance to the exterior were required. However, MedSea wanted to divide the land and sell the portion adjacent to the house; this portion currently being covered in trees. The property sold would be very suitable for up-market apartment blocks.

One of the conditions of the sale of the property to MedSea was that, while Mr Merman remained alive, the trees on the property could not be cut down as it would have caused him great distress to see such alterations to the family home. This clause in the contract would restrict the building of the apartment blocks. However, this restriction would not be enforceable on subsequent buyers of the property if MedSea wanted to sell the property in the future. A further issue affecting the building of the apartment blocks was that across one corner of the block there was a gas pipeline that was a part of the city infrastructure for the supply of gas facilities to London residents.

Required

Outline any provisions in IFRS 13 that relate to consideration of restrictions on the measurement of fair values of assets, and how in the situation described above the restrictions would affect the measurement of the fair value of the property by MedSea.

Exercise 3.5

REQUIREMENT FOR A STANDARD

★ Measurement at fair value has been available in accounting standards for a long period of time. However, it was only in 2011 that the IASB issued IFRS 13 *Fair Value Measurement*, providing an accounting standard in relation to fair value measurement.

Required

Discuss why such a standard was considered necessary.

Exercise 3.6

DEFINITION OF FAIR VALUE

★ IFRS 13 provides a definition of 'fair value'.

Required

Outline the key characteristics of this definition and explain the effects of the inclusion of each characteristic in the definition.

Exercise 3.7

ASSETS WITHOUT AN ACTIVE MARKET

★ Emily Chasan (2008) reported:

> 'It's ridiculous to apply fair value accounting to assets that have no market,' said Christopher Whalen, managing director of risk research firm Institutional Risk Analytics. 'All this volatility we now have in financial reporting and disclosure, it's just absolute madness.'
>
> 'Investors as a group have to get a better understanding of what the volatility means,' said Ed Nusbaum, chief executive of accounting firm Grant Thornton. 'They want to live in a perfect world. They'd like complete transparency and no surprises. But I think it's unlikely that the big write-downs that we've seen will reverse.'

Required

Discuss the issues associated with fair value accounting for assets without an active market.

Exercise 3.8

EXIT PRICES AS FAIR VALUE

★ Benston (2008) issued the following statement:

> Although the FASB has specified that fair values should be exit prices, many of the illustrative examples involve calculations of value-in-use or entrance values. This inconsistent application of the prescription of FAS 157 appears due to two factors. One is that the price another firm might pay for an asset depends on the value of the asset to that firm, its value in use. The other is perhaps the realization that when there is no potential purchaser, exit values would be zero or even negative if the firm would have to pay to dispose of an asset. The balance sheet would be decimated.

Required

Discuss whether Benston's criticisms of FAS 157 are applicable to IFRS 13.

Exercise 3.9

★

EXIT PRICES AS FAIR VALUE FOR CLASSES OF ASSETS

In its response to the IASB exposure draft, the G100 in Australia stated:

> The G100 does not believe that an exit price based measure of fair value is appropriate for all classes of assets. While such a measure may be appropriate for financial instruments we do not believe that an exit price based measure provides useful information for certain classes of non-financial assets such as property, plant and equipment where an entity-specific measure may be more appropriate.

Required

Discuss the use of entity-specific information in the generation of fair value numbers under IFRS 13.

Exercise 3.10

★★

MEASUREMENT OF FAIR VALUE

Ernst & Young (2005, p. 8) made the following statement:

> Nevertheless, the path the standard-setters have chosen is one where big swings in balance sheet and income statement numbers are inevitable. As a consequence, users of financial reports will need clear distinctions to be made between objective and subjective figures, between realised gains and losses, gains and losses based on real market process, and gains and losses based on hypothetical calculations.

Required

Discuss how IFRS 13 attempts to overcome these issues when providing information to users of financial reports.

Exercise 3.11

★★

FAIR VALUE OF WORK-IN-PROGRESS

In relation to fair value measurement, the following statement was made by Benston (2008):

> Since the exit price of raw materials will almost always be less than the price at which they were purchased and the exit value of partially finished goods probably is zero or negative, companies using the . . . definition of fair value would have to record a substantial expense . . . The situation is likely to be more drastic for fixed assets, particularly for special-purpose assets that have no value to other parties.

Required

Discuss the statement made by Benston.

Exercise 3.12

★★

MANAGEMENT BIAS ON FAIR VALUE MEASUREMENT

One of the concerns associated with fair value measurement is that management bias may affect the reliability of the information. IFRS 13 requires that fair values be based on market-based assumptions rather than entity-specific assumptions in order to overcome this issue.

Required

Compare the potential for management bias when making market-based or entity-specific assumptions.

Exercise 3.13

★★

FAIR VALUE HIERARCHY

IFRS 13 proposes a fair value hierarchy.

Required

Discuss the differences between the various levels in the hierarchy and whether prices produced under all levels should be described as 'fair values'.

Exercise 3.14

★★★

HIGHEST AND BEST USE

Royal Dutch Shell (2009) stated:

> 5.2 In practical terms, however, we doubt that an asset measured on any other basis than its intended use will provide more useful information to readers . . . the fact that, say, a site used for production would have a higher market value if it were redeveloped for retail purposes, is not relevant if the entity is not engaged in retail or, more obviously, needs the site in order to carry out its production operations.
>
> 5.3 The risk here is that the fair value measure, as redefined, results in irrelevant information.

Required

Discuss the issues associated with measuring the fair value of a site currently used for production but which also can be redeveloped for retail purposes.

References

Benston, GJ 2006, 'Fair value accounting: a cautionary tale from Enron', *Journal of Accounting and Public Policy*, 25(4), July, pp. 465–84.

—— 2008, 'The shortcomings of fair value accounting described in SFAS 157', *Journal of Accounting and Public Policy*, 27(2), March–April, pp. 101–14.

Chasan, E 2008, 'Is fair value accounting really fair?', Reuters, www.reuters.com, 26 February.

Ernst & Young 2005, *How fair is fair value?*, www.ey.com.

—— 2009, *Invitation to comment–fair value measurement*, www.ifrs.org.

Group of 100 2009, *ED/2009/5 Fair Value Measurement*, www.ifrs.org.

Hermann, D, Saudagaran, SM, & Thomas, WB 2006, 'The quality of fair value measures for property, plant and equipment', *Accounting Forum*, 30(1), January, pp. 43–59.

IASB 2009, IASB *Fair Value Measurements Roundtable Summary*, www.iasplus.com.

Nestlé 2009, *Comments on Exposure Draft ED/2009/5/Fair Value Measurement*, www.ifrs.org

Representatives of the Australian Accounting Profession 2009, *Comments on Exposure Draft ED/2009/5 Fair Value Measurement*, www.ifrs.org.

Royal Dutch Shell 2009, *Exposure Draft 2009/5 Fair Value Measurements*, www.ifrs.org.

Whittington, G 2008, 'Fair value and the IASB/FASB Conceptual Framework project: an alternative view', *Abacus*, 44(2), May, pp. 139–68.

4 Revenue

ACCOUNTING STANDARDS IN FOCUS

IAS 18 *Revenue*

LEARNING OBJECTIVES

After studying this chapter, you should be able to:

1 understand the background to the development of IAS 18 *Revenue*

2 understand the definition of 'income' under the *Conceptual Framework*

3 distinguish between the definitions of 'income' and 'revenue'

4 understand the scope of IAS 18

5 explain and apply the meaning of 'fair value' when applied to the measurement of revenue

6 explain and apply the recognition criteria for revenue, distinguishing between the sale of goods and the rendering of services

7 explain and apply the revenue recognition criteria for interest, royalties and dividends

8 understand the practical application of IAS 18

9 interpret and analyse the revenue recognition issues and disclosures arising in specific industries in practice

10 understand the relationship between IAS 18 and other standards and interpretations

11 describe the disclosure requirements of IAS 18

12 describe expected future developments in accounting for revenue.

4.1 INTRODUCTION TO IAS 18

IAS 18 *Revenue* was issued by the International Accounting Standards Committee (IASC) in December 1993. It replaced IAS 18 *Revenue Recognition* (issued in December 1982) and was confirmed as being included in the core set of standards to be issued by the International Accounting Standards Board (IASB) in April 2001.

IAS 18 was not amended substantially by the IASB when it was issued in 2001 and it, therefore, remains essentially a very old standard. Unfortunately, IAS 18 is not entirely consistent with the *Conceptual Framework for Financial Reporting (Conceptual Framework)* and is also internally inconsistent — with an Appendix that sometimes contradicts the body of the standard. Indeed, the original IAS 18 was written prior to the *Conceptual Framework* (which was issued in its original form in 1989). As a result, revenue recognition has been a problematic area for entities for many years. The IFRS Interpretations Committee (IFRIC) and its predecessor, the Standing Interpretations Committee (SIC), have received numerous requests for clarification of the standard and have issued six interpretations and numerous agenda decisions related to revenue since 1998.[1]

Understanding that revenue is such an important measure for entities and that it has been a problematic area for so long, the IASB, jointly with the Financial Accounting Standards Board (FASB) in the United States, added a significant project on revenue recognition to its agenda, finally issuing a discussion paper in December 2008, followed by an exposure draft (ED) in June 2010 that proposed a new model for revenue recognition. An overview of the ED is provided at the end of this chapter.

4.2 THE DEFINITION OF INCOME

The *Conceptual Framework*, paragraph 4.24 states that:

> Profit is frequently used as a measure of performance or as the basis for other measures, such as return on investment or earnings per share. The elements directly related to the measurement of profit are income and expenses.

Put simply, profit equals income less expenses. Income and expenses are the two *elements* of performance (as represented by the statement of profit or loss and other comprehensive income (also known as the statement of comprehensive income or the income statement)).

Paragraph 4.25(a) of the *Conceptual Framework* defines income as:

> increases in economic benefits during the accounting period in the form of inflows or enhancements of assets or decreases of liabilities that result in increases in equity, other than those relating to contributions from equity participants.

Put simply, an increase in an asset or a decrease in a liability will result in income, unless the increase or decrease results from an equity contribution (such as cash raised through share capital).

The definition of income is very broad, being based, in effect, on statement of financial position (balance sheet) movements. The elements of the statement of financial position (assets, liabilities and equity) are defined first in the *Conceptual Framework*, before the elements of the statement of profit or loss and other comprehensive income. Therefore, the statement of profit or loss and other comprehensive income is derived from the statement of financial position according to a strict reading of the *Conceptual Framework*. This is known as 'the asset/liability' model (see further discussion in section 4.6.1).

Because of this broad definition, income is further dissected into revenue and gains.

4.3 THE DISTINCTION BETWEEN INCOME AND REVENUE

4.3.1 Income dissected

Paragraph 4.29 of the *Conceptual Framework* states that income encompasses both revenue and gains:

> Revenue arises in the course of the ordinary activities of an entity and is referred to by a variety of different names including sales, fees, interest, dividends, royalties and rent.

---

[1] Agenda decisions indicate why IFRIC has not proceeded to issue an interpretation on an issue despite a request for clarification. This is usually because the request does not meet all the criteria for issuing an interpretation. Often IFRIC's agenda decision will explain where IFRIC thinks the answer to a particular question lies in the relevant standards.

Paragraph 4.30 of the *Conceptual Framework* states:

Gains represent other items that meet the definition of income and may, or may not, arise in the course of the ordinary activities of an entity. Gains represent increases in economic benefits and as such are no different in nature from revenue. Hence, they are not regarded as constituting a separate element in this *Conceptual Framework*.

Gains include, for example:
- gains on disposal of non-current assets (see chapter 11)
- unrealised gains on the upward revaluation of property, plant and equipment under IAS 16 *Property, Plant and Equipment* (see chapter 11)
- unrealised gains on the upward revaluation of financial assets that are classified as 'available-for-sale' under IAS 39 *Financial Instruments: Recognition and Measurement* (see chapter 7).

Because the definition of income includes both revenue and gains, these are not defined as separate elements under the *Conceptual Framework*. The only distinguishing feature of revenue in the *Conceptual Framework* is the reference to 'ordinary activities of an entity' in paragraph 4.29. Therefore, revenue is essentially a *classification* of income to distinguish between an entity's ordinary activities and other activities.

Despite the explanation in the *Conceptual Framework* as to why revenue needs no definition, IAS 18 *does* define revenue in paragraph 7 as:

the gross inflow of economic benefits during the period arising in the course of the ordinary activities of an entity when those inflows result in increases in equity, other than increases relating to contributions from equity participants.

This definition is consistent with the *Conceptual Framework*'s definition of income and its distinguishing feature of ordinary activities for revenue. However, it adds another distinguishing feature — gross inflows.

4.3.2 Ordinary activities and gross inflows

Ordinary activities are not defined in the *Conceptual Framework* or in IAS 18. In past accounting standards, a distinction was made between ordinary, abnormal and extraordinary items of income or expenses; however, this distinction and the concepts of abnormal or extraordinary items no longer exist under IFRSs. Thus, the meaning of 'ordinary' is left to entities to determine for themselves. Most entities interpret ordinary as relating to their core business operations, but this is not without some controversy.

Revenue is a gross concept, whereas gains tend to be net (although this is not always the case; for example, unrealised gains on the upward revaluation of certain assets can be gross). IAS 1, in the paragraphs dealing with offsetting, discusses this. Paragraph 34 states:

IAS 18 *Revenue* defines revenue and requires an entity to measure it at the fair value of the consideration received or receivable, taking into account the amount of any trade discounts and volume rebates the entity allows. An entity undertakes, in the course of its ordinary activities, other transactions that do not generate revenue but are incidental to the main revenue-generating activities. An entity presents the results of such transactions, when this presentation reflects the substance of the transaction or other event, by netting any income with related expenses arising on the same transaction. For example:

(a) An entity presents gains and losses on the disposal of non-current assets, including investments and operating assets, by deducting from the proceeds on disposal the carrying amount of the asset and related selling expenses

IAS 16 paragraph 68 *prohibits* gains from the disposal of property, plant and equipment from being classified as revenue. This is quite puzzling, considering that the netting requirement in IAS 1 applies also to the disposal of *operating* assets. Operating assets would be part of the entity's ordinary activities, so why would their disposal not meet the revenue classification? Presumably this is because the disposal of the asset would not be considered ordinary, whereas the continued operation of the asset would.

The logic for the link between ordinary activities and netting is not clearly articulated in IFRSs, and the potentially arbitrary nature of this distinction was highlighted in an issue presented to IFRIC in 2007. IFRIC was faced with the question of whether an entity could hold an asset for a dual purpose (both renting out and sale) as part of its ordinary activities. The question was posed by an entity in the automotive industry that rented out its cars but also sold those cars if customers wanted to purchase them. IAS 16 prohibited gains on the sale of those cars from being classified as revenue. IFRIC referred the matter to the IASB, which subsequently decided to amend IAS 16 in its 2007 Annual Improvements Process. The IASB amended IAS 16 to the extent that if an entity in the course of its ordinary activities routinely sells property, plant and equipment that it has held for rental to others, it should transfer such assets to inventories at their carrying amount when they cease to be rented and are held for sale. The proceeds of such assets should then be recognised as revenue in accordance with IAS 18 (IAS 16, paragraph 68A). As outlined in the IASB's 2007 ED on *Proposed Improvements to International Financial Reporting Standards*, in the IASB's view, the recognition of gross selling revenue, rather than a net gain or loss on sale of these assets, would better reflect the ordinary activities of such entities.

Once an item *is* classified as revenue, the question of gross or net can still arise. This is addressed in paragraph 8 of IAS 18, which states that revenue includes only the gross inflows received and receivable by the entity on its *own account*. Amounts collected on behalf of third parties, such as sales taxes, are not economic benefits that flow to the entity and do not result in increases in equity. This is because the amounts must be passed onto the third party. Therefore, they do not meet the definition of revenue. Similarly, in an agency relationship, amounts collected on behalf of the principal are not gross inflows flowing to the agent and thus do not meet the definition of revenue. Rather, the revenue is the amount of commission received or receivable by the agent. Further, IAS 18 requires revenue to be recognised net of trade discounts or volume rebates. This is nothing to do with an agency relationship and the *definition* of revenue but rather to do with how revenue is *measured* (see section 4.5).

Figure 4.1 summarises the distinction between income and revenue.

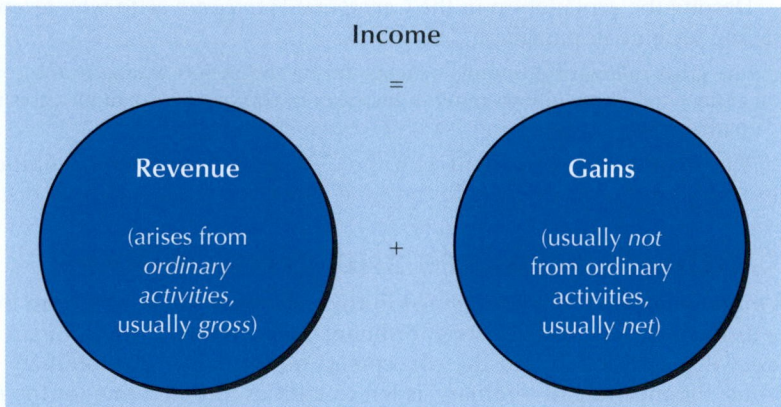

FIGURE 4.1 Distinguishing income from revenue

 LO4

4.4 THE SCOPE OF IAS 18

Paragraph 1 of IAS 18 states that the standard applies in:

accounting for revenue arising from the following transactions and events:
(a) the sale of goods;
(b) the rendering of services; and
(c) the use by others of entity assets yielding interest, royalties and dividends.

Goods include goods produced by the entity for the purpose of sale, such as products made by a manufacturer and goods purchased for resale, such as products purchased by a retailer or land held for resale.

The rendering of services typically involves the performance by an entity of a contractually agreed task over an agreed period of time. Examples include consulting services, maintenance services and accounting services. Services in respect of construction contracts are not included in the scope of IAS 18 but rather are included in the scope of IAS 11 *Construction Contracts*.

IAS 18 does not deal with revenue arising from:
(a) lease agreements (see IAS 17 *Leases* (refer chapter 12))
(b) dividends arising from investments which are accounted for under the equity method (see IAS 28 *Investments in Associates and Joint Ventures* (refer chapter 29))
(c) insurance contracts within the scope of IFRS 4 *Insurance Contracts*
(d) changes in the fair value of financial assets and financial liabilities or their disposal (see IAS 39 *Financial Instruments: Recognition and Measurement* (refer chapter 7))
(e) changes in the value of other current assets
(f) the initial recognition of and changes in the fair value of biological assets related to agricultural activity (see IAS 41 *Agriculture* (refer chapter 17))
(g) the initial recognition of agricultural produce (see IAS 41)
(h) the extraction of mineral ores.

4.5 MEASUREMENT AT FAIR VALUE

4.5.1 Measurement requirement

Paragraph 9 of IAS 18 states that:

> Revenue shall be measured at the fair value of the consideration received or receivable.

'Fair value' is defined in paragraph 7 as:

> the price that would be received to sell an asset or paid to transfer a liability in an orderly transaction between market participants at the measurement date. (See IFRS 13 *Fair Value Measurement*.)[2]

The amount of revenue arising from a transaction is usually determined by agreement between the entity and the buyer or user of the asset. Paragraph 10 states that:

> It is measured at the fair value of the consideration received or receivable taking into account the amount of any trade discounts and volume rebates allowed by the entity.

Illustrative example 4.1 illustrates the measurement of revenue where there are trade discounts or volume rebates.

ILLUSTRATIVE EXAMPLE 4.1 Measurement of revenue where there are trade discounts or volume rebates

Company Z sells packaging materials. Customers that purchase quantities in excess of a specified volume are entitled to a discount of 10% on their purchases. On 1 March 2013, Customer D purchased packaging materials in excess of the specified volume. The normal selling price per kilogram of packaging materials is $5 per kilogram. Customer D purchases 30 kilograms.

Without the volume discount, Customer D would have paid $150. With the volume discount, Customer D will pay $135. Company Z therefore measures its revenue from sales to Customer D at $135. Assuming it is a cash sale the journal entry would be:

Cash	Dr	135	
Revenue	Cr		135

If IAS 18 did not require the volume discount to be deducted in measuring the fair value of revenue, Company Z would need to record the following journal entry:

Cash	Dr	135	
Expenses (discount allowed)	Dr	15	
Revenue	Cr		150

The question of whether the expense could be netted against the revenue for disclosure purposes would then arise. Since IAS 18 requires a net measurement in the first place this question does not arise.

4.5.2 How to apply the fair value measurement requirement

In most cases, it is straightforward to calculate the fair value of the consideration received or receivable because usually the consideration is in the form of cash. The amount of cash to be paid is typically specified in an agreement.

---

[2] IFRS 13 *Fair Value Measurement* is a standard that combines all of the requirements in IFRSs regarding *how to* measure fair value into one place, rather than being dispersed throughout multiple IFRSs. IFRS 13 does *not* change any requirements regarding *when to* use fair value as the measurement basis.

Sometimes, however, the amount to be paid is deferred for a period of time. In other cases, the consideration may not be in the form of cash, but rather may be a swap for other goods or services. IAS 18 deals specifically with these cases.

Deferred consideration

Deferred consideration may take the form of interest-free credit provided to a buyer or acceptance of a note receivable bearing a below-market interest rate. In such cases, the fair value of the consideration will be less than the nominal amount of the cash receivable. IAS 18 specifies that these types of transactions are to be accounted for as financing transactions and that the fair value of the consideration should be determined by discounting all future receipts using an imputed rate of interest. The imputed rate of interest is the more clearly determinable of:

(a) the prevailing rate for a similar instrument of an issuer with a similar credit rating
(b) a rate of interest that discounts the nominal amount of the instrument to a current cash sales price of the goods or services.

The difference between the fair value and the nominal amount of the consideration is recognised as interest revenue in accordance with paragraphs 29 and 30 of IAS 18 and in accordance with IAS 39.

Illustrative example 4.2 illustrates how deferred consideration should be measured under IAS 18.

ILLUSTRATIVE EXAMPLE 4.2 Measurement of deferred consideration

Company B sells furniture and offers an interest-free period of 12 months to certain qualifying customers. Customer G qualifies for the interest-free period and purchases furniture on 30 June 2013. The current cash sales price of the furniture is $20 000. Customer G will pay $20 000 on 30 June 2014 (i.e. in 1 year's time).

The end of Company B's reporting period is 30 June. Company B determines that an appropriate discount rate for imputing interest to the transaction is 4% per annum. It determines that the present value of $20 000 to be received in 1 year's time is $19 230.

At 30 June 2013, Company B would record the following journal entry:

Receivable	Dr	20 000	
Revenue	Cr		19 230
Deferred Interest	Cr		770

For the year ended 30 June 2014, Company B would record the following journal entries:

Deferred Interest	Dr	770	
Interest Revenue	Cr		770
(To recognise interest earned on the transaction in the statement of profit or loss and other comprehensive income)			
Cash	Dr	20 000	
Receivable	Cr		20 000
(To recognise receipt of cash)			

Exchanges or swaps

The requirements for measuring consideration where goods or services are exchanged or swapped depend on whether the swap or exchange is for goods or services of a similar nature and value.

(a) If the swap or exchange *is* for goods or services of a similar nature and value, then IAS 18 states that this transaction does *not* generate revenue.
(b) If the swap or exchange *is not* for goods or services of a similar nature and value, then IAS 18 states that this transaction *does* generate revenue.

The rationale for this is not explained in the standard but can be deduced by applying the definition of revenue in IAS 18. In (a), there is no increase in equity because one asset is replaced by another with a similar value. In (b), there is an increase in equity to the extent that the replacement asset exceeds the value of the original asset. In the case of (b), IAS 18 requires the revenue to be measured at the fair value of the goods or services received, adjusted by the amount of any cash transferred.

Illustrative example 4.3 illustrates how swaps and exchanges are accounted for under IAS 18.

ILLUSTRATIVE EXAMPLE 4.3 Accounting for swaps and exchanges

Company S swaps a container of its milk for a container of milk of Company R in order to be able to deliver to a customer located closer to Company R's distribution centre. The value of the container of milk is $100, which is the same for both Company S and Company R. Company S would record the following journal entry.

Inventory – Container 2	Dr	100	
Inventory – Container 1	Cr		100

No revenue is recorded in this transaction because the swap or exchange is for goods of a similar nature and value.

The following week, Company S swaps a container of milk (with a value of $100) with Company D in exchange for a container of cream. The value of Company D's container of cream is $120. Company S also pays Company D $12. Company S would record the following journal entry:

Inventory – Container of Cream	Dr	120	
Revenue	Cr		108
Cash	Cr		12
Cost of Sales	Dr	100	
Inventory – Container of Milk	Cr		100

This transaction does generate revenue because the swap *is not* for goods of a similar nature and value. The revenue is measured gross, at the fair value of the goods received, adjusted by the amount of any cash transferred.

The requirements of IAS 18 are in contrast with those in IAS 16 *Property, Plant and Equipment*. IAS 16 (paragraph 24) addresses the measurement of the cost of property, plant and equipment acquired in an exchange transaction. It requires all exchanges to be measured at fair value unless (a) the exchange transaction lacks commercial substance or (b) the fair value of neither the asset received nor the asset given up is reliably measurable. IAS 38 *Intangible Assets* has similar requirements. However, neither of these standards addresses whether revenue arises on such exchanges. Arguably, as these exchanges are likely to be outside the ordinary activities of an entity, any difference between the two values will be treated as a gain (or loss), not as revenue.

SIC 31 *Revenue — Barter Transactions Involving Advertising Services* addresses an issue that arose during the 'dot.com' boom in the late 1990s. It deals with the circumstances under which a seller can reliably measure revenue at the fair value of advertising services received or provided in a barter transaction. It sets a number of tests that need to be met before the seller can recognise revenue at fair value, basically by reference to similar non-barter transactions.

4.6 THE RECOGNITION CRITERIA

IAS 18 sets out specific recognition criteria for the sale of goods, the rendering of services and interest, royalties and dividends.

Before considering these criteria, it is important to understand (1) the recognition criteria for income generally, (2) the main objective of IAS 18 and (3) the identification of the transaction to which the recognition criteria should be applied.

4.6.1 The recognition criteria for income generally

Paragraph 4.47 of the *Conceptual Framework* identifies the recognition criteria for income. It states:

> Income is recognised in the income statement when an increase in future economic benefits related to an increase in an asset or a decrease of a liability has arisen that can be measured reliably. This means, in effect, that recognition of income occurs simultaneously with the recognition of increases in assets or decreases in liabilities.

Theoretically, this means that once an asset is recognised or a liability reduced or derecognised, under the *Conceptual Framework*'s asset/liability model, income is recognised simultaneously.

Illustrative example 4.4 gives a simple example to illustrate the asset/liability model.

ILLUSTRATIVE EXAMPLE 4.4 Explaining the asset/liability model

Assume Company A sells goods to Customer B for $100. Customer B enters into an agreement to buy the goods from Company A on 1 February for $100. Company A delivers the goods on 15 February. Customer B pays for the goods on 28 February.

On the agreement date (1 February), Company A has undertaken to deliver the goods to Customer B and Customer B has promised to pay for them. Company A has an obligation to deliver the goods and a right to receive payment once delivery has been made. However, until Company A delivers the goods it does not have an asset under the *Conceptual Framework* because it does not control the right to receive payment until delivery. Similarly, Customer B has no liability under the *Conceptual Framework* because it has no obligation to pay until delivery has been made. The agreement is thus an executory contract (also known as an agreement equally proportionately unperformed) at agreement date because neither party to the contract has performed their obligations. In the case of such agreements, no asset or liability exists under the *Conceptual Framework*.

On the delivery date (15 February), Company A has performed under the agreement and is now entitled to receive payment. Company A thus has an asset under the *Conceptual Framework*. As the right to receive payment is not an equity contribution, the increase in the asset meets the definition of income, and Company A would record the following journal entry:

Asset – Receivable from Customer B	Dr	100
Income	Cr	100

On the payment date (28 February), Company A receives the cash from Customer B and records the following entry:

Cash	Dr	100
Asset – Receivable from Customer B	Cr	100

The right to receive cash is replaced by the cash received.

This example illustrates how basic accrual accounting fits within the asset/liability model of the *Conceptual Framework*.

Now assume that the agreement states that from 15 February, when Company A delivers the goods, it must continue to maintain them for a year for Customer B. Customer B still pays for the goods on 28 February; however, Customer B is entitled to a refund of 20% of the amount paid if Company A does not satisfactorily maintain the goods for the year as required.

Under the asset/liability model, Company A has an obligation to maintain the goods and to refund the cash as from 15 February. Thus, it would record the following entry:

Asset – Receivable from Customer B	Dr	100
Liability (obligation to maintain goods and refund cash)	Cr	20
Income	Cr	80

Under the *Conceptual Framework,* the definition of income is not met for 100% of the amount receivable because, while there has been an increase in an asset, there has also been an increase in a liability. The measurement of these amounts is not addressed in the *Conceptual Framework.*

On the payment date (28 February), Company A receives the cash from Customer B and records the following entry:

Cash	Dr	100	
Asset – Receivable from Customer B	Cr		100

The right to receive cash is replaced by the cash received as in the previous case. However, Company A still has a liability as described above. When this liability is settled, for example when the maintenance period is complete or over the period of the maintenance agreement (this is discussed further in section 4.6.5), Company A records the following entry:

Liability (obligation to maintain goods and refund cash)	Dr	20	
Income	Cr		20

The *definition* of income is met because there has been a reduction in a liability. The *recognition criteria* for income have also been met simultaneously with the reduction of the liability because the reduction of the liability can be reliably measured at that point.

Thus, under the asset/liability model, income is recognised in two parts — the first when the receivable from Customer B is recognised, and the second when the liability to Customer B is settled.

In practice, this is no different from traditional models such as an earnings model that 'defers' revenue in order to record revenue only when it is earned. In the example above, the liability to Customer B would likely be described as 'deferred income' under an earnings model and released to income either over the maintenance agreement period or at the end of the period depending on the terms of the agreement. Under the *Conceptual Framework,* 'deferred income' is not a liability; rather, the obligation to perform under the agreement is a liability. Because the measurement of this liability is not addressed in the *Conceptual Framework,* in practice, there is no difference between the asset/liability model and the earnings model in this case.

However, another approach that exists in practice is to record 100% of the revenue and then provide for the cost of meeting the obligation. This gives a different outcome from the asset/liability model.

Many of the difficulties that have arisen in practice stem from (1) lack of distinction between the *definition* of income and the *recognition* criteria and (2) lack of clarity as to what model applies under IAS 18. This is discussed further below.

4.6.2 The objective of IAS 18

We have seen that while there is a distinction between the *definition* of income and the *recognition criteria* for income under the *Conceptual Framework,* under the asset/liability model of the *Conceptual Framework,* the only key difference between the two is the test of reliable measurement. If there is an increase in an asset or a decrease in a liability resulting in an increase in equity, income *exists.* Provided it can be reliably measured, it is recognised there and then.

This is where IAS 18 comes into play. The key stated purpose of IAS 18 is to identity *when* revenue should be recognised (Objective paragraph). It states that:

Revenue is recognised when it is probable that future economic benefits will flow to the entity and these benefits can be measured reliably.

Note that these are also the recognition criteria for the recognition of assets. IAS 18 then goes on to specify the circumstances in which these criteria will be met.

This means that IAS 18 does not strictly follow the asset/liability model, because it imposes additional revenue recognition criteria beyond those in the *Conceptual Framework* for recognition of income. In illustrative example 4.4, for example, once the liability is settled, income is recognised immediately. IAS 18 sets out further criteria to determine whether, in fact, revenue is recognised at that point. However, this is not always inconsistent with the asset/liability model. In effect, consistent with the asset/liability model, it helps entities to determine *whether* the liability is settled at a point in time or over a period of time.

However, the wording used in IAS 18 is unhelpful in this regard because it mixes up definitions and recognition criteria as we will see shortly.

4.6.3 Identifying the transaction

Paragraph 13 deals with identification of the transaction to which the recognition criteria should be applied. It states:

> The recognition criteria in this Standard are usually applied separately to each transaction. However, in certain circumstances, it is necessary to apply the recognition criteria to the separately identifiable components of a single transaction in order to reflect the substance of the transaction.

Examples include the selling price of a product that includes an amount for subsequent servicing (as in illustrative example 4.4), and a sale agreement that includes a repurchase agreement such that the sale is effectively negated.

These types of arrangements are sometimes referred to as 'multiple element arrangements' and are discussed further in section 4.8.

4.6.4 Sale of goods

Paragraph 14 of IAS 18 states:

> Revenue from the sale of goods shall be recognised when all of the following conditions have been satisfied:
> (a) the entity has transferred to the buyer the significant risks and rewards of ownership of the goods;
> (b) the entity retains neither continuing managerial involvement to the degree usually associated with ownership nor effective control over the goods sold;
> (c) the amount of revenue can be measured reliably;
> (d) it is probable that the economic benefits associated with the transaction will flow to the entity; and
> (e) the costs incurred or to be incurred in respect of the transaction can be measured reliably.

Note that (a) and (b) fundamentally address whether the seller or the buyer has the asset in question that has purportedly been sold. In (a) a risks and rewards approach is applied to identifying whose asset it is, while in (b) a control approach is applied. Neither strictly applies the definition of an asset under the *Conceptual Framework*. These approaches are both currently used in IFRS literature, unfortunately not consistently. See figure 4.2.

Unfortunately 'control' is not defined in the *Conceptual Framework* and is used throughout IFRSs without consistency. Sometimes control refers to when an investor is exposed, or has rights, to variable returns from its involvement with an investee and has the ability to affect those returns through its power over the investee (IAS 27 — see chapter 29). In IAS 17 *Leases* (see chapter 12), the concept of control of an asset is linked to who has the risks and rewards incidental to ownership (even though this concept is not referred to as 'control'). In IAS 39 *Financial Instruments: Recognition and Measurement* (see chapter 7), there is a distinction between risks and rewards of ownership of an asset and control of that asset. Control in this case is referred to in terms of the entity's ability to sell the asset. If the entity is able to sell the asset then IAS 39 regards the entity as having control of the asset. In IAS 39, it is possible to *not* have the risks and rewards of ownership of an asset but still control it (paragraph 23). In IFRIC 4 *Determining whether an Arrangement contains a Lease*, the concept of *control of the use* of an asset is central. This is because a lease is defined as a *right of use* of an asset. IFRIC 4 contains conditions that must be met in order for an entity to control the right of use of an asset. These include the ability to operate the asset while obtaining more than a significant amount of output from the asset, or the ability to control physical access to the asset while obtaining more than a significant amount of output from the asset. Note, however, that these conditions will indicate whether or not the arrangement *is a lease* (i.e. whether a right of use has been given to an entity). Whether the lease transfers the risks and rewards of ownership of the asset to the entity (i.e. whether it is a finance lease or an operating lease) is a second question. Then we have to go back to IAS 17, which appears to equate risks and rewards of ownership with control!

FIGURE 4.2 Control vs. risks and rewards

The recognition criteria in the *Conceptual Framework* are repeated in (c) and (d). A new concept not included in the *Conceptual Framework* is introduced in (e) — reliable measurement of costs. The rationale for this criterion is not explained and it appears to have little to do with revenue.

Returning to our discussion of the asset/liability model, we can see that paragraph 14 has some similarities in that (c) and (d) are the same *recognition* criteria as for assets. The additional criteria in (a) and (b) deal with the asset purportedly sold and to some extent repeat the *definition* of an asset. However, by not using the same terminology as the *Conceptual Framework*, confusion is bound to arise, not to mention the fact that definitional concepts are mixed up in the recognition criteria in paragraph 14.

Paragraphs 15–19 discuss the recognition criteria in (a) and (d) in more detail. Most of the discussion relates to the transfer of the risks and rewards of ownership. In essence, the focus is on whether or not the asset has been transferred to the buyer.

Paragraph 15 states that, in most cases, the transfer of the risks and rewards of ownership coincides with the transfer of legal title or the passing of possession to the buyer. This is the case for most retail sales but not always.

Paragraph 16 states that if an entity retains significant risks of ownership, the transaction is not a sale and revenue is not recognised. Examples of such situations include:
(a) when the entity retains an obligation for unsatisfactory performance not covered by normal warranty provisions
(b) when the receipt of revenue by the seller is contingent on the buyer on-selling the goods
(c) when the goods are shipped subject to installation and the installation is a significant part of the contract which has not yet been completed by the entity
(d) when the buyer has the right to rescind the purchase.

Under the asset/liability model, these situations would result either in no asset recognised by the seller, or in a liability being recognised for all or some of the obligation or contingency created. This could result in the same outcome as IAS 18, but this depends on whether an asset is recognised and on whether any liability recognised equals the asset or is less than the asset. For example, in (a), IAS 18 prohibits any revenue recognition, whereas the asset/liability model would permit revenue recognition to the extent that the amount of the warranty obligation is less than the amount receivable from the customer. A similar situation applies in (c). However, in (b) and (d), both IAS 18 and the asset/liability model would result in no revenue recognition because under the asset/liability model a receivable from the customer would not be recognised (the definition of an asset would not be met).

Paragraph 17 states that if an entity retains only an insignificant risk of ownership, the transaction is a sale and revenue is recognised. For example a retailer may offer a refund if a customer is not satisfied.

> Revenue in such cases is recognised at the time of sale provided the seller can reliably estimate future returns and recognises a liability for returns based on previous experience and other relevant factors.

This approach is similar to the asset/liability model although it is not clear under paragraph 17 whether the liability is a liability for costs or an allocation of the amount of revenue received. This is discussed further in section 4.8.

Paragraph 18 addresses criterion (d) — the probability that economic benefits will flow to the entity. In some cases, economic benefits may not be probable until the consideration is received or until an uncertainty is removed.[3] A distinction needs to be made between an uncertainty that *precludes* revenue recognition and an uncertainty that affects the *measurement* of revenue. An example of an uncertainty that *precludes* revenue recognition would be a government restriction on remitting consideration from a sale in a foreign country. In this case, as under the asset/liability model, no receivable and thus no revenue is recognised until the government grants permission because the test of probability of inflow of economic benefits is not met until that point.

An example of an uncertainty that affects the *measurement* of revenue would be an uncertainty regarding the collectability of an amount already included in revenue. Such an amount is recognised as an expense (commonly referred to as an 'allowance for doubtful debts') rather than as an adjustment of the amount of revenue already recognised.

Paragraph 19 talks about the matching of revenue and expenses, which is somewhat of an antiquated concept and attempts to explain criterion (e) of the recognition criteria. It is curious that a standard on revenue recognition deals with cost deferral. This appears to be a derivation of US GAAP, which includes requirements in respect of cost deferral in some of its literature on revenue recognition.

---

[3] Note that 'probable' is not defined in the *Conceptual Framework*, but it is defined as meaning 'more likely than not' in IAS 37, paragraph 23.

4.6.5 Rendering of services

Paragraph 20 of IAS 18 states:

> When the outcome of a transaction involving the rendering of services can be estimated reliably, revenue associated with the transaction shall be recognised by reference to the stage of completion of the transaction at the end of the reporting period. The outcome of a transaction can be estimated reliably when all the following conditions are satisfied:
> (a) the amount of revenue can be measured reliably;
> (b) it is probable that the economic benefits associated with the transaction will flow to the entity;
> (c) the stage of completion of the transaction at the end of the reporting period can be measured reliably; and
> (d) the costs incurred for the transaction and the costs to complete the transaction can be measured reliably.

The recognition of revenue by reference to the stage of completion of a transaction is often referred to as the percentage of completion method. This method is applied in accounting for construction contracts under IAS 11 *Construction Contracts*. Under this method, revenue is recognised in the accounting periods in which the services are rendered.

Paragraphs (a) and (b) of the recognition criteria are the same as for the sale of goods. Paragraph 23 contains more guidance on 'reliable measurement' in respect of the rendering of services. It states:

> An entity is generally able to make reliable estimates after it has agreed to the following with the other parties to the transaction:
> (a) each party's enforceable rights regarding the service to be provided and received by the parties;
> (b) the consideration to be exchanged; and
> (c) the manner and terms of settlement.
> It is also usually necessary for the entity to have an effective internal financial budgeting and reporting system. The entity reviews and, when necessary, revises the estimates of revenue as the service is performed. The need for such revisions does not necessarily indicate that the outcome of the transaction cannot be estimated reliably.

Paragraph 24 sets out a number of methods that may be used to determine the stage of completion of a transaction. These include:

> (a) surveys of work performed
> (b) services performed to date as a percentage of total services to be performed
> (c) the proportion that costs incurred to date bear to the estimated total costs of the transaction.

In respect of (c), only costs that reflect services performed to date are included in costs incurred to date. Paragraph 24 also states that progress payments and advances received from customers often do *not* reflect the services performed.

Illustrative example 4.5 illustrates how the percentage of completion method is applied.

ILLUSTRATIVE EXAMPLE 4.5 Application of the percentage of completion method

On 1 March 2014, Company H enters into an agreement with Customer J to renovate Customer J's offices. The agreement states that the total consideration to be paid for the renovation will be $450 000. Company H expects that its total costs for the renovation will be $380 000. As at the end of its reporting period, 30 June 2014, Company H had incurred labour costs of $110 000 and materials costs of $150 000. Of the materials costs, $45 000 is in respect of materials that have not yet been used in the renovation. All labour costs are in respect of services performed on the renovation project. As at 30 June 2014, Customer J had made progress payments to Company H of $265 000.

Company H calculates the percentage of completion using paragraph 24(c) of IAS 18 as follows:

Total costs incurred to date	$260 000	
Less:		
Costs in respect of services not yet performed	(45 000)	
Total	215 000	(a)
Total estimated costs	380 000	(b)
Percentage complete	57%	(a) / (b)
Total estimated revenue under the agreement	450 000	(c)
Revenue to be recognised at 30 June 2014	254 605	57% × (c)

Note that payments made by Customer J cannot be used as a basis for calculating the percentage of completion under IAS 18 (paragraph 24). Also note that Company H will show a loss on this project as at 30 June 2014 (revenue of $254 605 less costs incurred to date of $260 000 equals a loss of $5395). This is because it has incurred materials costs of $45 000 that are not permitted to be used in the percentage of completion calculation because they are in respect of services that have not yet been performed. The materials will need to be used in the provision of future services on the project. However, under paragraph 19 of IAS 18, Company H could argue that it should defer the costs of $45 000 until the services are provided. If Company H deferred the costs, then it would recognise a profit of $39 605.

Sometimes it is not possible to calculate the percentage of completion of services provided as precisely as in illustrative example 4.5. For example, an entity might charge fees for admission to an event or for tuition over a period of time. Paragraph 25 of IAS 18 addresses this issue and states:

> For practical purposes, when services are performed by an indeterminate number of acts over a specified period of time, revenue is recognised on a straight-line basis over the specified period unless there is evidence that some other method better represents the stage of completion. When a specific act is much more significant than any other acts, the recognition of revenue is postponed until the significant act is executed.

So, for example, tuition fees would be recognised on a straight-line basis over the period of instruction. Admission fees to an event would be recognised when the event is staged.

How does this relate to the asset/liability model? Take the example of tuition fees. Assume an entity enters into an agreement to provide tuition for 1 year and charges an upfront fee of $12 000. Under the asset/liability model the entity would record the following journal entry on day 1 of the agreement.

Cash	Dr	12 000	
Liability (obligation to provide tuition)	Cr		12 000

As the services are provided, the entity would record the following entry:

Liability (obligation to provide tuition)	Dr	xxx	
Revenue	Cr		xxx

The asset/liability model does not prescribe how the various assets and liabilities are to be measured. Under IAS 18, the first entry would be the same except that the credit would likely be described as 'deferred revenue'. Under IAS 18, the second and following entries are also the same as under the asset/liability model (except for the description of the liability) and, in addition, IAS 18 prescribes that the amount recognised would be $1000 per month (i.e. on a straight-line basis over the period of the agreement).

In the asset/liability model, the credit recognised at inception of the agreement is known as a 'performance obligation'. While the terminology used is different, the concept of not recognising revenue until performance of the service has occurred is consistent between the two approaches.

The Appendix to IAS 18 provides numerous examples of transactions involving the rendering of services. From the examples, it is clear that the *performance of the service* is the critical requirement for revenue recognition.

Paragraph 26 addresses situations where the outcome of the transaction involving the rendering of services cannot be estimated reliably. If this is the case, then arguably one of the recognition criteria (paragraph 20(a)) is not met. Note that ALL the recognition criteria must be met in order for revenue to be recognised. Curiously, despite this, IAS 18 still permits revenue to be recognised in this case, but only to the extent of 'the expenses recognised that are recoverable'. The explanation for this is given partly in paragraph 27, which states that 'as the outcome of the transaction cannot be estimated reliably, no profit is recognised'. This directly contradicts the concept of revenue being a gross amount rather than the net gain or loss in a transaction. Arguably, if revenue is a gross concept, and one of the fundamental revenue recognition criteria is reliable measurement, if this criterion is not met then no revenue should be recognised at all. Paragraph 26 in effect focuses on cost recovery rather then revenue recognition and implies that recoverable costs can be deferred.

Paragraph 28 further exacerbates the problem by stating that if it is not probable that the costs incurred will be recovered, revenue is not recognised and the costs incurred are recognised as an expense. While these paragraphs attempt to address whether or not the outcome of a transaction can be reliably determined, by focusing on costs rather than revenue they create an inconsistency with the fundamental revenue recognition criteria.

4.7 INTEREST, ROYALTIES AND DIVIDENDS

Paragraph 29 of IAS 18 states:

> Revenue arising from the use by others of entity assets yielding interest, royalties and dividends shall be recognised on the basis set out in paragraph 30 when:
> (a) it is probable that the economic benefits associated with the transaction will flow to the entity; and
> (b) the amount of revenue can be measured reliably.

This merely repeats the revenue recognition criteria.

Paragraph 30 states:

> Revenue shall be recognised on the following bases:
> (a) interest shall be recognised using the effective interest method as set out in IAS 39, paragraphs 9 and AG5–AG8;
> (b) royalties shall be recognised on an accrual basis in accordance with the substance of the relevant agreement; and
> (c) dividends shall be recognised when the shareholder's right to receive payment is established.

The effective interest method is explained in chapter 7. Royalties accrue in accordance with the terms of the relevant agreement and are usually recognised on that basis unless it is more appropriate to recognise revenue on some other systematic basis (paragraph 33). For example, an agreement might state that an author is entitled to be paid royalties twice a year, that the author must deliver the manuscript by a certain date in order to earn the first royalty, and that the book must be published in order to earn the second royalty. In this case, there are two critical events that indicate when each royalty is earned, and revenue would be recognised on those dates. On the other hand, once the book has been published, royalties would be payable on an ongoing basis based on the sales of the book. Once a reliable measure for, say, each month's sales can be determined, royalties could be calculated on that basis and recognised as revenue on a monthly basis.

4.8 PRACTICAL EXAMPLES OF APPLYING IAS 18

The Appendix to IAS 18 (which is not a part of the standard) provides numerous examples of transactions involving the sale of goods and the rendering of services. Students should be cautious of some of the specific additional revenue recognition criteria provided in these examples because these are not always consistent with the standard and appear to be based on US GAAP rather than on IAS 18. For example, example 9 in the Appendix dealing with real estate sales indicated that the seller considers the ability of the buyer to complete payment. This example contradicted paragraph 24 of IAS 18. Example 9 was removed by IFRIC as part of interpretation IFRIC 15 *Agreements for the Construction of Real Estate*, which was issued in July 2008.

4.8.1 Examples in respect of the sale of goods

The following practical illustrative examples (4.6–4.12) further illustrate the application of IAS 18. In most of the examples one or two of the revenue recognition criteria in paragraph 14 are relatively more important to the transaction in question and these are highlighted in the examples. In all cases reliable measurement is assumed.

ILLUSTRATIVE EXAMPLE 4.6 Sales of goods where the buyer delays delivery

Company A sells goods to Customer B. Customer B requests Company A to hold delivery of the goods while it is preparing its site to be ready for delivery. Customer B formally accepts responsibility for the goods on the invoice date on the basis that that would be the usual delivery date.

Assuming the other revenue recognition criteria are met, Company A recognises revenue on the invoice date because at that date it has transferred the significant risks and rewards of ownership to Customer B and it is probable that future economic benefits will flow (i.e. Customer B will pay for the goods because it has formally accepted responsibility for them even though they have not yet been delivered).

Example 1 in the Appendix to IAS 18 provides further indicators of whether this transfer has occurred; however, these do not alter the fundamental revenue recognition criteria.

ILLUSTRATIVE EXAMPLE 4.7 Goods shipped subject to minor conditions

Company A sells goods to Customer B. On the delivery date, Company A invoices Customer B and is obliged to install the goods. The installation is minor and involves connecting the goods to an electric socket and testing that the goods perform when connected.

The key issue here is whether the installation requirement is a major or minor performance obligation of Company A. If it is a minor performance obligation with little likelihood that it will not be met then Company A has transferred the significant risks and rewards of ownership to Customer B on delivery, and it is probable that future economic benefits will flow (i.e. Customer B will pay for the goods even though installation is not complete because the installation is minor and unlikely to result in non-performance of the goods).

In this case, the performance obligation is minor and therefore Company A recognises revenue on the delivery date.

ILLUSTRATIVE EXAMPLE 4.8 Goods shipped subject to major conditions

Company A sells goods to Customer B. On the delivery date, Company A invoices Customer B and is obliged to install the goods. The installation is major and involves a few days' worth of work plus testing that the goods perform when installed.

In this case, the installation requirement is a major performance obligation. If Company A does not meet the obligation, Customer B would not accept the goods and would not pay for them. Thus, Company A has not transferred the significant risks and rewards of ownership to Customer B on delivery, and it is not probable that future economic benefits will flow (i.e. Customer B will not accept or pay for the goods until installation is complete because the installation is major and could result in non-performance of the goods if not properly performed).

In this case, the performance obligation is significant and therefore Company A does not recognise revenue until the installation is complete.

ILLUSTRATIVE EXAMPLE 4.9 Consignment sales

Company A sells goods to Customer B. The agreement between the two parties states that Customer B will hold those goods on consignment and will only pay for the goods to the extent that Customer B on-sells the goods to third parties.

In this case, Company A has not transferred the significant risks and rewards of ownership to Customer B on delivery, and it is not probable that future economic benefits will flow nor, indeed, can it be argued that revenue can be reliably measured because Customer B will only pay for those goods that it on-sells to third parties. Until Company B on-sells the goods, it has no requirement to pay anything to Company A.

Accordingly, Company A does not recognise any revenue until Customer B has on-sold the goods.

ILLUSTRATIVE EXAMPLE 4.10 Sales with a right of return

Company A sells goods to Customer B. The agreement between the two parties states that Customer B has the right to return the goods within 5 days of delivery.

The key issue here is whether the right of return is limited or unlimited. If it is a limited right, then Company A has transferred the significant risks and rewards of ownership to Customer B once that right expires, and at that date it is probable that future economic benefits will flow (i.e. Customer B will pay for the goods once the right of return period expires).

If it is an unlimited right (e.g. if Customer B can return the goods at any time in the future), then Company A has not transferred the significant risks and rewards of ownership to Customer B. In effect,

Customer B has the right to rescind the purchase and Company A is obliged to take the goods back at any time. Thus, Company A does not recognise any revenue. Example 5 in the Appendix to IAS 18 indicates that this should be accounted for as a financing transaction. This means that Company A will record the cash received for the 'sale' with the credit being recorded as a borrowing rather than as revenue (i.e. Dr Cash; Cr Borrowing).

ILLUSTRATIVE EXAMPLE 4.11 Instalment sales

Company A sells goods to Customer B. The agreement between the two parties states that Customer B pays for the goods in instalments, the first being paid on delivery and the rest being paid over 2 years from the date of delivery. The risks and rewards of the asset pass to Customer B at the date of delivery.

In this case, the revenue *recognition* criteria are met at the date of delivery. However, payment for the goods, other than the first instalment, is deferred. In accordance with IAS 18, paragraph 11, the *measurement* of the fair value of the consideration should be determined by discounting all future receipts using an imputed rate of interest.

Refer to illustrative example 4.2 for an illustration of how to apply this method.

ILLUSTRATIVE EXAMPLE 4.12 Payments in advance

Company A sells goods to Customer B. The agreement between the two parties states that Customer B pays for the goods in advance of delivery which will occur in 12 months' time. The risks and rewards of the goods pass to Customer B at the date of delivery.

Customer B pays $20 000 to Company A on 1 July 2013. Company A delivers the goods to Customer B on 1 July 2014.

Although this situation is not addressed in IAS 18, arguably it is exactly the reverse of the situation in illustrative example 4.11. Revenue is not recognised until the date of delivery and the advance payment should be treated as a financing transaction with interest accruing on it.

Company A would record the following journal entries, assuming the appropriate interest rate is 4%.

1 July 2013			
Cash	Dr	20 000	
Interest Expense	Dr	800	
Deferred Revenue (or obligation to deliver goods)	Cr		20 800
(To record the cash received in advance of delivery and accrued interest expense)			
1 July 2014			
Deferred Revenue	Dr	20 800	
Revenue	Cr		20 800
(To record the revenue recognised on the date of delivery at the fair value of the consideration which includes accrued interest)			

4.8.2 Examples in respect of the rendering of services

The following practical illustrative examples (4.13–4.17) further illustrate the application of IAS 18. In most of the examples one or two of the revenue recognition criteria in paragraph 20 are relatively more important to the transaction in question and these are highlighted in the examples. In all cases reliable measurement is assumed.

Company A sells goods to Customer B. Customer B enters into an agreement to buy the goods from Company A for $30 000 on 1 February. Company A delivers the goods on 15 February. Customer B pays for the goods on 28 February.

The agreement states that from 15 February, when Company A delivers the goods, it must continue to maintain them for a year for Customer B. Customer B still pays for the goods on 28 February; however, it is entitled to a refund of 20% of the amount paid if Company A does not satisfactorily maintain the goods for the year as required.

As discussed in illustrative example 4.4, under the asset/liability model, Company A has an obligation to maintain the goods and to refund the cash as from 15 February. Thus, it would record the following entry:

Asset – Receivable from Customer B	Dr
Liability (obligation to maintain goods and refund cash)	Cr
Revenue	Cr

Under the *Conceptual Framework*, the definition of income is not met for 100% of the amount receivable because, while there has been an increase in an asset, there has also been an increase in a liability. The measurement of these amounts is not addressed in the *Conceptual Framework*.

Under IAS 18, the same principle applies; however, the language used focuses on the stage of completion of the transaction rather than on any performance obligation. Example 11 in the Appendix to IAS 18 states that the identifiable amount for subsequent servicing is deferred and recognised as revenue over the period during which the service is performed. It also states that 'the amount deferred is that which will cover the expected costs of the services under the agreement, together with a reasonable profit on those services'. This requirement is presumably intended to achieve an estimate of the fair value of the services. Note that this does not equate to providing for the *cost* of meeting the obligation.

Thus, assuming Company A estimates the fair value of the services to be $8000, under IAS 18, Company A would record the following journal entries:

Feb. 15	Asset – Receivable from Customer B	Dr	30 000
	Deferred Revenue	Cr	8 000
	Revenue	Cr	22 000
	(To record the sale of goods to Customer B and the obligation to deliver services)		
Feb. 28	Cash	Dr	30 000
	Asset – Receivable from Customer B	Cr	30 000
	(To record the receipt of cash from Customer B)		

Over the period of the maintenance agreement Company A records the following entry:

Deferred Revenue	Dr	8 000
Revenue	Cr	8 000
(To record revenue as the services are provided to Customer B)		

ILLUSTRATIVE EXAMPLE 4.14 Commissions and upfront fees

Company A is an insurance agent and provides insurance advisory services to Customer B. Company A receives a commission from Insurance Company I when Company A places Customer B's insurance policy with Insurance Company I.

The key issue with commissions is whether the revenue is recognised in full upfront or over an actual or implied service period.

In this example, Company A would record its commission revenue in full upfront if its only service was to place the related insurance policy with Customer B. However, if Company A is required to render further services to Customer B over the life of the policy then part of the commission would be deferred and recognised as revenue over the period during which the policy is in force.

Usually it can be determined from the relevant arrangement whether further services are required. However, this is not always as simple as it sounds. In May 2006, IFRIC decided to take an item onto its agenda dealing with initial fees received by a fund manager. These fees are typically received by a fund manager when an investor makes an investment in a fund and are not refundable regardless of how long the investor remains in the relevant fund. Subsequent to the receipt of the initial fee, the fund manager will also receive an ongoing fee (usually a percentage of assets under management) from the fund for ongoing fund management. Units in the fund may be sold by an in-house adviser (i.e. belonging to the same group as the fund) or by an independent adviser.

The issue is whether the upfront fee should be recognised in full as revenue upfront or should be spread over the life of the investment.

IFRIC agreed that paragraph 13 of IAS 18 was relevant (refer section 4.6.3) and thus considered whether part of the upfront fee related to any actual or implied ongoing service obligation. The fact that the fee was not refundable did not necessarily mean that there was no ongoing service obligation. IFRIC noted that the upfront fee (usually a set percentage of the initial investment) was the same regardless of whether the investment was placed by an in-house manager or an independent adviser. If it was placed by an independent adviser, there was no link between the initial advice and the ongoing fund management. However, if it was placed by an in-house adviser there could be an implicit link between the initial advice and the ongoing fund management.

IFRIC was unable to reach agreement on this issue for various reasons, the key reason being that it was unable to determine whether the initial fee represented a separate service. The fact that an independent adviser earned the same fee as the in-house adviser did not necessarily mean that a separate service had been provided by the in-house adviser.

IFRIC agreed that if the upfront fee was clearly higher than the market rate for such a fee and was in substance related to ongoing services then the fee should be deferred. However it could not agree on the accounting in circumstances where the upfront fee was at market rate and how the link, if any, to ongoing services should be determined.

IFRIC removed the item from its agenda after debating it for three consecutive meetings because it was evident that it would be unable to reach a consensus. This discussion shows just how difficult revenue recognition issues can be in practice.

ILLUSTRATIVE EXAMPLE 4.15 Placement fees for arranging a loan[4]

Company A is a financial adviser and provides advisory services to Customer B. Company A receives a placement fee from Financial Services Company F when Company A places Customer B's loan with Company F.

In this case, the service is provided with the completion of a significant act (in accordance with paragraph 25 of IAS 18, i.e. the placement of the loan). As there is no further service obligation, Company A recognises its placement fee as at the date the loan is formally arranged.

ILLUSTRATIVE EXAMPLE 4.16 Membership fees

Company A is a sports club that charges membership fees. An upfront membership fee is payable on joining the club. In addition, an annual fee is also charged, at the commencement of each year. Both fees are non-refundable.

Again, the key question is whether the upfront fee contains any actual or implied ongoing service obligation. The upfront joining fee would usually not contain any ongoing service obligation and

---

[4] This chapter does not deal with more complex revenue recognition issues in the financial services industry. Chapter 7 addresses accounting for financial instruments which should be studied prior to considering this topic.

would provide membership only. If this is the case, then the joining fee would be recognised as revenue upfront. The annual fee would cover other services to be provided over the year — the key service being use of the facilities. Thus, the annual fee would be deferred and recognised as revenue over the year.

Note that example 17 in the Appendix to IAS 18 makes reference to collectability as a criterion for revenue recognition in the case of membership fees. This is inconsistent with paragraph 22 of IAS 18 which indicates that collectability is a *measurement* issue, not a *recognition* issue.

ILLUSTRATIVE EXAMPLE 4.17 Subscription fees

Company A is a publisher that charges non-refundable subscription fees. The subscription fee is payable each year in advance and entitles the customer to 12 magazines, one per month.

In this case, Company A clearly has an obligation to deliver the magazines each month and thus should recognise revenue when each month's magazine is despatched to the customer.

 4.9 REVENUE RECOGNITION ISSUES IN VARIOUS INDUSTRIES IN PRACTICE

Before addressing various industry issues, it is important to understand the principles for distinguishing between a principal and an agent in a transaction and for determining revenue in multiple-element transactions.

4.9.1 The principal/agent distinction

In 2009, the IASB added an additional example to IAS 18 (example 21) to clarify the distinction between an agent and a principal, following a submission to IFRIC. The example clarifies paragraph 8 of IAS 18 which states:

> in an agency relationship, the gross inflows of economic benefits include amounts collected on behalf of the principal and which do not result in increases in equity for the entity. The amounts collected on behalf of the principal are not revenue. Instead, revenue is the amount of commission.

Example 21 clarifies that the key distinction is whether the principal or agent is exposed to the significant risks and rewards associated with the sale of goods or the rendering of services. Table 4.1 explains the indicators that help make this distinction.

TABLE 4.1 Indicators of whether an entity is acting as an agent or principal in a transaction		
Feature of transaction	**Principal**	**Agent**
Responsibility for providing the goods and services	Primarily responsible for acceptable delivery of goods or services to the customer.	Not responsible for acceptability to the customer. If the customer is not satisfied the agent will have recourse to the principal.
Inventory risk — loss or damage, holding costs	Has inventory risk before or after the customer order and during shipping or on return.	Has no inventory risk.
Ability to set prices or provide additional goods or services.	Has latitude in setting prices, can offer additional goods or services.	Cannot amend prices or provide additional goods or services.
Customer's credit risk (risk that the customer will not be able to pay for the goods or services once delivered)	Bears the credit risk for the amount receivable from the customer.	Does not bear the credit risk.
Pre-determined fee or commission for services	Usually does not earn a pre-determined fee or commission.	Usually earns a pre-determined fee or commission.

4.9.2 Understanding multiple-element arrangements

In the telecommunications industry, it is common for entities to provide 'bundled' arrangements to customers. For example, a company might provide a telephone handset free of charge to a customer who subscribes for a service contract with the company. These types of arrangements are known as multiple-element arrangements and are addressed in paragraph 13 of IAS 18. Paragraph 13 requires the entity to identify the components of the transaction.

IFRIC 13 *Customer Loyalty Programmes*, which was published in June 2007 and effective for annual reporting periods beginning on or after 1 July 2008, makes it clear that paragraph 13 applies an *allocation* approach to revenue recognition. This means that the total amount of the consideration is allocated between the various components of the arrangement. Thus, if two or more goods or services are to be delivered at different times, paragraph 13 requires revenue to be allocated to each delivered and undelivered element of the transaction. The revenue in respect of the *delivered* element is recognised immediately, whereas the revenue in respect of the *undelivered* element is deferred and recognised when that element is delivered. This is in contrast to providing for the *costs* of items that have yet to be delivered. IFRIC clarified that paragraph 19 of IAS 18 applies to expected costs on items that *have already been delivered*. In other words, paragraph 19 does not deal with revenue recognition; it deals with expected costs to be incurred once revenue has already been recognised. This clarification is most helpful and alleviates some of the confusion referred to in illustrative example 4.4. Table 4.2 summarises the principles explained in IFRIC 13.

TABLE 4.2 Revenue allocation in multiple element arrangements, application of paragraphs 13 and 19 of IAS 18

	IAS 18 paragraph 13	IAS 18 paragraph 19
Key principle	Separate the transaction into its component parts. Identify the delivered and undelivered elements of the transaction. Allocate the total consideration between these elements.	Provide for the costs, if any, expected after the items have been delivered and revenue has been recognised.
Recognise revenue	For each component, when it is delivered.	N/A. Does not deal with revenue recognition.
Total amount of revenue	Equals the fair value of the consideration in accordance with paragraph 9 of IAS 18.	N/A. Does not deal with revenue recognition.
Does the total amount of revenue change over the life of the transaction?	No. The total amount determined at inception of the transaction is allocated to the various components. The timing of recognition may change but the total consideration does not change.	N/A. Does not deal with revenue recognition.

For example, assume Company A provides a bundled service offering to Customer B. It charges Customer B $3000 for upfront advice and two ongoing services — 'on-call' advice and access to Company A's databases over a 2-year period.

Customer B pays the $3000 upfront.

Company A determines that, if it were to charge a separate fee for each service if sold separately, the fee would be:

Upfront advice	$ 200
On-call advice	$2600
Access to databases	$ 800

While IFRIC 13 does not prescribe a method for allocating the consideration between the various components, a commonly accepted method is the relative fair value approach. In this example the approach results in the following allocation.

	Fair value of each component if sold separately $	Allocation of fair value to total consideration $	Allocated amount $
Upfront advice	200	200/3 600 × 3 000	166
On-call advice	2 600	2 600/3 600 × 3 000	2 167
Access to databases	800	800/3 600 × 3 000	667
Total	3 600		3 000

Company A would record the following journal entry at inception of the agreement:

Cash	Dr	3 000
Revenue – Upfront Advice	Cr	166
Deferred Revenue – On-call Advice	Cr	2 167
Deferred Revenue – Access to Databases	Cr	667

The deferred revenue for each of the undelivered elements (i.e. the on-call advice and the access to databases) will be recognised when those services are delivered. Because both the on-call advice and the access to databases are available to Customer B continuously over the period of the agreement, the revenue should be recognised in accordance with paragraph 25 of IAS 18 (i.e. on a straight-line basis).

Since this agreement is for 2 years, in each year (assuming the financial year coincides with the agreement year) Company A would record the following entry:

Deferred Revenue – On-call Advice	Dr	1 083.50
Deferred Revenue – Access to Databases	Dr	333.50
Revenue	Cr	1 417.00

By the end of the 2 years, Company A would have recorded a total of revenue of $3000, made up as follows:

Year 1	
Revenue – upfront advice	$ 166
Revenue – on-call advice and access to databases	1 417
Year 2	
Revenue – on-call advice and access to databases	1 417
Total	3 000

This equals the total consideration agreed to at the inception of the agreement. Therefore, the allocation process does not alter the *amount* of revenue recognised; it only affects the *timing* of revenue recognition.

(This should be distinguished from the case of deferred consideration where the amount of revenue *is* affected because the *payment is deferred* and this affects the fair value of the consideration).

4.9.3 Telecommunications

Numerous revenue recognition issues arise in the telecommunications industry, including multiple-element arrangements such as those described above, upfront connection fees, the sale of handsets via distributors and fees from third-party content providers.

Multiple-element arrangements

While IFRIC was asked to deal specifically with subscriber acquisition costs in the telecommunications industry in 2006, it declined to take the item onto its agenda on the basis that the IASB would address the issue more broadly as part of its revenue recognition project. The question posed was whether, in an arrangement where a handset is provided 'free' to a customer together with a contract for services, the cost of the handset to the provider could be recorded as a customer acquisition cost and capitalised as an asset. The principle articulated subsequently in IFRIC 13 discussed above makes it clear how the revenue side of the transaction should be accounted for but it does not address whether the costs can be deferred, nor does it specifically address how to determine whether components are separate or part of the multiple-element arrangement.

The key question is whether the provision of the handset forms part of a multiple-element arrangement or whether it is a separate transaction. This is often dependent on the facts and circumstances of the particular arrangement. If the provision of the handset is considered to be a separate transaction (e.g. because it is provided to the customer by a distributor who has no right of return to the telecommunications company and bears all the risks and rewards associated with the provision of the handset to the customer) then the cost of the handset to the telecommunications company should be treated as an expense when it is provided because there is no relationship to ongoing service revenue.

However, if the provision of the handset is considered to be an integral part of the service arrangement with the customer (e.g. because it is provided to the customer as part of its services agreement with the telecommunications company) then the cost of the handset to the telecommunications company could be deferred on the basis that the revenue from the entire arrangement is recognised over the period of the agreement.

Telstra Corporation Limited applies the former view in accounting policy note 2.12(d) to its 2010 financial statements, as illustrated in figure 4.3.

> **2. Summary of accounting policies (continued)**
> **2.12 Intangible assets (continued)**
> **(d) Deferred expenditure**
> Deferred expenditure mainly includes costs incurred for basic access installation and connection fees for in place and new services, and direct incremental costs of establishing a customer contract.
>
> Significant items of expenditure are deferred to the extent that they are recoverable from future revenue and will contribute to our future earning capacity. Any costs in excess of future revenue are recognised immediately in the income statement. Handset subsidies are considered to be separate units of accounting and expensed as incurred.
>
> We amortise deferred expenditure over the average period in which the related benefits are expected to be realised.

FIGURE 4.3 Deferred expenditure of Telstra Corporation
Source: Telstra (2010, p. 89).

The Deutsche Telekom Group also applies the former view as illustrated in its accounting policy note to its 2010 financial statements, as illustrated in figure 4.4

> The revenue and related expenses associated with the sale of mobile phones, wireless data devices, and accessories are recognized when the products are delivered and accepted by the customer.

FIGURE 4.4 Revenue recognition, Deutsche Telekom Group
Source: Deutsche Telekom (2010, p. 151).

Upfront connection fees

As explained in illustrative example 4.14, the key issue with fees received for connecting a customer to the telecommunications network is whether the revenue is recognised in full upfront or over an actual or implied service period. Most telecommunications companies consider the fee to form part of a multiple-element service arrangement with the customer, as illustrated in figures 4.5 and 4.6.

Sale of handsets via distributors

The key issue here is whether the distribution channels used by telecommunications companies are agents for the telecommunications company or whether they act in their own right as principals in a transaction with customers. Paragraph 8 of IAS 18 makes it clear that where an entity acts as an agent it recognises only its commission received and the key distinction between agent and principal is based on identifying who bears the risks and rewards of the goods or services to be provided (see section 4.9.1). Say, for example, a distributor sells handsets to customers and at the same time signs them up to a service agreement with the telecommunications company. The telecommunications company provides the handsets to the distributor and pays a commission to the distributor when it signs up a customer to a services agreement with the telecommunications company. The customer can return the handset to the distributor if it is faulty and the distributor must replace the handset at its own cost. This indicates that the distributor acts as a principal in respect of the handset but as an agent in respect of the services. From the telecommunications company's perspective, the revenue, if any, it receives from the sale of the handsets to the distributor is recognised at the date of sale (and related costs are expensed) rather than being recognised over the service period as discussed in the section on multiple-element arrangements above.

Fees from third-party content providers

The agent vs. principal question is also fundamental in cases where third parties provide content (such as ringtones, transport updates and games) to mobile phone customers. The content can either be purchased separately by the customer or included in a price plan.

The telecommunications company usually receives a fee from the third party content provider for every subscriber to that content. The question is whether the telecommunications company should record gross revenue from the sale of services including the content, with an expense for the cost of the content, or the net amount (i.e. the amount attributable to the content provided to the customer less the cost of the content to the telecommunications company).

The answer, again, lies in analysing the facts and circumstances of each arrangement. In general terms, where the telecommunications company is simply acting as a vehicle for the third party's content and the third party is directly responsible to the customer for issues such as accuracy of the data provided, then the telecommunications should only record the net amount as revenue.

Alternatively, if the telecommunications company brands the content as its own and takes full responsibility to the customer for its accuracy then it should record the revenue gross.

Summary of revenue recognition issues

The following extracts (figures 4.5 and 4.6) from the accounting policy notes to the financial statements of Telstra Corporation Limited and Deutsche Telekom Group provide a good summary of revenue recognition issues in the telecommunications industry.

FIGURE 4.5 Revenue recognition of Telstra Corporation

2.17 Revenue recognition
Our categories of sales revenue are recorded after deducting sales returns, trade allowances, discounts, sales incentives, duties and taxes.

(a) Rendering of services
Revenue from the provision of our telecommunications services includes telephone calls and other services and facilities provided, such as internet and data.
We record revenue earned from:
• telephone calls on completion of the call; and
• other services generally at completion, or on a straight line basis over the period of service provided, unless another method better represents the stage of completion.
Installation and connection fee revenues that are not considered to be separate units of accounting are deferred and recognised over the average estimated customer life. Incremental costs directly

(continued)

FIGURE 4.5 (continued)

related to these revenues are also deferred and amortised over the customer contract life in accordance with note 2.12(d).

In relation to basic access installation and connection revenue, we apply management judgement to determine the estimated customer contract life. Based on our reviews of historical information and customer trends, we have determined that our average estimated customer life is 5 years (2009: 5 years).

(b) Sale of goods

Our revenue from the sale of goods includes revenue from the sale of customer equipment and similar goods. This revenue is recorded on delivery of the goods sold.

Generally we record the full gross amount of sales proceeds as revenue, however if we are acting as an agent under a sales arrangement, we record the revenue on a net basis, being the gross amount billed less the amount paid to the supplier. We review the facts and circumstances of each sales arrangement to determine if we are an agent or principal under the sale arrangement.

(c) Rent of network facilities

We earn rent mainly from access to retail and wholesale fixed and mobile networks and from the rent of dedicated lines, customer equipment, property, plant and equipment and other facilities. The revenue from providing access to the network is recorded on an accrual basis over the rental period.

(d) Construction contracts

We record construction revenue on a percentage of contract completion basis. The percentage of completion of contracts is calculated based on estimated costs to complete the contract.

Our construction contracts are classified according to their type. There are two types of construction contracts, these being material intensive and short duration. Revenue is recognised on a percentage of completion basis using the appropriate measures as follows:
- for material intensive projects (actual costs/ planned costs) × planned revenue; and
- for short duration projects (which are those that are expected to be completed within a month), revenues and costs are recognised on completion.

(e) Advertising and directory services

Classified advertisements and display advertisements are published on a daily, weekly and monthly basis for which revenues are recognised at the time the advertisement is published.

All of our Yellow Pages and White Pages directory revenues are recognised on delivery of the published directories to customers' premises. Revenue from online directories is recognised over the life of service agreements, which is on average one year. Voice directory revenues are recognised at the time of providing the service to customers.

(f) Royalties

Royalty revenue is recognised on an accrual basis in accordance with the substance of the relevant agreements.

(g) Interest revenue

We record interest revenue on an accruals basis. For financial assets, interest revenue is determined by the effective yield on the instrument.

(h) Revenue arrangements with multiple deliverables

Where two or more revenue-generating activities or deliverables are sold under a single arrangement, each deliverable that is considered to be a separate unit of accounting is accounted for separately. When the deliverables in a multiple deliverable arrangement are not considered to be separate units of accounting, the arrangement is accounted for as a single unit.

We allocate the consideration from the revenue arrangement to its separate units based on the relative fair values of each unit. If the fair value of the delivered item is not available, then revenue is allocated based on the difference between the total arrangement consideration and the fair value of the undelivered item. The revenue allocated to each unit is then recognised in accordance with our revenue recognition policies described above.

Source: Telstra (2010, pp. 91–2).

FIGURE 4.6 Revenue recognition of Deutsche Telekom Group

Revenues include all revenues from the ordinary business activities of Deutsche Telekom. Revenues are recorded net of value-added tax and other taxes collected from customers that are remitted to governmental authorities. They are recognized in the accounting period in which they are earned in accordance with the realization principle. Customer activation fees are deferred and amortized over the estimated average period of customer retention, unless they are part of a multiple-element arrangement, in which case they are a component of the arrangement consideration to be paid by the customer. Activation costs and costs of acquiring customers are deferred, up to the amount of deferred customer activation fees, and recognized over the average customer retention period.

For **multiple-element arrangements**, revenue recognition for each of the units of accounting (elements) identified must be determined separately. Revenue is recognized on the basis of the fair value of the individual elements. Arrangements involving the delivery of bundled products or services shall be separated into individual elements, each with its own separate revenue contribution. Total arrangement consideration relating to the bundled contract is allocated among the different elements based on their relative fair values (i.e., a ratio of the fair value of each element to the aggregated fair value of the bundled deliverables is generated). The relative fair value of an individual element and thus the revenue recognized for this unit of accounting, however, is limited by that proportion of the total arrangement consideration to be provided by the customer, the payment of which does not depend on the delivery of additional elements. If the fair value of the delivered elements cannot be determined reliably but the fair value of the undelivered elements can be determined reliably, the total arrangement consideration provided by the customer is allocated by determining the fair value of the delivered elements as the difference between the total arrangement consideration and the fair value of the undelivered elements.

Payments to customers, including payments to dealers and agents (discounts, provisions) are generally recognized as a decrease in revenue. If the consideration provides a benefit in its own right and can be reliably measured, the payments are recognized as expenses.

Revenue recognition at Deutsche Telekom is as follows:

Revenue generated by the **mobile communications business** of the operating segments Germany, Europe, and United States includes revenues from the provision of mobile services, customer activation fees, and sales of mobile handsets and accessories. Mobile services revenues include monthly service charges, charges for special features, call charges, and roaming charges billed to T-Mobile customers, as well as other mobile operators. Mobile services revenue is recognized based upon minutes of use or other agreed calling plans less credits and adjustments for discounts. The revenue and related expenses association with the sale of mobile phones, wireless data devices, and accessories are recognized when the products are delivered and accepted by the customer.

The **fixed-network business** in the operating segments Germany and Europe provides narrow and broadband access to the fixed network as well as the Internet. Revenue generated from these types of access for the use of voice and data communications is recognized upon rendering of the service. The services rendered relate to use by customers (e.g., call minutes), availability over time (e.g., monthly service charges) or other agreed calling plans. Telecommunications equipment is also sold, leased, and serviced. Revenue and expenses associated with the sale of telecommunications equipment and accessories are recognized when the products are delivered, provided there are no unfulfilled company obligations that affect the customer's final acceptance of the arrangement. Revenue from rentals and operating leases is recognized monthly as the entitlement to the fees accrues. Revenues from customer activation fees are deferred over the average customer retention period. Revenues also result from charges for advertising and e-commerce. Advertising revenues are recognized in the period in which the advertisements are exhibited. Transaction revenues are recognized upon notification from the customer that qualifying transactions have occurred and collection of the resulting receivable is reasonably assured.

In the **Systems Solutions** operating segment, revenue is recognized when persuasive evidence of a sales arrangement exists, products are delivered or services are rendered, the sales price or fee is fixed or determinable and collectability is reasonably assured.

(continued)

FIGURE 4.6 *(continued)*

Revenue from Computing & Desktop Services is recognized as the services are provided using a proportional performance model. Revenue is recognized ratably over the contractual service period for fixed-price contracts and on an output or consumption basis for all other service contracts. Revenue from service contracts billed on the basis of time and material used is recognized at the contractual hourly rates as labor hours are delivered and direct expenses incurred.

Revenue from hardware sales or sales-type leases is recognized when the product is shipped to the customer, provided there are no unfulfilled company obligations that affect the customer's final acceptance of the arrangement. Any costs of these obligations are recognized when the corresponding revenue is recognized.

Telecommunication services include network services and hosting & ASP services. Contracts for network services, which consist of the installation and operation of communication networks for customers, have an average duration of approximately three years. Customer activation fees and related costs are deferred and amortized over the estimated average period of customer retention. Revenues for voice and data services are recognized under such contracts when used by the customer. When an arrangement contains a lease, the lease is accounted for separately in accordance with IFRIC 4 and IAS 17. Revenues from hosting & ASP services are recognized as the services are provided.

Revenue from rentals and leases is recognized on a straight-line basis over the rental period.

Source: Deutsche Telekom (2010, pp. 150–2).

4.9.4 Pharmaceutical

The following extracts (figures 4.7 and 4.8) from the financial statements of AstraZeneca PLC and Bayer AG provide a good summary of revenue recognition issues in the pharmaceutical industry. Note that some of the specific revenue recognition criteria for licence revenue recognition in multiple-element arrangements are based on US GAAP.

Revenue

Revenues comprise sales and income under co-promotion and co-development agreements.

Income under co-promotion and co-development agreements is recognised when it is earned as defined in the contract and can be reliably estimated. In general this is upon the sale of the co-promoted/developed product or upon the delivery of a promotional or developmental service.

Revenues exclude inter-company revenues and value-added taxes and represent net invoice value less estimated rebates, returns and settlement discounts. Revenues are recognised when the significant risks and rewards of ownership have been transferred to a third party.

In general, this is upon delivery of the products to wholesalers. In markets where returns are significant (currently only in the US), estimates of returns are accounted for at the point revenue is recognised. In markets where returns are not significant they are recorded when returned.

When a product faces generic competition particular attention is given to the possible levels of returns and, in cases where the circumstances are such that the level of returns (and, hence, revenue) cannot be measured reliably, revenues are only recognised when the right of return expires which is generally on ultimate prescription of the product to patients.

For the US market we estimate the quantity and value of goods which may ultimately be returned at the point of sale. Our returns accruals are based on actual experience over the preceding 12 months for established products together with market-related information such as estimated stock levels at wholesalers and competitor activity which we receive via third party information services. For newly launched products, we use rates based on our experience with similar products or a pre-determined percentage.

FIGURE 4.7 Revenue recognition of AstraZeneca
Source: AstraZeneca (2010, p. 143).

Net sales and other operating income

All revenues derived from the selling of products or rendering of services or from licensing agreements are recognized as sales. Other operational revenues are recognized as other operating income. Sales are recognized in the income statement when the significant risks and rewards of ownership of the goods have been transferred to the customer, the company retains neither continuing managerial involvement to the degree usually associated with ownership nor effective control over the goods sold, the amount of revenue and costs incurred or to be incurred can be measured reliably, and it is sufficiently probable that the economic benefits associated with the transaction will flow to the company.

Sales are stated net of sales taxes, other taxes and sales deductions at the fair value of the consideration received or to be received. Sales deductions are estimated amounts for rebates, cash discounts and product returns. They are deducted at the time the sales are recognized, and appropriate provisions are recorded. Sales deductions are estimated primarily on the basis of historical experience, specific contractual terms and future expectations of sales development. It is unlikely that factors other than these could materially affect sales deductions in the Bayer Group. Adjustments to provisions made in prior periods for rebates, cash discounts or product returns were of secondary importance for income before income taxes in the years under report.

Provisions for rebates in 2010 amounted to 1.9% of total net sales (2009: 1.8%). In addition to rebates, Group companies offer cash discounts for prompt payment in some countries. Provisions for cash discounts as of December 31, 2010 and December 31, 2009 were less than 0.1% of total net sales for the respective year.

Sales are reduced by the amount of the provisions for expected returns of defective goods or of saleable products that may be returned under contractual arrangements. The net sales are reduced on the date of sale or on the date when the amount of future returns can be reasonably estimated. Provisions for product returns amounted to 0.2% of total net sales for 2010, as in the previous year. If future product returns cannot be reasonably estimated and are significant to a sales transaction, the revenues and the related cost of sales are deferred until a reasonable estimate can be made or the right to return the goods has expired.

Some of the Bayer Group's revenues are generated on the basis of licensing agreements under which third parties are granted rights to products and technologies. Payments received, or expected to be received, that relate to the sale or outlicensing of technologies or technological expertise are recognized in income as of the effective date of the respective agreement if all rights relating to the technologies and all obligations resulting from them have been relinquished under the contract terms. However, if rights to the technologies continue to exist or obligations resulting from them have yet to be fulfilled, the payments received are deferred accordingly. Upfront payments and similar non-refundable payments received under these agreements are recorded as other liabilities and recognized in income over the estimated performance period stipulated in the agreement.

License or research and development collaboration agreements may consist of multiple elements and provide for varying consideration terms, such as upfront payments and milestone or similar payments. They therefore have to be assessed to determine whether sales revenues should be recognized for individually delivered elements of such arrangements, i.e. for more than one unit of account. The delivered elements are separated if they have value to the customer on a standalone basis, there is objective and reliable evidence of the fair value of the undelivered element(s) and the arrangement includes a general right of return relative to the delivered element(s) and delivery or performance of the as yet undelivered element(s) is probable and substantially within the control of the company. If all three criteria are fulfilled, the appropriate revenue recognition rule is then applied to each separate unit of account.

Other operating income may also arise from the exchange of intangible assets. The amount recognized is generally based on the fair value of the assets given up, which is generally calculated using the discounted cash flow method. If the assets given up are internally generated, the gain from the exchange normally equals their fair value.

FIGURE 4.8 Revenue recognition of Bayer Group
Source: Bayer (2010, pp. 156–7).

4.9.5 Retail

The following extracts (figures 4.9 and 4.10) from the financial statements of Esprit and Woolworths Limited provide a good summary of revenue recognition issues in the retail industry.

(p) Revenue recognition

Revenue comprises the fair value for the sale of goods and services, net of value-added tax, returns, rebates and discounts and after eliminating sales within the Group. Revenue is recognised as follows:

(i) Sales of goods — wholesale
Sales of goods are recognised on the transfer of risks and rewards of ownership, which generally coincides with the time when the goods are delivered to the customer and title has been passed.

(ii) Sales of goods — retail
Sales of goods are recognised on sale of a product to the customer. Retail sales are mainly in cash or by credit card.

(iii) Licensing income
Licensing income is recognised on an accrual basis in accordance with the substance of the relevant agreements.

(iv) Interest income
Interest income is recognised on a time proportion basis using the effective interest method.

FIGURE 4.9 Revenue recognition of Esprit
Source: Esprit (2010, p. 111).

(i) Sales revenue

Sales revenue represents the revenue earned from the provision of products and rendering of services to parties external to the consolidated entity and Company. Sales revenue is only recognised when the significant risks and rewards of ownership of the products, including possession, have passed to the buyer and for services when a right to be compensated has been attained and the stage of completion of the contract can be reliably measured.

Revenue is recognised on a commission only basis where Woolworths acts as an agent rather than a principal in the transaction. Revenue is recognised net of returns.

Revenue from the sale of customer gift cards is recognised when the card is redeemed and the customer purchases the goods by using the card.

(ii) Rental income
Rental income is recognised on a straight-line basis over the term of the lease.

(iii) Financing income
Interest income is recognised in the income statement as it accrues, using the effective interest method. Dividend income is recognised in the income statement on the date the entity's right to receive payment is established which in the case of quoted securities is the ex-dividend date.

FIGURE 4.10 Revenue recognition of Woolworths Limited
Source: Woolworths (2010, p. 95).

4.9.6 Airline

The airline industry has been significantly affected by the issue of IFRIC 13 *Customer Loyalty Programmes*. IFRIC 13 requires that when an entity offers customer loyalty award credits as part of a sales transaction the award credits must be identified as part of the sale transaction. The fair value of the consideration received or receivable in respect of the initial sale must be allocated between the award credits and the other components of the sale (paragraph 5). As discussed above, this is an *allocation* of the total fair value of the consideration between the amounts.

Note that IFRIC 13 only applies where the award credits are granted as *part of a sales transaction*. If, for example, a voucher is given to a customer regardless of a sale then that would be regarded as a marketing expense and would not be caught by IFRIC 13.

Some airlines previously accounted for their frequent flyer programs by providing for the incremental cost of flying the passenger when the award credits are redeemed, rather than by allocating the consideration between the components. This means the airlines recognised all the revenue at the time of the sales transaction and at the same time provided for the expected incremental cost.

The following extracts (figures 4.11, 4.12 and 4.13) illustrate the impact of IFRIC 13 on three different airlines. Qantas early adopted IFRIC 13 in its 2008 financial statements and clearly explained the impact of the change in its accounting policy. Singapore Airlines stated that it already applies the method required by IFRIC 13. British Airways stated that it would need to change its accounting policy in order to comply with IFRIC 13. Both Qantas and British Airways previously used the cost accrual method.

FIGURE 4.11 Revenue recognition of the Qantas Group

(G) Revenue Recognition

Passenger, Freight and Tours and Travel Revenue

Passenger, freight and tours and travel revenue is included in the Income Statement at the fair value of the consideration received net of sales discount, passenger and freight interline/IATA commission and goods and services tax (GST). Passenger recoveries (including fuel surcharge on passenger tickets) are disclosed as part of net passenger revenue. Freight fuel surcharge is disclosed as part of net freight revenue. Other sales commissions paid by Qantas are included in expenditure. Passenger, freight and tours and travel sales are credited to revenue received in advance and subsequently transferred to revenue when passengers or freight are uplifted or when tours and travel air tickets and land content are utilised. Unused tickets are recognised as revenue using estimates regarding the timing of recognition based on the terms and conditions of the ticket. Changes in these estimation methods could have a material impact on the financial statements of Qantas.

Frequent Flyer Revenue

Revenue received in relation to points earning flights is allocated, based on fair value, between the flight and points earned by members of the Qantas Frequent Flyer program. The value attributed to the awarded points is deferred as a liability, within revenue received in advance, until the points are ultimately utilised.

Revenue received from third parties for the issue of Qantas Frequent Flyer points is also deferred as a liability, within revenue received in advance.

As members of the program redeem points for an award, revenue is brought to account within the Income Statement. Revenue is recognised at point of redemption where non-flight rewards are awarded. Revenue in relation to flight awards is recognised when the passenger is uplifted.

The value attributed to points that are expected to expire (breakage) is recognised as revenue when the risk expires i.e. based on the number of points that have been redeemed relative to the total number expected to be redeemed.

Changes in breakage expectations are accounted for prospectively in accordance with Note 1(C). During the year, there has been no material change to breakage expectations.

Contract Work Revenue

Revenue from the rendering of services associated with contracts is included in contract work revenue.

Where services performed are in accordance with contractually agreed terms over a short period and are task specific, revenue is recognised when the service has been performed or when the resulting ownership of the goods passes to the customer.

Revenue on long-term contracts to provide goods or services is recognised in proportion to the stage of completion of the contract when the stage of contract completion can be reliably measured and otherwise on completion of the contract.

(continued)

FIGURE 4.11 *(continued)*

Other Income

Income resulting from claims for liquidated damages is recognised as other income when all performance obligations are met, including when a contractual entitlement exists, it can be reliably measured (including the impact of the receipt, if any, on the underlying assets' carrying value) and it is probable that the economic benefits will accrue to the Qantas Group.

Revenue from aircraft charter and leases, property income, Qantas Club membership fees, Frequent Flyer revenue relating to other carriers, freight terminal and service fees, commission revenue, age availed surplus revenue and other miscellaneous income is recognised as other income at the time service is provided.

Finance Income

Interest revenue is recognised as it accrues, taking into account the effective yield on the financial asset.

Asset Disposals

The gain or loss on the disposal of assets is recognised at the date the significant risks and rewards of ownership of the asset passes to the buyer, usually when the purchaser takes delivery of the asset. The gain or loss on disposal is calculated as the difference between the carrying amount of the asset at the time of disposal and the net proceeds on disposal.

Aircraft Financing Fees

Fees relating to linked transactions involving the legal form of a lease are recognised as revenue only when there are no significant obligations to perform, or refrain from performing, significant activities, management determines there are no significant limitations on use of the underlying asset and the possibility of reimbursement is considered remote. Where these criteria are not met, fees are brought to account as revenue or expenditure over the period of the respective lease or on a basis which is representative of the pattern of benefits derived from the leasing transactions, with the unamortised balance being held as a deferred lease benefit.

Dividend Revenue

Dividends/distributions from controlled entities are recognised as revenue by Qantas when dividends are declared by the controlled entities. Dividends/distributions from associates, jointly controlled entities and other investments are recognised when dividends are paid.

Dividend/distribution revenue is recognised net of any franking credits or withholding tax.

2. Change in Accounting Policy

On 1 July 2007, the Qantas Group revised its accounting policy in relation to accounting for Qantas Frequent Flyer points and their associated expiry. This accounting policy change effects the early adoption of Interpretation 13.

The previous accounting policy created a provision for the cost of the obligation to provide travel rewards to members arising from travel on points earning services. This provision excluded the costs of the number of points that were estimated to expire. The provision was calculated as the present value of the expected incremental direct cost (being the cost of meals and passenger expenses) of providing the travel rewards.

The new accounting policy requires revenue received in relation to points earning flights to be split. The allocation between the value of the flight and the value of the points awarded is undertaken at fair value. The value attributable to the flight is then recognised on passenger uplift, while the value attributed to the awarded points is deferred as a liability until the points are ultimately utilised.

The value attributed to the points that are expected to expire is recognised as revenue as the risk expires i.e. based on the number of points that have been redeemed relative to the total number expected to be redeemed.

The impact of the adoption of Interpretation 13 on the Balance Sheet as at 1 July 2006 and 30 June 2007 and the Income Statement for the year ended 30 June 2007 is shown in the following tables.

FIGURE 4.11 (continued)

Qantas Group	Previously Reported 1 July 2006 $m	Effect of Adoption of Interpretation 13 $m	Revised 1 July 2006 $m	Previously Reported 30 June 2007 $m	Effect of Adoption of Interpretation 13 $m	Revised 30 June 2007 $m
Total current assets[1]	4 948.4	—	4 948.4	5 587.4	—	5 587.4
Total non-current assets[1]	14 234.9	—	14 234.9	13 906.3	—	13 906.3
Total assets[1]	19 183.3	—	19 183.3	19 493.7	—	19 493.7
Current liabilities						
Payables	1 985.3	—	1 985.3	2 005.7	—	2 005.7
Revenue received in advance	2 282.8	481.0	2 763.8	2 533.6	515.7	3 049.3
Interest-bearing liabilities	440.8	—	440.8	863.7	—	863.7
Other financial liabilities	139.2	—	139.2	337.2	—	337.2
Provisions	469.0	(28.4)	440.6	534.4	(34.0)	500.4
Current tax liabilities	72.4	—	72.4	153.6	—	153.6
Deferred lease benefits/income	37.5	—	37.5	29.3	—	29.3
Total current liabilities	5 427.0	452.6	5 879.6	6 457.5	481.7	6 939.2
Non-current liabilities						
Revenue received in advance	708.5	312.6	1 021.1	701.5	348.2	1 049.7
Interest-bearing liabilities	5 334.8	—	5 334.8	4 210.9	—	4 210.9
Other financial liabilities	352.2	—	352.2	702.3	—	702.3
Provisions	479.7	(38.9)	440.8	481.9	(36.6)	445.3
Deferred tax liabilities	701.2	(217.9)	483.3	675.6	(238.1)	437.5
Deferred lease benefits/income	98.8	—	98.8	69.0	—	69.0
Total non-current liabilities	7 675.2	55.8	7 731.0	6 841.2	73.5	6 914.7
Total liabilities	13 102.2	508.4	13 610.6	13 298.7	555.2	13 853.9
Net assets	6 081.1	(508.4)	5 572.7	6 195.0	(555.2)	5 639.8
Equity						
Issued capital	4 382.2	—	4 382.2	4 481.2	—	4 481.2
Treasury shares	(23.8)	—	(23.8)	(32.6)	—	(32.6)
Reserves	329.3	—	329.3	148.2	—	148.2
Retained earnings	1 388.5	(508.4)	880.1	1 593.3	(555.2)	1 038.1

[1] Interpretation 13 has not impacted assets and accordingly the individual categories appearing on the face of the Balance Sheet have not been disclosed here.

(continued)

FIGURE 4.11 *(continued)*

Qantas Group	Previously Reported 1 July 2006 $m	Effect of Adoption of Interpretation 13 $m	Revised 1 July 2006 $m	Previously Reported 30 June 2007 $m	Effect of Adoption of Interpretation 13 $m	Revised 30 June 2007 $m
Equity attributable to members of Qantas	6 076.2	(508.4)	5 567.8	6 190.1	(555.2)	5 634.9
Minority interest	4.9	—	4.9	4.9	—	4.9
Total equity	6 081.1	(508.4)	5 572.7	6 195.0	(555.2)	5 639.8

Sales and Other Income	Previously Reported Year Ended 30 June 2007 $m	Effect of Adoption of Interpretation 13 $m	Revised Year Ended 30 June 2007 $m
Net passenger revenue[1]	11 968.2	(48.1)	11 920.1
Net freight revenue	902.5	—	902.5
Tours and travel revenue[1]	775.1	—	775.1
Contract work revenue	434.3	—	434.3
Other[1]	1 086.3	(57.9)	1 028.4
Sales and other income	15 166.4	(106.0)	15 060.4
Expenditure			
Manpower and staff related	3 334.7	—	3 334.7
Aircraft operating — variable[1]	2 608.4	—	2 608.4
Fuel	3 336.8	—	3 336.8
Selling and marketing[1]	726.7	(34.9)	691.8
Property	350.5	—	350.5
Computer and communication[1]	319.5	—	319.5
Tours and travel	641.7	—	641.7
Capacity hire	303.2	—	303.2
Ineffective and non-designated derivatives — closed positions	67.6	—	67.6
Other[1]	644.7	—	644.7
Depreciation and amortisation	1 362.7	—	1 362.7
Non-cancellable operating lease rentals	415.3	—	415.3
Share of net profit of associates and jointly controlled entities	(46.5)	—	(46.5)
Expenditure	14 065.3	(34.9)	14 030.4
Operating result	1 101.1	(71.1)	1 030.0
Ineffective and non-designated derivatives — open positions	(54.1)	—	(54.1)
Profit before related income tax expense and net finance costs	1 047.0	(71.1)	975.9

[1] Previously reported balances have been reclassified as a result of the implementation of a common chart of accounts throughout the Qantas Group.

FIGURE 4.11 *(continued)*

Sales and Other Income	Previously Reported Year Ended 30 June 2007 $m	Effect of Adoption of Interpretation 13 $m	Revised Year Ended 30 June 2007 $m
Finance income	244.0	—	244.0
Finance costs	(258.9)	4.1	(254.8)
Net finance costs	(14.9)	4.1	(10.8)
Profit before related income tax expense	1 032.1	(67.0)	965.1
Income tax expense	(312.5)	20.2	(292.3)
Profit for the year	719.6	(46.8)	672.8

Source: Qantas (2008, pp. 81–2, 87–8).

Note that the main impact is to reduce revenue recognised, increase revenue received in advance and reduce selling and marketing costs. This reflects the change from recognising all the revenue and accruing for costs versus recognising an element of the revenue and deferring the element relating to the award credits to be redeemed in the future.

FIGURE 4.12 Revenue recognition of Singapore Airlines

INT FRS 113: Customer Loyalty Programmes
The interpretation addresses accounting for loyalty award credits granted to customers who buy other goods or services, and the accounting for the entity's obligations to provide free or discounted goods or services to customers when the award credits are redeemed.

Loyalty award should be viewed as separately identifiable goods or services for which customers are implicitly paying and measured based on the allocated proceeds which represent the value of the award credits. The proceeds allocated to the award credits are deferred until the entity fulfils its obligations by supplying the free or discounted goods or services upon the redemption of the award credits.

The adoption of this interpretation should not result in a change in accounting policy of the Company as the current accounting treatment of the Company's award credits granted under the frequent flyer programme ('KrisFlyer') is closely aligned with the treatment as set out in the interpretation.

Source: Singapore Airlines (2008, p. 89).

FIGURE 4.13 Revenue recognition of British Airways

Revenue
Passenger and cargo revenue is recognised when the transportation service is provided. Passenger tickets net of discounts are recorded as current liabilities in the 'sales in advance of carriage' account until recognised as revenue. Unused tickets are recognised as revenue using estimates regarding the timing of recognition based on the terms and conditions of the ticket and historical trends. Other revenue is recognised at the time the service is provided. Commission costs are recognised at the same time as the revenue to which they relate and are charged to cost of sales.

(continued)

FIGURE 4.13 (*continued*)

Revenue recognition — mileage programmes

The Group operates two principal loyalty programmes. The airline frequent flyer programme operates through the airline's 'Executive Club' and allows frequent travellers to accumulate 'BA Miles' mileage credits that entitle them to a choice of various awards, primarily free travel. The estimated direct incremental cost of providing free redemption services, including British Airways' flights, in exchange for redemption of miles earned by members of the Group's 'Executive Club' is accrued as members of the scheme accumulate mileage. These costs are charged to cost of sales.

In addition, 'BA Miles' are sold to commercial partners to use in promotional activity. The fair value of the miles sold is deferred and recognised as revenue on redemption of the miles by the participants to whom the miles are issued. The cost of providing free redemption services is recognised when the miles are redeemed.

The Group also operates the AIRMILES scheme, operated by the Company's wholly-owned subsidiary Airmiles Travel Promotions Limited. The scheme allows companies to purchase miles for use in their own promotional activities. Miles can be redeemed for a range of benefits, including flights on British Airways and other carriers. The fair value of the miles sold is deferred and recognised as revenue on redemption of the miles by the participants to whom the miles are issued. The cost of providing free redemption services is recognised when the miles are redeemed.

New standards, amendments and interpretations not yet effective

The IASB and IFRIC issued the following standards and interpretations with an effective date after the date of these financial statements:

IFRIC 13 'Customer Loyalty Programmes', effective for annual periods beginning on or after July 1, 2008. IFRIC 13 addresses accounting by entities that operate or otherwise participate in customer loyalty programmes for their customers. IFRIC 13 applies to sales transactions in which the entities grant their customers award credits that, subject to meeting any further qualifying conditions, the customers can redeem in the future for free or discounted goods or services. The interpretation requires that an entity recognises credits that it awards to customers as a separately identifiable component of revenue, which would be deferred at the date of the initial sale. IRFIC 13 will become mandatory for the Group's consolidated financial statements beginning April 1, 2009 with earlier application permitted. The Group expects to early adopt IFRIC 13 from April 1, 2008 with initial adoption expected to result in a reduction in opening shareholders' equity.

Source: British Airways (2008, pp. 82, 87).

4.10 INTERACTION BETWEEN IAS 18 AND OTHER STANDARDS AND INTERPRETATIONS

We have seen in the foregoing sections that IAS 18 interacts with numerous standards and IFRIC interpretations, the most significant being IAS 39 in respect of the recognition of revenue for financial instruments (see chapter 7), IAS 1 in respect of disclosures, IAS 16 and IAS 38 in respect of gain recognition on the sale of non-current assets and accounting for exchanges or swaps of non-current assets, and IFRIC 13 in respect of the principle of revenue recognition in multiple-element arrangements. Another significant standard is IAS 11 *Construction Contracts*. IAS 11 requires use of the percentage of completion method of revenue recognition for construction contracts that fall within its scope. IAS 11, paragraph 3 defines a construction contract as 'a contract specifically negotiated for the construction of an asset or a combination of assets'. Typical construction contracts that meet this definition are contracts for the construction of residential houses. In these cases, the buyer usually owns the land and contracts with a builder to build a house on that land. The builder applies IAS 11 and recognises revenue on a percentage of completion basis (as described in illustrative example 4.5) as the house is being built.

In 2007, IFRIC was asked to address the situation described as 'pre-completion sales' of constructed assets. The typical example of this is where a developer builds a residential apartment block and sells the apartments 'off-the-plan' (i.e. before they are built). The question asked was whether these types of contracts were construction contracts to be accounted for under IAS 11 or whether they should be accounted for under the general requirements of IAS 18. In 2008, IFRIC issued an interpretation titled IFRIC 15 *Agreements for the Construction of Real Estate*.

The principles of the interpretation are as follows:

(a) Identify the components of the transaction by applying paragraph 13 of IAS 18.
(b) For the component that is a construction contract as defined in IAS 11, apply IAS 11 (i.e. percentage of completion method of revenue recognition).
(c) If the arrangement is not a construction contract but nevertheless the risks and rewards of ownership transfer to the buyer on a continuous basis, apply the percentage of completion method under IAS 18 (i.e. there is a continuous transfer of the risks and rewards of ownership and control of the goods in respect of which the services have been provided). This is to cater for situations where the substance of the arrangement is a construction contract but it does not meet the definition of a construction contract in IAS 11 (these situations are expected to be rare).
(d) If the arrangement is not a construction contract and the risks and rewards of ownership do not transfer on a continuous basis, then IAS 18 also applies, but the percentage of completion method of revenue recognition is not appropriate.

IFRIC had expressed some concerns with the concept of 'continuous transfer' and whether it was an acceptable interpretation of paragraph 14 of IAS 18 in respect of the sale of goods. The staff reported that IASB members have not objected to this notion. Nevertheless, IFRIC members believed that it was unlikely that many arrangements (that are not construction contracts) would meet the test of continuous transfer because all the conditions of paragraph 14 of IAS 18 would need to be met in respect of the partially completed work-in-progress. In other words, for example, if the tests in paragraph 14 were met, the buyer would be left with the partially completed work-in-progress should the developer fail and the buyer would have managerial control over the project. This is not the case in most off-the-plan sales where the buyer's risk is usually limited to their deposit. Notwithstanding these concerns, IFRIC agreed to retain the notion of 'continuous transfer', but expected that few arrangements would meet the required conditions.

Note that for many entities that undertake off-the-plan real estate sales, the effect of the interpretation will be to discontinue the percentage of completion method of revenue recognition. Revenue will only be recognised on completion and delivery of the apartments in accordance with paragraph 14 of IAS 18.

 ## 4.11 DISCLOSURE REQUIREMENTS OF IAS 18

Paragraph 35 of IAS 18 requires an entity to disclose:

(a) the accounting policies adopted for revenue recognition, including how it determined the stage of completion of transactions
(b) the amount of each significant category of revenue recognised during the period (i.e. sale of goods, rendering of services, interest, royalties and dividends)
(c) the amount of revenue arising from exchanges of goods and services.

Any related contingencies must also be disclosed in accordance with IAS 37 *Provisions, Contingent Liabilities and Contingent Assets*. These might include, for example, contingent liabilities arising from claims or penalties related to non-performance.

IAS 1 (refer chapter 18) requires revenue to be disclosed in the statement of profit or loss and other comprehensive income. The breakdown of revenue as required by IAS 18 may be disclosed in the statement or in the notes.

The example provided in figure 4.10 illustrates the comprehensive disclosures made in practice in respect of paragraph 35(a). Disclosures required in respect of paragraphs 11(b) and (c) are simple and do not cause any significant issues in practice.

 ## 4.12 EXPECTED FUTURE DEVELOPMENTS

As we have seen, accounting for revenue is a complex area, with IAS 18 being unhelpful in many respects.

Understanding that revenue is such an important measure for companies and that it has been a problematic area for so long, the IASB, jointly with the FASB, added a significant project on revenue recognition to its agenda, finally issuing a discussion paper in December 2008, followed by an ED titled *Revenue from Contracts with Customers* in June 2010. After an extensive round of further consultation and outreach, the Boards decided to re-expose the ED in November 2011, with a view to issuing a final standard in 2013.

The June 2010 ED focused on contracts with customers and thus excluded areas such as agriculture where fair value movements do not relate to contracts with customers.

The key principle in the ED was that when an entity becomes a party to a contract with a customer it should account for its rights and obligations under that contract on a net basis. The principle is based on the asset/liability model of the *Conceptual Framework* except that it prescribes a net basis for recognising assets and liabilities under the contract, whereas the *Conceptual Framework* implies a gross basis. The ED was also consistent with the asset/liability model in that it focuses on performance obligations rather than 'deferred revenue'.

The ED was also consistent with IFRIC 13 in that it proposed the revenue allocation method rather than the provision for future costs.

The ED identified five key steps that entities would apply in determining the appropriate timing and amount of revenue recognition:

1. Identify the contract with the customer.
2. Identify the separate performance obligations in the contract.
3. Determine the transaction price.
4. Allocate the transaction price to the separate performance obligations.
5. Recognise revenue when each performance obligation is satisfied.

While there was little objection to the five steps in the model, many respondents were concerned about some aspects of the detailed application of the model. These included lack of clarity about the notion of 'continuous transfer' (as discussed in section 4.10 of this chapter), greater use of subjective estimates where the consideration received is variable, application of the model to accounting for warranties and application of the guidance to onerous contracts. Some of these issues were addressed in the re-exposed ED.

SUMMARY

IAS 18 *Revenue* was issued by the IASC in December 1993 and was confirmed as being included in the core set of standards to be issued by the IASB in April 2001.

IAS 18 was not amended substantially by the IASB when it was issued in 2001. It, therefore, remains essentially a very old standard. Unfortunately, it is not entirely consistent with the *Conceptual Framework* and is also internally inconsistent — with an Appendix that sometimes contradicts the body of the standard. As a result, revenue recognition has been a problematic area for companies for many years, with many requests for interpretations by the SIC and IFRIC.

The definition of *income* in the *Conceptual Framework* is very broad, being based, in effect, on statement of financial position movements. This is known as 'the asset/liability' model. The definition of income includes both revenue and gains, with different criteria for each. IAS 18 deals only with revenue while other relevant standards deal with gains.

IAS 18 addresses revenue arising from:
(a) the sale of goods
(b) the rendering of services
(c) the use by others of entity assets yielding interest, royalties and dividends
with different recognition criteria for each category. In all cases, IAS 18 requires that revenue be measured at the fair value of the consideration received or receivable.

Many issues arise in the practice of applying IAS 18, including accounting for deferred consideration, swaps and exchanges of goods; identifying when services are provided; identifying whether multiple-element arrangements exist; accounting for upfront fees; and distinguishing between different types of real estate agreements. The IASB and FASB have engaged in a joint project to issue a revised standard on revenue in an attempt to address many of these issues.

Discussion questions

1. What are the key distinctions between 'income' and 'revenue'? Why do you think the IASB made these distinctions?
2. What is the 'asset/liability' model for the definition and recognition of income under the *Conceptual Framework*? Does it give a different outcome from other models permitted under IAS 18?
3. In what respects is IAS 18 inconsistent with the *Conceptual Framework*?
4. What are the recognition criteria for income under the *Conceptual Framework*? How do these differ from the key stated purpose of IAS 18?

5. What is a multiple-element transaction? Give two examples of these and discuss how IAS 18 applies to such transactions.
6. Compare and contrast the revenue recognition criteria for the sale of goods with those for the rendering of services.
7. Compare and contrast paragraphs 13 and 19 of IAS 18.
8. List the five steps in the IASB's proposed new revenue recognition model as set out in its June 2010 ED. Describe the areas within those steps that caused respondents concern.

Exercises

STAR RATING   ★ BASIC   ★★ MODERATE   ★★★ DIFFICULT

| Exercise 4.1 | **DEFINITIONS** |

★ State which of the following meets the definition of 'revenue' under IAS 18 for Company Z, a retailer of toys. Give reasons for your answer:
1. Sales tax collected on behalf of the taxing authority.
2. Gain on the sale of an investment property.
3. Amounts receivable from customers who have purchased toys.
4. Gain on the sale of equity securities held as investments.
5. Revaluation increase on the revaluation of operating properties under IAS 16.

| Exercise 4.2 | **DEFINITIONS, SCOPE** |

★ State whether each of the following is true or false:
1. 'Income' means the same as 'revenue'.
2. 'Gains' are always recognised net under IFRSs.
3. 'Revenue' must always be in respect of an entity's ordinary operations.
4. 'Gains' must always be outside of an entity's ordinary operations.
5. 'Deferred revenue' meets the definition of a liability under the *Conceptual Framework*.
6. Services provided under a construction contract are accounted for under IAS 18.

| Exercise 4.3 | **MEASUREMENT** |

★ State whether each of the following is true or false:
1. Revenue is measured at the fair value of the consideration given by the seller.
2. Revenue is measured at the price that would be received to sell an asset or paid to transfer a liability in an orderly transaction between market participants at the measurement date.
3. If payment for the goods or services is deferred, the fair value of the consideration will be less than the nominal amount of the cash receivable.
4. A swap or exchange for goods or services of a similar nature and value generates revenue.
5. Collectability of amounts due from customers is a measurement issue, not a recognition issue.

| Exercise 4.4 | **RECOGNITION** |

★ What is an 'executory contract'? How does this affect the dates on which revenue is recognised under the *Conceptual Framework*?

| Exercise 4.5 | **MEASUREMENT — DATES FOR RECOGNITION** |

★★ Company R sells plastic bottles. Wholesale customers that purchase more than 10 000 bottles per month are entitled to a discount of 6% on their purchases. On 1 March 2013, Customer P ordered 10 crates of bottles from Company R. Each crate contains 2000 bottles. The normal selling price per crate is $400. Company R delivered the 10 crates on 15 March 2013. Customer P paid for the goods on 15 April 2013. The end of Company R's reporting period is 30 June.

Required

Prepare the journal entries to record this transaction by Company R for the year ended 30 June 2013.

REVENUE RECOGNITION — SALE OF GOODS

★★ In each of the following situations, state at which date, if any, revenue will be recognised:

1. A contract for the sale of goods is entered into on 1 May 2013. The goods are delivered on 15 May 2013. The buyer pays for the goods on 30 May 2013. The contract contains a clause that entitles the buyer to rescind the purchase at any time. This is in addition to normal warranty conditions.
2. A contract for the sale of goods is entered into on 1 May 2013. The goods are delivered on 15 May 2013. The buyer pays for the goods on 30 May 2013. The contract contains a clause that entitles the buyer to return the goods up until 30 June 2013 if the goods do not perform according to their specification.
3. A contract for the sale of goods is entered into on 1 May 2013. The goods are delivered on 15 May 2013. The contract contains a clause that states that the buyer shall only pay for those goods that it sells to a third party for the period ended 31 August 2013. Any goods not sold to a third party by that date will be returned to the seller.
4. Retail goods are sold with normal provisions allowing the customer to return the goods if the goods do not perform satisfactorily. The goods are invoiced on 1 May 2013 and the customer pays cash for them on that date.

REVENUE RECOGNITION — RENDERING OF SERVICES

★★ On 1 February 2014, Company Z entered into an agreement with Customer S to develop a new database system (both hardware and software) for Customer S. The agreement states that the total consideration to be paid for the system will be $860 000. Company Z expects that its total costs for the system will be $670 000. As the end of its reporting period, 30 June 2014, Company Z had incurred labour costs of $130 000 and materials costs of $360 000. Of the materials costs, $60 000 is in respect of materials that have not yet been used on the system. Of the labour costs, $25 000 is an advance payment to a subcontractor who had not performed his work on the project as at 30 June 2014. As at 30 June 2014, Customer S had made progress payments to Company Z of $500 000.

Company Z has determined that IAS 11 does not apply to this transaction and calculates the percentage of completion using paragraph 24(c) of IAS 18.

Required

Calculate the revenue to be recognised by Company Z for the year ended 30 June 2014 and prepare the journal entries to record the transactions described. Assume all of Company Z's costs are paid for in cash.

AGENT VS. PRINCIPAL QUESTION

★★ Discuss how an entity would determine whether it acts as an agent or principal in sales transactions. In your answer, discuss the distinguishing features between an agency versus principal relationship and the consequences for revenue recognition.

MULTIPLE-ELEMENT ARRANGEMENT

★★ Company A provides a bundled service offering to Customer B. It charges Customer B $35 000 for initial connection to its network and two ongoing services — access to the network for 1 year and 'on-call troubleshooting' advice for that year.

Customer B pays the $35 000 upfront, on 1 July 2014. Company A determines that, if it were to charge a separate fee for each service if sold separately, the fee would be:

Connection fee	$ 5 000
Access fee	$12 000
Troubleshooting	$23 000

The end of Company A's reporting period is 30 June.

Required

Prepare the journal entries to record this transaction in accordance with IAS 18 for the year ended 30 June 2015, assuming Company A applies the relative fair value approach. Show all workings.

Exercise 4.10	**REVENUE RECOGNITION — RENDERING OF SERVICES**

★★★ In each of the following situations, state at which date(s), if any, revenue will be recognised:

1. A contract for the rendering of services is entered into on 1 May 2014. The services are delivered on 15 May 2014. The buyer pays for the services on 30 May 2014.
2. A contract for the rendering of services is entered into on 1 May 2014. The services are delivered continuously over a 1-year period commencing on 15 May 2014. The buyer pays for all the services on 30 May 2014.
3. A contract for the rendering of services is entered into on 1 May 2014. The services are delivered continuously over a 1-year period commencing on 15 May 2014. The buyer pays for the services on a monthly basis, commencing on 15 May 2014.
4. Company A is an insurance agent and provides insurance advisory services to Customer B. Company A receives a commission from Insurance Company I when Company A places Customer B's insurance policy with Insurance Company I, on 1 April 2014. Company A has no further obligation to provide services to Customer B.
5. Company A is an insurance agent and provides insurance advisory services to Customer B. Company A receives a commission from Insurance Company I when Company A places Customer B's insurance policy with Insurance Company I, on 1 April 2014. Company A is required to provide ongoing services to Customer B until 1 April 2015. Additional amounts are charged for these services. All amounts are at market rates.
6. Company A receives a non-refundable upfront fee from Customer B for investment advice, on 1 March 2014. Under the agreement with Customer B, Company A must provide ongoing management services until 1 March 2015. An additional amount is charged for these services. The upfront fee is higher than the market rate for equivalent initial investment advice services.

Exercise 4.11	**TELECOMMUNICATIONS MULTIPLE-ELEMENT ARRANGEMENT**

★★★ Company A is a telecommunications company that offers a variety of services to its customers including fixed-line telephone services, mobile phone services and Internet services. It uses numerous distributors to sell its mobile phone services. Customers purchase a phone handset from the distributor and at the same time can sign up to a contract with Company A for a period of 12 months or 24 months for the provision of network access for a fixed fee. Calls are charged separately if they exceed a certain limit per month. If the customer enters into a 12-month contract, the handset is sold to them for 40% less than the quoted market price. If the customer enters into a 24-month contract, the handset is sold to them for 50% less than the quoted market price. The distributor earns a commission from Company A based on a percentage of the consideration for each contract entered into — 12% for a 12-month contract and 15% for a 24-month contract.

Company A sells its handsets to its distributors at 50% less than fair value on the basis that the distributor will use the handset to entice customers to enter into the contracts with Company A.

If the customer has any problems with the handset during or after the period of the contract (up to a maximum of 2 years), the customer has recourse to the distributor who must replace the handset at its own cost. In the case of a handset manufactured by Company A, the distributor will source the handset from Company A, who will sell it to the distributor at 50% less than fair value.

The distributor sells handsets to customers even if they don't sign up to any services agreement with Company A. In such cases, the customers are charged the market price for the handsets. The distributor also sells other handsets (i.e. not only those of Company A).

Company A has determined that the distributor is acting as its agent in respect of the service contracts but not in respect of its handsets.

Additional information	
Handset cost to Company A	$100
Handset fair value	$160
12-month contract, price charged to customers	$50 per month, all paid upfront
24-month contract, price charged to customers	$40 per month, all paid upfront

Required

Discuss the revenue recognition issues that arise out of the transactions described (a) for Company A and (b) for the distributor. Ignore discounting.

References

AstraZeneca 2010, *Annual report 2010*, AstraZeneca PLC, London, www.astrazeneca.com.

Bayer Group 2010, *Annual report 2010*, Bayer AG, Germany, www.bayer.com.

British Airways 2008, *2007/08 annual report and accounts*, British Airways PLC, London, www.ba.com.

Deutsche Telekom Group 2010, *Annual report 2010*, Deutsche Telekom AG, Germany, www.deutschetelekom.com.

Esprit 2010, *Annual report 2010*, Esprit Holdings Limited, Bermuda, www.espritholdings.com.

—— 2006, *IFRIC Update*, March 2006, www.ifrs.org.

—— 2007, *IFRIC Update*, January 2007, www.ifrs.org.

IASB 2011, *Exposure Draft ED/2011/6 A revision of ED/2010/6 Revenue from Contracts with Customers*, IFRS Foundation, London, www.ifrs.org.

Qantas 2008, *Annual report 2008*, Qantas Airways Limited, www.qantas.com.

Singapore Airlines 2008, *Annual report 2007–08*, Singapore Airlines Limited, Singapore, www.singaporeair.com.

Telstra Corporation 2010, *Annual report 2010*, Telstra Corporation Limited, Australia, www.telstra.com.au.

Woolworths Limited 2010, *Annual report 2010*, Woolworths Limited, Australia, www.woolworthslimited.com.au.

5

Provisions, contingent liabilities and contingent assets

ACCOUNTING STANDARDS IN FOCUS

IAS 37 *Provisions, Contingent Liabilities and Contingent Assets*

LEARNING OBJECTIVES

After studying this chapter, you should be able to:

1 describe the background to IAS 37

2 identify which items are included within the scope of the standard

3 outline the concept of a provision

4 discuss how to distinguish provisions from other liabilities

5 outline the concept of a contingent liability

6 describe how to distinguish a provision from a contingent liability

7 explain when a provision should be recognised

8 explain how a provision, once recognised, should be measured

9 apply the definitions, recognition and measurement criteria for provisions and contingent liabilities to practical situations

10 outline the concept of a contingent asset

11 describe the disclosure requirements for provisions, contingent liabilities and contingent assets

12 compare the requirements of IFRS 3 regarding contingent liabilities with those of IAS 37

13 explain the expected future developments for IAS 37.

5.1 INTRODUCTION TO IAS 37

IAS 37 deals with the recognition, measurement and presentation of provisions, contingent liabilities and contingent assets. In 2005, the IASB added a project on amending IAS 37 to its agenda and subsequently issued a controversial exposure draft (see section 5.13). However, at the time of writing the board has paused the project due to other priorities. As a result, apart from some specific amendments made as a result of the issue and revision of IFRS 3 *Business Combinations* in 2004 and 2008 respectively and some other minor amendments, IAS 37 remains largely unchanged since its original issue date of 1998 by the International Accounting Standards Committee (IASC). This chapter addresses the standard in effect as at 1 January 2011.

The standard:

- defines provisions and specifies recognition criteria and measurement requirements for the recognition of provisions in financial statements
- defines contingent liabilities and contingent assets and prohibits their recognition in the financial statements but requires their disclosure when certain conditions are met
- requires that where provisions are measured using estimated cash flows the cash flows be discounted to their present value at the reporting date and specifies the discount rate to be used for this purpose
- prohibits providing for future operating losses
- defines onerous contracts and requires the estimated net loss under onerous contracts to be provided for
- specifies recognition criteria for restructuring provisions and identifies the types of costs that may be included in restructuring provisions
- requires extensive disclosures relating to provisions, recoveries, contingent liabilities and contingent assets.

5.2 SCOPE

IAS 37 prescribes the accounting and disclosure for all provisions, contingent liabilities and contingent assets except:

(a) those resulting from financial instruments (see chapter 7) and those arising in insurance entities from contracts with policyholders
(b) those resulting from executory contracts, except where the contract is onerous (Executory contracts are contracts under which neither party has performed any of its obligations or both parties have partially performed their obligations to an equal extent.)
(c) those specifically covered by another IAS/IFRS. For example, certain types of provisions are also addressed in standards on:
  - construction contracts (see IAS 11 *Construction Contracts*)
  - income taxes (see IAS 12 *Income Taxes*, covered in chapter 6)
  - leases (see IAS 17 *Leases*, covered in chapter 12. However, as IAS 17 contains no specific requirements to deal with operating leases that have become onerous, IAS 37 applies to such cases.)
  - employee benefits (see IAS 19 *Employee Benefits*)
  - insurance contracts (see IFRS 4 *Insurance Contracts*).

Some amounts sometimes described as provisions may relate to the recognition of revenue; for example, where an entity gives guarantees in exchange for a fee. This may also be described as 'deferred revenue'. IAS 37 does not address the recognition of revenue. IAS 18 *Revenue* identifies the circumstances in which revenue is recognised and provides practical guidance on the application of the recognition criteria (see chapter 4).

Sometimes the term 'provision' is also used in the context of items such as depreciation, impairment of assets and doubtful debts. These are adjustments to the carrying amounts of assets and are not addressed in IAS 37. Refer to IAS 36 *Impairment of Assets*, which is covered in chapter 15.

Other standards specify whether expenditures are treated as assets or as expenses. These issues are not addressed in IAS 37. Accordingly, IAS 37 neither prohibits nor requires capitalisation of the costs recognised when a provision is made. Refer to IAS 38 *Intangible Assets*, which deals partly with this issue, and is covered in chapter 13.

IAS 37 applies to provisions for restructuring (including discontinued operations). Where a restructure meets the definition of a discontinued operation, additional disclosures may be required by IFRS 5 *Non-current Assets Held for Sale and Discontinued Operations*. IFRS 3 *Business Combinations* deals with accounting for restructuring provisions arising in business combinations. This chapter covers the relevant requirements of IFRS 3.

5.3 DEFINITION OF A PROVISION

Paragraph 4.4 of the *Conceptual Framework for Financial Reporting* (*Conceptual Framework*) defines a liability as:

> a present obligation of the entity arising from past events, the settlement of which is expected to result in an outflow from the entity of resources embodying economic benefits.

This definition is repeated in paragraph 10 of IAS 37.

A provision is a subset of liabilities (i.e. it is a type of liability). Paragraph 10 of IAS 37 defines a provision as:

> a liability of uncertain timing or amount.

It is this *uncertainty* that distinguishes provisions from other liabilities.

The *Conceptual Framework* states that an essential characteristic of a liability is that the entity has a present obligation. An obligation is a duty or responsibility to act or perform in a certain way. Obligations may be legally enforceable as a consequence of a binding contract, for example. This is normally the case with amounts payable for goods or services received, which are described as 'payables' or 'trade creditors'. However, legal enforceability is not a necessary requirement to demonstrate the existence of a liability. An entity may have an equitable or constructive obligation, arising from normal business practice or custom, to act in an equitable manner. Alternatively, the obligation is construed from the circumstances. Determining whether an equitable or constructive obligation exists is often more difficult than identifying a legal obligation. IAS 37 does not specifically acknowledge the concept of an equitable obligation; however, it does define a constructive obligation, in paragraph 10, as:

> an obligation that derives from an entity's actions where:
> (a) by an established pattern of past practice, published policies or a sufficiently specific current statement, the entity has indicated to other parties that it will accept certain responsibilities; and
> (b) as a result, the entity has created a valid expectation on the part of those other parties that it will discharge those responsibilities.

A present obligation exists only where the entity has no realistic alternative but to make the sacrifice of economic benefits to settle the obligation (*Conceptual Framework* paragraph 4.16).

For example, assume that an entity makes a public announcement that it will match the financial assistance provided by other entities to victims of a natural disaster and, because of custom and moral considerations, has no realistic alternative but to provide the assistance. (In this case the events have already taken place — the natural disaster — and the public announcement is the obligating event.)

Importantly, a decision by the entity's management or governing body does not, by itself, create a constructive obligation. This is because the management or governing body would retain the ability to reverse that decision. A present obligation would come into existence when the decision was communicated publicly to those affected by it. This would result in the valid expectation that the entity would fulfil the obligation, thus leaving the entity with little or no discretion to avoid the sacrifice of economic benefits.

5.4 DISTINGUISHING PROVISIONS FROM OTHER LIABILITIES

A provision may arise from either a legal or constructive obligation. As stated previously, the key distinguishing factor is the uncertainty relating to either the timing of settlement or the amount to be settled.

Paragraph 11 of IAS 37 gives an example of the distinction between liabilities and provisions as follows. It states that trade payables and accruals are liabilities because:

> (a) trade payables are liabilities to pay for goods or services that have been received or supplied and have been invoiced or formally agreed with the supplier; and
> (b) accruals are liabilities to pay for goods or services that have been received or supplied but have not been paid, invoiced or formally agreed with the supplier, including amounts due to employees (for example, amounts relating to accrued vacation pay). Although it is sometimes necessary to estimate the amount or timing of accruals, the uncertainty is generally much less than for provisions.

Accruals are often reported as part of trade and other payables, whereas provisions are reported separately.

Note, however, that employee benefits are addressed specifically by IAS 19 *Employee Benefits*, and are not included in the scope of IAS 37.

Some examples of typical provisions include provisions for warranty, restructuring provisions and provisions for onerous contracts. These are discussed in more detail later in this chapter.

5.5 DEFINITION OF A CONTINGENT LIABILITY

Paragraph 10 of IAS 37 defines a contingent liability as:

(a) a possible obligation that arises from past events and whose existence will be confirmed only by the occurrence or non-occurrence of one or more uncertain future events not wholly within the control of the entity; or

(b) a present obligation that arises from past events but is not recognised because:

   (i) it is not probable that an outflow of resources embodying economic benefits will be required to settle the obligation; or

   (ii) the amount of the obligation cannot be measured with sufficient reliability.

The definition of a contingent liability is interesting because it encompasses two distinctly different concepts. The first, part (a) of the definition, is the concept of a *possible* obligation. This fails one of the essential characteristics of a liability — the requirement for the existence of a present obligation. If there is no present obligation, only a possible one, there is no liability. Hence, part (a) of the definition does not meet the definition of a liability such that one could argue that the term 'contingent *liability*' is misleading, because items falling into category (a) are not liabilities by definition.

Part (b) of the definition, on the other hand, deals with liabilities that fail the recognition criteria. They are present obligations, so they meet the essential requirements of the definition of liabilities, but they do not meet the recognition criteria (probability of outflow of economic benefits and reliability of measurement).

5.6 DISTINGUISHING A CONTINGENT LIABILITY FROM A PROVISION

Contingent liabilities are not recognised in the financial statements but must be disclosed in the financial statements unless the possibility of an outflow in settlement is remote.

Paragraph 12 of IAS 37 states that:

> In a general sense, all provisions are contingent because they are uncertain in timing or amount. However, within this Standard the term 'contingent' is used for liabilities and assets that are not recognised because their existence will be confirmed only by the occurrence or non-occurrence of one or more uncertain future events not wholly within the control of the entity. In addition, the term 'contingent liability' is used for liabilities that do not meet the recognition criteria.

The following example (figure 5.1) illustrates the difference between a contingent liability and a provision. Note, however, that financial guarantees are specifically covered by IAS 39 and must be accounted for in accordance with that standard or IFRS 4 (see chapter 7).

> When *Endeavour Limited* provides a guarantee to a bank in relation to a bank loan provided to *Tower Limited*:
> - If *Tower Limited* is solvent and able to repay the loan without breaching any debt covenants, a contingent liability exists and disclosure thereof is required in the notes to the financial statements of *Endeavour Limited*;
> - If *Tower Limited* has breached the debt covenants and it is probable that *Endeavour Limited* will be called upon as guarantor of the loan by the Bank, a provision should be recognised by *Endeavour Limited* for the amount likely to be paid to the Bank. This assumes that there is still uncertain 'timing or amount', otherwise the amount would be a liability.

FIGURE 5.1 Example of the difference between a provision and a contingent liability
Source: Ernst & Young (2002a).

5.7 THE RECOGNITION CRITERIA FOR PROVISIONS

The recognition criteria for provisions are the same as those for liabilities as set out in the *Conceptual Framework*. Curiously, IAS 37 also includes part of the definition of a liability in its recognition criteria for provisions (part (a) of the recognition criteria below). The reason for this is most likely the desire of the standard setters to distinguish between provisions and contingent liabilities, but it is arguable whether this needs to be done via the recognition criteria, since the definitions are sufficiently clear.

Paragraph 14 of IAS 37 states that a provision should be recognised when:

(a) an entity has a present obligation (legal or constructive) as a result of a past event;

(b) it is probable that an outflow of resources embodying economic benefits will be required to settle the obligation; and

(c) a reliable estimate can be made of the amount of the obligation.

If these conditions are not met, no provision shall be recognised.

The concept of probability is discussed in the *Conceptual Framework* and deals essentially with the likelihood of something eventuating. If it is more likely rather than less likely to eventuate, IAS 37 regards the outflow as probable. Probability is assessed for each obligation separately, unless the obligations form a group of similar obligations (such as product warranties) in which case the probability that an outflow will be required in settlement is determined by assessing the class of obligations as a whole.

Paragraphs 15 and 16 of IAS 37 discuss the concepts of a present obligation and probability, giving some useful examples:

15. In rare cases it is not clear whether there is a present obligation. In these cases, a past event is deemed to give rise to a present obligation if, taking account of all available evidence, it is more likely than not that a present obligation exists at the end of the reporting period.

16. In almost all cases it will be clear whether a past event has given rise to a present obligation. In rare cases, for example in a law suit, it may be disputed either whether certain events have occurred or whether those events result in a present obligation. In such a case, an entity determines whether a present obligation exists at the end of the reporting period by taking account of all available evidence, including, for example, the opinion of experts. The evidence considered includes any additional evidence provided by events after the end of the reporting period. On the basis of such evidence:

    (a) where it is more likely than not that a present obligation exists at the end of the reporting period, the entity recognises a provision (if the recognition criteria are met); and

    (b) where it is more likely that no present obligation exists at the end of the reporting period, the entity discloses a contingent liability, unless the possibility of an outflow of resources embodying economic benefits is remote [in which case no disclosure is made].

A past event that leads to a present obligation is called an obligating event. As discussed in the section on constructive obligations, for an event to be an obligating event the entity must have no realistic alternative to settling the obligation created by the event. In the case of a legal obligation this is because the settlement of the obligation can be enforced by law. In the case of a constructive obligation the event needs to create a valid expectation in other parties that the entity will discharge the obligation.

Reliable estimation is the final criterion for recognition of a provision. Although the use of estimates is a necessary part of the preparation of financial statements, in the case of provisions the uncertainty associated with reliable measurement is greater than for other liabilities. Accordingly, IAS 37 goes on to give more detailed guidance on measurement of provisions, which we will discuss later in the chapter. However, it is expected that except in very rare cases an entity will be able to determine a reliable estimate of the obligation.

Note the use of the concept of 'probability' in the recognition criteria for liabilities, including provisions, contrasted with the use of the concept of 'possibility' in determining whether or not a contingent liability should be disclosed. Paragraph 86 of IAS 37 requires contingent liabilities to be disclosed in the financial statements 'unless the possibility of an outflow in settlement is remote'. IAS 37 interprets 'probable' as meaning more likely than not to occur (IAS 37 paragraph 23). IAS 37 does not, however, provide any further guidance on what it means by 'possibility'. In plain English terms 'probability' addresses the likelihood of whether or not something will happen, whereas 'possibility' has a broader meaning — virtually anything is possible, but how probable is it? Given this distinction, we should assume that the intention of IAS 37 is that most contingent liabilities should be disclosed and that only in very rare circumstances is no disclosure appropriate.

Contingent liabilities need to be continually assessed to determine whether or not they have become actual liabilities. This is done by considering whether the recognition criteria for liabilities have been met. If it becomes probable that an outflow of economic benefits will be required for an item previously dealt with as a contingent liability, a provision is recognised in the financial statements in the period in which the change in probability occurs (IAS 37 paragraph 30).

5.7.1 Putting it all together — a useful decision tree

In sections 5.3 through 5.7 we discussed the definitions of provisions and contingent liabilities, the recognition criteria for provisions and when a contingent liability must be disclosed. The decision tree (figure 5.2) on the next page summarises this discussion. The decision tree is based on Appendix B of IAS 37 but has been modified to aid understanding.

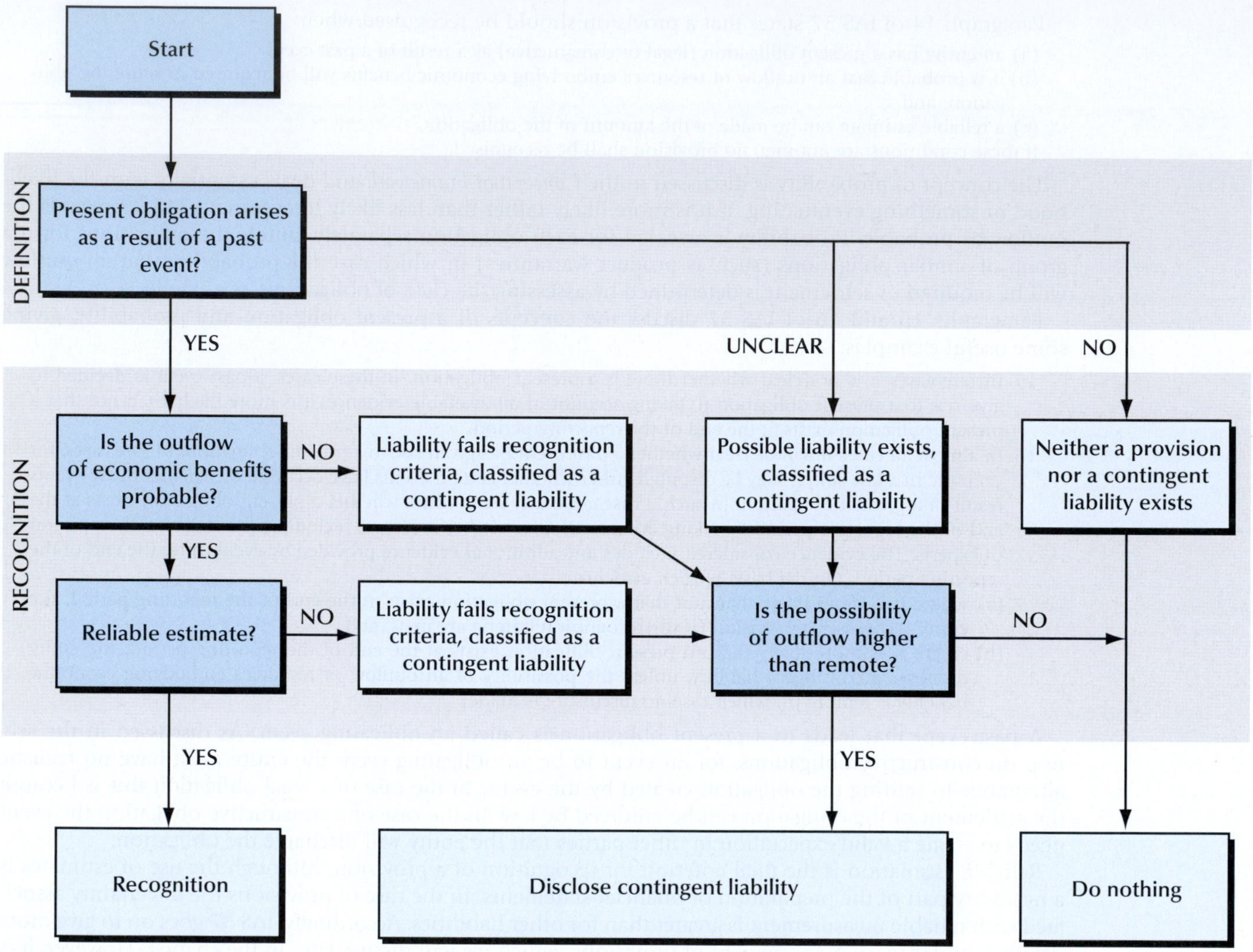

Decision tree flowchart:

DEFINITION

Start → Present obligation arises as a result of a past event?

- YES →
- UNCLEAR → Possible liability exists, classified as a contingent liability
- NO → Neither a provision nor a contingent liability exists

RECOGNITION

Is the outflow of economic benefits probable? — NO → Liability fails recognition criteria, classified as a contingent liability

YES ↓

Reliable estimate? — NO → Liability fails recognition criteria, classified as a contingent liability → Is the possibility of outflow higher than remote? — NO →

Is the possibility of outflow higher than remote?

YES ↓ (Reliable estimate) → Recognition

YES (Is the possibility of outflow higher than remote?) → Disclose contingent liability

NO → Do nothing

FIGURE 5.2 Decision tree
Source: Ernst & Young (2002b).

5.8 MEASUREMENT OF PROVISIONS

5.8.1 Best estimate

When measuring a provision, the amount recognised should be the *best estimate* of the consideration required to settle the present obligation at the end of the reporting period (IAS 37 paragraph 36). This amount is often expressed as the amount which represents, as closely as possible, what the entity would rationally pay to settle the present obligation at the end of the reporting period or to provide consideration to a third party to assume it. The fact that it is difficult to measure the provision and that estimates have to be used does not mean that the provision is not reliably measurable.

Paragraphs 39 and 40 of IAS 37 address the issue of how to deal with the uncertainties surrounding the amount to be recognised as a provision:

39. Uncertainties surrounding the amount to be recognised as a provision are dealt with by various means according to the circumstances. Where the provision being measured involves a large population of items, the obligation is estimated by weighting all possible outcomes by their associated probabilities. The name for this statistical method of estimation is 'expected value'. The provision will therefore be different depending on whether the probability of a loss of a given amount is, for example, 60 per cent or 90 per cent. Where there is a continuous range of possible outcomes, and each point in that range is as likely as any other, the mid-point of the range is used.

Example

An entity sells goods with a warranty under which customers are covered for the cost of repairs of any manufacturing defects that become apparent within the first six months after purchase. If minor defects were detected in all products sold, repair costs of 1 million would result. If major defects were detected in all products sold, repair costs of 4 million would result. The entity's past experience and future expectations indicate that, for the coming year, 75 per cent of the goods sold will have no defects, 20 per cent of the goods sold will have minor defects and 5 per cent of the goods sold will have major defects. In accordance with paragraph 24, an entity assesses the probability of an outflow for the warranty obligations as a whole.

The expected value of the cost of repairs is:

$$(75\% \text{ of nil}) + (20\% \text{ of 1m}) + (5\% \text{ of 4m}) = 400,000$$

40. Where a single obligation is being measured, the individual most likely outcome may be the best estimate of the liability. However, even in such a case, the entity considers other possible outcomes. Where other possible outcomes are either mostly higher or mostly lower than the most likely outcome, the best estimate will be a higher or lower amount. For example, if an entity has to rectify a serious fault in a major plant that it has constructed for a customer, the individual most likely outcome may be for the repair to succeed at the first attempt at a cost of 1,000, but a provision for a larger amount is made if there is a significant chance that further attempts will be necessary.

The provision is measured before tax. Any tax consequences are accounted for in accordance with IAS 12 *Income Taxes*.

The need to use judgement in determining the best estimate is clearly evident. Judgement is used in assessing, inter alia:
- what the likely consideration required to settle the obligation will be
- when the consideration is likely to be settled
- whether there are various scenarios that are likely to arise
- what the probability of those various scenarios arising will be.

The distinguishing characteristic of provisions — the uncertainty relating to either the timing of settlement or the amount to be settled — is clearly illustrated in the above discussion. Because of the extent of judgement required in measuring provisions, auditors focus more on auditing provisions than on other normal liabilities such as trade creditors and accruals. This is particularly the case if a change in one of the assumptions, such as the probability of a particular scenario eventuating or the likely consideration required to settle the obligation, would have a material impact on the amount recognised as a provision and thus on the financial statements.

5.8.2 Risks and uncertainties

IAS 37 (paragraph 42) requires that the risks and uncertainties surrounding the events and circumstances should be taken into account in reaching the best estimate of a provision. Paragraph 43 states:

Risk describes variability of outcome. A risk adjustment may increase the amount at which a liability is measured. Caution is needed in making judgements under conditions of uncertainty, so that income or assets are not overstated and expenses or liabilities are not understated. However, uncertainty does not justify the creation of excessive provisions or a deliberate overstatement of liabilities. For example, if the projected costs of a particularly adverse outcome are estimated on a prudent basis, that outcome is not then deliberately treated as more probable than is realistically the case. Care is needed to avoid duplicating adjustments for risk and uncertainty with consequent overstatement of a provision.

Disclosure of the uncertainties surrounding the amount or timing of expected outflows is required by paragraph 85(b) of the standard.

5.8.3 Present value

Provisions are required to be *discounted to present value* where the effect of discounting is material (IAS 37 paragraph 45). IAS 37 (paragraph 47) requires that the discount rate used must be a pre-tax rate that reflects current market assessments of the time value of money and the *risks specific to the liability*. Where future cash flow estimates have been adjusted for risk, the discount rate should not reflect this risk — otherwise the risk would be duplicated.

In practical terms it is often difficult to determine reliably a liability-specific discount rate. Usually entities use a rate available for a liability with similar terms and conditions or, if a similar liability is not available, a risk-free rate for a liability with the same term (e.g. a government bond[1] with a five-year term may be used as the basis for a company's specific liability with a five-year term) and this rate is then adjusted for the risks pertaining to the liability in question.

The higher the discount rate, the lower the amount that will be recognised as a liability. This seems counterintuitive — seemingly the higher the risk attached to the liability, the lower the amount at which it is recognised. However, a risk-adjusted rate for a liability would be a *lower* rate than the risk-free rate. This is demonstrated in illustrative example 5.1.

ILLUSTRATIVE EXAMPLE 5.1 Calculation of a risk-adjusted rate

A company has a provision for which the expected value of the cash outflow in three years' time is $150 and the risk-free rate is 5%. However, the possible outcomes lie within a range between $100 and $200. The company is risk-averse and would settle instead for a certain payment of, say, $160 in three years' time rather than being exposed to the risk of the actual outcome being as high as $200. The effect of risk in calculating present value can be expressed as either:

(a) discounting the risk-adjusted cash flow of $160 at the risk-free (unadjusted) rate of 5%, giving a present value of $138; or

(b) discounting the expected cash flow (which is unadjusted for risk) of $150 at a risk-adjusted rate that will give the present value of $138, i.e. a rate of 2.8%.

This outcome may seem surprising because the experience of most borrowers is that lenders will charge a higher rate of interest on loans that are assessed to be a higher risk to the lender. However, in the case of a provision, a lower rate reflects the elimination of the possibility of the actual cost being higher (i.e. the cost is capped at a certain amount above which it will not go), whereas in the case of a loan, the lender requires a premium to compensate it for the risk of not recovering the full value of the loan (i.e. the lender's asset is set at a floor below which it will not go). In other words, the discount rate for the asset (in this case the loan held by the lender) is increased to reflect the risk of recovering less and the discount rate for a provision is reduced to reflect the risk of paying more.

Source: Ernst & Young (2011, p. 1397).

Perhaps an easier way to factor in risk is to use it in assessing the probability of outcomes (as discussed in section 5.8.1) and then use a risk-free rate in discounting the cash flows. Paragraph 78 of IAS 19 *Employee Benefits* states that the discount rate for long-term employee benefit obligations should be determined by reference to market yields at the end of the reporting period on high-quality corporate bonds or, where there is no deep market in such bonds, the market yield on government bonds. The currency and term of the corporate bonds or government bonds should be consistent with the currency and estimated term of the employee benefit obligations. Although there may be some debate about how to determine the risk-free rate, market yields on high-quality corporate bonds or government bonds are reasonable approximations. It is unclear why IAS 37 and IAS 19 are inconsistent, but given that IAS 19 is a more recent standard than IAS 37, it is possible that IAS 37 may be modified to be consistent with IAS 19.

Illustrative example 5.2 shows the way a provision should be measured, taking into account risks and the time value of money.

ILLUSTRATIVE EXAMPLE 5.2 Measuring a provision

An entity estimates that the expected cash outflows to settle its warranty obligations at the end of the reporting period are as follows. (Note that the probability of cash outflows has already been adjusted for risk similarly to the example in section 5.8.1 and, accordingly, no further adjustment for risk is made to the discount rate.) The entity has used a discount rate based on government bonds with the same term and currency as the expected cash outflows.

---

[1] Assumed to be risk-free although this may not always be the case.

Expected cash outflow	Timing	Discount rate	Present value of cash outflow
$400 000	In 1 year	6.0%	$377 358
100 000	In 2 years	6.5%	88 166
20 000	In 3 years	6.9%	16 371
Present value			481 895

5.8.4 Future events

Anticipated future events expected to affect the amount required to settle the entity's present obligation must be reflected in the amount provided, when there is reliable evidence that they will occur.

As an example, paragraph 49 of IAS 37 states:

Expected future events may be particularly important in measuring provisions. For example, an entity may believe that the cost of cleaning up a site at the end of its life will be reduced by future changes in technology. The amount recognised reflects a reasonable expectation of technically qualified, objective observers, taking account of all available evidence as to the technology that will be available at the time of the clean-up. Thus it is appropriate to include, for example, expected cost reductions associated with increased experience in applying existing technology or the expected cost of applying existing technology to a larger or more complex clean-up operation than has previously been carried out. However, an entity does not anticipate the development of a completely new technology for cleaning up unless it is supported by sufficient objective evidence.

5.8.5 Expected disposal of assets

Gains from the expected disposal of assets must not be taken into account when measuring the amount of a provision (IAS 37 paragraph 51), even if the expected disposal is closely linked to the event giving rise to the provision. Rather, when the gain on disposal is made it should be recognised at that time in accordance with the relevant international accounting standard. Therefore, it is clear that only expected cash *outflows* must be taken into account in measuring the provision. Any cash inflows are treated separately from the measurement of the provision.

5.8.6 Reimbursements

When some of the amount required to settle a provision is expected to be recovered from a third party IAS 37 requires that the recovery be recognised as an asset, but only when it is *virtually certain* that the reimbursement will be received if the entity settles the obligation (paragraph 53). This differs from the normal asset recognition criteria, which require that the inflow of future economic benefits be *probable*. Presumably, the standard setters were concerned about an uncertain asset related to an uncertain liability, and therefore decided to make the recognition criteria stricter for these types of assets. When such an asset is recognised the amount should not exceed the amount of the provision. IAS 37 allows the income from the asset to be set off against the expense relating to the provision in the statement of profit or loss and other comprehensive income. However, it does not mention set off in the statement of financial position of the asset and the provision. One of the disclosures required, in paragraph 85(c), is the amount of any asset that has been recognised for expected reimbursements; therefore, it is reasonable to assume that IAS 37 did not intend for the provision and asset to be set off in the statement of financial position. This is alluded to in paragraph 56 of IAS 37.

5.8.7 Changes in provisions and use of provisions

IAS 37 requires provisions to be reviewed at the end of each reporting period and adjusted to reflect the current best estimate. If it is no longer probable that an outflow of resources embodying economic benefits will be required to settle the obligation, the provision should be reversed (IAS 37 paragraph 59).

Where discounting is used, the carrying amount of a provision increases in each period to reflect the passage of time. This increase is recognised as borrowing cost. This is similar to the way finance lease liabilities are accounted for under IAS 17 *Leases*, as shown in chapter 12.

A provision should be used only for expenditures for which the provision was originally recognised. Illustrative example 5.3 shows how a provision is accounted for where discounting is applied and where the provision is adjusted to reflect the current best estimate.

ILLUSTRATIVE EXAMPLE 5.3 Accounting for a provision

Company A estimates that it will be required to pay $100 000 in 3 years' time to settle a warranty obligation. The risk-free discount rate applied is 5.5%. The probability of cash outflows has been assessed (i.e. adjusted for risk) in determining the $100 000.

The following table shows how the provision is accreted over the 3 years:

A. Year	B. Present value at the beginning of the year	C. Interest expense at 5.5% (B × 5.5%)	D. Cash flows	E. Present value at the end of the year (B + C − D)
1	85 161	4 683	—	89 844
2	89 844	4 942	—	94 786
3	94 786	5 214	(100 000)	—

Journal entries are as follows:

On initial recognition in year 1:			
Warranty Expense	Dr	85 161	
Warranty Provision	Cr		85 161
On recognition of interest in year 1:			
Interest Expense	Dr	4 683	
Warranty Provision	Cr		4 683
On recognition of interest in year 2:			
Interest Expense	Dr	4 942	
Warranty Provision	Cr		4 942
On recognition of interest in year 3:			
Interest Expense	Dr	5 214	
Warranty Provision	Cr		5 214
On settlement of provision, end of year 3:			
Warranty Provision	Dr	100 000	
Cash	Cr		100 000

Now assume the same facts as above except that, at the end of year 2, Company A re-estimates the amount to be paid to settle the obligation at the end of year 3 to be $90 000. The appropriate discount rate remains at 5.5%.

The present value of $90 000 at the end of year 2 is $85 306. Company A thus adjusts the provision by $9480 ($94 786 − $85 306) to reflect the revised estimated cash flows.

Journal entries are as follows:

Revision of estimate at end of year 2:			
Warranty Provision	Dr	9 480	
Warranty Expense (statement of comprehensive income)	Cr		9 480
On recognition of interest in year 3:			
Interest Expense ($85 306 × 5.5% rounded)	Dr	4 694	
Warranty Provision	Cr		4 694

On settlement of provision, end of year 3:			
Warranty Provision	Dr	90 000	
Cash	Cr		90 000

The re-estimated cash flows are adjusted against the warranty expense recorded in the statement of comprehensive income, while the unwinding of the discount continues to be recorded as interest expense (IAS 37 paragraph 60). Any change in the discount rate used would also be adjusted against interest expense.

5.9 APPLICATION OF THE DEFINITIONS, RECOGNITION AND MEASUREMENT RULES

5.9.1 Future operating losses

IAS 37 states that provisions must not be recognised for future operating losses (paragraph 63). Even if a sacrifice of future economic benefits is expected, a provision for future operating losses is not recognised because a past event creating a present obligation has not occurred. This is because the entity's management will generally have the ability to avoid incurring future operating losses by either disposing of or restructuring the operation in question. An expectation of future operating losses may, however, be an indicator that an asset is impaired and the requirements of IAS 36 *Impairment of Assets* should be applied.

5.9.2 Onerous contracts

An onerous contract is defined in paragraph 10 of IAS 37 as:

> a contract in which the unavoidable costs of meeting the obligations under the contract exceed the economic benefits expected to be received under it.

If an entity is a party to an onerous contract, a provision for the present obligation under the contract must be recognised (IAS 37 paragraph 66). The reason these losses should be provided for is that the entity is contracted to fulfil the contract. Therefore, entry into an onerous contract gives rise to a present obligation.

Examples of onerous contracts include:
- where an electricity supplier has entered into a contract to supply electricity at a price lower than the price at which it is contracted to receive
- where a manufacturer has entered into a supply contract at a price below the costs of production.

IAS 37 does not go into a lot of detail regarding onerous contracts and the requirements of the standard are quite vague in this area. Therefore, judgement has to be applied on a case-by-case basis to assess whether or not individual contracts qualify as onerous contracts under the standard.

For the purpose of raising a provision in respect of an onerous contract, the amount to be recognised is the least net cost of exiting the contract; that is, the lesser of:
- the cost of fulfilling the contract, and
- any compensation or penalties arising from failure to fulfil the contract.

IAS 37 also requires that before a separate provision is made for an onerous contract, an entity must first recognise any impairment loss that has occurred on assets dedicated to that contract. This is illustrated in illustrative example 5.4.

ILLUSTRATIVE EXAMPLE 5.4 Accounting for an onerous contract

Company A enters into a supply agreement with Company B on 1 January 2014. The agreement states that Company A must supply Company B with 100 chairs at a price of $150 per chair. The agreement also states that if Company A cannot deliver the chairs on time and under the terms of the contract it must pay Company B a penalty of $12 000. The delivery date is 31 March 2014. Company A commences manufacturing the chairs on 1 March and experiences a series of production problems that result in the cost to produce each chair totalling $200 as at 31 March 2014. As at 31 March, Company A identifies an onerous contract in accordance with IAS 37 because the costs of fulfilling the contract (100 × $200 = $20 000) exceed the agreed amount to be received (100 × $150 = $15 000). The cost of the chairs is recognised as inventory as at 31 March 2014. Assuming the end of Company A's reporting period is 31 March, it must first recognise an impairment loss on the inventory. This would be calculated and recorded as $5000 (lower of cost and net realisable value (ignoring costs of disposal) under IAS 2 *Inventories* — see chapter 9). Once this impairment loss has been recognised, there is no amount to be recorded as a provision under the onerous contract. However, if Company A had not yet recorded any costs as inventory it would need to determine what amount to recognise as a provision for the onerous contract. This would be the lesser of the penalty required to be paid to Company B ($12 000) and the cost of fulfilling the contract (assume $20 000 if the costs have not yet been recognised). Thus, Company A would record a provision of $12 000.

5.9.3 Restructuring provisions

Perhaps the most controversial aspect of IAS 37 is the recognition criteria for restructuring provisions. IFRS 3 *Business Combinations* addresses restructuring provisions arising as part of a business combination, whereas IAS 37 addresses restructuring provisions arising other than as part of a business combination. Although the fundamental criteria are consistent, IFRS 3 has more prescriptive requirements than IAS 37. For ease of discussion, both types of restructuring provision are discussed here.

During the 1990s, standard setters in various jurisdictions set tougher rules on when a restructuring provision could be recognised, particularly when the provision related to the acquisition of a business. The reason for the crackdown was the tendency for companies to create restructuring provisions deliberately to avoid the recognition of an expense in future periods. Illustrative example 5.5 illustrates this point.

ILLUSTRATIVE EXAMPLE 5.5 Restructuring provisions

Assume Company A acquires Company B on 1 February 2013. The identifiable net assets and liabilities of Company B are $400 million and Company A pays $500 million cash as purchase consideration. The goodwill arising on acquisition is thus $100 million. Company A then decides to create a restructuring provision of $60 million for future possible restructuring activities related to Company B. Company A records the following additional entry as part of its acquisition accounting entries:

| Goodwill | Dr | 60 m | |
| Restructuring Provision | Cr | | 60 m |

Why does Company A have an incentive to record this entry? The entry increases the amount recorded as goodwill, and in the 1990s goodwill was required to be amortised in most jurisdictions. Why would Company A want to expose itself to future goodwill amortisation? The answer is that because the restructuring provision was recorded directly against goodwill, an expense for the restructuring will *never* be recorded. When Company A incurs the expenditure in the future, the outflows will be recorded against the provision. Company A would likely have been able to highlight goodwill amortisation as a separate item either in its statement of comprehensive income or the attached notes, and thus would have been satisfied that the amortisation expense was effectively quarantined from the rest of its reported profit. The benefit for Company A was that the restructuring expense never affected its profit, and thus the creation of the restructuring provision as part of the acquisition entries protected Company A's future profits.

Rules to make it more difficult to record restructuring provisions were introduced in the United States and the United Kingdom. In the United States, the requirements for the recognition of restructuring provisions are contained primarily in Emerging Issues Task Force (EITF) Consensus EITF 94-3 and EITF 95-3. In addition, the Securities and Exchange Commission (SEC) issued a staff accounting bulletin (SAB) 100, which clarified how the SEC interprets certain aspects of the EITFs previously mentioned.

In the United Kingdom, FRS 7 *Fair Values in Acquisition Accounting* addressed the required accounting for restructuring provisions.

IAS 37 and IAS 22 (superseded by IFRS 3) were the least prescriptive of these requirements but, when IFRS 3 *Business Combinations* superseded IAS 22, it came more into line with UK requirements.

Paragraph 70 of IAS 37 provides the following examples of events that may be considered as restructurings:

(a) sale or termination of a line of business;
(b) the closure of business locations in a country or region or the relocation of business activities from one country or region to another;
(c) changes in management structure, for example, eliminating a layer of management; and
(d) fundamental reorganisations that have a material effect on the nature and focus of the entity's operations.

In broad terms, to be able to raise a restructuring provision, three conditions need to be met. First, the entity must have a *present obligation (either legal or constructive)* to restructure such that it cannot realistically avoid going ahead with the restructuring and thus incurring the costs involved. Second, only costs that are *directly and necessarily* caused by the restructuring and *not associated with the ongoing activities* of the entity may be included in a restructuring provision. Third, if the restructuring involves the sale of an operation, no obligation is deemed to arise for the sale of an operation until the entity is committed to the sale by a *binding sale agreement*.

Each of these requirements is considered in more detail below.

Present obligation

Usually management initiates a restructuring and thus it is rare that a legal obligation will exist for a restructuring. IAS 37 therefore focuses on the conditions that need to be met for a constructive obligation to exist. As we saw earlier, a constructive obligation is defined in paragraph 10 as:

an obligation that derives from an entity's actions where:
(a) by an established pattern of past practice, published policies or a sufficiently specific current statement, the entity has indicated to other parties that it will accept certain responsibilities; and
(b) as a result, the entity has created a valid expectation on the part of those other parties that it will discharge those responsibilities.

In respect of restructuring provisions, paragraph 72 of IAS 37 states that a constructive obligation to restructure arises only when an entity:

(a) has a detailed formal plan for the restructuring identifying at least:
  (i) the business or part of a business concerned;
  (ii) the principal locations affected;
  (iii) the location, function, and approximate number of employees who will be compensated for terminating their services;
  (iv) the expenditures that will be undertaken; and
  (v) when the plan will be implemented; and
(b) has raised a valid expectation in those affected that it will carry out the restructuring by starting to implement that plan or announcing its main features to those affected by it.

Therefore, we see that the entity needs to have a *detailed formal plan* and must have raised a *valid expectation* in those affected. In respect of restructuring provisions arising as part of an acquisition, IAS 22 (now superseded by IFRS 3) went even further, with the following three additional requirements.

First, *at or before the date of acquisition*, the acquirer must have developed the *main features of a plan* that involves terminating or reducing the activities of the acquiree. The main features include items such as compensating employees for termination, closing facilities of the acquiree, eliminating product lines of the acquiree and terminating contracts of the acquiree that have become onerous because of the acquisition. Second, the main features of the plan must be *announced at or before the date of acquisition*, in order to meet the 'valid expectation' test in IAS 37. Third, the *detailed formal plan* required by IAS 37 must be developed by the *earlier of three months* after the date of acquisition and the date when the financial statements are authorised for issue.

IAS 22 allowed the restructuring provision to be recorded in the books of the *acquirer* (i.e. as part of the acquirer's acquisition entries), provided the criteria for recognition were met. This was in contrast to FRS 7. According to FRS 7, the identifiable assets and liabilities to be recognised should be only those of the *acquired entity* that existed at the acquisition date. FRS 7 was explicit in saying that provisions for restructuring would be recognised as identifiable liabilities only if the commitments had been made before the date of acquisition. It even went so far as to say that only if the acquired entity was demonstrably committed to the expenditure, whether or not the acquisition was completed, would it have a liability.

In October 1998 the Australian companies' regulator, the Australian Securities and Investments Commission (ASIC), issued a media release announcing that it had required St George Bank to adjust its financial statements for 1998 for a $120 million restructuring liability that had been recorded against goodwill in its 1997 financial statements. ASIC's view was that the restructuring provision could not be recognised because it did not relate to restructuring costs of the acquired entity. This was ASIC's interpretation of Urgent Issues Group (UIG) Abstract 8 *Accounting for Acquisitions — Recognition of Restructuring Costs as Liabilities* (ASIC 1998).

When the Australian Accounting Standards Board (AASB) issued its equivalent of IAS 37 (AASB 1044) in 2001, it amended the requirements of IAS 37 to reflect ASIC's view and required that the restructuring provision be a liability of the acquired entity. AASB 1044 was not very clear on this issue and it continued to be a controversial area for a number of years. Finally, in 2004, the IASB issued IFRS 3 *Business Combinations*, which amended IAS 22 to require that the liability be *a liability of the acquiree*, recognised in accordance with IAS 37. As a result, no additional criteria are required by IFRS 3, and the three additional requirements of IAS 22 were removed. In 2005, AASB 1044 was superseded by the Australian equivalent to IAS 37, AASB 137.

Recording restructuring provisions

Where a provision for restructuring costs arises on the acquisition of an entity, it must be recognised as a liability in the statement of financial position of the acquiree and not in the books of the acquirer or as a consolidation entry. The provision for the restructuring costs must be taken into account by the acquirer when measuring the fair value of the net assets acquired. Illustrative example 5.6 demonstrates this principle further.

ILLUSTRATIVE EXAMPLE 5.6 Recording restructuring provisions in the books of the acquiree

Assume Company X acquires Company Y, a manufacturing company that has a head office in the city centre and a manufacturing plant in an industrial area. As part of the acquisition plans, Company X decides to close Company Y's head office premises and move Company Y's staff to Company X's own city premises. Company Y will be paying for the office closure costs.

Assume that the cost of closing Company Y's office premises is $120 000. Company Y will record the following journal entry at or before the date of acquisition:

Restructuring Costs	Dr	120 000	
Restructuring Provision	Cr		120 000

In determining the fair value of the net assets acquired in Company Y (in accordance with IFRS 3), Company X will include the restructuring provision recorded by Company Y. On the other hand, if Company Y did not have an obligation to pay the restructuring costs, it would not have recorded them. Company X would *not* be permitted to create a provision for restructuring costs as part of its acquisition entries in accordance with IFRS 3.

We saw above that in order to satisfy the 'valid expectation' test in IAS 37, the entity needs to have started to implement the detailed formal plan or announced the main features to those affected by it. An entity can do this in the following ways:

- By the entity having already entered into firm contracts to carry out parts of the restructuring. These contracts would be of such a nature that they effectively force the entity to carry out the restructuring. This would be the case if they contained severe penalty provisions or the costs of not fulfilling the contract were so high that it would effectively leave the entity with no alternative but to proceed.
- By starting to implement the detailed restructuring. This could include, for example, selling assets, notifying customers that supplies will be discontinued, notifying suppliers that orders will be ceasing, dismantling plant and equipment, and terminating employees' service.
- By announcing the main features of the plan to those affected by it (or their representatives). There may be a number of ways in which such an announcement could be made. It could be through written communication, meetings or discussions with the affected parties.

It is important that the communication is made in such a way that it raises a valid expectation in the affected parties such that they can be expected to act as a result of the communication, and by them doing so the entity would be left with no realistic alternative but to go ahead with the restructuring. For example, affected employees would start looking for other employment and customers would seek alternative sources of supply.

Figure 5.3 provides examples of where a present obligation does and does not arise on a restructuring as a result of an acquisition.

Example 1

The acquired entity has developed a detailed plan for the restructuring. Details of the plan have not been made public but, as at the date of acquisition, agreement about key features of the plan has been reached with, or information about the plan has been disclosed to, relevant third parties. These parties include employee representatives, lessors and regulatory bodies. As at the acquisition date, no elements of the plan had begun to be implemented.

A present obligation exists because the key features of the plan have been communicated to those affected and a detailed plan has been developed. The fact that parts of the plan have not begun to be implemented at the acquisition date does not negate the constructive obligation. Importantly, the *acquired entity* has the obligation.

Example 2

The acquiring entity has developed a detailed plan for the restructuring as at the date of acquisition. That plan involves the closure of a number of operating sites if the acquisition is successful and the retrenchment of all employees at those sites. As at the date of acquisition, key features of the plan have not been made public; however, employee representatives have been informed. Lessors of premises that will no longer be required have been informed of the entity's intentions, and negotiations on potential lease-termination penalty costs have commenced. Expressions of interest have been sought regarding the sale of plant and equipment that will be surplus should the acquisition proceed. Preliminary commitments have been made, and, conditional on the acquisition proceeding, agreements have been reached with third parties regarding the relocation or alternative supply of certain goods and services currently provided from the sites to be closed. The planned restructuring is such that on closure of the sites the continued employment of affected employees is not possible.

A present obligation does not exist for the *acquired entity*, so no provision is permitted under IFRS 3.

FIGURE 5.3 Examples of the existence of a present obligation under IFRS 3 and IAS 37

Qualifying restructuring costs

The second requirement for recognition of a restructuring provision is that the provision can include only costs that are directly and necessarily caused by the restructuring and not associated with the ongoing activities of the entity (IAS 37 paragraph 80).

Examples of the types of costs that would be included in a restructuring provision include the costs of terminating leases and other contracts as a direct result of the restructuring; costs of operations conducted in effecting the restructuring, such as employee remuneration while they are engaged in such tasks as dismantling plant, disposing of surplus stocks and fulfilling contractual obligations; and costs of making employees redundant.

Paragraph 81 of IAS 37 specifically indicates that the types of costs excluded from provisions for restructuring would be the costs of retraining or relocating the continuing staff, marketing costs and costs related to investment in new systems and distribution networks. These types of costs relate to the future conduct of the entity and do not relate to present obligations.

These requirements relating to the types of costs that qualify as restructuring costs apply equally to internal restructurings as well as to restructurings occurring as part of an acquisition. Figure 5.4 provides examples of costs that qualify as restructuring costs and figure 5.5 provides examples of costs that *do not* qualify as restructuring costs.

FIGURE 5.4 Examples of costs that qualify as restructuring costs

Example 1

A restructuring plan includes discontinuing operations currently performed in a facility that is leased under an operating lease. A lease-cancellation penalty fee payable on terminating the lease is a restructuring cost.

(continued)

FIGURE 5.4 *(continued)*

Example 2

A restructuring plan includes relocating operations currently performed in a facility leased by the acquired entity to a site that is owned by the acquirer. The lessor will not release the acquired entity from the lease agreement and will not permit the acquirer or acquiree to sublease the facility. The acquirer does not intend to re-open the facility prior to the lease's expiration. The leased space provides no future benefit to the enterprise. The lease payments by the acquiree for the remaining non-cancellable term of the operating lease after operations cease are a restructuring cost.

Example 1

The acquired entity used to share computer resources with its previous parent company. Therefore, the restructuring plan includes activities to separate the acquired entity from its previous parent and establish independent computer resources. The costs include costs of installing a LAN, moving head office PCs, moving a call centre, moving dedicated systems and acquisitions of new software. Such costs are not restructuring costs because they are associated with the ongoing activities of the entity.

Example 2

The restructuring plan includes costs to hire outside consultants to identify future corporate goals and strategies for organisational structure. The consultants' costs are not restructuring costs because they are associated with the ongoing activities of the entity.

FIGURE 5.5 Examples of costs that do not qualify as restructuring costs

It is important to note that, although certain costs have occurred only because of restructuring (i.e. they would not have had to be incurred had the restructuring not taken place), this fact alone does not qualify them for recognition as restructuring costs. They also have to be costs that are not associated with the ongoing activities of the entity.

Binding sale agreement

The final requirement for recognition of a restructuring provision is that if the restructuring involves the sale of an operation, no obligation is deemed to arise for the sale until the entity is committed to the sale by a binding sale agreement (IAS 37 paragraph 78). Paragraph 79 explains:

> Even when an entity has taken a decision to sell an operation and announced that decision publicly, it cannot be committed to the sale until a purchaser has been identified and there is a binding sale agreement. Until there is a binding sale agreement, the entity will be able to change its mind and indeed will have to take another course of action if a purchaser cannot be found on acceptable terms. When the sale of an operation is envisaged as part of a restructuring, the assets of the operation are reviewed for impairment, under IAS 36. When a sale is only part of a restructuring, a constructive obligation can arise for the other parts of the restructuring before a binding sale agreement exists.

5.9.4 Other applications

The examples in figures 5.6 to 5.14, sourced from IAS 37 and modified to aid understanding, illustrate other applications of the recognition requirements of IAS 37.

FIGURE 5.6 Warranties

A manufacturer gives warranties at the time of sale to purchasers of its product. Under the terms of the contract for sale the manufacturer undertakes to make good, by repair or replacement, manufacturing defects that become apparent within three years from the date of sale. On past experience, it is probable (that is, more likely than not) that there will be some claims under the warranties.

FIGURE 5.6 *(continued)*

Present obligation as a result of a past obligating event — The obligating event is the sale of the product with a warranty, which gives rise to a legal obligation.

An outflow of resources embodying economic benefits in settlement — Probable for the warranties as a whole.

Conclusion — A provision is recognised for the best estimate of the costs of making good under the warranty products sold before the end of the reporting period.

Source: IAS 37, Appendix C, Example 1.

FIGURE 5.7 Contaminated land — legislation virtually certain to be enacted

An entity in the oil industry causes contamination but cleans up only when required to do so under the laws of the particular country in which it operates. One country in which it operates has had no legislation requiring cleaning up, and the entity has been contaminating land in that country for several years. At 31 December 2013, it is virtually certain that a draft law requiring a clean up of land already contaminated will be enacted shortly after the year end.

Present obligation as a result of a past obligating event — The obligating event is the contamination of the land (past event) which gives rise to a present obligation because of the virtual certainty of legislation requiring cleaning up.

An outflow of resources embodying economic benefits in settlement — Probable.

Conclusion — A provision is recognised for the best estimate of the costs of the clean-up.

Source: IAS 37, Appendix C, Example 2A.

FIGURE 5.8 Contaminated land and constructive obligation

An entity in the oil industry causes contamination and operates in a country where there is no environmental legislation. However, the entity has a widely published environmental policy in which it undertakes to clean up all contamination that it causes. The entity has a record of honouring this published policy.

Present obligation as a result of a past obligating event — The obligating event is the contamination of the land, which gives rise to a constructive obligation because the conduct of the entity has created a valid expectation on the part of those affected by it that the entity will clean up contamination.

An outflow of resources embodying economic benefits in settlement — Probable.

Conclusion — A provision is recognised for the best estimate of the costs of clean-up [the entity has a constructive obligation].

Source: IAS 37, Appendix C, Example 2B.

FIGURE 5.9 Offshore oilfield

An entity operates an offshore oilfield where its licensing agreement requires it to remove the oil rig at the end of production and restore the seabed. Ninety per cent of the eventual costs relate to the removal of the oil rig and restoration of damage caused by building it, and 10 per cent arise through the extraction of oil. At the end of the reporting period, the rig has been constructed but no oil has been extracted.

Present obligation as a result of a past obligating event — The construction of the oil rig creates a legal obligation under the terms of the licence to remove the rig and restore the seabed and is thus

(continued)

FIGURE 5.9 *(continued)*

an obligating event. At the end of the reporting period, however, there is no obligation to rectify the damage that will be caused by extraction of the oil.

An outflow of resources embodying economic benefits in settlement — Probable.

Conclusion — A provision is recognised for the best estimate of 90 per cent of the eventual costs that relate to the removal of the oil rig and restoration of damage caused by building it. These costs are included as part of the cost of the oil rig. The 10 per cent of costs that arise through the extraction of oil are recognised as a liability when the oil is extracted.

Source: IAS 37, Appendix C, Example 3.

FIGURE 5.10 Refunds policy

A retail store has a policy of refunding purchases by dissatisfied customers, even though it is under no legal obligation to do so. Its policy of making refunds is generally known.

Present obligation as a result of a past obligating event — The obligating event is the sale of the product, which gives rise to a constructive obligation because the conduct of the store has created a valid expectation on the part of its customers that it will refund purchases.

An outflow of resources embodying economic benefits in settlement — Probable, a proportion of goods are returned for refund.

Conclusion — A provision is recognised for the best estimate of the costs of refunds.

Source: IAS 37, Appendix C, Example 4.

FIGURE 5.11 Legal requirement to fit smoke filters

Under new legislation, an entity is required to fit smoke filters to its factories by 30 June 2013. The entity has not fitted the smoke filters.

(a) At the end of the reporting period, 31 December 2012:

Present obligation as a result of a past obligating event — There is no obligation because there is no obligating event either for the costs of fitting smoke filters or for fines under the legislation.

Conclusion — No provision is recognised for the cost of fitting the smoke filters.

(b) At the end of the reporting period, 31 December 2013:

Present obligation as a result of a past obligating event — There is still no obligation for the costs of fitting smoke filters because no obligating event has occurred (the fitting of the filters). However, an obligation might arise to pay fines or penalties under the legislation because the obligating event has occurred (the non-compliant operation of the factory).

An outflow of resources embodying economic benefits in settlement — Assessment of the probability of incurring fines and penalties by non-compliant operation depends on the details of the legislation and the stringency of the enforcement regime.

Conclusion — No provision is recognised for the costs of fitting smoke filters. However, a provision is recognised for the best estimate of any fines and penalties that are more likely than not to be imposed.

Source: Adapted from IAS 37, Appendix C, Example 6.

FIGURE 5.12 An onerous contract

An entity operates profitably from a factory that it has leased under an operating lease. During December 2013 the entity relocates its operations to a new factory. The lease on the old factory continues for the next four years, it cannot be cancelled and the factory cannot be re-let to another user.

FIGURE 5.12 (continued)

> **Present obligation as a result of a past obligating event** — The obligating event is the signing of the lease contract, which gives rise to a legal obligation.
>
> **An outflow of resources embodying economic benefits in settlement** — When the lease becomes onerous, an outflow of resources embodying economic benefits is probable. (Until the lease becomes onerous, the entity accounts for the lease under IAS 17 *Leases*.)
>
> **Conclusion** — A provision is recognised for the best estimate of the unavoidable lease payments.

Source: IAS 37, Appendix C, Example 8.

FIGURE 5.13 Repairs and maintenance: refurbishment costs — no legislative requirement

> Some assets require, in addition to routine maintenance, substantial expenditure every few years for major refits or refurbishment and the replacement of major components. IAS 16 *Property, Plant and Equipment* gives guidance on allocating expenditure on an asset to its component parts where these components have different useful lives or provide benefits in a different pattern.
>
> A furnace has a lining that needs to be replaced every five years for technical reasons. At the end of the reporting period, the lining has been in use for three years.
>
> **Present obligation as a result of a past obligating event** — There is no present obligation.
>
> **Conclusion** — No provision is recognised.
>
> The cost of replacing the lining is not recognised because, at the end of the reporting period, no obligation to replace the lining exists independently of the company's future actions — even the intention to incur the expenditure depends on the company deciding to continue operating the furnace or replace the lining. Instead of a provision being recognised, the depreciation of the lining takes account of its consumption, that is, it is depreciated over five years. The re-lining costs then incurred are capitalised with the consumption of each new lining shown by depreciation over the subsequent five years.

Source: IAS 37, Appendix C, Examples 11 and 11A.

FIGURE 5.14 Repairs and maintenance: refurbishment costs — legislative requirement

> An airline is required by law to overhaul its aircraft once every three years.
>
> **Present obligation as a result of a past obligating event** — There is no present obligation.
>
> **Conclusion** — No provision is recognised.
>
> The costs of overhauling aircraft are not recognised as a provision for the same reasons as the cost of replacing the lining is not recognised as a provision in Example 11A. Even a legal requirement to overhaul does not make the costs of overhaul a liability, because no obligation exists to overhaul the aircraft independently of the entity's future actions — the entity could avoid the future expenditure by its future actions, for example, by selling the aircraft. Instead of a provision being recognised, the depreciation of the aircraft takes account of the future incidence of maintenance costs, that is, an amount equivalent to the expected maintenance costs is depreciated over three years.

Source: IAS 37, Appendix C, Example 11B.

It is interesting to contrast figures 5.13 and 5.14 with figures 5.7 and 5.8. In figures 5.7 and 5.8, the entity had a present obligation for the costs of clean-up or removal, which were independent of the cost and useful life of the asset in question. In addition, in those examples the entity was unable to avoid the clean-up or removal, although it could be argued that it could avoid those actions and incur any resultant fines (as in figure 5.11). In that case, provision would be made for the best estimate of the costs of non-compliance with the relevant legislation.

5.10 CONTINGENT ASSETS

Paragraph 10 of IAS 37 defines a contingent asset as:

> a possible asset that arises from past events and whose existence will be confirmed only by the occurrence or non-occurrence of one or more uncertain future events not wholly within the control of the entity.

Paragraph 31 states that an entity shall *not recognise* a contingent asset. Paragraph 89 requires that a contingent asset be *disclosed* where an inflow of benefits is probable.

Note the lack of symmetry between the definition of a contingent asset and a contingent liability. The definition of a contingent liability includes both possible liabilities and liabilities that fail the recognition criteria. A contingent asset includes only possible assets. The standard setters were presumably concerned with overstatement of assets and therefore wanted to apply a more stringent test to the definition, although arguably an asset that fails the recognition criteria is more of an asset than a possible asset! Further, IAS 37 permits a contingent asset to be reclassified and recognised as an actual asset only when it has become virtually certain that an inflow of economic benefits will arise (paragraph 35). Contrast this with the test of probability, which is applied to asset recognition generally. It could be argued that IAS 37 is biased towards ensuring that contingent liabilities are disclosed in almost all circumstances and reclassified and recognised as actual liabilities as soon as they meet the liability recognition criteria. Contingent assets, however, can be disclosed only in rare circumstances and reclassified to actual assets only when they meet strict recognition criteria. This bias could be criticised as being against the IASB's *Conceptual Framework*. Paragraph BC3.27 in the Basis for Conclusions on *Chapter 3: Qualitative Characteristics of Useful Financial Information* states that:

> Chapter 3 does not include prudence or conservatism as an aspect of faithful representation because including either would be inconsistent with neutrality.

Note that the concept of *prudence* is no longer included in the *Conceptual Framework* as a result of the 2010 amendments to the *Conceptual Framework*. From this, it is clear that IAS 37, being a relatively old standard, has not kept pace with other changes in the *Conceptual Framework*. This is one of the reasons that the IASB added a project to amend IAS 37 to its agenda and issued an exposure draft in 2005 (see section 5.13).

An example of a contingent asset would be the possible receipt of damages arising from a court case, which has been decided in favour of the entity as at the end of the reporting period. The hearing to determine damages, however, will be held after the end of the reporting period. The outcome of the hearing is outside the control of the entity, but the receipt of damages is probable because the case has been decided in the entity's favour. The asset meets the definition of a contingent asset because it is possible that the entity will receive the damages and the hearing is outside its control. In addition, the contingent asset is disclosed because it is probable that the damages (the inflow of economic benefits) will flow to the entity.

5.11 DISCLOSURE

The disclosure requirements of IAS 37 are self-explanatory and are reproduced below:

84. For each class of provision, an entity shall disclose:
    (a) the carrying amount at the beginning and end of the period;
    (b) additional provisions made in the period, including increases to existing provisions;
    (c) amounts used (that is, incurred and charged against the provision) during the period;
    (d) unused amounts reversed during the period; and
    (e) the increase during the period in the discounted amount arising from the passage of time and the effect of any change in the discount rate.
    Comparative information is not required.
85. An entity shall disclose the following for each class of provision:
    (a) a brief description of the nature of the obligation and the expected timing of any resulting outflows of economic benefits;
    (b) an indication of the uncertainties about the amount or timing of those outflows. Where necessary to provide adequate information, an entity shall disclose the major assumptions made concerning future events, as addressed in paragraph 48; and
    (c) the amount of any expected reimbursement, stating the amount of any asset that has been recognised for that expected reimbursement.
86. Unless the possibility of any outflow in settlement is remote, an entity shall disclose for each class of contingent liability at the end of the reporting period a brief description of the nature of the contingent liability and, where practicable:
    (a) an estimate of its financial effect, measured under paragraphs 36–52;
    (b) an indication of the uncertainties relating to the amount or timing of any outflow; and
    (c) the possibility of any reimbursement.

89. Where an inflow of economic benefits is probable, an entity shall disclose a brief description of the nature of the contingent assets at the end of the reporting period, and, where practicable, an estimate of their financial effect, measured using the principles set out for provisions in paragraphs 36–52.

91. Where any of the information required by paragraphs 86 and 89 is not disclosed because it is not practicable to do so, that fact shall be stated.

92. In extremely rare cases, disclosure of some or all of the information required by paragraphs 84–89 can be expected to prejudice seriously the position of the entity in a dispute with other parties on the subject matter of the provision, contingent liability or contingent asset. In such cases, an entity need not disclose the information, but shall disclose the general nature of the dispute, together with the fact that, and reason why, the information has not been disclosed.

The disclosures required for contingent liabilities and assets necessarily involve judgement and estimation. Many analysts consider the contingent liabilities note to be one of the most important notes provided by a company because it helps the analyst to make his or her own decision about the likely consequences for the company and is useful in providing an overall view of the company's exposures. Thus, the use of the exemption permitted in paragraph 92 should be treated with caution because it could be interpreted as a deliberate concealing of the company's exposures.

An example of the disclosures required by paragraph 85 is included in Appendix D of IAS 37, shown in figure 5.15.

A manufacturer gives warranties at the time of sale to purchasers of its three product lines. Under the terms of the warranty, the manufacturer undertakes to repair or replace items that fail to perform satisfactorily for two years from the date of sale. At the end of the reporting period, a provision of 60 000 has been recognised. The provision has not been discounted as the effect of discounting is not material. The following information is disclosed:

A provision of 60 000 has been recognised for expected warranty claims on products sold during the last three reporting periods. It is expected that the majority of this expenditure will be incurred in the next financial year, and all will be incurred within two years of the end of the reporting period.

FIGURE 5.15 Warranties
Source: IAS 37, Appendix D, Example 1.

A good example of extensive disclosures of provisions, related assumptions and contingent liabilities is included in the annual report of Bayer AG, a global enterprise based in Germany, reporting under IFRS. Figure 5.16 is an extract from the contingencies note (note 31) and the first part of the note on legal risks (note 32). Students should refer to the annual report at www.bayer.com for the full note 32.

FIGURE 5.16 Example of disclosures of contingencies

31. Contingencies and other financial commitments
Contingent liabilities relate to potential future events which, although regarded as improbable on the reporting date, cannot be ruled out and would create an obligation if they occurred.

Contingent liabilities resulted entirely from commitments given to third parties and comprised:

Contingent Liabilities	Dec. 31, 2009	Dec. 31, 2010
	€ million	€ million
Warranties	74	53
Unpaid portion of the effective initial fund of Bayer–Pensionskasse	490	390
Miscellaneous	111	247
Total	675	690

(continued)

FIGURE 5.16 *(continued)*

In addition to provisions, other liabilities and contingent liabilities, there are also other financial commitments. These mainly related to leasing agreements and long-term rentals.

The non-discounted minimum future payments relating to operating leases totaled €595 million (2009: €606 million). The maturities of the respective payment obligations were as follows:

Operating Leases			
Maturing in	**Dec. 31, 2009**	**Maturing in**	**Dec. 31, 2010**
	€ million		€ million
2010	166	2011	182
2011	132	2012	132
2012	99	2013	94
2013	72	2014	71
2014	59	2015	49
2015 or later	78	2016 or later	67
Total	606	Total	595

Financial commitments resulting from orders already placed under purchase agreements related to planned or ongoing capital expenditure projects totaled €231 million (2009: €441 million). In addition, the Group has entered into research agreements with a number of third parties under which Bayer has agreed to fund various research projects or has assumed other payment obligations based on the achievement of certain milestones or other specific conditions. The total amount of such funding and other commitments was €1,132 million (2009: €661 million). As of December 31, 2010, the remaining payments expected to be made to these parties, assuming the milestones are reached or the other agreed conditions are met in the respective years, were as follows:

Other commitments			
Maturing in	**Dec. 31, 2009**	**Maturing in**	**Dec.31, 2010**
	€ million		€ million
2010	154	2011	119
2011	114	2012	235
2012	83	2013	154
2013	39	2014	200
2014	43	2015	120
2015 or later	228	2016 or later	304
Total	661	Total	1 132

32. Legal risks

As a global company with a diverse business portfolio, the Bayer Group is exposed to numerous legal risks, particularly in the areas of product liability, competition and antitrust law, patent disputes, tax

FIGURE 5.16 (continued)

assessments and environmental matters. The outcome of any current or future proceedings cannot be predicted. It is therefore possible that legal or regulatory judgments or future settlements could give rise to expenses that are not covered, or not fully covered, by insurers' compensation payments and could significantly affect our revenues and earnings.

Source: Bayer AG (2010, pp. 240–1).

5.12 COMPARISON BETWEEN IFRS 3 AND IAS 37 IN RESPECT OF CONTINGENT LIABILITIES

IFRS 3 *Business Combinations*, as revised in 2008, contains a number of requirements that are inconsistent with IAS 37. However, as discussed in section 5.9.3, the requirements in respect of restructuring provisions are consistent with IAS 37. The two areas of difference are in respect of contingent liabilities acquired in a business combination and contingent consideration.

5.12.1 Contingent liabilities acquired in a business combination

As discussed in section 5.6, IAS 37 states that contingent liabilities must *not* be recognised in the statement of financial position. Instead, they are disclosed if certain conditions are met. However, IFRS 3 (paragraph 23) states that the requirements of IAS 37 *do not apply* in determining which contingent liabilities to recognise at the acquisition date. Instead, the acquirer *must* recognise contingent liabilities assumed in a business combination — just as it must recognise all other liabilities assumed in a business combination. The only conditions for recognising the contingent liability are:
(a) it must be a present obligation arising from past events
(b) its fair value can be measured reliably.
Condition (a) means that contingent liabilities falling within part (a) of the contingent liability definition (i.e. a possible obligation — see section 5.5) are not recognised in a business combination — only those that fall within part (b) of the definition are eligible for recognition (i.e. there is a present obligation) provided their value can be reliably measured. This means that an acquirer must identify which contingent liabilities of the acquiree are present obligations that failed the recognition criteria from the perspective of the acquiree but which can be assigned a fair value by the acquirer. This is shown in illustrative example 5.7.

ILLUSTRATIVE EXAMPLE 5.7 Contingent liabilities in a business combination

Assume that an acquiree had identified damages payable in a lawsuit as a present obligation because it had lost the case, but it did not record the contingent liability as a liability because it could not reliably measure the amount payable. In this case, the acquirer would need to estimate the fair value of the amount payable and recognise it as one of the liabilities assumed in the business combination.

5.12.2 Contingent consideration in a business combination

Sometimes an acquirer may enter into an agreement with the vendor of the acquiree that entitles the vendor to additional consideration if certain conditions are met in the future. This is referred to as contingent consideration. IFRS 3 paragraph 39 requires the acquirer to include the fair value of that contingent consideration as part of the consideration transferred in exchange for the acquiree. This means that the acquirer must make an estimate, if necessary, to determine the fair value and would record a liability for the amount of the contingency. This is unless the contingent consideration is in the form of equity instruments — in which case the amount would be recorded as an equity instrument. This is demonstrated in illustrative example 5.8.

Company A acquires 100% of Company S from Company V. The purchase consideration is comprised of cash of $1 500 000 plus an agreement to pay a further $200 000 in cash to Company V if Company S achieves certain profit targets within three years of the acquisition date. The fair value of the identifiable assets and liabilities of Company S acquired is $1 200 000. Company A estimates the acquisition-date fair value of the contingent consideration to be $140 000 based on its expectations of Company S's future performance and the time value of money. Company A thus records the following journal entry at the date of acquisition (see chapter 14 for more details on how to account for a business combination):

Net Assets of Company S	Dr	1 200 000	
Goodwill	Dr	440 000	
Cash	Cr		1 500 000
Liability to Pay Company V	Cr		140 000

Note that if the contingent consideration was not recorded (i.e. if the requirements of IAS 37 were followed) goodwill would be lower. Companies wishing to minimise the amount of goodwill arising on acquisition would thus want to record a lower amount for contingent consideration.

Table 5.1 Summarises the similarities and differences between IFRS 3 and IAS 37.

TABLE 5.1 Similarities and differences between IFRS 3 and IAS 37

	IAS 37	IFRS 3	Same/Different
Contingent liabilities — part (a) of the definition of a contingent liability	Possible liabilities are not recognised by the entity.	Possible liabilities are not recognised by the acquirer.	Same
Contingent liabilities — part (b) of the definition of a contingent liability	A present obligation that fails *either* of the recognition criteria must not be recognised by the entity.	A present obligation whose fair value can be reliably measured must be recognised by the acquirer	Different
Contingent consideration	Contingent consideration is not specifically addressed, but applying the definition of a contingent liability would likely result in no amount being recognised by the entity.	Contingent consideration must be recognised by the acquirer at its acquisition date fair value.	Different
Restructuring provisions	A restructuring provision is recognised by the entity only if the criteria in IAS 37 are met.	A restructuring provision is recognised by the *acquiree* only if the criteria in IAS 37 are met.	Same

5.13 EXPECTED FUTURE DEVELOPMENTS

In June 2005, the IASB issued an exposure draft proposing significant changes to IAS 37 as part of its program to amend IFRS 3 (see chapter 14). The exposure draft proposed amendments to the title of IAS 37 (to 'Non-financial Liabilities'), new definitions of contingencies, and new recognition and measurement criteria. The proposed changes are so far-reaching that they attracted widespread concern by respondents to the exposure draft. At the time of writing, the project on non-financial liabilities is no longer on the board's active agenda. However, this may change subject to the IASB's agenda consultation process.[2] There is doubt as to whether the proposed changes will eventuate in their current form and therefore they will not be considered in more detail here.

SUMMARY

IAS 37 deals with the recognition, measurement and presentation of provisions and contingent assets and contingent liabilities. The standard contains specific requirements regarding the recognition of restructuring provisions and onerous contracts.

The standard:

- defines provisions and specifies recognition criteria and measurement requirements for the recognition of provisions in financial statements
- defines contingent liabilities and contingent assets and prohibits their recognition in the financial statements but requires their disclosure when certain conditions are met
- requires that where provisions are measured using estimated cash flows, that the cash flows be discounted to their present value at the reporting date and specifies the discount rate to be used for this purpose
- prohibits providing for future operating losses
- defines onerous contracts and requires the estimated net loss under onerous contracts to be provided for
- specifies recognition criteria for restructuring provisions and identifies the types of costs that may be included in restructuring provisions
- requires extensive disclosures relating to provisions, recoveries, contingent liabilities and contingent assets.

The standard differs from IFRS 3 *Business Combinations* in respect of the recognition of contingent liabilities and contingent consideration. However, it is consistent with IFRS 3 in respect of restructuring provisions.

Discussion questions

1. How is present value related to the concept of a liability?
2. Define (a) a contingency and (b) a contingent liability.
3. What are the characteristics of a provision?
4. Define a constructive obligation.
5. What is the key characteristic of a present obligation?
6. What are the recognition criteria for provisions?
7. At what point would a contingent liability become a provision?
8. Compare and contrast the requirements of IFRS 3 and IAS 37 in respect of restructuring provisions and contingent liabilities.

Exercises

STAR RATING   ★ BASIC   ★★ MODERATE   ★★★ DIFFICULT

| Exercise 5.1 | RECOGNISING A PROVISION — MEASUREMENT |

★ Explain how a borrowing cost could arise as part of the measurement of a provision. Illustrate your explanation with a simple example.

| Exercise 5.2 | RECOGNISING A PROVISION |

★ When should liabilities for each of the following items be recorded in the accounts of the business entity?
(a) Acquisition of goods by purchase on credit
(b) Salaries
(c) Annual bonus paid to management
(d) Dividends

---

[2] In July 2011, the IASB issued a consultation document seeking input on its post-2011 agenda.

RECOGNISING A PROVISION

★ The government introduces a number of changes to the value added tax system. As a result of these changes, Company A, a manufacturing company, will need to retrain a large proportion of its administrative and sales workforce in order to ensure continued compliance with the new taxation regulations. At the end of the reporting period, no retraining of staff has taken place.

Required

Should Company A provide for the costs of the staff training at the end of the reporting period?

RECOGNISING A PROVISION

★★ Company B, a listed company, provides food to function centres that host events such as weddings and engagement parties. After an engagement party held by one of Company B's customers in June 2013, 100 people became seriously ill, possibly as a result of food poisoning from products sold by Company B. Legal proceedings were commenced seeking damages from Company B, which disputed liability by claiming that the function centre was at fault for handling the food incorrectly. Up to the date of authorisation for issue of the financial statements for the year to 30 June 2013, Company B's lawyers advised that it was probable that Company B would not be found liable. However, two weeks after the financial statements were published, Company B's lawyers advised that, owing to developments in the case, it was probable that Company B would be found liable and the estimated damages would be material to the company's reported profits.

Required

Should Company B recognise a liability for damages in its financial statements at 30 June 2013? How should it deal with the information it receives two weeks after the financial statements are published?

RESTRUCTURING COSTS

★★ A division of an acquired entity will be closed and activities discontinued. The division will operate for 1 year after the date of acquisition, after which all divisional employees will be retrenched except for the retention of some employees retained to finalise closure of the division.

Required

Which of the following costs, if any, are restructuring costs?
(a) The costs of employees (salaries and benefits) to be incurred after operations cease and that are associated with the closing of the division.
(b) The costs of leasing the factory space occupied by the division for the year after the date of acquisition.
(c) The costs of modifying the division's purchasing system to make it consistent with that of the acquirer's.

RESTRUCTURING COSTS

★★ Company Z acquires Company Y. The restructuring plan, which satisfies the criteria for the existence of a present obligation under IAS 37 and IFRS 3, includes an advertising program to promote the new company image. The restructuring plan also includes costs to retrain and relocate existing employees of the acquired entity.

Required

Are these costs restructuring costs?

DISTINGUISHING BETWEEN LIABILITIES, PROVISIONS AND CONTINGENT LIABILITIES

★★ Identify whether each of the following would be a liability, a provision or a contingent liability, or none of the above, in the financial statements of Company A as at the end of its reporting period of 30 June 2013. Assume that Company A's financial statements are authorised for issue on 24 August 2013.
(a) An amount of $35 000 owing to Company Z for services rendered during May 2013.
(b) Long service leave, estimated to be $500 000, owing to employees in respect of past services.

(c) Costs of $26 000 estimated to be incurred for relocating employee D from Company A's head office location to another city. The staff member will physically relocate during July 2013.

(d) Provision of $50 000 for the overhaul of a machine. The overhaul is needed every 5 years and the machine was 5 years old as at 30 June 2013.

(e) Damages awarded against Company A resulting from a court case decided on 26 June 2013. The judge has announced that the amount of damages will be set at a future date, expected to be in September 2013. Company A has received advice from its lawyers that the amount of the damages could be anything between $20 000 and $7 million.

Exercise 5.8 CONTINGENT LIABILITIES — DISCLOSURE

★★ A customer filed a lawsuit against Company A in December 2014, for costs and damages allegedly incurred as a result of the failure of one of Company A's electrical products. The amount claimed was $3 million. Company A's lawyers have advised that the amount claimed is extortionate and that Company A has a good chance of winning the case. However, the lawyers have also advised that, if Company A loses the case, its expected costs and damages would be about $500 000.

Required

How should Company A disclose this event in its financial statements as at 31 December 2014?

Exercise 5.9 RECOGNISING A PROVISION

★★ In each of the following scenarios, explain whether or not Company G would be required to recognise a provision.

(a) As a result of its plastics operations, Company G has contaminated the land on which it operates. There is no legal requirement to clean up the land, and Company G has no record of cleaning up land that it has contaminated.

(b) As a result of its plastics operations, Company G has contaminated the land on which it operates. There is a legal requirement to clean up the land.

(c) As a result of its plastics operations, Company G has contaminated the land on which it operates. There is no legal requirement to clean up the land, but Company G has a long record of cleaning up land that it has contaminated.

Exercise 5.10 RISK AND PRESENT VALUE OF CASH FLOWS

★★ Using examples, explain how a liability-specific discount rate could cause the amount calculated for a provision to be lower when the risk associated with that provision is high. How could this problem be averted in practice?

Exercise 5.11 MEASURING A RESTRUCTURING PROVISION

★★ Company T's directors decided on 3 May 2014 to restructure the company's operations as follows:
• Factory Z would be closed down and put on the market for sale.
• 100 employees working in factory Z would be retrenched on 31 May 2014, and would be paid their accumulated entitlements plus three months wages.
• The remaining 20 employees working in factory Z would be transferred to factory X, which would continue operating.
• Five head-office staff would be retrenched on 30 June 2014, and would be paid their accumulated entitlements plus three months wages.

As at the end of Company T's reporting period, 30 June 2014, the following transactions and events had occurred:
• Factory Z was shut down on 31 May 2014. An offer of $4 million had been received for factory Z but there was no binding sales agreement.
• The 100 retrenched employees had left and their accumulated entitlements had been paid. However, an amount of $76 000, representing a portion of the three months wages for the retrenched employees, had still not been paid.

- Costs of $23 000 were expected to be incurred in transferring the 20 employees to their new work in factory X. The transfer is planned for 14 July 2014.
- Four of the five head-office staff who have been retrenched have had their accumulated entitlements paid, including the three months' wages. However, one employee, Jerry Perry, remains in order to complete administrative tasks relating to the closure of factory Z and the transfer of staff to factory X. Jerry is expected to stay until 31 July 2014. His salary for July will be $4000 and his retrenchment package will be $13 000, all of which will be paid on the day he leaves. He estimates that he would spend 60% of his time administering the closure of factory Z, 30% on administering the transfer of staff to factory X, and the remaining 10% on general administration.

Required

Calculate the amount of the restructuring provision recognised in Company T's financial statements as at 30 June 2014, in accordance with IAS 37.

Exercise 5.12   CALCULATION OF A PROVISION

In May 2013, Company A relocated employee R from Company A's head office to an office in another city. As at 30 June 2013, the end of Company A's reporting period, the costs were estimated to be $40 000. Analysis of the costs is as follows:

Costs for shipping goods	$ 3 000
Airfare	6 000
Temporary accommodation costs (May and June)	8 000
Temporary accommodation costs (July and August)	9 000
Reimbursement for lease break costs (paid in July; lease was terminated in May)	2 000
Reimbursement for cost-of-living increases (for the period 15 May 2013 – 15 May 2014)	12 000

Required

Calculate the provision for relocation costs for Company A's financial statements as at 30 June 2013. Assume that IAS 37 applies to this provision and that the effect of discounting is immaterial.

Exercise 5.13   RESTRUCTURING PROVISIONS ON ACQUISITION

Company A acquires Company B, effective 1 March 2014. At the date of acquisition, Company A intends to close a division of Company B. As at the date of acquisition, management has developed and the board has approved the main features of the restructuring plan and, based on available information, best estimates of the costs have been made. As at the date of acquisition, a public announcement of Company A's intentions has been made and relevant parties have been informed of the planned closure. Within a week of the acquisition being effected, management commences the process of informing unions, lessors, institutional investors and other key shareholders of the broad characteristics of its restructuring program. A detailed plan for the restructuring is developed within 3 months and implemented soon thereafter.

Required

Should Company A create a provision for restructuring as part of its acquisition accounting entries? Explain your answer. How would your answer change if all the circumstances are the same as those above except that Company A decided that, instead of closing a division of Company B, it would close down one of its own facilities?

Exercise 5.14   COMPREHENSIVE PROBLEM

ChubbyChocs Ltd, a listed company, is a manufacturer of confectionery and biscuits. The end of its reporting period is 30 June. Relevant extracts from its financial statements at 30 June 2014 are shown on the next page.

Current liabilities		
Provisions		
Provision for warranties		$270 000
Non-current liabilities		
Provisions		
Provision for warranties		160 715
Non-current assets		
Plant and equipment		
At cost	$2 000 000	
Accumulated depreciation	600 000	
Carrying amount	1 400 000	

Plant and equipment has a useful life of 10 years and is depreciated on a straight-line basis.

Note 36 — Contingent liabilities
ChubbyChocs is engaged in litigation with various parties in relation to allergic reactions to traces of peanuts alleged to have been found in packets of fruit gums. ChubbyChocs strenuously denies the allegations and, as at the date of authorising the financial statements for issue, is unable to estimate the financial effect, if any, of any costs or damages that may be payable to the plaintiffs.

The provision for warranties at 30 June 2014 was calculated using the following assumptions (there was no balance carried forward from the prior year):

Estimated cost of repairs — products with minor defects	$1 000 000
Estimated cost of repairs — products with major defects	$6 000 000
Expected % of products sold during FY 2014 having no defects in FY 2015	80%
Expected % of products sold during FY 2014 having minor defects in FY 2015	15%
Expected % of products sold during FY 2014 having major defects in FY 2015	5%
Expected timing of settlement of warranty payments — those with minor defects	All in FY 2015
Expected timing of settlement of warranty payments — those with major defects	40% in FY 2015, 60% in FY 2016
Discount rate	6%. The effect of discounting for FY 2015 is considered to be immaterial.

During the year ended 30 June 2015, the following occurred:
1. In relation to the warranty provision of $430 715 at 30 June 2014, $200 000 was paid out of the provision. Of the amount paid, $150 000 was for products with minor defects and $50 000 was for products with major defects, all of which related to amounts that had been expected to be paid in the 2015 financial year.
2. In calculating its warranty provision for 30 June 2015, ChubbyChocs made the following adjustments to the assumptions used for the prior year:

Estimated cost of repairs — products with minor defects	No change
Estimated cost of repairs — products with major defects	$ 5 000 000
Expected % of products sold during FY 2015 having no defects in FY 2016	85%

Expected % of products sold during FY 2015 having minor defects in FY 2016	12%
Expected % of products sold during FY 2015 having major defects in FY 2016	3%
Expected timing of settlement of warranty payments — those with minor defects	All in FY 2016
Expected timing of settlement of warranty payments — those with major defects	20% in FY 2016, 80% in FY 2017
Discount rate	No change. The effect of discounting for FY 2016 is considered to be immaterial.

3. ChubbyChocs determined that part of its plant and equipment needed an overhaul — the conveyer belt on one of its machines would need to be replaced in about May 2016 at an estimated cost of $250 000. The carrying amount of the conveyer belt at 30 June 2014 was $140 000. Its original cost was $200 000.
4. ChubbyChocs was unsuccessful in its defence of the peanut allergy case and was ordered to pay $1 500 000 to the plaintiffs. As at 30 June 2015, ChubbyChocs had paid $800 000.
5. ChubbyChocs commenced litigation against one of its advisers for negligent advice given on the original installation of the conveyer belt referred to in (4) above. In April 2015 the court found in favour of ChubbyChocs. The hearing for damages had not been scheduled as at the date the financial statements for 2015 were authorised for issue. ChubbyChocs estimated that it would receive about $425 000.
6. ChubbyChocs signed an agreement with BankSweet to the effect that ChubbyChocs would guarantee a loan made by BankSweet to ChubbyChocs' subsidiary, CCC Ltd. CCC's loan with BankSweet was $3 200 000 as at 30 June 2015. CCC was in a strong financial position at 30 June 2015.

Required

Prepare the relevant extracts from the financial statements (including the notes) of ChubbyChocs Ltd as at 30 June 2015, in compliance with IAS 37 and related International Financial Reporting Standards. Include comparative figures where required. Show all workings separately. Perform your workings in the following order:

(a) Calculate the warranty provision as at 30 June 2014. This should agree with the financial statements provided in the question.
(b) Calculate the warranty provision as at 30 June 2015.
(c) Calculate the movement in the warranty provision for the year.
(d) Calculate the prospective change in depreciation required as a result of the shortened useful life of the conveyer belt.
(e) Determine whether the unpaid amount owing as a result of the peanut allergy case is a liability or a provision.
(f) Determine whether the receipt of damages for the negligent advice meets the definition of an asset or a contingent asset.
(g) Determine whether the bank guarantee meets the definition of a provision or a contingent liability. (Ignore IAS 39 in this regard.)
(h) Prepare the financial statement disclosures.

References

ASIC 1998, *Media release 98/314*, Australian Securities and Investments Commission, October.
Bayer AG 2010, *Annual report 2010*, Bayer AG, Germany, www.bayer.com.
Ernst & Young 2002a, 'Provisions, contingent liabilities and contingent assets', *Accounting Brief*, January, Australia.
—— 2002b, AH 217 'Accounting for provisions', *Accounting handbook*, Australia.
—— 2011, *International GAAP 2011*, John Wiley & Sons, Inc., Chichester.

6 Income taxes

ACCOUNTING STANDARDS IN FOCUS

IAS 12 *Income Taxes*

LEARNING OBJECTIVES

After studying this chapter, you should be able to:

1. understand the nature of income tax
2. understand differences in accounting treatments and taxation treatments for a range of transactions
3. explain the concept of tax-effect accounting
4. calculate and account for current taxation expense
5. discuss the recognition requirements for current tax
6. account for the payment of tax
7. explain the nature of and accounting for tax losses
8. calculate and account for movements in deferred taxation accounts
9. apply the recognition criteria for deferred tax items
10. account for changes in tax rates
11. account for amendments to prior year taxes and identify other issues
12. explain the presentation requirements of IAS 12
13. implement the disclosure requirements of IAS 12.

6.1 THE NATURE OF INCOME TAX

Income taxes are levied by governments on income earned by individuals and entities in order to raise money to fund the provision of government services and infrastructure. The percentage payable and the determination of taxable income are governed by income tax legislation administered by a dedicated government body, such as the Australian Taxation Office. Tax payable is normally determined annually with the lodgement of a taxation document, although some jurisdictions may require payment by instalment, with estimates of tax payable being made on a periodic basis.

This chapter analyses the accounting standard IAS 12 *Income Taxes*. According to paragraph 1 of IAS 12, the standard applies in accounting for income taxes, including all domestic and foreign taxes based on taxable profits. It also applies to withholding taxes that are payable by a subsidiary, associate or joint arrangement on distributions to a reporting entity. The standard does not deal with methods of accounting for government grants or investment tax credits, but it does deal with accounting for tax effects arising in respect of such transactions.

At first glance, accounting for income tax appears to be a simple matter of calculating the liability owing, recognising the liability and expense, and recording the eventual payment of the amount outstanding. Such a simplistic approach applies only if accounting profit is the same amount as taxable profit and the respective profits have been determined by the same rules. Because this is generally not the case, accounting for income taxes can be a complicated exercise; hence the need for an accounting standard.

In each country there are different legal requirements for calculating taxable income. It is not the purpose of this chapter to deal with these requirements. Instead the focus is on the differences between the way in which income and expense are measured for accounting purposes and how they are measured for tax purposes. In general, it is assumed for simplicity that income and expense for tax purposes are based on cash flow in contrast to the use of the accrual method for accounting purposes. It is also assumed in this chapter that the company tax rate is 30%.

6.2 DIFFERENCES BETWEEN ACCOUNTING PROFIT AND TAXABLE PROFIT

Accounting profit is defined in IAS 12, paragraph 5, as 'profit or loss for a period before deducting tax expense', profit or loss being the excess (or deficiency) of revenues less expenses for that period. Such revenues and expenses would be determined and recognised in accordance with accounting standards and the *Conceptual Framework*. Taxable profit is defined in the same paragraph as the profit for a period, determined in accordance with the rules established by the taxation authorities, upon which income taxes are payable. Taxable profit is the excess of taxable income over taxation deductions allowable against that income. Thus, accounting profit and taxable profit — because they are determined by different principles and rules — are unlikely to be the same figure in any one period. Tax expense cannot be determined by simply multiplying the accounting profit by the applicable taxation rate. Instead, accounting for income taxes involves identifying and accounting for the differences between accounting profit and taxable profit. These differences arise from a number of common transactions and may be either permanent or temporary in nature.

6.2.1 Permanent differences

Permanent differences between accounting profit and taxable profit arise when the treatment of a transaction by taxation legislation and accounting standards is such that amounts recognised as part of accounting profit are never recognised as part of taxable profit, or vice versa. In some jurisdictions, for example, entities are allowed to deduct from their taxable income more than 100% of expenditure incurred on certain research and development activities undertaken during the taxation period. As a result of this extra deduction, taxable profit for the period is lower than accounting profit, and the extra amount is never recognised as an expense for accounting purposes. Other examples of permanent differences include income never subject to taxation, and expenditure incurred by an entity that will never be an allowable deduction. Where such differences exist, taxable profit will never equal accounting profit. No accounting requirements other than disclosure exist for these permanent differences (see section 6.13 of this chapter).

6.2.2 Temporary differences

Temporary differences between accounting profit and taxable profit arise when the period in which revenues and expenses are recognised for accounting purposes is different from the period in which such revenues and expenses are treated as taxable income and allowable deductions for tax purposes. Interest revenue recognised on an accrual basis, for example, may not be taxable income until it is received as cash. Similarly, insurance paid in advance may be tax-deductible when paid but is not recognised in calculating accounting profit as an expense until a later period. The key feature of these differences is that they are temporary, because sooner or later the amount of interest revenue will equal the amount of taxable interest income, and the amount deducted against taxable income for insurance will equal the insurance expense offset against accounting revenue. However, in any one individual accounting/taxation period, these amounts will differ when calculating accounting profit and taxable profit respectively.

Differences that result in the entity paying more tax in the future (e.g. when interest is received) are known as taxable temporary differences. Differences that result in the entity recovering tax via additional deductible expenses in the future (e.g. when accrued expenses are paid) are known as deductible temporary differences. The existence of such temporary differences means that income tax payable that is calculated on taxable profit will vary in the current period from that based on accounting profit, but tax payments will eventually catch up. This is demonstrated in illustrative example 6.1.

ILLUSTRATIVE EXAMPLE 6.1 Reversal of temporary difference

Assume that the accounting profit of Aster Ltd for the year ended 30 June 2013 was $150 000, including $5600 in interest revenue of which only $4000 had been received in cash. The company income tax rate is 30%.

If tax is not payable on interest until it has been received in cash, the company's taxable profit will differ from its accounting profit, and a taxable temporary difference will exist in respect of the $1600 interest receivable. If accounting profit for the next year is also $150 000 and the outstanding interest is received in August 2014, tax payable for the years ending 30 June 2013 and 2014 is calculated as follows:

	2013	2014
Accounting profit	$150 000	$150 000
Interest revenue	(1 600)	1 600
Taxable profit	$148 400	$151 600
Tax payable (30%)	44 520	45 480

Note that tax of $90 000, which is equal to 30% of $300 000 (being 2 × $150 000), is paid over the 2 years. The temporary difference created in 2013 is reversed in 2014. The same process occurs with all temporary differences although it may take a number of periods for a complete reversal to occur.

Appendix A to IAS 12 gives examples of temporary differences arising from different treatments of transactions for accounting and taxation purposes, some of which are listed below. These examples are not all-inclusive, so the relevant taxation legislation for specific jurisdictions should be consulted to determine if additional differences exist.

Circumstances that give rise to taxable temporary differences
Such circumstances include the following:
1. Interest revenue is received in arrears and is included in accounting profit on a time-apportionment basis but is included in taxable profit on a cash basis.
2. Revenue from the sale of goods is included in accounting profit when goods are delivered but is included in taxable profit only when cash is collected.
3. Depreciation of an asset is accelerated for tax purposes (the taxation depreciation rate is greater than the accounting rate).

4. Development costs are capitalised and amortised to the statement of profit or loss and other comprehensive income but are deducted in determining taxable profit in the period in which they are incurred.
5. Prepaid expenses have already been deducted on a cash basis in determining the taxable profit of the current or previous periods.
6. Depreciation of an asset is not deductible for tax purposes and no deduction will be available for tax purposes when the asset is sold or scrapped (see section 6.9 of this chapter).
7. A borrower records a loan at the proceeds received (which equal the amount due at maturity) less transaction costs, and the carrying amount of the loan is subsequently increased by amortising the transaction costs to accounting profit. The transaction costs are deducted for tax purposes in the period when the loan was first recognised.
8. A loan payable is measured on initial recognition at the amount of the net proceeds (net of transaction costs), and the transaction costs are amortised to accounting profit over the life of the loan. These transaction costs are not deductible in determining the taxable profit of future, current or prior periods (see section 6.9).
9. The liability component of a compound financial instrument (such as a convertible bond) is measured at a discount to the amount repayable on maturity, after assigning a portion of the cash proceeds to the equity component (see chapter 7 of this book). The discount is not deductible in determining taxable profit or loss.
10. Financial assets or investment property are carried at fair value, which exceeds cost, but no equivalent adjustment is made for tax purposes.
11. An entity revalues property, plant and equipment, but no equivalent adjustment is made for tax purposes.
12. The carrying amount of an asset is increased to fair value in a business combination that is an acquisition, but no equivalent adjustment is made for tax purposes.
13. Impairment of goodwill is not deductible in determining taxable profit, and the cost of the goodwill would not be deductible on disposal of the business (see section 6.9).

Temporary differences arising in circumstances 7, 8, 9 and 12 are beyond the scope of this chapter. The tax treatment of temporary differences arising from fair value accounting and revaluation to fair value (items 10 and 11) are discussed and illustrated in section 11.6.1 of this book.

Circumstances that give rise to deductible temporary differences

Such circumstances include the following:
1. Retirement benefit costs are deducted in determining accounting profit because service is provided by the employee, but are not deducted in determining taxable profit until the entity pays either retirement benefits or contributions to a fund. Similar temporary differences arise in relation to other accrued expenses — such as product warranties, leave entitlements and interest — which are deductible on a cash basis in determining taxable profit.
2. Accumulated depreciation of an asset in the financial statements is greater than the cumulative depreciation allowed up to the end of the reporting period for tax purposes. That is, the accounting depreciation rate is greater than the allowable taxation depreciation rate.
3. The cost of inventories sold before the end of the reporting period is deducted in determining accounting profit when goods or service are delivered, but is deducted in determining taxable profit only when cash is collected.
4. The net realisable value (see chapter 9 of this book) of an item of inventory, or the recoverable amount (see chapter 11) of an item of property, plant and equipment, is less than the previous carrying amount. The entity therefore reduces the carrying amount of the asset, but that reduction is ignored for tax purposes until the asset is sold.
5. Research costs (or organisation or other start-up costs) are recognised as an expense in determining accounting profit, but are not permitted as a deduction in determining taxable profit until a later period.
6. Income is deferred in the statement of financial position but has already been included in taxable profit in current or prior periods (for example, subscriptions received in advance).
7. A government grant that is included in the statement of financial position as deferred income will not be taxable in a future period (see section 6.9 of this chapter).
8. Financial assets or investment property is carried at fair value, which is less than cost, but no equivalent adjustment is made for tax purposes. (Temporary differences arising in these circumstances are beyond the scope of this chapter.)

In summary, income tax payable in any one period is affected by differences between items used to determine accounting profit and taxable profit. Some revenue items are not taxable, have already been taxed or will not be taxed until some future period(s). Some expense items are not deductible, have already been deducted or may be deducted in some future period(s). Additionally, extra deductions for which no expense will ever be incurred may be allowable under taxation legislation. The illustrative examples, exercises and problems in this chapter assume that the revenue from selling goods and services is taxable irrespective of whether cash has been received for the sale, and that the cost of sales is an allowable deduction irrespective of whether cash has been paid to acquire those goods.

6.3 ACCOUNTING FOR INCOME TAXES

As the objective paragraph of IAS 12 points out:

> The principal issue in accounting for income taxes is how to account for the current and future tax consequences of:
> (a) the future recovery (settlement) of the carrying amount of assets (liabilities) that are recognised in an entity's statement of financial position; and
> (b) transactions and other events of the current period that are recognised in an entity's financial statements.

IAS 12 requires the tax consequences of transactions and other events to be accounted for in the same manner and the same period as the transactions themselves. Thus, if a transaction is recognised in profit or loss for the period, so too is the related tax payable or tax benefit. Similarly, if a transaction is adjusted directly to equity, so too is the related tax effect. Differing accounting and taxation rules (as discussed in section 6.2) mean that the actual payment (deduction) of tax relating to revenue (expense) items may take place in both current and/or future accounting periods but IAS 12, paragraph 58, requires that the total income tax expense relating to transactions is recorded in the current year irrespective of when it will be paid or deducted.

To illustrate: an entity recognises interest revenue of $21 000 for the year ended 30 June 2014. Of this amount, $15 000 has been received in cash and a receivable asset has been raised for the remaining $6000. Tax legislation regards interest revenue as taxable only when it has been received. Therefore, the entity will pay tax of $4500 ($15 000 × 30%) in the current year and tax of $1800 ($6000 × 30%) in the following year when the $6000 receivable is paid. If the entity were to record only the current tax payable amount as income tax expense, the profit for the year would be overstated by $1800 given that $6300 of the interest revenue recognised for the year (not $4500) will eventually be paid to the taxation authorities and will not be available for use by the entity. To ensure that the profit after-tax figure for the year is both relevant and reliable, IAS 12 requires the entity to record an income tax expense of $6300 for the current year in respect to the interest revenue. This tax is payable via a current liability amount of $4500 and a deferred (future) liability of $1800.

The need to recognise both current and future tax consequences of current year transactions means that each transaction has two tax effects:
1. tax payable on profit earned for the year may be reduced or increased because the transaction is not taxable or deductible in the current year
2. future tax payable may be reduced or increased when that transaction becomes taxable or deductible.

If only current tax payable is recorded as an expense, then the profit for the current year will be understated or overstated by the amount of tax or benefit to be paid or received in future years. Similarly, in the years that the tax or benefit on these transactions is paid or received, income tax expense will include amounts relating to prior periods and therefore be understated or overstated. As IAS 12 requires income tax expense to reflect all tax effects of transactions entered into during the year regardless of when the effects occur, two calculations are required at the end of the reporting period:
• the calculation of current tax liability, which determines the amount of tax payable for the period
• the calculation of movements in deferred tax effects relating to assets and liabilities recognised in the statement of financial position, which determines the net effect of deferred taxes and deductions arising from transactions during the year.

Acknowledging the current and future tax consequences of all items recognised in the statement of financial position (subject to certain exceptions) should make the information about the tax implications of an entity's operations and financial position more relevant and reliable.

6.4 CALCULATION OF CURRENT TAX

Current tax is the recognition of taxes payable to the taxation authorities in respect of a particular period. The current tax calculation involves identifying differences between accounting revenues and taxable income, and between accounting expenses and allowable deductions, for transactions during the year, as well as reversing temporary differences from prior years that occur in the current period. Accounting profit for the period is adjusted by these differences to calculate taxable profit, which is then multiplied by the current tax rate to determine current tax payable.

When selecting the tax rate to apply, the requirements of IAS 12, paragraph 46, must be considered. This paragraph states:

> Current tax liabilities (assets) for the current and prior periods shall be measured at the amount expected to be paid to (recovered from) the taxation authorities, using the tax rates (and tax laws) that have been enacted or substantively enacted by the end of the reporting period.

Therefore, if a tax rate has changed — or, in some jurisdictions, if a change has been announced — the rate applicable to the taxable profit for the period must be applied.

Identifying permanent and temporary differences in the current year's profit is a relatively simple exercise. All revenues and expenses are reviewed for amounts that are not taxable or deductible. Identifying reversals of prior year temporary differences may require referring back to prior year worksheets, transactions posted to asset and liability accounts during the current year, or reconstructions of ledger accounts. (The latter method is used in this chapter.) Such reversals include, where applicable, accrued expenses that have been paid and are now deductible, bad debts written off and now deductible, accrued revenue that has been received and is now taxable, and prepaid expenses deducted in a prior period but now included in accounting profit.

Once the differences have been isolated, there are two ways that the current tax could be determined: (1) the net differences could be adjusted against accounting profit to derive taxable profit, or (2) the gross amounts of items with differences could be added back or deducted against accounting profit. (The latter method is adopted in this chapter.) A worksheet is used to perform this reconciliation between accounting profit and taxable profit using the following formula:

Accounting profit (loss)
+ (−) accounting expenses not deductible for tax
+ (−) accounting expenses where the amount differs from deductible amounts
+ (−) taxable income where the amount differs from accounting revenue
− (+) accounting revenues not subject to taxation
− (+) accounting revenue where the amount differs from taxable income
− (+) deductible amounts where the amount differs from accounting expense
= taxable profit

The current tax rate is then applied to taxable profit to derive the current tax payable.

ILLUSTRATIVE EXAMPLE 6.2 Determination of current tax worksheet

Iris Ltd's accounting profit for the year ended 30 June 2013 was $250 450. Included in this profit were the following items of revenue and expense:

Amortisation — development project	$30 000
Impairment of goodwill expense	7 000
Depreciation — equipment (15%)	40 000
Entertainment expense	12 450
Insurance expense	24 000
Doubtful debts expense	14 000
Proceeds on sale of equipment	30 000
Carrying amount of equipment sold	36 667
Rent revenue	25 000
Annual leave expense	54 000

At 30 June 2013, the company's draft statement of financial position showed the following balances:

	30 June 2013	30 June 2012
Assets		
Cash	$ 55 000	$ 65 000
Accounts receivable	295 000	277 000
Allowance for doubtful debts	(16 000)	(18 000)
Inventories	162 000	185 000
Prepaid insurance	30 000	25 000
Rent receivable	3 500	5 500
Development project	120 000	—
Accumulated amortisation	(30 000)	—
Equipment	200 000	266 667
Accumulated depreciation	(90 000)	(80 000)
Goodwill	35 000	35 000
Accumulated impairment expense	(14 000)	(7 000)
Deferred tax asset	?	24 900
Liabilities		
Accounts payable	310 500	294 000
Provision for annual leave	61 000	65 000
Mortgage loan	100 000	150 000
Deferred tax liability	?	57 150
Current tax liability	?	12 500

Additional information
1. Taxation legislation allows Iris Ltd to deduct 125% of the $120 000 spent on development during the year.
2. Iris Ltd has capitalised development expenditure relating to a filter project and amortises the balance over the period of expected benefit (4 years).
3. The taxation depreciation rate for equipment is 20%.
4. The equipment sold on 30 June 2013 cost $66 667 when it was purchased 3 years ago.
5. Neither entertainment expenditure nor goodwill impairment expense is deductible for taxation purposes.
6. The company income tax rate is 30%.

Calculation of current tax payable
Before completing the worksheet, all differences between accounting and taxation figures must be identified:

1. Development project
There are two differences here: a permanent difference arising from the extra 25% deduction allowed by tax legislation, and a temporary difference arising from the treatment of the development costs. For accounting purposes, the $120 000 has been capitalised and will be amortised over 4 years; for tax purposes, the entire expenditure is deductible in the current year. The tax deduction for development is therefore: $150 000 (being $120 000 + [25% × $120 000]).

2. Impairment of goodwill expense
No tax deduction is allowed for impairment expense, so the taxation deduction is nil. Paragraph 21 of IAS 12 does not permit the recognition of the deferred tax liability arising from the taxable temporary difference created (see section 6.9 of this chapter). Therefore, a permanent difference exists.

3. Depreciation expense — equipment
Because equipment is being depreciated at a faster rate for taxation purposes, a temporary taxable difference will exist. The amount of depreciation deductible is $53 333.40 (being $266 667 × 20%).

4. Entertainment expense
No deduction is allowed for entertainment expenditure, so the taxation deduction is nil and there is a permanent difference between accounting profit and taxable profit.

5. Insurance expense
Insurance expenditure is deductible when incurred. The existence of a prepaid insurance asset account in the statement of financial position indicates that the insurance payment and insurance expense figures are different. It is therefore necessary to reconstruct the asset account to identify if any part of the expense has already been deducted for taxation purposes. This is done as follows:

Prepaid Insurance			
Balance b/d	$25 000	Balance c/d	$30 000
Insurance Paid	29 000	Insurance Expense	24 000
	54 000		54 000

The insurance paid figure of $29 000 represents the deduction allowable in determining taxable profit. The expense figure of $24 000 shows that the payment made includes $5000 for insurance cover for the next accounting period. When this amount is expensed, no deduction will be available against taxable profit.

6. Allowance for doubtful debts
If, under taxation legislation, no deduction is allowed for bad debts until they have been written off, the taxation amount for doubtful debts will be nil. The draft statement of financial position shows that an allowance was raised in the previous year, so any debts written off against that allowance are deductible in the current year. To determine the amount (if any) of that write-off, the ledger account is reconstructed as follows:

Allowance for Doubtful Debts			
Balance b/d	$16 000	Balance c/d	$18 000
Bad Debts Written Off	16 000	Doubtful Debts Expense	14 000
	32 000		32 000

The allowable deduction for bad debts written off is therefore $16 000.

7. Proceeds on sale of equipment
All this revenue is taxable, so there is no permanent or temporary difference.

8. Carrying amount of equipment sold
The gain or loss on the sale of equipment is different for accounting and taxation purposes, and is calculated as shown in the following table.

	Accounting	Taxation
Cost	$66 667	$66 667
Accumulated depreciation	30 000	40 000
Carrying amount	36 667	26 667
Proceeds	30 000	30 000
Gain (loss)	$ (6 667)	$ 3 333

Because the sales proceeds are recognised for both accounting and taxation purposes, the difference in the loss or gain on sale is caused by the two methods recognising different carrying amounts for the asset sold. This difference is caused by the use of different depreciation rates. When preparing the current tax worksheet, adjusting for the different carrying amounts effectively adjusts for the difference in the gain or loss on sale.

9. Rent revenue
Rent revenue is taxable when received. The presence in the statement of financial position of a rent receivable asset indicates that part of the revenue has not yet been received as cash and is not taxable in the

current year. A temporary difference therefore exists in respect of rent, as demonstrated by reconstructing the ledger account:

Rent Receivable			
Balance b/d	$ 5 500	Balance c/d	$ 3 500
Rent Revenue	25 000	Cash Received	27 000
	30 500		30 500

In this instance, the cash received figure represents rent received for two different accounting periods: $5500 outstanding at the end of the prior year, and $21 500 for the current year. Thus, the taxable amount combines the reversal of last year's temporary difference and the tax payable on the current year's income. A temporary difference still exists for the $3500 rent for this year not yet received in cash.

10. Annual leave expense
Annual leave is deductible when paid in cash. The provision for annual leave indicates the existence of unpaid leave and therefore a taxation temporary difference. This is demonstrated by reconstructing the ledger account:

Provision for Annual Leave			
Balance c/d	$ 61 000	Balance b/d	$ 65 000
Leave Paid	58 000	Leave Expense	54 000
	119 000		119 000

The reconstruction reveals a payment of $58 000, which is deductible in the current year and represents a partial reversal of the temporary difference related to the opening balance. As none of the current year expense has been paid, no deduction is available this year and a further temporary difference is created.

This chapter assumes that sales revenue and cost of sales are taxable/deductible even when not received/paid in cash, so there are no differences with respect to the accounts receivable or accounts payable balances. If different assumptions applied, then the amounts of cash received for sales and cash paid for inventory would need to be determined in order to calculate the current tax payable.

Figure 6.1 contains the current worksheet used to calculate the current tax liability for Iris Ltd.

FIGURE 6.1 Completed current tax worksheet for Iris Ltd

IRIS LTD Current Tax Worksheet for the year ended 30 June 2013		
Accounting profit		$ 250 450
Add:		
Amortisation of development expenditure	$ 30 000	
Impairment of goodwill expense	7 000	
Depreciation expense	40 000	
Entertainment expense	12 450	
Insurance expense	24 000	
Doubtful debts expense	14 000	
Carrying amount of equipment sold (accounting)	36 667	
Annual leave expense	54 000	
Rent received (tax)	27 000	245 117
		495 567

(continued)

FIGURE 6.1 *(continued)*

Deduct:		
Rent revenue (accounting)	25 000	
Carrying amount of equipment sold (tax)	26 667	
Bad debts written off	16 000	
Insurance paid	29 000	
Development costs paid	150 000	
Annual leave paid	58 000	
Depreciation of equipment for tax	53 333	(358 000)
Taxable profit		137 567
Current liability @ 30%		$ 41 270

6.5 RECOGNITION OF CURRENT TAX

Paragraph 12 of IAS 12 states:

> Current tax for current and prior periods shall, to the extent unpaid, be recognised as a liability. If the amount already paid in respect of current and prior periods exceeds the amount due for those periods, the excess shall be recognised as an asset.

Additionally, paragraph 58 of the standard requires current tax to be recognised as income or an expense and included in the profit or loss for the period, except to the extent that the tax relates to a transaction recognised directly in equity or to a business combination. Therefore, the following journal entry is required to recognise the current tax payable for Iris Ltd at 30 June 2013:

30 June 2013			
Income Tax Expense (Current)	Dr	41 270	
Current Tax Liability	Cr		41 270
(Recognition of current tax liability)			

6.6 PAYMENT OF TAX

Taxation legislation may require taxation debts to be paid annually upon lodgement of a taxation return or at some specified time after lodgement (such as on receipt of an assessment notice, or at a set date or time). Alternatively, the taxation debt may be paid by instalment throughout the taxation year. In some jurisdictions, payments in advance relating to next year's estimated taxable profit may be required. Where one annual payment is required, the entry is:

Current Tax Liability	Dr	41 270	
Cash	Cr		41 270
(Payment of current liability)			

If payment by instalment is required, the process is a little more complicated. To pay by instalment, an estimate of taxable profit needs to be made; hence the reference in paragraph 12 of IAS 12 to amounts paid in excess of the amount due. To illustrate the process of payment by instalment, assume that Iris Ltd (from illustrative example 6.2) has to pay tax quarterly and has paid the following amounts for the first three quarters of the 2012–13 taxation year:

28 October 2012	$ 9 420
28 January 2013	10 380
28 April 2013	10 750

The journal entry to record the first payment is:

Income Tax Expense	Dr	9 420	
Cash	Cr		9 420
(Payment of first quarterly taxation instalment)			

Similar entries are passed at 28 January 2013 and 28 April 2013. At 30 June 2013, because the tax liability has been partially paid, an adjustment is required on the current tax worksheet to determine the balance of tax owing in relation to the 2012–13 year (see below).

IRIS LTD Current Tax Worksheet (extract) for the year ended 30 June 2013	
Taxable profit	$137 567
Tax payable @ 30%	41 270
Less: Tax already paid ($9 420 + $10 380 + $10 750)	(30 550)
Current tax liability	10 720

The adjusting journal entry becomes:

30 June 2013			
Income Tax Expense (Current)	Dr	10 720	
Current Tax Liability	Cr		10 720
(Recognition of current tax liability)			

LO7   6.7 TAX LOSSES

Tax losses are created when allowable deductions exceed taxable income. IAS 12 envisages three possible treatments for tax losses: they may be carried forward, carried back, or simply lost. Where taxation legislation allows tax losses to be carried forward and deducted against future taxable profits, the carry-forward may be either indefinite or for a limited number of years. Other restrictions — such as requiring losses to be deducted against non-taxable income on recoupment — may also apply. Carry-forward tax losses create a deductible temporary difference and therefore a deferred tax asset in that the company will pay less tax on future taxable profits. The recognition of a deferred tax asset for tax losses is discussed in detail in section 6.9.2 of this chapter.

ILLUSTRATIVE EXAMPLE 6.3 Creation and recoupment of carry-forward tax losses

The following information relates to Poppy Ltd for the year ended 30 June 2014:

Accounting loss	$ 7 600
Depreciation expense	14 700
Depreciation deductible for tax	20 300
Entertainment expense (not tax-deductible)	10 000
Income tax rate	30%

The calculation of the tax loss appears below:

POPPY LTD Current Tax Worksheet (extract) for the year ended 30 June 2014	
Accounting loss	$ (7 600)
Add:	
Depreciation expense	14 700
Entertainment expense	10 000
	17 100
Deduct:	
Depreciation deduction	(20 300)
Tax loss	(3 200)
Deferred tax asset @ 30%	$ 960

Assuming that recognition criteria are met, the adjusting journal entry is:

30 June 2014			
Deferred Tax Asset (Tax Losses)	Dr	960	
Income Tax Income	Cr		960
(Recognition of deferred tax asset from tax loss)			

If Poppy Ltd then makes a taxable profit of $23 600 for the year ending 30 June 2015, the loss is recouped as follows:

POPPY LTD Current Tax Worksheet (extract) for the year ended 30 June 2015	
Taxable profit before tax loss	$23 600
Tax loss recouped	(3 200)
Taxable profit	20 400
Current tax liability @ 30%	$ 6 120

The adjusting journal entry is:

30 June 2015			
Income Tax Expense (Current)	Dr	7 080	
Deferred Tax Asset (Tax Losses)	Cr		960
Current Tax Liability	Cr		6 120
(Recognition of current tax liability and reversal of deferred tax asset from tax loss)			

In jurisdictions where taxation legislation allows the current year's tax losses to be carried back, paragraph 13 of IAS 12 requires that: 'The benefit relating to a tax loss that can be carried back to recover current tax of a previous period shall be recognised as an asset'. Paragraph 14 further states that the recognition should take place in the period of the tax loss, because 'it is probable that the benefit will flow to the entity and the benefit can be reliably measured'.

Using the facts from illustrative example 6.3, the adjusting journal entry becomes:

30 June 2014			
Current Tax Asset	Dr	960	
Income Tax Expense	Cr		960
(Recognition of tax receivable on offset of tax loss against prior year taxable profit)			

6.8 CALCULATION OF DEFERRED TAX

As already explained, IAS 12 adopts the philosophy that the tax consequences of transactions that occur during a period should be recognised in income tax expense for that period. Where a transaction has two effects, both have to be recognised. The existence of temporary differences between accounting profit and taxable profit was identified earlier in the chapter. These temporary differences result in the carrying amounts of an entity's assets and liabilities being different from the amounts that would arise if a statement of financial position was prepared for the taxation authority. The latter are referred to as the tax base of an entity's assets and liabilities. At the end of the reporting period, a comparison of an entity's carrying amounts of assets and liabilities and their tax bases will reveal the temporary differences that exist, and adjustments will then be made to deferred assets and liabilities. (The reference to 'deferred' tax adjustments comes from the fact that assets and liabilities reflect future inflows and outflows to an entity. The deferred tax balances are related to these future flows, and hence are deferred to the future rather than affecting current tax.) For assets such as goodwill and entertainment costs payable, differences between their tax bases and carrying amounts may be caused by permanent differences. Such differences will not give rise to deferred tax adjustments.

The following steps are required to calculate deferred tax:

1. Determine the carrying amounts of items recognised in the statement of financial position and their tax bases.
2. Determine the assessable and deductible temporary differences relating to the future tax consequences of items recognised at the end of the current period.
3. Calculate and recognise the deferred tax assets and liabilities arising from these temporary differences after taking into account any relevant recognition exceptions (see section 6.8.5 of this chapter) and offset considerations (see section 6.12.1).
4. Recognise the net movement in deferred tax assets and liabilities during the period as deferred tax expense or income in profit or loss (unless an accounting standard requires recognition directly in equity or as part of a business combination).

The first three steps are carried out on a worksheet. The final step requires an adjusting journal entry.

6.8.1 Determining carrying amounts

Carrying amounts are asset and liability balances net of valuation allowances, accumulated depreciation, amortisation and impairment losses (for example, accounts receivable less allowance for doubtful debts).

6.8.2 Determining tax bases

Tax bases need to be calculated for assets and liabilities.

Tax bases of assets

The economic benefits embodied in an asset are normally taxable when recovered by an entity through the use or sale of that asset. The entity may then be able to deduct all or part of the cost or carrying amount of the asset against those taxable amounts when determining taxable profits.

Paragraph 7 of IAS 12 describes the tax base of an asset as:

> the amount that will be deductible for tax purposes against any taxable economic benefits that will flow to an entity when it recovers the carrying amount of the asset. If those economic benefits will not be taxable, the tax base of the asset is equal to its carrying amount.

The following formula can be applied to derive the tax base from the carrying amount of the asset:

Carrying amount − Future taxable amounts + Future deductible amounts = Tax base

Figure 6.2 contains examples of the calculation of tax bases for assets.

	Carrying amount	Future taxable amounts*	Future deductible amounts	Tax base
Prepayments $3000: fully deductible for tax when paid	$ 3 000	$(3 000)	$ 0	$ 0
Trade receivables less $2000 allowance for doubtful debts: sales revenue is already included in taxable profit	50 000	0	2 000	52 000
Plant and equipment costing $10 000 has a carrying value of $5400: accumulated depreciation at tax rates is $6500	5 400	(5 400)	3 500**	3 500
Loan receivable $25 000: loan repayment will have no tax consequences	25 000	0	0	25 000
Interest receivable $1000: recognised as revenue but not taxable until received	1 000	(1 000)	0	0

* Future taxable amounts are equal to carrying amounts unless economic benefits have already been included in taxable profit.
** The deductible amount represents the original cost of the asset less the accumulated depreciation based on taxation depreciation rates (being $10 000 − $6500 = $3500).

FIGURE 6.2 Calculation of the tax base of assets

The formula for calculating the tax base of an asset can be rearranged as follows:

Carrying amount − Tax base = Future taxable amounts − Future deductible amounts

In other words, a temporary difference (the difference between the carrying amount and the tax base) occurs when the future taxable amount is different from the future deductible amount.

Figure 6.2 illustrates the following situations:

- Where the future benefits are taxable, the carrying amount equals the future taxable amount. Hence, the tax base equals the future deductible amount. This can be seen in figure 6.2 for prepayments, plant and equipment, and interest receivable.
- Where there are no future taxable amounts, generally the deductible amount is zero and the tax base equals the carrying amount. In figure 6.2, this applies to the loan receivable. An exception is trade receivables where, although the future taxable amount is zero, the future deductible amount is not zero because of the existence of doubtful debts. In this case, the tax base equals the sum of the carrying amount and the future deductible amount.

Tax bases of liabilities

Liabilities, other than those relating to unearned revenue, do not create taxable amounts. Instead, settlement gives rise to deductible items.

Paragraph 8 of IAS 12 describes the tax base of a liability as:

its carrying amount, less any amount that will be deductible for tax purposes in respect of that liability in future periods. In the case of revenue which is received in advance, the tax base of the resulting liability is its carrying amount, less any amount of the revenue that will not be taxable in future periods.

The following formula can be applied to derive the tax base from the carrying amount of the liability:

Carrying amount + Future taxable amounts − Future deductible amounts = Tax base

Figure 6.3 contains examples of the calculation of the tax base for liabilities.

	Carrying amount	Future taxable amounts	Future deductible amounts	Tax base
Provision for annual leave $3900: not deductible for tax until paid	$ 3 900	$ 0	$(3 900)	$ 0
Trade payables $34 000: expense already deducted from taxable income	34 000	0	0	34 000
Subscription revenue received in advance $500: taxed when received	500	(500)	0	0
Loan payable $20 000: loan repayment will have no tax consequences	20 000	0	0	20 000
Accrued expenses $6 700: deductible when paid in cash	6 700	0	(6 700)	0
Accrued penalties $700: not tax-deductible	700	0	0	700

FIGURE 6.3 Calculation of the tax base of liabilities

Figure 6.3 illustrates two situations:
- Where the carrying amount equals the future deductible amount, the tax base is zero. This applies to provisions for annual leave and accrued expenses.
- Where there is no future deductible amount, the carrying amount equals the tax base. This applies to trade payables and the loan payable.

Some items may have a tax base but are not recognised as assets and liabilities in the statement of financial position. Paragraph 9 of IAS 12 provides the example of research costs that are recognised as an expense in determining accounting profit in the period in which they are incurred but are not allowed as a deduction in determining taxable profit until a later period. Additionally, under paragraph 52 the manner in which an asset/liability is recovered/settled may affect the tax base of that asset/liability in some jurisdictions.

6.8.3 Calculating temporary differences

When the carrying amount of an asset or liability is different from its tax base, a temporary difference exists. Temporary differences effectively represent the expected net future taxable amounts arising from the recovery of assets and the settlement of liabilities at their carrying amounts. Therefore, a temporary difference cannot exist where there are no future tax consequences from the realisation or settlement of an asset or liability at its carrying value.

Taxable temporary differences

A taxable temporary difference exists when the future taxable amount of an asset or liability exceeds any future deductible amounts. This is demonstrated in illustrative example 6.4.

ILLUSTRATIVE EXAMPLE 6.4 Calculation of a taxable temporary difference

An asset, which cost 150, has an accumulated depreciation of 50.
Accumulated depreciation for tax purposes is 90 and the tax rate is 25%.

Carrying amount	= 100
Future taxable amount	= 100
Future deductible amount	= 60
Tax base	= 100 − 100 + 60
	= 60 (= 150 cost less 90 tax depreciation)

Because the future taxable amount is greater than the future deductible amount, a temporary tax difference exists. In other words, the expectation is that the entity will pay income taxes in the future, when it recovers the carrying amount of the asset, because it expects to earn 100 but receive a tax deduction of 60. The entity has a liability to pay tax on that extra 40. As the payment occurs in the future, the liability is referred to as a 'deferred tax liability'.

Source: Adapted from IAS 12, paragraph 16.

Deductible temporary differences

A deductible temporary difference exists when the future taxable amount of an asset or liability is less than any future deductible amounts. This is demonstrated in illustrative example 6.5.

ILLUSTRATIVE EXAMPLE 6.5 Calculation of a deductible temporary difference

An entity recognises a liability of 100 for accrued product warranty costs. For tax purposes, the product warranty costs will not be deductible until the entity pays claims. The tax rate is 25%.

Carrying amount	= 100
Future taxable amount	= 0
Future deductible amount	= 100
Tax base	= 100 + 0 − 100
	= 0

As the future deductible amount is greater than the future taxable amount, a deductible temporary difference exists. In other words, in settling the liability for its carrying amount, the entity will reduce its future tax profits and hence its future tax payments. The entity then has an expected benefit relating to the future tax deduction. As the benefits are to be received in the future, the asset raised is referred to as a 'deferred tax asset'.

Source: Adapted from IAS 12, paragraph 25.

6.8.4 Calculating deferred tax liabilities and deferred tax assets

Paragraphs 15 and 24 of IAS 12 require (with some exceptions) that a deferred tax liability and a deferred tax asset be recognised for all taxable temporary differences and all deductible temporary differences, and that a total be determined for taxable temporary differences and for deductible temporary differences. An appropriate tax rate can then be applied to these totals to derive the balance of deferred tax liability and deferred tax asset at the end of the period. Paragraph 47 of the standard specifies that:

> Deferred tax assets and liabilities shall be measured at the tax rates that are expected to apply to the period when the asset is realised or the liability is settled, based on tax rates (and tax laws) that have been enacted or substantively enacted by the end of the reporting period.

Thus, if the tax rate is currently 30% but will rise to 32% in the next reporting period, deferred amounts should be measured at 32%. Should a change be enacted (or substantively enacted) between the end of the reporting period and the time of completion of the financial statements, no adjustment needs to be made to the tax balances recognised. However, disclosure of any material impacts should be made by note in compliance with IAS 10 *Events after the Reporting Period*.

Different tax rates may be required when temporary differences are expected to reverse in different periods and a change of tax rate is probable, or when temporary differences relate to different taxation jurisdictions. Additionally, consideration should be given to the manner in which an asset/liability is recovered/settled in jurisdictions where the manner of recovery/settlement determines the applicable tax rate (IAS 12 paragraph 52).

Before determining the amounts of deferred tax liabilities and deferred tax assets, consideration must be given to the recognition criteria mandated by the accounting standard. (See section 6.9 of this chapter.)

6.8.5 Excluded differences

Paragraphs 15 and 24 of IAS 12 mandate the following exceptions to the requirement that a deferred tax liability and a deferred tax asset (subject to probability assessment) be recognised for all taxable and deductible temporary differences:

    (a) the initial recognition of goodwill; or
    (b) the initial recognition of an asset or liability in a transaction which:
        (i) is not a business combination; and
        (ii) at the time of the transaction, affects neither accounting profit nor taxable profit (tax loss).

Goodwill

Goodwill is the excess of the cost of the business combination over the acquirer's interest in the net fair value of the identifiable assets, liabilities and contingent liabilities (see chapter 14). In jurisdictions where impairment of goodwill is not deductible, a taxable temporary difference is created because the tax base of goodwill is always nil. IAS 12 does not permit the recognition of the deferred tax liability relating to goodwill, because goodwill is a residual amount and recognising the deferred tax amount would increase the carrying amount of goodwill (IAS 12 paragraph 21). In jurisdictions where goodwill can be 'depreciated' for tax purposes, a deferred tax liability may be recognised if the carrying amount of the asset remains unimpaired.

Initial recognition of an asset or liability

A temporary difference may arise on the initial recognition of an asset or liability if the carrying amount is not equal to the tax base (e.g. if part or all of the cost of an asset is not deductible for tax purposes). The accounting treatment of the temporary difference depends on the nature of the transaction that created the asset or liability.

When deferred tax arises on the acquisition of an entity or business, and it has not been recognised by the acquiring or acquired entity before the acquisition, it must be recognised and taken into account in measuring the amount of goodwill or gain on bargain purchase. Deferred tax balances are recognised if they arise from temporary differences related to assets and liabilities that have affected pre-tax accounting profit or taxable profit at or before the time of initial recognition. This most commonly occurs when items are recognised for accounting and tax purposes in different reporting periods. Examples include prepayments, deferred income and accrued expenses.

If the exception provided in paragraph 15 of IAS 12 did not exist, an entity would be allowed to recognise the deferred tax liability or asset, and adjust the carrying amount of the asset or liability by the same amount, for a transaction that was not a business combination and affected neither accounting nor taxable profits. However, the standard setters considered that: 'Such adjustments would make the financial statements less transparent' (IAS 12 paragraph 22(c)), and so prohibited the recognition of such deferred tax amounts. Fortunately, such items are rare and would occur only where assets have a taxable value deemed by tax laws to be different from the cost of the asset. Such deferred amounts include:

- motor vehicles acquired where the total cost is in excess of a depreciation cost limit set by tax legislation
- the 'roll over' of the tax base of assets to an acquiring entity so that future tax deductions are limited to an amount that is different from the consideration paid
- a non-taxable government grant related to an asset that is deducted from the carrying amount of the asset, but for tax purposes is not deducted from the asset's depreciable amount (its tax base).

In addition to prohibiting the recognition of deferred tax amounts on the initial recognition of the asset or liability, IAS 12 also prohibits recognition of any subsequent changes to the unrecognised deferred tax liability or asset as the asset is depreciated (paragraph 22(c)).

6.8.6 Deferred tax worksheet

A deferred tax worksheet is shown in illustrative example 6.6. The purpose of the deferred tax worksheet is to calculate the movements in the deferred tax asset and the deferred tax liability accounts during the current period. Determining the temporary differences relating to assets and liabilities allows the closing balances of the deferred tax accounts to be calculated. A consideration of the beginning balances and movements during the year allows the calculation of the adjustments required to achieve those closing balances. All assets and liabilities may be included in the worksheet; alternatively, only those expected to have different accounting and tax bases could be shown.

Using the information provided in illustrative example 6.2, the deferred tax worksheet for Iris Ltd is shown in figure 6.4.

	Carrying amount	Future taxable amount	Future deductible amount	Tax base	Taxable temporary differences	Deductible temporary differences
IRIS LTD Deferred Tax Worksheet as at 30 June 2013						
Relevant assets						
Receivables[1]	$ 279 000	$ 0	$ 16 000	$ 295 000		$ 16 000
Prepaid insurance[2]	30 000	(30 000)	0	0	$ 30 000	
Rent receivable[3]	3 500	(3 500)	0	0	3 500	
Development project[4]	90 000	(90 000)	0	0	90 000	
Equipment[5]	110 000	(110 000)	80 000	80 000	30 000	
Goodwill[6]	21 000	(21 000)	0	0	21 000	
Relevant liabilities						
Provision for annual leave[7]	61 000	0	(61 000)	0		61 000
Total temporary differences					174 500	77 000
Excluded differences[8]					(21 000)	—
Temporary differences					153 500	77 000
Deferred tax liability[9]					46 050	
Deferred tax asset[9]						23 100
Beginning balances[10]					(17 150)	(24 900)
Movement during year[11]						
Adjustment[10]					28 900 Cr	(1 800) Cr

FIGURE 6.4 Deferred tax worksheet for Iris Ltd

1. The carrying amount of receivables $279 000 ($295 000 – 16 000) represents the cash that the company expects to receive after allowing for any doubtful debts. Tax on this amount has already been paid via sales revenue recognised in the current year, so the future taxable amount is zero. The allowance for doubtful debts raised as an expense in the current year is not deductible against taxable profit until the debts actually go 'bad' and are written out of the accounts receivable balance. Thus, there is a future deduction of $5000 available. The tax base for receivables is $283 000, being the total of all debts outstanding at 30 June 2013 (doubtful or otherwise). Because the future deductible amount is greater than the future taxable amount, a deductible temporary difference of $5000 exists in respect of receivables.
2. The prepaid insurance asset represents insurance monies that have been paid for insurance cover in the year ended 30 June 2014. The recovery of these benefits results in the flow of taxable economic benefits to Iris Ltd, giving a future taxable amount of $30 000. This amount was paid in the year ended 30 June 2013 and was allowed as a deduction against the taxable profit for that year. This means that no deduction is available when the $30 000 is expensed in the year ended 30 June 2014, giving a tax base for the asset of $0. As the future taxable amount exceeds the future deductible amount, a taxable temporary difference of $30 000 exists in respect of prepaid insurance.

3. The rent receivable asset represents monies to be received relating to revenue earned in the year ended 30 June 2013. The recovery of these benefits results in the flow of taxable economic benefits to Iris Ltd. Hence, a future taxable amount of $3500 exists. As this is a revenue item, no future deduction is available. The tax base is $0 because the cash received affects taxable profit in the year of receipt. As the future taxable amount exceeds the future deductible amount, a taxable temporary difference of $3500 exists in respect of the rent receivable.

4. The development project asset represents the future economic benefits expected to arise from development work undertaken in the current year. When those benefits are received, they are taxable. The total expenditure on development was deducted from taxable profit in the current year, so no future deduction is available. The tax base is $0 as the cash paid has already reduced taxable profit in the current year. As the future taxable amount exceeds the future deductible amount, a taxable temporary difference of $90 000 exists in respect of the development project.

5. The carrying amount of equipment represents the future economic benefits expected to be received from that asset over the remainder of its useful life, $110 000 ($200 000 − $90 000). When those benefits are received, they are taxable. Iris Ltd will be able to claim a deduction against those taxable benefits, but only to the extent of the carrying amount of the asset for taxation purposes. As the depreciation rate for tax purposes is greater than the accounting rate, the future deduction is only $80 000, being the original cost of $200 000 less $120 000 (i.e. 3 years' accumulated depreciation at 20% per annum). As the future taxable amount exceeds the future deductible amount, a taxable temporary difference of $30 000 exists in respect of equipment.

6. The carrying amount of goodwill represents the future economic benefits expected to be received. Those benefits are taxable when received but, unlike equipment, no deduction against the benefits is available. The tax base of goodwill is $0 as taxation law does not allow a deduction for any amounts paid to acquire goodwill. As the future taxable amount exceeds the future deductible amount, a taxable temporary difference of $21 000 exists in respect of goodwill.

7. The provision for annual leave represents leave accrued by employees as at the end of the reporting period. As the leave represents future payments, there is no future taxable amount. When those payments are made, they are fully deductible against taxable profit. The tax base at 30 June 2013 is $0 because leave payments are only deductible in the year of payment. As the future deductible amount exceeds the future taxable amount, a deductible temporary difference of $61 000 exists in respect of the annual leave provision.

8. The adjustment for excluded differences recognises that IAS 12 (paragraphs 15 and 24) has prohibited the recognition of deferred tax amounts relating to certain temporary differences (see section 6.9.2). Paragraph 15 prohibits the recognition of the taxable temporary difference relating to goodwill, so it is removed from the total temporary differences existing at 30 June 2013.

9. The deferred tax liability figure of $46 050 is the future tax payable as a result of the existence of taxable temporary differences of $153 500. The deferred tax asset figure of $23 100 is the future deductions available as a result of the existence of deductible temporary differences of $77 000. These figures represent the closing balances of the deferred tax accounts.

10. Deferred tax amounts may accumulate over time; for example, the taxable temporary difference for equipment represents 3 years differentials between accounting and taxation depreciation charges. This means that the deferred tax accounts have an opening balance representing prior year differences. If no adjustment is made for the opening balance, the deferred tax amounts are overstated. Accordingly, the opening balances are deducted from the total balances in order to determine the adjustment necessary to account for changes (additions and reversals) to deferred tax items during the current year. These adjustments are shown on the last line of the worksheet and form the basis of the adjusting journal entry for deferred tax. Positive figures are increases and negative figures are decreases in the account balances.

11. Normally, the deferred tax accounts are only adjusted at the end of each reporting period after the worksheet has been completed. Occasionally, however, adjustments are made to the deferred accounts during the year so the 'movements' line is used to adjust for such changes. Adjustments could be made for:
    - recoupment of prior year tax losses (see section 6.7)
    - a change in tax rates (see section 6.10)
    - an amendment to a prior year tax return (see section 6.11)
    - revaluation of property, plant and equipment items (see section 6.11.2)
    - business combinations (see section 6.11.3).

The flowcharts in figure 6.5 below summarise the measurement of deferred tax items according to IAS 12. While the flowcharts show the steps in the calculation of deferred tax items, they do not present the steps in determining whether the resultant deferred tax assets or deferred tax liabilities will be recognised. The criteria for the recognition of deferred tax assets and deferred tax liabilities are considered next, in section 6.9.

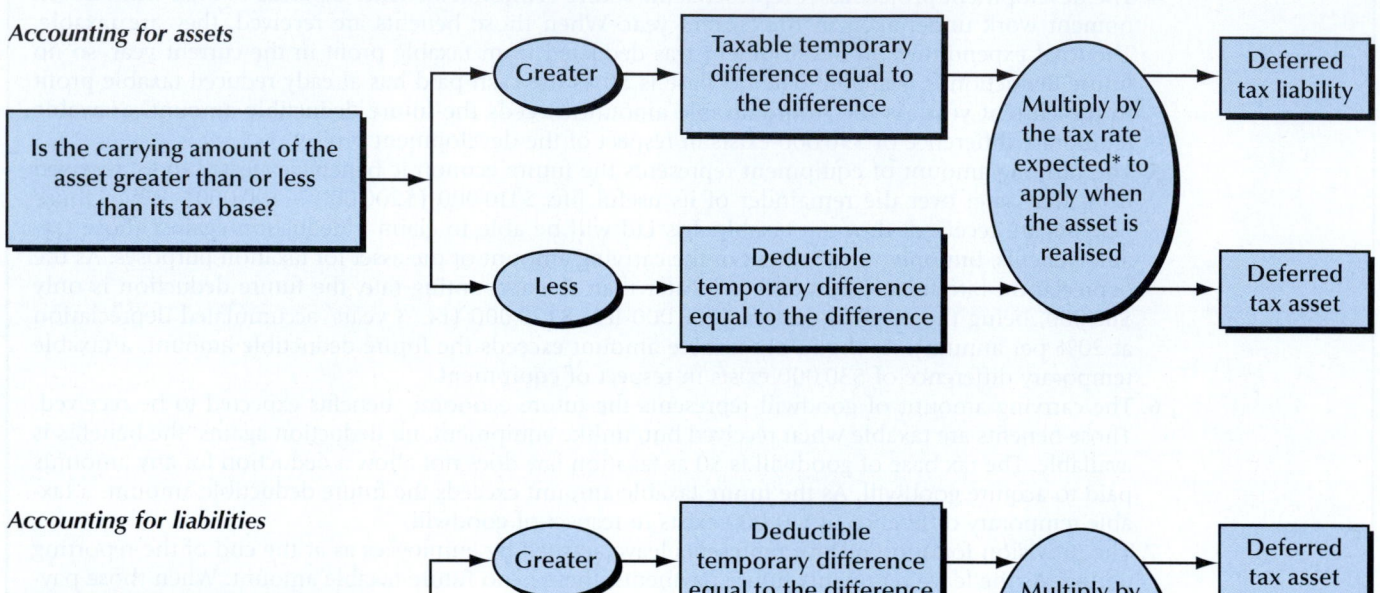

FIGURE 6.5 Accounting for deferred tax items
Note: *refers to the present tax rate or tax laws (tax rates) that have been enacted or substantively enacted by reporting date.
Source: CPA Australia (2010, p. 2).

6.9 RECOGNITION OF DEFERRED TAX LIABILITIES AND DEFERRED TAX ASSETS

The existence of temporary taxable and deductible differences may not result in the recognition of deferred tax assets and liabilities. Paragraphs 15 and 24 of IAS 12 specify recognition criteria that must be met before recognition occurs.

6.9.1 Deferred tax liabilities

Deferred tax liabilities must be recognised for all taxable temporary differences (except as outlined below). A liability is recognised when, and only when, it is probable that an outflow of resources embodying economic benefits will result from the settlement of a present obligation, and the amount at which the settlement will take place can be measured reliably (*Conceptual Framework* paragraph 4.46). There is no need to explicitly consider the recognition criteria for a deferred tax liability, because it is always probable that resources will flow from the entity to pay the tax associated with taxable temporary differences. As the carrying amount of the asset or liability giving rise to the taxable temporary difference is recovered or settled, the temporary difference will reverse and give rise to taxable amounts in future periods.

6.9.2 Deferred tax assets

Deferred tax assets must be recognised for all deductible temporary differences (subject to certain exceptions) and from the carry forward of tax losses, but only to the extent that is it *probable* that future taxable profits will be available against which the temporary differences can be utilised.

An asset is recognised when it is probable that the future economic benefits will flow to the entity, and the asset has a cost or value that can be measured reliably (*Conceptual Framework* paragraph 4.44). According to paragraph 4.40 of the *Conceptual Framework*, probability refers to the degree of uncertainty about whether the future economic benefits associated with the asset will flow to the entity. This probability must be assessed using the best evidence available based on the conditions at the end of the reporting period. The reversal of deductible temporary differences results in deductions against the taxable profits of future periods. Economic benefits in the form of reductions in tax payments will flow to the entity only if it earns sufficient taxable profits against which the deductions can be offset. Therefore, an entity recognises deferred tax assets only when it is probable that taxable profits will be available against which the deductible temporary differences can be utilised (IAS 12 paragraph 27). The realisation of a deferred tax asset would be probable where:

- there are sufficient taxable temporary differences relating to the same taxation authority and the same taxable entity that are expected to reverse in the same period as the deductible temporary differences, or in periods to which a tax loss arising from the deferred tax asset can be carried back or forward (paragraph 28)
- there would be taxable temporary differences arising if unrecognised increases in the fair values of assets were recognised
- it is probable that there will be other sufficient taxable profits arising in future periods against which to utilise the deductions
- other factors indicate that it is probable that the deductions can be realised.

If there are insufficient taxable temporary differences available against which to offset the deductible temporary differences, an entity can recognise a deferred tax asset only to the extent that sufficient taxable profits will be made in the future or that tax planning opportunities are available to create future taxable profits (IAS 12 paragraph 29). The following examples of tax planning opportunities that may be available in some jurisdictions are given in paragraph 30 of the standard:

- electing to have interest income taxed on either a received or a receivable basis
- deferring the claim for certain deductions from taxable profit
- selling, and perhaps leasing back, assets that have appreciated but for which the tax base has not been adjusted to reflect such appreciation
- selling an asset that generates non-taxable income in order to purchase another investment that generates taxable income.

A history of accounting losses, or the existence of unused tax losses, provides evidence that future taxable profits are unlikely to be available for the utilisation of deductible temporary differences. In these circumstances, the recognition of deferred tax assets would require either the existence of sufficient taxable temporary differences or convincing evidence that future taxable profits will be earned. In assessing the likelihood that tax losses will be utilised, the entity should consider whether:

- future budgets indicate that there will be sufficient taxable income derived in the foreseeable future
- the losses arise from causes that are unlikely to recur in the foreseeable future
- actions can be taken to create taxable amounts in the future
- there are existing contracts or sales backlogs that will produce taxable amounts
- there are new developments or favourable opportunities likely to give rise to taxable amounts
- there is a strong history of earnings other than those giving rise to the loss, and the loss was an aberration and not a continuing condition.

Where, on the balance of the evidence available, it is not probable that deductible temporary differences will be utilised in the future, no deferred tax asset is recognised. This probability assessment must also be applied to deferred tax assets that have previously been recognised and, if it is no longer probable that the benefits of such assets will flow to the entity, the carrying amount must be derecognised by passing the following entry:

30 June			
Income Tax Expense	Dr	xxx	
Deferred Tax Asset	Cr		xxx
(Derecognition of deferred tax assets where recovery is no longer probable)			

At the end of each reporting period, the entity should reassess the probability of recovery of all unrecognised deferred tax assets; it should recognise these assets to the extent that it is now probable that future taxable profit will allow the deduction of the temporary difference on its reversal. Changes in trading conditions, new taxation legislation, or a business combination may all contribute to improving the chance of recovering the deferred tax benefits. Paragraph 60 of IAS 12 requires that any adjustment to deferred tax be recognised in the statement of comprehensive income except to the extent that it relates to items previously charged or credited to equity.

ILLUSTRATIVE EXAMPLE 6.7 Recognition of deferred tax adjustments

Using the figures calculated in illustrative example 6.6 and assuming that the recognition criteria for deferred tax assets can be met, the adjusting journal for deferred tax movements is:

30 June 2013			
Income Tax Expense (Deferred)	Dr	30 700	
Deferred Tax Asset	Cr		1 800
Deferred Tax Liability	Cr		28 900
(Recognition of movements in deferred tax balances for the year)			

These movements can be checked back to the current worksheet as follows:
- Deferred tax assets arise in respect of doubtful debts and annual leave. In the current year, additional deductions of $2000 (doubtful debts) and $4000 (leave) are received. This indicates that more deductible temporary differences had been reversed than had been created, resulting in a decrease of $6000 in future deductions and a $1800 decrease in the deferred tax asset.
- Deferred tax liabilities arise in respect of development expenditure, equipment, insurance and rent. In the current year, additional deductions of $90 000 (development), $13 333 (depreciation) and $5000 (insurance) are offset by additional taxable amounts of $10 000 (sale of equipment) and $2000 (rent revenue), giving a net extra increase in taxable temporary differences and a $28 900 increase in the deferred tax liability.

The posting of this entry results in the deferred tax ledger accounts appearing as follows:

Deferred Tax Asset					
1/7/12	Balance b/d	24 900	30/6/13	Income Tax Expense	1 800
			30/6/13	Balance c/d	23 100
		24 900			24 900
1/7/13	Balance b/d	23 100			

Deferred Tax Liability					
30/6/13	Balance c/d	46 050	1/7/12	Balance b/d	17 150
			30/6/13	Income Tax Expense	28 900
		46 050			46 050
			1/7/13	Balance b/d	46 050

If the two taxation adjusting journals — current and deferred — are combined, then the total income tax expense recorded for the year ended 2013 by Iris Ltd is:

Income tax expense (current) (see section 6.5)	$ 41 270
Income tax expense (deferred) (see above)	30 700
Total	$ 71 970

This figure represents the total tax consequences of the transactions recorded in profit or loss for the year. It can be checked in this way: The accounting profit for the year is $250 450. All items of revenue and expense are taxable or deductible with the exception of goodwill impairment and entertainment expense. The development expenditure during the year gave rise to an 'extra' deduction of $30 000 against taxable profit. If the accounting profit adjusted for these permanent differences is multiplied by the tax rate, the result represents the total tax payable above (both now and in the future):

Accounting profit	$250 450
Add: Non-deductible amortisation	7 000
Add: Non-deductible entertainment expense	12 450
Less: Additional deduction for development	(30 000)
Taxable net profit	239 900
Tax @ 30%	$ 71 970

Thus, the income tax expense for the year has been reconciled.

6.9.3 Recognition of deferred amounts arising from investments

Where taxable or deductible temporary differences are associated with investments in subsidiaries, branches and associates, and interests in joint arrangements, the deferred tax liabilities and deferred tax assets associated with these temporary differences must be raised in accordance with paragraphs 39 and 44 of IAS 12. Temporary differences arise when the carrying amount of an investment or an interest in a joint arrangement differs from its tax base. Such differences may be caused by:
• the existence of undistributed profits of subsidiaries, branches, associates and interests in joint arrangements
• changes in foreign exchange rates when a parent and its subsidiary are based in different countries
• a reduction in the carrying amount of an investment in an associate to its recoverable amount.

The recognition of a deferred tax liability in relation to investments is required, by paragraph 39 of IAS 12, except where both of the following conditions are satisfied:

(a) the parent, investor, joint venturer or joint operator is able to control the timing of the reversal of the temporary difference; and
(b) it is probable that the temporary difference will not reverse in the foreseeable future.

Because there is no definition of or discussion about the meaning of the term 'foreseeable future', managerial judgement is required to determine whether the facts and circumstances associated with a particular investment satisfy the above criteria.

As both branches and subsidiaries are 'controlled' by the parent, the first condition would always be met for such investments. However, where the temporary difference arises with respect to undistributed profits in an associate and the investor cannot control the declaration of dividends from those profits, a deferred tax liability would be recognised.

Deferred tax assets associated with investments would normally arise when the investment has been written down to the recoverable amount, or when the application of fair value or equity accounting has written it down below its tax base. The recognition of such a deferred tax asset is allowed only to the extent that the temporary difference will reverse in the foreseeable future and taxable profit will be available against which the temporary difference can be utilised (IAS 12 paragraph 44).

LO10   6.10   CHANGE OF TAX RATES

When a new tax rate is enacted (or substantively enacted), the new rate should be applied in calculating the current tax liability and adjustments to deferred tax accounts during the year. It should also be applied to the deferred amounts recognised in prior years. A journal adjustment must be passed to increase or reduce the carrying amounts of deferred tax assets and liabilities, in order to reflect the new value of future taxable or deductible amounts. Paragraph 60 of IAS 12 requires the net amount arising from the restatement of deferred tax balances to be recognised in the statement of comprehensive income, except to the extent that the deferred tax amounts relate to items previously charged or credited to equity.

ILLUSTRATIVE EXAMPLE 6.8 Change of tax rate

As at 30 June 2013, the balances of deferred tax accounts for Carnation Ltd were:

Deferred tax asset	$29 600
Deferred tax liability	(72 800)

In September 2013, the government reduced the company tax rate from 40 cents to 30 cents in the dollar, effective from 1 July 2013. The recorded deferred tax balances represent the tax effect of future taxable amounts and future deductible amounts at 40 cents in the dollar, so they are now overstated and must be adjusted as follows:

	Deferred tax asset	Deferred tax liability
Opening balance	$29 600	$ 72 800
Adjustment for change in tax rate: ([40 − 30]/40)	(7 400)	(18 200)
Restated balance	$22 200	$ 54 600

The adjusting journal entry is:

Deferred Tax Liability	Dr	18 200	
Deferred Tax Asset	Cr		7 400
Income Tax Expense	Cr		10 800
(Recognition of the impact of a change of tax rate on deferred tax amounts)			

LO11   6.11   OTHER ISSUES

6.11.1   Amended prior year tax figures

In taxation jurisdictions where entities self-assess their taxable profit, it is possible that the taxation authority will amend that assessment by changing the amount of taxable or deductible items. This amendment could result in the entity being liable to pay extra tax or becoming eligible for a taxation refund. Upon receipt of an amended assessment, the entity should analyse the reason for the adjustment and consider whether both current and deferred tax are affected. For example, if an entity has used an incorrect taxation depreciation rate, then the amendment to the correct rate will change both the prior year taxable profit and future taxable profits across the economic life of the depreciable asset. If only current tax for the previous year has changed, the following journal entry would be passed:

Income Tax Expense	Dr	xxx	
Current Tax Liability	Cr		xxx
(Amendment to prior year current tax on receipt of amended assessment)			

If the amendment also changes a deferred item, the new temporary difference will need to be calculated and the carry-forward balance adjusted accordingly. In the depreciation example used above, the adjustment (assuming the accounting depreciation rate is lower than the rate used to calculate taxable income) is:

Income Tax Expense	Dr	xxx	
Deferred Tax Liability	Cr		xxx
Current Tax Liability	Cr		xxx
(Amendment to prior year current tax and deferred tax liability on receipt of amended assessment)			

Any amendment to the deferred tax liability or the deferred tax asset arising from amended assessments would appear on the deferred tax worksheet as a 'movement' adjustment.

6.11.2 Items recognised outside profit or loss

In general, the amount of current and deferred tax arising in a period must be recognised outside profit or loss if the tax relates to items that are recognised outside profit or loss (IAS 12 paragraph 61A). Examples of items that are recognised in other comprehensive income are:
- revaluation of items of property, plant and equipment to fair value (see chapter 11). At the time of revaluation, an adjustment may be required to be made to the balance of the deferred tax liability account. For example, if an item of plant is revalued upwards from $100 to $200 and the tax rate is 30%, the entity would pass the following journal entry:

Plant	Dr	100	
Gain on Revaluation of Plant (OCI)	Cr		100
(Revaluation of plant)			
Income Tax Expense – Gain on Revaluation of Plant (OCI)	Dr	30	
Deferred Tax Liability	Cr		30
(Recognition of tax effect of revaluation increase)			
Gain on Revaluation of Plant (OCI)	Dr	100	
Income Tax Expense (OCI)	Cr		30
Asset Revaluation Surplus	Cr		70
(Accumulation of net revaluation gain in equity)			

- exchange differences arising on the translation of the financial statements of a foreign entity (see chapter 28).

International Financial Reporting Standards also require or permit particular items to be credited directly to equity, for example:
- an adjustment to the opening balance of retained earnings resulting from either a change in accounting policy that is applied retrospectively or from the correction of an error
- amounts arising on the initial recognition of the equity component of a compound financial instrument (see chapter 7).

Where it is difficult to identify the amount of current or deferred tax relating to items recognised outside profit or loss, as may happen when graduated rates of income tax are applicable or a tax rate or rule has changed, a reasonable allocation should be made pro rata (IAS 12 paragraph 63).

6.11.3 Deferred tax arising from a business combination

The amount of deferred tax arising in relation to the acquisition of an entity or business is recognised (subject to the recognition criteria) and included as part of identifiable assets acquired and liabilities assumed when determining the goodwill or gain on bargain purchase arising on acquisition. (Further discussion of the determination of goodwill and gain on bargain purchase can be found in chapter 14.) When a deferred tax asset of the acquiree not recognised at the date of a business combination is subsequently recognised by the acquirer, the resulting deferred tax income is recognised in the statement of profit or loss and other comprehensive income. Additionally, paragraph 68 of IAS 12 requires that the amount of goodwill recognised on acquisition must be adjusted to the amount that would be recorded had the deferred tax asset been recognised on acquisition.

6.12 PRESENTATION IN THE FINANCIAL STATEMENTS

IAS 12 specifies the way in which tax items (revenues, expenses, assets and liabilities) are to be presented in the financial statements, including the circumstances in which items can be offset.

6.12.1 Tax assets and tax liabilities

Tax assets and tax liabilities must be classified as current and non-current as required by IAS 1 *Presentation of Financial Statements* (paragraph 60) and presented in the statement of financial position in accordance with IAS 1, paragraphs 54(n), 54(o) and 56. Paragraph 71 of IAS 12 allows current tax assets and current tax liabilities to be offset only when the entity has a legally enforceable right to offset the amount, and intends either to settle on a net basis or to realise the asset and settle the liability simultaneously. A legal right to set off the accounts would normally exist where the accounts relate to income taxes levied by the same taxing authority.

Deferred tax assets and deferred tax liabilities can be offset only if a legally enforceable right to offset current amounts exists; and the deferred items relate to income taxes levied by the same taxing authority on the same taxable entity, or on different taxable entities which intend either to settle on a net basis or to realise the asset and settle the liability simultaneously in each future period in which significant deferred amounts will reverse (IAS 12 paragraph 74).

Consequently, entities operating in a single country will normally offset both current and deferred tax assets and liabilities, and show only a net current tax liability or asset and a net deferred asset or liability.

6.12.2 Tax expense

The tax expense (or income) related to profit or loss for the period is required to be presented in the statement of profit or loss and other comprehensive income (IAS 12 paragraph 77).

6.13 DISCLOSURES

Paragraphs 79–82A of IAS 12 contain the required disclosures relating to income taxes. These disclosures are very detailed, and provide significant additional information about the makeup of income tax expense (or income), and both taxable and deductible temporary differences. Paragraph 79 requires the tax expense figure shown in the statement of profit or loss and other comprehensive income to be broken down into its various components (examples of which are listed in paragraph 80), such as current tax expense and deferred tax arising from temporary differences. Paragraph 81 requires a wide range of disclosures including tax relating to equity and discontinued operations, changes in tax rates, and unrecognised deferred tax assets and liabilities.

Paragraph 81 also requires two detailed reconciliations to be prepared:
- Paragraph 81(c) requires entities to disclose 'an explanation of the relationship between tax expense (income) and accounting profit'. This essentially reconciles expected tax — accounting profit multiplied by tax rate — to the actual tax expense recognised. The reconciliation enables financial statement users to understand why the relationship between accounting profit and income tax expense is unusual, the factors causing the variance, and factors that could affect the relationship in the future. Entities are allowed to reconcile in either or both of the following ways:
  – a numerical reconciliation between tax expense and expected tax
  – a numerical reconciliation between the average effective tax rate (tax expense divided by the accounting profit) and the applicable tax rate.

Irrespective of the reconciliation method used, entities must disclose the basis on which the applicable tax rate is computed.
- Paragraph 81(g) requires disclosure of the following information for deferred tax items recognised in the statement of financial position:

  in respect of each type of temporary difference, and in respect of each type of unused tax loss and unused tax credit:
    (i) the amount of the deferred tax assets and liabilities recognised in the statement of financial position for each period presented; and

(ii) the amount of the deferred tax income or expense recognised in profit or loss, if this is not apparent from the changes in the amounts recognised in the statement of financial position

Normally, the second part of the paragraph 81(g) disclosure is required only if a change in tax rate or legislation has occurred during the year, or if some other event causes an adjustment to a deferred account during the period.

When an entity has suffered tax losses in either the current or previous period, and recognised a deferred tax asset related to those losses that is dependent on earning future taxable profits in excess of those arising on the reversal of taxable temporary differences, paragraph 82 requires disclosure of the amount of the deferred tax asset and the nature of the evidence supporting its recognition.

Paragraph 82A applies only in those jurisdictions where tax rates vary according to the quantum of profit or retained earnings distributed as dividends. In this situation, paragraph 82A requires the entity to disclose the nature and amounts (to the extent practicable) of the potential income tax consequences that would result from the payment of dividends to its shareholders.

Figure 6.6 provides an illustration of the disclosures required by IAS 12.

FIGURE 6.6 Illustrative disclosures required by IAS 12

Note 4: Income tax expense	Notes	2013 $	2012 $	IAS 12 paragraph
Major components of income tax expense				*79*
Current tax expense		126 600	117 600	*80(a)*
Deferred tax from origination and reversal of temporary differences		(20 250)	11 320	*80(c)*
Deferred tax relating to tax rate change		250	—	*80(d)*
Benefit from unrecognised tax loss used to reduce current tax expense		(1 500)	—	*80(e)*
Income tax expense		105 100	128 920	*80(f)*
Tax relating to items charged (credited) direct to equity				
Deferred tax relating to revaluation of land		12 500	—	*80(h)*
Reconciliation of tax expense to prima facie tax on accounting profit				*81(b)*
The applicable tax rate is the company income tax rate of 30% (2012: 40%)				*81(c)(i)*
The prima facie tax on accounting profit differs from the tax expense provided in the accounts as follows:				
Accounting profit		402 000	397 000	
Prima facie tax at 30% (2012: 40%)		120 600	158 800	
Tax effect of non-deductible expenses				
Goodwill impairment		3 900	5 200	
Non-taxable revenue		(1 500)	(2 000)	
Entertainment		3 600	2 300	
		126 600	164 300	
Increase in beginning deferred taxes resulting from reduction in tax rate		250	—	
Reduction in current tax from recoupment of tax losses		(1 500)	—	
Tax effect of net movements in items giving rise to:*				
Deferred tax assets		(8 250)	3 200	
Deferred tax liabilities		(12 000)	(38 580)	
Tax expense		105 100	128 920	*81(d)*

* These figures represent the net effect of movements in assets and liabilities during the year which have increased or decreased current tax. The details can be found in disclosures required by paragraph 81(g)(ii).

(continued)

FIGURE 6.6 *(continued)*

Note 4: Income tax expense	Notes	2013 $	2012 $	IAS 12 paragraph
Change in tax rate As of 1 July 2012, the company tax rate changed from 40% to 30%				*81(d)*
Unrecognised deferred tax assets Tax losses in respect of which deferred tax has not been recognised as it is not probable that benefits will be received		20 000	40 000	*81(e)*
Unrecognised deferred tax liabilities Aggregate of temporary differences associated with investments in subsidiaries for which deferred tax liabilities have not been recognised		16 000	16 000	*81(f)*
Deferred tax assets and liabilities The following items have given rise to deferred tax assets:				
Accounts receivable		12 000	15 000	
Employee entitlements		24 000	22 000	
Total deferred tax assets		36 000	37 000	
The following items have given rise to deferred tax liabilities:				
Land		12 500	—	
Plant and equipment		15 000	36 000	
Total deferred tax liabilities		27 500	36 000	
Offset of deferred tax asset against liability		36 000	37 000	
Net deferred tax asset (liability)		8 500	(1 000)	*81(g) (i)*
Deferred tax expenses (income) recognised in the statement of comprehensive income for each type of temporary difference* Deferred tax expense in relation to:				
Plant and equipment		(12 000)	(38 580)	
Total deferred tax expense		(12 000)	(38 580)	
Deferred tax income in relation to:				
Accounts receivable		750	1 200	
Employee entitlements		7 500	2 000	
Total deferred tax income		8 250	3 200	*81(g) (ii)*

* This disclosure is required only if the movements in deferred items cannot readily be ascertained from other disclosures made with respect to deferred assets and liabilities. This is the case in this situation because the change in tax rate adjustments has obscured the movements in deferred items.

Figure 6.7 shows the income tax notes to the financial statements of the New Zealand company Fisher & Paykel Appliances Holdings Ltd for the reporting period ended 31 March 2011, which were prepared in accordance with International Financial Reporting Standards (IFRSs).

FIGURE 6.7 Income tax notes to the consolidated financial statements of Fisher & Paykel

9. Income tax expense

	Consolidated		Parent	
	31 March 2011 $'000	31 March 2010 $'000	31 March 2011 $'000	31 March 2010 $'000
(a) Income tax expense				
Current tax	23 259	(5 109)	66	739
Deferred tax	(8 684)	(14 831)	(101)	(127)
	14 575	(19 940)	(35)	612
Deferred income tax (credit)/expense included in income tax expense comprises:				
Decrease/(increase) in deferred tax assets (Note 18)	(8 313)	(11 920)	(101)	(127)
(Decrease)/increase in deferred tax liabilities (Note 24)	(371)	(2 911)	—	—
	(8 684)	(14 831)	(101)	(127)
(b) Numerical reconciliation of income tax expense to prima facie tax payable				
(Loss)/profit from continuing operations before income tax expense	48 120	(103 268)	112	(216)
Tax at the New Zealand tax rate of 30%	14 436	(30 980)	34	(65)
Tax effect of a change in New Zealand tax rate to 28%	1 116	—	16	—
Tax effect of amounts which are not deductible/ (taxable) in calculating taxable income:				
Other non-assessable income	(2 541)	(2290)	—	—
Forfeited NRWT and CFC income (2009/10 only) not sheltered by foreign tax credits	823	3 689	—	—
Unrealised losses/(gains) on New Zealand FC1 debenture	182	2 845	—	—
(Recognition)/Derecognition of deferred tax	(1 680)	—	—	—
Credits provided to /from Group companies	—	—	(151)	677
Other non-deductible amounts	3 144	8 699	—	—
	15 480	(18 307)	(101)	612
Difference in overseas tax rates	(126)	(1 496)	—	—
Under/(over) provision in prior years	(779)	(407)	66	—
	(905)	(1 903)	66	—
Income tax expense/(credit)	14 575	(19 940)	(35)	612

Tax legislation passed in 2010 reduced the New Zealand company tax rate from 30% to 28%, effective 1 April 2011. The weighted average applicable effective tax rate for the year ended 31 March 2011 was 30.3% (2010 31.2%). The decrease from the year ended 31 March 2010 is primarily due to prior year adjustments in New Zealand and the USA. The Group has estimated New Zealand tax losses available to carry forward of $15.9 million (2010 $18.9 million), subject to shareholder continuity being maintained as required by New Zealand tax legislation. In addition, the Group has unrecognized New Zealand tax losses of $0.8 million.

The Group has estimated North American tax losses available to carry forward of $14.8 million (2010 $8.9 million) and tax credits of $4.3 million. These are subject shareholder continuity being maintained as required by US tax legislation. In addition, the Group has unrecognized US tax losses and credits totalling $26.8 million.

(continued)

FIGURE 6.7 (continued)

18. Deferred tax assets

	Consolidated		Parent	
	31 March 2011 $'000	31 March 2010 $'000	31 March 2011 $'000	31 March 2010 $'000
The balance comprises temporary differences attributable to:				
Receivables provisions	8 216	209	—	—
Employee benefits	5 633	4 651	228	127
Inventories	2 429	10 145	—	—
Warranty provisions	4 130	4 430	—	—
Property, plant & equipment	9 969	(5 800)	—	—
Intangibles (excl DCS brand)	(21 425)	—	—	—
DCS brand	2 841	5 142	—	—
Cessation of business (Australian manufacturing)	—	2 649	—	—
Impairment of barter credits	4 230	4 667	—	—
Derivative financial instruments	2 005	(253)	—	—
USA energy tax credit*	4 260	4 941	—	—
Tax losses to carry forward*	30 605	39 989	—	—
Other temporary differences	2 964	5 436	—	—
	55 857	76 206	228	127
Movements:				
Opening balance at 1 April	76 206	67 830	127	—
Effect of a change in New Zealand tax rate to 28%	800	—	(16)	—
Credited (charged) to the Income Statement (Note 9)	8 313	11 920	101	127
Credited/(charged) to equity	(5 646)	1 999	—	—
Prior period adjustment	(5 140)	—	6	—
Transfer from Deferred tax liabilities	(19 487)	—	—	—
Foreign exchange differences	2 406	(5 543)	—	—
Other movements	(1 595)	—	10	—
Closing balance at 31 March	55 857	76 206	228	127
Expected settlement				
Within 12 months	17 167	11 851	204	55
In excess of 12 months	38 690	64 355	24	72
	55 857	76 206	228	127

* The utilisation of deferred tax assets is dependent on future taxable profits in excess of the profits arising from the reversal of existing taxable temporary differences and shareholder continuity being maintained in accordance with New Zealand tax legislation requirements. The recognition of these deferred tax assets is evidenced by forecasts of taxable income arising in the next ten years.

FIGURE 6.7 *(continued)*

24. Deferred tax liabilities

	Consolidated		Parent	
	31 March 2011 $'000	31 March 2010 $'000	31 March 2011 $'000	31 March 2010 $'000
The balance comprises temporary differences attributable to:				
Provisions	(876)	(9 283)	—	—
Property, plant & equipment	5 629	11 638	—	—
Intangible assets	4 008	24 780	—	—
Tax credits	(1 203)	—	—	—
Derivative financial instruments	(532)	—	—	—
Other temporary differences	(155)	595	—	—
Net deferred tax liabilities	6871	27 730	—	—
Movements:				
Opening balance at 1 April	27 730	32 421	—	—
Charged/(credited) to the Income Statement (Note 9)	(371)	(2 911)	—	—
Transfer to Deferred tax assets	(19 487)	—	—	—
Prior period adjustment	(426)	—	—	—
Foreign exchange differences	(129)	(1 780)	—	—
Other movements	(446)	—	—	—
Closing balance at 31 March	6 871	27 730	—	—
Expected settlement				
Within 12 months	(109)	(7 460)	—	—
in excess of 12 months	6 9810	35 190	—	—
	6 871	27 730	—	—

Source: Fisher & Paykel (2011, pp. 97, 114, 124).

SUMMARY

This chapter analyses the content of IAS 12 *Income Taxes* and provides guidance on its implementation. The principal issue in accounting for taxes is how to account for the current and future tax consequences of transactions and other events of the current period. The accounting standard requires entities to recognise (with limited exceptions) deferred tax liabilities and deferred tax assets when the recovery or settlement of an asset or liability will result in larger or smaller tax payments than would occur if such settlement or recovery had no tax consequence. The tax consequences of transactions are to be accounted for in the same way as the transaction to which they are related. Therefore, for transactions recognised in the statement of profit or loss and other comprehensive income, all related tax effects are also recognised in the statement of profit or loss and other comprehensive income. Where a transaction requires a direct adjustment to equity, so do any tax effects. Deferred tax assets, particularly those relating to tax losses, are recognised only if it is probable that the entity will have sufficient taxable profit in the future against which the tax benefit can be offset. All deferred tax liabilities must be recognised in full. IAS 12 requires extensive disclosures to be made in relation to both current and deferred tax items.

Discussion questions

1. What is the main principle of tax-effect accounting as outlined in IAS 12?
2. Explain the meaning of a temporary difference as it relates to deferred tax calculations and give three examples.
3. Explain how accounting profit and taxable profit differ, and how each is treated when accounting for income taxes.
4. In tax-effect accounting, the creation of temporary differences between the carrying amount and the tax base for assets and liabilities leads to the establishment of deferred tax assets and liabilities in the accounting records. List examples of temporary differences that create:
   (a) deferred tax assets
   (b) deferred tax liabilities.
5. In IAS 12, criteria are established for the recognition of a deferred tax asset and a deferred tax liability. Identify these criteria, and discuss any differences between the criteria for assets and those for liabilities.
6. What is a 'tax loss' and how is it accounted for?
7. 'Despite the fact that deferred tax liabilities and assets are recognised in respect of certain assets and liabilities, the income tax expense (or benefit) of such items is always recognised in the current year.' Is this statement true? Discuss.
8. What action should be taken when a tax rate or tax rule changes? Why?
9. Are all temporary differences that exist at the end of the reporting period recognised as deferred tax assets or deferred tax liabilities?
10. In determining whether deferred tax assets relating to tax losses are to be recognised, what factors should be taken into consideration?

Exercises

STAR RATING ★ BASIC ★★ MODERATE ★★★ DIFFICULT

| Exercise 6.1 | TAX EFFECTS OF A TEMPORARY DIFFERENCE |

★ The following information was extracted from the records of Protea Ltd for the year ended 30 June 2013:

PROTEA LTD
Deferred Tax Worksheet (extract)
as at 30 June 2013

	Carrying amount	Future taxable amount	Future deductible amount	Tax base	Taxable temporary differences	Deductible temporary differences
Relevant assets Equipment	$60 000	$(60 000)	$108 000	$108 000		$48 000

Equipment is depreciated at 25% p.a. straightline for accounting purposes, but the allowable rate for taxation is 20% p.a.

Required

Assuming that no equipment is purchased or sold during the years ended 30 June 2014 and 30 June 2015, calculate:
(a) the accounting expense and tax deduction for each year
(b) the impact of depreciation on the taxable profit for each year
(c) the movement in the temporary difference balance for each year.

| Exercise 6.2 | CALCULATION OF CURRENT TAX |

★ Thistle Ltd made an accounting profit before tax of $40 000 for the year ended 30 June 2014. Included in the accounting profit were the following items of revenue and expense.

Donations to political parties (non-deductible)	5 000
Depreciation — machinery (20%)	15 000
Annual leave expense	5 600
Rent revenue	12 000

For tax purposes the following applied:

Depreciation rate for machinery	25%
Annual leave paid	6 500
Rent received	10 000
Income tax rate	30%

Required

1. Calculate the current tax liability for the year ended 30 June 2014, and prepare the adjusting journal entry.
2. Explain your treatment of rent items in your answer to requirement 1.

Exercise 6.3   **CALCULATION OF DEFERRED TAX**

★   The following information was extracted from the records of Orchid Ltd for the year ended 30 June 2014:

ORCHID LTD Statement of Financial Position (extract) as at 30 June 2014		
Assets		
Accounts receivable	$ 25 000	
Allowance for doubtful debts	(2 000)	$23 000
Machines	100 000	
Accumulated depreciation — machines	(25 000)	75 000
Liabilities		
Interest payable		1 000

Additional information
(a) The accumulated depreciation for tax purposes at 30 June 2014 was $50 000.
(b) The tax rate is 30%.

Required

Prepare a deferred tax worksheet to identify the temporary differences arising in respect of the assets and liabilities in the statement of financial position, and to calculate the balance of the deferred tax liability and deferred tax asset accounts at 30 June 2014. Assume the opening balance of the deferred tax accounts was $0.

Exercise 6.4   **CALCULATION OF CURRENT TAX**

★   Daisy Ltd recorded an accounting profit before tax of $100 000 for the year ended 30 June 2015. Included in the accounting profit were the following items of revenue and expense.

Entertainment expenses (non-deductible)	$ 2 000
Depreciation — vehicles (10%)	17 000
Rent revenue	2 500
For tax purposes the following applied:	
Depreciation rate — vehicles	15%
Rent received	$ 3 000
Income tax rate	30%

Required

1. Use a current tax worksheet to calculate the current tax liability for the year ended 30 June 2015. Prepare the adjusting journal entry.
2. Explain the future tax effect of the adjustment made in part 1 for rent received/revenue.

<table>
<tr><td>**Exercise 6.5**</td><td>**CURRENT AND DEFERRED TAX**</td></tr>
</table>

★ Myrtle Ltd has determined its accounting profit before tax for the year ended 30 June 2013 to be $256 700. Included in this profit are the items of revenue and expense shown below.

Royalty revenue (non-taxable)	$ 8 000
Proceeds on sale of building	75 000
Entertainment expense	1 700
Depreciation expense — buildings	7 600
Depreciation expense — plant	22 500
Carrying amount of building sold	70 000
Doubtful debts expense	4 100
Annual leave expense	46 000
Insurance expense	4 200
Development expense	15 000

The company's draft statement of financial position at 30 June 2013 showed the following assets and liabilities:

Assets		
Cash		$ 2 500
Accounts receivable	$ 21 500	
Less: Allowance for doubtful debts	(4 100)	17 400
Inventory		31 600
Prepaid insurance		4 500
Land		75 000
Buildings	170 000	
Less: Accumulated depreciation	(59 500)	110 500
Plant	150 000	
Less: Accumulated depreciation	(67 500)	82 500
Deferred tax asset (opening balance)		9 600
		333 600
Liabilities		
Accounts payable		25 000
Provision for annual leave		10 000
Deferred tax liability (opening balance)		6 000
Loan		140 000
		$ 181 000

Additional information

(a) Quarterly income tax instalments paid during the year were:

28 October 2012	$ 18 000
28 January 2013	17 500
28 April 2013	18 000

with the final balance due on 28 July 2013.

(b) The tax depreciation rate for plant (which cost $150 000 3 years ago) is 20%. Depreciation on buildings is not deductible for taxation purposes.

(c) The building sold during the year had cost $100 000 when acquired 6 years ago. The company depreciates buildings at 5% p.a., straight-line. Any gain (loss) on sale of buildings is not taxable (i.e. not deductible).

(d) During the year, the following cash amounts were paid:

Annual leave	$52 000
Insurance	3 700

(e) Bad debts of $3500 were written off against the allowance for doubtful debts during the year.

(f) The $15 000 spent (and expensed) on development during the year is not deductible for tax purposes until 30 June 2014.

(g) Myrtle Ltd has tax losses amounting to $12 500 carried forward from prior years.

(h) The company tax rate is 30%.

Required

1. Determine the balance of any current and deferred tax assets and liabilities for Myrtle Ltd as at 30 June 2013.
2. Prepare any necessary journal entries.

Exercise 6.6

CALCULATION OF MOVEMENTS IN DEFERRED TAX ACCOUNTS

★ The statements of financial position of Acacia Ltd at 30 June 2014 showed the following net assets:

	2014	2013
Assets		
Cash	80 000	85 000
Inventory	170 000	155 000
Receivables	500 000	480 000
Allowance for doubtful debts	(55 000)	(40 000)
Plant	500 000	500 000
Accumulated depreciation	(260 000)	(210 000)
Deferred tax asset	?	40 500
Liabilities		
Accounts payable	290 000	260 000
Provision for long-service leave	60 000	45 000
Rent received in advance	25 000	20 000
Deferred tax liability	?	38 100

Additional information

(a) Accumulated depreciation of plant for tax purposes was $315 000 at 30 June 2013, and depreciation for tax purposes for the year ended 30 June 2014 amounted to $75 000.

(b) The tax rate is 30%.

Required

Prepare a worksheet to calculate the end of reporting period adjustment to deferred tax asset and liability accounts as at 30 June 2014, and show the necessary journal entry.

Exercise 6.7

CALCULATION OF CURRENT TAX LIABILITY AND ADJUSTING JOURNAL ENTRY

★ The profit before tax, as reported in the statement of profit or loss and other comprehensive income of Violet for the year ended 30 June 2014, amounted to $60 000, including the following revenue and expense items:

Rent revenue	$3 000
Government grant received (non-taxable)	1 000
Bad debts expense	6 000

Depreciation of plant	5 000
Annual leave expense	3 000
Entertainment costs (non-deductible)	1 800
Depreciation of buildings (non-deductible)	800

The statement of financial position of the company at 30 June 2014 showed the following net assets.

	2014	2013
Assets		
Cash	8 000	8 500
Inventory	17 000	15 500
Receivables	50 000	48 000
Allowance for doubtful debts	(5 500)	(4 000)
Office supplies	2 500	2 200
Plant	50 000	50 000
Accumulated depreciation	(26 000)	(21 000)
Buildings	30 000	30 000
Accumulated depreciation	(14 800)	(14 000)
Goodwill (net)	7 000	7 000
Deferred tax asset	?	4 050
Liabilities		
Accounts payable	29 000	26 000
Provision for long-service leave	6 000	4 500
Provision for annual leave	4 000	3 000
Rent received in advance	2 500	2 000
Deferred tax liability	?	3 150

Additional information

(a) Accumulated depreciation of plant for tax purposes was $31 500 at 30 June 2013, and depreciation for tax purposes for the year ended 30 June 2014 amounted to $7500.

(b) The tax rate is 30%.

Required

Prepare a worksheet to calculate taxable income and the company's current tax liability as at 30 June 2014, and prepare the end of reporting period adjustment journal.

Exercise 6.8	**CALCULATION OF CURRENT TAX, AND PRIOR YEAR AMENDMENT**

★★ The accounting profit before tax of Jasmine Ltd for the year ended 30 June 2014 was $22 240. It included the following revenue and expense items:

Government grant (non-taxable)	$ 3 600
Proceeds from sale of plant	33 000
Carrying amount of plant sold	30 000
Entertainment expense (non-deductible)	11 100
Doubtful debts expense	8 100
Depreciation expense — plant	24 000
Insurance expense	12 900
Annual leave expense	15 400

The draft statement of financial position as at 30 June 2014 included the following assets and liabilities:

	2014	2013
Accounts receivable	$ 156 000	$ 147 500
Allowance for doubtful debts	(6 800)	(5 200)
Prepaid insurance	3 400	5 600
Plant	240 000	290 000
Accumulated depreciation — plant	(134 400)	(130 400)
Deferred tax asset	?	9 990
Provision for annual leave	14 100	9 700
Deferred tax liability	?	9 504

Additional information
(a) In November 2013, the company received an amended assessment for the year ended 30 June 2013 from the taxing authority. The amendment notice indicated that an amount of $4500 claimed as a deduction had been disallowed. Jasmine Ltd has not yet adjusted its accounts to reflect the amendment.
(b) For tax purposes, the carrying amount of plant sold was $26 000. This sale was the only movement in plant for the year.
(c) The tax deduction for plant depreciation was $28 800. Accumulated depreciation at 30 June 2013 for taxation purposes was $156 480.
(d) In the previous year, Jasmine Ltd had made a tax loss of $18 400. Jasmine Ltd recognised a deferred tax asset in respect of this loss.
(e) The tax rate is 30%.

Required

Show all workings.
1. Prepare the journal entry necessary to record the amendment to the prior year's taxation return.
2. Prepare the current tax worksheet and journal entry/entries to calculate and record the current tax for the year ended 30 June 2014.
3. Justify your treatment of annual leave expense in the current tax worksheet.
4. Calculate the temporary difference as at 30 June 2014 for each of the following assets. Explain how these differences arise and why you have classified them as either deductible temporary differences or taxable temporary differences:
   (a) plant
   (b) accounts receivable.

Exercise 6.9	CURRENT AND DEFERRED TAX WITH TAX RATE CHANGE

★★ You have been asked by the accountant of Fennel Ltd to prepare the tax-effect accounting adjustments for the year ended 30 June 2014. Investigations revealed the following information:
(a) In September 2012, the government reduced the company tax rate from 40 cents to 30 cents in the dollar, effective from 1 July 2013.
(b) The profit for the year ended 30 June 2014 was $920 000.
(c) The assets and liabilities at 30 June were:

	2014	2013
Accounts receivable	$ 235 000	$ 200 000
Allowance for doubtful debts	(13 000)	(12 000)
Inventory	250 000	220 000
Land	100 000	100 000
Buildings	800 000	800 000
Accumulated depreciation — buildings	(99 000)	(70 000)
Plant	600 000	600 000

(continued)

	2014	2013
Accumulated depreciation — plant (accounting)	$(190 000)	$(120 000)
Development expenditure		
— costs incurred	320 000	200 000
— accumulated amortisation	(144 000)	(80 000)
Deferred tax asset	?	29 600
Goodwill (net)	—	20 000
Accounts payable	170 000	150 000
Deferred tax liability	?	72 000
Provision for long-service leave	36 000	28 000
Provision for warranty claims	32 000	34 000

(d) The company is entitled to claim a tax deduction of 125% for development expenditure in the year of expenditure. The company has adopted the accounting policy of capitalising and then amortising the expenditure over five years.

(e) Revenue for the year included:
Non-taxable income $126 000

(f) Expenses brought to account included:

Depreciation — buildings	$ 29 000
Depreciation — plant	70 000
Impairment — goodwill (non-deductible)	20 000
Amortisation — development expenditure	64 000

(g) Accumulated depreciation on plant for tax purposes was $180 000 on 30 June 2013, and $285 000 on 30 June 2014.

(h) Bad debts of $14 000 were written off during the year, and warranty repairs to the value of $22 000 were carried out. There was no tax deduction for long-service leave in the current year.

(i) Buildings are depreciated in the accounting records but no deduction is allowed for tax purposes.

Required

1. Prepare the journal entry to account for the change in the income tax rate in September 2012.
2. Prepare the worksheets and journal entries to calculate and record the current tax liability, and any movements in deferred tax assets and liabilities in accordance with IAS 12, for the year ended 30 June 2014.

Exercise 6.10 **RECOGNITION OF DEFERRED TAX ASSETS**

★★ Tulip Ltd incurred an accounting loss of $7560 for the year ended 30 June 2013. The current tax calculation determined that the company had incurred a tax loss of $12 500. Taxation legislation allows such losses to be carried forward and offset against future taxable profits. The company had the following temporary differences:

	30 June 2013	30 June 2012	Expected period of reversal
Deductible temporary differences:			
Accounts receivable	$12 000	$10 000	2014
Plant and equipment	5 000	7 500	2014/2015 equally
Taxable temporary differences:			
Interest receivable	1 500	2 500	2014
Prepaid insurance	10 000	20 000	2014

At 30 June 2012, Tulip Ltd had recognised a deferred tax liability of $6750 and a deferred tax asset of $5250 with respect to temporary differences existing at that date. No adjustment has yet been made for temporary differences existing at 30 June 2013.

Required

1. Discuss the factors that Tulip Ltd should consider in determining the amount (if any) to be recognised for deferred tax assets at 30 June 2013.

2. Calculate the amount (if any) to be recognised for deferred tax assets at 30 June 2013. Justify your
answer.

CURRENT AND DEFERRED TAX

★★ The accounting profit before tax for the year ended 30 June 2013 for Lily Ltd amounted to $18 500 and
included:

Depreciation — motor vehicle (25%)	$ 4 500
Depreciation — equipment (20%)	20 000
Rent revenue	16 000
Royalty revenue (non-taxable)	5 000
Doubtful debts expense	2 300
Entertainment expense (non-deductible)	1 500
Proceeds on sale of equipment	19 000
Carrying amount of equipment sold	18 000
Annual leave expense	5 000

The draft statement of financial position at 30 June 2013 contained the following assets and liabilities:

	2013	2012
Assets		
Cash	$ 11 500	$ 9 500
Receivables	12 000	14 000
Allowance for doubtful debts	(3 000)	(2 500)
Inventory	19 000	21 500
Rent receivable	2 800	2 400
Motor vehicle	18 000	18 000
Accumulated depreciation — motor vehicle	(15 750)	(11 250)
Equipment	100 000	130 000
Accumulated depreciation — equipment	(60 000)	(52 000)
Deferred tax asset	?	6 450
		136 100
Liabilities		
Accounts payable	15 655	21 500
Provision for annual leave	4 500	6 000
Current tax liability	?	7 600
Deferred tax liability	?	2 745
		37 845

Additional information
(a) The company can claim a deduction of $15 000 (15%) for depreciation on equipment, but the
motor vehicle is fully depreciated for tax purposes.
(b) The equipment sold during the year had been purchased for $30 000 2 years before the date of sale.
(c) The company tax rate is 30%.

Required

1. Determine the balance of any current and deferred tax assets and liabilities for Lily Ltd as at 30 June
2013, using appropriate worksheets. Show all workings.
2. Prepare any necessary journal entries.

DISCLOSURES

★★ The following taxation worksheets relate to Mint Ltd's taxation adjustments for the years ending 30 June 2013 and 30 June 2014. Using these worksheets, prepare appropriate notes to the financial statements for 30 June 2014 in accordance with IAS 12 disclosure requirements.

MINT LTD Current Tax Worksheet for the year ended 30 June 2013		
Accounting profit before tax		$ 2 042 686
Add:		
Depreciation building — non-deductible	$108 000	
Entertainment expense — non-deductible	86 800	
Legal expense — non-deductible	$ 79 200	
Political donations — non-deductible	9 900	
Penalty — non-deductible	20 800	
Doubtful debts expense	123 000	
Depreciation expense — equipment	120 000	
Depreciation expense — furniture and fittings	720 000	
Depreciation expense — motor vehicles	160 000	
Annual leave expense	680 000	
Insurance expense	254 200	
Long-service leave expense	22 000	
Amortisation — patent	100 000	
Rent expense	309 600	
Interest expense	28 000	
Supplies expense	404 800	
Carrying amount of equipment sold	550 000	
Interest received for tax purposes	187 550	3 963 850
		6 006 536
Deduct:		
Interest revenue	186 050	
Political donations deductible	100	
Carrying amount of equipment sold — taxation	400 000	
Debts written off	92 300	
Depreciation — equipment (taxation)	150 000	
Depreciation — furniture and fittings (taxation)	960 000	
Depreciation — motor vehicles (taxation)	200 000	
Annual leave paid	495 000	
Interest paid	28 000	
Insurance paid	256 400	
Development expenditure — additional deduction	25 000	
Amortisation — patent (taxation)	150 000	
Supplies purchased	402 200	
Rent paid	312 500	(3 657 550)
Taxable income		2 348 986
Total tax payable (35%)		822 145
Less: Tax already paid		(546 271)
Current tax liability		$ 275 874

MINT LTD
Deferred Tax Worksheet
as at 30 June 2013

	Carrying amount	Future taxable amount	Future deductible amount	Tax base	Taxable temporary differences	Deductible temporary differences
Relevant assets						
Accounts receivable (net)	$2 406 000	$ 0	$ 123 000	$2 259 000		$ 123 000
Interest receivable	18 000	(18 000)	0	0	$ 18 000	
Consumable supplies	118 400	(118 400)	0	0	118 400	
Prepaid insurance	59 400	(59 400)	0	0	59 400	
Prepaid rent	12 900	(12 900)	0	0	12 900	
Building	3 492 000	(3 492 000)	0	2 560 000	3 492 000	
Furniture and fittings	3 470 000	(3 470 000)	2 560 000	450 000	910 000	
Motor vehicles	520 000	(520 000)	450 000	150 000	70 000	
Equipment	240 000	(240 000)	150 000	50 000	90 000	
Patent	200 000	(200 000)	50 000		150 000	
Relevant liabilities						
Interest payable	7 000	0	(7 000)	0		7 000
Provision for long-service leave	220 800	0	(220 800)	0		220 800
Provision for annual leave	704 000	0	(704 000)	0		704 000
Temporary differences					4 920 700	1 054 800
Excluded differences					3 492 000	
Net temporary differences					1 428 700	1 054 800
Deferred tax liability (35%)					500 045	
Deferred tax asset (35%)						369 180
Beginning balances					(397 080)	(326 840)
Movement during year (tax rate)					49 635	40 855
Adjustment					$ 152 600	$ 83 195
					Credit	Debit

MINT LTD
Current Tax Worksheet
for the year ended 30 June 2014

Accounting profit before tax		$ 1 900 591
Add:		
Depreciation building — non-deductible	$ 168 000	
Entertainment expense — non-deductible	95 600	
Legal expense — non-deductible	87 000	
Political donations — non-deductible	10 900	
Amortisation — development expenditure	40 000	
Doubtful debts expense	160 600	
Depreciation expense — equipment	135 000	
Depreciation expense — furniture and fittings	963 750	
Depreciation expense — motor vehicles	160 000	
Annual leave expense	652 000	

(continued)

Add: (continued)		
Insurance expense	$ 276 300	
Long-service leave expense	48 400	
Amortisation — patent	100 000	
Rent expense	356 400	
Supplies expense	458 300	
Carrying amount of equipment sold	90 000	
Interest received for tax purposes	140 650	$ 3 942 900
		5 843 491
Deduct:		
Interest revenue	150 650	
Political donations — deductible	100	
Carrying amount of equipment sold — taxation	37 500	
Debts written off	123 000	
Depreciation — equipment (taxation)	168 750	
Depreciation — furniture and fittings (taxation)	1 285 000	
Depreciation — motor vehicles (taxation)	200 000	
Annual leave paid	680 000	
Insurance paid	282 600	
Research and development paid (125%)	150 000	
Amortisation — patent (taxation)	50 000	
Supplies purchased	504 400	
Rent paid	358 350	(3 990 350)
Taxable income		1 853 141
Total tax payable (35%)		648 599
Less: Tax already paid		(475 000)
Current tax liability		173 599

MINT LTD
Deferred Tax Worksheet
as at 30 June 2014

	Carrying amount	Assessable amount	Deductible amount	Tax base	Taxable temporary differences	Deductible temporary differences
Relevant assets						
Accounts receivable (net)	$ 2 588 400	$ 0	$ 160 600	$ 2 749 000		$ 160 600
Interest receivable	8 000	(8 000)	0	0	$ 8 000	
Consumable supplies	164 500	(164 500)	0	0	164 500	
Prepaid insurance	65 700	(65 700)	0	0	65 700	
Prepaid rent	14 850	(14 850)	0	0	14 850	
Building	6 424 000	(6 424 000)	0	0	6 424 000	
Furniture and fittings	3 406 250	(3 406 250)	2 175 000	2 175 000	1 231 250	
Motor vehicles	360 000	(360 000)	250 000	250 000	110 000	
Equipment	465 000	(465 000)	393 750	393 750	71 250	
Patent	100 000	(100 000)	0	0	100 000	
Development expenditure	80 000	(80 000)	0	0	80 000	

	Carrying amount	Assessable amount	Deductible amount	Tax base	Taxable temporary differences	Deductible temporary differences
Relevant liabilities						
Interest payable	7 000	0	(7 000)	0		7 000
Provision for long-service leave	269 200	0	(269 200)	0		269 200
Provision for annual leave	676 000	0	(676 000)	0		676 000
Temporary differences					8 269 550	1 112 800
Excluded differences					(6 424 000)	
Net temporary differences					1 845 550	1 112 800
Deferred tax liability (35%)					645 943	
Deferred tax asset (35%)						389 480
Beginning balances					(500 045)	(369 180)
Movement during year						
Adjustment					145 898	20 300
					Credit	Debit

Exercise 6.13 **CREATION AND REVERSAL OF TEMPORARY DIFFERENCES**

★★ The following are all independent situations. Prepare the journal entries for deferred tax on the creation or reversal of any temporary differences. Explain in each case the nature of the temporary difference. Assume a tax rate of 30%.

1. The entity has an allowance for doubtful debts of $10 000 at the end of the current year relating to accounts receivable of $125 000. The prior year balances for these accounts were $8500 and $97 500 respectively. During the current year, debts worth $9250 were written off as uncollectable.
2. The entity sold a vehicle at the end of the current year for $15 000. The vehicle cost $100 000 when purchased 3 years ago, and had a carrying amount of $25 000 when sold. The taxation depreciation rate for equipment of this type is 33%.
3. The entity has recognised an interest receivable asset with a beginning balance of $17 000 and an ending balance of $19 500 for the current year. During the year, interest of $127 000 was received in cash.
4. At the end of the current year, the entity has recognised a liability of $4000 in respect of outstanding fines for non-compliance with safety legislation. Such fines are not tax-deductible.

Exercise 6.14 **CREATION AND REVERSAL OF A TEMPORARY DIFFERENCE**

★★ Rose Ltd purchased equipment on 1 July 2011 at a cost of $25 000. The equipment had an expected economic life of five years and was to be depreciated on a straight-line basis. The taxation depreciation rate for equipment of this type is 15% p.a. straight-line. On 30 June 2013, Rose Ltd reassessed the remaining economic life of the equipment from 3 years to 2 years, and the accounting depreciation charge was adjusted accordingly. The equipment was sold on 30 June 2014 for $15 000. The company tax rate is 30%.

Required

For each of the years ended 30 June 2012, 2013 and 2014, calculate the carrying amount and the tax base of the asset and determine the appropriate deferred tax entry. Explain your answer.

Exercise 6.15 **PAYMENT OF INCOME TAX AND AMENDED ASSESSMENT**

★★ Dover Ltd calculated its current tax liability at 30 June 2013 to be $57 500. This tax was paid in instalments as shown in the following table.

28 October 2012	$13 200
28 January 2013	11 600
28 April 2013	15 200
28 July 2013	17 500

On 1 November 2013, an amended assessment notice was received from the taxing authority. It disallowed a donation for $1500 claimed as a deduction, and amended the taxation depreciation rate used for vehicles from 50% to 30%. The accounting depreciation rate is 25%. As a result, further tax of $1950 was paid on 31 December 2013. The company tax rate is 30%.

Required

Prepare all journal entries necessary to record the taxation transactions for the period to 31 December 2013.

Exercise 6.16 · CALCULATION OF DEFERRED TAX, AND ADJUSTMENT ENTRY

★★★ The following information was extracted from the records of Bulb Ltd as at 30 June 2013:

Asset (liability)	Carrying amount	Tax base
Accounts receivable	$150 000	$175 000
Motor vehicles	165 000	125 000
Provision for warranty	(12 000)	0
Deposits received in advance	(15 000)	0

The depreciation rates for accounting and taxation are 15% and 25% respectively. Deposits are taxable when received, and warranty costs are deductible when paid. An allowance for doubtful debts of $25 000 has been raised against accounts receivable for accounting purposes, but such debts are deductible only when written off as uncollectable.

Required

1. Calculate the temporary differences for Bulb Ltd as at 30 June 2013. Justify your classification of each difference as either a deductible temporary difference or a taxable temporary difference.
2. Prepare the journal entry to record deferred tax for the year ended 30 June 2013 assuming no deferred items had been raised in prior years.

Exercise 6.17 · CURRENT AND DEFERRED TAX WITH PRIOR YEAR LOSSES

★★★ The accounting profit before tax of Gardenia Ltd was $175 900. It included the following revenue and expense items:

Government grant (non-taxable)	$ 3 600
Interest revenue	11 000
Long-service leave expense	7 000
Doubtful debts expense	4 200
Depreciation — plant (15% p.a., straight-line)	33 000
Rent expense	22 800
Entertainment expense (non-deductible)	3 900

The draft statement of financial position as at 30 June 2013 included the following assets and liabilities:

	2013	2012
Cash	$ 9 000	$ 7 500
Accounts receivable	83 000	76 800
Allowance for doubtful debts	(5 000)	(3 200)
Inventory	67 100	58 300

Interest receivable	1 000	—
Prepaid rent	2 800	2 400
Plant	220 000	220 000
Accumulated depreciation — plant	(99 000)	(66 000)
Deferred tax asset	?	30 360
Accounts payable	71 200	73 600
Provision for long-service leave	64 000	61 000
Deferred tax liability	?	720

Additional information
(a) The tax depreciation rate for plant is 10% p.a., straight-line.
(b) The tax rate is 30%.
(c) The company has $15 000 in tax losses carried forward from the previous year. A deferred tax asset was recognised for these losses. Taxation legislation allows such losses to be offset against future taxable profit.

Required

1. Prepare the worksheets and journal entries to calculate and record the current tax liability and the movements in deferred tax accounts for the year ended 30 June 2013.
2. Justify your treatment of the interest revenue in the current tax worksheet. Explain how and why this leads to the deferred tax consequence shown in the deferred tax worksheet.

References

CPA Australia 2010, *International Financial Reporting Standards (IFRS) Fact Sheet — IAS 12 Income Taxes*, CPA Australia, February, www.cpaaustralia.com.au.
Fisher & Paykel Appliances Holdings Ltd 2011, *Annual report for the year ending 31 March 2011*, New Zealand, www.fisherpaykel.co.nz.

7 Financial instruments

ACCOUNTING STANDARDS IN FOCUS

IAS 32 *Financial Instruments: Presentation*

IFRS 7 *Financial Instruments: Disclosures*

IAS 39 *Financial Instruments: Recognition and Measurement*

IFRS 9 *Financial Instruments (replacement of IAS 39)*

LEARNING OBJECTIVES

After studying this chapter, you should be able to:

1 describe the background to the development of accounting standards on financial instruments

2 define a financial instrument

3 outline and apply the definitions of financial assets and financial liabilities

4 explain the concept of a derivative

5 distinguish between equity instruments and financial liabilities

6 explain the concept of a compound financial instrument

7 determine the classification of revenues and expenses arising from financial instruments

8 determine when financial assets and financial liabilities may be offset

9 describe the main disclosure requirements of IFRS 7

10 describe the scope of IAS 39

11 explain the concept of an embedded derivative

12 distinguish between the four categories of financial instruments specified in IAS 39

13 apply the recognition criteria for financial instruments

14 understand and apply the measurement criteria for each category of financial instrument

15 outline the rules of hedge accounting set out in IAS 39 and be able to apply the rules to simple common cash flow and fair value hedges

16 briefly describe the requirements of IFRS 9

17 briefly describe expected future developments with respect to accounting for financial instruments.

7.1 INTRODUCTION TO IAS 32, IFRS 7, IAS 39 AND IFRS 9

Accounting for financial instruments was the most controversial area in the development of the IASB's 'stable platform' of standards adopted in 2005. Indeed, the controversy surrounding IAS 39 in particular almost derailed the IASB's plans for adopting IFRSs in Europe for financial years beginning on or after 1 January 2005. As late as 30 June 2004, IAS 39 had still not been completed because changes continued to be proposed or made in response to lobbying from various European interested parties, notably the banks. The controversial aspects of the standards at that time were largely those relating to hedge accounting. The controversy continued during the financial crisis of 2008 as a consequence of which the IASB was put under enormous pressure to amend IAS 39. In this case there was pressure to allow entities to move away from using a fair value measurement basis and to change the requirements for impairment of financial assets. As a result, the IASB amended the reclassification rules of IAS 39 and then proceeded to issue very quickly a new standard to replace IAS 39. This standard, IFRS 9 *Financial Instruments*, was issued in November 2009. However, by the end of 2011, IFRS 9 had still not been endorsed by the European parliament for a number of reasons (discussed in section 7.16). As a result, very few entities currently apply IFRS 9 and thus this chapter focuses on IAS 39.

Figure 7.1 provides an extract from the Report of the Financial Crisis Advisory Group,[1] which illustrates the controversy and complexity surrounding the accounting for financial instruments at the time of the 2008 financial crisis.

FIGURE 7.1 Effective financial reporting

Report of the Financial Crisis Advisory Group

While the post-mortems are still being written, it seems clear that accounting standards were not a root cause of the financial crisis. At the same time, it is clear that the crisis has exposed weaknesses in accounting standards and their application. These weaknesses reduced the credibility of financial reporting, which in part contributed to the general loss of confidence in the financial system. The weaknesses primarily involved (1) the difficulty of applying fair value ('mark-to-market') accounting in illiquid markets; (2) the delayed recognition of losses associated with loans, structured credit products, and other financial instruments by banks, insurance companies and other financial institutions; (3) issues surrounding the broad range of off-balance sheet financing structures, especially in the US; and (4) the extraordinary complexity of accounting standards for financial instruments, including multiple approaches to recognizing asset impairment. Some of these weaknesses also highlighted areas in which International Financial Reporting Standards ('IFRS') and US generally accepted accounting principles ('US GAAP') diverged.

In the early part of the crisis, the principal criticism of financial reporting focused on fair value accounting. This criticism contended that fair value accounting contributed to the pro-cyclicality of the financial system. Prior to the crisis, it is argued, fair value accounting led to significant overstatement of profits; however, during the crisis, it was supposed to have led to a severe overstatement of losses and the consequent 'destruction of capital'. Thus, the argument went, a vicious cycle ensued: falling asset prices led to accounting write-downs; the write-downs led to forced asset sales by institutions needing to meet capital adequacy requirements; and the forced sales exacerbated the fall in asset prices. In the US, moreover, critics singled out the other-than-temporary impairment standards for available-for-sale and held-to-maturity securities as being particularly 'destructive' because institutions were forced to take charges against earnings as a consequence of what they believed to be temporary 'market irrationality'.

Proponents of fair value accounting do not deny that indeed mark-to-market accounting shows the fluctuations of the market, but they maintain that these cycles are a fact of life and that the use of fair value accounting does not exacerbate these cycles. Moreover, they argue that fair value accounting standards provided 'early warning' signals by revealing the market's discomfort with inflated asset values. In their view, this contributed to a more timely recognition of problems and mitigation of the crisis.

---

[1] Report of the Financial Crisis Advisory Group, July 28, 2009

FIGURE 7.1 *(continued)*

Whatever the final outcome of the debate over fair value accounting, it is unlikely that, on balance, accounting standards led to an understatement of the value of financial assets. While the crisis may have led to some understatement of the value of mark-to-market assets, it is important to recognize that, in most countries, a majority of bank assets are still valued at historic cost using the amortized cost basis. Those assets are not marked to market and are not adjusted for market liquidity. By now it seems clear that the overall value of these assets has not been understated — but overstated. The incurred loss model for loan loss provisioning and difficulties in applying the model — in particular, identifying appropriate trigger points for loss recognition — in many instances has delayed the recognition of losses on loan portfolios. (The results of the US stress tests seem to bear this out.) Moreover, the off-balance sheet standards, and the way they were applied, may have obscured losses associated with securitizations and other complex structured products. Thus, the overall effect of the current mixed attribute model by which assets of financial institutions have been measured, coupled with the obscurity of off-balance sheet exposures, has probably been to understate the losses that were embedded in the system.

Even if the overall effect of accounting standards may not have been pro-cyclical, we consider it imperative that the weaknesses in the current standards be addressed as a matter of urgency. Improvements in accounting standards cannot 'cure' the financial crisis by resolving underlying economic and governance issues (for example, the massive overleveraging of the global economy, excessive risk taking, and the undercapitalization of the banking sector). However, as demonstrated by the positive market reaction to disclosure of the results of the US stress tests, improvements in standards that enhance transparency and reduce complexity can help restore the confidence of financial market participants and thereby serve as a catalyst for increased financial stability and sound economic growth. Conversely, any changes in financial reporting that reduce transparency and allow the impact of the crisis to be obscured would likely have the opposite effect, by further reducing the confidence of market participants and thereby prolonging the crisis or by laying the foundation for future problems.

Source: Financial Crisis Advisory Group (2009).

In sections 7.16 and 7.17 of this chapter we'll discuss the extent to which, by the end of 2011, the IASB had addressed the matters raised in this report.

Because IAS 32, IFRS 7 and IAS 39 are complex standards, this chapter aims to provide an overall explanation of the requirements. It emphasises those areas most commonly affecting the majority of reporting entities, and places less emphasis on specialised areas.

IAS 32 was developed before IAS 39. It set out the definitions of financial instruments, financial assets and financial liabilities, distinguished between financial liabilities and equity instruments, and prescribed detailed disclosures. The standard was developed separately from IAS 39 because consensus on the recognition, derecognition, measurement and hedging rules for financial instruments was difficult to achieve. Therefore, the standard setters first established classification and disclosure rules, anticipating that increased disclosure by reporting entities would provide more information, not only for users, but also for the standard setters. Increased disclosure helps to provide standard setters with information that assists in developing further standards.

In 2006, IAS 32 was renamed *Financial Instruments: Presentation* and a new standard, IFRS 7 *Financial Instruments: Disclosures*, was introduced, applicable to annual periods beginning on or after 1 January 2007. IFRS 7 contains many of the disclosure requirements that were originally in IAS 32 and also introduced a number of new requirements. It also includes some of the requirements that were in IAS 30 *Disclosures in the Financial Statements of Banks and Similar Financial Institutions* and supersedes that standard.

IAS 39 was originally based largely on the similar FASB standard in the United States, Statement of Financial Accounting Standards No. 133 (SFAS 133) *Accounting for Derivative Instruments and Hedging Activities*. FASB standards have historically been rule-based rather than principle-based, and this explains why IAS 39 is considerably more rule-based than other IASB standards. As IAS 39 was amended repeatedly during 2003 and 2004 and then again in 2008, it moved further away from SFAS 133 but still reflects many of the same rules.

Each standard is addressed separately in this chapter. IAS 32, IFRS 7 and IAS 39 each contain Application Guidance, which is abbreviated in this chapter as AG. IFRS 7 and IAS 39 also contain Implementation Guidance.

7.2 WHAT IS A FINANCIAL INSTRUMENT?

7.2.1 Definition of a financial instrument

IAS 32, paragraph 11, defines a financial instrument as:

> any contract that gives rise to a financial asset of one entity and a financial liability or equity instrument of another entity.

Financial assets and financial liabilities are terms defined in IAS 32 (see sections 7.3.1 and 7.3.2 of this chapter). Financial assets are defined from the perspective of the *holder* of the instrument, whereas financial liabilities and equity instruments are defined from the perspective of the *issuer* of the instrument.

An equity instrument is defined in paragraph 11 as:

> any contract that evidences a residual interest in the assets of an entity after deducting all of its liabilities.

The most common type of equity instrument is an ordinary share of a company. The holder of the shares is not entitled to any fixed return on or of its investment; instead, the holder receives the residual after all liabilities have been settled. This applies both to periodic returns (where dividends are paid after interest on liabilities has been paid) and capital returns (when a company is wound up, all liabilities are settled before shareholders are entitled to any return of their investment).

7.2.2 Two sides to the story

Note that the definition of a financial instrument is two-sided — the contract must always give rise to a financial asset of one party, with a corresponding financial liability or equity instrument of another party. For example, a contract that gives the seller of a product the right to receive cash from the purchaser creates a receivable for the seller (a financial asset) and a payable for the purchaser (a financial liability).

7.2.3 Common types of financial instruments

Financial instruments include primary instruments such as cash, receivables, investments and payables, as well as derivative financial instruments such as financial options and forward exchange contracts. Derivative financial instruments, or derivatives, are instruments that *derive* their value from another underlying item such as a share price or an interest rate. (The definition of a derivative is discussed in section 7.4 of this chapter.)

7.2.4 Contracts to buy or sell non-financial instruments

Financial instruments do *not* include non-financial assets such as property, plant and equipment, or non-financial liabilities such as provisions for restoration. Contracts to buy or sell non-financial items are also usually not financial instruments. Many commodity contracts fall into this category (contracts to buy or sell oil, cotton, wheat and so on). These commodity contracts are thus outside the scope of IAS 32. However, IFRS 7 requires reporting entities with commodity contracts that are within the scope of IAS 39 to follow the disclosure requirements of IFRS 7. Certain commodity contracts are, however, included within the scope of IAS 32. These include contracts to buy or sell non-financial items that can be settled net (in cash) or by exchanging financial instruments, or in which the non-financial item is readily convertible into cash. Contracts to buy or sell gold might fall into the latter category and hence might be caught by IAS 32 (IAS 32 paragraph 8) and IAS 39 (IAS 39 paragraph 5).

7.2.5 Other items that are *not* financial instruments

Note also that the definition of a financial instrument requires there to be a contractual right or obligation. Therefore liabilities or assets that are not contractual — such as income taxes that are created as a result of statutory requirements imposed by governments, or constructive obligations as defined in IAS 37 *Provisions, Contingent Liabilities and Contingent Assets* (see chapter 5) — are not financial instruments.

In addition, certain financial assets and liabilities lie outside the scope of the standard (IAS 32 paragraph 4). These include employee benefits accounted for under IAS 19, and investments in subsidiaries, associates and joint ventures that are accounted for under IFRS 10 *Consolidated Financial Statements*, IAS 27 *Separate Financial Statements*, IAS 28 *Investments in Associates and Joint Ventures* and IFRS 11 *Joint Arrangements*.

7.3 FINANCIAL ASSETS AND FINANCIAL LIABILITIES

7.3.1 Financial assets

A financial asset is defined in paragraph 11 of IAS 32 as follows:

any asset that is:
(a) cash;
(b) an equity instrument of another entity;
(c) a contractual right:
   (i) to receive cash or another financial asset from another entity; or
   (ii) to exchange financial assets or financial liabilities with another entity under conditions that are potentially favourable to the entity; or
(d) a contract that will or may be settled in the entity's own equity instruments and is:
   (i) a non-derivative for which the entity is or may be obliged to receive a variable number of the entity's own equity instruments; or
   (ii) a derivative that will or may be settled other than by the exchange of a fixed amount of cash or another financial asset for a fixed number of the entity's own equity instruments. For this purpose the entity's own equity instruments do not include puttable financial instruments classified as equity instruments in accordance with paragraphs 16A and 16B, instruments that impose on the entity an obligation to deliver to another party a pro rata share of the net assets of the entity only on liquidation and are classified as equity instruments in accordance with paragraphs 16C and 16D, or instruments that are contracts for the future receipt or delivery of the entity's own equity instruments.

Examples of common financial assets in each of the categories of the definition include:
(a) cash — either cash on hand or the right of the depositor to obtain cash from the financial institution with which it has deposited the cash
(b) an equity instrument of another entity — ordinary shares held in another entity, commonly known as share investments
(c) a contractual right
   (i) to receive cash or another financial asset — trade accounts receivable, notes receivable, loans receivable
   (ii) to exchange under potentially favourable conditions — an option held by the holder to purchase shares in a specified company at less than the market price.

Part (d) of the definition was added in amendments made to IAS 39 in 2003, 2004 and 2007. The amendments were made in response to issues arising from the classification of certain complex financial instruments as liabilities or equity. (Liability/equity classification is discussed in section 7.5 of this chapter.)

7.3.2 Financial liabilities

A financial liability is defined in paragraph 11 of IAS 32 as follows:

any liability that is:
(a) a contractual obligation:
   (i) to deliver cash or another financial asset to another entity; or
   (ii) to exchange financial assets or financial liabilities with another entity under conditions that are potentially unfavourable to the entity; or
(b) a contract that will or may be settled in the entity's own equity instruments and is:
   (i) a non-derivative for which the entity is or may be obliged to deliver a variable number of the entity's own equity instruments; or
   (ii) a derivative that will or may be settled other than by the exchange of a fixed amount of cash or another financial asset for a fixed number of the entity's own equity instruments. For this purpose, rights, options or warrants to acquire a fixed number of the entity's own equity instruments for a fixed amount of any currency are equity instruments if the entity offers the rights, options or warrants pro rata to all of its existing owners of the same class of its own non-derivative equity instruments. Also, for these purposes the entity's own equity instruments do not include puttable financial instruments that are classified as equity instruments in accordance with paragraphs 16A and 16B, instruments that impose on the entity an obligation to deliver to another party a pro rata share of the net assets of the entity only on liquidation and are classified as equity instruments in accordance with paragraphs 16C and 16D, or instruments that are contracts for the future receipt or delivery of the entity's own equity instruments.

As an exception, an instrument that meets the definition of a financial liability is classified as an equity instrument if it has all the features and meets the conditions in paragraphs 16A and 16B or paragraphs 16C and 16D.

Examples of common financial liabilities in each of the categories of the definition include:

(a) a contractual obligation
(i) to deliver cash or another financial asset — trade accounts payable, notes payable, loans payable
(ii) to exchange under potentially unfavourable conditions — an option written (i.e. issued) by the issuer to sell shares in a specified company at less than the market price.

Part (b) of the definition was added in amendments made to IAS 39 in 2003, 2004 and 2007. The amendments were made in response to issues arising from the classification of certain complex financial instruments as liabilities or equity. (Liability/equity classification is discussed in section 7.5 of this chapter.) Table 7.1 contains a summary of common financial instruments.

TABLE 7.1 Summary of common financial instruments		
Financial assets	**Financial liabilities**	**Equity instruments**
Cash	Bank overdraft	Ordinary shares
Accounts receivable	Accounts payable	Certain preference shares
Notes receivable	Notes payable	
Loans receivable	Loans payable	
Derivatives with potentially favourable exchange conditions	Derivatives with potentially unfavourable exchange conditions	
	Certain preference shares	

7.4 DEMYSTIFYING DERIVATIVES

The concept of a derivative may appear daunting because there are numerous derivative financial instruments in the market that seem complex and difficult to understand. However, as already noted, fundamentally all derivatives simply *derive* their value from another underlying item such as a share price or an interest rate. Derivative financial instruments create rights and obligations that have the effect of transferring between the parties to the instrument one or more of the financial risks inherent in an underlying primary financial instrument. On inception, derivative financial instruments give one party a contractual right to exchange financial assets or financial liabilities with another party under conditions that are potentially favourable, while the other party has a contractual obligation to exchange under potentially unfavourable conditions.

Figure 7.2 provides an option contract as an example of a derivative.

FIGURE 7.2 How an option contract works

An option contract

Party A buys an option that entitles it to purchase 1000 shares in Company Z at $3 a share, at any time in the next 6 months. The shares in Company Z are the *underlying* financial instruments from which the option derives its value. The option is thus the derivative financial instrument. The amount of $3 a share is called the *exercise price* of the *option*.

Party B sells the option to Party A. Party A is called the *holder* of the option, and Party B is called the *writer* of the option. Party A will usually pay an amount called a *premium* to purchase the option. The amount of the premium is less than what Party A would have to pay for the shares in Company Z.

Assume that at the date of the option contract the market price of shares in Company Z is $2.60.

The financial instrument created by this transaction is a contractual right of Party A to purchase the 1000 shares in Company Z at $3 a share (a financial asset of Party A), and a contractual obligation of Party B to sell the shares in Company Z to Party A at $3 a share (a financial liability of Party B). Party A's right is a financial asset because it has the right to exchange under potentially favourable conditions to itself. Thus, if the share price of Company Z rises above $3, Party A will exercise its

FIGURE 7.2 *(continued)*

option and require Party B to deliver the shares at $3 a share. Party A will have benefited from this transaction by acquiring the shares in Company Z at less than the market price. Conversely, Party B's obligation is a financial liability because it has the obligation to exchange under potentially unfavourable conditions to itself. Thus, if the shares in Company Z rise to $3.20, Party A will purchase the shares from Party B for $3000. If Party A had had to purchase the shares on the market, it would have paid $3200.

Party B may have made a loss from this transaction, depending on whether it already held the shares in Company Z, or had to go out and buy them for $3200 and then sell them to Party A for $3000, or had entered into other derivative contracts with other parties enabling it to purchase the shares at less than $3000.

What if the share price in Company Z never exceeds $2.60 over the 6-month term of the option? In this case, Party A will not exercise the option and the option will lapse. The option is termed 'out-of-the-money' from Party A's perspective — it has no value to Party A because the exercise price is higher than the market price. Once the share price rises above $3, the option is termed 'in-the-money'. Party A is not compelled to exercise its option, even if it is in-the-money. From Party A's perspective, it has a right to exercise the option should it so choose. However, if Party A exercises its option, Party B is then compelled to deliver the shares under its contractual obligation.

IAS 32, AG 17, notes that the nature of the holder's right and of the writer's obligation is not affected by the likelihood that the option will be exercised.

In simple terms, parties to derivative financial instruments are taking bets on what will happen to the underlying financial instrument in the future. In the example in figure 7.2, Party A was taking a bet that the share price in Company Z would rise above $3 within 6 months, and Party B was taking a bet that it would not. Party B would most likely hedge its bet by doing something to protect itself should the market price rise above $3. It could do this by entering into another derivative with another party, enabling Party B to purchase shares from that other party at $3. Often a chain of derivative financial instruments will be created in this way. Party A will probably not know anything about the chain created. (Hedging is discussed in section 7.15 of this chapter.)

IAS 32 does not prescribe recognition and measurement rules for derivatives; these are addressed in IAS 39. Instead, IAS 32 includes derivatives in the definition of financial instruments. Other types of derivatives include interest rate swaps, forward exchange contracts and futures contracts.

7.5 DISTINGUISHING FINANCIAL LIABILITIES FROM EQUITY INSTRUMENTS

IAS 32 is very prescriptive in the area of distinguishing between financial liabilities and equity instruments. This area, commonly known as the debt versus equity distinction, is of great concern to many reporting entities because instruments classified as liabilities rather than equity affect:

- a company's gearing and solvency ratios
- debt covenants with financial institutions (usually a requirement that specified financial ratios of the borrower do not exceed predetermined thresholds; if they do exceed the thresholds, the financial institution has a right to require repayment of the loan)
- whether periodic payments on these instruments are treated as interest or dividends
- regulatory requirements for capital adequacy (banks and other financial institutions are required by their regulators to maintain a certain level of capital, which is calculated by reference to assets and equity).

Accordingly, reporting entities are often motivated, when raising funds, to issue instruments that are classified as equity for accounting purposes. In the years since IAS 32 was first issued, many complex instruments were devised by market participants specifically to achieve equity classification under IAS 32. Some of these instruments were liabilities in substance but were able to be classified technically as equity, notwithstanding a 'substance over form' test in IAS 32. As a result, the standard setters amended IAS 32 in 2003–04 to create specific rules designed to address these complex instruments. Unfortunately, the rules are now more complicated than the instruments themselves, so this section will address the key principles of liability versus equity classification only.

7.5.1 The rules

IAS 32, paragraph 15, states:

> The issuer of a financial instrument shall classify the instrument, or its component parts, on initial recognition as a financial liability, a financial asset or an equity instrument in accordance with the substance of the contractual arrangement and the definitions of a financial liability, a financial asset and an equity instrument.

To avoid any doubt, paragraph 16 goes on to repeat and clarify the definition of a financial liability. It states that an instrument shall be classified as an equity instrument if, and only if, *both* conditions (a) and (b) below are met:

(a) The instrument includes no contractual obligation:
    (i) to deliver cash or another financial asset to another entity; or
    (ii) to exchange financial assets or financial liabilities with another entity under conditions that are potentially unfavourable to the issuer.
(b) If the instrument will or may be settled in the issuer's own equity instruments, it is:
    (i) a non-derivative that includes no contractual obligation for the issuer to deliver a variable number of its own equity instruments; or
    (ii) a derivative that will be settled only by the issuer exchanging a fixed amount of cash or another financial asset for a fixed number of its own equity instruments.

Part (a) is clearly referring to the definition of a financial liability. Part (b) helps to clarify the amendments to the definitions of a financial asset and a financial liability (discussed in section 7.3 of this chapter). In essence, the rules in part (b) are trying to establish who bears 'equity risk' in complex transactions where an entity issues a financial instrument that will or may be settled in its own shares.

The concept of equity risk is useful for both part (b) of the test and generally in determining whether an instrument is equity or a liability. Note, however, that part (a) of the test turns only on whether or not the issuer has a contractual obligation.

Part (a) of the equity/liability test: contractual obligation

The examples in figure 7.3 apply part (a) of the equity/liability test, together with the equity risk concept.

Paragraph 17 of IAS 32 reiterates that a critical feature in differentiating a financial liability from an equity instrument is the existence of a contractual obligation of the issuer. Paragraph 18 then goes on to state that the substance of a financial instrument, rather than its legal form, governs its classification on the entity's statement of financial position. Some financial instruments, such as the preference shares in example 3 of figure 7.3, take the legal form of equity but are liabilities in substance. Other financial instruments, such as the preference shares in example 4 of figure 7.3, may combine features associated with equity instruments and those associated with financial liabilities. Sometimes the combined features result in the financial instrument being split into its component parts (see section 7.6 of this chapter).

FIGURE 7.3 Applying part (a) of the equity/liability test

Example 1: Ordinary shares

Company A wants to raise funds of $1 million. It does so by issuing ordinary shares to the public. The holders of those shares are exposed to equity risk (they are not entitled to any fixed return on or of their investment, and receive the residual left over after all liabilities have been settled) in respect of both periodic payments and capital returns. If there is no profit after interest on liabilities and other contractual obligations have been paid, then there are no dividends. If, on winding up, there are no assets after all liabilities have been settled, there is nothing returned to the shareholders. This is the fundamental nature of equity risk. The ordinary shares issued by Company A are equity instruments of Company A. Under part (a) of the test, Company A has no contractual obligation to its ordinary shareholders.

Company A would record the following journal entry on initial recognition:

Cash (financial asset)	Dr	1 000 000
Ordinary Share Capital (equity)	Cr	1 000 000

FIGURE 7.3 *(continued)*

Example 2: Non-cumulative, non-redeemable preference shares

Company A decides to issue preference shares instead of ordinary shares. It issues one million preference shares for $1 each. Each preference shareholder is entitled to a non-cumulative dividend of 5% annually. (A non-cumulative dividend means that, if in any year a dividend is not paid, the shareholder forfeits it.) The preference shareholders rank ahead of ordinary shareholders on the winding-up of the company. The preference shares are non-redeemable (the holders of the shares cannot get their money back).

Under part (a) of the test, Company A has no contractual obligation to the preference shareholders, either to pay dividends or to return the cash. Therefore the preference shares are equity instruments of Company A. In addition, applying the concept of equity risk reveals that the preference shareholders are exposed to equity risk, although it is lower than for the ordinary shareholders.

Company A would record the following journal entry on initial recognition:

| Cash (financial asset) | Dr | 1 000 000 | |
| Preference Share Capital (equity) | Cr | | 1 000 000 |

Example 3: Cumulative, redeemable preference shares

Company A issues one million preference shares for $1 each, and each preference shareholder is entitled to a *cumulative* dividend of 5% annually. The preference shareholders rank ahead of ordinary shareholders on the winding-up of the company. The preference shares are redeemable for cash *at the option of the holder*.

Under part (a) of the test, Company A now has a contractual obligation to the preference shareholders — both in respect of dividends and to return the cash. Company A must pay the dividends and, if in any period it cannot pay, it must make up the payment with the next dividend. Furthermore, Company A must repay the money whenever the holder demands repayment. Therefore, the preference shares are financial liabilities of Company A. In addition, applying the concept of equity risk reveals that the preference shareholders are not exposed to equity risk — they are guaranteed a periodic return of 5% and they can require that their cash be returned. They bear the same risk as would a lender to the Company. A lender's risk is generally credit risk (the risk that Company A will fail to discharge its obligations) and liquidity risk (the risk that Company A will fail to raise funds to enable it to redeem the liability on demand).

Company A would record the following journal entry on initial recognition:

| Cash (financial asset) | Dr | 1 000 000 | |
| Preference Share Liability (financial liability) | Cr | | 1 000 000 |

Example 4: Cumulative, redeemable preference shares

Company A issues one million preference shares for $1 each, and each preference shareholder is entitled to a *cumulative* dividend of 5% annually. The preference shareholders rank ahead of ordinary shareholders on the winding-up of the company. The preference shares are redeemable for cash *at the option of Company A*.

Under part (a) of the test, Company A now has a contractual obligation to the preference shareholders, but only in respect of dividends. It cannot be required to return the cash, since redemption is at its own option. In addition, applying the concept of equity risk reveals that the preference shareholders are partially exposed to equity risk — they are guaranteed a periodic return of 5% but they cannot require that their cash be returned. IAS 32, AG 25, confirms that preference shares redeemable at the option of the issuer are not financial liabilities. IAS 32, AG 26, clarifies that, when preference shares are non-redeemable, the other rights that attach to them determine the appropriate classification. It states that when distributions, whether cumulative or non-cumulative, are at the discretion of the issuer, the shares are equity instruments.

However, neither AG 25 nor AG 26 is particularly useful in helping decide what to do if the distributions are not discretionary. Is it possible for the preference share to be part liability and part

(continued)

FIGURE 7.3 *(continued)*

equity? The answer, in theory, is yes. IAS 32 contains a section on compound financial instruments (discussed in section 7.6 of this chapter). In practice, though, such splitting of the instrument would be difficult to achieve. This is further complicated by having to split the 'dividend' into an interest component and a dividend component (see section 7.7). The discussion in AG 26 implies that cumulative dividends, on their own, would not be sufficient to cause a preference share to be classified as a liability, and that the overall substance of the arrangement must be considered. Unfortunately, it then goes on to give examples of where the distribution payments create a financial liability in substance, but says that even then the cumulative dividends do not create a liability. Therefore, in this example, the preference shares are equity instruments of Company A.

Company A would record the following journal entry on initial recognition:

Cash (financial asset)	Dr	1 000 000	
Preference Share Capital (equity)	Cr		1 000 000

Another example (added to IAS 32 in the 2003–04 revisions) of a financial instrument whose legal form may be equity but whose accounting classification is a financial liability is a puttable instrument. A puttable instrument gives the holder the right to put the instrument back to the issuer for cash or another financial asset. This is so even when the amount of cash/other financial asset is determined on the basis of an index or another amount that may increase or decrease. For example, certain mutual funds, unit trusts and partnerships provide their unit holders or members with a right to redeem their interests in the issuer at any time for cash equal to their proportionate share of the net asset value of the issuer. Traditionally, unit holder funds have been classified as equity because the legal form of their interest was equity. However, under paragraph 18 of the revised IAS 32, it is clear that these are financial liabilities. This caused a significant change to the presentation of financial statements for unit trusts. In 2008, the IASB amended IAS 32 to modify the definition of a financial liability so that such puttable instruments would not automatically result in liability classification.

Paragraphs 19 and 20 of IAS 32 go on to explain that an entity has a contractual obligation to deliver cash/other financial assets notwithstanding:

- any restrictions on the entity's ability to meet its obligation (such as access to foreign currency)
- that the obligation may be conditional on the counterparty exercising its redemption right (as in example 3 of figure 7.3 — redemption is at the option of the holder and therefore could be considered to be conditional on the holder exercising its right to redeem. However, this does not negate the fact that the issuer has a contractual obligation to redeem the shares, because it cannot avoid its obligation should it be required to redeem by the holder.)
- that the financial instrument does not explicitly establish a contractual obligation to deliver cash/other financial assets. A contractual obligation may be implied in the terms and conditions of the instrument. Unfortunately, the guidance in paragraph 20 contradicts the guidance on preference shares in AG 26. AG 26 states that non-redeemable preference shares are equity instruments, notwithstanding a term that prevents ordinary share dividends from being paid if the preference share dividend is not paid, or from being paid on the issuer's expectation of profit or loss for a period. A fairly common term in certain non-redeemable preference shares is that the dividend is 'discretionary' but, if the preference dividend is not paid, then ordinary dividends cannot be paid. If these terms exist in the preference shares of highly profitable companies, one could argue under paragraph 20 of IAS 32 that the implicit terms and conditions of the preference shares require the dividend to be paid. However, AG 26 states that such conditions do not create a financial liability of the issuer.

Part (b) of the equity/liability test: settlement in the entity's own equity instruments

Paragraph 21 of IAS 32 states that a contract is not an equity instrument solely because it may result in the receipt or delivery of the entity's own equity instruments. As noted earlier in this section, such an instrument can be classified as an equity instrument under paragraph 16(b) of IAS 32 only if it is:

(i) a *non*-derivative that includes *no* contractual obligation for the issuer to deliver a *variable* number of its own equity instruments; or

(ii) a derivative that will be settled only by the issuer exchanging a *fixed* amount of cash or another financial asset for a *fixed* number of its own equity instruments.

Part (i) will be examined first. Assume listed Company A has an obligation to deliver to Party B as many of Company A's own ordinary shares as will equal $100 000. The number of shares that Company A will have to issue will vary depending on the market price of its own shares. If Company A's shares are each worth $1 at the date of settlement of the contract, it will have to deliver 100 000 shares. If Company A's shares are each worth 50c at the date of settlement of the contract, it will have to deliver 200 000 shares. Company A has a contractual obligation at all times to deliver $100 000 to Party B; that is, the value is fixed, and so the number of shares to be delivered will vary. Therefore, Company A's financial instrument fails the test in part (i) and the instrument is a financial liability. Applying the concept of equity risk, the *holder* of the financial instrument (Party B) is not exposed to equity risk because it will always receive $100 000 regardless of the market price of Company A's shares. A true equity risk-taker will be exposed to share price fluctuations — this reflects the residual nature of an equity risk-taker's investment.

Now examine part (ii). Assume listed Company A issues a share option to Party B that entitles Party B to buy 100 000 shares in Company A at $1 each in 3 months' time. This financial instrument meets the conditions for equity classification under part (ii) because it is a derivative that will be settled by issuing a fixed number of shares for a fixed amount. Assume that, at the date of the grant of the option, Company A's share price is $1. If in 3 months' time Company A's share price exceeds $1, Party B will exercise its option and Company A must issue its shares to Party B for $100 000. If, however, in 3 months' time Company A's share price falls below $1, Party B will not exercise its option and Company A will not issue any shares. Applying the concept of equity risk reveals that the *holder* of the financial instrument (Party B) is exposed to equity risk because it is not guaranteed to receive $100 000 in value. Whether or not it receives $100 000 is entirely dependent on the market price of Company A's shares. As a true equity risk-taker, it is exposed to share price fluctuations; this reflects the residual nature of an equity risk-taker's investment. Party B will have paid a premium to Company A for the option. Paragraph 22 of IAS 32 states that this premium is added directly to Company A's equity, consistent with the classification of the instrument as an equity instrument.

7.5.2 Contingent settlement provisions and settlement options

Sometimes, when a financial instrument requires an entity to deliver cash/other financial assets, the terms of settlement are dependent on the occurrence or non-occurrence of uncertain future events that are beyond the control of both the issuer and the holder. Examples of such events include changes in a share market index, the consumer price index or the issuer's future revenues. The issuer of such an instrument does not have the unconditional right to avoid delivering the cash/other financial assets, so paragraph 25 of IAS 32 requires such instruments to be classified as financial liabilities unless they meet certain rare exceptions. For example, assume that Company A issues preference shares to Party B, the terms of which entitle Party B to redeem the preference shares for cash if Company A's revenues fall below a specified level. Because neither Company A nor Party B can control the level of Company A's revenues, the settlement provision is considered to be contingent. However, because Company A cannot avoid repaying Party B should Company A's revenues fall below the specified level, Company A does not have an unconditional right to avoid repayment. Thus the preference shares are a financial liability of Company A.

It is common for financial instruments to contain a choice of settlement. For example, preference shares may be redeemed for cash or for the issuer's ordinary shares. Sometimes the choice is the issuer's; sometimes it is the holder's. Paragraph 26 of IAS 32 requires that, when a *derivative* financial instrument gives one party a choice over how it is settled, it is a financial asset or a financial liability unless all of the settlement alternatives would result in it being an equity instrument. An example is a share option that the issuer can decide to settle net in cash or by exchanging its own shares for cash. Because not all of the settlement options would result in an equity instrument being issued, the option must be classified as a financial asset or liability. Note that the likely outcome is not taken into account; the fact that cash settlement may be required is sufficient to create a financial asset or liability.

Paragraph 26 does not address *non-derivative* financial instruments. Therefore, where a non-derivative financial instrument such as a preference share may be redeemed for cash or for the issuer's own ordinary shares, paragraph 26 does not apply. Instead, paragraph 16 would be applied to determine whether or not there is (a) a contractual obligation to deliver cash/other financial assets, or (b) a contractual obligation to deliver a variable number of the issuer's ordinary shares. Note that both (a) and (b) must be answered in the negative for equity classification to apply. So, for example, if the *issuer* of the preference share has the option to redeem for cash or for a variable number of its ordinary shares, the first question to ask is: Does the issuer have a contractual obligation to deliver cash? If redemption is at the issuer's option, the issuer has *no* contractual obligation to redeem *at all* and therefore arguably the second question about the number of ordinary shares is irrelevant. Indeed, paragraph 16(b) asks whether or not the issuer has a contractual obligation to deliver a variable number of its own shares and, since redemption is at the issuer's option, it has no such contractual obligation, even though the number of shares that potentially will be issued is variable. Therefore, all other things being equal, the preference shares will be classified as equity. On the other hand, if redemption is at the *holder's* option, the instrument would be classified as a liability, because the issuer has a contractual obligation to deliver cash/other financial assets or ordinary shares because the holder has the right to call for redemption. This is so even if the number of ordinary shares is fixed, because the holder's right to redeem for cash means that paragraph 16(a) is met.

 LO6

7.6 COMPOUND FINANCIAL INSTRUMENTS

Paragraph 28 of IAS 32 requires an issuer of a non-derivative financial instrument to determine whether it contains both a liability and an equity component. Such components must be classified separately as financial liabilities, financial assets or equity instruments.

Paragraph 29 goes on to explain that this means that an entity recognises separately the components of a financial instrument that (a) creates a financial liability of the entity, and (b) grants an option to the holder of the instrument to convert it into an equity instrument of the entity. A common example of such a financial instrument is a convertible bond or note that entitles the holder to convert the note into a fixed number of ordinary shares of the issuer. From the perspective of the *issuer*, such an instrument comprises two components: (a) a financial liability, being a contractual obligation to deliver cash/other financial assets in the form of interest payments and redemption of the note; and (b) an equity instrument, being an option issued to the holder entitling it to the right, for a specified period of time, to convert the note into a fixed number of ordinary shares of the issuer. Note that the number of shares to be issued must be fixed, otherwise the option would not meet the definition of an equity instrument under paragraph 16(b) as discussed on pages 221–5.

Classification of the liability and equity components is made on initial recognition of the financial instrument and is not revised as a result of a change in the likelihood that the conversion option may be exercised. This is because, until such time as the conversion option is either exercised or lapses, the issuer has a contractual obligation to make future payments.

How does the issuer measure the separate liability and equity components? Paragraphs 31 and 32 of IAS 32 prescribe that the financial liability must be calculated first, with the equity component by definition being the residual. The example in figure 7.4 illustrates how this is done.

FIGURE 7.4 A convertible note, allocating the components between liability and equity

Example 5: Compound financial instrument — a convertible note

Company A issues 2000 convertible notes on 1 July 2013. The notes have a 3-year term and are issued at par with a face value of $1000 per note, giving total proceeds at the date of issue of $2 million. The notes pay interest at 6% annually in arrears. The holder of each note is entitled to convert the note into 250 ordinary shares of Company A at any time up to maturity.

When the notes are issued, the prevailing market interest rate for similar debt (similar term, similar credit status of issuer and similar cash flows) without conversion options is 9%. This rate is higher than the convertible note's rate because the holder of the convertible note is prepared to accept a lower interest rate given the implicit value of its conversion option.

The issuer calculates the contractual cash flows using the market interest rate (9%) to work out the value of the holder's option, as follows:

Present value of the principal: $2 million payable in 3 years' time:	$ 1 544 367
Present value of the interest: $120 000 ($2 million × 6%) payable annually in arrears for 3 years	303 755
Total liability component	1 848 122
Equity component (by deduction)	151 878
Proceeds of the note issue	$ 2 000 000

FIGURE 7.4 *(continued)*

The journal entries at the date of issue are as follows:

Cash	Dr	2 000 000	
Financial Liability	Cr		1 848 122
Equity	Cr		151 878

The equity component is not remeasured (IAS 32 paragraph 22) and thus remains at $151 878 until the note is either converted or redeemed. If the note is converted, the remaining liability component is transferred to equity. If the note is redeemed, the equity component remains in equity despite redemption.

Source: Adapted from IAS 32, Illustrative Example 9, paragraphs IE35–IE36.

7.6.1 Putting it all together

The liability/equity distinction rules in IAS 32 can rarely be applied in isolation. Unfortunately, IAS 32 does not contain a clear hierarchy to assist in determining which rules take precedence. Is it the substance over form rule in paragraph 15? Is it the definition rule in paragraph 15? Is it the contractual obligation rule in paragraph 16? Is it the 'settlement in own equity' rules? Is it the settlement options or contingent settlement provisions rules? Is it the components rule in paragraph 28?

Take our redeemable preference shares in example 4 of figure 7.3. Company A issued one million preference shares for $1 each, and each preference shareholder is entitled to a *cumulative* dividend of 5% annually. The preference shareholders rank ahead of ordinary shareholders on the winding-up of the company. The preference shares are redeemable for cash *at the option of Company A*. Assume that a few more terms and conditions have been added. Instead of the shares being redeemable only for cash, they are redeemable for cash or *for a fixed number of ordinary shares* at the option of Company A, at any time after 5 years. The shares also contain a conversion option, entitling the holder to convert to a fixed number of ordinary shares of Company A at any time up to 5 years. In addition, although the dividends are cumulative, they can be paid only if Company A's profit exceeds $250 000, indexed annually.

Table 7.2 helps to answer the questions, taking each set of 5 years separately.

TABLE 7.2 Applying the various liability/equity rules as a whole		
Liability/equity rules	**First 5 years**	**After 5 years**
Contractual obligation to deliver cash?	No	No (issuer's option)
Contractual obligation to exchange under potentially unfavourable conditions?	No	No
Derivative or non-derivative?	Non-derivative	Non-derivative
If a non-derivative, contractual obligation to deliver shares?	Yes (holder's option to convert)	No (issuer's option to redeem)
Are shares to be delivered fixed or variable?	Fixed, therefore equity classification	Fixed
If a derivative, settled by fixed cash/fixed number of shares?	N/A	N/A
Contingent settlement provisions?	Yes — the dividends are paid only if profit targets are met[1]	Yes — the dividends are paid only if profit targets are met

(continued)

TABLE 7.2 (continued)

Liability/equity rules	First 5 years	After 5 years
If a derivative, terms of settlement options?	N/A	N/A
Compound financial instrument?	Yes — holder has the option to convert to a fixed number of ordinary shares	No
Substance over form?	Equity[2]	Equity
Classification	Equity	Equity

Notes:
1. Under paragraph 25 of IAS 32, the dividend conditions meet the contingent settlement definition and would require liability classification, but AG 26 refutes this by stating that the dividends are at the discretion of the issuer.
2. Although the instrument is a compound instrument for the first 5 years, there is no liability component because the substance of the entire instrument is equity given the other terms and conditions. This assumes that the dividend payments are discretionary. Therefore no splitting into component parts is required.

7.7 INTEREST, DIVIDENDS, GAINS AND LOSSES

Paragraph 35 of IAS 32 requires the statement of profit or loss and other comprehensive income classification of items relating to financial instruments to match their statement of financial position classification. Thus, statement of profit or loss and other comprehensive income items relating to financial liabilities and financial assets are classified as income or expenses, or gains or losses. These are usually interest expense, interest income and dividend income. Distributions to holders of equity instruments are debited directly to equity. Usually these are dividends. These principles also apply to the component parts of a compound financial instrument.

Table 7.3 summarises these principles.

TABLE 7.3 Classification of revenues, expenses and equity distributions

Statement of financial position classification	Statement of profit or loss and other comprehensive income classification	Statement of changes in equity
Equity instrument		Dividends distributed
Financial liability	Interest expense	
Financial asset	Interest income, dividend income	

The transaction costs of an equity transaction are deducted from equity, but only to the extent to which they are incremental costs directly attributable to the equity transaction that otherwise would have been avoided (IAS 32 paragraph 37). Examples of such costs include registration and other regulatory fees, legal and accounting fees and stamp duties. These costs are required to be shown separately under IAS 1 *Presentation of Financial Statements*.

7.8 OFFSETTING A FINANCIAL ASSET AND A FINANCIAL LIABILITY

Paragraph 42 of IAS 32 states that a financial asset and a financial liability shall be offset and the net amount presented when, and only when, an entity:

(a) currently has a legally enforceable right to set off the recognised amounts; and
(b) intends either to settle on a net basis, or to realise the asset and settle the liability simultaneously.

The underlying rationale of this requirement is that when an entity has the right to receive or pay a single net amount and intends to do so, it has effectively only a single financial asset or financial liability.

Note that the right of set-off must be legally enforceable and therefore usually stems from a written contract between two parties. In rare cases, there may be an agreement between three parties allowing a debtor to apply an amount due from a third party against the amount due to a creditor. Assume, for example, that Company A owes Company B $1000, and Company Z owes Company A $1000. Company A has therefore recorded in its books the following:

Amount Receivable from Company Z	Dr	1 000
Amount Owing to Company B	Cr	1 000

Provided there is a legal right of set-off allowing Company A to offset the amount owing to Company B against the amount owed by Company Z, the amounts may be offset in Company A's accounts. Both Company B and Company Z must be parties to this legal right of set-off with Company A.

The conditions for offsetting are strict and essentially require written legal contracts resulting in net cash settlement. Many arrangements that create 'synthetic' (manufactured) offsetting are not permitted under IAS 32. Paragraph 49 provides examples of common cases where offsetting is not permitted.

7.9 DISCLOSURES

IFRS 7 contains many pages dealing with disclosures, but only relatively few 'black letter' requirements. This chapter does not address these requirements in detail, and readers are expected to have a general understanding of the requirements only.

The purpose of the disclosure requirements is to provide information to enhance understanding of the significance of financial instruments to an entity's financial position, performance and cash flows; and to assist in assessing the amounts, timing and certainty of future cash flows associated with those instruments.

Transactions in financial instruments may result in an entity assuming or transferring to another party one or more of the financial risks described in table 7.4. The purpose of the required disclosures is to assist users in assessing the extent of such risks related to financial instruments.

TABLE 7.4 Financial risks pertaining to financial instruments	
Type of risk	**Description**
Market risk	• *Currency risk* — the risk that the value of a financial instrument will fluctuate because of changes in foreign exchange rates • *Interest rate risk* — the risk that the value of a financial instrument will fluctuate because of changes in market interest rates. For example, the issuer of a financial liability that carries a fixed rate of interest is exposed to decreases in market interest rates, such that the issuer of the liability is paying a higher rate of interest than the market rate. • *Other price risk* — the risk that the value of a financial instrument will fluctuate as a result of changes in market prices (other than those arising from interest rate risk or currency risk) Market risk embodies the potential for both loss and gain.
Credit risk	The risk that one party to a financial instrument will fail to discharge an obligation and cause the other party to incur a financial loss
Liquidity risk	The risk that an entity will encounter difficulty in meeting obligations associated with financial liabilities. This is also known as funding risk. For example, as a financial liability approaches its redemption date, the issuer may experience liquidity risk if its available financial assets are insufficient to meet its obligations.

Illustrative examples are included in Ernst & Young's publication, *IFRS 7 Financial Instruments: Disclosures*, *second edition* (2007).

IFRS 7 applies to all entities for all types of financial instruments, other than those specifically excluded from its scope. Scope exclusions include:
• interest in subsidiaries, associates and joint ventures accounted for under IFRS 10, IAS 27, or IAS 28
• employers' rights and obligations arising from employee benefit plans, to which IAS 19 *Employee Benefits* applies

- insurance contracts as defined in IFRS 4 *Insurance Contracts*
- share-based payment transactions to which IFRS 2 *Share-based Payment* applies.

IFRS 7 applies to both recognised and unrecognised financial instruments. For example, loan commitments not within the scope of IAS 39 are within the scope of IFRS 7.

IFRS 7 requires disclosure of financial instruments grouped by *class*. A class of financial instrument is a lower level of aggregation than a category, such as 'available-for-sale' or 'loans and receivables' (see section 7.12). For example, government debt securities, equity securities, or asset-backed securities could all be considered classes of financial instruments (see Ernst & Young (2007)).

IFRS 7 is divided into two main sections. The first section requires disclosure of the significance of financial instruments for financial position and performance. These disclosures are grouped into:

1. the statement of financial position
2. the statement of profit or loss and other comprehensive income
3. other disclosures.

The second section requires disclosure about the nature and extent of risks arising from financial instruments. These include both quantitative and qualitative disclosures. The risks are grouped into the three categories noted above, that is, market risk, credit risk and liquidity risk. The Application Guidance (paragraph B6) states that these risk disclosures shall be given either in the financial statements or incorporated by cross-reference from the financial statements to some other statement, such as a management commentary or risk report.

Examples of the types of disclosures required in each of the sections are provided in tables 7.5 and 7.6.

TABLE 7.5 Significance of financial instruments for financial position and performance

Statement of financial position

Overall requirement	Summary of details required
Categories of financial assets and financial liabilities (paragraph 8)	• The carrying amount of specified categories, as defined in IAS 39, for example, financial assets at fair value through profit or loss, held-to-maturity investments.
Financial assets or financial liabilities at fair value through profit or loss (paragraphs 9, 10 and 11)	• If an entity has designated loans or receivables at fair value through profit or loss, specified details are required including the maximum exposure to credit risk, the amount by which any credit derivatives or similar instruments mitigate that exposure, the amount of the change in fair value that is attributable to changes in the credit risk and the amount of the change in the fair value of any credit derivatives or similar instruments. • If an entity has designated a financial liability at fair value through profit or loss, specified details are required including the amount of the change in fair value that is attributable to changes in the credit risk and the difference between the carrying amount of the liability and the amount the entity would be contractually required to pay at maturity. An example of this would be a long-dated financial liability whose creditworthiness has deteriorated.
Reclassification (paragraph 12)	• Disclosure is required of the amount and reason for reclassification to or from the cost or amortised cost and fair value categories (see section 7.14.3).
Derecognition (paragraph 13)	• Specified disclosures are required where an entity has transferred financial assets in such a way that part or all of the financial assets do not qualify for derecognition.
Collateral (paragraphs 14 and 15)	• Collateral given: an entity must disclose the carrying amount of financial assets it has pledged as collateral (security) for liabilities or contingent liabilities. The terms and conditions of the pledge must also be disclosed. • Collateral received: specified details must be disclosed where an entity holds collateral (of financial and non-financial assets) and is permitted to sell or repledge that collateral.

TABLE 7.5 *(continued)*

Overall requirement	Summary of details required
Allowance for credit losses (paragraph 16)	• When financial assets are impaired by credit losses and the entity records the impairment in a separate account (rather than deducting the loss directly from the asset concerned), it must disclose a reconciliation of that account.
Compound financial instruments with multiple embedded derivatives (paragraph 17)	• Disclosure is required of the existence of such features in compound financial instruments.
Defaults and breaches (paragraphs 18 and 19)	• For loans payable, disclosure is required of any defaults during the period, the carrying amount of loans payable in default at the end of the reporting period and whether the default was remedied before the financial statements were authorised for issue.
Statement of profit or loss and other comprehensive income	
Items of income, expense, gains or losses (paragraph 20)	• Net gains or losses for each category of financial asset and financial liability. • Total interest income and total interest expense for financial assets or liabilities that are not at fair value through profit or loss. • Fee income and expense arising from financial assets or liabilities not at fair value through profit or loss, and from trust and other fiduciary activities. • Interest income on impaired financial assets. • The amount of any impairment loss for each class of financial asset.

It should be noted that IFRS 7 does not prescribe how statement of profit or loss and other comprehensive income amounts are determined. For example, interest income on financial instruments carried at fair value through profit or loss may be included in total interest income or it may be included in net gains or losses for that category.

TABLE 7.6 Significance of financial instruments for other disclosures

Other disclosures	
Overall requirement	**Summary of details required**
Accounting policies (paragraph 21)	• Disclose relevant accounting policies. Where the accounting methods are prescribed in the relevant standards (e.g. in IAS 39) then the entity should not repeat these but rather disclose where it has applied choices available, for example, what criteria it used in designating financial assets as available-for-sale, or what criteria it used to determine whether there is objective evidence of impairment of financial assets.
Hedge accounting (paragraphs 22, 23 and 24)	• For each type of hedge identified in IAS 39 (i.e. fair value hedges, cash flow hedges and hedges of net investments in foreign operations), disclose a description of each type, the financial instruments designated as hedging instruments and their fair values at the reporting date and the nature of the risks being hedged. • Additional details are required for cash flow hedges, including the periods when the cash flows are expected to occur, forecast transactions not expected to occur, the ineffectiveness recognised in profit or loss and the amount recognised in and removed from equity during the period. • Additional details are required for fair value hedges: the gains or losses on the hedging instrument and on the hedged item.
Fair value (paragraphs 25–30)	• For each class of financial assets and liabilities, disclose the fair value of that class in a way that permits it to be compared with its carrying amount. • Disclose the methods and assumptions used in determining fair value.

(continued)

TABLE 7.6 *(continued)*

Overall requirement	Summary of details required
	• If fair values are determined using valuation techniques (rather than quoted market prices) a sensitivity analysis is required. This means the entity is required to quantify the effect on profit or loss if one or more of the assumptions used, if changed, would change fair value significantly. • Other details are required in respect of gains or losses arising on initial recognition of certain financial instruments.

Table 7.7 shows the disclosure requirements for the risks arising from financial instruments.

TABLE 7.7 Nature and extent of risks arising from financial instruments

Qualitative disclosures

Overall requirement	Summary of details required
For each type of risk (credit risk, liquidity risk and market risk) disclose... (paragraph 33)	(a) the exposures to risk and how they arise (b) the entity's objectives, policies and processes for managing the risk and the methods used to measure the risk (c) any changes in (a) or (b) from the previous period. The policies and processes an entity uses would normally include the structure and organisation of its risk management function, the policies for hedging or otherwise mitigating risks, processes for monitoring hedge effectiveness, and policies and processes for avoiding large concentrations of risk.
For each type of risk (credit risk, liquidity risk and market risk) disclose... (paragraph 34)	(a) summary quantitative data about its exposure to that risk at the end of the reporting period. This disclosure must be based on the information provided internally to key management personnel of the entity (as defined in IAS 24 *Related Party Disclosures*) (b) the disclosures required by paragraphs 36–42 (see below) to the extent not provided in (a) (c) concentrations of risk if not apparent from (a) and (b). AG B8 states that concentrations of risk arise from financial instruments that have similar characteristics and are affected similarly by changes in economic or other conditions. For example, a risk concentration may be by geographic area, by industry or by currency.
Credit risk — disclose by class of financial instrument... (paragraph 36)	(a) the amount that best represents its maximum exposure to credit risk at the end of the reporting period without taking into account any collateral held (this amount would typically be the gross carrying amount of the asset, after deduction of any impairment losses) (b) a description of any collateral held in (a) (c) information about the credit quality of financial assets that are neither past due (past due is defined in appendix A as being when a counterparty has failed to make a payment when contractually due) or impaired
Credit risk — financial assets that are either past due or impaired, disclose by class of financial asset... (paragraph 37)	(a) an analysis of the age of financial assets that are past due as at the end of the reporting period but not impaired (b) an analysis of financial assets that are individually determined to be impaired as at the end of the reporting period
Credit risk — collateral and other credit enhancements obtained (paragraph 38)	Specified details are required to be disclosed when an entity obtains financial or non-financial assets during the period by taking possession of collateral it holds as security.

TABLE 7.7 (continued)	
Overall requirement	**Summary of details required**
Liquidity risk (paragraph 39)	(a) a maturity analysis for financial liabilities that shows the remaining contractual maturities (b) a description of how the entity manages the liquidity risk inherent in (a). An entity must use judgement to determine the appropriate time bands for a maturity analysis, that is, for when amounts fall due. For example, an entity might determine that the following time bands are appropriate: • not later than 1 month • between 1 month and 3 months • between 3 months and 6 months • later than 6 months. The Application Guidance (B11D) states that the amounts disclosed in the maturity analysis must be the contractual undiscounted cash flows. This could be problematic for liabilities that mature later than 1 year because the amounts disclosed in the note would likely not reconcile to the statement of financial position where the discounted amount would be shown. Examples of how an entity might manage liquidity risk include: • having access to undrawn loan commitments • holding readily liquid financial assets than can be sold to meet liquidity needs • having diverse funding sources.
Market risk — sensitivity analysis (paragraphs 40 and 41)	An entity must disclose (a) for each type of market risk (i.e. currency risk, interest rate risk and other price risk) a sensitivity analysis showing how profit or loss or equity would have been affected by changes in the relevant risk variable that were reasonably possible at the end of the reporting period (b) the methods and assumptions used in preparing the sensitivity analysis (c) changes from the previous period in the methods and assumptions used. For example, if an entity has a floating interest rate (i.e. variable) liability at the end of the year, the entity would disclose the effect on interest expense for the current year if interest rates had varied by reasonably possible amounts. This effect could be disclosed as a range, for example, the entity could state that had the interest rate varied by between 0.25–0.5% then total interest expense would have increased by an amount of between \$xx and \$xy. If an entity prepares a sensitivity analysis that analyses the interdependencies between market risk variables (e.g. between interest rate risk and currency risk) then it need not make the disclosures in (a) but must rather disclose its own interdependent risk analysis.

 ## 7.10 THE SCOPE OF IAS 39 *FINANCIAL INSTRUMENTS: RECOGNITION AND MEASUREMENT*

The stated objective of IAS 39 (see paragraph 1) is to establish principles for recognising and measuring financial assets, financial liabilities and some contracts to buy or sell non-financial items. Arguably, IAS 39 establishes rules rather than principles. Because the standard is very complex, particularly in its application to financial institutions, this chapter addresses only the more common applications of IAS 39 and aims to provide a general understanding of its requirements.

7.10.1 The exceptions

IAS 39 applies to all entities and to all types of financial instruments, with ten exceptions set out in paragraph 2. The exceptions in themselves are complicated, so only an overview of them will be provided. The exceptions are:

1. Investments in subsidiaries, associates and joint ventures that are accounted for under IFRS 10, IFRS 11 or IAS 28. However, certain investments in such entities may be accounted for under IAS 39 if so permitted

by IAS 27 or IAS 28. For example, IAS 27 permits investments in subsidiaries, associates and joint ventures to be carried at cost or, under IAS 39, in the investor's own separate (not consolidated) financial statements. Also, investments in subsidiaries, associates and joint ventures are measured under IFRS 5 *Non-current Assets Held for Sale and Discontinued Operations* if they are held exclusively for disposal.

2. Rights and obligations under leases to which IAS 17 *Leases* applies. However, certain lease receivables and finance lease payables are subject to the derecognition and impairment provisions of IAS 39. Also, embedded derivatives in leases are subject to IAS 39.

3. Employers' rights and obligations under employee benefit plans to which IAS 19 *Employee Benefits* applies.

4. Rights and obligations arising under insurance contracts, with certain exceptions. Insurance contracts are covered by their own standard, but contracts issued by insurers that are not insurance contracts (such as investment contracts) are covered by IAS 39. Contracts that require a payment based on climatic, geological or other physical variables are commonly used as insurance policies and payment is made based on the amount of loss to the insured entity. These contracts are caught by the standard on insurance contracts and are outside the scope of IAS 39 under this exemption. However, if the payment under the contract is unrelated to the insured entity's loss, then IAS 39 applies. IAS 39 also covers embedded derivatives in such contracts.

5. Financial instruments issued by the entity that meet the definition of an equity instrument in IAS 32. This applies only to the *issuer* of the equity instrument. The *holder* of such an instrument will have a financial asset that is covered by IAS 39.

6. Financial guarantee contracts, such as letters of credit, that provide for specified payments to be made to reimburse the holder of the contract for a loss it incurs because a specified debtor fails to make payment when due under a debt instrument are measured either under IFRS 4 *Insurance Contracts* or IAS 39 at the election of the issuer.

7. Loan commitments that cannot be settled net in cash or another financial instrument, unless the loan commitment is measured at fair value through profit or loss (see section 7.12 of this chapter) under IAS 39, in which case it is covered by IAS 39. Loan commitments outside the scope of IAS 39 are measured under IAS 37.

8. Contracts between an acquirer and a vendor in a business combination to buy or sell an acquiree at a future date.

9. Financial instruments to which IFRS 2 *Share-based Payment* applies.

10. Rights to payments to reimburse the entity for expenditure it is required to make to settle a liability that it recognises as a liability under IAS 37.

As discussed in section 7.2.4 of this chapter, contracts to buy or sell *non-financial* items are generally not financial instruments. Certain commodity contracts are, however, included within the scope of IAS 32. These include contracts to buy or sell non-financial items that can be settled net (in cash) or by exchanging financial instruments, or in which the non-financial item is readily convertible into cash.

7.10.2 'Own use' contracts

Similarly, IAS 39 includes within its scope contracts to buy or sell *non*-financial items that can be settled net (in cash) or by another financial instrument, or by exchanging financial instruments. The exception to this is contracts entered into and that continue to be held for the purpose of the receipt or delivery of a non-financial item in accordance with the entity's expected purchase, sale or usage requirements (paragraph 5).

For example, an entity may enter into a contract to buy a machine in 2 months' time for $50 000. The entity places an order and agrees to pay cash for the machine on standard credit terms after delivery. This contract is a contract for the purchase of a non-financial item and is settled *gross* in cash. The entity would not record any liability to pay for the machine until delivery of the machine because, until that time, it does not have a contractual obligation to pay the supplier since the supplier has *not* yet supplied the machine. Such a contract is outside the scope of IAS 39. However, if the entity is owed an amount of $45 000 by the supplier, and agrees to settle the purchase of the machine *net* by paying $5000 on delivery, IAS 39 catches the contract. Under IAS 39, the entity has a financial liability at the date of entering into the contract even though the machine has not yet been delivered.

The required journal entry on initial recognition of the amount owing by the supplier would be:

| Amount Owed by Supplier | Dr | 45 000 | |
| Revenue | Cr | | 45 000 |

At the date of entering into the contract to settle net, the journal entry would be:

Right to Receive Machine	Dr	5 000	
Financial Liability	Cr		5 000

On delivery of the machine, the journal entries would be:

Cost of Machine	Dr	45 000	
Amount Owed by Supplier	Cr		45 000
Financial Liability	Dr	5 000	
Cash	Cr		5 000
Cost of Machine	Dr	5 000	
Right to Receive Machine	Cr		5 000

This accounting would be required unless the entity can prove that the contract was entered into and continues to be held for the purpose of the receipt or delivery of a non-financial item in accordance with the entity's expected purchase, sale or usage requirements. In the example above this would usually be the case. However, ideally, such terms should be explicitly written into these contracts in order to avoid any doubt.

This example shows how far reaching the scope of IAS 39 is and demonstrates that it applies to contracts equally proportionately unperformed (where both parties to the contract have equal unperformed rights and obligations) unless they are specifically scoped out. Traditionally, contracts equally proportionately unperformed have not been accounted for. Common examples of such contracts are normal purchase and sale agreements, such as the purchase of the machine described above. A purchaser does not usually account for the right to receive a machine and the corresponding obligation to pay for it at the date of making a purchase order. Similarly, the supplier does not usually account for the right to receive payment for the machine, and a corresponding obligation to deliver it, at the date of receiving the purchase order. Both parties commence recognition at the date of delivery, which is the date at which the equally unperformed rights and obligations are performed. IAS 39 clearly requires accounting on a rights and obligations basis unless the contracts giving rise to those rights and obligations are scoped out of the standard — hence the scoping out of normal purchases and sales of non-financial items. However, as soon as the contract becomes something other than normal, with terms that embody financial assets and liabilities (as in the example above), a rights-and-obligations approach is required.

 7.11 DERIVATIVES AND EMBEDDED DERIVATIVES

7.11.1 Three required characteristics

Paragraph 9 of IAS 39 defines a derivative. As explained in section 7.4 of this chapter, derivatives *derive* their value from another underlying item such as a share price or an interest rate. The definition requires *all* of the following three characteristics to be met:
- its value must change in response to a change in an underlying variable such as a specified interest rate, price, or foreign exchange rate
- it must require no initial net investment or an initial net investment that is smaller than would be required for other types of contracts with similar responses to changes in market factors
- it is settled at a future date.

7.11.2 Examples of derivatives

Typical examples of derivatives are futures and forward, swap and option contracts. A typical option contract was discussed in section 7.4. A derivative usually has a notional amount, which is an amount of currency, a number of shares or other units specified in a contract. However, a derivative does not require the holder or writer to invest or receive the notional amount at the inception of the contract. In the example in figure 7.2, where Party A buys an option that entitles it to purchase 1000 shares in Company Z at $3 a share at any time in the next 6 months, the 1000 shares is the notional amount. However, a notional amount is not an essential feature of a derivative. For example, a contract may require a fixed payment of $2000 if a specified interest rate increases by a specified percentage. Such a contract is a derivative even though there is no notional amount (IAS 39, AG 9).

Many option contracts require a premium to be paid to the writer of the option. The premium is less than what would be required to purchase the underlying shares or other underlying financial instruments and thus option contracts meet the definition of a derivative.

7.11.3 Embedded derivatives

Derivatives may exist on a stand-alone basis, or they may be embedded in other financial instruments. An embedded derivative is a component of a combined (or 'hybrid') instrument that also includes a non-derivative host contract, with the effect that some of the cash flows of the combined instrument vary in a way similar to a stand-alone instrument (IAS 39 paragraph 10). An embedded derivative cannot be contractually detached from the host contract, nor can it have a different counterparty from that of the host instrument.

For example, section 7.6 of this chapter showed that a common example of a compound financial instrument is a convertible bond or note that entitles the holder to convert the note into a fixed number of ordinary shares of the issuer. From the perspective of the *issuer*, such an instrument comprises two components: (a) a financial liability, being a contractual obligation to deliver cash/other financial assets in the form of interest payments and redemption of the note; and (b) an equity instrument, being an option issued to the holder entitling it to the right, for a specified period of time, to convert the note into a fixed number of ordinary shares of the *issuer*. The equity instrument is an embedded derivative. The issuer of the convertible note records the embedded derivative as an equity instrument under IAS 32 and this is specifically excluded from the scope of IAS 39 (paragraph 2(d)). The holder of the convertible note records the embedded derivative, being a derivative embedded in its financial asset, under IAS 39.

Separation of embedded derivatives

Paragraph 11 of IAS 39 requires an embedded derivative to be separated from the host contract if, and only if, the following three conditions are met:
- the economic characteristics and risks of the embedded derivative are *not closely related* to the economic characteristics and risks of the host contract
- a separate instrument with the same terms as the embedded derivative would meet the definition of a derivative
- the combined instrument is not measured at fair value through profit or loss. This means that a derivative embedded in a combined financial instrument measured at fair value through profit or loss is not separated, even if it could be separated. This is because the separated embedded derivative would be required to be measured at fair value through profit or loss anyway.

If an embedded derivative is separated, it is generally required to be measured at fair value. If fair value cannot be reliably measured, then the entire contract must be measured at fair value through profit or loss (IAS 39 paragraphs 12 and 9).

The following are examples of instruments where the economic characteristics and risks of the embedded derivative are *not closely related* to the economic characteristics and risks of the host contract:
- a put option embedded in a debt instrument that allows the holder to require the issuer to reacquire the instrument for an amount of cash that varies on the basis of the change in an equity or commodity price or index. This is because the host is a debt instrument and the variables are not related to the debt instrument
- an equity conversion feature embedded in a host convertible debt instrument (as discussed in section 7.6 of this chapter)
- an option to extend the remaining term to maturity of a debt instrument without a concurrent adjustment to the market rate of interest at the time of the extension
- commodity-indexed interest or principal payments embedded in a host debt instrument or insurance contract by which the amount of interest or principal is indexed to the price of the commodity (such as gold).

IAS 39, AG 30, contains other examples of such instruments. AG 33 goes on to give examples of instruments where the economic characteristics and risks of the embedded derivative *are* closely related to the economic characteristics and risks of the host contract. These examples are very prescriptive and not clearly principle-based.

LO12 7.12 **THE FOUR CATEGORIES OF FINANCIAL INSTRUMENTS**

The four categories of financial instruments are set out in paragraph 9 of IAS 39. Table 7.8 summarises the requirements of paragraph 9 and provides common examples of financial instruments likely to fall into each of the four categories.

TABLE 7.8 The four categories of financial instruments

Category	Characteristics	Other requirements	Examples
A financial asset or financial liability *at fair value through profit or loss*	(a) It is classified as *held for trading*; or (b) Upon initial recognition it *is designated by the entity as at fair value through profit or loss.* Any financial asset or financial liability may be so designated, provided certain conditions are met, except for investments in equity instruments that do not have a quoted market price.	In order to be classified as held for trading, a financial asset or financial liability must be: (i) acquired or incurred principally for the purpose of selling or repurchasing it in the near term; (ii) part of a portfolio of identified financial instruments that are managed together and for which there is evidence of a recent actual pattern of short-term profit-taking; or (iii) a derivative (except for a derivative that is a financial guarantee contract or a hedging instrument).	Share portfolio held for short-term gains; forward exchange contract; interest rate swap; call option
Held-to-maturity investments	(a) Are *non-derivative* financial assets with *fixed or determinable payments and fixed maturity*; and (b) The entity has the *positive intention and ability to hold these investments to maturity.*	Excludes investments • designated as at fair value through profit or loss • designated as available-for-sale • that meet the definition of loans and receivables. Note that the ability to designate an investment as held-to-maturity relies heavily on management intent. Accordingly, IAS 39 contains a 'punishment' for managers who do not act according to their intent: if an entity sells or reclassifies more than an insignificant amount of held-to-maturity investments during the current financial year or the two preceding financial years, then the entity shall not classify any financial assets as held-to-maturity.	Commercial bill investments; government bonds; corporate bonds; converting notes (that will convert at a fixed date in future); fixed-term/maturity debentures
Loans and receivables	*Non-derivative* financial assets with *fixed or determinable payments* that are *not quoted* in an active market	Excludes loans and receivables: • designated as at fair value through profit or loss • intended to be sold in the near term, which must be classified as held-for-trading • designated as available-for-sale • those for which the holder may not recover substantially all of its initial investment, other than because of credit deterioration, which must be classified as available-for-sale.	Accounts receivable; loans to other entities; mortgage loans (financial institutions); credit card receivables
Available-for-sale financial assets	*Non-derivative financial assets* that are designated as available-for-sale and do not fall into any of the above three categories		Ordinary share investments; convertible notes; preference share investments

Note that only the first category in table 7.8 is applicable to financial assets and financial liabilities. All the other categories apply to financial assets only.

 7.13 THE RECOGNITION CRITERIA

Paragraph 14 of IAS 39 states that an entity shall recognise a financial asset or a financial liability on its statement of financial position when, and only when, the entity becomes a party to the contractual provisions of the instrument. (This requirement to recognise rights and obligations arising under contractual agreements was discussed in section 7.10.2 of this chapter.) AG 35 provides other examples of applying the recognition criteria, as follows:

- Unconditional receivables and payables are recognised as assets or liabilities when the entity becomes a party to the contract and, as a consequence, has a legal right to receive or a legal obligation to pay cash. Normal trade debtors and trade creditors would fall into this category.
- Assets to be acquired and liabilities to be incurred under a firm commitment to purchase or sell goods or services are generally not recognised until at least one of the parties has performed under the agreement. However, this is subject to the rules set out in the scope paragraph of IAS 39 (discussed in section 7.10 of this chapter). Thus, if a firm commitment to buy or sell non-financial items is within the scope of IAS 39, its net fair value is recognised as an asset or liability on the commitment date.
- A forward contract within the scope of the standard is also recognised as an asset or liability at the commitment date. When an entity becomes party to a forward contract, the rights and obligations at the commitment date are often equal, so that the net fair value of the forward is zero. The example in figure 7.5 illustrates how a forward foreign exchange contract is accounted for on initial recognition.

Accounting for a forward foreign exchange contract on initial recognition

Company A enters into a forward foreign exchange contract with Company B to receive US$10 000 in 3 months' time, at a forward rate of A$1.00 = US$0.70.

At the date of entering into the contract, the exchange rate (the spot rate at that date) was A$1.00 = US$0.68.

At the date of entering into the contract, Company A must recognise its rights and obligations under the contract, which are:
- a right to receive US$10 000 at the forward rate in 3 months' time, which equals A$14 285
- an obligation to pay for the US$10 000 in 3 months' time by delivering A$14 285.

Accordingly, Company A records the following journal entries on initial recognition:

| Forward Foreign Exchange Receivable | Dr | 14 285 | |
| Forward Foreign Exchange Payable | Cr | | 14 285 |

However, because the net fair value of the contract is zero on initial recognition, no asset or liability is recognised.

FIGURE 7.5 Accounting for a forward foreign exchange contract on initial recognition

Note the following:
- Option contracts within the scope of the standard are recognised as assets or liabilities when the holder or writer becomes a party to the contract.
- Planned future transactions, no matter how likely, are not assets and liabilities because the entity has not become a party to a contract.

 7.14 MEASUREMENT

The measurement rules in IAS 39 address:
1. initial measurement
2. subsequent measurement
3. reclassifications

4. gains and losses

5. impairment and uncollectability of financial assets.

The rules are applied distinctly to each of the four categories of financial instruments discussed in section 7.12 of this chapter.

7.14.1 Initial measurement

Paragraph 43 of IAS 39 requires that, on initial recognition, financial assets and financial liabilities must be measured at fair value. Fair value is defined in paragraph 9 as:

> the price that would be received to sell an asset or paid to transfer a liability in an orderly transaction between market participants at the measurement date. (See IFRS 13.)

The concept of fair value is discussed in chapter 3 of this book.

In addition, paragraph 43 requires that transaction costs directly attributable to the acquisition or issue of the financial asset or liability must be added to the fair value, except for financial assets and liabilities measured at fair value through profit or loss. Transaction costs are defined in paragraph 9 as:

> incremental costs that are directly attributable to the acquisition, issue or disposal of a financial asset or financial liability (see Appendix A paragraph AG13). An incremental cost is one that would not have been incurred if the entity had not acquired, issued or disposed of the financial instrument.

IAS 39, AG 13, provides further guidance. Examples of transaction costs include fees and commissions paid to agents, advisers, brokers and dealers; levies by regulatory agencies and securities exchanges; and transfer taxes and duties (such as stamp duties). Transaction costs do not include debt premiums or discounts, financing costs or internal administrative or holding costs.

The fair value of a financial instrument on initial recognition is normally the transaction price (the fair value of the consideration given or received). However, if part of the consideration given or received is for something other than the financial instrument, then the fair value must be estimated using valuation techniques. For example, if a company provides an interest-free loan to its employees, part of the consideration is given in the form of recognition of employee services or loyalty rather than for the entire loan itself. The fair value of the loan must be calculated by discounting the future cash flows using a market rate of interest for a similar loan (similar as to currency, term and credit rating). Any additional amount lent is accounted for as an expense unless it qualifies for recognition as some other type of asset. Figure 7.6 provides an example.

Initial measurement of an interest-free loan

Company Z provides interest-free loans to 10 employees for a 5-year term, payable at the end of 5 years. The total loan amount is $200 000. A market rate of interest for a similar 5-year loan is 5%. The present value of this receivable, being the future cash flows discounted at 5%, is approximately $157 000. Therefore, $43 000 is an expense to Company Z on initial recognition of the loan.

Company Z would record the following journal entries:

Loans Receivable	Dr	157 000	
Expenses	Dr	43 000	
Cash	Cr		200 000

FIGURE 7.6 Initial measurement of an interest-free loan

7.14.2 Subsequent measurement

Subsequent measurement depends on whether or not the item is a financial asset or financial liability, and on which of the categories applies.

Financial assets are measured as follows (IAS 39 paragraph 45):

1. 'At fair value through profit or loss' — at fair value. This includes all derivatives, other than those subject to the hedge accounting rules (see section 7.15 of this chapter).

2. Held-to-maturity investments — at amortised cost.

3. Loans and receivables — at amortised cost.

4. Available-for-sale financial assets — at fair value.

An exception is given for investments in equity instruments that do not have a quoted market price in an active market and whose fair value cannot be measured reliably. Such equity instruments, and any linked derivatives, must be measured at cost. Furthermore, if any of these financial assets are hedged items, they are subject to the hedge accounting measurement rules (see section 7.15 of this chapter).

Amortised cost is defined in paragraph 9 of IAS 39 as follows:

> the amount at which the financial asset or financial liability is measured at initial recognition minus principal repayments, plus or minus the cumulative amortisation using the effective interest method of any difference between that initial amount and the maturity amount, and minus any reduction (directly or through the use of an allowance account) for impairment or uncollectibility.

The effective interest method is defined in paragraph 9 as:

> a method of calculating the amortised cost of a financial asset or a financial liability . . . and of allocating the interest income or interest expense over the relevant period.

The effective interest rate is defined in paragraph 9 as:

> the rate that exactly discounts estimated future cash payments or receipts through the expected life of the financial instrument or, when appropriate, a shorter period to the net carrying amount of the financial asset or financial liability.

The effective interest rate must be calculated considering all contractual terms of the instrument. It includes all fees, transaction costs, premiums and discounts. (A calculator with a finance function is needed to calculate the effective interest rate.)

Illustrative example 7.1 provides an example of how amortised cost is calculated.

ILLUSTRATIVE EXAMPLE 7.1   Calculation of amortised cost (based on IAS 39, Implementation Guidance B.26)

Company A purchases a debt instrument with a 5-year term for its fair value of $1000 (including transaction costs). The instrument has a principal amount of $1250 (the amount payable on redemption) and carries fixed interest of 4.7% annually. The annual cash interest income is thus $59 ($1250 × 0.047). Using a financial calculator, the effective interest rate is calculated as 10%. The debt instrument is classified as a held-to-maturity investment.

The following table sets out the cash flows and interest income for each period, using the effective interest rate of 10%:

A. Year	B. Amortised cost at beginning of year	C. Interest income $(B \times 10\%)$	D. Cash flows	E. Amortised cost at end of year $(B + C - D)$
2012	1 000	100	59	1 041
2013	1 041	104	59	1 086
2014	1 086	109	59	1 136
2015	1 136	113	59	1 190
2016	1 190	119	59 + 1 250	—

The journal entries to record this transaction on initial recognition and throughout the life of the instrument are as follows:

On initial recognition in 2012:

Held-to-Maturity Investment	Dr	1 000
Cash	Cr	1 000

On recognition of interest in 2012:

Held-to-Maturity Investment	Dr	41
Cash	Dr	59
Interest Income	Cr	100

On recognition of interest in 2013:

Held-to-Maturity Investment	Dr	45	
Cash	Dr	59	
Interest Income	Cr		104

On recognition of interest in 2014:

Held-to-Maturity Investment	Dr	50	
Cash	Dr	59	
Interest Income	Cr		109

On recognition of interest in 2015:

Held-to-Maturity Investment	Dr	54	
Cash	Dr	59	
Interest Income	Cr		113

On recognition of interest in 2016:

Held-to-Maturity Investment	Dr	60	
Cash	Dr	59	
Interest Income	Cr		119

On redemption of investment in 2016:

Cash	Dr	1 250	
Held-to-Maturity Investment	Cr		1 250

Financial liabilities are measured subsequent to initial recognition at amortised cost except for those designated as 'at fair value through profit or loss', which must be measured at fair value (IAS 39 paragraph 47). There are four exceptions to this rule:
1. Derivative liabilities linked to investments in equity instruments that do not have a quoted market price in an active market and whose fair value cannot be measured reliably. Such linked derivatives must be measured at cost. This mirrors the exemption for derivative assets.
2. Financial liabilities arising in certain circumstances when a financial asset is transferred under the derecognition rules. These are outside the scope of this chapter.
3. Financial guarantee contracts (see section 7.10). These are initially measured at fair value and subsequently at the *higher* of
   (i) the amount determined in accordance with IAS 37 and
   (ii) the amount initially recognised less, where appropriate, cumulative amortisation recognised in accordance with IAS 18 *Revenue*.
   A common example of a financial guarantee contract is when a parent company guarantees the debts of its subsidiary to an external financier. The parent undertakes to pay the financier in the event that the subsidiary is unable to pay.
4. Commitments to provide a loan at a below-market interest rate. The measurement rules are the same as for (3) above.
   If any of these financial liabilities are hedged items, they are subject to the hedge accounting measurement rules (see section 7.15 of this chapter).
   Illustrative example 7.2 provides an example of a financial liability measured at amortised cost.

Company L enters into an agreement with Company B to lend it $1 million (plus transaction costs of $25 000) on 1 July 2012. The interest to be paid is 5% for each of the first 2 years and 7% for each of the next 2 years, annually in arrears. The loan must be repaid after 4 years. The annual cash interest expense is thus $50 000 ($1 million $\times$ 0.05) for each of the first 2 years and $70 000 ($1 million $\times$ 0.07) for each of the next 2 years. Using a financial calculator, the effective interest rate is calculated as 6.67%. Company B measures the financial liability at fair value on initial recognition and subsequently at amortised cost in accordance with IAS 39, paragraphs 43 and 47.

The following table sets out the cash flows and interest expense for each period, using the effective interest rate of 6.67%.

A. Year	B. Amortised cost at beginning of year	C. Interest expense ($B \times 6.67\%$)	D. Cash flows	E. Amortised cost at end of year ($B + C - D$)
2012	975 000	65 014	50 000	990 014
2013	990 014	66 015	50 000	1 006 029
2014	1 066 029	67 083	70 000	1 003 112
2015	1 003 112	66 888	70 000 + 1 000 000	—

The journal entries to record this transaction on initial recognition and throughout the life of the instrument in the books of Company B are as follows:

On initial recognition in 2012:

Cash	Dr	975 000	
Bond – Liability	Dr	25 000	
Bond – Liability	Cr		1 000 000

On recognition of interest in 2012:

Interest Expense	Dr	65 014	
Bond – Liability	Cr		15 014
Cash	Cr		50 000

On recognition of interest in 2013:

Interest Expense	Dr	66 015	
Bond – Liability	Cr		16 015
Cash	Cr		50 000

On recognition of interest in 2014:

Interest Expense	Dr	67 083	
Bond – Liability	Dr	2 917	
Cash	Cr		70 000

On recognition of interest in 2015:

Interest Expense	Dr	66 888	
Bond – Liability	Dr	3 112	
Cash	Cr		70 000

On repayment of liability in 2015:

Interest Expense	Dr	0	
Bond – Liability	Dr	1 000 000	
Cash	Cr		1 000 000

7.14.3 Reclassifications

IAS 39 contains various prescriptive rules on the reclassification of financial instruments. The rules are aimed at preventing inconsistent gain or loss recognition and the use of arbitrage between the categories. In summary:

- Paragraph 50 of IAS 39 generally requires that an entity shall not reclassify a financial instrument into or out of the fair value through profit or loss category while it is held or issued.
- Held-to-maturity items can or must be reclassified to the available-for-sale category. This may occur because of a change in management's intention, or because of breaking the rules allowing held-to-maturity classification (see table 7.8).
- In rare circumstances, a financial instrument may be reclassified from a fair value measurement basis to a cost basis. These are set out in paragraph 54.

In response to the financial crisis of 2007–08, in October 2008, the IASB approved and published amendments to IAS 39 and IFRS 7 to allow reclassifications of certain financial assets (1) out of the 'fair value through profit or loss' category to either the loan and receivables, available-for-sale or held-to-maturity categories, and (2) out of the 'available-for-sale' category to the loans and receivables or held-to-maturity categories. The rationale for these amendments was that, because of the lack of liquidity in financial markets, certain financial assets that were primarily traded in active markets could no longer be so traded.

The amendments (in paragraphs 50A–50F of IAS 39) were made in response to requests by regulators to enable banks to record financial assets that are no longer traded in an active market at amortised cost. The IASB suspended its normal due process in order to make the amendments quickly as it was under intense pressure to do so.

Strict conditions needed to be met in order for these new reclassifications to be made. The effective date of the amendments was 1 July 2008.

7.14.4 Gains and losses

A gain or loss arising from the change in fair value or otherwise of a financial instrument that is *not* part of a hedging relationship (see section 7.15 of this chapter) is recognised, in accordance with the four categories, as follows (IAS 39 paragraph 55):

1. 'At fair value through profit or loss' — in profit or loss.
2. Held-to-maturity investments — in profit or loss. This occurs when the asset is derecognised or impaired, and through the amortisation process.
3. Loans and receivables — in profit or loss. This occurs when the asset is derecognised or impaired, and through the amortisation process.
4. Available-for-sale financial assets — directly in equity, through the statement of changes in equity. When the financial instrument is derecognised, the cumulative amount remaining in equity is removed from equity and 'recycled' back to profit or loss. This rule is subject to four exceptions, all of which must be recognised in profit or loss:
    (a) impairment losses
    (b) foreign exchange gains and losses
    (c) interest calculated using the effective interest rate method
    (d) dividends on available-for-sale equity instruments.

7.14.5 Impairment and uncollectability of financial assets

Paragraph 58 of IAS 39 states that an entity shall assess at each balance date whether there is *objective evidence* that a financial asset is impaired. Objective evidence includes observable data about the following loss events (IAS 39 paragraphs 58–61):

(a) significant financial difficulty of the issuer
(b) a breach of contract or default in interest or principal payments

(c) a lender granting concessions to the borrower that the lender would not otherwise consider

(d) it becoming probable that a borrower will enter bankruptcy or other financial reorganisation (such as administration)

(e) the disappearance of an active market for the financial asset because of financial difficulties

(f) observable data indicating that there is a measurable decrease in the estimated future cash flows from a group of financial assets since the original recognition of those assets. This applies mainly to large groups of receivables where companies determine whether a provision for doubtful debts is required for the group. Traditionally, entities such as banks have made a 'general provision' for impairment of a group of receivables because individual customers in that group are relatively small. IAS 39 limits the creation of such general provisions to circumstances where there are observable and directly correlating data. Such data may include, for example, an increased number of delayed payments or customers reaching their maximum credit limit in the group; national or local economic conditions that correlate with defaults on the assets within the group, such as a decrease in property prices for mortgages in the relevant area; a decrease in oil prices for loans to oil producers; or an increase in the unemployment rate in the geographical area of the borrowers

(g) in respect of investments in equity instruments, significant changes with an adverse effect that have taken place in the technological, market, economic or legal environment in which the issuer operates.

Under paragraph 60, the following events are *not*, on their own, objective evidence that a financial asset is impaired:

(a) the disappearance of an active market because an entity's financial instruments are no longer actively traded

(b) a downgrade of an entity's credit rating

(c) a decline in the fair value of a financial asset below its cost/amortised cost. For example, a decline in the fair value of an investment in a fixed-term *debt instrument* that results from an increase in the risk-free interest rate does not necessarily mean that the investment is impaired, if the investment is being held to maturity. However, a significant or prolonged decline in the fair value of an investment in an *equity instrument* below its cost *is* objective evidence of impairment.

Impairment losses are recognised, in accordance with the four categories, as follows (IAS 39 paragraphs 63–70):

(a) 'At fair value through profit or loss' — not applicable — the impairment rules do not apply to such instruments.

(b) Held-to-maturity investments — the amount of the loss is measured as the difference between the asset's carrying amount and the present value of expected future cash flows discounted at the asset's original effective interest rate. The carrying amount of the asset is reduced either directly or through use of an allowance account (traditionally termed a 'provision'). The amount of the loss must be recognised in profit or loss. An impairment loss should be reversed only if there is objective evidence of an event after the impairment was recognised, such as an improvement of the debtor's credit rating. The reversal is recognised in profit or loss. The reversal must not result in the carrying amount of the asset exceeding what the amortised cost would have been had the impairment not been recognised at the date the impairment is reversed.

(c) Loans and receivables — as for held-to-maturity investments.

(d) Available-for-sale financial assets — the cumulative loss that has been recognised directly in equity must be removed from equity and recognised in profit or loss. This includes any decline in fair value already recognised in equity plus the impairment loss. Reversals of impairment losses are permitted only for investments in *debt* instruments. The requirement for objective evidence of a reversal is the same as for categories (b) and (c) above, but there is no limit on the upward reversal because the asset is measured at fair value. Reversals of impairment losses for investments in *equity* instruments through profit or loss are not permitted. Effectively, this means that the cost of the equity investment must be reset at the impaired value, and any future upward changes in fair value must be recorded directly in equity.

Once a financial asset has been written down as a result of an impairment loss, interest income is recognised thereafter using the rate of interest used to discount the future cash flows for the purpose of measuring the impairment loss (IAS 39, AG 93).

Illustrative example 7.3 builds on illustrative example 7.1 by demonstrating the calculation of an impairment loss for a held-to-maturity investment.

Company A purchases a debt instrument with a 5-year term for its fair value of $1000 (including transaction costs). The instrument has a principal amount of $1250 (the amount payable on redemption) and carries fixed interest of 4.7% annually. The annual cash interest income is thus $59 ($1250 × 0.047). Using a financial calculator, the effective interest rate is calculated as 10%. The debt instrument is classified as a held-to-maturity investment. During 2014, the issuer of the instrument is in financial difficulties and it becomes probable that the issuer will be put into administration by a receiver. The fair value of the instrument is estimated to be $636 at the end of 2014, calculated by discounting the expected future cash flows at 10%. No cash flows are received during 2015. At the end of 2015, the issuer is released from administration and Company A receives a letter from the receiver stating that the issuer will be able to meet all of its remaining obligations, including interest and repayment of principal.

The following table sets out the cash flows and interest income for each period, using the effective interest rate of 10%:

A. Year	B. Amortised cost at beginning of year	C. Interest income (B × 10%)	D. Cash flows	E. Amortised cost at end of year (B + C − D)
2012	1 000	100	59	1 041
2013	1 041	104	59	1 086
2014	1 086	109	59	1 136
2015	1 136	113	59	1 190
2016	1 190	119	59 + 1 250	—

The journal entries for 2012, 2013 and 2014 are the same as set out in illustrative example 7.1. At the end of 2014, Company A records the following journal entry:

| Expense (profit or loss) | Dr | 500 | |
| Held-to-Maturity Investment | Cr | | 500 |

The asset's carrying value is now $636:

A. Year	B. Amortised cost, less impairment losses, at beginning of year	C. Interest income (B × 10%)	D. Cash flows	E. Amortised cost at end of year (B + C − D)
2015	636	64	—	700

During 2015, Company A records interest as 10% of $636 in accordance with IAS 39, paragraph AG 93:

| Held-to-Maturity Investment | Dr | 64 | |
| Interest Income | Cr | | 64 |

At the end of 2015, Company A has objective evidence that the impairment loss has been reversed. The limit on the amount of the reversal is what the amortised cost of the asset would have been at the date of reversal had the impairment loss not been recorded. According to the first table above, this amount would have been $1190 at the end of 2015. The asset's carrying value at the end of 2015 was $700, so the reversal of the impairment loss is $490 ($1190 − $700). The journal entry is as follows:

| Held-to-Maturity Investment | Dr | 490 | |
| Income (profit or loss) | Cr | | 490 |

The journal entries for 2016 are then the same as shown in illustrative example 7.1.

Illustrative example 7.4 shows the calculation of an impairment loss on an available-for-sale investment in a debt instrument and in an equity instrument.

ILLUSTRATIVE EXAMPLE 7.4 Impairment loss on an available-for-sale investment

Part A: In a debt instrument

Company A invests in a debt instrument on 1 July 2012. At this date, the cost and fair value of the instrument is $100 000. The instrument is classified as available-for-sale and so is measured at fair value, and changes in fair value are recorded directly in equity. The following table sets out the changes in the fair value of the debt instrument, and the nature of the change in each year.

Year	Fair value change	Nature of change
2013	($10 000)	No objective evidence of impairment
2014	($20 000)	Objective evidence of impairment
2015	$15 000	Objective evidence of reversal of impairment

The journal entries (ignoring interest income) recorded by Company A are shown below:

On initial recognition on 1 July 2012:

Available-for-Sale Investment	Dr	100 000	
Cash	Cr		100 000

Change in fair value for 2013:

Equity	Dr	10 000	
Available-for-Sale Investment	Cr		10 000

Impairment loss for 2014:

Expense (profit or loss)	Dr	30 000	
Available-for-Sale Investment	Cr		20 000
Equity	Cr		10 000

(The above entry is necessary because paragraph 67 of IAS 39 requires the cumulative loss recognised in equity to be transferred to profit or loss.)

Reversal of impairment loss in 2015:

Available-for-Sale Investment	Dr	15 000	
Income (profit or loss)	Cr		15 000

Part B: In an equity instrument

Assume exactly the same facts as in part A, except that the investment is in an equity instrument. All the journal entries will be the same, except for the entry in 2015, which will be as follows:

Increase in fair value in 2015 (not a reversal of an impairment loss):

Available-for-Sale Investment	Dr	15 000	
Equity	Cr		15 000

7.14.6 Summary of the measurement rules of IAS 39

Table 7.9 summarises the measurement rules of IAS 39 discussed earlier in this section of the chapter.

TABLE 7.9 Summary of the measurement rules in IAS 39

Category of financial asset/ liability	Initial measurement	Subsequent measurement	Reclassifications	Gains and losses	Impairment
A financial asset or financial liability *at fair value through profit or loss*	Fair value	Fair value, unless a hedging instrument[1] or hedged item	Not permitted except in limited specified circumstances	Recognised in profit or loss, unless a hedging instrument[1] or hedged item	Not applicable
Held-to-maturity investments	Fair value plus transaction costs	Amortised cost, unless a hedged item	May or must be reclassified to available-for-sale	Recognised in profit or loss, unless a hedged item	Loss, recognised in profit or loss. Reversal of impairment loss permitted subject to conditions. Limit on extent of reversal.
Loans and receivables	Fair value plus transaction costs	Amortised cost, unless a hedged item	Not permitted	Recognised in profit or loss, unless a hedged item	Loss, recognised in profit or loss. Reversal of impairment loss permitted subject to conditions. Limit on extent of reversal.
Available-for-sale financial assets	Fair value plus transaction costs	Fair value, unless a hedged item	Permitted in rare circumstances	Recognised in equity, unless a hedged item. Four exceptions where gains/losses must be recognised in profit or loss. Amounts in equity are recycled to profit or loss when the asset is derecognised	Loss, recognised in profit or loss. This includes any decline in fair value already recorded in equity. Reversal of impairment loss permitted only for debt investments, subject to conditions. No limit on extent of reversal. Reversal of impairment loss through profit or loss prohibited for equity investments.
Other financial liabilities	Fair value plus transaction costs with four exceptions	Amortised cost, unless a hedged item	Not permitted	Recognised in profit or loss, unless a hedged item	Not applicable

Note:
1. This category includes derivatives that may be effective hedging instruments. The financial assets in the other categories may be hedged items (the item being hedged) but cannot be hedging instruments.

7.15 HEDGE ACCOUNTING

Entities enter into hedge arrangements for economic reasons; namely, to protect themselves from the types of risks discussed in section 7.9 — currency risk, fair value interest rate risk, price risk and so on. Hedge accounting generally results in a closer matching of the statement of financial position effect with the profit or loss effect, and protects the statement of profit or loss and other comprehensive income from volatility caused by changes in fair value from period to period. The hedge accounting rules in IAS 39 are very prescriptive. They are best put into perspective by remembering that the standard is based heavily on

SFAS 133, and that the standard's implicit preference is for fair value measurement so that, in order to qualify for hedge accounting, entities need to meet strict specified criteria.

Two important concepts need to be understood:
1. the hedging instrument
2. the hedged item.

7.15.1 The hedging instrument

Paragraph 9 of IAS 39 defines a hedging instrument as:

> a designated derivative or (for a hedge of the risk of changes in foreign currency exchange rates only) a designated non-derivative financial asset or non-derivative financial liability whose fair value or cash flows are expected to offset changes in the fair value or cash flows of a designated hedged item...

An instrument must meet eight essential criteria for it to be classified as a hedging instrument:
1. It must be *designated* as such. This means that management must document the details of the hedging instrument and the item it is hedging, at the inception of the hedge.
2. It *must* be a *derivative* unless criterion 3 is met.
3. It is hedging *foreign currency* exchange risk, in which case it can be a non-derivative.
4. It must be expected to *offset changes* in the fair value or cash flows of the hedged item.
5. It must be with a party *external* to the reporting entity — external to the consolidated group or individual entity being reported on (paragraph 73). There is one exception to this rule in respect of intra-group monetary items when certain conditions are met (paragraph 80).
6. It *cannot be split* into component parts, except for separating the time value and intrinsic value in an option contract, and the interest element and spot price in a forward contract (paragraph 74).
7. A proportion of the entire hedging instrument, such as 50% of the notional amount, may be designated as the hedging instrument. However, a hedging relationship may *not be designated for only a portion of the time* period during which the hedging instrument remains outstanding (paragraph 75).
8. A single hedging instrument may be designated as a hedge of more than one type of risk provided that (a) the risks hedged can be identified clearly, (b) the effectiveness of the hedge can be demonstrated, and (c) there is specific designation of the hedging instrument and different risk positions (paragraph 76).

Examples of hedging instruments are forward foreign currency exchange contracts, interest rate swaps and futures contracts. Written options cannot be hedging instruments of the writer because the potential exposure to loss is greater than the potential gain on the hedged item (IAS 39, AG 94), so they do not meet criterion 4.

7.15.2 The hedged item

IAS 39 provides the following definitions:
- a hedged item (paragraph 9)

  > an asset, liability, firm commitment, highly probable forecast transaction or net investment in a foreign operation that (a) exposes the entity to risk of changes in fair value or future cash flows and (b) is designated as being hedged...

- a forecast transaction (paragraph 9)

  > an uncommitted but anticipated future transaction.

  An example of a forecast transaction is expected future sales or purchases.

- a firm commitment (paragraph 9)

  > a binding agreement for the exchange of a specified quantity of resources at a specified price on a specified future date or dates.

An example of a firm commitment is a purchase order to buy a machine for $50 000 in 3 months' time.

Paragraph 78 of IAS 39 permits groups of assets, liabilities and so on to be the hedged item, provided they have similar risk characteristics and proportionate fair value changes (paragraph 83). However, under paragraph 84, a net position cannot be hedged (e.g. the net of a group of similar assets and similar liabilities). Certain exceptions to this were introduced in mid 2004 to meet the concerns of financial institutions that routinely hedge net positions as part of their asset/liability management. This was one of the reasons that financial institutions were initially so opposed to the introduction of IAS 39, as it would affect their standard hedging practices.

The hedged item can be a financial item or a non-financial item. If it is a *financial item*, such as an interest-bearing investment, the risk being hedged may be only *part of the total risks* in that item, provided that effectiveness can be measured (paragraph 81). For example, an interest-bearing investment potentially exposes the holder to interest rate risk, credit risk and price risk. The holder may choose to hedge only the interest rate exposure, or only the credit risk, and so on. The reason for this is that the component risks of financial items can be readily identified.

Note that a held-to-maturity investment cannot be a hedged item with respect to interest rate risk or prepayment risk because, by definition, the investment must be held to maturity and thus these risks should not eventuate (paragraph 79). However, such an instrument may be a hedged item with respect to foreign currency risk and credit risk.

However, if the hedged item is a *non-financial item*, the risk being hedged must be the *total risks* because of the difficulty in isolating and measuring the component risks in non-financial items. The only exception to this is foreign currency risk, which may be separately hedged (paragraph 82).

Derivatives cannot be designated as hedged items because they are deemed held for trading and measured at fair value through profit or loss.

7.15.3 The conditions for hedge accounting and the three types of hedge

Hedge accounting recognises the offsetting effects on profit or loss of changes in the fair values of the hedging instrument and the hedged item. Paragraph 88 of IAS 39 sets out the five conditions that must be met in order for hedge accounting to be applied:

1. At the inception of the hedge, there must be formal *designation and documentation* of the hedging relationship and the entity's risk-management objective and strategy for undertaking the hedge. That documentation must include identification of:
   - the hedging instrument
   - the hedged item
   - the nature of the risk being hedged
   - how the entity will assess hedge effectiveness.
2. The hedge must be expected to be *highly effective* in achieving offsetting changes in fair value or cash flows attributable to the hedged risk. 'Highly effective' is elaborated on in AG 105 of IAS 39, which explains that changes must almost fully offset each other and actual results must be within a range of 80%–125%. For example, if actual results are a loss on a hedging instrument of $120 and a corresponding gain on the hedged item of $100, offset can be measured by 100/120 (being 83%) or by 120/100 (being 120%). Effectiveness is assessed, at a minimum, at the time an entity prepares its interim or annual financial statements (AG 106).
3. For cash flow hedges (discussed below), a forecast transaction that is the subject of the hedge must be highly probable and must present an exposure to variations in cash flows that could affect profit or loss. 'Highly probable' is explained further in the Implementation Guidance at F3.7 as meaning a much greater likelihood than 'more likely than not' (the meaning of 'probable').
4. The effectiveness of the hedge can be reliably measured.
5. The hedge is assessed on an ongoing basis and must be determined actually to have been highly effective throughout the financial reporting periods for which the hedge was designated.

   Hedge effectiveness is defined in paragraph 9 as:

   > the degree to which changes in the fair value or cash flows of the hedged item that are attributable to a hedged risk are offset by changes in the fair value or cash flows of the hedging instrument.

The three types of hedging relationships are:
- fair value hedge
- cash flow hedge
- hedge of a net investment in a foreign operation as defined in IAS 21. This is accounted for in a similar manner to cash flow hedges, but will not be discussed further in this chapter.

  Note the following points:
- A fair value hedge is a hedge of the exposure to changes in fair value of an asset, liability or unrecognised firm commitment.
- A cash flow hedge is a hedge of the exposure to variability in cash flows of a recognised asset or liability, or a highly probable forecast transaction.
- Paragraph 87 of IAS 39 states that a hedge of the foreign currency risk of a firm commitment may be accounted for as either a fair value hedge or a cash flow hedge.
- A simple way of remembering the difference between the two types of hedge is that a cash flow hedge locks in future cash flows, whereas a fair value hedge does not.
- The most commonly occurring hedge transactions for average reporting entities are interest rate hedges and foreign currency hedges.

As an example of a simple cash flow hedge, assume that Company B has a borrowing with lender Bank L that carries a variable rate of interest. Company B is worried about its exposure to future increases in the variable rate of interest and decides to enter into an interest rate swap with bank S. The borrowing is the hedged item, and the risk being hedged is interest rate risk. Under the interest rate swap, bank S pays Company B the variable interest rate, and Company B pays bank S a specified fixed interest rate. The interest rate swap is the hedging instrument. The net cash flows for Company B are its payments of a fixed interest rate, so it has locked in its cash flows. This is therefore a cash flow hedge, assuming all the required criteria of IAS 39 are met. Figure 7.7 illustrates this example of a simple cash flow hedge.

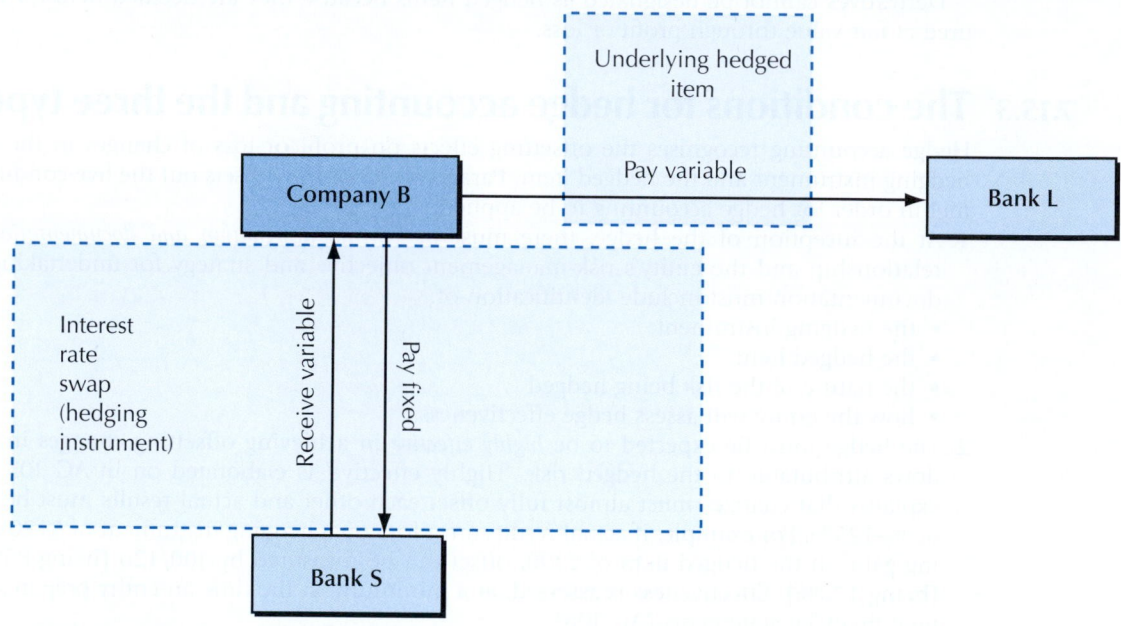

FIGURE 7.7 A simple cash flow hedge

There is no exchange of principal in an interest rate swap — the cash flows are simply calculated using the principal as the basis for the calculation. For the example illustrated in figure 7.7, assume that the hedged item is a borrowing of $100 000 with a variable interest rate, currently 5%. The fixed rate under the interest rate swap is 6%. For the relevant period, Company B will pay Bank L $100 000 × 5% = $5000. Under the swap, Company B will pay a net $1000 (receive $100 000 × 5% and pay $100 000 × 6%). Thus, Company B's net cash outflow is $5000 + $1000 = $6000, which is the fixed rate. Note that Bank L is not a party to the swap — it continues to receive payments from Company B under its borrowing arrangement. Company B has locked in its cash flows at $6000, and has certainty that this is what it will pay over the term of the swap. Currently the cash flows are higher than what it would pay under a variable rate, but Company B has entered into the swap in the expectation that the variable rate will rise.

Table 7.10 sets out the main requirements for fair value hedges and cash flow hedges.

TABLE 7.10 Summary of the main requirements of IAS 39 for fair value hedges and cash flow hedges		
	Fair value hedge	**Cash flow hedge**
Hedged item	Fair value exposures in a recognised asset or liability or unrecognised firm commitment (paragraph 86)	Cash flow variability exposures in a recognised asset or liability or highly probable forecast transaction (paragraph 86)
Gain or loss on hedging instrument	Recognised immediately in profit or loss (paragraph 89)	Fully effective portion recognised directly in equity (paragraph 95). Ineffective portion recognised immediately in profit or loss (paragraph 95)

TABLE 7.10 *(continued)*

	Fair value hedge	**Cash flow hedge**
Gain or loss on hedged item	Adjust hedged item and recognise in profit or loss (paragraph 89). This applies even if the hedged item is otherwise measured at cost.[1] It also applies to available-for-sale investments (see exception to general rule of gain/loss recognition in section 7.14.4 of this chapter).	Not applicable because the exposure being hedged is future cash flows that are not recognised
Hedge ineffectiveness is recorded in profit or loss	Automatically, since the entire gain or loss on both the hedged item and the hedging instrument is recorded in profit or loss	Must be calculated and separated from the amount recorded in equity
Timing of recycling of hedge gains/losses in equity to profit or loss (paragraphs 97–100)	Not applicable	Hedge of a forecast transaction that subsequently results in the recognition of a *financial* asset or financial liability: during the periods in which said asset/liability affects profit or loss, e.g. when the interest income or expense is recognised (paragraph 97) Hedge of a forecast transaction that subsequently results in the recognition of a *non-financial* asset or non-financial liability: either (a) during the periods in which said asset/liability affects profit or loss, e.g. when the depreciation expense is recognised; or (b) include immediately in the initial cost of said asset/liability (paragraph 98). In this case, the amount is not included in profit or loss Entities must choose between (a) or (b) as their adopted accounting policy and must apply consistently to all such transactions (paragraph 99)

Note:
1. If the hedged item is measured at amortised cost, then the fair value adjustment is amortised to profit or loss, using a recalculated effective interest rate (paragraph 92).

A simple fair value hedge is demonstrated in illustrative example 7.5.

ILLUSTRATIVE EXAMPLE 7.5 A simple fair value hedge

Company Z has an investment in an equity instrument classified as an available-for-sale investment. The cost of the investment on 1 July 2012 was $250 000. On 1 September 2012, Company Z enters into a derivative futures contract to hedge the fair value of the investment. All the conditions for hedge accounting are met, and the hedge qualifies as a fair value hedge because it is a hedge of an exposure to changes in the fair value of a recognised asset. At the next reporting date, 30 September 2012, the fair value of the investment (hedged item) was $230 000, based on quoted market bid prices. The fair value of the derivative (hedging instrument) at that date was $18 000. Company Z would record the journal entries shown below.

On initial recognition of the investment 1 July 2012:

Available-for-Sale Investment	Dr	250 000	
Cash	Cr		250 000

On entering into the futures contract 1 September 2012:

No entries because the net fair value is zero.

On remeasurement at 30 September 2012:

Expense (profit or loss)	Dr	20 000	
Available-for-Sale Investment	Cr		20 000
Futures Contract	Dr	18 000	
Income (profit or loss)	Cr		18 000

The hedge is within the effectiveness range of 85%–120% (actual range is 90%–111%), so the hedge accounting may continue. The net effect of the hedge is that Company Z records a net loss in profit or loss of $2000. The ineffective portion of the hedge ($2000) is recorded automatically in profit or loss. Note that the decline in fair value of the available-for-sale investment is recorded in profit or loss, even though the normal accounting for such investments is to recognise fair value changes directly in equity. This exception is made specifically for hedge accounting, to enable the matching effect of the hedging instrument with the hedged item in profit or loss to occur.

A cash flow hedge of a firm commitment is demonstrated in illustrative example 7.6.

ILLUSTRATIVE EXAMPLE 7.6   Cash flow hedge of a firm commitment (based on IAS 39, Implementation Guidance F.5.6)

On 30 June 2012, Company A enters into a forward exchange contract to receive foreign currency (FC) of 100 000 and deliver local currency (LC) of 109 600 on 30 June 2013. It designates the forward exchange contract as a hedging instrument in a cash flow hedge of a firm commitment to purchase a specified quantity of paper on 31 March 2013, and the resulting payable. Payment for the paper is due on 30 June 2013. All hedge accounting conditions in IAS 39 are met.

Note that a hedge of foreign currency risk in a firm commitment may be either a cash flow hedge or a fair value hedge (IAS 39 paragraph 87). Company A has elected to account for it as a cash flow hedge. Company A has also elected to apply IAS 39, paragraph 98(b), and adjust the cost of non-financial items acquired as a result of hedged forecast transactions.

The following table sets out the spot rate, forward rate and fair value of the forward contract at relevant dates.

Date	Spot rate	Forward rate to 30 June 2013	Fair value of forward contract
30 June 2012	1.072	1.096	—
31 December 2012	1.080	1.092	(388)[1]
31 March 2013	1.074	1.076	(1 971)
30 June 2013	1.072	—	(2 400)

1. This can be calculated if the applicable yield curve in the local currency is known. Assuming the rate is 6%, the fair value is calculated as follows: $([1.092 \times 100\,000] - 109\,600)/(1 + 0.06 \times 6/12)$.

Journal entries are shown below:

At 30 June 2012:

Forward Contract	Dr	LC0	
Cash	Cr		LC0
(Initial recognition of forward contract)			

On initial recognition, the forward contract has a fair value of zero (IAS 39 paragraph 43).

At 31 December 2012:

Equity	Dr	LC388	
Forward Contract (liability)	Cr		LC388
(Recording the change in the fair value of the forward contract)			

At 31 March 2013:

Equity	Dr	LC1 583	
Forward Contract (liability)	Cr		LC1 583
(Recording the change in the fair value of the forward contract)			
Paper (purchase price)	Dr	LC107 400	
Paper (hedging loss)	Dr	LC1 971	
Equity	Cr		LC1 971
Payable	Cr		LC107 400

The last entry recognises the purchase of the paper at the spot rate (1.074 × FC100 000), and removes the cumulative loss that has been recognised in equity and includes it in the initial measurement of the purchased paper (IAS 39 paragraph 98(b)). The paper is thus recognised effectively at the forward rate, and the hedge has been 100% effective.

At 30 June 2013:

Payable	Dr	LC107 400	
Cash	Cr		LC107 200
Profit or Loss	Cr		LC200
(Recording settlement of the payable at the spot rate and associated exchange gain)			
Profit or Loss	Dr	LC429	
Forward Contract	Cr		LC429
(Recording loss on forward contract between 1 April 13 and 30 June 13)			

The forward contract has been effective in hedging the commitment and the payable up to this date. However, the loss on the contract is recognised in profit or loss because the hedge is no longer of a firm commitment but of the fair value of a recognised liability (the payable). The movement must be recorded in profit or loss because the hedge arrangement is now a fair value hedge.

Forward Contract	Dr	LC2 400	
Cash	Cr		LC2 400
(Recording net settlement of forward contract)			

If this transaction had been designated as a fair value hedge, then the entries recorded in equity for the cash flow hedge would instead be recorded as an asset or liability (IAS 39 paragraph 93). Paragraph 94 then requires the initial carrying amount of the asset acquired to be adjusted for the cumulative amount recognised in the statement of financial position. The adjusted journal entries would be as follows:

At 31 December 2012:

Asset	Dr	LC388	
Forward Contract (liability)	Cr		LC388
(Recording change in fair value of forward contract)			

At 31 March 2013:

Asset	Dr	LC1 583	
Forward Contract (liability)	Cr		LC1 583
(Recording change in fair value of forward contract)			
Paper (purchase price)	Dr	LC107 400	
Paper (hedging loss)	Dr	LC1 971	
Asset	Cr		LC1 971
Payable	Cr		LC107 400
(Recording purchase of paper and transferring cumulative amount recognised as an asset to the cost of the paper)			

7.15.4 Discontinuing hedge accounting

Under paragraph 91 of IAS 39, a fair value hedge must be discontinued prospectively if one of the following occurs:

(a) The hedging instrument expires or is sold, terminated or exercised.

(b) The hedge no longer meets the criteria for hedge accounting.

(c) The entity revokes the designation.

Under paragraph 101 of IAS 39, a cash flow hedge must be discontinued prospectively if one of the following occurs:

(a) The hedging instrument expires or is sold, terminated or exercised. In this case, the cumulative gain or loss that remains recognised in equity from the period when the hedge was effective should remain in equity until the forecast transaction occurs. When the transaction occurs, paragraphs 97, 98 or 100 apply.

(b) The hedge no longer meets the criteria for hedge accounting. In this case, the cumulative gain or loss that remains recognised in equity from the period when the hedge was effective should remain in equity until the forecast transaction occurs. When the transaction occurs, paragraphs 97, 98 or 100 apply.

(c) The forecast transaction is no longer expected to occur. In this case, the cumulative gain or loss that remains recognised in equity from the period when the hedge was effective should be recognised in profit or loss.

(d) The entity revokes the designation. In this case, the cumulative gain or loss that remains recognised in equity from the period when the hedge was effective should remain in equity until the forecast transaction occurs or is no longer expected to occur. When the transaction occurs, paragraphs 97, 98 or 100 apply. If the forecast transaction is no longer expected to occur, the cumulative gain or loss that remains recognised in equity from the period when the hedge was effective should be recognised in profit or loss.

The rationale behind these requirements is that hedge accounting is required for the time that the hedge was effective. If the forecast transaction occurs, then the transaction benefits from the hedge for the time that the hedge was effective. If the forecast transaction does not occur, then there is no transaction to benefit from the hedge.

7.16 IFRS 9 — OVERVIEW

As noted in section 7.1 of this chapter, during the financial crisis of 2008, the IASB came under enormous pressure to amend IAS 39. The reclassification amendment (see section 7.14.3) was made in order to allow banks to cease using fair value accounting for certain financial assets. The normal due process required of the IASB was suspended in order to allow the amendment to be made urgently in October 2008. Part of the global response to the financial crisis was the creation of the Group of Twenty (G20) which met (and continues to meet) to address issues on a global, rather than national, basis. At its London summit in April 2009, the G20 called for a number of changes to accounting standards. A key theme was a call for convergence between US GAAP and IFRSs. A second key theme was a call for amendments to the financial instruments standards in three main respects — (1) to reduce complexity; (2) to address the impairment rules; and (3) to address off-balance sheet entities. Item (3) has been dealt with through the amendments to the consolidation standards (IFRS 10, IAS 27, and IFRS 12) which were issued in 2011 — see chapters 23 to 27. Item (1) was addressed through the rapid development and issuance of IFRS 9. Item (2) is still in progress although it has been partially addressed by IFRS 9.

The IASB decided to tackle the G20's challenge in phases. The first phase was to reduce the complexity of IAS 39 with respect to financial assets. IFRS 9 was issued in November 2009, dealing only with financial assets and was added to in October 2010 to address financial liabilities. During 2011 and 2012, the IASB continued to work on new impairment and hedging rules that will eventually be incorporated into IFRS 9 and thus IAS 39 will be superseded. The effective date of IFRS 9 was originally for financial years beginning on or after 1 January 2013, but was amended to 1 January 2015 because of the delay in finalising the impairment and hedging requirements. IFRS 9 was not endorsed in Europe and very few entities currently apply it.

7.16.1 Financial assets under IFRS 9

Figure 7.8 summarises the requirements of IFRS 9 in respect of financial assets.

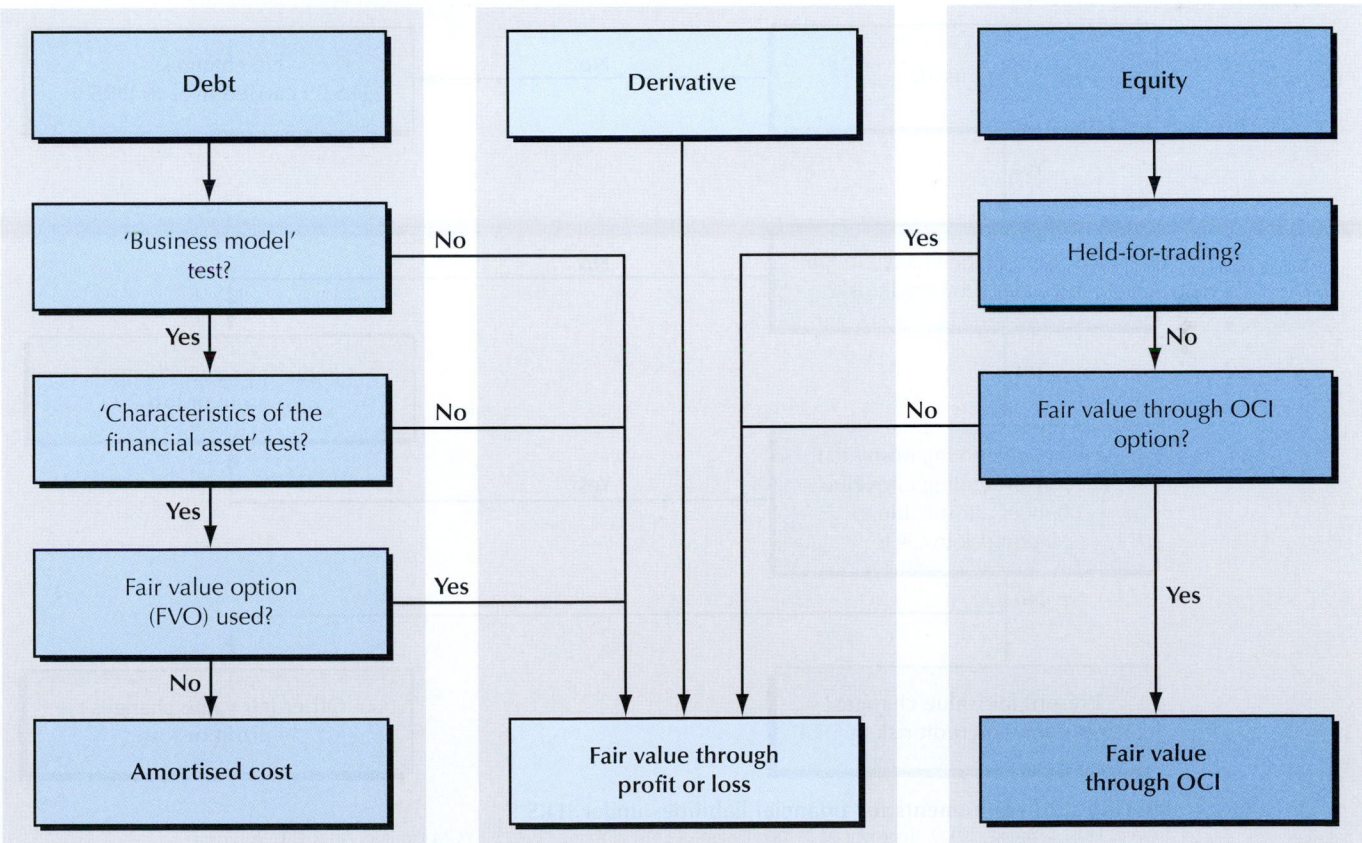

FIGURE 7.8 Requirements for financial assets under IFRS 9
Source: Ernst & Young (2011). Reproduced by permission of Ernst & Young © 2012 EYGM Limited. All Rights Reserved.

IFRS 9 is considerably more simplified than IAS 39. It has removed the concept of separating embedded derivatives from host contracts and reduced the categories of financial assets. Further, it has reduced complexity with respect to impairment of equity securities since these are either measured at fair value through profit or loss (in which case impairment rules are not needed) or through equity (other comprehensive income (OCI)), with no recycling of profits or losses permitted. This means that fair value movements of an investment in an equity security which is measured at fair value through OCI are *never* recognised in profit or loss and impairment rules are thus unnecessary. This aspect of IFRS 9 remains unpopular and was one of the reasons why it was not endorsed in Europe, but it was seen by the IASB as the only way to avoid the complexity of the impairment rules and at the same time allow entities to keep the impact of equity investments 'quarantined' from profit or loss. At the time of the financial crisis of 2008, many entities argued that they should not have to impair their investments in equity securities because they intended to hold them for the long term. This is not an acceptable argument under IAS 39 (see section 7.14.5). In addition, because impairment losses on equity securities cannot be reversed under IAS 39, entities were concerned about taking the loss to profit or loss but having to take any subsequent increase in fair value to equity. The solution in IFRS 9 is to keep *all* movements in fair value of equity securities quarantined — if an entity chooses to do so. Effectively, the IASB is asserting that if entities believe that their equity investments are long-term and fair value movements should not affect profit, then they should *never* affect profit, even when they are sold. Originally, to keep true to this principle, the IASB had proposed to not allow dividends received from such investments to be recognised in profit or loss, but changed this in the final standard after objections from constituents.

7.16.2 Financial liabilities under IFRS 9

Figure 7.9 summarises the classification and measurement requirements of IFRS 9 in respect of financial liabilities.

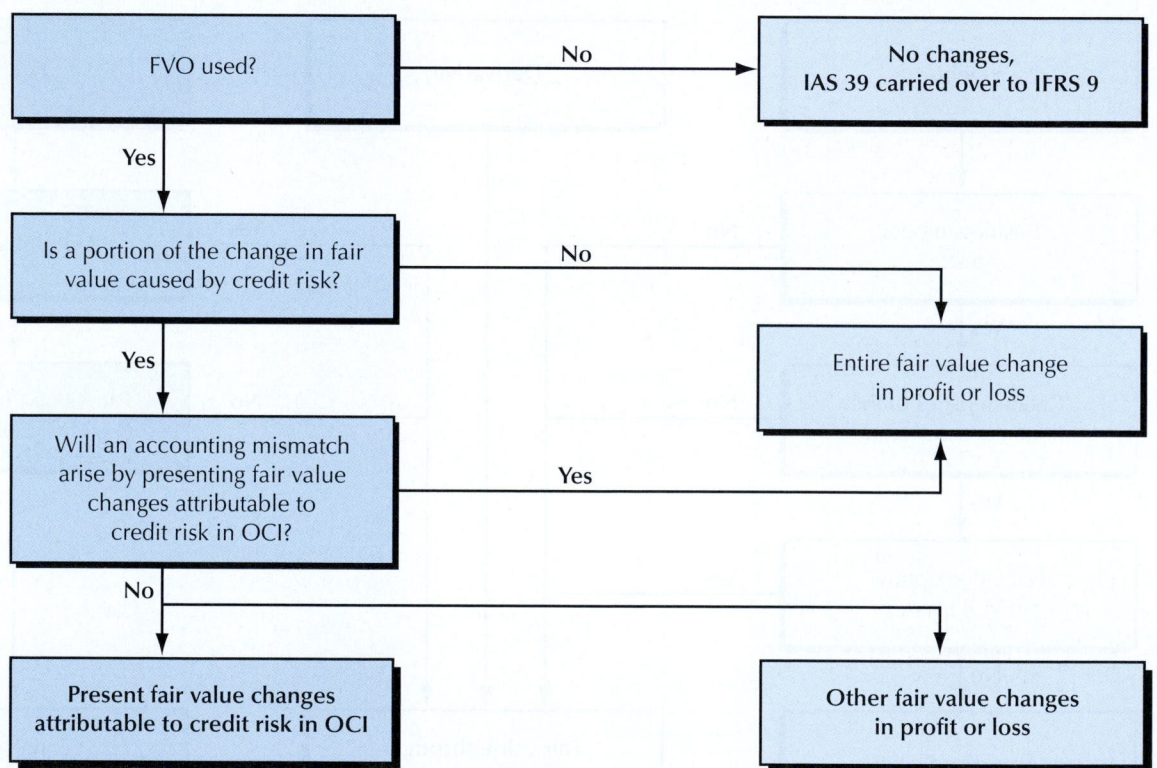

FIGURE 7.9 Requirements for financial liabilities under IFRS 9
Source: Ernst & Young (2011). Reproduced by permission of Ernst & Young © 2012 EYGM Limited. All Rights Reserved

7.17 EXPECTED FUTURE DEVELOPMENTS

As noted in section 7.16 above, the IASB intends to supersede IAS 39 with IFRS 9 once the hedging and impairment requirements are finalised. As at the time of writing, these had still not been completed but is expected that the hedging rules will be considerably simplified and that the impairment rules will allow for earlier recognition of impairment losses (on financial assets measured at amortised cost) than is currently allowed under IAS 39. This should address one of the criticisms raised during the financial crisis (see section 7.1), namely that impairment losses were not recognised sufficiently early. The criticisms surrounding the ability to determine fair value in illiquid or inactive markets has been addressed by the issue of IFRS 13 *Fair Value Measurement* in 2011, which specifically addresses how to determine fair values in such situations. This leaves the liability versus equity complexity (IAS 32 — see section 7.5) still to be tackled and we have yet to see how the IASB will deal with this. Originally the IASB and FASB had indicated that they would work on this as a joint project, but as at the beginning of 2012, work on this project had been deferred indefinitely.

Thus, to a large extent, many of the criticisms of the efficacy of the financial instruments standards should, at least according to the IASB, have been addressed by 2012. Whether IFRS 9 will be endorsed by the European Union parliament once all the new hedging and impairment requirements are incorporated, remains to be seen.

As an interesting contrast to those who argued that accounting, and particularly fair value accounting, was responsible for the financial crisis, it is instructive to read the speech by Andrew G. Haldane of the Bank of England, given on 19 December 2011. In his speech he supports fair value accounting principles as the appropriate means of measuring and managing financial risk and argues against suspending fair value when markets fall.

He states that, historically, fair value accounting principles have gained ground when the going has been good, and lost it when it has got tough. He cites examples — US President Roosevelt in 1938 suspended fair valuation of investment bank assets, President Bush in the 1990s granted the SEC authority to suspend fair value rules, and pressure in 2008 on the FASB and IASB to 'ease back' fair value accounting rules (the reclassification amendment that allowed banks to reclassify financial assets held at fair value through profit or loss out of that category in 'rare circumstances'). He states that in hard times fair values are seen as 'more troublemaker than matchmaker'. From a financial stability perspective, he argues, this is a cause for concern because potential losses are hidden from view. He goes even further and argues that *all* bank assets should be measured at fair value. This is step further than IFRS 9, which allows certain assets to be measured at amortised cost. Whether his argument gains any support remains to be seen, but one thing is certain — controversy surrounding the accounting for financial instruments seems set to continue.

SUMMARY

IAS 32 defines financial instruments, financial assets, financial liabilities and derivatives and distinguishes between financial liabilities and equity instruments. IFRS 7 prescribes disclosures. IAS 32 sets prescriptive rules for distinguishing financial liabilities from equity instruments, and for accounting for compound financial instruments that have elements of both. It requires that interest, dividends, gains and losses be accounted for consistent with the statement of financial position classification of the related financial assets and financial liabilities. It also sets prescriptive requirements for offsetting a financial asset and a financial liability.

IAS 39 requires all financial instruments including derivatives to be initially recorded at fair value. It defines an embedded derivative and establishes rules for separating an embedded derivative from the host contract. It creates four categories of financial instruments. Each category has its own rules for measurement, including initial and subsequent measurement, reclassifications, gains and losses and impairment.

IAS 39 permits hedge accounting provided that strict criteria are met. These include meeting specified conditions before hedge accounting can be applied, meeting the definition of a hedging instrument and a hedged item, and identifying which of the three types of hedge the hedge transaction meets. IAS 39 prescribes when hedge accounting must be discontinued and how the discontinuation must be accounted for. It also contains rules for the derecognition of financial instruments, but these are not addressed in this chapter.

Criticism of the standards for financial instruments emerged during the financial crisis in 2008. In response the IASB rapidly amended IAS 39 in 2008 and issued IFRS 9 in 2009. While IFRS 9 is not yet complete, the remaining parts dealing with hedging and impairment are expected to be finalised during 2012.

Accounting for financial instruments remains controversial.

Discussion questions

1. Discuss the concept of 'equity risk' and how it is useful in determining whether a financial instrument is a financial liability or an equity instrument of the issuer.
2. Discuss why the standard setters first set rules on presentation and disclosure of financial instruments before tackling recognition and measurement. Do you think the earlier creation of IAS 32 assisted in the development of IAS 39?

3. Does IAS 32 contain a clear hierarchy to be used in determining whether a financial instrument is a financial liability or an equity instrument of the issuer? Explain your answer.
4. What is the purpose of IFRS 7's disclosure requirements?
5. Describe the main risks that pertain to financial instruments.
6. Explain how a concentration of credit risk may arise for trade accounts receivable.
7. IAS 39 applies a 'rights and obligations approach' to the recognition of financial instruments. Discuss.
8. Explain what an economic hedge is. Will hedge accounting always result in the same outcome as an economic hedge?
9. Distinguish, explain and discuss the meaning of 'highly effective' and 'highly probable' in the context of the hedge accounting rules in IAS 39.
10. Identify the main criticisms of accounting for financial instruments that emerged during the financial crisis. To what extent had the IASB addressed these by the end of 2011?
11. Describe the three categories of financial asset under IFRS 9. How is each category accounted for?

Exercises

STAR RATING   ★ BASIC   ★★ MODERATE   ★★★ DIFFICULT

| Exercise 7.1 | CLASSIFICATION OF REVENUES AND EXPENSES |

★ Classify the following items as statement of profit or loss and other comprehensive income/statement of changes in equity.
(a) Dividends paid on non-redeemable preference shares
(b) Dividends paid on preference shares redeemable at the holder's option
(c) Interest paid on a 5-year, fixed interest note
(d) Interest paid on a convertible note classified as a compound instrument

| Exercise 7.2 | SCOPE OF IAS 32 |

★ Which of the following are financial instruments (i.e. a financial asset, financial liability, or equity instrument in another entity) within the scope of IAS 32? Give reasons for your answer.
(a) Cash
(b) Investment in a debt instrument
(c) Investment in a subsidiary
(d) Provision for restoration of a mine site
(e) Buildings owned by the reporting entity
(f) Forward contract entered into by a bread manufacturer to buy wheat
(g) Forward contract entered into by a gold producer to hedge the future sales of gold
(h) General sales tax payable

| Exercise 7.3 | SCOPE OF IAS 39 |

★ Which of the following are financial instruments (i.e. a financial asset, financial liability, or equity instrument in another entity) within the scope of IAS 39? Give reasons for your answer.
(a) Provision for employee benefits
(b) Deferred revenue
(c) Prepayments
(d) Forward exchange contract
(e) 3% investment in private company
(f) A percentage interest in an unincorporated joint venture
(g) A non-controlling interest in a partnership
(h) A non-controlling interest in a discretionary trust
(i) An investment in an associate
(j) A forward purchase contract for wheat to be used by the entity to make flour
(k) As for part (j), but the entity regularly settles the contracts net in cash or takes delivery of the underlying wheat and sells it shortly after making a dealer's margin
(l) Leases
(m) Trade receivables

Exercise 7.4	IMPAIRMENT

★ State whether each of the following statements is true or false.

(a) Financial assets measured 'at fair value through profit or loss' must be tested annually for impairment.

(b) A reversal of an impairment loss on a held-to-maturity investment is recognised in profit or loss.

(c) A reversal of an impairment loss on an available-for-sale investment in a debt instrument is not permitted.

(d) A reversal of an impairment loss on an available-for-sale investment in an equity instrument is not permitted.

Exercise 7.5	HEDGING

★ State whether each of the following statements is true or false.

(a) In any hedge relationship there needs to be a hedged item and a hedging instrument.

(b) A hedging instrument must always be a derivative.

(c) A cash flow hedge locks in a reporting entity's future cash flows.

(d) A forecast transaction is an uncommitted but anticipated future transaction.

(e) In order to qualify for hedge accounting, there must be formal designation and documentation of the hedging relationship and the entity's risk-management objective and strategy for undertaking the hedge.

(f) The documentation and designation in (e) may occur at any time.

Exercise 7.6	DISTINGUISHING FINANCIAL LIABILITIES FROM EQUITY INSTRUMENTS (1)

★ Company A issues 100 000 $1 convertible notes. The notes pay interest at 7%. The market rate for similar debt without the conversion option is 9%. The note is not redeemable, but it converts at the option of the holder into however many shares that will have a value of exactly $100 000.

Required

Determine whether this financial instrument should be classified as a financial liability or equity instrument of Company A. Give reasons for your answer.

Exercise 7.7	CATEGORISING COMMON FINANCIAL INSTRUMENTS UNDER IAS 32

★★ Categorise each of the following common financial instruments as financial assets, financial liabilities or equity instruments — of the issuer or the holder, as specified.

(a) Loans receivable (holder)

(b) Loans payable (issuer)

(c) Ordinary shares of the issuer

(d) The holder's investment in the ordinary shares in part (c)

(e) Redeemable preference shares of the issuer, redeemable at any time at the option of the holder

(f) The holder's investment in the preference shares in part (e)

Exercise 7.8	CATEGORISING COMMON FINANCIAL INSTRUMENTS UNDER IAS 39

★★ Categorise each of the following common financial instruments in one of the four categories specified in IAS 39. Assume that the entity does not elect the 'at fair value through profit or loss category'.

(a) Loans receivable (holder)

(b) Loans payable (issuer)

(c) Ordinary shares of the issuer

(d) The holder's investment in the ordinary shares in part (c)

(e) Redeemable preference shares of the issuer, redeemable at any time at the option of the holder

(f) The holder's investment in the preference shares in part (e)

Exercise 7.9	OFFSETTING A FINANCIAL ASSET AND A FINANCIAL LIABILITY

★★ In each of the situations below, state whether the financial asset and financial liability must be offset in the books of Company A as at 30 June 2012, and explain why.

(a) Company A owes Company B $500 000, due on 30 June 2013. Company B owes Company A $300 000, due on 30 June 2013. A legal right of set-off between the two companies is documented in writing, and the parties have indicated their intent to settle the amounts on a net basis.

(b) Company A owes Company B $500 000, due on 30 June 2013. Company B owes Company A $300 000, due on 31 March 2013. A legal right of set-off between the two companies is documented in writing, and the parties have indicated their intent to settle the amounts on a net basis whenever possible.

(c) Company A owes Company B $500 000, due on 30 June 2013. Company C owes Company A $300 000, due on 30 June 2013.

(d) Company A owes Company B $500 000, due on 30 June 2013. Company C owes Company A $500 000, due on 30 June 2013. A legal right of set-off between the three companies is documented in writing, and the parties have indicated their intent to settle the amounts on a net basis.

(e) Company A owes Company B $500 000, due on 30 June 2013. Company A has plant and equipment with a fair value of $500 000 that it pledges to Company B as collateral for the debt.

| Exercise 7.10 | FINANCIAL INSTRUMENTS CATEGORIES AND MEASUREMENT |

★★ Identify which of the four categories specified in IAS 39 each of the following items belongs to in the books of Company H, the holder. Also identify how each item will be measured.

(a) Forward exchange contract
(b) 5-year government bond paying interest of 5%
(c) Trade accounts receivable
(d) Trade accounts payable
(e) Mandatory converting notes paying interest of 6% (the notes must convert to a variable number of ordinary shares at the expiration of their term)
(f) Investment in a portfolio of listed shares held for capital growth
(g) Investment in a portfolio of listed shares held for short-term gains
(h) As in part (e), except that in the previous year Company H sold the majority of its held-to-maturity investments to Company Z
(i) Borrowings of $1 million, carrying a variable interest rate

| Exercise 7.11 | DISTINGUISHING FINANCIAL LIABILITIES FROM EQUITY INSTRUMENTS |

★★ Company A issues 100 000 $1 redeemable convertible notes. The notes pay interest at 5%. They convert at any time at the option of the holder into 100 000 ordinary shares. The notes are redeemable at the option of the holder for cash after 5 years. Market rates for similar notes without the conversion option are 7%.

Required

Determine whether this financial instrument should be classified as a financial liability or equity instrument of Company A. Give reasons for your answer.

| Exercise 7.12 | DISTINGUISHING FINANCIAL LIABILITIES FROM EQUITY INSTRUMENTS |

★★★ Company A issues 100 000 $1 redeemable convertible notes. The notes pay interest at 5%. They convert at any time at the option of the holder into 100 000 ordinary shares. The notes are redeemable at the option of the issuer for cash after 5 years. If after 5 years the notes have not been redeemed or converted, they cease to carry interest. Market rates for similar notes without the conversion option are 7%.

Required

Determine whether this financial instrument should be classified as a financial liability or equity instrument of Company A. Give reasons for your answer.

| Exercise 7.13 | DISTINGUISHING FINANCIAL LIABILITIES FROM EQUITY INSTRUMENTS |

★★★ Company A issues 100 000 $1 redeemable convertible notes. The notes pay interest at 5%. The notes are redeemable after 5 years at the option of the issuer for cash or for a variable number of shares (calculated according to a formula). If after 5 years the notes have not been redeemed or converted, they continue to carry interest at a new market rate to be determined at the expiration of the 5 years.

Required

Determine whether this financial instrument should be classified as a financial liability or equity instrument of Company A. Give reasons for your answer.

Exercise 7.14	**DISTINGUISHING FINANCIAL LIABILITIES FROM EQUITY INSTRUMENTS**

★★★ Company A issues redeemable preference shares with a fixed maturity date. The shares are redeemable only on maturity at the option of the holder. The shares carry a cumulative 6% dividend.

Required

Determine whether this financial instrument should be classified as a financial liability or equity instrument of Company A. Give reasons for your answer.

Exercise 7.15	**DISTINGUISHING FINANCIAL LIABILITIES FROM EQUITY INSTRUMENTS**

★★★ Company A issues redeemable preference shares. The shares are redeemable for cash at the option of the issuer. The shares carry a cumulative 6% dividend. In addition, the preference share dividend can be paid only if a dividend on ordinary shares is paid for the relevant period. Company A is highly profitable and has a history of paying ordinary dividends at a yield of about 4% annually without fail for the past 25 years. Company A issued the preference shares after considering various options to raise finance for building a new factory. The market interest rate for long-term debt at the time the preference shares were issued was 7%.

Required

Determine whether this financial instrument should be classified as a financial liability or equity instrument of Company A. Give reasons for your answer.

Exercise 7.16	**ACCOUNTING FOR A COMPOUND FINANCIAL INSTRUMENT**

★★★ The facts from example 5 of figure 7.4 are repeated below:

Company A issues 2000 convertible notes on 1 July 2012. The notes have a 3-year term and are issued at par with a face value of $1000 per note, giving total proceeds at the date of issue of $2 million. The notes pay interest at 6% annually in arrears. The holder of each note is entitled to convert the note into 250 ordinary shares of Company A at any time up to maturity.

When the notes are issued, the prevailing market interest rate for similar debt (similar term, similar credit status of issuer and similar cash flows) without conversion options is 9%. This rate is higher than the convertible note's rate because the holder of the convertible note is prepared to accept a lower interest rate given the implicit value of its conversion option.

The issuer calculates the contractual cash flows using the market interest rate (9%) to work out the value of the holder's option, as follows:

Present value of the principal: $2 million payable in 3 years' time:	$1 544 367
Present value of the interest: $120 000 ($2 million × 6%) payable annually in arrears for 3 years	303 755
Total liability component	1 848 122
Equity component (by deduction)	151 878
Proceeds of the note issue	$2 000 000

Required

Prepare the journal entries to account for this transaction for each year of its term under each of the following circumstances.
(a) The holders exercise their conversion option at the expiration of the note's term.
(b) The holders do not exercise their option and the note is repaid at the end of its term.
(c) The holders exercise their option at the end of year 2.

Exercise 7.17	**AMORTISED COST, JOURNAL ENTRIES**

★★★ Company B issues a bond with a face value of $500 000 on 1 July 2012. Transaction costs incurred amount to $12 000. The bond pays interest at 6% per annum, in arrears. The bond must be repaid after 5 years.

Required

Prepare the journal entries to record this transaction on initial recognition and throughout the life of the bond in the books of Company B.

EMBEDDED DERIVATIVES

★★★   Identify which of the following embedded derivatives must be separated from the relevant host contract. In each case, state also how the host contract and the embedded derivative should be measured in the books of the holder. Assume that the host instrument is not measured at fair value through profit or loss.

(a) An equity conversion feature embedded in a convertible debt instrument

(b) An embedded derivative in an interest-bearing host debt instrument, where the embedded derivative derives its value from an underlying interest rate index and can change the amount of interest that would otherwise be paid on the host debt instrument

(c) An embedded cap (upper limit) on the interest rate on a host debt instrument, where the cap is at or above the market rate of interest when the debt instrument is issued

(d) As in part (c), except that the cap is below the market rate of interest

References

Ernst & Young 2007, *IFRS 7 Financial Instruments: disclosures, second edition*, www.ey.com/ifrs.

—— 2011, *Implementing Phase 1 of IFRS 9 (Second Edition)*, www.ey.com/ifrs.

Financial Crisis Advisory Group 2009, *Report of the Financial Crisis Advisory Group*, 28 July, www.ifrs.org.

Haldane, AG 2011, *Accounting for bank uncertainty*, Bank of England, 19 December, www.bankofengland.co.uk/publications/speeches.

8 Share-based payment

ACCOUNTING STANDARDS IN FOCUS

IFRS 2 *Share-based Payment*

LEARNING OBJECTIVES

After studying this chapter, you should be able to:

1 explain the objective and scope of IFRS 2

2 distinguish between cash-settled and equity-settled share-based payment transactions

3 demonstrate how equity-settled and cash settled share-based payment transactions are recognised

4 explain how equity-settled share-based payment transactions are measured

5 explain the concept of vesting through differentiating between vesting and non-vesting conditions

6 explain the concept of a share option reload feature

7 explain how modifications to granted equity instruments are treated

8 demonstrate how cash-settled share-based payment transactions are measured

9 describe and apply the disclosure requirements of IFRS 2.

INTRODUCTION

The purpose of this chapter is to examine share-based payments. The International Financial Reporting Standard (IFRS) covering share-based payments is IFRS 2 *Share-based Payment*. Under IFRS 2, all transactions with employees or other parties — whether to be settled in cash (or settled in other assets) or settled in the equity instruments of an entity — must now be recognised in the entity's financial statements. The standard adopts the view that all share-based payment transactions ultimately lead to expense recognition, and entities must reflect the effects of such transactions in their profit or loss.

Organisations use various mechanisms to encourage their managers and employees to make decisions that improve the returns to shareholders, including offering remuneration that is linked to the share price of the organisation. This reflects a view that the behaviour of employees can be directed and controlled through the use of remuneration and other similar incentives. It is theorised that remuneration incentives linked to accounting and other performance measures will encourage managers and employees to take decisions and actions that positively impact the financial performance of the organisation and, in turn, the interests of shareholders of the organisation.

Share plans and share option plans are an increasingly common feature of remuneration for directors, senior managers and executives, and many other employees as a means of aligning employees' interests with those of the shareholders, and encouraging employee retention. The remuneration report provided by the Australian arm of Woolworths (Woolworths Limited) in its 2011 annual report presents a rationale for engaging in share-based payment transactions with employees. It also provides examples of the types of incentives and conditions that might be incorporated into some employee share plans.

Woolworths Limited's remuneration policy and structure recognises that it operates in a competitive environment and that corporate performance and the interests of its shareholders depend on the quality of its employees. The overall approach and key elements embodied in Woolworths Limited's remuneration policy are summarised in figure 8.1.

Remuneration Report

2. Remuneration policy

Remuneration policy is aligned with both our financial and strategic business objectives and recognises that people are a major contributor to sustained improvements in performance. Woolworths' approach to remuneration is in line with principles endorsed by the Australian Institute of Company Directors, Australian Employee Ownership Association and Australian Shareholders Association.

Woolworths' remuneration policy for all senior executives ensures:
- Remuneration is market competitive and designed to attract, motivate and retain key executives;
- Demanding performance measures are applied to both short and long term 'at risk' remuneration;
- Short term performance is linked to both financial and non-financial performance measures; and
- Long term performance is measured through the creation of value for shareholders.

Company protection and employment stability is provided through pre-established employment agreements limiting the amount of termination payments and providing restrictive covenants on future employment by competitors.

FIGURE 8.1 Woolworths Limited's remuneration principles
Source: Woolworths Ltd (2011, p. 46).

Companies have been criticised over the size of executive remuneration, for failing to align executive incentives more closely with shareholder returns, and for using short terms (one to three years) for share incentives to vest rather than longer-term incentives (five to ten years). A review of Woolworths Limited's approach shows the inclusion of a long-term incentive component in its remuneration strategy. Companies have also been criticised for failure to disclose details of their executive performance hurdles, such as return on equity rates, which they usually justify on the basis of commercial sensitivity. Details of required disclosures and examples of actual disclosures are presented in section 8.9.

Some entities may also issue shares or share options to pay for the purchase of property or for professional advice or services. Before the issue of IFRS 2, there was no requirement to identify the expenses associated with this type of transaction or to measure and recognise such transactions in the financial statements of an entity. Accounting standard setters have decided that recognising the cost of share-based payments in the financial statements of entities should improve the relevance, reliability and comparability of financial information and help users of financial information to understand the economic transactions affecting entities.

8.1 APPLICATION AND SCOPE

IFRS 2 applies to share-based payment transactions. The standard was first issued with an effective date for financial statements covering periods beginning on or after 1 January 2005. IFRS 2 has since been amended for vesting conditions and cancellations, with an effective date for these amendments of 1 January 2009. Equity instruments issued in a business combination in exchange for control of the acquiree are not within the scope of IFRS 2; they are accounted for under IFRS 3 *Business Combinations*. However, IFRS 2 applies to the cancellation, replacement or modification of share-based payments arising because of a business combination or restructuring.

Also excluded under paragraph 6 of IFRS 2 are share-based payments in which the entity receives or acquires goods or services under a contract within the scope of paragraphs 8–10 of IAS 32 *Financial Instruments: Presentation*. Also excluded are share-based payments in which the entity receives goods or services under a contract within the scope of paragraphs 5–7 of IAS 39 *Financial Instruments: Recognition and Measurement*; for example, contracts to buy or sell a non-financial item such as a building, that can be settled net in cash or another financial instrument, or by the exchange of financial instruments.

8.2 CASH-SETTLED AND EQUITY-SETTLED SHARE-BASED PAYMENT TRANSACTIONS

IFRS 2 applies to share-based payments in which an entity acquires or receives goods or services. Goods can include inventory, consumables, property, plant or equipment, intangibles and other non-financial forms of assets; services, such as the provision of labour, are usually consumed immediately.

Measurement principles and specific requirements for three forms of share-based payments are dealt with in IFRS 2. These three forms are defined in paragraph 2 and Appendix A to IFRS 2 and are summarised as follows:

1. *equity-settled* share-based payment transactions, in which the entity receives goods or services as consideration for its own equity instruments (including shares or share options)
2. *cash-settled* share-based payment transactions, in which the entity acquires goods or services by incurring liabilities to transfer cash or other assets to the supplier (counterparty) for amounts that are based on the value (price) of the shares or other equity instruments of the entity
3. *other* transactions in which the entity receives or acquires goods or services, and the terms of the arrangement provide either the entity or the counterparty of the goods or services with a choice of settling the transaction in cash (or other assets) or equity instruments.

The accounting treatment for these transactions differs depending on the form of settlement. The three forms and the essential features of share-based payment transactions are summarised in table 8.1.

TABLE 8.1 Form and features of share-based payment transactions

Form	Features
Equity-settled share-based payment	Entity receives goods or services as consideration for its own equity instruments
Cash-settled share-based payment	Entity acquires goods or services by incurring liabilities for amounts based on the value of its own equities
Other	Entity receives or acquires goods or services and the entity, or the counterparty, has the choice of whether the transaction is settled in cash or equity

Any transfers of an entity's equity instruments by its shareholders to parties that have supplied goods or services to the entity are considered, under paragraph 3A of IFRS 2, to be share-based payments (unless the transfer is clearly for a purpose other than payment for goods or services supplied to the entity). This treatment also applies to transfers of equity instruments of the entity's parent, or equity instruments of another entity in the same group as the entity, to parties that have supplied goods or services.

A transaction with an employee who holds equity instruments of the employing entity is not within the scope of IFRS 2 (paragraph 4). If, for example, the employee holds equity in the employer and is granted the right to acquire additional equity at a price that is less than fair value (e.g. a rights issue), the granting or exercise of that right by the employee is not governed by IFRS 2.

LO3 8.3 RECOGNITION

Paragraph 7 of IFRS 2 requires goods or services received in a share-based payment transaction to be recognised when they are received. A corresponding increase in equity must be recognised if the goods or services were received in an equity-settled share-based payment transaction. An increase in a liability must be recognised if the goods or services were acquired in a cash-settled share-based payment.

Usually an expense arises from the consumption of goods or services. For example, as services are normally consumed immediately, an expense is recognised as the service is rendered. If goods are consumed over a period of time or, as in the case of inventories, sold at a later date, an expense will not be recognised until the goods are consumed or sold. Sometimes it may be necessary to recognise an expense before the goods or services are consumed or sold because they do not qualify for recognition as assets. For example, this may occur if goods are acquired as part of the research phase of a project. Even though the goods may not have been consumed, they will not qualify for recognition as assets under other accounting standards. When the goods or services received in a share-based payment do not qualify for recognition as an asset, they must be expensed (IFRS 2 paragraph 8).

A share-based payment transaction would, depending on the principles for asset or liability recognition, be recognised in journal entries as shown below.

Asset or Expense	Dr	xxx
Equity	Cr	xxx
(Recognition of an equity-settled share-based payment)		
Asset or Expense	Dr	xxx
Liability	Cr	xxx
(Recognition of a cash-settled share-based payment)		

A significant feature of IFRS 2 is the accounting treatment it applies to transactions settled in cash, which is different to the treatment it applies to equity-settled transactions. If a share-based payment is settled in cash, the general principle employed in IFRS 2 is that the goods or services received and the liability incurred are measured at the fair value of the liability (IFRS 2 paragraph 10). The fair value of the liability must be remeasured at the end of each reporting period and at the date of settlement, and any changes in fair value are recognised in profit or loss (IFRS 2 paragraph 30). For share-based payment transactions that are equity-settled, the general principle is that the goods or services received and the corresponding increase in equity are measured at the date the goods or services are received, using the fair value of those goods or services. If the fair value cannot be measured reliably, the goods or services are measured indirectly by reference to the fair value of the equity instruments granted.

Under this approach a differential accounting treatment of changes in the fair value of equity instruments occurs, based on whether a transaction is classified as a liability or as equity. The fair value of transactions classified as equity is measured at the date the goods or services are received and subsequent value changes are ignored. In contrast, the fair value of transactions classified as liabilities (debt) are adjusted to fair value at the end of each reporting period and the resulting profit or loss is included in income.

LO4 8.4 EQUITY-SETTLED SHARE-BASED PAYMENT TRANSACTIONS

The goods or services received in equity-settled share-based payments and the corresponding increase in equity must be measured at the fair value of the goods or services unless that fair value cannot be estimated reliably (IFRS 2 paragraph 10). For transactions with parties other than employees, there is a rebuttable presumption in IFRS 2 (paragraph 13) that the fair value of goods or services can be estimated reliably. In the unusual cases where the fair value cannot be reliably estimated, paragraph 10 requires that the goods or services and the corresponding increase in equity are to be measured indirectly by reference to the fair value of the equity instruments granted at the date the goods are obtained or the service is rendered.

It is normally considered that the fair value of services received in transactions with employees cannot be reliably measured. Thus, the fair value of the services received from employees is measured by reference to the equity instruments granted. In summary, under IFRS 2, equity-settled share-based payments are measured and recognised as follows:

Asset or Expense	Dr	Fair value of goods or
Equity	Cr	services received or acquired
(Recognition of a share-based payment in which fair value of goods or services can be reliably estimated)		
Asset or Expense	Dr	Fair value of the equity
Equity	Cr	instruments granted
(Recognition of a share-based payment where fair value of goods or services cannot be reliably estimated)		

8.4.1 Transactions in which services are received

Certain conditions may need to be satisfied before the counterparty in a share-based payment transaction becomes entitled to receive cash (or other assets) or equity instruments of the entity. When the conditions have been satisfied, the counterparty's entitlement has *vested*. Under a share-based payment arrangement, a counterparty's right to receive cash, other assets or equity instruments of the entity vests when the counterparty's entitlement is no longer conditional on the satisfaction of any vesting conditions (IFRS 2 Appendix A).

If the equity instruments vest immediately, the counterparty is not required to serve a specified period of service before becoming unconditionally entitled to the equity instruments (IFRS 2 paragraph 14). On grant date, the services received are recognised in full together with a corresponding increase in equity. However, if the equity instruments do not vest until a period of service has been completed, under paragraph 15 the services and the corresponding increase in equity are accounted for across the vesting period as the services are rendered.

The granting of equity instruments in the form of share options to employees conditional on completing a 2-year period of service accounted for over the 2-year vesting period is demonstrated in illustrative example 8.1.

ILLUSTRATIVE EXAMPLE 8.1 Recognition of share options as services are rendered across the vesting period

Wang Ltd grants 100 share options to each of its 50 employees. Each grant is conditional upon the employee working for Wang Ltd for the next 2 years. It is assumed that each employee will satisfy the vesting conditions. At grant date, the fair value of each share option is estimated as $25.

According to IFRS 2, paragraph 15(a), Wang Ltd will recognise the following amounts during the vesting period for the services received from the employees as consideration for the share options granted.

Year	Calculation	Remuneration expense for period $	Cumulative remuneration expense $
1	(100 × 50 options) × $25 × 1/2 years	62 500	62 500
2	(100 × 50 options) × $25 − $62 500	62 500	125 000

8.4.2 Transactions measured by reference to the fair value of the equity instruments granted

Determining the fair value of equity instruments granted

Paragraph 11 of IFRS 2 states that, if share-based payments are with employees and others providing similar services, it is not usually possible to measure the fair value of services received. If it is not possible to reliably estimate the value of goods or services received, then the transaction is measured by reference to the fair value of the equity instruments granted. If market prices are not available, or if the equity instruments are subject to terms and conditions that do not apply to traded equity instruments, then a valuation technique must be used to estimate what the price of the equity instruments would have been, in an arm's length transaction, on the measurement date.

While IFRS 2 (appendix B11–41) discusses the inputs to option-pricing models such as the Black–Scholes–Merton formula, the choice of model is left to the entity. The valuation technique chosen must be consistent with generally accepted valuation methodologies for pricing financial instruments. It must also incorporate the terms and conditions of the equity instruments (e.g. whether or not an employee is entitled to receive dividends during the vesting period), and any other factors and assumptions that knowledgeable, willing market participants would consider in setting the price (IFRS 2 paragraph 17). For instance, many employee share options have long lives, and they are usually exercisable after the vesting period and before the end of the option's life. Option-pricing models calculate a theoretical price by using key determinants of the options.

Appendix B6 of IFRS 2 supplies the following list of factors that option-pricing models take into account as a minimum:
- exercise price of the option
- life of the option
- current price of the underlying shares
- expected volatility of the share price
- dividends expected on the shares
- risk-free interest rate for the life of the option.

Expected *volatility* is a measure of the amount by which a price is expected to fluctuate during a period. Volatility is typically expressed in annualised terms, for example, daily, weekly or monthly price observations. Often there is likely to be a range of reasonable expectations about future volatility, dividends and exercise date behaviour. If so, an expected value would be calculated by weighting each amount within the range by its associated probability of occurrence.

Expectations about the future are generally based on experience and modified if the future is reasonably expected to differ from the past. For instance, if an entity with two distinctly different lines of business disposes of the one that was significantly less risky than the other, historical volatility may not be the best information on which to base reasonable expectations for the future. In other circumstances, historical information may not be available. For example, unlisted entities will have no historical share price data; likewise, newly listed entities will have little share price data available.

Whether expected dividends should be taken into account when measuring the fair value of shares or options granted depends on whether the counterparty is entitled to dividends. Generally, the assumption about expected dividends is based on publicly available information.

The *risk-free* interest rate is the implied yield currently available on zero-coupon government issues of the country in whose currency the exercise price is expressed, with a remaining term equal to the expected term of the option (IFRS 2 appendix B37). It may be necessary to use an appropriate substitute if no such government issues exist or if circumstances indicate that the implied yield on zero-coupon government issues is not representative of the risk-free interest rate (e.g. in high inflation economies).

Woolworths Limited (discussed earlier in this chapter) discloses its use of an option pricing model in the determination of the fair value of options and performance rights. A relevant extract from Woolworths Limited's 2011 annual report appears in figure 8.2. In this extract Woolworths limited explains that its chosen option pricing model incorporates market conditions.

(iv) Share-based payment transactions
… Fair value is measured at grant date using a Monte-Carlo simulation option pricing model performed by an independent valuer which takes into account market based performance conditions. The fair value per instrument is multiplied by the number of instruments expected to vest based on achievement of non-market based performance conditions (e.g. service conditions) to determine the total cost.

FIGURE 8.2 Woolworths Limited's use of option pricing models
Source: Woolworths Ltd (2011, p. 101).

8.5 VESTING

8.5.1 Treatment of vesting conditions

If a grant of equity instruments is conditional on satisfying certain vesting conditions such as remaining in the entity's employment for a specified period of time, then the vesting conditions are not taken into account when estimating the fair value of the equity instruments. Instead, the vesting conditions are accounted for by adjusting the number of equity instruments included in the measurement of the transaction amount. Thus, the amount recognised for goods or services received as consideration for the equity instrument is based on the number of equity instruments that eventually vest. On a cumulative basis, this means that if a vesting condition is not satisfied then no amount is recognised for goods or services received.

A situation where employees leave during the vesting period, the number of equity instruments expected to vest varies. This is demonstrated in illustrative example 8.2.

ILLUSTRATIVE EXAMPLE 8.2 Grant where the number of equity instruments expected to vest varies

Seers Company grants 100 share options to each of its 50 employees. Each grant is conditional on the employee working for the company for the next 3 years. The fair value of each share option is estimated as $25. On the basis of a weighted average probability, the company estimates that 10% of its employees will leave during the 3-year period and therefore forfeit their rights to the share options.

During the year immediately following grant date (year 1) three employees leave, and at the end of year 1 the company revised its estimate of total employee departures over the full 3-year period from 10% (five employees) to 16% (eight employees).

During year 2 a further two employees leave, and the company revised its estimate of total employee departures across the 3-year period down to 12% (six employees). During year 3 a further employee leaves, making a total of six (3 + 2 + 1) employees who have departed. A total of 4400 share options (44 employees × 100 options per employee) vested at the end of year 3.

Year	Calculation	Remuneration expense for period $	Cumulative remuneration expense $
1	(5000 options × 84%) × $25 × 1/3 years	35 000	35 000
2	([5000 options × 88%] × $25 × 2/3 years) − $35 000	38 333	73 333
3	(4400 options × $25) − $73 333	36 667	110 000

Source: Adapted from IFRS 2, IG11.

In addition to continuing in service with the entity, employees may be granted equity instruments that are conditional on the achievement of a performance condition. Where the length of the vesting period varies according to when the performance condition is satisfied, the estimated length of the vesting period, at grant date, is based on the most likely outcome of the performance condition (IFRS 2 paragraph 15(b)).

A grant of shares with a performance condition linked to the level of an entity's earnings and in which the length of the vesting period varies is demonstrated in illustrative example 8.3.

ILLUSTRATIVE EXAMPLE 8.3 Grant with a performance condition linked to earnings

At the beginning of year 1 Benning Ltd grants 100 shares to each of its 50 employees, conditional on the employee remaining in the company's employ during the 3-year vesting period. The shares have a fair value of $20 per share at grant date. No dividends are expected to be paid over the 3-year period. Additionally, the vesting conditions allow the shares to vest at the end of:
- year 1 if the company's earnings have increased by more than 18%
- year 2 if earnings have increased by more than 13% averaged across the 2-year period
- year 3 if earnings have increased by more than 10% averaged across the 3-year period.

By the end of year 1, Benning Ltd's earnings have increased by only 14% and three employees have left. The company expects that earnings will continue to increase at a similar rate in year 2 and the shares will vest at the end of year 2. It also expects that a further three employees will leave during year 2, and therefore that 44 employees will vest in 100 shares each at the end of year 2.

Year	Calculation	Remuneration expense for period $	Cumulative remuneration expense $
1	(44 employees × 100 shares) × $20 × 1/2 years	44 000	44 000

By the end of year 2 the company's earnings have increased by only 10%, resulting in an average of only 12% ([14% + 10%]/2) and so the shares do not vest. Two employees left during the year. The company expects that another two employees will leave during year 3 and that its earnings will increase by at least 6%, thereby achieving the average of 10% per year.

Year	Calculation	Remuneration expense for period $	Cumulative remuneration expense $
2	([43 employees × 100 shares] × $20 × 2/3 years) − $44 000	13 333	57 333

Another three employees leave during year 3 and the company's earnings have increased by 8%, resulting in an average increase of 10.67% over the 3-year period. Therefore, the performance condition has been satisfied. The 42 remaining employees (50 − [3 + 2 + 3]) are entitled to receive 100 shares each at the end of year 3.

Year	Calculation	Remuneration expense for period $	Cumulative remuneration expense $
3	([42 employees × 100 shares] × $20) − $57 333	26 667	84 000

Source: Adapted from IFRS 2, IG12.

An entity may also grant equity instruments to its employees with a performance condition, and where the exercise price varies. This particular situation is demonstrated in illustrative example 8.4.

Because the exercise price varies depending on the outcome of a performance condition that is not a market condition, the effect of the performance condition (in this case, the possibility that the exercise price might be either $40 or $30) is not taken into account when estimating the fair value of the share options at grant date. Instead, the entity estimates the fair value of the share options at grant date and ultimately revises the transaction amount to reflect the outcome of the performance condition.

ILLUSTRATIVE EXAMPLE 8.4 Grant of equity instruments where the exercise price varies

At the beginning of year 1 Phillipe Ltd granted 5000 share options with an exercise price of $40 to a senior executive, conditional upon the executive remaining with the company until the end of year 3. The exercise price drops to $30 if Phillipe Ltd's earnings increase by an average of 10% per year over the 3-year period. On grant date the estimated fair value of the share options with an exercise price of $40 is $12 per option and, if the exercise price is $30, the estimated fair value of the options is $16 per option.

During year 1 the company's earnings increased by 12% and they are expected to continue to increase at this rate over the next 2 years. During year 2 the company's earnings increased by 13% and the company continued to expect that the earnings target would be achieved. During year 3 the company's earnings increased by only 3%. The earnings target was therefore not achieved and so the 5000 vested share options will have an exercise price of $40. The executive completed 3 years' service and so satisfied the service condition.

Year	Calculation	Remuneration expense for period $	Cumulative remuneration expense $
1	5000 options × $16 × 1/3 years	26 667	26 667
2	(5000 options × $16 × 2/3 years) − $26 667	26 666	53 333
3	(5000 options × $12) − $53 333	6 667	60 000

Source: Adapted from IFRS 2, IG12.

Paragraph 21 of IFRS 2 requires that market conditions (such as a target share price) be taken into account when estimating the fair value of equity instruments. The goods or services received from a counterparty that satisfies all other vesting conditions (such as remaining in service for a specified period of time) are recognised whether or not the market condition is satisfied.

A grant of equity instruments with a market condition is demonstrated in illustrative example 8.5.

ILLUSTRATIVE EXAMPLE 8.5 Grant with a market condition

At the beginning of year 1 Smallville Ltd grants 5000 share options to a senior executive, conditional on that executive remaining in the company's employ until the end of year 3. The share options cannot be exercised unless the share price has increased from $15 at the beginning of year 1 to above $25 at the end of year 3. If the share price is above $25 at the end of year 3, the share options can be exercised at any time during the next 7 years (that is, by the end of year 10). The company applies an option-pricing model that takes into account the possibility that the share price will exceed $25 at the end of year 3 and the possibility that the share price will not exceed $25 at the end of year 3. It estimates the fair value of the share options with this embedded market condition to be $9 per option. The executive completes 3 years' service with Smallville Ltd.

Year	Calculation	Remuneration expense for period $	Cumulative remuneration expense $
1	5000 options × $9 × 1/3 years	15 000	15 000
2	(5000 options × $9 × 2/3 years) − $15 000	15 000	30 000
3	(5000 options × $9) − $30 000	15 000	45 000

Source: Adapted from IFRS 2, IG13.

As noted earlier, because the executive has satisfied the service condition, the company is required to recognise these amounts irrespective of the outcome of the market condition.

8.5.2 Treatment of non-vesting conditions

IFRS 2 was amended in 2008 to clarify vesting conditions. The amendments clarify that vesting conditions comprise service and performance conditions only, and that other features of a share-based payment are not vesting conditions.

The amendments take into account all non-vesting conditions when estimating the fair value of equity instruments granted (paragraph 21A, effective 1 January 2009). Under this provision, for grants of equity with non-vesting conditions, an entity must recognise the goods or services received from a counterparty that satisfies all vesting conditions that are not market conditions (such as services from an employee who remains in service for a specified period of time). This applies whether or not the non-vesting conditions are satisfied.

The process of determining whether or not a condition is a non-vesting condition, or a service or performance condition, is illustrated in the flowchart in figure 8.3.

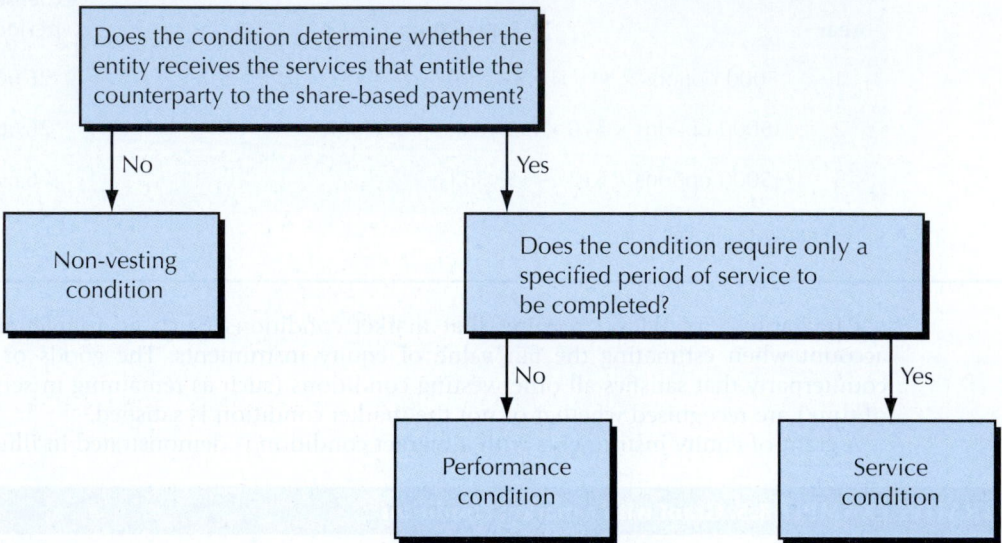

FIGURE 8.3 Distinguishing vesting and non-vesting conditions
Source: Adapted from AASB 2008–1, IG11.

8.6 TREATMENT OF A RELOAD FEATURE

Employee share options often include features that are not found in exchange-traded options. One such feature is a *reload* which entitles the employee to be automatically granted new options when the previously granted options are exercised using shares rather than cash to satisfy the exercise price. Although a reload feature can add considerably to an option's value, it is not considered feasible to value the reload feature at grant date. Under paragraph 22 of IFRS 2, a reload feature is not taken into account when estimating the fair value of the options granted at measurement date. Instead, a reload feature is accounted for as a new option if and when a reload option is subsequently granted.

After vesting date

Having recognised the goods or services received and a corresponding increase in equity, paragraph 23 of IFRS 2 prevents an entity from making a subsequent adjustment to total equity after vesting date. For example, if an amount is recognised for services received from an employee, it may not be reversed if the vested equity instruments are later forfeited or, in the case of share options, if the options are not subsequently exercised. This restriction applies only to total equity; it does not preclude an entity from transferring amounts from one component of equity to another.

If the fair value of the equity instruments cannot be estimated reliably

In the event that the fair value of equity instruments cannot be reliably estimated, they must instead be measured at their *intrinsic* value (IFRS 2 paragraph 24(a)). Intrinsic value is measured at the date goods are obtained or services are rendered, at the end of each subsequent reporting period, and at the date of final settlement. Any change in intrinsic value must be recognised in profit or loss. For a grant of share options, the share-based payment arrangement is finally settled when the options are exercised, forfeited, or when they lapse. The amount to be recognised for goods or services is based on the number of equity instruments that ultimately vest or are exercised. The estimate must be revised if subsequent information indicates that the number of share options expected to vest differs from previous estimates. On vesting date, the estimate is then revised to equal the number of equity instruments that ultimately vest.

Illustrative example 8.6 provides an example of the application of the intrinsic value method of accounting for share-based payments.

At the beginning of year 1, Brown Ltd granted 100 share options each to its 50 employees. The share options will vest at the end of year 3 if the employees remain employed by the company at that date. The share options have a life of 5 years. The exercise price is $60, which is also Brown Ltd's share price at the grant date. The company concludes that it cannot reliably estimate the fair value of the share options at the grant date.

Brown Ltd's share price during years 1–5 and the number of share options exercised during years 4–5 are set out below. Share options may be exercised only at year-end.

Year	Share price at year-end	Number of share options exercised at year-end
1	63	0
2	65	0
3	75	0
4	88	2 600
5	100	1 700

A   At the end of year 1 three employees have left, and the company estimates that a further seven employees will leave during years 2 and 3. Hence, only 80% of the share options are expected to vest.

Year	Calculation	Remuneration expense for period $	Cumulative remuneration expense $
A 1	(50 × 100 options × 80%) × ($63 − $60) × 1/3 years	4 000	4 000

B   Two employees left during year 2, and the company revises its estimate of the number of share options expected to vest to 86%.
C   Two more employees leave during year 3, so there are 4300 share options vested at the end of year 3 (100 × [50 − (3 + 2 + 2)]).

Year	Calculation	Remuneration expense for period $	Cumulative remuneration expense $
B 2	(50 × 100 options × 86% × [$65 − $60] × 2/3 years) − $4000	10 333	14 333
C 3	(43 × 100 options × [$75 − $60]) − $14 333	50 167	64 500

In accordance with paragraph 24 of IFRS 2, Brown Ltd will recognise the following amounts in years 4 and 5:

Year	Calculation	Remuneration expense for period $	Cumulative remuneration expense $
4	(1700 outstanding options × [$88 − $75]) + (2600 exercised options × [$88 − $75])	55 900	120 400
5	(1700 exercised options × [$100 − $88])	20 400	140 800*

*(1700 options × [$100 − $60]) + (2600 options × [$88 − $60])

Source: Adapted from IFRS 2, IG16.

If share options are forfeited after vesting date or lapse at the end of the share option's life, then paragraph 24(b) of IFRS 2 requires the amount previously recognised for goods or services to be reversed.

Paragraph 25 requires that if a grant of equity instruments is settled during the vesting period, the settlement must be accounted for as an acceleration of vesting. The amount that would otherwise have been recognised for services received over the remainder of the vesting period is, instead, recognised immediately. Any payment made by the entity on settlement is accounted for as the repurchase of equity instruments (a deduction from equity). Any excess of payment amount over the intrinsic value of the equity instrument measured at repurchase date must be recognised as an expense.

8.7 MODIFICATIONS TO TERMS AND CONDITIONS ON WHICH EQUITY INSTRUMENTS WERE GRANTED

An entity might choose to modify the terms and conditions on which it granted equity instruments. For example, it might change (reprice/retest) the exercise price of share options previously granted to employees at prices that were higher than the current price of the entity's shares. It might accelerate the vesting of share options to make the options more favourable to employees; or it might remove or alter a performance condition. If the exercise price of options is modified, the fair value of the options changes. A reduction in the exercise price would increase the fair value of share options. Irrespective of any modifications to the terms and conditions on which equity instruments are granted, paragraph 27 of IFRS 2 requires the services received, measured at the grant-date fair value of the equity instruments, to be recognised unless those equity instruments do not vest.

Although some companies provide for retesting to allow for the potential volatility of earnings and the cyclical nature of the market, many companies limit the retesting opportunities and others do not allow retesting at all. Billabong International Limited does not allow retesting of performance targets (see figure 8.4).

Remuneration Report

Variable remuneration components

Executive Performance Share Plan (EPSP)/Long Term Incentive (LTI) plan
At the end of each performance period, the Human Resources and Remuneration Committee considers the EPS performance of the Company and determines to what extent the awards should vest.

Each year prior to awards being granted, the Human Resources and Remuneration Committee considers the market environment, the Group's business strategy, performance expectations and shareholder expectations and sets the performance targets for the awards to be granted that year. No retesting is permitted.

FIGURE 8.4 Retesting (repricing) Billabong International Limited
Source: Billabong International Ltd (2011, p. 27).

The incremental effects of modifications that increase the total fair value of the share-based payment arrangement, or that are otherwise beneficial to the employee, must also be recognised. The incremental fair value is the difference between the fair value of the modified equity instrument and that of the original equity instrument, both estimated at the date of modification (IFRS 2 appendix B43(a)). Similarly, if the modification increases the number of equity instruments granted, the fair value of the additional equity instruments, measured at the date of modification, must be included in the amount recognised for services received.

If the modification occurs during the vesting period, the incremental fair value is included in the measurement of the amount recognised for services received from the modification date until the date when the modified equity instruments vest. This is in addition to the amount based on the grant-date fair value of the original equity instruments that is recognised over the remainder of the original vesting period. If the modification occurs after the vesting date, the incremental fair value is recognised immediately, or over the vesting period if the employee is required to complete an additional period of service before becoming unconditionally entitled to the modified equity instruments.

The terms or conditions of the equity instruments granted may be modified in a manner that reduces the total fair value of the share-based payment arrangement or that is not otherwise beneficial to the employee. If this occurs, then IFRS 2 (appendix B44) requires the services received as consideration to be accounted for as if that modification had not occurred (i.e. the decrease in fair value is not to be taken into account).

8.7.1 Repurchases

If vested equity instruments are repurchased, IFRS 2 (paragraph 29) specifies that the payment made to the employee is accounted for as a deduction from equity. If the payment exceeds the fair value of the equity instruments repurchased, the excess is recognised as an expense.

Illustrative example 8.7 demonstrates the accounting treatment of a repricing modification to the terms and conditions of share options.

ILLUSTRATIVE EXAMPLE 8.7 Grant of equity instruments that are subsequently repriced

Merton Ltd grants 100 share options to each of its 50 employees, conditional upon the employee remaining in service over the next 3 years. The company estimates that the fair value of each option is $15. On the basis of a weighted average probability, the company also estimates that 10 employees will leave during the 3-year vesting period and therefore forfeit their rights to the share options.

A   Four employees leave during year 1, and the company estimates that a further seven employees will leave during years 2 and 3. By the end of year 1 the company's share price has dropped, and it decides to reprice the share options. The repriced share options will vest at the end of year 3. At the date of repricing, Merton Ltd estimates that the fair value of each of the original share options is $5 and the fair value of each repriced share option is $8. The incremental value is $3 per share option, and this amount is recognised over the remaining 2 years of the vesting period along with the remuneration expense based on the original option value of $15.

Year	Calculation	Remuneration expense for period $	Cumulative remuneration expense $
A 1	(50 − 11) employees × 100 options × $15 × 1/3 years	19 500	19 500

B   During year 2 a further four employees leave, and the company estimates that another four employees will leave during year 3 to bring the total expected employee departures over the 3-year vesting period to 12 employees.

Year	Calculation	Remuneration expense for period $	Cumulative remuneration expense $
B 2	([50 − 12] employees × 100 options) × ([$15 × 2/3 years] + [$3 × 1/2 years]) − $19 500	24 200	43 700

C   A further three employees leave during year 3. For the remaining 39 employees (50 − [4 + 4 + 3]), the share options vested at the end of year 3.

Year	Calculation	Remuneration expense for period $	Cumulative remuneration expense $
C 3	([50 − 11] employees × 100 options × [$15 + $3]) − $43 700	26 500	70 200

Source: Adapted from IFRS 2, IG15.

LO8 8.8 CASH-SETTLED SHARE-BASED PAYMENT TRANSACTIONS

Paragraphs 30–33 of IFRS 2 set out the requirements for share-based payments in which an entity incurs a liability for goods or services received, based on the price of its own equity instruments. These are known as *cash-settled* share-based payments. The fair value of the liability involved is remeasured at the end of each reporting period and the date of settlement, and any changes in the fair value are recognised in profit or loss for the period. In contrast, the fair value of *equity-settled* share-based payments is determined at grant date, and remeasurement of the granted equity instruments at the end of each subsequent reporting period and settlement date does not occur.

Examples of cash-settled share-based payments included in paragraph 31 of IFRS 2 are share appreciation rights that might be granted to an employee as part of a remuneration package. Share appreciation rights entitle the holder to a future cash payment (rather than an equity instrument) based on increases in the share price. Another example is where an employee is granted rights to shares that are redeemable, providing the employee with a right to receive a future cash payment.

There is a presumption in IFRS 2 that the services rendered by employees in exchange for the share appreciation rights have been received. Where share appreciation rights vest immediately, the services and the associated liability must also be recognised immediately. Where the share appreciation rights do not vest until the employees have completed a specified period of service, the services received and the associated liability to pay for those services are recognised as the service is rendered. The liability is measured, initially and at the end of each reporting period until settled, at the fair value of the share appreciation rights by applying an option-pricing model that takes into account the terms and conditions on which share appreciation rights were granted, and the extent to which employees have rendered service (paragraph 33).

Illustrative example 8.8 provides an example of the accounting treatment for cash-settled share appreciation rights.

ILLUSTRATIVE EXAMPLE 8.8 Cash-settled share appreciation rights

Brierley Ltd grants 100 share appreciation rights (SARs) to each of its 50 employees, conditional upon the employee staying with the company for the next 3 years. The company estimates the fair value of the SARs at the end of each year as shown below. The intrinsic values of the SARs at the date of exercise (which equal the cash paid out) at the end of years 3, 4 and 5 are also shown. All SARs held by employees remaining at the end of year 3 will vest.

Year	Fair value	Intrinsic value
1	$14.40	
2	$15.50	
3	$18.20	$15.00
4	$21.40	$20.00
5		$25.00

A During year 1 three employees leave and the company estimates that six more will leave during years 2 and 3.

B Four employees leave during year 2, and the company estimates that three more will leave during year 3.

Year	Calculation	Expense $	Liability $
A 1	(50 − 9) employees × 100 SARs × $14.40 × 1/3 years	19 680	19 680
B 2	([50 − 10] employees × 100 SARs × $15.50 × 2/3 years) − $19 680	21 653	41 333

C Two employees leave during year 3.
D At the end of year 3, 15 employees have exercised their SARs.
E Another 14 employees exercise their SARs at the end of year 4.
F The remaining 12 employees exercise their SARs at the end of year 5.

Year	Calculation	Expense $	Liability $
C 3	([50 – 9 – 15] employees × 100 SARs × $18.20) – $41 333	5 987	47 320
D	15 employees × 100 SARs × $15	22 500	
E 4	([26 – 14] employees × 100 SARs × $21.40) – $47 320	(21 640)	25 680
	14 employees × 100 SARs × $20	28 000	
F 5	(0 employees × 100 SARs × $25) – $25 680	(25 680)	0
	12 employees × 100 SARs × $25	30 000	
	Total	80 500	

Source: Adapted from IFRS 2, IG19.

8.8.1 Share-based payment transactions with cash alternatives

Some share-based payments may provide either the entity or the counterparty with the choice of having the transaction settled in cash (or other assets) or the issue of equity instruments. If the entity has incurred a liability to settle in cash or other assets, the transaction is treated as a cash-settled share-based payment. If no liability has been incurred, paragraph 34 of IFRS 2 requires that the transaction be treated as an equity-settled share-based payment.

Share-based payment transactions where the counterparty has settlement choice

If the counterparty to a share-based payment has the right to choose whether a transaction is settled in cash or equity instruments, a compound financial instrument has been created that includes a debt component and an equity component. The debt component represents the counterparty's right to demand a cash settlement, and the equity component represents the counterparty's right to demand settlement in equity instruments.

IFRS 2 (paragraphs 35, 36) requires that transactions with employees be measured at fair value on measurement date, by taking into account the terms and conditions on which rights to cash and equity were granted. For transactions with others in which the fair value of goods or services is measured directly, the equity component is measured as the difference between the fair value of the goods or services received and the fair value of the debt component at the date they are received. The fair value of the debt component is measured before the fair value of the equity component (paragraph 37), as the counterparty must forfeit the right to receive cash in order to receive equity instruments. The measurement of compound financial instruments with employees (and other counterparties) is summarised in table 8.2.

TABLE 8.2 Measurement of compound financial instruments	
Counterparty	**Measurement approach**
Employees	Measure fair value (FV) of the debt component then FV of the equity component, at measurement date, taking into account the terms and conditions on which rights to cash or equity were granted
Parties other than employees	Equity component is the difference between FV of goods or services received and FV of the debt component, at the date the goods or services are received

The goods or services received in respect of each component of the compound financial instrument must be accounted for separately. For the debt component, the goods or services and a liability to pay for them is recognised as the counterparty supplies the goods or services, in the same manner as other cash-settled share-based payments. For the equity component, the goods or services received and the increase in equity are recognised as the counterparty supplies the goods or services, in the same manner as other equity-settled share-based payments.

At settlement date, the liability must be remeasured to fair value (IFRS 2 paragraph 39). If equity instruments are issued rather than a cash settlement paid, the liability must be transferred directly to equity as consideration for the equity instruments. If the counterparty takes cash settlement, the payment is applied in settlement of the liability. Any equity component previously recognised remains within equity although it can be transferred within equity.

A grant of shares with a cash alternative subsequently added that provides an employee with a settlement choice is demonstrated in illustrative example 8.9.

ILLUSTRATIVE EXAMPLE 8.9 Grant of shares with a cash alternative subsequently added

At the beginning of year 1 Scotland Ltd granted 10 000 shares with a fair value of $24 per share to a senior manager, conditional on the manager remaining in the company's employ for 3 years. By the end of year 2 the share price had dropped to $15 per share. At that date the company added a cash alternative to the grant, giving the manager the right to choose whether to receive the 10 000 shares or cash equal to the value of the shares on vesting date. On vesting date the share price had dropped to $12.

Year	Calculation	Asset/expense $	Equity $	Liability $
1	10 000 shares × $24 × 1/3 years	80 000	80 000	

The addition of the cash alternative at the end of year 2 created an obligation to settle in cash. Scotland Ltd must recognise the liability to settle in cash based on the fair value of the shares at the modification date and the extent to which the specified services have been received. The liability must be remeasured at the end of each subsequent reporting period and at the date of settlement.

Year	Calculation	Asset/expense $	Equity $	Liability $
2	(10 000 shares × $24 × 2/3 years) − $80 000	80 000	80 000	
	10 000 shares × $15 × 2/3 years		(100 000)	100 000*

Year	Calculation	Asset/expense $	Equity $	Liability $
3	(10 000 shares × $24) − $160 000	80 000	30 000	50 000*
	(10 000 shares × $12) − $150 000	(30 000)		(30 000)
	Total	210 000	90 000	120 000**

* At the date of modification when the cash alternative is added the total liability is $150 000 ($15 × 10 000 shares). At this date a potential liability must be recognised.

** Total liability at date of settlement is $120 000 ($12 × 10 000 shares).

Source: Adapted from IFRS 2, IG15.

An example of a share-based payment transaction in which an employee has a right to choose either a cash settlement or an equity settlement is demonstrated in illustrative example 8.10.

ILLUSTRATIVE EXAMPLE 8.10 Share-based payment transaction where employee has settlement choice

Norden Ltd grants to each of its 10 executives a choice of receiving a cash payment equivalent to 1000 shares or receiving 1200 shares. The grant is conditional on the completion of 3 years' service with the company. If the share alternative is chosen, the shares must be held for 2 years after vesting date. At the grant date the company's share price is $25 per share. At the end of years 1, 2 and 3 the share price is $27, $28 and $30 respectively. The company does not expect to pay dividends in the next 3 years. After taking into account the effects of post-vesting transfer restrictions, the company estimates that the grant-date fair value of the share alternative is $24 per share.

The fair value of the cash alternative is $250 000 (10 × 1000 shares × $25), and the fair value of the equity alternative is $288 000 (10 × 1200 shares × $24). Therefore, the fair value of the equity component of the compound instrument is $38 000 ($288 000 − $250 000). Norden Ltd will recognise the following amounts:

Year	Calculation	Asset/expense $	Equity $	Liability $
1	Liability component (10 × 1000 × $27 × 1/3 years)	90 000		90 000
	Equity component ($38 000 × 1/3 years)	12 667	12 667	
2	Liability component (10 × 1000 × $28 × 2/3 years) − $90 000	96 667		96 667
	Equity component ($38 000 × 1/3 years)	12 667	12 667	
3	Liability component (10 × 1000 × $30) − $186 667	113 333		113 333
	Equity component ($38 000 × 1/3 years)	12 666	12 666	

At the end of year 3, the employees must choose whether to take the cash or shares. At settlement, the liability must be remeasured to its full value. If all employees choose the cash settlement, the liability is $300 000 (10 × 1000 × $30). If cash is paid on settlement it must be applied to settle the liability in full, with any previously recognised equity instrument remaining within equity.

Year	Calculation	Asset/expense $	Equity $	Liability $
End year 3	Choice 1: Cash equivalent to 10 × 1000 shares × $30 Cash settlement of $300 000 paid			(300 000)
	Totals	338 000	38 000	0

If the employees choose to receive shares, the liability is transferred direct to equity (IFRS 2 paragraph 39) as the consideration for the equity instruments that were issued. If all employees choose the equity alternative, the amount of the liability transferred to equity is $300 000.

Year	Calculation	Asset/expense $	Equity $	Liability $
End year 3	Choice 2: Equity issue of 10 × 1200 shares 12 000 shares issued		300 000	(300 000)
	Totals	338 000	338 000	0

Source: Adapted from IFRS 2, IG21.

Share-based payment transactions where the entity has settlement choice

Where an entity has a choice of settling in cash or equity instruments, it must determine whether it has a present obligation to settle in cash. Paragraph 41 of IFRS 2 states that an entity has a present obligation to settle in cash if the choice of settlement in equity instruments has no commercial substance (perhaps the entity is legally prohibited from issuing shares), it has a past practice or a stated policy of settling in cash, or if it generally settles in cash whenever the counterparty asks for cash settlement. If a present obligation exists, the transaction must be accounted for as a cash-settled share-based payment. If a present obligation to settle in cash does not exist, the transaction is accounted for as an equity-settled arrangement.

On settlement, if the entity elects to settle in cash, paragraph 43(a) of IFRS 2 requires the cash payment to be accounted for as the repurchase of an equity interest, resulting in a deduction from equity. Where there is an equity settlement, no further accounting adjustments are required. If, on settlement, the entity selects the settlement alternative with the higher fair value, an additional expense for the excess value given must be recognised. The excess value is either the difference between the cash paid and the fair value of the equity instruments that would have been issued, or the difference between the fair value of the equity instruments issued and the amount of cash that would have been paid, whichever is applicable.

8.9 DISCLOSURE

The global financial crisis which emerged in 2008 has resulted in much criticism about the inadequacy of disclosure in regard to performance hurdles and incentives used in share-based payment transactions. Corporate executives, on the other hand, complain about the onerous reporting and disclosure requirements necessary under the accounting rules. One difficulty faced by regulators is how to reduce the volume of required information yet still retain meaningful and useful disclosure.

Paragraphs 44–52 of IFRS 2 prescribe various disclosures relating to share-based payments. The objective of these disclosures is to provide significant additional information to assist financial statement users to understand the nature and extent of share-based payment arrangements that existed during the reporting period. The three principles that underpin the disclosures required by IFRS 2 are shown in table 8.3.

TABLE 8.3 Principles underpinning the disclosures in IFRS 2

Disclosure principle	IFRS 2 paragraph
The nature and extent of the share-based payment arrangements.	44
How the fair value of goods or services received, or the fair value of equity instruments granted during the period, was determined.	46
The effect of share-based payment transactions on the entity's profit or loss for the period and on its financial position.	50

Paragraph 45 of IFRS 2 specifies the disclosures necessary to give effect to the principle in paragraph 44 as including at least the following:
- a description of each type of share-based payment arrangement that existed at any time during the period, including the general terms and conditions of each arrangement, such as vesting requirements, the maximum term of options granted, and the methods of settlement.

An entity with substantially similar types of share-based payments may aggregate this information unless separate disclosure of each arrangement is necessary to enable users to understand the nature and extent of the arrangements.

Other specific disclosures required by paragraph 45 are the number and weighted average exercise prices of share options for options that:
- are outstanding at the beginning of the period
- are granted during the period
- are forfeited during the period
- are exercised during the period
- have expired during the period
- are outstanding at the end of the period
- are exercisable at the end of the period.

In relation to share options exercised during the period, the weighted average share price at the date of exercise must be disclosed. If the options were exercised on a regular basis throughout the period, the weighted average share price during the period may be disclosed instead. For share options outstanding at the end of the period, the range of exercise prices and weighted average remaining contractual life must be disclosed. If the range of exercise prices is wide, the outstanding options must be divided into ranges that are meaningful for assessing the number and timing of additional shares that may be issued and the cash that may be received upon exercise of those options.

If the fair value of goods or services received as consideration for equity instruments of the entity has been measured indirectly by reference to the fair value of the equity instruments granted, the following information must be disclosed (paragraph 47):

- the weighted average fair value of share options granted during the period, at the measurement date, and information on how the fair value was measured including:
  - the option-pricing model used and the inputs to that model including the weighted average share price, exercise price, expected volatility, option life, expected dividends, the risk-free interest rate, and any other inputs to the model including the assumptions made to incorporate the effects of expected early exercise
  - how expected volatility was determined, including an explanation of the extent to which expected volatility was based on historical volatility
  - whether, and how many, other features of the option grant (such as a market condition) were incorporated into the measurement of fair value
- for equity instruments other than share options granted during the period, the number and weighted average fair value at the measurement date, and information on how that fair value was measured, including:
  - if not measured on the basis of an observable market price, how fair value was determined
  - whether and how expected dividends were incorporated
  - whether and how any other features of the equity instruments were incorporated
- for share-based payment arrangements that were modified during the period:
  - an explanation of the modifications
  - the incremental fair value granted as a result of the modifications and information on how the incremental fair value granted was measured.

If the entity has measured the fair value of goods or services received during the period directly, it is required to disclose how that fair value was determined (e.g. at market price).

If the entity has rebutted the assumption that the fair value of goods or services received can be estimated reliably, it is required to disclose that fact (paragraph 49) together with an explanation of why the presumption was rebutted.

Paragraph 51 gives effect to the principle that an entity must disclose information that enables financial statement users to understand the effect of share-based payments on the entity's profit or loss for the period and on its financial position. This paragraph requires disclosure of at least the following:

- the total expense recognised for the period arising from share-based payments in which the goods or services received did not qualify for recognition as assets, including separate disclosure of that portion of the total expense that arises from transactions accounted for as equity-settled share-based payments
- for liabilities arising from share-based payment transactions:
  - the total carrying amount at the end of the period
  - the total intrinsic value at the end of the period of liabilities for which the counterparty's right to cash or other assets had vested by the end of the period.

Finally, paragraph 52 requires the disclosure of such other additional information as may be needed to enable the users of the financial statements to understand the nature and extent of the share-based payment arrangements; how the fair value of goods or services received, or the fair value of equity instruments granted was determined; and the effect of share-based payments on the entity's profit or loss and on its financial position.

A review of the corporate annual reports shows the large volume of space devoted to share-based payment disclosure. For example, Billabong International Limited's 2011 remuneration report covers 30 pages (2010: 17 pages).

An extract relating to share-based payment disclosures for Billabong International Limited appears in figure 8.5.

FIGURE 8.5 Accounting policy note for share-based payments

1 Summary of significant accounting policies
(y) Employee and executive share plans
Equity-based compensation benefits are provided to employees via the Billabong Executive Performance Share Plan and the Executive Performance and Retention Plan.

(continued)

FIGURE 8.5 *(continued)*

Billabong Executive Performance Share Plan

Share-based compensation benefits are provided to the executive team via the Billabong Executive Performance Share Plan. Information relating to this Plan is set out in note 42.

The market value of shares issued to employees for no cash consideration under the employee share scheme is recognised as an employee benefit expense with a corresponding increase in equity when the employees become entitled to the shares.

The fair value of equity instruments granted under the Billabong Executive Performance Share Plan is recognised as an employee benefit expense over the period during which the employees become unconditionally entitled to the instruments. There is a corresponding increase in equity, being recognition of an option reserve. Once the employees become unconditionally entitled to the instruments the option reserve is set-off against the treasury shares vested.

The fair value of equity instruments granted is measured at grant date and is determined by reference to the Billabong International Limited share price at grant date, taking into account the terms and conditions upon which the rights were granted. . .

Billabong Executive Performance and Retention Plan

Share-based compensation benefits are also provided to the executive team via the Billabong Executive Performance and Retention Plan. Information relating to this Plan is set out in note 42.

The fair value of the options granted under the Billabong Executive Performance and Retention Plan is recognised as an employee benefit expense with a corresponding increase in equity. The fair value is measured at grant date and recognised over the period during which the executive team becomes unconditionally entitled to the options.

The fair value at grant date is independently determined using the Monte-Carlo simulation valuation technique that takes into account the exercise price, the term of the option, the share price at grant date and expected price volatility of the underlying share, the expected dividend yield and the risk free interest rate for the term of the option.

The fair value of the options granted is adjusted to reflect market vesting conditions, but excludes the impact of any non-market vesting conditions (for example, profitability and sales growth targets). Non-market vesting conditions are included in assumptions about the number of options that are expected to become exercisable. At each reporting date, the entity revises its estimate of the number of options that are expected to become exercisable. The employee benefit expense recognised each period takes into account the most recent estimate. The impact of the revision to original estimates, if any, is recognised in the income statement with a corresponding adjustment to equity.

Source: Billabong International Ltd (2011, pp. 68–9).

SUMMARY

IFRS 2 deals with the recognition and measurement of share-based payment transactions. Share-based payments are arrangements in which an entity receives or acquires goods or services as consideration for, or based on the price of (respectively) its own equity instruments. The main features of the standard are that it:

- requires financial statement recognition of the goods or services acquired or received under share-based payment arrangements, regardless of whether the settlement is cash or equity or whether the counterparty is an employee or another party.
- employs the general principle for cash-settled transactions that the goods or services received and the liability incurred are measured at the fair value of the liability; and, until it is settled, the fair value of the liability is remeasured at the end of each reporting period and at the date of settlement and any changes in fair value are recognised in profit or loss.
- employs the general principle for equity-settled transactions that the goods or services received and the corresponding increase in equity are measured at the grant date, and at the fair value of the goods or services received; and if the fair value cannot be measured reliably, the goods or services are measured indirectly by reference to the fair value of the equity instruments granted.
- allows an entity to choose appropriate option-valuation models to determine fair values and to tailor those models to suit the entity's specific circumstances.

- includes a lengthy set of disclosure requirements aimed at enabling financial statement users to understand the nature, extent and effect of share-based payments, and how the fair value of goods or services received or equity instruments granted was determined.

Discussion questions

1. Why do standard setters formulate rules on the measurement and recognition of share-based payment transactions?
2. What is the difference between equity-settled and cash-settled share-based payment transactions?
3. What is the different accounting treatment for instruments classified as debt and those classified as equity?
4. Outline the accounting treatment for the recognition of an equity-settled share-based payment transaction.
5. Explain when a counterparty's entitlement to receive equity instruments of an entity vests.
6. What are the minimum factors required under IFRS 2 to be taken into account in option-pricing models?
7. Distinguish between vesting and non-vesting conditions.
8. Explain what the 'retesting' of share options means.
9. Explain the measurement approach for cash-settled share-based payment transactions.
10. Are the following statements true or false?
    (a) Goods or services received in a share-based payment transaction must be recognised when they are received.
    (b) Historical volatility provides the best basis for forming reasonable expectations of the future price of share options.
    (c) Share appreciation rights entitle the holder to a future equity instrument based on the profitability of the issuer.

Exercises

STAR RATING ★ BASIC ★★ MODERATE ★★★ DIFFICULT

Exercise 8.1 — SCOPE OF IFRS 2

★ Which of the following is a share-based payment transaction within the scope of IFRS 2? Give reasons for your answer.
(a) Goods acquired from a supplier (counterparty) by incurring a liability based on the market price of the goods
(b) An invoiced amount for professional advice provided to an entity, charged at an hourly rate, and to be settled in cash
(c) Services provided by an employee to be settled in equity instruments of the entity
(d) Supply of goods in return for cash or equity instruments at the discretion of the counterparty
(e) Dividend payment to employees who are holders of an entity's shares

Exercise 8.2 — RECOGNITION PRINCIPLES

★ Zebra Ltd, a listed company, organises major sporting events. It acquires crowd control equipment in return for a liability for an amount based on the price of 1000 of its own shares.

Required

Is this a share-based payment transaction? Should Zebra Ltd recognise the acquisition cost as an asset or an expense? Explain.

Exercise 8.3 — CATEGORISING

★ An entity grants 10 000 shares to a senior manager in return for services rendered.

Required

Should the entity recognise the cost of these services as a liability or a component of equity? Explain.

Exercise 8.4   EQUITY-SETTLED SHARE-BASED PAYMENT TRANSACTIONS

★ On 1 January 2013, Park Ltd announces a grant of 250 share options to each of its 20 senior executives. The grant is conditional on the employee continuing to work for Park Ltd for the next 3 years. The fair value of each share option is estimated to be $14. On the basis of a weighted average probability, Park Ltd estimates that 10% of its senior executives will leave during the vesting period.

Required

Prepare a schedule setting out the annual and cumulative remuneration expense to be recognised by Park Ltd for services rendered as consideration for the share options granted.

Exercise 8.5   CASH-SETTLED SHARE-BASED PAYMENT TRANSACTIONS

★ An entity receives inventory from a counterparty in exchange for a liability based on the price of 5000 of the entity's own shares. At the date of receiving the inventory, the entity's shares have a market value of $9.50 each.

Required

Measure the value of this transaction and prepare an appropriate journal entry to recognise it.

Exercise 8.6   MODIFICATIONS TO EQUITY-SETTLED SHARE-BASED PAYMENT TRANSACTIONS

★★ At the beginning of year 1, Iona Ltd grants 50 share options to each of its 120 employees, conditional on the employee remaining in the employ of Iona Ltd over the next 2 years. The company estimates that the fair value of the options on grant date is $12. On the basis of a weighted average probability, Iona Ltd estimates that 15% of its employees will leave during the vesting period. At the end of year 1 eight employees have left, and Iona Ltd estimates that a further nine will leave during year 2. By the end of year 1 the company's share price has dropped, and it decides to reprice the share options. It estimates that the fair value of the original share options is $7 and the fair value of the repriced share options is $10. Nine employees leave during year 2.

Required

Prepare a schedule setting out the remuneration expense to be recognised at the end of years 1 and 2.

Exercise 8.7   ACCOUNTING FOR A GRANT WHERE THE NUMBER OF EQUITY INSTRUMENTS EXPECTED TO VEST VARIES

★★ Tiger Ltd grants 80 share options to each of its 200 employees. Each grant is conditional on the employee working for the company for the 3 years following the grant date. On grant date, the fair value of each share option is estimated to be $12. On the basis of a weighted average probability, the company estimates that 20% of its employees will leave during the 3-year vesting period.

During year 1, 15 employees leave and the company revises its estimate of total employee departures over the full 3-year period from 20% to 22%.

Required

Prepare a schedule setting out the annual and cumulative remuneration expense for year 1.

Exercise 8.8   ACCOUNTING FOR A GRANT OF SHARE OPTIONS WHERE THE EXERCISE PRICE VARIES

★★ At the beginning of 2015, Whistler Ltd grants 3000 employee share options with an exercise price of $45 to its newly appointed chief executive officer, conditional on the executive remaining in the company's employ for the next 3 years. The exercise price drops to $35 if Whistler Ltd's earnings increase by an average of 10% per year over the 3-year period. On grant date, the estimated fair value of the employee share options with an exercise price of $35 is $22 per option. If the exercise price is $45, the options have an estimated fair value of $17 each.

During 2015, Whistler Ltd's earnings increased by 8% and are expected to continue to increase at this rate over the next 2 years.

Required

Prepare a schedule setting out the annual remuneration expense to be recognised by Whistler Ltd and the cumulative remuneration expense for 2015.

ACCOUNTING FOR A GRANT WITH A MARKET CONDITION

★★ At the beginning of 2013, Bay Ltd grants 10 000 share options to a senior marketing executive, conditional on that executive remaining in the company's employ until the end of 2015. The share options cannot be exercised unless the share price has increased from $20 at the beginning of 2013 to above $30 at the end of 2015. If the share price is above $30 at the end of 2013, the share options can be exercised at any time during the following 5 years. Bay Ltd applies a binomial option-pricing model that takes into account the possibility that the share price will exceed $30 at the end of 2015 and the possibility that the share price will not exceed $30 at the end of 2015. The fair value of the share options with this market condition is estimated to be $14 per option.

Required

Calculate the annual and cumulative remuneration expense to be recognised by Bay Ltd for 2013.

DISCLOSURE

★★ Bentley Ltd operates a share option plan for its officers, employees and consultants for up to 10% of its outstanding shares. Under this plan, the exercise price of each option equals the closing market price of the shares on the day before the grant. Each option has a term of 5 years and vests one-third on each of the 3 years following grant date. Before this financial period, Bentley Ltd has accounted for its share option plan on settlement date and no expense has been recognised.

Required

Prepare an appropriate memorandum outlining the disclosures that will need to be made in Bentley Ltd's financial statement following the adoption of IFRS 2.

APPLICATION OF THE INTRINSIC VALUE METHOD

★★★ At the beginning of 2013, Atlas Ltd grants 2000 share options to each of its 50 most senior executives. The share options have a life of 5 years and will vest at the end of year 3 if the executives remain in service until then. The exercise price is $50 and Atlas Ltd's share price is also $50 at the grant date. As the company's share options have characteristics significantly different from those of other traded share options, the use of option-pricing models will not provide a reliable measure of fair value at grant date.

The company's share price during years 1–3 is shown below.

Year	Share price at year-end	Estimated number of executives departing in each year	Number of executives remaining at year-end	Number of share options exercised at year-end
1	53	3	46	0
2	55	2	44	0
3	65	1	43	0

Required

Calculate the annual and cumulative remuneration expense to be recognised by Atlas Ltd for each of the 3 years.

SHARE-BASED PAYMENT WITH A NON-VESTING CONDITION

★★★ An employee is offered the opportunity to contribute 10% of his annual salary of $3000 across the next 2 years to a plan under which he receives share options. The employee's accumulated contributions to the plan may be used to exercise the options at the end of the 2-year period. The estimated annual expense for this share-based payment arrangement is $200.

Required

Prepare the necessary journal entry or entries to recognise this arrangement at the end of the first year.

ACCOUNTING FOR CASH-SETTLED SHARE-BASED PAYMENT TRANSACTIONS

★★★ Abernethy Ltd grants 1000 share appreciation rights (SARs) to 10 senior managers, to be taken in cash within 2 years of vesting date on condition that the managers do not leave in the next 3 years. The SARs vest at the end of year 3. Abernethy Ltd estimates the fair value of the SARs at the end of each year in which a liability exists as shown below. The intrinsic value of the SARs at the date of exercise at the end of year 3 is also shown.

Year	Fair value	Intrinsic value	Number of managers who exercised their SARs
1	$ 4.40		
2	$ 5.50		
3	$10.20	$ 9.00	4

During year 1, one employee leaves and Abernethy Ltd estimates that a further two will leave before the end of year 3. One employee leaves during year 2 and the corporation estimates that another employee will depart during year 3. One employee leaves during year 3. At the end of year 3, four employees exercise their SARs.

Required

Prepare a schedule setting out the expense and liability that Abernethy Ltd must recognise at the end of each of the first 3 years.

References

Billabong International Ltd 2011, *2010/2011 Full financial report*, Billabong International Limited, Australia, www.billabongbiz.com.

International Accounting Standards Board 2009, *IFRS 2 Share-based Payments*, IFRS Foundation, London, www.ifrs.org.

Woolworths Ltd 2011, *Annual report 2011*, Woolworths Limited, Australia, www.woolworthslimited.com.au.

9 Inventories

ACCOUNTING STANDARDS IN FOCUS

IAS 2 *Inventories*

LEARNING OBJECTIVES

After studying this chapter, you should be able to:

1 discuss the nature of inventories

2 explain how to measure inventories

3 explain what is included in the cost of inventory

4 account for inventory transactions using both the periodic and the perpetual methods

5 explain and apply end-of-period procedures for inventory under both periodic and perpetual methods

6 explain why cost flow assumptions are required and apply both FIFO and weighted average cost formulas

7 explain the net realisable value basis of measurement and account for adjustments to net realisable value

8 identify the amounts to be recognised as inventory expenses

9 implement the disclosure requirements of IAS 2.

9.1 THE NATURE OF INVENTORIES

For retailing and manufacturing entities inventory is the most active asset, and may make up a significant proportion of current assets. The cost of sales during the period is normally the largest expense of such entities.

The main accounting standard analysed in this chapter is IAS 2 *Inventories*. The standard was first issued as IAS 2 in October 1975, revised in 1993, amended in 1999 and 2000, exposed in May 2002 as a part of the *Exposure Draft of Proposed Improvements to International Accounting Standards,* and issued in its present form in 2003.

According to paragraph 2 of IAS 2, the standard applies in accounting for all inventories except work in progress arising under construction contracts (covered by IAS 11 *Construction Contracts*) and financial instruments and biological assets related to agricultural activity and agricultural produce at the point of harvest (IAS 41 *Agriculture*).

Paragraph 6 of IAS 2 defines inventories as follows:

> Inventories are assets:
> (a) held for sale in the ordinary course of business;
> (b) in the process of production for such sale; or
> (c) in the form of materials or supplies to be consumed in the production process or in the rendering of services.

Note the following points arising from this definition:

1. The assets are held for sale in the ordinary course of business. The accounting standards do not define 'ordinary', but IFRS 5 *Non-current Assets Held for Sale and Discontinued Operations* requires that non-current assets held for sale are to be distinguished from inventories. This indicates that the term 'inventories' should be applied only to those assets that are always intended for sale or use in producing saleable goods or services.

2. Accounting for assets held for use by the entity is covered by other accounting standards according to their nature. IAS 16 *Property, Plant and Equipment* covers tangible assets such as production equipment; IAS 38 *Intangible Assets* covers intangible assets such as patents.

3. Supplies or materials such as stationery would not be treated as inventories unless they are held for sale or are used in producing goods for sale.

4. IAS 16, paragraph 8, states that 'spare parts and servicing equipment are usually carried as inventory' unless those spare parts are expected to be used during more than one period, or can be used only in conjunction with an item of property, plant and equipment. This standard clearly envisages that spare parts as inventory are those items consumed regularly during the production process, such as bobbin winders on commercial sewing machines.

5. In the case of a service provider, inventories include the costs of the service for which the entity has not yet recognised the related revenue (IAS 2 paragraph 8).

6. The assets are current assets because they satisfy the following criteria for classification as 'current' set out in paragraph 66 of IAS 1 *Presentation of Financial Statements*:
   • it is expected to be realised in, or is intended for sale or consumption in the entity's normal operating cycle
   • it is held primarily for the purpose of being traded
   • it is expected to realise the asset within 12 months after the reporting period, or
   • the asset is cash or a cash equivalent as defined in IAS 7 *Statement of Cash Flows*.

The operating cycle of an entity is the time between the acquisition of assets for processing and their realisation in cash or cash equivalents. In some industries, such as retailing, the operating cycle may be very short, but for others, like winemaking, the operating cycle could cover a number of years. When the entity's operating cycle is not clearly identifiable, its duration is assumed to be 12 months (IAS 1 paragraph 69).

To illustrate: Nokia Corporation, based in Finland, prepares its financial statements in accordance with International Financial Reporting Standards (IFRSs). The extract from Nokia's notes to the consolidated financial statements at 31 December 2010, as shown in figure 9.1, indicates what is contained in inventories.

In this chapter, accounting for inventory is considered as follows:
• initial recognition of inventory — determining the cost of inventory acquired or made
• recording of inventory transactions using either the periodic or perpetual inventory methods, including end-of-period procedures and adjustments
• assignment of costs to inventory using the FIFO or weighted average cost flow assumptions

- measurement subsequent to initial recognition — determining the amount at which the asset is reported subsequent to acquisition, including any write-down to net realisable value.

18 INVENTORIES	2010 EURm	2009 EURm
Raw materials, supplies and other	762	409
Work in progress	642	681
Finished goods	1 119	775
Total	2 523	1 865

FIGURE 9.1 Extract from the consolidated financial statements of Nokia
Source: Nokia (2011, p. 45).

9.2 MEASUREMENT OF INVENTORY UPON INITIAL RECOGNITION

According to paragraph 9 of IAS 2, 'Inventories shall be measured at the lower of cost and net realisable value'. As the purpose of acquiring or manufacturing inventory items is to sell them at a profit, inventory will initially be recognised at cost. Two specific industry groups have been exempted from applying the lower of cost and net realisable value rule, namely:

(a) producers of agricultural and forest products, agricultural produce after harvest and minerals and mineral products, to the extent that they are measured at net realisable value in accordance with well-established practices in those industries

(b) commodity broker-traders who measure their inventories at fair value less costs of disposal.

In these cases, movements in net realisable value or fair value less any costs of disposal incurred during the period are recognised in the statement of profit or loss and other comprehensive income. Where inventories in these industries are measured by reference to historical cost, the lower of cost and net realisable value rule mandated by paragraph 9 would still apply.

9.3 DETERMINATION OF COST

The first step in accounting for inventory is its initial recognition at cost. IAS 2, paragraph 10, specifies three components of cost:

- costs of purchase
- costs of conversion
- other costs incurred in bringing the inventories to their present location and condition.

Costs of conversion apply only to manufacturing entities where raw materials and other supplies are purchased and then converted to other products.

9.3.1 Costs of purchase

Paragraph 11 of IAS 2 states that the costs of purchase comprise the purchase price, import duties and other taxes (other than those subsequently recoverable by the entity from the taxing authorities), transport, handling and other costs directly attributable to the acquisition of finished goods, materials and services. Trade discounts, rebates and other similar items are deducted in determining the costs of purchase.

Terms of sale

In identifying the costs of purchase, consideration must be given to the terms of sale relating to inventory items because such terms determine the treatment of transport costs associated with purchase. If goods are sold FOB (free on board) shipping point, freight costs incurred from the point of shipment are paid by the buyer, and are included in the costs of purchase. If goods are sold FOB destination, the seller pays all freight costs.

Transaction taxes

Many countries levy taxes on transactions involving the exchange of goods and services, and require entities engaging in such activities to collect and remit the tax to the government. If such a 'goods and services tax' or 'value added tax' exists, care must be taken to exclude these amounts from the costs of purchase if they are recoverable by the entity from the taxing authorities.

Trade and cash discounts

Trade discounts are reductions in selling prices granted to customers. Such discounts may be granted as an incentive to buy, as a means to quit ageing inventory or as a reward for placing large orders for goods. Because the discount reduces the purchase cost, it is deducted when determining the cost of inventory. Cash or settlement discounts are offered as incentives for early payment of amounts owing on credit sales. Credit terms appear on invoices or contracts and often take the form '2/7, n/30', which means that the buyer will receive a 2% discount if the invoice is paid within seven days of the invoice date or will get 30 days to pay without discount. Some entities may also impose an interest penalty for late payment.

Divergent accounting practices have arisen over time in respect of settlement discounts, with some countries treating the discount as a reduction in the cost of inventories and others treating the discount as revenue. This issue was settled when the International Financial Reporting Interpretations Committee (IFRIC) stated in November 2004 that 'settlement discounts should be deducted from the cost of inventories' (IASB 2004). Thus, discounts received are to be treated as a deduction from the cost of inventories rather than as discount revenue. On the other hand, rebates that specifically and genuinely refund selling expenses are not to be deducted from the cost of inventories.

Deferred payment terms

Where an item of inventory is acquired for cash or short-term credit, determination of the purchase price is relatively straightforward. One variation that may arise is that some or all of the cash payment is deferred. In this case, as noted in paragraph 18 of IAS 2, the purchase cost contains a financing element — the difference between the amount paid and a purchase on normal credit terms — which must be recognised as interest expense over the period of deferral.

9.3.2 Costs of conversion

IAS 2, paragraph 12, identifies costs of conversion as being the costs directly related to the units of production, such as direct labour, plus a systematic allocation of fixed and variable production overheads that are incurred in converting materials into finished goods. Variable overheads are indirect costs of production that vary directly with the volume of production and are allocated to each unit of production on the basis of actual use of production facilities. Fixed overheads, such as depreciation of production machinery, remain relatively constant regardless of the volume of production and are allocated to the cost of inventory on the basis of normal production capacity. Where a production process simultaneously produces one or more products, the costs of conversion must be allocated between products on a systematic and rational basis (paragraph 14). Costing methodologies are a managerial accounting issue and outside the scope of this book.

9.3.3 Other costs

Other costs can be included only if they are 'incurred in bringing the inventories to their present location and condition' (IAS 2 paragraph 15). Such costs could include specific design expenses incurred in producing goods for individual customers. IAS 23 *Borrowing Costs* allows borrowing costs such as interest to be included in the cost of inventories but only where such inventories are a qualifying asset; that is, one which takes a substantial period of time to get ready for its intended use or sale. Inventory items would rarely meet this criterion.

9.3.4 Excluded costs

The following costs are specifically listed in paragraph 16 of IAS 2 as costs that cannot be included in the cost of inventories and must be recognised as expenses when incurred:
- abnormal amounts of wasted materials, labour or other production costs
- storage costs, unless necessary in the production process before a further production stage
- administrative overheads that do not contribute to bringing inventories to their present location and condition
- selling costs.

9.3.5 Cost of inventories of a service provider

Service providers, such as cleaners, would normally measure any inventories at the cost of production. Because a service is being provided, such costs would consist primarily of labour and other personnel costs for those employees directly engaged in providing the service. The costs of supervisory personnel and directly attributable overheads may also be included, but paragraph 19 of IAS 2 prohibits the inclusion of labour and other costs relating to sales and general administrative personnel. Profit margins or non-attributable overheads that are built into the prices charged by service providers cannot be factored into the value of inventories. Such inventory assets would be recognised only for services 'in-progress' at the end of the reporting period for which the service provider has not as yet recognised any revenue (e.g. where a catering firm has provided meals for 10 days as at the end of the reporting period but bills the client on a fortnightly basis).

ILLUSTRATIVE EXAMPLE 9.1 Determination of cost

Western Ltd, an Australian company, received the following invoice from De Ferrari Garments Ltd, an Italian garment manufacturer.

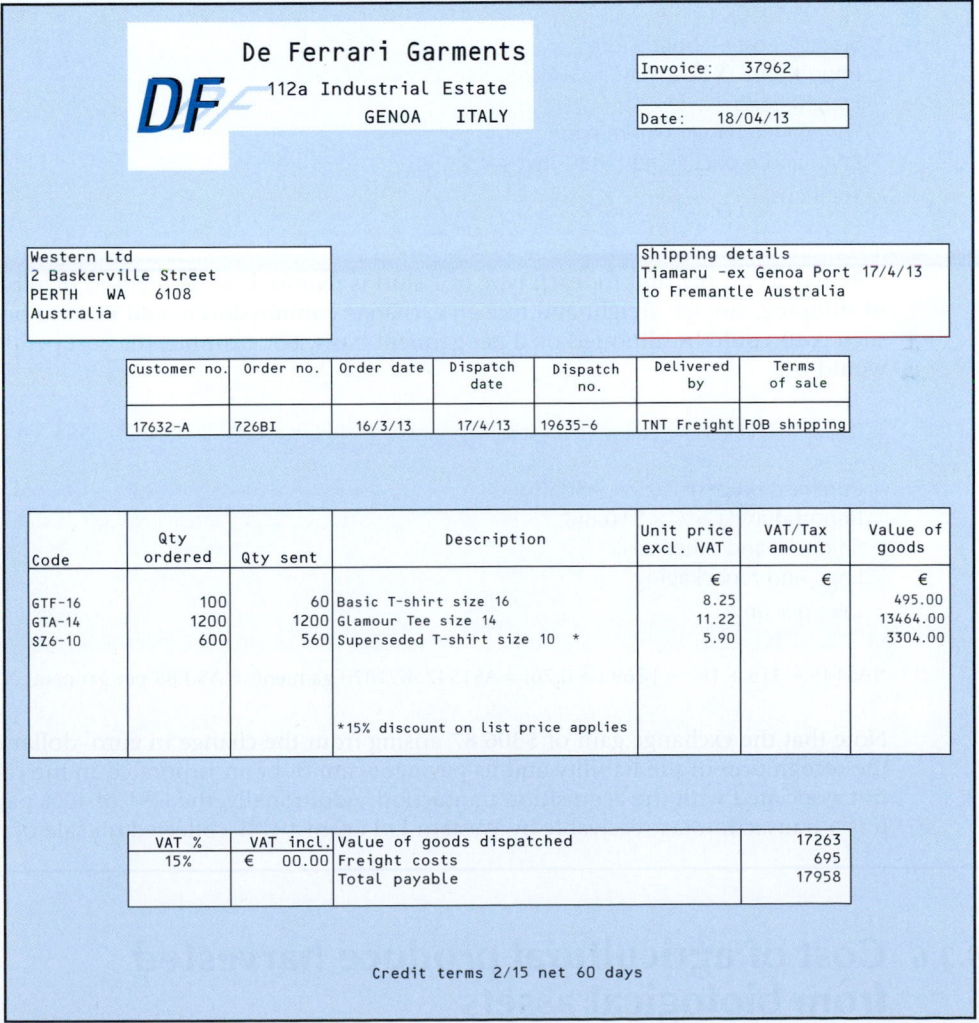

The goods arrived at Fremantle port on 29 May 2013 and were held in a bond store pending payment of import duties and taxes. After the payment of storage costs of A$145, import duty at 1.5% of the total value of goods in Australian dollars, goods and services tax (GST) of 10% and local freight charges of A$316, the goods were finally delivered to Western Ltd's warehouse on 6 June 2013. The invoice was received on 8 June and a liability of $A23 628.95 recorded using the exchange rate of A$1 = €0.76 at that date. The invoice was paid in full on 8 July by the remittance of $A23 322.08 (at an exchange rate of A$1 = €0.77). Western Ltd paid A$167 to acquire the euros. Upon receipt of the goods, Western Ltd attaches its own logo to the T-shirts and repackages them for sale. The cost of this further processing is A$2.54 per T-shirt.

Problem

What is the cost of this inventory?

Solution

The cost of inventory would include the following amounts:

Purchase price	€17 263.00
Shipping costs	695.00
	€17 958.00
Conversion to Australian dollars:	
€17 958 ÷ 0.76	23 628.95
Storage costs – bond store	145.00
Import duty ($22 714.47 × 1.5%)	340.72
Freight costs	316.00
Foreign exchange commission	167.00
Logo and repackaging (1820 items × $2.54)	4 622.80
Total cost	A$29 220.47

Where a cost per unit for each type of T-shirt is required, some method of allocating the 'generic' costs of shipping, storage, freight and foreign exchange commission would need to be employed. In this case, such costs could be allocated on a per garment basis. For example, the cost per unit for the Basic T-shirts would be:

	A$
Purchase price (€8.25 ÷ A$0.76)	10.86
Import duty (1.5% × $10.86)	0.16
Shipping and other costs*	0.85
Logo and repackaging	2.54
Cost per unit	$14.41

*(A$145 + 316 + 167 + [€695 ÷ 0.76] = A$1542.47/1820 garments = A$0.85 per garment)

Note that the exchange gain of $306.87 arising from the change in euro–dollar exchange rates between the recognition of the liability and its payment cannot be incorporated in the calculation of cost as it is not associated with the acquisition transaction. Additionally, the GST of 10% payable is not included as it is a transaction tax receivable by Western Ltd against GST collected on sale of inventory.

9.3.6 Cost of agricultural produce harvested from biological assets

IAS 41 *Agriculture* requires inventories of agricultural produce, such as wheat and oranges, to be measured at their fair value less costs to sell at the point of harvest. IAS 2, paragraph 20, deems this value to be 'cost' for the purposes of applying the requirements of the inventory standard.

9.3.7 Estimating cost

Techniques for determining cost such as the standard cost method or the retail method may be used for convenience so long as the resulting values approximate cost. Manufacturing entities determine a 'standard' value of materials, direct and indirect labour and overheads for each product based on normal levels of efficiency and capacity utilisation. Adjustments are made at the end of the reporting period to account for variances between standard and actual costs. Standard costs must be regularly reviewed and amended as required. The retail method is used to measure inventories of large numbers of rapidly changing items with similar margins for which it is impractical to use other costing methods. Supermarket and department store chains most often employ this method of approximating cost. Cost is determined by reducing the sales value of the inventory by an appropriate percentage gross margin or an average percentage margin. In applying this method, care must be taken to ensure that gross margins are adjusted for goods that have been discounted below their original selling price.

9.4 ACCOUNTING FOR INVENTORY

There are two main methods of accounting for inventory: the periodic method and the perpetual method.

9.4.1 Periodic method

Under the periodic method, the amount of inventory is determined periodically (normally annually) by conducting a physical count and multiplying the number of units by a cost per unit to value the inventory on hand. This amount is then recognised as a current asset. This balance remains unchanged until the next count is taken. Purchases and returns of inventory during the reporting period are posted directly to expense accounts. Cost of sales during the year is determined as follows:

> Cost of sales = Opening inventory + Purchases + Freight inwards − Purchase returns − Cash discounts received − Closing inventory

Accounting for inventory using the periodic method is cost effective and easy to apply, but its major disadvantage is that the exact quantity and cost of inventory cannot be determined on a day-to-day basis, and this might result in lost sales or unhappy customers. Additionally, it is not possible to identify stock losses or posting errors, resulting in accounting figures that might be inaccurate or misleading.

9.4.2 Perpetual method

Under the perpetual method, inventory records are updated each time a transaction involving inventory takes place. Thus, up-to-date information about the quantity and cost of inventory on hand will always be available, enabling the entity to provide better customer service and maintain better control over this essential asset. This system is more complicated and expensive than the periodic method but, with the advent of user-friendly computerised accounting packages and point-of-sale machines linked directly to accounting records, most businesses today can afford to and do use the perpetual method.

The perpetual method requires a subsidiary ledger to be maintained, either manually or on computer, with a separate record for each inventory item detailing all movements in both quantity and cost. This subsidiary record is linked to the general ledger account for inventory, and regular reconciliations are carried out to ensure the accuracy and completeness of the accounting records. This reconciliation process is discussed in section 9.5 of this chapter.

ILLUSTRATIVE EXAMPLE 9.2 Comparing the periodic and the perpetual inventory methods

Kotka Ltd sells garden furniture settings. This example illustrates the journal entries necessary to record the normal inventory transactions that would occur during an accounting period, and the reporting of gross profit from the sale of inventory under both accounting systems.

The inventory account in the general ledger of Kotka Ltd at the beginning of the year under both methods is shown on the next page.

Inventory		
1/7/13 Balance b/d	6 700	
(10 units @ $670)		

The following transactions took place during the year:

(a) Purchased 354 settings (FOB shipping) at $670 each on credit terms of 2/10, n/30 from Grimstad Pty Ltd.

(b) Sold, on credit, 352 settings for $975 each.

(c) Returned four settings to the supplier.

(d) Seven settings were returned by customers.

The journal entries necessary to record these transactions under both inventory accounting methods are shown below.

KOTKA LTD
Journal entries

Perpetual inventory method   *Periodic inventory method*

(a) Purchased 354 settings (FOB shipping) at $670 each on credit terms of 2/10, n/30 from Grimstad Pty Ltd.

	Dr	Cr		Dr	Cr
Inventory	237 180		Purchases	237 180	
A/cs Payable		237 180	A/cs Payable		237 180

(b) Sold, on credit, 352 settings for $975 each.

	Dr	Cr		Dr	Cr
A/cs Receivable	343 200		A/cs Receivable	343 200	
Sales Revenue		343 200	Sales Revenue		343 200
Cost of Sales	235 840				
Inventory		235 840			

(c) Returned four settings to the supplier.

	Dr	Cr		Dr	Cr
A/cs Payable	2 680		A/cs Payable	2 680	
Inventory		2 680	Purchase Returns		2 680

(d) Seven settings were returned by customers.

	Dr	Cr		Dr	Cr
Sales Returns	6 825		Sales Returns	6 825	
A/cs Receivable		6 825	A/cs Receivable		6 825
Inventory	4 690				
Cost of Sales		4 690			

Important differences to note between the two methods of accounting for inventory are as follows:

• Purchases are posted directly to the asset account under the perpetual method, and are posted to expense accounts under the periodic method.

• When goods are sold, a second entry is necessary under the perpetual method to transfer the cost of those goods from the inventory account to the expense account, cost of sales.

• When goods are returned to suppliers, the return is adjusted directly to inventory under the perpetual method, and is posted to a purchase returns account under the periodic method.

- When goods are returned from customers, a second journal entry is necessary under the perpetual method to transfer the cost of these goods out of the cost of sales account and back into the inventory account.
- Under the periodic method, freight is normally posted to a separate account. Under the perpetual method, freight is included in the cost of inventory unless the amounts are immaterial, in which case freight costs would be accumulated in a separate expense account.
- If inventory items being returned to the supplier have been paid for, an accounts receivable account would be opened pending a cash refund from the supplier.
- If sales returns have been paid for, an accounts payable entry would be raised to recognise the need to refund cash to the customer.
- Under the periodic method, cash settlement discounts would be posted to a separate ledger account. Under the perpetual method, settlement discounts would be deducted from the cost of inventory.

After posting the journal entries, the general ledger account would appear as shown below.

Perpetual inventory method

Inventory			
1/7/13 Balance b/d	6 700	Cost of Sales	235 840
A/cs Payable	237 180	A/cs Payable	2 680
Cost of Sales	4 690	Balance c/d	10 050
	248 570		248 570
Balance b/d	10 050		

Periodic inventory method

Inventory		
1/7/13 Balance b/d	6 700	

Assuming that the physical count at the end of the reporting period found 15 settings on hand at a cost of $670 each, the gross profit earned on these would be determined as follows:

KOTKA LTD
Determination of Gross Profit

Perpetual inventory method

Sales revenue	343 200
Less: Sales returns and allowances	(6 825)
Net sales revenue	336 375
Cost of sales	(231 150)
Gross profit	$ 105 225

Periodic inventory method

Sales revenue		343 200
Less: Sales returns		(6 825)
Net sales revenue		336 375
Cost of sales		
Opening inventory	6 700	
Add: Purchases	237 180	
	243 880	
Less: Purchase returns	(2 680)	
Goods available for sale	241 200	
Less: Closing inventory	(10 050)	
Cost of sales		(231 150)
Gross profit		$ 105 225

Note that, in this example, the same gross profit is reported irrespective of the inventory recording method adopted. However, where adjustments are made for damaged or lost inventory, the gross profit will be different under the perpetual method.

LO5

9.5 END-OF-PERIOD ACCOUNTING

To ensure that reported figures for inventory, cost of sales and other expenses are accurate and complete, certain procedures must be carried out at the end of each accounting period. It is essential that good internal controls be instituted to ensure that inventory is protected from fraud or loss and that inventory figures are complete and accurate. This section examines the physical count, end-of-year cut-off and essential reconciliation procedures.

9.5.1 Physical count

Under the periodic method, inventory must be counted at the end of each accounting period to determine the value of closing inventory. Periodic counts are made under the perpetual method to verify the accuracy of recorded quantities for each inventory item, although not necessarily at the end of the reporting period, if inventory differences are historically found to be immaterial.

The way in which the physical count is conducted will depend on the type of inventory and the accounting system of the entity. Stockpiled inventory such as mineral sands may require the use of surveyors to measure quantities on hand and assay tests to determine mineral content.

The following are some steps that are generally taken to ensure the accuracy of a physical count:
- The warehouse, retail store or storage facility should be arranged so as to facilitate counting and clearly segregate non-inventory items.
- Cut-off procedures should be put in place and final numbers of important documents such as dispatch notes and invoices are recorded. (Cut-off procedures are discussed in greater detail in section 9.5.2.)
- Prenumbered count sheets, tags or cards should be produced detailing inventory codes and descriptions. A supervisor should record all numbers used and account for spoiled documents to ensure that the count details are complete. Alternatively, where inventory items have bar codes, electronic scanners can be used to record the count.
- Counting should be done in teams of at least two people: one counter and one checker. All team members should sign the count records.
- Any damaged or incomplete items located during the count should be clearly listed on the count records.
- The supervisor should ensure that all goods have been counted before the count sheets are collected.

Perpetual method

Once the physical count is complete, under the perpetual method the quantities on hand are then compared to recorded quantities and all discrepancies investigated. Recording errors cause discrepancies; for example, the wrong code number or quantity might have been entered, or a transaction might not have been processed in the correct period. Alternatively, discrepancies may reveal losses of goods caused by damage or fraud. Recording errors can be corrected but the value of goods that have been lost should be written off using the following entry:

Inventory Losses	Dr	5 000	
Inventory	Cr		5 000
(Recognition of inventory losses during the period)			

Unless they are immaterial, inventory losses must be disclosed separately in the notes to the financial statements (see section 9.9 of this chapter).

Periodic method

Once the count is completed, under this method the count quantities are then costed and the value of inventory brought to account. This adjustment can be done in a number of ways, but the simplest is to post the following two journal entries:

Opening Inventory (Cost of Sales)	Dr	79 600	
Inventory	Cr		79 600
(Transfer of opening balance to expense)			

Inventory	Dr	87 100	
Closing Inventory (Cost of Sales)	Cr		87 100
(Recognition of final inventory balance)			

Under the periodic method, inventory losses and fraud cannot be identified and recorded as a separate expense. The movement in inventory balances plus the cost of purchases is presumed to represent the cost of sales during the reporting period.

9.5.2 Cut-off procedures

Under both periodic and perpetual methods there is a need to ensure that, when a physical count is conducted, there is a proper cut-off of the record keeping so that the accounting records reflect the results of the physical count and include all transactions relevant to the accounting period, while excluding those that belong to other periods. For all inventory transactions (sales, purchases and returns), it is possible for inventory records to be updated before transaction details are posted to the general ledger accounts. For example, goods are normally entered into inventory records when the goods are received, but accounts payable records will not record the liability until the invoice arrives because shipping documents may not record price details. Under the periodic method, there is a need to ensure a proper cut-off between the general ledger recording of goods received, shipped and returned, and the inventory counted. Under the perpetual method, there is a need to ensure that all inventory movements are properly recorded in the perpetual records, so a valid comparison is made between inventory counted and the perpetual record quantities. Further, if the perpetual method is not integrated with the general ledger, there is also a need to ensure a proper cut-off between the general ledger and the perpetual records. Thus, at the end of the reporting period it is essential that proper cut-off procedures be implemented.

The following cut-off errors could arise:
- Goods have been received into inventory, but the purchase invoice has not been processed.
- Goods have been returned to a supplier, and deleted from inventory, but the credit note has not been processed.
- Goods have been sold and dispatched to a customer, but the invoice has not been raised.
- Goods have been returned by a customer, but the credit note has not been issued.

If inventory movements have been processed before invoices and credit notes, adjusting entries are needed to bring both sides of the transaction into the same accounting period.

9.5.3 Goods in transit

Accounting for goods in transit at the end of the reporting period will depend upon the terms of trade. Where goods are purchased on an FOB shipping basis, the goods belong to the purchaser from the time they are shipped, and should be included in inventory/accounts payable at the end of the reporting period. All such purchases in transit will need to be identified and the following adjusting journal entry posted:

Goods in Transit (Inventory)	Dr	1 500	
Accounts Payable	Cr		1 500
(Recognition of inventory in transit at the end of the reporting period)			

If goods are purchased on FOB destination terms, no adjustment will be required because the goods still legally belong to the supplier.

If goods are sold on FOB destination terms, they belong to the entity until they arrive at the customer's premises. Because the sale will have been recorded in the current year, the following adjusting entries will be required to remove that sale and reinstate the inventory:

Inventory	Dr	3 000	
Cost of Sales	Cr		3 000
(Reversal of sale for goods in transit at the end of the reporting period)			

Sales Revenue	Dr	4 500	
Accounts Receivable	Cr		4 500
(Reversal of sale for goods in transit at the end of the reporting period)			

9.5.4 Consignment inventory

Care must be taken in the treatment of consignment inventory. Under a consignment arrangement, an agent (the consignee) agrees to sell goods on behalf of the consignor on a commission basis. The transfer of goods to the consignee is not a legal sale/purchase transaction. Legal ownership remains with the consignor until the agent sells the goods to a third party. Steps must be taken to ensure that goods held on consignment are not included in the physical count. Equally, goods owned by the entity that are held by consignees must be added to the physical count.

9.5.5 Control account/subsidiary ledger reconciliation

This end-of-period procedure is required only under the perpetual method. The general ledger account balance must be reconciled with the total of the subsidiary ledger (manual or computerised). Recording errors and omissions will cause the reconciliation process to fail. Any material discrepancies should be investigated and corrected. This process will identify only amounts that have not been posted to both records; it cannot identify errors within the subsidiary records, such as posting a purchase to the wrong inventory item code. However, the physical count/recorded figure reconciliation will isolate these errors.

ILLUSTRATIVE EXAMPLE 9.3 End-of-period adjustments

Bob Smith, trading as Honefoss Pty Ltd, completed his first year of trading as a toy wholesaler on 30 June 2014. He is worried about his end-of-year physical and cut-off procedures.

The inventory ledger account balance at 30 June 2014, under the perpetual inventory method, was $78 700. His physical count, however, revealed the cost of inventory on hand at 30 June 2014 to be only $73 400. While Bob expected a small inventory shortfall due to breakage and petty theft, he considered this shortfall to be excessive.

Upon investigating reasons for the inventory 'shortfall', Bob discovered the following:
- Goods costing $800 were sold on credit to R Finn for $1300 on 26 June 2014 on FOB destination terms. The goods were still in transit at 30 June 2014. Honefoss Pty Ltd recorded the sale on 26 June 2014 but did not include these goods in the physical count.
- Included in the physical count were $2200 of goods held on consignment.
- Goods costing $910 were purchased on credit from Lapua Ltd on 25 June 2014 and received on 28 June 2014. The purchase was unrecorded at 30 June 2014 but the goods were included in the physical count.
- Goods costing $400 were purchased on credit from Kuovola Supplies on 23 June 2014 on FOB shipping terms. The goods were delivered to the transport company on 27 June 2014. The purchase was recorded on 27 June 2014 but, as the goods had not yet arrived, Honefoss Pty Ltd did not include these goods in the physical count.
- At 30 June 2014 Honefoss Pty Ltd had unsold goods costing $3700 out on consignment. These goods were not included in the physical count.
- Goods costing $2100 were sold on credit to Vetlonda Ltd for $3200 on 24 June 2014 on FOB shipping terms. The goods were shipped on 28 June 2014. The sale was unrecorded at 30 June 2014 and Honefoss Pty Ltd did not include these goods in the physical count.
- Goods costing $1500 had been returned to Ruovesi Garments on 30 June 2014. A credit note was received from the supplier on 5 July 2014. No payment had been made for the goods prior to their return.

These transactions and events must be analysed to determine if adjustments are required to the ledger accounts (general and subsidiary) and/or the physical count records as follows:

Workings

	Recorded balance $	Physical count $
Balance prior to adjustment	78 700	73 400
Add: Goods sold, FOB destination and in transit at 30 June	800	800
Less: Goods held on consignment	—	(2 200)
Add: Unrecorded purchase	910	—
Add: Goods purchased, FOB shipping and in transit at 30 June	—	400
Add: Goods out on consignment	—	3 700
Less: Unrecorded sale	(2 100)	—
Less: Unrecorded purchase returns	(1 500)	—
	$76 810	$76 100

If, after all adjustments are made, the recorded balance cannot be reconciled to the physical count, the remaining discrepancy is presumed to represent inventory losses and a final adjustment is made as follows:

Adjusted balances	76 810	76 100
Inventory shortfall	(710)	—
	$76 100	$76 100

The following journal entries are necessary on 30 June 2014 to correct errors and adjust the inventory ledger accounts:

HONEFOSS PTY LTD General Journal			
2014 30 June			
Sales Revenue	Dr	1 300	
Accounts Receivable (R Finn)	Cr		1 300
(Correction of sale recorded in error)			
Inventory (Item X)	Dr	800	
Cost of Sales	Cr		800
(Correction of sale recorded in error)			
Inventory (Item Y)	Dr	910	
Accounts Payable (Lapua Ltd)	Cr		910
(Correction of unrecorded purchase)			
Accounts Receivable (Vetlonda Ltd)	Dr	3 200	
Sales Revenue	Cr		3 200
(Correction of unrecorded sale)			
Cost of Sales	Dr	2 100	
Inventory (Item Z)	Cr		2 100
(Correction of unrecorded sale)			
Accounts Payable (Ruovesi Garments)	Dr	1 500	
Inventory (Item W)	Cr		1 500
(Correction of unrecorded purchase return)			

(continued)

Inventory Losses and Write-Downs	Dr	710	
Inventory	Cr		710
(Unexplained variance (physical/records) written off)			

9.6 ASSIGNING COSTS TO INVENTORY ON SALE

The nature of inventory held by an entity does not affect its initial recognition at cost but has a significant impact when that inventory is sold. As shown in illustrative example 9.2, under the perpetual system the cost of inventory items is transferred to a 'Cost of Sales' expense account on sale, and under the periodic system a 'Cost of Sales' figure is calculated at the end of the reporting period. This is an easy task if the nature of inventory is such that it is possible to clearly identify the exact inventory item that has been sold and its cost, but what if it is not possible to identify exactly the cost of the item sold? How can you measure the cost of a tonne of wheat when it is extracted from a stockpile consisting of millions of tonnes acquired at different prices over the accounting period?

IAS 2 addresses this problem by mandating two different rules for the assigning of cost to inventory items sold.

The rules differ depending on the nature of inventory held. Paragraph 23 states that:

> The cost of inventories of items that are not ordinarily interchangeable and goods or services produced and segregated for specific projects shall be assigned by using specific identification of their individual costs.

Thus, if the inventory held consists of items that can be individually identified because of their unique nature or by some other means, or cannot be individually identified but have been acquired for a specific project, then the exact cost of the item sold must be recorded as cost of sales expense.

Paragraph 25 states that:

> The cost of inventories, other than those dealt with in paragraph 23, shall be assigned by using the first-in, first-out (FIFO) or weighted average cost formula.

This means that, where a specific cost cannot be identified because of the nature of the item sold, then some method has to be adopted to estimate that cost. This process is known as 'assigning' cost. Most inventory items fall into this category; for example, identical items of food and clothing and bulk items like oil and minerals. There are many methods of assigning a cost to inventory items sold but IAS 2 restricts entities to a choice between two methods — FIFO and weighted average.

9.6.1 First-in, first-out (FIFO) cost formula

The FIFO formula assumes that items of inventory that were purchased or produced first are sold first, and the items remaining in inventory at the end of the period are those most recently purchased or produced (IAS 2 paragraph 27). Thus, more recent purchase costs are assigned to the inventory asset account, and older costs are assigned to the cost of sales expense account.

Consider this example: there are 515 Blu-ray players on hand at 30 June 2014, and recent purchase invoices showed the following costs:

28 June	180 players at $49.00
15 June	325 players at $48.50
31 May	200 players at $47.00

The value of ending inventory is found by starting with the most recent purchase and working backwards until all items on hand have been priced (on the assumption that it is not known when any particular Blu-ray player was sold). The value of ending inventory would be $25 052.50 (being 180 players at $49 + 325 players at $48.50 + 10 players at $47).

Many proponents of the FIFO method argue that this method best reflects the physical movement of inventory, particularly perishable goods or those subject to changes in fashion or rapid obsolescence (as in the case of Blu-ray players). If the oldest goods are normally sold first, then the oldest costs should be assigned to expense.

9.6.2 Weighted average cost formula

Under the weighted average cost formula, the cost of each item sold is determined from the cost of similar items purchased or produced during the period. The average may be calculated on a periodic basis (weighted average), or as each additional shipment is received (moving average).

Using a periodic basis, the cost of inventory on hand at the beginning of the period plus all inventory purchased during the year is divided by the total number of items available for sale during the period (opening quantity plus purchased quantity). This produces the cost per unit. For example: inventory on hand at 1 January 2015 was valued at $3439.78, consisting of 134 units at an average of $25.67 each. During the year the following purchases were made:

$$200 \text{ units at } \$27.50 = \$5\,500.00$$
$$175 \text{ units at } \$28.35 = \$4\,961.25$$
$$300 \text{ units at } \$29.10 = \$8\,730.00$$
$$120 \text{ units at } \$29.00 = \$3\,480.00$$

At the end of the year, the weighted average cost of inventory would be calculated as:

$$\$3\,439.78 + \$5\,500.00 + \$4\,961.25 + \$8\,730.00 + \$3\,480.00 = \$26\,111.03 \div 929 \text{ units} = \$28.11 \text{ per unit}$$

Using the *moving weighted average method*, the average unit cost is recalculated each time there is an inventory purchase or purchase return. This is demonstrated in illustrative example 9.4.

ILLUSTRATIVE EXAMPLE 9.4 Application of cost formulas

The following information has been extracted from the records of Savonlinna Parts about one of its products. Savonlinna Parts uses the perpetual inventory method and its reporting period ends on 31 December.

		No. of units	Unit cost $	Total cost $
2014				
01/01	Beginning balance	800	7.00	5 600
06/01	Purchased	300	7.05	2 115
05/02	Sold @ $12.00 per unit	1 000		
19/03	Purchased	1 100	7.35	8 085
24/03	Purchase returns	80	7.35	588
10/04	Sold @ $12.10 per unit	700		
22/06	Purchased	8 400	7.50	63 000
31/07	Sold @ $13.25 per unit	1 800		
04/08	Sales returns @ $13.25 per unit	20		
04/09	Sold @ $13.50 per unit	3 500		
06/10	Purchased	500	8.00	4 000
27/11	Sold @ $15.00 per unit	3 100		

Required

1. Calculate the cost of inventory on hand at 31 December 2014 and the cost of sales for the year ended 31 December 2014, assuming:
   (a) the FIFO cost flow assumption
   (b) the moving average cost flow assumption (round the average unit costs to the nearest cent, and round the total cost amounts to the nearest dollar).
2. Prepare the trading section of the statement of profit or loss and other comprehensive income for the year ended 31 December 2014, assuming:
   (a) the FIFO cost flow assumption
   (b) the moving average cost flow assumption.

Part 1. (a) First-in, first-out cost formula

Date	Details	Purchases No. units	Purchases Unit cost	Purchases Total cost	Cost of sales No. units	Cost of sales Unit cost	Cost of sales Total cost	Balance[1] No. units	Balance[1] Unit cost	Balance[1] Total cost
01/01	Inventory balance							800	7.00	5 600
06/01	Purchases	300	7.05	2 115				800 300	7.00 7.05	5 600 2 115
05/02	Sales				800 200	7.00 7.05	5 600 1 410	100	7.05	705
19/03	Purchases	1 100	7.35	8 085				100 1 100	7.05 7.35	705 8 085
24/03	Purchase returns	(80)	7.35	(588)				100 1 020	7.05 7.35	705 7 497
10/04	Sales				100 600	7.05 7.35	705 4 410	420	7.35	3 087
22/06	Purchases	8 400	7.50	63 000				420 8 400	7.35 7.50	3 087 63 000
31/07	Sales				420 1 380	7.35 7.50	3 087 10 350	7 020	7.50	52 650
04/08	Sales returns[2]				(20)	7.50	(150)	7 040	7.50	52 800
04/09	Sales				3 500	7.50	26 250	3 540	7.50	26 550
06/10	Purchases	500	8.00	4 000				3 540 500	7.50 8.00	26 550 4 000
22/11	Sales				3 100	7.50	23 250	440 500	7.50 8.00	3 300 4 000
				76 612			74 912			

Notes:
1. As it is assumed the earliest purchases are sold first, a separate balance of each purchase at a different price must be maintained.
2. The principle of 'last-out, first-in' is applied to sales returns.

Part 1. (b) Moving average cost formula

Date	Details	Purchases No. units	Purchases Unit cost	Purchases Total cost	Cost of sales[2] No. units	Cost of sales[2] Unit cost	Cost of sales[2] Total cost	Balance No. units	Balance Unit cost[1]	Balance Total cost
01/01	Inventory balance							800	7.00	5 600
06/01	Purchases	300	7.05	2 115				1 100	7.01	7 715
05/02	Sales				1 000	7.01	7 010	100	7.01	705
19/03	Purchases	1 100	7.35	8 085				1 200	7.33	8 790
24/03	Purchase returns	(80)	7.35	(588)				1 120	7.32	8 202
10/04	Sales				700	7.32	5 124	420	7.32	3 078

Date	Details	Purchases No. units	Purchases Unit cost	Purchases Total cost	Cost of sales[2] No. units	Cost of sales[2] Unit cost	Cost of sales[2] Total cost	Balance No. units	Balance Unit cost[1]	Balance Total cost
22/06	Purchases	8 400	7.50	63 000				8 820	7.49	66 078
31/07	Sales				1 800	7.49	13 482	7 020	7.49	52 596
04/08	Sales returns				(20)	7.49	(150)	7 040	7.49	52 746
04/09	Sales				3 500	7.49	26 215	3 540	7.49	26 531
06/10	Purchases	500	8.00	4 000				4 040	7.56	30 531
22/11	Sales				3 100	7.56	23 436	940	7.56	7 095
				76 612			75 117			

Notes:
1. The average cost per unit is recalculated each time there is a purchase or a purchase return at a different cost.
2. The 'average' cost on the date of sale is applied to calculate the 'cost of sales'.

Part 2

SAVONLINNA PARTS
Statement of Profit or Loss and Other Comprehensive Income (extract)
for the year ended 31 December 2014

	FIFO $	Moving average $
Sales revenue	138 070	138 070
Less: Sales returns	(265)	(265)
Net sales	137 805	137 805
Less: Cost of sales	(74 912)	(75 117)
Gross profit	$ 62 893	$ 62 688

Because the purchase price has been rising throughout the year, using the FIFO formula produces a lower cost of sales (higher gross profit) and a higher inventory balance than the moving average formula.

9.6.3 Which cost formula to use?

The choice of method is a matter for management judgement and depends upon the nature of the inventory, the information needs of management and financial statement users, and the cost of applying the formulas. For example, the weighted average method is easy to apply and is particularly suited to inventory where homogeneous products are mixed together, like iron ore or spring water. On the other hand, first-in, first-out may be a better reflection of the actual physical movement of goods, such as those with use-by dates where the first produced must be sold first to avoid loss due to obsolescence, spoilage or legislative restrictions. Entities with diversified operations may use both methods because they carry different types of inventory. Using diverse methods is acceptable under IAS 2, but paragraph 26 cautions that 'a difference in geographical location of inventories (or in the respective tax rules), by itself, is not sufficient to justify the use of different cost formulas'. The nature of the inventory itself should determine the choice of formula.

9.6.4 Consistent application of costing methods

Once a cost formula has been selected, management cannot randomly switch from one formula to another. Because the choice of method can have a significant impact on an entity's reported profit and asset figures, particularly in times of volatile prices, indiscriminate changes in formulas could result in the reporting of financial information that is neither comparable nor reliable. Accordingly, paragraph 13 of IAS 8 *Accounting Policies, Changes in Accounting Estimates and Errors* requires that accounting policies be consistently applied to ensure comparability of financial information. Changes in accounting policies are allowed (IAS 8 paragraph 14) only when required by an accounting standard or where the change results in reporting more relevant and reliable financial information. Therefore, unless the nature of inventory changes, it is unlikely that the cost formulas will change. A switch from the FIFO to the weighted average method must be disclosed in accordance with the requirements of IAS 8, in particular paragraph 19. This paragraph requires the change to be applied retrospectively, and the information disclosed as if the new accounting policy had always been applied. Hence, a change from the FIFO method to the weighted average method would require adjustments to the financial statements to show the information as if the weighted average method had always been applied. Adjustments can be taken through the opening balance of retained earnings. Comparative information would also need to be restated.

9.7 NET REALISABLE VALUE

As the measurement rule mandated by IAS 2 for inventories is the 'lower of cost and net realisable value' (paragraph 9), an estimate of net realisable value must be made to determine if inventory must be written down. Normally, this estimate is done before preparing the financial statements but, where management become aware during the reporting period that goods or services can no longer be sold at a price above cost, inventory values should be written down to net realisable value. The rationale for this measurement rule, according to paragraph 28 of IAS 2, is that 'assets should not be carried in excess of amounts expected to be realised from their sale or use'.

Net realisable value is the net amount that an entity expects to realise from the sale of inventory in the ordinary course of business. It is defined in paragraph 6 of IAS 2 as 'the estimated selling price in the ordinary course of business less the estimated costs of completion and the estimated costs necessary to make the sale'. Net realisable value is specific to an individual entity and is not necessarily equal to fair value less selling costs. Fair value is defined as 'the price that would be received to sell an asset or paid to transfer a liability in an orderly transaction between market participants at the measurement date. (See IFRS 13 *Fair Value Measurement*.)' (IAS 2 paragraph 6).

Net realisable value may fall below cost for a number of reasons including:
- a fall in selling price (e.g. fashion garments)
- physical deterioration of inventories (e.g. fruit and vegetables)
- product obsolescence (e.g. computers and electrical equipment)
- a decision, as part of an entity's marketing strategy, to manufacture and sell products for the time being at a loss (e.g. new products)
- miscalculations or other errors in purchasing or production (e.g. over-stocking)
- an increase in the estimated costs of completion or the estimated costs of making the sale (e.g. air-conditioning plants).

9.7.1 Estimating net realisable value

Estimates of net realisable value must be based on the most reliable evidence available at the time the estimate is made (normally the end of the reporting period) of the amount that the inventories are expected to realise. Thus, estimates must be made of:
- expected selling price
- estimated costs of completion (if any)
- estimated selling costs.

These estimates take into consideration fluctuations of price or cost occurring after the end of the reporting period to the extent that such events confirm conditions existing at the end of the reporting period. The purpose for which inventory is held should be taken into account when reviewing net realisable values. For example, the net realisable value of inventory held to satisfy firm sales or service contracts is based on the contract price. If the sales contracts are for less than the inventory quantities held, the net realisable value of the excess is based on general selling prices. Estimated selling costs include all costs likely to be incurred in securing and filling customer orders such as advertising costs, sales personnel salaries and operating costs, and the costs of storing and shipping finished goods.

It is possible to use formulas based on predetermined criteria to initially estimate net realisable value. These formulas normally take into account, as appropriate, the age, past movements, expected future movements and estimated scrap values of the inventories. However, the results must be reviewed in the light of any special circumstances not anticipated in the formulas, such as changes in the current demand for inventories or unexpected obsolescence.

9.7.2 Materials and other supplies

IAS 2, paragraph 32, states that materials and other supplies held for use in the production of inventories are not written down below cost if the finished goods in which they will be incorporated are expected to be sold at or above cost. When the sale of finished goods is not expected to recover the costs, then materials are to be written down to net realisable value. IAS 2 suggests that the replacement cost of the materials or other supplies is probably the best measure of their net realisable value.

9.7.3 Write-down to net realisable value

Inventories are usually written down to net realisable value on an item-by-item basis. Paragraph 29 of IAS 2 states that 'it is not appropriate to write inventories down on the basis of a classification of inventory, for example, finished goods, or all the inventories in a particular operating segment'. Where it is not practical to separately evaluate the net realisable value of each item within a product line, the write-down may be applied on a group basis provided that the products have similar purposes or end uses, and are produced and marketed in the same geographical area. IAS 2 generally requires that service providers apply the measurement rule only on an item-by-item basis, as each service ordinarily has a separate selling price.

The journal entry to process the write-down would be:

Inventory Write-Down Expense	Dr	800	
Inventory	Cr		800
(Write-down to net realisable value)			

9.7.4 Reversal of prior write-down to net realisable value

If the circumstances that previously caused inventories to be written down below cost change, or if a new assessment confirms that net realisable value has increased, the amount of a previous write-down can be reversed (subject to an upper limit of the original write-down). This could occur if an item of inventory written down to net realisable value because of falling sales prices is still on hand at the end of a subsequent period and its selling price has recovered.

The journal entry to process the reversal would be:

Inventory	Dr	800	
Inventory Write-Down Expense	Cr		800
(Write-up to revised net realisable value)			

ILLUSTRATIVE EXAMPLE 9.5 Application of measurement rule

Vastervick Pty Ltd retails gardening equipment and has four main product lines: mowers, vacuum blowers, edgers and garden tools. At 30 June 2013, cost and net realisable values for each line were as shown below.

Application of lower of cost and net realisable value measurement rule				
Inventory item	Quantity	Cost per unit $	NRV per unit $	Lower of cost and NRV $
Mowers	16	215.80	256.00	3 452.80
Vacuum blowers	113	62.35	60.00	6 780.00
Edgers	78	27.40	36.00	2 137.20
Garden tools	129	12.89	11.00	1 419.00
Inventory at the lower of cost and net realisable value				$13 789.00

The following journal entry would be required to adjust inventory values to net realisable value:

30 June 2013			
Inventory Write-Down Expense	Dr	509.36	
Inventory	Cr		509.36
(Write-down to net realisable value — vacuum blowers			
$265.55 (113 × $2.35) and garden tools $243.81 (129 × $1.89))			

9.8 RECOGNITION AS AN EXPENSE

Paragraph 34 of IAS 2 requires the following items to be recognised as expenses:
- carrying amount of inventories in the period in which the related revenue is recognised, in other words, cost of sales
- write-down of inventories to net realisable value and all losses
- reversals of write-downs to net realisable value.

The only exception to this rule relates to inventory items used by an entity as components in self-constructed property, plant or equipment. The cost of these items would be capitalised and recognised as an expense via depreciation.

9.9 DISCLOSURE

Paragraph 36 of IAS 2 contains the required disclosures relating to inventories. Before preparing the disclosure note, inventories on hand will need to be classified into categories because paragraph 36(b) requires 'the carrying amount in classifications appropriate to the entity' to be disclosed. Common classifications suggested in paragraph 37 are merchandise, production supplies, materials, work in progress and finished goods. Figure 9.2 provides an illustration of the disclosures required by IAS 2.

FIGURE 9.2 An example of illustrative disclosures required by IAS 2

			IAS 2 Paragraph
Note 1: Summary of accounting policies (extract)			
Inventories			
Inventories are valued at the lower of cost and net realisable value. Costs incurred in bringing each product to its present location and condition are accounted for as follows: • raw materials — purchase cost on a first-in, first-out basis • finished goods and work in progress — cost of direct material and labour and proportion of manufacturing overheads based on normal operating capacity • production supplies — purchase cost on a weighted average cost basis.			*36(a)*
Note 6: Inventories			
	2013 $'000	2012 $'000	
Inventories carried at lower of cost and net realisable value			
At cost:			*36(b)*
Raw materials	1 257	1 840	
Work in progress	649	721	
Finished goods	3 932	4 278	
Production supplies	385	316	
Total carrying amount	6 223	7 155	

FIGURE 9.2 (*continued*)

Inventories carried at net realisable value			
Obsolete goods	269	174	*36(c)*
Less: Costs of disposal	(31)	(18)	
Total carrying amount	238	156	
In respect to inventory, the following items have been recognised as expenses during the period:			
Cost of sales	11 674	10 543	*36(d)*
Write-down to net realisable value	26	18	*36(e)*
Reversal of write-down(a)	(3)	—	*36(f)*
(a) A prior year write-down was reversed during the current period as a result of an increase in selling price for that inventory item.			*36(g)*
Inventory with a carrying amount of $570 000 has been pledged as security for loans to the company.			*36(h)*

SUMMARY

The purpose of this chapter is to analyse the content of IAS 2 *Inventories* and provide guidance on its implementation. The principal issue in accounting for inventories is the determination of cost and its subsequent recognition as an expense, including any write-down to net realisable value (IAS 2 paragraph 1). One key decision in recognising inventory is the selection of an appropriate method for allocating costs between individual items of inventory to determine the cost of sales and the cost of inventory on hand. Following the initial recognition of the inventory, cost must be compared to net realisable value, and the value of inventory written down where net realisable value falls below cost. IAS 2 requires disclosures to be made in relation to the inventories held by an entity and the accounting policies adopted with respect to these assets.

Discussion questions

1. Define 'cost' as applied to the valuation of inventory.
2. What is meant by the term 'net realisable value'? Is this the same as fair value? If not, why not?
3. Explain the concept of lower of cost and net realisable value for inventory.
4. Which is more expensive to maintain: a perpetual inventory system, or a periodic inventory system? Why?
5. In what circumstances must assumptions be made in order to assign a cost to inventory items when they are sold?
6. 'Estimating the value of inventory is not sufficiently accurate to justify using such an approach. Only a full physical count can give full accuracy.' Discuss.
7. What is the difference between the first-in, first-out method and the weighted average method of assigning cost?
8. Compare and contrast the impact on the reported profit and asset value for an accounting period of the first-in, first-out method and the weighted average method.
9. Why is the lower of cost and net realisable value rule used in the accounting standard? Is it permissible to revalue inventory upwards? If so, when?
10. What impact do the terms of trade have on the determination of the quantity and value of inventory on hand where goods are in transit at the end of the reporting period?

Exercises

STAR RATING ★ BASIC ★★ MODERATE ★★★ DIFFICULT

Exercise 9.1	**CONSIGNMENT OF INVENTORY**
★	Arend al Ltd reported in a recent financial statement that approximately $12 million of merchandise was received on consignment. Should the company recognise this amount on its statement of financial position? Explain.

SELECTION OF COST ASSUMPTION

★ Under what circumstances would each of the following inventory cost methods be appropriate?
(a) Specific identification
(b) Last-in, first-out
(c) Average cost
(d) First-in, first-out
(e) Retail inventory

Exercise 9.3 **STATEMENT OF FINANCIAL POSITION CLASSIFICATION**

★ Where, if at all, should the following items be classified on a statement of financial position?
(a) Goods out on approval to customers
(b) Goods in transit that were recently purchased FOB destination
(c) Land held by a real estate firm for sale
(d) Raw materials
(e) Goods received on consignment
(f) Stationery supplies

Exercise 9.4 **DISCLOSURES RELATING TO INVENTORY**

★ Jokela Pty Ltd reported inventory in its statement of financial position as follows:

| Inventories | $11 247 900 |

What additional disclosures might be necessary to present the inventory fairly?

Exercise 9.5 **RECORDING INVENTORY TRANSACTIONS**

★ Henry Halmstad began business on 1 March 2014. Henry balances the books at month-end and uses the periodic inventory system. Henry's transactions for March 2014 are detailed below.

March	1	Henry invested $16 000 cash and $10 000 office equipment into the business.
	2	Purchased merchandise from B Askoy on account for $4800 on terms of 2/15, n/30.
	5	Sold merchandise to S Stavanger on account for $1200 on terms of 2/10, n/30.
	8	Purchased merchandise for cash, $860 on cheque no. 003.
	12	Purchased merchandise from N Kurikka on account for $2000 on terms of 2/10, n/30.
	14	Paid B Askoy for 2 March purchase on cheque no. 004.
	15	Received $1176 from S Stavanger in payment of the account.
	21	Sold merchandise to Alesund Ltd on account for $1600 on terms of 2/10, n/30.
	21	Paid N Kurikka for 12 March purchase on cheque no. 005.
	22	Purchased merchandise from B Kimito on account for $2400 on terms of 2/15, n/30.
	23	Sold merchandise for $1300 cash.
	25	Returned defective merchandise that cost $600 to B Kimito.
	28	Paid salaries of $1400 on cheque no. 006.

Required

Prepare journal entries for March 2014, using the pro-forma journals provided.

Cash Receipts Journal

Date	Account	Ref.	Cash	Disc. all.	Sales	A/c rec.	Other

Cash Payments Journal

Date	Account	Ch.	Ref.	Other	A/c pay.	Purch.	Cash	Disc. rec.

Purchases Journal

Date	Account	Terms	Ref.	Amount

Sales Journal

Date	Account	Terms	Ref.	Amount

General Journal

Date	Account	Ref.	Dr	Cr

Exercise 9.6   **DETERMINING INVENTORY COST AND COST OF SALES (PERIODIC)**

★ *Select the correct answer. Show any workings required and provide reasons to justify your choice.*

1. The cost of inventory on hand at 1 January 2013 was $25 000 and at 31 December 2013 was $35 000. Inventory purchases for the year amounted to $160 000, freight outwards expense was $500, and purchase returns were $1400. What was the cost of sales for the year ended 31 December 2013?

   (a) $148 100
   (b) $148 600
   (c) $149 100
   (d) $150 000

2. The following inventory information relates to K Rauma, who uses a periodic inventory system and rounds the average unit cost to the nearest dollar:

Beginning inventory	10 units @ average cost of $25 each = $250
January purchase	10 units @ $24 each
July purchase	39 units @ $26 each
October purchase	20 units @ $24 each
Ending inventory	25 units

   What is the cost of ending inventory using the weighted average costing method?

   (a) $625
   (b) $620
   (c) $618.75
   (d) $610

Exercise 9.7   **ASSIGNING COST (PERPETUAL)**

★ *Select the correct answer. Show any workings required and provide reasons to justify your choice.*

Arvika uses the perpetual inventory method. Arvika's inventory transactions for August 2014 were as follows:

		No.	Unit cost	Total cost
Aug. 1	Beginning inventory	20	$4.00	$80.00
7	Purchases	10	$4.20	$42.00
10	Purchases	20	$4.30	$86.00
12	Sales	15	?	?
16	Purchases	20	$4.60	$92.00
20	Sales	40	?	?
28	Sales returns	3	?	?

1. Using this information, assume that Arvika uses the FIFO cost flow method and that the sales returns relate to the 20 August sales. The sales return should be costed back into inventory at what unit cost?

   (a) $4.00
   (b) $4.20
   (c) $4.30
   (d) $4.60

2. Assuming that Arvika uses the moving average cost flow method, the 12 August sales should be costed at what unit cost?
   (a) $4.16
   (b) $4.07
   (c) $4.06
   (d) $4.00

ASSIGNMENT OF COST (PERIODIC AND PERPETUAL)

★ *Select the correct answer. Show any workings required and provide reasons to justify your choice.*
Malmo Ltd's inventory transactions for April 2014 are shown below.

Date	Purchases			Cost of sales			Balance		
	No. units	Unit cost	Total cost	No. units	Unit cost	Total cost	No. units	Unit cost	Total cost
April 1							20	$8.00	$160.00
4	90	$8.40	$756.00						
7	100	$8.60	$860.00						
10				50					
13	(20)	$8.60	($172.00)						
18				70					
21				(5)					
29				40					

1. If Malmo Ltd uses the perpetual inventory system with the moving average cost flow method, the 18 April sale would be costed at what unit cost?
   (a) $8.60
   (b) $8.46
   (c) $8.44
   (d) $8.42
2. If Malmo Ltd uses the periodic inventory system with the FIFO cost flow method, what would be the cost of sales for April?
   (a) $1303.00
   (b) $1508.60
   (c) $1310.00
   (d) $1324.00
3. If Malmo Ltd uses the perpetual inventory system with the FIFO cost flow method, the 21 April sale return (relating to the 18 April sale) would be costed at what unit cost?
   (a) $8.00
   (b) $8.60
   (c) $8.40
   (d) $8.50
4. If Malmo Ltd uses the periodic method with the weighted average cost flow method, what would be the value of closing inventory at 30 April 2011? (Round average cost to the nearest cent.)
   (a) $295.40
   (b) $301.00
   (c) $253.20
   (d) $297.50

END-OF-PERIOD ADJUSTMENTS

★★ An extract from Uppsala Ltd's unadjusted trial balance as at 30 June 2013 appears below. Uppsala Ltd's reporting period ends on 30 June and uses the perpetual method to record inventory transactions.

	$	$
Inventory	194 400	
Sales		631 770
Sales returns	6 410	
Cost of sales	468 640	
Inventory losses	12 678	

Additional information

- On 24 June 2013, Uppsala Ltd recorded a $1320 credit sale of goods costing $1200. These goods, which were sold on FOB destination terms and were in transit at 30 June 2013, were included in the physical count.
- Inventory on hand at 30 June 2013 (determined via physical count) had a cost of $195 600 and a net realisable value of $194 740.

Required

1. Prepare any adjusting journal entries required on 30 June 2013.
2. Prepare the trading section of the statement of profit or loss and other comprehensive income for the year ended 30 June 2013.

Exercise 9.10	END-OF-PERIOD ADJUSTMENTS

★★ A physical count of inventory at 31 December 2013 revealed that Brunnsberg Pty Ltd had inventory on hand at that date with a cost of $441 000. Brunnsberg Pty Ltd uses the periodic method to record inventory transactions. Inventory at 1 January 2013 was $397 000. The annual audit identified that the following items were excluded from this amount:

- Merchandise of $61 000 is held by Brunnsberg Pty Ltd on consignment. The consignor is Angelholm Ltd.
- Merchandise costing $38 000 was shipped by Brunnsberg Pty Ltd FOB destination to a customer on 31 December 2013. The customer was expected to receive the goods on 6 January 2014.
- Merchandise costing $46 000 was shipped by Brunnsberg Pty Ltd FOB shipping to a customer on 29 December 2013. The customer was scheduled to receive the goods on 2 January 2014.
- Merchandise costing $83 000 shipped by a vendor FOB destination on 31 December 2013 was received by Brunnsberg Pty Ltd on 4 January 2014.
- Merchandise costing $51 000 purchased FOB shipping was shipped by the supplier on 31 December 2013 and received by Brunnsberg Pty Ltd on 5 January 2014.

Required

1. Based on the above information, calculate the amount that should appear for inventory on Brunnsberg Pty Ltd's statement of financial position at 31 December 2013.
2. Prepare any journal entries necessary to adjust the Inventory general ledger account to the amount calculated in requirement 1.

Exercise 9.11	APPLYING THE LOWER OF COST AND NRV RULE

★★ The following information relates to the inventory on hand at 30 June 2013 held by Vaasa Ltd.

Item No.	Quantity	Cost per unit $	Cost to replace $	Estimated selling price $	Cost of completion and disposal $
A1458	600	2.30	2.41	3.75	0.49
A1965	815	3.40	3.26	3.50	0.55
B6730	749	7.34	7.35	10.00	0.95
D0943	98	1.23	1.14	1.00	0.12
G8123	156	3.56	3.56	5.70	0.67
W2167	1 492	6.12	6.15	7.66	0.36

Required

Calculate the value of inventory on hand at 30 June 2013 in accordance with the requirements of IAS 2.

END-OF-REPORTING-PERIOD ADJUSTMENTS

Norway Outfitters sells outdoor adventure equipment. The entity uses the perpetual inventory method to account for inventory transactions and assigns costs using the moving average method. All purchases and sales are made on FOB destination, 30-day credit terms.

At 30 June 2014, the balance of the Inventory control account in the general ledger was $248 265 after the special journal totals were posted but before the balance-date adjusting entries were prepared and posted.

A physical count showed goods worth $256 100 to be on hand. Investigations of the discrepancy between the general ledger account balance and the count total revealed the following:

- Damaged ropes worth $1200 were returned to the supplier on 29 June, but this transaction has not yet been recorded.
- During the stocktake, staff found that a box of leather gloves worth $595 had suffered water damage during a recent storm. The gloves were damaged beyond repair and so were not included in the count, but they are still recorded in the inventory records.
- Equipment worth $1500, which was sold for $2500 on 29 June, was still in transit to the customer on 30 June. The sale was recorded on 29 June and the equipment was not included in the physical count.
- An error occurred when posting the purchase journal totals for May 2014. The correct total of $25 100 was erroneously posted as $21 500.
- The physical count included goods worth $7600 that were being held on consignment for All Weather Gear Pty Ltd.
- An all-terrain kit worth $1570 was returned by a customer on 28 June. The sales return transaction was correctly journalised and posted to the ledgers, but the kit was not returned to the warehouse and therefore was not included in the physical count.

Required

Adjust and reconcile the inventory control ledger account balance to the physical account (adjusted as necessary).

ALLOCATING COST (WEIGHTED AVERAGE), REPORTING GROSS PROFIT AND APPLYING THE NRV RULE

Oslo Ltd wholesales bicycles. It uses the perpetual inventory method and allocates cost to inventory on a moving average basis. The company's reporting period ends on 31 March. At 1 March 2014, inventory on hand consisted of 350 bicycles at $82 each and 43 bicycles at $85 each. During the month ended 31 March 2014, the following inventory transactions took place (all purchase and sales transactions are on credit):

March	1	Sold 300 bicycles for $120 each.
	3	Five bicycles were returned by a customer. They had originally cost $82 each and were sold for $120 each.
	9	Purchased 55 bicycles at $91 each.
	10	Purchased 76 bicycles at $96 each.
	15	Sold 86 bicycles for $135 each.
	17	Returned one damaged bicycle to the supplier. This bicycle had been purchased on 9 March.
	22	Sold 60 bicycles for $125 each.
	26	Purchased 72 bicycles at $98 each.
	29	Two bicycles, sold on 22 March, were returned by a customer. The bicycles were badly damaged so it was decided to write them off. They had originally cost $91 each.

Required

1. Calculate the cost of inventory on hand at 31 March 2014 and the cost of sales for the month of March. (Round the average unit cost to the nearest cent, and round the total cost amounts to the nearest dollar.)
2. Show the Inventory general ledger control account (in T-format) as it would appear at 31 March 2014.
3. Calculate the gross profit on sales for the month of March 2014.

ASSIGNING COST AND REPORTING GROSS PROFIT USING DIFFERENT COST METHODS

★★ The following information has been extracted from the records of Lillehammer Trading about one of its products. Lillehammer Trading uses the perpetual inventory system and its reporting period ends on 30 September.

		No. of units	Unit cost $	Total cost $
2013				
01/10	Beginning balance	1 600	14.00	22 400
06/10	Purchased	600	14.10	8 460
05/11	Sold @ $24.00 per unit	2 000		
19/12	Purchased	2 200	14.70	32 340
24/12	Purchase returns	160	14.70	2 352
10/01	Sold @ $24.20 per unit	1 400		
22/03	Purchased	16 800	15.00	252 000
30/04	Sold @ $26.50 per unit	3 600		
04/05	Sales returns @ $26.50 per unit	40		
04/06	Sold @ $27.00 per unit	7 000		
06/08	Purchased	1 000	16.00	16 000
27/09	Sold @ $30.00 per unit	6 200		

Required

1. Calculate the cost of inventory on hand at 30 September 2013 and the cost of sales for the year ended 30 September 2013, using:
   (a) the FIFO cost method
   (b) the moving average cost method (round the average unit costs to the nearest cent, and round the total cost amounts to the nearest dollar).
2. Prepare the trading section of the statement of profit or loss and other comprehensive income for the year ended 30 September 2013, using:
   (a) the FIFO cost method
   (b) the moving average cost method.

END-OF-YEAR ADJUSTMENTS

★★ The inventory control account balance of Johnkoping Fashions at 30 June 2013 was $221 020 using the perpetual inventory method. A physical count conducted on that day found inventory on hand worth $220 200. Net realisable value for each inventory item held for sale exceeded cost. An investigation of the discrepancy revealed the following:
- Goods worth $6600 held on consignment for Swede Accessories had been included in the physical count.
- Goods costing $1200 were purchased on credit from Vetlanda Ltd on 27 June 2013 on FOB shipping terms. The goods were shipped on 28 June 2013 but, as they had not arrived by 30 June 2013, were not included in the physical count. The purchase invoice was received and processed on 30 June 2013
- Goods costing $2400 were sold on credit to Iceland Pty Ltd for $3900 on 28 June 2013 on FOB destination terms. The goods were still in transit on 30 June 2013. The sales invoice was raised and processed on 29 June 2013.
- Goods costing $2730 were purchased on credit (FOB destination) from Finn Handbags on 28 June 2013. The goods were received on 29 June 2013 and included in the physical count. The purchase invoice was received on 2 July 2013.

- On 30 June 2013, Johnkoping Fashions sold goods costing $6300 on credit (FOB shipping) terms to Viking Boutique for $9600. The goods were dispatched from the warehouse on 30 June 2013 but the sales invoice had not been raised at that date.
- Damaged inventory items valued at $2650 were discovered during the physical count. These items were still recorded on 30 June 2013 but were omitted from the physical count records pending their write-off.

Required

Prepare any journal entries necessary on 30 June 2013 to correct any errors and to adjust inventory.

Exercise 9.16
★★★

Note: Exercises 9.16, 9.17 and 9.18 concern the same entity, Sweden Emporium, because they have been designed so that they can be combined to form a single comprehensive problem.

ASSIGNMENT OF COST

Sweden Emporium is a gift shop situated in a small fishing village. The business carries a range of merchandise that it accounts for under the perpetual inventory method. Cost is assigned using the FIFO cost flow method. All purchases are on FOB shipping terms, with 30 days credit. The end of the reporting period is 30 June.

The following information lists the transactions during October 2013 for one item of inventory (wall plaques):

Date	Detail	Number	Unit cost
Oct. 1	Opening balance	45	6.40
4	Purchase	50	6.50
8	Sale	60	
11	Purchase	70	6.60
14	Purchase return	10	6.60
19	Sale	70	
24	Sale return (on 19 Oct. sale)	5	
28	Purchase	40	6.70

Required

For the inventory item (wall plaques), calculate October's cost of sales expense and the cost of inventory on hand at 31 October 2013. Round all figures to the nearest cent.

Exercise 9.17
★★★

END-OF-REPORTING-PERIOD RECONCILIATION AND NRV

Sweden Emporium is a gift shop situated in a small fishing village. The business carries a range of merchandise that it accounts for under the perpetual inventory method. Cost is assigned using the FIFO cost flow method. All purchases are on FOB shipping terms, with 30 days credit. The end of the reporting period is 30 June.

A physical count of inventory at 30 June 2014 found inventory worth $189 650. The inventory control ledger account at that date had a balance of $193 700. Investigations of the discrepancy between these two figures revealed the following:

- An unopened carton containing posters worth $420 had not been included in the count.
- Seven large conch shells were found to be damaged beyond repair and were not recorded in the count. The shells, worth $220, are still recorded in the inventory records.
- Goods costing $590 were ordered on 27 June 2014 and delivered to the transport company by the supplier on 29 June. As the goods were in transit on 30 June, they were not included in the count. The purchase was recorded when the goods arrived at the shop on 2 July 2014.
- Sweden Emporium has a number of paintings on display in local restaurants on a consignment basis. The paintings are worth $4200 and were not included in the count.
- A brass telescope had been sold for $1200 on 30 June. As the telescope was still in the shop awaiting collection by the owner, it was included in the count. The telescope cost $950.
- Five missing dolphin statues worth $160 could not be located and are presumed to have been stolen from the shop.

1. Reconcile the Inventory control ledger account balance with the physical count figure (adjust both figures as necessary).
2. Prepare any journal entries necessary to achieve the reconciliation.

| Exercise 9.18 | **END-OF-REPORTING-PERIOD RECONCILIATION AND NRV** |

★★★ Sweden Emporium is a gift shop situated in a small fishing village. The business carries a range of merchandise that it accounts for under the perpetual inventory method. Cost is assigned using the FIFO cost flow method. All purchases are on FOB shipping terms, with 30 days credit. The end of the reporting period is 30 June.

IAS 2 requires inventory to be recorded at the lower of cost and net realisable value. C Bligh, the owner of Sweden Emporium, assessed the net realisable value of her inventory at 30 June 2014 and concluded that the net realisable value of all items (except barometers) exceeded cost. The six barometers on hand cost $150 each, but C Bligh is of the opinion that they will need to be discounted to $90 in order to sell them.

Required

Explain what is meant by the term 'net realisable value' and detail the action C Bligh must take in respect to the wall barometers.

| Exercise 9.19 | **ALLOCATING COST (FIFO), REPORTING GROSS PROFIT AND APPLYING THE NRV RULE** |

★★★ Stockholm Ltd wholesales bicycles. It uses the perpetual inventory method and allocates cost to inventory on a first-in, first-out basis. The company's reporting period ends on 31 March. At 1 March 2013, inventory on hand consisted of 350 bicycles at $82 each and 43 bicycles at $85 each. During the month ended 31 March 2013, the following inventory transactions took place (all purchase and sales transactions are on credit):

March	1	Sold 300 bicycles for $120 each.
	3	Five bicycles were returned by a customer. They had originally cost $82 each and were sold for $120 each.
	9	Purchased 55 bicycles at $91 each.
	10	Purchased 76 bicycles at $96 each.
	15	Sold 86 bicycles for $135 each.
	17	Returned one damaged bicycle to the supplier. This bicycle had been purchased on 9 March.
	22	Sold 60 bicycles for $125 each.
	26	Purchased 72 bicycles at $98 each.
	29	Two bicycles, sold on 22 March, were returned by a customer. The bicycles were badly damaged so it was decided to write them off. They had originally cost $91 each.

Required

1. Calculate the cost of inventory on hand at 31 March 2013 and the cost of sales for the month of March.
2. Show the Inventory general ledger control account (in T-format) as it would appear at 31 March 2013.
3. Calculate the gross profit on sales for the month of March 2013.
4. IAS 2 requires inventories to be measured at the lower of cost and net realisable value. Identify three reasons why the net realisable value of the bicycles on hand at 31 March 2013 may be below their cost.
5. If the net realisable value is below cost, what action should Stockholm Ltd take?

| Exercise 9.20 | **ASSIGNING COSTS AND END-OF-PERIOD ADJUSTMENTS** |

★★★ Lund Retailing Ltd is a food wholesaler that supplies independent grocery stores. The company operates a perpetual inventory system, with the first-in, first-out method used to assign costs to inventory items. Freight costs are not included in the calculation of unit costs. Transactions and other related information regarding two of the items (baked beans and plain flour) carried by Lund Ltd are given below for June 2013, the last month of the company's reporting period.

	Baked beans	Plain flour
Unit of packaging	Case containing 25 × 410 g cans	Box containing 12 × 4 kg bags
Inventory @ 1 June 2013	350 cases @ $19.60	625 boxes @ $38.40
Purchases	1. 10 June: 200 cases @ $19.50 plus freight of $135 2. 19 June: 470 cases @ $19.70 per case plus freight of $210	1. 3 June: 150 boxes @ $38.45 2. 15 June: 200 boxes @ $38.45 3. 29 June: 240 boxes @ $39.00
Purchase terms	2/10, n/30, FOB shipping	n/30, FOB destination
June sales	730 cases @ $28.50	950 boxes @ 40.00
Returns and allowances	A customer returned 50 cases that had been shipped in error. The customer's account was credited for $1425.	As the June 15 purchase was unloaded, 10 boxes were discovered damaged. A credit of $384.50 was received by Lund Retailing Ltd.
Physical count at 30 June 2013	326 cases on hand	15 boxes on hand
Explanation of variance	No explanation found — assumed stolen	Boxes purchased on 29 June still in transit on 30 June
Net realisable value at 30 June 2013	$29.00 per case	$38.50 per box

Required

1. Calculate the number of units in inventory and the FIFO unit cost for baked beans and plain flour as at 30 June 2013 (show all workings).
2. Calculate the total dollar amount of the inventory for baked beans and plain flour, applying the lower of cost and net realisable rule on an item-by-item basis. Prepare any necessary journal entries (show all workings).

Exercise 9.21	**ALLOCATING COST (MOVING AVERAGE), END-OF-PERIOD ADJUSTMENTS AND WRITE-DOWNS TO NRV**
★★★	**Part A**

Mario Gothenburg uses the perpetual inventory method and special journals, balances the books at month-end and uses control accounts and subsidiary ledgers for all accounts receivable and accounts payable. All sales and purchases are made on 2/10, n/30, FOB destination terms. The moving average method is used to assign cost to inventory items.

The information below and overleaf has been extracted from Mario's books and records for May and June 2014.

	$
Inventory control ledger account balance at 31 May	20 367.30
Accounts payable control ledger account balance at 31 May	7 973.60
Inventory purchases on credit during June	11 248.90
Cash paid to trade creditors during June	15 123.40
Discount received during June	438.90
Inventory sales on credit during June	15 020.00

(continued)

Inventory ledger card balances at 1 June:
Pool filters   43 @ $232.50   9 997.50
Pool pumps   21 @ $493.80   10 369.80
                                                                                                              20 367.30

The credit inventory purchases during June comprised the following:
June   4   5 pool pumps @ $476.10 each   2 380.50
        17   3 pool pumps @ $491.30 each   1 473.90
        18   12 pool filters @ $236.70 each   2 840.40
        24   2 pool pumps @ $491.30 each   982.60
        29   15 pool filters @ $238.10 each   3 571.50
                                                                                                              11 248.90

The credit inventory sales during June comprised the following:
June   1   1 pool pump @ $520 and 1 pool filter @ $300   820
         5   18 pool filters @ $300 each   5 400
        18   4 pool pumps @ $550 each   2 200
        23   15 pool filters @ $330 each   4 950
        28   5 pool filters @ $330 each   1 650
                                                                                                              15 020

Other movements in inventory during June were:
June   9   2 pool filters, sold 5 June (not paid for) were returned by the customer
        20   3 pool filters purchased 18 June (not paid for) were returned to the supplier
        26   1 pool pump, purchased 4 June (paid for) was returned to the supplier

Required

1. Prepare the perpetual inventory records for June 2014.
2. Prepare the inventory control and accounts payable control general ledger accounts (in T-format) for the month of June 2014.

Part B

At 30 June 2014, Mario conducted a physical stocktake that found 14 pool filters and 26 pool pumps on hand. An investigation of discrepancies between the inventory card balances and the physical count showed that the 15 pool filters purchased on 29 June 2014 were still in transit from the supplier's factory on 30 June 2014, and one pool pump, sold on 18 June, had been returned by a customer on 30 June. No adjustment has been made in the books for the sales return. The customer had not paid for the returned pump.

Required

Prepare any general journal entries necessary to correct the Inventory control general ledger account balance as at 30 June 2014. (Narrations are not required, but show all workings.) Do not adjust the perpetual inventory records prepared in Part A.

Part C

On 30 June 2014, Mario determined that his inventory items have the following net realisable values:

Pool filters	$232 each
Pool pumps	$546 each

Required

1. What does the term 'net realisable value' mean?
2. What sources of evidence could Mario examine to determine net realisable value?
3. What action should Mario take as at 30 June 2014 with respect to these net realisable values? Why?

References

IASB 2004, *IFRIC Update*, November, IASB, www.ifrs.org.
Nokia 2011, *Nokia in 2010*, Nokia Corporation, Finland, www.nokia.com.

10 Employee benefits

ACCOUNTING STANDARDS IN FOCUS

IAS 19 *Employee Benefits*

LEARNING OBJECTIVES

After studying this chapter, you should be able to:

1 outline the principles applied in accounting for employee benefits

2 discuss the scope and purpose of IAS 19

3 discuss the definition of employee benefits

4 prepare journal entries to account for short-term liabilities for employee benefits, such as wages and salaries, sick leave and annual leave

5 compare defined benefit and defined contribution post-employment benefit plans

6 prepare entries to account for expenses, assets and liabilities arising from defined contribution post-employment plans

7 prepare entries to record expenses, assets and liabilities arising from defined benefit post-employment plans

8 explain how to measure and record other long-term liabilities for employment benefits, such as long service leave

9 explain when a liability should be recognised for termination benefits and how it should be measured.

10.1 INTRODUCTION TO ACCOUNTING FOR EMPLOYEE BENEFITS

Employee benefits typically constitute a significant component of an entity's expenses, particularly in the services sector. For example, Billabong International Ltd reports in its 2011 financial statements that 'selling, general and administrative expenses' of $599 million include 'employee benefits expense' of $283 million. Employees are remunerated for the services they provide. Employee remuneration is not limited to wages, which may be paid weekly, fortnightly or monthly, but often includes entitlements to be paid, such as sick leave, annual leave, long service leave and post-employment benefits; that is, contributions for superannuation plans or pension plans. The measurement of short-term liabilities for employee benefits, such as sick leave and annual leave, is relatively straightforward. However, the measurement of other types of employee benefits, including post-employment benefits, other long-term benefits, such as long service leave, and termination benefits, is more complex because it requires estimation and present value calculations.

10.2 SCOPE AND PURPOSE OF IAS 19

IAS 19 *Employee Benefits* applies to all employee benefits except those to which IFRS 2 *Share-based Payment* applies. Employee benefits arise from formal agreements, which are often referred to as workplace agreements, between an entity and its individual employees. Alternatively, employee benefits may arise from agreements between an entity and groups of employees or their representatives. These agreements are often referred to as enterprise bargaining agreements. Employee benefits also include requirements specified by legislation or industry arrangements for employers to contribute to an industry, state or national plan. Informal practices that generate a constructive obligation, such as payment of annual bonuses, also fall within the scope of employee benefits under IAS 19. Share-based employee benefits are beyond the scope of IAS 19. Chapter 8 considers share-based payments, including share-based employee remuneration.

The purpose of IAS 19 is to prescribe the measurement and recognition of expenses, assets and liabilities arising from services provided by employees. Liabilities arise when employees provide services in exchange for benefits to be provided later by the employer. Accounting for employee benefits is complicated because some benefits may be provided many years after employees have provided services. The measurement of liabilities for employee benefits is made more difficult because the payment of some employee benefits for past services may be conditional upon the continuation of employment.

10.3 DEFINING EMPLOYEE BENEFITS

Paragraph 8 of IAS 19 defines employee benefits as:

> all forms of consideration given by an entity in exchange for service rendered by employees or for the termination of employment.

Employee benefits are usually paid to employees but the term also includes amounts paid to their dependants or to other parties.

Wages, salaries and other employee benefits are usually recognised as expenses. However, the costs of employee benefits may be allocated to assets in accordance with other accounting standards. For example, the cost of labour used in the manufacture of inventory is included in the cost of inventory in accordance with IAS 2 *Inventories*. The cost of an internally generated intangible asset recognised in accordance with IAS 38 *Intangible Assets*, such as the development of a new production process, includes the cost of employee benefits for staff, such as engineers, employed in generating the new production process.

10.4 SHORT-TERM EMPLOYEE BENEFITS

Short-term employee benefits are expected to be settled wholly within one year after the end of the annual reporting period in which the employee renders the service. Examples of short-term employee benefits include wages, salaries, bonuses and profit-sharing arrangements. They also include various forms of paid leave entitlements for which employees may be eligible. Sick leave and annual leave are common forms of paid leave entitlements. IAS 19 refers to various forms of leave entitlements as paid absences.

Short-term employee benefits also include non-monetary benefits, which are often referred to as 'fringe benefits'. Non-monetary benefits include the provision of health insurance, housing and motor vehicles. For example, non-monetary employee benefits received by Billabong International Ltd executives include health insurance, car allowances and clothing allowances. An entity may offer non-monetary benefits to attract staff. For example, a mining company may provide housing to employees where there are no major towns located near its mining sites. Non-monetary benefits may also arise from salary sacrifice arrangements, otherwise referred to as salary packaging. A salary sacrifice arrangement involves the employee electing to forgo some of his or her salary or wages in return for other benefits, such as a motor vehicle, provided by the employer.

10.4.1 Payroll

The subsystem for regular recording and payment of employee benefits is referred to as the payroll. The payroll involves:
- recording the amount of wages or salaries for the pay period
- updating personnel records for the appointment of new employees
- updating personnel records for the termination of employment contracts
- calculating the amount to be paid to each employee, net of deductions
- remitting payment of net wages or salaries to employees
- remitting payment of deductions to various external parties
- complying with regulatory requirements, such as reporting to taxation authorities.

Businesses may process several payrolls. For example, a business may process a payroll each fortnight for employees who are paid on a fortnightly basis and process a separate monthly payroll for employees paid on a monthly basis.

In return for providing services to the employer, employees regularly receive benefits, or remuneration, in the form of wages or salaries. Employers are typically required to deduct income tax from employees' wages and salaries. Thus the employee receives a payment that is net of tax, and the employer subsequently pays the amount of income tax to the taxation authority.

Employers may offer a service of deducting other amounts from employees' wages and salaries and paying other parties on their behalf. For example, the employer may deduct union membership fees from employees' wages and make payments to the various unions on behalf of the employees. Similarly, the employer may deduct health insurance premiums from the employees' wages, and remit payments to the various health insurance funds that its employees have joined.

Payments made on behalf of an employee from amounts deducted from the employee's wages or salaries form part of the entity's wages and salaries expense. As these amounts are typically remitted in the month following the payment of wages and salaries, they represent a short-term liability for employee benefits at the end of each month.

Paragraph 11(a) of IAS 19 requires short-term employee benefits for services rendered during the period to be recognised as a liability after deducting any amounts already paid. Short-term liabilities for employee benefits must be measured at the nominal (undiscounted) amount that the entity expects to pay.

10.4.2 Accounting for the payroll

Illustrative example 10.1 demonstrates accounting for the payroll, including deductions from employees' remuneration, the remittance of payroll deductions and the measurement of resulting liabilities at the end of the period.

ILLUSTRATIVE EXAMPLE 10.1 Accounting for the payroll

Curtin Ltd pays its managers on a monthly basis. All of Curtin Ltd's salaries are recognised as expenses. Curtin Ltd's employees can elect to have their monthly health insurance premiums deducted from their salaries and paid to their health insurance fund on their behalf. The company provides a similar service for the payment of union membership fees. Curtin Ltd also operates a giving scheme under which employees can elect to have donations to nominated charities deducted from their salaries and wages and remitted on their behalf to the selected charities. Figure 10.1 summarises the managerial payrolls for May and June 2013.

	May 2013		June 2013	
	$	$	$	$
Gross payroll for the month		2 400 000		2 500 000
Deductions payable to:				
Taxation authority	530 000		600 000	
Total Care Health Fund	40 000		40 000	
National Health Fund	20 000		20 000	
UNICEF	3 000		3 000	
National Heart Research Fund	4 000		4 000	
Union fees	12 000		12 500	
Total deductions for the month		609 000		679 500
Net salaries paid		1 791 000		1 820 500

FIGURE 10.1 Summary of Curtin Ltd's payroll

Each time the monthly payroll is processed, the cost of the salaries is charged to expense accounts and a liability is accrued for the gross wages payable. Payments of net wages and salaries and remittance of payroll deductions to taxation authorities and other parties reduce the payroll liability account.

The managerial payroll is processed on the second Monday of the month and net salaries are paid to employees on the following Tuesday. During May, managers earned salaries of $2.4 million. After deducting amounts for income tax, union membership fees, contributions to health funds and donations, Curtin Ltd paid its managers a net amount of $1 791 000 during May. All of the deductions are paid to the various external bodies in the following month. Health insurance deductions and union subscriptions are remitted on the first Friday of the following month. Thus, the deductions for health insurance and union subscriptions for the May payroll are remitted on Friday 7 June. Income tax withheld is remitted on the 20th of the following month. Deductions for donations are paid on the 21st of the following month.

The balance of Curtin Ltd's Accrued Managerial Payroll account at 1 June 2013 is $609 000, being the deductions from managers' salaries for income tax, health insurance premiums, union fees and donations for May 2013. These amounts are paid during June 2013.

During June 2013, Curtin Ltd's managers earned gross salaries of $2.5 million. The managers actually received $1 820 500, being the net wages and salaries after deductions for income tax, health insurance premiums, union fees and donations to charities. In total, $679 500 was deducted from managers' salaries for June 2013. This amount is a liability at the end of June 2013. The amounts deducted from employees' salaries during June 2013 are remitted during July 2013.

The journal entries to record Curtin Ltd's payroll and remittances for June 2013 are as follows:

June 7	Accrued Payroll	Dr	40 000	
	Bank	Cr		40 000
	(Payment of May payroll deductions for Total Health Care Fund)			
	Accrued Payroll	Dr	20 000	
	Bank	Cr		20 000
	(Payment of May payroll deductions for National Health Fund)			
	Accrued Payroll	Dr	12 000	
	Bank	Cr		12 000
	(Payment of May payroll deductions for union fees)			
June 10	Salaries Expense	Dr	2 500 000	
	Accrued Payroll	Cr		2 500 000
	(Managerial payroll for June)			

			Dr	1 820 500	
June 11	Accrued Payroll		Dr	1 820 500	
	Bank		Cr		1 820 500
	(Payment of net salaries for June)				
June 20	Accrued Payroll		Dr	530 000	
	Bank		Cr		530 000
	(Payment of May payroll deductions for withheld income tax)				
June 21	Accrued Payroll		Dr	3 000	
	Bank		Cr		3 000
	(Payment of May payroll deductions for UNICEF)				
	Accrued Payroll		Dr	4 000	
	Bank		Cr		4 000
	(Payment of May payroll deductions for National Heart Research Fund)				

10.4.3 Accrual of wages and salaries

The end of the payroll period often differs from the end of the reporting period because payrolls are usually determined on a weekly or fortnightly basis. Accordingly, it is usually necessary to recognise an expense and a liability for employee benefits for the business days between the last payroll period and the end of the reporting period. This is demonstrated in illustrative example 10.2.

ILLUSTRATIVE EXAMPLE 10.2 Accrual of wages and salaries

Canterbury Ltd pays its employees on a fortnightly basis. The last payroll in the year ended 30 September 2013 was for the fortnight (10 working days) ended Friday 27 September 2013. There was one business day between the end of the final payroll period and the end of the reporting period. Assuming the cost of employee benefits for the remaining day was $120 000, Canterbury Ltd would record the following accrual:

Wages and Salaries Expense	Dr	120 000	
Accrued Wages and Salaries	Cr		120 000
(Accrual of wages and salaries)			

The accrued wages and salaries is a liability for short-term employee benefits. Paragraph 16 of IAS 19 requires accrued short-term employee benefits to be measured at nominal value, that is, the amount expected to be paid to settle the obligation.

10.4.4 Short-term paid absences

Employees may be entitled to be paid during certain absences, such as annual recreational leave or short periods of illness. Some entities also offer other forms of paid leave, including maternity leave, parental leave, carers' leave and bereavement leave. Entitlements to short-term paid absences are those entitlements that are expected to be settled within 12 months after the end of the reporting period.

Short-term paid absences may be either accumulating or non-accumulating. Non-accumulating paid absences are leave entitlements that the employee may not carry forward to a future period. For example, an employment agreement may provide for 5 days of paid, non-cumulative sick leave. If the employee does not take sick leave during the year, the unused leave lapses; that is, it does not carry forward to an increased entitlement in the following year.

Accumulating paid absences are leave entitlements that the employee may carry forward to a future period if unused in the current period. For example, an employment agreement may provide for 20 days of paid annual leave. If the employee only takes 15 days of annual leave during the year, the remaining 5 days may be carried forward and taken in the following year.

Accumulating paid absences may be vesting or non-vesting. If accumulating paid absences are vesting, the employee is entitled, upon termination of employment, to cash settlement for unused leave. If accumulating paid absences are non-vesting, the employee has no entitlement to cash settlement of unused leave. For example, an employment contract may provide for cumulative annual leave of 20 days, vesting to a maximum of 30 days, and non-vesting cumulative sick leave of 10 days per annum. After 2 years of service, the employee would have been entitled to take 40 days of annual leave and 20 days of sick leave, but if the employee resigned after 2 years of employment, during which no annual leave or sick leave had been taken, the termination settlement would include payment for 30 days' unused annual leave (the maximum allowed by the employment agreement). There would be no cash settlement of the unused sick leave because it was non-vesting.

Paragraph 13 of IAS 19 requires expected short-term accumulating paid absences to be recognised when the employee renders services that increase the entitlement. For example, if its employees are entitled to 2 weeks of cumulative sick leave for every year of service, the entity is required to accrue the sick leave throughout the year. The employee benefit; that is, the accumulated leave, is measured as the amount that the entity expects to pay to settle the amount that has accumulated at the end of the reporting period. If the leave is cumulative but non-vesting, it is possible that there will not be a future settlement. The sick leave might remain unused when the employment contract is terminated. However, the sick leave must still be accrued throughout the period of employment because an obligation arises when the employee provides services that give rise to the leave entitlement. If the leave is non-vesting, it is necessary to estimate the amount of accumulated paid absence that the entity expects to pay.

For non-accumulating short-term paid absences, paragraph 13 requires the entity to recognise the employee benefit when the paid absence occurs. A liability is not recognised for unused non-accumulating leave entitlements because the employee is not entitled to carry them forward to a future period.

The alternative forms of short-term paid absences and the corresponding recognition and measurement requirements are depicted in figure 10.2.

Accumulation	Vesting/non-vesting	Recognition	Liability measurement
Accumulating — employee may carry forward unused entitlement	Vesting — employee is entitled to cash settlement of unused leave	Recognised as employee provides services giving rise to entitlement	Nominal, amount expected to be paid, i.e. total vested accumulated leave
	Non-vesting — no cash settlement of unused leave	Recognised as employee provides services giving rise to entitlement	Nominal, amount expected to be paid, requires estimation of amount that will be used
Non-accumulating — unused entitlement lapses each period		Recognised when paid absences occur	No liability is recognised

FIGURE 10.2 Short-term paid absences

The following illustrative examples demonstrate accounting for short-term paid absences. First, illustrative example 10.3 demonstrates accounting for annual leave.

ILLUSTRATIVE EXAMPLE 10.3 Accounting for annual leave

Southern Ltd has four employees in its Manchester branch. Each employee is entitled to 20 days of paid recreational leave per annum, referred to as annual leave (AL). At 1 July 2012, the balance of the provision for annual leave was $4360. During the year employees took a total of 70 days of annual leave, which cost Southern Ltd $9160. After annual leave taken during the year had been recorded, the provision for annual leave account had a debit balance of $4800 in the trial balance at 30 June 2013 before end-of-period adjustments. All annual leave accumulated at 30 June 2013 is expected to be paid by 30 June 2014. The following information is obtained from the payroll records for the year ended 30 June 2013:

Employee	Wage per day	AL 1 July 2012 in days	Increase in entitlement in days	AL taken in days
East	$120	9	20	16
North	$160	7	20	16
South	$180	8	20	14
West	$ 90	8	20	24

A liability must be recognised for accumulated annual leave at 30 June 2013. This is measured as the amount that is expected to be paid. As annual leave is vesting, all accumulated leave is expected to be paid. The first step in measuring the liability is to calculate the number of days of accumulated annual leave for each employee at 30 June 2013. Although this calculation would normally be performed by payroll software, we will manually calculate the number of days to enhance your understanding of the process. The next step is to multiply the number of days of accumulated annual leave by each employee's daily wage.

Employee	AL 1 July 2012 in days	Increase in entitlement in days	AL taken in days	Accumulated AL 30 June 2013	Liability for AL 30 June 2013 $
East	9	20	16	13	1 560
North	7	20	16	11	1 760
South	8	20	14	14	2 520
West	8	20	24	4	360
					6 200

The calculation of accumulated annual leave in days and the resultant liability are as follows:

East: 9 + 20 − 16 = 13 days × $120 per day = $1560
North: 7 + 20 − 16 = 11 days × $160 per day = $1760
South: 8 + 20 − 14 = 14 days × $180 per day = $2520
West: 8 + 20 − 24 = 4 days × $90 per day = $360

The above calculations show that a liability of $6200 should be recognised for annual leave at 30 June 2013. After recording annual leave taken during the year, the unadjusted trial balance shows a debit balance of $4800 for the provision for annual leave. Thus, a journal entry is required to record an increase of $11 000.

Wages and Salaries Expense	Dr	11 000	
Provision for Annual Leave	Cr		11 000
(Accrual of liability for annual leave)			

In illustrative example 10.3, an annual adjustment was made to the provision for annual leave. Some entities make accruals for annual leave more frequently to facilitate more comprehensive internal reporting to management. This is easily achieved with electronic accounting systems or payroll software.

Accounting for accumulating sick leave is demonstrated in illustrative example 10.4. In this illustration, the accumulating sick leave is non-vesting.

Massey Ltd has 10 employees who are each paid $500 per week for a 5-day working week (i.e. $100 per day). Employees are entitled to 5 days of accumulating non-vesting sick leave each year. At 1 July 2012, the accumulated sick leave brought forward from the previous year was 10 days in total. During the year ended 30 June 2013, employees took 35 days of paid sick leave and 10 days of unpaid sick leave. One employee resigned at the beginning of the year. At the time of her resignation she had accumulated 5 days of sick leave. It is estimated that 60% of the unused sick leave will be taken during the following year and that the remaining 40% will not be taken at all.

After recording sick leave taken during the year, the unadjusted trial balance shows that the balance of the provision for sick leave at 30 June 2013 is $3000 Dr.

The following table is constructed to assist in calculating the amount of the provision for sick leave that Massey Ltd should recognise at 30 June 2013:

		Sick leave			% of leave expected to be taken	
No. of employees	Base pay/day $	Balance b/d 1 July 2012 Days	Accumulated in 2013 Days	Taken or lapsed Days	Within 12 months %	After 1 year %
10	100	10	50	40	60	0

The 10 employees who were employed for all of the year ended 30 June 2013 became entitled to 5 days of sick leave during the year. Thus the total increase in entitlement during the year is 50 days. During the year, 35 days of paid sick leave were taken and 5 days of sick leave entitlement lapsed because an employee with 5 days' accumulated sick leave resigned without having used her entitlement. Thus, the aggregate sick leave entitlement reduced by 40 days during the year.

The amount of the liability at 30 June 2013 is measured by first calculating the number of days of accumulated sick leave entitlement at 30 June 2013.

	Days
Brought forward July 2012	10
Increase in entitlement for services provided in the current year	50
Sick leave entitlement taken or lapsed during the year	(40)
Sick leave carried forward 30 June 2013	20

The number of days of accumulated sick leave at the end of the reporting period is multiplied by the proportion of days expected to be taken, in this case, 60%. This amount, 12 days, is then multiplied by the current rate of pay per day:

$$20 \text{ days} \times 60\% \times \$100 \text{ per day} = \$1200$$

Thus a provision for sick leave of $1200 Cr should be recognised at 30 June 2013. The unadjusted balance of the provision for sick leave is $3000 Dr. Accordingly, the provision must be increased by $4200 as follows:

Wages and Salaries Expense	Dr	4 200	
Provision for Sick Leave	Cr		4 200
(Accrual of liability for sick leave)			

For simplicity, the accrual adjustment to recognise sick leave is made at the end of the year in this example. Many companies make such adjustments throughout the year to provide more complete internal reporting to management. This is facilitated by payroll software that automates the calculation of accumulated entitlements.

10.4.5 Profit-sharing and bonus plans

Employers may offer profit-sharing arrangements and bonuses to their employees. Bonuses may be determined as a lump-sum amount or based on accounting or market-based measures of performance. Many large companies use bonuses in management incentive schemes. For example, the remuneration received by the senior executives of Billabong International Ltd includes base salary, bonuses linked to performance (incentive-based remuneration) and superannuation benefits. The components of remuneration for the chief executive officer (CEO) for 2009 to 2011 are shown in figure 10.3. As can be seen, the decline in total remuneration in 2011 resulted from lower incentive-based remuneration. This occurred because certain performance targets pertaining to the Billabong Group profit after tax and working capital were not met in that year.

Name: D. O'Neill Position: Chief executive officer (CEO)	2011 $'000	2010 $'000	2009 $'000
Base salary	1 261	1 142	1 144
Short-term incentives	—	1 119	578
Non-monetary benefits (e.g. car allowance, health insurance)	3	5	3
Long-term incentives — value vested during the year	—	—	525
Superannuation	15	14	13
Total remuneration realised	1 279	2 280	2 263

FIGURE 10.3 Billabong International Ltd CEO Remuneration
Source: Billabong International Ltd (2011, pp. 18, 30; 2010, p. 21).

The bonus forms part of a management remuneration package designed to align the interests of the manager with the interests of the entity or its owners. However, as seen in figure 10.4, the Human Resource and Remuneration Committee of the Board of Directors of Billabong International Ltd revised the remuneration scheme in response to shareholder concerns.

The Board took seriously the shareholder concerns raised at the October 2010 Annual General Meeting regarding Billabong's remuneration policies and approach. Subsequently, consultation with shareholders took place to ensure the Board fully understood your concerns so they could be considered and addressed as part of the review process.

The Board values shareholder feedback and your views have helped shape our decisions with regard to future executive remuneration. Specifically, in 2010–11 the Board has responded to shareholder concerns by making the following changes:
- the adoption of a second performance measure for Billabong's Long Term Incentive (LTI), the Executive Performance Share Plan (EPSP); and
- that dividends on unvested EPSP shares be held in trust, payable only if performance targets are met and shares vest.

FIGURE 10.4 Letter from Human Resource and Remuneration Committee Chair (extract)
Source: Billabong International Ltd (2011, p. 12).

Paragraph 19 of IAS 19 requires an entity to recognise the expected cost of profit-sharing and bonus payments if:

(a) the entity has a present legal or constructive obligation to make such payments as a result of past events; and
(b) a reliable estimate of the obligation can be made.
A present obligation exists when, and only when, the entity has no realistic alternative but to make the payments.

Although the entity may have no legal obligation to pay the bonus, a constructive obligation arises if the entity has a well-established practice of paying the bonus and it has no realistic alternative but to pay the bonus. For instance, non-payment may be harmful to the entity's relations with its employees.

Liabilities for short-term profit-sharing arrangements and bonuses are measured at the nominal (i.e. undiscounted) amount that the entity expects to pay. Thus, if payment under a profit-sharing arrangement is subject to the employee still being employed when the payment is due, the amount recognised as a liability is reduced by the amount that is expected to go unpaid due to staff turnover. For example, assume an entity has a profit-sharing arrangement in which it is obligated to pay 1% of profit for the period to employees and the amount becomes payable 3 months after the end of the reporting period. Based on staff turnover in prior years, the entity estimates that only 95% of employees will be eligible to receive a share of profit 3 months after the end of the reporting period. Accordingly, the amount of the liability that should be recognised for the profit-sharing scheme is equal to 0.95% of the entity's profit for the period. In this simple example it is assumed the bonus is distributed equally among employees.

 ## 10.5 POST-EMPLOYMENT BENEFITS

Post-employment benefits are benefits, other than termination benefits (which are considered in section 10.7), that are payable after completion of employment, typically after the employee retires. Where post-employment benefits involve significant obligations, it is common (and in some countries compulsory) for employers to contribute to a post-employment benefit plan for employees. For example, in Australia, it is compulsory for most private sector employers to contribute to a superannuation plan for employees.

Post-employment benefit plans are defined in paragraph 8 of IAS 19 as:

> formal or informal arrangements under which an entity provides post-employment benefits for one or more employees.

Post-employment benefit plans are also referred to as superannuation plans, employee retirement plans and pension plans. The employer makes payments to a fund. The fund, which is a separate entity, typically a trust, invests the contributions and provides post-employment benefits to the employees, who are the members of the fund. Figure 10.5 shows the relations between the employer, the superannuation fund (plan) and the employees (members of the fund).

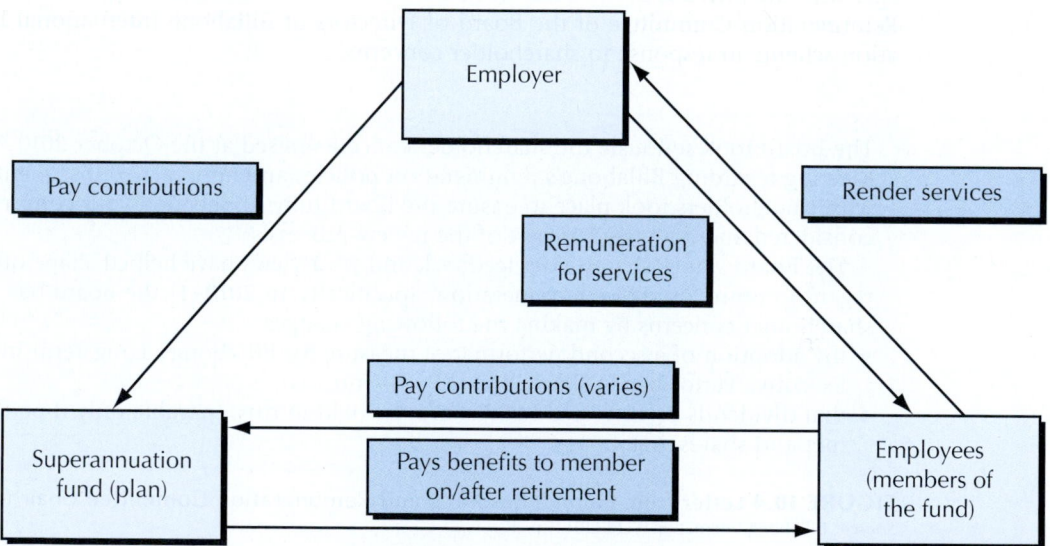

FIGURE 10.5 Relationships between the employer, the superannuation fund (plan) and the employees

The two types of post-employment benefit plans are defined benefit plans and defined contribution plans, including multi-employer plans.

Paragraph 8 of IAS 19 refers to defined contribution plans as post-employment plans for which an entity pays fixed contributions into a separate entity. The contributions are normally based on the wages and salaries paid to employees. The contributing entity has no legal or constructive obligation to pay further contributions if the fund does not hold sufficient assets to pay all employee benefits relating to employees' service in the current and prior periods. The amount received by employees on retirement is dependent upon the level of contributions and the return earned by the fund on its investments.

In paragraph 8 of IAS 19, defined benefit plans are defined as post-employment plans other than defined contribution plans. If a post-employment plan is not classified as a defined contribution plan, by default, it is a defined benefit plan. Critical to the definition of a defined contribution post-employment benefit plan is the absence of an obligation for the employer to make further payments if the fund is unable to pay all the benefits accruing to members for their past service. Thus, defined benefit post-employment plans are those in which the employer has some obligation to pay further contributions to enable the fund to pay members' benefits. In a defined benefit post-employment plan, the benefit received by members on retirement is determined by a formula reflecting their years of service and level of remuneration. It is not dependent upon the performance of the fund. If the performance of the fund is insufficient to pay members' post-employment benefits, the trustee of the fund will require the employer, who is the sponsor of the fund, to make additional payments to the fund. Similarly, if the fund achieves higher returns than are required to pay members' post-employment benefits, the employer may be able to take a 'contribution holiday'.

Most private sector (and many public sector) post-employment benefit plans are defined contribution plans. Employers often prefer defined contribution plans because there is no risk of liability for further contributions if the fund fails to earn an adequate return.

IAS 19 prescribes accounting treatment for contributions to post-employment benefit funds and assets and liabilities arising from post-employment benefit plans from the perspective of the employer. It does not prescribe accounting requirements for the post-employment benefit fund.

10.6 ACCOUNTING FOR DEFINED CONTRIBUTION POST-EMPLOYMENT PLANS

As described above, entities that participate in defined contribution post-employment plans make payments to a post-employment benefit fund, such as a superannuation fund. The amount is determined as a percentage of remuneration paid to employees who are members of the fund. Contributions payable to defined contribution funds are recognised in the period the employee renders services. The contributions payable during the period are recognised as expenses unless another standard permits the cost of employment benefits to be allocated to the carrying amount of an asset, such as internally constructed plant in accordance with IAS 16 *Property, Plant and Equipment*.

If the amount paid to the defined contribution fund by the entity during the year is less than the amount payable in relation to services rendered by employees, a liability for unpaid contributions must be recognised at the end of the period. The liability is measured at the undiscounted amount payable to the extent that contributions are due within 12 months after the reporting period. Paragraph 52 of IAS 19 requires discounting of liabilities for contributions to defined contribution plans that are due more than 12 months after the reporting period in which the employee provides the related services. The discount rate used to discount a post-employment benefit obligation is determined by reference to market yields on high-quality corporate bonds in accordance with IAS 19 paragraph 83. If the obligation is to be settled in a country that does not have a deep market in high-quality corporate bonds, the market yield on government bonds must be used.

If the amount paid to the defined contribution fund by the entity during the year is greater than the amount of contributions payable in relation to services rendered by employees, the entity recognises an asset to the extent that it is entitled to a refund or reduction in future contributions. In this situation, the asset would be a prepayment, or prepaid expenses.

ILLUSTRATIVE EXAMPLE 10.5 Accounting for defined contribution post-employment plans

Monash Ltd provides a defined contribution superannuation plan for its employees. Under the plan, Monash Ltd is required to contribute 9% of gross wages, salaries and commissions payable for services rendered by employees. Monash Ltd makes quarterly payments of $80 000 to the superannuation plan. Monash Ltd's annual reporting period ends on 30 June. If the amount paid to the superannuation fund during the financial year is less than 9% of gross wages, salaries and commissions for that year, Monash Ltd must pay the outstanding contributions by 30 September of the following financial year. If the amount paid during the financial year is more than 9% of the gross wages, salaries and bonuses for the year, the excess contributions are deducted from amounts payable in the following year.

Monash Ltd's employee benefits for the year ended 30 June 2013 comprise:

	$
Gross wages and salaries	3 900 000
Gross commissions	100 000
	4 000 000

The deficit in Monash Ltd's superannuation contributions for the year ended 30 June 2013 is determined as follows:

	$
Contributions payable:	
9% × gross wages, salaries and bonuses	360 000
Contributions paid during 2013: $80 000 × 4	320 000
Superannuation contribution payable	40 000

Monash Ltd must recognise a liability for the unpaid superannuation contributions. The liability is not discounted because it is a short-term liability for employee benefits. Monash Ltd would record the following entry for 30 June 2013:

Wages and Salaries Expense	Dr	40 000	
Superannuation Payable	Cr		40 000
(Accrual of liability for unpaid superannuation contributions)			

LO7 10.7 ACCOUNTING FOR DEFINED BENEFIT POST-EMPLOYMENT PLANS

As described in section 10.5, the employer pays contributions to a fund, which is a separate entity from the employer. The fund accumulates assets through contributions and returns on investments. The accumulated assets are used to pay post-employment benefits to members (retired employees). The return on investments held by the superannuation fund comprises dividend and interest income and changes in the fair value of investments. The benefits paid to members are a function of their remuneration levels while employed and the number of years of service. If there is a shortfall in the fund's capacity to pay benefits to members, the trustee of the fund may require the employer to make additional contributions. Thus, the employer effectively underwrites the actuarial and investment risks of the plan. In other words, the entity bears the risk of the fund being unable to pay benefits.

The assets of the superannuation plan, which are mostly investments, do not always equal its obligation to pay post-employment benefits to members. The superannuation plan has a deficit to the extent that the present value of the defined benefit obligation (i.e. post-employment benefits that are expected to be paid to employees for their services up to the end of the reporting period) exceeds the fair value of the plan assets. Conversely, a surplus arises when the fair value of the plan assets exceeds the present value of the defined benefit obligation.

Whether the deficit (surplus) of the defined benefit superannuation plan is a liability (asset) of the sponsoring employer is debatable. Some argue that the surplus in the superannuation plan does not satisfy all of the characteristics of an asset. Arguably, the assets of the plan are not controlled by the employer because they cannot be used for its benefit. For example, the employer may not use the surplus of the defined benefit superannuation plan to pay its debts; the assets of the plan are only used to generate cash flows to pay post-employment benefits to the members of the plan. Although the surplus is expected to result in future cash savings, such as lower contributions in future, it could be argued that the employer has not obtained control over those benefits through a past event where the reduction in superannuation contributions is at the discretion of the trustee of the superannuation fund.

Similarly, it has been argued that a deficit in the defined benefit superannuation fund is not a liability of the sponsoring employer because it does not have a present obligation to make good the shortfall. For instance, the employer may modify the post-employment benefits payable so as to avoid some of the obligation.

The perspective adopted in IAS 19 is that the surplus or deficit of the defined benefit superannuation plan is an asset, or liability, respectively, of the sponsoring employer. In some cases, the entity might not have a legal obligation to make good any shortfall in the fund's assets. For example, the terms of the trust deed may allow the employer to change or terminate its obligation under the plan. Although the employer might not have a legal obligation to make up any shortfall, it typically has a constructive obligation because terminating its obligations under the plan may make it difficult to retain and recruit staff. Accordingly, the accounting treatment prescribed by IAS 19 for an entity's obligations arising from sponsorship of a defined benefit plan assumes that the entity will continue to promise the post-employment benefits over the remaining working lives of its employees. Similarly, the Standard reflects the view that any surplus of the fund represents expected future inflows, in the form of reduced contributions, arising from having contributed more than is needed in the past. The Standard and Basis for Conclusions focus on how to measure the resulting asset rather than justifying whether it meets the definition and recognition criteria.

If adopting the view that a deficit or surplus of the defined benefit superannuation plan is a liability or asset of the sponsoring employer, the next issue to resolve is whether it should be recognised and, if so, how it should be measured. Before looking at how the standard setters resolved these issues, we will consider the possibilities, which are shown in figure 10.6. At one extreme, the deficit or surplus is not recognised in the financial statements of the entity that sponsors the defined benefit superannuation plan. In other words, the superannuation deficit or surplus is 'off-balance sheet'. At the other extreme, referred to as 'net capitalisation', the deficit (surplus) of the fund is recognised as a liability (asset) on the statement of financial position of the entity that sponsors the defined benefit superannuation plan. Under net capitalisation, the net superannuation liability or asset is usually measured as the difference between the present value of post-employment benefits earned by employees for services in the current and prior periods and the fair value of plan assets. Between these two extremes are various partial capitalisation methods in which some amount of the surplus or deficit of the fund remains off-balance sheet. For example, the previous version of IAS 19 permitted increments in the defined benefit obligation resulting from prior periods (referred to as past service costs) to be recognised progressively over the average remaining period until they become vested.

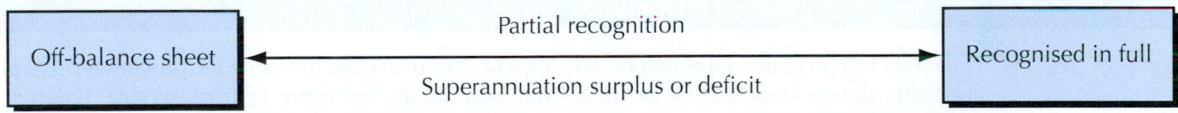

FIGURE 10.6 Alternative approaches to accounting for defined benefit superannuation plans

In the absence of accounting regulation, preparers were able to select different approaches to accounting for defined benefit post-employment benefits, ranging from off-balance sheet to net capitalisation. For instance, many companies in the United States kept their obligations for defined benefit pension plans off-balance sheet prior to the introduction of FAS 158: Defined Benefit Pension and other Post-retirement Pension Plans in 2006. In Australia, the adoption of the previous version of IAS 19 permitted net capitalisation and alternative partial capitalisation approaches.

Obviously, the use of different methods of accounting for post-employment benefits reduces the comparability of financial statements. Concerns were also raised about delays in recognition of liabilities which were perpetuated by partial capitalisation methods. Untimely recognition of assets or liabilities arising under post-employment benefit plans results in misleading information in the statement of financial position which is not adequately resolved by additional disclosures in the notes. There is evidence that users of financial statements did not fully understand the information provided by entities about their obligations or promises for post-employment benefits. For example, Sengupta and Wang (2011) provide evidence that bond market participants make inadequate use of note disclosures about off-balance sheet employee benefit obligations. The IASB and the FASB jointly undertook a project to enhance the comparability and transparency of accounting for post-employment benefits (IASB 2008). The outcome of that project was a revised version of IAS 19 *Employee Benefits*. We will now turn to the requirements of IAS 19 for accounting for defined benefit post-employment benefits.

The net capitalisation approach is adopted by IAS 19. Thus, the sponsoring employer recognises a net defined benefit liability or asset, representing its exposure to the defined benefit superannuation fund at the end of the reporting period. Contributions paid into the fund by the employer increase the assets of the fund, and thus increase a surplus or reduce any deficit of the fund. The employer accounts for its contributions to the fund as a decrease in the net defined benefit liability, or an increase in the net defined benefit asset. The employer recognises expenses in relation to its sponsorship of the defined benefit superannuation fund when service costs and interest costs are incurred, rather than when contributions are paid. This will become clear as we work through the revised requirements of IAS 19 for accounting for defined benefit superannuation funds.

The key steps involved in accounting by the employer for a defined benefit post-employment fund in accordance with IAS 19 (paragraph 57) are:
1. determining the deficit or surplus of the fund
2. determining the amount of the net defined benefit liability (asset), which is the amount of the deficit or the surplus, adjusted for any effect of limiting a net-defined benefit asset to the asset ceiling, which is explained below
3. determining the amounts to be recognised in profit or loss for current service cost, any past service cost and net interest expense (income) on the net defined benefit liability (asset)
4. determining the remeasurement of the net defined benefit liability (asset) to be recognised in other comprehensive income, which comprises actuarial gains and losses, return on plan assets (other than amounts included in net interest), and any change in the effect of the asset ceiling (other than amounts included in net interest).

We will now take a closer look at each step.

10.7.1 Step 1: Determining the deficit or surplus of the fund

There are two elements to determining the deficit or surplus of the fund — the obligation to pay benefits and any plan assets. Paragraph 67 of IAS 19 requires an entity to use the projected unit credit method to determine the present value of post-employment benefits earned by employees for services in the current and prior periods. Other names for the projected unit credit method include the *accrued benefit method pro-rated on service* and the *benefits/years of service method*. The projected unit credit method, which attributes a proportionate amount of additional benefit to each period of service, is shown in illustrative example 10.6.

ILLUSTRATIVE EXAMPLE 10.6 Determining the present value of the defined benefit obligation using the projected unit credit method

Dickens Ltd provides a defined benefit superannuation plan in which employees receive post-employment benefits determined as 1% of their final year salary, for every year of service. Salaries are expected to increase by 5% (compound) each year. The accountant has determined that the appropriate discount rate is 10% p.a. Charles commenced working for Dickens Ltd on 1 July 2013 with an annual salary of $40 000 and is expected to retire on 30 June 2016. For simplicity, this example ignores the additional adjustment that would be necessary to reflect the probability that Charles will resign or retire at a different date. The fair value of plan assets is $400, $800 and $1350 at the end of 2014, 2015 and 2016, respectively.

To understand the table below, you will need to read the following explanation which commences with the figure in the bottom right cell. At 30 June 2016 Charles will be entitled to 3% of his final year salary for three years of service. If his salary increases by 5% p.a., his salary for the year ended 30 June 2016 will be $44 100. At 3% of final year salary, Charles' post-employment benefit will be $1323 ($44 100 × 3%). Note that this is the amount in the 'Total current and prior years' of the column labelled 'Year ended 30/6/16'. The benefit attributed to each year is $1/n$ of the total benefit payable after n years. In this example, the amount attributed to each year is $441, being 1/3 of $1323. The amount of $441 is the amount in the row labelled 'current year' in the column for each year. The total current and prior year amount for each year is carried forward in the table as the prior year amount in the next year.

Schedule of changes in the defined benefit obligation			
	Year ended 30/6/14 $	**Year ended 30/6/15** $	**Year ended 30/6/16** $
Prior year	0	441	882
Current year	441	441	441
Total current and prior years	441	882	1 323

The obligation is measured as the present value of the accumulated post-employment benefit at the end of each period. In this example a discount rate of 10% is used. Each period the present value increases partly as a result of current year benefits relating to service, and partly because the discounting period is reduced as the time to settlement decreases. The present value of the accrued benefits increases as the expected settlement time approaches because the expected settlement is discounted over a shorter period of time. The difference in the present value attributable to discounting over a shorter period is accounted for as interest expense. The interest component is calculated for each period by multiplying the opening balance of the liability by the interest rate.

The following table illustrates the increase in the defined benefit obligation over the three-year period, differentiating between the service cost and interest elements. The opening obligation is the present value of the benefit attributed to Charles' prior years. The interest cost for the year ended 30 June 2014 is nil because the opening balance of the obligation is nil. The interest cost for the year ended 30 June 2015 is $36, being $365 × 10%. The current service cost is the present value of the defined benefit attributed to the current year. For example, for the year ended 30 June 2014, the benefit attributed to current service is $441, as per the table on page 332. This is the increase in Charles' defined benefit entitlements attributable to his services during the year ended 30 June 2014. This amount is expected to be settled on 30 June 2016, that is, two years later. Accordingly, the current service cost for the year ended 30 June 2014; that is, the present value of the benefit attributed to the year ended 30 June 2014, is calculated as $441/(1 + 0.1)^2$. The closing obligation is the present value of the benefit attributed to current and prior years.

Schedule of current service cost, interest and present value of the defined benefit obligation			
	Year ended 30/6/14 $	Year ended 30/6/15 $	Year ended 30/6/16 $
Opening obligation	0	365	802
Interest at 10%	0	36	80
Current service cost	365	401	441
Closing obligation	365	802	1 323

To complete the first step, it is necessary to determine the difference between the fair value of plan assets and the present value of the defined benefit obligation. The excess of the defined benefit obligation over the fair value of the plan assets is the deficit of the fund. Conversely, any excess of the fair value of plan assets over the present value of the defined benefit obligation is a surplus of the defined benefit superannuation fund. The previous example is based on an individual to simplify the calculations of accrued benefits. However, the fund would typically provide multiple members and the plan assets would generate cash inflows to be used to settle obligations to all members.

ILLUSTRATIVE EXAMPLE 10.7 Determining the deficit or surplus of the defined benefit superannuation fund

To illustrate the calculation of the deficit or surplus of the defined benefit superannuation fund, we will assume the following information about the assets and obligations for post-employment benefits of Dickens Employees Superannuation Fund:

	30/6/14 $	30/6/15 $	30/6/16 $
Closing obligation	4 900	5 700	6 550
Fair value of plan assets	4 500	5 400	6 600
Deficit (surplus) of the fund	400	300	(50)

The closing obligation is the present value of the defined benefit obligation at the end of each reporting period. The fund has a deficit of $400 at 30 June 2014. This amount is calculated as '$4900 – $4500', which is the amount by which the present value of the defined benefit obligation exceeds the fair value of plan assets. At 30 June 2015, the fund has a deficit of $300, being the excess of the obligation of $5700 over the fair value of plan assets, $5400. At 30 June 2016, the fair value of plan assets exceeds the defined benefit obligation. Accordingly, the defined benefit superannuation fund has a surplus of $50, being the fair value of plan assets, $6600, less the defined benefit obligation, $6550.

Obligations to pay pensions during employees' lives or that of their eligible dependants can further complicate the measurement of accrued benefits because the total payment is dependent upon the mortality rate of the employees and their eligible beneficiaries. Companies often rely on actuarial assessments to estimate the defined benefit obligation and the level of investment required to enable the fund to pay accumulated benefits as and when they fall due. Actuaries apply mathematical, statistical, economic and financial analysis to assess risks associated with contracts, such as insurance contracts and superannuation funds. Actuarial estimates rely on assumptions, such as the employee retention rates and the rate at which salaries are expected to increase. Actuaries also provide financial planning advice, on matters such as the level of investment needed to generate sufficient future cash flows to meet the expected obligations as and when they fall due. Some companies employ their own actuaries, while many others engage actuaries as professional consultants.

10.7.2 Step 2: Determining the amount of the net defined benefit liability (asset)

A net defined benefit liability arises when the defined benefit superannuation fund has a deficit. The net defined benefit liability is measured as the amount of the deficit of the defined benefit superannuation fund, which is calculated following the procedure described in step 1. For example, in illustrative example 10.7 the amount of the net defined benefit liability for the year ended 30 June 2015 is $300.

A net defined benefit asset arises when the defined benefit superannuation fund has a surplus. The net defined benefit asset is measured as the amount of the surplus, adjusted for any effect of limiting a net defined benefit asset to the asset ceiling. The asset ceiling is defined in paragraph 8 of IAS 19 as 'the present value of any economic benefits available in the form of refunds from the plan or reductions in future contributions to the plan'. The net defined benefit asset is the lower of the surplus of the defined benefit superannuation fund and the asset ceiling. For example, if we assume that the present value of reductions in Dickens Ltd's future contributions to the plan at 30 June 2016 were $60, the net defined benefit asset of Dickens Ltd would be measured as $50, being the lower of the surplus of the defined benefit fund and the asset ceiling. However, if the present value of reductions in Dickens Ltd's future contributions to the plan at 30 June 2016 were only $40, its net defined benefit asset would be measured as $40.

10.7.3 Step 3: Determining the amounts to be recognised in profit or loss

The amount of the net defined benefit liability (asset) is affected by the present value of the defined benefit obligation and the fair value of plan assets. The present value of the defined benefit obligation is affected by the service cost, which comprises current service cost, past service cost and any gain or loss on settlement of the defined benefit.

Current service cost is 'the increase in the present value of defined benefit obligation resulting from employee service in the current period' (IAS 19 paragraph 8). The service cost for each year in illustrative example 10.6 is a current service cost to Dickens Ltd because it is the increase in the present value of the defined benefit obligation attributed to employment services rendered by Charles during each year.

Past service cost is defined in paragraph 8 of IAS 19 as the change in the present value of the defined benefit obligation for employee service in prior periods, resulting from a plan amendment or a curtailment. Illustrative example 10.8 draws on the same information as used in illustrative example 10.6, with the addition of an amendment to the terms of the superannuation plan on 1 July 2015.

Paragraph 8 of IAS 19 defines the *net interest on the net defined benefit liability (asset)* as the change in the net defined benefit liability (asset) that arises from the passage of time. The net interest on net defined benefit liability (asset) is measured by multiplying the discount rate that is used to measure the defined benefit obligation at the beginning of the period by the net defined benefit liability (asset) (IAS 19 paragraph 123). Paragraph 83 requires the discount rate to be determined with reference to market yields on high-quality corporate bonds. In jurisdictions in which there is no deep market in such bonds, the market yield on government bonds should be used instead. The standard requires contributions received by the fund and benefits paid to be taken into account when calculating interest. This would involve recalculating interest for part of the year each time the plan assets were increased by a contribution or where payment of benefits resulted in settlement gains or losses, giving rise to change in the net defined benefit liability or asset. Throughout this text, this process is simplified by applying the discount rate to the opening balance of the net defined benefit liability (asset), effectively assuming contributions and benefits are paid at the end of each year.

When the superannuation fund pays benefits to a member, both the plan assets and the defined benefit obligation are reduced. If, at the time of settlement, the carrying amount of the obligation to the member is equal to the amount actually payable, the settlement will have no effect on the surplus or deficit of the fund. However, the carrying amount of the defined benefit obligation results from numerous actuarial estimates, resulting in potential inaccuracy in measurement. Differences between the carrying amount of the defined benefit obligation of the fund and the amount actually paid to a member give rise to a gain or loss on settlement, which is a service cost recognised in profit or loss.

ILLUSTRATIVE EXAMPLE 10.8 Modifications to a defined benefit superannuation plan

On 1 July 2015, Dickens Ltd modified the terms of the defined benefit superannuation plan from 1% of final year salary per year of service to 0.9% of final year salary per year of service. The modification applies retrospectively to services rendered before 1 July 2015. Accordingly, after the modification the defined benefit payable at 30 June 2016 is expected to be 2.7% of final year salary instead of 3% of final salary, which had been used in the measurement of the defined benefit obligation at 30 June 2015.

The revised defined benefit payable to Charles after three years; that is, at 30 June 2016, is expected to be $1191. This is calculated as 2.7% of Charles' final year salary (2.7% × $44 100 = $1191). Applying the projected credit method, the annual service cost is $397.

Schedule of changes in the defined benefit obligation			
Benefit attributed to:	Year ended 30/6/14 $	Year ended 30/6/15 $	Year ended 30/6/16 $
Prior year	0	397	794
Current year	397	397	397
Total current and prior years	397	794	1 191

The following schedule shows the current service cost, interest cost and present value of the defined benefit obligation on the basis of the revised terms of the plan, under which the benefit payable is 0.9% of salary for each year of service. The present value of the increase in the defined benefit obligation attributed to current service cost is $328 and $361 in the years ended 30 June 2014 and 30 June 2015, respectively. These present values are determined using the discount rate of 10%.

Schedule of current service cost, interest and present value of the defined benefit obligation			
	Year ended 30/6/14 $	Year ended 30/6/15 $	Year ended 30/6/16 $
Opening obligation	0	328	722
Interest at 10%	0	33	72
Current service cost	328	361	397
Closing obligation	328	722	1 191

Workings:

30/6/2014 Current service cost = $397/(1 + 0.1)^2 = $328
30/6/2015 Current service cost = $397/(1 + 0.1)^1 = $361; Interest cost = $328 × 10% = $33
30/6/2016 Interest cost = $722 × 10% = $72

Recall that the terms of the defined benefit superannuation plan were modified on 1 July 2015. Until 30 June 2015, the measurement of the present value of the defined benefit obligation had been based on a benefit of 1% of final salary for each year of service. This yielded a present value of $802 at 30 June 2015 as shown in illustrative example 10.6. From 1 July 2015, the amount of the present value of the defined benefit obligation should be remeasured based on a benefit of only 0.9% of final year salary for each year of service. This yields a present value of $722 as shown in the immediately preceding schedule. Accordingly, the opening obligation for the year ended 30 June 2016 should be adjusted for a past service cost of ($80) as follows:

	Year ended 30/6/15 $	Year ended 30/6/16 $
Opening obligation	365	802
Past service costs arising from modifications to the plan	—	(80)
Adjusted obligation		722
Interest at 10%	36	72
Current service cost	401	397
Closing obligation	802	1 191

Current and past service cost, interest income or expense and settlement gains or losses are recognised in profit or loss.

10.7.4 Step 4: Determining the remeasurements of the net defined benefit liability (asset) to be recognised in other comprehensive income

The effects of remeasurements of the net defined benefit liability (asset) are recognised in other comprehensive income. Changes in the net defined benefit liability (asset) that result from remeasurements comprise actuarial gains and losses, return on plan assets (other than amounts included in net interest), and any change in the effect of the asset ceiling (excluding amounts included in net interest).

Actuarial gains and losses occur when changes in actuarial assumptions or experience adjustments affect the present value of the defined benefit obligation. The measurement of the defined benefit obligation is sensitive to assumptions such as employee turnover and the rate of increase in salaries. For example, an increase in the rate of salary increase used in measuring the defined benefit obligation would increase the expected future settlement and, hence, the present value of the defined benefit obligation. An increase in the rate of salary increase results in an actuarial loss because it increases the present value of the defined benefit obligation. Another example of a change in an actuarial assumption is a change in the discount rate used to determine the present value of the obligation. An increase in the discount rate results in an actuarial gain because it reduces the present value of the defined benefit obligation.

Experience adjustments refer to differences between the actual results and previous actuarial estimates used to measure the defined benefit obligation. An example is the difference between the estimated employee turnover for the year and the actual employee turnover during the year. Experience adjustments may also relate to early retirement, mortality rates and the rate of increase in salaries.

The return on plan assets is determined after deducting the costs of managing the plan assets and tax payable by the superannuation fund on its income derived from plan assets. Other administration costs are not deducted from the return on plan assets (IAS 19 paragraph 130).

Classification of actuarial gains and losses as items of other comprehensive income shields reported profit from the volatility that would arise from the recognition of actuarial gains and losses.

ILLUSTRATIVE EXAMPLE 10.9 Accounting for a defined benefit plan

Flinders Ltd has a defined benefit superannuation plan for its senior managers. Members of the plan had been entitled to 10% of their average salary for every year of service.

The following information is available about the Flinders DB Superannuation Fund:

		$'000
30 June 2013		
Present value of defined benefit obligation at 30 June 2013		26 000
Fair value of plan assets at 30 June 2013		30 000
Asset ceiling at 30 June 2013		4 200
Interest rate used to measure the defined benefit obligation 30 June 2013	7%	
1 July 2013		
Past service costs		5 000
Year ended 30 June 2014		
Current service cost		4 000
Contributions received by the fund		4 500
Benefits paid by the fund		Nil
Return on plan assets		800
Actuarial gain resulting from change in the discount rate, 30 June 2014		1 470
Present value of defined benefit obligation at 30 June 2014		35 700
Fair value of plan assets at 30 June 2014		37 400
Asset ceiling at 30 June 2014		2 500
Interest rate used to measure the defined benefit obligation 30 June 2014	8%	

Additional information
(a) The current service cost is given as $4 million. This estimation is based on actuarial advice and provided by the manager of the superannuation fund.
(b) Actuarial advice has been obtained for the present value of the defined benefit obligation at 30 June 2013 and 30 June 2014.
(c) On 1 July 2013 Flinders Ltd revised its defined benefits and increased the entitlement to 11% of average salary. The revision to the defined benefit plan resulted in an increase in the defined benefit obligation of $5 million on 1 July 2013.
(d) During the year ended 30 June 2014, Flinders Ltd contributed $4 800 000 to the fund. All of the contributions to the Flinders DB Superannuation Fund are paid by Flinders Ltd. The senior managers of Flinders Ltd, who are the members of the fund, do not pay any superannuation contributions.
(e) The discount rate used to measure the defined benefit obligation was increased from 7% to 8% on 30 June 2014, resulting in a decrease of $1 470 000 in the present value of the defined benefit obligation.
(f) The fair value of plan assets is derived from valuations performed by Hope & Moore Valuers as at 30 June 2014.

The information shown above is used to prepare the journal entries to account for Flinders Ltd's superannuation liability (asset) for the year ended 30 June 2014 in accordance with IAS 19. But first we will determine the amount of the net defined benefit liability (asset) at 30 June 2013.

Flinders DB Superannuation Fund had a surplus of $4 000 000, being the excess of the fair value of plan assets over the present value of the defined benefit obligation, at 30 June 2013. Flinders Ltd recognised a net defined benefit asset of $4 000 000, being the lesser of the surplus and the asset ceiling of $4 200 000.

Next we will consider the four steps involved in accounting by the employer for a defined benefit post-employment fund identified by IAS 19 (paragraph 57). The defined benefit worksheet, which is shown below for the Flinders DB Superannuation Fund, incorporates the four steps and provides workings for the summary journal entries to account for the defined benefit post-employment fund in the books of the employer and provides a basis for the disclosure requirements required by IAS 19.

FLINDERS DB SUPERANNUATION FUND
Defined Benefit Worksheet
for the year ended 30 June 2014

	Flinders Ltd				Flinders DB Superannuation Fund	
	Profit/loss $'000	OCI $'000	Bank $'000	Net DBL(A) $'000	DBO $'000	Plan Assets $'000
Balance 30/6/13				4 000 Dr	26 000 Cr	30 000 Dr
Past service cost	5 000 Dr				5 000 Cr	
Revised balance 1/7/13				1 000 Cr	31 000 Cr	30 000 Dr
Net interest at 7%	70 Dr				2 170 Cr	2 100 Dr
Current service cost	4 000 Dr				4 000 Cr	
Contributions to the fund			4 500 Cr			4 500 Dr
Benefits paid by the fund					0	0
Return on plan assets		800 Cr				800 Dr
Actuarial gain: DBO		1 470 Cr			1 470 Dr	
Journal entry	**9 070 Dr**	**2 270 Cr**	**4 500 Cr**	**2 300 Cr**		
Balance 30/6/14				1 700 Dr	35 700 Cr	37 400 Dr
Adjustment for asset ceiling if < deficit				Not applicable		
Balance 30/6/14				**1 700 Dr**	**35 700 Cr**	**37 400 Dr**

Step 1: Determining the deficit or surplus of the fund

At 30 June 2014, the Flinders DB Superannuation Fund has a surplus of $1 700 000. This is shown in the last row of the defined benefit worksheet, and can be calculated as the excess of the fair value of plan assets ($37 400 000) over the present value of the defined benefit obligation (DBO) ($35 700 000).

Step 2: Determining the amount of the net defined benefit liability (asset)

The net defined benefit asset is $1 700 000, being the lesser of the surplus of $1 700 000 and the asset ceiling of $2 500 000.

Step 3: Determining the amounts to be recognised in profit or loss

The increase in the DBO of $5 000 000 resulting from the past service cost is recognised as an expense in profit or loss. The revised balance of the net defined benefit liability (asset) is calculated as the deficit of the fund, being the excess of the DBO over the fair value of plan assets after accounting for the past service cost. The revised balance of the defined benefit liability (asset) is shown to facilitate the calculation of the interest cost.

The net interest is $70 000 determined as 7% of the net defined benefit liability after taking into account the past service cost, as shown in the defined benefit worksheet. The net interest is recognised in profit or loss. The interest component of the increase in the DBO and the fair value of plan assets is $2 170 000 and $2 100 000, respectively.

The current service cost of $4 000 000 increases the DBO. The current service cost is recognised in profit or loss. These three items correspond to step 3.

Thus the three items recognised in profit or loss, the past service cost, the net interest and the current service cost, amount to $9 070 000 as shown in the journal entry line of the defined benefit worksheet.

Step 4: Determining the amount of remeasurements to be recognised in other comprehensive income

There are two remeasurements of the net defined benefit asset during the year ended 30 June 2014. One of the remeasurements results from the return on plan assets exceeding the interest income included in net interest recognised in profit or loss. The return on plan assets affects the fair value of plan assets as shown in the defined benefit worksheet. The other remeasurement results from the increase in the discount rate used to measure the present value of the DBO. This remeasurement affects the DBO as shown in the defined benefit worksheet. The effects of the remeasurements are recognised in other comprehensive income (OCI) as shown in the defined benefit worksheet.

The payment of contributions during the year ended 30 June 2014 increases the net defined benefit asset and increases the plan assets of the fund.

Any benefits paid to members during the period would reduce both the plan assets and the DBO. It appears in the fund columns only because it is a transaction of the fund, and not a transaction of the sponsoring employer.

The defined benefit worksheet provides working papers for the journal entries to account for the defined benefit superannuation plan in the books of Flinders Ltd. The summary journal entries are shown below.

Summary entry	Superannuation Expense (P/L)	Dr	9 070 000	
	Superannuation Gain (OCI)	Cr		2 270 000
	Bank	Cr		4 500 000
	Net Superannuation Asset	Cr		2 300 000
	(Payment of superannuation contributions and recognition of changes in net superannuation asset)			

The defined benefit worksheet also provides a basis for preparation of notes to the financial statements for some of the disclosures required by IAS 19 in respect of defined benefit post-employment plans. Paragraph 140 includes a requirement for a reconciliation of the opening balance to the closing balance of the net defined benefit liability (asset), showing separate reconciliations for plan assets, the present value of the defined benefit obligation and the effect of the asset ceiling. Each reconciliation is required to show the effect, if applicable, of past service cost and gains and losses arising on settlement, current service cost, interest income or expense, and remeasurement of the net defined liability (asset), showing separately return on plan assets excluding amounts included in interest, actuarial gains arising from changes in demographic assumptions, actuarial gains and losses arising from changes in financial assumptions and changes in the effect, if any, of the asset ceiling (IAS 19 paragraph 141). Paragraph 141 also requires disclosure of contributions, distinguishing between those paid by the employer and those paid by the members of the plan, and benefits paid. Other reconciliation items include the effects of changes in foreign exchange rates and the effects of business combinations and disposals.

The net capitalisation method can result in large gains and losses being recognised in profit or loss, or other comprehensive income, due to changes in the surplus or deficit of the fair value of plan assets over the present value of accrued benefits. For instance, the present value of the defined benefit obligation increases if employee retention is greater than the amount assumed in the previous actuarial estimate, which may result in a deficit in the superannuation fund. Similarly, an unexpected decline in the return on investment of plan assets may cause the plan assets to grow at a slower rate than the present value of the defined benefit obligation, giving rise to an increase in the superannuation liability recognised by the employer. The net capitalisation method is unpopular with some preparers of financial statements who would prefer less volatility of earnings.

There is ongoing debate as to how an employer should account for post-employment benefits, including pension funds, and the adequacy of disclosures in corporate financial statements. For further reading on research in this area refer to Gallery (2003), Gordon (2005), Skaife et al. (2007) and Sengupta and Wang (2011).

 10.8 OTHER LONG-TERM EMPLOYEE BENEFITS

Long-term employee benefits are benefits for services provided in the current period that will not be paid until more than 12 months after the end of the period. Post-employment benefits were considered in section 10.5. This section considers long-term employee benefits that are provided to employees during the period of their employment. A common form of long-term employee benefits is long service leave, which is a paid absence after the employee has provided a long period of service, such as 3 months of paid leave after 10 years of continuous employment.

Long service leave accrues to employees as they provide service to the entity. The principle adopted by IAS 19 is that an obligation arises for long service leave when the employees provide services to the employer, even though the employees may have no legal entitlement to the leave. Thus, a liability is recognised for long service leave as it accrues. Long service leave payments reduce the long service leave liability.

Accounting for other long-term employee benefits is similar to accounting for defined-benefit post-employment plans except that the effects of remeasurements are not recognised in other comprehensive income (IAS 19 paragraphs 154–55). Thus the net liability (asset) for long-term employee benefits is measured as the net of the present value of the defined benefit obligation at the reporting date minus the fair value at the reporting date of plan assets (if any) out of which the obligations are to be settled directly, subject to adjustment of a net asset for the effects of an asset ceiling, if applicable.

In some countries it is extremely unusual to establish plan assets to provide for the payment of long service leave benefits to employees. Thus, the accounting treatment for long service leave benefits is usually confined to the recognition of the present value of the obligation measured in accordance with the projected unit credit method.

The projected unit credit method measures the obligation for long-term employee benefits by calculating the present value of the expected future payments that will result from employee services provided to date. The measurement of the present value of the obligation for long service leave payments is complicated by the need to make several estimates. These include estimation of when the leave will be taken, projected salary levels, and the proportion of employees who will continue in the entity's employment long enough to become entitled to long service leave. Actuarial advice is often used in the measurement of long service leave obligations.

The steps involved in the measurement of a liability for long service leave are as follows:

1. *Estimate the number of employees who are expected to become eligible for long service leave.* The probability that employees will become eligible for long service leave generally increases with the period of employment. For example, if an entity provides long service leave after 10 years of employment, the probability that employees who have already been working for the entity for 7 years will continue in employment for another 3 years is very high, as the closer proximity to long service leave entitlement provides an incentive to employees to stay with their current employer. Thus, the proportion of employees who are expected to become eligible for long service leave is usually calculated separately for employees with different levels of prior service.

2. *Estimate the projected wages and salaries at the time that long service leave is expected to be paid.* This step involves the application of expected inflation rates or other cost adjustment rates over the remaining period before long service leave is paid. Applying an estimated inflation rate:

$$\text{Projected salaries} = \text{current salaries} \times (1 + \text{inflation rate})^n$$
where n = number of years until long service leave is expected to be paid.

For example, for employees who have 3 years remaining before long service leave is expected to be paid, current salaries are projected over a period of 3 years.

3. *Determine the accumulated benefit.* The projected unit credit is determined as the proportion of projected long service leave attributable to services that have already been provided by the employee. The accumulated benefit is calculated as:

$$\frac{\text{Years of employment}}{\text{Years required for LSL}} \times \frac{\text{weeks of paid leave}}{52} \times \text{projected salaries}$$

4. *Measure the present value of the accumulated benefit.* The accumulated benefit is discounted at a rate determined by reference to market yields on high-quality corporate bonds, in accordance with paragraph 83. If the country in which the long service leave entitlement will be paid does not have a deep market in high-quality corporate bonds, the government bond rate is used.

$$\text{Present value} = \frac{\text{accumulated benefit}}{(1 + i)^n}$$
where i is the interest rate on high-quality corporate bonds maturing n years later.

The liability for long service leave is a provision. After determining the amount of the obligation for long service leave at the end of the period, following steps 1 to 4 above, the provision is increased or decreased as required.

Illustrative example 10.10 demonstrates the measurement of the obligation for long service leave, applying the projected unit credit method in accordance with IAS 19, and the entries to account for changes in the provision for long service leave.

ILLUSTRATIVE EXAMPLE 10.10 Accounting for long service leave

Auckland Sails Ltd commenced operations on 1 July 2012 and had 150 employees. Average salaries were $60 000 per annum for the year. Auckland Sails Ltd accounts for all recognised employee costs as expenses. Employees are entitled to 13 weeks of long service leave after 10 years of employment. The following information is based on advice received from actuarial consultants at 30 June 2013:

Number of years unit credit	1 year
Number of years until long service leave is expected to be paid	9 years
Probability that long service leave will be taken (proportion of employees expected to stay long enough to become entitled to long service leave)	50%
Expected increase in salaries (based on inflation)	2% p.a.
Yield on 9-year high-quality corporate bonds at 30/6/2013	10%

The discount rate is determined using 9-year bonds because the long service leave is expected to be paid 9 years after the end of the reporting period.

Step 1: Estimate the number of employees who are expected to become eligible for long service leave.

$$50\% \times 150 \text{ employees} = 75 \text{ employees}$$

Step 2: Estimate the projected salaries.

$$= \text{Salary} \times (1 + \text{inflation rate})^n$$
$$= \$60\,000 \times 75 \text{ employees} \times (1 + 0.02)^9 = \$5\,377\,917$$

The current salary is inflated over 9 years because employees are expected to take long service leave nine years after the end of the reporting period.

Step 3: Determine the accumulated benefit.

$$= \frac{\text{Years of employment}}{\text{Years required for LSL}} \times \frac{\text{week of paid leave}}{52} \times \text{projected salaries}$$
$$= \frac{1}{10} \times \frac{13}{52} \times \$5\,377\,917 = \$134\,448$$

Step 4: Measure the present value of the accumulated benefit.

$$= \frac{\text{Accumulated benefit}}{(1 + i)^n}$$
$$= \$134\,448/(1 + 0.1)^9 \text{ [or } \$134\,448 \times 0.4241 \text{ from present value tables]}$$
$$= \$57\,019$$

The change in the provision for long service leave is recorded by the following journal entry:

2013				
June 30	Long Service Leave Expense	Dr	57 019	
	Provision for Long Service Leave	Cr		57 019
	(Increase in provision for long service leave)			

Note there was no beginning of period provision for long service leave as this is the first year.

During the following year, Auckland Sails Ltd's 150 employees continued to work for the company. Average salaries increased to $68 000 per annum for the year. The following information is based on advice received from actuarial consultants at 30 June 2014:

Number of years unit credit	2 years
Number of years until long service leave is expected to be paid	8 years
Probability that LSL will be taken (proportion of employees expected to stay long enough to be entitled)	55%
Expected increase in salaries (based on inflation)	2% p.a.
Yield on 8-year high-quality corporate bonds 30/6/2014	9%

The discount rate is determined using 8-year bonds because the long service leave is expected to be paid 8 years after the end of the reporting period.

Step 1: Estimate the number of employees who are expected to become eligible for long service leave.

$$55\% \times 150 \text{ employees} = 82.5 \text{ employees}$$

Step 2: Estimate the projected salaries.

$$= \text{Salary} \times (1 + \text{inflation rate})^n$$
$$= \$68\,000 \times 82.5 \text{ employees} \times (1 + 0.02)^8 = \$6\,573\,009$$

The current salary is inflated over 8 years because employees are expected to take long service leave 8 years after the end of the reporting period.

Step 3: Determine the accumulated benefit.

$$= \frac{\text{Years of employment}}{\text{Years required for LSL}} \times \frac{\text{week of paid leave}}{52} \times \text{projected salaries}$$
$$= \frac{2}{10} \times \frac{13}{52} \times \$6\,573\,009 = \$328\,650$$

Step 4: Measure the present value of the accumulated benefit.

$$= \frac{\text{Accumulated benefit}}{(1 + i)^n}$$
$$= \$328\,650/(1 + 0.09)^8 \text{ [or } \$328\,650 \times 0.50187 \text{ from present value tables]}$$
$$= \$164\,939$$

The increase in the long service leave can be calculated as $164 939 less $57 019 because there have been no long service leave payments during the year to reduce the provision from the amount recognised at the end of the previous year. The change in the provision for long service leave is recorded by the following journal entry:

2014				
June 30	Long Service Leave Expense	Dr	107 920	
	Provision for Long Service Leave	Cr		107 920
	(Increase in provision for long service leave)			

The increase in the provision for long service leave during 2014 can be attributed to several factors:
- an increase in unit credit accumulated by employees. In the first year, the employees' accumulation was 10% of the leave, but, by the end of the second year, 20% had been accumulated because the employees had completed 2 of the 10 years of service required to become eligible for long service leave.
- the interest cost, being the increase in the present value arising from discounting the future cash flows over a shorter period.
- an increase in projected salaries resulting from an increase in remuneration. That is, salaries increased beyond the projected 2% during 2014.
- a reduction in the interest rate used from 10% at 30 June 2013 to 9% at 30 June 2014.

10.9 TERMINATION BENEFITS

When an employee is retrenched or made redundant, the employer may be obliged to pay termination benefits. For example, a downturn in the economy may cause a manufacturer to reduce the scale of its operations, resulting in some portion of the entity's workforce being made redundant. Termination benefits are typically lump sum payments. Paragraph 8 of IAS 19 refers to termination benefits as employee benefits that are payable as a result of either:

(a) an entity's decision to terminate an employee's employment before the normal retirement date; or
(b) an employee's decision to accept an offer of benefits in exchange for the termination of employment.

Thus, termination benefits can be distinguished from other forms of employee benefits because the obligation to pay termination benefits arises from the termination of an employment contract, rather than from past services provided by the employee. Although the obligation arises from a decision to terminate employment, the extent of past services provided by each employee is usually a factor in determining the amount of the payment.

The decision to undertake a redundancy program is not sufficient for the recognition of a liability for termination benefits. Merely deciding to undertake a redundancy program does not create an obligation to a third party and does not, therefore, meet the definition of a liability in accordance with the *Conceptual Framework*.

Paragraph 165 of IAS 19 requires an entity to recognise an expense and a liability for termination benefits at the earlier of the following dates:

(a) when the entity can no longer withdraw the offer of the benefits; and
(b) when the entity recognises costs for a restructuring that is within the scope of IAS 37 and that involves the payment of termination benefits.

Paragraphs 166 and 167 of IAS 19 elaborate on when an entity can no longer withdraw from an offer. Paragraph 166 refers to termination benefits that become payable as a result of the employee accepting an offer of benefits in exchange for the termination of employment, such as a voluntary redundancy arrangement. Once the employee accepts, the entity can no longer withdraw the offer. Further, the entity may be prevented from withdrawing an offer by existing regulations, contracts or laws. The entity can no longer withdraw an offer once such restrictions take effect.

Paragraph 167 is concerned with termination benefits that become payable as a result of the entity's decision to terminate employment. This situation differs from the circumstances in the preceding paragraph because the termination decision is made by the employer and the employee does not have a choice. When the termination benefits result from the entity's decision to terminate an employee's employment, the offer can no longer be withdrawn when the entity has communicated to affected employees a plan of termination that meets all the following criteria (IAS 19 paragraph 167):

(a) actions required to complete the plan indicate that significant changes to the plan are unlikely
(b) the plan identifies the location, function or job classification, the number of employees whose services are to be terminated, and the expected completion date

(c) the plan establishes the termination benefits payable in sufficient detail to enable employees to determine the type and amount of benefits they will receive.

If at the time of initial recognition termination benefits are expected to be settled wholly within 12 months after the end of the annual reporting period, they are measured using the same principles as other short-term employee benefits. That is, the termination benefits are measured at the nominal (undiscounted) amount that the entity expects to pay. However, if the termination benefits are not expected to be settled wholly within 12 months after the end of the reporting period, they must be measured at present value. The expected payments required to settle the obligation are discounted at a rate determined by reference to market yields on high-quality corporate bonds, in accordance with paragraph 83. This is consistent with the measurement of other long-term employee benefits.

ILLUSTRATIVE EXAMPLE 10.11 Termination benefits

During June 2012, the board of directors of Universal Ltd approved a plan to outsource its data processing operations. The closure of the data processing operations is expected to result in the retrenchment of 180 employees throughout Australia and New Zealand. The chief financial officer provided an estimate of redundancy costs of A$1.2 million. The board expected that it would take at least 6 months to select a contractor for outsourcing the data processing and that it would take a further 3 months for training before internal data processing operations could be discontinued.

During May 2013, redundancy packages were negotiated with trade union representatives and communicated to employees. Data processing operations were to be transferred to an external service provider in India on 1 October 2013.

When should Universal Ltd recognise an expense and liability for the redundancy payments?

2012

The termination benefits become payable as a result of Universal Ltd's decision to terminate employment, rather than as a result of an offer being accepted by employees. Accordingly, Universal Ltd must recognise a liability for termination benefits when it can no longer withdraw from a plan of termination communicated to affected employees, and that plan meets the criteria specified in paragraph 167 of IAS 19.

At 30 June 2012, the termination plan meets some of the criteria. Management had specified the location (Australia and New Zealand) and function (data processing) of the employees becoming redundant, and estimated their number at 180. The termination benefit payable for each job specification is likely to have formed the basis of the estimated redundancy costs of $1.2 million. However, until Universal Ltd has identified an alternative source of data processing, it will not be able to decide on a time at which the redundancy plan should be implemented. Further, although the decision to discontinue the internal data processing operation had been made by Universal Ltd's board of directors, it has not been communicated to the employees. Therefore, Universal Ltd should not recognise an expense and liability for termination benefits in association with the planned closure of its data processing operations at 30 June 2012 in accordance with IAS 19.

2013

By June 2013, the company had completed the formal detailed termination plan by specifying when it is to be implemented. The negotiations with unions over the amount of redundancy payments and entering into a contract with an external provider demonstrate that it is unlikely that significant changes will be made to the amount or timing of the redundancy plan. The termination plan has been communicated to affected employees. Accordingly, Universal Ltd should recognise an expense and a liability for termination benefits in association with the planned closure of its data processing operations in its financial statements for the period ended 30 June 2013 in accordance with IAS 19.

SUMMARY

Employee benefit costs are a significant expense for most reporting entities. Accounting for employee benefits is complicated by the diversity of arrangements for remuneration for services provided by employees. This area of accounting is further complicated by the different methods prescribed by IAS 19 to account for various forms and categories of employee benefits. Liabilities for short-term employee benefits, such as salaries, wages, sick leave, annual leave and bonuses payable within 12 months after the reporting period, are measured at the undiscounted amount that the entity expects to pay. Long-term liabilities for defined benefits, such as long service leave, are measured at the present value of the defined benefit obligations less the fair value of plan assets, if any, out of which the obligation is to be settled. The obligation for long service leave is measured using the projected unit credit method. IAS 19 also prescribes accounting treatment for post-employment benefit plans. Accounting for defined contribution post-employment plans is relatively straightforward: a liability is recognised by the entity for contributions payable for the period in excess of contributions paid. Conversely, an asset is recognised if contributions paid exceed the contributions payable to the extent that the entity expects the excess contributions to be refunded or deducted from future contributions. An entity's net exposure to a defined benefit post-employment plan is measured at the present value of the defined benefit obligations less the fair value of plan assets. If the defined benefit fund has a surplus, the net defined benefit asset recognised by the entity is subject to an asset ceiling. In this chapter, we have also considered termination benefits. The measurement of a liability for termination benefits depends on whether they are expected to be settled wholly within 12 months of the annual reporting period in which they were first recognised. The principles for the measurement of the termination benefits liability are consistent with those for short-term employee benefits and other long-term employee benefits.

Discussion questions

1. What is a paid absence? Provide an example.
2. What is the difference between accumulating and non-accumulating sick leave? How does the recognition of accumulating sick leave differ from the recognition of non-accumulating sick leave?
3. What is the difference between vesting and non-vesting sick leave? How does the recognition of vesting sick leave differ from the recognition of non-vesting sick leave?
4. Explain how a defined contribution superannuation plan differs from a defined benefit superannuation plan.
5. During October 2008, there was a sudden global decline in the price of equity securities and credit securities. Many superannuation funds made negative returns on investments during this period. How would this event affect the wealth of employees and employers? Consider both defined benefit and defined contribution superannuation funds in your answer to this question.
6. Explain how an entity should account for its contribution to a defined contribution superannuation plan in accordance with IAS 19.
7. Compare the off-balance sheet approach to accounting for a defined benefit post-employment plan with the net capitalisation approach adopted by IAS 19. Can these approaches be explained by different underlying views as to whether a deficit or surplus in the fund meets the definition of a liability or asset of the sponsoring employer?
8. In relation to defined benefit post-employment plans, paragraph 56 of IAS 19 states, 'the entity is, in substance, underwriting the actuarial and investment risks associated with the plan'. Evaluate whether the requirements for the recognition and measurement of the net defined benefit liability reflect the underlying assumptions about the entity's risks.
9. Identify and discuss the assumptions involved in the measurement of a provision for long service leave. Assess the consistency of these requirements with the fundamental qualitative characteristics of financial information prescribed by the *Conceptual Framework for Financial Reporting*.
10. Explain the projected unit credit method of measuring and recognising an obligation for long-term employee benefits. Illustrate your answer with an example.
11. The board of directors of City Scooters Ltd met in June 2013 and decided to close down a branch of the company's operations when the lease expired in the following February. The chief financial officer advised that termination benefits of $2.0 million are likely to be paid. Should the company recognise a liability for termination benefits in its financial statements for the year ended June 2013? Justify your judgement with reference to the requirements of IAS 19.

Exercises

STAR RATING ★ BASIC ★★ MODERATE ★★★ DIFFICULT

| Exercise 10.1 | ACCOUNTING FOR THE PAYROLL |

★ Adelaide Ltd pays its employees on a monthly basis. The payroll is processed on the 6th day of the month and payable on the 7th day of the month. Gross salaries for July were $500 000, from which $125 000 was deducted in tax. All of Adelaide Ltd's salaries are accounted for as expenses. Deductions for health insurance were $10 000. Payments for health insurance and employee withheld income taxes are due on the 15th day of the following month.

Required

1. Prepare all journal entries to record the July payroll, the payment of July salaries and the remittance of deductions.
2. Calculate the balance of the Accrued Payroll account at the end of July.

Exercise 10.2 **ACCRUAL OF WAGES AND SALARIES**

★ London Ltd has a weekly payroll of $125 000. The last payroll processed before the end of the annual reporting period was for the week ended Friday 24 June. Employees do not work during weekends.

Required

Prepare a journal entry to accrue the weekly payroll as at 30 June.

Exercise 10.3 **ACCOUNTING FOR SICK LEAVE**

★ Huang Ltd has 100 employees who each earn a gross wage of $150 per day. In an attempt to reduce absenteeism, Huang Ltd introduced a new workplace agreement providing all employees with entitlement to 5 days of non-vesting, accumulating sick leave per annum, effective from 1 July 2012. Under the previous workplace agreement, all sick leave was non-cumulative. During the year ended 30 June 2013, 300 days of paid sick leave were taken by employees. It is estimated that 60% of unused sick leave will be taken during the year ended 30 June 2014 and that 40% will not be taken at all.

Required

Prepare a journal entry to recognised Huang Ltd's liability, if any, for sick leave at 30 June 2013.

Exercise 10.4 **ACCOUNTING FOR SICK LEAVE**

★ Auckland Ltd has 200 employees who each earn a gross wage of $140 per day. Auckland Ltd provides 5 days of paid non-accumulating sick leave for each employee per annum. During the year, 150 days of paid sick leave and 20 days of unpaid sick leave were taken. Staff turnover is negligible.

Required

Calculate the employee benefits expense for sick leave during the year and the amount that should be recognised as a liability, if any, for sick leave at the end of the year.

Exercise 10.5 **ACCOUNTING FOR ANNUAL LEAVE**

★ Newcastle Ltd provides employees with 4 weeks (20 days) of annual leave for each year of service. The annual leave is accumulating and vesting up to a maximum of 6 weeks. Thus, all employees take their annual leave within 6 months after the end of each reporting period so that it does not lapse. Employees are paid only their regular wage while taking annual leave. Refer to the following extract from Newcastle Ltd's payroll records for the year ended 30 June 2013:

Employee	Wage/day	AL 1 July 2012 days	Increase in entitlement days	AL taken days
Chand	$160	6	20	15
Kim	$125	3	20	16
Smith	$150	2	20	13
Zhou	$100	4	20	17

Required

Calculate the amount of annual leave that should be accrued for each employee.

ACCOUNTING FOR PROFIT-SHARING ARRANGEMENTS

Wellington Ltd has a profit-sharing arrangement in which 1% of profit for the period is payable to employees, paid 3 months after the end of the reporting period. Employees' entitlements under the profit-sharing arrangement are subject to their continued employment at the time the payment is made. Based on past staff turnover levels, it is expected that 95% of the share of profit will be paid. Wellington Ltd's profit for the period was $70 million.

Required

Prepare a journal entry to record Wellington Ltd's liability for employee benefits arising from the profit-sharing arrangement at the end of the reporting period.

ACCOUNTING FOR LONG SERVICE LEAVE

Victoria Ltd provides long service leave entitlement of 13 weeks of paid leave after 10 years of continuous employment. The provision for long service leave had a credit balance of $140 000 at 30 June 2013. During the year ended 30 June 2014, long service leave of $25 000 was paid. At the end of the year, the present value of the defined benefit obligation for long service leave was $150 000.

Required

Prepare all journal entries in relation to long service leave for the year ended 30 June 2014.

ACCOUNTING FOR DEFINED CONTRIBUTION SUPERANNUATION PLANS

Southern Isle Ltd provides a defined contribution superannuation fund for its employees. The company pays contributions equivalent to 10% of annual wages and salaries. Contributions of $50 000 per month were paid for the year ended 30 June 2013. Actual wages and salaries were $7 million. Three months after the reporting period, there is a settlement of the difference between the amount paid and the annual amount payable determined with reference to Southern Isle Ltd's audited payroll information. The settlement at 30 September involves either an additional contribution payment by Southern Isle Ltd or a refund of excess contributions paid.

Required

Prepare all journal entries required during June 2013 for Southern Isle Ltd's payment of, and liability for, superannuation contributions.

ACCOUNTING FOR THE PAYROLL AND ACCRUAL OF WAGES AND SALARIES

Lavender Ltd pays its employees on a fortnightly basis. All employee benefits are recognised as expenses. The following information is provided for its July and August payrolls:

	July		August	
	$	$	$	$
Fortnightly payroll		580 000		700 000
		720 000		600 000
Gross payroll for the month		1 300 000		1 300 000
Deductions payable to:				
Taxation authority	250 000		245 000	
Health Fund	20 000		20 000	
Community Charity	4 000		4 000	
Union fees	6 500		6 500	
Total deductions for the month		280 500		275 500
Net wages and salaries paid				
14 July, 11 August	458 775		553 230	
28 July, 25 August	560 725	1 019 500	471 270	1 024 500
		1 300 000		1 300 000

The two fortnightly payrolls in August were for the fortnight ended Friday, 7 August and Friday, 21 August. The payrolls were processed and paid on the following Monday and Tuesday respectively. Payroll deductions are remitted as follows:

Health fund deductions	3rd day of the following month
Union fees	3rd day of the following month
Taxation authority	15th day of the following month
Community charity	21st day of the following month

Required

1. Prepare all journal entries to account for the August payroll and all payments relating to employee benefits during August.
2. Prepare a journal entry to accrue wages for the remaining days in August not included in the final August payroll. Use the same level of remuneration as per the final payroll for August.

Exercise 10.10   **ACCOUNTING FOR ANNUAL LEAVE**

★ Tulip Ltd provides 4 weeks (20 days) of accumulating vested annual leave for each year of service. The company policy is that annual leave must be taken within 6 months of the end of the period in which it accrues. Annual leave is paid at the base salary rate (which excludes commissions, bonuses and overtime).

The following summary data is derived from Tulip Ltd's payroll records for the year ended 30 June 2013. Base pay rates have increased during the year. The amounts shown are applicable at 30 June 2013.

		Annual leave		
Employee category	Base pay/day $	Balance b/d 1 July 2012 days	Accumulated during year days	Taken during year days
Managers	440	100	200	260
Sales staff	220	150	600	630
Office workers	110	120	400	387
Other	100	60	200	240

Additional information
After leave taken during the year had been recorded, Tulip Ltd's trial balance revealed that the provision for annual leave had a debit balance of $223 370 at 30 June 2013.

Required

Prepare journal entries to account for the liability for annual leave at 30 June 2013.

Exercise 10.11   **ACCOUNTING FOR SICK LEAVE**

★ Daffodil Ltd opened a call centre on 1 July 2012. The company provides 1 week (5 days) of sick leave entitlement for the employees working at the call centre. The following information has been obtained from Daffodil Ltd's payroll records and actuarial assessments for the year ended 30 June 2013. The column headed 'Term. in 2013' indicates the leave entitlement pertaining to service of employees whose employment was terminated during the year. The actuary has estimated the percentage of unused leave that would be taken within 12 months if Daffodil Ltd allowed leave to accumulate. Due to high staff turnover, the remaining leave would lapse (or be settled in cash, if vesting) within 1 year after the end of the reporting period.

Employee category	Base pay/day $	Current service days	Leave taken in 2013 days	Term. in 2013 days	Estimated leave used 2013 %	Estimated termination 2013 %
Supervisors	100	30	20	3	90	10
Operators	80	500	400	60	70	30

Required

Calculate the employee benefits expense for sick leave for the year and the amount that should be recognised as a liability for sick leave at 30 June 2013, assuming that sick leave entitlements are:
(a) non-accumulating
(b) accumulating and non-vesting
(c) accumulating and vesting.

Exercise 10.12 | **ACCOUNTING FOR DEFINED BENEFIT SUPERANNUATION PLANS**

★★ Sydney Ltd provides a defined benefit superannuation plan for its managers. The assistant accountant has completed some sections of the defined benefit worksheet based on information provided in an actuary's report on the Sydney DB Superannuation Fund for the year ended 30 June 2014:

SYDNEY DB SUPERANNUATION FUND Defined Benefit Worksheet for the year ended 30 June 2014						
	Sydney Ltd				Sydney DB Superannuation Fund	
	Profit/loss $'000	OCI $'000	Bank $'000	Net DBL(A) $'000	DBO $'000	Plan Assets $'000
Balance 30/6/13				1 000 Cr	6 000 Cr	5 000 Dr
Net interest at 10%						
Current service cost					400 Cr	
Contributions to the fund			600 Cr			600 Dr
Benefits paid by the fund					100 Dr	100 Cr
Actuarial loss: DBO					300 Cr	
Journal Entry						
Balance 30/6/14					7 200 Cr	6 000 Dr
Adjustment for asset ceiling if < deficit						
Balance 30/6/14						

Additional information
The asset ceiling was $600 000 at 30 June 2014.

Required

1. Determine the surplus or deficit of the fund at 30 June 2014.
2. Determine the net defined benefit asset or liability at 30 June 2014.
3. Calculate the net interest and distinguish between the interest expense component of the defined benefit obligation and the interest income component of the change in the fair value of plan assets for the year ended 30 June 2014.
4. Determine the amount to be recognised in profit or loss in relation to the defined benefit superannuation plan for the year ended 30 June 2014.
5. Determine the amount to be recognised in other comprehensive income in relation to the defined benefit superannuation plan for the year ended 30 June 2014.

Exercise 10.13 | **ACCOUNTING FOR DEFINED BENEFIT SUPERANNUATION PLANS**

★★ Which of the following items in relation to a defined benefit fund are recognised in (i) profit or loss and (ii) other comprehensive income in accordance with IAS 19?
(a) current service cost
(b) past service cost incurred during the period
(c) net interest
(d) return on plan assets excluding amounts recognised in net interest

(e) benefits paid to members
(f) current period actuarial gains in relation to the defined benefit obligation
(g) current period actuarial losses in relation to the defined benefit obligation
(h) current period actuarial gains in relation to the assets of the plan
(i) current period actuarial losses in relation to the assets of the plan
(j) contributions paid.

Exercise 10.14 ACCOUNTING FOR DEFINED BENEFIT SUPERANNUATION PLANS

★★ For each of the following scenarios, determine (i) the surplus or deficit in the defined benefit super-annuation fund and (ii) the net defined benefit liability or asset that should be recognised by the sponsoring employer in accordance with IAS 19:

	Present value of DBO	Fair value of plan assets	Asset ceiling
(a)	$1 300 000	$1 000 000	$Nil
(b)	$1 550 000	$1 200 000	$Nil
(c)	$2 000 000	$2 200 000	$100 000
(d)	$2 400 000	$2 500 000	$250 000

Exercise 10.15 ACCOUNTING FOR SICK LEAVE

★★ Rose Ltd provides 1 week (5 days) of accumulating non-vesting sick leave for each year of service. Sick leave is paid at the base pay rate, which does not include commissions, bonuses and overtime. The proportion of accumulated sick leave that will be taken is estimated for each category of employee due to differences in staff turnover rates. The following summary data is derived from Rose Ltd's payroll records for the year ended 30 June 2013.

Employee category	Base pay/day $	Sick leave Balance b/d 1 July 2012 Days	Sick leave Increase in leave for current service Days	Sick leave Leave taken or lapsed Days	% of unused leave expected to be taken Within 12 months %	% of unused leave expected to be taken 1 year later %	% of unused leave expected to be taken 2 years later %
Managers	450	120	50	10	20	10	5
Consultants	300	110	100	90	75	10	0
Clerical staff	100	80	100	70	65	9	0

Additional information
The yield on high-quality corporate bonds at 30 June 2013 is 7% for one-year bonds and 8% for two-year bonds. After leave taken during the year had been recorded Rose Ltd's trial balance at 30 June 2013 revealed the provision for sick leave had a credit balance of $13 000.

Required
1. Prepare journal entries to account for the liability for sick leave at 30 June 2013.
2. State how much of the provision should be classified as a non-current liability.

Exercise 10.16 ACCOUNTING FOR BONUSES AND DEFINED CONTRIBUTION SUPERANNUATION PLANS

★★ Orchid Ltd contributes to a defined contribution superannuation plan for its employees. Contributions have been established as 10% of wages and salaries, including bonuses, actually paid during the year. Contributions based on budgeted payroll costs were set at $100 000 per month. There is annual net settlement of superannuation contributions payable or refundable based on actual audited payroll information. The net settlement occurs on 30 September for the preceding year ended 30 June.

Managers are entitled to a bonus calculated at 5% of their base salary if Orchid Ltd's profit before tax (excluding the bonus) is more than 20% of market capitalisation of the company at the beginning of the year. The profit target was achieved in 2012 and 2013. The bonus is payable 6 months after the end of the reporting period, provided the manager has remained in the company's employment.

	2013 $	2012 $
Managerial salaries expense	4 500 000	4 000 000
Other salaries and wages	8 000 000	7 800 000
	12 500 000	11 800 000
Accrued wages and salaries	300 000	250 000
Accrued managerial bonuses	?	400 000

At 30 June 2012, Orchid Ltd correctly anticipated that all managers would be eligible for the bonus because staff turnover among managers had been very low. However, by 30 June 2013, the company had moved to new premises and one manager, with a salary of $800 000, indicated that the additional travel was causing him to reconsider his position. The directors estimated that there was a 50% probability that the manager would resign by 31 December 2013, and an 80% probability that he would resign by 30 June 2014.

Required

1. Prepare the journal entry to record the contribution to the superannuation plan for June 2013.
2. Prepare a journal entry to record the liability, if any, arising from the bonus plan at 30 June 2013.
3. Prepare a journal entry to account for the superannuation asset or liability, if any, at 30 June 2013.

Exercise 10.17

ACCOUNTING FOR LONG SERVICE LEAVE

★★ Geranium Ltd provides long service leave for its retail staff. Long service leave entitlement is determined as 13 weeks of paid leave for 10 years of continued service. The following information is obtained from Geranium Ltd's payroll records and actuarial reports for its retail staff at 30 June 2013:

Unit credit (years)	No. of employees	% expected to become entitled	Annual salary per employee	No. of years until vesting	Yield on HQ corporate bonds
1	60	20%	$27 000	9	10%
2	50	30%	$27 000	8	9%
3	30	50%	$27 000	7	9%
4	10	60%	$27 000	6	9%

Additional information
(a) The estimated annual increase in retail wages is 1% p.a. for the next 10 years, reflecting expected inflation.
(b) The provision for long service leave for retail staff at 30 June 2012 was $22 000.
(c) No employees were eligible to take long service leave during the year ended 30 June 2013.

Required

Prepare the journal entry to account for Geranium Ltd's provision for long service leave at 30 June 2013.

Exercise 10.18

ACCOUNTING FOR LONG SERVICE LEAVE

★★ Bluebell Ltd provides credit services. Bluebell Ltd provides the employees with long service leave entitlements of 13 weeks of paid leave for every 10 years of continuous service. As the company has been operating for only 5 years, no employees have become entitled to long service leave. However, the company recognises a provision for long service leave using the projected unit credit approach required by IAS 19.

The following information is obtained from Bluebell Ltd's payroll records and actuarial reports for the non-managerial staff of its debt collection business at 30 June 2013:

Unit credit (years)	No. of employees	% expected to become entitled	Average annual salary	No. of years until vesting	Yield on govt. corporate bonds
1	100	20%	$40 000	9	6%
2	85	26%	$42 000	8	6%
3	40	35%	$44 000	7	5%
4	32	50%	$46 500	6	5%
5	25	65%	$49 600	5	5%

Additional information
(a) The estimated annual increase in retail wages is 5% p.a. for the next 10 years, reflecting Bluebell Ltd's policy of increasing salaries of its debt collection staff for each year of additional experience.
(b) At 30 June 2012, the provision for long service leave for non-managerial debt collection staff was $132 000.

Required

Prepare the journal entry to account for Bluebell Ltd's provision for long service leave at 30 June 2013 in relation to the non-managerial employees of the company's debt collection business.

Exercise 10.19	ACCOUNTING FOR DEFINED BENEFIT SUPERANNUATION PLANS

★★★ Lily Ltd provides a defined benefit superannuation plan for its managers. The following information is available in relation to the plan.

	2013 $
Present value of the defined benefit obligation 1 July 2012	10 000 000
Fair value of plan assets 1 July 2012	9 500 000
Current service cost	1 150 000
Contributions paid by Lily Ltd to the fund during the year	1 000 000
Benefits paid by the fund during the year	1 200 000
Present value of the defined benefit obligation 30 June 2013	10 750 000
Fair value of plan assets at 30 June 2013	10 047 500

Additional information
(a) No past service costs were incurred during the year ended 30 June 2013.
(b) The interest rate used to measure the present value of defined benefits at 30 June 2012 was 9%.
(c) The interest rate used to measure the present value of defined benefits at 30 June 2013 was 10%.
(d) There was an actuarial gain pertaining to the present value of the defined benefit obligation as a result of an increase in the interest rate.
(e) The only remeasurement affecting the fair value of plan assets is the return on plan assets.
(f) The asset ceiling was nil at 30 June 2012 and 30 June 2013.
(g) All contributions received by the funds were paid by Lily Ltd. Employees make no contributions.

Required

1. Determine the surplus or deficit of Lily Ltd's defined benefit plan at 30 June 2013.
2. Determine the net defined benefit asset or liability that should be recognised by Lily Ltd at 30 June 2013.
3. Calculate the net interest for the year ended 30 June 2013.
4. Calculate the actuarial gain or loss for the defined benefit obligation for the year ended 30 June 2013.

5. Calculate the return on plan assets, excluding any amount recognised in net interest, for the year ended 30 June 2013.
6. Present a reconciliation of the opening balance to the closing balance of the net defined benefit liability (asset), showing separate reconciliations for plan assets and the present value of the defined benefit obligation.
7. Prepare a summary journal entry to account for the defined benefit superannuation plan in the books of Lily Ltd for the year ended 30 June 2013.

| Exercise 10.20 | **ACCOUNTING FOR DEFINED BENEFIT SUPERANNUATION PLANS** |
| ★★★ | |

Some years ago, Wattle Ltd established a defined benefit superannuation plan for its employees. The company has since introduced a defined contribution plan, which all new staff join when commencing employment with Wattle Ltd. Although the defined benefit plan is now closed to new recruits, the fund continues to provide for employees who have been with the company for a long time. The following actuarial report has been received for the defined benefit plan:

	2013 $
Present value of the defined benefit obligation 1 Jan.	20 000 000
Past service cost	2 000 000
Net interest	?
Current service cost	800 000
Benefits paid	2 100 000
Actuarial loss on DBO	100 000
Present value of the defined benefit obligation 31 Dec.	$ 23 000 000
Fair value of plan assets at 1 Jan.	19 000 000
Return on plan assets	?
Contributions paid to the fund during the year	1 000 000
Benefits paid by the fund during the year	2 100 000
Fair value of plan assets at 30 June 2013	$ 20 130 000

Additional information
(a) All contributions received by the funds were paid by Wattle Ltd. Employees make no contributions.
(b) The interest rate used to measure the present value of the defined benefit obligation was 10% at 31 December 2012 and 31 December 2013.
(c) The asset ceiling was nil at 31 December 2012 and 31 December 2013.

Required

1. Determine the surplus or deficit of Wattle Ltd's defined benefit plan at 31 December 2013.
2. Determine the net defined benefit asset or liability that should be recognised by Wattle Ltd at 31 December 2013.
3. Calculate the net interest and the return on plan assets for the year ended 31 December 2013.
4. Present a reconciliation of the opening balance to the closing balance of the net defined benefit liability (asset), showing separate reconciliations for plan assets and the present value of the defined benefit obligation.
5. Prepare a summary journal entry to account for the defined benefit superannuation plan in the books of Wattle Ltd for the year ended 31 December 2013.

References

Billabong International Ltd 2010, *2009/2010 Full financial report*, Billabong International Limited, Australia, www.billabongbiz.com.
—— 2011, *2010/2011 Full financial report*, Billabong International Limited, Australia, www.billabongbiz.com.

Gallery, N 2003, 'Are superannuation disclosures in company financial reports useful?', *Australian Accounting Review*, vol. 13, no. 2, pp. 60–72.

Gordon, I 2005, 'Accrual accounting catches up with employers sponsoring defined benefit plans', *Financial Reporting, Regulation and Governance*, vol. 4, no. 1, www.cbs.curtin.edu.au.

IASB 2008, *Discussion paper: Preliminary views on amendments to IAS 19 Employee Benefits*, www.ifrs.org.

Sengupta, P & Wang, Z 2011, 'Pricing of off-balance sheet debt: How do bond market participants use the footnote disclosures on operating leases and postretirement benefits', *Accounting and Finance*, vol. 51, no. 3, pp. 787–808.

Skaife, HA, Bradshaw, MT, Davis-Friday, PY, Gordon, ED, Hopkins, PE, Laux, R, Nelson, KK, Rajgopal, S, Ramesh, K, Uhl, R & Vrana, G (American Accounting Association's Financial Accounting Standards Committee) 2007, 'Response to FASB exposure draft: Employers' accounting for defined benefit pension and other post-retirement plans: An amendment of FASB Statements No. 87, 88, 106, and 132(R)', *Accounting Horizons*, vol. 21, no. 2, pp. 201–13.

11

Property, plant and equipment

ACCOUNTING STANDARDS IN FOCUS

IAS 16 *Property, Plant and Equipment*

LEARNING OBJECTIVES

After studying this chapter, you should be able to:

1 understand the nature of property, plant and equipment

2 understand the recognition criteria for initial recognition of property, plant and equipment

3 understand how to measure property, plant and equipment on initial recognition

4 explain the alternative ways in which property, plant and equipment can be measured subsequent to initial recognition

5 explain the cost model of measurement and understand the nature and calculation of depreciation

6 explain the revaluation model of measurement

7 understand the factors to consider when choosing which measurement model to apply

8 account for derecognition

9 implement the disclosure requirements of IAS 16.

LO1 | 11.1 THE NATURE OF PROPERTY, PLANT AND EQUIPMENT

The accounting standard analysed in this chapter is IAS 16 *Property, Plant and Equipment*. The standard was first issued by the International Accounting Standards Board (IASB) in March 1982, amended on numerous occasions, exposed in May 2002 as part of the IASB project on improvements to international accounting standards (IASs), and issued in its present form in 2004. As a result of this process, the IASB has clarified selected matters and provided additional guidance. It has not reconsidered the fundamental approach to the accounting for property, plant and equipment contained in IAS 16.

According to paragraph 2 of IAS 16, the standard applies in accounting for property, plant and equipment except where another standard requires or permits a different accounting treatment. IAS 16 does not apply to property, plant and equipment classified as held for sale in accordance with IFRS 5 *Non-current Assets Held for Sale and Discontinued Operations*; biological assets related to agricultural activity as these are accounted for under IAS 41 *Agriculture*; or mineral rights and mineral reserves such as oil, gas and similar non-regenerative resources. However, IAS 16 does apply to property, plant and equipment used to develop or maintain biological assets and mineral rights and reserves.

Paragraph 6 of IAS 16 defines property, plant and equipment as follows:

Property, plant and equipment are tangible items that:
(a) are held for use in the production or supply of goods or services, for rental to others, or for administrative purposes; and
(b) are expected to be used during more than one period.

Note the following:

- The assets are 'tangible' assets. The distinction between tangible and intangible assets is discussed in depth in chapter 13. However, a key feature of tangible assets is that they are physical assets, such as land, rather than non-physical, such as patents and trademarks.
- The assets have specific uses within an entity; namely, for use in production/supply, rental or administration. Assets that are held for sale, including land, or held for investment are not included under property, plant and equipment. Instead, assets held for sale are accounted for in accordance with IFRS 5.
- The assets are non-current assets, the expectation being that they will be used for more than one accounting period.

Property, plant and equipment may be divided into classes for disclosure purposes, a class of assets being a grouping of assets of a similar nature and use in an entity's operations. Examples of classes of property, plant and equipment are land, machinery, motor vehicles and office equipment. The notes to the statement of financial position of Billabong International Ltd, at 30 June 2011, as shown in figure 11.1, provide an indication of what is contained in that category as well as the reasons for the movements in this category of assets.

In this chapter, accounting for property, plant and equipment is considered as follows:

- recognition of the asset — the point at which the asset is brought into the accounting records
- initial measurement of the asset — determining the initial amount at which the asset is recorded in the accounts
- measurement subsequent to initial recognition — determining the amount at which the asset is reported subsequent to acquisition, including the recording of any depreciation of the asset
- derecognition of the asset.

FIGURE 11.1 Property, plant and equipment

Note 14. Non-current assets — Property, plant and equipment				
	Land and buildings $'000	Furniture, fittings and equipment $'000	Leased plant and equipment $'000	Total $'000
At 30 June 2009				
Cost or fair value	43 821	235 957	11 917	291 695
Accumulated depreciation	(2 505)	(122 592)	(4 782)	(129 879)
Net book amount	41 316	113 365	7 135	161 816

FIGURE 11.1 *(continued)*

	Land and buildings $'000	Furniture, fittings and equipment $'000	Leased plant and equipment $'000	Total $'000
Year ended 30 June 2010				
Opening net book amount	41 316	113 365	7 135	161 816
Additions from acquisitions (note 35)	—	1 117	—	1 117
Additions	11 416	40 816	22	52 254
Disposals	—	(848)	(64)	(912)
Depreciation charge	(1 219)	(32 874)	(830)	(34 923)
Exchange differences	(534)	(7 183)	(1 158)	(8 875)
Closing net book amount	50 979	114 393	5 105	170 477
At 30 June 2010				
Cost or fair value	54 520	258 689	9 690	322 899
Accumulated depreciation	(3 541)	(144 296)	(4 585)	(152 422)
Net book amount	50 979	114 393	5 105	170 477

	Land and buildings $'000	Furniture fittings and equipment $'000	Leased plant and equipment $'000	Total $'000
Year ended 30 June 2011				
Opening net book amount	50 979	114 393	5 105	170 477
Additions from acquisitions (note 35)	—	27 532	—	27 532
Additions	—	41 858	56	41 914
Disposals	—	(1 198)	—	(1 198)
Depreciation charge	(1 149)	(38 323)	(660)	(40 132)
Exchange differences	(1 535)	(11 926)	(280)	(13 741)
Closing net book amount	48 295	132 336	4 221	184 852
At 30 June 2011				
Cost or fair value	51 442	291 999	9 083	352 524
Accumulated depreciation	(3 147)	(159 663)	(4 862)	(167 672)
Net book amount	48 295	132 336	4 221	184 852

Source: Billabong International Ltd (2011, p. 88).

 LO2 ## 11.2 INITIAL RECOGNITION OF PROPERTY, PLANT AND EQUIPMENT

Paragraph 7 of IAS 16 contains the principles for recognition of property, plant and equipment:

> The cost of an item of property, plant and equipment shall be recognised as an asset if, and only if:
> (a) it is probable that future economic benefits associated with the item will flow to the entity; and
> (b) the cost of the item can be measured reliably.

This is a *general* recognition principle for property, plant and equipment. It applies to the initial recognition of an asset, when parts of that asset are replaced, and when costs are incurred in relation to that asset during its useful life. To recognise a cost as an asset, the outlay must give rise to the expectation of future economic benefits.

The criteria for recognition in paragraph 7 differ from the recognition criteria for the elements of financial statements in paragraph 4.38 of the *Conceptual Framework*. Under the *Conceptual Framework*, an asset can be recognised when the cost or value can be measured with reliability; under IAS 16, recognition can occur only if the *cost* can be measured reliably. Assets for which the cost cannot be reliably measured but whose initial fair value can be measured reliably cannot be recognised in the entity's records.

11.2.1 Asset versus expense

For most items of property, plant and equipment, the entity will incur some initial expenditure. One of the key problems for the entity is determining whether the outlay should be expensed or capitalised as an asset. As paragraph 7 of IAS 16 states, the elements of that decision relate to whether the entity expects there to be future economic benefits, whether the receipt of those benefits is probable, and whether the benefits will flow specifically to the entity. As noted in paragraph 4.45 of the *Conceptual Framework*, the expensing of outlays:

> does not imply either that the intention of management in incurring expenditure was other than to generate future economic benefits for the entity or that management was misguided. The only implication is that the degree of certainty that economic benefits will flow to the entity beyond the current accounting period is insufficient to warrant the recognition of an asset.

As property, plant and equipment consists of physical assets such as land and machinery, such assets are normally traded in a market. One test of the existence of future benefits is then to determine whether there exists a market for the item in question. A problem with some assets is that once items have been acquired and installed, there is no normal market for them. However, in many cases, the expected economic benefits arise because of the use of that asset in conjunction with other assets held by the entity. At a minimum, the future benefits would be the scrap value of the item. Where the assets are intangible, such as costs associated with the generation of software, the absence of a physical asset causes more problems in terms of asset recognition. Chapter 13 discusses in detail the problems associated with the recognition of intangible assets.

11.2.2 Separate assets — significant parts

The total property, plant and equipment of an entity may be broken down into separate assets. This is sometimes referred to as a 'significant parts' approach to asset recognition. An entity allocates the amount initially recognised in respect of an asset to its significant parts and accounts for each part separately. Paragraph 9 of IAS 16 notes that the identification of what constitutes a separate item of plant and equipment requires the exercise of judgement, because the standard does not prescribe the unit of measure for recognition. The key element in determining whether an asset should be further subdivided into its significant parts is an analysis of what is going to happen in the future to that asset. Having identified an asset, the entity wants to recognise the expected benefits as they are consumed by the entity, with the recognition being in the period in which the benefits are received. Hence, if an asset has a number of significant parts that have different useful lives then, in order for there to be an appropriate recognition of benefits consumed, significant parts with different useful lives need to be identified and accounted for separately.

For example, consider an aircraft as an item of property, plant and equipment. Is it sufficient to recognise the aircraft as a single asset? An analysis of the aircraft may reveal that there are various parts of the aircraft that have different useful lives. Parts of the aircraft include the engines, the frame of the aircraft and the fittings (seats, floor coverings and so on). It may be necessary to refit the aircraft every 5 years, whereas the engines may last twice as long. Similarly, an entity that deals with the refining of metals may have a blast furnace, the lining of which needs to be changed periodically. The lining of the blast furnace therefore needs to be separated from the external structure in terms of asset recognition and subsequent accounting for the asset. Further, as noted in paragraph 9 of IAS 16, it may be appropriate to aggregate individually insignificant items (such as moulds, tools and dies) and apply the criteria to the aggregate value.

11.2.3 Generation of future benefits

Paragraph 11 of IAS 16 notes that certain assets may not of themselves generate future benefits, but instead it may be necessary for the entity itself to generate future benefits. For example, some items of property, plant and equipment may be acquired for safety or environmental reasons, such as equipment associated with the safe storage of dangerous chemicals. The entity's generation of the benefits from use of the chemicals can occur only if the safety equipment exists. Hence, even if the safety equipment does not of itself generate cash flows, its existence is necessary for the entity to be able to use chemicals within the business.

 11.3 INITIAL MEASUREMENT OF PROPERTY, PLANT AND EQUIPMENT

Having established that an asset can be recognised, the entity must then assign to it a monetary amount. Paragraph 15 of IAS 16 contains the principles for initial measurement of property, plant and equipment: 'An item of property, plant and equipment that qualifies for recognition as an asset shall be measured at its cost.' Paragraph 16 specifies three elements of cost, namely:

- purchase price
- directly attributable costs
- initial estimate of the costs of dismantling and removing the item or restoring the site on which it is located.

These elements are considered separately in the following sections.

11.3.1 Purchase price

'Purchase price' is not defined in IAS 16, but paragraph 16(a) states that the purchase price includes import duties and non-refundable purchase taxes, and is calculated after deducting any trade discounts and rebates. The essence of what constitutes purchase price is found in the definition of cost in paragraph 6 of the standard, which states: 'Cost is the amount of cash or cash equivalents paid or the fair value of the other consideration given to acquire an asset at the time of its acquisition or construction.'

Where an item of property, plant and equipment is acquired for cash, determination of the purchase price is relatively straightforward. One variation that may arise is that some or all of the cash payment is deferred. In this case, as noted in paragraph 23 of IAS 16, the cost is the cash price equivalent at the recognition date, determined by measuring the cash payments on a present value basis (done by discounting the cash flows). Interest is then recognised as the payments are made.

More difficulties arise where the exchange involves assets other than cash. In a non-cash exchange, the acquiring entity receives a non-cash asset and in return provides a non-cash asset to the seller. In measuring the cost of the asset acquired, the question is whether the measurement should be based on the value of the asset given up by the acquirer, or by reference to the value of the asset acquired from the seller. In relation to the application of the cost principle of measurement, note the following:

1. Cost is determined by reference to the fair value of what is given up by the acquirer rather than by the fair value of the item acquired. The cost represents the sacrifice made by the acquirer. This principle is inherent in the definition of cost in paragraph 6 of IAS 16. Further, paragraph 26 states that where both the fair value of what is given up by the acquirer and the asset received are reliably measurable, then the fair value of the asset given up is used to measure the cost of the asset received, unless the fair value of the asset received is more clearly evident. 'More clearly evident' presumably relates to the cost and difficulty of determining the fair value as, in the paragraph 26 example, the fair values of both the asset received and the asset given up can be measured reliably.

2. Cost is measured by reference to fair value (paragraph 24). The term fair value is defined in paragraph 6 of IAS 16 as 'the price that would be received to sell an asset or paid to transfer a liability in an orderly transaction between market participants at the measurement date'.

   Fair value is an exit price. The process of determining fair value necessarily involves judgement and estimation. The acquiring company is not actually trading the items given up in the marketplace for cash, but is trying to estimate what it would get for those items if it did so. Hence, the determination of fair value is only an estimation. A further practical problem in determining fair value is that the nature of the market in which the goods given up are normally traded may make estimation difficult. The market may be highly volatile with prices changing daily, or the market may be relatively inactive. Chapter 3 contains detailed information on the measurement of fair value.

   If the acquirer gives up an asset at fair value, and the carrying amount of the asset is different from the fair value, then the entity will recognise a gain or a loss. According to paragraph 34 of IAS 1 *Presentation of Financial Statements*, gains and losses on the disposal of non-current assets are reported by deducting from the proceeds on disposal the carrying amount of the asset and related selling expenses.

Assume then that an entity acquires a piece of machinery and gives in exchange a block of land. The land is carried by the entity at original cost of $100 000 and has a fair value of $150 000. The journal entry to record the acquisition of the machinery is:

Machinery	Dr	150 000	
Gain on Sale of Land	Cr		50 000
Land	Cr		100 000

Alternatively, the entry could be shown as:

Machinery	Dr	150 000	
Proceeds on Sale of Land	Cr		150 000
(Sale of land in exchange for machinery)			
Carrying Amount of Land Sold	Dr	100 000	
Land	Cr		100 000
(Carrying amount of land sold)			

The entity then reports a gain on sale of land of $50 000.

If, instead of giving land in exchange, the entity issued shares having a fair value of $150 000, the journal entry is:

Machinery	Dr	150 000	
Share Capital	Cr		150 000
(Acquisition of machinery by issue of shares)			

Further discussion on the measurement of the fair value of equity instruments issued by the acquirer in exchange for assets is found in chapter 14.

3. Paragraph 24 of IAS 16 requires the use of fair value to measure the cost of an asset received unless the exchange transaction lacks commercial substance. Commercial substance is concerned with whether the transaction has a discernible effect on the economics of an entity. Paragraph 25 states that an exchange transaction has commercial substance if:
   (a) *the configuration (risk, timing and amount) of the cash flows of the asset received differs from the configuration of the cash flows of the asset transferred.* This would not occur if similar assets (e.g. an exchange of commodities such as oil or milk) were exchanged as would occur where, for example, suppliers exchanged inventories in various locations to fulfil demand on a timely basis in a particular location; or
   (b) *the entity-specific value of the portion of the entity's operations affected by the transaction changes as a result of the exchange.* Paragraph 6 defines entity-specific value as 'the present value of the cash flows an entity expects to arise from the continuing use of an asset and from its disposal at the end of its useful life or expects to incur when settling a liability'. If there is no change in the expected cash flows to the entity as a result of the exchange, as in the case of the exchange of similar items, then the transaction lacks commercial substance; and
   (c) *the difference in (a) or (b) is significant relative to the fair value of the assets exchanged.* In both (a) and (b), the change in cash flows or configuration must be material, with materiality being measured in relation to the fair value of the assets exchanged.
   Where the transaction lacks commercial substance, the asset acquired is measured at the carrying amount of the asset given up.
4. Paragraph 24 of IAS 16 also covers the situation where, in an exchange of assets, neither the fair value of the assets given up nor the fair value of the assets acquired can be measured reliably. Such situations could occur where the assets exchanged are both traded in weak markets where market transactions are infrequent. In this situation, the acquirer measures the cost of the asset acquired at the carrying amount of the asset given up.

Acquisition date

One of the problems in recording the acquisition of an item of property, plant and equipment relates to the determination of the fair values of the assets involved in the exchange. As noted above, accounting for the asset exchange requires that potentially both the fair values of the assets acquired and assets given up must be determined. However, where the markets for these assets are volatile, choosing the appropriate fair value may be difficult. This can be seen where an entity issues shares in exchange for an asset. The fair value of the shares issued may change on a daily basis. At what point in time should the fair values be measured?

Some likely dates that may be considered are:
- the date the contract to exchange the assets is signed
- the date the consideration is paid
- the date on which the assets acquired are received by the acquirer
- the date on which an offer becomes unconditional.

The advantage of these dates is that they relate to a point of time that can be determined objectively, such as the date the item of property, plant and equipment arrives at the acquirer's premises. A problem is that there may be a number of dates involved if, for example, an item of equipment arrives in stages or payment for the equipment is to be made in instalments over time.

The date on which the fair values should be measured is the date on which the acquirer *obtains control of the asset or assets acquired* — hereafter referred to as the 'acquisition date'. The definition of cost in paragraph 6 of IAS 16 refers to the 'time of its [the asset's] acquisition'. There is no specific date defined in the standard. In IFRS 3 *Business Combinations*, acquisition date is defined as 'the date on which the acquirer obtains control of the acquiree'.

The measurement of the fair value relates to the date the assets acquired are recognised in the records of the acquirer. At this date, the acquirer must be able to reliably measure the cost of the asset. Recognition of an asset requires the acquirer to have control of expected future benefits. Hence, when the item acquired becomes the asset of the acquirer (i.e. when the expected benefits come under the control of the acquirer), this is the point in time when the measurements of the fair values of assets acquired and given up are made. Paragraph 23 of IAS 16 states that the cost of an item of property, plant and equipment is the cash price equivalent at the 'recognition date'. Recognition date is normally the same as acquisition date.

Acquisition of multiple assets

The above principles as stated in IAS 16 apply to the acquisition of individual items of property, plant and equipment. However, an acquisition may consist of more than one asset, such as a block of land and a number of items of machinery. The acquirer may acquire the assets as a group, paying one total amount for the bundle of assets. The cost of acquiring the bundle of assets is determined as per IAS 16, namely by measuring the fair value of what is given up by the acquirer to determine the purchase price, and adding to this any directly attributable costs. However, even if the total cost of the bundle of assets can be determined, for accounting purposes it is necessary to determine the cost of each of the separate assets as they may be in different classes, or some may be depreciable and others not. No guidance is given in this standard for determining the costs of each of the assets. However, IFRS 3 *Business Combinations* paragraph 2(b) states:

> The cost of the group shall be allocated to the individual identifiable assets and liabilities on the basis of their relative *fair values* at the date of purchase. Such a transaction or event does not give rise to goodwill.

In this situation, the cost of each asset to be recorded separately is calculated by allocating the cost of the bundle of assets over the assets acquired in proportion to the fair values of the assets acquired. To illustrate this allocation procedure, assume an entity acquired land, buildings and furniture at a total cost of $300 000 cash. In order to separately record each asset acquired at cost, the entity determines the fair value of each asset, for example:

Land	$ 40 000
Buildings	200 000
Furniture	80 000
	$320 000

The total cost of $300 000 is then allocated to each asset on the basis of these fair values as follows:

Land	$40 000/$320 000 × $300 000	=	$ 37 500
Buildings	$200 000/$320 000 × $300 000	=	187 500
Furniture	$80 000/$320 000 × $300 000	=	75 000
			$300 000

The acquisition of the three assets is recorded by the entity as follows:

Land	Dr	37 500	
Buildings	Dr	187 500	
Furniture	Dr	75 000	
Cash	Cr		300 000
(Acquisition of assets for cash)			

Under IAS 16, the basic principle of recording assets acquired is to record at cost. Where a bundle of assets is acquired, the cost of the separate assets must be estimated, and the fair values of the assets acquired can be used in this process. Where the cost of the assets in total is less than the sum of the fair values of the assets acquired, a bargain purchase has been made. However, as the assets are to be recognised initially at cost, no gain is recognised on acquisition.

11.3.2 Directly attributable costs

The key feature of those costs included in the cost of acquisition is that they are directly attributable *to bringing the asset to the location and condition necessary for it to be capable of operating in the manner intended by management* (IAS 16 paragraph 16(b)).

Costs to be included

Paragraph 17 of IAS 16 provides examples of directly attributable costs:
- costs of employee benefits arising directly from the construction or acquisition of the item of property, plant and equipment
- costs of site preparation
- initial delivery and handling costs
- installation and assembly costs — where buildings are acquired, associated costs could be the costs of renovation
- costs of testing whether the asset is functioning properly
- professional fees.

It can be seen that all these costs are incurred before the asset is used, and are necessary in order for the asset to be usable by the entity. Note, however, the use of the word 'necessary'. There may be costs incurred that were not necessary; for example, the entity may have incurred fines, or a concrete platform may have been placed in the wrong position and had to be destroyed and a new one put in the right place. These costs should be written off to an expense rather than being capitalised as part of the cost of the acquired asset.

A further cost that may be capitalised into the cost of an item of property, plant and equipment is that of borrowing costs. Borrowing costs (i.e. interest and other costs associated with the borrowing of funds) are accounted for under IAS 23 *Borrowing Costs*. Paragraph 8 of IAS 23 states that borrowing costs that are directly attributable to the acquisition, construction or production of a qualifying asset must be capitalised as part of the cost of the asset. (A qualifying asset is one that necessarily takes a substantial period of time to get ready for its intended use or sale, such as a building.)

Costs not to be included

Paragraphs 19 and 20 of IAS 16 contain examples of costs that should not be included in directly attributable costs:
- *costs of opening a new facility*. These costs are incurred after the item of property, plant and equipment is capable of being used; the opening ceremony, for example, does not enhance the operating ability of the asset.

- *costs of introducing a new product or service, including costs of advertising and promotional activities.* These costs do not change the location or working condition of the asset.
- *costs of conducting business in a new location or with a new class of customer (including costs of staff training).* Unless the asset is relocated, there is no change in the asset's ability to operate.
- *administration and other general overhead costs.* These costs are not directly attributable to the asset, but are associated generally with the operations of the entity.
- *costs incurred while an item capable of operating in the manner intended by management has yet to be brought into use or is operated at less than full capacity.* These costs are incurred because of management's decisions regarding the timing of operations rather than being attributable to getting the asset in a position for operation.
- *initial operating losses, such as those incurred while demand for the item's output builds up.* These are not incurred before the asset is ready for use.
- *costs of relocating or reorganising part or all of the entity's operations.* If a number of currently operating assets are relocated to another site, then the costs of relocation are general, and not directly attributable to the item of property, plant and equipment.

Income earned

Paragraph 17(e) of IAS 16 notes that the cost of the asset should be determined after deducting the net proceeds from selling any items produced when bringing the asset to that location and condition, such as proceeds from the sale of samples produced during the testing process. The principle here is that any flows, whether in or out, that occur before the asset is in a position to operate as management intends must be taken into account in determining the cost of the asset. The testing process is a necessary part of readying the asset for its ultimate use. Paragraph 21 provides an example of where income may be earned before the asset is ready for use but should not be included in the calculation of the cost of the asset. The example given is of income earned from the use of the construction site as a car park while there is a delay before the construction of a building. These revenues have nothing to do with the creation of the asset. They are incidental to the development activity, and should be separately recognised.

Acquisition for zero or nominal cost

An entity may acquire an asset for zero cost, or be required to pay an amount substantially different from the fair value of the asset. For example, an entity may be given a computer for no charge, or be required to pay only half price for a block of land or a building. Applying IAS 16, where there is zero cost, the entity receiving the asset would not record the asset. In the case of a heavily discounted asset, the asset would be recorded at the cost, namely the purchase price paid plus the directly attributable costs.

11.3.3 Costs of dismantling, removal or restoration

At the date an asset is initially recognised, an entity is required to estimate any costs necessary to eventually dismantle and remove the asset and restore its site. For example, when an asset such as an offshore oil platform is constructed, an entity knows that in the future it is required by law to dismantle and remove the platform in such a manner that the environment is cared for. The construction of the platform gives rise to a liability for restoration under IAS 37 *Provisions, Contingent Liabilities and Contingent Assets*. The expected costs, measured on a present value basis, are capitalised into the cost of the platform as the construction of the platform brings with it the responsibility of disposing of it. Acceptance of the liability for dismantling and removal is an essential part of bringing the asset to a position of intended use. As with directly attributable costs, the dismantling and removal costs are depreciated over the life of the asset. There may be restoration costs associated with the use of land, such as where the land is used for mining or farming. These costs are capitalised into the cost of the land at the acquisition date and, although the land is not depreciated, the restoration costs are depreciated over the period in which the benefits from use of the land are received.

As explained in paragraphs BC14–BC15 of the Basis for Conclusions on IAS 16, because of the limited scope of the revisions undertaken during the Improvements project, the IASB concentrated on the initial estimate of the costs of dismantling, removal and restoration. Issues relating to changes in that estimate, changes in interest rates, and the emergence of obligations subsequent to the asset's acquisition are not covered in IAS 16. However, the IASB did note that, regardless of whether the obligation is incurred when the item is acquired or when it is being used, the obligation's underlying nature and its association with the asset are the same. Hence, where obligations arise because of the use of an asset, these should be included in the cost of the asset.

LO4 11.4 MEASUREMENT SUBSEQUENT TO INITIAL RECOGNITION

At the point of initial recognition of an item of property, plant and equipment, the asset is measured at cost, which is the purchase price plus directly attributable costs and removal and/or restoration costs. After this initial recognition, an entity has a choice on the measurement basis to be adopted. IAS 16 paragraph 29 recognises two possible measurement models:

- the cost model
- the revaluation model.

The choice of model is an accounting policy decision. That policy is not applied to individual assets but to an entire class of property, plant and equipment. Hence, for each class of assets, an entity must decide the measurement model to be used. Having chosen a particular measurement model for a specific class of assets, the entity may later change to the alternative basis. For example, an entity that initially chose the revaluation model may at a later date change to the cost model. In order to change from one basis to another, the principles of IAS 8 *Accounting Policies, Changes in Accounting Estimates and Errors* must be applied. Paragraph 14 of IAS 8 states:

> An entity shall change an accounting policy only if the change:
> (a) is required by an IFRS; or
> (b) results in the financial statements providing reliable and more relevant information about the effects of transactions, other events or conditions on the entity's financial position, financial performance or cash flows.

It is part (b) that establishes the principle for change. The key is whether the change in measurement basis will make the financial statements more useful to users; in particular, will the information be more relevant and/or more reliable? In general, a change from the cost model to the revaluation model would be expected to increase the relevance of information provided because more current information is being made available. However, the change may make the information less reliable, as the determination of fair value requires estimation to occur. The entity would need to assess the overall benefit of the change in order to justify the change. In contrast, changing from the revaluation model would generally lead to a decrease in the relevance of the information. However, it may be that the determination of fair value has become so unreliable that the fair values determined have little meaning. Again, a judgement of the relative trade-offs between relevance and reliability needs to be made.

Paragraph 17 of IAS 8 notes that the accounting for a change from the cost model to the revaluation model constitutes a change in accounting policy, but the accounting for such a change is done in accordance with the principles in IAS 16 rather than those in IAS 8, namely by applying the principles of the revaluation model. No such statement is made about a change from fair value back to cost. It would appear that the accounting for this is based on IAS 8, paragraph 22 in particular. This paragraph requires the change to be applied retrospectively, and the information disclosed as if the new accounting policy had always been applied. Hence, a change from the revaluation model to the cost model would require adjustments to the accounting records to show the information as if the cost model had always been applied. Adjustments can be taken through the opening balance of retained earnings. Comparative information would also need to be restated.

LO5 11.5 THE COST MODEL

Paragraph 30 of IAS 16 states:

> After recognition as an asset, an item of property, plant and equipment shall be carried at its cost less any accumulated depreciation and any accumulated impairment losses.

The cost is as described in section 11.3 of this chapter, and includes outlays incurred up to the point where the asset is at the location and in the working condition to be capable of operating in the manner intended by management. Note that this entails management determining a level of operations, a capacity of production or a use for the item of property, plant and equipment. In getting a machine to an appropriate working condition, management may need to undertake certain outlays to keep the machine running efficiently at that level. In relation to a vehicle that is needed to take a driver from point A to point B, the car needs to run efficiently and at a required safety level, without breaking down. In order for this to occur, the car needs to be regularly serviced, have tune-ups and incur any other routine checks. Costs associated with keeping the item of property, plant and equipment at the required working condition are expensed, and not added to the depreciable cost of the asset. These costs are generally referred to as repairs and maintenance.

Similar examples can be seen with other assets, such as escalators that need to be regularly maintained to ensure they achieve the basic task of moving passengers from one level to another. Most items of plant with moving parts require some form of regular maintenance. Paragraph 12 of IAS 16 notes the existence of these 'repairs and maintenance' costs, stating that these costs should not be capitalised into the cost of the asset. These costs relate to the day-to-day servicing of the asset and consist mainly of labour and consumables, but may also include the cost of small parts. Costs of repairs and maintenance are expensed as incurred.

After acquisition, management may also outlay funds refining the ability of the asset to operate. These are not outlays associated with repairs, maintenance or replacement. Examples of such expenditures relate to outlays designed to increase the remaining useful life of the asset, increase its capacity, improve the quality of the output, and adjust the asset to reduce operating costs.

A decision to capitalise these outlays requires the application of the recognition principle in paragraph 7 of IAS 16. Capitalisation requires there to be an increase in probable future economic benefits associated with the asset; that is, it should be probable that the expenditure increases the future economic benefits embodied in the asset in excess of its standard of performance assessed at the time the expenditure is made. Note the timing of the assessment process: at the time the expenditure is increased. The comparison is not with the original capacity to operate or the expected future benefits at acquisition, but with the capacity existing at the time the subsequent expenditure is incurred. Hence, if the capacity of the asset had reduced over time, expenditure to revive the asset to its original capacity would be capitalised. The assessment of capacity requires judgement, and needs to take into account matters such as the level of maintenance performed before the incurrence of the subsequent expenditure. The latter could not include the costs of any as yet unperformed maintenance work.

11.5.1 Depreciation

Under the cost model, after initial recognition, an asset continues to be recorded at its original cost. The subsequent carrying amount is determined after adjustments are made only for depreciation and impairment losses. (Impairment losses are discussed in chapter 15.) The main point of the following discussion is to determine the depreciation in relation to an item of property, plant and equipment.

In order to understand the accounting principles for depreciation, it is necessary to consider the definitions of depreciation, depreciable amount, useful life and residual value contained in paragraph 6 of IAS 16:

Depreciation is the systematic allocation of the depreciable amount of an asset over its useful life.

Depreciable amount is the cost of an asset, or other amount substituted for cost, less its residual value.

The *residual value* of an asset is the estimated amount that an entity would currently obtain from disposal of the asset, after deducting the estimated costs of disposal, if the asset were already of the age and in the condition expected at the end of its useful life.

Useful life is:
(a) the period over which an asset is expected to be available for use by an entity; or
(b) the number of production or similar units expected to be obtained from the asset by an entity.

Process of allocation

Depreciation is a process of allocation. Assets by definition are expected future benefits and, as noted in section 11.2, the initial recognition of an item of property, plant and equipment requires that it is probable that the future benefits will flow to the entity. On acquiring these benefits, an entity will have expectations as to the period over which these benefits are to be received and the pattern of these benefits (e.g. they could be received evenly over the life of the asset). The purpose of determining the depreciation charge for the period is to measure the consumption of benefits allocable to the current period, ensuring that, over the useful life of the asset, each period will be allocated its fair share of the cost of the asset acquired. This principle is found in paragraphs 50 and 60 of IAS 16:

50 The depreciable amount of an asset shall be allocated on a systematic basis over its useful life.

60 The depreciation method used shall reflect the pattern in which the asset's future economic benefits are expected to be consumed by the entity.

It could be argued that there are two concepts of depreciation, namely:
• a process of allocation
• a change in the value of an asset.

There are at least three variables that cause a change in value of an asset over the period:
1. a reduction in value owing to the use of the asset over the period
2. an increase/decrease in the value owing to a change in the general price level
3. a change in the specific price level for this type of asset.

When depreciation is calculated as an allocation of the cost of the asset, what is being measured is variable (1). If an asset is measured at a revalued amount such as its fair value, and if depreciation is measured as the change in the fair value over the period, then the amount calculated will be a mixture of all the variables. If the increase in price levels is so high that the fair value of an asset increases over the period, then there will be no depreciation calculated at all.

By describing depreciation as a process of allocation, the IASB is effectively arguing that an increase in value is not sufficient justification for not depreciating an asset. The IASB wants to consider separately the consumption of benefits and the changes in value over a period. In its 1996 discussion paper, *Measurement of Tangible Fixed Assets*, the Accounting Standards Board in the United Kingdom provided the following example (paragraph 5.15) to illustrate the difference between consumption and changes in value:

> Even where there are no general price changes, a change in the value of a tangible asset might still not reflect the consumption of economic benefits of the asset. For example, the drop in value of a new car during its first year would be unlikely to equate to the consumption of economic benefits of the car during the same period resulting from the use of the car. This difference occurs because the price change reflects the market's evaluation of the decline in economic benefits, which may differ from that made by a business. In this example the price change reflects the market's evaluation of the additional economic benefits a new car has over a second-hand car (e.g. the purchaser of a new car can specify exactly what features he wants while the purchaser of a second-hand car cannot, a new car has a known history etc.), but does not reflect the business's evaluation of the remaining economic benefits.

Under IAS 16, the depreciation charge for the period reflects the consumption of the economic benefits over the period and ignores the fall in the asset's fair value. As paragraph 52 of the standard states, depreciation is recognised even if the fair value of an asset is greater than its carrying amount (which is the amount at which an asset is recognised after deducting any accumulated depreciation and accumulated impairment losses). However, depreciation is not recognised if the asset's residual value exceeds the carrying amount.

As noted later in this chapter, where a revalued amount is used rather than cost, the depreciation charge affects current period income, and an increase in the value of the asset affects revaluation surplus. If both amounts affected income, then it would be important to determine whether it is useful to try to measure separately the two components of the change in value of the asset. If depreciation is capitalised into the cost of production, it may be argued that only the amount relating to the consumption of benefits should affect the cost of inventory produced.

Methods of depreciation

The accounting policy that an entity must adopt for depreciation is specified in paragraphs 50 and 60 of IAS 16, namely the systematic allocation of the cost or other revalued amount of an asset over its useful life in a manner that reflects the pattern in which the asset's future economic benefits are expected to be consumed. There are many methods of allocation, depending on the pattern of benefits. Paragraph 62 of the standard notes three methods:

- *Straight-line method.* This is used where the benefits are expected to be received evenly over the useful life of the asset. The depreciation charge for the period is calculated as:

$$\frac{\text{Depreciable amount}}{\text{Useful life}} = \frac{\text{Cost } less \text{ residual value}}{\text{Useful life}}$$

If an item of plant had an original cost of $100 000, a residual value of $10 000, and a useful life of 4 years, the depreciation charge each year is:

$$\text{Depreciation expense p.a.} = \tfrac{1}{4}(\$100\,000 - \$10\,000)$$
$$= \$22\,500$$

The journal entry is:

Depreciation Expense – Plant		Dr	22 500
Accumulated Depreciation – Plant		Cr	22 500
(Depreciation on plant per annum)			

Note that both the residual value and the useful life may change during the life of the asset as expectations change.

- *Diminishing-balance method.* This method is used where the pattern of benefits is such that more benefits are received in the earlier years in the life of the asset. As the asset increases in age, the benefits each year are expected to reduce.

  It is possible to calculate a rate of depreciation that would result in the depreciable amount being written off over the useful life, with the depreciation charge each year being calculated by multiplying the rate by the carrying amount at the beginning of the year. The formula is:

$$\text{Depreciation rate} = 1 - \sqrt[n]{\frac{r}{c}}$$

where n = useful life
         r = residual value
         c = cost or other revalued amount

Using the same information as in the example for the straight-line method, the depreciation rate under the diminishing-balance method is:

$$\text{Depreciation rate} = 1 - \sqrt[4]{\frac{10\,000}{100\,000}}$$

$$= 44\% \text{ approximately}$$

The depreciation expense each year following acquisition of the item of plant at the beginning of the first year is:

Year 1 depreciation expense = 44% × $100 000	= $ 44 000
Year 2 depreciation expense = 44% × $56 000	= $ 24 640
Year 3 depreciation expense = 44% × $31 360	= $ 13 798
Year 4 depreciation expense = $13 798 − $10 000	= $ 3 798

The depreciation charge then reflects a decreasing pattern of benefits over the asset's useful life.

- *Units-of-production method.* This method is based on the expected use or output of the asset. Variables used could be production hours or production output.

  Using the above example again, assume that over the 4-year life of the asset the expected output of the asset is as follows:

Year 1	17 000 units
Year 2	15 000 units
Year 3	12 000 units
Year 4	6 000 units
	50 000 units

The depreciation expense in each of the 4 years is:

Year 1 depreciation expense = 17/50 × $90 000 = $ 30 600
Year 2 depreciation expense = 15/50 × $90 000 = $ 27 000
Year 3 depreciation expense = 12/50 × $90 000 = $ 21 600
Year 4 depreciation expense = 6/50 × $90 000 = $ 10 800
$ 90 000

IAS 16 does not specify the use of any specific method of depreciation. The method chosen by an entity should be based on which method most closely reflects the expected pattern of consumption of the future economic benefits embodied in the asset.

Paragraph 61 of IAS 16 requires an entity to review the depreciation method chosen to ensure that it is providing the appropriate systematic allocation of benefits. The review process should occur at least at the end of each financial year. If there has been a change in the pattern of benefits such that the current method is inappropriate, the method should be changed to one that reflects the changed pattern of benefits. This change is not a change in an accounting policy, simply a change in accounting method. As such it is accounted for as a change in an accounting estimate, with the application of IAS 8. Under paragraph 36 of IAS 8, the change is recognised prospectively with adjustments being made to the amounts recognised in the current period and future periods as appropriate.

The depreciation method is applied from the date the asset is available for use; that is, when it is in the location and condition necessary for it to perform as intended by management. As noted in paragraph 55 of IAS 16, depreciation continues even if the asset is temporarily idle, dependent on movements in residual value and expected useful life. However, under methods such as the units-of-production method, no depreciation is recognised where production ceases.

Useful life

Determination of useful life requires estimation on the part of management, because the way in which an item of property, plant and equipment is used and the potential for changes in the market for that item affect estimates of useful life. Paragraph 56 of IAS 16 provides the following list of factors to consider in determining useful life:

(a) the *expected usage* of the asset by the entity; this is assessed by reference to the asset's expected capacity or physical output
(b) the expected *physical wear and tear*, which depends on operational factors such as the number of work shifts for which the asset will be used and the repair and maintenance program of the entity, and the care and the maintenance of the asset while it is idle
(c) *technical or commercial obsolescence* arising from changes or improvements in production, or from a change in the market demand for the product or service output of the asset. For example, computers may be regarded as having a relatively short useful life. The actual period over which they may be expected to work is probably considerably longer than the period over which they may be considered to be technologically efficient. The useful life for depreciation purposes is related to the period over which the entity intends to use them, which is probably closer to their technological life than the period over which they would be capable of being used
(d) *legal or similar limits* on the use of the asset, such as expiry dates of related leases.

There is no necessary relationship between useful life to the entity and the economic life of the asset. Management may want to hold only relatively new assets, and a policy of replacement after specified periods of time may mean that assets are held for only a proportion of their economic lives. In other words, useful life for the purpose of calculating depreciation is defined in terms of the asset's expected usefulness to the entity. As noted earlier, the useful life of an asset covers the entire time the asset is available for use, including the time the asset is idle but available for use.

As noted in paragraph 58 of IAS 16, land is a special type of asset. Unless the land is being used for a purpose where there is a limited life imposed on the land, such as a quarry, it is assumed to have an unlimited life. Such land is not subject to depreciation. Hence, when accounting for land and buildings, these assets are dealt with separately so that buildings are made subject to depreciation. If, however, the cost of land includes the expected costs of dismantling, removal or restoration, then these costs are depreciated over the period in which the benefits from use of the land are received.

Just as the depreciation method requires a periodic review, so the useful life of an asset is subject to review. According to paragraph 51 of IAS 16, the review should occur at least at each financial year-end. A change in the assessment of the useful life will result in a change in the depreciation rate used. As this is a change in accounting estimate, changes are made prospectively in accordance with IAS 8 paragraph 36.

ILLUSTRATIVE EXAMPLE 11.1 Assessment of useful life

An entity is in the business of making camera lenses. The machine used in this process is very well made, and could be expected to provide a service in making the lenses currently demanded for another 20 years. As the machine is computer-driven, the efficiency of making lenses is affected by the sophistication of the computer program to define what is required in a lens. Technological advances are being made all the time, and it is thought that a new machine with advanced technology will be available within the next 5 years. The type of lens required is also a function of what cameras are considered to be in demand by consumers. Even if there is a change in technology, it is thought that cameras with the old style lens could still be marketable for another 7 years.

Required

What useful life should management use in calculating depreciation on the machine?

Solution

Three specific time periods are mentioned:
- physical life: 20 years
- technical life: 5 years
- commercial life: 7 years.

A key element in determining the appropriate life is assessing the strategy used by management in marketing its products. If management believes that to retain market share and reputation it needs to be at the cutting edge of technology, 5 years will be appropriate. If, however, the marketing strategy is aimed at the general conusmer, 7 years will be appropriate. In essence, management needs to consider at what point it expects to replace the machine.

Residual value

Note again the definition of residual value in paragraph 6 of IAS 16:

> The *residual value* of an asset is the estimated amount that the entity would currently obtain from disposal of the asset, after deducting the estimated costs of disposal, if the asset were already of the age and in the condition expected at the end of its useful life.

Residual value is an estimate based on what the entity would currently obtain from the asset's disposal; that is, what could be obtained at the time of the estimate — not at the expected date of disposal at the end of the useful life. The estimate is based on what could be obtained from disposal of similar assets that are currently, at the date of the estimate, at the end of their useful lives, and which have been used in a similar fashion to the asset being investigated. Where assets are unique, this estimation process is much more difficult than for assets that are constantly being replaced. For an asset such as a vehicle, which may have a useful life of 10 years, the residual value of a new vehicle is the net amount that could be obtained now for a 10-year-old vehicle of the same type as the one being depreciated. In many cases, the residual value will be negligible or scrap value.

This form of assessment means that the residual value will not be adjusted for expected changes in prices. Basing the residual value calculation on current prices relates to the adoption in IAS 16 of depreciation as a process of allocating economic benefits. If the residual value were adjusted for future prices, then there may be no measure of benefits consumed during the period as the residual value may exceed the carrying amount at the beginning of the period. It is also debatable whether the residual value should take into account possible technological developments. In relation to computers it may reasonably be expected that there will be such changes within a relatively short period of time, whereas with motor vehicles, trying to predict cars being powered with something other than oil is more difficult. Management is not required to be a predictor of future inventions. Expectations of technological change are already built into current second-hand asset prices. Management should then take into account reasonable changes in technological development and the effect on prices. Where assets are expected to be used for the whole or the majority of their useful lives, the residual values are zero or immaterial in amount.

In paragraphs BC28–BC29 of the Basis for Conclusions on IAS 16, the IASB raises the issue of why an entity deducts an asset's residual value from the cost of the asset for measurement of depreciation. Two reasons are proposed. First, the objective is one of precision; that is, reducing the amount of depreciation so that it reflects the item's net cost. The second is one of economics; that is, stopping depreciation if the entity expects the asset to increase in value by an amount greater than that by which it will diminish. The IASB did not adopt either the net cost or the economic objective completely. Expected increases in value do not override the need to depreciate an asset. An increase in the expected residual value of an asset because of past events affects the depreciable amount; expectations of future changes in residual value other than the effects of expected wear and tear will not.

Where residual values are material, an entity must, under paragraph 51 of IAS 16, review the residual value at each financial year-end. If a change is required, again the change is a change in estimate and is accounted for prospectively as an adjustment to future depreciation.

It is possible that the review of the residual value of an asset may lead to depreciation 'credits'. Consider the following situation:

Asset at cost	$100
Useful life	4 years
Depreciation method	Straight-line
Residual value at acquisition	$60

The entity would then charge depreciation at $10 p.a. If at the start of year 3 the residual value is estimated to be $90, what should the depreciation charge be in years 3 and 4?

At the end of year 2, the carrying amount of the asset is $80, being cost of $100 less 2 years depreciation of $10 p.a. At the start of year 3, there is a change in an estimate, namely to the residual value. Under IAS 8, the change in estimate must be adjusted against the current period and any future periods affected by the change. In this case, both years 3 and 4 are equally affected by the change in the estimated residual value. Hence, in both these years the entity should recognise a depreciation credit of $5 (50% of $90 − $80), with a corresponding debit to accumulated depreciation. The depreciation credit reduces the entity's total depreciation expense for the period.

Significant parts depreciation

It has been mentioned previously in this chapter that a significant parts approach requires an entity to allocate the cost of an asset to its significant parts and account for each part separately; for example, the cost of an aeroplane is allocated to such parts as the frame, the engines and the fittings. According to paragraph 43 of IAS 16, *each part* of an item of property, plant and equipment with a *cost that is significant* in relation to the total cost of the item must be depreciated *separately*. In other words, an entity is required to separate each item of property, plant and equipment into its significant parts, with each part being separately depreciated. Any remainder is also depreciated separately.

Paragraph 13 of the standard discusses the replacement or renewal of the parts of an asset:

> Under the recognition principle in paragraph 7, an entity recognises in the carrying amount of an item of property, plant and equipment the cost of replacing part of such an item when that cost is incurred if the recognition criteria are met. The carrying amount of those parts that are replaced is derecognised in accordance with the derecognition provisions of this Standard (see paragraphs 67–72).

As is consistent with accounting for all separate items of property, plant and equipment, once an acquired asset is separated into the relevant significant parts, if one of those parts needs regular replacing or renewing, the part is generally accounted for as a separate asset. The replaced asset is depreciated over its useful life, and derecognised on replacement.

To illustrate the accounting for parts, consider the case of a building with a roof that periodically needs replacing. If the roof is accounted for as a separate part, then the roof is accounted for as a separate asset and is depreciated separately. On replacement, paragraph 13 of IAS 16 is applied, and the carrying amount (if any) of the old roof is written off. In order for this derecognition to occur, it is necessary to know the original cost of the roof and the depreciation charged to date. The new roof is accounted for as the acquisition of a new asset, assessed under paragraph 7 and, if capitalised as an asset, subsequently depreciated. If, however, the roof is not treated as a separate part from the acquisition date of the building, then on replacement of the roof, the recognition principle in paragraph 7 and the derecognition principle in paragraph 13 also apply. An entity cannot carry both the replacement and the replaced portion as assets. Calculation of the amount to be derecognised is more difficult where no separate part is recognised because the depreciation of the building has not been separated from the depreciation of the roof.

Another example of dealing with a part of an asset arises where assets are subject to regular major inspections to ensure that they reach the requisite safety and quality requirements. Under paragraph 14 of IAS 16, such major inspections may be capitalised as a replacement part. In order for the cost of the inspection to be capitalised, the recognition criteria in paragraph 7 of the standard must be met. In particular, it must be probable that future economic benefits associated with the outlay will flow to the entity. For example, if there is a 5-year inspection of aircraft by a specific party, and this is required every 5 years in order for the plane not to be grounded, then the cost of the inspection provides benefits to the owner of the aircraft for that period of time by effectively providing a licence to continue flying. The capitalised amount is then depreciated over the relevant useful life, most probably the time until the next inspection.

11.6 THE REVALUATION MODEL

Use of the revaluation model of measurement is the alternative treatment to the cost model. Paragraph 31 of IAS 16 states:

> After recognition as an asset, an item of property, plant and equipment whose fair value can be measured reliably shall be carried at a revalued amount, being its fair value at the date of the revaluation less any subsequent accumulated depreciation and subsequent accumulated impairment losses. Revaluations shall be made with sufficient regularity to ensure that the carrying amount does not differ materially from that which would be determined using fair value at the end of the reporting period.

In relation to this paragraph, note the following points:

1. The measurement basis is fair value, defined in Appendix A of IFRS 13 *Fair Value Measurement* as 'the price that would be received to sell an asset or paid to transfer a liability in an orderly transaction between market participants at the measurement date'. Fair value is an exit price and is measured in accordance with IFRS 13. Under this standard, there are a number of methods that may be used to measure fair value such as the market approach, the cost approach and the income approach. There are also a variety of inputs to these valuation techniques which are prioritised into three levels — Level 1, Level 2 and Level 3. This fair value hierarchy gives highest priority to observable inputs rather than unobservable inputs. See chapter 3 for more information on fair value measurement.

2. IAS 16 does not specify how often revaluations must take place. The principle established is that the revaluations must be of sufficient regularity such that the carrying amount of the asset does not materially differ from fair value. The frequency of revaluations depends on the nature of the assets themselves. For some assets, frequent revaluations are necessary because of continual change in the fair values owing to a volatile market. For other assets, revaluation every 3 or 5 years may be appropriate (paragraph 34). Paragraph 38 notes that assets may be revalued on a rolling basis provided that the total revaluation is completed within a short period of time, and that at no time is the total carrying amount of the class of assets materially different from fair value.

3. To understand the type of information that might be observed in determining whether there is a need to revalue an asset, it is useful to note the inputs into the valuation techniques. For example, in paragraph B35(g) of IFRS 13, in relation to buildings held and used, it is noted that a Level 2 input would be the price per square metre for the building derived from observable market data; for example, multiples derived from process in observed transactions involving comparable or similar buildings in similar locations.

Paragraph 36 of IAS 16 notes that the revaluation model is not applied to individual items of property, plant and equipment; instead, the accounting policy is applied to a class of assets. Hence, for each class of assets, management must choose whether to apply the cost model or the revaluation model.

A class of property, plant and equipment 'is a grouping of assets of a similar nature and use in an entity's operations' (IAS 16 paragraph 37). Examples of separate classes are:

- land
- land and buildings
- machinery
- ships
- aircraft
- motor vehicles
- furniture and fixtures
- office equipment.

There are two purposes for requiring revaluation to be done on a class rather than on an individual asset basis. First, this limits the ability of management to 'cherry-pick' or selectively choose which assets to revalue. Second, the requirement to have all assets within the class measured on a fair value basis means that there is consistent measurement for the same type of assets in the entity.

According to paragraph 31 of IAS 16, where an asset is carried at a revalued amount, recognition of the asset should occur only when the fair value can be measured reliably. One question arising here is that, if a class of assets is being carried at fair value but there are assets within that class for which the fair value cannot be reliably measured, should those assets be written off because the recognition criteria cannot be met? The problem is that writing off these assets provides less relevant information than including the assets at cost.

The question then is whether, in order to be able to adopt the revaluation model, the fair values need to be capable of being reliably measured for all assets within the class. The problem with allowing some assets within a class to be at fair value and others at cost is that an entity can cherry-pick which assets are going to be measured at what amount. This amounts to selective revaluation. The only way to stop selective revaluation is for the standard setters to require the use of the fair value method only where *all* assets within the class can be reliably measured at fair value.

11.6.1 Applying the revaluation model: revaluation increases

Paragraphs 39 and 40 of IAS 16 contain the principles for applying the fair value method to revaluation increases. These paragraphs apply to individual items of property, plant and equipment. In other words, even though revaluations are done on a class-by-class basis, the accounting is done on an asset-by-asset basis.

The first part of paragraph 39 states:

> If an asset's carrying amount is increased as a result of a revaluation, the increase shall be recognised in other comprehensive income and accumulated in equity under the heading of revaluation surplus.

Note two points here:

1. *The increase is recognised in comprehensive income.* In the statement of profit or loss and other comprehensive income, the comprehensive income for a period is divided into profit or loss (P/L) for the period and other comprehensive income (OCI). Revaluation increases are recognised in other comprehensive income, not profit or loss. An example of a statement of profit or loss and other comprehensive income showing the disclosure of profit for the year separately from the other comprehensive income items is given in figure 11.2.

FIGURE 11.2 Statement of profit or loss and other comprehensive income

XYZ GROUP Statement of Profit or Loss and Other Comprehensive Income for the year ended 31 December 20X7		
(illustrating the presentation of profit or loss and other comprehensive income in one statement and the classification of expenses within profit by function) *(in thousands of currency units)*		
	20X7	**20X6**
Revenue	390 000	355 000
Cost of sales	(245 000)	(230 000)
Gross profit	145 000	125 000
Other income	20 667	11 300
Distribution costs	(9 000)	(8 700)
Administrative expenses	(20 000)	(21 000)
Other expenses	(2 100)	(1 200)
Finance costs	(8 000)	(7 500)
Share of profit of associates	35 100	30 100
Profit before tax	161 667	128 000
Income tax expense	(40 417)	(32 000)
Profit for the year from continuing operations	121 250	96 000
Loss for the year from discontinued operations	—	(30 500)
Profit for the year	121 250	65 500
Other comprehensive income		
Items that will not be reclassified to profit or loss		
Gains on property revaluation	933	3 367
Actuarial gains (losses) on defined benefit pension plans	(667)	1 333
Share of gain (loss) on property revaluation of associates	400	(700)
Income tax relating to items that will not be reclassified	(166)	(1 000)
	500	3 000

FIGURE 11.2 *(continued)*

	20X7	20X6
Items that may be reclassified subsequently to profit or loss		
Exchange differences on translating foreign operations	5 334	10 667
Available-for-sale financial assets	(24 000)	26 667
Cash flow hedges	(667)	(4 000)
Income tax relating to items that may be reclassified	4 833	(8 334)
	(14 500)	25 000
Other comprehensive income for the year, net of tax	(14 000)	28 000
TOTAL COMPREHENSIVE INCOME FOR THE YEAR	107 250	93 500

Source: IASB (2011, p. B1026).

Hence the initial journal entry for a revaluation increase is:

Asset	Dr	xxx	
Gain on Revaluation of Non-Current Asset (OCI)	Cr		xxx
(Revaluation of asset)			

In accordance with paragraph 42 of IAS 16, the effects of any taxes on income need to be accounted for in accordance with IAS 12 *Income Taxes*. A revaluation of an asset causes a change between the tax base and the carrying amount of the asset, giving rise to a temporary difference, and a deferred tax liability needs to be raised (see paragraph 20 of IAS 1). Paragraph 90 of IAS 1 *Presentation of Financial Statements* requires the disclosure of 'the amount of income tax relating to each item of other comprehensive income'. To reflect the tax effect of the gain, the required entry is:

Income Tax Expense – Gain on Revaluation of Asset (OCI)	Dr	xxx	
Deferred Tax Liability	Cr		xxx
(Recognition of tax effect of revaluation increase)			

The reason for the immediate recognition of the deferred tax effect is because, as explained below, the gain on revaluation of non-current assets is accumulated in equity.

2. Having recognised the gain in other comprehensive income, the gain, net of tax, is transferred to equity under the heading of revaluation surplus. The required entry is:

Gain on Revaluation of Non-Current Asset (OCI)	Dr	xxx	
Income Tax Expense (OCI)	Cr		xxx
Asset Revaluation Surplus	Cr		xxx
(Accumulation of net revaluation gain in equity)			

The asset revaluation surplus is disclosed in the reserve section of the statement of financial position.

ILLUSTRATIVE EXAMPLE 11.2 Revaluation increases and tax effect

On 1 January 2014, an entity carries an item of land at a cost of $100 000, this amount also being the tax base of the asset. The land is revalued to $120 000. The tax rate is 30%.

The tax base of the asset is $100 000 and the new carrying amount is $120 000, giving rise to a taxable temporary difference of $20 000. A deferred tax liability of $6000 must be raised to account for the expected tax to be paid in relation to the increase in expected benefits from the asset. The asset revaluation surplus raised will be the net after-tax increase in the asset ($20 000 − $6000 = $14 000). The appropriate accounting entries on revaluation of the asset are shown in figure 11.3.

Land	Dr	20 000	
Gain on Revaluation of Land (OCI)	Cr		20 000
(Recognition of revaluation increase: $120 000 – $100 000)			
Income Tax Expense (OCI)	Dr	6 000	
Deferred Tax Liability	Cr		6 000
(Tax effect of revaluation of land)			
Gain on Revaluation of Land (OCI)	Dr	20 000	
Income Tax Expense (OCI)	Cr		6 000
Asset Revaluation Surplus	Cr		14 000
(Accumulation of net revaluation gain in equity)			

FIGURE 11.3 Journal entries for revaluation with associated tax effect

Where the item of property, plant and equipment is depreciable, there are two possible accounting treatments under paragraph 35 of IAS 16:

1. restate proportionately with the change in the gross carrying amount of the asset so that the carrying amount of the asset after revaluation equals its revalued amount; or
2. eliminate the accumulated depreciation balance against the gross carrying amount of the asset and then restate the net amount to the fair value of the asset. This method is applied in this chapter.

ILLUSTRATIVE EXAMPLE 11.3 Revaluation increases and depreciable assets

On 30 June 2013, an item of plant has a carrying amount of $42 000, being the original cost of $70 000 less accumulated depreciation of $28 000. The fair value of the asset is $50 000. The tax rate is 30%. The entries are shown in figure 11.4.

The revaluation is done in two steps:
The *first* step is to write off the accumulated depreciation of the plant, reducing the asset to its carrying amount of $42 000.

Accumulated Depreciation	Dr	28 000	
Plant	Cr		28 000
(Write down asset to its carrying amount)			

The *second* step is to adjust the carrying amount of $42 000 to the fair value of the asset, $50 000, being an increase of $8000. This increase is tax-effected, and the net gain accumulated to equity.

Plant	Dr	8 000	
Gain on Revaluation of Plant (OCI)	Cr		8 000
(Revaluation of asset to fair value)			
Income Tax Expense (OCI)	Dr	2 400	
Deferred Tax Liability	Cr		2 400
(Tax effect of revaluation increase)			
Gain on Revaluation of Plant (OCI)	Dr	8 000	
Income Tax Expense (OCI)	Cr		2 400
Asset Revaluation Surplus	Cr		5 600
(Accumulation of net revaluation gain in equity)			

FIGURE 11.4 Revaluation increase and depreciable assets

Assume that the depreciable asset in illustrative example 11.3 was acquired for $70 000 on 1 July 2012 to be used in the business. Depreciation rates are on a straight-line basis at 20% p.a. for accounting and 35% for tax. The tax rate is 30%.

On 30 June 2013, the carrying amount and the tax base of the asset are as follows:

	Accounting	Tax
Original cost	$ 70 000	$ 70 000
Accumulated depreciation	(14 000)	(24 500)
Net amount	56 000	45 500

Hence, the taxable temporary difference at 30 June 2013 is $10 500 ($56 000 – $45 500), with a deferred tax liability of $3150 being recognised.

On 30 June 2014, the asset has a carrying amount and tax base as follows:

	Accounting	Tax
Original cost	$ 70 000	$ 70 000
Accumulated depreciation	(28 000)	(49 000)
Net amount	42 000	21 000

Assume that on this date the asset is revalued to $50 000. The appropriate entries are:

2014				
June 30	Accumulated Depreciation	Dr	28 000	
	Plant	Cr		28 000
	(Write down asset to its carrying amount)			
	Plant	Dr	8 000	
	Gain on Revaluation of Plant (OCI)	Cr		8 000
	(Revaluation of asset to fair value)			
	Income Tax Expense (OCI)	Dr	2 400	
	Deferred Tax Liability	Cr		2 400
	(Tax effect of revaluation increase)			
	Gain on Revaluation of Plant (OCI)	Dr	8 000	
	Income Tax Expense (OCI)	Cr		2 400
	Asset Revaluation Surplus	Cr		5 600
	(Accumulation of net revaluation gain in equity)			

For the purpose of determining required entries for tax-effect accounting at the end of the year, the carrying amount of the asset on 30 June 2014 in the accounting records is now $50 000, but its tax base is unchanged at $21 000. This gives a taxable temporary difference of $29 000, and a total deferred tax liability of $8700 at a 30% tax rate. Since $2400 of the deferred tax liability is already recognised in the revaluation entry above, the total credit to the deferred tax liability needs to be only $6300. As the beginning deferred tax liability for the year is $3150, the adjustment required in the current year ending 30 June 2014 is $3150 ($6300 – $3150). In order to recognise the adjustment to the deferred tax liability, the appropriate entry is as follows:

2014				
June 30	Income Tax Expense	Dr	3 150	
	Deferred Tax Liability	Cr		3 150
	(Recognition of deferred tax liability)			

The tax-effect worksheet is shown in figure 11.5.

	Carrying amount	Taxable amount	Deductible amount	Tax base	Taxable temporary differences	Deductible temporary differences
Plant	$50 000	$(50 000)	$21 000	$21 000	$29 000	
Temporary difference					29 000	
Deferred tax liability — closing balance					8 700 Dr	
Beginning balance					3 150 Cr	
Movement during the year					2 400 Cr	
Adjustment					3 150 Cr	

FIGURE 11.5 Tax-effect worksheet on revaluation of assets

Revaluation increase reversing previous revaluation decrease

The full text of paragraph 39 of IAS 16 is as follows:

> If an asset's carrying amount is increased as a result of a revaluation, the increase shall be recognised in other comprehensive income and accumulated in equity under the heading of revaluation surplus. However, the increase shall be recognised in profit or loss to the extent that it reverses a revaluation decrease of the same asset previously recognised in profit or loss.

Hence, a revaluation increase is credited to an asset revaluation surplus unless the increase reverses a revaluation decrease previously recognised as an expense. The accounting treatment for revaluation decreases is discussed in the next section, and illustrative example 11.7 on pages 378–9 demonstrates entries for this situation.

11.6.2 Applying the revaluation model: revaluation decreases

Paragraph 40 of IAS 16 states:

> If an asset's carrying amount is decreased as a result of a revaluation, the decrease shall be recognised in profit or loss. However, the decrease shall be recognised in other comprehensive income to the extent of any credit balance existing in the revaluation surplus in respect of that asset.

As with revaluation increases, this paragraph covers two situations: a revaluation decrease, and a revaluation decrease following a previous revaluation increase.

The accounting for a revaluation decrease involves an immediate recognition of a loss in the period of the revaluation. As the change in the carrying amount of the asset directly affects income, the tax effect is dealt with in the normal workings of tax-effect accounting. Hence, no extra tax-effect entries outside those generated via the tax-effect worksheet are necessary in accounting for revaluation decrease.

ILLUSTRATIVE EXAMPLE 11.5 Revaluation decrease

Assume an item of plant has a carrying amount of $50 000, being original cost of $60 000 less accumulated depreciation of $10 000. If the asset is revalued downwards to $24 000, the appropriate journal entries are:

Accumulated Depreciation	Dr	10 000	
Plant	Cr		10 000
(Write down asset to its carrying amount of $50 000)			
Loss – Downward Revaluation of Plant (P/L)	Dr	26 000	
Plant	Cr		26 000
(Revaluation of asset from carrying amount of $50 000 to fair value of $24 000)			

In relation to the tax-effect worksheet, if the carrying amount and the tax base in this example were the same immediately before the revaluation, then there would be a deductible temporary difference of $26 000. A deferred tax asset of $7800 would be raised via the tax-effect worksheet analysis at the end of the reporting period.

Decrease reversing previous revaluation increase

Where an asset revaluation surplus has been raised via a previous revaluation increase, in accounting for a subsequent revaluation decrease for the same asset, the surplus must be eliminated before any expense is recognised. In adjusting for the previous revaluation increase, both the asset revaluation surplus and the related deferred tax liability must be reversed.

ILLUSTRATIVE EXAMPLE 11.6 Decrease reversing previous increase

Assume an entity has a block of land with a carrying amount of $200 000. When the land was revalued upwards from $100 000, the following entries were passed:

Land	Dr	100 000	
Gain on Revaluation of Land (OCI)	Cr		100 000
(Revaluation of asset to fair value)			
Income Tax Expense (OCI)	Dr	30 000	
Deferred Tax Liability	Cr		30 000
(Tax effect of revaluation increase)			
Gain on Revaluation of Land (OCI)	Dr	100 000	
Income Tax Expense (OCI)	Cr		30 000
Asset Revaluation Surplus	Cr		70 000
(Accumulation of net revaluation gain in equity)			

If the asset is *revalued downwards* to $160 000, the $40 000 write-down is a partial reversal of the previous upward revaluation. The accounting entries then reflect:
- a recognition of the decrease on other comprehensive income, and
- a decrease in accumulated equity, namely, asset revaluation surplus.

Loss on Revaluation of Land (OCI)	Dr	40 000	
Land	Cr		40 000
(Revaluation downwards of land)			
Deferred Tax Liability	Dr	12 000	
Income Tax Expense (OCI)	Cr		12 000
(Tax effect of revaluation decrease)			
Asset Revaluation Surplus	Dr	28 000	
Income Tax Expense (OCI)	Dr	12 000	
Loss on Revaluation of Land (OCI)	Cr		40 000
(Reduction in accumulated equity due to revaluation decrease on land)			

If the asset is *revalued downwards to $80 000*, which is a reduction of $120 000, the asset is written down to an amount $20 000 less than the original cost of the asset.

In accordance with paragraph 40, the downward revaluation requires a loss to be recognised in profit or loss, as well as a decrease to be recognised in other comprehensive income. Effectively this will result in the elimination of the deferred tax liability and the asset revaluation surplus previously raised. The appropriate entries are:

Loss on Revaluation of Land (P/L)	Dr	20 000	
Loss on Revaluation of Land (OCI)	Dr	100 000	
Land	Cr		120 000
(Revaluation downwards of land)			
Deferred Tax Liability	Dr	30 000	
Income Tax Expense (OCI)	Cr		30 000
(Tax effect of loss on revaluation of land)			
Asset Revaluation Surplus	Dr	70 000	
Income Tax Expense (OCI)	Dr	30 000	
Loss on Revaluation of Land (OCI)	Cr		100 000
(Reduction in accumulated equity due to revaluation decrease on land)			

The tax-effect worksheet, assuming the original revaluation increase occurred in a previous period, is shown in figure 11.6.

	Carrying amount	Taxable amount	Deductible amount	Tax base	Taxable temporary differences	Deductible temporary differences
Land	$80 000	$(80 000)	$100 000	$100 000		$20 000
Temporary difference						20 000
Deferred tax liability — closing balance						
Deferred tax asset — closing balance						6 000 Cr
Beginning balance					$30 000 Cr	
Movement during the year					30 000 Dr	
Adjustment						6 000 Dr

FIGURE 11.6 Tax-effect worksheet on revaluation of assets

The tax-effect worksheet shows that the entity would recognise a deferred tax asset of $6000, reflecting the fact that the carrying amount of the asset is $20 000 less than the tax base.

Net revaluation increase reversing previous revaluation decrease

Where an asset is revalued upwards, an asset revaluation surplus is credited except where the increase reverses a revaluation decrease previously recognised as a loss. In this case, the revaluation increase must be recognised as a gain.

ILLUSTRATIVE EXAMPLE 11.7 Revaluation increase reversing previous decrease

Assume an entity has an item of plant whose current carrying amount is $200 000 (accumulated depreciation being $20 000). The asset had cost $300 000. It was revalued downwards from a carrying amount of $270 000 to $220 000, with the following accounting entries being passed:

Accumulated Depreciation	Dr	30 000	
Plant	Cr		30 000
(Write down asset to its carrying amount of $270 000)			

Loss – Downward Revaluation of Plant (P/L) Plant (Revaluation of asset from carrying amount of $270 000 to fair value of $220 000)	Dr Cr	50 000	50 000

If the asset is assessed as having a *fair value* of $230 000, there is a revaluation increase of $30 000. However as there was a previous decrease of $50 000, the appropriate revaluation entry must reverse part of this previously recognised revaluation loss. The entries are:

Accumulated Depreciation Plant (Write down asset to its carrying amount of $200 000)	Dr Cr	20 000	20 000
Plant Gain on Revaluation of Plant (P/L) (Revaluation of asset from carrying amount of $200 000 to fair value of $230 000, subsequent to prior write-down of the asset)	Dr Cr	30 000	30 000

If the asset is assessed as having a *fair value* of $280 000, the accounting entries recognise the increase of $80 000 as consisting of two parts:
1. the reversal of the previously recognised write-down loss of $50 000; the reversal is recognised as a gain, and disclosed in profit or loss
2. the $30 000 increase recognised in other comprehensive income and accumulated in asset revaluation surplus.

The entries are:

Accumulated Depreciation Plant (Write down asset to its carrying amount of $200 000)	Dr Cr	20 000	20 000

Plant
   Gain on Revaluation of Plant (P/L)
   Gain on Revaluation of Plant (OCI)
(Revaluation of plant from carrying amount of $200 000 to fair value of $280 000)
	Dr
	Cr
	Cr
		80 000	50 000
			30 000

Income Tax Expense (OCI) Deferred Tax Liability (Tax effect of revaluation gain)	Dr Cr	9 000	9 000

Gain on Revaluation of Plant (OCI)
   Income Tax Expense (OCI)
   Asset Revaluation Surplus
(Accumulation of revaluation gain in equity)
	Dr
	Cr
	Cr
		30 000	9 000
			21 000

11.6.3 Effects of accounting on an asset-by-asset basis

If the fair value basis of measurement is chosen, IAS 16 requires it to be applied to items of property, plant and equipment on a class-by-class basis. However, in accounting for revaluation increases and decreases, the accounting is done on an individual asset basis within the class. Practising accountants and standard setters have often argued that a better accounting treatment would be to account for revaluation increases and decreases on a class-by-class basis. The rationale for this is that under IAS 16 revaluation increases [gains] are recognised in other comprehensive income and accumulated in equity while revaluation decreases [losses] are recognised in profit or loss in the period the revaluation occurs. If revaluation was done on a class-by-class basis, then it would be the net increase that would be accounted for, providing a netting of the gains and losses. Figure 11.7 illustrates this.

Assets	Carrying amount $	Fair value $	increase/(decrease) $
Plant A	1 500 000	2 000 000	500 000
Plant B	1 500 000	1 200 000	(300 000)
Total	3 000 000	3 200 000	200 000

FIGURE 11.7 Revaluation by asset or class of asset?

Applying IAS 16, both Plant A and Plant B, being in the one class of assets, have to be revalued to fair value if the revaluation model is applied to plant. However, in accounting for the movements in fair value, each asset is dealt with separately. With Plant A, as there is a revaluation increase of $500, the increase results in a $500 gain being recognised in other comprehensive income and $350 (assuming a tax rate of 30%) being accumulated in equity affecting an asset revaluation surplus. With Plant B, the revaluation decrease of $300 is recognised as an expense affecting current period profit or loss. For those who argue that revaluations should be accounted for on a class-by-class basis, the net revaluation increase on plant is $200. Accounting on a class basis would result in recognising a $200 gain in other comprehensive income and then accumulating $140 in an asset revaluation surplus with no effect on current period profit or loss. The argument for the class method of accounting is that it reduces the biased effect that the IAS 16 method has on current period profit or loss. However the two methods produce the same total comprehensive income for the period.

11.6.4 Applying the revaluation model: transfers from asset revaluation surplus

Paragraph 41 of IAS 16 covers the accounting for the asset revaluation surplus subsequent to its creation. There are two circumstances where the asset revaluation surplus may be transferred to retained earnings. Note that there is no requirement that the asset revaluation surplus must be transferred, only a specification of situations where it may be transferred. The *first* situation is where the asset is derecognised (i.e. removed from the statement of financial position, for example, by sale of the asset). In this case, the whole or part of the surplus may be transferred. The *second* situation is where an asset is being used up over its useful life, a proportion of the revaluation surplus may be transferred to retained earnings, the proportion being in relation to the depreciation on the asset. In this case, the amount of the surplus transferred would be equal to the difference between depreciation based on the original cost, and depreciation based on the revalued amount, adjusted for the tax effect relating to the surplus. This second situation is shown in illustrative example 11.8.

ILLUSTRATIVE EXAMPLE 11.8 Transferring revaluation surplus to retained earnings

Assume an item of plant is acquired for $100 000. The plant is immediately revalued to $120 000. The asset has a useful life of 10 years and the tax rate is 30%.
The revaluation entries are:

Plant	Dr	20 000	
Gain on Revaluation of Plant (OCI)	Cr		20 000
(Revaluation of plant from $100 000 to $120 000)			
Income Tax Expense (OCI)	Dr	6 000	
Deferred Tax Liability	Cr		6 000
(Tax effect of revaluation of plant)			

Gain on Revaluation of Plant (OCI)	Dr	20 000	
Income Tax Expense (OCI)	Cr		6 000
Asset Revaluation Surplus	Cr		14 000
(Accumulation of revaluation gain in equity)			

At the end of the following year, depreciation expense of $12 000 is recorded. As the asset is being used up at 10% p.a., the entity may transfer 10% of the asset revaluation surplus to retained earnings. The entry is:

Asset Revaluation Surplus	Dr	1 400	
Transfer From Asset Revaluation Surplus	Cr		1 400
(Transfer from asset revaluation surplus to retained earnings)			

Transfers from the asset revaluation surplus may also occur where a bonus issue of share capital is made from the asset revaluation surplus. As the surplus is created only via an upward revaluation of assets, it is expected that the standard setters would not allow reinstatement once transfers from the asset revaluation surplus have been made.

ILLUSTRATIVE EXAMPLE 11.9 Bonus share issue from asset revaluation surplus

Assume an entity has an item of plant that was previously revalued from $100 000 to $200 000, giving rise to an asset revaluation surplus of $70 000 and a deferred tax liability of $30 000.

The entity then used $30 000 of the asset revaluation surplus to issue bonus shares, leaving a balance of $40 000 in the asset revaluation surplus. The plant was subsequently written down from a carrying amount of $150 000 to $70 000, a reduction of $80 000. The appropriate journal entries for the downward revaluation are:

Accumulated Depreciation	Dr	50 000	
Plant	Cr		50 000
(Write off accumulated depreciation on revaluation of plant)			

Loss on Revaluation of Plant (OCI)	Dr	80 000	
Plant	Cr		80 000
(Write down of plant from $150 000 to $70 000)			

Deferred Tax Liability	Dr	24 000	
Income Tax Expense (OCI)	Cr		24 000
(Tax effect of loss on revaluation of plant)			

Asset Revaluation Surplus	Dr	40 000	
Income Tax Expense (OCI)	Dr	24 000	
Loss on Revaluation of Plant (P/L)	Dr	16 000	
Loss on Revaluation of Plant (OCI)	Cr		80 000
(Accumulation of revaluation loss to equity)			

In relation to these entries, note the following:
- The balance of $40 000 in the asset revaluation surplus is totally written off. If there had been no prior bonus issue of shares from the asset revaluation surplus, a total of $56 000 would have been debited to the surplus, being 70% × $80 000. However, as the surplus has been reduced due to the bonus issue, the balance of $40 000 is totally written off.
- The deferred tax liability raised when the asset was revalued upwards was unaffected by the bonus issue. Hence, on writing the asset down by $80 000, the deferred tax liability is reduced by $24 000.
- The $16 000 balance in the last entry arises because of the use of the asset revaluation surplus in the bonus issue. It is accounted for as a loss.

A further problem arising from transfers from the asset revaluation surplus in situations such as a bonus issue of shares occurs where a number of assets are being revalued. IAS 16 requires the accounting for the asset revaluation surplus to be done on an asset-by-asset basis. Where there is a bonus issue from the asset revaluation surplus, the entity will have to identify which assets are being affected by the use of the asset revaluation surplus for the bonus issue. Any basis of choosing which assets are affected is purely arbitrary.

11.6.5 Applying the revaluation model: depreciation of revalued assets

Section 11.5.1 of this chapter discusses the accounting treatment for depreciation under IAS 16. As noted, the term 'depreciable amount' includes 'other amount substituted for cost'. This includes fair value. Paragraph 50 of IAS 16 notes that depreciation is a process of allocation. Hence, even though an asset is measured at fair value, depreciation is not determined simply as the change in fair value of the asset over a period. As with the cost method, depreciation for a period is calculated after considering the pattern of economic benefits relating to the asset and the residual value of the asset.

ILLUSTRATIVE EXAMPLE 11.10 Depreciation of revalued assets

Assume an entity has an item of plant that was revalued to $1000 at 30 June 2014. The asset is expected to have a remaining useful life of 5 years, with benefits being received evenly over that period. The residual value is calculated to be $100. Consider two situations.

Situation 1

At 30 June 2015, no formal revaluation occurs and the management of the entity assess that the carrying amount of the plant is not materially different from fair value.
  The appropriate journal entry for the 2014–15 period is:

2015				
June 30	Depreciation Expense	Dr	180	
	Accumulated Depreciation	Cr		180
	(Depreciation on plant 1/5[$1000 − $100])			

  The asset is reported in the statement of financial position at a carrying amount of $820, equal to a gross amount of $1000 less accumulated depreciation of $180, the carrying amount being equal to fair value.

Situation 2

At 30 June 2015, a formal revaluation occurs and the external valuers assess the fair value of the plant to be $890. Tax rate is 30%.
  The appropriate journal entries for the 2014–15 period are:

2015				
June 30	Depreciation Expense	Dr	180	
	Accumulated Depreciation	Cr		180
	(Depreciation on plant 1/5[$1000 − $100])			
	Accumulated Depreciation	Dr	180	
	Plant	Cr		180
	(Write down asset to its carrying amount)			
	Plant	Dr	70	
	Gain on Revaluation of Plant (OCI)	Cr		70
	(Revaluation of plant from $820 to $890)			

Income Tax Expense (OCI)	Dr	21	
Deferred Tax Liability	Cr		21
(Tax effect of revaluation of plant)			
Gain on Revaluation of Plant (OCI)	Dr	70	
Income Tax Expense (OCI)	Cr		21
Asset Revaluation Surplus	Cr		49
(Accumulation of net revaluation gain in equity)			

In other words, there is a two-step process. Depreciation is allocated in accordance with normal depreciation principles. Then, as a formal revaluation occurs, the accumulated depreciation is written off and the asset revalued to fair value. The asset is reported in the statement of financial position at fair value of $890 with no associated accumulated depreciation.

It may be argued that the accounting in situation 2 is inappropriate. Whereas the depreciation charge affects profit or loss, the gain on the revaluation of the asset affects other comprehensive income. The economic benefits in relation to the asset for the period are not only those achieved by consumption of the asset, but also those obtained by changes in the market value of the asset. However, these are accounted for differently under IAS 16. It could then be argued that the appropriate depreciation in situation 2 should be the change in fair value over the period, namely $110 ($1000 – $890), with the journal entry being:

Depreciation Expense	Dr	110	
Accumulated Depreciation	Cr		110
(Depreciation on plant)			

No revaluation entry is then necessary. Note, however, that this entry is not allowed under IAS 16.

Subsequent to revaluation, the entity should reassess the useful life and residual value of the revalued asset because these may change as a result of economic changes affecting the entity and its use of assets. Using the example in scenario 2, following the revaluation at 30 June 2015, assume the entity determines that the residual value is $110 and the remaining useful life is 4 years. In the 2015–16 period, the depreciation entry is:

Depreciation Expense	Dr	195	
Accumulated Depreciation	Cr		195
(Depreciation on plant 1/4[$890 – $110])			

LO7   11.7   CHOOSING BETWEEN THE COST MODEL AND THE REVALUATION MODEL

Given that IAS 16 allows entities a choice between the cost model and the revaluation model, it is of interest to consider what motivates entities to choose between the two measurement models.

Arguments relating to the choice of models generally claim that a current price (a fair value) will provide more relevant information than a past price (the original cost), and that the costs associated with continuously determining the present price reduces the incentive, on a cost–benefit basis, to move to current values. Certainly the requirement under IAS 16 to continuously adjust the carrying amounts of assets measured at fair value so that they are not materially different from current fair values provides a cost disincentive to management to adopt the revaluation model. Costs associated with adopting the revaluation model include the cost of employing valuers, annual costs associated with reviewing the carrying amounts to assess whether a revaluation is necessary, extra record-keeping costs associated with the revaluations, including accounting for the associated revaluation increases and decreases, and increased audit costs relating to the review of changing revalued amounts. In January 2002, Ernst & Young in Australia reported on entities changing valuation methods when it became a requirement in that country for entities using the fair value basis to adopt the equivalent of the current IAS 16 accounting procedures. Previously, entities could revalue assets on an irregular basis rather than keeping the fair values continuously current. Ernst & Young (2002) reported that:

- of the entities surveyed, 40% reported a change in measurement basis for one or more classes of non-current assets
- of those entities reporting a change in the measurement basis, all changed from the fair value basis to the cost basis. No entities changed from the cost basis to the fair value basis.

Ernst & Young (p. 8) argued:

> [t]he number of entities changing measurement basis to cost would appear to indicate that the costs associated with keeping the revaluations up to date at each reporting period outweighs the perceived benefits associated with improved relevance and reliability of financial information by recognising fair value adjustments.

A further factor that influences some entities' measurement choice in favour of the cost model is harmonisation with US GAAP, which does not allow the revaluation of non-current assets.

Another factor that entities have to consider when choosing their measurement bases for classes of property, plant and equipment is the effect of the model on the statement of profit or loss and other comprehensive income. Where assets are measured on a fair value basis, the depreciation per annum is expected to be higher as the depreciable amount is higher. In the 2002 Ernst & Young study (p. 3), it was reported:

> [o]f those entities reverting to original cost as the measurement basis for a class of non-current asset, a reduction in annual depreciation expense (and therefore an increase in profit) ranging from $500 000 to $1.1 million resulted.

Besides the effect of lower depreciation, there will be the effect on the disposal of the asset. Where an asset is measured at fair value, there is expected to be an immaterial amount of profit or loss on sale as, at the time of sale, the recorded amount of the asset should be close to that of the market price. For an asset measured at cost, any gain or loss on sale will be reported in the statement of profit or loss and other comprehensive income.

What, apart from increased relevance and reliability arguments, are the incentives for management to use the revaluation model? The effect of adopting the revaluation model is to increase the entity's assets and equities (via the revaluation surplus). Hence, entities that need to report higher amounts in these areas would consider adoption of the revaluation model. The incentives for entities to adopt fair value measures then tend to be entity-specific because the entities face pressures relating to external circumstances. Examples of such pressures are:

- Entities with debt covenants generally have constraints relating to their debt–asset ratios, such as the requirement that the debt–asset ratio must not exceed 50%. Hence, for an entity with increasing debt, adoption of the revaluation model for a class of assets that is increasing in value will ease pressures on the debt–asset ratio by increasing the asset base of the entity. This assumes that the debt covenant allows revaluations to be taken into account in measuring assets.
- An entity's reported profit figure may be under scrutiny from a specific source, such as a trade union seeking reasons to support claims for higher pay, or regulators looking at monopoly control within an industry.

Where there are pressures to report lower profits, adoption of the revaluation model provides scope for higher depreciation charges. These are reflected in the profit or loss for the period. The increases in the values of the non-current assets do not affect profit or loss but are reported in other comprehensive income. If ratios such as rates of return on assets or equity are based on profit rather than comprehensive income, lower reported profits and higher asset/equity bases will result in an entity being seen in a less favourable light.

However, as noted above, the incentives relating to playing with profit and asset numbers tend to rely on users of the information having no knowledge of accounting rules or movements in prices within industries or sectors, or being unable to make comparisons across entities within an industry segment. One of the key elements of analysing entities within an industry is comparability of information. If all entities in the sector are applying the cost model, analysts can make their judgements by comparing the information between the entities and applying information from sources other than accounting reports, such as movements in price indexes. The entity then has less reason to incur the costs of adopting the revaluation model of measurement.

 ## 11.8 DERECOGNITION

As noted in paragraph 3 of IAS 16, the standard does not apply to non-current assets classified as held for sale and accounted for under IFRS 5. IAS 16 then deals with the disposal of non-current assets that have not previously been classified as held for sale.

Paragraph 67 of IAS 16 identifies two occasions where derecognition of an item of property, plant and equipment should occur:

- on disposal, such as the sale of the asset
- when no future economic benefits are expected, either from future use or from disposal.

When items of property, plant and equipment are sold, regardless of whether there are many or few remaining economic benefits, the selling entity will recognise a gain or loss on the asset, this being determined as the difference between the net proceeds from sale and the carrying amount of the asset at the time of sale (IAS 16 paragraph 71). In calculating the net proceeds from sale, any deferred consideration must be discounted, and the proceeds calculated at the cash price equivalent (IAS 16 paragraph 72). As the carrying amount is net of depreciation and impairment losses, it is necessary to calculate the depreciation from the beginning of the reporting period to the point of sale. Failing to do this, whether under the cost model or the revaluation model, would be out of step with the key principle established in IAS 16 that depreciation is a process of allocation and each period must bear its fair share of the cost or revalued amount of the asset.

The gain or loss on sale is included in the profit or loss for the period. Note paragraph 34 of IAS 1 *Presentation of Financial Statements*:

> IAS 18 *Revenue* defines revenue and requires an entity to measure it at the fair value of the consideration received or receivable, taking into account the amount of any trade discounts and volume rebates the entity allows. An entity undertakes, in the course of its ordinary activities, other transactions that do not generate revenue but are incidental to the main revenue-generating activities. An entity presents the results of such transactions, when this presentation reflects the substance of the transaction or other event, by netting any income with related expenses arising on the same transaction. For example:
> (a) an entity presents gains and losses on the disposal of non-current assets, including investments and operating assets, by deducting from the proceeds on disposal the carrying amount of the asset and related selling expenses; . . .

Paragraph 34 requires only the disclosure of the gain or loss on sale, as opposed to separate disclosure of the income and the carrying amount of the asset (see also paragraph 98(c) of IAS 1). The argument for the netting of the income and expense is that gains/losses on the disposal of property, plant and equipment result from activities that are not considered to be the main revenue-generating activities of an entity.

In paragraph BC35 of the Basis of Conclusions on IAS 16, the IASB argued:

> users of financial statements would consider these gains and the proceeds from an entity's sale of goods in the course of its ordinary activities differently in their evaluation of an entity's past results and their projections of future cash flows. This is because revenue from the sale of goods is typically more likely to recur in comparable amounts than are gains from sales of items of property, plant and equipment. Accordingly, the Board concluded that an entity should not classify as revenue gains on disposals of items of property, plant and equipment.

However, in preparing a cash flow statement, proceeds from the sale of property, plant and equipment are normally shown as a cash flow from investing activities.

ILLUSTRATIVE EXAMPLE 11.11 Disposals of assets

An entity acquired an item of plant on 1 July 2013 for $100 000. The asset had an expected useful life of 10 years and a residual value of $20 000. On 1 January 2016, the entity sold the asset for $81 000.

Required

Prepare the journal entries relating to this asset in the year of sale.

At the point of sale, the depreciation on the asset must be calculated for that part of the year for which the asset was held before the sale. Hence, for the half-year before the sale, under the straight-line method, depreciation of $4000 (i.e. $0.5 \times 1/10[\$100\,000 - \$20\,000]$) must be charged as an expense. The entry is:

Depreciation Expense	Dr	4 000	
Accumulated Depreciation	Cr		4 000
(Depreciation charge up to point of sale)			

The gain or loss on sale is the difference between the proceeds on sale of $81\,000 and the carrying amount at time of sale of $80\,000 (i.e. $\$100\,000 - 2.5[1/10 \times \$80\,000]$), which is $1000. The required journal entry is:

Cash	Dr	81 000	
Accumulated Depreciation	Dr	20 000	
Plant	Cr		100 000
Gain on Sale of Plant	Cr		1 000
(Gain on sale of asset)			

Alternatively, the following entries could be used:

Cash	Dr	81 000	
Proceeds on Disposal of Asset	Cr		81 000
(Sale of asset)			
Carrying Amount of Asset Sold	Dr	80 000	
Accumulated Depreciation	Dr	20 000	
Plant	Cr		100 000
(Carrying amount of asset sold)			

In this example, the asset was sold for $81\,000. Assume that the asset, now referred to as Plant A, was traded in for another asset, Plant B. Plant B had a fair value of $280\,000, with the entity making a cash payment of $202\,000 as well as giving up Plant A. The trade-in amount is then $78\,000. The journal entries to record this transaction are:

Plant B	Dr	280 000	
Loss on Sale of Plant A (P/L)	Dr	2 000	
Accumulated Depreciation – Plant A	Dr	20 000	
Plant A	Cr		100 000
Cash	Cr		202 000
(Acquisition of Plant B and trade-in of Plant A)			

11.9 DISCLOSURE

Paragraphs 73–79 of IAS 16 contain the required disclosures relating to property, plant and equipment. Information in paragraph 73 is required on a class-by-class basis, and paragraph 77 relates only to assets stated at revalued amounts. Paragraph 79 contains information that entities are encouraged to disclose, but are not required to do so. Figure 11.8 provides an illustration of the disclosures required by IAS 16.

FIGURE 11.8 Illustrative disclosures required by IAS 16

			IAS 16 paragraph

Note 1: Summary of accounting policies (extract)
Property, plant and equipment

Freehold land and buildings on freehold land are measured on a fair value basis. At the end of each reporting period, the value of each asset in these classes is reviewed to ensure that it does not differ materially from the asset's fair value at that date. Where necessary, the asset is revalued to reflect its fair value. In June 2014, revaluations were carried out by an independent valuer; since then valuations have been made internally. The basis for the assessment of fair value has been by reference to observable transactions in the property market, including an analysis of prices paid in recent market transactions for similar properties. No other valuation techniques were used. *73(a) 77(a) 77(b) 77(a)*

All other classes of property, plant and equipment are measured at cost. *73(a)*

Depreciation
Depreciation is provided on a straight-line basis for all property, plant and equipment, other than freehold land. *73(b)*
The useful lives of the assets are: *73(c)*

	2016	2015
Freehold buildings	40 years	40 years
Plant and equipment	5 to 15 years	5 to 15 years

Note 10: Property, plant and equipment

	Land and buildings		Plant and equipment		IAS 16 paragraph
	2016	2015	**2016**	2015	
	$'000	$'000	**$'000**	$'000	
Balance at beginning of year	**1 861**	1 765	**2 840**	2 640	*73(d)*
Accumulated depreciation	**(400)**	(364)	**(732)**	(520)	
Carrying amount	**1 461**	1 401	**2 108**	2 120	
Additions	**—**	123	**755**	372	*73(e)(i)*
Disposals	**(466)**	(18)	**(181)**	(158)	*73(e)(ii)*
Acquisitions via business combinations	**739**	—	**412**	—	*73(e)(iii)*
Impairment losses	**—**	—	**(100)**	—	*73(e)(v)*
Depreciation	**(20)**	(36)	**(161)**	(212)	*73(e)(vii)*
Transfer to assets held for sale	**(438)**	—	**(890)**	—	*73(e)(ix)*
Net exchange differences	**11**	(9)	**8**	(14)	*73(e)(viii)*
Carrying amount at end of year	**1 287**	1 461	**1 951**	2 108	*73(d)*
Property, plant and equipment:					
At cost	**1 707**	1 861	**2 944**	2 840	
Accumulated depreciation and impairment losses	**(420)**	(400)	**(993)**	(732)	
Carrying amount at end of year	**1 287**	1 461	**1 951**	2 108	*73(d)*

For the freehold land and buildings measured at fair value, the carrying amount that would have been recognised if they had been carried at cost is: *77(e)*

	2016	2015
	$'000	$'000
Carrying amount at end of year	**942**	824

Plant and equipment of $420 000 have been pledged as security for loans to the company. *74(a)*

(continued)

FIGURE 11.8 (continued)

The company has entered into a contract to acquire $640 000 of plant equipment over the next two years.	74(c)
Activity in the revaluation surplus for land and buildings is as follows:	77(f)

	2016	2015
	$'000	$'000
Balance at beginning of year	309	303
Revaluation of gains on land and buildings	42	9
Deferred tax liability	(13)	(3)
Balance at end of year	338	309

There are no restrictions on the distribution of the balance of the surplus to shareholders.

SUMMARY

'Property, plant and equipment' covers a wide range of assets such as vehicles, aircraft, all types of buildings, and specific structures such as oil and gas offshore platforms. These assets have a variety of useful lives, expected benefits, risk of receipt of benefits, movements in value over time, and expected value at point of derecognition. In some cases at derecognition, assets such as oil platforms require entities to incur costs rather than receive a residual value on sale. IAS 16, although recognising this variety, provides common principles to be applied to all items of property, plant and equipment.

Initial recognition occurs when the recognition criteria are met and assets are then recorded at cost. Subsequent to initial recognition, entities have a choice of measurement model, namely the cost model and the revaluation model. Under both measurement models, assets are subject to depreciation, this being a process of allocation and not a process of change in value. The measurement of depreciation requires judgements to be made by the accountant, including useful lives, residual values and pattern of receipt of benefits. Use of the revaluation model has additional accounting complications with revaluation increases and decreases potentially affecting asset revaluation surplus accounts, and having tax-effect consequences. Because of the judgements having to be made, IAS 16 requires extensive disclosures to be made.

DEMONSTRATION PROBLEM 11.1 Movements in assets, depreciation

Munich Manufacturing Ltd's post-closing trial balance at 30 June 2015 included the following balances:

Machinery control (at cost)	$244 480
Accumulated depreciation – machinery control	113 800
Fixtures (at cost; purchased 2 December 2012)	308 600
Accumulated depreciation – fixtures	134 138

The Machinery Control and Accumulated Depreciation – Machinery Control accounts are supported by subsidiary ledgers. Details of machines owned at 30 June 2015 are as follows:

Machine	Acquisition date	Cost	Estimated useful life	Estimated residual value
1	28 April 2011	$74 600	5 years	$3800
2	4 February 2013	82 400	5 years	4400
3	26 March 2014	87 480	6 years	5400

Additional information
(a) Munich Manufacturing Ltd uses the general journal for all journal entries, records depreciation to the nearest month, balances its books every 6 months, and records amounts to the nearest dollar.

(b) The company uses straight-line depreciation for machinery and diminishing-balance depreciation at 20% per annum for fixtures.

The following transactions and events occurred from 1 July 2015 onwards:

2015	
July 3	Exchanged items of fixtures (having a cost of $100 600; a carrying amount at exchange date of $56 872; and a fair value at exchange date of $57 140) for a used machine (Machine 4). Machine 4's fair value at exchange date was $58 000. Machine 4 originally cost $92 660 and had been depreciated by $31 790 to exchange date in the previous owner's accounts. Munich Manufacturing Ltd estimated Machine 4's useful life and residual value to be 3 years and $4580 respectively.
Oct. 10	Traded in Machine 2 for a new machine (Machine 5) that cost $90 740. A trade-in allowance of $40 200 was received and the balance was paid in cash. Freight charges of $280 and installation costs of $1600 were also paid in cash. Munich Manufacturing Ltd estimated Machine 5's useful life and residual value to be 6 years and $5500 respectively.
2016	
April 24	Overhauled Machine 3 at a cash cost of $16 910, after which Munich Manufacturing Ltd revised its residual value to $5600 and extended its useful life by 2 years.
May 16	Paid for scheduled repairs and maintenance on the machines of $2370.
June 30	Recorded depreciation and scrapped Machine 1.

Required

1. Prepare journal entries to record the above transactions and events.
2. Prepare the Accumulated Depreciation – Machinery Control and Accumulated Depreciation – Fixtures ledger accounts for the period 30 June 2015 to 30 June 2016.

Solution

1. *Journal entries*

Calculate the depreciation on each of the depreciable assets so that when events such as a sale occur, depreciation up to the date of the transaction can be calculated. Depreciation is calculated as:

$$\text{(Cost – residual value)/expected useful life}$$

For the three items of machinery, the depreciation per month is calculated as follows:

Machine 1 depreciation = ($74 600 – $3800)/60 months = $1180 per month
Machine 2 depreciation = ($82 400 – $4400)/60 months = $1300 per month
Machine 3 depreciation = ($87 480 – $5400)/72 months = $1140 per month

On 3 July, the company exchanges items of fixtures for a machine. After assessing that the transaction has commercial substance, the first journal entry derecognises the fixtures by eliminating both the asset account and the accumulated depreciation. The carrying amount represents the expense to be matched with the proceeds on sale to determine a gain/loss on sale.

2015				
July 3	Accumulated Depreciation – Fixtures*	Dr	43 728	
	Carrying Amount – Fixtures	Dr	56 872	
	Fixtures	Cr		100 600
	*$100 600 – $56 872			

The second journal entry recognises the acquired machine (Machine 4) at cost. Cost is measured using the fair value of the consideration given by the acquirer. As cost is the measurement used, the fair value of the machine is not relevant. Similarly, the carrying amount of the asset in the seller's records is also not relevant. The entry also records the proceeds on sale, as it is the machinery that is being received in exchange for the fixtures.

	Machinery (M4)	Dr	57 140	
	Proceeds on Sale – Fixtures	Cr		57 140

The depreciation per month for M4 is then calculated:

Machine 4 depreciation = ($57 140 – $4580)/36 months = $1460 per month

On 10 October, Machine 2 is traded in for Machine 5. Depreciation up to point of sale on Machine 2 is determined, being $1300 per month for the 3 months from July to September.

Oct. 10	Depreciation – Machinery (M2)*	Dr	3 900	
	Accumulated Depreciation – Machinery (M2)	Cr		3 900
	*$1300 × 3 months			

Machine 2 is derecognised with the machine and related accumulated depreciation being written out of the records. The carrying amount is used to determine a gain or loss on sale.

	Accumulated Depreciation – Machinery (M2)*	Dr	41 600	
	Carrying Amount – Machinery (M2)**	Dr	40 800	
	Machinery (M2)	Cr		82 400
	*$1300 × 32 months			
	**$82 400 – $41 600			

Machine 5 is recorded at cost. Cost is determined as the sum of the purchase price and directly attributable costs. Purchase price is the fair value of consideration given up by the acquirer. In the absence of a fair value for Machine 2, the consideration is based on the fair value of Machine 5, namely $90 740. The directly attributable costs are the freight charges of $280 and installation costs of $1600, both being necessarily incurred to get the asset into the condition for management's intended use.

The trade-in allowance is used as the selling price of the asset, in the absence of a fair value of the asset. The cash outlay is then the sum of the balance paid to the seller of Machine 5 and the directly attributable costs.

	Machinery (M5)*	Dr	92 620	
	Proceeds on Sale – Machinery (M2)	Cr		40 200
	Cash	Cr		52 420
	*$90 740 + $280 + $1600			

The depreciation per month for Machine 5 is then calculated:

Machine 5 depreciation = ($92 620 – $5500)/72 months = $1210 per month

On 24 April 2016, Machine 3 received an overhaul. This resulted in a change in the capacity of the machine, which increased the residual value and extended its useful life. Because this results in a change in the depreciation per month, depreciation based on the rate before the overhaul for the period up to the date of the overhaul is recorded.

2016 April 24	Depreciation – Machinery (M3)*	Dr	11 400	
	Accumulated Depreciation – Machinery (M3).	Cr		11 400
	*$1140 × 10 months			

Because the overhaul increases the expected benefits from the asset — that is, the outlay for the overhaul results in probable future benefits, the cost of the overhaul is capitalised, increasing the overall cost of the asset.

Machinery (M3)		Dr	16 910	
Cash		Cr		16 910

The overhaul results in a change in expectations, so it is necessary to calculate a revised depreciation per month:

M3:	New depreciable amount	= $87 480 + $16 910 − $5600	= $98 790
	Accumulated depreciation balance	= $1140 × 25 months	= $28 500
	Carrying amount to be depreciated	= $98 790 − $28 500	= $70 290
	New useful life	= 72 months − 25 months + 24 months = 71 months	
	Revised depreciation	= $70 290/71 months	= $990 per month

Because outlays on repairs and maintenance do not lead to increased future benefits, these outlays are expensed.

May 16	Repairs and Maintenance Expense	Dr	2 370	
	Cash	Cr		2 370

At the end of the reporting period, depreciation is accrued on all depreciable assets:

Machinery:	M1	$1180 × 10 months	$ 11 800
	M3	$990 × 2 months	1 980
	M4	$1460 × 12 months	17 520
	M5	$1210 × 9 months	10 890
			$ 42 190*
Fixtures:	$308 600 − $100 600		$208 000
	Less: $134 138 − $43 728		(90 410)
			$117 590
	20% × $117 590		$ 23 518**

June 30	Depreciation – Machinery*	Dr	42 190	
	Depreciation – Fixtures**	Dr	23 518	
	Accumulated Depreciation – Machinery	Cr		42 190
	Accumulated Depreciation – Fixtures	Cr		23 518

Machine 1 is scrapped, so the asset is derecognised by writing off the asset and related accumulated depreciation. The undepreciated amount is recognised as an expense. A residual value of $3800 was expected but not received, so the company incurs a loss of $3800.

	Accumulated Depreciation – Machinery (M1)*	Dr	70 800	
	Carrying Amount – Machinery (M1)**	Dr	3 800	
	Machinery (M1)	Cr		74 600
	*$1180 × 60 months			
	**$74 600 − $70 800			

2. *Ledger accounts*

Accumulated Depreciation – Machinery Control

10/10/15	Machinery	41 600	30/6/15	Balance b/d	113 800
31/12/15	Balance c/d	76 100	10/10/15	Depreciation	3 900
		117 700			117 700
30/6/16	Machinery	70 800	31/12/15	Balance b/d	76 100
	Balance c/d	58 890	24/4/16	Depreciation	11 400
			30/6/16	Depreciation	42 190
		129 690			129 690
			30/6/16	Balance b/d	58 890

Accumulated Depreciation – Fixtures

3/7/15	Fixtures	43 728	30/6/15	Balance b/d	134 138
31/12/15	Balance c/d	90 410			
		134 138			134 138
			31/12/15	Balance b/d	90 410
30/6/16	Balance c/d	113 928	30/6/16	Depreciation	23 518
		113 928			113 928
			30/6/16	Balance b/d	113 928

On 1 July 2014, Weinheim Ltd acquired a number of assets from Berlin Ltd. The assets had the following fair values at that date:

Plant A	$300 000
Plant B	180 000
Furniture A	60 000
Furniture B	50 000

In exchange for these assets, Weinheim Ltd issued 200 000 shares with a fair value of $2.95 per share. The directors of Weinheim Ltd decided to measure plant at fair value under the revaluation model and furniture at cost. The plant was considered to have a further 10-year life with benefits being received evenly over that period, whereas furniture is depreciated evenly over a 5-year period.

At 31 December 2014, Weinheim Ltd assessed the carrying amounts of its assets as follows:
- Plant A was valued at $296 000, with an expected remaining useful life of 8 years.
- Plant B was valued at $168 000, with an expected remaining useful life of 8 years.
- Furniture A's carrying amount was considered to be less than its recoverable amount.
- Furniture B's recoverable amount was assessed to be $40 000, with an expected remaining useful life of 4 years.

Appropriate entries were made at 31 December 2014 for the half-yearly accounts.

On 15 February 2015, Weinheim Ltd made a bonus issue of shares: 5600 shares fully paid to $1 per share were issued from the Plant A asset revaluation surplus.

At 30 June 2015, Weinheim Ltd assessed the carrying amounts of its assets as follows:
- Plant A was valued at $274 000.
- Plant B was valued at $161 500.
- The carrying amounts of furniture were less than their recoverable amounts.

The tax rate is 30%.

Required

Prepare the journal entries passed during the 2014–15 period in relation to the non-current assets in accordance with IAS 16 *Property, Plant and Equipment*.

Solution

The assets acquired are recorded at cost. The total cost of the assets is the fair value of the shares issued, namely $590 000 (i.e. 200 000 shares at $2.95 per share). This exactly equals the sum of the fair values of the assets acquired, hence the cost of each of the assets acquired is assumed to be equal to its fair value. If the amount were different from $590 000, say $550 000, then the cost of each asset would be determined based on the proportion of fair value to total fair value.

2014				
July 1	Plant A	Dr	300 000	
	Plant B	Dr	180 000	
	Furniture A	Dr	60 000	
	Furniture B	Dr	50 000	
	Share Capital	Cr		590 000
	(Acquisition of assets)			

At the end of each reporting period, depreciation is calculated and recorded. The next two entries record the depreciation on Plant A and Plant B after 6 months, at 31 December 2014.

Dec. 31	Depreciation Expense – Plant A	Dr	15 000	
	Accumulated Depreciation	Cr		15 000
	(Depreciation, 10% × ½ × $300 000)			
	Depreciation Expense – Plant B	Dr	9 000	
	Accumulated Depreciation	Cr		9 000
	(Depreciation, 10% × ½ × $180 000)			

Plant is measured using the revaluation model. At 31 December, the fair values of plant are assessed. In relation to Plant A, the carrying amount of the asset is $285 000 (i.e. $300 000 − $15 000). The fair value is assessed to be $296 000. There is then a revaluation increase of $11 000. The first journal entry is to write off any accumulated depreciation at the point of revaluation:

	Accumulated Depreciation – Plant A	Dr	15 000	
	Plant A	Cr		15 000
	(Write down Plant A to its carrying amount)			

The second journal entry recognises the increase in other comprehensive income:

	Plant A	Dr	11 000	
	Gain on Revaluation of Plant (OCI)	Cr		11 000
	(Revaluation of Plant A from carrying amount of $285 000 to fair value of $296 000)			

The third entry recognises the tax effect of the gain:

	Income Tax Expense (OCI)	Dr	3 300	
	Deferred Tax Liability	Cr		3 300
	(Tax effect of gain on revaluation of plant)			

The fourth entry accumulates the after-tax gain in equity, in the asset revaluation surplus account:

Gain on Revaluation of Plant (OCI)	Dr	11 000
Income Tax Expense (OCI)	Cr	3 300
Asset Revaluation Surplus – Plant A	Cr	7 700
(Accumulation of net revaluation gain in equity)		

Assets are revalued by class. However, accounting for revaluations is on an asset-by-asset basis. It is therefore important to associate any revaluation surplus with the asset that created that surplus. Accordingly, in the above entry the surplus is associated with Plant A.

With Plant B, the carrying amount at 31 December is $171 000 (i.e. $180 000 – $9000). The fair value is assessed to be $168 000. The revaluation decrease is $3000. This amount is recognised as a loss in current period profit or loss.

Accumulated Depreciation – Plant B	Dr	9 000
Plant B	Cr	9 000
(Write down Plant B to its carrying amount)		
Loss on Revaluation of Plant (P/L)	Dr	3 000
Plant B	Cr	3 000
(Revaluation of Plant B from carrying amount of $171 000 to fair value of $168 000)		

Furniture is measured under the cost model. Depreciation for the 6-month period is calculated based on an allocation of the cost over a 5-year period:

Depreciation Expense – Furniture A	Dr	6 000
Accumulated Depreciation	Cr	6 000
(Depreciation, $\frac{1}{5} \times \frac{1}{2} \times \$60\,000$)		
Depreciation Expense – Furniture B	Dr	5 000
Accumulated Depreciation	Cr	5 000
(Depreciation, $\frac{1}{5} \times \frac{1}{2} \times \$50\,000$)		

The carrying amount of Furniture B at 31 December is $45 000 (i.e. $50 000 – $5000). The recoverable amount is $40 000. The asset is written down to recoverable amount, with the write-down being added to the accumulated depreciation account, and reported as an impairment loss.

Impairment Loss – Furniture B	Dr	5 000
Accumulated Depreciation and Impairment Losses – Furniture B	Cr	5 000
(Write-down of asset to recoverable amount)		

On 2 February 2015 the company made a bonus issue of $5600. This increased share capital, and was appropriated from the asset revaluation surplus related to Plant A. Note that revaluation increases and decreases are treated on an asset-by-asset basis, and so any transfers from revaluation surplus must be associated with specified surplus accounts.

2015			
Feb. 15	Asset Revaluation Surplus – Plant A	Dr	5 600
	Share Capital	Cr	5 600
	(Issue of bonus shares, 5600 × $1)		

At 30 June, depreciation is recorded for plant assets based on an allocation of the fair values at 31 December 2014.

June 30	Depreciation Expense – Plant A Accumulated Depreciation (Depreciation, $^{1}/_{8} \times ^{1}/_{2} \times \$296\,000$)	Dr Cr	18 500	18 500
	Depreciation Expense – Plant B Accumulated Depreciation (Depreciation, $^{1}/_{8} \times ^{1}/_{2} \times \$168\,000$)	Dr Cr	10 500	10 500

The fair value of Plant A is assessed to be $274 000. Since the carrying amount is $277 500 (i.e. $296 000 – $18 500), there is a revaluation decrease of $3500. Before recognising any expense on the revaluation decrease, there needs to be a reversal of the effects of any previous revaluation increase. For Plant A, at 31 December 2014, there was a revaluation increase of $11 000 which resulted in the recording of a $3300 deferred tax liability and a $7700 asset revaluation surplus. Hence, with the revaluation decrease of $3500, the normal adjustment would be to debit the deferred tax liability with $1050 (being 30% × $3500) and debit the asset revaluation surplus with $2450 (being 70% × $3500). However, because of the bonus dividend, the balance in the asset revaluation surplus for Plant A is only $2100 (i.e. $7700 – $5600). There is a deficiency of $350 in relation to the surplus.

The required journal entries at 30 June 2015 for Plant A are:

- *the elimination of the accumulated depreciation account*

Accumulated Depreciation – Plant A Plant A (Write down Plant A to its carrying amount)	Dr Cr	18 500	18 500

- *the recognition of the revaluation decrease in other comprehensive income:*

Loss on Revaluation of Plant (OCI) Plant A (Revaluation of Plant A from carrying amount of $277 500 to fair value of $274 000)	Dr Cr	3 500	3 500

- *the tax effect of the revaluation write-down:*

Deferred Tax Liability Income Tax Expense (OCI) (Tax effect of loss on revaluation of plant)	Dr Cr	1 050	1 050

- *the accumulation of the loss on revaluation to equity; as the asset revaluation surplus for Plant A has been reduced because of the bonus issue of shares, the deficiency is recognised as a loss:*

Asset Revaluation Surplus – Plant A Income Tax Expense (OCI) Loss on Revaluation of Plant (P/L) Loss on Revaluation of Plant (OCI) (Accumulation of revaluation loss to equity)	Dr Dr Dr Cr	2 100 1 050 350	3 500

For Plant B, the carrying amount is $157 500 (i.e. $168 000 – $10 500). The fair value is $161 500. There is a revaluation increase of $4000. The accounting for this increase requires a reversal of any prior decrease. With Plant B at 31 December 2014, an expense of $3000 was recognised as a result of a revaluation decrease. The reversal of the previous decrease requires the recognition of income of $3000. The $1000 balance of the current increase (i.e. $4000 − $3000) is accounted for as other comprehensive income with a deferred tax liability and asset revaluation surplus being recognised.

The required journal entries for Plant B are:

- *the elimination of the accumulated depreciation account*

Accumulated Depreciation – Plant B	Dr	10 500	
Plant B	Cr		10 500
(Write down Plant B to its carrying amount)			

- *the recognition of both a gain in profit or loss (for the reversal of the prior decrease) and a gain in other comprehensive income on the revaluation of Plant B*

Plant B	Dr	4 000	
Gain on Revaluation of Plant (OCI)	Cr		1 000
Gain on Revaluation of Plant (P/L)	Cr		3 000
(Recognition of revaluation increase in profit or loss and other comprehensive income)			

- *tax effect of revaluation gain*

Income Tax Expense (OCI)	Dr	300	
Deferred Tax Liability	Cr		300
(Tax effect of gain on revaluation of plant)			

- *accumulation of the revaluation gain in equity*

Gain on Revaluation of Plant (OCI)	Dr	1 000	
Income Tax Expense (OCI)	Cr		300
Asset Revaluation Surplus – Plant B	Cr		700
(Accumulation of net revaluation gain in equity)			

Furniture at cost is depreciated for the final 6 months of the year.

Depreciation Expense – Furniture A	Dr	6 000	
Accumulated Depreciation	Cr		6 000
(Depreciation, $\frac{1}{5} \times \frac{1}{2} \times \$60\,000$)			
Depreciation Expense – Furniture B	Dr	5 000	
Accumulated Depreciation	Cr		5 000
(Depreciation, $\frac{1}{4} \times \frac{1}{2} \times \$40\,000$)			

Discussion questions

1. What assets constitute property, plant and equipment?
2. What are the recognition criteria for property, plant and equipment?
3. How should items of property, plant and equipment be measured at point of initial recognition, and would gifts be treated differently from acquisitions?
4. How is cost determined?

5. What choices of measurement model exist subsequent to assets being initially recognised?
6. What factors should entities consider in choosing alternative measurement models?
7. What is meant by 'depreciation expense'?
8. How is useful life determined?
9. What is meant by 'residual value' of an asset?
10. How does an entity choose between depreciation methods, for example, straight-line versus diminishing-balance models?
11. What is meant by 'significant parts depreciation'?
12. Under the revaluation model, how is a revaluation increase accounted for?
13. Under the revaluation model, how is a revaluation decrease accounted for?
14. When, and why, must tax effect be considered in accounting for revaluation increases and decreases?
15. Should accounting for revaluation increases and decreases be done on an asset-by-asset basis or on a class-of-assets basis?
16. What differences occur between asset-by-asset or class-of-asset bases in accounting for revaluation increases and decreases?
17. When should property, plant and equipment be derecognised?

Exercises

STAR RATING ★ BASIC ★★ MODERATE ★★★ DIFFICULT

Exercise 11.1 | FAIR VALUE BASIS FOR MEASUREMENT

★ The management of an entity has decided to use the fair value basis for the measurement of its equipment. Some of this equipment is very hard to obtain and has in fact increased in value over the current period. Management is arguing that, as there has been no decline in fair value, no depreciation should be charged on these pieces of equipment. Discuss.

Exercise 11.2 | ANNUAL DEPRECIATION CHARGE

★ A company is in the movie rental business. Movies are generally kept for 2 years and then either sold or destroyed. However, management wants to show increased profits, and believes that the annual depreciation charge can be lowered by keeping the movies for 3 years. Discuss.

Exercise 11.3 | DECLINE IN VALUE OF ASSETS

★ A new accountant has been appointed to the firm of Gutenberg Ltd, which owns a large number of depreciable assets. Upon analysing the firm's depreciation policy, the accountant has implemented a new policy based on the principle that the depreciation rate for particular assets should measure the decline in the value of the assets. Discuss this policy change.

Exercise 11.4 | DEPRECIATION CHARGES

★ The management of Carlsberg Ltd has been analysing the financial reports provided by the accountant, who has been with the firm for a number of years. Management has expressed its concern over depreciation charges being made in relation to the company's equipment. In particular, it believes that the depreciation charges are not high enough in relation to the factory machines because new technology applied in that area is rapidly making the machines obsolete. Management's concern is that the machines will have to be replaced in the near future and, with the low depreciation charges, the fund will not be sufficient to pay for the replacement machines. Discuss.

Exercise 11.5 | REVALUATION OF ASSETS

★ In the 30 June 2014 annual report of Sonner Ltd, the equipment was reported as follows:

Equipment (at cost)	$ 500 000
Accumulated Depreciation	(150 000)
	350 000

The equipment consisted of two machines, Machine A and Machine B. Machine A had cost $300 000 and had a carrying amount of $180 000 at 30 June 2014, and Machine B had cost $200 000 and was carried at $170 000. Both machines are measured using the cost model, and depreciated on a straight-line basis over a 10-year period.

On 31 December 2014, the directors of Sonner Ltd decided to change the basis of measuring the equipment from the cost model to the revaluation model. Machine A was revalued to $180 000 with an expected useful life of 6 years, and Machine B was revalued to $155 000 with an expected useful life of 5 years.

At 30 June 2015, Machine A was assessed to have a fair value of $163 000 with an expected useful life of 5 years, and Machine B's fair value was $136 500 with an expected useful life of 4 years.

The tax rate is 30%.

Required

1. Prepare the journal entries during the period 1 July 2014 to 30 June 2015 in relation to the equipment.
2. According to accounting standards, on what basis may management change the method of asset measurement, for example from cost to fair value?

Exercise 11.6 **REVALUATION OF ASSETS**

★ On 30 June 2014, the statement of financial position of Meezen Ltd showed the following non-current assets after charging depreciation:

Building	$ 300 000	
Accumulated Depreciation	(100 000)	$200 000
Motor Vehicle	120 000	
Accumulated Depreciation	(40 000)	80 000

The company has adopted fair value for the valuation of non-current assets. This has resulted in the recognition in previous periods of an asset revaluation surplus for the building of $14 000. On 30 June 2014, an independent valuer assessed the fair value of the building to be $160 000 and the vehicle to be $90 000. The income tax rate is 30%.

Required

1. Prepare any necessary entries to revalue the building and the vehicle as at 30 June 2014.
2. Assume that the building and vehicle had remaining useful lives of 25 years and 4 years respectively, with zero residual value. Prepare entries to record depreciation expense for the year ended 30 June 2015 using the straight-line method.

Exercise 11.7 **STRAIGHT-LINE DEPRECIATION VS DIMINISHING-BALANCE DEPRECIATION**

★★ Surfers Ltd uses tractors as a part of its operating equipment, and it applies the straight-line depreciation method to depreciate these assets. Surfers Ltd has just taken over Paradise Ltd, which uses similar tractors in its operations. However, Paradise Ltd has been using a diminishing-balance method of depreciation for these tractors. The accountant in Surfers Ltd is arguing that for both entities the same depreciation method should be used for tractors. Provide arguments for and against this proposal.

Exercise 11.8 **DEPRECIATION CHARGES**

★★ A new accountant has been appointed to Dettum Ltd and has implemented major changes in the calculation of depreciation. As a result, some parts of the factory have much larger depreciation charges. This has incensed some operations managers who believe that, as they take particular care with the maintenance of their machines, their machines should not attract large depreciation charges that reduce the profitability of their operations and reflect badly on their management skills. The operations managers plan to meet the accountant and ask for change. How should the new accountant respond?

Exercise 11.9 **BUILDING COSTS**

★★ Trabitz Ltd has acquired a new building. Which of the following items should be included in the cost of the building?

(a) Stamp duty

(b) Real estate agent's fees

(c) Architect's fees for drawings for internal adjustments to the building to be made before use

(d) Interest on the bank loan to acquire the building, and an application fee to the bank to get the loan, which is secured on the building

(e) Cost of changing the name on the building

(f) Cost of changing the parking bays

(g) Cost of refurbishing the lobby to the building to attract customers and make it more user friendly

Exercise 11.10 **CAPITALISATION**

★★ Rennau Ltd has acquired a new machine, which it has had installed in its factory. Which of the following items should be capitalised into the cost of the building?

(a) Labour and travel costs for managers to inspect possible new machines and for negotiating for a new machine

(b) Freight costs and insurance to get the new machine to the factory

(c) Costs for renovating a section of the factory, in anticipation of the new machine's arrival, to ensure that all the other parts of the factory will have easy access to the new machine

(d) Cost of cooling equipment to assist in the efficient operation of the new machine

(e) Costs of repairing the factory door, which was damaged by the installation of the new machine

(f) Training costs of workers who will use the machine

Exercise 11.11 **EXPENSING OF COSTS**

★★ Mehna Ltd has acquired a new building for $500 000. It has incurred incidental costs of $10 000 in the acquisition process for legal fees, real estate agent's fees and stamp duties. Management believes that these costs should be expensed because they have not increased the value of the building and, if the building was immediately resold, these amounts would not be recouped. In other words, the fair value of the building is considered to still be $500 000. Discuss how these costs should be accounted for.

Exercise 11.12 **DEPRECIATION**

★★ Plaaz Ltd was formed on 1 July 2012 to provide delivery services for packages to be taken between the city and the airport. On this date, the company acquired a delivery truck from Frensdorf Trucks. The company paid cash of $50 000 to Frensdorf Trucks, which included government charges of $600 and registration of $400. Insurance costs for the first year amounted to $1200. The truck is expected to have a useful life of 5 years. At the end of the useful life, the asset is expected to be sold for $24 000, with costs relating to the sale amounting to $400.

The company went extremely well in its first year, and the management of Plaaz Ltd decided at 1 July 2013 to add another vehicle, a flat-top, to the fleet. This vehicle was acquired from a liquidation auction at a cash price of $30 000. The vehicle needed some repairs for the elimination of rust (cost $2300), major servicing to the engine (cost $480) and the replacement of all tyres (cost $620). The company believed it would use the flat-top for another 2 years and then sell it. Expected selling price was $15 000, with selling costs estimated to be $400. On 1 July 2013, both vehicles were fitted out with a radio communication system at a cost per vehicle of $300. This was not expected to have any material effect on the future selling price of either vehicle. Insurance costs for the 2013–14 period were $1200 for the first vehicle and $900 for the newly acquired vehicle.

All went well for the company except that, on 1 August 2014, the flat-top that had been acquired at auction broke down. Plaaz Ltd thought about acquiring a new vehicle to replace this one but, after considering the costs, decided to repair the flat-top instead. The vehicle was given a major overhaul at a cost of $6500. Although this was a major expense, management believed that the company would keep the vehicle for another 2 years. The estimated selling price in 3 years time is $12 000, with selling costs estimated at $300. Insurance costs for the 2014–15 period were the same as for the previous year.

Required

Prepare the journal entries for the recording of the vehicles and the depreciation of the vehicles for each of the 3 years. The financial year ends on 30 June.

Exercise 11.13 | **DEPRECIATION**

★★ Heilbach Ltd constructed a building for use by the administration section of the company. The completion date was 1 July 2007, and the construction cost was $840 000. The company expected to remain in the building for the next 20 years, at which time the building would probably have no real salvage value and have to be demolished. It is expected that demolition costs will amount to $15 000. In December 2013, following some severe weather in the city, the roof of the administration building was considered to be in poor shape so the company decided to replace it. On 1 July 2014, a new roof was installed at a cost of $220 000. The new roof was of a different material to the old roof, which was estimated to have cost only $140 000 in the original construction, although at the time of construction it was thought that the roof would last for the 20 years that the company expected to use the building. Because the company had spent the money replacing the roof, it thought that it would delay construction of a new building, thereby extending the original life of the building from 20 years to 25 years.

Required

Discuss how you would account for the depreciation of the building and how the replacement of the roof would affect the depreciation calculations.

Exercise 11.14 | **DEPRECIATION CALCULATION**

★★ On 1 July 2014, Bergfeld Airlines acquired a new aeroplane for a total cost of $10 million. A breakdown of the costs to build the aeroplane was given by the manufacturers:

Aircraft body	$ 3 000 000
Engines (2)	4 000 000
Fitting out of aircraft:	
Seats	1 000 000
Carpets	50 000
Electrical equipment — passenger seats	200 000
— cockpit	1 500 000
Food preparation equipment	250 000

All costs include installation and labour costs associated with the relevant part.

It is expected that the aircraft will be kept for 10 years and then sold. The main value of the aircraft at that stage is the body and the engines. The expected selling price is $2.1 million, with the body and engines retaining proportionate value.

Costs in relation to the aircraft over the next 10 years are expected to be as follows:

(a) *Aircraft body.* This requires an inspection every 2 years for cracks and wear and tear, at a cost of $10 000.

(b) *Engines.* Each engine has an expected life of 4 years before being sold for scrap. It is expected that the engines will be replaced in 2018 for $4.5 million and again in 2022 for $6 million. These engines are expected to incur annual maintenance costs of $300 000. The manufacturer has informed Bergfeld Airlines that a new prototype engine with an extra 10% capacity should be on the market in 2020, and that existing engines could be upgraded at a cost of $1 million.

(c) *Fittings.* Seats are replaced every 3 years. Expected replacement costs are $1.2 million in 2017 and $1.5 million in 2023. The repair of torn seats and faulty mechanisms is expected to cost $100 000 p.a. Carpets are replaced every 5 years. They will be replaced in 2019 at an expected cost of $65 000, but will not be replaced again before the aircraft is sold in 2021. Cleaning costs amount to $10 000 p.a. The electrical equipment (such as the TV) for each seat has an annual repair cost of $15 000. It is expected that, with the improvements in technology, the equipment will be totally replaced in 2020 by substantially better equipment at a cost of $350 000. The electrical equipment in the cockpit is tested frequently at an expected annual cost of $250 000. Major upgrades to the equipment are expected every 2 years at expected costs of $250 000 (in 2013), $300 000 (in 2015),

$345 000 (in 2017) and $410 000 (in 2022). The upgrades will take into effect the expected changes in technology.

(d) *Food preparation equipment.* This incurs annual costs for repair and maintenance of $20 000. The equipment is expected to be totally replaced in 2020.

Required

1. Discuss how the costs relating to the aircraft should be accounted for.
2. Determine the expenses recognised for the 2014–15 financial year.

Exercise 11.15 | **REVALUATION OF ASSETS AND TAX-EFFECT ACCOUNTING**

★★ Almdorf Ltd acquired a machine on 1 July 2012 at a cost of $100 000. The machine has an expected useful life of 5 years, and the company adopts the straight-line basis of depreciation. The tax depreciation rate for this type of machine is 12.5% p.a. The company tax rate is 30%.

Almdorf Ltd measures this asset at fair value. Movements in fair values are as follows:

30 June 2013	$85 000	Remaining useful life: 4 years
30 June 2014	60 000	Remaining useful life: 3 years
30 June 2015	45 000	

Owing to a change in economic conditions, Almdorf Ltd sold the machine for $45 000 on 30 June 2015. The asset was revalued to fair value immediately before the sale.

Required

1. Provide the journal entries used to account for this machine over the period 2012 to 2015.
2. For each of the 3 years ended 30 June 2013, 2014 and 2015, calculate the carrying amount and the tax base of the asset, and determine the appropriate tax-effect entry in relation to the machine. Explain your answer.

Exercise 11.16 | **ACQUISITION AND SALE OF ASSETS, DEPRECIATION**

★★ Thader Turf Farm owned the following items of property, plant and equipment as at 30 June 2014:

Land (at cost)		$120 000
Office building (at cost)	150 000	
Accumulated depreciation	(23 375)	126 625
Turf cutter (at cost)	65 000	
Accumulated depreciation	(42 367)	22 633
Water desalinator (at fair value)		189 000

Additional information (at 30 June 2014)

(a) The straight-line method of depreciation is used for all depreciable items of property, plant and equipment. Depreciation is charged to the nearest month and all figures are rounded to the nearest dollar.

(b) The office building was constructed on 1 April 2010. Its estimated useful life is 20 years and it has an estimated residual value of $40 000.

(c) The turf cutter was purchased on 21 January 2011, at which date it had an estimated useful life of 5 years and an estimated residual value of $3200.

(d) The water desalinator was purchased and installed on 2 July 2013 at a cost of $200 000. On 30 June 2014, the plant was revalued upwards by $7000 to its fair value on that day. Additionally, its useful life and residual value were re-estimated to 9 years and $18 000 respectively.

The following transactions occurred during the year ended 30 June 2015:

(*Note:* All payments are made in cash.)

(e) On 10 August 2014, new irrigation equipment was purchased from Pond Supplies for $37 000. On 16 August 2014, the business paid $500 to have the equipment delivered to the turf farm. Thomas Schwazer was contracted to install and test the new system. In the course of installation, pipes worth $800 were damaged and subsequently replaced on 3 September. The irrigation system was fully operational by 19 September and Thomas Schwazer was paid $9600 for his services. The system has an estimated useful life of 4 years and a residual value of $0.

(f) On 1 December 2014, the turf cutter was traded in on a new model worth $80 000. A trade-in allowance of $19 000 was received and the balance paid in cash. The new machine's useful life and residual value were estimated at 6 years and $5000 respectively.

(g) On 1 January 2015, the turf farm's owner Helmut Dorf decided to extend the office building by adding three new offices and a meeting room. The extension work started on 2 February and was completed by 28 March at a cost of $49 000. The extension is expected to increase the useful life of the building by 4 years and increase its residual value by $5000.

(h) On 30 June 2015, depreciation expense for the year was recorded. The fair value of the water desalination plant was $165 000.

Required

(Show all workings and round amounts to the nearest dollar.)

Prepare general journal entries to record the transactions and events for the reporting period ended 30 June 2015 (narrations are not required).

Exercise 11.17 ★★ **ACQUISITIONS, DISPOSALS, DEPRECIATION**

Meerbeck Ltd purchased equipment on 1 July 2013 for $39 800 cash. Transport and installation costs of $4200 were paid on 5 July 2013. Useful life and residual value were estimated to be 10 years and $1800 respectively. Meerbeck Ltd depreciates equipment using the straight-line method to the nearest month, and reports annually on 30 June. The company tax rate is 30%.

In June 2015, changes in technology caused the company to revise the estimated total life from 10 years to 5 years, and the residual value from $1800 to $1200. This revised estimate was made before recording the depreciation for the financial year ended 30 June 2015.

On 30 June 2015, the company adopted the revaluation model to account for equipment. An expert valuation was obtained showing that the equipment had a fair value of $30 000 at that date.

On 30 June 2016, depreciation for the year was charged and the equipment's carrying amount was remeasured to its fair value of $16 000.

On 30 September 2016, the equipment was sold for $8400 cash.

Required

(Show all workings and round amounts to the nearest dollar.)

Prepare general journal entries to record the transactions and events for the period 1 July 2013 to 30 September 2016. (Narrations are not required.)

Exercise 11.18 ★★ **REVALUATION OF ASSETS**

On 1 July 2012, Themar Ltd acquired two assets within the same class of plant and equipment. Information on these assets is as follows:

	Cost	Expected useful life
Machine A	$100 000	5 years
Machine B	60 000	3 years

The machines are expected to generate benefits evenly over their useful lives. The class of plant and equipment is measured using fair value.

At 30 June 2013, information about the assets is as follows:

	Fair value	Expected useful life
Machine A	$84 000	4 years
Machine B	38 000	2 years

On 1 January 2014, Machine B was sold for $29 000 cash. On the same day, Themar Ltd acquired Machine C for $80 000 cash. Machine C has an expected useful life of 4 years. Themar Ltd also made a bonus issue of 10 000 shares at $1 per share, using $8000 from the general reserve and $2000 from the asset revaluation surplus created as a result of measuring Machine A at fair value.

At 30 June 2014, information on the machines is as follows:

	Fair value	Expected useful life
Machine A	$61 000	3 years
Machine C	68 500	1.5 years

The income tax rate is 30%.

Required

Prepare the journal entries in the records of Themar Ltd to record the described events over the period 1 July 2012 to 30 June 2014, assuming the ends of the reporting periods are 30 June 2013 and 30 June 2014.

Exercise 11.19

★★

DETERMINING THE COSTS OF ASSETS

Nassau Ltd uses many kinds of machines in its operations. It constructs some of these machines itself and acquires others from the manufacturers. The following information relates to two machines that it has recorded in the 2013–14 period. Machine A was acquired, and Machine B was constructed by Nassau Ltd itself:

Machine A	
Cash paid for equipment, including GST of $8000	$ 88 000
Costs of transporting machine — insurance and transport	3 000
Labour costs of installation by expert fitter	5 000
Labour costs of testing equipment	4 000
Insurance costs for 2013–14	1 500
Costs of training for personnel who will use the machine	2 500
Costs of safety rails and platforms surrounding machine	6 000
Costs of water devices to keep machine cool	8 000
Costs of adjustments to machine during 2013–14 to make it operate more efficiently	7 500

Machine B	
Cost of material to construct machine, including GST of $7000	$ 77 000
Labour costs to construct machine	43 000
Allocated overhead costs — electricity, factory space etc.	22 000
Allocated interest costs of financing machine	10 000
Costs of installation	12 000
Insurance for 2013–14	2 000
Profit saved by self-construction	15 000
Safety inspection costs prior to use	4 000

Required

Determine the amount at which each of these machines should be recorded in the records of Nassau Ltd. For items not included in the cost of the machines, note how they should be accounted for.

Exercise 11.20

★★

CLASSIFICATION OF ACQUISITION COSTS

Alsbach Ltd began operations on 1 July 2012. During the following year, the company acquired a tract of land, demolished the building on the land and built a new factory. Equipment was acquired for the factory and, in March 2013, the factory was ready. A gala opening was held on 18 March, with the local parliamentarian opening the factory. The first items were ready for sale on 25 March.

During this period, the following inflows and outflows occurred:

(a) While searching for a suitable block of land, Alsbach Ltd placed an option to buy with three real estate agents at a cost of $100 each. One of these blocks of land was later acquired.

(b) Payment of option fees	$300
(c) Receipt of loan from bank	400 000
(d) Payment to settlement agent for title search, stamp duties and settlement fees	10 000
(e) Payment of arrears in rates on building on land	5 000
(f) Payment for land	100 000
(g) Payment for demolition of current building on land	12 000
(h) Proceeds from sale of material from old building	5 500
(i) Payment to architect	23 000
(j) Payment to council for approval of building construction	12 000
(k) Payment for safety fence around construction site	3 400
(l) Payment to construction contractor for factory building	240 000
(m) Payment for external driveways, parking bays and safety lighting	54 000
(n) Payment of interest on loan	40 000
(o) Payment for safety inspection on building	3 000
(p) Payment for equipment	64 000
(q) Payment of freight and insurance costs on delivery of equipment	5 600
(r) Payment of installation costs on equipment	12 000
(s) Payment for safety fence surrounding equipment	11 000
(t) Payment for removal of safety fence	2 000
(u) Payment for new fence surrounding the factory	8 000
(v) Payment for advertisements in the local paper about the forthcoming factory and its benefits to the local community	500
(w) Payment for opening ceremony	6 000
(x) Payments to adjust equipment to more efficient operating levels subsequent to initial operation	3 300

Required

Using the information provided, determine what assets Alsbach Ltd should recognise and the amounts at which they would be recorded.

Exercise 11.21 **ACQUISITIONS, DISPOSALS, TRADE-INS, OVERHAULS, DEPRECIATION**

★★ Axel Schulz is the owner of Wremen Fishing Charters. The business's final trial balance on 30 June 2012 (end of the reporting period) included the following balances:

Processing Plant (at cost, purchased 4 April 2010)	$ 148 650
Accumulated Depreciation — Processing plant	(81 274)
Charter Boats	291 200
Accumulated Depreciation — Boats	(188 330)

The following boats were owned at 30 June 2012:

Boat	Purchase date	Cost	Estimated useful life	Estimated residual value
1	23 February 2008	$62 000	5 years	$3 000
2	9 September 2008	$66 400	5 years	$3 400
3	6 February 2009	$78 600	4 years	$3 600
4	20 April 2010	$84 200	6 years	$3 800

Additional information

Wremen Fishing Charters calculates depreciation to the nearest month using straight-line depreciation for all assets except the processing plant, which is depreciated at 30% on the diminishing-balance method. Amounts are recorded to the nearest dollar.

Part A

The following transactions and events occurred during the year ended 30 June 2013:

2012	
July 26	Traded in Boat 1 for a new boat (Boat 5) which cost $84 100. A trade-in allowance of $8900 was received and the balance was paid in cash. Registration and stamp duty costs of $1500 were also paid in cash. Axel Schulz estimated Boat 5's useful life and residual value at 6 years and $4120 respectively.
Dec. 4	Overhauled the processing plant at a cash cost of $62 660. As the modernisation significantly expanded the plant's operating capacity and efficiency, Axel Schulz decided to revise the depreciation rate to 25%.
2013	
Feb. 6	Boat 3 reached the end of its useful life but no buyer could be found, so the boat was scrapped.
June 30	Recorded depreciation.

Required

Prepare general journal entries (narrations are required) to record the transactions and events for the year ended 30 June 2013.

Part B

On 26 March, Axel Schulz was offered fish-finding equipment with a fair value of $9500 in exchange for Boat 2. The fish-finder originally cost its owner $26 600 and had a carrying value of $9350 at the date of offer. The fair value of Boat 2 was $9100.

Required

If Axel Schulz accepts the exchange offer, what amount would the business use to record the acquisition of the fish-finding equipment? Why? Justify your answer by reference to the requirements of IAS 16 relating to the initial recognition of a property, plant and equipment item.

Exercise 11.22

★★

ACQUISITIONS, REVALUATIONS, REPLACEMENTS, DEPRECIATION

Hamburg Trading operates in a very competitive field. To maintain its market position, it purchased two new machines for cash on 1 January 2013. It had previously rented its machines. Machine A cost $40 000 and Machine B cost $100 000. Each machine was expected to have a useful life of 10 years, and residual values were estimated at $2000 for Machine A and $5000 for Machine B.

On 30 June 2014, Hamburg Trading adopted the revaluation model to account for the class of machinery. The fair values of Machine A and Machine B were determined to be $32 000 and $90 000 respectively on that date. The useful life and residual value of Machine A were reassessed to 8 years and $1500. The useful life and residual value of Machine B were reassessed to 8 years and $4000.

On 2 January 2015, extensive repairs were carried out on Machine B for $66 000 cash. Hamburg Trading expected these repairs to extend Machine B's useful life by 3.5 years, and it revised Machine B's estimated residual value to $9450.

Owing to technological advances, Hamburg Trading decided to replace Machine A. It traded in Machine A on 31 March 2015 for new Machine C, which cost $64 000. A $28 000 trade-in was allowed for Machine A, and the balance of Machine C's cost was paid in cash. Transport and installation costs of $950 were incurred in respect to Machine C. Machine C was expected to have a useful life of 8 years and a residual value of $8000.

Hamburg Trading uses the straight-line depreciation method, recording depreciation to the nearest month and the nearest dollar. The end of its reporting period is 30 June.

On 30 June 2015, fair values were determined to be $140 000 and $65 000 for Machines B and C respectively.

Required

Prepare general journal entries to record the above transactions and the depreciation journal entries required at the end of each reporting period up to 30 June 2013. (Narrations are not required but show all workings.)

Exercise 11.23 **DEPRECIATION CALCULATION**

★★★ Elben Ltd operates a factory that contains a large number of machines designed to produce knitted garments. These machines are generally depreciated at 10% p.a. on a straight-line basis. In general, machines are estimated to have a residual value on disposal of 10% of cost. At 1 July 2013, Elben Ltd had a total of 64 machines, and the statement of financial position showed a total cost of $420 000 and accumulated depreciation of $130 000. During 2013–14, the following transactions occurred:
(a) On 1 September 2013, a new machine was acquired for $15 000. This machine replaced two other machines. One of the two replaced machines was acquired on 1 July 2010 for $8200. It was traded in on the new machine, with Elben Ltd making a cash payment of $8800 on the new machine. The second replaced machine had cost $9000 on 1 April 2011 and was sold for $7300.
(b) On 1 January 2014, a machine that had cost $4000 on 1 July 2004 was retired from use and sold for scrap for $500.
(c) On 1 January 2014, a machine that had been acquired on 1 January 2011 for $7000 was repaired because its motor had been damaged from overheating. The motor was replaced at a cost of $4800. It was expected that this would increase the life of the machine by an extra 2 years.
(d) On 1 April 2014, Elben Ltd fitted a new form of arm to a machine used for putting special designs onto garments. The arm cost $1200. The machine had been acquired on 1 April 2011 for $10 000. The arm can be used on a number of other machines when required and has a 15-year life. It will not be sold when any particular machine is retired, but retained for use on other machines.

Required

1. Record each of the transactions. The end of the reporting period is 30 June.
2. Determine the depreciation expense for Elben Ltd for 2013–14.

Exercise 11.24 **REVALUATION OF ASSETS AND TAX-EFFECT ACCOUNTING**

★★★ For Bornholt Ltd, profit before income tax for the year ended 30 June 2013 amounted to $375 000, including the following expenses:

Depreciation of plant	$50 000
Goodwill impairment*	13 000
Long-service leave	40 000
Holiday pay	30 000
Doubtful debts	55 000
Entertainment*	12 000
Depreciation of furniture	5 000
*Non-deductible for taxation	

The statement of financial position of Bornholt Ltd at 30 June 2012 and 2013 showed the assets and liabilities of the company as follows:

Assets	2012	2013
Cash	$ 73 000	$ 82 000
Inventory	127 000	158 000
Receivables	430 000	585 000
Allowance for doubtful debts	(20 000)	(40 000)
Plant (net)	350 000	320 000

Assets (continued)	2012	2013
Furniture (net)	$ 75 000	$ 65 000
Goodwill	63 000	50 000
Deferred tax asset	21 000	?
Liabilities		
Payables	247 000	265 000
Provision for long-service leave	30 000	50 000
Provision for holiday pay	20 000	30 000
Deferred tax liability	11 250	?

Additional information
(a) Plant and furniture are different classes of assets. Both are measured at fair value. The furniture was revalued downward to $65 000 at 30 June 2013. Furniture had not previously been revalued upwards. Tax depreciation for the year ended 30 June 2013 was $7500, giving a carrying amount for tax purposes at 30 June 2013 of $55 000. The plant was revalued upwards at 30 June 2013 to $320 000. Tax depreciation on plant was $75 000, giving a carrying amount for tax purposes at 30 June 2013 of $250 000.
(b) Total bad debts written off for the 2012–13 year were $35 000.
(c) The tax rate is 30%.

Required

1. Calculate, by using worksheets, the amounts of income tax expense and current and deferred income tax assets/liabilities for the reporting period ended 30 June 2013.
2. Prepare the deferred tax asset and deferred tax liability accounts.

Exercise 11.25	**COST OF ACQUISITION**

★★★ Borod Ltd started business early in 2013. During its first 9 months, Borod Ltd acquired real estate for the construction of a building and other facilities. Operating equipment was purchased and installed, and the company began operating activities in October 2013. The company's accountant, who was not sure how to record some of the transactions, opened a Property ledger account and recorded debits and (credits) to this account as follows.

(a)	Cost of real estate purchased as a building site	$ 170 000
(b)	Paid architect's fee for design of new building	23 000
(c)	Paid for demolition of old building on building site purchased in (a)	28 000
(d)	Paid land tax on the real estate purchased as a building site in (a)	1 700
(e)	Paid excavation costs for the new building	15 000
(f)	Made the first payment to the building contractor	250 000
(g)	Paid for equipment to be installed in the new building	148 000
(h)	Received from sale of salvaged materials from demolishing the old building	(6 800)
(i)	Made final payment to the building contractor	350 000
(j)	Paid interest on building loan during construction	22 000
(k)	Paid freight on equipment purchased	1 900
(l)	Paid installation costs of equipment	4 200
(m)	Paid for repair of equipment damaged during installation	2 700
	Property ledger account balance	$1 009 700

Required

1. Prepare a schedule with the following column headings. Analyse each transaction, enter the payment or receipt in the appropriate column, and total each column.

Item no.	Land	Land improvements	Building	Manufacturing equipment	Other

2. Prepare the journal entry to close the $1 009 700 balance of the Property ledger account.

DEPRECIATION

Springs Manufacturing, which started operations on 1 September 2010, is owned by Alice Ltd. Alice Ltd's accounts at 31 December 2013 included the following balances:

Machinery (at cost)	$91 000
Accumulated Depreciation – Machinery	(48 200)
Vehicles (at cost; purchased 21 November 2012)	46 800
Accumulated Depreciation – Vehicles	(19 656)
Land (at cost; purchased 25 October 2010)	81 000
Building (at cost; purchased 25 October 2010)	185 720
Accumulated Depreciation – Building	(28 614)

Details of machines owned at 31 December 2013 are as follows:

Machine	Purchase date	Cost	Useful life	Residual value
1	7 October 2010	$43 000	5 years	$2 500
2	4 February 2011	$48 000	6 years	$3 000

Additional information

(a) Alice Ltd calculates depreciation to the nearest month and balances the records at month-end. Recorded amounts are rounded to the nearest dollar, and the end of the reporting period is 31 December.

(b) Alice Ltd uses straight-line depreciation for all depreciable assets except vehicles, which are depreciated on the diminishing balance at 40% p.a.

(c) The vehicles account balance reflects the total paid for two identical delivery vehicles, each of which cost $23 400.

(d) On acquiring the land and building, Alice Ltd estimated the building's useful life and residual value at 20 years and $5000 respectively.

The following transactions occurred from 1 January 2014:

2014		
Jan.	3	Bought a new machine (Machine 3) for a cash price of $57 000. Freight charges of $442 and installation costs of $1758 were paid in cash. The useful life and residual value were estimated at 5 years and $4000 respectively.
June	22	Bought a second-hand vehicle for $15 200 cash. Repainting costs of $655 and four new tyres costing $345 were paid for in cash.
Aug.	28	Exchanged Machine 1 for office furniture that had a fair value of $12 500 at the date of exchange. The fair value of Machine 1 at the date of exchange was $11 500. The office furniture originally cost $36 000 and, to the date of exchange, had been depreciated by $24 100 in the previous owner's books. Alice Ltd estimated the office furniture's useful life and residual value at 8 years and $540 respectively.
Dec.	31	Recorded depreciation.

2015		
April	30	Paid for repairs and maintenance on the machinery at a cash cost of $928.
May	25	Sold one of the vehicles bought on 21 November 2012 for $6600 cash.
June	26	Installed a fence around the property at a cash cost of $5500. The fence has an estimated useful life of 10 years and zero residual value. (Debit the cost to a land improvements asset account.)
Dec.	31	Recorded depreciation.

2016	
Jan. 5	Overhauled Machine 2 at a cash cost of $12 000, after which Alice Ltd estimated its remaining useful life at 1 additional year and revised its residual value to $5000.
June 20	Traded in the remaining vehicle bought on 21 November 2012 for a new vehicle. A trade-in allowance of $3700 was received and $22 000 was paid in cash. Stamp duty of $500 and registration and third-party insurance of $800 were also paid for in cash.
Oct. 4	Scrapped the vehicle bought on 22 June 2014, as it had been so badly damaged in a traffic accident that it was not worthwhile repairing it.
Dec. 31	Recorded depreciation.

Required

Prepare general journal entries to record the above transactions.

Exercise 11.27

★★★

DEPRECIATION

Chorin Ltd started operations on 1 October 2010. Its accounts at 30 June 2013 included the following balances:

Machinery (at cost)	$98 000
Accumulated Depreciation – Machinery	(47 886)
Vehicles (at cost; purchased 20 February 2011)	160 000
Accumulated Depreciation – Vehicles	(89 440)
Land (at cost; purchased 20 March 2013)	75 000
Building (at cost; purchased 20 March 2013)	290 600
Accumulated Depreciation – Building	(3 420)
Land Improvements (at cost; purchased 20 March 2013)	18 000
Accumulated Depreciation – Land Improvements	(300)

Details of machines owned at 30 June 2013 were:

Machine	Purchase date	Cost	Useful life	Residual value
1	2 October 2010	$25 000	4 years	$2 500
2	27 December 2010	42 000	5 years	4 000
3	29 July 2011	31 000	4 years	3 000

Additional information
(a) Chorin Ltd calculates depreciation to the nearest month and balances the records at month-end. Recorded amounts are rounded to the nearest dollar, and the end of the reporting period is 30 June.
(b) Chorin Ltd uses straight-line depreciation for all depreciable assets except vehicles, which are depreciated on the diminishing balance at 30% p.a.
(c) The Vehicles account balance reflects the total paid for four identical delivery vehicles, which cost $40 000 each.
(d) On acquiring the land and building, Chorin Ltd estimated the building's useful life and residual value at 20 years and $17 000 respectively.
(e) The Land Improvements account balance reflects a payment of $18 000 made on 20 March 2013 for driveways and a car park. On acquiring these land improvements, Chorin Ltd estimated their useful life at 15 years with no residual value.

The following transactions occurred from 1 July 2013:

2013		
Aug.	3	Purchased a new machine (Machine 4) for a cash price of $36 000. Installation costs of $1800 were also paid. Chorin Ltd estimated the useful life and residual value at 5 years and $3500 respectively.
Nov.	15	Paid vehicle repairs of $600.
Dec.	30	Exchanged one of the vehicles for items of fixtures that had a fair value of $17 000 at the date of exchange. The fair value of the vehicle at the date of exchange was $16 000. The fixtures originally cost $50 000 and had been depreciated by $31 000 to the date of exchange in the previous owner's books. Chorin Ltd estimated the fixtures' useful life and residual value at 5 years and $2500 respectively.
2014		
March	10	Sold Machine 1 for $5000 cash.
June	30	Recorded depreciation expense.
Sept.	20	Traded in Machine 3 for a new machine (Machine 5). A trade-in allowance of $10 000 was received for Machine 3 and $34 000 was paid in cash. Chorin Ltd estimated Machine 5's useful life and residual value at 6 years and $5000 respectively.
Dec.	30	Scrapped Machine 2, as it was surplus to requirements and no buyer could be found for it.
2015		
Feb.	8	Paid $8000 to overhaul Machine 4, after which Machine 4's useful life was estimated at 2 remaining years and its residual value was revised to $5000.
June	30	Recorded depreciation expense.

Required

Prepare general journal entries to record the above transactions.

References

Accounting Standards Board 1996, *Measurement of tangible fixed assets*, discussion paper, Accounting Standards Board UK.

Billabong International Ltd 2011, *2010/2011 Full financial report*, Billabong International Limited, Australia, www.billabongbiz.com.

Ernst & Young 2002, *The impact of AASB 1041 'Revaluation of Non-current Assets': A survey of corporate Australia's adoption of the new standard*, Ernst & Young Australia, January.

International Accounting Standards Board (IASB) 2011, *IASB documents published to accompany International Accounting Standard 1 Presentation of Financial Statements*, IASB, www.ifrs.org.

12 Leases

ACCOUNTING STANDARDS IN FOCUS

IAS 17 *Leases*

LEARNING OBJECTIVES

After studying this chapter, you should be able to:

1 discuss the characteristics of a lease

2 explain the difference between a finance lease and an operating lease

3 understand and apply the guidance necessary to classify leases

4 discuss the incentives to misclassify leases

5 account for finance leases from the perspective of a lessee

6 account for finance leases from the perspective of a lessor

7 account for finance leases by manufacturer or dealer lessors

8 account for operating leases from the perspective of both lessors and lessees

9 recognise and account for sale and leaseback transactions

10 discuss possible future changes to lease accounting.

INTRODUCTION

The rapid growth of leasing as a means of gaining access to the economic benefits embodied in assets during the 1970s led to a concern among standard setters worldwide that the credibility of financial reports was compromised by extensive use of such 'off-balance-sheet' arrangements. Accordingly, the 1980s saw the issue of leasing standards by both international and national standard-setting bodies. These standards adopted similar accounting treatments based on the premise that, when a lease transfers substantially all of the risks and rewards incidental to ownership to the lessee, that lease is in substance equivalent to the acquisition of an asset on credit by the lessee, and to a sale or financing by the lessor. The mandatory recognition of the asset/liability relating to the lease is justified by two arguments.

First, IAS 17 *Leases* paragraph 21 states:

> Although the legal form of a lease agreement is that the lessee may acquire no legal title to the leased asset, in the case of finance leases the substance and financial reality are that the lessee acquires the economic benefits of the use of the leased asset for the major part of its economic life in return for entering into an obligation to pay for that right an amount approximating, at the inception of the lease, the fair value of the asset and the related finance charge.

Second, paragraph 22 states:

> If such lease transactions are not reflected in the lessee's statement of financial position, the economic resources and the level of obligations of an entity are understated, thereby distorting financial ratios.

Interestingly, these justifications for the recognition of lease assets and liabilities make no reference to the *Conceptual Framework* definitions and recognition criteria, but concentrate on the substance of the exchange of benefits and the reliability of financial information. This rationale seems to view the lease transaction as the quasi-purchase of an asset, in the sense that it records the acquisition of an asset even though no transfer of legal title takes place.

The leasing standards remained unchanged over time even though there were many calls for major change. In July 1996, the International Accounting Standards Board (IASB) and the Financial Accounting Standards Board (FASB) in the United States established a joint international working group on leasing and commenced a review of the current leasing standards. In March 2009, the IASB issued a discussion paper (DP) entitled *Leases — Preliminary Views*. Comments were required to be sent to the IASB by 17 July 2009. In August 2010, the IASB issued an exposure draft (ED) on leases with a comment period ending December 2010. Subsequently, in July 2011, the FASB and IASB announced they would re-expose the ED as a result of their revised proposals due to the comments received. At June 2012, no new standard on leases has been issued.

12.1 WHAT IS A LEASE?

Paragraph 4 of IAS 17 defines a lease as:

> an agreement whereby the lessor conveys to the lessee in return for a payment or series of payments the right to use an asset for an agreed period of time.

Thus, under a lease agreement the lessee acquires, not the asset itself, but the *right* to use the asset for a set time. Leased assets range from physical assets such as land, plant and vehicles, through to intangible assets such as patents, copyright and mineral rights. Lease agreements may also result in the eventual transfer of ownership from lessor to lessee. For example, under a hire purchase agreement, the lessee will use the asset while paying for its acquisition. The agreed period of time may vary from a short period, such as the daily hire of a motor vehicle, to a longer period, such as the rental of office space by a company. The key feature of leases is the existence of an asset owned by one party (the lessor) but used, for some or all of its economic life, by another party (the lessee).

Service agreements relating to the provision of services, such as cleaning or maintenance, between two parties are not regarded as leases because the contract does not involve the use of an asset. These agreements are regarded as executory contracts — that is, both parties are still to perform to an equal degree the actions required by the contract. Thus, each party is regarded as having a right and obligation to participate in a future exchange or, alternatively, to compensate or be compensated for the consequences of not doing so. A cleaning contract entitles an entity to receive cleaning services on a regular basis and creates an obligation to pay for those services after they have been received. The key issue is the performance of the service. Until the cleaning services are delivered, the contract is merely an exchange of promises, not of future economic benefits. The existence of a non-cancellable service agreement or one that includes significant penalties for non-performance may, however, result in the service recipient acquiring control over future economic benefits (the right to receive cleaning services) that are likely to be delivered and can be reliably measured — in other words, an asset.

Accounting for leases is complicated by the fact that there are two parties involved — the lessor and the lessee.

12.1.1 Scope of application of IAS 17

Paragraph 2 of IAS 17 excludes the following types of leases from the scope of the accounting standard:
- lease agreements to explore for or use minerals, oil, natural gas and similar non-regenerative resources
- licensing agreements for such items as motion picture films, video recordings, plays, manuscripts, patents and copyrights.

No explanation is given for the exclusion of resource exploitation rights and licensing agreements, which means that the standard applies only to leases for assets with physical substance. Ironically, paragraph 3 states that the standard 'applies to agreements that transfer the right to use assets'. An agreement allowing a licensee to use a patented process provides future economic benefits to that licensee and meets the *Conceptual Framework*'s definition of an asset in just the same way as a motor vehicle lease. The exclusion of these agreements from the scope of the standard is difficult to justify. Presumably, the expectation is that accounting standards on extractive industries, self-generating and renewable assets and intangibles will deal with leases of this type.

Additionally, paragraph 2 of IAS 17 prescribes that the standard must not be applied as the basis of measurement for leased investment properties or leased biological assets, because the measurement rules for such assets are contained in IAS 40 *Investment Property* and IAS 41 *Agriculture* respectively.

12.2 CLASSIFICATION OF LEASES

Paragraph 8 of IAS 17 requires both lessees and lessors to classify each lease arrangement as either an *operating lease* or a *finance lease* and to make this classification at the inception of the lease (paragraph 13), which is defined in paragraph 4 as 'the earlier of the date of the lease agreement and the date of commitment by the parties to the principal provisions of the lease'. This classification process is vitally important because the accounting treatment and disclosures prescribed by the standard for each type of lease differ significantly.

IAS 17 paragraph 4 defines a finance lease as:

a lease that transfers substantially all the risks and rewards incidental to ownership of an asset. Title may or may not eventually be transferred.

An operating lease is simply defined as:

a lease other than a finance lease.

The key criterion of a finance lease is the transfer of substantially all the risks and rewards without a transfer of ownership. The classification process therefore consists of three steps. First, the potential rewards and potential risks associated with the asset must be identified. Second, the lease agreement must be analysed to determine what rewards and risks are transferred from the lessor to the lessee. Third, an assessment must be made as to whether the risks and rewards associated with the asset have been substantially passed to the lessee.

The *risks* of ownership include:
- unsatisfactory performance, with the asset unable to provide benefits or service at the expected level or quality
- obsolescence, particularly with regard to the development of more technically advanced items
- idle capacity
- decline in residual value or losses on eventual sale of the asset
- uninsured damage and condemnation of the asset.

The *rewards* include:
- any benefits obtained from using the asset to provide benefit or service to the entity
- appreciation in residual value or gains on the eventual sale of the asset.

The risks and rewards relating to movements in realisable value are the most difficult to transfer without transferring the title. If the leased asset is to be returned to the lessor, then the risk of an adverse movement in realisable value has not been transferred unless the lessee guarantees some or all of the value of the asset at the end of the lease term.

IAS 17 does not define the term 'substantially' or prescribe classification criteria. This is left as a judgement call. By omitting quantitative examples, the IASB has placed the classification decision back in the hands of managers, who must decide what is 'substantial' for their entity and particular circumstances. The disadvantage of this approach is that similar or even identical lease agreements may be classified differently because of varying interpretations of what the terms 'major part' and 'substantially all' mean.

12.3 CLASSIFICATION GUIDANCE

To help account preparers in the classification process, paragraphs 10 and 11 of IAS 17 provide the following series of situations that individually or in combination would normally lead to a lease transaction being classified as a finance lease:
- The lease transfers ownership of the asset by the end of the lease term.
- The lessee has the option to purchase the asset at a price that is expected to be sufficiently lower than the fair value at the date the option becomes exercisable for it to be reasonably certain that the option will be exercised.
- The lease term is for the major part of the economic life of the asset even if title is not transferred.
- At the inception of the lease, the present value of the minimum lease payments amounts to substantially all of the fair value of the leased asset.
- The leased assets are of such a specialised nature that only the lessee can use them without major modification.
- If the lessee can cancel the lease, the lessor's losses associated with the cancellation are borne by the lessee.
- Gains or losses from the fluctuation in the fair value of the residual accrue to the lessee.
- The lessee has the ability to continue the lease for a secondary period at a rental that is substantially less than market rent.

Note that these pointers are guidelines in assessing whether substantially all the risks and rewards are transferred. Each pointer then relates to some measure of risk or reward.

For the purpose of analysis, the guidelines have been restated as five main questions, as represented in figure 12.1, to aid in classifying lease arrangements as either operating leases or finance leases.

Therefore when classifying leases, managers will need to examine three main conditions of the lease agreement:
- cancellability of the lease
- extent of the asset's economic life transferred to the lessee
- present value of minimum lease payments.

12.3.1 Cancellability of the lease

A non-cancellable lease locks both parties into the agreement and ensures that the exchange of risks and rewards will occur. A lease from which both or either party could walk away at any time may result in only a limited transfer of risks and rewards. However, the application of this classification guidance is not a simple cancellable/non-cancellable choice. The definition of a non-cancellable lease provided in paragraph 4 of IAS 17 introduces shades of grey into the equation by deeming cancellable leases with the following characteristics to be 'non-cancellable':
- leases that can be cancelled only upon the occurrence of some remote contingency
- leases that can be cancelled only with the permission of the lessor
- leases where the lessee, upon cancellation, is committed to enter into a further lease for the same or equivalent asset with the same lessor
- leases that provide that the lessee, upon cancellation, incurs a penalty large enough to discourage cancellation in normal circumstances.

A careful examination of the lease agreement is necessary to ensure that cancellable leases are correctly designated.

It would appear that the standard setters have based the assessment of the probability that future risks and rewards have been transferred on whether or not a lease can be cancelled. That is, if a lease can be cancelled at any time without penalty, then there is no certainty that the transfer will be completed.

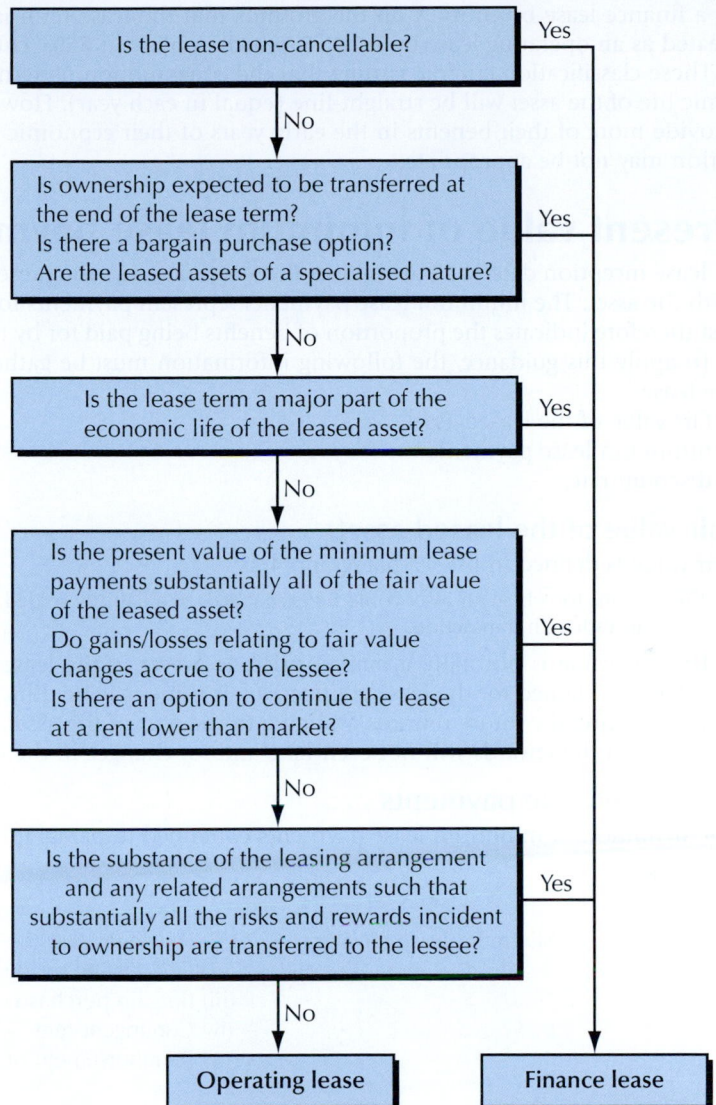

FIGURE 12.1 Guidelines for classifying a lease

12.3.2 Extent of the asset's economic life transferred to the lessee

This classification guidance requires measurement of the lease term against the asset's economic useful life. Paragraph 4 of IAS 17 defines an asset's economic life as either:

(a) the period over which an asset is expected to be economically usable by one or more users; or
(b) the number of production or similar units expected to be obtained from the asset by one or more users.

The lease term is defined as the 'non-cancellable period for which the lessee has contracted to lease the asset' (paragraph 4).

This test represents an attempt to measure the extent of the transfer of rewards to the lessee. If title to the asset is transferred to the lessee at the end of the lease, or if there is a reasonable expectation at lease inception date that the lessee will purchase the asset (via a favourable purchase option clause) at the end of the lease term, then the lessee effectively holds the asset for all (or the balance remaining) of the asset's economic life. Where the asset is to be returned to the lessor at the end of the lease term, then judgement must be applied. What percentage of the asset's economic life represents a 'major' part — 60%? 70%? 80%? The lack of clear guidance in the accounting standard could result in differing classifications of similar lease arrangements. For example, a 6-year lease of an asset with an economic life of 8 years could be classified as a finance lease by entity A on the grounds that the lease term is 74% of the asset's economic life, but treated as an operating lease by entity B, which applies an 85% 'cut off'.

These classification criteria assume that the consumption pattern of economic benefits across the economic life of the asset will be straight-line (equal in each year). However, some assets, such as vehicles, may provide more of their benefits in the early years of their economic lives, so a time-based classification criterion may not be appropriate.

12.3.3 Present value of minimum lease payments

At lease inception date, the fair value of the asset measures the present value of the total benefits associated with the asset. The minimum lease payments represent payments for benefits transferred to the lessee. This test therefore indicates the proportion of benefits being paid for by the lessee.

To apply this guidance, the following information must be gathered or determined at the inception of the lease:
- fair value of the leased asset
- minimum lease payments
- discount rate.

Fair value of the leased asset

Fair value is defined in IAS 17 paragraph 4 as:

> the amount for which an asset could be exchanged, or a liability settled, between knowledgeable, willing parties in an arm's length transaction.

The fair value is normally a market price. However, if the lease relates to specialised equipment constructed or obtained for the lease contract, a fair value may be difficult to obtain. The fair value is regarded as representing the future rewards available to the user of the asset, discounted by the market to allow for the risk that the rewards will not eventuate and for changes in the purchasing power of money over time.

Minimum lease payments

The definition of minimum lease payments contained in paragraph 4 of the standard can be expressed as follows:

Minimum lease payments =	(i) Payments over the lease term
+	(ii) Guaranteed residual value
+	(iii) Bargain purchase option
−	(iv) Contingent rent
−	(v) Reimbursement of costs paid by the lessor

(i) The lease payments are simply the total amounts payable under the lease agreement.

(ii) The guaranteed residual value is that part of the residual value of the leased asset guaranteed by the lessee or a third party related to the lessee (paragraph 4). The lessor will estimate the residual value of the leased asset at the end of the lease term based on market conditions at the inception of the lease, and the lessee will guarantee that, when the asset is returned to the lessor, it will realise at least that amount. The guarantee may range from 1% to 100% of the residual value and is a matter for negotiation between lessor and lessee. If the guarantee is provided by a party related to the lessor rather than the lessee, that part of the residual value is regarded, for the purposes of IAS 17, as unguaranteed. Where a lessee guarantees some or all of the residual value of the asset, the lessor has transferred risks associated with movements in the residual value to the lessee.

(iii) A bargain purchase option is a clause in the lease agreement allowing the lessee to purchase the asset at the end of the lease for a preset amount, significantly less than the expected residual value at the end of the lease term; hence, the 'bargain' description. In paragraph 4 of IAS 17, within the definition of minimum lease payments, the option price is described as one:

> that is expected to be sufficiently lower than the fair value at the date the option becomes exercisable for it to be reasonably certain, at the inception of the lease, that the option will be exercised.

Together, amounts (i), (ii) and (iii) above represent the maximum possible payment the lessee is legally obliged to make under the lease agreement, assuming that the guaranteed amount must be paid in full or the purchase option will be exercised.

(iv) Scheduled lease payments may be increased or decreased during the lease term by the occurrence of events specified in the lease agreement. Additional payments arising from such changes are called contingent rent. For example, an agreement to lease a photocopier may specify an additional charge where the number of copies made in a month exceed 100 000; or a motor vehicle lease charge may be decreased if the vehicle is driven only on sealed metropolitan roads. These charges/reductions relate to the use of the leased asset but, as the occurrence of the contingent event is uncertain at lease inception date, they are ignored when calculating the minimum lease payments.

(v) Lease payments may include two components: a charge for using the asset, and a charge to *reimburse the lessor for operating expenses* paid on behalf of the lessee. These operating amounts include insurance, maintenance, consumable supplies, replacement parts and rates. These costs are given the generic title executory costs in this chapter. Amounts paid to reimburse such costs are excluded from minimum lease payments because they do not relate to the value of the asset transferred between lessor and lessee. Payments for such items give rise to equally unperformed contracts.

Discount rate

The minimum lease payments are discounted to present value by applying an appropriate discount rate. Discounting is not necessary if the lease contains a bargain purchase option or a 100% guaranteed residual value because, in both cases, the present value of the minimum lease payments will equal the fair value of the leased asset. Hence, a complete transfer of risks and rewards is deemed to have taken place.

To discount the minimum lease payments, the lessee/lessor will need to ascertain the interest rate implicit in the lease. This is defined in paragraph 4 of IAS 17 as:

> the discount rate that, at the inception of the lease, causes the aggregate present value of:
> (a) the minimum lease payments; and
> (b) the unguaranteed residual value
> to be equal to the sum of:
> (i) the fair value of the leased asset, and
> (ii) any initial direct costs of the lessor.

Initial direct costs (IDC) are incremental costs that are directly attributable to negotiating and arranging a lease, except for such costs incurred by manufacturer or dealer lessors (paragraph 4). Examples include commission and legal fees and internal costs, but exclude general overheads such as those incurred by a sales and marketing team (paragraph 38). Initial direct costs incurred by a manufacturer/dealer lessor are excluded from the definition of initial direct costs (paragraph 38) because, according to paragraph 46, the costs of negotiating and arranging a finance lease are 'mainly related to earning the manufacturer's or dealer's selling profit'. How the IASB reached this conclusion is hard to understand. Thus, for the purposes of determining the interest rate implicit in the lease, any initial direct costs incurred by a lessee or a manufacturer/dealer lessor are ignored.

The interest rate implicit in the lease is determined at the inception date of the lease, and this may differ from the commencement date of the lease term, which is a date set by the agreement. This may lead to the use of a distorted discount rate if the inception date of the lease differs from the commencement of the lease term, as this is the date from which the lessee is entitled to exercise its right to use the leased asset and presumably the date from which the lessee is entitled to receive the lease payments. As (a) and (b) from the paragraph 4 definition equal the future economic rewards obtainable from the asset, the interest rate is that used by the market to determine the fair value. From this comes the notion that the rate is implicit in the terms of the agreement.

If it is not possible to determine the fair value of the asset at the inception of the lease or the residual value at the end of the lease term, then the interest rate implicit in the lease cannot be calculated. In this situation, paragraph 20 of IAS 17 states that the lessee's (rather than the lessor's) incremental borrowing rate should be used to discount the minimum lease payments. The incremental borrowing rate is the rate of interest the lessee would have to pay on a similar lease or, if this is not determinable, the rate that (at the inception of the lease) the lessee would incur to borrow over a similar term, and with a similar security, the funds necessary to purchase the asset (paragraph 4).

Substantial transfer?

The present value of the minimum lease payments can be determined as a percentage of the fair value of the leased asset and a judgement made as to whether this represents the transfer of 'substantially all' of the fair value of the asset from the lessor to the lessee. Again, a lack of quantitative guidelines may result in the inconsistent classification of similar lease arrangements.

On 30 June 2014, Gisborne Ltd leased a vehicle to Tauranga Ltd. Gisborne Ltd had purchased the vehicle on that day for its fair value of $89 721. The lease agreement, which cost Gisborne Ltd $1457 to have drawn up, contained the following:

Lease term	4 years
Annual payment, payable in advance on 30 June each year	$23 900
Economic life of vehicle	6 years
Estimated residual value at end of lease term	$15 000
Residual value guaranteed by lessee	$7 500

The lease is cancellable, but cancellation will incur a monetary penalty equivalent to 2 years rental payments. Included in the annual payment is an amount of $1900 to cover reimbursement for the costs of insurance and maintenance paid by the lessor. The directors of Tauranga Ltd have indicated that they intend to return the asset to Gisborne Ltd at the end of the lease term.

IAS 17 requires the lease to be classified as either a finance lease or an operating lease, based on the extent to which the risks and rewards associated with the vehicle have been effectively transferred from Gisborne Ltd to Tauranga Ltd.

Is the lease non-cancellable?
The lease agreement is cancellable, but a significant monetary penalty equal to 2 years rental payments will apply. This meets part (d) of the definition of non-cancellable in IAS 17 paragraph 4. Therefore, the lease is deemed to be non-cancellable.

Is ownership expected to be transferred at the end of the lease term?
The expectation is that the asset will be returned to the lessor.

Is the lease term a major part of the economic life of the leased asset?
The lease term is 4 years, which is only 60% of the asset's economic life of 6 years. If expected benefits were receivable evenly over the asset's useful life, it would be doubtful that the lease arrangement is not for the major part of the asset's life.

Is the present value of the minimum lease payments substantially all of the fair value of the leased asset?

Minimum lease payments
The minimum lease payments consist of:
- lease payments net of cost reimbursement — there is an immediate payment of $22 000 (being $23 900 – $1900) and four subsequent payments of $22 000
- contingent rental — which does not arise in this example
- guaranteed residual value — an amount of $7500 is guaranteed at the end of the fourth year.
The unguaranteed residual value is $7500.

Interest rate implicit in the lease
The discount rate is the rate that discounts the minimum lease payments and the unguaranteed residual value to the aggregate of the asset's fair value and any initial indirect costs of the lessor. In this example, the discount rate is the rate that discounts the lessee rental payments and the residual value to $91 178, which is the sum of the asset's fair value at 1 July 2014 of $89 721 and the initial direct costs of $1457 incurred by the lessor. This rate is found by trial and error using present value tables or a financial calculator.

The implicit interest rate in this example is 7%, that is:

$$\text{Present value} = \$22\,000 + (\$22\,000 \times 2.6243\ [T_2\ 7\%\ 3y]) + (\$15\,000 \times 0.7629\ [T_1\ 7\%\ 4y])$$
$$= \$22\,000 + \$57\,735 + \$11\,443$$
$$= \$91\,178$$

where T = present value table
    y = years

Note the following:
- As the first payment is made at the inception of the lease, it is not discounted.
- The discount factor used is an annuity factor based on three equal payments of $22 000 for the next 3 years at 7%.
- The discount factor used is based on a single payment of $15 000 (the residual value) at the end of the lease term in 4 years time at a rate of 7%. The $15 000 comprises $7500 guaranteed by the lessee plus the unguaranteed balance of $7500.

The present value is equal to the fair value (FV) plus initial direct costs (IDC), so the interest rate implicit in the lease is 7%.

Present value of minimum lease payments (PV of MLP)

PV of MLP	= $22 000 + ($22 000 × 2.6243 [T_2 7% 3y]) + ($7500 × 0.7629 [$T_1$ 7% 4y])
	= $22 000 + $57 735 + $5 722
	= $85 457
FV + IDC	= $91 178
PV/(FV + IDC)	= ($85 457/$91 178) × 100%
	= 93.7%

Therefore, at a 93.7% level, the present value of the minimum lease payments is considered to be substantially all of the fair value of the leased asset.

Classification of the lease

Application of the guidelines provides mixed signals. The key criterion in classifying leases is whether substantially all the risks and rewards incident to ownership have been transferred. This requires an overall analysis of the situation, but insufficient information is given in the example to do this. The different signals coming from the lease term test and the present value test may be due to the fact that the majority of the rewards will be transferred in the early stages of the life of the asset, as with motor vehicles. This is reflected in the relatively low residual value at the end of the lease term. These mixed signals demonstrate that the guidelines must be used for guidance only and not treated as specific criteria that must be met.

Further, an analysis of the substance of the lease arrangement must be undertaken to ensure that it is not just the form of the lease agreement that is being accounted for (see section 12.5 of this chapter for more details).

Given no extra information, it is concluded that the lease agreement should be classified as a finance lease because substantially all the risks and rewards incident to ownership have been passed to the lessee.

12.4 SUBSTANCE OVER FORM: INCENTIVES TO MISCLASSIFY LEASES

The classification of lease arrangements as either finance leases or operating leases determines the accounting treatment of transactions associated with the lease. For finance leases, the lessee recognises an asset and liability at the inception of the lease. The leased asset is subsequently depreciated and the liability is reduced through rental payments. An annual interest charge is recognised in respect of the liability. For operating leases, the lessee treats rental payments as expenses.

These divergent accounting treatments provide an incentive to managers to classify lease arrangements as operating leases. Finance leases may have the following adverse impacts on a lessee entity's financial statements or on decisions made by users of those statements.
- The capitalisation of the leased asset increases the value of reported non-current assets and reduces the return on assets ratio.
- Recognition of the present value of future lease payments as a liability increases reported current and non-current liabilities. This adversely affects debt–equity ratios and liquidity–solvency ratios,

such as the current ratio (current assets/current liabilities). Reporting increased liabilities may result in entities breaching debt covenants, thereby causing debts to become due and payable immediately.

- Subsequent depreciation and interest expenses may exceed rental payments and result in lower profits being reported in the early years of the lease.
- Depreciation and interest expenses are not deductible for tax purposes, so additional liabilities may have to be recognised under IAS 12 *Income Taxes* when these expenses are less than the deduction for rental payments.
- More onerous disclosure requirements are prescribed for finance leases.

The ability to manipulate gearing ratios and thereby possibly reduce the cost of capital or increase the availability of finance for an entity is the most significant reward of keeping financing arrangements off the statement of financial position by classifying them as operating leases. As a result, since the release of IAS 17, the leasing industry has been geared towards promoting lease structures or arrangements that meet the guidelines for classification as operating leases. As noted in paragraph 21 of IAS 17, classification and the subsequent accounting must be based on substance and financial reality and not merely legal form. Hence, after considering the guidelines, which concentrate on the form of the lease agreement, the process of classifying a lease must include an analysis of the substance of the lease arrangement.

Features of lease arrangements that can be manipulated include the lease term (in particular, using short terms with options to renew), residual values, economic life estimates and bargain price options.

McGregor (1996, appendix 2, pp. 33–4) gives the following examples of finance leases structured as operating leases:

- *Novated motor vehicle leases.* Under this arrangement, employees enter into finance lease arrangements with a lessor finance company to finance motor vehicles. The employer and employee then enter into a sublease. When the ultimate risk rests with the employee, the arrangement is an operating lease. However, if the employer assumes the risk by, for example, guaranteeing the lease payments, the lease may be in substance a finance lease.
- *Rolling stock sale and leaseback.* In Australia, public sector entities have entered into offshore sale and leaseback arrangements in respect of public transport. Typically, the leases are for periods of 4 to 7 years with options for renewal, and are classified as operating leases. Assets involved include suburban trains, locomotives, light rail vehicles and buses. The unique rail gauges and other user-specific characteristics of this type of equipment make it unlikely that it would find a ready secondary market at the expiration of the lease term, and therefore underline the implausibility of any contention that the leases would not be renewed.
- *Private funding of public infrastructure.* Such funding arrangements often involve the establishment of a special-purpose company by a financier to raise private sector finance by the issue of debt securities for the construction of buildings such as police stations and courthouses. Apart from special-purpose fitting out, the buildings are of a generic type for which alternative uses would therefore be readily available. The buildings are then leased to a government department or other public sector operator. The leases are invariably classified as operating leases by the government department or other public sector operator. An integral feature of most of these arrangements is that the government guarantees the debt securities, thereby ensuring that the bondholders are fully indemnified. Often the government also agrees to a pricing structure that ensures that capital as well as all other costs of the project will be recouped by the investor. Therefore, the risks and rewards of ownership are effectively transferred to the lessee (the government).
- *Separate arrangements for bargain purchase options or guaranteed residual values.* Some leases have been structured to include bargain purchase options or guaranteed residual values that are not specified directly as part of the lease agreements. For example, a bargain purchase option may be specified in an agreement completely separate from the lease agreement itself, and may be portrayed as unrelated to the lease agreement. Alternatively, a trust may be interposed between the lessor and lessee, with the lessee subscribing for units in the trust that are to be drawn against in the event of a shortfall in residual value. In these situations, the very existence of these arrangements may be difficult to detect and, even if detected, may be claimed to be unrelated to the lease and therefore not relevant to the lease classification process.

Shanahan (1989) described another scheme using an interposed entity. Under this arrangement, the lessor leases the asset to the interposed entity, which is owned 50/50 by the lessor and lessee, in the form of a finance lease. The interposed entity then subleases the asset to the ultimate lessee via a series of short-term operating leases, with options to renew. The lessor normally holds a 'put' option, whereby the lessor can force the lessee to buy its share of the interposed entity should the lessee fail to renew the operating lease. The lessee would then control the interposed entity and must consolidate its accounts (including the finance lease) with those of the lessee.

Tolling agreements (a non-lease) may also be used whereby the lessee has no right to use the leased equipment, but pays a toll to the lessor for provision of an asset *and* an operator for the asset. As the lessor's operator uses the asset, it is argued by those not wanting to recognise lease assets and liabilities that no lease as defined by IAS 17 exists.

The fact that managers can circumvent the requirements of the accounting standard and keep leases off the statement of financial position by using such contrivances means that the comparability and usefulness of financial reports is considerably diminished. As McGregor (1996, p. 3) points out:

> standards which do not require the recognition of assets and liabilities in respect of rights and obligations arising under certain financing arrangements have become a motivating factor in the selection of that type of financing arrangement over other forms of arrangement.

All the arrangements described above are finance leases in substance, and a strict application of the IAS 17 definition of a finance lease should result in the classification of the arrangement as a finance lease. However, the notion of what is substantial is capable of a wide range of interpretations, and the lack of clear quantitative guidance in the accounting standard may allow unethical managers to manipulate the lease classification process.

12.4.1 SIC Interpretation 27

In December 2001, the Standing Interpretations Committee (the interpretative committee of the IASB's predecessor body) issued SIC Interpretation 27 *Evaluating the Substance of Transactions Involving the Legal Form of a Lease* in an attempt to provide authoritative guidance to assist in the classification decision. SIC Interpretation 27 requires that a series of transactions that includes a lease should be accounted for as a single transaction 'when the overall economic effect cannot be understood without reference to the series of transactions as a whole' (paragraph 3). This merely reiterates the 'substance over form' approach adopted by IAS 17. However, paragraph 5 of SIC Interpretation 27 also provides the following indicators of arrangements that do not in substance involve a lease:

(a) an entity retains all the risks and rewards incident to ownership of an underlying asset and enjoys substantially the same rights to its use as before the arrangement;

(b) the primary reason for the arrangement is to achieve a particular tax result, and not to convey the right to use an asset; and

(c) an option is included on terms that make its exercise almost certain (e.g. a put option that is exercisable at a price sufficiently higher than the expected fair value when it becomes exercisable).

Thus, the interpretation clearly details transactions that are *not* leases but does little to assist the classification of leases as either financing or operating.

12.4.2 IFRIC Interpretation 4

To further assist account preparers, the IFRS Interpretation Committee (formerly IFRIC) issued IFRIC Interpretation 4 *Determining whether an Arrangement contains a Lease* in February 2004. This interpretation was issued to assist account preparers in determining whether arrangements that are *not* in the legal form of a lease may in fact convey the right to use an item for an agreed period of time in return for a series of payments, and should therefore be treated as a lease for accounting purposes. Such arrangements may include:

- outsourcing arrangements
- arrangements in the telecommunications industry where suppliers of network capacity enter into contracts to provide purchases with rights to capacity
- take-or-pay contracts in which purchasers must make specified payments irrespective of whether they take delivery of services or products.

The assessment of whether an arrangement contains a lease must be done at the inception of the arrangement using the information available at that time. If the provisions of the arrangement are subsequently changed, a reassessment will be made. Using the definition of a lease as an agreement whereby the lessor conveys to the lessee the right to use an asset for an agreed period of time in return for a payment or series of payments (IAS 17 paragraph 4), two criteria were developed to identify the lease component within an arrangement. These are stated in IFRIC Interpretation 4, paragraph 6:

(a) fulfilment of the arrangement is dependent on the use of a specific asset or assets (the asset); and
(b) the arrangement conveys a right to use the asset.

IFRIC Interpretation 4 uses an illustrative example of a purchaser who enters into a take-or-pay arrangement with an industrial gas supplier. If that supplier provides the gas from a plant that is built on the purchaser's premises and used solely to provide gas under the arrangement then, applying the above criteria, this lease is a 'de facto' lease of the gas plant.

If an arrangement does contain a lease component, then that part of the arrangement must be segregated and accounted for in accordance with IAS 17. This would require classification as an operating or financing lease at the inception of the arrangement. Payments made under the arrangement would need to be separated into lease payments and payments for other services on the basis of their relative fair values (IFRIC Interpretation 4 paragraph 13).

12.5 ACCOUNTING FOR FINANCE LEASES BY LESSEES

Once an arrangement has been classified as a finance lease, the asset and liability arising from it must be determined and recognised in the accounts.

12.5.1 Initial recognition

When a lease has been classified as a finance lease, paragraph 20 of IAS 17 requires the lessee to recognise, at the commencement of the lease term, an asset and a liability, each determined at the inception of the lease, equal in amount to the fair value of the leased property or, if lower, the present value of the minimum lease payments. The form of the entry is:

Lease Asset	Dr	PV of MLP	
Lease Liability	Cr		PV of MLP

The commencement of the lease term is the date from which the lessee is entitled to exercise its right to use the leased asset, and may be the same date as the inception of the lease or a later date. If not already determined as part of the classification process, the value of the asset or liability needs to be calculated at the inception of the lease by reference to the terms of the lease agreement. If the lessee incurs initial direct costs associated with the negotiation and securing of the lease arrangements then, according to paragraph 24 of IAS 17, these costs are added to the amount recognised as an asset. The journal entry is:

Lease Asset	Dr	PV of MLP + IDC	
Lease Liability	Cr		PV of MLP
Cash	Cr		IDC

12.5.2 Subsequent measurement

After initial recognition, IAS 17 prescribes differing accounting treatments for the lease asset and the lease liability.

Leased assets

Paragraph 27 of IAS 17 states:

The depreciation policy for depreciable leased assets shall be consistent with that for depreciable assets that are owned, and the depreciation recognised shall be calculated in accordance with IAS 16 *Property, Plant and Equipment* and IAS 38 *Intangible Assets*.

Depreciable assets are those whose future benefits are expected to expire over time or by use. The asset is depreciated over its useful life in a pattern reflecting the consumption or loss of the rewards embodied in the asset. The length of a leased asset's useful life depends on whether or not ownership of the asset will transfer at the end of the lease term. If the asset is to be returned to the lessor, then its useful life is the lease term. If ownership is reasonably certain to transfer to the lessee, then its useful life is its economic life or remainder thereof. Additionally, to determine whether a leased asset has become impaired, the lessee must apply IAS 36 *Impairment of Assets*.

Lease liability

Because lease payments are made over the lease term, paragraph 25 of IAS 17 requires the payments to be divided into the following components:
- reduction of the lease liability
- reimbursement of lessor costs
- interest expense incurred
- payment of contingent rent.

The second two are easily determined by reference to the lease agreement, but the first two need to be calculated. The lease liability recognised at the commencement of the lease term represents the present value of future lease payments relating to the use of the asset. This present value is determined by applying the interest rate implicit in the lease. Thus, the interest expense can be obtained by applying the same rate to the outstanding lease liability at the beginning of the payment period. A payments schedule can be used to determine the interest expense and the reduction in the liability over the lease period.

Accounting for the reimbursement of lessor costs and contingent rent

Paragraph 25 of IAS 17 requires contingent rent to be recognised as an expense of the year in which it is incurred. The accounting standard is silent about the component of lease payments that represents a reimbursement of costs incurred by the lessor. However, as the cost of such items is effectively borne by the lessee, the payment should be recognised as an expense. Consideration must be given to the pattern of consumption relating to those expenses and normal prepayment and accrual rules apply.

ILLUSTRATIVE EXAMPLE 12.2 Accounting for finance leases by lessees

Using the facts from illustrative example 12.1, the lease payments schedule prepared by Tauranga Ltd, based on annual payments of $22 000 for the vehicle and an interest rate of 7%, would be:

TAURANGA LTD
Lease Payments Schedule

	Minimum lease payments[a]	Interest expense[b]	Reduction in liability[c]	Balance of liability[d]
30 June 2014[e]				$85 457[f]
30 June 2014	$22 000	$ —	$22 000	63 457
30 June 2015	22 000	4 442	17 558	45 899
30 June 2016	22 000	3 213	18 787	27 112
30 June 2017	22 000	1 898	20 102	7 010
30 June 2018	7 500	490	7 010	—
	$95 500	$10 043	$85 457	

(a) Four annual payments of $22 000 payable in advance on 30 June of each year, plus a guaranteed residual value of $7500 on the last day of the lease.
(b) Interest expense = balance of liability each year multiplied by 7%. No interest expense is incurred in the first year because payment is made at the commencement of the lease.
(c) Reduction in liability = minimum lease payments less interest expense. The total of this column must equal the initial liability, which may require rounding the final interest expense figure.
(d) The balance is reduced each year by the amount in column 3.
(e) At lease inception.
(f) Initial liability = present value of minimum lease payments. As the present value of minimum lease payments is less than the fair value of the asset, paragraph 20 of IAS 17 requires the lower amount to be recognised.

The payment schedule is used to prepare lease journal entries and disclosure notes each year. The journal entries recorded by Tauranga Ltd for the 4 years of the lease in accordance with IAS 17 are:

TAURANGA LTD General Journal			
Year ended 30 June 2014			
30 June 2014:			
Leased Vehicle	Dr	85 457	
Lease Liability	Cr		85 457
(Initial recording of lease asset/liability)			
Lease Liability	Dr	22 000	
Prepaid Executory Costs*	Dr	1 900	
Cash	Cr		23 900
(First lease payment)			
*Executory costs have been capitalised because the insurance and maintenance benefits will not be received until the next reporting period.			
Year ended 30 June 2015			
1 July 2014:			
Executory Costs	Dr	1 900	
Prepaid Executory Costs	Cr		1 900
(Reversal of prepayment)			
30 June 2015:			
Lease Liability	Dr	17 558	
Interest Expense	Dr	4 442	
Prepaid Executory Costs	Dr	1 900	
Cash	Cr		23 900
(Second lease payment)			
Depreciation Expense	Dr	19 489	
Accumulated Depreciation	Cr		19 489
(Depreciation charge for the period [$85 457 − $7500]/4)*			
*Because the asset will be returned at the end of the lease term, the useful life is the lease term of 4 years and the depreciable amount is the cost less the guaranteed residual value.			
Year ended 30 June 2016			
1 July 2015:			
Executory Costs	Dr	1 900	
Prepaid Executory Costs	Cr		1 900
(Reversal of prepayment)			
30 June 2016:			
Lease Liability	Dr	18 787	
Interest Expense	Dr	3 213	
Prepaid Executory Costs	Dr	1 900	
Cash	Cr		23 900
(Third lease payment)			
Depreciation Expense	Dr	19 489	
Accumulated Depreciation	Cr		19 489
(Depreciation charge for the period [$85 457 − $7500]/4)			
Year ended 30 June 2017			
1 July 2016:			
Executory Costs	Dr	1 900	
Prepaid Executory Costs	Cr		1 900
(Reversal of prepayment)			

30 June 2017:			
Lease Liability	Dr	20 102	
Interest Expense	Dr	1 898	
Prepaid Executory Costs	Dr	1 900	
Cash	Cr		23 900
(Fourth lease payment)			
Depreciation Expense	Dr	19 489	
Accumulated Depreciation	Cr		19 489
(Depreciation charge for the period [$85 457 − $7500]/4)			

Year ended 30 June 2018

1 July 2017:			
Executory Costs	Dr	1 900	
Prepaid Executory Costs	Cr		1 900
(Reversal of prepayment)			
30 June 2018:			
Lease Liability	Dr	7 010	
Interest Expense	Dr	490	
Leased Vehicle*	Cr		7 500
(Return of leased vehicle)			
Depreciation Expense	Dr	19 490	
Accumulated Depreciation	Cr		19 490
(Depreciation charge for the period [$85 457 − $7500]/4)			
Accumulated Depreciation	Dr	77 957	
Leased Vehicle	Cr		77 957
(Fully depreciated asset written off)			

*The final 'payment' is the return of the asset at its guaranteed residual value. If the asset is being purchased, this entry will record a cash payment. Another entry will then be required to reclassify the undepreciated balance of the asset from a 'leased' asset to an 'owned' asset.

12.5.3 Disclosures required

Paragraph 31 of IAS 17 requires that, in addition to meeting the requirements of IFRS 7 *Financial Instruments: Disclosures*, the following information must be disclosed by lessees:

- the carrying amount of each class of leased asset as at the end of the reporting period
- a reconciliation between the total future minimum lease payments at the end of the reporting period and their present value
- the total of future minimum lease payments at the end of the reporting period and their present value for each of the following periods:
  - not later than 1 year
  - later than 1 year and not later than 5 years
  - later than 5 years
- contingent rents recognised as an expense in the period
- the total of future minimum sublease payments expected to be received under non-cancellable subleases at the end of the reporting period
- a general description of the lessee's material leasing arrangements.

Future minimum lease payments include all future amounts payable under the lease agreement less reimbursements of the lessor's costs and any known contingent rents. This reconciliation provides some information about future cash flows to financial statement users.

Figure 12.2 shows the leasing accounting policy disclosures and extracts from the commitments note to the financial statements of the Qantas Group for the year ended 30 June 2011.

FIGURE 12.2 Note extracts from the Qantas Group annual report 30 June 2011

THE QANTAS GROUP
Notes to the Financial Statements
for the year ended 30 June 2011

1. Statement of significant accounting policies
(P) Property, Plant and Equipment
Finance Leased and Hire Purchase Assets

Leased assets under which the Qantas Group assumes substantially all the risks and benefits of ownership are classified as finance leases. Other leases are classified as operating leases.

Linked transactions involving the legal form of a lease are accounted for as one transaction when a series of transactions are negotiated as one or take place concurrently or in sequence and cannot be understood economically alone.

Finance leases are capitalised. A lease asset and a lease liability equal to the present value of the minimum lease payments and guaranteed residual value are recorded at the inception of the lease. Any gains and losses arising under sale and leaseback arrangements are deferred and depreciated over the lease term. Capitalised leased assets are depreciated on a straight-line basis over the period in which benefits are expected to arise from the use of those assets. Lease payments are allocated between the reduction in the principal component of the lease liability and the interest element.

The interest element is charged to the Consolidated Income Statement over the lease term so as to produce a constant periodic rate of interest on the remaining balance of the lease liability.

Fully prepaid leases are classified in the Consolidated Balance Sheet as hire purchase assets, to recognise that the financing structures impose certain obligations, commitments and/or restrictions on the Qantas Group, which differentiate these aircraft from owned assets.

Leases are deemed to be non-cancellable if significant financial penalties associated with termination are anticipated.

Operating Leases

Rental payments under operating leases are charged to the Consolidated Income Statement on a straight-line basis over the term of the lease.

With respect to any premises rented under long-term operating leases, which are subject to sub-tenancy agreements, provision is made for any shortfall between primary payments to the head lessor less any recoveries from sub-tenants. These provisions are determined on a discounted cash flow basis, using a rate reflecting the cost of funds.

28. Commitments
(A) FINANCE LEASE AND HIRE PURCHASE COMMITMENTS

	Qantas Group	
	2011 $M	2010 $M
AS LESSEE		
Finance lease and hire purchase liabilities included in the Consolidated Financial Statements at the present value of future rentals		
Aircraft and engines — payable:		
Not later than one year	46	44
Later than one year but not later than five years	427	482
Later than five years	—	—
	473	526
Less: future lease and hire purchase finance charges and deferred lease benefits	15	17
Total finance lease and hire purchase liabilities	458	509
Finance lease and hire purchase liabilities included in the Consolidated Financial Statements		
Current liabilities (refer to Note 21)	51	54
Non-current liabilities (refer to Note 21)	407	455
Total finance lease and hire purchase liabilities	458	509

FIGURE 12.2 *(continued)*

The Qantas Group leases aircraft under finance leases with expiry dates between one and five years. Most finance leases contain purchase options exercisable at the end of the lease term. The Qantas Group has the right to negotiate extensions on most leases.

(B) OPERATING LEASE COMMITMENTS

AS LESSEE

Non-cancellable operating lease commitments not provided for in the Consolidated Financial Statements

Aircraft — payable:

Not later than one year	632	698
Later than one year but not later than five years	1 718	2 212
Later than five years	450	705
	2 800	3 615

Non-aircraft — payable:

Not later than one year	171	152
Later than one year but not later than five years	527	433
Later than five years	404	344
	1 102	929
Less: provision for potential under-recovery of rentals on unused premises available for sub-lease (included in onerous contract provision — refer to note 22)	7	9
	1 095	920

Total operating lease commitments not provided for in the Consolidated Financial Statements

	3 895	4 535

The Qantas Group leases aircraft, buildings and plant and equipment under operating leases with expiry dates between one and 32 years.

The Qantas Group has the right to negotiate extensions on most leases.

AS LESSOR

Operating lease receivables not recognised in the Consolidated Financial Statements

Receivable:

Not later than one year	12	12
Later than one year but not later than five years	47	47
Later than five years	32	44

Total operating lease receivables not recognised in the Consolidated Financial Statements

	91	103

Qantas leases out freighter aircraft under long-term operating leases with rentals received monthly.

Source: The Qantas Group (2011, pp. 59, 87–8).

Figure 12.3 provides an illustration of the disclosures required by IAS 17, and is based on the figures used in illustrative example 12.2.

FIGURE 12.3 Illustrative disclosures required by IAS 17 for lessees of finance leases

	IAS 17 paragraph
Note 1: Summary of accounting policies (extract) **Leasing** Leases are classified as finance leases whenever the terms of the lease transfer substantially all the risks and rewards of ownership to the lessee. All other leases are classified as operating leases.	*31(e)*
The entity as a lessee Assets held under finance leases are recognised as assets of the entity at their fair value at the date of acquisition or, if lower, at the present value of the minimum lease payments.	

(continued)

FIGURE 12.3 *(continued)*

The corresponding liability to the lessor is included in the statement of financial position as a finance lease liability. Lease payments are apportioned between finance charges and reduction of the lease liability to achieve a constant rate of interest on the remaining balance of the liability. Finance charges are charged directly against income unless they are directly attributable to qualifying assets, in which case they are capitalised in accordance with the entity's general policy on borrowing costs.

Note 16: Property, plant and equipment (extract)
The carrying amount of the entity's plant and equipment includes an amount of $46 479 (2015: $65 968) relating to leased assets.)

Note 36: Finance lease liabilities

	Minimum lease payments 2016	PV of payments 2016	Minimum lease payments 2015	PV of payments 2015	
Amounts payable under finance leases:					31(b)
Within 1 year	22 000	20 102	22 000	18 787	
After 1 year but not more than 5 years	7 500	7 010	29 500	27 112	
Total minimum lease payments	29 500	27 112	51 500	45 899	
Less: Finance charges	(2 388)		(5 601)		
Present value of minimum lease payments	27 112		45 899		

In respect of finance leases, the following item has been recognised as an expense during the period:			31(c)
	2016	**2015**	
Contingent rent	1 200	—	

12.6 ACCOUNTING FOR FINANCE LEASES BY LESSORS

When a lease is classified as a finance lease, the lessor will need to 'derecognise' the leased asset and record a lease receivable.

12.6.1 Initial recognition

In theory, the classification process required by IAS 17 should result in identical classifications by both lessors and lessee. In reality, differing circumstances may result in the same lease being classified differently; for example, where the lessor benefits from a residual value guarantee provided by a party unrelated to the lessee (paragraph 9).

Paragraph 36 of IAS 17 requires the lessor to recognise assets held under a finance lease in its statement of financial position and present them as a receivable at an amount equal to the net investment in the lease. The net investment in the lease is defined in paragraph 4 as the gross investment in the lease discounted at the interest rate implicit in the lease, with the gross investment being equal to:

(a) the minimum lease payments receivable by the lessor under a finance lease, and
(b) any unguaranteed residual value accruing to the lessor.

This value would normally equate to the fair value of the asset at the inception of the lease. Initial direct costs, except those incurred by manufacturer or dealer lessors, are included in the initial measurement of the finance lease receivable and reduce the amount of interest revenue recognised over the lease term. The definition of interest rate implicit in the lease automatically includes initial direct costs in the finance lease receivable, so there is no need to add them separately (paragraph 38). Lessees are required to recognise assets and liabilities associated with finance leases at the commencement of the lease term but no date for recognition is specified for lessors; presumably, it would be the same date.

The recognition of the fair value of the leased asset as a receivable raises an interesting issue in that the 'receivable', for those leases with no purchase option, has both a monetary component (the rent payments) and non-monetary component (the return of the asset). The problem with this 'combination asset' is that IFRS 7 requires specific disclosures to be made for the rent part of the receivable, which is a financial asset as defined by that standard, but does not require disclosures with respect to the non-monetary component. Additionally, these components are subject to different risks, and recording both as an ostensible financial asset may mislead financial statements users.

12.6.2 Subsequent measurement

As the lease payments are received from the lessee over the lease term, the receipts need to be analysed into the following components:
- reduction of the lease receivable
- interest revenue earned
- reimbursement of costs paid on behalf of the lessee
- receipt of contingent rent.

The latter two are easily determined by reference to the lease agreement, but the first two need to be calculated in a similar fashion to that used by the lessor. The lease receivable recognised at the commencement of the lease term represents the present value of future lease payments relating to the use of the asset. This present value is determined by applying the interest rate implicit in the lease. Thus, the interest revenue can be obtained by applying the same rate to the outstanding lease receivable at the beginning of the payment period. A receipts schedule can be used to determine the interest revenue and the reduction in the receivable over the lease period.

12.6.3 Accounting for executory costs and contingent rentals

IAS 17 is silent on the treatment of contingent rent and the reimbursements of costs incurred on behalf of the lessee. However, as these receipts meet the definition of income in the *Conceptual Framework*, contingent rents should be recognised as revenue in the period they were earned, and reimbursements should be recorded as revenue in the same period in which the related expenses are incurred.

ILLUSTRATIVE EXAMPLE 12.3 Accounting for finance leases by lessors

On 30 June 2014, Gisborne Ltd leased a vehicle to Tauranga Ltd. Gisborne Ltd had purchased the vehicle on that day for its fair value of $89 721. The lease agreement, which cost Gisborne Ltd $1457 to have drawn up, contained the following:

Lease term	4 years
Annual payment, payable in advance on 30 June each year	$23 900
Economic life of vehicle	6 years
Estimated residual value at end of economic life	$2 000
Estimated residual value at end of lease term	$15 000
Residual value guaranteed by lessee	$7 500

The lease is cancellable, but cancellation will incur a monetary penalty equivalent to 2 years rental payments. Included in the annual payment is an amount of $1900 to cover reimbursement for the costs of insurance and maintenance paid by the lessor. The directors of Tauranga Ltd have indicated that they will return the asset to Gisborne Ltd at the end of the lease term.

Classification of the lease by the lessor
Gisborne Ltd would apply IAS 17 guidelines and classify the lease as a finance lease. See illustrative example 12.1 for workings.

The lease receipts schedule based on annual payments of $22 000 for the vehicle and an interest rate implicit in the lease of 7% shows:

GISBORNE LTD Lease Receipts Schedule				
	Minimum lease receipts[(a)]	Interest revenue[(b)]	Reduction in receivable[(c)]	Balance of receivable[(d)]
30 June 2014				$91 178[(e)]
30 June 2014	$ 22 000	$ —	$22 000	69 178
30 June 2015	22 000	4 842	17 158	52 020
30 June 2016	22 000	3 641	18 359	33 661
30 June 2017	22 000	2 356	19 644	14 017
30 June 2018	15 000	983	14 017	—
	$103 000	$11 822	$91 178	

(a) Four annual receipts of $22 000 payable in advance on 30 June of each year, plus a residual value of $15 000 (of which $7500 is guaranteed by the lessee) on the last day of the lease.
(b) Interest revenue = balance of receivable each year multiplied by 7%. No interest revenue is earned in the first year because the payment is received at the inception of the lease.
(c) Reduction in receivable = minimum lease receipts less interest revenue. The total of this column must equal the initial receivable, which may require rounding the final interest revenue figure.
(d) The balance is reduced each year by the amount in column 3.
(e) Initial receivable = fair value of $89 721 plus initial direct costs of $1457. This figure equals the present value of minimum lease payments receivable and the present value of the unguaranteed residual value.

The lease receipts schedule is used to prepare lease journal entries and disclosure notes each year, as shown below:

GISBORNE LTD General Journal			
Year ended 30 June 2014 30 June 2014:			
Vehicle	Dr	89 721	
Cash	Cr		89 721
(Purchase of motor vehicle)			
Lease Receivable	Dr	89 721	
Vehicle	Cr		89 721
(Lease of vehicle to Tauranga Ltd)			
Lease Receivable	Dr	1 457	
Cash	Cr		1 457
(Payment of initial direct costs)			
Cash	Dr	23 900	
Lease Receivable	Cr		22 000
Reimbursement in Advance*	Cr		1 900
(Receipt of first lease payment)			
*The reimbursement of executory cost has been carried forward to 2015, when Gisborne Ltd will pay the costs.			
Year ended 30 June 2015 1 July 2014:			
Reimbursement in Advance	Dr	1 900	
Reimbursement Revenue	Cr		1 900
(Reversal of accrual)			

30 June 2015:			
Insurance and Maintenance	Dr	1 900	
Cash	Cr		1 900
(Payment of costs on behalf of lessee)			
Cash	Dr	23 900	
Lease Receivable	Cr		17 158
Interest Revenue	Cr		4 842
Reimbursement in Advance	Cr		1 900
(Receipt of second lease payment)			
Year ended 30 June 2016			
1 July 2015:			
Reimbursement in Advance	Dr	1 900	
Reimbursement Revenue	Cr		1 900
(Reversal of accrual)			
30 June 2016:			
Insurance and Maintenance	Dr	1 900	
Cash	Cr		1 900
(Payment of costs on behalf of lessee)			
Cash	Dr	23 900	
Lease Receivable	Cr		18 359
Interest Revenue	Cr		3 641
Reimbursement in Advance	Cr		1 900
(Receipt of third lease payment)			
Year ended 30 June 2017			
1 July 2016:			
Reimbursement in Advance	Dr	1 900	
Reimbursement Revenue	Cr		1 900
(Reversal of accrual)			
30 June 2017:			
Insurance and Maintenance	Dr	1 900	
Cash	Cr		1 900
(Payment of costs on behalf of lessee)			
Cash	Dr	23 900	
Lease Receivable	Cr		19 644
Interest Revenue	Cr		2 356
Reimbursement in Advance	Cr		1 900
(Receipt of fourth lease payment)			
Year ended 30 June 2018			
1 July 2017:			
Reimbursement in Advance	Dr	1 900	
Reimbursement Revenue	Cr		1 900
(Reversal of accrual)			
30 June 2018:			
Insurance and Maintenance	Dr	1 900	
Cash	Cr		1 900
(Payment of costs on behalf of lessee)			
Vehicle	Dr	15 000	
Interest Revenue	Cr		983
Lease Receivable	Cr		14 017
(Return of vehicle at end of lease)			

12.6.4 The initial direct costs anomaly

The inclusion (by the standard setters) of initial direct costs incurred by lessors in the definition of the interest rate implicit in the lease creates an interest rate differential between lessee and lessor where a lease agreement transfers all of the risks and rewards related to an asset.

To illustrate: consider the same situation as described in illustrative example 12.3 but increasing the guaranteed residual value to $15 000 (100% of the residual), which effectively transfers all of the benefits of the vehicle from Gisborne Ltd to Tauranga Ltd. The present value of the minimum lease payments would then be:

$$\begin{aligned} \text{PV of MLP} &= \$22\,000 + (\$22\,000 \times 2.6243 \; [T_2\; 7\%\; 3y]) + (\$15\,000 \times 0.7629 \; [T_1\; 7\%\; 4y]) \\ &= \$22\,000 + \$57\,735 + \$11\,443 \\ &= \$91\,178 \end{aligned}$$

This figure equals the fair value of the asset, $89 721, plus the initial direct costs incurred by the lessor of $1457.

However, paragraph 20 of IAS 17 requires lessees to recognise, at the inception of the lease, an asset and a liability equal to the fair value of the leased asset or, if *lower*, the present value of the minimum lease payments. As the present value of the minimum lease payments using the 7% interest rate implicit in the lease is *higher* than the asset's fair value, it cannot be recognised by the lessee even though it would be recognised by the lessor. The lessee, Tauranga Ltd, can only recognise a lease asset and liability of $89 721, and must recalculate the interest rate implicit in the lease in order to determine interest expense charges over the lease term.

The interest rate that discounts the lease payments to $89 721 is 8%, so Tauranga Ltd will calculate its interest at 8% and Gisborne Ltd will calculate its interest revenue at 7%. The difference represents the recovery of the initial direct costs by Gisborne Ltd via the lease payments received.

12.6.5 Disclosures required

Paragraph 47 of IAS 17 requires that, in addition to disclosures required by IFRS 7, the following information must be disclosed separately in the financial statements in respect of finance leases:

- a reconciliation between the gross investment in the lease and the present value of the minimum lease payments at the end of the reporting period
- the gross investment in the lease and the present value of minimum lease payments receivable at the end of the reporting period, for each of the following periods:
  - not later than 1 year
  - later than 1 year and not later than 5 years
  - later than 5 years
- unearned finance income
- the unguaranteed residual values accruing to the benefit of the lessor
- the accumulated allowance for uncollectable minimum lease payments receivable
- contingent rents recognised as income in the period
- a general description of the lessor's material leasing arrangements.

Figure 12.4 provides an illustration of the disclosures required by IAS 17. The information used in this figure is derived from the Gisborne Ltd lease shown in illustrative example 12.3.

FIGURE 12.4 Illustrative disclosures required by IAS 17 for lessors of finance leases

	IAS 17 paragraph
Note 1: Summary of accounting policies (extract) **Leasing** Leases are classified as finance leases whenever the terms of the lease transfer substantially all the risks and rewards of ownership to the lessee. All other leases are classified as operating leases.	*47(f)*

FIGURE 12.4 (continued)

The entity as a lessor
Amounts due from lessees under finance leases are recorded as a receivable at the amount of the entity's net investment in the leases. Finance lease income is allocated to accounting periods, so as to reflect a constant periodic rate of return on the entity's net investment outstanding in respect of the leases.

Note 36: Finance lease receivables

	Investment in lease 2016	PV of receivables 2016	Investment in lease 2015	PV of receivables 2015	
Amounts receivable under finance leases:					47(a)
Within 1 year	22 000	19 644	22 000	18 359	
After 1 year but not more than 5 years	15 000	14 017	37 000	33 661	
Total minimum lease payments receivable	37 000	33 661	59 000	52 020	
Less: Unearned finance income	(3 339)		(6 980)		47(b)
Present value of minimum lease payments	33 661		52 020		

Unguaranteed residual values of assets leased under finance leases at the end of the reporting period are estimated at $7500 (2015: $7500)
47(c)

In respect of finance leases, contingent rents amounting to $1200 (2015: nil) were recognised as income during the period.
47(e)

12.7 ACCOUNTING FOR FINANCE LEASES BY MANUFACTURER OR DEALER LESSORS

When manufacturers or dealers offer customers the choice of either buying or leasing an asset, a lease arrangement gives rise to two types of income:
- profit or loss equivalent to the outright sale of the asset being leased
- finance income over the lease term.

Accounting for the lease is identical to that required by non-manufacturer/dealer lessors except for an initial entry to recognise profit or loss and the fact that initial direct costs are not included in the lease receivable amount.

IAS 17 paragraph 42 requires manufacturer and dealer lessors to recognise selling profit or loss at the commencement of the lease, in accordance with the policy followed by the entity for outright sales. Where artificially low interest rates have been offered to entice the customer to enter the lease, the selling profit recorded must be restricted to that which would apply if a market rate of interest had been charged.

Hence, as well as recognising the lease receivable, the manufacturer or dealer records the profit or loss on sale (at market interest rates) at the commencement of the lease. The sales revenue recognised is equal to the fair value of the asset or, if lower, the minimum lease payments calculated at a market rate of interest. The cost of sale expense is the cost or carrying amount of the leased property less the present value of any unguaranteed residual value. Sales revenue less cost of sales expense equals selling profit or loss. Additionally, paragraph 42 of IAS 17 requires the initial direct costs incurred by the manufacturer or dealer in negotiating and arranging the lease to be recognised as an expense when the profit is recognised. Such costs are regarded as part of earning the profit on sale rather than a cost of leasing (paragraph 46).

12.8 ACCOUNTING FOR OPERATING LEASES

Operating leases are those where substantially all the risks and rewards incident to ownership remain with the lessor. IAS 17 requires such arrangements to be treated as rental agreements, with all payments treated as income or expense by the respective parties.

12.8.1 Accounting treatment

Lessees

Paragraph 33 of IAS 17 requires the lessee to recognise lease payments as an expense on a straight-line basis over the lease term unless another systematic basis is more representative of the time pattern of the user's benefit.

Lessors

Lease receipts

Paragraph 50 of IAS 17 requires lessors to account for receipts from operating leases as income on a straight-line basis over the lease term unless another systematic basis is more representative of the time pattern in which the benefit derived from the leased asset is diminished.

Initial direct costs

Any initial direct costs incurred by lessors in negotiating operating leases are to be added to the carrying amount of the leased asset and recognised as an expense over the lease term on the same basis as the lease income (IAS 17 paragraph 52). The initial direct costs are then capitalised into a deferred costs account and disclosed as follows:

Asset	$ xxx
Less: Accumulated depreciation	(xxx)
	xxx
Plus: Initial direct costs	xxx
	xxx

Because the IAS 17 definition of initial direct costs excludes costs incurred by manufacturers and dealers in negotiating and executing a lease, paragraph 52 applies only to costs incurred by non-dealer/manufacturer lessors.

Depreciation of leased assets

Paragraph 49 of IAS 17 requires the leased asset to be presented in the statement of financial position according to the nature of the asset. According to paragraph 53, depreciation of assets provided under operating leases should be consistent with the lessor's normal depreciation policy for similar assets, and should be calculated in accordance with IAS 16 and IAS 38.

ILLUSTRATIVE EXAMPLE 12.5 Accounting for operating leases

On 1 July 2014, Rotorua Ltd leased a bobcat from Palmerston Ltd. The bobcat cost Palmerston Ltd $35 966 on that same day. The finance lease agreement, which cost Palmerston Ltd $381 to have drawn up, contained the following:

Lease term	3 years
Estimated economic life of the bobcat	10 years
The lease is cancellable	
Annual rental payment, in arrears (commencing 30/6/15)	$3 900
Residual value at end of the lease term	$24 500
Residual guaranteed by Rotorua Ltd	$0
Interest rate implicit in lease	6%

IAS 17 requires the lease to be classified as either a finance lease or an operating lease based on the extent to which the risks and rewards associated with the vehicle have been effectively transferred between Rotorua Ltd and Palmerston Ltd.

Is the lease non-cancellable?
The lease agreement is cancellable; either party can walk away from the arrangement without penalty.

Is ownership expected to be transferred at the end of the lease term?
Rotorua Ltd expects to return the bobcat to Palmerston Ltd.

Is the lease term a major part of the economic life of the leased asset?
The lease term is 3 years, which is only 30% of the bobcat's economic life of 10 years. Therefore, it would appear that the lease arrangement is not for the major part of the asset's life.

Is the present value of the minimum lease payments substantially all of the fair value of the leased asset?
Minimum lease payments
The minimum lease payments consist of three payments, in arrears, of $3900. There are no contingent rentals, executory costs or guaranteed residual value.
Present value of minimum lease payments

$$\text{PV of MLP} = \$3900 \times 2.6730 \text{ [3 years } T_2 \text{ 6\%]}$$
$$= \$10\,425$$
$$\text{PV/FV} = \$10\,425/\$35\,966$$
$$= 29\%$$

Is the substance of the transaction such that substantially all the risks and rewards incident to ownership have been transferred?

The shortness of the lease term compared with the asset's economic life indicates that it is, in substance, an operating lease.

Classification of the lease

On the basis of the evidence available, there has not been an effective transfer of substantially all the risks and rewards associated with the bobcat to the lessee. Hence, the lease should be classified and accounted for as an *operating lease*.

Journal entries

The following journal entries would be passed in the books of both the lessor and the lessee for the year ended 30 June 2015:

ROTORUA LTD General Journal			
30 June 2015: Lease Expense Cash (Payment of first year's rental)	Dr Cr	3 900	3 900

PALMERSTON LTD General Journal			
1 July 2014: Plant and Equipment Cash (Purchase of bobcat)	Dr Cr	35 966	35 966
Deferred Initial Direct Costs – Plant and Equipment Cash (Initial direct costs incurred for lease)	Dr Cr	381	381
30 June 2015: Cash Lease Income (Receipt of first year's rental)	Dr Cr	3 900	3 900
Lease Expense Deferred Initial Direct Costs – Plant and Equipment (Recognition of initial direct cost: $381/3 years)	Dr Cr	127	127
Depreciation Expense Accumulated Depreciation (Depreciation charge for the period: $35 966/10)	Dr Cr	3 597	3 597

12.8.2 Disclosures required

Lessees

Paragraph 35 of IAS 17 requires lessees, in addition to meeting the requirements of IFRS 7, to disclose the following information in respect of operating leases:

(a) the total of future minimum lease payments under non-cancellable operating leases for each of the following periods:
  (i) not later than one year;
  (ii) later than one year and not later than five years;
  (iii) later than five years;
(b) the total of future minimum sublease payments expected to be received under non-cancellable subleases at the end of the reporting period;

(c) lease and sublease payments recognised as an expense in the period, with separate amounts for minimum lease payments, contingent rents, and sublease payments;

(d) a general description of the lessee's significant leasing arrangements . . .

The key feature of these disclosures is the identification of future commitments with respect to those operating leases which are non-cancellable. This information allows users of financial statements to factor in lease expenses against expected future profits, and alerts potential creditors to the fact that some future cash flows are not available to service new liabilities.

Figure 12.5 provides an illustration of the disclosures required by IAS 17.

	IAS 17 paragraph
Note 1: Summary of accounting policies (extract)	
Leasing Leases are classified as finance leases whenever the terms of the lease transfer substantially all the risks and rewards of ownership to the lessee. All other leases are classified as operating leases.	35(d)
The entity as a lessee Rentals payable under operating leases are charged to income on a straight-line basis over the term of the relevant lease.	
Note 43: Operating lease arrangements Minimum lease payments recorded as expense amounted to $167 500 (2014: $152 100) for the period.	35(c)
Future minimum lease payments under non-cancellable operating leases are as follows:	

	2015	2014	
Within 1 year	70 000	51 700	35(a)
After 1 year but not more than 5 years	115 500	100 000	
More than 5 years	76 200	64 800	
	261 700	216 500	

FIGURE 12.5 Illustrative disclosures required by IAS 17 for lessees of operating leases

Lessors

Paragraph 56 of IAS 17 requires lessors to make the following disclosures, in addition to those required by IFRS 7, with respect to operating leases:

(a) the future minimum lease payments under non-cancellable operating leases in the aggregate and for each of the following periods:
  (i)   not later than one year;
  (ii) later than one year and not later than five years;
  (iii) later than five years.
(b) total contingent rents recognised as income in the period.
(c) a general description of the lessor's leasing arrangements.

Figure 12.6 provides an illustration of the disclosures required by IAS 17.

FIGURE 12.6 Illustrative disclosures required by IAS 17 for lessors of operating leases

	IAS 17 paragraph
Note 1: Summary of accounting policies (extract)	
Leasing Leases are classified as finance leases whenever the terms of the lease transfer substantially all the risks and rewards of ownership to the lessee. All other leases are classified as operating leases.	56(c)

(continued)

FIGURE 12.6 *(continued)*

The entity as a lessor
Rental income from operating leases is recognised on a straight-line basis over the term of the relevant lease.

Note 43: Operating lease arrangements
Future minimum lease payments receivable under non-cancellable operating leases are as follows:

	2012	**2011**	
Within 1 year	81 000	60 200	*56(a)*
After 1 year but not more than 5 years	317 900	324 000	
More than 5 years	153 900	228 800	
	552 800	613 000	

Contingent rent income amounting to $15 600 (2014: nil) was recognised during the period.   *56(b)*

12.8.3 Accounting for lease incentives

In order to induce prospective lessees to enter into non-cancellable operating leases, lessors may offer lease incentives such as rent-free periods, upfront cash payments or contributions towards lessee expenses such as fit-out or removal costs. However attractive these incentives appear, it is unlikely that they are truly free because the lessor will structure the rental payments so as to recover the costs of the incentives over the lease term. Thus, rental payments will be higher than for leases that do not offer incentives.

IAS 17 is silent about incentives, and deals only with accounting for the rental payments made under the operating lease agreement. As a result, SIC Interpretation 15 *Operating Leases — Incentives* was issued in December 1998 to provide guidance on accounting for incentives by both lessors and lessees. Paragraph 3 of this interpretation requires that all incentives associated with an operating lease should be regarded as part of the net consideration agreed for the use of the leased asset, irrespective of the nature or form of the incentive or the timing of the lease payments.

- For lessors — the aggregate cost of the incentives is treated as a reduction in rental income over the lease term on a straight-line basis.
- For lessees — the aggregate benefit of incentives is treated as a reduction in rental expense over the lease term on a straight-line basis.

In both cases, another systematic basis can be used if it better represents the diminishment of the leased asset.

ILLUSTRATIVE EXAMPLE 12.6 Accounting for lease incentives

As an incentive to enter a 4-year operating lease for a warehouse, Nelson Ltd receives an upfront cash payment of $600 upon signing an agreement to pay Hutt Ltd an annual rental of $11 150.

Nelson Ltd will make the following journal entries with respect to the lease incentive:

At inception of the lease			
Cash	Dr	600	
Incentive from Lessor	Cr		600
(Recognition of liability to lessor)			
Payment entry (year 1)			
Lease Expense	Dr	11 000	
Incentive from Lessor*	Dr	150	
Cash	Cr		11 150
(Record payment of rent and reduction in liability)			
*Being 600/4.			

Hutt Ltd will make the following journal entries with respect to the lease incentive:

At inception of the lease			
Incentive to Lessee	Dr	600	
Cash	Cr		600
(Recognition of receivable)			
Receipt entry (year 1)			
Cash	Dr	11 150	
Incentive to Lessee*	Cr		150
Rent income	Cr		11 000
(Record receipt of rent and reduction in receivable)			
Being 600/4.			

This broad-brush approach assumes that all incentives are the same, but a number of issues need to be resolved:
- the need to distinguish between 'capital' incentives such as property fit-outs, particularly in the retail industry, and 'cash' incentives such as rent-free periods
- the need to distinguish between property fit-outs that became part of the structure of a leased property and were owned by the lessor, and fit-outs that were owned by the lessee
- the difficulty of determining in practice whether market rentals were being paid by major tenants who had received incentives to lease space in a property
- the need to exclude incentives provided to achieve a desired tenancy mix aimed at improving rentals under future leases of the property.

To date, these matters have not been considered by the IASB.

12.9 ACCOUNTING FOR SALE AND LEASEBACK TRANSACTIONS

A 'sale and leaseback' is a lease transaction that creates an accounting problem for lessees. Effectively, this type of arrangement involves the sale of an asset that is then leased back from the purchaser for all or part of its remaining economic life. Hence, the original owner becomes the lessee but the asset itself does not move. In substance, the lessee gives up legal ownership but still retains control over some or all of the asset's future economic benefits via the lease agreement. Generally, the asset is sold at a price equal to or greater than its fair value, and is leased back for lease payments sufficient to repay the purchaser for the cash invested plus a reasonable return. Therefore, the lease payment and the sale price are usually interdependent because they are negotiated as a package (IAS 17 paragraph 58).

Entities normally enter into sale and leaseback arrangements to generate immediate cash flows while still retaining the use of the asset. Such arrangements are particularly attractive where the fair value of an asset is considerably higher than its carrying amount, or where a large amount of capital is tied up in property and plant.

The major accounting issue revolves around the sale rather than the lease component of the transaction. The lease is classified and accounted for in exactly the same fashion as normal lease transactions, but accounting for the sale transaction differs according to whether the lease is classified as a finance lease or an operating lease.

12.9.1 Finance leases

According to IAS 17 paragraph 59:

> If a sale and leaseback transaction results in a finance lease, any excess of sales proceeds over the carrying amount shall not be immediately recognised as income by a seller-lessee. Instead, it shall be deferred and amortised over the lease term.

This accounting treatment is justified on the basis that the leaseback of the asset negates the sale transaction. In other words, there was a finance agreement between the lessor and the lessee — not a sale — with the asset used as security. Paragraph 60 of IAS 17 states that for this reason 'it is not appropriate to regard an excess of sales proceeds over the carrying amount as income'. The accounting standard provides no guidance on how the deferred income is to be classified in the statement of financial position. In this chapter, any deferred income is recognised separately and classified as 'other' liabilities on the statement of financial position. Amortisation is on a straight-line basis over the lease term.

ILLUSTRATIVE EXAMPLE 12.7 Sale and leaseback

In an attempt to alleviate its liquidity problems, Napier Ltd entered into an agreement on 1 July 2014 to sell its processing plant to Timaru Ltd for $3.5 million (which is the fair value of the plant). At the date of sale, the plant had a carrying amount of $2.75 million. Timaru Ltd immediately leased the processing plant back to Napier Ltd. The terms of the lease agreement were:

Lease term	6 years
Economic life of plant	8 years
Annual rental payment, in arrears (commencing 30/6/15)	$700 000
Residual value of plant at end of lease term (fully guaranteed)	$500 000
Interest rate implicit in the lease	10%

The lease is non-cancellable. The annual rental payment includes $35 000 to reimburse the lessor for maintenance costs incurred on behalf of the lessee.

Accounting for the sale of the processing plant

Step 1 — Classify the leaseback
Napier Ltd must determine whether the leaseback has resulted in the company retaining substantially all of the risks and rewards associated with the processing plant, even though legal title has passed to Timaru Ltd, before classifying the lease as a finance lease in accordance with IAS 17 requirements.

Based on the following evidence, both lessor and lessee should conclude that the lease should be classified as a *finance lease*:
- the lease is non-cancellable
- ownership is not expected to be transferred at the end of the lease term
- the lease term is a major part of the economic life of the leased asset
- the present value of the minimum lease payments is substantially all of the fair value of the leased asset. It was calculated as follows:

$$
\begin{aligned}
\text{PV of MLP} &= (\$665\,000 \times 4.3553) + (\$500\,000 \times 0.5645) \\
&= \$2\,896\,275 + \$282\,250 \\
&= \$3\,178\,525 \\
\text{PV/FV} &= \$3\,178\,525/\$3\,500\,000 \\
&= 90.8\%
\end{aligned}
$$

Step 2 — Record the 'sale' transaction
This illustrative example shows only those journal entries relating to the sale of the processing plant to Timaru Ltd. The lease is recorded as shown in illustrative example 12.2.

NAPIER LTD General Journal			
Year ended 30 June 2015 1 July 2014:			
Cash	Dr	3 500 000	
Deferred Gain on Sale	Cr		750 000
Processing Plant	Cr		2 750 000
(Sale of plant under sale and leaseback agreement)			

30 June 2015:		
Deferred Gain on Sale	Dr	125 000
Gain on Sale of Leased Plant	Cr	125 000
(Amortisation of deferred gain: $750 000/6)		

The deferred gain is recognised as income on a straight-line basis over the lease term.

12.9.2 Operating leases

All operating leases are accounted for in the same way regardless of whether a sale and leaseback transaction is involved. The only accounting issue involves the initial recognition of the sale transaction.

The accounting treatment of the gain or loss on sale is determined by the relationship between the sale price of the asset and the asset's fair value on the date of sale. Essentially, a gain or loss on sale can be recognised immediately only when it equates to the gain or loss that would have been earned on a sale at fair value. Excess or reduced gains or losses are to be deferred and amortised over the lease term. Table 12.1 is part of the Implementation Guidance to IAS 17, and sets out the alternative treatments as required by paragraphs 61–63 of the standard.

Table 12.1 Alternative treatments of gain or loss on sale

	Carrying amount equal to fair value	Carrying amount less than fair value	Carrying amount above fair value
Sale price at fair value (paragraph 61)			
Profit	No profit	Recognise profit immediately	Not applicable
Loss	No loss	Not applicable	Recognise loss immediately
Sale price below fair value (paragraph 61)			
Profit	No profit	Recognise profit immediately	No profit (note 1)
Loss not compensated for by future lease payments at below market price	Recognise loss immediately	Recognise loss immediately	(note 1)
Loss compensated for by future lease payments at below market price	Defer and amortise loss	Defer and amortise loss	(note 1)
Sale price above fair value (paragraph 61)			
Profit	Defer and amortise profit	Defer and amortise excess of selling price over fair value. Recognise any excess of fair value over carrying amount immediately (note 3)	Defer and amortise profit (note 2)
Loss	No loss	No loss	(note 1)

Notes:
1. These parts of the table represent circumstances dealt with in paragraph 63 of the standard. Paragraph 63 requires the carrying amount of an asset to be written down to fair value where it is subject to a sale and leaseback. This therefore results in a carrying amount equal to fair value.
2. Profit is the difference between the fair value and sale price because the carrying amount would have been written down to fair value in accordance with paragraph 63.
3. The excess profit (the excess of selling price over fair value) is deferred and amortised over the period for which the asset is expected to be used. Any excess of fair value over the carrying amount is recognised immediately.

Source: Adapted from IAS 17 Implementation Guidance, pp. B890–1.

12.9.3 Disclosures required

Sale and leaseback transactions are subject to the same disclosure requirements prescribed for lessees and lessors in relation to both operating and finance leases. Unique or unusual provisions of the agreement should be disclosed as part of the required description of material leasing arrangements. Additionally, sale and leaseback transactions may fall under the separate disclosure criteria in IAS 1 *Presentation of Financial Statements* with respect to gains or losses on the sale of assets.

12.9.4 Deferral and amortisation — some theoretical concerns

The accounting treatment prescribed by IAS 17 paragraphs 59 and 61 relating to any gain or loss on the sale of an asset in a sale and leaseback transaction may result in the deferral of such gains or losses and their amortisation over the lease term. The *Conceptual Framework* does not support this accounting treatment, because it results in reporting debit and credit balances in the statement of financial position that do not meet the definitions of assets and liabilities. In illustrative example 12.7, Napier Ltd records a 'deferred gain' of $750 000 on 1 July 2014, but is this a liability? The *Conceptual Framework* in paragraph 4.4(b) defines a liability as:

> a present obligation of the entity arising from past events, the settlement of which is expected to result in an outflow from the entity of resources embodying economic benefits.

The $750 000 credit balance recorded by the lessee certainly arises from a past event — the sale of the asset — but, as there is no future outflow in respect of this amount, it should not be classified and reported as a liability. Income is defined in paragraph 4.25 of the *Conceptual Framework* as follows:

> Income is increases in economic benefits during the accounting period in the form of inflows or enhancements of assets or decreases of liabilities that result in increases in equity, other than those relating to contributions from equity participants.

The sale of its asset by Napier Ltd provides a cash inflow of $3.5 million and the loss of $2.75 million in future benefits, resulting in a net increase in equity of $750 000. This transaction clearly gives rise to income. The accounting treatment prescribed by IAS 17 paragraphs 59 and 61 results in entities incorrectly reporting income as liabilities, or expenses as assets. Accordingly, the profit reported in the statement of profit or loss and other comprehensive income will be incorrect, as will the total asset and liability figures reported on the statement of financial position. This 'error' situation will continue throughout the lease term as the 'deferred credit' or 'deferred debit' balances are amortised to profit and loss. Again, the rationale for this accounting treatment seems to be based on the notion that a lease is a quasi-sale transaction. There can be only one 'sale' recorded for a finance leaseback, and only a 'real' profit recorded for an operating leaseback. The reality, of course, is that the two transactions should be treated independently and recorded in accordance with the *Conceptual Framework*.

12.10 PROPOSALS TO CHANGE THE LEASING STANDARD

Accounting for leases by most countries is very comparable, in that most countries require the application of principles similar to those in IAS 17. However, it is also recognised that the accounting principles applied are flawed.

In July 2006, as a result of the agreement between the IASB and the FASB to converge accounting standards, a joint working party was formed between the two bodies to propose a new accounting standard on leases. The aims of the project were stated as:

- to produce an improved accounting standard that faithfully reports the economics of leasing transactions
- to develop a principles-based standard
- to produce a converged standard that can be applied internationally.

As noted in the information provided for observers at the IASB meeting in July 2008, the main concerns about the current IAS 17 were:

- the dividing line between finance and operating leases is hard to define in a principled way
- any dividing line means that similar transactions are accounted for differently
- obligations under non-cancellable leases are little different from borrowings, but for operating leases they are not recognised as liabilities

- assets used in the business that are held under operating leases are not shown on the statement of financial position, thereby overstating return on assets
- leases are scoped out of the financial instruments standards, leading to inconsistencies between leases and similar transactions
- lessor accounting is based on a deferral and matching model that is inconsistent with the direction the revenue recognition project is likely to take.

Currently, leases are classified into finance and operating leases. The IASB staff produced five reasons why the requirement to classify leases should be removed:

- All leases give rise to a right to use the leased item that meets the definition of an asset; a single conceptual model to account for all leases is preferable.
- The removal of classification would result in a simpler accounting standard.
- Classification is a difficult process, often resulting in similar transactions being accounted for differently. Removal of classification would result in similar transactions being accounted for in the same way.
- Retaining the classification may result in inconsistencies in how the minimum lease payments are determined for classification purposes. For example, contingent rentals may be included for finance leases but not operating leases.
- Any differences between current accounting requirements for finance leases and any new model developed for operating leases are unlikely to justify the additional complexity of a classification requirement.

In March 2009, the IASB issued a discussion paper entitled *Leases — Preliminary Views*. Comments were required to be sent to the IASB by 17 July 2009. In August 2010, the IASB issued an exposure draft (ED) on leases with a comment period ending December 2010. In the Introduction to the ED, the IASB explained the main proposals of the proposed standard as follows:

> The exposure draft proposes that lessees and lessors should apply a right-of-use model in accounting for all leases (including leases of right-of-use assets in a sublease) other than leases of biological and intangible assets, leases to explore for or use natural resources, and leases of some investment properties. For leases within the scope of the draft IFRS, this means that:
>
> (a) a lessee would recognise an asset representing its right to use the leased ('underlying') asset for the lease term (the 'right-of-use' asset) and a liability to make lease payments.
>
> (b) a lessor would recognise an asset representing its right to receive lease payments and, depending on its exposure to risks or benefits associated with the underlying asset, would either:
>
> (i) recognise a lease liability while continuing to recognise the underlying asset (a performance obligation approach); or
>
> (ii) derecognise the rights in the underlying asset that it transfers to the lessee and continue to recognise a residual asset representing its rights to the underlying asset at the end of the lease term (a derecognition approach).
>
> Assets and liabilities recognised by lessees and lessors would be measured on a basis that:
>
> (a) assumes the longest possible lease term that is more likely than not to occur, taking into account the effect of any options to extend or terminate the lease.
>
> (b) uses an expected outcome technique to reflect the lease payments, including contingent rentals and expected payments under term option penalties and residual value guarantees, specified by the lease.
>
> (c) is updated when changes in facts or circumstances indicate that there would be a significant change in those assets or liabilities since the previous reporting period.
>
> For contracts that combine service and lease components, the right to receive lease payments and the liability to make lease payments would exclude payments arising from distinct service components and non-distinct service components for lessors that apply the derecognition approach.
>
> For leases of twelve months or less, lessees and lessors would be able to apply simplified requirements.
>
> The exposure draft also proposes disclosures based on stated objectives, including disclosures about the amounts recognised in the financial statements arising from leases and the amount, timing and uncertainty of cash flows arising from those contracts.

These proposals would have a major effect on lessees that have a large number of operating leases as these would now be accounted for in the same way as finance leases. Also, all lessees would be affected by the proposed changes in accounting for lease options and contingent rentals. For lessors, as the ED proposes two different methods for accounting for leases held by lessors, the effect would depend on the lessor's exposure to risks and benefits under the lease.

Debate continues on accounting for leases. In July 2011, the FASB and IASB announced they would re-expose the ED as a result of their revised proposals due to the comments received. At July 2012, no new standard on leases has been issued.

SUMMARY

Leases are arrangements whereby the right to use an asset is transferred to a lessee but ownership is retained by the lessor. By definition, finance leases transfer substantially all of the risks and rewards incidental to ownership from the lessor to the lessee. Operating leases do not. All leases must be classified as either operating leases or finance leases at the inception of the lease.

For finance leases, lessees must record a lease asset and a lease liability measured at the lower of the fair value of the leased property and the present value of the minimum lease payments. The asset is subsequently depreciated over the lease term or its economic life if ownership is to be transferred at the end of the lease. The liability is reduced as lease payments are made.

For finance leases, lessors must transfer their net investment in the lease to a receivable account which is subsequently reduced by lease receipts and the eventual return of the asset at the end of the lease. Manufacturer and dealer lessors must also record a profit or loss on sale of the asset at the beginning of the lease term.

Operating leases are treated as a rental arrangement with lessors recording rental revenue and lessees recording rental expense over the term of the lease.

Some of the accounting treatments required by IAS 17, notably those relating to sale and leaseback arrangements, create assets and liabilities which are not in accordance with the *Conceptual Framework*'s definitions. Accordingly, the IASB is reviewing the accounting standard with a view to removing such anomalies.

DEMONSTRATION PROBLEM 12.1 Manufacturer lessor

On 1 July 2014, Greymouth Ltd leased a photocopier from Stewart Ltd, a company that manufactures, retails and leases copiers. The photocopier had cost Stewart Ltd $30 000 to make but had a fair value on 1 July 2014 of $35 080. The lease agreement contained the following provisions:

Lease term	3 years
Annual payment, payable in advance on 1 July each year	$14 500
Economic life of the copier	4 years
Estimated residual value at the end of the lease term when the copier is returned to Stewart Ltd	$3 000
Residual value guaranteed by Greymouth Ltd	$1 500
Interest rate implicit in the lease	10%
The lease is cancellable, provided another lease is immediately entered into.	

The annual payment included an amount of $2500 p.a. to reimburse Stewart Ltd for the cost of paper and toner supplied to Greymouth Ltd. Stewart Ltd's solicitor prepared the lease agreement for a fee of $1365.

On 30 June 2017, at the end of the lease term, Greymouth Ltd returned the copier to Stewart Ltd, which sold the copier for $3000.

Required

Part A

1. Classify the lease for both the lessor and the lessee. Justify your answer.
2. Prepare the following:
   (a) *for the lessee:* the lease payment schedule and the journal entries for the year ended 30 June 2017 only
   (b) *for the lessor:* the lease receipts schedule and the journal entries for the year ended 30 June 2015 only.

Part B

Assume that the lease term is for 2 years, payments are $12 000 immediately and a further $12 000 in 12 months' time, and no residual value has been guaranteed by Greymouth Ltd on return of the asset to Stewart Ltd.

1. Classify the lease for both the lessor and the lessee. Justify your answer.
2. Prepare the journal entries for both lessor and lessee for the year ended 30 June 2015 only.

Solution

Part A

1. *Classify the lease.*
   (a) Determine whether the lessor is a financier or a manufacturer/dealer. This is essential as it changes the accounting treatment for initial direct costs paid by the lessor and the definition of the interest rate implicit in the lease.
   Stewart Ltd is a manufacturer lessor. Accordingly, the initial direct costs are treated as part of cost of sales and are not included in calculating the interest rate implicit in the lease.
   (b) Examine the terms of the lease agreement to determine whether substantially all of the risks and rewards associated with ownership of the copier have been transferred to the lessee.
      (i) *Is the lease non-cancellable?* The lease is cancellable provided that another lease is immediately entered into. Such an arrangement is deemed to be non-cancellable under part (c) of the definition of a 'non-cancellable lease' in IAS 17 paragraph 4.
      (ii) *Is ownership expected to be transferred at the end of the lease term?* No, the copier will be returned to the lessor at the end of the lease term, but the lessee has partially guaranteed its residual value at that date.
      (iii) *Is the lease term for all or a major part of the asset's economic life?* The lease term at 3 years is 75% of the copier's economic life. This represents a major part of that economic life.
      (iv) *Is the present value of the minimum lease payments equal to substantially all of the fair value of the asset at the inception of the lease?* (Minimum lease payments are the payments over the lease term that the lessee is required to make excluding contingent rent and executory costs together with any guaranteed residual value.) Annual payments of $14 500 are required but included in these is an amount of $2500 p.a. to cover operational costs paid by the lessor. Thus, the minimum lease payments for the copier are one payment of $12 000 immediately, two future payments of $12 000 and a guaranteed residual value of $1500.

Interest rate implicit in the lease

The interest rate which discounts the minimum lease payments and the unguaranteed residual value of $1500 to the aggregate of the fair value of the copier ($35 080) at the inception of the lease is 10%.

   Applying the discount rate to the minimum lease payments, we find the present value to be 97%, which is substantially all of the fair value of the copier.

$$\text{PV of MLP} = \$12\,000 + (\$12\,000 \times 1.7355 \; [T_2 \; 10\% \; 2y]) + (\$1500 \times 0.7513 \; [T_1 \; 10\% \; 3y])$$
$$= \$12\,000 + \$20\,826 + \$1127$$
$$= \$33\,953/\$35\,080 = 96.8\%$$

Given the above, both companies will classify the transaction as a finance lease.

2. (a) *Prepare a lease payments schedule and journal entries for the lessee for the year ended 30 June 2017 only.*

	MLP	Interest expense	Reduction in liability	Balance of liability
GREYMOUTH LTD (Lessee)				
Lease Payments Schedule				
1 July 2014				$33 953[a]
1 July 2014	$12 000	—[b]	$12 000	21 953[c]
1 July 2015	12 000	$2 195[d]	9 805[e]	12 148
1 July 2016	12 000	1 215	10 785	1 363
30 June 2017	1 500	137	1 363	—
	$37 500	$3 547	$33 953	

(a) The lower of PV of MLP and fair value of the copier as required by IAS 17 paragraph 20.
(b) Because the first payment is made immediately it is not discounted.
(c) The balance is reduced as each lease payment is made.
(d) Equals the balance of the liability $21 953 × 10%, the interest rate implicit in the lease.
(e) The payment must be split into interest expense and reduction of the lease liability as per IAS 17 paragraph 25.

GREYMOUTH LTD
Journal Entries
for year ended 30 June 2017

2016				
July 1	Lease Liability	Dr	10 785	
	Interest Payable	Dr	1 215	
	Executory Costs	Dr	2 500	
	Cash	Cr		14 500
	(Recording the third and final lease payment)			
2017				
June 30	Depreciation Expense	Dr	10 817	
	Accumulated Depreciation	Cr		10 817
	(Recognition of the depreciation of the leased asset for the year as per paragraph 27 [$33 953 − $1 500/3])			
	Lease Liability	Dr	1 363	
	Interest Expense	Dr	137	
	Accumulated Depreciation	Dr	32 453	
	Leased Asset	Cr		33 953
	(Return of the copier at the end of the lease term)			

2. (b) *Prepare a lease receipts schedule and journal entries for the lessor for the year ended 30 June 2015 only.*

STEWART LTD (Lessor)
Lease Receipts Schedule

	MLR	Interest revenue	Reduction in receivable	Balance of receivable
1 July 2014				$35 080[(a)]
1 July 2014	$12 000	—[(b)]	$12 000	23 080[(c)]
1 July 2015	12 000	$2 308[(d)]	9 692[(e)]	13 388
1 July 2016	12 000	1 339	10 661	2 727
30 June 2017	3 000	273	2 727	—
	$39 000	$3 920	$35 080	

(a) Net investment in the lease = fair value of the copier as required by IAS 17 paragraph 36.
(b) Because the first receipt occurs immediately it is not discounted.
(c) The balance is reduced as each lease receipt is recorded.
(d) Equals the balance of the receivable $23 080 × 10%, the interest rate implicit in the lease.
(d) The receipt must be split into interest revenue and reduction of the lease receivable as per IAS 17 paragraph 37.

Because Stewart Ltd is a manufacturer lessor, the first journal entry must record the profit or loss on sale of the asset as required by IAS 17 paragraph 42.

STEWART LTD
Journal Entries
for year ended 30 June 2015

2014				
July 1	Lease Receivable	Dr	35 080	
	Sales Revenue*	Cr		33 953
	Cost of Sales**	Dr	28 873	
	Inventory	Cr		30 000
	(Recognition of lease receivable and recording sale of copier)			
	*PV of MLP			
	**Cost less PV of unguaranteed residual ($1 500 × 0.7513)			

	Lease Costs	Dr	1 365	
	Cash	Cr		1 365
	(Payment of initial direct costs)			
	Cash	Dr	14 500	
	Lease Receivable	Cr		12 000
	Reimbursement Revenue	Cr		2 500
	(Receipt of first payment)			
2015				
June 30	Paper and Toner Expense	Dr	2 500	
	Cash	Cr		2 500
	(Payment of executory costs)			
	Interest Receivable	Dr	2 308	
	Interest Revenue	Cr		2 308
	(Interest expense accrual)			

Solution

Part B

1. *Classify the lease.*
    (a) Determine whether the lessor is a financier or a manufacturer/dealer. This is essential as it changes the accounting treatment for initial direct costs paid by the lessor and also the definition of the interest rate implicit in the lease.

    Stewart Ltd is a manufacturer lessor. Accordingly, the initial direct costs are treated as part of cost of sales and are not included in calculating the interest rate implicit in the lease.
    (b) Examine the terms of the lease agreement to determine whether substantially all the risks and rewards associated with ownership of the copier have been transferred to the lessee.
        (i) *Is the lease non-cancellable?* The lease is cancellable provided that another lease is immediately entered into. Such an arrangement is deemed to be non-cancellable under part (c) of the definition of a 'non-cancellable lease' in IAS 17 paragraph 4.
        (ii) *Is ownership expected to be transferred at the end of the lease term?* No, the copier will be returned to the lessor at the end of the lease term.
        (iii) *Is the lease term for all or a major part of the asset's economic life?* The lease term at 2 years is 50% of the copier's economic life. At this level, it does not represent a major part of that economic life.
        (iv) *Is the present value of the minimum lease payments equal to substantially all of the fair value of the asset at the inception of the lease? (Minimum lease payments are the payments over the lease term that the lessee is required to make excluding contingent rent and executory costs together with any guaranteed residual value.)* Annual payments of $14 500 are required but included in these is an amount of $2500 p.a. to cover operational costs paid by the lessor. Thus, the minimum lease payments for the copier are one payment of $12 000 immediately and one payment of $12 000 next year.

Interest rate implicit in the lease
The interest rate which discounts the minimum lease payments and the unguaranteed residual value of $1500 to the aggregate of the fair value of the copier ($35 080) at the inception of the lease is 10%.

Applying the discount rate to the minimum lease payments, we find the present value is 65%, and not substantially all of the fair value of the copier.

$$\text{PV of MLP} = \$12\,000 + (\$12\,000 \times 0.9091 \ [T_1 \ 10\% \ 1y])$$
$$= \$12\,000 + \$10\,909$$
$$= \$22\,909/\$35\,080 = 65.3\%$$

Given the above, both companies will classify the transaction as an operating lease.

2. *Prepare the journal entries for both lessor and lessee for the year ended 30 June 2015 only.*

GREYMOUTH LTD (Lessee)
Journal Entries
for year ended 30 June 2015

2014				
July 1	Rent Expense	Dr	12 000	
	Cash	Cr		12 000
	(Recording the first lease payment)			

STEWART LTD (Lessor)
Journal Entries
for year ended 30 June 2015

2014				
July 1	Cash	Dr	12 000	
	Rental Income	Cr		12 000
	(Recording the first lease receipt)			
2015				
June 30	Depreciation Expense – Copier	Dr	7 500	
	Accumulated Depreciation	Cr		7 500
	(Depreciation on copier for the year [$30 000/4])			

DEMONSTRATION PROBLEM 12.2 Financier lessor

On 30 June 2014, Cambridge Ltd leased a vehicle to Awamutu Ltd. Cambridge Ltd had purchased the vehicle on that day for its fair value of $89 721. The lease agreement, which cost Cambridge Ltd $1457 to have drawn up, contained the following provisions:

Lease term	4 years
Annual payment, payable in advance on 30 June each year	$23 900
Economic life of vehicle	6 years
Estimated residual value at end of economic life	$2 000
Estimated residual value at end of lease term	$15 000
Residual value guaranteed by lessee	$15 000
Interest rate implicit in the lease	7%

The lease is cancellable, but cancellation will incur a monetary penalty equivalent to 2 years rental payments. Included in the annual payment is an amount of $1900 to cover reimbursement for the costs of insurance and maintenance paid by the lessor. The directors of Awamutu Ltd have indicated that they are interested in acquiring the asset at the end of the lease.

Required

1. Explain why both Awamutu Ltd and Cambridge Ltd classify the above transaction as a finance lease.
2. Prepare the following for the lessor, Cambridge Ltd:
   (a) the lease receipts schedule (show all workings)
   (b) the journal entries for the year ended 30 June 2014 and 30 June 2015.
3. Prepare the following for the lessee, Awamutu Ltd:
   (a) the lease payments schedule (show all workings)
   (b) the journal entries for the year ended 30 June 2014 and 30 June 2015.

Solution

1. *Classify the lease.*

    (a) Determine whether the lessor is a financier or a manufacturer/dealer. This is essential as it changes the accounting treatment for initial direct costs paid by the lessor and the definition of the interest rate implicit in the lease.

        Cambridge Ltd is a financier lessor. Accordingly, the initial direct costs are treated as part of the lease receivable and are included in calculating the interest rate implicit in the lease.

    (b) Examine the terms of the lease agreement to determine whether substantially all of the risks and rewards associated with ownership of the copier have been transferred to the lessee.

        (i) *Is the lease non-cancellable?* The lease is cancellable, but cancellation will incur a monetary penalty equivalent to 2 years' rental payments. Such an arrangement is deemed to be non-cancellable under part (d) of the definition of a 'non-cancellable lease' in IAS 17 paragraph 4.

        (ii) *Is ownership expected to be transferred at the end of the lease term?* Yes, the directors of Awamutu Ltd have indicated that they are interested in acquiring the asset at the end of the lease term. Additionally, they have guaranteed all of its residual value at that date.

        (iii) *Is the lease term for all or a major part of the asset's economic life?* The lease term at 4 years is 67% of the copier's economic life. At this level, the lease term is not a major part of that economic life.

        (iv) *Is the present value of the minimum lease payments equal to substantially all of the fair value of the asset at the inception of the lease? (Minimum lease payments are the payments over the lease term that the lessee is required to make excluding contingent rent and executory costs together with any guaranteed residual value.)* Annual payments of $23 900 are required but included in these is an amount of $1900 p.a. to cover operational costs paid by the lessor. Thus, the minimum lease payments for the copier are one payment of $22 000 immediately, three future payments of $22 000, and a guaranteed residual value of $15 000.

Interest rate implicit in the lease

The interest rate, which discounts the minimum lease payments and the unguaranteed residual value of $1500 to the aggregate of the fair value of the vehicle ($89 721) and the initial direct costs incurred by Cambridge Ltd ($1457) at the inception of the lease, is 7% as shown below:

$$= \$22\,000 + (\$22\,000 \times 2.6243\ [T_2\ 7\%\ 3y]) + (\$15\,000 \times 0.7629\ [T_1\ 7\%\ 4y])$$
$$= \$22\,000 + \$57\,735 + \$11\,443$$
$$= \$89\,721\ \text{(fair value)} + \$1457\ \text{(initial direct costs)}$$
$$= \$91\,178$$

Therefore 7% is the interest rate implicit in the lease.

    Since the lessee has guaranteed all of the residual value at the end of the lease term, substantially all the risks and rewards relating to the vehicle have been transferred to the lessee.

    Given the above, both companies have classified the transaction as a finance lease.

2. (a) *Prepare the lease receipts schedule for the lessor, Cambridge Ltd.*

CAMBRIDGE LTD
Lease Receipts Schedule

	MLR	Interest revenue	Reduction in receivable	Balance of receivable
30 June 2014				$91 178
30 June 2014	$ 22 000	—	$22 000	69 178
30 June 2015	22 000	$ 4 842	17 158	52 020
30 June 2016	22 000	3 641	18 359	33 661
30 June 2017	22 000	2 356	19 644	14 017
30 June 2018	15 000	983	14 017	—
	$103 000	$11 822	$91 178	

    (b) *Prepare the journal entries for Cambridge Ltd for years ended 30 June 2014 and 30 June 2015.*

Since Cambridge Ltd is a financier lessor, the initial direct costs are included in the lease receivable.

CAMBRIDGE LTD
Journal Entries
for years ended 30 June 2014 and 2015

Year ending 2014

Vehicle	Dr	89 721	
Cash	Cr		89 721
(Purchase of vehicle to be leased)			
Lease Receivable	Dr	91 178	
Vehicle	Cr		89 721
Cash	Cr		1 457
(Lease of vehicle and payment of initial direct costs)			
Cash	Dr	23 900	
Lease Receivable	Cr		22 000
Unearned Executory Revenue	Cr		1 900
(Receipt of first payment)			

Year ending 2015

Insurance and Maintenance	Dr	1 900	
Cash	Cr		1 900
(Costs paid on behalf of lessee)			
Unearned Executory Revenue	Dr	1 900	
Reimbursement Revenue	Cr		1 900
(Transfer of reimbursement revenue)			
Cash	Dr	23 900	
Interest Revenue	Cr		4 842
Lease Receivable	Cr		17 158
Unearned Executory Revenue	Cr		1 900
(Receipt of second payment)			

3. (a) *Prepare the lease payments schedule for the lessee, Awamutu Ltd.*

Paragraph 20 of IAS 17 requires the lessee to record a lease liability measured at the lower of fair value of the leased asset and the PV of MLP at the inception of the lease. In this situation, the PV of MLP discounted at the 7% interest rate used by the lessor is greater than fair value, hence the lessee must recalculate the interest rate based on the fair value of the asset as below:

$$= \$22\,000 + (\$22\,000 \times 2.5771 \; [T_2 \; 8\% \; 3y]) + (\$15\,000 \times 0.7350 \; [T_1 \; 8\% \; 4y])$$
$$= \$22\,000 + \$56\,696 + \$11\,025$$
$$= \$89\,721 \; \text{(fair value)}$$

Therefore 8% is the interest rate implicit in the lease for the lessee.

AWAMUTU LTD
Lease Payments Schedule

	MLP	Interest expense	Reduction in liability	Balance of liability
30 June 2014				$89 721
30 June 2014	$ 22 000	—	$ 22 000	67 721
30 June 2015	22 000	$ 5 418	16 582	51 139
30 June 2016	22 000	4 091	17 909	33 230
30 June 2017	22 000	2 658	19 342	13 888
30 June 2018	15 000	1 112	13 888	—
	$103 000	$13 279	$ 89 721	

(b) *Prepare the journal entries for Awamutu Ltd for the years ended 30 June 2014 and 2015.*

AWAMUTU LTD Journal Entries for years ended 30 June 2014 and 2015			
Year ending 2014			
Leased Vehicle	Dr	89 721	
Lease Liability	Cr		89 721
(Recognition of lease)			
Lease Liability	Dr	22 000	
Prepaid Executory Costs	Dr	1 900	
Cash	Cr		23 900
(First lease payment)			
Year ending 2015			
Executory Costs	Dr	1 900	
Prepaid Executory Costs	Cr		1 900
(Executory costs expired during the year)			
Depreciation Expense	Dr	14 620	
Accumulated Depreciation	Cr		14 620
(Depreciation of leased asset for the year			
($89 721 − 2 000)/6 (use economic life as ownership may			
be transferred))			
Lease Liability	Dr	16 582	
Interest Expense	Dr	5 418	
Prepaid Executory Costs	Dr	1 900	
Cash	Cr		23 900
(Second lease payment)			

Discussion questions

1. Leases are classified on the basis of 'substance over form'. What does this criterion mean and how does it relate to the capitalisation of finance leases?
2. What are 'minimum lease payments'?
3. If a lease agreement states that 'the lessee guarantees a residual value, at the end of the lease term, of $20 000', what does this mean?
4. What is meant by 'the interest rate implicit in a lease'?
5. Where a lessor incurs initial direct costs in establishing a lease agreement, how are these costs to be accounted for by the lessor?
6. Identify three possible adverse effects on a lessee entity's financial statements arising from the classification of a lease arrangement as a finance lease.
7. How, according to IAS 17 requirements, are finance leases to be accounted for by lessees?
8. How, according to IAS 17 requirements, are finance leases to be accounted for by lessors?
9. How does the accounting treatment for a finance lease change if the lessor is a manufacturer/dealer lessor?
10. How, according to IAS 17 requirements, are operating leases accounted for by lessees?
11. How, according to IAS 17 requirements, are operating leases to be accounted for by lessors?
12. In the context of operating leases, what are lease incentives and how are they accounted for?
13. Explain how a profit made by a lessee on a sale and leaseback transaction is to be accounted for.
14. 'The accounting treatment required by IAS 17 paragraph 59 is not in accordance with the *Conceptual Framework*'. Discuss.
15. What changes to accounting for leases are proposed in future versions of the standard?

Exercises

STAR RATING ★ BASIC ★★ MODERATE ★★★ DIFFICULT

Exercise 12.1   IDENTIFICATION OF LEASES

★ For the following arrangements, discuss whether they are 'in substance' lease transactions, and thus fall under the ambit of IAS 17.

(a) Entity A leases an asset to Entity B, and obtains a non-recourse loan from a financial institution using the lease rentals and asset as collateral. Entity A sells the asset subject to the lease and the loan to a trustee, and leases the same asset back.

(b) Entity A enters into an arrangement to buy petroleum products from Entity B. The products are produced in a refinery built and operated by Entity B on a site owned by Entity A. Although Entity B could provide the products from other refineries which it owns, it is not practical to do so. Entity B retains the right to sell products produced by the refinery to other customers but there is only a remote possibility that it will do so. The arrangement requires Entity A to make both fixed unavoidable payments and variable payments based on input costs at a target level of efficiency to Entity B.

(c) Entity A leases an asset to Entity B for its entire economic life and leases the same asset back under the same terms and conditions as the original lease. The two entities have a legally enforceable right to set off the amounts owing to one another, and an intention to settle these amounts on a net basis.

(d) Entity A enters into a non-cancellable 4-year lease with Entity B for an asset with an expected economic life of 10 years. Entity A has an option to renew the lease for a further 4 years at the end of the lease term. At the conclusion of the lease arrangement, the asset will revert back to Entity B. In a separate agreement, Entity B is granted a put option to sell the asset to Entity A should its market value at the end of the lease be less than the residual value.

Exercise 12.2   FINANCE LEASES VS OPERATING LEASES

★ Timaru Ltd runs a successful chain of fashion boutiques, but has been experiencing significant cash flow problems. The directors are examining a proposal made by an accounting consultant that all the shops currently owned by the company be sold and either leased back or the businesses moved to alternative leased shops. The directors are keen on the plan but are puzzled by the consultant's insistence that all lease agreements for the shops be 'operating' rather than 'finance' leases.

Required

1. Explain the difference between a finance lease and an operating lease.
2. Explain, by reference to the requirements of IAS 17, why the consultant prefers operating to finance leases.
3. Describe three disadvantages to the company of entering into finance lease agreements.

Exercise 12.3   LEASE CLASSIFICATION AND DETERMINATION OF INTEREST RATES

★ *This exercise contains four multiple-choice questions. Select the correct answer and show any workings required.*

1. Pukekohe Ltd sells land that originally cost $150 000 to Taupo Ltd for $230 000 when the land's fair value is $215 000, and then enters into a cancellable lease agreement to use the land for 2 years at an annual rental of $2000. In the current year, how much profit would Pukekohe Ltd record on the sale of the land?
   (a) $15 000
   (b) $80 000
   (c) $65 000
   (d) Nil

2. Using the information from part 1 above, how would Taupo Ltd record the annual cash received from Pukekohe Ltd?
   (a) As rental revenue
   (b) As a reduction of the lease receivable
   (c) As rental expense
   (d) As interest revenue and a reduction of the lease receivable

3. On 1 July 2014, Masterton Ltd leases a machine with a fair value of $109 445 to Tokoroa Ltd for 5 years at an annual rental (in advance) of $25 000, and Tokoroa Ltd guarantees in full the estimated residual value of $15 000 on return of the asset. What would be the interest rate implicit in the lease?
   (a) 10%
   (b) 12%
   (c) 9%
   (d) 14%
4. Using the information from part 3, how would Tokoroa Ltd classify the lease?
   (a) As an operating lease
   (b) As a finance lease
   (c) As a sale and leaseback
   (d) As a lease incentive

Exercise 12.4 **LEASE INCENTIVES**

★ As an incentive to enter a non-cancellable operating lease for office premises for 10 years, the lessor has offered the lessee a rent-free period of 2 years. Rental payments under the lease beginning in year 3 are $5000 p.a.

Required

Prepare journal entries to account for the lease payment in year 3 of the lease in the records of both the lessor and the lessee.

Exercise 12.5 **FINANCE LEASE**

★ If a lease has been capitalised as a finance lease, identify two circumstances in which the lease receivable raised by the lessor will differ from the lease asset raised by the lessee.

Exercise 12.6 **FINANCE LEASE — LESSOR**

★ On 1 July 2013, Jane Plum decided she needed a new car. She went to the local car yard, North Ltd, run by Fred Peach. Jane discussed the price of a new Roadster Special with Fred, and they agreed on a price of $37 000. As North Ltd had acquired the vehicle from the manufacturer for $30 000, Fred was pleased with the deal. On learning that Jane wanted to lease the vehicle, Fred agreed to arrange for South Ltd, a local finance company, to set up the lease agreement. North Ltd then sold the car to South Ltd for $37 000.

South Ltd wrote a lease agreement, incurring initial direct costs of $1410 as a result. The lease agreement contained the following provisions:

Initial payment on 1 July 2013	$13 000
Payments on 1 July 2014 and 1 July 2015	$13 000
Guaranteed residual value at 30 June 2016	$10 000
Implicit interest rate in the lease	6%
The lease is non-cancellable.	

South Ltd agreed to pay for the insurance and maintenance of the vehicle, the latter to be carried out by North Ltd at regular intervals. The cost of these services is valued at $3000 p.a.

The vehicle had an expected useful life of 4 years. The expected residual value of the vehicle at 30 June 2016 was $12 000.

Costs of maintenance and insurance incurred by South Ltd over the years ended 30 June 2014 to 30 June 2016 were $2810, $3020 and $2750 respectively. At 30 June 2016, Jane returned the vehicle to South Ltd, which sold the car for $9000 on 5 July 2016 and invoiced Jane for the appropriate balance. Jane subsequently paid the debt on 13 July 2016.

Required

1. Assuming the lease is classified as a finance lease, prepare the journal entries in the books of South Ltd in relation to the lease from 1 July 2013 to 31 July 2016.
2. In relation to finance leases, explain why the balance of the asset account raised by the lessee at the inception of the lease may differ from the balance of the receivable asset raised by the lessor.

Exercise 12.7 — LEASE CLASSIFICATION; ACCOUNTING BY LESSEE

★ On 1 July 2013, Otago Ltd leased a plastic-moulding machine from Nelson Ltd. The machine cost Nelson $130 000 to manufacture and had a fair value of $154 109 on 1 July 2013. The lease agreement contained the following provisions:

Lease term	4 years
Annual rental payment, in advance on 1 July each year	$41 500
Residual value at end of the lease term	$15 000
Residual guaranteed by lessee	nil
Interest rate implicit in lease	8%
The lease is cancellable only with the permission of the lessor.	

The expected useful life of the machine is 6 years. Otago Ltd intends to return the machine to the lessor at the end of the lease term. Included in the annual rental payment is an amount of $1500 to cover the costs of maintenance and insurance paid for by the lessor.

Required

1. Classify the lease for both lessee and lessor based on the guidance provided in IAS 17. Justify your answer.
2. Prepare (a) the lease schedules for the lessee (show all workings), and (b) the journal entries in the books of the lessee for the year ended 30 June 2014.

Exercise 12.8 — LEASE CLASSIFICATION; ACCOUNTING BY LESSOR

★ Use the information contained in exercise 12.7 to complete the following:
1. Classify the lease for both lessee and lessor based on the guidance provided in IAS 17. Justify your answer.
2. Prepare (a) the lease schedules for the lessor (show all workings) and (b) the journal entries in the books of the lessor for the year ended 30 June 2014.

Exercise 12.9 — ACCOUNTING BY LESSEE AND LESSOR

★ On 1 July 2014, Christchurch Ltd leased a processing plant to Wellington Ltd. The plant was purchased by Christchurch Ltd on 1 July 2014 for its fair value of $467 112. The lease agreement contained the following provisions:

Lease term	3 years
Economic life of plant	5 years
Annual rental payment, in arrears (commencing 30/6/2015)	$150 000
Residual value at end of the lease term	$90 000
Residual guaranteed by lessee	$60 000
Interest rate implicit in lease	7%
The lease is cancellable only with the permission of the lessor.	

Wellington Ltd intends to return the processing plant to the lessor at the end of the lease term. The lease has been classified as a finance lease by both the lessee and the lessor.

Required

1. Prepare:
   (a) the lease payment schedule for the lessee (show all workings)
   (b) the journal entries in the records of the lessee for the year ended 30 June 2016.
2. Prepare:
   (a) the lease receipt schedule for the lessor (show all workings)
   (b) the journal entries in the records of the lessor for the year ended 30 June 2016.

FINANCE LEASE — LESSEE

★ Hamilton Ltd prepares the following lease payments schedule for the lease of a machine from Hutt Ltd. The machine has an economic life of 6 years. The lease agreement requires four annual payments of $33 000, and the machine will be returned to Hutt Ltd at the end of the lease term. The lease payments schedule is:

	MLP	Interest expense (10%)	Reduction in liability	Balance of liability
1 July 2012				$98 512
1 July 2013	$ 30 000	$ 9 851	$ 20 149	78 363
1 July 2014	30 000	7 836	22 164	56 199
1 July 2015	30 000	5 620	24 380	31 819
1 July 2016	35 000	3 181	31 819	—
	$125 000	$26 488	$98 512	

The following five multiple-choice questions relate to the information provided above. Select the correct answer and show any workings required.

1. In its notes to the accounts at 30 June 2014, Hamilton Ltd would disclose future lease payments of what amount?
   (a) $95 000
   (b) $65 000
   (c) $99 000
   (d) $104 000

2. For the year ended 30 June 2013, what would Hamilton Ltd record in relation to the lease?
   (a) An interest payable of $26 488
   (b) An interest payable of $nil
   (c) An interest payable of $9851
   (d) An interest payable of $7836

3. How much annual depreciation expense would Hamilton Ltd record?
   (a) $24 628
   (b) $16 419
   (c) $15 585
   (d) $23 378

4. If Hutt Ltd (the lessor) records a lease receivable of $102 327, the variance between this receivable and the liability of $98 512 recorded by Hamilton Ltd could be due to what?
   (a) Initial direct costs paid by Hutt Ltd
   (b) An unguaranteed residual value
   (c) Both of the above
   (d) Neither of the above

5. Assume that the 1 July 2013 lease payment included an additional amount of $3000 for exceeding a limit for machine usage hours specified in the lease agreement. Hamilton Ltd would account for this charge by recognising it as what?
   (a) An expense and disclosing the amount in the notes (if material)
   (b) Additional executory costs
   (c) Revenue
   (d) A reduction in the lease liability

LEASE CLASSIFICATION

★★ New Ltd manufactures specialised moulding machinery for both sale and lease. On 1 July 2014, New Ltd leased a machine to Zealand Ltd. The machine being leased cost New Ltd $195 000 to make and its fair value at 1 July 2014 is considered to be $212 515. The terms of the lease are as follows:

The lease term is for 5 years, starting on	1 July 2014
Annual lease payment, payable on 30 June each year	$57 500
Estimated useful life of machine (scrap value $2500)	8 years
Estimated residual value of machine at end of lease term	$37 000

(continued)

| Residual value guaranteed by Zealand Ltd | $25 000 |
| Interest rate implicit in the lease | 10% |

The annual lease payment includes an amount of $7500 to cover
annual maintenance and insurance costs.
Zealand Ltd may cancel the lease but only with the permission of the lessor.
Zealand Ltd intends to lease a new machine at the end of the lease term.

Required

Classify the lease for both New Ltd and Zealand Ltd. Justify your answer.

Exercise 12.12   LEASE SCHEDULES AND JOURNAL ENTRIES (YEAR 1)

★★ On 1 July 2014, Island Ltd leased a crane from Pacific Ltd. The crane cost Pacific Ltd $120 307, considered to be its fair value on that same day. The finance lease agreement contained the following provisions:

The lease term is for 3 years, starting on	1 July 2014
The lease is non-cancellable	
Annual lease payment, payable on 30 June each year	$39 000
Estimated useful life of crane	4 years
Estimated residual value of crane at end of lease term	$22 000
Residual value guaranteed by Island Ltd	$16 000
Interest rate implicit in the lease	7%
The lease was classified as a finance lease by both Island Ltd and Pacific Ltd at 1 July 2014.	

Required

1. Prepare the lease schedules for both the lessee and the lessor.
2. Prepare the journal entries in the records of the lessee only for the year ended 30 June 2015.

Exercise 12.13   FINANCE LEASE — LESSEE (INCLUDING DISCLOSURES)

★★ Dunedin Ltd decided to lease from Rotorua Ltd a motor vehicle that had a fair value at 30 June 2012 of $38 960. The lease agreement contained the following provisions:

Lease term (non-cancellable)	3 years
Annual rental payments (commencing 30/6/12)	$11 200
Guaranteed residual value (expected fair value at end of lease term)	$12 000
Extra rental per annum if the car is used outside the metropolitan area	$1 000

The expected useful life of the vehicle is 5 years. At the end of the 3-year lease term, the car was returned to the lessor, which sold it for $10 000. The annual rental payments include an amount of $1200 to cover the cost of maintenance and insurance arranged and paid for by the lessor. The car was used outside the metropolitan area in the 2013–14 year. The lease is considered to be a finance lease.

Required

1. Prepare the journal entries for Dunedin Ltd from 30 June 2012 to 30 June 2015.
2. Prepare the relevant disclosures required under IAS 17 for the years ending 30 June 2013 and 30 June 2014.
3. How would your answer to requirement 1 change if the guaranteed residual value was only $10 000, and the expected fair value at the end of the lease term was $12 000?

Exercise 12.14   SALES AND LEASEBACK

★★ Ultramarine Ltd is asset rich but cash poor. In an attempt to alleviate its liquidity problems, it entered into an agreement on 1 July 2013 to sell its processing plant to Wanganui Ltd for $467 100. At the date of sale, the plant had a carrying amount of $400 000 and a future useful life of 5 years. Wanganui Ltd immediately leased the processing plant back to Ultramarine Ltd. The terms of the lease agreement were:

Lease term	3 years
Economic life of plant	5 years
Annual rental payment, in arrears (commencing 30/6/14)	$165 000
Residual value of plant at end of lease term	$90 000
Residual value guaranteed by Ultramarine Ltd	$60 000
Interest rate implicit in the lease	6%
The lease is cancellable, but only with the permission of the lessor.	

At the end of the lease term, the plant is to be returned to Wanganui Ltd. In setting up the lease agreement Wanganui Ltd incurred $9414 in legal fees and stamp duty costs. The annual rental payment includes $15 000 to reimburse the lessor for maintenance costs incurred on behalf of the lessee.

Required

1. Classify the lease for both lessor and lessee. Justify your answer.
2. Prepare a lease payments schedule and the journal entries in the records of Ultramarine Ltd for the year ending 30 June 2014. Show all workings.
3. Prepare a lease receipts schedule and the journal entries in the records of Wanganui Ltd for the year ending 30 June 2014. Show all workings.
4. Explain how and why your answers to requirements 1 and 2 would change if the lease agreement could be cancelled at any time without penalty.
5. Explain how and why your answer to requirements 1, 2 and 3 would change if the processing plant had been manufactured by Wanganui Ltd at a cost of $400 000.

Exercise 12.15	**SALE AND LEASEBACK ARRANGEMENTS**
★★★	

Kapiti Ltd is a company involved in a diverse range of activities involving power generation, machinery retailing and agriculture. The accounting policy note attached to the 2010 financial statements included the following under the heading 'Leases':

> During the year the company entered into a refinancing arrangement which involved the sale of the Lilac Mountain power station under a sale and leaseback arrangement. The difference between the carrying amount of the power station and its original cost has been included in profit and disclosed as a gain on sale of a non-current asset. Sales proceeds in excess of the original cost have been treated as deferred income in the statement of financial position. The amount of deferred income will be systematically amortised over the term of the lease.

The power station is a unique asset in that the licence to generate power from that station is held by Kapiti Ltd and cannot be transferred. The leaseback period is for the remaining 20 years economic life of the power station and Kapiti Ltd has guaranteed its expected residual value at that time of $55 000.

Required

1. Does the Kapiti Ltd sale and leaseback arrangement involve a finance lease or an operating lease? Justify your choice.
2. Critically evaluate the accounting treatment adopted by Kapiti Ltd with respect to the sale and leaseback agreement. Refer, where necessary, to relevant sections of IAS 17.
3. Compare the resulting deferred income account with the *Conceptual Framework's* definitions of and recognition criteria for the elements of financial statements.

Exercise 12.16	**LEASE CLASSIFICATION; ACCOUNTING AND DISCLOSURES**
★★★	

Birkenhead Ltd has entered into an agreement to lease a D9 bulldozer to Albert Ltd. The lease agreement details are as follows:

Length of lease	5 years
Commencement date	1 July 2013
Annual lease payment, payable 30 June each year commencing 30 June 2014	$8 000
Fair value of the bulldozer at 1 July 2013	$34 797

(continued)

Estimated economic life of the bulldozer	8 years
Estimated residual value of the plant at the end of its economic life	$2000
Residual value at the end of the lease term, of which 50% is guaranteed by Albert Ltd	$7200
Interest rate implicit in the lease	9%

The lease is cancellable, but a penalty equal to 50% of the total lease payments is payable on cancellation. Albert Ltd does not intend to buy the bulldozer at the end of the lease term. Birkenhead Ltd incurred $1000 to negotiate and execute the lease agreement. Birkenhead Ltd purchased the bulldozer for $34 797 just before the inception of the lease.

Required

1. State how both companies should classify the lease. Give reasons for your answer.
2. Prepare a schedule of lease payments for Albert Ltd.
3. Prepare a schedule of lease receipts for Birkenhead Ltd.
4. Prepare journal entries to record the lease transactions for the year ended 30 June 2014 in the records of both companies.
5. Prepare an appropriate note to the financial statements of both companies as at 30 June 2014.

Exercise 12.17 — FINANCE LEASE WITH GRV AND LEASEBACK VARIATIONS

★★★ On 1 July 2013, Porirua Ltd acquired an item of plant for $31 864. On the same date, Porirua Ltd entered into a lease agreement with Hastings Ltd in relation to the asset. According to the lease agreement, Hastings Ltd agreed to pay $12 000 immediately, with a further two payments of $12 000 on 1 July 2014 and 1 July 2015.

At 30 June 2016, the asset is to be returned to the lessor and its residual value is expected to be $6000. Hastings Ltd has agreed to guarantee the expected residual value at 30 June 2013. All insurance and maintenance costs are to be paid by Porirua Ltd and are expected to amount to $2000 p.a. The costs of preparing the lease agreement amounted to $360. The interest rate implicit in the lease is 9%. The lease is classified as a finance lease. Plant is depreciable on a straight-line basis.

Required

1. Prepare a schedule of lease receipts for Porirua Ltd and the journal entries for the year ended 30 June 2014.
2. Prepare a schedule of lease payments for Hastings Ltd and the journal entries for the year ended 30 June 2014.
3. Assume that Hastings Ltd guaranteed a residual value of only $4000. Prepare a lease schedule for both Porirua Ltd and Hastings Ltd.
4. Instead of acquiring the plant for $31 864, assume that Porirua Ltd manufactured the plant at a cost of $29 500 before entering into the lease agreement with Hastings Ltd. Prepare a schedule of lease receipts for Porirua Ltd and the journal entries for the year ended 30 June 2014.
5. Assume that Hastings Ltd manufactured the plant itself at a cost of $29 500 and sold the plant to Porirua Ltd for $31 864. Hastings Ltd then leased it back under the original terms of the finance lease, with Hastings Ltd guaranteeing a residual value of $4000. Prepare a lease schedule and journal entries for both Porirua Ltd and Hastings Ltd for the year ended 30 June 2014.

Exercise 12.18 — FINANCE LEASE — MANUFACTURER LESSOR

★★★ Auckland Ltd manufactures specialised moulding machinery for both sale and lease. On 1 July 2013, Auckland Ltd leased a machine to Christchurch Ltd, incurring $1500 in costs to prepare and execute the lease document. The machine being leased cost Auckland Ltd $195 000 to make and its fair value at 1 July 2013 is considered to be $212 515. The terms of the lease agreement are as follows:

Lease term commencing on 1 July 2013	5 years
Annual lease payment commencing on 1 July 2014	$57 500
Estimated useful life of machine (scrap value $2500)	8 years
Estimated residual value of machine at end of lease term	$37 000
Residual value guaranteed by Christchurch Ltd	$25 000
Interest rate implicit in the lease	10%
The lease is classified as a finance lease.	

The annual lease payment includes an amount of $7500 to cover annual maintenance and insurance costs. Actual executory costs for each of the 5 years were:

2013–14	$7 200
2014–15	7 700
2015–16	7 800
2016–17	7 100
2017–18	7 000

Christchurch Ltd may cancel the lease but will incur a penalty equivalent to 2 years payments if it does so. Christchurch Ltd intends to lease a new machine at the end of the lease term. The end of the reporting period for both companies is 30 June.

Required

1. Prepare a schedule of lease receipts for Auckland Ltd.
2. Prepare the general journal entries to record the lease transactions for the year ended 30 June 2014 in the records of Auckland Ltd.

Exercise 12.19

★★★

FINANCE LEASE — LESSEE AND LESSOR

On 1 July 2014, Wellington Ltd acquired a new car. The manager of Wellington Ltd, Jack Wellington, went to the local car yard, Hamilton Autos, and discussed the price of a new Racer Special with John Hamilton. Jack and John agreed on a price of $37 876. As Hamilton Autos had acquired the vehicle from the manufacturer for $32 000, John was pleased with the deal. On discussing the financial arrangements in relation to the car, Jack decided that a lease arrangement was the most suitable. John agreed to arrange for Dunedin Ltd, a local finance company, to set up the lease agreement. Hamilton Autos then sold the car to Dunedin Ltd for $37 876.

Dunedin Ltd wrote a lease agreement, incurring initial direct costs of $534 in the process.

The lease agreement contained the following clauses:

Initial payment on 1 July 2014	$13 000
Payments on 1 July 2015 and 1 July 2016	$13 000
Interest rate implicit in the lease	6%

The lease agreement also specified for Dunedin Ltd to pay for the insurance and maintenance of the vehicle, the latter to be carried out by Hamilton Autos at regular intervals. A cost of $3000 per annum was included in the lease payments to cover these services.

Jack wanted the lease to be considered an operating lease for accounting purposes. To achieve this, the lease agreement was worded as follows:

- The lease is cancellable by Wellington Ltd at any stage. However, if the lease is cancelled, Wellington Ltd agrees to lease, on similar terms, another car from Dunedin Ltd.
- Wellington Ltd is not required to guarantee the payment of any residual value. At the end of the lease term, 30 June 2017, or if cancelled earlier, the car automatically reverts to the lessor with no payments being required from Wellington Ltd.

The vehicle had an expected economic life of 6 years. The expected fair value of the vehicle at 30 June 2017 was $12 000. Because of concern over the residual value, Dunedin Ltd required Jack to sign another contractual arrangement separate from the lease agreement which gave Dunedin Ltd the right to sell the car to Wellington Ltd if the fair value of the car at the end of the lease term was less than $10 000.

Costs of maintenance and insurance paid by Dunedin Ltd to Hamilton Autos over the years ended 30 June 2015 to 30 June 2017 were $2810, $3020 and $2750.

At 30 June 2017, Jack returned the vehicle to Dunedin Ltd. The fair value of the car was determined by to be $9000. Dunedin Ltd invoked the second agreement. With the consent of Wellington, Dunedin Ltd sold the car to Hamilton Autos for a price of $9000 on 5 July 2017, and invoiced Wellington Ltd for $1000. Wellington Ltd subsequently paid this amount on 13 July 2017.

Required

Assuming the lease is classified as a finance lease, prepare:
1. a schedule of lease payments for Wellington Ltd
2. journal entries in the records of Wellington Ltd for the years ending 30 June 2015, 30 June 2017 and 30 June 2018
3. a schedule of lease receipts for Dunedin Ltd
4. journal entries in the records of Dunedin Ltd for the years ending 30 June 2015, 30 June 2017 and 30 June 2018.

References

Accounting Standards Board UK 1999, *Leases: implementation of a new approach*, discussion paper prepared for the IASC, ASB Publications, Central Milton Keynes, UK.

IASB 2012, *Project report*, International Accounting Standards Board UK, www.ifrs.org.

McGregor, W 1996, *Accounting for leases: a new approach — recognition by lessees of assets and liabilities arising under lease contracts*, FASB, July. Quoted material sourced from this publication.

Qantas 2011, *Annual report 2011*, Qantas Airways Limited, Australia, www.qantas.com.au.

Shanahan, J 1989, '$1 plus $1 equals a million-dollar lease', *Australian Business*, 14 June, pp. 79–80.

13 Intangible assets

ACCOUNTING STANDARDS IN FOCUS

IAS 38 *Intangible Assets*

LEARNING OBJECTIVES

After studying this chapter, you should be able to:

1 understand the key characteristics of an intangible asset

2 explain the criteria relating to the initial recognition of intangible assets and their measurement at point of initial recognition, distinguishing between acquired and internally generated intangibles

3 explain how to measure intangibles subsequent to initial recognition, including the principles relating to the amortisation of intangibles

4 explain the accounting for retirement and disposal of intangible assets

5 apply the disclosure requirements of IAS 38

6 discuss changes to IAS 38 proposed in the Australian Accounting Standards Board discussion paper (2008)

7 discuss innovative suggestions for improving the reporting of intangible assets.

INTRODUCTION

Chapter 11 discusses the accounting standards for the tangible assets of property, plant and equipment. This chapter examines the standards for intangible assets. The International Accounting Standards Board (IASB) believes it is necessary to distinguish between tangible assets (such as property, plant and equipment) and intangible assets (such as patents and brand names). In analysing the accounting for intangible assets, the question that must always be kept in mind is whether there should be any difference in the accounting treatment for tangible and intangible assets. What is it that is different about intangible assets that makes a separate accounting standard, and presumably different accounting rules, for intangible and tangible assets necessary?

Historically, it is common for entities to report all their tangible assets on the statement of financial position/balance sheet but be less consistent in the reporting of intangible assets. As a result, there are sometimes large differences between the market value of an entity and its recorded net assets. As Jenkins and Upton (2001, p. 4) noted:

> The problem that confronts businesses, users of business and financial reporting, standard-setters and regulators is how best to understand and communicate the difference between the value of a company (usually expressed as the market capitalisation) and the accounting book value of that company.

To assist in understanding the difference between these two numbers, Jenkins and Upton (2001, p. 5) provided the analysis shown in figure 13.1. Item 6 in this figure is not an area that accounting can directly address, although the quality of the accounting may affect the degree to which it exists. At 31 December 2000, the market-to-book gap of Enron was approximately $64 billion. However, Lev (2002, pp. 133–4) argued that this was not related to intangibles:

> The best evidence that Enron lacked substantial intangibles is that its demise made hardly a ripple in the energy trading market, and had practically no effect on electricity prices. Intangibles, by definition, are unique factors of production that cannot be quickly imitated by competitors. The fact that Enron's competitors quickly stepped in to fill the gap is inconsistent with the existence of intangibles conferring on their owners sustained competitive advantages.
>
> So the answer to the question posed at the opening of this note — where have Enron's intangibles gone? — is a simple one. Nowhere. Enron did not have substantial intangibles, that is, if hype, glib, and earnings manipulation do not count as intangibles.

1. Accounting book value	$xxx
2. + Market assessments of differences between accounting measurement and underlying value of recognised assets and liabilities	xxx
3. + Market assessments of the underlying value of items that meet the definition of assets and liabilities but are not recognised in financial statements (e.g. patents developed through internal research and development)	xxx
4. + Market assessments of intangible value drivers or value impairers that do not meet the definition of assets and liabilities (e.g. employee morale)	xxx
5. + Market assessments of the entity's future plans, opportunities and business risks	xxx
6. + Other factors, including puffery, pessimism and market psychology	xxx
7. Market capitalisation	$xxx

FIGURE 13.1 Differences between market capitalisation and accounting book value
Source: Jenkins and Upton (2001, p. 5). © 2001. Reproduced with the permission of CPA Australia Ltd.

How can accounting assist in providing more information about what causes the gap between accounting book value and market capitalisation numbers? How much information should be provided about all the assets and liabilities of an entity? What should be in the financial statements and what should be in the notes to those statements? These are questions for accounting standard setters to solve.

The standards on accounting for intangibles are contained in IAS 38 *Intangible Assets*. In its 2004 revision, the IASB did not attempt to revisit all areas of accounting for intangibles. Its emphasis in this revision was to reflect changes as a result of decisions made in the Business Combinations project, particularly relating to accounting for intangibles acquired as part of a business combination. Hence, there still may be areas of inconsistency between accounting for intangibles obtained outside a business combination and those acquired as part of a business combination.

IAS 38 covers the accounting for all intangible assets except, as detailed in paragraphs 2 and 3, those specifically covered by another accounting standard: financial assets; and mineral rights and expenditure on exploration for, or development and extraction of, minerals, oil, natural gas and similar non-regenerative resources. Other intangible assets specifically covered by standards other than IAS 38 are:

- intangible assets held by an entity for sale in the ordinary course of business (see IAS 2 *Inventories* and IAS 11 *Construction Contracts*)
- intangible assets arising from insurance contracts with policyholders (IFRS 4 *Insurance Contracts*)
- deferred tax assets (IAS 12 *Income Taxes*)
- leases within the scope of IAS 17 *Leases*
- assets arising from employee benefits (IAS 19 *Employee Benefits*)
- goodwill acquired in a business combination (IFRS 3 *Business Combinations*)
- non-current intangible assets held for sale (IFRS 5 *Non-current Assets Held for Sale and Discontinued Operations*).

An example of the assets that are being considered in this chapter is shown in figure 13.2 which contains the intangible assets disclosed by Christian Dior in its 2010 annual report. Note that brands and trade names comprise the majority of the intangible assets but other intangibles include licences and computer software.

FIGURE 13.2 Examples of intangible assets

NOTE 3 — BRANDS, TRADE NAMES AND OTHER INTANGIBLE ASSETS

(EUR millions)	2010			2009	2008[1]
	Gross	Amortization and impairment	Net	Net	Net
Brands	9 806	(426)	9 380	9 152	8 920
Trade names	3 339	(1 362)	1 977	1 853	1 909
License rights	32	(30)	2	15	15
Leasehold rights	373	(236)	137	117	121
Software	490	(346)	144	111	110
Other	289	(157)	132	122	124
TOTAL	14 329	(2 557)	11 772	11 370	11 199
of which: assets held under finance leases	14	(14)	—	—	—

(1) See Note 1.2 Application of IAS 38 as amended.

3.3 Brands and trade names
The breakdown of brands and trade names by business group is as follows:

(EUR millions)	2010			2009	2008
	Gross	Amortization and impairment	Net	Net	Net
Christian Dior Couture	34	—	34	34	47
Wines and Spirits	2 980	(35)	2 945	2 937	2 755
Fashion and Leather Goods	3 895	(338)	3 557	3 543	3 565
Perfumes and Cosmetics	1 286	(22)	1 264	1 262	1 264
Watches and Jewelry	1 386	(6)	1 380	1 167	1 166
Selective Retailing	3 292	(1 316)	1 976	1 853	1 909
Other activities	272	(71)	201	209	123
BRANDS AND TRADE NAMES	13 145	(1 788)	11 357	11 005	10 829

(continued)

FIGURE 13.2 *(continued)*

The brands and trade names recognized in the table above are those that the Group has acquired. The principal acquired brands and trade names as of December 31, 2010 are:

- Wines and Spirits: Hennessy, Moët & Chandon champagnes, Veuve Clicquot, Krug, Château d'Yquem, Château Cheval Blanc, Belvedere, Glenmorangie, Newton Vineyards and Numanthia Termes;
- Fashion and Leather Goods: Louis Vuitton, Fendi, Donna Karan New York, Céline, Loewe, Givenchy, Kenzo, Thomas Pink, Berluti and Pucci;
- Perfumes and Cosmetics: Parfums Christian Dior, Guerlain, Parfums Givenchy, Make Up for Ever, Benefit Cosmetics, Fresh and Acqua di Parma;
- Watches and Jewelry: TAG Heuer, Zenith, Hublot, Chaumet and Fred;
- Selective Retailing: DFS Galleria, Sephora, Le Bon Marché;
- Other activities: the publications of the media group Les Echos-Investir and the Royal Van Lent-Feadship brand.

These brands and trade names are recognized in the balance sheet at their value determined as of the date of their acquisition by the Group, which may be much less than their value in use or their net selling price as of the closing date for the consolidated financial statements of the Group. This is notably the case for the brands Louis Vuitton, Christian Dior Couture, Veuve Clicquot, and Parfums Christian Dior, or the trade name Sephora, with the understanding that this list must not be considered as exhaustive.

Brands developed by the Group, notably Dom Pérignon as well as the De Beers jewelry trade name developed as a joint-venture with the De Beers group, are not capitalized in the balance sheet.

Please refer also to Note 5 for the impairment testing of brands, trade names and other intangible assets with indefinite useful lives.

Source: Christian Dior (2011, pp. 117, 119).

13.1 THE NATURE OF INTANGIBLE ASSETS

Paragraph 8 of IAS 38 defines an intangible asset as follows:

> an identifiable non-monetary asset without physical substance

Other writers have similar definitions. For example, Lev stated (2001, p. 5):

> An intangible asset is a claim to future benefits that does not have a physical or financial (a stock or bond) embodiment.

According to the IAS 38 definition, there are three key characteristics of an intangible asset: identifiable, non-monetary in nature and without physical substance. Each characteristic is there for a reason, generally to exclude certain assets from being classified as intangible assets.

13.1.1 Non-monetary in nature

Monetary assets are defined in IAS 38 as 'money held and assets to be received in fixed or determinable amounts of money'. The reason for including 'non-monetary' in the definition of intangible assets is to exclude financial assets such as loans and receivables from being classified as intangible assets. The accounting for financial assets is covered in IFRS 9 *Financial Instruments* and IAS 39 *Financial Instruments: Recognition and Measurement*.

13.1.2 Identifiable

IAS 38 does not contain a definition of 'identifiable'. However, paragraph 12 of this standard sets down two criteria, either of which must be met for an asset to be classified as an intangible asset. Paragraph 12 states:

> An asset is identifiable if it either:
> (a) is separable, i.e. is capable of being separated or divided from the entity and sold, transferred, licensed, rented or exchanged, either individually or together with a related contract, identifiable asset or liability, regardless of whether the entity intends to do so; or
> (b) arises from contractual or other legal rights, regardless of whether those rights are transferable or separable from the entity or from other rights and obligations.

There are thus two parts to the concept of identifiability.

First, consider the criterion of separability. Separability tests whether an entity can divide an asset from other assets and transfer it to another party. Some examples of assets that do not meet this criterion were identified by the Australian Accounting Standards Board (AASB) (2008, paragraph 15):

> For example, the identifiability criterion scopes out customer service capability, presence in geographic markets or locations, strong labour relations, ongoing training or recruiting programs, knowledge capital, ecological attitudes, outstanding credit ratings and access to capital markets, and favourable government relations ...

Assets such as high staff morale and customer relationships may be capable of being named and discussed, and actions may be taken to adjust the levels of them within an entity, but such assets cannot be transferred to another entity.

Why was the criterion of separability included in the definition of an asset? The answer is reliability of measurement. If an asset can be transferred to another entity, then probably a market exists for that asset. If no transfer can occur, then there will be no market. If there is no market, there is no market price. It would seem that the standard setters are afraid that preparers of financial statements will include assets such as staff morale on their balance sheet at some form of non-market valuation, and they are concerned about the reliability of such measurements. By including separability in the definition of intangible assets, there is a limit placed on the assets that could potentially appear on a balance sheet.

As noted by the AASB (2008, paragraph 36):

> Assets that have descriptions implying they are tangible assets, such as land, may include an intangible component. For example, the (intangible) view from a block of land is inextricably linked to the land and in practice it is not separated nor typically explicitly acknowledged for financial reporting purposes.

Similarly, some land is available for residential purposes while other land is only available for industrial purposes. The right to erect a particular type of building on a block of land is rarely valued separately from the land itself. The AASB (2008, paragraph 37) further notes that in many financial reports a number of intangible assets are grouped together under the one heading; for example, the descriptor 'brand' may comprise a trademark, a trade name, formulas, recipes and technological expertise. The trademark 'Coca-Cola' has no value unless it is combined with the formula to make the drink itself.

The second criterion to the concept of identifiability is if it 'arises from contractual or other legal rights'. As noted earlier, this criterion is an alternative to separability. Hence there are some intangible assets that are not separable but meet the definition of an intangible asset because of part (b) in paragraph 12 of IAS 38. In paragraph BC10 of the Basis for Conclusions on IAS 38, the IASB stated:

> Some contractual-legal rights establish property interests that are not readily separable from the entity as a whole. For example, under the laws of some jurisdictions some licences granted to an entity are not transferable except by sale of the entity as a whole.

Examples of assets fitting into this category generally relate to situations where a government gives or sells a right to an entity, such as:

- an entity has a right to use two million litres of water per annum in its production process
- an entity has a right to emit a specified quantity of greenhouse gases into the atmosphere per annum.

A condition of receiving this right is that the right cannot be transferred between entities; hence, if an entity used only one million litres of water, it could not sell/transfer the remaining right to one million litres of water to another entity. The right is then not separable. However the IASB believed that these assets could be distinguished from other assets held by an entity and should be disclosed as intangible assets. Separability was then not seen as the only criterion for identifiability.

In his discussion of the interrelationship between tangible and intangible assets, Upton (2001, p. 61) commented: 'With control comes the ability to buy, sell, or withhold from the market — characteristics of the everyday notion of an asset.' Upton then interpreted the meaning of 'control' to require identifiability, implying that expected benefits cannot be controlled if the benefits are not separable, and the entity does not have the ability to transfer them to another entity. He also noted (p. 62):

> The definition of an asset is derived from sensible economics and everyday use of language. The more complex answer is that monetary measurement is impossible without a notion like control.

Non-physical assets cannot be recognised unless they are identifiable. The reason for this restriction is that it makes the subsequent measurement of assets easier. However, as noted by the AASB (2008, paragraph 86), embedding the notice of 'identifiability' in the definition of intangible assets perpetuates the perception that intangible assets are fundamentally different from tangible assets for recognition purposes.

Figure 13.3 contains a list of assets that could potentially meet the identifiability criteria. The list is part of the illustrative examples that accompany IFRS 3 *Business Combinations* (2008).

CLASS	BASIS
Marketing-related intangible assets	
Trademarks, trade names, service marks, collective marks and certification marks	Contractual
Trade dress (unique colour, shape or package design)	Contractual
Newspaper mastheads	Contractual
Internet domain names	Contractual
Non-competition agreements	Contractual
Customer-related intangible assets	
Customer lists	Non-contractual
Order or production backlog	Contractual
Customer contracts and related customer relationships	Contractual
Non-contractual customer relationships	Non-contractual
Artistic-related intangible assets	
Plays, operas and ballets	Contractual
Books, magazines, newspapers and other literary works	Contractual
Musical works such as compositions, song lyrics and advertising jingles	Contractual
Pictures and photographs	Contractual
Video and audiovisual material, including motion pictures or films, music videos and television programs	Contractual
Contract-based intangible assets	
Licensing, royalty and standstill agreements	Contractual
Advertising, construction, management, service or supply contracts	Contractual
Lease agreements (whether the acquiree is the lessee or lessor)	Contractual
Construction permits	Contractual
Franchise agreements	Contractual
Operating and broadcast rights	Contractual
Servicing contracts, such as mortgage servicing contracts	Contractual
Employment contracts	Contractual
Use rights, such as drilling, water, air, timber cutting and route authorities	Contractual
Technology-based intangible assets	
Patented technology	Contractual
Computer software and mask works	Contractual
Unpatented technology	Non-contractual
Databases, including title plants	Non-contractual
Trade secrets, such as secret formulas, processes and recipes	Contractual

FIGURE 13.3 Identifiable intangible assets

As noted earlier, one of the problems with non-separable assets is the ability to measure them. Some assets, such as an excellent workforce and a high level of customer satisfaction, are interrelated in that very good employees will lead to high customer satisfaction. To recognise these as separate assets would raise difficulties in determining the value of one separately from the other. With the measurement of tangible assets, the emphasis is generally not on measuring the benefits from the asset, but on recording the cost of the asset. Benefits from assets are often measured at the level of a cash-generating unit rather than at the individual asset level, as is the case when determining impairment of assets (see chapter 15 of this book).

13.1.3 Lack of physical substance

Lack of physical substance is the third characteristic in the definition of an intangible asset. It is the characteristic that separates assets such as property, plant and equipment from intangible assets, in that property, plant and equipment would generally meet both the other criteria of an intangible asset; that is, IAS 16 *Property, Plant and Equipment* provides accounting policies for identifiable, non-monetary assets.

Note at the outset that some intangible assets may be associated with a physical item, such as software contained on a computer disk. However, the asset is really the software and not the disk itself. As noted in paragraph 4 of IAS 38, judgement in some cases is required to determine which element, tangible or intangible, is most important to the classification of the asset. Use of the physical substance characteristic is interesting in that paragraph 4.11 of the *Conceptual Framework* states:

> physical form is not essential to the existence of an asset; hence patents and copyrights, for example, are assets if future economic benefits are expected to flow from them to the entity and if they are controlled by the entity.

If physical substance is not intrinsic to the determination of assets, why then is it necessary to distinguish between physical and non-physical assets?

The differences between physical and non-physical assets and the need to distinguish between them was highlighted by then US Federal Reserve Board chairman Alan Greenspan in a report to Congress (27 February 2002), as reported by Lev (2002, pp. 131–2):

> But an economy in which concepts (intangibles) form an important share of valuation has its own vulnerabilities.
> As the recent events surrounding Enron have highlighted, a firm is inherently fragile if its value added emanates more from conceptual as distinct from physical assets. A physical asset, whether an office building or an automotive assembly plant, has the capability of producing goods even if the reputation of the managers of such facilities falls under a cloud. The rapidity of Enron's decline is an effective illustration of the vulnerability of a firm whose market value largely rests on capitalized reputation. The physical assets of such a firm comprise a small proportion of its asset base. Trust and reputation can vanish overnight. A factory cannot.

Lev (2002, p. 132) then noted that Greenspan had highlighted a major macroeconomic attribute of intangibles, namely 'the fact that concepts cannot be held as inventories means a greater share of GDP is not subject to a type of dynamics that amplifies cyclical swings'. Hence, according to Lev, an intangibles-intensive economy has a greater chance of recovery in bad economic times — competitors have equal access to physical assets whereas intangibles are the drivers of value and growth. These assets still remain of value even in bad times (Lev, 2002, p. 134):

> Hypothetically, would a tarnished reputation of Microsoft, Pfizer, or DuPont's management destroy the ability of these and similarly innovative companies to continuously introduce new products and services and maintain dominant competitive positions? Of course not. Even when companies collapse, valuable patents, brands, R&D laboratories, trained employees, and unique information systems will find eager buyers.

It is then necessary to carefully ensure that our accounting systems can deal successfully with both assets of physical substance and those without.

Many writers in the accounting literature do not agree that separating assets on a physical/non-physical basis is useful in subclassifying assets. For example:

> Indeed, once we agree that assets are future economic benefits, tangibility and even legal ownership are irrelevant for accountants; it is only some confused 'physicalist' prejudice that might persuade them otherwise (Napier & Power 1992, pp. 85–95).

> [T]he *lack of physical existence* is not of itself a satisfactory criterion for distinguishing a tangible from an intangible asset. Such assets as bank deposits, accounts receivable, and long-term investments lack physical substance, yet accountants classify them as tangible assets (Kieso & Weygandt 1992, p. 589).

There are a number of problems with defining intangible assets in terms of physical existence. The *first* problem is that it conflicts with the way in which accountants have traditionally classified assets. Non-monetary items such as investments in equity or debt instruments, leases, and deferred costs such as research and development expenditure have not generally been classified as intangible assets. Monetary items such as receivables, prepayments and deferred tax assets are similarly not classified as intangible assets.

The *second* problem relates to why accountants would want to classify assets on the basis of whether they have physical substance. There are an infinite number of ways of classifying items, such as by colour, size or shape. The choice of classification must have a purpose. Are preparers or users of accounts interested in how many assets can be touched and how many cannot be touched? It is doubtful that this is the case. In determining the appropriate criterion for classifying assets, there must be an explanation for the relevance of the classification. If useful information is the purpose of the classification, accountants' actions in practice and lack of supporting logic in the accounting literature raise doubts as to whether physical substance is the appropriate basis for classifying assets.

The *third* problem with using the physical substance criterion is the potential conflict with the *Conceptual Framework* as quoted above. Based on the definition of assets as future economic benefits, all assets are intangible in that they represent a collection of perceived economic benefits. Thus, it is not the block of land or item of plant that is the asset; it is the economic benefits embodied in that physical item that constitutes the asset. A key example of this is leased assets. It is not the physical leased motor vehicle that is the asset, but the economic benefits from that physical item that constitute the asset. In relation to leased items, Stevenson (1989, p. 5) noted, 'we can quickly slip back to physical concepts of assets if we are not careful'.

The *fourth* problem with the criterion of physical substance is that tangibility is not an indication of the worth of an asset. As James (2001) noted:

> Accounting for new-economy organisations is often problematic, because much of the value lies in intangibles: brands, customer relationships and knowledge. Spotless Services is an example. The company has maintained a relatively stable share price during a period when its tangible assets (NTA) went negative (the NTA is now positive). The reason is that Spotless's assets are mostly intangible; in recognition of this, the company no longer includes the NTA in its public accounts because, according to the company secretary, it is not relevant.

Interestingly, IAS 38 has no discussion on the characteristic of 'physical substance', yet four paragraphs are devoted to the control characteristic of an asset.

Why, then, distinguish non-physical assets? Lev (2001, p. 5) provides some answers. He defined an intangible asset as 'a claim to future benefits that does not have a physical or financial (a stock or a bond) embodiment'. He then used the terms 'intangibles', 'knowledge assets' and 'intellectual capital' interchangeably, as he saw the term 'intangibles' being used by accountants, 'knowledge assets' by economists, and 'intellectual capital' in the management and legal literature. He summarised (p. 7) intangible assets as being non-physical sources of value (claims to future benefits) generated by innovation (or discovery, relating to innovations, research and development), unique organisational designs (relating to brands, organisational structures and marketing savvy), or human resource practices (relating to unique personnel and compensation policies, recruitment successes and low turnover of employees).

The reason for distinguishing between physical and non-physical assets is that the very nature of a non-physical asset means that the accounting standards for the recognition and measurement of non-physical assets may have to be different from those for tangible assets. What are these unique characteristics and how do they cause a problem? Consider the following characteristics raised by Lev (2001):

- *Intangible assets are non-rival assets* (p. 22). They can be used at the same time for multiple purposes, such as an airline reservation system that can serve many customers. There is no opportunity cost of using the asset.
- *The assets are characterised by large fixed (sunk) costs and negligible marginal (incremental) cost* (pp. 22–3). Examples of this are the development of a headache tablet and the creation of a computer software program.
- *Many intangibles are not subject to the diminishing returns characteristic of physical assets* (p. 23). Production of more computer disks does not reduce the worth of the software asset. There may be increasing returns to scale. For example, a university may develop a software program for student enrolment that can be valuable for ongoing use by the university and may also be sold to other universities, thereby increasing the return on the original investment.
- *Intangibles may have network effects* (p. 26). The value of the item increases as the number of people using the item increases. The utility of such items as a computer game console (Xbox 360 or Playstation 3), a telephone network (Vodafone or Nokia), or a computer program (Microsoft Word or Excel spreadsheets) increases as more people use the same item.
- *Intangibles may be more difficult to manage and operate than tangible assets* (p. 32). Physical assets such as buildings are harder to steal and copy.
- *Property rights are harder to determine* (p. 33). Investments in employee training and advertising are areas where it is hard to exclude others from securing some of the benefits.
- *The relationship between the investment and the ultimate benefits is hard to track.* Are the extra sales the result of the training of employees, or because the item has become trendy?
- *The relationship between the investment and the return is skewed* (p. 39). Many investments in intangibles result in failure while some are a huge success. The investment is then often high risk. As Lev noted, a key element in intangibles is that success relies on a discovery. Investments in tangible assets tend to occur after the discovery, and alternative uses including the sale of the assets do not depend on discovery.
- *There is in general an absence of organised and competitive markets* (p. 42). Intangibles such as brand names may be sold but, given the unique nature of most intangibles, there is no active market for them. The sale of a brand name in one industry has no bearing on the potential for sale of another brand, even in the same industry. Lev (p. 47) argues that markets in intangibles lack *transparency*, so,

'details of licensing deals and alliances are generally not made public, and acquired intangibles are usually bundled with other assets'.

- *There is a high degree of uncertainty regarding the future benefits of intangible assets*. This is a general statement as there are some physical assets that also exhibit uncertainty in relation to expected benefits. As Egginton (1990, p. 194) stated:

> For example, there could be more uncertainty over the future benefits of the tangible oil and gas reserves of a section of ocean than over the future benefits of the intangible European rights to the Coca-Cola brand name.

Lev (2001, p. 47) summarised the above discussion as follows:

> Intangibles are inherently difficult to trade. Legal property rights are often hazy, contingent contracts are difficult to draw, and the cost structure of many intangibles (large sunk costs, negligible marginal costs) is not conducive to stable pricing. Accordingly, at present there are no active, organized markets in intangibles. This could soon change with the advent of Internet-based exchanges, but it will require specific enabling mechanisms, such as valuation and insurance schemes. Private trades in intangibles in the form of licensing and alliances proliferate, but they do not provide information essential for the measurement and valuation of intangibles.

Because non-physical assets have the above characteristics, they cause particular problems for accountants. The two key activities for accountants in relation to assets are the recognition and measurement of the assets. With non-physical assets, the determination of when they should be recognised (Should one wait for a point of discovery? Does an asset exist when the investment is made? Is there an asset at the point employee training occurs?), and how they should be measured (Where is the market? Can the specific benefits be isolated? Are the property rights over the expected benefits fuzzy?) is in general more difficult. Hence, the need for a specific standard on non-physical assets arises from the need for extra guidance on the recognition and measurement of those assets — not because such assets are of any greater or lesser value than physical assets. With physical assets, where there are thin markets or where the assets are of a specialised nature, the guidance in IAS 38 could be considered to be equally applicable to tangible assets.

13.1.4 Why have intangibles become important?

For quite some time, writers in the business press have noted a change in the factors that cause a company to be valuable. As far back as 1987, Gottliebsen (1987, p. 6) noted a change in the composition of valuable assets in modern entities:

> Around the world, Japanese manufacturers established brands such as Sony, Toyota, Nissan, National, Honda and Mazda that have become household names. Their plans to move a vast amount of their productive capacity from Japan to the US reveal that the really fragile asset is the so-called 'tangible asset' — the bricks, mortar and plant that represented the old manufacturing capacity, now to be scrapped. The real tangible asset that endured was the brands — now to be produced for the US market from a different place.

More recently, Lev (2002, p. 132) made similar observations:

> Pfizer's value comes from its discovery activities (drug developments, patents, trademarks), and from an unusually effective sales force (human capital, training), and not from its lab equipment or pill production facilities. Wal-Mart's incredible competitiveness derives from unique organizational processes, such as those shifting inventory management to suppliers, rather than from brick and mortar.

An analysis of the price-to-book ratio over time can provide evidence of the increasing importance of intangibles. Figure 13.4 shows a graph of the Standard and Poor's (S&P) 500 companies over a 30-year period. It can be seen that in the early 1980s the net assets reported by companies were not much less than the market capitalisation of those companies. However, subsequently the market capitalisation increased relative to book values, peaking at a ratio of 6:1 in March 2001, which meant that for every six dollars of market value, only one dollar appeared on the statement of financial position, while the remaining five dollars represented intangible assets. This economic phenomenon occurred despite the development of an increasing number of accounting standards attempting to ensure reported financial information would be more relevant and faithfully represented. As Karsan (2009) noted in an analysis of the information in figure 13.4:

> Furthermore, there has been a shift when it comes to industries in the S&P 500, with manufacturing companies playing a decreasing role while knowledge-based companies (e.g. software, consulting, other services etc.), where hard-assets are not a determining factor, comprise a larger portion of the index.

S&P 500 Price/Book Ratio

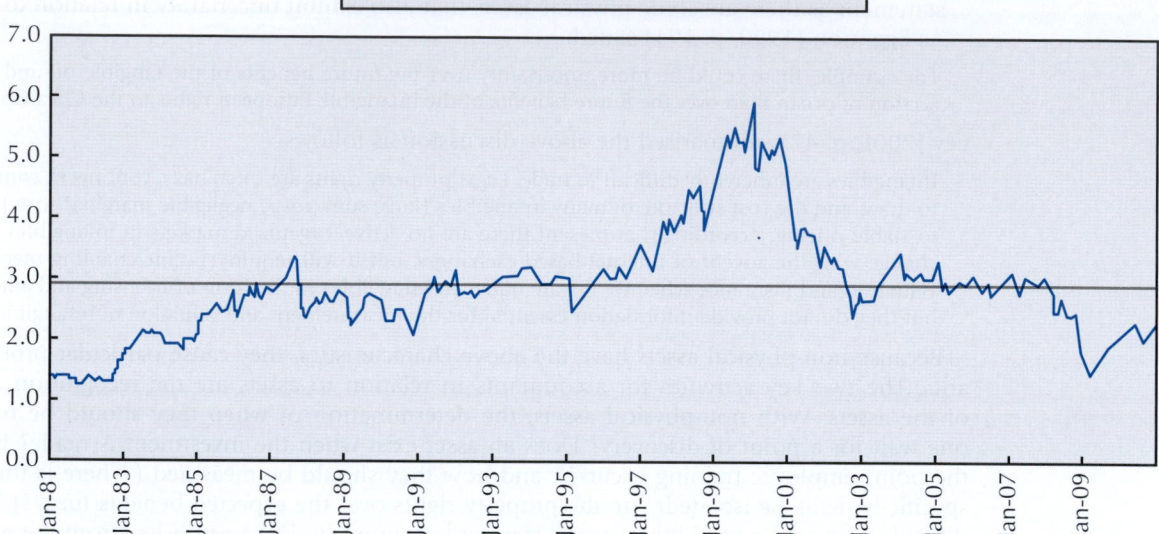

FIGURE 13.4 Average price-to-book ratio of the S&P 500 companies
Source: Sadan (2010).

The increasing investment in intangible assets was also noted by Corrado and Hulten (2010):

> Tangible investment dropped from 11.1% of business output in 1947 to 10.0% in 2007, while intangible investment increased from 4.5% of business output to 13.7% during the same period.

They produced the graph in figure 13.5.

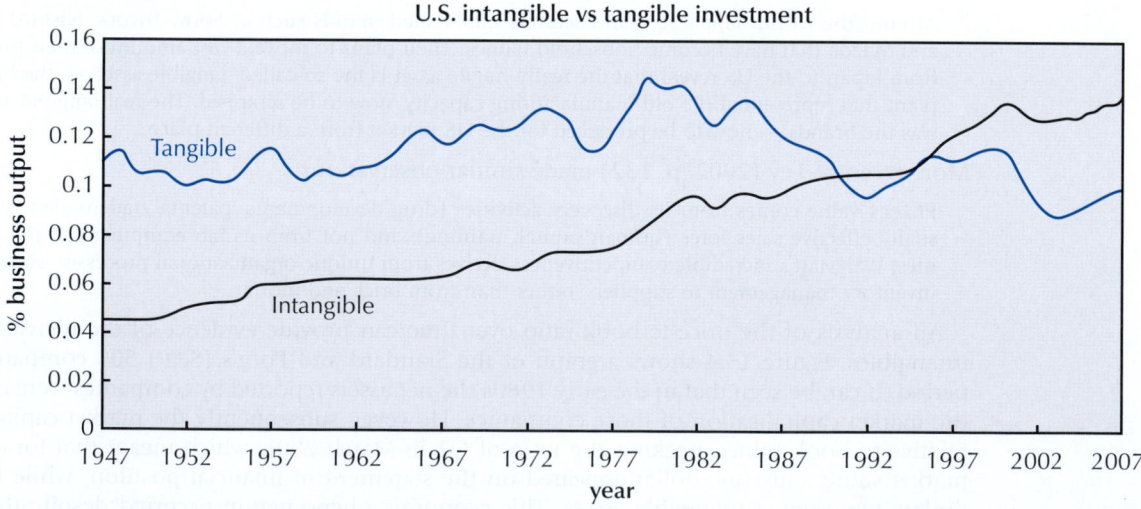

FIGURE 13.5 Tangible vs intangible investment
Source: Corrado & Hulten (2010).

Lev (2001, pp. 8–9) asked why intangibles are more important now than in the 1960s, 1970s and 1980s. He argued that the surge in intangibles was driven by the 'unique combination of two related economic forces' — intensified business competition and the advent of information technologies. He provided numerous examples to support his case, and the diagram in figure 13.6 illustrates his argument.

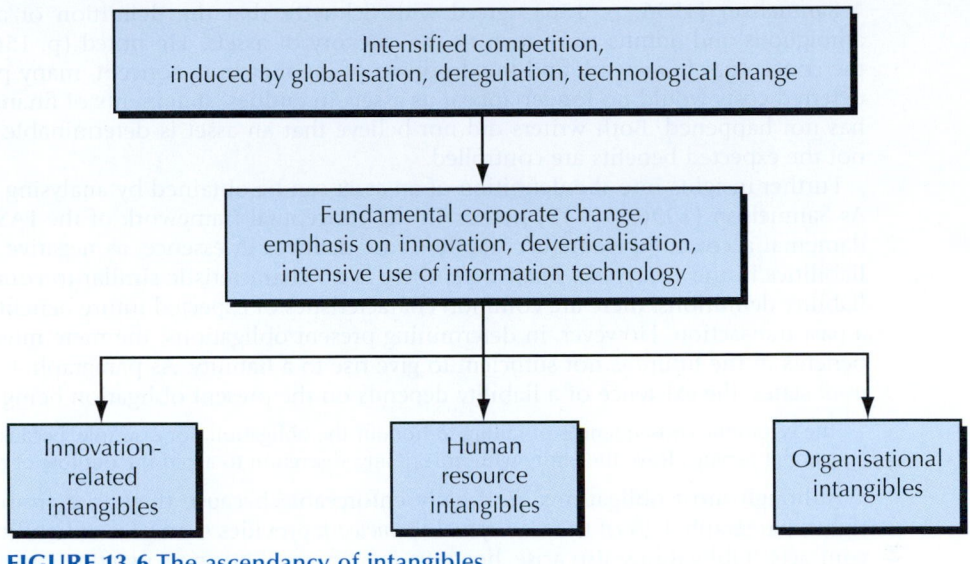

FIGURE 13.6 The ascendancy of intangibles
Source: Lev (2001, p. 18).

On the basis of Lev's 2001 analysis, intangible assets can be classified into four groups (see Lev, Radhakrishnan & Zhang (2009)):

1. *Discovery/learning intangibles* — technology, know-how, patents and other assets emanating from the discovery (R&D) and learning (e.g. reverse engineering) processes of business enterprises, universities and national laboratories.
2. *Customer-related intangibles* — brands, trademarks and unique distribution channels (e.g. internet-based sales), which create abnormal (above cost of capital) earnings.
3. *Human-resource intangibles* — specific human resource practices such as training and compensation systems, which enhance employee productivity and reduce turnover.
4. *Organisation capital* — unique structural and organisational designs and business processes generating sustainable competitive advantages.

13.1.5 The definition of an asset and identifying intangible assets

Paragraph 4.4 of the *Conceptual Framework* describes an asset as 'a resource controlled by the entity'. Paragraphs 13–16 of IAS 38 discuss the application of the characteristic of 'control' and the classification of certain items as intangible assets.

The crux of the debate is whether items (as noted earlier by the FASB) that probably do not meet the identifiability criterion — such as effective advertising programs, trained staff, favourable government relations and fundraising capabilities — qualify as assets. According to paragraphs 13–16 of IAS 38, items such as market and technical knowledge (paragraph 14), staff skills, specific management or technical talent (paragraph 15) and a portfolio of customers, market share, customer relationships and customer loyalty (paragraph 16) do not meet the definition of intangible assets. The key reason for excluding such items as assets is the interpretation of the term 'control' as used in the definition of an asset. According to paragraph 13 of IAS 38, control normally stems from 'legal rights that are enforceable in a court of law'. In the absence of legal rights, it is more difficult to demonstrate control.

An outspoken critic of the definition of an asset has been Walter Schuetze, former chief accountant of the Securities and Exchange Commission (SEC) in the United States and former member of the FASB. He argued (1993, p. 67): 'FASB's definition is so complex, so abstract, so open-ended, so all-inclusive, and so vague that we cannot use it to solve problems.' He further stated (2001, p. 12):

> The definition does not discriminate and help us to decide whether something or anything on the margin is an asset. That definition describes an empty box. A large empty box. A large empty box with sideboards.

Because of this, he proposed that assets are defined as 'cash, contractual claims to cash or services, and items that can be sold separately for cash'. This definition incorporates ideas of separability/exchangeability and legal contracts for benefits. He considered the concept of control to be too vague to be operational.

Samuelson (1996, p. 156) agreed with Schuetze that the definition of assets is 'too complex and ambiguous and admits too much to the category of assets'. He noted (p. 156) that, with the advent of the conceptual framework and the dropping of the matching concept, many people expected that several deferred costs would no longer appear as assets in entities' statements of financial position. However, this has not happened. Both writers did not believe that an asset is determinable by considering whether or not the expected benefits are controlled.

Further insights into the definition of an asset can be obtained by analysing the definition of a liability. As Samuelson (1996, p. 147) noted: 'In the conceptual framework of the FASB, assets are the most fundamental accounting elements. Liabilities are defined, in essence, as negative assets'. In the definition of liabilities in the *Conceptual Framework*, there is no characteristic similar to control. Yet, for both asset and liability definitions, there are common characteristics of expected future benefits/outflows and existence of a past transaction. However, in determining present obligations, the mere intention to sacrifice economic benefits in the future is not sufficient to give rise to a liability. As paragraph 4.16 of the *Conceptual Framework* states, the existence of a liability depends on the present obligation being such that:

> the economic consequences of failing to honour the obligation, for example, because of the existence of a substantial penalty, leave the entity with little, if any, discretion to avoid the outflow of resources to another party.

Although most obligations are legally enforceable because they arise from contractual or other legal rights, paragraph 4.15 of the *Conceptual Framework* provides examples of liabilities where there are no legal contracts: 'Obligations also arise, however, from normal business practice, custom and a desire to maintain good business relations or act in an equitable manner.' For example, a provision for long-service leave and a deferred tax liability can be recognised as liabilities well before there is any legal enforceability, presumably on the grounds of past experience and/or normal business practice. Both are based on expectations of what might occur. With long-service leave provisions, provisions are based on expected retention rates because employees may change jobs before becoming eligible for payment.

Compare this with an entity that invests in its future staff by outlaying funds on training programs. The entity has invested in its staff, but it has no control over whether staff remain employed by it. Nevertheless, it has an expectation that it will receive most if not all of the benefits from the training programs. If the staff stay, the entity has control over the benefits from the increased sales that arise from the training programs. Access to the future benefits that arise from the well-trained staff who stay with the entity can be denied to other entities. Not all the expected benefits may eventuate but, if they do, they belong to the entity. In fact, if past experience indicates that the entity has a fine record of retaining staff, it can be inferred or construed from the facts in the particular situation that the benefits will flow to the entity. So, if custom and usual business practice are a guide, the benefits will flow to the entity. Although the staff could decide to go to another entity and provide it with the benefits of their training, that entity cannot argue that there are any grounds, such as normal business practice, for suggesting that this will occur. The second entity may form an expectation that the other entity's staff will change employment but there are no legal, equitable or constructive reasons for suggesting that its expectation is any more than a hope.

As noted in the Conceptual Framework Project Update on the IASB's website www.ifrs.org, the FASB and IASB have decided to adopt the following working definition of an asset:

> An *asset* of an entity is a present economic resource to which the entity has a right or other access that others do not have.

A right or other access that others do not have is enforceable by legal or equivalent means, such as a professional association. This emphasis on legally enforceable rights could further narrow the recognition of resources as assets.

The debate over the 'real' assets of today's entities is heightened with the existence of Internet or dot.com entities. Some of these entities have high values but very little in non-current assets or inventory. As King and Henry (1999) noted, the value of these entities lies in their intellectual capital: 'In fact, a common saying about them is that "the assets walk out the door every night".' King and Henry did not even question whether these items were assets, being more interested in the question of reliability of measurement. They noted:

> Major banks, such as BT Commercial (part of Bankers Trust, now Deutsche Bank), have lent literally hundreds of millions of dollars to companies like Zenith, Strohs, and Florsheim with the firms' trade names and patents as collateral... Appraisals are relevant and reliable enough for America's largest banks, so they should also be relevant and reliable for individual investors.

Such difficulties in determining whether certain intangibles meet the definition of an asset caused the standard setters to introduce the further test of identifiability. By requiring identifiability for recognition of intangibles, they diffused the debate as to whether an item such as good staff relations is an asset. Regardless of whether it is an asset, it is not an intangible asset because it does not meet the identifiability criterion, and so can only be recognised, if at all, as part of goodwill. However, reducing the number of assets recognised in the financial statements because of measurement problems may also reduce the relevance of the information provided in those financial statements.

13.2 RECOGNITION AND INITIAL MEASUREMENT

IAS 38 establishes standards in relation to the recognition and initial measurement of intangible assets. In order to provide some questions to consider when analysing these standards, it is worthwhile examining some issues raised by Upton (2001). This is done in the following section.

13.2.1 Measurement and relevance issues

In his analysis of intangibles, Upton (2001, p. 53) noted that there are four criteria to consider in determining the information that should be recognised in the financial statements:
- *Definitions* — does the item meet the definition of one of the elements of financial statements?
- *Measurability* — does the item have an attribute that is measurable with sufficient reliability?
- *Relevance* — is the information about the item capable of making a difference in user decisions?
- *Reliability* — is the information representationally faithful, verifiable and neutral?

He noted further that these criteria were also subject to a cost–benefit constraint.

In this context, Upton (2001, p. 54) observed that FASB Statement No. 2 *Accounting for Research and Development* required all outlays on research and development to be charged to expense. Similarly, in IAS 38, the IASB requires all outlays on research to be expensed, and specific criteria must be met before outlays on development can be capitalised. In FASB Statement No. 2, the following reasons were given for the decision to expense outlays:
- uncertainty of future benefits
- lack of causal relationship between outlay and eventual outcome
- inability to measure future benefits
- lack of usefulness of information about capitalised costs in assessing future performance of an entity.

As Upton noted, these reasons go to the heart of the measurement and relevance issues associated with recognising items in the financial statements. He made a number of insightful comments concerning the issues of measurement and relevance, as discussed in the following section.

Issues of measurement

Upton (2001) made the following observations:
- *Without a clear boundary, there is a risk that any measurement will double-count.* One problem in recognising and measuring intangible assets is the possibility that the same benefits are also included in the measurement of another intangible. For example, if an entity has good staff morale, this will contribute as well to a high level of customer satisfaction. Both lead to the increase in the profitability of an entity. However, measuring these two items separately creates the danger of valuing the same income stream twice. If measurements are based purely on the capitalisation of costs, this is less likely to happen.
- *Retrospective capitalisation may be a useful measure.* If all outlays on areas such as research are initially expensed, it may be useful to allow the retrospective capitalisation of these outlays when a level of success is achieved. Whether the capitalisation of all past outlays is appropriate is, however, questionable.
- *Recognition of in-process assets may be a useful measure.* When an entity outlays funds to either develop some software or find a cure for some disease, the expected results are highly uncertain. One possibility in terms of overcoming the 'expense everything' syndrome is to have a class of in-process assets, and to accumulate costs into in-process accounts. There is no doubt that some in-process information is valuable. In fact, effort expended to date is information for which other entities are willing to pay. An analogy can be made with financial options, for which there may be no value at expiration date.
- *Cross-fertilisation and multigenerational factors.* In some research programs, such as the development of medical cures, it is possible that research will never be totally wasted. The researcher may not find the desired cure for HIV/AIDS but, as a result of the research, the information discovered about blood may assist in providing solutions for other medical problems. Expensing purely because no cure for

HIV/AIDS was found is being too prescriptive in relation to relating outlays to specified outcomes. Similarly, amounts may be spent on developing software that is continuously being updated. However, elements of the software in the first generation device may still be an important foundation in subsequent devices. To expense all previous outlays just because a new version of the asset is developed is again short-sighted.

- *There are two 'gaps' that frustrate attempts to recognise intangible assets.* The first is the 'time gap', which is the gap between the outlay and the determination of the outcome. The longer the gap, the more reluctant standard setters will be to allow capitalisation. The second is the 'correlation gap', which relates the expense to the eventual outcome. For example, were outlays on the HIV/AIDS cure related to the information obtained on blood clotting?

Issues of relevance

Upton (2001) also made the following observations:

- *Relevance of capitalised cost information.* An adage popular in the oil industry is 'What you spend doesn't matter. What you find does.' With many intangible assets, the level of expenditure is not proportional to the eventual worth of the outcome. To capitalise costs, then, does not indicate the potential worth of the outcome or the asset, assuming it has any.
- *Uncertainty does not mean irrelevance.* Accounting does not require certainty for information to be useful. As noted earlier, companies are willing to pay for in-process assets, even though the eventual result is uncertain. It is also true that any entity that does not spend money on developing software or finding medical cures will not produce these products. In terms of causal relationships, entities doing drug research will find drug cures even if they are not the ones originally sought. Potentially causal relationships should not be sought on individual research projects but rather on a combination of research projects.
- *Cost information may not be as relevant as fair value but may be more reliable.* One of the problems of accumulating costs is that the asset may be overstated because the level of costs does not directly relate to the level of benefits. However, the accumulation of costs is at least a reliable measure. If an entity attempts to measure the fair value of an intangible asset, even though the fair value may be more relevant the measure may be less reliable. To choose between accumulated costs and fair value is to trade off relevance and reliability. However, just because something can be measured reliably should not mean that this is what should be disclosed. The measurement attribute must be a relevant one.
- *Volatility of information.* The worth of an entity is affected by events such as a safety recall, a shift in customer tastes, or the success of rival entities and their brands. If information about these events is not disclosed and disclosure is limited to the physical assets, can users obtain a real view of what is happening to the entity? The information on these items may be volatile, but to exclude them may create a financial impression that the entity is in a constantly steady state.

As Upton noted, the determination of relevance and reliable measurement is subject to a cost–benefit test. The costs of any rules on intangibles are borne by the entities preparing the financial statements and by the auditors. The users of the financial statements also incur costs relating to keeping up with accounting rules and adapting their financial analysis models. Unfortunately, although the costs may be quantifiable, the benefits in terms of the incremental information to the users are difficult to measure. Although some research has shown that disclosure of capitalised research and development costs is useful, the benefits relative to the costs have not been empirically demonstrated.

13.2.2 Criteria for recognition and initial measurement

After determining that an asset exists and that it meets the definition of an intangible asset, the asset must meet the two criteria in paragraph 21 of IAS 38 before it can be recognised. The criteria are:

- it is *probable* that the future economic benefits attributable to the asset will flow to the entity
- the *cost* of the asset can be measured *reliably*.

These criteria are the same as those for the recognition of property, plant and equipment in IAS 16 *Property, Plant and Equipment*. If the cost of the asset cannot be reliably measured, but the fair value is determinable, an asset cannot be recognised under either IAS 16 or IAS 38 because both standards require initial measurement at cost. As noted later, this has consequences for the recognition of intangible assets that are internally generated rather than acquired, as well as causing differences in the statements of financial position of entities that internally generate assets and those that acquire assets.

In relation to the initial measurement of an intangible asset, paragraph 24 of IAS 38 states:

> An intangible asset shall be measured initially at cost.

With the reliable measurement of cost as one of the recognition criteria, this cost forms the basis for initial measurement.

These recognition criteria and the requirement for initial measurement should be viewed as general principles only. Having established these criteria, IAS 38 then proceeds to examine the accounting for intangibles based upon how these assets were generated. The standard analyses intangibles in terms of four ways in which an entity could have obtained the assets:

- separate acquisition
- acquisition as part of a business acquisition
- acquisition by way of a government grant
- internally generated assets.

For each of these situations, IAS 38 provides specific recognition criteria and measurement rules. It is these that are applied in accounting for intangibles rather than the general criteria noted in paragraphs 21 and 24. Presumably the standard setters considered that there were particular measurement issues that arose under each of these situations requiring different principles to be established for each situation.

13.2.3 Separate acquisition

In recognising assets acquired separately, paragraph 25 of IAS 38 notes that:

> the probability recognition criterion in paragraph 21(a) is always considered to be satisfied for separately acquired intangible assets.

The standard setters argue that the price paid for the asset automatically takes into account the probability of the expected benefits being received; hence, it is unnecessary to apply a further probability test. For example, if an asset had expected cash inflows of $1000, and the probability of these inflows being received was 40%, then an acquirer would pay $400 for the asset. The standard setters argue that these benefits are now automatically probable. Further, paragraph 26 of IAS 38 states:

> In addition, the cost of a separately acquired intangible asset can usually be measured reliably. This is particularly so when the purchase consideration is in the form of cash or other monetary assets.

The measurement of cost may, however, be more difficult if the exchange involves the acquirer giving up non-monetary assets rather than cash.

An intangible asset acquired separately is initially measured at cost. As with property, plant and equipment, the cost of an asset is the sum of the purchase price and the directly attributable costs (IAS 38 paragraph 27). The purchase price is measured as the fair value of what is given up by the acquirer in order to acquire the asset, and the directly attributable costs are those necessarily incurred to get the asset into the condition where it is capable of operating in the manner intended by management. (These concepts are discussed further in this book in sections 11.3.1 and 11.3.2 of chapter 11 in relation to property, plant and equipment.) The principles of accounting for separately acquired intangibles and property, plant and equipment are the same.

In summary, where a for-profit entity acquires an intangible asset as a separate asset, there is only one recognition criterion to be applied, namely reliable measurement of the cost of the asset.

13.2.4 Acquisition as part of a business combination

Where assets are acquired as part of a business combination, IFRS 3 *Business Combinations* is applied. Appendix A of this standard contains a definition of a 'business combination' and a 'business'. This standard is discussed in detail in chapter 14 of this book. In this section, a reference to a business combination indicates that the acquiring entity has acquired a group of assets rather than a single asset and one of the assets in that group is an intangible asset. The group of assets could be an operating division or a segment of another entity. The key issue is then how to account for the acquisition of an intangible asset when it is acquired as part of a group of assets rather than as a single asset. Note, however, that IFRS 3 prescribes different accounting for the acquisition of a group of assets that constitutes a business and for a group that does not constitute a business. In applying the principles in IAS 38 relating to acquisition of assets as part of a business combination, it is first necessary to ensure that the group of assets being acquired is a business.

With respect to recognition criteria to apply when intangible assets are acquired in a business combination, IAS 38 states that *no* recognition criteria need be applied. Provided the assets meet the definition of an intangible asset, they must be recognised as separate assets. As with separately acquired intangible assets, paragraph 33 of IAS 38 provides that, where intangible assets are acquired as part of a business combination, the effect of probability is reflected in the measurement of the asset. Hence, the probability recognition criterion is automatically met. Further, it is argued in paragraph 33 of IAS 38 that the requirement for reliability of measurement is always met as sufficient information always exists to measure reliably the fair value of the asset. This non-application of recognition criteria in accounting for intangibles acquired in a business combination is also seen in IFRS 3 where paragraphs 11 and 12 note that the recognition conditions for the identifiable assets must meet the definition of an asset in the *Conceptual Framework*, as well as be a part of what the acquirer and the acquiree exchanged in the business combination transaction.

In dissenting from the issue of IAS 38, Professor Whittington (one of the IASB members) argued that the probability test in paragraph 21(a) should be applied in testing the recognition of all intangibles, stating that issues relating to the recognition criteria in the *Conceptual Framework* should be resolved before having different recognition criteria for intangible assets acquired in a business combination. The justification for different criteria is presumably that there is an increased relevance of information in reporting the separate intangible assets rather than subsuming them into goodwill.

The application of these recognition requirements means that an acquirer must, in recognising separately the acquiree's intangible assets, recognise intangible assets that the acquiree has not recognised in its records, such as in-process research and development that cannot be recognised under IAS 38 as internally generated assets (discussed later in this section). As noted in paragraph 34, recognition by an acquirer of an acquiree's in-process research and development project only depends on whether the project meets the definition of an intangible asset. It can be seen that entities that acquire intangible assets in a business combination will be able, and in fact are required, to recognise intangible assets that are not separately recognisable when acquired by other means.

The measurement of intangible assets acquired in a business combination is established in paragraph 33 of IAS 38:

> In accordance with IFRS 3 *Business Combinations*, if an intangible asset is acquired in a business combination, the cost of that intangible asset is its fair value at the acquisition date.

Note firstly that it is IFRS 3 that determines the measurement of assets acquired in a business combination. Under IFRS 3 acquired assets are measured at fair value. Hence, intangible assets acquired in a business combination must be measured at initial recognition at fair value. This is then a departure from the general measurement rule in paragraph 24. Paragraph 33 of IAS 38 does say that 'the cost . . . is its fair value'; however, the acquiring entity does not attempt to measure the cost, rather it measures the fair value.

The measurement of fair value is determined in accordance with IFRS 13 *Fair Value Measurement*. IFRS 13 defines fair value in Appendix A as:

> The price that would be received to sell an asset or paid to transfer a liability in an orderly transaction between market participants at the measurement date.

Chapter 3 of this book provides information on the measurement of fair value under IFRS 13.

13.2.5 Acquisition by way of a government grant

According to paragraph 44 of IAS 38, some intangible assets, such as licences to operate radio or television stations, are allocated to entities via government grants. These intangibles are accounted for in accordance with IAS 20 *Accounting for Government Grants and Disclosure of Government Assistance*, whereby an entity may choose to initially recognise both the intangible asset and the grant at fair value. If an entity does not choose to use the fair value measurement option, it will recognise the asset initially at a nominal amount plus directly attributable costs.

13.2.6 Internally generated intangible assets

The recognition criteria and measurement rules are different for intangible assets acquired as a separate asset or acquired in a business combination. The approach taken in accounting for internally generated assets is different again. The recognition criteria in paragraph 21 are not applied at all. The measurement approach used is one of capitalisation of outlays incurred by the entity.

This continuous change in accounting for intangible assets leaves the standard setters open to criticism for lack of consistency in the accounting for acquired intangibles versus internally generated intangibles.

As Jenkins and Upton (2001, p. 6) noted, genealogy is not an essential characteristic of an asset. Therefore, the accounting should not automatically be different according to whether an asset arises from a business combination or is internally generated.

The problem from an accounting point of view with internally generated intangibles is determining at what point in time an asset should be recognised. An entity may outlay funds in an exploratory project, such as developing software to overcome a specific problem, or designing a tool for a special purpose. There is no guarantee of success at the start of the project. The program may not work or the tool may be unsatisfactory for the purpose. Should the accountant capitalise the costs from the beginning of the project, or wait until there is some indication of success? A further problem with some intangible assets such as brand names is whether the costs outlaid relate solely to increasing the worth of the brand name or simply to enhancing the overall reputation of the entity.

The standard setters' solution to the problem of when to begin capitalising costs is to classify the generation of the asset into two phases: the research phase and the development phase. These terms are defined in paragraph 8 of IAS 38 as follows:

> Research is original and planned investigation undertaken with the prospect of gaining new scientific or technical knowledge and understanding.

> Development is the application of research findings or other knowledge to a plan or design for the production of new or substantially improved materials, devices, products, processes, systems or services before the start of commercial production or use.

It can be seen from these definitions that the earlier stages of a project are defined as research and, at some point in time, the project moves from a research phase to a development phase. Examples of research activities are given in paragraph 56 of IAS 38, such as the search for new knowledge or for alternatives for materials, devices, products, processes, systems or services. Examples of development activities are found in paragraph 59, such as the design, construction and operation of a non-commercial pilot plant, and the design of pre-production prototypes and models. From an accounting perspective, expenditure on research is expensed when incurred (paragraph 54), and expenditure on development is capitalised as an intangible asset. It is obviously important to be able to distinguish one phase from the other.

Paragraph 57 of IAS 38 is the key paragraph in this regard. It contains a list of criteria, all of which must be met in order for a development outlay to be capitalised. In order to capitalise development outlays, an entity must be able to demonstrate all of the following:

(a) the technical feasibility of completing the intangible asset so that it will be available for use or sale;
(b) its intention to complete the intangible asset and use or sell it;
(c) its ability to use or sell the intangible asset;
(d) how the intangible asset will generate probable future economic benefits. Among other things, the entity can demonstrate the existence of a market for the output of the intangible asset or the intangible asset itself or, if it is to be used internally, the usefulness of the intangible asset;
(e) the availability of adequate technical, financial and other resources to complete the development and to use or sell the intangible asset; and
(f) its ability to measure reliably the expenditure attributable to the intangible asset during its development.

Given the degree of difficulty in distinguishing research activities from development activities, it seems simpler to disregard any attempt to distinguish between the two activities and just allow capitalisation when the criteria in paragraph 57 are met. In other words, for an entity to decide whether to capitalise an outlay, the decision will not be based on an application of the definitions of research and development, but rather on whether the criteria in paragraph 57 are met. If the criteria are met, it will then be decided that the project is in the development stage. The definitions of research and development are then superfluous. The recognition criteria for an internally generated intangible asset are then those contained in paragraphs 18, 21 and 57 of IAS 38.

The criteria in paragraph 57 are designed to help determine whether, in relation to a project, it is probable that there will be future benefits flowing to the entity. If there are markets for the output, the project is feasible, and the resources are available to complete the project, then it becomes probable that there will be future cash inflows. The criteria in paragraph 57 are then an elaboration — the provision of more detailed requirements — on the criteria in paragraph 18. This approach in IAS 38 provides more certainty in obtaining comparable accounting across entities than simply relying on an accounting principle that states that, if there are probable expected future benefits, an entity should capitalise the outlay.

If the criteria in paragraph 57 are all met, IAS 38 requires the intangible asset to be measured at cost. This cost is not, however, the total cost relating to the project. The amount to be capitalised is the 'sum of expenditure incurred from the date when the intangible asset first meets the recognition criteria in paragraphs 21, 22 and 57' (paragraph 65). Paragraph 71 explicitly prohibits the reinstatement of amounts previously expensed. Recognition of an asset that is not yet available for use requires an entity to subject that asset to an annual impairment test as per IAS 36 *Impairment of Assets*. Paragraphs 66–67 of IAS 38 note that the cost comprises all directly attributable costs necessary to create, produce and prepare the asset to be capable of operating in a manner intended by management, and provide examples of such costs as well as items that are not components of the cost.

In his discussion of this issue, Lev argued that the immediate expensing of all outlays distorted current and future earnings. He stated (2001, p. 124):

> Given the heightened uncertainty, it makes sense to recognize intangible investments when the uncertainty about benefits is considerably resolved.

His solution to the problem was to have a recognition principle based on the achievement of technological feasibility. He argued (p. 125):

> A major advantage of the proposed asset recognition is its allowance of managers to convey important information about the progress and success of the development program. Indiscriminate capitalization of all expenditures on intangibles does not provide such information.

It can be seen that the criteria in IAS 38 are in line with Lev's views, although the feasibility expressed in the standard require both technological and economic feasibility.

Upton (2001, p. 66) viewed the identification of such a recognition principle as 'interesting', but was still concerned that entities could manipulate the criteria to suit their ends:

> Might some managers conjure assets from thin air in an attempt to pump up the balance sheet? Might others turn a blind eye to discovered assets in an attempt to pump up future operating results (by avoiding amortization)? Both possibilities are real, and either could damage the credibility of financial reporting.

Jenkins and Upton (2001, p. 8) noted, first, that the conceptual framework does not require certainty of future benefits before the recognition of an asset and, second, that there is evidence that companies are willing to pay for in-process research and development even though the ultimate result may be uncertain. Upton's suggestion (2001, p. 66) for resolving the problem was to couple the criterion of technological feasibility with a requirement for retrospective capitalisation or value-based measurement. In either case, management would be required to establish the asset, rather than having no asset because all outlays were expensed, and subsequent periods would bear their share of the amortisation of the asset as well as recognition of the benefits.

It may seem that the use of the terms 'research' and 'development', which may be associated with such assets as patents and software development, are not applicable to all internally generated intangibles, such as brand names. However, it needs to be remembered that all intangible assets must meet the identifiability criterion, one part of which is separability, which is the capability of being separated and sold or transferred. In relation to certain assets, paragraph 63 of IAS 38 provides a major exclusion in an entity's ability to capitalise internally generated intangibles:

> Internally generated brands, mastheads, publishing titles, customer lists and items similar in substance shall not be recognised as intangible assets.

The standard setters concluded that, even though the criteria in paragraph 57(a)–(f) are met, the listed items in paragraph 63 cannot be recognised. As paragraph 64 states, the standard setters do not believe that the costs associated with developing the listed assets can be distinguished from the cost of developing the business as a whole. For example, it may be argued that funds spent on developing a brand name also enhance the overall image of the entity, and therefore the outlays cannot be solely attributable to the brand name.

13.2.7 Explaining the non-recognition of internally generated assets

There are a number of problems associated with the treatment of internally generated assets versus that required for acquired intangibles. In particular, there are inconsistencies in the accounting for internally generated intangibles and intangibles acquired in a business combination. Note, in this regard:

(a) *The initial recognition of intangible assets.* IAS 38 requires intangible assets to be initially recognised at cost. However, for assets acquired in a business combination, an intangible asset can be recognised at fair value. Internally generated intangibles cannot be recognised, even if the fair value can be reliably measured. For example, outlays on research cannot be recognised as an asset. However, if an entity acquires another entity that has in-process research, an intangible asset can be recognised if the fair value can be measured reliably. Further, the research so recognised can be revalued if this class of asset is measured at fair value. The AASB (2008, paragraph 97) noted that not all users of financial statements agreed with different treatments for intangible assets:

> Some of the Analysts Representative Group meeting with the IASB in February 2007 expressed a view that, irrespective of whether assets are acquired or internally generated, they should be treated in the same way. They noted that it would seem odd to recognise more, or fewer, intangible assets in an acquisition than an entity would recognise prior to the acquisition.

(b) *The measurement of fair value.* One of the reasons given in paragraph BCZ38(c) of the Basis for Conclusions on IAS 38 for disallowing the recognition of intangible assets is the impossibility of determining the fair value of an intangible asset reliably if no active market exists for the asset, and active markets are unlikely to exist for internally generated intangible assets. However, for intangible assets recognised in a business combination, it is assumed that fair value can be measured (reliably, it is hoped) without the existence of active markets. IAS 38 allows the use of other measurement techniques or even what an entity would have paid based on the best information available. Hence, in a business combination, the fair values of intangibles can be measured reliably using measures determined outside an active market, but these same measures cannot be used to measure the fair values of internally generated assets for asset recognition purposes. As a protection, the requirements of IAS 36 *Impairment of Assets* can be applied to both acquired and internally generated intangible assets.

The AASB (2008, paragraph 101) stated that some argue that business combinations are unique types of transactions and that the principles developed for business combinations should not be applied in other circumstances. Some arguments given in paragraph 101 to support this proposition were:

- The extent of due diligence typically associated with a business combination provides a cost-effective context for recognising intangible assets only in those circumstances.
- The recognition of an intangible asset acquired in a business combination would not increase the assets of the acquirer. It merely substitutes one asset (an intangible asset) for what would otherwise be recognised as another asset (goodwill). The risks of undermining the quality of financial statements by overstating assets are arguably higher if an internally generated intangible asset is recognised.
- In a business combination, tangible assets such as property, plant and equipment are accounted for differently from internally generated intangible assets.

(c) *Brands, mastheads, publishing titles and customer lists.* Paragraph 63 of IAS 38 prohibits the recognition of internally generated brands and items similar in substance. However, such assets can be recognised when acquired in a business combination (as well as if acquired as a separate asset). As far as the measurement of the fair value of these assets goes, the argument presented in point (b) applies — if the fair value of a brand can be determined in a business combination then it can be determined if internally generated. Further, it has been noted previously that the reason given in paragraph 64 of IAS 38 for non-recognition of internally generated brands is that the cost of these items 'cannot be distinguished from the cost of developing the business as a whole'. If this argument is true for internally generated brands, then surely it is equally true for acquired brands. How is it possible in a business combination to distinguish acquired brands from acquired goodwill? How can the cost of acquiring a brand in a business combination be distinguished from acquiring a business as a whole?

Lev (2001, pp. 85–91) believed that the non-capitalisation of internally generated intangibles is a question of politics, stating:

> The main reason for the intangibles' information failure lies, in my opinion, in the complex web of motives of the major players in the information arena: managers, auditors, and well-connected financial analysts.

He argued:

- *Managers prefer to inflate future profits.* Where major investments in research and development are written off, this is a guarantee that future revenues and earnings derived from these acquisitions will be reported unencumbered by the major expense item, the amortisation of the intangible asset. The effects on ratios such as rates of return on assets and equity are better in the future if write-offs occur now rather than periodic amortisations later.
- *Investors generally consider write-offs as one-time items, of no consequence for valuation.* A number of large hits is considered better than periodic amortisation. Investors discount the effect of one-time write-offs and cheer the improved profitability of subsequent years.

- *Immediate expensing obviates the need to provide explanations in case of failure.* Writing off assets denotes failure, and managers prefer to avoid questions and lawsuits. Further failure always attracts more attention than success.

Upton (2001, pp. 80–3) raised further arguments to support the non-recognition of intangible assets:

- *Cost and benefit.* Accounting rules involve entities in incurring costs, such as those for running analytical models, measuring fair values, and paying auditors to review the measures.
- *Lack of relevance of capitalised numbers.* Is there a sufficient link between the capitalised costs and the expected future benefits? For knowledge-based assets, the measurement of the benefits may be impossible.

The AASB (2008, paragraph 102(c)) provides the following quotation from a PricewaterhouseCoopers (2007, p. 7) study that found that 74% of respondents described the term 'intangible assets' recognised in the balance sheet as 'not useful':

> None of the respondents uses balance sheet information on acquired intangible assets — for example, customer lists or brands. The majority of the interviewees believe that the current allocation of purchase price, required under both IFRS and US GAAP, does not provide useful information.

- *Volatility.* Recognising intangible assets in the statement of financial position produces a subtle source of volatility in, or at least reduced control over, reported income. If intangible assets are recognised and amortised, the amortisation continues without regard to current activity.

13.2.8 Recognition of an expense

Paragraphs 68–71 of IAS 38 cover the issue of when expenditure on an intangible asset should be expensed. However, if the previous rules in IAS 38 are followed, then the appropriate outlays are expensed when the criteria are not met. These paragraphs add nothing particularly new to the accounting for intangible assets. However, paragraph 69 provides a list of other examples of outlays that should always be recognised as an expense when incurred, these being expenditures on:

- start-up activities
- training activities
- advertising and promotional activities
- relocating or reorganising part or all of an entity.

Provision of this list ensures no asset will be recognised in relation to these activities, taking the judgement away from preparers of the financial statements.

Paragraph 71 has major import. This paragraph prohibits the recognition at a later date of past expenditure as assets. In other words, if amounts relating to research have been expensed, these amounts cannot then be capitalised, nor can appropriate adjustments to equity be made, when an intangible asset is created at the development stage. As noted earlier, Upton suggested a possible role for the retroactive capitalisation of expenses, because it forced entities to recognise and subsequently amortise their assets. Upton (2001, p. 64) also noted that retroactive capitalisation did not offer a solution to the non-capitalisation of assets such as brands, as these assets lack a series of discrete expenditures. It may be that acceptance of fair value as well as historical cost measures is necessary to solve some of these issues.

13.2.9 Internally generated goodwill

Paragraph 49 of IAS 38 states categorically that internally generated goodwill is not recognised as an asset. Hence, goodwill can be recognised only when it is acquired as part of a business combination and measured in accordance with IFRS 3 *Business Combinations*.

The reason given in paragraph 49 of IAS 38 for non-recognition is that goodwill is not identifiable; that is, it is not separable, nor does it arise from contractual or other legal rights. A second reason given for non-recognition, as stated in paragraph 49, is that the cost of internally generated goodwill cannot be reliably determined. The fair value of goodwill could be determined by comparing the fair value of the entity as a whole and subtracting the sum of the fair values of the identifiable assets and liabilities of the entity. However, under IAS 38, the principle for recognition is that identifiable intangible assets as well as goodwill must initially be measured at cost, not at fair value. As is discussed in more detail in the next section, this principle makes the recognition of internally generated intangibles harder than the recognition of acquired intangibles.

13.3 MEASUREMENT SUBSEQUENT TO INITIAL RECOGNITION

13.3.1 Measurement basis

Consistent with IAS 16, after the initial recognition of an intangible asset at cost, an entity must choose for each class of intangible asset whether to measure the assets using the *cost model* or the *revaluation model* — see paragraph 72. (These models are discussed in greater detail in chapter 11 of this book.)

Cost model

Under the cost model, the asset is recorded at the initial cost of acquisition and is then subject to amortisation (see section 13.3.3 of this chapter) and impairment testing (see chapter 15 of this book).

Revaluation model

Under the revaluation model, the asset is carried at fair value, and is subject to amortisation and impairment charges. As with property, plant and equipment, if this model is chosen, revaluations are made with sufficient regularity so that the carrying amount of the asset does not materially differ from the current fair value at the end of the reporting period.

One specification that applies to intangible assets but is not required for property, plant and equipment is how the fair value is to be measured. Under paragraph 75 of IAS 38, the fair value must be measured by reference to an active market. An active market is defined in IFRS 13 as a market in which transactions for the asset or liability take place with sufficient frequency and volume to provide pricing information on an ongoing basis. This means that an intangible asset acquired in a business combination and measured at fair value using some measurement technique cannot subsequently use that same measurement technique if it adopts the revaluation model. In the absence of an active market, the intangible asset would be kept at the fair value determined at the date of the business combination and accounted for by the cost basis. As paragraph 76 notes, the choice of revaluation model does not allow the recognition of intangible assets that cannot be recognised initially at cost. However, paragraph 77 allows an asset for which only part of the cost was recognised to be fully revalued to fair value.

Paragraph 78 of IAS 38 states that intangibles such as brands, newspaper mastheads, patents and trademarks cannot be measured at fair value, as there is no active market for these assets because they are unique. As with the recognition of these types of intangible assets, the standard setters have stated specifically that they can be measured only at cost.

Selection of the revaluation model requires all assets in the one class to be measured at fair value. Because of the insistence on using active markets for the measurement of fair value, the standard recognises that there will be cases where fair values cannot be determined for all assets within one class. Hence, under paragraph 81 of IAS 38, where there is no active market for an asset, the asset can be measured at cost even if the class is measured using the revaluation model. Further, if the ability to measure the asset at fair value disappears because the market for the asset no longer meets the criteria to be classified as active, the asset is carried at the latest revalued amount and effectively accounted for under the cost model. If the market again becomes active, the revaluation model can be resumed.

Accounting for intangible assets measured using the revaluation model is exactly the same as for property, plant and equipment (see chapter 11). Where there is a revaluation increase, the asset is increased and the increase is credited directly to a revaluation surplus. However, if the revaluation increase reverses a previous revaluation decrease relating to the same asset, the revaluation increase is recognised as income (IAS 38 paragraph 85). Any accumulated amortisation is eliminated at the time of revaluation.

Where there is a revaluation decrease, the decrease is recognised as an expense unless there has been a previous revaluation increase. In the latter case, the adjustment must first be made against any existing revaluation surplus before recognising an expense (IAS 38 paragraph 86). Any accumulated amortisation is eliminated at the time of the revaluation.

As with a revaluation surplus on property, plant and equipment, paragraph 87 of IAS 38 states that the revaluation surplus may be transferred to retained earnings when the surplus is realised on the retirement or disposal of the asset. Alternatively, the revaluation surplus may progressively be taken to retained earnings in proportion to the amortisation of the asset.

13.3.2 Subsequent expenditures

Paragraph 20 of IAS 38 discusses subsequent expenditures in general. It is argued in this paragraph that the unique nature of intangibles means that subsequent expenditures should be expensed rather than capitalised. Subsequent expenditures maintain expected benefits rather than increase them. Further, with many subsequent expenditures, it may be difficult to attribute them to specific intangible assets rather than to the entity as a whole. Paragraph 20 notes that with the paragraph 63 intangibles, whether acquired or internally generated, subsequent expenditures are always expensed.

Paragraph 42 provides specific guidance on subsequent expenditures relating to acquired in-process research and development projects. Effectively, the same criteria for initially recognising an asset and expensing are applied to account for subsequent expenditures. The results of this application are:

- to expense research outlays
- to expense development outlays not meeting the criteria in paragraph 57
- to add to the acquired in-process research or development project if the development expenditure satisfies the paragraph 57 criteria.

13.3.3 Amortisation of intangible assets

Useful life

A key determinant in the amortisation process for intangible assets is whether the useful life is finite or indefinite. If finite, then the asset has to be amortised over that life. If the asset has an indefinite life, then there is no annual amortisation charge. Paragraph 88 of IAS 38 states:

> An entity shall assess whether the useful life of an intangible asset is finite or indefinite and, if finite, the length of, or number of production or similar units constituting, that useful life. An intangible asset shall be regarded by the entity as having an indefinite useful life when, based on an analysis of all the relevant factors, there is no foreseeable limit to the period over which the asset is expected to generate net cash inflows for the entity.

The term 'indefinite' does not mean that the asset has an infinite life; that is, that it is going to last forever. As paragraph 91 notes, an indefinite life means that, with the proper maintenance, there is no foreseeable end to the life of the asset. Paragraph 90 provides a list of factors that should be considered in determining the useful life of the asset:

- the expected use of the asset by the entity and whether the asset could be managed efficiently by another management team
- typical product life cycles for the asset, and public information on estimates of useful lives of similar assets that are used in a similar way
- technical, technological, commercial or other types of obsolescence
- the stability of the industry, and changes in market demand
- expected actions by competitors
- the level of maintenance expenditure required and the entity's ability and intent to reach such a level
- the period of control over the asset and legal or similar limits on the use of the asset
- whether the useful life of the asset depends on the useful lives of other assets of the entity.

Paragraph 94 of IAS 38 notes that, as a general rule, assets whose lives depend on contractual or legal lives will be amortised over those lives or shorter periods in some cases. If renewal is possible, then the useful life applied can include the renewal period providing there is evidence to support renewal by the entity without significant cost.

Figure 13.7 contains two examples from those in the illustrative examples accompanying IAS 38 in relation to the assessment of useful lives.

Rather than considering the existence of an indefinite life for intangible assets, the standard setters could have set a maximum useful life such as 40 years. However, as noted in paragraph BC63 of the Basis for Conclusions on IAS 38, the IASB considers that writing standards in such a fashion would not accord with the principle that the accounting numbers should be representationally faithful. The principles in IAS 38 provide management with more discretion but allow for the provision of more relevant information. In order for an intangible asset (such as a trademark) to have an indefinite life, an entity is required to outlay funds on an annual basis to maintain the trademark. Consider in this regard the annual expenditure by soft-drink companies to maintain the value of their trademarks. The annual profit figure is then affected by these outlays. To require amortisation charges to be levied as well, when the asset is being maintained, would be to affect the statement of profit or loss and other comprehensive income twice.

Example: An acquired broadcasting licence that expires in 5 years

The broadcasting licence is renewable every 10 years if the entity provides at least an average level of service to its customers and complies with the relevant legislative requirements. The licence may be renewed indefinitely at little cost and has been renewed twice before the most recent acquisition. The acquiring entity intends to renew the licence indefinitely and evidence supports its ability to do so. Historically, there has been no compelling challenge to the licence renewal. The technology used in broadcasting is not expected to be replaced by another technology at any time in the foreseeable future. Therefore, the licence is expected to contribute to the entity's net cash inflows indefinitely.

The broadcasting licence would be treated as having an indefinite useful life because it is expected to contribute to the entity's net cash inflows indefinitely. Therefore, the licence would not be amortised until its useful life is determined to be finite. The licence would be tested for impairment under IAS 36 annually and whenever there is an indication that it may be impaired.

Example: An acquired trademark used to identify and distinguish a leading consumer product that has been a market-share leader for the past 8 years

The trademark has a remaining legal life of 5 years but is renewable every 10 years at little cost. The acquiring entity intends to renew the trademark continuously and evidence supports its ability to do so. An analysis of (1) product life cycles, (2) market, competitive and environmental trends, and (3) brand extension opportunities provides evidence that the trademarked product will generate net cash inflows for the acquiring entity for an indefinite period.

The trademark would be treated as having an indefinite useful life because it is expected to contribute to net cash inflows indefinitely. Therefore, the trademark would not be amortised until its useful life is determined to be finite. It would be tested for impairment under IAS 36 annually and whenever there is an indication that it may be impaired.

FIGURE 13.7 Examples of indefinite lives for intangible assets

Intangible assets with finite useful lives

Paragraph 97 of IAS 38 states the principles relating to the amortisation period and choice of amortisation method. In general, the principles of amortisation are the same as those for depreciating property, plant and equipment under IAS 16. In both cases, the process involves the allocation of the depreciable amount on a systematic basis over the useful life, with the method chosen reflecting the pattern in which the expected benefits are expected to be consumed by the entity. Paragraph 98 notes that an amortisation method will rarely result in an amortisation charge that is lower than if a straight-line method had been used. Further, in accordance with paragraph 104, the amortisation period and amortisation method should be reviewed at least at the end of each annual reporting period, which is the same for property, plant and equipment.

However, IAS 38 contains a number of rules that are specific to intangible assets, presumably because of the relative uncertainty associated with intangible assets:

- Where the pattern of benefits cannot be determined reliably, the straight-line method is to be used (paragraph 97). This is, presumably, to bring some consistency and comparability into the calculations.
- The residual value is assumed to be zero unless there is a commitment by a third party to purchase the asset at the end of its useful life, *or* there is an active market for the asset, and:
  - residual value can be determined by reference to that market and
  - it is probable that such a market will exist at the end of the asset's useful life (paragraph 100).

Any changes in residual value, amortisation method or useful life are changes in accounting estimates, and accounted for prospectively with an effect on the current and future amortisation charges.

Intangible assets with indefinite useful lives

As noted earlier, where an intangible asset has an indefinite useful life, there is no amortisation charge (IAS 38 paragraph 107). As with finite useful lives, the useful life of an intangible that is not being amortised must be reviewed each period (paragraph 109). Any change from indefinite to finite useful life for an asset is treated as a change in estimate and affects the amortisation charge in current and future periods. Intangible assets with indefinite useful lives are subject to annual impairment tests (see chapter 15).

LO4 13.4 RETIREMENTS AND DISPOSALS

Accounting for the retirements and disposals of intangible assets is identical to that for property, plant and equipment under IAS 16. In particular, under IAS 38:

- intangible assets are to be derecognised on disposal or when there are no expected future benefits from the asset (paragraph 112)
- gains or losses on disposal are calculated as the difference between the proceeds on disposal and the carrying amount at point of sale, with amortisation calculated up to the point of sale (paragraph 113)
- amortisation of an intangible with a finite useful life does not cease when the asset becomes temporarily idle or is retired from active use (paragraph 117).

LO5 13.5 DISCLOSURE

Paragraph 118 of IAS 38 requires disclosures for each class of intangibles, and for internally generated intangibles to be distinguished from other intangibles. Examples of separate classes are given in paragraph 119:

- brand names
- mastheads and publishing titles
- computer software
- licences and franchises
- copyrights, patents and other industrial property rights, service and operating rights
- recipes, formulas, models, designs and prototypes
- intangible assets under development.

Disclosures required by paragraph 118(a) and (b) would be contained in note 1 to the financial statements, as illustrated in figure 13.8. Disclosures required by paragraphs 118 and 122 of IAS 38 are illustrated in figure 13.9.

Note 1: Summary of significant accounting policies (extract)	IAS 38 paragraph 118
Intangible assets Intangible assets are initially recognised at cost. Intangible assets that have indefinite useful lives are tested for impairment on an annual basis. Intangible assets that have finite useful lives are amortised over those lives on a straight-line basis.	*(b)*

Patents and copyrights
These have all been acquired by the company. Costs relating to these assets are capitalised and amortised on a straight-line basis over the following periods:
    Patent — packaging   5 years
    Patent — tools   10 years
    Copyright   10 years
	(b)

Licence The licence relating to television broadcasting rights is determined to be indefinite.	*(a)*

Research and development
Research costs are expensed as incurred. Development costs are expensed except those that it is probable will generate future economic benefits, this being determined by an analysis of factors such as technical feasibility and the existence of markets. Such costs are currently being amortised on a straight-line basis over the following periods:
    Tool design project   5 years
    Water cooling project   10 years
	(a)
	
	(b)

FIGURE 13.8 Illustrative disclosures required by paragraph 118(a) and (b) of IAS 38

Other disclosures required, where relevant, by paragraph 118 of IAS 38 are:

- the line item in the statement of profit or loss and other comprehensive income in which any amortisation of intangible assets is included (paragraph 118(d))
- increases or decreases during the period resulting from revaluations under paragraphs 75, 85 and 86 and from impairment losses recognised or reversed directly in equity (paragraph 118(e)(iii))
- impairment losses reversed in profit or loss during the period (paragraph 118(e)(v)).

Note 11: Intangible assets					IAS 38 paragraph 122

Details about the Company's intangible assets are provided below. All intangibles are considered to have finite useful lives except for a patent held for a tool used in the manufacture of steel windmills. As this tool is able to substantially lessen the cost of manufacturing windmills, and all entities manufacturing windmills acquire the special tool from the company for use in their production process, the continued use of the tool in the manufacturing process is considered to be infinite. Hence, the patent is considered to have an indefinite life. The tool has a carrying amount of $155 000 [2013: $155 000]. *(a)*

Apart from the above, the main items constituting the intangible assets of the Company are:

	Carrying amount		Remaining amortisation period		
	2014 $'000	2013 $'000	2014 years	2013 years	*(b)*
Patents and copyrights					
Patent — packaging	31	45	7	8	
Patent — tools	52	66	5	6	
Copyright — manuals	15	24	3	4	
Deferred development expenditure					
Tool design	322	312	5	6	
Packaging design	95	110	3	4	

	Patents and copyrights		Deferred development expenditure		*paragraph 118*
	2014 $'000	2013 $'000	2014 $'000	2013 $'000	
Balance at beginning of year, at cost	576	545	592	361	*(c)*
Accumulated amortisation	276	234	166	110	
Carrying amount at beginning of year	300	311	426	251	
Additions:					*(e)(i)*
Acquisition of subsidiary	—	22	—	54	
Internal development	—	—	72	182	
Acquired separately	10	15	—	—	
Disposals	(15)	—	—	—	*(e)(ii)*
Amortisation	(38)	(32)	(52)	(44)	*(e)(vi)*
Impairment	—	(10)	—	(12)	*(e)(iv)*
Exchange differences	5	(6)	5	(5)	*(e)(vii)*
Carrying amount at end of year	262	300	451	426	
Intangible assets:					
At cost	557	576	669	592	*(c)*
Accumulated amortisation	295	276	218	166	
Carrying amount at end of year	262	300	451	426	

FIGURE 13.9 Illustrative disclosures required by paragraphs 118 and 122 of IAS 38

Paragraph 122 of IAS 38 also requires the following disclosures, if relevant:
- for intangible assets acquired by way of a *government grant* and initially recognised at fair value (paragraph 122(c)):
  - the fair value initially recognised for these assets
  - their carrying amount
  - whether they are measured after recognition under the cost model or the revaluation model.
- the existence and carrying amounts of intangible assets whose *title is restricted* and the carrying amounts of intangible assets *pledged as security* for liabilities (paragraph 122(d)).
- the amount of *contractual commitments* for the acquisition of intangible assets (paragraph 122(e)).

Paragraph 124 details further disclosures where intangible assets are carried at revalued amounts. An example of this disclosure is contained in figure 13.10.

	IAS 38 paragraph 124
Intangibles carried at revalued amounts	
The company has recognised its Internet domain name as an intangible asset. The asset was recognised initially at cost in 2012. The revaluation model was used to measure this asset from 1 January 2013. At the end of the reporting period, 31 December 2014, the carrying amount of this asset is $52 500. If the cost method had continued to be applied, the carrying amount would have been $33 600.	(a)(i) (a)(ii) (a)(iii)

The revaluation surplus in relation to this asset is as follows:

(b)

	2014	2013
Balance at beginning of year	$48 000	$45 000
Increase	4 500	3 000
Balance at end of year	$52 500	$48 000

There are no restrictions on the distribution of this balance to shareholders.

FIGURE 13.10 Disclosures required by paragraph 124 of IAS 38

Paragraph 126 requires disclosure of the aggregate amount of research and development expenditure recognised as an expense during the period. Disclosures in paragraph 128 that are encouraged but not required include a description of any fully amortised intangible asset that is still in use, and a brief description of significant intangible assets controlled by the entity but not recognised as assets because they did not meet the recognition criteria in IAS 38.

An example of disclosure of intangible assets is in figure 13.11, which shows the intangible assets disclosed by Fisher & Paykel in its 2011 annual report.

FIGURE 13.11 Example of disclosure of intangible assets

17. Intangible assets

	Development costs $'000	Goodwill $'000	Patents & trademarks $'000	Computer software $'000	Brands $'000	Licences $'000	Customer Relationships $'000	Total $'000
1 April 2009								
Cost	19 479	136 030	7 879	35 149	73 856	151 017	44 271	467 681
Accumulated amortisation & impairment	(4 659)	(69 689)	(3 522)	(23 384)	—	(56 039)	(12 543)	(169 836)
Net book amount	14 820	66 341	4 357	11 765	73 856	94 978	31 728	297 845
Year ended 31 March 2010								
Opening net book amount	14 820	66 341	4 357	11 765	73 856	94 978	31 728	297 845
Additions	5 240	—	470	2 306	—	—	—	8 016
Disposals	—	—	—	(228)	—	—	—	(288)
Amortisation charge	(3 273)	—	(1 685)	(3 277)	—	(5 963)	(3 968)	(18 166)
Impairment charge*	(4 918)	—	—	—	(36 682)	—	—	(41 600)
Exchange differences	(1 638)	(5 357)	(20)	95	(15 073)	8	(5 651)	(27 636)
Closing net book amount	10 231	60 984	3 122	10 661	22 101	89 023	22 109	218 231
31 March 2010								
Cost	23 820	117 422	6 579	34 844	22 101	147 430	35 853	388 049
Accumulated amortisation & impairment	(13 589)	(56 438)	(3 457)	(24 183)	—	(58 407)	(13 744)	(169 818)
Net book amount	10 231	60 984	3 122	10 661	22 101	89 023	22 109	218 231

* In the year ended 31 March 2010, the Elba brand allocated to the factory operations Italy cash generating unit and capitalised development costs held in New Zealand were impaired, further details are shown in sub-Notes (b)(iv) & (c) following.

FIGURE 13.11 *(continued)*

	Development costs $'000	Goodwill $'000	Patents & trademarks $'000	Computer software $'000	Brands $'000	Licences $'000	Customer Relationships $'000	Total $'000
Year ended 31 March 2011								
Opening net book amount	10 231	60 984	3 122	10 661	22 101	89 023	22 109	218 231
Additions	7 588	—	497	4 618	—	4	—	12 707
Disposals	—	—	(157)	—			—	(157)
Amortisation charge	(3 228)	—	(614)	(2 836)	—	(6 555)	(3 426)	(16 659)
Exchange differences	(476)	(765)	36	(228)	(1 241)	(89)	(411)	(3 174)
Closing net book amount	14 115	60 219	2 884	12 215	20 860	82 383	18 272	210 948
31 March 2011								
Cost	32 609	115 890	6 104	39 899	20 860	147 091	35 366	397 819
Accumulated amortisation & impairment	(18 494)	(55 671)	(3 220)	(27 684)	—	(64 708)	(17 094)	(186 871)
Net book amount	14 115	60 219	2 884	12 215	20 860	82 383	18 272	210 948

Source: Fisher & Paykel (2011, p. 110).

 13.6 PROPOSALS FOR CHANGES IN ACCOUNTING FOR INTANGIBLE ASSETS

In 2008, the AASB published a discussion paper (DP) entitled *Initial Accounting for Internally Generated Intangible Assets*. The research by the AASB on accounting for intangible assets was initially at the request of the IASB. In 2007, the IASB and the FASB declined to take an intangibles project onto their active agendas. The IASB Chairman suggested that the AASB continue this work under the sponsorship of the National Standard Setters (NSS), which is a global group of representatives of national accounting standard setters and related organisations whose main role is to assist the IASB in its work, primarily through research and commenting on project priorities.

This section will present some of the proposals for change in the accounting for intangible assets raised in the DP. The primary focus of the DP is on accounting for internally generated intangible assets. A concern raised in the DP about the current requirements of IAS 38 is that the requirements for recognition of intangibles when acquired via a business combination are less restrictive than those currently required for recognition of internally generated intangible assets.

13.6.1 Techniques for recognition of internally generated intangibles

IAS 38 currently requires outlays relating to internally generated intangibles to be classified as research and development, with paragraph 57 providing criteria that must be met before any development outlays can be capitalised. The DP analyses different ways in which internally generated assets could be recognised, and proposes three techniques that could be used: planned versus unplanned, a hypothetical business combination or the use of indicators.

Planned vs unplanned assets

Internally generated assets could be divided into planned and unplanned assets. Paragraph 41 of the DP defines these as follows:

(a) 'planned internally generated intangible assets', being those created out of a discrete plan, the primary purpose of which is to create the assets; and

(b) 'unplanned internally generated intangible assets', being other internally generated intangible assets that arise from the day-to-day operations of a business.

The identification of a planned asset would be associated with the incurrence of costs reliably attributable to the asset from inception of the plan. For example, there might be a discrete plan to develop a brand for which costs can be reliably attributed as the plan is implemented. Hence, in-process assets could be recognised by an entity as it implements its plan. The existence of the plan identifies the unit of account and enables the reliable measurement of the cost of the asset to occur. With unplanned activities, even if costs are associated with these activities, it is less likely that there would be sufficient evidence to reliably attribute the costs to any specific asset.

If this technique were acceptable to the standard setters, the ability to 'demonstrate technical and commercial feasibility of completion' could be replaced with 'the existence of evidence of a discrete plan that is being or has been implemented'.

A hypothetical business combination

With this technique, an entity is assumed to be an acquirer (as per IFRS 3) at reporting date; that is, it acts as if it is the acquirer of its own entity in a hypothetical business combination. The object is to account for all the assets of the entity that would be recognised by an acquirer in a business combination. In paragraph 53 of the DP, the authors refer to an article by Britton Manasco who reported that Dow Chemical undertook an exercise for internal management purposes that included the identification of patents, and was planning to undertake a similar exercise for 'know-how'. An exercise by an entity conducted as a hypothetical business combination could be demanding but could provide valuable information. In a friendly business combination, an acquirer is able to conduct a thorough due diligence to determine what is being acquired. Presumably an entity knows more about its existing internally generated intangible assets than the tangible assets it acquires in a business combination, particularly if it were a hostile business combination.

Application of this technique would mean that intangible assets could be recognised when their fair values could be reliably measured via a hypothetical business combination exercise being undertaken. A technique based on a hypothetical business combination may be difficult and costly the first time it is adopted; however, subsequent analyses could rely on information previously generated and documented.

Use of indicators

Intangible assets could be recognised if there is an indication that such assets exist at reporting date. Examples of possible indicators are:
- a documented discrete plan
- a documented strategy to manage an asset which has been identified by management as worthy of its attention
- an external source, such as an uninvited offer from a third party to acquire an internally generated intangible asset that has not been previously identified by management.

One advantage of this approach is that it is less costly than the hypothetical business combination approach. A disadvantage is that it relies on the judgements of management which may result in a lack of comparability across entities.

If the standard setters allow use of any of the above techniques, paragraphs 63 and 64 of the current IAS 38 would have to be deleted.

13.6.2 Measurement of fair value

A further question discussed in the DP relates to whether or not fair values for intangible assets can be reliably measured. The DP recognises that Level 1 or Level 2 inputs may not be available for intangible assets (see chapter 3 for a discussion of the levels of inputs in measuring fair value). Reliance may then need to be placed on Level 3 inputs. Those interviewed by the authors of the DP indicated that measurement techniques such as the capitalisation of discounted cash flows and excess of profits and capitalisation of earnings multiples approaches could provide measurements that are reliable, dependent on the quality and availability of entity-specific information. Further, one of the financial analysts interviewed by the authors of the DP commented that markets are emerging as increasingly more transactions in internally generated assets, such as brand names, occur.

The DP also provides anecdotal evidence that indicates that there have been business combinations where internally generated intangible assets were central to the negotiations and that the market effectively valued these items prior to the takeover (DP, paragraph 158):

Two examples of business combinations where internally generated intangible assets were a significant focus of the negotiations and had an observable impact on the acquisition price include the business combination of the German telephone company Mannesmann Mobilfunk by British Vodaphone in 2000 (customer contracts and intellectual property) and the business combination between America Online and Time Warner in 2001 (subscriber lists and customer contracts).

13.6.3 A disclosure-only reporting approach

The accounting for internally generated intangible assets is a controversial area. Many people have doubts about the usefulness of providing financial information about such assets. Some argue that increased disclosure rather than specific recognition and measurement is the answer. The DP (paragraph 244) quotes a 2007 PricewaterhouseCoopers study in which 74% of the interviewees described the balance sheet item 'Intangibles' as 'not useful'. PricewaterhouseCoopers concluded that investors are more interested in the nature of and expenditure on intangible assets than in the treatment of intangible assets in the financial statements. The DP noted that the Danish Agency for Trade and Industry in 2000 proposed that companies should prepare intellectual capital statements that report on a company's efforts to obtain, develop, share and anchor the knowledge resources required to ensure future results. (For more information on the construction of intellectual capital statements in Denmark, see Bukh, Laresen and Mouritsen (2001) who analysed the development of intellectual capital statements in 19 Danish firms.)

Many users believe that note disclosures do not give due prominence to items that are critical to an entity's operations. Note disclosures also do not lead to comparability between entities. Further, the levels of disclosure and audit risks associated with providing note disclosure is comparable to the levels of disclosure and audit risks associated with recognising the same information in the financial statements. As a consequence, there is no reason to prefer disclosure over recognition.

 ## 13.7 INNOVATIVE MEASURES OF INTANGIBLES

It has already been noted that there is often a large difference between the capitalised value of an entity and the identifiable assets and liabilities reported by that entity. Even with the adoption of IAS 38, the strictness of the rules relating to the recognition of internally generated intangibles means that there will not be an expansion in the recognition of intangible assets by entities. In some cases, there will be a reduction where, before the adoption of IAS 38, internally generated assets such as brand names and mastheads were recognised in the accounts. The purpose of this section is to note the existence of an ever-increasing volume of literature suggesting new ideas in reporting about the value of entities. Many of these innovative ideas are concerned with providing information about the content of the unreported assets of an entity. This section suggests that the accounting profession needs to ensure that it does not get left behind by other information professionals in the provision of information about the value of an entity and the variables that determine that value.

Figure 13.6 (p. 471) shows Lev's breakdown of intangibles into innovation-related, human resource and organisational intangibles. The analysis of the composition of intangibles has been undertaken by a number of writers and organisations. In 2008, Marr investigated ways of making 'the invisible visible' by identifying intellectual capital. Marr asserted that intellectual capital included all non-tangible resources attributed to an organisation and which contributed to the delivery of organisational strategy. It divided intangible resources into three components, namely human capital, structural capital and relational capital. These relationships between and variables of these components are shown in figure 13.12 overleaf.

When analysing how the relationships and variables may be reported, the major point to consider is this: the purpose of the reports is to provide more information about variables in the organisation that management believes add value to the organisation. For example, under IAS 38, an assembled workforce is not allowed to be capitalised as an asset, even within a business combination, and funds spent on training employees must be expensed. Hence, the financial statements do not recognise any attempts by management to increase the human capital of the organisation. The question for accountants to consider is whether there are ways in which human capital can be measured, and whether the measures are sufficiently reliable (and relevant) to be included in the financial statements. There have been many attempts to measure human capital. Mayo (2001) provides an excellent summary of proposed measures in chapter 3 of his book.

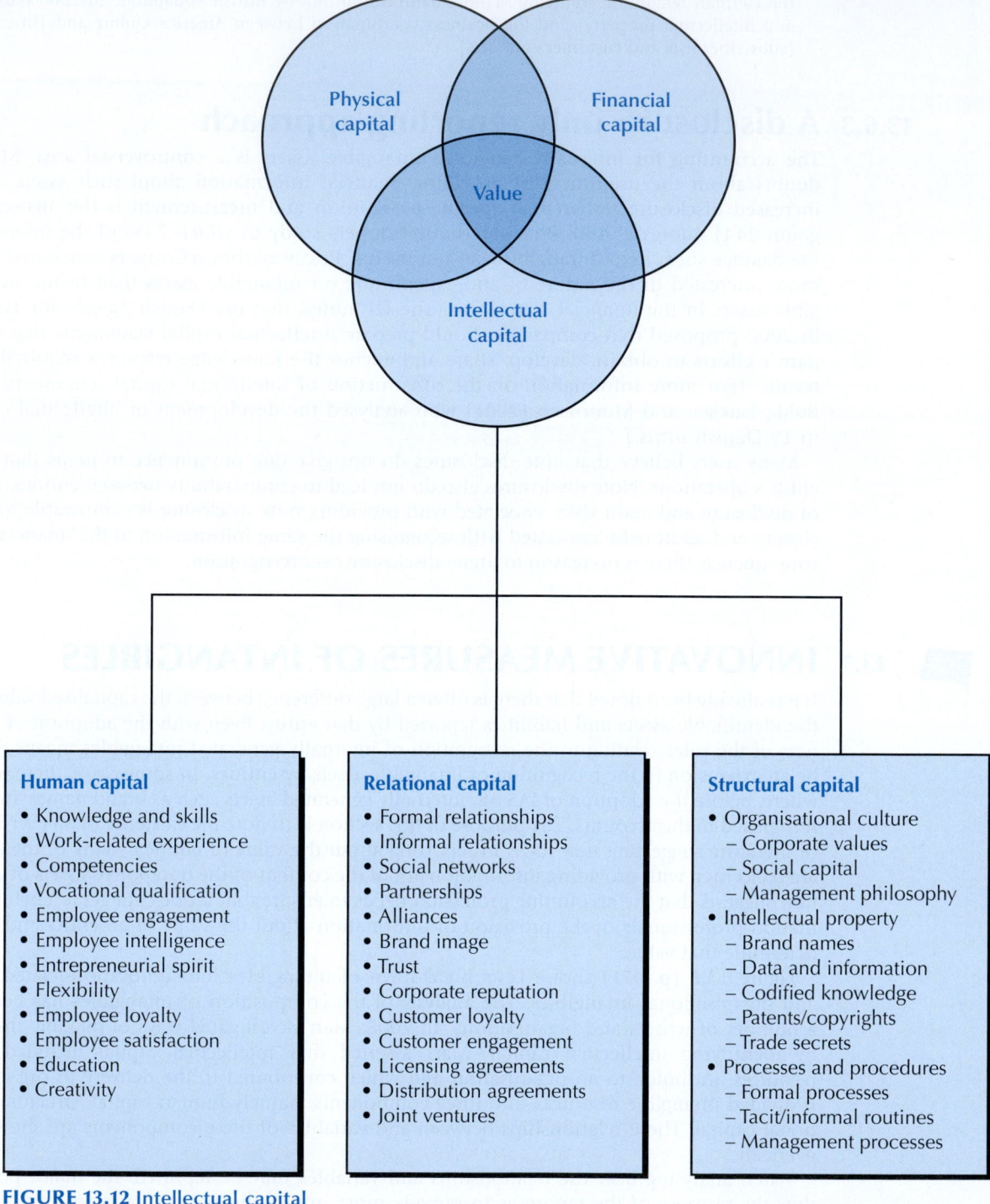

Physical
capital

Financial
capital

Value

Intellectual
capital

Human capital
- Knowledge and skills
- Work-related experience
- Competencies
- Vocational qualification
- Employee engagement
- Employee intelligence
- Entrepreneurial spirit
- Flexibility
- Employee loyalty
- Employee satisfaction
- Education
- Creativity

Relational capital
- Formal relationships
- Informal relationships
- Social networks
- Partnerships
- Alliances
- Brand image
- Trust
- Corporate reputation
- Customer loyalty
- Customer engagement
- Licensing agreements
- Distribution agreements
- Joint ventures

Structural capital
- Organisational culture
  - Corporate values
  - Social capital
  - Management philosophy
- Intellectual property
  - Brand names
  - Data and information
  - Codified knowledge
  - Patents/copyrights
  - Trade secrets
- Processes and procedures
  - Formal processes
  - Tacit/informal routines
  - Management processes

FIGURE 13.12 Intellectual capital
Source: Adapted from Marr (2008).

Most measures are, however, not directed at including the information in financial statements. A key element in analysing the measures is to determine the variables that various authors see as important and the different ways these are measured. For example, Mayo (2001, pp. 58–60) reviewed the Balanced Scorecard approach as developed by Kaplan and Norton in 1992. He noted that, in terms of employee capabilities, the three outcome measurements identified were employee satisfaction, employee retention and employee productivity, with these being driven by enablers such as staff competencies, technology infrastructure, and the climate for action.

Such measures are not suitable for inclusion in financial statements. It is expected that, in the foreseeable future, information on aspects of capital other than financial capital will not be included in the financial statements themselves. However, companies will endeavour to plug the information gap by providing additional reports. Some accounting firms have become involved with these reports; for example, the Systematic 2004 *Intellectual capital report* was audited by Deloitte in Denmark.

In the Systematic report, the following comment was made:

> Better train people and risk they leave than do nothing and they stay.

Perhaps this can be adapted for the accounting profession as follows:

> Better become involved in the measurement of intangibles than risk being left out of the information provision business.

SUMMARY

Intangible assets are considered to be sufficiently different from other assets such as property, plant and equipment for the standard setters to provide a separate standard. The reason for having such a standard is that the nature of intangibles is such that there are particular measurement problems associated with these assets that require specific accounting principles to be established. IAS 38 *Intangible Assets* is concerned with the definition, recognition, measurement and disclosure of intangibles.

The characteristic of 'identifiability' is critical to the identification of intangibles, and is the same concept that arises in IFRS 3 *Business Combinations* in relation to identifiable assets, liabilities and contingent liabilities recognised by the acquirer. In considering the accounting for intangibles, it is important to consider the differences in accounting depending on the source of the intangibles. Intangible assets acquired within a business combination are easier to recognise than those internally generated by the entity. This is because within a business combination the measurement issues are limited by the amount of the cost of the combination.

Amortisation of intangibles raises particular issues in terms of the useful lives of assets. The potential to assess some intangible assets as having indefinite useful lives and hence not subject to amortisation makes the decision on what is the useful life of an asset very significant. It is important to understand how to make such a decision. Aspects of that decision process are required to be specifically disclosed.

DEMONSTRATION PROBLEM 13.1 Development outlays

This demonstration problem illustrates the application of the criteria in paragraph 57 of IAS 38, determining when development outlays are capitalised or expensed.

Pretoria Ltd is a highly successful engineering company that manufactures filters for airconditioning systems. Due to its dissatisfaction with the quality of the filters currently available, on 1 January 2014 it commenced a project to design a more efficient filter. The following notes record the events relating to that project:

2014	
January	Paid $145 000 in salaries of company engineers and consultants who conducted basic tests on available filters with varying modifications.
February	Spent $165 000 on developing a new filter system, including the production of a basic model. It became obvious that the model in its current form was not successful because the material in the filter was not as effective as required.
March	Acquired the fibres division of Durban Ltd for $330 000. The fair values of the tangible assets of this division were: property, plant and equipment, $180 000; inventories, $60 000. This business was acquired because one of the products it produced was a fibrous compound sold under the brand name Springbok, that Pretoria Ltd considered would be excellent for including in the filtration process.

	By buying the fibres division, Pretoria Ltd acquired the patent for this fibrous compound. Pretoria Ltd valued the patent at $50 000 and the brand name at $40 000, using a number of valuation techniques. The patent had a further 10-year life but was renewable on application. Further costs of $54 000 were incurred on the new filter system during March.
April	Spent a further $135 000 on revising the filtration process to incorporate the fibrous compound. By the end of April, Pretoria Ltd was convinced that it now had a viable product because preliminary tests showed that the filtration process was significantly better than any other available on the market.
May	Developed a prototype of the filtration component and proceeded to test it within a variety of models of airconditioners. The company preferred to sell the filtration process to current manufacturers of airconditioners if the process worked with currently available models. If this proved not possible, the company would then consider developing its own brand of airconditioners using the new filtration system. By the end of May, the filtration system had proved successful on all but one of the currently available commercial models. Costs incurred were $65 000.
June	Various airconditioner manufacturers were invited to demonstrations of the filtration system. Costs incurred were $25 000, including $12 000 for food and beverages for the prospective clients. The feedback from a number of the companies was that they were prepared to enter negotiations for acquiring the filters from Pretoria Ltd. The company now believed it had a successful model and commenced planning the production of the filters. Ongoing costs of $45 000 to refine the filtration system, particularly in the light of comments by the manufacturers, were incurred in the latter part of June.

Required

Explain the accounting for the various outlays incurred by Pretoria Ltd.

Solution

The main problem in accounting for the costs is determining at what point of time costs can be capitalised. This is resolved by applying the criteria in paragraph 57 of IAS 38:

- *Technical feasibility.* At the end of April, the company believed that the filtration process was technically feasible.
- *Intention to complete and sell.* At the end of April, the company was not yet sure that the system was adaptable to currently available models of airconditioners. If it wasn't adaptable, the company would have to test whether development of its own brand of airconditioners would be a commercial proposition. Hence, it was not until the end of May that the company was convinced it could complete the project and had a product that it could sell.
- *Ability to use or sell.* By the end of May, the company had a product that it believed it had the ability to sell. Being a filter manufacturer, it knew the current costs of competing products and so could make an informed decision about the potential for the commercial sale of its own filter.
- *Existence of a market.* The market comprised the airconditioning manufacturers. By selling to the manufacturers, the company had the potential to generate probable future cash flows. This criterion was met by the end of May.
- *Availability of resources.* From the beginning of the project, the company was not short of resources, being a highly successful company in its own right.
- *Ability to measure costs reliably.* Costs are readily attributable to the project throughout its development.

On the basis of the above analysis, the criteria in paragraph 57 of IAS 38 were all met at the end of May. Therefore, costs incurred before this point are expensed, and those incurred after this point are capitalised. Hence, the following costs would be written off as incurred:

January	$ 145 000
February	165 000
March	54 000
April	135 000
May	65 000

In acquiring the fibres division from Durban Ltd, Pretoria Ltd would pass the following entry:

Property, plant and equipment	Dr	180 000	
Inventories	Dr	60 000	
Brand	Dr	40 000	
Patent	Dr	50 000	
Cash	Cr		330 000
(Acquisition of assets)			

The patent would initially be depreciated over a 10-year useful life. However, this would need to be reassessed upon application of the fibrous compound to the airconditioning filtration system. This alternative use may extend the expected useful life of the product, and hence of the patent. The brand name would be depreciated over the same useful life of the patent, because it is expected that the brand has no real value unless backed by the patent.

The company would then capitalise development costs of $45 000 in June.

The marketing costs incurred in June of $25 000 would be expensed because they are not part of the development process.

Discussion questions

1. What are the key characteristics of an intangible asset?
2. Explain what is meant by 'identifiability'.
3. How do the principles for amortisation of intangible assets differ from those for depreciation of property, plant and equipment?
4. Explain what is meant by an 'active market'.
5. How is the useful life of an intangible asset determined?
6. What intangibles can never be recognised if internally generated? Why?
7. Explain the difference between 'research' and 'development'.
8. Explain when development outlays can be capitalised.
9. Explain how intangible assets are initially measured, and whether the measurement differs depending on whether the assets are acquired in a business combination or internally generated by an entity.
10. Give two ways in which it is easier to recognise intangibles that are acquired in a business combination than those that are internally generated.
11. What are the recognition criteria for intangible assets?
12. Explain why managers may prefer to expense outlays on intangibles rather than capitalise them.
13. Explain why capitalisation of outlays may not provide relevant information about the intangible assets held by an entity.
14. Explain the application of the revaluation model for intangible assets.
15. Explain the use of fair values in the accounting for intangible assets.

Exercises

STAR RATING ★ BASIC ★★ MODERATE ★★★ DIFFICULT

Exercise 13.1 | **USEFUL TRADEMARK LIFE**

★ X Ltd holds a trademark that is well known within consumer circles and has enabled the company to be a market leader in its area. The trademark has been held by the company for 9 years. The legal life of the trademark is 5 years, but is renewable by the company at little cost to it.

Required

Discuss how the company should determine the useful life of the trademark, noting in particular what form of evidence it should collect to justify its selection of useful life.

Exercise 13.2 | **ACCOUNTING FOR USEFUL LIFE**

★ A company that sells DVDs by sending emails to prospective customers has acquired a customer list from another company that also markets its products in a similar fashion. The company estimates that it will generate sales from the list for a minimum of 2 years and a maximum of 3 years. The company intends to add names to the list from answers to a questionnaire attached to each of the emails. This should extend the useful life of the list for another year.

Required

Discuss how the company should account for the cost of the customer list. If the cost is capitalised, discuss the determination of the useful life over which the asset is amortised.

Exercise 13.3   **IMPORTANCE OF INTANGIBLE ASSETS**

★ In its 2005 annual report, Compusoft Corporation reported £352 million of intangibles and total assets of £80 652 million. Note 8 to the report disclosed details about the entity's intangible assets, including the following breakdown:

June 30 in £ millions	Gross carrying amount	Accumulated amortisation
Contract-based	566	(382)
Technology-based	240	(131)
Marketing-based	42	(11)
Customer-related	31	(3)
	879	(527)

Required

Discuss the importance of intangible assets to computing and software companies such as Compusoft, and analyse whether there are aspects of IAS 38 that prevent such companies from disclosing more information about their intangible assets.

Exercise 13.4   **RECOGNITION OF BRANDS**

★ Simon Evans (2003) reported that a small Victorian wine producer was planning to raise up to $7 million and list on the Australian Securities Exchange. The report stated that Warrenmang Ltd, based in the Pyrenees region in north-west Victoria, had been set up to acquire the Warrenmang, Bazzini and Masoni business and brands. The company hoped to list on the Australian Securities Exchange in February 2004.

Required

Discuss potential problems associated with the recognition of brands by the acquiring entity.

Exercise 13.5   **BRANDS AND FORMULAS**

★ Wayne Upton (2001, p. 71) in his discussion of the lives of intangible assets noted that the formula for Coca-Cola has grown more valuable over time, not less, and that Sir David Tweedie, former chairman of the IASB, joked that the brand name of his favourite Scotch whisky is older than the United States of America — and, in Sir David's view, the formula for Scotch whisky has contributed more to the sum of human happiness.

Required

Outline the accounting for brands under IAS 38, and discuss the difficulties for standard setters in allowing the recognition of all brands and formulas on the statement of financial position.

Exercise 13.6   **FINANCIAL STATEMENTS AND INTANGIBLES**

★ Upton (2001, p. 50) notes:

> There is a popular view of financial statements that underlies and motivates many discussions of intangible assets. That popular view often sounds something like this:
>
> If accountants got all the assets and liabilities into financial statements, and they measured all those assets and liabilities at the right amounts, stockholders' equity would equal market capitalization. Right?

Required

Comment on the truth of this 'popular view'.

Exercise 13.7

★★

VALUATION OF INTERNALLY GENERATED INTANGIBLES

In its 2008 discussion paper, the AASB reached the following conclusion in paragraph 113:

> We conclude that, under a valuation-based model, internally generated intangible assets that satisfy the definition of an intangible asset in IAS 38/IFRS 3 should be subject to the same recognition requirements for intangible assets acquired in a business combination, using a technique based on a hypothetical business combination. Accordingly, all internally generated intangible assets that would be recognised if acquired in a business combination under IFRS 3 should be recognised. While less onerous identification techniques or recognition criteria could be adopted, they have significant conceptual shortcomings.

Required

Critically analyse these conclusions.

Exercise 13.8

★★

RESEARCH AND DEVELOPMENT

Because of the low level of rainfall in Simonstown, householders find it difficult to keep their gardens and lawns sufficiently watered. As a result, many householders have installed bores that allow them to access underground water suitable for using on the garden. This is a cheaper option than incurring excess water bills by using the government-provided water system. One of the problems with much of the bore water is that its heavy iron content leaves a brown stain on paths and garden edges. This can make homes look unsightly and lower their value.

Noting this problem, Strand Laboratories believed that it should research the problem with the goal of developing a filter system that could be attached to a bore and remove the effects of the iron content in the water. This process, if developed, could be patented and filters sold through local reticulation shops.

In 2011, Strand commenced its work on the problem, resulting in August 2015 in a patent for the NoMoreIron filter process. Costs incurred in this process were as shown below.

2011–12	Research conducted to develop filter	$ 125 000
2012–13	Research conducted to develop filter	132 000
2013–14	Design and construction of prototype	152 000
2014–15	Testing of models	51 000
2015–16	Fees for preparing patent application	12 000
2016–17	Research to modify design	34 000
2017–18	Legal fees to protect patent against cheap copies	15 000

Required

Discuss how the company should account for each of these outlays.

Exercise 13.9

★★

RECOGNITION OF INTANGIBLES

Soweto Ltd is unsure of how to obtain computer software. Four possibilities are:
1. Purchase computer software externally, including packages for payroll and general ledger.
2. Contract to independent programmers to develop specific software for the company's own use.
3. Buy computer software to incorporate into a product that the company will develop.
4. Employ its own programmers to write software that the company will use.

Required

Discuss whether the accounting will differ depending on which method is chosen.

Exercise 13.10

★★

AMORTISATION OF INTANGIBLES

Nick Tabakoff (1999) stated:

> News Corporation is far from convinced of the merits of the standard [IAS 38]. At the Australian division, News Limited, finance director and deputy chief executive Peter McCourt says: 'The reason you get standards like that is that they are prepared by people who are not really responsible to anybody. The business community gains nothing from writing off the value of intangibles over a limited time frame. If the standard comes in, the market will simply add back the amortisation.'

McCourt believes the standard penalises companies that are acquisitive when it comes to intangible assets. He can see no reason for the existence of the standard. 'Who is it aimed at, who is being better informed by taking that charge? I don't think it gets you anywhere.'

He is not alone in getting worked up about preventing accountants from minimising the values placed on intangibles. Even the legendary Berkshire Hathaway chief Warren Buffett has strong views on the issue. He has been quoted as saying: 'Amortisation of intangibles is rubbish. It distorts true cashflows and thus economic reality. For example, the economic earnings of Disney are much greater than reported earnings. Accounting is pushing people to do things that are nuts.'

These comments were made before the latest revisions to IAS 38.

Required

Comment on whether the current IAS 38 has resolved the issues raised in this article.

Exercise 13.11 **HUMAN RESOURCE ACCOUNTING**

★★ In the following article, Whiting and Chapman (2003) consider whether the value of rugby players, being a team's most valuable asset, should be placed on the balance sheet (statement of financial position).

Sporting glory — the great intangible

While rugby stars are heroes to many, when checking the books they become a complex intangible. Rosalind Whiting and Kyla Chapman investigate the merits of Human Resource Accounting in professional sport.

Australia, New Zealand and rugby union — a combination guaranteed to stir patriotic feelings across the Tasman! But what if we add accounting to this equation? Rugby players are the teams' most valuable assets, so should we be placing their value on the balance sheet? And if so, does it make any difference to the decisions that users of financial statements make?

Human resource accounting in professional sport

Professional sport has been prevalent in the United Kingdom and the United States for nearly 200 years. However, professional sport arrived later to Australia and New Zealand. In particular, the Kiwis only entered this arena in 1995 when the New Zealand Rugby Football Union (NZRFU) signed the Tri Nations sponsorship deal and removed all barriers preventing rugby union players being paid for their services. Player contract expenses in New Zealand now amount to over NZ$20 million annually, according to the NZRFU.

In the United Kingdom and the United States, the professional teams' financial accounts quite often incorporate human resource accounting (HRA). HRA is basically an addition to traditional accounting, in which a value for the employees is placed on the balance sheet and is amortised over a period of time, instead of expensing costs such as professional development.

There is debate about the merits of this process and the arguments are in line with those we have been hearing about intangibles in general. More recently, there has been worldwide movement towards recognising acquired identifiable intangible assets at fair value in the financial statements. So why not include an organisation's human resources? While (thankfully) most people agree that employees are valuable, there are accounting difficulties with the concept of ownership or control of the employees (asset definition) and the reliability of measurement.

Despite these concerns, one area where HRA does have some international acceptability is in accounting for professional sport, mainly because of the measurable player transfer costs. But there is still some variability in the reporting of human resource value, ranging from the capitalisation of signing and transfer fees through to player development costs or valuations.

To the authors' knowledge, HRA is not currently practised with Australia and New Zealand's professional sports teams. The absence of transfer fees between clubs when trading players may explain this.

Decision making

Accountants are required to provide information that assists users in assessing an organisation's financial and service performance and in making decisions about providing resources to, or doing business with the firm.

The big question is whether HRA information is more useful to the decision maker than the alternative expensing treatment. Supporters of HRA argue that capitalised information is useful for strategic planning and management of employees, and provides a more accurate measure of the firm's status and total performance.

Those against HRA say it is too subjective to be useful and that it just imposes another cost on the organisation. Some detractors argue that it makes unprofitable organisations appear profitable simply because smart people work there. But those who believe in the efficiency of the market would argue that investors are not naive, and decisions would be unaffected by the way in which human resource information is presented.

Past research has shown that sophisticated users of financial information do make significantly different decisions with the different presentations. With this in mind we decided to test this outcome in New Zealand.

The New Zealand study

In June 2001, 64 members of the New Zealand professional body, the Institute of Chartered Accountants of New Zealand (ICANZ) responded to our postal questionnaire. This constituted a 20 per cent response rate from the 300 randomly selected ICANZ members.

All respondents were provided with the CEO's report, and the financial statements and notes of the fictitious Gladiator Super Twelve rugby franchise.

Half of the respondents were sent financial statements in which player training and development costs were expensed in the year that they were incurred.

The other half received an identical set of statements; however, the team was capitalised on the balance sheet.

It was stated in the notes to the accounts that the team was periodically revalued every five years, and then annual player training and development costs were capitalised and added to the valuation and subsequently amortised over a period of three years (average contract length). Respondents were asked a series of decision making questions and then the answers from the two groups (expensing and capitalising) were statistically compared.

Generally, the presentation of the human resource information made no difference to the assessments and decisions made by our respondents. They assessed financial position and performance, risk and future financial performance to be at the same level regardless of the presentation. And even when presented with an investment decision where they had to divide $100 000 between the franchise and a fixed term New Zealand bank investment, there was no difference in the levels of investment between the two groups.

In most cases respondents in the two groups gave similar reasons for their assessments.

However, when assessing current performance, the group with the expensed player development costs mainly used statement of financial performance information, whereas the group with the capitalised statements also used the statement of financial position. This suggests that they understood the nature of the information with which they were provided.

Differences in opinion

Women and men showed no overall differences in their responses. However, it was with investment experience that we uncovered some contrasting results. Most of our respondents fell into two groups, those with limited investment experience (less than one year) and those having extensive experience (five or more years).

We felt that the experienced group would more closely represent the sophisticated users as studied in previous research.

We found some differences in assessments between the experienced and the limited experience group. The groups rated financial performance and risk of the franchise differently and invested significantly different amounts in the franchise. Interestingly, members of the limited experience group rated growth as a more important reason for their investment decisions — whereas the experienced group said net profit levels were more important.

Of greater interest was whether experience level affected respondents' ability to cope with the different presentations of human resource information. In most cases it did not. However, limited experience investors did make significantly different assessments of the risk and future performance of the franchise according to the presentation of the human resource information. In these situations the limited experience expensing group acted like the experienced group of investors, whereas the limited experience capitalising group did not.

The capitalised information may have confused the less experienced investors.

In general, the users (sophisticated and unsophisticated) were unaffected in their assessments and decisions by the presentation of the human resource information. This conflicts with prior studies, which found that HRA did make a difference to decision making. This variation could be due to accountants now having a better understanding of the issues surrounding

(continued)

intangibles recognition and the effect of accounting method choice on financial statement numbers and ratios. Also accountants are spending less time in accounting number preparation and more time in interpretation and business advice.

However, our exercise only explored one type of decision-making process, that of an investment. Prior studies may have been of a wider nature, which could explain the differing result.

Overall, our study shows that generally accountants will make the same investment decisions regardless of whether human resource information is expensed or capitalised. If HRA is to follow the international trends emerging in intangibles reporting, then capitalised human resource information may become more prevalent. This study suggests that this won't negatively affect those accountants who provide interpretative and investment advice.

Required

Critically analyse the arguments made in the article and assess whether there should be any changes made to IAS 38 as a result.

Exercise 13.12	RESEARCH AND DEVELOPMENT

★★ Stellenbosch Laboratories Ltd manufactures and distributes a wide range of general pharmaceutical products. Selected audited data for the reporting period ended 31 December 2014 are as follows:

Gross profit	$ 17 600 000
Profit before income tax	1 700 000
Income tax expense	(500 000)
Profit for the period	1 200 000
Total assets:	
Current	7 300 000
Non-current	11 500 000

The company uses a standard mark-up on cost.

From your audit files, you ascertain that total research and development expenditure for the year amounted to $4 700 000. This amount is substantially higher than in previous years and has eroded the profitability of the company. Mr Bosch, the company's finance director, has asked for your firm's advice on whether it is acceptable accounting practice for the company to carry forward any of this expenditure to a future accounting period.

Your audit files disclose that the main reason for the significant increase in research and development costs was the introduction of a planned 5-year laboratory program to attempt to find an antidote for the common cold. Salaries and identifiable equipment costs associated with this program amounted to $2 350 000 for the current year.

The following additional items were included in research and development costs for the year:

(a) Costs to test a new tamper-proof dispenser pack for the company's major selling line (20% of sales) of antibiotic capsules — $760 000. The new packs are to be introduced in the 2013 financial year.

(b) Experimental costs to convert a line of headache powders to liquid form — $590 000. The company hopes to phase out the powder form if the tests to convert to the stronger and better handling liquid form prove successful.

(c) Quality control required by stringent company policy and by law on all items of production for the year — $750 000.

(d) Costs of a time and motion study aimed at improving production efficiency by redesigning plant layout of existing equipment — $50 000.

(e) Construction and testing of a new prototype machine for producing hypodermic needles — $200 000. Testing has been successful to date and is nearing completion. Hypodermic needles accounted for 1% of the company's sales in the current year, but it is expected that the company's market share will increase following introduction of this new machine.

Required

Respond to Mr Bosch's question for each of these items.

Exercise 13.13

★★

RECOGNITION OF INTANGIBLES

Ladysmith Ltd has recently diversified by taking over the operations of Kimberley Ltd at a cost of $10 million. Kimberley Ltd manufactures and sells a cleaning cloth called the 'Supaswipe', which was developed by Kimberley Ltd's highly trained and innovative research staff. The unique nature of the coating used on the 'Supaswipe' has resulted in Kimberley Ltd acquiring a significant share of the South African market. A recent expansion into the Equatorial African market has proved successful. As a result of the takeover, Ladysmith Ltd acquired the following assets:

	Fair value (at date of acquisition)
Land and buildings	$ 3 200 000
Production machinery	2 000 000
Inventory	1 800 000
Accounts receivable	700 000
	$ 7 700 000

In addition to the above, Kimberley Ltd owned, but had not recognised, the following:
- trademark — 'Supaswipe'
- patent — formula for the special coating.

The research staff of Kimberley Ltd have agreed to join the staff of Ladysmith Ltd and will continue to work on a number of projects aimed at producing specialised versions of the 'Supaswipe'.

The directors have requested your assistance in accounting for the acquisition of Kimberley Ltd. In particular, they are uncertain as to the treatment of the $2.3 million discrepancy between the assets recorded by Kimberley Ltd and the price paid for the company.

Required

Write to the directors outlining the alternative courses of action available in relation to the $2.3 million discrepancy. Your reply should cover the issues of asset recognition, measurement, classification and subsequent accounting treatment.

Exercise 13.14

★★

RESEARCH AND DEVELOPMENT

Capetown Ltd has been involved in a project to develop an engine that runs on extracts from sugar cane. It started the project in February 2014. Between the starting date and 30 June 2014, the end of the reporting period for the company, Capetown Ltd spent $254 000 on the project. At 30 June 2014, there was no indication that the project would be commercially feasible, although the company had made significant progress and was sufficiently sure of future success that it was prepared to outlay more funds on the project.

After spending a further $120 000 during July and August, the company had built a prototype that appeared to be successful. The prototype was demonstrated to a number of engineering companies during September, and several of these companies expressed interest in the further development of the engine. Convinced that it now had a product that it would be able to sell, Capetown Ltd spent a further $65 000 during October adjusting for the problems that the engineering firms had pointed out. On 1 November, Capetown Ltd applied for a patent on the engine, incurring legal and administrative costs of $35 000. The patent had an expected useful life of 5 years, but was renewable for a further 5 years upon application.

Between November and December 2014, Capetown Ltd spent an additional amount of $82 000 on engineering and consulting costs to develop the project such that the engine was at manufacturing stage. This resulted in changes in the overall design of the engine, and costs of $5000 were incurred to add minor changes to the patent authority.

On 1 January 2015, Capetown Ltd invited tenders for the manufacture of the engine for commercial sale.

Required

Discuss how Capetown Ltd should account for these costs. Provide journal entries with an explanation of why these are the appropriate entries.

Exercise 13.15	ACCOUNTING FOR BRANDS

★★★ Jon West Ltd is a leading company in the sale of frozen and canned fish produce. These products are sold under two brand names. Fish caught in southern Australian waters are sold under the brand 'Arctic Fresh', which is the brand the company developed when it commenced operations and which is still used today. Fish caught in the northern oceans are sold under the brand name 'Tropical Taste', the brand developed by Fishy Tales Ltd. Jon West Ltd acquired all the assets and liabilities of Fishy Tales Ltd a number of years ago when it took over that company's operations.

Jon West Ltd has always marketed itself as operating in an environmentally responsible manner, and is an advocate of sustainable fishing. The public regards it as a dolphin-friendly company as a result of its previous campaigns to ensure dolphins are not affected by tuna fishing. The marketing manager of Jon West Ltd has noted the efforts of the ship, the *Steve Irwin*, to disrupt and hopefully stop the efforts of Japanese whalers in the southern oceans and the publicity that this has received. He has recommended to the board of directors that Jon West Ltd strengthen its environmentally responsible image by guaranteeing to repair any damage caused to the *Steve Irwin* as a result of attempts to disrupt the Japanese whalers. He believes that this action will increase Jon West Ltd's environmental reputation, adding to the company's goodwill. He has told the board that such a guarantee will have no effect on Jon West Ltd's reported profitability. He has explained that, if any damage to the *Steve Irwin* occurs, Jon West Ltd can capitalise the resulting repair costs to the carrying amounts of its brands, as such costs will have been incurred basically for marketing purposes. Accordingly, as the company's net asset position will increase, and there will be no effect on the statement of profit or loss and other comprehensive income, this will be a win–win situation for everyone.

Required

The chairman of the board knows that the marketing manager is very effective at selling ideas but knows very little about accounting. The chairman has, therefore, asked you to provide him with a report advising the board on how the proposal should be accounted for under International Financial Reporting Standards and how such a proposal would affect Jon West Ltd's financial statements.

Exercise 13.16	PATENTS

★★★ Song Ltd has recently obtained some patents considered useful in its manufacture of men's shoes. The patents consist of:
- Patent XC456, acquired from a leather manufacturing firm for $425 000.
- Patent CU254, obtained as part of a bundle of assets acquired from the conglomerate U-Beaut Fashions.

Song Ltd is also in the process of preparing an application for a patent for a new process of softening leather. It has spent a number of years refining this process.

The accountant for Song Ltd is unsure how to account for patents under IFRSs. He has asked you to prepare a *detailed* report for him on the principles of how to account for patents, using the examples above to illustrate the appropriate accounting procedures.

Required

Prepare a report for Song Ltd's accountant.

References

Australian Accounting Standards Board, 2008, *Initial Accounting for Internally Generated Intangible Assets*, discussion paper, Australian Accounting Standard Board, www.aasb.com.au.

Bukh, PN, Larsen, HT, & Mouritsen, J 2001, 'Constructing intellectual capital statements', *Scandinavian Journal of Management*, vol. 17, pp. 87–108.

Christian Dior 2011, *2010 Annual report*, France, www.dior-finance.com.

Corrado, CA & Hulten, CR 2010, 'How do you measure a "technological revolution"?', *American Economic Review*, vol. 100, no. 2, May, pp. 99–104.

Egginton, DA 1990, 'Towards some principles for intangible asset accounting', *Accounting and Business Research*, Summer, pp. 193–205.

Evans, S 2003, 'Winery presses ahead with float', *The Australian Financial Review*, 9 December.

Fisher & Paykel 2011, *Annual report for the year ended 31 March 2011*, Fisher & Paykel Appliances Holdings Ltd, New Zealand, www.fisherpaykel.co.nz.

Gottliebsen, R 1987, 'Recognising the value of intangible assets', *Business Review Weekly*, 13 February, p. 6.

James, D 2001, 'Intangible virtues', *Business Review Weekly*, 4 May.

Jenkins, E & Upton, W 2001, 'Internally generated intangible assets: framing the discussion', *Australian Accounting Review*, vol. 11, no. 2, pp. 4–11.

Karsan, S 2009, *S&P Price to Book*, blog, 15 October, www.barelkarsan.com.

Kieso, DE & Weygandt, JJ 1992, *Intermediate accounting*, 7th edn, John Wiley, New York.

King, AM & Henry, JM 1999, 'Valuing intangible assets through appraisals', *Strategic Finance*, vol. 81, no. 5, pp. 32–7. Quoted material sourced from this publication.

Lev, B 2001, *Intangibles: management, measurement, and reporting*, Brookings Institution Press, Washington, DC.

—— 2002, 'Where have all of Enron's intangibles gone?' *Journal of Accounting and Public Policy*, vol. 21, pp. 131–135.

—— 2003, 'Remarks on the measurement, valuation and reporting of intangible assets', *The Economic Review*, vol. 9, no. 3, pp. 66–70.

Lev, B, Radhakrishnan, S & Zhang, W 2009, 'Organization capital', *Abacus*, vol. 45, no.3, pp. 275–98.

Manasco, B 1997, 'Dow Chemical Capitalizes on Intellectual Assets', *Knowledge Inc*, March.

Marr, B 2008, 'Management accounting guideline — impacting future value: How to manage your intellectual capital', *Management, Strategy and Measurement*, The Society of Management Accountants of Canada (CMA Canada), the American Institute of Certified Public Accountants, Inc. (AICPA) and The Chartered Institute of Management Accountants (CIMA), available at http://media.journalofaccountancy.com/JOA/Issues/2008/09/MAG%20IntCapital-Eng.pdf.

Mayo, A 2001, *The human value of the enterprise*, Nicholas Brealey Publishing, London.

Napier, C & Power, M 1992, 'Professional research, lobbying and intangibles: a review essay', *Accounting and Business Research*, Winter, pp. 85–95.

Sadan, Y 2010, 'S&P 500–summary of valuation metrics', *The Hard Trade*, 17 October, http://thehardtrade.com.

Samuelson, RA 1996, 'The concept of an asset in accounting theory', *Accounting Horizons*, vol. 10, no. 3, pp. 147–57. Quoted material sourced from this publication.

Schuetze, WP 1993, 'What is an asset?', *Accounting Horizons*, vol. 7, no. 3, pp. 66–70. Quoted material sourced from this publication.

—— 2001, 'What are assets and liabilities? Where is true north? (Accounting that my sister would understand)', *Abacus*, vol. 37, no. 1, pp. 1–25. Quoted material sourced from this publication.

Stevenson, K 1989, 'The precedent in Australian thinking', paper presented at the accounting forum on off-balance-sheet structures, conducted by the Australian Accounting Research Foundation and sponsored by Coopers & Lybrand, Sydney.

Systematic 2004, *Intellectual capital report*, www.systematic.com.

Tabakoff, N 1999, 'Assets: standard deviation', *Business Review Weekly*, 21 May.

Upton, WS 2001, *Business and financial reporting, challenges from the new economy*, Financial Accounting Series No. 219-A, Financial Accounting Standards Board, Norwalk, Connecticut, USA.

Whiting, R & Chapman, K 2003, 'Sporting glory — the great intangible', *Australian CPA*, February.

14

Business combinations

LEARNING OBJECTIVES

After studying this chapter, you should be able to:

1 understand the nature of a business combination and its various forms
2 explain the basic steps in the acquisition method of accounting for a business combination
3 account for a business combination in the records of the acquirer
4 recognise and measure the assets acquired and liabilities assumed in the business combination
5 understand the nature of and the accounting for goodwill and gain from bargain purchase
6 account for shares acquired in the acquiree
7 prepare the accounting records of the acquiree
8 account for subsequent adjustments to the initial accounting for a business combination
9 provide the disclosures required under IFRS 3.

14.1 THE NATURE OF A BUSINESS COMBINATION

The accounting standard relevant for accounting for business combinations is IFRS 3 *Business Combinations* issued by the International Accounting Standards Board (IASB) in January 2008. In IFRS 3, Appendix A contains the defined terms, while Appendix B contains application guidance — both Appendices are an integral part of IFRS 3. The IASB has also published a Basis for Conclusions on IFRS 3, but this is not an integral part of the standard.

A business combination is defined in Appendix A to IFRS 3 as:

> A transaction or other event in which an acquirer obtains control of one or more businesses.

For a business combination to occur there has to be an economic transaction between two entities in which the control of a business is transferred from one business to another. The meaning of control is the same as in IFRS 10 *Consolidated Financial Statements*. Control exists when an investor is exposed, or has rights, to variable returns from its involvement with the investee and has the ability to affect those returns through its power over the investee.

The term business is defined in Appendix A as:

> An integrated set of activities and assets that is capable of being conducted and managed for the purpose of pro-viding a return in the form of dividends, lower costs or other economic benefits directly to investors or other owners, members or participants.

The purpose of defining a business is to distinguish between the acquisition of a group of assets that does not constitute a business — such as a number of desks, bookcases and filing cabinets — and the acquisition of a business. A group of assets that *does not* constitute a business is accounted for under IFRS 16 *Property, Plant and Equipment*, while a group of assets that *does* constitute a business is accounted for under IFRS 3 *Business Combinations*. Where a group of assets not constituting a business is acquired, these assets are measured at cost (IFRS 3 paragraph 2(b)). In contrast, as explained later in this chapter, where a business is acquired, the assets are measured at fair value.

For a group of assets to constitute a business, they must be capable of providing a return. In order to pro-vide a return, a business will normally consist of inputs, processes and outputs; for example, an entity will acquire raw materials which will be processed to produce finished goods that will be sold to customers. The assets of the entity, then, integrate to generate the return to the entity. Note, however, that the definition of business in IFRS 3 does not require the entity to create outputs. The definition only requires that the assets be *capable* of providing a return. Hence, an entity which is in the development stage, such as a mining operation that has not yet produced ore for sale, can still be classified as a business. It is also not necessary that the entity actually be producing outputs at the time of the acquisition, or even that the acquirer plans to use the assets in a particular fashion immediately. As long as the assets are capable of producing a return, the assets constitute a business. Note also the use of the phrase 'integrated set of activities'. As is explained in more detail later in the chapter in the analysis of the nature of goodwill, goodwill arises where there exists synergy between assets. Goodwill can only be recognised when assets are acquired as part of a business (IFRS 3 paragraph 2(b)).

Consider the situation in figure 14.1 in which entity A acquires a mining division from entity B by issuing its shares to entity B. In this situation, entity A is considered to be the acquirer, as it obtains control of the mining business from entity B. In analysing the substance of the transaction, entity A is acquiring a business from entity B and selling shares in itself to entity B. Entity B is acquiring shares from entity A and selling a mining division to entity A. However, entity B is not undertaking a business combination. It is acquiring a single asset, shares in entity A. In contrast, entity A is acquiring a business, namely the mining division, from entity B. Both entity A and entity B are acquiring assets and giving up some form of consideration. However, only entity A is undertaking a business combination.

The combination of separate businesses requires joining the assets and liabilities of the acquirer with those acquired from the acquiree. Assuming the existence of two companies, A Ltd and B Ltd, the following general forms of business combinations are covered in this chapter:

1. A Ltd acquires all the assets and liabilities of B Ltd.
   B Ltd continues as a company, holding shares in A Ltd.
2. A Ltd acquires all the assets and liabilities of B Ltd.
   B Ltd liquidates.
3. C Ltd is formed to acquire all the assets and liabilities of A Ltd and B Ltd.
   A Ltd and B Ltd liquidate.
4. A Ltd acquires a group of net assets of B Ltd, the group of net assets constituting a business, such as a division, branch or segment, of B Ltd.
   B Ltd continues to operate as a company.

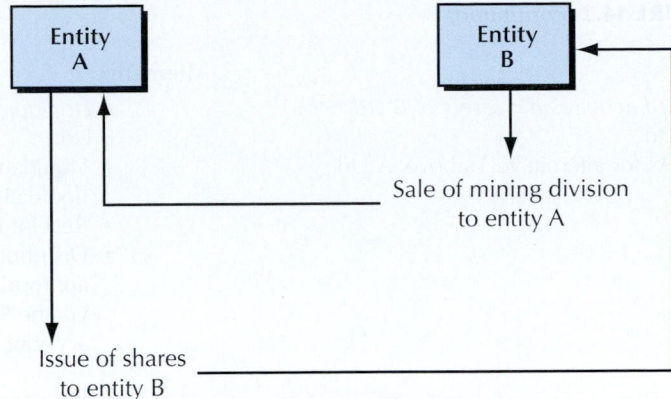

FIGURE 14.1 Identification of a business combination

Obtaining control over the net assets of another entity could be achieved by one entity acquiring the shares of another entity on the open market and, because of the quantity of shares acquired, being able to control the financial and operating policies of the other entity. Accounting for this form of business combination requires the application of the principles discussed in this chapter, but the application further involves the preparation of consolidated financial statements. Accounting for these forms of business combinations is discussed in chapters 23 to 27.

A business combination could also occur without any exchange of assets or equity between the entities involved in the exchange. For example, a business combination could occur where two entities merged under a contract. The shareholders of the two entities could agree to adjust the rights of each of their shareholdings so that they receive a specified share of the profits of both the combined entities. As a result of the contract, both entities would be under the control of a single management group. Business combinations are also not restricted to transactions involving companies. Mutual entities (see the definition in IFRS 3 Appendix A) such as credit unions and mutual insurance companies which combine together, for example to increase their market share and to lower their risk, may also have to account for the combination under IFRS 3.

There are many other forms of business combinations that can occur, such as A Ltd acquiring the assets only of B Ltd, and B Ltd paying off the liabilities and then liquidating. Alternatively, A Ltd may acquire all the assets and only some of the liabilities of B Ltd, and B Ltd pays the remaining liabilities before liquidating. The number of possible arrangements is quite large, but most situations are covered by consideration of the three alternatives in figure 14.2.

IFRS 3 applies to all business combinations except those listed in paragraph 2 of the standard, namely:
- *Where the business combination results in the formation of a joint venture.* Such a business combination is accounted for under IFRS 11 *Joint Arrangements*.
- *Where the business combination involves entities or businesses under common control.* According to Appendix B, such a business combination occurs where all of the combining entities or businesses ultimately are controlled by the same party or parties both before and after the combination, and where control is not transitory. This situation could arise where P Ltd owns 100% of the shares of S Ltd. The directors of P Ltd form a new entity, X Ltd, wholly owned by P Ltd, which acquires all the issued shares of S Ltd in an internal reconstruction. All the combining entities are controlled by P Ltd both before and after the reconstruction.

FIGURE 14.2 General forms of business combinations

Alternative 1	
A Ltd acquires net assets of B Ltd	*B Ltd continues, holding shares in A Ltd*
A Ltd:	B Ltd:
• Receipt of assets and liabilities of B Ltd	• Sale of assets and liabilities to A Ltd
• Consideration transferred, e.g. shares, cash or other consideration	• Gain or loss on sale
	• Receipt of consideration transferred, e.g. shares, cash or other consideration

(continued)

FIGURE 14.2 *(continued)*

Alternative 2

A Ltd acquires net assets of B Ltd
A Ltd:
• As for alternative 1 above, A Ltd

B Ltd liquidates
B Ltd:
• Liquidation account, including gain/loss on liquidation
• Receipt of purchase consideration
• Distribution of consideration to appropriate parties, including shareholders via the Shareholders' Distribution account

Alternative 3

C Ltd formed
C Ltd:
• Formation of C Ltd with issue of shares
• Acquisition of assets and liabilities of A Ltd and B Ltd
• Payment for net assets of A Ltd and B Ltd via cash outlays or issue of shares in C Ltd

A Ltd and B Ltd liquidate
A Ltd and B Ltd:
• As for alternative 2 above, B Ltd

14.2 ACCOUNTING FOR A BUSINESS COMBINATION — BASIC PRINCIPLES

The required method of accounting for a business combination under paragraph 4 of IFRS 3 is the *acquisition method*. The four key steps in this method are noted in paragraph 5 of the standard:
1. Identify the acquirer.
2. Determine the acquisition date.
3. Recognise and measure the identifiable assets acquired, the liabilities assumed, and any non-controlling interest in the acquiree.
4. Recognise and measure goodwill or a gain from a bargain purchase.

The acquisition method is applied on the acquisition date, which is the date the acquirer obtains control of the acquiree. On this date, the business combination occurs. IFRS 3 also provides requirements for the subsequent measurement and accounting for assets and liabilities recognised initially at acquisition date.

14.2.1 Identifying the acquirer [step 1]

Paragraph 7 of IFRS 3 states that the acquirer is 'the entity that obtains *control* of another entity, i.e. the acquiree'. Appendix A of IFRS 3 provides the following definitions:

acquiree: The business or businesses that the acquirer obtains control of in a business combination.
acquirer: The entity that obtains control of the acquiree.

The key criterion, then, in identifying an acquirer is that of control. This term is the same as that used in IFRS 10 *Consolidated Financial Statements* for identifying a parent–subsidiary relationship (see chapter 23 of this book). Control of an investee is defined as existing when 'the investor is exposed, or has rights, to variable returns from its involvment with the investee and has the ability to affect those returns through its power over the investee'. In some situations, it is very easy to identify an acquirer. For example, if entity A acquires more than half the shares of entity B, then entity A will have control over entity B because its majority shareholding will give entity A more than half of the voting rights of entity B as well as control of entity B's board.

In other situations, identification of an acquirer requires judgement. Consider the situation where entity A combines with entity B. To effect the combination, a new company (entity C) is formed, which issues shares to acquire all the shares of both entities A and B. The subsequent organisation structure is as shown below:

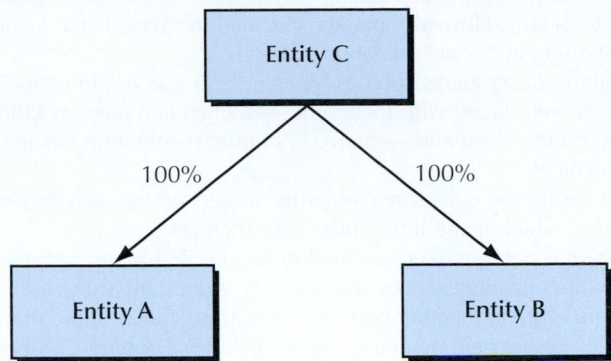

As entity C is created solely to formalise the organisation structure, it is not the acquirer although it may be considered to be the legal parent of both the other entities. As noted in paragraph B18 of Appendix B to IFRS 3, one of the entities that existed before the combination must be identified as the acquirer, as entity C is not a party to the decisions associated with the business combination, just a part of the form of the organisation structure created to facilitate the combination. As noted earlier, if entity A is identified as the acquirer, then the assets and liabilities of entity B (the acquiree) are measured at fair value at acquisition date.

Paragraphs B14–B18 of Appendix B to IFRS 3 provide some indicators to assist in assessing which entity is the acquirer:

- *What are the relative voting rights in the combined entity after the business combination?* The acquirer is usually the entity whose owners have the largest portion of the voting rights in the combined entity. As noted in paragraph B19, in a reverse acquisition, entity X may issue its shares to acquire the shares of entity Y. However, because of the greater number of X shares given to the former Y shareholders relative to those held by the shareholders in entity X before the combination, the former shareholders in entity Y may have the majority of shares in entity X and be able to determine the operating and financial policies of the combined entities.
- *Is there a large minority voting interest in the combined entity?* As discussed in chapter 23 of this book, the acquirer is usually the entity that has the largest minority voting interest in an entity that has a widely dispersed ownership.
- *What is the composition of the governing body of the combined entity?* The acquirer is usually the combining entity whose owners have the ability to elect or appoint or to remove a majority of the members of the governing body of the combined entity.
- *What is the composition of the senior management that governs the combined entity subsequent to the combination?* This is an important indicator given that the criterion for identification of an acquirer is that of control. If X and Y combine, is the senior management group of the combined entity dominated by former senior managers of X or Y?
- *What are the terms of the exchange of equity interests?* Has one of the combining entities paid a premium over the pre-combination fair value of one of the combining entities, an amount paid in order to gain control?
- *Which entity is the larger?* This could be measured by reference to the fair value of each of the combining entities, or relative revenues or profits. In a takeover, it is normally the larger company that takes over the smaller company (that is, the larger company is the acquirer). For example, if the global company Microsoft Ltd combines with Barrow Computers, a small computing company operating in only one Australian city, then it is most likely that Microsoft Ltd is the acquirer. An example of a small Chinese company acquiring a larger company in the same industry is shown in figure 14.3. The acquisition followed a scandal in the industry, so the circumstances were unusual. However, it needs to be noted that the indicators are only guidelines that require judgement when being applied.
- *Which entity initiated the exchange?* Normally the entity that is the acquirer is the one that undertakes action to take over the acquiree.

Determining the controlling entity is the key to identification of the acquirer. However, doing so may not be straightforward in many business combinations, and the accountant might be required to make a reasoned judgement based on the circumstances.

Minnow of milk trade poised to swallow giant

The central government is asking Beijing Sanyuan Foods to look into an acquisition but did not name a target company. However, market speculation says it is the Sanlu Group, whose products triggered the snow-balling milk contamination scandal . . .

While industry giants such as Mengniu, Yili and Bright Dairy lost consumer confidence because their products were laced with melamine — a chemical that has killed four babies and sickened at least 54 000 on the mainland — Sanyuan's brand recognition has improved because its products were clear of the chemical.

As a result, the dairy, once regarded as second tier, saw its share price surge. It closed up 10 per cent on Thursday, which is the limit under exchange rules.

There has been market speculation that Beijing-based Sanyuan will acquire Sanlu . . .

Sanyuan's products accounted for only 2 per cent of the mainland milk market. By comparison, Mengniu and Yili together comprise about two-thirds of the market.

Sanlu, 43 per cent owned by New Zealand's Fonterra Co-operative Group, has strong production capability and distribution channels.

'Had the crisis not happened, it should be Sanlu to acquire Sanyuan,' Mr Yang said.

FIGURE 14.3 Small company acquires a large company
Source: Jasmine Wang, *South China Morning Post* (2008, p. A7).

Paragraph 6 requires an acquirer to be identified in every business combination. It has been argued by some accountants that there are business combinations where it is impossible to identify an acquirer. For example, in its response to the Amendments ED, the Accounting Standards Board in the United Kingdom (2005, p. 8) stated:

> We have reservations about requiring the acquisition method for *all* business combinations. In certain circumstances it may not be possible to identify an acquirer and therefore the use of acquisition accounting (which reflects acquisition of one entity by another) may not faithfully represent the business combination. We consider that 'true' mergers do occur.

Accounting for combinations achieved by contract alone was introduced in the 2007 issue of IFRS 3 — previously such combinations were excluded from the application of IFRS 3. As noted in paragraph BC79 of the Basis for Conclusions on IFRS 3, determination of an acquirer in such circumstances may be difficult as there may be no exchange of readily measurable consideration. However, difficulties in identifying an acquirer are not a sufficient reason for justifying a different accounting treatment. As explained later (see section 14.4 of this chapter), the acquisition method requires the assets and liabilities of the *acquiree* to be measured at fair value. It is then necessary in a business combination to determine which entity is the acquirer and which is the acquiree. Consider a situation where entity A enters into a business combination with entity B. If entity A were identified as the acquirer, then it would be the assets and liabilities of entity B that would be measured at fair value; whereas, if entity B were identified as the acquirer, it would be entity A's assets and liabilities that would be recorded at fair value.

14.2.2 Determining the acquisition date [step 2]

Acquisition date is defined in Appendix A to IFRS 3 as follows:

> The date on which the **acquirer** obtains control of the **acquiree**.

A business combination involves the joining together of assets under the control of a specific entity. Therefore, the business combination occurs at the date the assets or net assets are under the control of the acquirer. This date is the acquisition date.

Other dates that are important during the process of the business combination may be:

- the date the contract is signed
- the date the consideration is paid
- a date nominated in the contract
- the date on which assets acquired are delivered to the acquirer
- the date on which an offer becomes unconditional.

These dates may be important, but determination of acquisition date does not depend on when the acquirer receives physical possession of the assets acquired, or actually pays out the consideration to the acquiree. The use of control as the key criterion to determine acquisition date ensures that the substance of the transaction determines the accounting rather than the form of the transaction. For example, assets acquired may be delivered in stages, or payments made for these assets may be made over a period of time with a number of payments being required. As noted in paragraph 9 of IFRS 3, on the closing date of the combination, the acquirer legally transfers the consideration — cash or shares — and acquires the assets and assumes the liabilities of the acquiree. However, in some cases this may not be the acquisition date.

The definition of acquisition date then relates to the point in time when the net assets of the acquiree become the net assets of the acquirer — in essence, the date on which the acquirer can recognise the net assets acquired in its own records. This approach is consistent with the *Conceptual Framework* in that an asset is defined in terms of future economic benefits that are controlled by an entity.

There are four main areas where the selection of the date affects the accounting for a business combination:
- The identifiable assets acquired and liabilities assumed by the acquirer are measured at the fair value at the acquisition date. The choice of fair value is affected by the choice of the acquisition date.
- The consideration paid by the acquirer is determined as the sum of the fair values of assets given, equity issued and/or liabilities undertaken in exchange for the net assets or shares of another entity. The choice of date affects the measure of fair value. For example, in the case of shares listed on a stock exchange, the market price of these shares may fluctuate on a daily basis. The choice of the acquisition date affects the choice of which particular quoted price is used in calculating the fair value of shares issued by the acquirer as consideration.
- The acquirer may acquire only some of the shares of the acquiree. The owners of the balance of the shares of the acquiree are called the non-controlling interest — defined in Appendix A as 'the equity in a subsidiary not attributable, directly or indirectly, to a parent'. This non-controlling interest is also measured at fair value at acquisition date.
- The acquirer may have previously held an equity interest in the acquiree prior to obtaining control of the acquiree. For example, entity X may have previously acquired 20% of the shares of entity Y, and now acquires the remaining 80% giving it control of entity Y. The acquisition date is the date when entity X acquired the 80% interest. The 20% share holding will be recorded as an asset in the records of entity X. At acquisition date, the fair value of this investment is measured.

The effect of determining the acquisition date is that the financial position of the combined entity at acquisition date should report the assets and liabilities of the acquiree at that date, and any profits reported as a result of the acquiree's operations within the business combination should reflect profits earned after the acquisition date.

14.3 ACCOUNTING IN THE RECORDS OF THE ACQUIRER

Where the acquirer purchases assets and assumes liabilities of another entity, it has to consider:
(a) the recognition and measurement of the identifiable assets acquired and the liabilities assumed (step 3 of the acquisition method)
(b) the recognition and measurement of goodwill or a gain from a bargain purchase (step 4 of the acquisition method).

As noted in section 14.1, accounting for business combinations where the acquirer purchases the shares of the acquiree is covered in chapters 23 to 27. In this chapter, for such business combinations, only the recognition and measurement of the investment by the acquirer is covered (see section 14.6).

14.4 RECOGNITION AND MEASUREMENT OF ASSETS ACQUIRED AND LIABILITIES ASSUMED [STEP 3]

14.4.1 Recognition

Paragraph 10 of IFRS 3 states:

> As of the acquisition date, the acquirer shall recognise, separately from goodwill, the identifiable assets acquired, the liabilities assumed and any non-controlling interest in the acquiree. Recognition of identifiable assets acquired and liabilities assumed is subject to the conditions specified in paragraphs 11 and 12.

Paragraph 4.38 of the *Conceptual Framework* specifies two recognition criteria for assets and liabilities, stating that recognition occurs if:
- it is probable that any future economic benefit will flow to or from the entity
- the item has a cost or value that can be reliably measured.

In deciding whether to recognise an asset or liability, in a business combination it is assumed that the probability test for the assets acquired and liabilities undertaken in a business combination is unnecessary and that these assets and liabilities will always be able to be measured reliably. Use of estimates simply means the measure may involve uncertainty, but does not mean the measure is unreliable.

In relation to the probability criterion, paragraph BC126 of the Basis for Conclusions on IFRS 3 states explicitly that the acquirer is required 'to recognise identifiable assets acquired and liabilities assumed regardless of the degree of probability of an inflow or outflow of economic benefits'. The assets acquired and liabilities assumed are measured at fair value. That fair value will reflect expectations about the probability of inflows or outflows of benefits. The effects of probability are then built into the measurement of the fair value, and that amount is always expected to be received for assets or paid out for liabilities. The probability criterion is then unnecessary where fair values are used as the measurement method.

Paragraph 10 requires the recognition of any non-controlling interest in the acquiree. Non-controlling interests are discussed in chapter 26.

In paragraphs 11 and 12 of IFRS 3, there are two conditions that have to be met prior to the recognition of assets and liabilities acquired in the business combination:

Firstly, at the acquisition date, the assets and liabilities recognised by the acquirer must meet the definitions of assets and liabilities in the *Conceptual Framework*. Any expected future costs cannot be included in the calculation of assets acquired and liabilities assumed.

One area affected by this condition is the accounting for contingent liabilities. IAS 37 *Provisions, Contingent Liabilities and Contingent Assets* paragraph 10 contains the following definition of a contingent liability:

(a) a possible obligation that arises from past events and whose existence will be confirmed only by the occurrence or non-occurrence of one or more uncertain future events not wholly within the control of the entity; or

(b) a present obligation that arises from past events but is not recognised because:
  (i) it is not probable that an outflow of resources embodying economic benefits will be required to settle the obligation; or
  (ii) the amount of the obligation cannot be measured with sufficient reliability.

Note that there are two types of contingent liabilities — real liabilities (present obligations) that are not recognised because of a failure to meet the recognition criteria, and non-liabilities (possible obligations). As the contingent liabilities under (b) above are real liabilities, they are recognised by the acquirer in a business combination and measured at fair value. The requirements in terms of the recognition criteria in IAS 37 do not apply for a business combination. However, the contingent liabilities under (a) are not real liabilities and therefore are not recognised in a business combination. It is expected that forthcoming changes to IAS 37 will eliminate the concept of contingent liabilities.

Secondly, the item acquired or assumed must be part of the business acquired rather than the result of a separate transaction. This recognition principle is an example of the application of substance over form in that the entities involved in the transaction may link another transaction with the business combination, but in substance it is a separate transaction. Paragraphs 51–52 of IFRS 3 contain examples of such transactions. One example is where the business combination transaction settles pre-existing relationships between the acquirer and the acquiree. Paragraph BC122 explains this by providing the example where a potential acquiree has a receivable for an unresolved claim against the potential acquirer. As part of the agreement to combine, the acquirer agrees to settle the claim with the acquiree, and part of the consideration transferred is for that purpose. It is then necessary to separate the two transactions and separate out of the consideration transferred the amount paid to settle the claim.

As noted in paragraph 13 of IFRS 3, a possible result of applying the principles of IFRS 3 is that there may be assets and liabilities recognised as a result of the business combination that were not recognised by the acquiree. One example of this is internally generated intangibles that were not recognised by the acquiree on the application of IAS 38 *Intangible Assets*; for example, internally generated brands would not be recognised by an acquiree but would be recognised by the acquirer. The acquirer would measure these at fair value.

In recognising the assets and liabilities, it is necessary to classify or designate them. Paragraph 15 requires that the acquirer do this on the basis of the contractual terms, economic conditions, its operating or accounting policies and other pertinent conditions that exist at acquisition date. One example of this is the classification of financial instruments, for example, as financial assets at fair value or at amortised cost.

As a part of the illustrative examples accompanying IFRS 3, the IASB provided examples of items acquired in a business combination that would meet the definition of an intangible asset (see figure 14.4).

CLASS	BASIS
Marketing-related intangible assets	
Trademarks, trade names, service marks, collective marks and certification marks	Contractual
Trade dress (unique colour, shape or package design)	Contractual
Newspaper mastheads	Contractual
Internet domain names	Contractual
Non-competition agreements	Contractual
Customer-related intangible assets	
Customer lists	Non-contractual
Order or production backlog	Contractual
Customer contracts and related customer relationships	Contractual
Non-contractual customer relationships	Non-contractual
Artistic-related intangible assets	
Plays, operas and ballets	Contractual
Books, magazines, newspapers and other literary works	Contractual
Musical works such as compositions, song lyrics and advertising jingles	Contractual
Pictures and photographs	Contractual
Video and audiovisual material, including motion pictures or films, music videos and television programs	Contractual
Contract-based intangible assets	
Licensing, royalty and standstill agreements	Contractual
Advertising, construction, management, service or supply contracts	Contractual
Lease agreements (whether the acquiree is the lessee or lessor)	Contractual
Construction permits	Contractual
Franchise agreements	Contractual
Operating and broadcasting rights	Contractual
Servicing contracts such as mortgage servicing contracts	Contractual
Employment contracts	Contractual
Use rights, such as drilling, water, air, timber cutting and route authorities	Contractual
Technology-based intangible assets	
Patented technology	Contractual
Computer software and mask works	Contractual
Unpatented technology	Non-contractual
Databases including title plants	Non-contractual
Trade secrets such as secret formulas, processes and recipes	Contractual

FIGURE 14.4 Intangible assets, IFRS 3 Illustrative Examples

14.4.2 Measurement

Paragraph 18 requires an acquirer to measure the identifiable assets acquired and the liabilities assumed at their fair values on acquisition date.

Fair value is defined in Appendix A to IFRS 3 as follows:

the price that would be received to sell an asset or paid to transfer a liability in an orderly transaction between market participants at the measurement date.

Fair value is basically a market-based measure in a transaction between unrelated parties. However, the process of determining fair value necessarily involves judgement and estimation. The acquiring entity is not actually trading the items in the marketplace for cash, but is trying to estimate what the exchange price would be if it did so. Hence, the determination of fair value involves estimation.

Fair value is measured in accordance with IFRS 13 *Fair Value Measurement* issued by the IASB in 2011. Fair value is defined as an exit price and is determined after the specific asset or liability has been identified, the principal (or most advantageous) market has been determined, the assumptions that market participants would make in pricing an asset or liability have been identified, and — for a non-financial asset — the highest and best use of the asset has been determined.

IFRS 13 describes three valuation techniques that an entity might use to determine fair value:

- *the market approach*: using prices generated by market transactions involving identical or comparable assets or liabilities
- *the income approach*: converting future amounts such as cash flows to a current, discounted amount
- *the cost approach*: determining an amount which reflects the amount currently needed to replace the service capacity of an asset.

IFRS 13 also identifies a three-level hierarchy for the inputs to the valuation techniques:

- Level 1 inputs are fully observable and are unadjusted quoted prices in an active market for identical assets and liabilities.
- Level 2 inputs are directly or indirectly observable inputs other than Level 1 inputs.
- Level 3 inputs are unobservable.

Chapter 3 provides detailed information on IFRS 13 and the measurement of fair value of assets and liabilities.

Figure 14.5 contains an extract from the 2006 annual report of Danisco Ltd, a Danish company that is one of the world's leading producers of ingredients for food and other consumer products. Danisco acquired Genencor International Inc. Ltd in 2004–05 and in its 2006 financial report provided an explanation of the fair value measurements used in accounting for this acquisition. Different measurement methods were used to measure the fair values of different assets.

---

22 Purchase of enterprises and activities

2005/06

Genencor International Inc.

The measurement of the acquired assets and liabilities was concluded in 2005/06, and the basis for their recognition and the calculation of goodwill was established. The measurement of the intangible assets was based on identification of cash generating values. Where it has been possible to relate the values directly to the earnings of the business, this has been used as the basis of the measurement. For technologies and other values not directly related to the cash flows of earnings, the measurement has been determined on the basis of replacement cost. The calculations are based on a WACC of 9%.

The fair value measurements have resulted in identification of total intangible assets of DKK 514 million and a consequent fair value adjustment against the carrying amounts of DKK 264 million. The most important identified intangible assets are patents of DKK 178 million, technology related to enzyme production of DKK 103 million, and customer contracts, licenses and other intangible assets of DKK 225 million.

The measurement of property, plant and equipment has for all major buildings and plant been based on external valuations. Production equipment and other non-current assets have primarily been measured by the company's own production engineers.

The fair value measurements have resulted in writedowns of DKK 366 million of property, plant and equipment, mainly buildings and production equipment in the USA, Belgium and Finland, which due to geographical location, wear and tear and reduced useful lives carry a lower fair value.

The fair value adjustment of deferred tax and tax payable is related to the above adjustments of intangible and tangible assets and to estimated tax liabilities associated with events before the date of acquisition.

FIGURE 14.5 Alternative measures of fair value
Source: Danisco (2006, p. 70).

Why did the IASB choose fair value as the measurement principle? The IASB provided an answer in paragraph BC198 of the Basis for Conclusions on IFRS 3:

In developing the measurement principle in the revised standards, the boards concluded that fair value is the most *relevant* attribute for assets acquired and liabilities assumed in a business combination. Measurement at fair value also provides information that is more *comparable* and *understandable* than measurement at cost or on the basis of allocating the total cost of an acquisition. [emphasis added]

One of the problems that may arise in measuring the assets and liabilities of the acquiree is that the initial accounting for the business combination may be incomplete by the end of the reporting period. For example, the acquisition date may be 20 June and the end of the reporting period may be 30 June. In this situation, in accordance with paragraph 45 of IFRS 3, the acquirer must report provisional amounts in its financial statements. The provisional amounts will be best estimates and will need to be adjusted to fair values when those amounts can be determined after the end of the reporting period. The measurement period in which the adjustments can be made cannot exceed one year after the acquisition date. In Note 27 of its 2008 annual report, Wesfarmers Limited disclosed the provisional fair values of identifiable assets in its acquisition of Coles Group Limited. This information is shown in figure 14.6. Also in figure 14.6 is Note 27 of the 2009 annual report which shows the results of finalisation of the provisional accounting, including adjustments to goodwill.

FIGURE 14.6 Provisional measurements of fair value

27 BUSINESS COMBINATIONS [Annual report 2008]

Acquisitions

During the period, Wesfarmers completed several acquisitions, the most significant being:

On 23 November 2007, Wesfarmers Limited, through its controlled entity Wesfarmers Retail Holdings Pty Ltd, acquired, through a Scheme of Arrangement ('the Scheme'), 89.4% of the voting shares of Coles group Limited ('Coles group'), a publicly listed company and its subsidiaries. Combined with the initial interest of 10.6% purchased in April 2007 at a total cost of $2077 million, Wesfarmers held 100% of the voting shares in Coles group on 23 November 2007.

Coles group is based in Australia and operates retail businesses in Australia and New Zealand. The Scheme consideration consisted of 152.6 million Wesfarmers ordinary shares, 152.6 million Wesfarmers partially protected shares and $4328 million in cash. The cost of the acquisition totalled $19 307 million.

The provisional fair value of identifiable assets and liabilities recognised on acquisition of Coles group has decreased $238 million compared to the fair value amounts previously reported. This reduction is due largely to a decrease in plant and equipment and an increase in provisions recognised on acquisition. The reduction in the fair value of identifiable assets and liabilities results in a corresponding increase to goodwill recognised on acquisition. At 30 June 2008, the acquisition accounting balances are provisional due to ongoing work finalising valuations and tax related matters which may impact acquisition accounting entries.

On 1 September 2007, the Group's chemicals and fertilisers subsidiary, CSBP Limited, acquired 100% of Australian Vinyls Corporation, a privately owned company, which is the only manufacturer of poly vinyl chloride in the Australian market. The cost of the acquisition totalled $142 million.

	CONSOLIDATED	
	RECOGNISED ON ACQUISITION $m	BOOK CARRYING VALUE $m

Details of the provisional fair value of identifiable assets of the Coles group and the Group's other acquisitions as at the date of acquisitions are:

Assets		
Cash and cash equivalents	505	505
Trade and other receivables	525	551
Inventories	3 662	3 659
Investment in associate	8	8
Property, plant and equipment	3 279	3 443
Investment property	6	8
Intangible assets	4 295	709
Assets held for sale	40	26
Deferred tax assets	378	458
Other assets	53	53
	12 751	9 420

(continued)

FIGURE 14.6 *(continued)*

	CONSOLIDATED	
	RECOGNISED ON ACQUISITION $m	BOOK CARRYING VALUE $m
Liabilities		
Trade and other payables	3 305	3 297
Interest bearing borrowings	2 013	2 079
Provisions	1 543	1 070
Other liabilities	223	277
	7 084	6 723
Fair value of identifiable net assets	5 667	2 697
Goodwill arising on acquisition	13 846	
	19 513	
Cost of combinations		
Cash paid to shareholders	6 604	
Shares issued to shareholders	12 733	
Costs associated with the acquisitions	176	
	19 513	
Cash outflow on acquisitions		
Net cash acquired — operating accounts	502	
Net cash acquired — broking trust accounts	3	
Cash paid for initial holding in Coles group (in prior reporting period)	2 077	
Cash paid	(6 780)	
Net cash outflow	(4 198)	

From the date of acquisition, the Coles group and other acquisitions contributed $475 million to the net profit after tax of the Group.

If the combinations had taken place at the beginning of the period, the revenue from continuing operations for the Group would have been $49 427 million. It is considered impracticable to obtain robust normalised pre-acquisition results from 1 July 2007 due to the differences in reporting periods and the timing of accounting period end adjustments recognised by the Coles group prior to acquisition.

The goodwill of $13 846 million arising on consolidation includes goodwill attributable to the Coles group acquisition of $13 801 million and is attributable to various factors, including the ability to provide improved products and services to customers, the value of growth opportunities and inseparable intangible assets.

27 BUSINESS COMBINATIONS [Annual report 2009]
Finalisation of acquisition accounting

Australian Vinyls Corporation

On 31 August 2008, the provisional acquisition accounting period ended for the acquisition of Australian Vinyls Corporation. There were no significant adjustments to the fair value of identifiable assets and liabilities which were provisionally disclosed at 30 June 2008.

Coles Group Limited ('Coles group')

On 22 November 2008, the provisional acquisition accounting period ended for the acquisition of the Coles group. Adjustments were made in finalising the acquisition accounting, resulting in the fair value of identifiable assets recognised on acquisition increasing by $118 million compared to the provisional fair value amounts previously reported at 30 June 2008. This increase is due largely to an increase in deferred tax assets, relating to property, plant and equipment, and provisions, as a result of finalising the tax effect accounting. The increase in the fair value resulted in a corresponding decrease to goodwill recognised on acquisition.

Retained earnings as at 30 June 2008 has increased by $19 million as a result of the above changes. This is due largely to a decrease in income tax expense. The impact to net profit after tax for the 12 months to 30 June 2009 is not considered by the Company to be significant.

Source: Wesfarmers (2008, pp. 114–15; 2009, p. 120).

After the end of the reporting period, as new information and facts are gathered, the acquirer will progressively adjust the assets and liabilities acquired to fair value. This process may also result in the recognition of new assets and liabilities previously not recognised. The adjustments in assets and liabilities are recognised by means of an increase or decrease in goodwill (IFRS 3 paragraph 48).

14.5 GOODWILL AND GAIN ON BARGAIN PURCHASE [STEP 4]

Paragraph 32 of IFRS 3 states:

> The acquirer shall recognise goodwill as of the acquisition date measured as the excess of (a) over (b) below:
> (a) the aggregate of:
>   (i) the consideration transferred measured in accordance with this IFRS, which generally requires acquisition-date fair value (see paragraph 37);
>   (ii) the amount of any non-controlling interest in the acquiree measured in accordance with this IFRS; and
>   (iii) in a business combination achieved in stages (see paragraphs 41 and 42), the acquisition-date fair value of the acquirer's previously held equity interest in the acquiree.
> (b) the net of the acquisition-date amounts of the identifiable assets acquired and the liabilities assumed measured in accordance with this IFRS.

In relation to parts (a)(ii) and (iii) in paragraph 32, these will affect calculations only where the acquirer obtains control by acquiring shares in the acquiree. This is discussed in chapters 23 to 27 of this book. This means that for business combinations discussed in this chapter, goodwill is determined by comparing the consideration transferred by the acquirer with the net fair value of the identifiable assets and liabilities acquired.

The net fair value of the identifiable assets and liabilities acquired is determined as step 3. The first part of step 4 is then the measurement of consideration transferred.

14.5.1 Consideration transferred

According to paragraph 37, the consideration transferred:
- is measured at fair value at acquisition date
- is calculated as the sum of the acquisition-date fair values of the assets transferred by the acquirer, the liabilities incurred by the acquirer to former owners of the acquiree, and the equity interest issued by the acquirer.

In a specific exchange, the consideration transferred to the acquiree could include just one form of consideration, such as cash, but could equally well consist of a number of forms such as cash, other assets, shares and contingent consideration. These are considered in the following pages.

Cash or other monetary assets

The fair value is the amount of cash or cash equivalent dispersed. The amount is usually readily determinable. One problem that may occur arises when the settlement is deferred to a time after the acquisition date. For a deferred payment, the fair value to the acquirer is the amount the entity would have to borrow to settle the debt immediately. The discount rate used is the entity's incremental borrowing rate.

Use of cash, including a deferred payment, to acquire net assets results in the acquirer recording the following form of entry at the acquisition date:

Net assets	Dr	xxx	
Cash	Cr		xxx
Payable to Acquiree	Cr		xxx
(Acquisition of net assets with partially deferred payment)			

When the deferred payment is made to the acquiree, the interest component needs to be recognised:

Payable to Acquiree	Dr	xxx	
Interest Expense	Dr	xxx	
Cash	Cr		xxx
(Payment of deferred amount)			

Non-monetary assets

Non-monetary assets are assets such as property, plant and equipment, investments, licences and patents. Chapter 3 discusses how fair values are determined.

The acquirer is effectively selling the non-monetary asset to the acquiree. Hence, it is earning income equal to the fair value on the sale of the asset. Where the carrying amount of the asset in the records of the acquirer is different from fair value, a gain or loss on the asset is recognised at acquisition date. This principle is explained in paragraph 38 of IFRS 3: 'the acquirer shall remeasure the transferred assets or liabilities to their fair values as of the acquisition date and recognise the resulting gains or losses, if any, in profit or loss'.

Use of a non-monetary asset such as plant as part of the consideration to acquire net assets results in the acquirer recording the following entries (assume a cost of plant of $180, a carrying amount of $150 and fair value of $155):

Accumulated Depreciation	Dr	30	
Plant	Cr		25
Gain	Cr		5
(Remeasurement as part of consideration transferred in a business combination)			
Net Assets Acquired	Dr	xxx	
Plant	Cr		155
Other Consideration Payable	Cr		xxx
(Acquisition of net assets)			

The acquirer recognises a gain on the non-current asset and the asset is then included in the consideration transferred at fair value.

Equity instruments

If an acquirer issues its own shares as consideration, it needs to determine the fair value of those shares at the acquisition date. For listed entities, reference is made to the quoted prices of the shares. As noted in paragraph BC342 of the Basis for Conclusions on IFRS 3, 'equity instruments issued as consideration in a business combination should be measured at their fair values on the acquisition date'.

There has been considerable ongoing debate within the accounting community about which date should be used to measure the fair value of equity instruments issued. As noted in paragraph BC342, the IASB and the Financial Accounting Standards Board (FASB) have discussed two alternative models, namely the acquisition date model (equity instruments would be measured on the date the acquirer obtains control over the business acquired), and the agreement date model (equity instruments would be measured on the date a substantive agreement is reached between the acquirer and the target's management).

The IASB noted there were valid arguments for both models. It subsequently voted to support acquisition date, being the date that control passes from the acquiree to the acquirer, in the interests of convergence with the FASB. Two of the reasons given were:
- the consideration given and the assets acquired and liabilities assumed would be measured on the same date, including the residual goodwill
- the parties to a business combination are likely to take into account expected changes between the agreement date and the acquisition date in the fair value of the acquirer and the market price of the acquirer's securities issued as consideration.

Liabilities assumed

The fair values of liabilities assumed are best measured by the present values of expected future cash outflows. Future losses or other costs expected to be incurred as a result of the combination are not liabilities of the acquirer and are therefore not included in the calculation of the fair value of consideration paid.

Costs of issuing debt and equity instruments

Paragraph 53 of IFRS 3 indicates costs to issue debt and equity instruments are accounted for in accordance with IAS 32 *Financial Instruments: Presentation* and IAS 39 *Financial Instruments: Recognition and Measurement*. In issuing equity instruments such as shares as part of the consideration paid, transaction costs such as stamp duties, professional advisers' fees, underwriting costs and brokerage fees may be incurred. Paragraph 35 of

IAS 32 states that these outlays should be treated as a reduction in the share capital of the entity as such costs reduce the proceeds from the equity issue, net of any related income tax benefit. Hence, if costs of $1000 are incurred in issuing shares as part of the consideration paid, the journal entry in the records of the acquirer is:

Share Capital	Dr	1 000	
Cash	Cr		1 000
(Costs of issuing equity instruments)			

Similarly, the costs of arranging and issuing financial liabilities are an integral part of the liability issue transaction. These costs are included in the initial measurement of the liability. According to paragraph 43 of IAS 39, a financial liability is measured at its fair value plus, in the case of a financial liability not at fair value through profit or loss, transaction costs that are directly attributable to the issue of the financial liability. Financial liabilities are discussed further in chapter 7.

Contingent consideration

Appendix A to IFRS 3 provides the following definition of contingent consideration:

> Usually, an obligation of the **acquirer** to transfer additional assets or **equity interests** to the former owners of an **acquiree** as part of the exchange for **control** of the **acquiree** if specified future events occur or conditions are met. However, contingent consideration also may give the **acquirer** the right to the return of previously transferred consideration if specified conditions are met.

Consider two examples of contingencies. The first is where, because the future income of the acquirer is regarded as uncertain, the agreement contains a clause that requires the acquirer to provide additional consideration to the acquiree if the income of the acquirer is not equal to or exceeds a specified amount over some specified period. The second situation is where the acquirer issues shares to the acquiree and the acquiree is concerned that the issue of these shares may make the market price of the acquirer's shares decline over time. Therefore, the acquirer may offer additional cash or shares if the market price falls below a specified amount over a specified period of time.

According to paragraph 39 of IFRS 3, consistent with other measurements in transferred consideration, the acquirer shall recognise the acquisition-date fair values of contingent consideration as part of the consideration transferred.

Some respondents on the exposure draft to IFRS 3 expressed concern about the ability of preparers of financial statements to measure reliably the fair value of assets and liabilities arising from contingencies. However, as noted in paragraph BC228 of the Basis for Conclusions on IFRS 3, standard setters believe that this measurement should be no more difficult than measuring other fair values at acquisition date. There should be sufficient information at acquisition date based upon discussions undertaken and information collected prior to acquisition date during the acquisition negotiations and process to enable fair value to be measured.

14.5.2 Acquisition-related costs

In addition to the consideration transferred by the acquirer to the acquiree, a further item to be considered in determining the cost of the business combination is the costs directly attributable to the combination, which includes costs such as 'finder's fees; advisory, legal, accounting, valuation and other professional or consulting fees; [and] general administrative costs, including the costs of maintaining an internal acquisitions department' (IFRS 3 paragraph 53).

In IAS 16 *Property, Plant and Equipment* and IAS 38 *Intangible Assets*, directly attributable costs are considered as a part of the cost of acquisition and capitalised into the cost of the asset acquired. In contrast, the acquisition-related costs associated with a business combination are accounted for as expenses in the periods in which they are incurred and the services are received. The key reasons given for this approach are provided in paragraph BC366 of the Basis for Conclusions on IFRS 3:
- Acquisition-related costs are not part of the fair value exchange between the buyer and seller.
- They are separate transactions for which the buyer pays the fair value for the services received.
- These amounts do not generally represent assets of the acquirer at acquisition date because the benefits obtained are consumed as the services are received.

The IFRS 3 accounting for these outlays is a result of the decision to record the identifiable assets acquired and liabilities assumed at fair value. In contrast, under IAS 16 and IAS 38, the assets acquired are initially recorded at cost.

The trial balance below represents the financial position of Whiting Ltd at 1 January 2013.

WHITING LTD
Trial Balance
as at 1 January 2013

	Debit	Credit
Share capital		
Preference — 6000 fully paid shares		$ 6 000
Ordinary — 30 000 fully paid shares		30 000
Retained earnings		21 500
Equipment	$42 000	
Accumulated depreciation – equipment		10 000
Inventory	18 000	
Accounts receivable	16 000	
Patents	3 500	
Debentures		4 000
Accounts payable		8 000
	$79 500	$79 500

At this date, the business of Whiting Ltd is acquired by Salmon Ltd, with Whiting Ltd going into liquidation. The terms of acquisition are as follows:

1. Salmon Ltd is to take over all the assets of Whiting Ltd as well as the accounts payable of Whiting Ltd.
2. Costs of liquidation of $350 are to be paid by Whiting Ltd with funds supplied by Salmon Ltd.
3. Preference shareholders of Whiting Ltd are to receive two fully paid preference shares in Salmon Ltd for every three shares held or, alternatively, $1 per share in cash payable at acquisition date.
4. Ordinary shareholders of Whiting Ltd are to receive two fully paid ordinary shares in Salmon Ltd for every share held or, alternatively, $2.50 in cash, payable half at the acquisition date and half on 31 December 2013.
5. Debenture holders of Whiting Ltd are to be paid in cash out of funds provided by Salmon Ltd. These debentures have a fair value of $102 per $100 debenture.
6. All shares being issued by Salmon Ltd have a fair value of $1.10 per share. Holders of 3000 preference shares and 5000 ordinary shares elect to receive the cash.
7. Costs of issuing and registering the shares issued by Salmon Ltd amount to $40 for the preference shares and $100 for the ordinary shares.
8. Costs associated with the business combination and incurred by Salmon Ltd were $1000.

The calculation of the consideration transferred in the business combination to Salmon Ltd is shown in figure 14.7. The incremental borrowing rate for Salmon Ltd is 10% p.a.

Consideration transferred:		Fair value
Cash: Costs of liquidation	$ 350	
Preference shareholders (3000 × $1.00)	3 000	
Ordinary shareholders		
– payable immediately (1/2 × 5000 × $2.50)	6 250	
– payable later (1/2 × 5000 × $2.50 × 0.909091)*	5 682	
Debentures, including premium ($4000 × 1.02)	4 080	$19 362
Shares: Preference shareholders (2000 × $1.10)	2 200	
Ordinary shareholders (50 000 × $1.10)	55 000	57 200
Consideration transferred		$76 562

* $5682 is the cash payable in one year's time discounted at 10% p.a.

FIGURE 14.7 Consideration transferred in the business combination

In acquiring the net assets of Whiting Ltd, Salmon Ltd passes the journal entries shown in figure 14.8.

2013				
Jan. 1	Net Assets Acquired	Dr	76 562	
	Consideration Payable	Cr		19 362
	Share Capital – Preference	Cr		2 200
	Share Capital – Ordinary	Cr		55 000
	(Acquisition of the net assets of Whiting Ltd)			
	Consideration Payable	Dr	13 680	
	Cash	Cr		13 680
	(Payment of cash consideration to Whiting Ltd: $19 362 less $5682 payable later)			
	Share Capital – Ordinary	Dr	100	
	Share Capital – Preference	Dr	40	
	Cash	Cr		140
	(Share issue costs)			
	Acquisition-Related Expenses	Dr	1 000	
	Cash	Cr		1 000
	(Acquisition-related expenses)			
Dec. 31	Consideration Payable	Dr	5 682	
	Interest Expense	Dr	568	
	Cash	Cr		6 250
	(Balance of consideration paid)			

FIGURE 14.8 Journal entries in the acquirer's records

14.5.3 Goodwill

As noted at the beginning of section 14.5, goodwill is the excess of the consideration transferred over the net fair value of the identifiable assets acquired and liabilities assumed.

> Goodwill = Consideration transferred
> *less*
> Acquirer's interest in the net fair value of the acquiree's identifiable assets and liabilities

Goodwill is accounted for as an asset and is defined in Appendix A to IFRS 3 as:

> An asset representing the future economic benefits arising from other assets acquired in a **business combination** that are not individually identified and separately recognised.

The criterion of 'being individually identified' relates to the characteristic of 'identifiability' as used in IAS 38 *Intangible Assets* to distinguish intangible assets from goodwill. Note paragraph 11 of IAS 38 in this regard:

> The definition of an intangible asset requires an intangible asset to be identifiable to distinguish it from goodwill. Goodwill recognised in a business combination is an asset representing future economic benefits arising from other assets acquired in a business combination that are not individually identified and separately recognised. The future economic benefits may result from synergy between the identifiable assets acquired or from assets that, individually, do not qualify for recognition in the financial statements.

In order to be identifiable, an asset must be capable of being separated or divided from the entity, or arise from contractual or other legal rights. The notion of being 'separately recognised' is also then a part of the criterion of 'identifiability'. This criterion is discussed further in chapter 13.

Goodwill is then a residual, after the acquirer's interest in the identifiable tangible assets, intangible assets, and liabilities of the acquiree is recognised.

The components of goodwill

Johnson and Petrone (1998, p. 295) identified six components of goodwill:

1. *Excess of the fair values over the book values of the acquiree's recognised assets.* In a business acquisition, as assets acquired are measured at fair value, these excesses should not exist. Subsequent to the acquisition, the acquiree's goodwill could include such excesses where assets are measured at cost.
2. *Fair values of other net assets not recognised by the acquiree.* The assets of concern here are those tangible assets which are incapable of reliable measurement by the acquiree, and non-physical assets that do not meet the identifiability criteria for intangible assets.
3. *Fair value of the 'going concern' element of the acquiree's existing business.* This represents the ability of the acquiree to earn a higher return on an assembled collection of net assets than would be expected from those net assets operating separately. This reflects synergies of the assets, as well as factors relating to market imperfections such as an ability of an entity to earn a monopoly profit, or where there are barriers to competitors entering a particular market.
4. *Fair value from combining the acquirer's and acquiree's businesses and net assets.* This stems from the synergies that result from the combination, the value of which is unique to each combination.
5. *Overvaluation of the consideration paid by the acquirer.* This relates to errors in valuing the consideration paid by the acquirer, and may arise particularly where shares are issued as consideration with differences in prices for small parcels of shares as opposed to controlling parcels of shares. There could also be overvaluation of the fair values of the assets acquired. This component could then relate to all errors in measuring the fair values in the business combination.
6. *Overpayment (or underpayment) by the acquirer.* This may occur if the price is driven up in the course of bidding; conversely, goodwill could be understated if the acquiree's net assets were obtained through a distress or fire sale.

In paragraph BC130 of the Basis for Conclusions on IFRS 3, the IASB recognised that components 1 and 2 are not conceptually part of goodwill. Johnson and Petrone (1998, p. 295) and the IASB (paragraph BC131) recognised that components 5 and 6 in the above list also are not conceptually part of goodwill, but rather relate to measurement errors. The two components that are seen as part of goodwill are components 3 and 4, described by Johnson and Petrone (p. 296) as 'going-concern goodwill' and 'combination goodwill' respectively, with the combination of the components being referred to as 'core goodwill'. This is represented diagrammatically in figure 14.9.

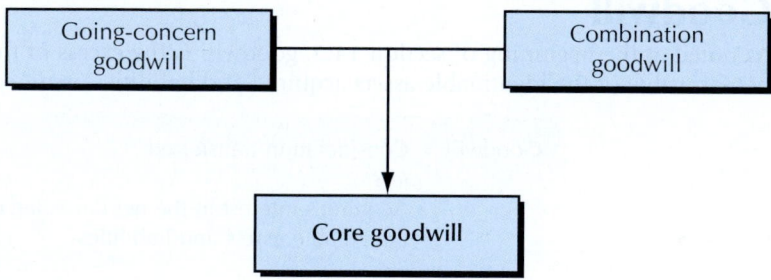

FIGURE 14.9 Core goodwill
Source: Data derived from Johnson and Petrone (1998).

It is this 'core goodwill' that the IASB is concerned with in determining how to account for goodwill. The IASB in paragraph BC137 of the Basis for Conclusions on IFRS 3 notes how IFRS 3 tries to avoid subsuming the first, second and fifth components into the amount calculated as goodwill by requiring an acquirer to make every effort to:
- measure the consideration accurately (eliminating or reducing component 5)
- recognise the identifiable net assets acquired at their fair values rather than their carrying amounts (eliminating or reducing component 1)
- recognise all acquired intangible assets (reducing component 2).

Figure 14.10 contains extracts from Nokia and Christian Dior's annual reports relating to acquisitions made by those entities. Note the descriptions of the items that are expected to generate goodwill.

Is goodwill an asset?

IFRS 3 accounts for goodwill as an asset. Whether core goodwill is an asset is considered in detail in Johnson and Petrone (1998, pp. 296–302) and in Miller and Islam (1988). There are many other articles in the

In April 2008, the group acquired the entire share capital of the Swiss watchmaker Hublot for total consideration of 306 million euros (486 million Swiss francs), including 2 million euros in acquisition costs. The purchase price allocation included an allocation of 219 million euros to Brand, and 122 million euros to goodwill. The goodwill mainly represents the company's expertise in designing and manufacturing timepieces, and the synergies arising from the brand's integration into the distribution network of the Watches and Jewelry business group.

In October 2008, the Group acquired a 90% equity stake in Royal Van Lent, the Dutch designer and builder of yachts sold under the Royal Van Lent — Feadship brand, with the remaining 10% stake of the share capital being subject to a purchase commitment. The final allocation of the purchase price of 362 million euros included 92 million euros to the brand and other intangible assets and 263 million euros to goodwill. Goodwill represents the company's know-how in the design and building of luxury yachts, as well as its relations with customers forged over time.

Source: Christian Dior (2011, pp. 114, 115).

During 2010, the group completed several minor acquisitions that did not have a material impact on the consolidated financial statements. The purchase consideration paid and the total goodwill arising from these acquisitions amounted to EUR 108 million and EUR 82 million, respectively. The goodwill arising from these acquisitions is attributable to assembled workforce and post acquisition synergies.

Source: Nokia Corporation (2010, p. 37).

FIGURE 14.10 Components of goodwill

accounting literature that discuss this issue, because it has been a source of much debate. Of the accounting standard-setting bodies that have considered the issue, the Accounting Standards Board in the United Kingdom in 1997, in its Financial Reporting Standard 10 *Goodwill and Intangible Assets*, took the view that goodwill is not an asset (Summary, paragraph b):

> Goodwill arising on acquisition is neither an asset like other assets nor an immediate loss in value. Rather, it forms the bridge between the cost of an investment shown as an asset in the acquirer's own financial statements and the values attributed to the acquired assets and liabilities in the consolidated financial statements. Although purchased goodwill is not in itself an asset, its inclusion amongst the assets of the reporting entity, rather than as a deduction from shareholders' equity, recognises that goodwill is part of a larger asset, the investment, for which management remains accountable.

As defined in the *Conceptual Framework*, an asset has essentially three characteristics: (1) expected future economic benefits, (2) control by the owner over the benefits, and (3) the benefits arise as the result of a past event. There is little debate over whether goodwill is a repository of expected future economic benefits, as this is evidenced by the fact that the acquirer has been prepared to pay extra consideration over and above an amount equal to the fair value of the acquiree's identifiable net assets. Similarly, the existence of the business combination is seen as a past event. The key area of debate is whether the entity has control over the benefits.

The meaning of 'control' in relation to intangibles is discussed in chapter 13 of this book. It is argued there that the IASB, because of the debates over whether items such as well-trained employees or marketing outlays are assets, introduces the identifiability criterion to ensure that the only items recognised as intangible assets are those that are separable or arise from contractual or other legal rights. Paragraph BC323 of the Basis for Conclusions on IFRS 3 recognises that goodwill arises in part because of factors such as having a well-trained workforce and loyal customers not being seen as controllable by the entity and therefore not being assets.

The problem with goodwill is that it is a unique asset. It arises as a residual. As Leo, Hoggett and Radford (1995, pp. 44–7) noted, the key difference between identifiable net assets and goodwill is measurement:

> The difference between the measurement method used for goodwill and that for measurement of all other assets of the business is whether the method involves determining the value of the business as a whole or part thereof.

The authors defined unidentifiable assets (p. 46) as those assets that meet the recognition criteria and cannot be measured without measuring the total net assets of a business entity. The existence of goodwill depends on the measurement of the entity as a whole. In recognising this, the IASB argued in paragraph BC323 of the Basis for Conclusions on IFRS 3:

> control of core goodwill is provided by means of the acquirer's power to direct the policies and management of the acquiree. Therefore, both the IASB and the FASB concluded that core goodwill meets the conceptual definition of an asset.

Accounting for goodwill

As noted earlier, goodwill is calculated as the excess of the consideration transferred in the business combination over the acquirer's interest in the net fair value of the identifiable assets acquired and liabilities assumed from the acquiree. Hence, to calculate goodwill as a part of the acquisition analysis it is necessary to calculate the consideration transferred and the net fair value of the identifiable assets acquired and liabilities assumed. A comparison of these two amounts determines the existence of goodwill. The acquirer then recognises goodwill as an asset in the same way as for all other identifiable assets acquired.

ILLUSTRATIVE EXAMPLE 14.2 Acquisition analysis

Using the figures from illustrative example 14.1 on pages 518–19, assume that Salmon Ltd assesses the fair values of the identifiable assets and liabilities of Whiting Ltd to be as follows:

Equipment	$36 000
Inventory	20 000
Accounts receivable	9 000
Patents	10 000
Accounts payable	8 000

To determine the entries to be passed by the acquirer, prepare an acquisition analysis that compares the consideration transferred with the net fair value of the identifiable assets, liabilities and contingent liabilities acquired. The analysis for this example is shown in figure 14.11.

Acquisition analysis

Net fair value of identifiable assets acquired and liabilities assumed:

Equipment	$36 000
Inventory	20 000
Accounts receivable	9 000
Patents	10 000
	75 000
Accounts payable	8 000
Net fair value	$67 000

Consideration transferred:
This was calculated in figure 14.7 on page 518 as $76 562.

Goodwill acquired:
Net fair value acquired   = $67 000
Consideration transferred = $76 562
Goodwill   = $76 562 − $67 000
        = $9 562

FIGURE 14.11 Acquisition analysis by the acquirer

The journal entries for Salmon Ltd at acquisition date are as shown in figure 14.12.

FIGURE 14.12 Journal entries of the acquirer, including recognition of goodwill, at acquisition date

Equipment	Dr	36 000	
Inventory	Dr	20 000	
Accounts Receivable	Dr	9 000	
Patents	Dr	10 000	
Goodwill	Dr	9 562	
Accounts Payable	Cr		8 000
Consideration Payable	Cr		19 362
Share Capital – Preference	Cr		2 200
Share Capital – Ordinary	Cr		55 000
(Acquisition of the assets and liabilities of Whiting Ltd)			

Consideration Payable	Dr	13 680	
Cash	Cr		13 680
(Payment of cash consideration)			
Acquisition-Related Expenses	Dr	1 000	
Cash	Cr		1 000
(Acquisition-related costs)			
Share Capital – Ordinary	Dr	100	
Share Capital – Preference	Dr	40	
Cash	Cr		140
(Share issue costs)			

14.5.4 Accounting for a gain on bargain purchase

Where the acquirer's interest in the net fair value of the acquiree's identifiable assets and liabilities is greater than the consideration transferred, the difference is called a gain on a bargain purchase. In equation format, it can be represented as follows:

Gain on bargain purchase = Acquirer's interest in the net fair value of the acquiree's identifiable assets and liabilities

less

Consideration transferred

The existence of a bargain purchase is considered by the standard setters (paragraph BC371) as an anomalous transaction as parties to the business combination do not knowingly sell assets at amounts lower than their fair value. However, because the acquirer has excellent negotiation skills, or because the acquiree has made a sale for other than economic reasons or is forced to sell owing to specific circumstances such as cash flow problems, such situations do arise.

The standard setters adopt the view that most business combinations are an exchange of equal amounts, given markets in which the parties to the business combinations are informed and willing participants in the transaction. Therefore, the existence of a bargain purchase is expected to be an unusual or rare event.

Paragraph 36 of IFRS 3 requires that before a gain is recognised, the acquirer must reassess whether it has correctly:
• identified all the assets acquired and liabilities assumed
• measured at fair value all the assets acquired and liabilities assumed
• measured the consideration transferred.

The objective here is to ensure that all the measurements at acquisition date reflect all the information that is available at that date.

Note that one effect of recognising a bargain purchase is that there is no recognition of goodwill. A gain on bargain purchase and goodwill cannot be recognised in the same business combination.

ILLUSTRATIVE EXAMPLE 14.3 Gain on bargain purchase

Using the information regarding the consideration transferred in a business combination from illustrative examples 14.1 and 14.2, assume the fair values of the identifiable assets and liabilities of Whiting Ltd are assessed to be:

Equipment	$45 000
Inventory	25 000
Accounts receivable	9 000
Patents	11 000
	90 000
Accounts payable	8 000
	$82 000

The *acquisition analysis* now shows:

Net fair value of assets and liabilities acquired	= $82 000
Consideration transferred	= $76 562
Gain on bargain purchase	= $82 000 − $76 562
	= $5438

Assuming that the reassessment process did not result in any changes to the fair values calculated, the first journal entry in Salmon Ltd to record the acquisition of the net assets of Whiting Ltd is:

Equipment	Dr	45 000	
Inventory	Dr	25 000	
Accounts Receivable	Dr	9 000	
Patents	Dr	11 000	
Accounts Payable	Cr		8 000
Consideration Payable	Cr		19 362
Share Capital – Preference	Cr		2 200
Share Capital – Ordinary	Cr		55 000
Gain (Profit or Loss)	Cr		5 438
(Acquisition of assets and liabilities acquired from Whiting Ltd, and the gain on bargain purchase)			

14.5.5 Application of IFRS 3 in practice

According to paragraph BC158 of the Basis for Conclusions on IFRS 3, both the IASB and the FASB believed that the decision usefulness of financial statements would be enhanced if intangible assets acquired in a business combination were distinguished from goodwill. In its report on the application of the FASB's Statement of Financial Accounting Standards No. 141 from 2002–07, Intangible Business (see www.intangiblebusiness.com) gave many examples of US business combinations in which there was a reluctance to separate intangibles from goodwill. Two examples are shown in figures 14.13 and 14.14.

Walt Disney acquisition of Pixar in 2006 ($7.5 bn)

Walt Disney paid $7.5 billion for the digital animation studio, Pixar, which brought you Toy Story, Finding Nemo and other movie classics. The intangible assets, mainly trademarks and tradenames, were given a value of just $0.2 billion while goodwill was $5.6 billion. Of course, the skilled workforce of Pixar would be a key asset that Walt Disney wanted to acquire and both the US and IFRS standards on business combinations specifically exclude workforce from recognizable intangible assets. Nevertheless we do not believe that the value of other recognizable intangible assets is actually as low as that reported by Walt Disney.

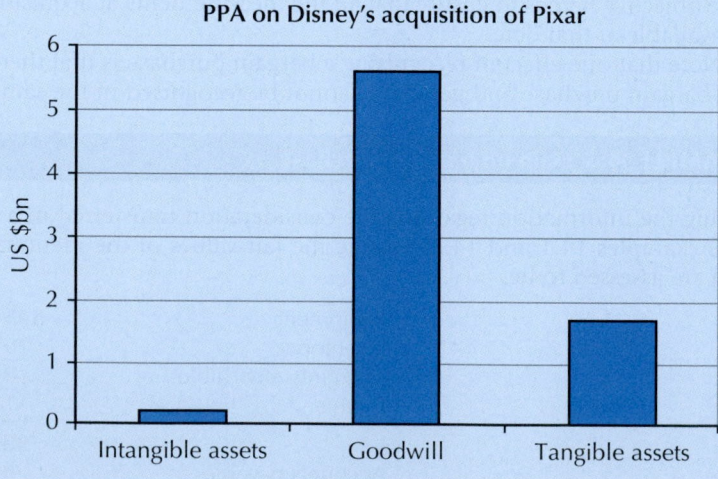

FIGURE 14.13 Separation of identifiable intangibles from goodwill (1)
Source: Intangible Business (2007, p. 21).

Google acquisition of YouTube ($1.2 bn)

Google acquired YouTube, the Internet video sharing company, in 2006 for $1.2 billion, of which $0.2 billion was allocated to intangible assets and $1.1 billion to goodwill (net tangible assets were negative). YouTube is the destination of choice for youngsters who want to share video content online. As such it depends largely on its brand name to attract subscribers. We are surprised that such a small proportion of the purchase price has been allocated to the brand. A possible conclusion from this is that the value given to the intangibles is too low or too much was paid for YouTube.

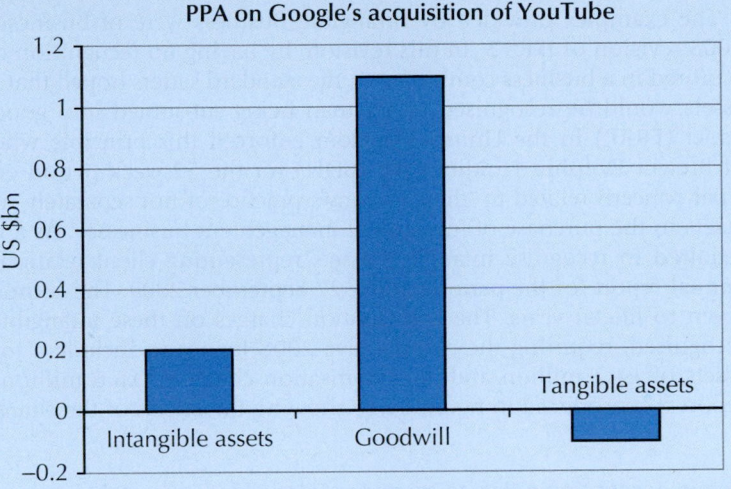

FIGURE 14.14 Separation of identifiable intangibles from goodwill (2)
Source: Intangible Business (2007, p. 22).

To provide a contrast, Intangible Business showed the results of PepsiCo's acquisition of the UK snack brand Wotsits. Figure 14.15 shows the dollars allocated to intangibles was far greater than those to goodwill.

PepsiCo's acquisition of Wotsits ($351 m)

Pepsi-Cola acquired the UK snack brand Wotsits and other smaller brands in 2002 for $0.4 billion, of which $0.2 billion was allocated to the brand and less than $0.1 billion to goodwill. Identified intangibles were 86% of total intangibles. The brand accounting for half the acquisition price seems a reasonable position and is significantly greater than the average of 28%.

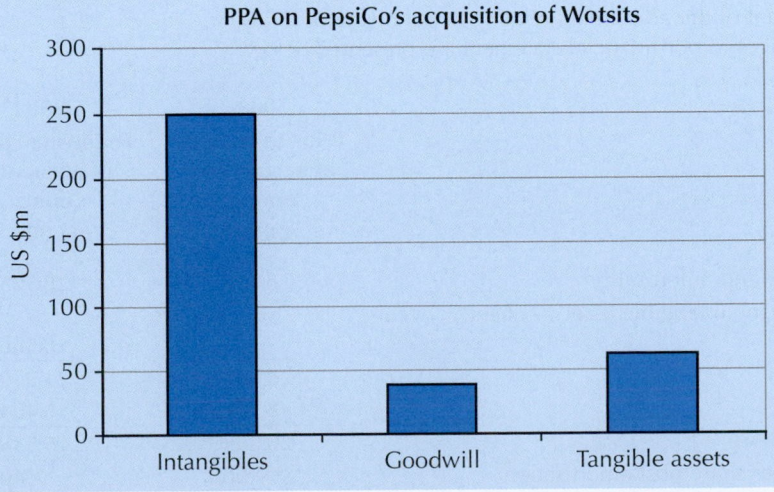

FIGURE 14.15 Separation of identifiable intangibles from goodwill (3)
Source: Intangible Business (2007, p. 15).

It may be argued that the application of IFRS 3 has made a difference. However, Forbes (2007, p. 9) states:

We analysed intangible asset values reported by the FTSE [Financial Times Stock Exchange] 100 companies in their most recent published reports and accounts. Of these companies, 89 had reported under IFRS. We analysed 84 of them, which valued assets and liabilities underlying business combinations with a total deal value of £39.8 billion. The relative allocation was goodwill — 53%; intangible assets — 30%; and tangible assets less liabilities — 17%.

The reason for not wanting to reduce goodwill and increase the recognition of intangibles, hopefully, is not simply that goodwill is not subject to amortisation under IFRS whereas most identifiable intangibles do not have indefinite useful lives.

The examples provided by Intangible Business were of business combinations occurring prior to the 2008 revision of IFRS 3. In this revision, by having no recognition criteria in relation to identifiable assets acquired in a business combination, the standard setters hoped that preparers would ensure that intangible assets would be recognised rather than being subsumed into goodwill. The Financial Reporting Review Panel (FRRP) in the United Kingdom enforced this principle when reviewing the report and accounts of Brewin Dolphin Holdings plc (BDH) for the 52-week period ending 30 June 2007. The FRRP's principal concern related to 'the company's practice of not separately recognising customer related intangible assets in the purchase of investment management businesses'. As a result of the FRRP's findings, BDH was required to recognise intangible assets representing client relationships separately from goodwill in its annual report for the period ending 27 September 2009. The company amortises client relationships over seven to fifteen years. The amortisation charges on these intangibles since they were acquired were also recognised, requiring the comparative 2008 figures to include a total amortisation charge for intangible assets of £4.2 million and an amortisation charge of £6.6 million in 2009. Note 4 of the 2009 annual report is reproduced in figure 14.16 showing the effects of the change in the company's policy.

FIGURE 14.16 Change in accounting policy to recognise intangibles separately from goodwill

4. Change in accounting policy

After a long and constructive dialogue with the Financial Reporting Review Panel the Group has considered the additional clarification which the forthcoming standard IFRS 3 (2008) brings to the recognition of intangible assets and the various practices currently applied by other firms in the purchase of investment management businesses, and has retrospectively changed its accounting policy. Payments to acquire teams of investment managers, bringing with them funds under management, have been re-classified as the intangible asset — client relationships, rather than goodwill. Similarly intangible assets representing client relationships acquired as part of business combinations have been recognised separately to goodwill. The new accounting policy is considered preferable as it brings us into line with our peers and is more transparent.

This new accounting policy has been applied retrospectively from the date of the Group's transition to IFRS and the comparative figures for 2008 in these financial statements have been restated.

Opening retained earnings as at 1 October 2007 have been reduced by £2.2m after deferred taxation which is the cumulative amount of the adjustment relating to periods prior to 2008.

The main changes to our financial statement are presented below:

	2009 Prior to change of accounting policy £000	2009 Following change of accounting policy £000	2008 Previously reported £000	2008 As restated £000
Profit before tax and amortisation	28 505	28 505	36 202	36 202
Amortisation of the intangible asset — client relationships	—	(6 566)	—	(4 244)
Profit before tax	28 505	21 939	36 202	31 958
Taxation	(8 242)	(6 404)	(11 127)	(9 939)
Profit after taxation	20 263	15 535	25 075	22 019
Basic earning per share post amortisation	9.6p	7.4p	12.2p	10.7p
Fully diluted earning per share post amortisation	9.4p	7.2p	11.7p	10.3p

FIGURE 14.16 (continued)

	2009 Prior to change of accounting policy £000	2009 Following change of accounting policy £000	2008 Previously reported £000	2008 As restated £000
Net assets	128 230	118 219	125 176	119 893
Intangible assets				
Goodwill	99 095	48 438	93 023	48 376
Client relationships	—	36 753	—	37 309
	99 095	85 191	93 023	85 685
Deferred tax asset/(liability)	(3 041)	852	(3 993)	(1 938)

Source: Brewin Dolphin Holdings plc (2009, p. 45).

14.6 SHARES ACQUIRED IN THE ACQUIREE

Where an entity acquires shares in another entity, rather than the net assets of that entity, the measurement of the initial investment in these financial assets is in accordance with IAS 39 *Financial Instruments: Recognition and Measurement*, i.e. at fair value plus transaction costs.

Transaction costs are defined in paragraph 9 of IAS 39 *Financial Instruments: Recognition and Measurement*, and according to paragraph AG13 of Appendix A of IAS 39 include fees and commission paid to agents, advisers, brokers and dealers; levies by regulatory agencies and securities exchanges; and transfer taxes and duties such as stamp duties.

If the investment in the other entity is such that the entity is classified as a subsidiary, an associate or an interest in a joint arrangement, then the investment is measured at the fair value of the consideration transferred. It is expected that in most exchanges the fair value of the shares acquired will equal the fair value of the consideration transferred.

Where an acquirer issued shares and gave up cash in exchange for the shares of an acquiree, the journal entry in the records of the acquirer is:

Shares in Acquiree	Dr	xxx	
Share Capital	Cr		xxx
Cash	Cr		xxx
(Acquisition of shares in another entity)			

ILLUSTRATIVE EXAMPLE 14.4 Acquisition of shares in an acquiree

Assume that on 1 January 2013 Salmon Ltd acquired all the issued shares in Whiting Ltd for $80 000, giving in exchange $10 000 cash and 20 000 shares in Salmon Ltd; the latter having a fair value of $3.50 per share. Transaction costs of $500 were paid in cash. Share issue costs were $1000. The journal entries in the records of Salmon Ltd at the acquisition date are as shown in figure 14.17.

Shares in Whiting Ltd	Dr	80 000	
Cash	Cr		10 000
Share Capital	Cr		70 000
(Acquisition of shares in Whiting Ltd)			
Shares in Whiting Ltd	Dr	500	
Cash	Cr		500
(Transaction costs)			
Share Capital	Dr	1 000	
Cash	Cr		1 000
(Costs of issuing shares to Whiting Ltd)			

FIGURE 14.17 Accounting for the acquisition of shares

14.6.1 Existence of a previously held equity interest

In illustrative example 14.4, the acquirer acquired all issued shares of the acquiree in one transaction. An alternative situation could occur where the acquirer obtained its controlling interest in the acquirer by acquiring further shares and thereby adding to its previously held equity interest. For example, in illustrative example 14.4, Salmon Ltd may have previously held 20% of the shares in Whiting Ltd on 1 January 2013, and at that date acquired the remaining 80% of the shares of Whiting Ltd. As a business combination occurs when the acquirer obtains control of the acquiree, it is on the date of the second acquisition of shares that the business combination occurs. In IFRS 3, this is referred to as a business combination achieved in stages — sometimes called a step acquisition. Obviously, there may be a number of step purchases of shares in the acquiree prior to the obtaining of control. Each of the steps prior to the date where the acquirer obtains control will be accounted for as in illustrative example 14.4; that is, the acquirer will recognise an investment in the acquiree with each step acquisition being measured at fair value.

It is also possible, of course, that the acquirer may obtain control of the acquiree without making a further step acquisition. For example, the composition of the non-controlling interest may change such that the acquirer becomes the controlling entity — see chapter 23 for further discussion on control.

The accounting for a step acquisition is given in paragraph 42 of IFRS 3:

> In a business combination achieved in stages, the acquirer shall remeasure its previously held equity interest in the acquiree at its acquisition-date fair value and recognise the resulting gain or loss, if any, in profit or loss or other comprehensive income, as appropriate.

Using the situation in illustrative example 14.4, but assuming that prior to acquiring 80% of the shares of Whiting on 1 January 2013, Salmon Ltd had acquired 20% of Whiting Ltd's shares on 1 January 2012 for $10 000 and this investment had a $16 000 fair value at 1 January 2013, at 1 January 2013 Salmon Ltd would then record the following entry to revalue its previously held investment in Whiting Ltd:

Shares in Whiting Ltd	Dr	6 000	
Gain (Profit or loss)	Cr		6 000
(Remeasurement of previously held equity interest on business combination)			

As noted in paragraph 42 of IFRS 3, where the acquirer presents subsequent changes in fair value of the investment in other comprehensive income, then the accounting for the amounts recognised in equity will be the same as if the equity interest was sold — in essence transferred to profit or loss. According to IAS 1 *Presentation of Financial Statements*, paragraph 7, amounts transferred to profit or loss in the current period that were recognised in other comprehensive income in the current or previous periods are called reclassification adjustments.

Figure 14.18 contains the information provided in Note 5 to the 30 June 2009 financial report of the Royal Automobile Club of Western Australia concerning its step acquisition of RAC Insurance Pty Ltd.

FIGURE 14.18 Step acquisition

Note 5

Business combination

(a) Summary of acquisition

On 5 August 2008 RACI Pty Ltd acquired the remaining 50% of the issued shares in RAC Insurance Pty Ltd, a personal lines general insurer, for a cash consideration of $104 650 000 (excluding direct costs). RACI Pty Ltd now owns 100% of the issued shares of RAC Insurance Pty Ltd.

Details of the purchase consideration [consideration transferred], the fair value of the assets and liabilities acquired and goodwill are as follows:

	$'000
Purchase consideration (refer to (b) below):	
Cash paid	104 650
Total consideration transferred	104 650
Fair value of equity interest in RAC Insurance Pty Ltd held before the business combination (refer to (d) below)	104 650
Total net assets	**209 300**
Acquisition related costs (included in consulting expenses) in the income statement for the year ended 30 June 2009	2 425

FIGURE 14.18 (continued)

The fair value of net identifiable assets and goodwill have been recognised in the balance sheet at 100% in accordance with AASB 3 [equivalent to IFRS 3] and a fair value gain on revaluation of the initial 50% shareholding recognised in the income statement.

(b) Purchase consideration

	Consolidated	
	2009	2008
	$'000	$'000
Outflow of cash to acquire subsidiary net of cash acquired		
Cash consideration	104 650	—
Less: Balances acquired		
Cash	3 047	
Outflow of cash	101 603	

(c) Assets and liabilities acquired

. . .

(d) Fair value gain on revaluation of equity accounted joint venture

	$'000
Acquisition date fair value of 50% equity interest immediately before acquisition date (refer (a) above)	104 650
Less: equity accounted investment value as at 5 August 2008	(43 310)
Fair value gain on revaluation of equity accounted joint venture included in income statement	61 340

Source: RAC WA (2009, pp. 59–69).

14.7 ACCOUNTING IN THE RECORDS OF THE ACQUIREE

Where the acquirer purchases the acquiree's assets and liabilities, the acquiree may continue in existence or may liquidate. The acquiree accounts affected by the business combination will differ according to the actions of the acquiree.

14.7.1 Acquiree does not liquidate

In the situation where the acquiree disposes of a business, the journal entries required in the records of the acquiree are shown in figure 14.19. Under IAS 16 *Property, Plant and Equipment*, when an item of property, plant and equipment is sold, gains or losses are recognised in the statement of profit or loss and other comprehensive income. Similarly, on the sale of a business, the acquiree recognises a gain or loss.

FIGURE 14.19 Journal entries of acquiree on sale of business

Receivable from Acquirer	Dr	xxx	
Liability A	Dr	xxx	
Liability B	Dr	xxx	
Liability C	Dr	xxx	
Asset A	Cr		xxx
Asset B	Cr		xxx
Asset C	Cr		xxx
Gain on Sale of Operation	Cr		xxx
(Sale of operation)			

(continued)

FIGURE 14.19 *(continued)*

Shares in Acquirer	Dr	xxx	
Cash	Dr	xxx	
Receivable from Acquirer	Cr		xxx
(Receipt of consideration from acquirer)			

14.7.2 Acquiree liquidates

The entries required in the records of the acquiree when it sells *all* its net assets to the acquirer are shown in figure 14.20. The accounts of the acquiree are transferred to two accounts, the Liquidation account and the Shareholders' Distribution account.

To the *Liquidation account* are transferred:
- all assets taken over by the acquirer, including cash if relevant, as well as any assets not taken over and which have a zero value, including goodwill
- all liabilities taken over
- the expenses of liquidation if paid by the acquiree
- additional expenses to be paid by the acquiree but not previously recognised by the acquiree
- consideration from the acquirer as proceeds on sale of net assets
- all reserves, including retained earnings.

The balance of the Liquidation account is then transferred to the Shareholders' Distribution account.

FIGURE 14.20 Journal entries of acquiree on liquidation after sale of net assets

Liquidation	Dr	xxx	
Asset A	Cr		xxx
Asset B	Cr		xxx
Asset C	Cr		xxx
(Transfer of all assets acquired by acquirer, at their carrying amounts)			
Liability A	Dr	xxx	
Liability B	Dr	xxx	
Liability C	Dr	xxx	
Liquidation	Cr		xxx
(Transfer of all liabilities assumed by the acquirer)			
Liquidation	Dr	xxx	
Cash	Cr		xxx
(Liquidation and other expenses not recognised previously, if paid by the acquiree)			
Receivable from Acquirer	Dr	xxx	
Liquidation	Cr		xxx
(Consideration for net assets sold)			
Cash	Dr	xxx	
Shares in Acquirer	Dr	xxx	
Receivable from Acquirer	Cr		xxx
(Receipt of consideration)			
Other Reserves	Dr	xxx	
Retained Earnings	Dr	xxx	
Liquidation	Cr		xxx
(Transfer of reserves)			
Liquidation	Dr	xxx	
Shareholders' Distribution	Cr		xxx
(Transfer of balance of liquidation)			

FIGURE 14.20 (continued)

Share Capital	Dr	xxx	
Shareholders' Distribution	Cr		xxx
(Transfer of share capital)			
Shareholders' Distribution	Dr	xxx	
Cash	Cr		xxx
Shares in Acquirer	Cr		xxx
(Distribution of consideration to shareholders)			

To the *Shareholders' Distribution* account are transferred:
- the balance of share capital
- the balance of the Liquidation account
- the portion of the consideration received from the acquirer that is distributed to the shareholders. Some of the consideration received by the acquiree may be used to pay for liabilities not assumed by the acquirer, and for liquidation expenses.

ILLUSTRATIVE EXAMPLE 14.5 Entries in the acquiree's records

Using the information from illustrative example 14.1 on pages 518–19, the entries in the records of Whiting Ltd are shown in figure 14.21.

FIGURE 14.21 Liquidation of acquiree

Liquidation	Dr	69 500	
Accumulated Depreciation – Equipment	Dr	10 000	
Equipment	Cr		42 000
Inventory	Cr		18 000
Accounts Receivable	Cr		16 000
Patents	Cr		3 500
(Assets taken over)			
Accounts Payable	Dr	8 000	
Liquidation	Cr		8 000
(Liabilities taken over)			
Liquidation	Dr	350	
Liquidation Expenses Payable	Cr		350
(Liquidation expenses payable by acquiree)			
Liquidation	Dr	80	
Debenture Holders Payable	Cr		80
(Premium expense on debentures to be paid on redemption)			
Receivable from Salmon Ltd	Dr	76 562	
Liquidation	Cr		76 562
(Consideration receivable)			
Cash	Dr	13 680	
Shares in Salmon Ltd	Dr	57 200	
Receivable from Salmon Ltd	Cr		70 880
(Receipt of consideration from acquirer)			
Retained Earnings	Dr	21 500	
Liquidation	Cr		21 500
(Transfer of retained earnings)			

(continued)

FIGURE 14.21 *(continued)*

Liquidation	Dr	36 132	
Shareholders' Distribution	Cr		36 132
(Balance of liquidation account transferred to shareholders' distribution)			
Share Capital – Ordinary	Dr	30 000	
Share Capital – Preference	Dr	6 000	
Shareholders' Distribution	Cr		36 000
(Transfer of share capital)			
Debentures	Dr	4 000	
Debenture Holders Payable	Cr		4 000
(Transfer of debentures to payable account)			
Liquidation Expenses Payable	Dr	350	
Debenture Holders Payable	Dr	4 080	
Cash	Cr		4 430
(Payment of liabilities)			
Shareholders' Distribution	Dr	72 132	
Cash	Cr		9 250
Shares in Salmon Ltd	Cr		57 200
Receivable from Salmon Ltd	Cr		5 682
(Payment to shareholders)			

14.7.3 Acquirer buys only shares in the acquiree

When the acquirer buys only shares in the acquiree, there are no entries in the records of the acquiree because the transaction is between the acquirer and the shareholders of the acquiree entity. The acquiree itself is not involved.

14.8 SUBSEQUENT ADJUSTMENTS TO THE INITIAL ACCOUNTING FOR A BUSINESS COMBINATION

Three areas where adjustments may need to be made subsequent to the initial accounting after acquisition date are:
- goodwill
- contingent liabilities
- contingent consideration.

Goodwill

Having recognised goodwill arising in the business combination, the subsequent accounting is directed from other accounting standards:
- goodwill is not subject to amortisation but is subject to an annual impairment test as detailed in IAS 36 *Impairment of Assets* (see chapter 15).
- goodwill cannot be revalued because IAS 38 *Intangible Assets* does not allow the recognition of internally generated goodwill.

Contingent liabilities

Having recognised any contingent liabilities of the acquiree as liabilities, the acquirer must then determine a subsequent measurement for the liability. The liability is initially recognised at fair value. Subsequent to acquisition date, according to paragraph 56 of IFRS 3, the liability is measured as the higher of:

(a) the amount that would be recognised in accordance with IAS 37; and
(b) the amount initially recognised less, if appropriate, cumulative amortisation recognised in accordance with IAS 18 *Revenue*.

Under IAS 37 paragraph 36, the liability would be measured at the best estimate of the expenditure required to settle the present obligation at the end of the reporting period. This would be used, for example, where a liability was recognised in relation to a court case. However, the IASB was also concerned about contingent liabilities such as guarantees or other financial liabilities. Under IAS 39 paragraph 47, the subsequent measurement of financial liabilities requires preparers to use the higher of the IAS 37 measurements and the amount initially recognised subject to amortisation in line with IAS 18. In order for IFRS 3 to be consistent with IAS 39, the measurement method to be used in subsequent accounting for contingent liabilities was made the same as that in IAS 39.

Contingent consideration

At acquisition date, the contingent consideration is measured at fair value, and is classified either as equity (e.g. the requirement for the acquirer to issue more shares subject to subsequent events) or as a liability (e.g. the requirement to provide more cash subject to subsequent events). Subsequent to the business combination, paragraph 54 of IFRS 3 requires the accounting for contingent consideration to be in accordance with the accounting standard that would normally apply to these accounts. However, IFRS 3 provides guidance on the measures to be used.

Where the contingent consideration is classified as equity, no remeasurement is required, and the subsequent settlement is accounted for within equity (IFRS 3 paragraph 58(a)). This means that if extra equity instruments are issued they are effectively issued for no consideration and there is no change to share capital.

Where the contingent consideration is a financial liability, it will be accounted for under IAS 39 and measured at fair value with movements being accounted for in accordance with that standard. If it is a liability not within the scope of IAS 39, it is accounted for in accordance with IAS 37. So, if there were changes in the amount of an expected cash outflow, the liability would be adjusted and an amount recognised in profit or loss.

It should be noted that the subsequent accounting for contingent consideration is to treat it as a post-acquisition event; that is, not affecting the measurements made at acquisition date. Hence, any subsequent adjustments do not affect the goodwill calculated at acquisition date.

ILLUSTRATIVE EXAMPLE 14.6 Comprehensive example

Labrador Ltd's major business is in the pet food industry. It makes a number of canned pet foods, mainly for cats and dogs, as well as having a very promising line in dry dog food. It has been interested for some time in the operations of Pelican Ltd, an entity that deals with the processing of grain products for a number of other industries including flour-processing, health foods and, in more recent times, the production of grain products for feeding birds. Given its interest in the pet food industry and its desire to stay as one of the leaders in this area, Labrador Ltd began negotiations with Pelican Ltd to acquire its birdseed product division.

Negotiations began in July 2013. After months of discussion between the relevant parties of both companies, an agreement was reached on 15 February 2014 for Labrador Ltd to acquire the birdseed division. The agreement document was taken to the board of directors of Pelican Ltd who ratified the agreement on 1 March 2014. The net assets were exchanged on this date.

The net assets of the birdseed division at 1 March 2014, showing the carrying amounts at that date and the fair values as estimated by Labrador Ltd from documentation supplied by Pelican Ltd, were as shown below:

	Carrying amount	Fair value
Plant and equipment	$160 000	$167 000
Land	70 000	75 000
Motor vehicles	30 000	32 000
Inventory	24 000	28 000
Accounts receivable	18 000	16 000
Total assets	302 000	318 000
Accounts payable	35 000	35 000
Bank overdraft	55 000	55 000
Total liabilities	90 000	90 000
Net assets	$212 000	$228 000

Details of the consideration Labrador Ltd agreed to provide in exchange for the net assets of the division are described below:

- 100 000 shares in Labrador Ltd — movements in the share price were as follows:

1 July 2013	$1.00
1 October 2013	1.10
1 January 2014	1.15
1 February 2014	1.30
15 February 2014	1.32
16 February 2014	1.45
1 March 2014	1.50

- Because of doubts as to whether it could sustain a share price of at least $1.50, Labrador Ltd agreed to supply cash to the value of any decrease in the share price below $1.50 for the 100 000 shares issued, this guarantee of the share price lasting until 31 July. Labrador Ltd believed that there was a 90% chance that the share price would remain at $1.50 or higher and a 10% chance that it would fall to $1.48.
- Cash of $40 000, half to be paid on the date of acquisition and half in one year's time.
- Supply of a patent relating to the manufacture of packing material. This has a fair value of $60 000 but has not been recognised in the records of Labrador Ltd because it resulted from an internally generated research project.
- Pelican Ltd was currently being sued for damages relating to a claim by a bird breeder who had bought some seed from the company, and claimed that this resulted in the death of some prime breeding pigeons. Labrador Ltd agreed to pay any resulting damages in relation to the court case. The expected damages were $40 000. Lawyers estimated that there was only a 20% chance of losing the case.

Labrador Ltd supplied the cash on the acquisition date as well as surrendering the patent. The shares were issued on 5 March, and the costs of issuing the shares amounted to $1000. The incremental borrowing rate for Labrador Ltd is 10% p.a. Acquisition-related costs paid by Labrador Ltd in relation to the acquisition amounted to $5000.

On 31 July the share price of Labrador Ltd's shares was $1.52.

Required

Prepare the journal entries in the records of the acquirer.

Solution

Acquisition analysis

Net fair value of assets acquired and liabilities assumed		
Plant and equipment		$167 000
Land		75 000
Motor vehicles		32 000
Inventory		28 000
Accounts receivable		16 000
		318 000
Accounts payable		35 000
Bank overdraft		55 000
Provision for damages (20% × $40 000)		8 000
		98 000
		$220 000
Consideration transferred		
Purchase consideration:		
Shares:	100 000 × $1.50	$150 000
Guarantee:	10% ($1.50 − $1.48) × 100 000	200
Cash:	Payable now	20 000
	Deferred ($20 000 × 0.909 091)	18 182
Patent		60 000
		$248 382
Goodwill ($248 382 − $220 000)		$ 28 382

The journal entries of the acquirer, Labrador Ltd, are shown in figure 14.22.

2014				
March 1	Plant and Equipment	Dr	167 000	
	Land	Dr	75 000	
	Motor Vehicles	Dr	32 000	
	Inventory	Dr	28 000	
	Accounts Receivable	Dr	16 000	
	Goodwill	Dr	28 382	
	Accounts Payable	Cr		35 000
	Bank Overdraft	Cr		55 000
	Provision for Damages	Cr		8 000
	Share Capital	Cr		150 000
	Provision for Loss in Value of Shares	Cr		200
	Cash	Cr		20 000
	Consideration Payable	Cr		18 182
	Gain on Sale of Patent	Cr		60 000
	(Acquisition of birdseed division from Pelican Ltd)			
	Acquisition-Related Expenses	Dr	5 000	
	Cash	Cr		5 000
	(Acquisition-related costs)			
March 5	Share Capital	Dr	1 000	
	Cash	Cr		1 000
	(Costs of issuing shares)			
July 31	Provision for Loss in Value of Shares	Dr	200	
	Gain	Cr		200
	(Contingency not having to be paid)			

FIGURE 14.22 Journal entries of the acquirer

14.9 DISCLOSURE — BUSINESS COMBINATIONS

Paragraphs 59–63 of IFRS 3 contain information on disclosures required in relation to business combinations. To meet these disclosure requirements it is necessary to apply Appendix B of IFRS 3, which is an integral part of IFRS 3 containing application guidance.

Paragraph 59 requires entities to disclose information about the nature and financial effect of business combinations occurring during the current reporting period, or after the end of the reporting period but before the financial statements are authorised for issue. Paragraphs B64–B66 contain information to assist preparers to meet the disclosure objective in paragraph 59.

Note the qualitative information required to be disclosed under paragraph B64. In particular, note B64(d) which requires disclosure of the primary reasons for the business combination as well as a description of how the acquirer obtained control of the acquiree. This information should assist users to evaluate the success of the business combination and judge the ability of management to make investment decisions.

Also note that paragraph B64(e) requires disclosure of 'a qualitative description of the factors that make up goodwill recognised, such as expected synergies from combining operations of the acquiree and the acquirer, intangible assets that do not qualify for separate recognition or other factors'. Goodwill is not to be considered just a residual calculation. As explained in section 14.5.3, core goodwill can consist of elements such as combination goodwill and going-concern goodwill. An understanding of where the synergies exist will assist management in managing the earnings from goodwill as well as in any later impairment tests of goodwill (see chapter 15 for more details concerning impairment testing). Unrecognised intangible assets may also be included in goodwill (see chapter 13 for information on accounting for intangible assets in a business combination).

Paragraph 61 of IFRS 3 requires the disclosure of information to assist in the evaluation of the financial effects of adjustments recognised in the current period that relate to business combinations occurring in previous periods. Paragraph B67 details disclosures required in meet the information objective in paragraph 61.

An example of the required disclosures is provided in figure 14.23.

FIGURE 14.23 Disclosures required by Labrador Ltd under IFRS 3

26. Business combinations			IFRS 3 paragraph
Acquisition of division from Pelican Ltd			
During the current reporting period, the company acquired the birdseed division of Pelican Ltd. The acquisition date was 1 March 2014. The company has not had to dispose of any operations as a result of this combination. The primary reason for the business combination was to gain synergies in terms of the sales outlets for products sold by both entities.			*B64(a)* *B64(b)* *B64(d)*
The consideration transferred to Pelican Ltd was $248 382. The components of the cost were:			*B64(f)*
Shares in the company		$150 000	
Cash paid and payable		38 182	
Patent for packaging		60 000	
Guarantee relating to the maintenance of the company's share price		200	*B64(g)(i)*
The contingent consideration — the guarantee — was measured at acquisition date at $200 being based on an analysis of probable movements in share prices and budgeted information on future sales. The company issued 100 000 shares, determining a fair value of $1.50 based on the current market price of the company at 1 March 2014 as reported by the stock exchange.			*B64(g)(ii)* *B64(f)(iv)*
The assets acquired and liabilities assumed from Pelican Ltd were, as at 1 March 2014:			*B64(i)*

	Carrying amount	Fair value	
Plant and equipment	$160 000	$167 000	
Land	70 000	75 000	
Motor vehicles	30 000	32 000	
Inventory	24 000	28 000	
Accounts receivable	18 000	16 000	
	302 000	318 000	
Accounts payable	35 000	35 000	
Bank overdraft	55 000	55 000	
	90 000	90 000	
Contingent liability acquired	8 000	8 000	
		98 000	
Net assets acquired		$220 000	

Goodwill of $28 382 was recognised in the acquisition, the extra consideration being paid due to the excellent reputation and customer following relating to the quality of the birdseed products.			*B64(e)*
An adjustment of $2000 was made to the fair value of the plant and equipment and goodwill subsequent to the acquisition due to the provisional nature of the fair value of some of the specialised equipment determined at acquisition date.			*B67(a)*
The contingent liability acquired related to a court case involving a claim from a customer that certain bird food was of poor quality. If the court case were lost, which is not expected, the damages could be $40 000. A present obligation is regarded as existing at the end of the reporting period.			*B64(j)*

FIGURE 14.23 *(continued)*

Subsequent to the end of the reporting period, the provision in relation to the company's guarantee in relation to maintenance of the share price expired. No extra payment was required, as the share price had been maintained.	*B64(g)(iii)*
Acquisition-related costs amounted to $5 000, all of which was recognised as an expense against the line item 'operating expenses'. Share issue costs of $1000 were treated as a reduction in share capital.	*B64(m)*

Acquisition of shares in Cages Ltd

On 1 August 2013, the company acquired 100% of the shares in Cages Ltd, a company involved mainly in manufacturing bird cages, for $100 000. The primary reason for acquiring the company was to expand the variety of products sold to customers in the same industry. The consideration paid was cash.   *B64(a),(b),(c)*   *B64(d)*   *B64(f)*

The assets and liabilities of Cages Ltd at acquisition date were: *B64(i)*

	Carrying amount	Fair value
Plant and equipment	$ 82 000	$ 88 000
Vehicles	22 000	20 000
Cash	12 000	12 000
Accounts receivable	8 000	7 000
	124 000	127 000
Accounts payable	32 000	32 000
Net assets	$ 92 000	$ 95 000

Goodwill of $5000 was acquired, attributable to a quality, well-trained workforce. The consolidated revenue for the consolidated group is $952 000. If the business combinations occurring during the year had occurred on 1 July 2013 instead of during the year, it is estimated that consolidated revenue would have been $985 000. The consolidated profit under the same assumption would have been $322 000 instead of $299 000.   *B64(e)*   *B64(q)*

27. Goodwill

	2014	2013	
Gross amount at beginning of period	$20 600	$19 600	*B67(d)(i)*
Accumulated impairment losses	500	300	
	20 100	19 300	
Goodwill acquired	35 380	3 000	*B67(d)(ii)*
	55 480	22 300	
Adjustments — tax assets recognised	—	2 000	*B67(d)(iii)*
		20 300	
Impairment losses for current period	—	200	*B67(d)(iv)*
Carrying amount at end of period	$55 480	$20 100	
Consisting of:			*B67(d)(viii)*
Gross amount at end of period	$55 980	$20 600	
Accumulated impairment losses	500	500	
	$55 480	$20 100	

Figure 14.24 contains the disclosures provided by the Billabong International Limited in its 2011 annual report concerning its business combinations.

FIGURE 14.24 Disclosures of business combinations

Note 35. Business combinations

Purchase consideration — cash outflow

	2011 $'000	2010 $'000
Outflow of cash to acquire subsidiary, net of cash acquired		
Cash consideration	203 610	9 894
Less: Cash balances acquired	(258)	(434)
Add-back: Bank overdraft	3 461	—
	206 813	9 460
Payments relating to prior year acquisitions and other immaterial current year acquisitions	8 251	40 131
Outflow of cash — investing activities	215 064	49 591

Acquisition related costs

Acquisition related costs of $8.8 million (2010: $3.9 million) are included in 'other expenses' in the income statement and in 'operating activities' in the cash flow statement. Of this amount $3.2 million relates to the acquisition of 'West 49 Inc.' and $5.2 million relates to the 'Bay Action, RVCA, Surfection, SDS/Jetty Surf and Rush Surf' acquisitions disclosed in aggregate below. The remaining $0.4 million relates to other immaterial current year acquisitions.

2011

West 49 Inc.

(a) Summary of acquisitions

On 1 September 2010 Billabong International Limited acquired 100% of the shares of West 49 Inc., a leading Canadian specialty retailer of apparel, footwear, accessories and equipment related to the youth action sports lifestyle. The acquisition has increased the Group's market share in Canada.

Details of the purchase consideration, the net assets acquired and goodwill are as follows:

	$'000
Purchase consideration:	
Cash paid	94 038
Total purchase consideration	94 038

The assets and liabilities recognised as a result of the acquisition are as follows:

	Fair value $'000
Other receivables	1 224
Inventory	36 590
Plant and equipment	19 894
Prepayments	704
Deferred tax assets	1 262
Bank overdrafts	(3 461)
Trade and other payables	(54 640)
Provision for contingent tax liabilities	(19 581)
Identifiable intangible assets	286
Net identifiable assets acquired	(17 722)
Add: Goodwill	111 760
Net assets acquired	94 038

Provision for contingent tax liabilities represents contingent liabilities recognised at fair value. The assessment of the amount of contingent tax liabilities involves the exercise of management judgements concerning potential future events.

FIGURE 14.24 *(continued)*

Goodwill is attributable to the workforce and synergies expected to arise after the acquisition of the business.

The above accounting in regards to the 'West 49 Inc.' acquisition has been determined provisionally pending a review of the fair value of identifiable assets and liabilities.

The acquired business contributed revenues of $152.8 million and net loss after tax (including $3.2 million of acquisition related costs) of $5.6 million to the Group for the period from acquisition to 30 June 2011.

Bay Action, RVCA, Surfection, SDS/Jetty Surf and Rush Surf

(a) Summary of acquisitions

On 2 July 2010 GSM (Operations) Pty Ltd and Pineapple Trademarks Pty Ltd acquired the assets and certain liabilities of Bay Action Pty Ltd, Byron Concepts Pty Ltd, Big Kahoona Pty Ltd and the Timperley Partnership, a number of retail stores primarily featuring surf and related lifestyle apparel and accessories. The acquisition has increased the Group's market share in the Australian retail sector.

On 21 July 2010 Seal Trademarks Pty Ltd, GSM Add 2, Inc. and GSM Investments Ltd acquired the assets and certain liabilities of RVCA Corporation, RVCA Platform, LLC, VASF LLC and RVCA LA, LLC, a progressive art and design-driven brand. The acquisition has provided the opportunity to further expand the North American and international sales representation through the Group's distribution network.

On 23 September 2010 GSM (Operations) Pty Ltd acquired 50% of the issued share capital of Surfection Pty Ltd, a retail chain primarily featuring surf and related lifestyle apparel and accessories, and control of the entity through the acquisition of greater than 50% of the voting rights. The acquisition has increased the Group's market share in the Australian retail sector. Surfection Pty Ltd has been fully consolidated from the date on which control was transferred to the Group.

On 8 November 2010 Board Sports Retail Pty Ltd and Pineapple Trademarks Pty Ltd acquired the assets and certain liabilities of Jetty Surf Pty Ltd, a retail chain operating under the banners SDS and Jetty Surf, primarily featuring surf and related lifestyle apparel and accessories. The acquisition has increased the Group's market share in the Australian retail sector.

On 26 November 2010 GSM (Operations) Pty Ltd and Pineapple Trademarks Pty Ltd acquired the assets and certain liabilities of Rush Lifestyle Australia Pty Ltd, Rush Lifestyle Clothing Australia Pty Ltd and W R James Pty Ltd, a retail chain primarily featuring surf and related lifestyle apparel and accessories. The acquisition has increased the Group's market share in the Australian retail sector.

	$'000
Purchase consideration:	
Cash paid	109 572
Deferred consideration	37 783
Contingent consideration	40 388
Total purchase consideration	187 743

The assets and liabilities recognised as a result of the acquisitions are as follows:

	Fair value $'000
Cash and cash equivalents	258
Trade and other receivables	6 200
Inventory	30 776
Plant and equipment	7 638
Prepayments	230
Deferred tax assets	5 428
Employee entitlements	(1 248)
Trade and other payables	(29 064)
Deferred tax liabilities	(13)
Identifiable intangible assets	30 293
Net identifiable assets acquired	50 498
Less: Non-controlling interests	(3 649)
Add: Goodwill	140 894
Net assets acquired	187 743

(continued)

FIGURE 14.24 *(continued)*

Goodwill is attributable to the workforce and synergies expected to arise after the acquisition of the businesses. Goodwill is only deductible in the United States of America for tax purposes. For acquisitions that occurred in the year ended 30 June 2011, up to $75.8 million will be deductible for tax purposes.

The acquired businesses contributed revenues of $160.5 million and net profit after tax and non-controlling interests (including $5.2 million of acquisition related costs) of $5.2 million to the Group for the period from the date of each acquisition to 30 June 2011.

(i) Deferred and contingent consideration

In relation to the acquisition of the assets and certain liabilities of RVCA Corporation, RVCA Platform, LLC, VASF LLC and RVCA LA, LLC, additional deferred and contingent consideration will be payable in cash on or after 1 July 2015 based on the earnings achieved for the year ending 30 June 2015. In relation to the acquisition of the assets and certain liabilities of Jetty Surf Pty Ltd, additional pre-determined deferred consideration will be payable in cash from 1 November 2013. As at their respective acquisition dates a present value amount totalling $78.2 million was recognised as a non-current deferred consideration liability for these acquisitions of which $37.8 million is deferred and $40.4 million is contingent consideration. The aggregated range of the contingent consideration is a minimum of nil and there is no prescribed maximum.

(ii) Acquired receivables

The fair value of acquired trade and other receivables is $7.4 million. The gross contractual amount of the acquired trade receivables is $9.9 million and an amount of $2.5 million is considered to be uncollectible as at the acquisition date.

(iii) Non-controlling interests

The Group elected to recognise the non-controlling interests for Surfection Pty Ltd at fair value.

(iv) Revenue and profit contribution

If the acquisitions had occurred on 1 July 2010, consolidated revenue and consolidated net profit after tax and non-controlling interests (including acquisition related costs) for the year ended 30 June 2011 would have been $1770.5 million and $114.0 million respectively based on best estimates.

2010

(a) Summary of acquisition

On 1 November 2009 GSM Online Retail, Inc. and Seal Trademarks Pty Ltd acquired the assets and certain liabilities of Swell Commerce, Inc., a leading online retailer in the US boardsport sector. The acquisition has increased the Group's market share in the US online boardsports retail sector.

On 1 December 2009 GSM (Operations) Pty Ltd acquired 20% of the issued share capital of Surfstitch Pty Ltd, a leading Australian online boardsport retailer, and control of the entity through the acquisition of greater than 50% of the voting rights. The acquisition has increased the Group's market share in the Australian online boardsports retail sector.

Surfstitch Pty Ltd has been fully consolidated from the date on which control was transferred to the Group. GSM (Operations) Pty Ltd has put and call options to acquire the remaining 80% of the business.

From 1 January 2010 GSM (Europe) Pty Ltd has acquired the DaKine distribution rights from distributors of DaKine products in Austria, Belgium, France, Germany and Luxembourg. GSM (Europe) Pty Ltd now has exclusive rights to distribute DaKine products in these countries.

On 23 April 2010 GSM (Europe) Pty Ltd and GSM Czech Republic s.r.o. acquired the assets and certain liabilities of OTTY s.r.o. a company duly established and existing in accordance with the laws of the Czech Republic. The acquisition has increased the Group's market share in Europe.

On 1 May 2010 Billabong Retail, Inc. and Seal Trademarks Pty Ltd acquired the assets and certain liabilities of Becker Surf Boards, Inc., a US retail chain featuring surf and related lifestyle apparel and accessories. The acquisition has increased the Group's market share in the US retail sector.

FIGURE 14.24 *(continued)*

Details of the aggregated purchase consideration, the net assets acquired and goodwill are as follows:

	$'000
Purchase consideration:	
Cash paid	9 894
Estimated cash payable	2 699
Contingent consideration	7 277
Total purchase consideration	19 870

The assets and liabilities recognised as a result of the acquisition are as follows:

	Fair value $'000
Cash and cash equivalents	434
Trade receivables	122
Inventory	6 194
Plant and equipment	1 117
Prepayments	476
Deferred tax assets	203
Employee entitlements	(162)
Trade and other payables	(5 745)
Deferred tax liabilities	(112)
Identifiable intangible assets	212
Net identifiable assets acquired	2 739
Less: Non-controlling interests	(1 642)
Add: Goodwill	18 773
Net assets acquired	19 870

Goodwill is attributable to the workforce and synergies expected to arise after the acquisition of the businesses. Goodwill is only deductible in the United States of America for tax purposes. For acquisitions that occurred in the year ended 30 June 2010, up to US$10.1 million will be deductible for tax purposes.

(i) Contingent consideration
In relation to the acquisition of the assets and certain liabilities of Swell Commerce, Inc., in the event that certain pre-determined earnings targets are achieved for the year ended 30 June 2012, additional consideration of between US$0 and up to a maximum of US$7 million may be payable in cash.

(ii) Acquired receivables
The fair value of acquired trade receivables is $0.1 million. The gross contractual amount is equal to the fair value of the acquired trade receivables. There were no acquired trade receivables that are expected to be uncollectible.

(iii) Non-controlling interests
In accordance with the accounting policy set out in note 1(h), the Group elected to recognise the non-controlling interests in Surfstitch Pty Ltd as its proportionate share of the acquired net identifiable assets.

(iv) Option to acquire
In February 2010, the Group entered into an exclusive 10-year agreement to license the California-based skateboard brand, Plan B. In addition to the license agreement, on 25 February 2010 Seal Trademarks Pty Ltd and CMDW, Inc signed a Purchase Option Agreement for the purchase of the Intellectual Property of

(continued)

FIGURE 14.24 *(continued)*

Plan B Skateboards. The option period is from the date of the agreement, being 25 February 2010, until 5:00 pm on the day 10 years later, unless earlier lapsed and can be exercised by Seal Trademarks Pty Ltd at any time during the option period.

(v) Revenue and profit contribution
The acquired businesses contributed revenues of $22.0 million and net profit after tax and non-controlling interests of $2.3 million to the Group for the period from each acquisition to 30 June 2010.

   If the acquisitions had occurred on 1 July 2009, consolidated revenue and consolidated net profit after tax and non-controlling interests for the year ended 30 June 2010 would have been $1502.5 million and $145.7 million respectively based on best estimates.

Source: Billabong International Ltd (2011, pp. 113–17).

SUMMARY

IFRS 3 was issued in January 2008 on completion of a major project on business combinations undertaken by the IASB. IFRS 3 specifies accounting standards that have implications not only for the exchanges of assets between entities but also for the accounting for subsidiaries and associated entities. The standard specifies how an acquirer accounts for the assets and liabilities acquired as well as the measurement of the consideration transferred. In making these calculations, the acquirer must determine the acquisition date as all fair value measurements are made at acquisition date. The standard interacts with other standards such as IAS 38 *Intangible Assets* and IAS 37 *Provisions, Contingent Liabilities and Contingent Assets* because the acquirer has to recognise intangible assets and liabilities acquired in a business combination. The nature and calculation of goodwill is also covered in this accounting standard, as is the treatment of a gain on a bargain purchase.

   Entities commonly trade with each other, exchanging one set of assets for another. When a grouping of assets constitutes a business, the accounting for the exchange transaction is determined by IFRS 3. IFRS 3 requires the application of the acquisition method under which the accountant must be able to identify which of the entities involved in the combination is the acquirer. The identifiable assets and liabilities acquired are measured at fair value at the acquisition date.

   Goodwill or the gain on a bargain purchase is determined as a residual which, for the business combinations considered in this chapter, is generally determined by comparing the consideration transferred and the net fair value of the identifiable assets and liabilities acquired. Where the acquirer acquires the shares in the acquiree and where the acquirer already holds some shares in the acquiree at the acquisition date, the determination of goodwill is more involved. Understanding the nature of goodwill is essential to understanding how to account for it. With the existence of the accounting standard on impairment of assets, goodwill is not required to be amortised. Where a bargain purchase arises, the gain is recognised in current period income.

DEMONSTRATION PROBLEM 14.1 Acquisition analyses

On 1 January 2013, Trevally Ltd concluded agreements to take over the operations of Mackerel Ltd and to acquire the rest of the shares of Perch Ltd. The statements of financial position of the three companies as at that date were:

	Trevally Ltd	Mackerel Ltd	Perch Ltd
Cash	$ 20 000	$ 1 000	$ 12 500
Accounts receivable	35 000	19 000	30 000
Inventory	52 000	26 500	40 000
Property, plant and equipment (net)	280 500	149 500	107 500
Shares in Perch Ltd (15 000 shares)	19 000	—	—
Debentures in Hangi Ltd	45 000	18 000	—
	$451 500	$214 000	$190 000

	Trevally Ltd	Mackerel Ltd	Perch Ltd
Accounts payable	$ 78 000	$ 76 000	$ 27 500
Loan payable	—	40 000	—
$10 debentures — nominal value	—	—	50 000
Share capital — issued at $1	300 000	80 000	70 000
Retained earnings	73 500	18 000	42 500
	$451 500	$214 000	$190 000

Mackerel Ltd included in the notes to its accounts a contingent liability relating to a guarantee for a loan. Although a present obligation existed, a liability was not recognised by Mackerel Ltd because of the difficulty of measuring the ultimate amount to be paid.

The details of the acquisition agreements are as follows.

Mackerel Ltd

Trevally Ltd is to acquire all the assets (except cash) and all the liabilities of Mackerel Ltd. In exchange for every four shares in Mackerel Ltd, shareholders are to receive three shares in Trevally Ltd *and* $1.00 in cash. Each share in Trevally Ltd has a fair value of $1.80. Trevally Ltd is to pay additional cash to Mackerel Ltd to cover the total liquidation expenses of Mackerel Ltd which are expected to amount to $6000. The cash already held by Mackerel Ltd is to go towards the liquidation costs. The assets of Mackerel Ltd are all recorded in Mackerel Ltd's records at cost (depreciated if applicable). The fair values of Mackerel Ltd's assets are:

Receivables	$ 17 500
Inventory	32 000
Property, plant and equipment	165 500
Debentures in Hangi Ltd	19 000

Mackerel Ltd had been undertaking research into new manufacturing machinery, and had expensed a total of $10 000 research costs. Trevally Ltd determined that the fair value of this in-process research was $2000 at acquisition date. The contingent liability relating to the guarantee was considered to have a fair value of $1500.

External accounting advice and valuers fees amounted to $3000.

Perch Ltd

Trevally Ltd is to acquire the remaining issued capital of Perch Ltd. In exchange, the shareholders in Perch Ltd are to receive four shares in Trevally Ltd for every five shares held in Perch Ltd. The shares already held in Perch Ltd are valued at $21 600. They have been measured at fair value with movements in fair value being recognised in profit or loss.

The legal costs incurred by Trevally Ltd in issuing its shares to Mackerel Ltd and Perch Ltd amounted to $1300 and $800 respectively.

Required

Prepare the acquisition analyses and journal entries necessary to record the acquisition of both Mackerel Ltd and Perch Ltd in the records of Trevally Ltd.

Solution

Prepare acquisition analyses and journal entries
The first step is to analyse the nature of the business combination, in particular what happens to each entity involved in the transactions. In this example, Trevally Ltd is the acquirer. It acquires assets and liabilities of Mackerel Ltd, probably with the latter entity going into liquidation. With Perch Ltd, Trevally Ltd acquires only shares in that entity; hence, the transaction is between Trevally Ltd and the shareholders of Perch Ltd and not with Perch Ltd.

Considering the combination between Trevally Ltd and Mackerel Ltd, the first step is to prepare an acquisition analysis. This involves looking at the two sides of the transaction, determining the fair value of the identifiable assets acquired and liabilities assumed and calculating the consideration transferred. The difference between these two amounts will be goodwill or gain on bargain purchase.

1. *Acquisition analysis — Trevally Ltd and Mackerel Ltd*

Trevally Ltd acquired all the assets except cash, and assumed all the liabilities of Mackerel Ltd. These assets and liabilities are now measured at fair value.

Accounts receivable	$ 17 500
Inventory	32 000
Property, plant and equipment	165 500
Debentures in Hangi Ltd	19 000
In-process research	2 000
	236 000
Provision for guarantee	1 500
Loan payable	40 000
Accounts payable	76 000
	117 500
Net fair value	$ 118 500

Consideration transferred

The consideration transferred is the purchase consideration payable to Mackerel Ltd and is measured as the sum of the fair values of shares issued, liabilities undertaken and assets given up by the acquirer. In this example, Trevally Ltd issues shares and gives up cash. The share price is the fair value of the shares at the acquisition date.

Consideration transferred			
Shares:	Share capital of Mackerel Ltd	$80 000	
	Shares issued by Trevally Ltd (3/4)	60 000 × $1.80	$108 000
Cash:	80 000/4 × $1.00	20 000	
	Liquidation costs	6 000	
Less:	Held by Mackerel Ltd	(1 000)	25 000
Consideration transferred			$133 000

The consideration transferred is then compared with the net fair value of the identifiable assets and liabilities acquired to determine whether goodwill or a gain arises. In this case the consideration transferred is greater, hence, goodwill has been acquired.

$$\text{Goodwill} = \$133\,000 - \$118\,500 = \$14\,500$$

2. *Acquisition analysis — Trevally Ltd and Perch Ltd*

In this situation, Trevally Ltd acquires the shares in the acquiree rather than the actual assets and liabilities. Note that Trevally Ltd can gain control over the net assets of another entity by either buying the actual net assets or by acquiring a controlling interest in the entity that holds those net assets. The acquisition of the shares as an asset is not a business combination. However, by acquiring the shares, a business combination may have occurred, and a set of consolidated financial statements is prepared for the combined businesses using the principles of IFRS 3.

Cost of shares acquired	
Share capital of Perch Ltd	$70 000
Already held by Trevally Ltd	15 000
To acquire	$ 55 000
Trevally Ltd to issue 55 000 × 4/5 × $1.80 =	$ 79 200

The shares already held by Trevally Ltd in Perch Ltd are recorded at $19 000 at acquisition date. The fair value is $21 600. The investment is revalued at acquisition date to fair value, and the difference between these two amounts, $2600, is recorded as a gain.

The general journal entries in Trevally Ltd can then be read from the acquisition analysis. Note that when shares are issued the relevant account is 'Share Capital'.

Accounts Receivable	Dr	17 500	
Inventory	Dr	32 000	
Property, Plant and Equipment	Dr	165 500	
Debentures in Hangi Ltd	Dr	19 000	
In-process Research	Dr	2 000	
Goodwill	Dr	14 500	
Accounts Payable	Cr		76 000
Loan Payable	Cr		40 000
Provision for Guarantee	Cr		1 500
Share Capital	Cr		108 000
Payable to Mackerel Ltd	Cr		25 000
(Acquisition of net assets of Mackerel Ltd)			
Payable to Mackerel Ltd	Dr	25 000	
Cash	Cr		25 000
(Payment of consideration transferred)			
Acquisition-Related Expenses	Dr	3000	
Cash	Cr		3000
(Acquisition-related costs)			
Shares in Perch Ltd	Dr	2 600	
Gain on Revaluation of Investment	Cr		2 600
(Revaluation of investment to fair value)			
Shares in Perch Ltd	Dr	79 200	
Share Capital	Cr		79 200
(Purchase of remaining shares in Perch Ltd)			
Share Capital	Dr	2 100	
Cash	Cr		2 100
(Share issue costs incurred)			

Note that the costs of share issue reduce the Share Capital account which shows the net proceeds from share issues.

DEMONSTRATION PROBLEM 14.2 Acquisition and liquidation

On 1 July 2014, Barramundi Ltd and Bay Ltd sign an agreement whereby the operations of Bay Ltd are to be taken over by Barramundi Ltd. Bay Ltd will liquidate after the transfer is complete. The statements of financial position of the two companies on that day were as shown below.

	Barramundi Ltd	Bay Ltd
Cash	$ 50 000	$ 20 000
Accounts receivable	75 000	56 000
Inventory	46 000	29 000
Land	65 000	—
Plant and equipment	180 000	167 000
Accumulated depreciation — plant and equipment	(60 000)	(40 000)
Patents	10 000	—
Shares in Cape Ltd	—	26 000
Debentures in Brett Ltd (nominal value)	10 000	—
	$376 000	$258 000

	Barramundi Ltd	Bay Ltd
Accounts payable	$ 62 000	$ 31 000
Mortgage loan	75 000	21 500
10% debentures (face value)	100 000	30 000
Contributed equity:		
Ordinary shares of $1, fully paid	100 000	—
A class shares of $2, fully paid	—	40 000
B class shares of $1, fully paid		60 000
Retained earnings	39 000	75 500
	$376 000	$258 000

Barramundi Ltd is to acquire all the assets of Bay Ltd (except for cash). The assets of Bay Ltd are recorded at their fair values except for:

	Carrying amount	Fair value
Inventory	$ 29 000	$ 39 200
Plant and equipment	127 000	155 000
Shares in Cape Ltd	26 000	22 500

In exchange, the A class shareholders of Bay Ltd are to receive one 7% debenture in Barramundi Ltd, redeemable on 1 July 2015, for every share held in Bay Ltd. The fair value of each debenture is $3.50. Barramundi Ltd will also provide one of its patents to be held jointly by the A class shareholders of Bay Ltd and for which they will receive future royalties. The patent is carried at $4000 in the records of Barramundi Ltd, but is considered to have a fair value of $5000.

The B class shareholders of Bay Ltd are to receive two shares in Barramundi Ltd for every three shares held in Bay Ltd. The fair value of each Barramundi Ltd share is $2.70. Costs to issue these shares amount to $900. Additionally, Barramundi Ltd is to provide Bay Ltd with sufficient cash, additional to that already held, to enable Bay Ltd to pay its liabilities. The outstanding debentures are to be redeemed at a 10% premium. Annual leave entitlements of $16 200 outstanding at 1 July 2013 and expected liquidation costs of $5000 have not been recognised by Bay Ltd. Costs incurred in arranging the business combination amounted to $1600.

Required

1. Prepare the journal entries in the records of Barramundi Ltd to record the acquisition of Bay Ltd.
2. Prepare the Liquidation, Liquidator's Cash and Shareholders' Distribution ledger accounts in the records of Bay Ltd.

Solution

1. Prepare the journal entries of Barramundi Ltd
The nature of the transaction in this question is that the acquirer, Barramundi Ltd, is acquiring the operations (assets and liabilities) of Bay Ltd with the acquiree going into liquidation.

The first step is to prepare the acquisition analysis, which is a comparison of the fair value of the identifiable assets acquired and liabilities assumed with the consideration transferred.

Acquisition analysis — Barramundi Ltd and Bay Ltd
Note that all the assets acquired and the liabilities assumed by the acquirer are measured at fair value.

Accounts receivable	$ 56 000
Inventory	39 200
Plant and equipment	155 000
Shares in Cape Ltd	22 500
	$272 700

Consideration transferred
The consideration transferred is measured by calculating the fair value of the assets given up, liabilities undertaken and shares issued by the acquirer. In this example, the acquirer issues shares and debentures in itself, gives up a patent and provides cash.

Purchase consideration

Shareholders				
Debentures:	A shares of Bay Ltd	20 000		
	Debentures in Barramundi (1/1)	20 000 × $3.50		$ 70 000
Shares:	B shares of Bay Ltd	60 000		
	Shares in Barramundi (2/3)	40 000 × $2.70		108 000
Patent				5 000
Creditors		30 000		
Cash:	Debentures issued		$ 3 000	
	Plus premium (10%)		33 000	
	Accounts payable		31 000	
	Mortgage loan		21 500	
	Liquidation costs		5 000	
	Annual leave		16 200	
	Total cash required		106 700	
	Less: Already held		(20 000)	86 700
Total consideration transferred				$269 700

Because the total consideration transferred is less than the net fair value of the identifiable assets and liabilities acquired, the acquirer has to assess the measurements undertaken in the acquisition analysis. Having been assured that all relevant assets and liabilities have been included and that the fair values are reliable, the difference is then accounted for as a bargain purchase, and is included in current period income.

Gain on bargain purchase [$272 700 − $269 700]	$3 000

The general journal entries can then be read from the acquisition analysis. Note that when shares are issued the relevant account is 'Share Capital'.

In relation to the patent, prior to accounting for the business combination, the acquirer remeasures the asset to fair value.

Patent	Dr	1000	
Gain	Cr		1000
(Remeasurement to fair value as part of consideration transferred on business combination)			
Accounts Receivable	Dr	56 000	
Inventory	Dr	39 200	
Property, Plant and Equipment	Dr	155 000	
Shares in Cape Ltd	Dr	22 500	
Payable to Bay Ltd	Cr		156 700
Share Capital	Cr		108 000
Patent	Cr		5 000
Gain on Bargain Purchase	Cr		3 000
(Acquisition of Bay Ltd)			
Payable to Bay Ltd	Dr	156 700	
7% Debentures	Cr		70 000
Cash	Cr		86 700
(Payment of consideration)			

Acquisition-Related Expenses	Dr	1 600	
Cash	Cr		1600
(Acquisition-related costs)			
Share Capital	Dr	900	
Cash	Cr		900
(Payment of share issue costs)			

Note that the costs of share issue reduce the share capital issued with the Share Capital account then showing the net proceeds from share issues.

2. *Prepare the ledger accounts of Bay Ltd*

The Liquidation account effectively records the sale of the assets and the receipt of the purchase consideration.

- All items being sold by the acquiree — whether assets or a package of assets and liabilities — are taken at their carrying amount to the Liquidation account.
- Any amounts arising during the liquidation process and not previously recorded by the acquiree are also taken to the Liquidation account. In this example, there are three such items: premium on debentures, annual leave payable and liquidation costs. The relevant amounts are debited to the Liquidation account and liabilities are raised in relation to these items.
- Any reserves recognised by the acquiree — in this example it is retained earnings — are taken to the Liquidation account.
- The consideration transferred is credited to the Liquidation account, with the recognition of assets received, namely cash, patent, shares in Barramundi Ltd and debentures in Barramundi Ltd.

The balance of the Liquidation account is transferred to the Shareholders' Distribution account.

Liquidation			
Receivables	56 000	Retained Earnings	75 500
Inventory	29 000	Accumulated Depreciation	40 000
Plant and Equipment	167 000	Receivable from Barramundi Ltd	269 700
Shares in Cape Ltd	26 000		
Debentures – Premium	3 000		
Annual Leave Payable	16 200		
Liquidation Costs Payable	5 000		
Shareholders' Distribution	83 000		
	385 200		385 200

The cash received via the consideration transferred and the balance originally held by the acquiree is used to pay the liabilities of the acquiree, including liabilities such as liquidation costs payable raised during the liquidation process.

Liquidator's Cash			
Opening balance	20 000	Accounts Payable	31 000
Receivable from Barramundi Ltd	86 700	Debentures	33 000
		Mortgage Loan	21 500
		Liquidation Costs Payable	5 000
		Annual Leave Payable	16 200
	106 700		106 700

The capital balances of the acquiree, in this example the capital relating to both A and B shares issued by the acquiree, are taken to the credit side of the Shareholders' Distribution account. The assets to be distributed to the former shareholders of the acquiree are transferred to the debit side of the account. In this case they consist of the debentures and shares in Barramundi Ltd and the patent, all these having been received as part of the consideration transferred from the acquirer. The account balances when the balance transferred from the Liquidation account is included. At this stage, all accounts of the acquiree are closed.

Shareholders' Distribution			
Debentures in Barramundi Ltd	70 000	Share Capital – A Shares	40 000
Shares in Barramundi Ltd	108 000	Share Capital – B Shares	60 000
Patent	5 000	Liquidation	83 000
	183 000		183 000

Discussion questions

1. What is meant by a 'business combination'?
2. Discuss the importance of identifying the acquisition date.
3. What is meant by 'contingent consideration' and how is it accounted for?
4. Explain the key components of 'core' goodwill.
5. What recognition criteria are applied to assets acquired and liabilities assumed in a business combination?
6. How is an acquirer identified?
7. Explain the key steps in the acquisition method.
8. How is the consideration transferred calculated?
9. If an acquiree liquidates, what are the key accounts raised by the acquiree and which accounts are transferred to these accounts?
10. How is a gain on bargain purchase accounted for?
11. Why is it important to identify an acquirer in a business combination?

Exercises

STAR RATING ★ BASIC ★★ MODERATE ★★★ DIFFICULT

Exercise 14.1 APPLYING IFRS 3

★ Bass Ltd has recently undertaken a business combination with Bream Ltd. At the start of negotiations, Bass Ltd owned 30% of the shares of Bream Ltd. The current discussions between the two entities concerned Bass Ltd's acquisition of the remaining 70% of shares of Bream Ltd. The negotiations began on 1 January 2013 and enough shareholders in Bream Ltd agreed to the deal by 30 September 2013. The purchase agreement was for shareholders in Bream Ltd to receive in exchange shares in Bass Ltd. Over the negotiation period, the share price of Bass Ltd shares reached a low of $5.40 and a high of $6.20.

The accountant for Bass Ltd, Mr Spencer, knows that IFRS 3 has to be applied in accounting for business combinations. However, he is confused as to how to account for the original 30% investment in Bream Ltd, what share price to use to account for the issue of Bass Ltd's shares, and how the varying dates such as the date of exchange and acquisition date will affect the accounting for the business combination.

Required

Provide Mr Spencer with advice on the issues that are confusing him.

Exercise 14.2 ACCOUNTING BY THE ACQUIRER

★ On 1 July 2013, New Ltd acquired the following assets and liabilities from Day Ltd:

	Carrying amount	Fair value
Land	$300 000	$350 000
Plant (cost $400 000)	280 000	290 000
Inventory	80 000	85 000
Cash	15 000	15 000
Accounts payable	(20 000)	(20 000)
Loans	(80 000)	(80 000)

In exchange for these assets and liabilities, New Ltd issued 100 000 shares that had been issued for $1.20 per share but at 1 July 2013 had a fair value of $6.50 per share.

Required

1. Prepare the journal entries in the records of New Ltd to account for the acquisition of the assets and liabilities of Day Ltd.
2. Prepare the journal entries assuming that the fair value of New Ltd shares was $6 per share.

Exercise 14.3   ACCOUNTING BY AN ACQUIRER

★   Light Ltd acquired all the assets and liabilities of Sound Ltd on 1 July 2014. At this date, the assets and liabilities of Sound Ltd consisted of:

	Carrying amount	Fair value
Current assets	$1 000 000	$ 980 000
Non-current assets	4 000 000	4 220 000
	5 000 000	5 200 000
Liabilities	500 000	500 000
	$4 500 000	$4 700 000
Share capital — 100 000 shares	$3 000 000	
Reserves	1 500 000	
	$4 500 000	

In exchange for these net assets, Light Ltd agreed to:

• issue 10 Light Ltd shares for every Sound Ltd share — Light Ltd shares were considered to have a fair value of $10 per share; costs of share issue were $500
• transfer a patent to the former shareholders of Sound Ltd — the patent was carried in the records of Light Ltd at $350 000 but was considered to have a fair value of $1 million
• pay $5.20 per share in cash to each of the former shareholders of Sound Ltd.
Light Ltd incurred $10 000 in costs associated with the acquisition of these net assets.

Required

1. Prepare an acquisition analysis in relation to this acquisition.
2. Prepare the journal entries in Light Ltd to record the acquisition.

Exercise 14.4   ACQUISITION OF SHARES IN ACQUIREE

★   On 1 January 2014, Desert Ltd acquired all the issued shares of Island Ltd. At this date the equity of Island Ltd consisted of:

Share capital — 100 000 shares issued at $5 per share	$500 000
General reserve	200 000
Asset revaluation surplus	100 000
Retained earnings	50 000

In exchange for these shares, Desert Ltd agreed to pay the former shareholders of Island Ltd two shares in Desert Ltd, these having a fair value of $4 per share, plus $1.50 cash for each share held in Island Ltd. The costs of issuing the shares were $800.

Required

Prepare the journal entries in the records of Desert Ltd to record these events.

ACCOUNTING BY AN ACQUIRER

★ Lower Ltd acquired the assets and liabilities of Higher Ltd on 1 July 2014. These net assets measured at fair value consisted of:

Equipment	$ 50 000
Land	80 000
Trucks	40 000
Current assets	10 000
Current liabilities	(16 000)

Required

Prepare the journal entries in Lower Ltd to record this business combination assuming that, to acquire these net assets, Lower Ltd:
1. issued 100 000 shares at $1.80 per share
2. issued 100 000 shares at $1.60 per share.

LIQUIDATION OF THE ACQUIREE

★ Hamilton Ltd acquired all the assets and liabilities of Daydream Ltd, giving in exchange 100 000 shares, these having a fair value of $2.80 per share, and $50 000 cash.

At the acquisition date, the statement of financial position of Daydream Ltd was as follows:

Cash	$ 10 000
Accounts receivable	20 000
Land	80 000
Plant	240 000
Vehicles	50 000
	$400 000
Accounts payable	$ 40 000
Loans	60 000
	$100 000
Share capital	$200 000
General reserve	40 000
Retained earnings	60 000
	$300 000

Costs of liquidation amounted to $1000.

Required

Prepare the journal entries to liquidate Daydream Ltd.

DETERMINING THE FAIR VALUE OF EQUITY ISSUED BY THE ACQUIRER

★ On 1 December 2014, Trout Ltd acquired all the assets and liabilities of Dory Ltd, with Trout Ltd issuing 100 000 shares to acquire them. The fair values of Dory Ltd's assets and liabilities at this date were:

Cash	$ 50 000
Furniture and fittings	20 000
Accounts receivable	5 000
Plant	125 000
Accounts payable	15 000
Current tax liability	8 000
Annual leave payable	2 000

The financial year for Trout Ltd is January to December.

1. Prepare the journal entries for Trout Ltd to record the business combination at 1 December 2014, assuming the fair value of each Trout Ltd share at acquisition date is $1.90. Prepare any note disclosures for Trout Ltd at 31 December 2014 in relation to the business combination.
2. Assume the fair value of each Trout Ltd share at acquisition date is $1.90. At acquisition date, the acquirer could only determine a provisional fair value for the plant. On 1 March 2015, Trout Ltd received the final value from the independent appraisal, the fair value at acquisition date being $131 000. Assuming the plant had a further 5-year life from the acquisition date, explain how Trout Ltd will account for the business combination both at acquisition date and in the financial statements for 2015.
3. Prepare the journal entries for Trout Ltd to record the business combination at 1 December 2014, assuming the fair value of each Trout Ltd share at acquisition date is $1.70.

| Exercise 14.8 | DETERMINING THE FAIR VALUE OF EQUITY ISSUED BY THE ACQUIRER |

★ The following are the statements of financial position at 30 September 2013 of Shark Ltd and Squid Ltd.

Shark Ltd			
Share capital — 80 000 shares	$ 80 000	Non-current assets (at valuation less	
Asset revaluation surplus	140 000	depreciation)	$190 000
General reserve	60 000	Current assets	148 000
Retained earnings	30 000		
Creditors and provisions	28 000		
	$338 000		$338 000

Squid Ltd			
Share capital — 60 000 shares	$ 60 000	Non-current assets (at cost less	
General reserve	20 000	depreciation)	$ 50 000
Retained earnings	25 000	Current assets	65 000
Creditors and provisions	10 000		
	$115 000		$115 000

Additional information
(a) During September the shares of the companies were selling on the stock exchange at or near the following prices:

Shark Ltd $5.80   Squid Ltd $1.80

(b) On 30 September the directors of Shark Ltd made an offer to the shareholders of Squid Ltd to acquire their shares on the basis of one fully paid share at $1 in Shark Ltd for every two fully paid shares at $1 in Squid Ltd.
    The offer was open for 1 month and was contingent upon being accepted by the holders of at least 75% of Squid Ltd's capital.
(c) Immediately after the announcement, Shark Ltd's shares rose in price on the stock exchange to $6.20 and the shares of Squid Ltd rose to $3. The shares of both companies stayed at or close to this price throughout October.
(d) By the end of October, holders of 90% of Squid Ltd shares accepted the Shark Ltd offer and the latter company proceeds to acquire these shares on the agreed basis.
(e) By mid-November, Shark Ltd shares dropped in price on the stock exchange to $5.50.
(f) Costs of issuing and registering shares issued by Shark Ltd amounted to $2000.

Required
1. Give the journal entries necessary to record the transactions. (Show clearly to which company particular entries relate.)
2. State briefly why you selected the value adopted in recording the acquisition, and whether you consider there is any acceptable alternative recording value.
3. Show the statement of financial position of Shark Ltd after the entries have been recorded.

ACCOUNTING FOR GOODWILL

★★ Silver Ltd has acquired a major manufacturing division from Fern Ltd. The accountant, Ms Ball, has shown the board of directors of Silver Ltd the financial information regarding the acquisition. Ms Ball calculated a residual amount of $45 000 to be reported as goodwill in the accounts. The directors are not sure whether they want to record goodwill on Silver Ltd's statement of financial position. Some directors are not sure what goodwill is or why the company has bought it. Other directors even query whether goodwill is an asset, with some being concerned with future effects on the statement of profit or loss and other comprehensive income.

Required

Prepare a report for Ms Ball to present to the directors to help them understand the nature of goodwill and how to account for it.

IDENTIFYING THE ACQUIRER

★★ White Ltd has been negotiating with Cloud Ltd for several months, and agreements have finally been reached for the two companies to combine. In considering the accounting for the combined entities, management realises that, in applying IFRS 3, an acquirer must be identified. However, there is debate among the accounting staff as to which entity is the acquirer.

Required

1. What factors/indicators should management consider in determining which entity is the acquirer?
2. Why is it necessary to identify an acquirer? In particular, what differences in accounting would arise if White Ltd or Cloud Ltd were identified as the acquirer?

ACCOUNTING FOR RESEARCH

★★ Tall Ltd has acquired all the net assets of Blacks Ltd with the latter going into liquidation. Both companies operate in the area of testing and manufacturing pharmaceutical products. One of the main reasons that Tall Ltd sought to acquire Blacks Ltd was that the latter company had an impressive record in the development of drugs for the cure of some mosquito-related diseases. Blacks Ltd employed a number of scientists who were considered to be international experts in their area and at the leading edge of research in their field. Much of the recent work undertaken by these scientists was classified for accounting purposes as research and, as per IAS 38 *Intangible Assets*, was expensed by Blacks Ltd. However, in deciding what it would pay to take over Blacks Ltd, Tall Ltd had paid a sizeable amount of money for the ongoing research being undertaken by Blacks Ltd as it was expected that it would be successful eventually.

The accountant for Tall Ltd, Mr Basket, has suggested that the amount paid by Tall Ltd for this research should be shown as goodwill in the company's statement of financial position. However, the directors of the company do not believe that this faithfully represents the true nature of the assets acquired in the business combination, and want to recognise this as an asset separately from goodwill. Mr Basket believes that this will not be in accordance with IAS 38.

Required

Provide the directors with advice on the accounting for the aforementioned transaction.

ACCOUNTING FOR ACQUISITION-RELATED COSTS

★★ One of the responsibilities of the Group Accountant for Southland Ltd, Ms Bluff, is to explain the accounting principles applied by the company in preparing the annual report to the company's Board of Directors. Having analysed IFRS 3, Ms Bluff is puzzled by the requirement in paragraph 53 of IFRS 3 that any acquisition-related costs such as fees for lawyers and valuers should be expensed. Ms Bluff has analysed other accounting standards such as IAS 16 *Property, Plant and Equipment* and notes that under this standard such costs are capitalised into the cost of any property, plant and equipment acquired. She therefore believes that to expense such costs in accounting for a business combination would not be consistent with accounting for acquisitions of other assets.

Further, Ms Bluff believes that to expense such costs would result in a loss being reported in the statement of profit or loss and other comprehensive income in the period the business combination occurs. She is not sure how she will explain to the board of directors that the company makes a loss every time it enters a business combination. She believes the directors will wonder why the company enters into business combinations if immediate losses occur — surely losses indicate that bad decisions have been made by the company.

Required

Prepare a report for Ms Bluff on how she should explain the accounting for acquisition-related costs to the board of directors.

Exercise 14.13   **LIQUIDATION OF ACQUIREE, ACCOUNTING BY ACQUIRER**

★★   Marlin Ltd, a supplier of snooker equipment, agreed to acquire the business of a rival firm, Crab Ltd, taking over all assets and liabilities as at 1 June 2013.

The price agreed on was $60 000, payable $20 000 in cash and the balance by the issue to the selling company of 16 000 fully paid shares in Marlin Ltd, these shares having a fair value of $2.50 per share.

The trial balances of the two companies as at 1 June 2013 were as follows:

	Marlin Ltd		Crab Ltd	
	Dr	Cr	Dr	Cr
Share capital		$100 000		$ 90 000
Retained earnings		12 000	$ 24 000	
Accounts payable		2 000		20 000
Cash	$ 30 000		—	
Plant (net)	50 000		30 000	
Inventory	14 000		26 000	
Accounts receivable	8 000		20 000	
Government bonds	12 000		—	
Goodwill	—		10 000	
	$114 000	$114 000	$110 000	$110 000

All the identifiable net assets of Crab Ltd were recorded by Crab Ltd at fair value except for the inventory, which was considered to be worth $28 000 (assume no tax effect). The plant had an expected remaining life of 5 years.

The business combination was completed and Crab Ltd went into liquidation. Costs of liquidation amounted to $1000. Marlin Ltd incurred incidental costs of $500 in relation to the acquisition. Costs of issuing shares in Marlin Ltd were $400.

Required

1. Show the Liquidation account and the Shareholders' Distribution account in the records of Crab Ltd.
2. Prepare the journal entries in the records of Marlin Ltd to record the business combination.
3. Show the statement of financial position of Marlin Ltd after completion of the business combination.
4. On 31 July 2013, Marlin Ltd became aware that there had been an error in measuring the fair value of the plant at 1 June 2013. It had in fact a fair value at that date of $36 000. Explain how Marlin Ltd is required to adjust for that error. Marlin Ltd's reporting period ends on 30 June.

Exercise 14.14   **CONSIDERATION TRANSFERRED**

★★   On 1 September 2014, the directors of Jewfish Ltd approached the directors of Cod Ltd with the following proposal for the acquisition of the issued shares of Cod Ltd, conditional on acceptance by 90% of the shareholders of Cod Ltd by 30 November 2014:
- Two fully paid ordinary shares in Jewfish Ltd plus $3.10 cash for every preference share in Cod Ltd, payable at acquisition date.
- Three fully paid ordinary shares in Jewfish Ltd plus $1.20 cash for every ordinary share in Cod Ltd. Half the cash is payable at acquisition, and the other half in one year's time.

By 30 November, 90% of the ordinary shareholders and all of the preference shareholders of Cod Ltd had accepted the offer. The directors of Jewfish Ltd decided *not* to acquire the remaining ordinary shares. Share transfer forms covering the transfer were dated 30 November 2014, and showed a price per Jewfish Ltd ordinary share of $4.20. Jewfish Ltd's incremental borrowing rate is 8% p.a.

The statement of financial position of Cod Ltd at 30 November 2014 was as follows:

COD LTD Statement of Financial Position as at 30 November 2014		
Current assets		$ 120 000
Non-current assets		
Land and buildings	$203 000	
Plant and equipment	168 000	
Less: Accumulated depreciation	(45 000)	
Shares in other companies listed on stock exchange at cost		
(market $190 000)	30 000	
Government bonds, at cost	50 000	
Total non-current assets		406 000
Total assets		526 000
Current liabilities		30 000
Net assets		$ 496 000
Equity		
Share capital		
80 000 ordinary shares fully paid	$160 000	
50 000 6% preference shares fully paid	100 000	$ 260 000
Retained earnings		236 000
Total equity		$ 496 000

Jewfish Ltd then appointed a new board of directors of Cod Ltd. This board took office on 1 December 2014 and immediately:
- revalued the asset Shares in Other Companies to its market value (assume no tax effect)
- used the surplus so created to make a bonus issue of $32 000 to ordinary shareholders, each shareholder being allocated two ordinary shares for every ten ordinary shares held.

Required

Prepare all journal entries (in general form) to record the transactions in the records of (a) Jewfish Ltd and (b) Cod Ltd.

| Exercise 14.15 | LIQUIDATION OF ACQUIREE, ACCOUNTING BY ACQUIRER |

★★ Hastings Ltd is seeking to expand its share of the widgets market and has negotiated to take over the operations of Flounder Ltd on 1 January 2014. The statements of financial position of the two companies as at 31 December 2013 were as follows:

	Hastings Ltd	Flounder Ltd
Cash	$ 23 000	$ 12 000
Accounts receivable	25 000	34 700
Inventory	35 500	27 600
Freehold land	150 000	100 000
Buildings (net)	60 000	30 000
Plant and equipment (net)	65 000	46 000
Goodwill	25 000	2 000
	$383 500	$252 300

(continued)

	Hastings Ltd	Flounder Ltd
Accounts payable	$ 56 000	$ 43 500
Mortgage loan	50 000	40 000
Debentures	100 000	50 000
Share capital — 100 000 shares	100 000	—
— 60 000 shares	—	60 000
Other reserves	28 500	26 800
Retained earnings	49 000	32 000
	$383 500	$252 300

Hastings Ltd is to acquire all the assets, except cash, of Flounder Ltd. The assets of Flounder Ltd are all recorded at fair value except:

	Fair value
Inventory	$ 39 000
Freehold land	130 000
Buildings	40 000

In exchange, Hastings Ltd is to provide sufficient extra cash to allow Flounder Ltd to repay all of its outstanding debts and its liquidation costs of $2400, plus two fully paid shares in Hastings Ltd for every three shares held in Flounder Ltd. The fair value of a share in Hastings Ltd is $3.20. An investigation by the liquidator of Flounder Ltd reveals that at 31 December 2013 the following debts were outstanding but had not been recorded:

Accounts payable	$1 600
Mortgage interest	4 000

The debentures issued by Flounder Ltd are to be redeemed at a 5% premium. Costs of issuing the shares were $1200.

Required

1. Prepare the acquisition analysis and journal entries to record the business combination in the records of Hastings Ltd.
2. Prepare the Liquidation, Liquidator's Cash, and Shareholders' Distribution accounts for Flounder Ltd.

Exercise 14.16
★★

ACCOUNTING FOR BUSINESS COMBINATION BY ACQUIRER, LIQUIDATION ACCOUNTS OF ACQUIREE

On 1 July 2013, two companies — New Starfish Ltd and Tuna Ltd — sign an agreement whereby the operations of Tuna Ltd are to be taken over by New Starfish Ltd. Tuna Ltd is to liquidate after the transfer is complete. The statements of financial position of the two companies on that day were as follows:

	New Starfish Ltd	Tuna Ltd
Cash	$ 50 000	$ 20 000
Accounts receivable	75 000	56 000
Inventory	56 000	29 000
Land	65 000	—
Plant and equipment	180 000	167 000
Accumulated depreciation — plant and equipment	(60 000)	(40 000)
Shares in Sefton Ltd	—	26 000
Debentures in Akaroa Ltd (face value)	10 000	—
	$376 000	$258 000

	New Starfish Ltd	Tuna Ltd
Accounts payable	$ 62 000	$ 31 000
Mortgage loan	75 000	21 500
10% debentures (face value)	100 000	30 000
Share capital:		
Ordinary shares of $1, fully paid	100 000	—
A class shares of $2, fully paid	—	40 000
B class shares of $1, fully paid		60 000
Retained earnings	39 000	75 500
	$376 000	$258 000

Acquisition of Tuna Ltd

New Starfish Ltd is to acquire all of the assets of Tuna Ltd (except for cash). The assets of Tuna Ltd are recorded at their fair values except for the following:

	Carrying amount	Fair value
Inventory	$ 29 000	$ 39 200
Plant and equipment	127 000	140 000
Shares in Sefton Ltd	26 000	22 500

In exchange, the A class shareholders of Tuna Ltd are to receive one 7% debenture in New Starfish Ltd, redeemable on 1 July 2015, for every share held in Tuna Ltd. The fair value of each debenture is $3.50. The B class shareholders of Tuna Ltd are to receive two shares in New Starfish Ltd for every three shares held in Tuna Ltd. The fair value of each New Starfish Ltd share is $2.70. Costs to issue these shares will amount to $900.

Additionally, New Starfish Ltd is to provide Tuna Ltd with sufficient cash, additional to that already held, to enable Tuna Ltd to pay its liabilities. The outstanding debentures are to be redeemed at a 10% premium. Annual leave entitlements of $16 200 outstanding at 1 July 2013 and expected liquidation costs of $5000 have not been recognised by Tuna Ltd. Costs associated with undertaking the acquisition amounted to $1600.

Required

1. Prepare the acquisition analysis and journal entries in the books of New Starfish Ltd to record the acquisition of Tuna Ltd.
2. Prepare the Liquidation, Liquidator's Cash, and Shareholders' Distribution ledger accounts in the records of Tuna Ltd.

Exercise 14.17
★★

ACCOUNTING FOR BUSINESS COMBINATION BY ACQUIRER, JOURNAL ENTRIES FOR LIQUIDATION OF ACQUIREE

Ling Ltd and Morwong Ltd are small family-owned companies engaged in vegetable growing and distribution. The Spencer family owns the shares in Morwong Ltd and the Rokocoko family own the shares in Ling Ltd. The head of the Spencer family wishes to retire but his two sons are not interested in carrying on the family business. Accordingly, on 1 July 2014, Ling Ltd is to take over the operations of Morwong Ltd, which will then liquidate. Ling Ltd is asset-rich but has limited overdraft facilities so the following arrangement has been made.

Ling Ltd is to acquire all of the assets, except cash, delivery trucks and motor vehicles, of Morwong Ltd and will assume all of the liabilities except accounts payable. In return, Ling Ltd is to give the shareholders of Morwong Ltd a block of vacant land, two delivery vehicles and sufficient additional cash to enable the company to pay off the accounts payable and the liquidation costs of $1500. The land and vehicles had the following values at 30 June 2014:

	Carrying amount	Fair value
Freehold land	$ 50 000	$120 000
Delivery trucks	30 000	28 000

On the liquidation of Morwong Ltd, Mr Spencer is to receive the land and the motor vehicles and his two sons are to receive the delivery trucks.

The statements of financial position of the two companies as at 30 June 2014 were as follows:

	Ling Ltd	Morwong Ltd
Cash	$ 3 500	$ 2 000
Accounts receivable	25 000	15 000
Freehold land	250 000	100 000
Buildings (net)	25 000	30 000
Cultivation equipment (net)	65 000	46 000
Irrigation equipment	16 000	22 000
Delivery trucks	45 000	36 000
Motor vehicles	25 000	32 000
	$454 500	$283 000
Accounts payable	$ 26 000	$ 23 500
Loan — Bank of NZ	150 000	80 000
Loan — Trevally Bros	35 000	35 000
Loan — Long Cloud	70 000	52 500
Share capital — 100 000 shares	100 000	—
— 60 000 shares	—	60 000
Reserves	28 500	—
Retained earnings	45 000	32 000
	$454 500	$283 000

All the assets of Morwong Ltd are recorded at fair value, with the exception of:

	Fair value
Freehold land	$120 000
Buildings	40 000
Cultivation equipment	40 000
Motor vehicle	34 000

Required

1. Prepare the acquisition analysis and the journal entries to record the acquisition of Morwong Ltd's operations in the records of Ling Ltd.
2. Prepare the journal entries to record the liquidation of Morwong Ltd.
3. Prepare the statement of financial position of Ling Ltd after the business combination, including any notes relating to the business combination.

ACCOUNTING FOR BUSINESS COMBINATION BY ACQUIRER

★★ Sweetlip Ltd and Warehou Ltd are two family-owned flax-producing companies in New Zealand. Sweetlip Ltd is owned by the Wood family and the Bradbury family owns Warehou Ltd. The Wood family has only one son and he is engaged to be married to the daughter of the Bradbury family. Because the son is currently managing Warehou Ltd, it is proposed that, after the wedding, he should manage both companies. As a result, it is agreed by the two families that Sweetlip Ltd should take over the net assets of Warehou Ltd.

The statement of financial position of Warehou Ltd immediately before the takeover is as follows:

	Carrying amount	Fair value
Cash	$ 20 000	$ 20 000
Accounts receivable	140 000	125 000
Land	620 000	840 000
Buildings (net)	530 000	550 000

	Carrying amount	Fair value
Farm equipment (net)	$ 360 000	$364 000
Irrigation equipment (net)	220 000	225 000
Vehicles (net)	160 000	172 000
	$2 050 000	
Accounts payable	$ 80 000	80 000
Loan — Trevally Bank	480 000	480 000
Share capital	670 000	
Retained earnings	820 000	
	$2 050 000	

The takeover agreement specified the following details:
- Sweetlip Ltd is to acquire all the assets of Warehou Ltd except for cash, and one of the vehicles (having a carrying amount of $45 000 and a fair value of $48 000), and assume all the liabilities except for the loan from the Trevally Bank. Warehou Ltd is then to go into liquidation. The vehicle is to be transferred to Mr and Mrs Bradbury.
- Sweetlip Ltd is to supply sufficient cash to enable the debt to the Trevally Bank to be paid off and to cover the liquidation costs of $5500. It will also give $150 000 to be distributed to Mr and Mrs Bradbury to help pay the costs of the wedding.
- Sweetlip Ltd is also to give a piece of its own prime land to Warehou Ltd to be distributed to Mr and Mrs Bradbury, this eventually being available to be given to any offspring of the forthcoming marriage. The piece of land in question has a carrying amount of $80 000 and a fair value of $220 000.
- Sweetlip Ltd is to issue 100 000 shares, these having a fair value of $14 per share, to be distributed via Warehou Ltd to the soon to-be-married-daughter of Mr and Mrs Bradbury, who is currently a shareholder in Warehou Ltd.

The takeover proceeded as per the agreement, with Sweetlip Ltd incurring incidental acquisition costs of $25 000 and $18 000 share issue costs.

Required

Prepare the acquisition analysis and the journal entries to record the acquisition of Warehou Ltd in the records of Sweetlip Ltd.

Exercise 14.19	ACCOUNTING FOR A BUSINESS COMBINATION BY BOTH THE ACQUIRER AND THE ACQUIREE

★★★ Saratoga Ltd was finding difficulty in raising finance for expansion. Kingfish Ltd was interested in achieving economies by marketing a wider range of products.

The following shows the financial positions of the companies at 30 June 2013.

	Saratoga Ltd	Kingfish Ltd
Share capital		
40 000 shares	$ 40 000	
90 000 shares		$ 90 000
Retained earnings	12 000	30 000
	52 000	120 000
Liabilities		
Debentures (secured by floating charge)	20 000	—
Accounts payable	42 000	12 000
	62 000	12 000
Total equity and liabilities	$114 000	$132 000

(continued)

	Saratoga Ltd	Kingfish Ltd
Assets		
Cash	$ 12 000	$ 24 000
Accounts receivable	18 000	20 000
Inventory (at cost)	43 000	47 000
Land and buildings (at cost)	23 000	19 000
Plant and machinery (at cost)	52 000	41 000
Accumulated depreciation on plant and machinery	(34 000)	(19 000)
Total assets	**$114 000**	**$132 000**

It was agreed that it would be mutually advantageous for Saratoga Ltd to specialise in manufacturing, and for marketing, purchasing and promotion to be handled by Kingfish Ltd. Accordingly, Kingfish Ltd sold *part* of its assets to Saratoga Ltd on 1 July 2013, the identifiable assets acquired having the following fair values:

Inventory	$22 000 (cost $15 000)
Land and buildings	$34 000 (carrying amount $10 000)
Plant and machinery	$27 000 (cost $38 000, accumulated depreciation $18 000)

The acquisition was satisfied by the issue of 40 000 'A' ordinary shares (fully paid) in Saratoga Ltd.

Required

1. Show the journal entries to record the above transactions in the records of Saratoga Ltd:
   (a) if the fair value of the 'A' ordinary shares of Saratoga Ltd was $2 per share
   (b) if the fair value of the 'A' ordinary shares of Saratoga Ltd was $2.20 per share. (Assume the assets acquired constitute a business entity.)
2. Show the journal entries in the records of Kingfish Ltd under (a) and (b) in requirement 1.
3. Show the statement of financial position of Saratoga Ltd after the transactions, assuming the fair value of Saratoga's Ltd's 'A' ordinary shares was $2.20 per share. Provide the notes to the financial statements relating to the business combinations.

Exercise 14.20

ACCOUNTING FOR ACQUISITIONS OF A BUSINESS AND SHARES IN ANOTHER ENTITY

★★★ Tailor Ltd is seeking to expand its share of the pet care market and has negotiated to acquire the operations of Flathead Ltd and the shares of Octopus Ltd.

At 1 July 2013, the trial balances of the three companies were:

	Tailor Ltd	Flathead Ltd	Octopus Ltd
Cash	$ 145 000	$ 5 200	$ 84 000
Accounts receivable	34 000	21 300	12 000
Inventory	56 000	30 000	25 400
Shares in listed companies	16 000	22 000	7 000
Land and buildings (net)	70 000	40 000	36 000
Plant and equipment (net)	130 000	105 000	25 000
Goodwill (net)	6 000	5 000	5 600
	$ 457 000	$ 228 500	$ 195 000
Accounts payable	$ 65 000	$ 40 000	$ 29 000
Bank overdraft	0	0	1 500
Debentures	50 000	0	100 000
Mortgage loan	100 000	30 000	0
Contributed equity:			
Ordinary shares of $1, fully paid	200 000	150 000	60 000
Other reserves	15 000	6 500	2 500
Retained earnings (30/6/13)	27 000	2 000	2 000
	$ 457 000	$ 228 500	$ 195 000

Flathead Ltd

Tailor Ltd is to acquire all assets (except cash and shares in listed companies) of Flathead Ltd. Acquisition-related costs are expected to be $7600. The net assets of Flathead Ltd are recorded at fair value except for the following:

	Carrying amount	Fair value
Inventory	$ 30 000	$ 26 000
Land and buildings	40 000	80 000
Shares in listed companies	22 000	18 000
Accounts payable	(40 000)	(49 100)
Accrued leave	0	(29 700)

In exchange, the shareholders of Flathead Ltd are to receive, for every three Flathead Ltd shares held, one Tailor Ltd share worth $2.50 each. Costs to issue these shares are $950. Additionally, Tailor Ltd will transfer to Flathead Ltd its 'Shares in listed companies' asset, which has a fair value of $15 000. These shares, together with those already owned by Flathead Ltd, will be sold and the proceeds distributed to the Flathead Ltd shareholders. Assume that the shares were sold for their fair values.

Tailor Ltd will also give Flathead Ltd sufficient additional cash to enable Flathead Ltd to pay all its creditors. Flathead Ltd will then liquidate. Liquidation costs are estimated to be $8700.

Octopus Ltd

Tailor Ltd is to acquire all the issued shares of Octopus Ltd. In exchange, the shareholders of Octopus Ltd are to receive one Tailor Ltd share, worth $2.50, and $1.50 cash for every two Octopus Ltd shares held.

Required

1. Prepare the acquisition analysis and journal entries to record the acquisitions in the records of Tailor Ltd.
2. Prepare the Liquidation account and Shareholders' Distribution account for Flathead Ltd.
3. Explain in detail why, if Flathead Ltd has recorded a goodwill asset of $5000, Tailor Ltd calculates the goodwill acquired via an acquisition analysis. Why does Tailor Ltd not determine a fair value for the goodwill asset and record that figure as it has done for other assets acquired from Flathead Ltd?
4. If Tailor Ltd subsequently receives a dividend cheque for $1500 from Octopus Ltd, paid from retained earnings earned before its acquisition of the shares in Octopus Ltd, how should Tailor Ltd account for that cheque? Why?
5. Shortly after the business combination, the liquidator of Flathead Ltd receives a valid claim of $25 000 from a creditor. As Tailor Ltd has agreed to provide sufficient cash to pay all the liabilities of Flathead Ltd at acquisition date, the liquidator requests and receives a cheque for $25 000 from Tailor Ltd. How should Tailor Ltd record this payment? Why?

Exercise 14.21	ACQUISITION OF TWO BUSINESSES

★★★ Queenfish Ltd is a manufacturer of specialised industrial machinery seeking to diversify its operations. After protracted negotiations, the directors decided to purchase the assets and liabilities of Blackfish Ltd and the spare parts retail division of Teraglin Ltd.

At 30 June 2014 the statements of financial position of the three entities were as follows:

	Queenfish Ltd	Blackfish Ltd	Teraglin Ltd
Land and buildings (net)	$ 60 000	$ 25 000	$ 40 000
Plant and machinery (net)	100 000	36 000	76 000
Office equipment (net)	16 000	4 000	6 000
Shares in listed companies	24 000	15 000	20 800
Debentures in listed companies	20 000	—	—
Accounts receivable	35 000	26 000	42 000
Inventory	150 000	54 000	30 200

(continued)

	Queenfish Ltd	Blackfish Ltd	Teraglin Ltd
Cash	$ 59 000	$ 11 000	$ 9 000
Goodwill	—	7 000	—
	$ 464 000	$ 178 000	$ 224 000
Accounts payable	26 000	14 000	27 000
Current tax liability	21 000	6 000	7 000
Provision for leave	36 000	10 000	17 500
Bank loan	83 000	16 000	43 500
Debentures	60 000	50 000	—
Share capital (issued at $1, fully paid)	200 000	60 000	90 000
Retained earnings	38 000	22 000	39 000
	$ 464 000	$ 178 000	$ 224 000

The acquisition agreement details are as follows:

Blackfish Ltd
Queenfish Ltd is to acquire all the assets (other than cash) and liabilities (other than debentures, provisions and tax liabilities) of Blackfish Ltd for the following purchase consideration:
- Shareholders in Blackfish Ltd are to receive three shares in Queenfish Ltd, credited as fully paid, in exchange for every four shares held. The shares in Queenfish Ltd are to be issued at their fair value of $3 per share. Costs of share issue amounted to $2000.
- Queenfish Ltd is to provide sufficient cash which, when added to the cash already held, will enable Blackfish Ltd to pay out the current tax liability and provision for leave, to redeem the debentures at a premium of 5%, and to pay its liquidation expenses of $2500.

The fair values of the assets and liabilities of Blackfish Ltd are equal to their carrying amounts with the exception of the following:

	Fair value
Land and buildings	$60 000
Plant and machinery	50 000

Incidental costs associated with the acquisition amount to $2500.

Teraglin Ltd
Queenfish Ltd is to acquire the spare parts retail business of Teraglin Ltd. The following information is available concerning that business, relative to the whole of Teraglin Ltd:

	Total amount	Spare parts division	
	Carrying amount	Carrying amount	Fair value
Land and buildings (net)	$40 000	$20 000	$30 000
Plant and machinery (net)	76 000	32 000	34 500
Office equipment (net)	6 000	2 000	2 500
Accounts receivable	42 000	21 000	20 000
Inventory	30 200	12 000	12 000
Accounts payable	27 000	14 000	14 000
Provision for leave	17 500	7 000	7 000

The divisional net assets are to be acquired for $10 000 cash, plus 11 000 ordinary shares in Queenfish Ltd issued at their fair value of $3, plus the land and buildings that have been purchased from Blackfish Ltd.
Incidental costs associated with the acquisition are $1000.

Required

1. Prepare the acquisition analysis for the acquisition transactions of Queenfish Ltd.
2. Prepare the liquidation account for Blackfish Ltd.
3. Prepare the journal entries for the acquisition transactions in the records of Queenfish Ltd and Teraglin Ltd.

References

Accounting Standards Board UK 2005, Letter of comment (no. 130) on *Exposure Draft of Proposed Amendments to IFRS 3 Business Combinations*, 28 October, www.fasb.org.

Billabong International Ltd 2011, *2010/2011 Full financial report*, Billabong International Limited, Australia, www.billabongbiz.com.

Brewin Dolphin Holdings plc 2009, *Annual report and accounts 2009*, Brewin Dolphin Holdings plc, United Kingdom, www.brewindolphinholdings.co.uk.

Christian Dior 2011, *2010 Annual report*, France, www.dior-finance.com.

Danisco 2006, *Annual report 2005/06*, Danisco Corporation, Denmark, www.danisco.com.

Forbe, T 2007, 'The failure of IFRS 3', *Intellectual Asset Management*, issue 21, December–January 2007, pp. 8–12.

Intangible Business 2007, *SFAS 141: The first 5 years*, Intangible Business Ltd, United Kingdom, www.intangiblebusiness.com.

Johnson, LT & Petrone, KR 1998, 'Is goodwill an asset?', *Accounting Horizons*, vol. 12, no. 3, pp. 293–303.

Leo, KJ, Hoggett, JR & Radford, J 1995, *Accounting for identifiable intangibles and goodwill*, Australian Society of Certified Practising Accountants, Melbourne.

Miller, M & Islam, A 1988, *The definition and recognition of assets*, Accounting Theory Monograph No. 7, Australian Accounting Research Foundation, Melbourne.

Nokia 2011, *Nokia in 2010*, Nokia Corporation, Finland, www.nokia.com.

RAC WA 2009, 'RAC Concise Financial Report for the financial year ended 30 June 2009', *horizons*, issue 14, October–November 2009, pp. 59–69.

Wang, J 2008, 'Minnow of milk trade poised to swallow giant', *South China Morning Post*, 27 September, p. A7.

Wesfarmers 2008, *2008 Annual report*, Wesfarmers Limited, Australia, www.wesfarmers.com.au.

—— 2009, *2009 Annual report*, Wesfarmers Limited, Australia, www.wesfarmers.com.au.

15

Impairment of assets

ACCOUNTING STANDARDS IN FOCUS

IAS 36 *Impairment of Assets*

LEARNING OBJECTIVES

After studying this chapter, you should be able to:

1 understand the purpose of the impairment test for assets

2 understand when to undertake an impairment test

3 explain how to undertake an impairment test for an individual asset

4 identify a cash-generating unit, and account for an impairment loss for a cash-generating unit — not including goodwill

5 account for the impairment of goodwill

6 account for reversals of impairment losses

7 apply the disclosure requirements of IAS 36.

15.1 INTRODUCTION TO IAS 36

Chapters 11 and 13 discuss the measurement and recognition criteria for property, plant and equipment, and intangibles. These assets are measured at cost or revalued amount and, for each asset, the cost or revalued amount is allocated over its useful life. The exception is where intangible assets have indefinite useful lives, in which case no amortisation is charged. In the statement of financial position (balance sheet) at the end of a reporting period, the assets are reported at cost or revalued amount less the accumulated depreciation/amortisation. Because there are many judgements in the depreciation/amortisation process — estimates of useful life, residual values and the pattern of benefits — the question to be asked at the end of the reporting period is whether the carrying amounts of the assets in the statement of financial position overstate the worth of the assets. In other words, can an entity expect to recover in future periods the carrying amounts of an entity's assets? Recovery can be from future use of the asset and/or from the eventual disposal of the asset. If an entity does not expect to recover the carrying amount of an asset, the entity has an impairment loss in relation to that asset. Paragraph 6 of IAS 36 *Impairment of Assets* defines an impairment loss as follows:

> An impairment loss is the amount by which the carrying amount of an asset or a cash-generating unit exceeds its recoverable amount.

This chapter examines the impairment test for assets. The accounting standard covering impairment is IAS 36 *Impairment of Assets*. The standard was issued initially by the International Accounting Standards Board (IASB) in July 1998, amended on numerous occasions, exposed for further amendment in December 2002, and issued in its present form in 2004.

Under IAS 36, an entity is required to conduct impairment tests for its assets to see whether it has incurred any impairment losses. The purpose of the impairment test is to ensure that assets are not carried at amounts that exceed their recoverable amounts or, more simply, that assets are not overstated.

Key questions in relation to the impairment test are:

- How does the test work?
- Is the test the same for all assets?
- Should the test apply to individual assets or to groups of assets? If to groups, which groups?
- Is the accounting treatment the same for assets measured at cost and for those measured at revalued amount?
- When should the test be carried out? Should it be done annually, every 3 years or some other time?
- Can the results of the impairment test be reversed; that is, if an asset is written down because it is impaired, can later events lead to the reversal of that write-down?

15.1.1 Scope of IAS 36

Paragraph 2 of IAS 36 notes that the standard does not apply to all assets; that is, not all assets are subject to impairment testing. Assets to which IAS 36 does not apply are:

- inventories — IAS 2 *Inventories*
- assets arising from construction contracts — IAS 11 *Construction Contracts*
- deferred tax assets — IAS 12 *Income Taxes*
- assets arising from employee benefits — IAS 19 *Employee Benefits*
- financial assets — IAS 39 *Financial Instruments: Recognition and Measurement*
- investment properties measured at fair value — IAS 40 *Investment Property*
- biological assets measured at fair value less costs to sell — IAS 41 *Agriculture*
- deferred acquisition costs and intangible assets relating to insurance contracts — IFRS 4 *Insurance Contracts*
- non-current assets or disposal groups classified as held for sale — IFRS 5 *Non-current Assets Held for Sale and Discontinued Operations*.

The accounting standards listed contain the principles for recognition and measurement of the particular assets covered by those standards. Note that in some of these standards the assets are required to be recorded at fair value, or fair value less costs of disposal. Fair value is discussed in detail in chapter 3. Where assets are recorded at fair value, there is no need to test for recoverability of the carrying amount of the asset. Under IAS 2, inventory is recorded at the lower of cost and net realisable value. As net realisable value is defined in terms of estimated selling price, IAS 2 has an inbuilt impairment test requiring inventory to be written down when the cost is effectively greater than the recoverable amount.

15.2 WHEN TO UNDERTAKE AN IMPAIRMENT TEST

As noted earlier, the purpose of the impairment test is to ensure that disclosed assets do not have carrying amounts in excess of their recoverable amounts. However, under IAS 36 it is not necessary at the end of each reporting period to test each asset in order to determine whether it is impaired. The only assets that need to be tested at the end of the reporting period are those where there is any *indication* that an asset may be impaired (see paragraph 9 of IAS 36). An entity therefore must determine by looking at various sources of information whether there is sufficient evidence to suspect that an asset may be impaired. If there is no such evidence, then an entity can assume that impairment has not occurred.

For most assets, the need for an impairment test can be assessed by analysing sources of evidence. However, there are some assets for which an impairment test *must* be undertaken every year. Paragraph 10 identifies these assets:

- intangible assets with indefinite useful lives
- intangible assets not yet available for use
- goodwill acquired in a business combination.

The reason for singling out these assets for automatic impairment testing is that the carrying amounts of these assets are considered to be more uncertain than those of other assets. For intangible assets with indefinite useful lives, there is no annual amortisation charge, and hence no ongoing reduction in the carrying amounts of the assets. As the assets are not being reduced via amortisation, it is considered essential that the carrying amounts be tested against the recoverable amounts. Goodwill is calculated as a residual amount when a business combination occurs. (This is discussed in more detail later in this chapter.) Goodwill is also not subject to annual amortisation; instead, it is subject to an annual impairment test. However, impairment testing does not absolve management from being aware of events that may cause impairment to occur within an accounting period and accounting for such impairments as they occur.

Another important reason for remeasuring assets and testing for impairment relates to the concept of depreciation adopted by the IASB. As noted in chapter 11, depreciation is viewed as a process of allocation rather than as a valuation process, even when an asset is measured at a revalued amount. Hence, the carrying amount of an asset reflects the unallocated measure of the asset rather than the benefits to be derived from the asset in the future. The impairment test relates to the assessment of recoverability of the asset, which is not a feature of the depreciation allocation process.

15.2.1 Collecting evidence of impairment

The purpose of the impairment test is to determine whether the carrying amount of an asset exceeds its recoverable amount. The evidence of impairment relates to variables that may support the belief that the asset under investigation is not worth as much as it was previously. The indicators noted in IAS 36 are only the minimum that an entity's management should look at. Management should take into account the nature and use of a specific asset and determine the factors that may indicate deterioration in the asset's worth. The minimum indicators listed in IAS 36 are described in two groups: external sources of information, and internal sources of information.

External sources of information

Paragraph 12 of IAS 36 lists four sources of information relating to the external environment in which the entity operates:

1. *Asset's value*. Has the asset's value declined more than would normally be expected during the period? This may occur for many reasons relating to changes in expectations concerning the operation of the entity. For example, there may have been a significant reduction in the entity's sales when new products or technologies that the entity planned to introduce within a certain timeframe are not introduced within that timeframe. Further, there may have been movements in key personnel that affect the productivity of the entity itself and bring increased pressure from competitors who employed those people.
2. *Entity's environment/market*. Have significant adverse changes occurred or will they occur in the technological, market, economic or legal environment in which the entity operates, or in the market to which the asset is dedicated? For example, a competitor may have developed a product or technology that is likely to cause or has caused a significant and permanent reduction in the entity's market share.
3. *Interest rates*. Have market interest rates or market rates of return increased during the period, with potential changes in the interest rate used in assessing an entity's present value of future cash flows?
4. *Market capitalisation*. Is the carrying amount of the net assets of the entity greater than the market capitalisation of the entity?

Internal sources of information

Paragraph 12 of IAS 36 lists three sources of information based on events within the entity itself:

1. *Obsolescence or physical damage.* Does an analysis of the asset reveal physical damage or obsolescence?
2. *Changed use within the entity.* Is the asset expected to be used differently within the entity? For example, the asset may become idle; there may be a restructure in the entity that changes the use of the asset; there may be plans to sell the asset; or the useful life of an intangible may be changed from indefinite to finite.
3. *Economic performance of the asset.* Do internal reports indicate that the economic performance of the asset is worse than expected? Evidence of this consists of:
   - actual cash flows for maintenance or operating the asset may be significantly higher than expected
   - actual cash inflows or profits may be lower than expected
   - expected cash flows for maintenance of operations may have increased, or expected profits may be lower.

In analysing the information from the above sources, paragraph 15 of IAS 36 notes that materiality must be taken into account. If, in previous analyses, the carrying amount of an asset was significantly lower than the asset's recoverable amount, minor movements in the factors listed above may cause the recoverable amount to be closer to the carrying amount but not large enough to expect the carrying amount to be greater than the recoverable amount. For example, if short-term interest rates changed, this may not be expected to affect long-term interest rates.

In its notes to the 2010 consolidated financial statements, Nokia (2010, pp. 14–15) provided details of the factors that trigger an impairment review for the entity (see figure 15.1).

> **Assessment of the recoverability of long-lived assets, intangible assets and goodwill**
> For the purposes of impairment testing, goodwill is allocated to cash-generating units that are expected to benefit from the synergies of the acquisition in which the goodwill arose.
>
> The Group assesses the carrying amount of goodwill annually or more frequently if events or changes in circumstances indicate that such carrying amount may not be recoverable. The Group assesses the carrying amount of identifiable intangible assets and long-lived assets if events or changes in circumstances indicate that such carrying amount may not be recoverable. Factors that could trigger an impairment review include significant underperformance relative to historical or projected future results, significant changes in the manner of the use of the acquired assets or the strategy for the overall business and significant negative industry or economic trends.

FIGURE 15.1 Indicators of impairment for Nokia Corporation
Source: Nokia Corporation (2010, p. 23).

15.3 IMPAIRMENT TEST FOR AN INDIVIDUAL ASSET

The impairment test involves comparing the carrying amount of an asset with its recoverable amount. To understand the nature of this test, it is necessary to understand a number of definitions given in paragraph 6 of IAS 36:

> The recoverable amount of an asset or a cash-generating unit is the higher of its fair value less costs of disposal and its value in use.
>
> Fair value is the price that would be received to sell an asset or paid to transfer a liability in an orderly transaction between market participants at the measurement date. (See IFRS 13 *Fair Value Measurement.*)
>
> Costs of disposal are incremental costs directly attributable to the disposal of an asset or cash-generating unit, excluding finance costs and income tax expense.
>
> Value in use is the present value of the future cash flows expected to be derived from an asset or cash-generating unit.

Note the phrase 'an asset or cash-generating unit' in the above definitions. The discussion in this section focuses on an individual asset, and it is assumed that, for the asset being tested for impairment, there are specific cash flows that can be associated with the asset. Cash-generating units are discussed in section 15.4.

From the definition of recoverable amount, there are two possible amounts against which the carrying amount can be tested for impairment: (1) fair value less costs of disposal and (2) value in use. Although the definition of recoverable amount refers to the 'higher' of these two amounts, an impairment occurs if the carrying amount exceeds recoverable amount (paragraph 8). However, it is not always necessary to measure both amounts when testing for impairment. If either one of these amounts is greater than carrying amount, the asset is not impaired (paragraph 19). Where there are active markets, determining fair value less costs of disposal is probably easier than calculating value in use. However, where the carrying amount exceeds the fair value less costs of disposal, it is necessary to calculate the value in use. Figure 15.2 is a diagrammatic representation of the impairment test.

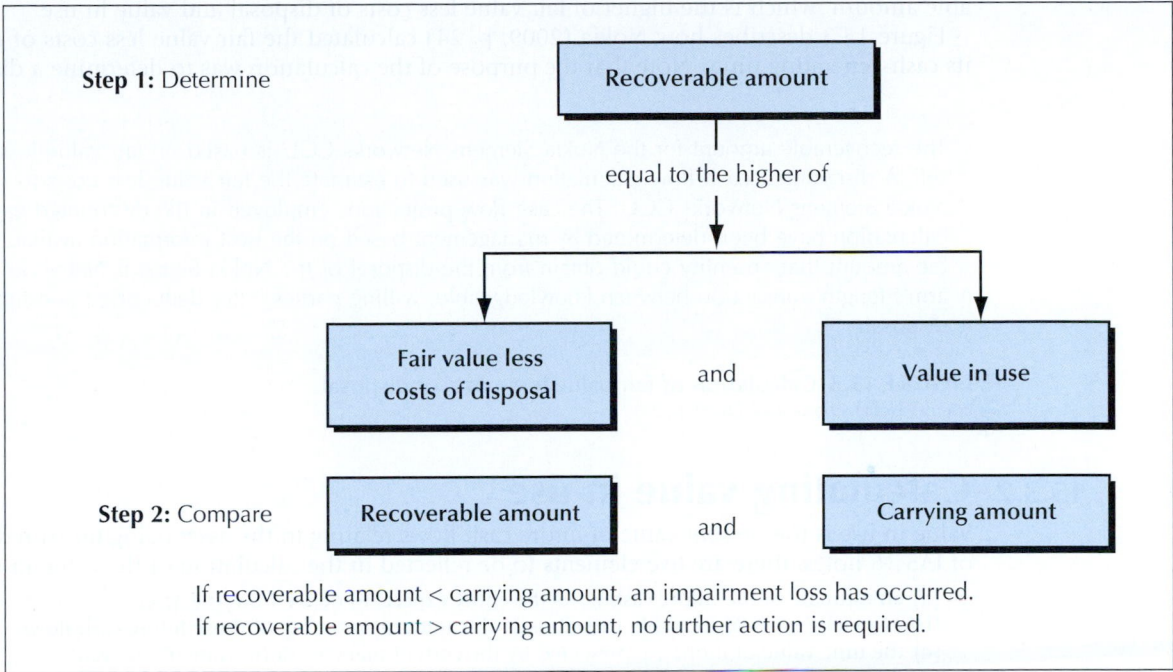

FIGURE 15.2 The impairment test

In calculating either fair value less costs of disposal or value in use, paragraph 23 of IAS 36 notes that in 'some cases, estimates, averages and computational shortcuts may provide reasonable approximations', rather than an entity having to perform in-depth calculations annually. It is also possible to use the most recent detailed calculation of recoverable amount made in a preceding year (paragraph 24) in the case of an intangible asset with an indefinite useful life. The latter is possible if *all* the following criteria are met:
- for the intangible asset, if tested as part of a cash-generating unit (see section 15.4 of this chapter), the other assets and liabilities in the unit have not changed significantly
- in the preceding year's calculation, the difference between the carrying amount and recoverable amount was substantial
- an analysis of all evidence relating to events affecting the asset suggests that the likelihood of the recoverable amount being less than carrying amount is remote.

15.3.1 Calculating fair value less costs of disposal

There are two parts to the determination of fair value less costs of disposal, namely *fair value* and *costs of disposal*. Fair value is measured in accordance with IFRS 13 *Fair Value Measurement* and is discussed in detail in chapter 3. Fair value is defined as an exit price and can be measured using a number of valuation techniques using various observable or unobservable inputs.

Paragraph 28 of IAS 36 provides the following examples of costs of disposal: legal costs, stamp duty and similar transaction taxes, costs of removing the asset, and direct incremental costs to bring the asset into condition for sale. The costs must be directly associated with either the sale of the asset or getting the asset ready for sale. Any costs arising after the sale of the asset, even if arising as a result of the sale, are not regarded as costs of disposal.

Paragraph 5 of IAS 36 provides guidance where an asset is measured under the alternative accounting treatment in IAS 16, namely at a revalued amount (i.e. fair value). Fair value as a measure does not include a consideration of disposal costs. Hence, if an asset's fair value is equal to its market value, the difference between fair value and fair value less costs of disposal is the disposal costs of the asset. If the disposal costs are immaterial, then there is no significant difference between fair value and fair value less costs of disposal. Therefore, where an asset is measured at fair value, revaluation decreases are not distinguishable from impairment losses. If the disposal costs are material, then fair value less costs of disposal is less than the carrying amount (i.e. fair value). The asset's value in use would then need to be calculated to determine whether it was less than fair value. If so, the asset is impaired and must be written down to recoverable amount, which is the higher of fair value less costs of disposal and value in use.

Figure 15.3 describes how Nokia (2009, p. 24) calculated the fair value less costs of disposal of one of its cash-generating units. Note that the purpose of the calculation was to determine a disposal price.

The recoverable amount for the Nokia Siemens Networks CGU is based on fair value less costs to sell. A discounted cash flow calculation was used to estimate the fair value less costs to sell of the Nokia Siemens Networks CGU. The cash flow projections employed in the discounted cash flow calculation have been determined by management based on the best information available to reflect the amount that an entity could obtain from the disposal of the Nokia Siemens Networks CGU in an arm's length transaction between knowledgeable, willing parties, after deducting the estimated costs of disposal.

FIGURE 15.3 Calculation of fair value less costs of disposal
Source: Nokia Corporation (2009, p. 24).

15.3.2 Calculating value in use

Value in use is the present value of future cash flows relating to the asset being measured. As paragraph 30 of IAS 36 notes, there are five elements to be reflected in the calculation of the value in use:

(a) an estimate of the future cash flows the entity expects to derive from the asset;
(b) expectations about possible variations in the amount or timing of those future cash flows;
(c) the time value of money, represented by the current market risk-free rate of interest;
(d) the price for bearing the uncertainty inherent in the asset; and
(e) other factors, such as illiquidity, that market participants would reflect in pricing the future cash flows the entity expects to derive from the asset.

The object is to measure the present value of the cash flows relating to the asset, in other words, to determine the cash flows and apply a discount rate. Some of the elements noted above — particularly (b), (d) and (e) — may affect either the measurement of the cash flows or the discount rate. Figure 15.4 shows a calculation of value in use based on Example 2 in the Illustrative Examples accompanying IAS 36.

Year	Long-term growth rates	Future cash flows	Present value factor at 15% discount rate	Discounted future cash flows
2012		$230*	0.869 57	$ 200
2013		253*	0.756 14	191
2014		273*	0.657 52	180
2015		290*	0.571 75	166
2016		304*	0.497 18	151
2017	3%	313**	0.432 33	135
2018	−2%	307**	0.375 94	115
2019	−6%	289**	0.326 90	94
2020	−15%	245**	0.284 26	70
2021	−25%	184**	0.247 19	45
2022	−67%	61**	0.214 94	13
Value in use				$1360

* Based on management's best estimate of net cash flow projections.
** Based on an extrapolation from preceding year cash flow using declining growth rates.

FIGURE 15.4 Calculation of value in use

As can be seen from figure 15.4, the calculation of value in use requires the estimation of future cash flows and a discount rate applied to these future cash flows.

Paragraph 53A of IAS 36 *Impairment of Assets* notes that fair value differs from value in use. In particular, whereas fair value reflects market participants' assumptions when pricing an asset, value in use reflects factors that are specific to an entity. Paragraph 53A also provides a number of factors that would not be reflected in fair value:

(a) additional value derived from the grouping of assets (such as the creation of a portfolio of investment properties in different locations);

(b) synergies between the asset being measured and other assets;

(c) legal rights or legal restrictions that are specific only to the current owner of the asset; and

(d) tax benefits or tax burdens that are specific to the current owner of the asset.

Determining future cash flows

Paragraphs 33–54 of IAS 36 provide guidance in measuring future cash flows. Some important guidelines are:

- Cash flow projections should be based on *management's best estimate* of the range of economic conditions that will exist over the remaining useful life of the asset. These should be tempered by an analysis of past cash flows and management's success in the past in predicting future cash flows accurately. Where external evidence is available, this should be given greater weight than simple reliance on management's expectations.

- Cash flow projections should be based on the most recent *financial budgets and forecasts*. These projections should cover a maximum period of five years unless a longer period can be justified. For most entities, a detailed analysis of future operations rarely extends beyond five years.

- For years after the 5-year budget projection, reliance should be placed on a steady or declining *growth rate*, unless there are specific reasons for predicting an increasing growth rate. In cases where an entity is doing particularly well, expectations of competitors entering the industry must be taken into consideration. The growth rate used should not exceed the long-term growth rate for the products, industries or country in which the entity operates. See figure 15.4 for an example of this.

- The cash inflows should include those from *continuing use* of the asset over its expected useful life as well as those expected to be received on *disposal* of the asset. Further, any cash *outflows* necessary to achieve the projected inflows must be taken into account. This may be particularly applicable at the time of the asset's disposal, where outlays are incurred to prepare the asset for disposal.

- Projected cash flows must be estimated for the asset in its *current* condition (paragraph 44). Where there is an expected restructuring of the entity in future periods, or where there are possibilities for improving or enhancing the performance of the asset by subsequent expenditure, projections of cash flows will not take these possible events into consideration. In the Illustrative Examples accompanying IAS 36, Examples 5 and 6 demonstrate how cash flows are determined when restructuring and capital expenditure are made to enhance performance. In both cases, if the value in use is being determined at 2015, and the restructuring/capital expenditure will not occur until 2019, the value in use at 2015 is determined by excluding the cash inflows/outflows relating to these future events. Once the entity is committed to the restructure, for example in 2017, the value in use calculated at that date could include the benefits from the restructure, such benefits being an increase in the expected cash flows. In the example of capital expenditure, using an aircraft as an example, management may include in its 2015 budget capital expenditure for 2018 that is necessary to renew the operating capacity of the aircraft. However, the value in use at 2015 excludes expected renewal costs and subsequent benefits. When the capital expenditure is incurred in 2018, the increased benefits from the capital expenditure can be included in the calculation in order to determine the value in use at the end of that period. Day-to-day servicing costs are included in the outflows used to measure value in use, as are the costs of major inspections.

- Cash flows relating to *financing activities* or *income tax* are not included in the calculations of future cash flows. As the discount rate is based on a pre-tax basis, the future cash flows must also be on a pre-tax basis.

- In assessing cash flows from *disposal*, the expected disposal price will take into account specific future price increases/decreases, and be based on an analysis of prices prevailing at the date of the estimate for similar assets in conditions similar to those expected for the asset under consideration at the end of its useful life.

- Appendix A to IAS 36, described as an 'integral part of the standard', contains guidance on the use of present value techniques in measuring value in use. In paragraph A2, two approaches to calculating present value are noted. The first is the 'traditional' approach. It adjusts for expectations about possible variations in cash flow, the price for bearing uncertainty, and other factors used in pricing the asset by making the adjustments in the discount rate. The second is the 'expected cash flow' approach. It makes adjustments for these variables in arriving at risk-adjusted expected cash flows. The expected cash flows are based on consideration of all possible cash flows rather than just the most likely cash flow. Paragraph A7 provides the example of a situation where the possible cash flows and their related probabilities are:

	Cash flow	Probability	Expected cash flow
Cash flow 1	$100	10%	$ 10
Cash flow 2	200	60%	120
Cash flow 3	300	30%	90
Expected cash flow			$220

It is also possible for the expected cash flow to take into account probabilities of being received in different years. As noted in paragraph A7, a cash flow of $1000 may be received in 1 year, 2 years or 3 years, with probabilities of 10%, 60% and 30% respectively:

	Present value	Probability	Expected cash flow
$1000 in 1 year at 5%	$952.38	10%	$ 95.24
$1000 in 2 years at 5%	907.03	60%	544.22
$1000 in 3 years at 5%	863.84	30%	259.15
Expected present value			$898.61

A further refinement could be to apply different discount rates for different future periods where value in use is sensitive to a difference in risk for different periods or to the term structure of interest rates (paragraph A8):

	Present value	Probability	Expected cash flow
$1000 in 1 year at 5%	$952.38	10%	$ 95.24
$1000 in 2 years at 5.25%	902.73	60%	541.64
$1000 in 3 years at 5.5%	851.61	30%	255.48
Expected present value			$892.36

Undertaking this level of detail in measuring the expected cash flows must always be subject to a cost–benefit constraint (paragraph A12).

Paragraph A6 notes that there are further disadvantages with using the traditional approach because it relies on finding an interest rate that is commensurate with the risk. This requires isolating an asset existing in the market that has similar characteristics to the one being measured, and being able to observe the discount rate. The expected cash flow approach does not rely on finding such an asset but incorporates variations in risk and cash flows into the calculations of the expected cash flows. A range of possible outcomes is then built into the model, reducing the reliance on a single most likely outcome.

Determining the discount rate

Paragraph 55 of IAS 36 notes that the discount rate should:
- reflect the time value of money
- reflect the risks specific to the asset for which the future cash flow estimates have not been adjusted.

The rate may be determined by viewing rates used for similar assets in the market, or from the weighted average cost of capital of a listed entity that has a single asset, or portfolio of assets, similar to the asset under review (paragraph 56).

Paragraph A3 of Appendix A notes that a general principle in choosing a discount rate is that the interest rate 'should reflect assumptions that are consistent with those inherent in the estimated cash flows'. Not to do so could lead to double-counting. The example given in paragraph A3(a) to illustrate this is as follows:

> For example, a discount rate of 12 per cent might be applied to contractual cash flows of a loan receivable. That rate reflects expectations about future defaults from loans with particular characteristics. That same 12 per cent rate should not be used to discount expected cash flows because those cash flows already reflect assumptions about future defaults.

Further advice contained in paragraphs A15–A21 of Appendix A includes the following:
- As a starting point in choosing a discount rate, an entity may consider the current rates affecting it, such as the entity's weighted cost of capital, the entity's incremental borrowing rate and other market borrowing rates.
- The rate must reflect specific risks affecting the entity, with consideration being given to risks such as country risk, currency risk and price risk.
- The way the entity is financed as a whole, and the way the entity specifically financed the acquisition of the asset in question, should not affect the determination of the discount rate.

Figure 15.5 contains information provided in Note 19 to the financial statements in the 2011 annual report of Amcor Ltd (2011, p. 114). Note in particular the information provided about the calculation of the recoverable amount using value-in-use calculations.

FIGURE 15.5 Calculation of value in use

(b) Impairment tests for goodwill

For the purpose of impairment testing, goodwill acquired in a business combination is allocated to cash-generating units or groups of cash-generating units (CGUs) according to the level at which management monitors goodwill.

The goodwill amounts allocated below are tested annually or semi-annually if there are indicators of impairment, by comparison with the recoverable amount of each CGU or group of CGUs assets. Recoverable amounts for CGUs are measured at the higher of fair value less costs to sell and value in use. Value in use is calculated from cash flow projections for five years using data from the consolidated entity's latest internal forecasts. The key assumptions for the value in use calculations are those regarding discount rates, growth rates and expected changes in margins.

The forecasts used in the value in use calculations are management estimates in determining income, expenses, capital expenditure and cash flows for each asset and CGU. Changes in selling prices and direct costs are based on past experience and management's expectation of future changes in the markets in which the consolidated entity operates. Cash flows beyond the five year period are extrapolated using estimated growth rates.

The following table presents a summary of the goodwill allocation and the key assumptions used in determining the recoverable amount of each CGU:

CGU	Goodwill Allocation 2011 $ million	Goodwill Allocation 2010 $ million	Discount Rate 2011 %	Discount Rate 2010 %	Growth Rate 2011 %	Growth Rate 2010 %
Rigid Plastics						
Rigid Plastics	626.7	712.3	9.5	10.8	3.0	3.0
Australasia and Packaging Distribution						
Australasia	62.9	63.8	10.9	10.4	—	2.0
Packaging Distribution	92.3	113.4	8.6	9.8	—	—
Flexibles						
Flexibles Europe & Americas	478.8	402.3	8.1	8.8	0.5	—
Tobacco Packaging	231.3	201.6	8.1	8.8	—	—
Flexibles Asia Pacific	40.1	40.7	16.0	10.4	3.0	3.0
	1532.1	1534.1				

Following the restructure and integration of activities of the newly acquired Alcan Packaging business, a reassessment of CGUs was performed during the current financial year. Comparative information has been adjusted on a consistent basis.

(continued)

FIGURE 15.5 *(continued)*

The discount rate used in performing the value in use calculations reflects the consolidated entity's weighted average cost of capital, as adjusted for specific risks relating to each geographical region in which the CGUs operate. The pre-tax discount rates are disclosed above.

The growth rate represents the average rate applied to extrapolate CGU cash flows beyond the five year forecast period. These growth rates are determined with regard to the long term performance of each CGU in their respective market and are not expected to exceed the long term average growth rates in the applicable market.

Source: Amcor Ltd (2011, p. 114).

15.3.3 Recognition and measurement of an impairment loss for an individual asset

Paragraphs 58–64 of IAS 36 provide the principles for recognition and measurement of an impairment loss for an individual asset. If the recoverable amount of an asset is less than its carrying amount, an impairment loss occurs, and the asset must be written down from its carrying amount to the recoverable amount.

Where an asset is measured using the *cost model*, according to paragraph 60 of IAS 36 an impairment loss is recognised immediately in profit or loss. In relation to the other side of the accounting entry to the loss, reference should be made to paragraph 73(d) of IAS 16 *Property, Plant and Equipment*. According to this paragraph, for items of property, plant and equipment 'the gross carrying amount and the accumulated depreciation (aggregated with accumulated impairment losses) at the beginning and end of the period' should be disclosed. When impairment occurs, there is no need to write off any existing accumulated depreciation or create a separate accumulated impairment account. The impairment write-down can be included in accumulated depreciation, preferably referred to as 'Accumulated Depreciation and Impairment Losses'.

Hence, if an asset having a carrying amount of $100 (original cost $160) has a recoverable amount of $90, the appropriate journal entry to account for the impairment loss is:

Impairment Loss	Dr	10	
Accumulated Depreciation and Impairment Losses	Cr		10
(Impairment loss on asset)			

Where an asset is measured using the *revaluation model* (i.e. at fair value), according to paragraph 60 of IAS 36 any impairment loss is treated as a revaluation increase and accounted for as set out in IAS 16. If an asset at the end of an accounting period has a carrying amount of $100, being previously calculated as fair value of $120 less accumulated depreciation of $20, and the asset's recoverable amount (and possibly its fair value) at the end of the period is determined to be $90, the accounting entry is:

Accumulated Depreciation	Dr	20	
Asset	Cr		20
(Write-down of asset)			
Loss – Downward Revaluation of Asset (P/L)	Dr	10	
Asset	Cr		10
(Revaluation of asset)			

If the revalued asset had a previous revaluation increase of $20, giving rise to a revaluation surplus of $14 and a deferred tax liability (using a tax rate of 30%) of $6, then the entry to write the asset down to a recoverable amount of $90 requires an adjustment directly against the revaluation surplus:

Accumulated Depreciation	Dr	20	
Asset Revaluation Surplus	Dr	7	
Deferred Tax Liability	Dr	3	
Asset	Cr		30
(Write-down of asset to recoverable amount)			

574 PART 2 Elements

Regardless of whether the cost model or the revaluation model is used, once the impairment loss is recognised, any subsequent depreciation/amortisation is based on the new recoverable amount. In accordance with paragraph 63 of IAS 36, the depreciation charge is that necessary to allocate the asset's revised carrying amount (the recoverable amount) less its residual value (if any) on a systematic basis over its remaining useful life. Consider the example of the asset recorded at cost of $160 less accumulated depreciation of $60 and having a recoverable amount of $90. The impairment loss of $10 is recognised, the remaining useful life of the asset is assessed (assume 3 years, with equal benefits each year), and the residual value is determined (assume zero). Hence, in the year following recognition of the impairment loss, depreciation of $30 (i.e. $\frac{1}{3} \times \$90$) is recognised.

It is possible that the recoverable amount is negative owing to large expected future cash outflows relating to the asset, so the impairment loss could be greater than the carrying amount of the asset. According to paragraph 62 of IAS 16, a liability for the excess should be raised only if another standard requires it.

Figure 15.6 contains information disclosed in Note 8 to the 2010 financial statements of Nokia Corporation relating to its impairment of specific assets.

FIGURE 15.6 Impairment of assets

8. Impairment

EURm	2010	2009	2008
Goodwill	—	908	—
Other intangible assets	—	56	—
Property, plant and equipment	—	1	77
Inventories	—	—	13
Investments in associated companies	—	19	8
Available-for-sale investments	107	25	43
Other non-current assets	3	—	8
Total	110	1 009	149

Other intangible assets

In 2010 and 2008, the Group did not recognise any impairment charges on other intangible assets. In conjunction with the Group's decision to refocus its activities around specified core assets, the Group recorded impairment charges in 2009 totalling EUR 56 million for intangible assets arising from the acquisitions of Enpocket and Intellisync and the asset acquisition of Twango. The impairment charge was recognised in other operating expense and is included in the Devices & Services segment.

Property, plant and equipment and inventories

In 2010, the Group did not recognise any impairment charges with respect to property, plant and equipment and inventories. In 2008, resulting from the Group's decision to discontinue the production of mobile devices in Germany, an impairment loss was recognised amounting to EUR 55 million. The impairment loss related to the closure and sale of production facilities at Bochum, Germany during 2008 and is included in the Devices & Services segment.

In 2008, Nokia Siemens Networks recognised an impairment loss amounting to EUR 35 million relating to the sale of its manufacturing site in Durach, Germany. The impairment loss was determined as the excess of the book value of transferring assets over the fair value less costs to sell for the transferring assets. The impairment loss was allocated to property, plant and equipment and inventories.

Investments in associated companies

In 2010, the Group did not recognise any impairment charges on its investments in associated companies. After application of the equity method, including recognition of the Group's share of results of associated companies, the Group determined that recognition of impairment losses of EUR 19 million in 2009 and EUR 8 million in 2008 was necessary to adjust the Group's investment in associated companies to its recoverable amount.

(continued)

FIGURE 15.6 *(continued)*

Available-for-sale investments

The Group's investment in certain equity securities held as non-current available-for-sale suffered a permanent decline in fair value resulting in an impairment charge of EUR 107 million in 2010 (EUR 25 million in 2009. EUR 43 million in 2008). These impairment amounts are included within financial expenses and other operating expenses in the consolidated income statement. See also note 11.

Source: Nokia Corporation (2010, pp. 36, 37).

 15.4 CASH-GENERATING UNITS — EXCLUDING GOODWILL

The discussion in section 15.3 focuses on individual assets and whether they have been impaired. The impairment test in such cases involves the determination of recoverable amount, and this requires the measurement of fair value less costs of disposal and value in use of the asset being tested for impairment. However, for some assets, fair value less costs of disposal may be determinable, because the asset is separable and a market for that asset exists, but it may be impossible to determine the value in use. Value in use requires determining the expected cash flows to be received from an asset.

Some assets do not individually generate cash flows because the cash flows generated are the result of a combination of several assets. For example, a motor vehicle used by a manager does not by itself generate cash flows. Similarly, a machine in a factory works in conjunction with the rest of the assets in the factory to produce inventory which, when sold, creates cash inflows for an entity. For such assets, if the carrying amount exceeds the fair value less costs of disposal, some other measure relating to value in use must be used. Figure 15.7 reproduces an example provided in IAS 36 paragraph 67.

Example

A mining entity owns a private railway to support its mining activities. The private railway could be sold only for scrap value and it does not generate cash inflows that are largely independent of the cash inflows from the other assets of the mine.

It is not possible to estimate the recoverable amount of the private railway because its value in use cannot be determined and is probably different from scrap value. Therefore, the entity estimates the recoverable amount of the cash-generating unit to which the private railway belongs, i.e. the mine as a whole.

FIGURE 15.7 Cash flows and individual assets

The private railway described in figure 15.7 'could be sold only for scrap value', but this information is unimportant in determining the cash-generating unit. Even if the railway could be sold for a reasonable amount of money, the answer to what constitutes the cash-generating unit is the same. The key question is whether the cash flows expected to be received by the entity as a whole can be allocated to the various parts of the entity. The railway by itself does not generate cash flows; the cash flows are generated by the combination of the mine and the railway. Hence, the railway is not a separate cash-generating unit. Because the railway is being used by the mining entity, there are no expected cash flows from disposal of the railway, so any consideration of the proceeds on sale of the railway is irrelevant.

Paragraph 66 of IAS 36 requires that, where there is any indication an asset may be impaired, if possible the recoverable amount should be estimated for the individual asset.

However, if this is not possible, the entity should 'determine the recoverable amount of the cash-generating unit to which the asset belongs'. In other words, the impairment test is applied to a cash-generating unit rather than to an individual asset. Paragraph 6 contains the following definition of a cash-generating unit:

A cash-generating unit is the smallest identifiable group of assets that generates cash inflows that are largely independent of the cash inflows from other assets or groups of assets.

15.4.1 Identifying a cash-generating unit

The identification of a cash-generating unit requires judgement. As is stated in the definition, the key is to determine the 'smallest identifiable group of assets', and this group must create 'independent' cash flows from continuing use. Guidelines given in paragraphs 67–73 of IAS 36 include the following:

• Consider how management monitors the entity's operations, such as by product lines, businesses, individual locations, districts or regional areas.

- Consider how management makes decisions about continuing or disposing of the entity's assets and operations.
- If an active market exists for the output of a group of assets, this group constitutes a cash-generating unit.
- Even if some of the output of a group is used internally, if the output could be sold externally, then these prices can be used to measure the value in use of the group of assets.
- Cash-generating units should be identified consistently from period to period for the same group of assets.

Figure 15.8 contains examples adapted from those in the Illustrative Examples (accompanying IAS 36) relating to the identification of cash-generating units.

A. Retail store chain

Cool Surf City Store belongs to a retail store chain, Cool Surf Enterprises, which sells clothing under the Cool Surf brand. City Store makes all its retail purchases through Cool Surf Enterprises' purchasing centre. Pricing, marketing, advertising and human resource policies (except for hiring City Store's cashiers and salespeople) are decided by Cool Surf Enterprises. Cool Surf Enterprises also owns five other stores in the same city as Cool Surf City Store and 20 other stores in other cities. All stores are managed in the same way. Is Cool Surf City Store a cash-generating unit?

Analysis

- *An entity should consider whether internal management reporting is organised to measure performance on a store-by-store basis, and whether the business is run on a store-by-store profit basis, or on a region/city basis.*
- *All Cool Surf Enterprises' stores are in different suburbs, and probably have different customer bases. So, although City Store is managed at a corporate level, it generates cash inflows that are largely independent of those of other Cool Surf stores. Therefore, it is likely that the City Store is a cash-generating unit.*

B. Magazine titles

A publisher owns 150 magazine titles of which 70 were acquired and 80 were self-created. The price paid for a purchased magazine title is recognised as an intangible asset. The costs of creating magazine titles and maintaining existing titles are recognised as an expense as incurred. Cash inflows from direct sales and advertising are identifiable for each magazine title. Titles are managed by customer segments. The level of advertising income for a magazine title depends on the range of titles in the customer segment to which the magazine title relates. Management has a policy of abandoning old titles before the end of their economic lives and replacing them immediately with new titles for the same customer segment. Does an individual magazine title represent a separate cash-generating unit?

Analysis

- *It is likely that the recoverable amount of an individual magazine title can be assessed. Even though the level of advertising income for a title is influenced, to a certain extent, by the other titles in the customer segment, cash inflows from direct sales and advertising are identifiable for each title. In addition, although titles are managed by customer segments, decisions to abandon titles are made on an individual title basis.*
- *It is likely that individual magazine titles generate cash inflows that are largely independent of each other and that each magazine title is a separate cash-generating unit.*

C. Building half-rented to others and half-occupied for own use

Biscuits Ltd is a manufacturing company. It owns a headquarters building that used to be fully occupied for internal use. After downsizing, half the building is now used internally and half is rented to third parties. The lease agreement with the tenant is for 5 years. Is the building a cash-generating unit?

Analysis

- *The main purpose of the building is to serve as a corporate asset, supporting Biscuits Ltd's manufacturing activities. The building as a whole cannot be considered to generate cash inflows that are largely independent of the biscuit-making activities. It is likely that the cash-generating unit for the building is Biscuits Ltd as a whole.*
- *The building is not held as an investment. Therefore, it would not be appropriate to determine the value in use of the building based on projections of future market-related rents.*

FIGURE 15.8 Identifying cash-generating units, IAS 36, Illustrative Examples, Example 1

One of the problems with using a cash-generating unit is that the identification of a particular unit within an entity is arbitrary. It requires judgement on the part of management, and the factors used in the determination will vary from entity to entity. There is no question of comparability between entities, because the cash-generating unit is used for internal accounting purposes and not external reporting disclosures. However, there is the issue of whether management will select cash-generating units with an eye to which assets may decrease in value, and ensure that such assets are included in units in which other assets increase in value.

One alternative to the cash-generating unit is the segment concept as in IFRS 8 *Operating Segments*. Although determination of segments is also arbitrary, an accounting standard covers the identification of segments, which should improve the comparability across entities, and the identified segments are reported to the public. Note, however, that IAS 36 allows a segment to be used as the cash-generating unit only if the segment equates to the smallest identifiable group of assets that generate independent cash flows. Figure 15.9 shows how in Wesfarmers Note 16 to its 2011 financial statements (2011, p. 125) reported the company's allocation of goodwill to its cash-generating units.

Allocation of goodwill to groups of cash generating units	Consolidated	
	2011 $m	2010 $m
Carrying amount of goodwill		
Chemicals, Energy and Fertilisers	15	15
Home Improvement and Office Supplies		
– Bunnings	850	848
– Officeworks	799	799
Industrial and Safety		
– Blackwoods Australia	308	308
– Coregas	252	252
– Other	156	149
Insurance		
– Lumley Australia	434	434
– Other	493	493
Coles	10 228	10 216
Kmart	273	273
Target	2 419	2 419
	16 227	16 206

FIGURE 15.9 Allocation of goodwill to cash-generating units
Source: Wesfarmers Ltd (2011, p. 125).

15.4.2 Impairment loss for a cash-generating unit — excluding goodwill

An impairment loss occurs when the carrying amount of the assets of a cash-generating unit exceeds their recoverable amount.

Determining the impairment loss

In determining the carrying amount of the assets, all those assets that are directly attributable to the cash-generating unit and that contribute to generating the cash flows used in measuring recoverable amount must be included. There must be consistency between what is being measured for recoverable amount — namely cash flows relating to a group of assets — and the measurement of the carrying amount of those assets.

The principles for determining the recoverable amount of a cash-generating unit are the same as those described for an individual asset in section 15.3 of this chapter. However, note that paragraph 76(b) of IAS 36 requires that the carrying amount of a cash-generating unit does not include the carrying amount of any recognised liability. This is because, as stated in paragraph 43(b), the calculation of the future cash flows of the cash-generating unit does not include cash outflows that relate to obligations that have been recognised as liabilities, such as payables and provisions.

Accounting for an impairment loss in a cash-generating unit

If an impairment loss is recognised in a cash-generating unit that has not recorded any goodwill, paragraph 104 of IAS 36 states that the impairment loss should be allocated to reduce the carrying amount of the assets of the unit by allocating the impairment loss on a pro rata basis based on the carrying amount of each asset in the unit. The reduction in each carrying amount relates to each specific asset, and should be treated as an impairment of each asset, even though the impairment loss was based on an analysis of a cash-generating unit. The loss is accounted for in the same way as that for an individual asset as described in section 15.3, with losses relating to an asset measured at cost being recognised immediately in profit or loss.

Paragraph 105 of IAS 36 places some restrictions on an entity's ability to write down assets as a result of the allocation of the impairment loss across the carrying amounts of the assets of the cash-generating unit. For each asset, the carrying amount should not be reduced below the highest of:

(a) its fair value less costs of disposal (if measurable);
(b) its value in use (if determinable); and
(c) zero.

If there is an amount of impairment loss allocated to an asset, but a part of it would reduce the asset below, say, its fair value less costs of disposal, then that part is allocated across the other assets in the cash-generating unit on a pro rata basis (see illustrative example 15.1). However, as paragraph 106 notes, if the recoverable amount of each of the assets cannot be estimated without undue costs or effort, then an arbitrary allocation of the impairment loss between the assets of the unit will suffice because all the assets of a cash-generating unit work together.

ILLUSTRATIVE EXAMPLE 15.1 Impairment of a cash-generating unit

A cash-generating unit has been assessed for impairment and it has been determined that the unit has incurred an impairment loss of $12 000. The carrying amounts of the assets and the allocation of the impairment loss on a proportional basis are as shown below.

	Carrying amount	Proportion	Allocation of impairment loss	Net carrying amount
Buildings	$ 500 000	5/12	$ 5 000	$495 000
Equipment	300 000	3/12	3 000	297 000
Land	250 000	2.5/12	2 500	247 500
Fittings	150 000	1.5/12	1 500	148 500
	$1 200 000		$12 000	

However, if the fair value less costs of disposal of the buildings was $497 000, then this is the maximum to which these assets could be reduced. Hence, the balance of the allocated impairment loss to buildings of $2000 (i.e. $5000 – [$500 000 – $497 000]) has to be allocated across the other assets:

	Carrying amount	Proportion	Allocation of impairment loss	Net carrying amount
Buildings				$497 000
Equipment	$297 000	297/693	$ 857	296 143
Land	247 500	247.5/693	714	246 786
Fittings	148 500	148.5/693	429	148 071
	$693 000		$2 000	

The journal entry to reflect the recognition of the impairment loss is:

Impairment Loss	Dr	12 000	
Accumulated Depreciation and Impairment			
Losses – Buildings	Cr		3 000
Accumulated Depreciation and Impairment			
Losses – Equipment	Cr		3 857
Land	Cr		3 214
Accumulated Depreciation and Impairment			
Losses – Fittings	Cr		1 929

Corporate assets

One problem that arises when dividing an entity into separate cash-generating units is dealing with corporate assets. Corporate assets, such as the headquarters building or the information technology support centre, are integral to all cash-generating units generating cash flows but do not by themselves independently generate cash flows. Paragraph 102 of IAS 36 sets out how corporate assets should be dealt with in determining impairment losses for an entity:

Step 1: If any corporate assets can be allocated on a reasonable and consistent basis to cash-generating units, then this should be done. Each unit is then, where appropriate, tested for an impairment loss. Where a loss occurs in a cash-generating unit, the loss is allocated pro rata across the assets including the portion of the corporate asset allocated to the unit.

Step 2: If some corporate assets cannot be allocated across the cash-generating units, the entity:
- compares the carrying amount of each unit being tested (excluding the unallocated corporate asset) with its recoverable amount and recognises any impairment loss by allocating the loss across the assets of the unit
- identifies the smallest cash-generating unit that includes the unit under review and to which a portion of the unallocated corporate asset can be allocated on a reasonable and consistent basis
- compares the carrying amount of the larger cash-generating unit, including the portion of the corporate asset, with its allocated amount. Any impairment loss is then allocated across the assets of the larger cash-generating unit.

Illustrative example 15.2 provides the accounting for corporate assets.

ILLUSTRATIVE EXAMPLE 15.2 Accounting for corporate assets

An entity has two cash generating units, A and B. The assets of the two units are as follows:

	Unit A	Unit B
Plant	$500	$400
Land	300	220

The entity has two corporate assets: the headquarters building and a research centre. The headquarters is assumed to be used equally by both units. The carrying amount of the research centre cannot be allocated on a reasonable basis to the two units. The headquarters building has a carrying amount of $160. The research centre's assets consist of furniture of $100 and equipment of $160. Neither of the corporate assets produces cash flows for the entity.

The recoverable amounts of the two cash-generating units are:

Unit A	$900
Unit B	$665

The *first* step is to calculate the impairment losses for each of the cash generating units. To do this, the carrying amount of the headquarters building is allocated equally between the two units as it is used equally by those units. Impairment losses are then as follows:

	Unit A	Unit B
Plant	$ 500	$ 400
Land	300	220
Headquarters building	80	80
	880	700
Recoverable amount	900	665
Impairment loss	$ 0	$ 35

The impairment loss of $35 for Unit B is then allocated across all non-excluded assets in that unit:

	Carrying amount	Proportion of loss	Loss	Adjusted carrying amount
Plant	$400	400/700	$20	$380
Land	220	220/700	11	209
Headquarters building	80	80/700	4	76
			$35	

The *second* step is to deal with the research centre. This requires the determination of any impairment loss for the smallest cash generating unit that includes the research centre. In this case, the smallest cash generating unit is the entity as a whole. The impairment loss is calculated as follows:

Unit A	
Plant	$ 500
Land	300
Headquarters building [$80 + $76]	156
Unit B	
Plant	380
Land	209
Research Centre	
Furniture	40
Equipment	30
	1 615
Recoverable amount [$900 + $665]	1 565
Impairment loss	$ 50

This impairment loss is then allocated across these assets on a pro rata basis:

	Carrying amount	Proportion of loss	Loss	Adjusted carrying amount
Unit A				
Plant	$ 500	500/1 615	$15	$485
Land	300	300/1 615	9	291
Headquarters building [$80 + $76]	156	156/1 615	5	151

	Carrying amount	Proportion of loss	Loss	Adjusted carrying amount
Unit B				
Plant	380	380/1 615	12	368
Land	209	209/1 615	7	202
Research Centre				
Furniture	40	40/1 615	1	39
Equipment	30	30/1 615	1	29
	$1 615		$50	

15.5 CASH-GENERATING UNITS AND GOODWILL

In accounting for impairment losses for cash-generating units, one of the assets that may be recorded by an entity is goodwill. IAS 36 contains specific requirements for accounting for goodwill and how its existence affects the allocation of impairment losses across the assets of a cash-generating unit.

Goodwill is recognised only when it is acquired in a business combination. As discussed in chapter 13, IAS 38 *Intangible Assets* does not allow the recognition of internally generated goodwill, or the revaluation of any acquired goodwill. In accounting for a business combination, goodwill is calculated as a residual, involving calculation of variables including the consideration transferred and the net fair value of the identifiable assets and liabilities acquired. (See chapter 14 for more information on business combinations.) Goodwill then consists of those assets that cannot be individually identified or separately recognised.

Goodwill is an accumulation of assets, and may arise from synergy between the assets in the combined businesses or from assets that individually do not qualify for recognition. The assets that constitute goodwill increase the wealth of the entity and add to the expected future cash flows of the entity. However, for specific assets to be included in goodwill, either the cash flows associated with the specific assets cannot be reliably measured or the cash flows are earned in conjunction with other assets. Hence, it is not possible to determine a fair value less costs of disposal for goodwill, or to identify a set of cash flows that relates specifically to goodwill.

Accounting for goodwill acquired in a business combination is specified in paragraph 32 of IFRS 3 *Business Combinations*. The acquirer measures goodwill acquired in a business combination at cost less any accumulated impairment losses. Goodwill is not subject to amortisation. Instead, the acquirer tests the carrying amount of goodwill annually in accordance with IAS 36.

When a business combination occurs, and goodwill is calculated as part of accounting for that combination, the goodwill acquired is allocated to one or more cash-generating units (IAS 36 paragraph 80). Even though goodwill was acquired in relation to the entity as a whole, the cash flow earning capacity of goodwill must be allocated across the cash-generating units. The aim is to allocate all assets, whether corporate assets or goodwill, to the cash-generating units so they can be associated with the cash flows received by those units.

When deciding which units should have goodwill allocated to them, consideration should be given to how internal management monitors the goodwill. According to paragraph 80, the goodwill should be allocated to the *lowest level* at which management monitors the goodwill. When the business combination occurred, the acquirer would have analysed the earning capacity of the entity it proposed to acquire, and would have equated aspects of goodwill to various cash-generating units. It is possible that the allocation of goodwill would be made to each of the segments identified by management under the application of IFRS 8 *Operating Segments*. Paragraph 80 of IAS 36 states that the units to which goodwill is allocated should not be larger than a segment based on either the entity's primary or secondary reporting format. This is due to the fact that IFRS 8 requires the determination of business and geographical segments based on areas that are subject to different risks and return, and the internal financial reporting system within the entity is used as a basis for identifying these segments.

In its response to the Financial Accounting Standards Board (FASB) in the United States in relation to the board's deliberations on the impairment testing of goodwill, as reported in the FASB Summary of

Comment Letters, Technology Network suggested that goodwill should be tested at the enterprise level in all cases, or at least that option should be permitted:

> Many acquisitions are integrated into existing businesses for internal reporting purposes with many companies recording the goodwill at an operating or business unit level. However, over time, successful acquisitions frequently (and hopefully) create synergies with other internal reporting units and throughout an enterprise.
>
> The only way to ensure that this value is captured may be to perform impairment testing at the enterprise level. While we recognize that the Board has rejected such an approach, we believe that testing at the enterprise level would be appropriate in limited circumstances. For example, in the software industry, the acquired goodwill frequently becomes so integrated into the company's entire product line that it essentially becomes a new company platform. Thus, we do not believe there should be any firm rule prohibiting enterprise level testing. It should be allowed in appropriate circumstances.

The IASB (paragraph BC139 of the Basis for Conclusions on IAS 36) considered this argument and rejected impairment testing of goodwill at the level of the entity itself. It saw the important link as being the level at which goodwill is tested, with the level of internal reporting reflecting the management and reporting of goodwill that occurs within the entity itself.

As noted in paragraph BC139, the IASB was concerned that entities did not resort to testing the goodwill at the level of the entity itself. It stated:

> There should be a link between the level at which goodwill is tested for impairment and the level of internal reporting that reflects the way an entity manages its operations and with which the goodwill naturally would be associated.

In that sense, the allocation of goodwill should not be an arbitrary process. As noted in paragraph 82 of IAS 36, developing additional reporting systems should not normally be necessary.

Under IFRS 3, there is an allowance for a provisional initial accounting for the business combination. Paragraph 84 of IAS 36 therefore provides, consistent with IFRS 3, that where the allocation of goodwill cannot be completed before the end of the annual period in which the business combination occurred, the initial allocation is to be completed before the end of the first annual period beginning after the acquisition date.

15.5.1 Impairment testing of goodwill

A cash-generating unit that has goodwill allocated to it must be tested for impairment *annually* or more frequently if there is an indication the unit may be impaired (IAS 36 paragraph 90). As with other impairment tests, this involves comparing the carrying amount of the unit's assets, including goodwill, with the recoverable amount of the unit's assets.

Recoverable amount exceeds carrying amount

If the recoverable amount exceeds the carrying amount, there is no impairment loss. In particular, there is no impairment of goodwill. The goodwill balance remains unadjusted; that is, it is not reduced due to impairment loss.

Note that this test is not a robust test of the amount of goodwill recorded by the unit. Under this test, the goodwill is protected or 'cushioned' against impairment by:

- *internally generated goodwill:* the benefits relating to the acquired goodwill may have been received by the entity, but unrecognised internally generated goodwill may exist in the entity. The internally generated goodwill may have arisen subsequent to the business combination, or could consist of that existing in the acquirer itself prior to the business combination.
- *unrecognised identifiable net assets:* intangibles may exist which do not meet the recognition criteria under IAS 38 *Intangible Assets*. These are not included in the measure of the carrying amount of the assets of the cash-generating unit, yet the cash flows generated by these assets increase the recoverable amount of the unit.
- *excess value over carrying amount of recognised assets:* the impairment test uses the carrying amount of the unit's recognised assets. If the fair values of these assets are greater than their carrying amounts, the extra benefits relating to these assets increase the recoverable amount of the unit.

The IASB recognises that the above test provides a cushion against recognising impairment losses for goodwill. In paragraph BC135 of the Basis for Conclusions on IAS 36, it notes that the carrying amount of goodwill will always be shielded from impairment by internally generated goodwill. The impairment test for goodwill is at best ensuring that the carrying amount of goodwill is recoverable from cash flows generated by both acquired and internally generated goodwill. Such a cushion works, of course, only if the recoverable amount is being maintained; that is, if the value of the assets both identifiable and unidentifiable are being maintained by the entity. If the assets of the unit are being well managed then, in most cases, the goodwill of the unit is also being maintained. The test is then a screening mechanism. However, one advantage of the screening test is that it significantly reduces the cost of applying an impairment test, particularly in comparison to other tests that require a remeasurement of goodwill by measuring the net fair values of the identifiable assets and liabilities of the unit on an annual basis.

Figure 15.10 is an extract from Note 15 to the 2010 annual report of Boral Ltd, explaining how the company conducted its impairment tests for goodwill.

Impairment Tests for Goodwill

Goodwill and other intangible assets that have an indefinite useful life are not subject to amortisation but are tested annually for impairment. Goodwill is allocated to the Group's Cash Generating Units (CGUs) identified according to business type and Country of operation.

Key Assumptions

The recoverable amount of CGUs is the higher of the asset's fair value less costs to sell and its value in use. Value in use calculations use pre-tax cash flow projections based on financial budgets and plans approved by management covering a five year period. Recognising that the Group operates in cyclical markets, cash flow projections covering periods of up to 10 years are used where this period more appropriately reflects a full business cycle. Cash flows beyond the projection period are extrapolated using growth rates of between 0.8% and 2.5% which do not exceed the long-term average growth rate for the industry in which the CGU operates.

The Group's weighted cost of capital is used as a starting point for determining the discount rate with appropriate adjustments for the risk profile relating to the relevant segments and the countries in which they operate. The discount rates applied to pre-tax cash flows range from 12% to 14%.

The key assumptions relate to housing starts and market share, with the most sensitive assumption arising from forecast housing starts. These assumptions have been determined with reference to current performance and taking into account external forecasts. Housing starts forecasts utilised in the cash flow projections do not exceed historical experiences in the relevant geographies.

Certain US businesses recoverable amounts have been determined based on fair value less costs to sell based on external information.

The recoverable amount of CGUs exceeds their carrying values as at 30 June 2010. Management believes that any reasonable change in the key assumptions on which the estimates are based would not cause the aggregate carrying amount to exceed the recoverable amount of these CGUs.

Write-Down of Goodwill

At 30 June 2009, the Group wrote down the value of goodwill by $48.0 million. In the United States of America, goodwill arising on the acquisition of construction materials businesses in Colorado and Oklahoma was written down by $30.8 million due to weak market volumes. The write-down was calculated on a value in use basis utilising a pre-tax discount rate of 13.9%. The Group also wrote down the value of goodwill by $17.2 million relating to the precast panels business. The write-down was calculated on a value in use basis utilising a pre-tax discount rate of 12.0%.

Segment summary of goodwill	Consolidated	
	2010 $ millions	2009 $ millions
Boral Construction Materials	67.9	76.8
Cement Division	2.3	2.3
Boral Building Products	43.4	43.4
United States of America	161.4	169.5
	275.0	292.0

FIGURE 15.10 Impairment testing of goodwill
Source: Boral Ltd (2010, pp. 90–1).

Carrying amount exceeds recoverable amount

If the carrying amount exceeds the recoverable amount, there is an impairment loss, and this loss is recognised in accordance with paragraph 104 of IAS 36. This paragraph states that the impairment loss must be allocated to reduce the carrying amount of the assets of the unit, or group of units, in the following order:

- firstly, to reduce the carrying amount of any goodwill allocated to the cash-generating unit
- then, to the other assets of the unit pro rata on the basis of the carrying amount of each asset in the unit.

These reductions in carrying amounts are treated as impairment losses on the individual assets of the unit and recognised as any other impairment losses on assets.

However, paragraph 105 of IAS 36 provides some restrictions on the write-downs to individual assets:

In allocating an impairment loss in accordance with paragraph 104, an entity shall not reduce the carrying amount of an asset below the highest of:
(a) its fair value less costs of disposal (if measurable);
(b) its value in use (if determinable); and
(c) zero.
The amount of the impairment loss that would otherwise have been allocated to the asset shall be allocated pro rata to the other assets of the unit (group of units).

Illustrative example 15.3 provides an example of accounting for an impairment loss for a cash-generating unit that contains goodwill.

ILLUSTRATIVE EXAMPLE 15.3 Impairment of CGUs

An entity has two cash generating units, A and B. A comparison of the assets of these units at the date of the impairment test including allocated goodwill and their recoverable amounts is as follows:

	Unit A	Unit B
Identifiable assets	$ 1 000	$ 900
Goodwill	200	150
	1 200	1 050
Recoverable amount	1 300	880
Impairment loss	$ 0	$ 170

In accounting for the impairment loss of Unit B, the first step is to write-off the goodwill:

Impairment loss		Dr	150
Goodwill		Cr	150
(Impairment of goodwill)			

If only some of the goodwill had been written off, the credit entry would be taken to the account: Accumulated Impairment Losses – Goodwill.

The remaining $20 impairment loss would be allocated across the identifiable assets of Unit B on a pro rata basis.

There has been much controversy over the goodwill impairment test. In fact, three IASB members dissented on the issue of IAS 36, mainly over aspects of this test.

The advantage of the procedure used in IAS 36 is that it is not complex or costly, leading to a belief that the benefits outweigh the costs — see paragraph BC170 of the Basis for Conclusions on IAS 36.

The criticism of the test is that it *does not measure whether goodwill has been impaired*. Using the example in illustrative example 15.3, although there is an impairment loss of $150, there is no subsequent test to determine whether the goodwill has been impaired or whether some of the identifiable assets have been impaired. The method arbitrarily allocates the impairment loss firstly to goodwill — it assumes goodwill has been impaired. In the exposure draft to IAS 36, the impairment test suggested was a two-step approach, the second step of which is outlined in figure 15.11.

Once an impairment loss is determined, the *second step* requires three actions:

Action 1: Calculate the implied value of goodwill
The implied value of goodwill is calculated as follows:

Recoverable amount of the   *less*   net fair value of the identifiable assets, liabilities,
cash-generating unit   and contingent liabilities the entity would recognise
                                         if it acquired the cash-generating unit in a business
                                         combination on the date of the impairment test excluding
                                         any identifiable asset acquired in a business combination
                                         but not recognised separately from goodwill at the
                                         acquisition date.

Note that this measure of implied goodwill reduces the cushions. The assets and liabilities measured are not just those recorded by the entity, but those that would be recognised in an acquisition at the date the impairment test is made. Implied goodwill is, then, not protected by unrecognised identifiable assets because, under IFRS 3, these can be recognised in a business combination. Nor is it protected by excess values of the recognised assets because these assets are now measured at fair value rather than at carrying amount. If the object of the second step of the impairment test is to measure the current value of goodwill, then failing to exclude these other assets means the implied value of goodwill would consist of 'real' goodwill and identifiable assets.

The goodwill figure is still cushioned by internally generated goodwill, but it is not possible to distinguish between acquired goodwill and internally generated goodwill. There also does not seem any point in doing so because, if the purpose of the impairment test is to ensure that assets are not overstated, then whether the goodwill is 'old acquired' or 'new internally generated' does not matter. The question is whether at the time of the impairment test the unit has the carrying amount of goodwill as shown in the accounts.

Action 2: Compare the carrying amount of goodwill with the implied value of goodwill
If the carrying amount is *less than* the implied value, goodwill is not impaired, and no impairment loss needs to be recognised for goodwill. The impairment loss on the cash-generating unit then relates to the other assets of the unit. If the carrying amount is *greater than* the implied value, an impairment loss for goodwill has occurred and would be recognised immediately in profit or loss.

Action 3: Allocate the balance (if any) of the impairment loss to the other assets of the unit on a pro rata basis according to the carrying amount of each asset in the unit
The accounting for the balance of the impairment loss is the same as for an impairment loss in a cash-generating unit where there is no goodwill.

FIGURE 15.11 Impairment loss in a cash-generating unit with allocated goodwill — the three actions of the second step

Using the information provided in illustrative example 15.3, having determined an impairment loss for Unit B of $170, the implied goodwill of Unit B is measured. This is done by measuring the fair value of the identifiable assets of Unit B at the date of the impairment test. Assuming the fair value is $800, implied goodwill will be $80, being recoverable amount of $880 less $800. Therefore, goodwill should be reduced by $80, leaving a balance of $70. The remaining balance of the impairment loss of $90 is used to reduce the identifiable assets to $810, this being done on a pro rata basis.

Note in figure 15.11 that the process endeavours to measure the goodwill of the cash-generating unit, something IAS 16 does not do. The problem with the two-step process is that the calculation of the implied value for goodwill requires measuring the fair values of the assets, liabilities and contingent liabilities of the cash-generating unit. This is seen by the IASB (paragraph BC166 of the Basis for Conclusions on IAS 36) as costly and impracticable. The field tests conducted by the IASB led it to change from the two-step method to the one-step method. An example of one company's opinion of the costliness of the approach is found in the comments of the Dow Chemical Company in its submission to the FASB on goodwill impairment, as reported in the Summary of Comment letters. The Dow Chemical Company's comments were considered by the FASB to be representative of the majority of comments on this issue:

> The mechanics of the impairment test will be cost prohibitive to undertake. The Board cannot seriously expect companies to regularly estimate the fair value of its assets and liabilities in attempting to calculate the implied fair value of goodwill. Our experience with obtaining such appraisals in the context of business acquisitions has led us to believe that any benefit from such precise impairment measurements is far outweighed by the prohibitive costs of retaining and regularly engaging outside valuation experts whose opinions can vary widely in their professional assessment. As a practical and cost-effective alternative, we strongly recommend the use of *book values* of reported assets for this purpose.

Timing of impairment tests

As noted earlier, goodwill has to be tested for impairment annually. However, the test does not have to occur at the end of the reporting period. As paragraph 96 of IAS 36 notes, the test may be performed at any time during the year, provided it is performed at the same time every year. According to paragraph BC171 of the Basis for Conclusions on IAS 36, this measure was allowed as a means of reducing the costs of applying the test. However, if a business combination has occurred in the current period, and an allocation has been made to one or more cash-generating units, all units to which goodwill has been allocated must be tested for impairment before the end of that year — see paragraph 96 of IAS 36 in this regard.

It is not necessary for all cash-generating units to be tested for impairment at the same time. If there are two units being tested for impairment, one being a smaller cash-generating unit within a larger unit and the larger unit contains an allocation of goodwill, it is necessary to test the smaller unit for impairment first. This ensures that, if necessary, the assets of the smaller unit are adjusted before the testing of the larger unit. Similarly, if the assets of a cash-generating unit containing goodwill are being tested at the same time as the unit, then the assets must be tested first.

One of the reasons for requiring annual testing for both goodwill and intangibles with an indefinite life, apart from the uncertainty of measuring these assets, relates to the depreciation concept adopted by the standard setters, discussed in chapter 11 of this book. Depreciation is seen as a 'process of allocation'. Hence, to have assets such as goodwill and indefinite life intangibles permanently on the records with no allocation to accounting periods seems to depart from the allocation process and to move to a valuation concept. The IASB (paragraph BC121 of the Basis for Conclusions on IAS 36) noted that 'non-amortisation of an intangible asset increases the reliance that must be placed on impairment reviews of that asset to ensure that its carrying amount does not exceed its recoverable amount'. However, in accordance with paragraph 10(a) for indefinite life intangibles and paragraph 96 for goodwill, both may be tested at any time during the year, provided the test is performed at the same time every year. It must also be remembered that, as stated in paragraph BC122 of the Basis for Conclusions on IAS 36, annual testing is not a substitute for management being aware of events or changing circumstances that may indicate possible impairment and the need for additional testing.

Other impairment issues relating to goodwill

IAS 36 raises a number of other issues that need to be considered in accounting for the impairment of goodwill within a cash-generating unit:

- *Disposal of an operation within a cash-generating unit.* Where the cash-generating unit has a number of distinct operations and goodwill has been allocated to the unit, if one of the operations is disposed of, it is necessary to consider whether any of the goodwill relates to the operation disposed of. If it does, the amount of goodwill is measured on the basis of the relative values of the operation disposed of and the portion of the cash-generating unit retained, unless the entity can demonstrate that some other method better reflects the goodwill associated with the operation disposed of. In calculating the gain or loss on disposal of the operation, the allocated portion of the goodwill is included in the carrying amount of the assets sold (paragraph 86).

  For example, if part of a cash-generating unit was sold for $200 and the recoverable amount of the remaining part of the unit is $600, then it is assumed that 25% (200/[200 + 600]) of the goodwill has been sold and is included in the carrying amount of the operation disposed of.

- *Reorganisation of the entity.* Where an entity containing a number of cash-generating units restructures, changing the composition of the cash-generating units, and where goodwill has been allocated to the original units, paragraph 87 requires the reallocation of the goodwill to the new units. The allocation is done on a relative value basis similar to that used where a cash-generating unit is disposed of, again unless the entity can demonstrate that some other method better reflects the goodwill associated with the operation disposed of.

 15.6 REVERSAL OF AN IMPAIRMENT LOSS

An impairment loss is recognised after an entity analyses the future prospects of an individual asset or a cash-generating unit. Subsequent to an impairment loss occurring because of doubts about the performance of assets, it is possible for circumstances to change such that, when the recoverable amount of the assets increases, consideration can be given to a reversal of a past impairment loss. Paragraph 110 of IAS 36 requires an entity to assess *at the end of each reporting period* whether there are indications that an impairment loss recognised in previous periods may not exist or may have decreased. If such indications exist, the entity should estimate the recoverable amount of the asset or unit.

Similar to the assessment of whether there is an indication of an impairment loss, an entity needs to look at internal and external evidence to determine the existence of evidence for a reversal of the previous loss. Paragraph 111 of IAS 36 requires an entity to assess specific internal and external sources of information. These indicators are effectively the same as those for assessing the existence of a loss except that the indicators for a reversal relate to improvements in the entity's prospects. The indicators noted in paragraph 111 are (with italics added):

External sources of information
(a) there are observable indications that the asset's value has increased significantly during the period;
(b) significant changes with a *favourable effect* on the entity have taken place during the period, or will take place in the near future, in the technological, market, economic or legal environment in which the entity operates or in the market to which the asset is dedicated;
(c) market interest rates or other market rates of return on investments have *decreased* during the period, and those decreases are likely to affect the discount rate used in calculating the asset's value in use and increase the asset's recoverable amount materially;

Internal sources of information
(d) significant changes with a *favourable effect* on the entity have taken place during the period, or are expected to take place in the near future, in the extent to which, or manner in which, the asset is used or is expected to be used. These changes include costs incurred during the period to improve or enhance the asset's performance or restructure the operation to which the asset belongs; and
(e) evidence is available from internal reporting that indicates that the economic performance of the asset is, or will be, *better* than expected.

It is possible, as envisaged by paragraph 113 of IAS 36, that a review of the evidence will not result in a reversal of a previous impairment loss, but instead may lead to changes in the depreciation/amortisation measure of an asset. The review may lead to changes in expectations about useful life, residual value, and the pattern of benefits to be received.

If the evidence is such that there is a change in the estimates in relation to an asset (and only if there has been a change in the estimates), a reversal of impairment loss can be recognised. The reversal process requires the recognition of an increase in the carrying amount of the asset to its recoverable amount.

The ability to recognise a reversal of an impairment loss and the accounting for that reversal depend on whether the reversal relates to an individual asset, a cash-generating unit or goodwill.

15.6.1 Reversal of an impairment loss — individual asset

Where the recoverable amount is greater than the carrying amount of an individual asset (other than goodwill), the reversal of a previous impairment loss requires adjusting the carrying amount of the asset to recoverable amount. In determining the amount by which the carrying amount is to be adjusted, one limitation, as outlined in paragraph 117 of IAS 36, is that the carrying amount cannot be increased to an amount in excess of the carrying amount that would have been determined had no impairment loss been recognised. Hence, for a depreciable asset, if there were changes made to the useful life, residual value or pattern of benefits as a result of the impairment loss in the previous period, then there needs to be a calculation of carrying amount using the depreciation variables applied before the impairment loss to determine what the carrying amount would have been if there had been no impairment loss. This latter amount is the maximum to which the actual carrying amount can be increased.

If the individual asset is recorded under the *cost model*, then the increase in the carrying amount is recognised immediately in profit or loss:

Accumulated Depreciation/Amortisation and Impairment Losses	Dr	xxx	
Income – Impairment Loss Reversal	Cr		xxx
(Reversal of impairment loss)			

After the reversal of the impairment loss and the adjustment of the asset to its new carrying amount, in accordance with paragraph 121 of IAS 36 the depreciation/amortisation charge must be adjusted so that the revised carrying amount, less any residual value, is allocated across the remaining useful life on a systematic basis.

In Note 17 of its 2011 annual report, Amcor Ltd reported information relating to reversals of previous impairment write-downs as shown in figure 15.12.

(c) Non-current asset impairment reversals

30 June 2011

During the year ended 30 June 2011 the Other/Investments segment recognised a reversal of impairment of $0.6 million that had previously been recognised on plant and equipment in the Glass Tubing business. This business has subsequently been sold and therefore the impairment reversed.

30 June 2010

During the year ended 30 June 2010 Amcor Flexibles recognised a reversal of impairment of $0.7 million that had previously been recognised on property, plant and equipment as part of the repositioning of the business as announced in April 2007. Two plants within this original process have subsequently been sold and therefore the impairment reversed.

FIGURE 15.12 Impairment reversals
Source: Amcor Ltd (2011, p. 110).

15.6.2 Reversal of an impairment loss — cash-generating unit

If the reversal of the impairment loss relates to a cash-generating unit, in accordance with paragraph 122 of IAS 36 the reversal of the impairment loss is allocated pro rata to the assets of the unit, except for goodwill, with the carrying amounts of those assets. These reversals will then relate to the specific assets of the cash-generating unit and will be accounted for as detailed above for individual assets. In relation to those individual assets, the carrying amount of an asset cannot, as per paragraph 123 of IAS 36, be increased above the lower of its recoverable amount (if determinable) and the carrying amount that would have been determined had no impairment loss been recognised for the asset in previous periods.

If the situation envisaged in paragraph 123 occurs, then the amount of impairment loss reversal that cannot be allocated to an individual asset is then allocated on a pro rata basis to the other assets of the cash-generating unit, except for goodwill.

15.6.3 Reversal of an impairment loss — goodwill

Paragraph 124 of IAS 36 states that an impairment loss recognised for goodwill shall *not* be reversed in a later period. The reasons for this decision by the standard setters are detailed in paragraphs BC187–BC191 of the Basis for Conclusions on IAS 36.

The key principle driving the accounting for goodwill in a reversal of impairment loss situation is that established in IAS 38 *Intangibles*, namely that internally generated goodwill cannot be recognised. Where there is a reversal of an impairment loss, in order to be able to allocate some of the reversal amount to goodwill it would be necessary to establish that the old acquired goodwill still existed, rather than the increase in goodwill being recognition of internally generated goodwill. Because of the nature of goodwill, it is not possible to determine how much of any goodwill existing in an entity is remaining acquired goodwill or goodwill internally generated since the acquisition. To allow an impairment reversal to increase the carrying amount of goodwill is potentially allowing the recognition of internally generated goodwill, or, as described in paragraph BC190, 'backdoor' capitalisation of internally generated goodwill — hence the prohibition in IAS 36.

Some IASB members saw a potential inconsistency with disallowing the reinstatement of goodwill based on the grounds of non-recognition of internally generated goodwill and the allowance in IAS 36 of internally generated goodwill to act as a cushion to recognition of an impairment loss on goodwill. The standard setters, however, concluded that to shield or cushion an impairment loss is not as bad as direct recognition of internally generated goodwill in a reversal situation. However, there is probably some truth in the accusation that inconsistent accounting is allowed because the entity that has acquired goodwill is effectively allowed to recognise internally generated goodwill via the cushion effect in the impairment test, while at the same time those entities that have not acquired goodwill are not allowed to recognise internally generated goodwill.

Illustrative example 15.4 provides an example of a reversal of a previous period impairment loss within a cash-generating unit to which goodwill has been allocated.

ILLUSTRATIVE EXAMPLE 15.4 Reversal of impairment loss

At 30 June 2015, Entity A incurred an impairment loss of $5000, of which $3000 was used to write off the goodwill and $2000 to write down the assets. The allocation of the impairment loss to the assets was as follows:

	Carrying amount	Proportion of loss	Loss	Adjusted carrying amount
Land	$10 000	1/5	$ 400	$ 9 600
Plant	40 000	4/5	1 600	38 400
	$50 000		$2 000	

The plant had previously cost $100 000 and was being depreciated at 10% per annum, requiring a depreciation charge of $10 000 per annum. Subsequent to the impairment, the asset was depreciated on a straight-line basis over three years, at $12 800 per annum.

At 30 June 2016, the business situation had improved and the entity believed that it should reverse past impairment losses. A comparison of the carrying amounts of the assets at 30 June 2016 and their recoverable amounts revealed:

Land	$ 9 600
Plant [$38 400 − $12 800]	25 600
Furniture	800
	36 000
Recoverable amount	38 800
Excess of recoverable amount over carrying amount	$ 2 800

The excess cannot be allocated to the goodwill as impairment losses on goodwill can never be reversed.

If the excess were allocated to the assets it can only be allocated to the assets existing at the previous impairment write-down as assets cannot be written up above their original cost. The excess of recoverable amount is then allocated to the relevant assets on a pro rata basis:

	Carrying amount	Share of loss	Adjusted carrying amount
Land	$ 9 600	$ 764	$10 364
Plant	25 600	2 036	27 636
	$35 200	$ 2800	

These assets cannot be written up above the amounts that they would have been recorded at if there had been no previous impairment. These amounts would be:

Land	$10 000
Plant	$30 000 [$40 000 less $10 000 depreciation for the 2015–16 financial year]

As the land cannot be written up above $10 000, $364 of the $764 that was allocated to it must be reallocated to the plant. This would increase the carrying amount of the plant to $28 000 (being $27 636 + $364). This is still less than the maximum of $30 000. The journal entry to record the reversal of the impairment loss is:

Land	Dr	400	
Accumulated Depreciation and Impairment Loss – Plant	Dr	2 400	
Income – Reversal of Impairment Loss	Cr		2 800
(Reversal of impairment loss)			

15.7 DISCLOSURE

Paragraph 126 of IAS 36 requires the following disclosures for each class of assets:

   (a) the amount of impairment losses recognised in profit or loss during the period and the line item(s) of the statement of comprehensive income in which those impairment losses are included;

   (b) the amount of reversals of impairment losses recognised in profit or loss during the period and the line item(s) of the statement of comprehensive income in which those impairment losses are reversed;

   (c) the amount of impairment losses on revalued assets recognised in other comprehensive income during the period; and

   (d) the amount of reversals of impairment losses on revalued assets recognised in other comprehensive income during the period.

As noted in chapter 11 of this book, paragraph 73(e) of IAS 16 *Property, Plant and Equipment* requires, in relation to the reconciliation of the carrying amount at the beginning and end of the period for each class of property, plant and equipment, disclosure of:

• increases or decreases during the period resulting from impairment losses recognised or reversed in other comprehensive income

• impairment losses recognised in profit or loss during the period

• impairment losses reversed in profit or loss during the period.

Similar disclosures are required for intangibles under paragraph 118 of IAS 38 *Intangible Assets* for each class of intangible asset.

As paragraph 128 of IAS 36 states, the disclosures required by paragraph 126 may be presented or included in a reconciliation of the carrying amount of assets at the beginning and end of the period. (Such disclosures were illustrated in chapter 11.) For parts (a) and (b) of paragraph 126, disclosure is required of the relevant line item(s) used. If these were included in other expenses or other income then information relating to impairment losses or reversals would be required in the note to the statement of profit or loss and other comprehensive income relating to these line items in the statement of profit or loss and other comprehensive income. For example, the note to other expenses may be as shown in figure 15.13.

Paragraph 129 of IAS 36 details information to be disclosed for each reportable segment where an entity applies IFRS 8 *Operating Segments*.

Disclosures required by paragraph 130 of IAS 36 are illustrated in figure 15.14. If impairment losses relate to items of property, plant and equipment, such a note can be included in the note detailing disclosures of property, plant and equipment. Disclosures concerning impairment losses for a cash-generating unit may be provided in a separate note, or if applicable attached to the segment report. In figure 15.14, an impairment note is used because the information is given for both individual assets as well as a cash-generating unit.

NOTE 5: Expenses			IAS 36 paragraph
Other operating expenses			
	2017 $'000	2016 $'000	
Amortisation of intangibles	521	435	
Impairment losses:			
Plant and equipment	100	—	*126(a)*
Land and buildings	—	—	
Trade receivables	52	21	
Patents	64	—	

FIGURE 15.13 Disclosures required by paragraph 126(a) of IAS 36

14. Impairment	IAS 36 paragraph 130
The company incurred an impairment loss of $10 000 in relation to property held by the entity for future expansion, the item being written down to recoverable amount due to the pending closure of the plant. The value of the property was reduced due to there being environmental concerns over future development in that area.	*(b)* *(c)(i)* *(a)*
Impairment losses were also recognised in the current period in relation to the pet food division. This division is one of the company's cash-generating units as well as being a reportable segment of the company. The reason for the write-downs was the expected fall in future cash flows due to increased competition in the area, particularly given the lowering of government restrictions on imported products. The recoverable amount of the cash-generating unit is based on a value-in-use calculation. The discount rate used in the calculation of value in use was 10%, compared with the 11% rate used for a previous value-in-use calculation made in 2008. There has been no change in the aggregation of assets in the cash-generating unit since 2011. The impairment loss amounted to $2 600 000 and was allocated as follows:	*(d)(i)* *(a)* *(e)* *(g)* *(d)(iii)* *(b)* *(d)(ii)*

Land and buildings	$ 500 000
Leasehood improvements	420 000
Plant and equipment	310 000
Leased plant and equipment	—
Patents and licences	480 000
Research and development	370 000
Goodwill	520 000
	$2 600 000

FIGURE 15.14 Disclosures required by paragraph 130 of IAS 36

Paragraph 133 of IAS 36 requires disclosures in relation to any goodwill that has not been allocated to a cash-generating unit at the end of the reporting period. In particular, an entity must disclose the amount of the unallocated goodwill and the reasons that amount has not been allocated to the cash-generating units in the entity.

Because the calculation of recoverable amount requires assumptions and estimates relating to future cash flows, IAS 36 requires disclosures relating to the calculation of recoverable amount. Paragraph 132 encourages, but does not require, disclosure of *key assumptions* used to determine the recoverable amounts of assets or cash-generating units.

Paragraph 134 of IAS 36 requires disclosures about the *estimates* used to measure the recoverable amount of a cash-generating unit when goodwill or an intangible asset with an indefinite life is included in the carrying amount of the unit, and the carrying amount of goodwill or intangible assets with indefinite useful lives allocated to that unit is *significant* in comparison with the entity's total carrying amount of goodwill or intangible assets with indefinite useful lives. Where the carrying amount of goodwill or intangible assets is not significant for a unit, paragraph 135 requires that fact to be disclosed. If, for a number of such units, the recoverable amounts are based on the same key assumptions and the aggregate carrying amount of goodwill or intangible assets with indefinite lives is significant in comparison to the total for the entity, paragraph 135 requires similar, but not as extensive, disclosures to those in paragraph 134.

Figure 15.15 contains the disclosures required for Entity M by paragraph 134 of IAS 36.

FIGURE 15.15 Disclosures required by paragraphs 134 and 135 of IAS 36

15. Impairment: goodwill and intangible assets	Paragraph
Goodwill has been allocated for impairment testing purposes to three individual cash-generating units — two in Europe (units A and B) and one in North America (unit C) — and to one group of cash-generating units (operation XYZ) in Asia. The carrying amount of goodwill allocated to unit C and operation XYZ is significant in comparison with the total carrying amount of goodwill, but the carrying amount of goodwill allocated to each of units A and B is not. Nevertheless, the recoverable amounts of units A and B are based on some of the same key assumptions, and the aggregate carrying amount of goodwill allocated to those units is significant. Unit C also has an intangible asset with an indefinite useful life for which the carrying amount is significant in comparison with the entity's total carrying amount of such assets.	*135*
Operation XYZ The carrying amount of goodwill allocated to this cash-generating unit is $1200. The recoverable amount of operation XYZ has been determined to be $2.4m based on a value-in-use calculation. The recoverable amount calculations are most sensitive to changes in the following assumptions: • gross margin during the budget period (5 years) • Japanese yen/dollar exchange rate during the budget period • market share during the budget period • growth rate used to extrapolate cash flows beyond the budget period.	*134* *(a)* *(c)* *(d)(i)*
Management relies on past experience as well as reference to published market indicators and economists' forecasts to determine the values assigned to these key assumptions.	*(d)(ii)*
The calculation of recoverable amount uses cash flow projections based on financial budgets approved by management covering a 5-year period, and a discount rate of 8.4%.	*(d)(iii)* *(d)(v)*
Cash flows beyond that 5-year period have been extrapolated using a steady 6.3% growth rate. This growth rate does not exceed the long-term average growth rate for the market in which XYZ operates. Management believes that any reasonably possible change in the key assumptions on which XYZ's recoverable amount is based would not cause XYZ's carrying amount to exceed its recoverable amount.	*(d)(iv)* *(f)*
Unit C The carrying amount of goodwill allocated to this unit is $1200.	*(a)* *(b)*
The unit has an intangible asset, being the brand name *Chanell*, which has a carrying amount of $1000.	*(c)*
The recoverable amount of unit C has been determined to be $3.6m based on a value-in-use calculation. That calculation is most sensitive to changes in the following assumptions: • 5-year government bond rate during the budget period (5 years) • raw materials price inflation during the budget period	*(d)(i)*

(continued)

FIGURE 15.15 *(continued)*

• market share during the budget period	
• growth rate used to extrapolate cash flows beyond the budget period.	*(d)(ii)*
Management relies on past experience as well as reference to published market indicators and economists' forecasts to determine the values assigned to these key assumptions.	
The calculation uses cash flow projections based on financial budgets approved by management covering a 5-year period, and a discount rate of 8.4%.	*(d)(iii)* *(d)(v)*
Cash flows beyond that 5-year period have been extrapolated using a steady 6.3% growth rate. This growth rate does not exceed the long-term average growth rate for the market in which XYZ operates. Management believes that any reasonably possible change in the key assumptions on which XYZ's recoverable amount is based would not cause XYZ's carrying amount to exceed its recoverable amount.	*(d)(iv)*

Units A and B — *135*

Units A and B have an aggregate carrying amount of goodwill of $700 allocated to them. — *(a)*

The recoverable amounts of units A and B have been determined on the basis of value-in-use calculations. Those units produce complementary products and their recoverable amounts are based on some of the same key assumptions. These assumptions are:
- gross margin during the budget period (4 years) — *(c)*
- raw materials price inflation during the budget period
- market share during the budget period
- growth rate used to extrapolate cash flows beyond the budget period.

Management relies on past experience as well as reference to published market indicators and economists' forecasts to determine the values assigned to these key assumptions. — *(d)*

Management believes that any reasonably possible change in any of these key assumptions would not cause the aggregate carrying amount of A and B to exceed the aggregate recoverable amount of those units. — *(e)*

In the example used in figures 15.14 and 15.15, the recoverable amount is based on value in use. Similar information is required to be disclosed if recoverable amount is based on fair value less costs of disposal — see paragraph 134(e) of IAS 36 for details.

Figure 15.16 provides information contained in Note 14 of the 2011 annual report of Pacific Brands about the impairment tests conducted by the company.

FIGURE 15.16 Disclosures concerning impairment

Impairment tests for CGUs containing goodwill and indefinite life intangible assets

The following CGUs have significant carrying amounts of goodwill and indefinite life intangible assets:

	Consolidated			
	Goodwill		Brand names	
	2011 $'000	2010 $'000	2011 $'000	2010 $'000
Omni Apparel[1]	200 220	200 220	84 541	84 541
Bonds[1]	186 519	186 519	188 500	188 500
Workwear	177 763	177 763	99 980	99 980
Footwear, Outerwear & Sport	—	137 103	—	28 790
Homewares	106 435	153 039	30 344	30 344
	670 937	854 644	403 365	432 155

[1] Omni Apparel and Bonds operating segments form the Underwear & Hosiery reportable segment

FIGURE 15.16 *(continued)*

Impairments during the year

During the year, the Consolidated Entity recognised impairment losses with respect to the Footwear, Outerwear & Sport CGU. The impairment resulted from underperformance and uncertainty with respect to future performance in key markets in which the CGU operates, which in turn adversely impacted expected returns and estimated cash flows to be recovered through use. The Consolidated Entity impaired the carrying amount of goodwill, brand names and other intangible assets by $174.8 million.

The Consolidated Entity has also written off $39.9 million of intangible assets attributable to the divestment of the Sleepmaker and Dunlop Foams businesses. This one off impairment loss was required to bring the assets in line with their fair value less costs to sell. The impairment loss was recognised in other expenses. The net loss on disposal recognised on completion of the sale was $2.3 million (recognised in other expenses).

Recoverable amount

The recoverable amounts of the CGUs above were determined using value in use calculations. Separate value in use calculations are prepared for each of the CGUs that make up the Consolidated Entity. The CGUs are consistent with the operating segments of the Consolidated Entity. Those calculations use cash flow projections based on Board approved budgets and forecasts for a further four year period which are extrapolated in perpetuity.

The recoverable amount as determined by the value in use calculation is materially sensitive to the sales growth rates applied in the forecasted period, terminal value growth rate that is applied into perpetuity and the discount rate applied. The sales growth rates applied in the value in use calculation for the forecasted period range between 2% and 4% (2010: 3% and 8%). Terminal value growth rates range from 1% to 4% (2010: 2% to 3%) and a pre-tax discount rate of 14% (2010: 14%) has been used in discounting the projected cash flows. The pre-tax discount rate was estimated based on the Consolidated Entity's weighted average cost of capital which is determined with regard to various external market indices.

A reduction in the pre-tax free cash flows used in the value in use by 10%, or a reduction in the terminal value growth rate of 2%, or a 1% increase in the discount rate could result in impairment for a CGU within the group.

Source: Pacific Brands Ltd (2011, p. 65).

SUMMARY

It is important that users of financial statements can rely on the information provided. In particular they need to be assured that the assets in the statement of financial position are not stated at amounts greater than an entity could expect to recover from those assets. It needs to be recognised that an entity can obtain cash flows from two sources in relation to any asset: (1) by using the asset or (2) by selling the asset. One of these involves an ongoing use of the asset whereas the other relates to an immediate sale of the asset. Any test of the carrying amounts of assets against their recoverable amounts must take both sources of cash flows into account.

For an entity to conduct an impairment test, there must be indications of impairment. Entities then need to continuously obtain information about factors that may indicate that assets are impaired. These sources of information may consist of an analysis of economic factors external to the organisation, such as actions of competitors, or economic factors within the entity itself, such as the performance of the entity's property, plant and equipment over time. When there are indications of impairment, an entity conducts an impairment test, comparing the carrying amounts of relevant assets and their recoverable amounts. The latter involves measurement of value in use and fair value less costs of disposal.

In many cases, single assets do not produce cash flows for the entity. Instead, the assets of the entity are allocated to units, called cash-generating units, as each unit produces independent cash flows for an entity. In such cases, impairment tests are conducted on the cash-generating units, rather than on individual assets. Where an impairment loss occurs, the loss must be allocated across the assets of the unit, with goodwill being the first asset affected. Where corporate assets such as research facilities exist, it may be necessary to combine a number of cash-generating units together in order to test for impairment of the corporate asset.

Having written down assets as a result of impairment tests, entities may see potential improvement in the recoverable amounts of assets by observing the same indicators used for detecting impairment losses. In such cases, where the recoverable amounts of assets have increased, impairment losses may be reversed, subject to constraints. Impairment losses relating to goodwill, however, can never be reversed.

DEMONSTRATION PROBLEM 15.1 Impairment losses, no corporate assets

Kakadu Ltd has two divisions, Killmore and Katherine, each of which is a separate cash-generating unit (CGU). Kakadu Ltd adopts a decentralised management approach whereby unit managers are expected to operate their units. However, there is one corporate asset, the information technology network, which is centrally controlled and provides a computer network to the company as a whole. The information technology network is not a depreciable asset.

At 30 June 2014 the net assets of each division, including its allocated share of the information technology network, were as follows:

	Killmore	Katherine
Information technology (IT) network	$ 284 000	$ 116 000
Land	450 000	290 000
Plant (20% p.a. straight-line depreciation)	1 310 000	960 000
Accumulated depreciation (plant)	(917 000)	(384 000)
Goodwill	46 000	32 000
Patent (10% straight-line amortisation)	210 000	255 000
Accumulated amortisation (patent)	(21 000)	(102 000)
Cash	20 000	12 000
Inventory	120 000	80 000
Receivables	34 000	40 000
	1 536 000	1 299 000
Liabilities	(276 000)	(189 000)
Net assets	$1 260 000	$1 110 000

Additional information as at 30 June 2014:
- Killmore's land had a fair value less costs of disposal of $437 000.
- Katherine's patent had a carrying amount below fair value less costs of disposal.
- Katherine's plant had a fair value less costs of disposal of $540 000.
- Receivables were considered to be collectable.
- The IT network is not depreciated, as it is assumed to have an indefinite life.

Kakadu Ltd's management undertook impairment testing at 30 June 2014 and determined the recoverable amount of each cash-generating unit to be: $1 430 000 for Killmore and $1 215 000 for Katherine.

Required

Prepare any journal entries necessary to record the results of the impairment testing for each of the CGUs.

Solution

The first step is to determine whether either CGU has an impairment loss. This is done by comparing the carrying amount of the assets of each CGU with the recoverable amount of these assets. Note that it is the carrying amount of the *assets* not the net assets that is used — the test is for the impairment of assets, not net assets.

	Killmore	Katherine
Carrying amount of assets	$1 536 000	$1 299 000
Recoverable amount	1 430 000	1 215 000
Impairment loss	$ (106 000)	$ (84 000)

As a result of the comparison, both CGUs have suffered impairment losses.

For each CGU, the impairment loss is used to write off any goodwill and then to allocate any balance across the other assets in proportion to their carrying amounts.

Killmore CGU

Killmore has goodwill of $46 000. Therefore, the first step is to write off goodwill of $46 000.

The second step is to allocate the remaining impairment loss of $60 000 (i.e. $106 000 − $46 000).

Note that although all the assets are included in the calculation to determine whether the CGU has incurred an impairment loss, the allocation of that loss is only to those assets that will be written down as a result of the allocation process. Cash and receivables are not written down as they are recorded at amounts equal to fair value. The inventory is recorded under IAS 2 at the lower of cost and net realisable value, and as such is excluded from the impairment test write-down under IAS 36. The allocation of the balance of the impairment loss is done on a pro rata basis, in proportion to the assets' carrying amounts.

	Carrying amount	Proportion	Allocation of loss	Adjusted carrying amount
IT network	$ 284 000	284/1 316	$12 948	$271 052
Land	450 000	450/1 316	20 517	429 483
Plant	393 000	393/1 316	17 918	375 082
Patent	189 000	189/1 316	8 617	180 383
	$1 316 000		$60 000	

After the initial allocation across the assets, a check has to be made on the amount of each write-down as IAS 36 places limitations on the amount to which assets can be written down. Paragraph 105 of IAS 36 states that for each asset the carrying amount should not be reduced below the highest of the following:

- its fair value less costs of disposal
- its value in use
- zero.

In this example, the land has a fair value less costs of disposal of $437 000. Hence it cannot be written down to $429 483 as per the above allocation table. Only $13 000 (to write the asset down from $450 000 to $437 000) of the impairment loss can be allocated to it. Therefore, the remaining $7517 allocated loss (i.e. $20 517 − $13 000) must be allocated to the other assets. This allocation is based on the adjusted carrying amounts, the right-hand column of the table above.

	Carrying amount	Proportion	Allocation of loss	Adjusted carrying amount
IT Network	$271 052	271 052/826 517	$2 465	$268 587
Plant	375 082	375 082/826 517	3 411	371 671
Patent	180 383	180 383/826 517	1 641	178 742
	$826 517		$7 517	

The impairment loss for each asset is then based, where relevant, on the accumulation of both allocations. With non-depreciable assets such as land, the asset is simply written down, whereas with depreciable assets such as plant, the account increased is the accumulated depreciation and impairment losses account.

The journal entry for Killmore is:

Impairment Loss	Dr	106 000	
Goodwill	Cr		46 000
Land	Cr		13 000
IT Network [$12 948 + $2 465]	Cr		15 413
Accumulated Depreciation and Impairment			
Losses – Plant [$17 918 + $3 411]	Cr		21 329
Accumulated Depreciation and Impairment			
Losses – Patent [$8 617 + $1 641]	Cr		10 258

Katherine CGU

As with the Killmore CGU, the impairment loss is used to write off the goodwill balance, $32 000, and then the balance of the impairment loss, $52 000 (i.e. $84 000 − $32 000), is allocated across the remaining assets, except for cash, receivables and inventory. Further, as the patent's carrying amount is below fair value less costs of disposal, no impairment loss can be allocated to it.

	Carrying amount	Proportion	Allocation of loss	Adjusted carrying amount
IT network	$116 000	116/982	$ 6 143	$109 857
Land	290 000	290/982	15 356	274 644
Plant	576 000	576/982	30 501	545 499
	$982 000		$52 000	

Because the plant has a fair value less costs of disposal of $540 000 and this is below the adjusted carrying amount of $545 499, the full impairment loss of $30 501 can be allocated to it.

The journal entry for Katherine is:

Impairment Loss	Dr	84 000	
Goodwill	Cr		32 000
IT Network	Cr		6 143
Land	Cr		15 356
Accumulated Depreciation and Impairment			
Losses – Plant	Cr		30 501

DEMONSTRATION PROBLEM 15.2 Impairment losses, corporate asset

Parkes Ltd has three CGUs, a head office and a research facility. The carrying amounts of the assets and their recoverable amounts are as follows:

	Unit A	Unit B	Unit C	Head office	Research facility	Parkes Ltd
Carrying amount	$100	$150	$200	$150	$50	$650
Recoverable amount	129	164	271			584

The assets of the head office are allocable to the three units as follows:
- Unit A: $19
- Unit B: $56
- Unit C: $75

The assets of the research facility cannot be reasonably allocated to the CGUs.

Required

Assuming all assets can be adjusted for impairment, prepare the journal entry relating to any impairment of the assets of Parkes Ltd.

Solution

For each unit there needs to be a comparison between the carrying amounts of the assets of the units and their recoverable amounts to determine which, if any, of the CGUs is impaired. As the asset of the head office can be allocated to each of the units, the carrying amounts of each of the units must then include the allocated part of the head office.

Calculation of impairment losses for units

	Unit A	Unit B	Unit C
Carrying amount	$119	$206	$275
Recoverable amount	129	164	271
Impairment loss	$ —	$ 42	$ 4

Because the assets of Unit A are not impaired, no write-down is necessary. For Units B and C, the impairment losses must be allocated to the assets of the units. The allocation is in proportion to the carrying amounts of the assets.

Allocation of impairment loss

	Unit B		Unit C	
To head office	$11	[42 × 56/206]	$1	[4 × 75/275]
To other assets	31	[42 × 150/206]	3	[4 × 200/275]
	$42		$4	

In relation to the research centre, the assets of the centre cannot be allocated to the units, so the impairment test is based on the smallest CGU that contains the research centre, which in this case is the entity as a whole, Parkes Ltd. For this calculation, the carrying amounts of the assets of the units as well as the head office are reduced by the impairment losses already allocated. The total assets of Parkes Ltd consist of all the assets of the entity.

Impairment testing for CGU as a whole

	Unit A	Unit B	Unit C	Head office	Research centre	Parkes Ltd
Carrying amount	100	150	200	150	50	650
Impairment loss	–	31	3	12	—	46
Net	**100**	**119**	**197**	**138**	**50**	**604**
Recoverable amount						**584**
Impairment loss						20

Because the carrying amount of the assets of Parkes Ltd is greater than the recoverable amount of the entity, the entity has incurred an impairment loss. This loss is allocated across all the assets of the entity in proportion to their carrying amounts.

Allocation of impairment loss

	Carrying amount	Proportion	Allocation of loss	Adjusted carrying amount
Unit A	$100	100/604 × 20	$ 3	$ 97
Unit B	119	119/604 × 20	4	116
Unit C	197	197/604 × 20	6	191
Head office	138	138/604 × 20	5	132
Research centre	50	50/604 × 20	2	48
	$604		$20	

Journal entry for impairment loss

The journal entry for the impairment loss recognises the reduction in each of the assets. As the composition of the assets is not detailed in this question, the credit adjustments are made against the asset accounts. They could also have been made against an accumulated depreciation and impairment losses account. Obviously if the composition of each of the assets of each unit had been given, the impairment loss would have been allocated to specific assets rather than assets as a total category as in the solution here.

Impairment Loss	Dr	66	
Assets – Unit A	Cr		3
Assets – Unit B	Cr		34
Assets – Unit C	Cr		9
Assets – Head Office	Cr		18
Assets – Research Facility	Cr		2

Discussion questions

1. What is an impairment test?
2. Why is an impairment test considered necessary?
3. When should an entity conduct an impairment test?
4. What are some external indicators of impairment?
5. What are some internal indicators of impairment?
6. What is meant by recoverable amount?
7. How is an impairment loss calculated in relation to a single asset accounted for?
8. What are the limits to which an asset can be written down in relation to impairment losses?
9. What is a cash-generating unit?
10. How are impairment losses accounted for in relation to cash-generating units?
11. Are there limits in adjusting assets within a cash-generating unit when impairment losses occur?
12. How is goodwill tested for impairment?
13. What is a corporate asset?
14. How are corporate assets tested for impairment?
15. When can an entity reverse past impairment losses?
16. What are the steps involved in reversing an impairment loss?

Exercises

STAR RATING ★ BASIC ★★ MODERATE ★★★ DIFFICULT

Exercise 15.1 CASH-GENERATING UNITS

★ Fresh Milk Ltd owns a large number of dairy farms. It has a number of factories that are used to produce milk products that are then sent to other factories to be converted into milk-based products such as yoghurt and custard. In applying IAS 36 *Impairment of Assets*, the accountant for Fresh Milk Ltd is concerned about correctly identifying the cash-generating units (CGUs) for the company, and has sought your advice on such questions as to whether the milk production section is a separate CGU even though the company does not sell milk directly to other parties, or whether it should be included in the milk-based products CGU.

Required

Write a report to the accountant of Fresh Milk Ltd, including the following:
1. Define a CGU.
2. Explain why impairment testing requires the use of CGUs, rather than being based on single assets.
3. Explain the factors that the accountant should consider in determining the CGUs for Fresh Milk Ltd.

Exercise 15.2 IMPAIRMENT TESTING AND GOODWILL

★ At 30 June 2014, Longreach Ltd is considering undertaking an impairment test. Having only recently adopted the international accounting standards, the management of Longreach Ltd seeks your advice in relation to this test under IAS 36 *Impairment of Assets*.

Required

Write a report to management, specifically explaining:
1. the purpose of the impairment test

2. how the existence of goodwill will affect the impairment test
3. the basic steps to be followed in applying the impairment test.

Exercise 15.3   FREQUENCY OF IMPAIRMENT TEST

★ In setting up its systems to apply IAS 36 *Impairment of Assets*, management of Mildura Ltd wants to know how often the company needs to apply an impairment test on its assets, and what information it needs to generate to determine whether a test is needed.

Required

Prepare a response to management.

Exercise 15.4   DETERMINATION OF CGUs

★ The Rennes City Council contracts out the bus routes in Rennes to various subcontractors based on a tender arrangement. Some routes, such as the Express to City routes, are profitable, while others, such as those collecting schoolchildren from remote areas, are unprofitable. As a result, the city council requires tenderers to take a package of routes, some profitable, some less so. The Le Bon Bus Company has won the contract to operate its buses with a package of five separate routes, one of which operates at a significant loss. Specific buses are allocated by the Le Bon Bus Company to each route, and cash flows can be isolated to each route because drivers and takings are specific to each route.

Required

Discuss the determination of cash-generating units for the Le Bon Bus Company.

Exercise 15.5   IMPAIRMENT LOSS

★ Tambo Ltd has determined that its fine china division is a cash-generating unit. The carrying amounts of the assets at 30 June 2013 are as follows:

Factory	$ 210 000
Land	150 000
Equipment	120 000
Inventory	60 000

Tambo Ltd calculated the recoverable amount of the division to be $510 000.

Required

Provide the journal entry(ies) for the impairment loss, assuming that the fair value less costs of disposal of the land are (a) $140 000 and (b) $145 000.

Exercise 15.6   IMPAIRMENT LOSS, GOODWILL

★ On 1 January 2014, Narrabri Ltd acquired all the assets and liabilities of Oakey Ltd. Oakey Ltd has a number of operating divisions, including one whose major industry is the manufacture of toy trains, particularly those of historical significance. The toy trains division is regarded as a cash-generating unit. In paying $2 million for the net assets of Oakey Ltd, Narrabri Ltd calculated that it had acquired goodwill of $240 000. The goodwill was allocated to each of the divisions, and the assets and liabilities acquired measured at fair value at acquisition date.

At 31 December 2016, the carrying amounts of the assets of the toy train division were:

Factory	$ 250 000
Inventory	150 000
Brand — 'Froggy'	50 000
Goodwill	50 000

There is a declining interest in toy trains because of the aggressive marketing of computer-based toys, so the management of Narrabri Ltd measured the recoverable amount of the toy train division at 31 December 2016, determining it to be $423 000.

Required

Prepare the journal entries to account for the impairment loss at 31 December 2016.

Exercise 15.7

IMPAIRMENT LOSS, GOODWILL, PARTLY OWNED SUBSIDIARY

★ Winton Ltd acquired 60% of the issued shares of Wodonga Ltd on 1 January 2014 for $426 000. At this date, the net fair value of the identifiable assets and liabilities of Wodonga Ltd was $660 000.

At 31 December 2014, the tangible assets and liabilities of Wodonga Ltd as included in the consolidated financial statements of Winton Ltd were as follows:

Property, plant and equipment	$ 863 000
Accumulated depreciation	(120 000)
	743 000
Inventory	55 000
Cash	22 000
	820 000
Liabilities	(50 000)
	$ 770 000

Goodwill had not been written down over the year.

In conducting an impairment test on Wodonga Ltd as a cash-generating unit, Winton Ltd assessed the recoverable amount of Wodonga Ltd to be $800 000.

Required

1. Explain how the impairment loss in relation to Wodonga Ltd should be allocated. Prepare journal entry(ies) in relation to the assets of Wodonga Ltd at 31 December 2014 as a result of the impairment test.
2. Explain the accounting for the impairment (if any) if the recoverable amount was $860 000.

Exercise 15.8

EFRAG RESPONSE TO PROPOSED AMENDMENTS

★★ Read the following comments made by the European Financial Reporting Advisory Group (EFRAG) in its response, dated 4 April 2003 (pp. 4–5), to the IASB on the proposed amendments to IAS 36:

Impairment test

The proposed impairment test does not distinguish between acquired goodwill and pre-existing goodwill of the acquirer nor between acquired goodwill and goodwill internally generated after the combination. This results in 'cushions', so avoiding recognition of real impairment losses of goodwill in certain situations when the impairment test is performed. We believe that this undermines the reliability of the information obtained.

The Board claims that there seems to be no alternative design for the impairment test to avoid this. This may be true for the replacement of acquired goodwill by self-generated goodwill of the acquired business but we believe a stronger effort should be made to eliminate the cushion provided by the pre-acquisition self-generated goodwill of the acquirer. The current UK accounting standard FRS 11 *Impairment of Fixed Assets and Goodwill* attempts to make such a distinction.

We urge the Board to delete the second step of the impairment test (paragraph 86). We believe that the second step, which measures the amount of goodwill impairment by comparing its carrying amount with its implied value, is costly and does not improve the quality of the information.

In our view it suffices to allocate the identified impairment firstly to goodwill and then to intangible assets with indefinite useful lives that are part of the cash-generating unit and any remainder to other assets on a pro rata basis.

Required

Evaluate the comments made by EFRAG.

Exercise 15.9	**DELOITTE TOUCHE TOHMATSU RESPONSE**

★★ Read the following comments made by Deloitte Touche Tohmatsu (4 April 2003, p. 7) on the proposed amendments to IAS 36:

> We agree with the conclusion that goodwill acquired in a business combination should be recognised as an asset. With regard to the accounting for goodwill after initial recognition, we generally agree with the Board's proposal. However, we note that there may be circumstances where goodwill has a finite life. For example, this may be the case when an entity has a specified life. In certain jurisdictions such as the People's Republic of China (the PRC), foreign investment is made by means of certain legal structures that expire after a specified number of years. At the end of the agreed period, the assets will revert to the PRC partner. In such circumstances, any goodwill will have an implied value of zero at the end of the entity's life.
>
> Consequently, we believe that, in accounting for goodwill after initial recognition, there should be a rebuttable presumption that goodwill has an indefinite life and, therefore, accounted for at cost less any accumulated impairment losses. However, in those cases where that presumption is rebutted and sufficient persuasive evidence exists indicating that goodwill has a finite life, we believe that a method of systematic amortisation is preferable to 'impairment only' accounting. In such cases, we believe that goodwill, consistently with other intangible assets that have a finite life, should be amortised and tested for impairment when an indicator exists. The impairment test applied to goodwill with a definite life should be the same test as goodwill with an indefinite life.

Required

Evaluate the comments made by Deloitte Touche Tohmatsu.

Exercise 15.10	**IDENTIFICATION OF CGUs**

★★ Burger Queen is a chain of fast-food restaurants — most reasonably sized towns in the country have a Burger Queen outlet. The key claim to fame of the Burger Queen restaurants is that their fried chips are extra crunchy. Also, to ensure that there is a consistent standard of food and service across the country, the management of the chain of restaurants conducts spot checks on restaurants. Failure to provide the high standard expected by Burger Queen management can mean that the franchise to a particular location can be taken away from the franchisee. Burger Queen management is responsible for the television advertising across the country as well as the marketing program, including the special deals that may be available at any particular time.

Each restaurant is responsible for its own sales, cooking of food, training of staff, and general matters such as cleanliness of the store. However, all material used in the making of the burgers and other items sold are provided at a given cost from the central management, which can thereby control the quality and the price.

Required

Identify the cash-generating unit(s) in this scenario. Give reasons for your conclusions.

Exercise 15.11	**IDENTIFICATION OF CGUs**

★★ Marla Macalister is in the business of making rubber tubing that comes in all sorts of sizes and shapes. Marla has established three factories in the north, south and east parts of the city. Each factory has a large machine that can be adjusted to produce all the varieties of tubing that Marla sells. Each machine is capable of producing around 100 000 metres of tubing a week, depending on diameter and shape. Marla's current sales amount to about 250 000 metres a week. Each factory is never worked to full capacity. However, sales are sufficiently high that Marla cannot afford to shut one of the factories.

In order to satisfy customer demand as quickly as possible, all orders are directed to Marla, who allocates the jobs to the various factories depending on the current workload of each factory. This also ensures that efficient runs of particular types of tubing can be done at the same time. Each factory is managed individually in terms of maintenance of the machines, the hiring of labour and the packaging and delivery of the finished product.

Required

Identify the cash-generating unit(s) in this scenario. Give reasons for your conclusions.

Exercise 15.12	**IDENTIFICATION OF CGUs**

★★ Fad Furniture Ltd has three separate operating divisions. The first, the timber division, is in charge of producing milled timber. This division manages a number of timber plantations and timber mills from which the finished timber is produced. The majority of the timber is sold, at an internal transfer price, to the second area of operations in Fad Furniture, the parts division. Any excess timber is sold to external parties. The parts division is responsible for turning the timber into parts for the making of timber furniture, both indoor and outdoor. These parts are suitable only for the manufacture of the furniture produced by Fad Furniture. The parts are then transferred at internal transfer prices to the third area of operations, the furniture division. This division assembles the furniture and delivers it to the various outlets that retail Fad Furniture's products.

Required

1. Identify the cash-generating unit(s) in this scenario, giving reasons for your conclusions.
2. Would the determination of the cash-generating units be affected if the parts division was also responsible for kit furniture, where the parts are made available to customers for self-assembly?

Exercise 15.13 VALUE IN USE

★★ Management is assessing the future cash flows in relation to an entity's assets, and considers that there are two possible scenarios for future cash flows. The first, for which there is a 70% probability of occurrence, would provide future cash flows of $5 million. The second, which has a probability of occurrence of 30%, would provide future cash flows of $8 million. Management has decided that the calculation of value in use should be based on the most likely scenario, namely the one that will produce cash flows of $5 million.

Required

Evaluate management's decision.

Exercise 15.14 WRITE-DOWN

★★ Mildura Enterprises Ltd acquired a building in which to conduct its operations at a cost of $10 million. The building generates no cash flows on its own and is considered a part of the cash-generating unit, which is the firm as a whole. Since the building was acquired, the value of inner-city properties has declined owing to an overabundance of office space and the downturn in the economy. The company would receive only $8 million dollars if it decided to sell the building now. However, the company believes the building is serving its purpose and the profits are high, so there is no current intention of selling the building.

Required

Discuss whether the building should be written down to $8 million. Provide any journal entries necessary.

Exercise 15.15 ASSET IMPAIRMENT

★★ Parkes Ltd acquired a network facility for its administration section on 1 July 2014. The network facility cost $550 000 and was depreciated using a straight-line method over a 5-year period, with a residual value of $50 000. On 30 June 2016, the company assessed the current market value of the facility given that there was an active market for such facilities as many companies used a similar network. The value was determined to be $300 000.

Required

Discuss whether the network facility asset is impaired and whether it should be written down to $300 000. Provide any journal entries necessary.

Exercise 15.16 IMPAIRMENT LOSS FOR A CASH-GENERATING UNIT, REVERSAL OF IMPAIRMENT LOSS

★★ One of the cash-generating units of Broome Ltd is associated with the manufacture of wine barrels. At 30 June 2013, Broome Ltd believed, based on an analysis of economic indicators, that the assets of the unit were impaired. The carrying amounts of the assets and liabilities of the unit at 30 June 2013 were:

Buildings	$ 420 000
Accumulated depreciation — buildings*	(180 000)
Factory machinery	220 000
Accumulated depreciation — machinery**	(40 000)
Goodwill	15 000
Inventory	80 000

		$	40 000
Receivables		$	40 000
Allowance for doubtful debts			(5 000)
Cash			20 000
Accounts payable			30 000
Loans			20 000

   * Depreciated at $60 000 p.a.
  ** Depreciated at $45 000 p.a.

Broome Ltd determined the value in use of the unit to be $535 000. The receivables were considered to be collectable, except those considered doubtful. The company allocated the impairment loss in accordance with IAS 36.

During the 2013–14 period, Broome Ltd increased the depreciation charge on buildings to $65 000 p.a., and to $50 000 p.a. for factory machinery. The inventory on hand at 1 July 2013 was sold by the end of the year. At 30 June 2014, Broome Ltd, because of a return in the market to the use of traditional barrels for wines and an increase in wine production, assessed the recoverable amount of the cash-generating unit to be $30 000 greater than the carrying amount of the unit. As a result, Broome Ltd recognised a reversal of the impairment loss.

Required

1. Prepare the journal entries for Broome Ltd at 30 June 2013 and 2014.
2. What differences would arise in relation to the answer in requirement 1 if the recoverable amount at 30 June 2014 was $20 000 greater than the carrying amount of the unit?
3. If the recoverable amount of the buildings at 30 June 2014 was $175 000, how would this change the answer to requirement 2?

Exercise 15.17   **ALLOCATION OF CORPORATE ASSETS**

★★   Hay Ltd has three cash-generating units, Hebel Division, Hawker Division and Hillston Division. The head office is in the city, and the infrastructure for the divisions is located outside the city centre. Because of the potential for the company to have problems of an environmental nature or in relation to social justice, particularly with its mix of employees, Hay Ltd has recently established a social responsibility centre (SRC), which interacts with the divisions, generating information and statistics for the production of a triple-bottom-line social responsibility report.

At 30 June 2014, the net assets relating to each of the divisions as well as the headquarters section and the SRC were as follows:

	Hebel Division	Hawker Division	Hillston Division	Head office	SRC
Land	$ 120 000	$ 140 000	$ 80 000	$10 000	$ 5 000
Plant and equipment	420 000	310 000	270 000	40 000	15 000
Accumulated depreciation	(120 000)	(100 000)	(80 000)	(5 000)	(4 000)
Inventories	150 000	110 000	100 000	0	0
Accounts receivable	90 000	80 000	50 000	0	0
	660 000	540 000	420 000	45 000	16 000
Liabilities	60 000	50 000	50 000	0	0
Net assets	$ 600 000	$ 490 000	$370 000	$45 000	$16 000

Hay Ltd believes that the corporation's headquarters supplies approximately equal service to the three divisions, and an immaterial amount to the SRC. Because the SRC has been established only recently, it is not possible at this stage to allocate the assets of the SRC to the three divisions. Economic indicators suggest that the company's assets may have been impaired, so management has determined the value in use of each of the divisions — the head office and the SRC do not generate cash inflows. The recoverable amount of the three divisions were calculated to be:

Hebel Division	$720 000
Hawker Division	500 000
Hillston Division	400 000

Required

Determine how Hay Ltd should account for any impairment loss to the entity.

Exercise 15.18 ALLOCATION OF CORPORATE ASSETS AND GOODWILL

★★ Quilpie Ltd acquired all the assets and liabilities of Roma Ltd on 1 January 2014. Roma Ltd's activities were run through three separate businesses, namely the Sandstone Unit, the Sapphire Unit and the Silverton Unit. These units are separate cash-generating units. Quilpie Ltd allowed unit managers to effectively operate each of the units, but certain central activities were run through the corporate office. Each unit was allocated a share of the goodwill acquired, as well as a share of the corporate office.

At 31 December 2014, the assets allocated to each unit were as follows:

	Sandstone	Sapphire	Silverton
Factory	$ 820	$ 750	$ 460
Accumulated depreciation	(420)	(380)	(340)
Land	200*	300**	150*
Equipment	300	410	560
Accumulated depreciation	(60)	(320)	(310)
Inventory	120	80	100*
Goodwill	40	50	30
Corporate property	200	150	120

* These assets have carrying amounts less than fair value less costs of disposal.
** This asset has a fair value less costs of disposal of $293.

Quilpie Ltd determined the recoverable amount of each of the business units at 31 December 2014:

Sandstone	$1 170
Sapphire	900
Silverton	800

Required

Determine how Quilpie Ltd should allocate any impairment loss at 31 December 2014.

Exercise 15.19 IMPAIRMENT, TWO CASH-GENERATING UNITS

★★ Miles Ltd has two divisions, Jericho and Jackson. Each of these is regarded as a separate cash-generating unit. At 31 December 2013, the carrying amounts of the assets of the two divisions were:

	Jericho	Jackson
Plant	$1 500	$1 200
Accumulated depreciation	(650)	(375)
Patent	240	
Inventory	54	75
Receivables	75	82
Goodwill	25	20

The receivables were regarded as collectable, and the inventory's fair value less costs of disposal was equal to its carrying amount. The patent had a fair value less costs of disposal of $220. The plant at Jericho was depreciated at $300 p.a., and that at Jackson was depreciated at $250 p.a.

Miles Ltd undertook impairment testing at 31 December 2013, and determined the recoverable amounts of the two divisions to be:

Jericho	$1 044
Jackson	990

As a result, management increased the depreciation of the Jericho plant from $300 to $350 p.a. for the year 2013.

By 31 December 2014, the performance in both divisions had improved, and the carrying amounts of the assets of both divisions and their recoverable amounts were as follows:

	Jericho	Jackson
Carrying amount	$1 322	$1 433
Recoverable amount	1 502	1 520

Required

Determine how Miles Ltd should account for the results of the impairment tests at both 31 December 2013 and 31 December 2014.

Exercise 15.20

★★

CORPORATE ASSETS

Albury Ltd recently conducted an impairment test on the company. It determined that it had two cash-generating units, Division One and Division Two. Both divisions were considered to be impaired, with Division One having an impairment loss of $25 000 and Division Two having an impairment loss of $30 000. These losses were allocated to the assets of the divisions in accordance with IAS 36 *Impairment of Assets*, with the assets and liabilities of the divisions after the allocation being recorded as follows:

	Division One	Division Two
Cash	$ 5 000	$ 8 000
Inventory	30 000	40 000
Receivables	20 000	8 000
Plant	320 000	300 000
Accumulated depreciation	(120 000)	(120 000)
Land	80 000	50 000
Buildings	110 000	100 000
Accumulated depreciation	(40 000)	(60 000)
Furniture & fittings	40 000	30 000
Accumulated depreciation	(15 000)	(10 000)
Total assets	430 000	346 000
Provisions	20 000	40 000
Borrowings	30 000	66 000
Total liabilities	50 000	106 000
Net assets	$ 380 000	$ 240 000

Albury Ltd also recorded goodwill of $14 000 (net of accumulated impairment losses of $12 000) and had corporate assets consisting of a head office building carried at $150 000 (net of depreciation of $50 000) and furniture and fittings of $80 000 (net of depreciation of $20 000).

Albury Ltd determined that the recoverable amount of the entity's assets was $950 000.

The management of Albury Ltd then completed the accounting for impairment losses. The receivables in both divisions were considered to be collectable.

Required

Prepare a table of the assets and liabilities of Albury Ltd, using the headings 'Division One', 'Division Two' and 'Corporate', after the completion of accounting for impairment losses.

Exercise 15.21   **CORPORATE ASSET**

★★   Fiery Ltd is a company that is operated through two divisions, namely Green Ltd and Dragon Ltd. These divisions were regarded as separate cash-generating units. The assets of the two divisions at 30 June 2013 were as follows:

	Green Ltd	Dragon Ltd
Land	$100 000	$ 64 000
Plant	280 000	145 000
Accumulated depreciation	(60 000)	(30 000)
Equipment	160 000	220 000
Accumulated depreciation	(40 000)	(20 000)
Inventory	60 000	36 000
Goodwill	20 000	15 000
	$520 000	$430 000

Fiery Ltd had a corporate headquarters carried at an amount of $100 000. This asset could not be allocated on a reasonable basis to the cash-generating units.

At 30 June 2013 there were indications that the assets of the company may be impaired. The company calculated the recoverable amounts to be as follows:

Fiery Ltd	$973 000
Green Ltd	$478 000
Dragon Ltd	$420 000

The inventory had fair values less costs of disposal greater than the current carrying amounts. The land held by Green Ltd had fair value less costs of disposal of $97 000.

Required

Prepare the journal entries at 30 June 2013 to record the accounting for the impairment losses.

Exercise 15.22   **REVERSAL OF IMPAIRMENT LOSSES**

★★   At 30 June 2013, Reacher Ltd reported the following assets:

Land	$ 50 000
Plant	250 000
Accumulated depreciation	(50 000)
Goodwill	8 000
Inventory	40 000
Cash	2 000

All assets are measured using the cost model.

At 30 June 2013, the recoverable amount of the entity, considered to be a single cash-generating unit, was $272 000.

For the period ending 30 June 2014, the depreciation charge on plant was $18 400. If the plant had not been impaired the charge would have been $25 000.

At 30 June 2014, the recoverable amount of the entity was calculated to be $13 000 greater than the carrying amount of the assets of the entity. As a result, Reacher Ltd recognised a reversal of the previous year's impairment loss.

Required

Prepare the journal entries relating to impairment at 30 June 2013 and 2014.

Exercise 15.23 **ALLOCATION OF CORPORATE ASSET AND GOODWILL**

★★★ Perth Ltd has two cash-generating units, Division One and Division Two. At 30 June 2014, the net assets of the two divisions were as follows:

	Division One	Division Two
Cash	$ 12 000	$ 8 000
Inventory	30 000	40 000
Receivables	20 000	8 000
Plant	320 000	0
Accumulated depreciation (Plant)	(120 000)	0
Land	90 000	150 000
Buildings	110 000	140 000
Accumulated depreciation (Buildings)	(40 000)	(60 000)
Furniture & fittings	0	30 000
Accumulated depreciation (Furniture & fittings)	0	(10 000)
Total assets	422 000	306 000
Provisions	20 000	40 000
Borrowings	30 000	66 000
Total liabilities	50 000	106 000
Net assets	$ 372 000	$ 200 000

Additional information regarding the divisions' assets is as follows:
- the receivables of both divisions were considered to be collectable
- Division Two's land had a fair value less costs of disposal of $135 000 at 30 June 2014.

At 30 June 2014 Perth Ltd also had the following corporate assets, which Perth's management decided to allocate equally to the two divisions:
- goodwill of $14 000
- a head office building with a carrying amount of $160 000 (net of $50 000 accumulated depreciation).

Perth Ltd's management conducted impairment testing on the company's assets at 30 June 2014 and determined that Division One's recoverable amount was $415 000 and Division Two's recoverable amount was $310 000.

Required

Prepare the journal entries required at 30 June 2014 to account for any impairment losses.

Exercise 15.24 **CORPORATE ASSETS, ALLOCATED AND UNALLOCATED**

★★★ Ararat Ltd has three divisions, Aramac, Alpha and Amby, which operate independently of each other to produce milk products. The company has a headquarters and a research centre located in Albury, with the divisions located throughout Australia. The research centre interacts with all the divisions to assist in the improvement of the manufacturing process and the quality of the products manufactured by the entity.

There is not as yet any basis on which to determine how the work of the research centre will be allocated to each of the three divisions, as this will depend on priorities of the company overall and issues that arise in each division. The company headquarters provides approximately equal services to each of the divisions, but an immaterial amount to the research centre.

Neither the headquarters nor the research centre generates cash inflows.

On 30 June 2014, the net assets of Ararat Ltd were as follows:

	Aramac	Alpha	Amby	Head office	Research centre
Land	$ 440 000	$ 280 000	$ 160 000	$110 000	$ 67 000
Plant & equipment	840 000	620 000	540 000	80 000	45 000
Accumulated depreciation	(240 000)	(200 000)	(160 000)	(10 000)	(12 000)
Inventories	240 000	180 000	140 000	0	0
Accounts receivable	120 000	100 000	60 000	0	0
	$1 400 000	$ 980 000	$ 740 000	$180 000	$100 000
Liabilities	120 000	100 000	100 000	0	0
Net assets	$1 280 000	$ 880 000	$ 640 000	$180 000	$100 000

Management of Ararat Ltd believes there are economic indicators to suggest that the company's assets may have been impaired. Accordingly, they have had recoverable amount assessed for each of the divisions:

Aramac	$1 550 000
Alpha	1 000 000
Amby	750 000

The land held by Aramac Ltd was measured at fair value using the revaluation model because of the specialised nature of the land. At 30 June 2014, the fair value was $440 000. The land held by Alpha Ltd was measured at cost, and had a fair value less costs of disposal of $270 264 at 30 June 2014.

Required

Determine how Ararat Ltd should account for any impairment of the entity. Justify your decisions and complete any required journal entries.

Exercise 15.25 **IMPAIRMENT LOSS**

★★★ Casey Ltd prepared the following draft statement of financial position at 30 June 2014:

Cash	$ 5 000	Share capital	$1 000 000
Receivables	15 000	Retained earnings	280 000
Land (at fair value 1/7/13)	160 000	General reserve	120 000
Company headquarters	1 000 000		1 400 000
Accumulated depreciation	(180 000)	Long-term loans	400 000
Factories	1 790 000	Provisions	40 000
Accumulated depreciation	(910 000)	Other liabilities	160 000
Goodwill	60 000		600 000
Accumulated impairment losses	(40 000)		
Intangibles	150 000		
Accumulated amortisation	(50 000)		
Total assets	2 000 000	Equity and liabilities	2 000 000

At the end of the reporting period, after undertaking an analysis, management determined that it was probable that the assets of the entity were impaired. Management conducted an impairment test, determining that the recoverable amount for the entity's assets was $1 820 000. The whole entity was regarded as a cash-generating unit.

Land is measured by Casey Ltd at fair value, while all other assets are accounted for by the cost model. At 30 June 2014, the fair value of the land was determined to be $150 000. The land had previously been revalued upwards by $20 000. The tax rate is 30%.

Required

(Show all workings.)

1. Prepare the journal entries required on 30 June 2014 in relation to the measurement of the assets of Casey Ltd.
2. Assume that, as the result of the allocation of the impairment loss, the factories were to be written down to $800 000. If the fair value less costs of disposal of the factories was determined to be $750 000, outline the adjustments, if any, that would need to be made to the journal entries you prepared in requirement 1, and explain why adjustments are or are not required.

References

Amcor 2011, *Annual report 2011*, Amcor Limited, Australia, www.amcor.com.au.

Boral Ltd 2010, *Annual report 2010*, Boral Limited, Australia, www.boral.com.au.

Deloitte Touche Tohmatsu 2003, *Comments of Deloitte Touche Tohmatsu on Exposure Draft 3 Business Combinations*, 4 April, p. 7, www.iasplus.com.

European Financial Reporting Advisory Group 2003, *Comments of EFRAG on Exposure Draft 3 Business Combinations*, 4 April, p. 10, www.iasplus.com.

FASB 2003, *Summary of Comment Letters, Exposure Draft (Revised) Business Combinations and Intangible Assets — Accounting for Goodwill*, www.ifrs.org.

Nokia 2009, *Nokia in 2009*, Nokia Corporation, Finland, www.nokia.com.

—— 2010, *Nokia in 2010*, Nokia Corporation, Finland, www.nokia.com.

Pacific Brands 2011, *Annual report 2011*, Pacific Brands Limited, Australia, www.pacificbrands.com.au.

Wesfarmers 2011, *Annual report 2011*, Wesfarmers Limited, Australia, www.wesfarmers.com.au.

16

Accounting for mineral resources

IFRS 6 *Exploration for and Evaluation of Mineral Resources*

After studying this chapter, you should be able to:

1 understand the background behind the issuance of IFRS 6

2 understand the scope of IFRS 6

3 understand the range of industry accounting policies applied to the recognition of exploration and evaluation assets

4 explain how to measure exploration and evaluation assets

5 understand the impairment procedures applicable to exploration and evaluation assets

6 implement the presentation and disclosure requirements of IFRS 6

7 discuss the possible future developments related to the accounting for the extractive industries.

16.1 INTRODUCTION TO IFRS 6 *EXPLORATION FOR AND EVALUATION OF MINERAL RESOURCES*

IFRS 6 *Exploration for and Evaluation of Mineral Resources* was issued by the International Accounting Standards Board (IASB) in December 2004. Historically, the IASB has tended to avoid industry-specific standard setting. However, the extractive industries, which include industries involved in the seeking, finding and extracting of minerals, oil and gas, represent a significant economic contributor to the global economy and, due to the unique accounting issues faced by these industries, are routinely excluded from the scope of many International Financial Reporting Standards (IFRSs).

In November 2000, the IASB's predecessor, the International Accounting Standards Committee (IASC), published an issues paper, *Extractive Industries Issues Paper*, which was meant to be the first step in the process of developing a comprehensive IFRS for the extractive industries. However, the economic strength of entities in the extractive industries also gives them significant political influence and, as a result, they tend to be very effective lobbyists. This, along with the reformation of the IASC into the IASB, resulted in the issuance of IFRS 6, which merely grandfathers current industry practice to a large extent.

The issuance of IFRS 6 was, and still remains, a much debated political exercise. Some would say IFRS 6 reflects the significant influence the various extractive industries' lobby groups exert. Others would say it was merely issued because something was needed in time for the 2005 wave of IFRS adopters, given the extra time that development of comprehensive guidance would likely have required. The effort to develop such comprehensive guidance continues even today, as discussed in section 16.7 of this chapter.

16.2 SCOPE OF IFRS 6

The scope of IFRS 6 is specifically limited to accounting for exploration and evaluation (E&E) expenditures incurred by an entity in connection with the 'exploration for and evaluation of mineral resources', which the standard defines as '[t]he search for mineral resources, including minerals, oil, natural gas and similar non-regenerative resources after the entity has obtained legal rights to explore in a specific area, as well as the determination of the technical feasibility and commercial viability of extracting the mineral resource'.

The IASB deliberately decided not to expand the scope of IFRS 6 to avoid pre-empting the outcome of its extractive activities project, as well as to avoid any significant delay in the issuance of E&E expenditure guidance, which would have resulted from an expanded scope. Therefore, the accounting policies applicable under IFRSs for other aspects of extractive industries activities should be determined in accordance with paragraphs 7 to 12 of IAS 8 *Accounting Policies, Changes in Accounting Estimates and Errors*. As explained in chapter 18, that means:

1. If a transaction, other event or condition is specifically covered by an existing IFRS, that Standard should be applied in determining the appropriate accounting policy. For example, the acquisition of equipment to be used in the extraction of mineral resources is not covered by IFRS 6 because that extraction occurs after the technical feasibility and commercial viability of extracting the mineral resource is demonstrated in the first place. However, acquisition of property, plant and equipment is addressed by IAS 16 *Property, Plant and Equipment* so IAS 16 should be applied in arriving at the accounting policy to apply to the acquisition of the plant and equipment.

2. If there is no specific IFRS that applies to a transaction, other event or condition, the entity's management must apply its judgement in determining an appropriate accounting policy to result in information that is (IAS 8 paragraph 10):

   (a) relevant to the economic decision-making needs of users; and
   (b) reliable, in that the financial statements:
     (i) represent faithfully the financial position, financial performance and cash flows of the entity;
     (ii) reflect the economic substance of transactions, other events and conditions, and not merely the legal form;
     (iii) are neutral, that is, free from bias;
     (iv) are prudent; and
     (v) are complete in all material respects.

3. In applying this judgement, management should consider the requirements and guidance in IFRSs dealing with similar and related issues, followed by the definitions, recognition criteria and measurement concepts for assets, liabilities, income and expenses in the *Conceptual Framework for Financial Reporting* (the *Conceptual Framework*).

4. Management may also consider the most recent pronouncements of other standard-setting bodies that use a similar conceptual framework to develop accounting standards, other accounting literature and accepted industry practices, to the extent that these do not conflict with IFRSs or the *Conceptual Framework*.

The difficulty for entities in the extractive industries is that mineral resources are excluded from the scope of a number of standards including:

- IAS 2 *Inventories*
- IAS 16 *Property, Plant and Equipment*
- IAS 17 *Leases*
- IAS 18 *Revenue*
- IAS 38 *Intangible Assets*
- IAS 40 *Investment Property*
- IFRIC Interpretation 4 *Determining whether an Arrangement contains a Lease.*

This is further complicated by the fact that these scope exclusions are not complete. For example, IAS 16 does not apply to 'the recognition and measurement of exploration and evaluation assets' (i.e. they are covered by IFRS 6) or 'mineral rights and mineral reserves such as oil, natural gas and similar non-regenerative resources'. However, it does apply to property, plant and equipment used to develop or maintain E&E assets, mineral rights and mineral reserves. IFRS 6 at least addresses the accounting for one significant activity undertaken at some stage by all entities in the extractive industries: exploration and evaluation. Figure 16.1 illustrates the scope of IFRS 6.

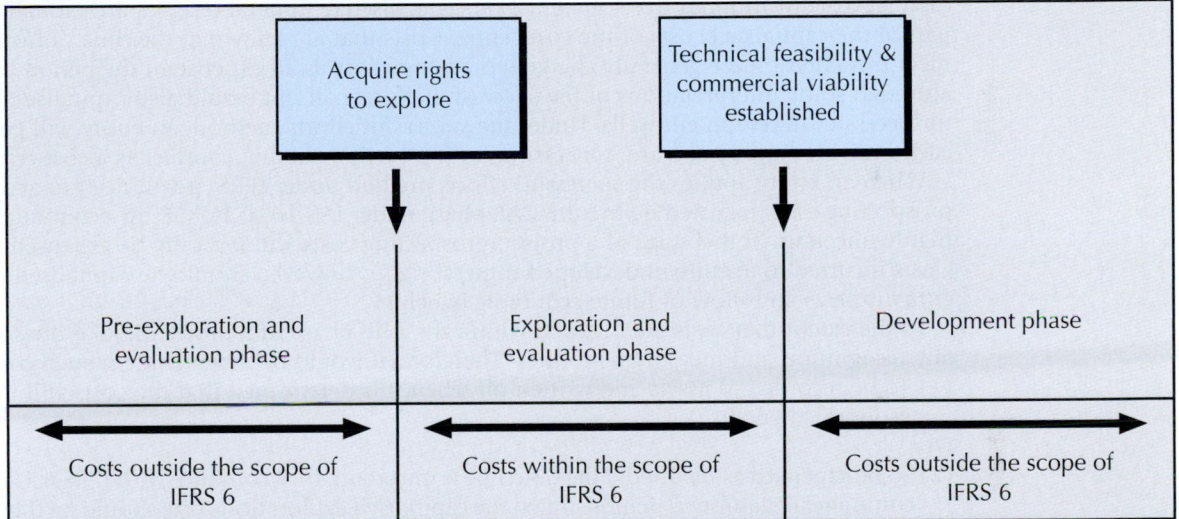

FIGURE 16.1 Scope of IFRS 6

As figure 16.1 shows, entities engaged in the exploration for and evaluation of mineral resources should not apply IFRS 6 to expenditures incurred before the E&E phase (i.e. before the rights to explore the area have been obtained) or after the E&E phase (i.e. after the technical feasibility and commercial viability of extracting the resource are demonstrable). Rather, in these phases, management must apply appropriate judgement in determining which accounting policies should apply to such costs by considering the requirements of IAS 8, as previously noted.

 16.3 RECOGNITION OF E&E ASSETS

16.3.1 Application of previous accounting policies

E&E assets are merely those E&E expenditures that have been capitalised as assets in accordance with the entity's accounting policy. In line with the IASB's objective of minimising disruptions caused by the adoption of IFRSs by entities involved in E&E activities, IFRS 6 provides a temporary exemption from application of the hierarchy in paragraphs 11 and 12 of IAS 8 to E&E assets and instead only requires the application of paragraph 10 of IAS 8. This means that management must apply their judgement as set out in item 2 of section 16.2 but are not required to consider items 3 and 4 in applying that judgement.

This temporary exemption has the effect of allowing the accounting practices that existed prior to the issuance of IFRS 6 to continue to the extent they meet the requirements of item 2. This means that the entity's accounting policy for recognition of E&E assets need not be fully compliant with the *Conceptual Framework* and, as a result, some costs may be capitalised earlier than would normally be allowed under the *Conceptual Framework*. For example, when an entity obtains the rights to explore an area, costs incurred to undertake such exploration (e.g. equipment rental, engineering costs, contractor fees) would not normally meet the asset definition and recognition criteria contained in the *Conceptual Framework* until the existence of probable future economic benefits has been established (i.e. until the entity has established the existence of mineral resources in the area and confirmed the probability of being able to economically benefit from those resources). However, under IFRS 6, if an entity previously had a policy of capitalising such costs, they are allowed to continue with that policy. This means entities will show more assets and less costs as a result of the application of IFRS 6 than they otherwise would be able to under the *Conceptual Framework*.

The main issue in accounting for E&E expenditures is whether such expenditures should be expensed as incurred or capitalised and, if they are capitalised, which costs qualify for such capitalisation and at what point in the operating cycle capitalisation should commence. Two common methods used globally by entities involved in extractive activities to account for E&E costs are the 'successful efforts' method and the 'full cost' method. Figure 16.2 provides a description of these two methods.

FIGURE 16.2 Description of the successful efforts method and the full cost method

Exploration, evaluation and development costs
Successful efforts method
Within the context of a 'successful efforts' approach, only those costs that lead directly to the discovery, acquisition, or development of specific discrete mineral reserves are capitalised and become part of the capitalised costs of the cost centre. Costs that are known at the time of incurrence to fail to meet this criterion are generally charged to profit or loss as an expense in the period they are incurred, although some interpretations of the successful efforts concept would also capitalise the cost of unsuccessful development wells. Under the successful efforts method, an entity will generally consider each individual mineral lease, concession, or production sharing contract as a cost centre.

When an entity applies the successful efforts method under IFRS, it will need to account for prospecting costs incurred before the E&E phase under IAS 16 or IAS 38. As economic benefits are highly uncertain at this stage of a project, prospecting costs will typically be expensed as incurred. Costs incurred to acquire undeveloped mineral rights, however, should be capitalised under IFRS if an entity expects an inflow of future economic benefits.

To the extent that costs are incurred within the E&E phase of a project, IFRS 6 does not prescribe any recognition and measurement rules. Therefore, it would be acceptable for such costs:
(1) To be recorded as assets and written off when it is determined that the costs will not lead to economic benefits

Or

(2) To be expensed as incurred if the outcome is uncertain. In accordance with IFRS 6.17, once commercial viability is demonstrated the capitalised exploration costs should be transferred to property, plant and equipment or intangibles, as appropriate, after being assessed for impairment.

If commercial viability is uncertain or not immediately obvious, then costs can remain capitalised while a company is still actively engaged in the exploration or evaluation effort. If the exploration or evaluation effort has ceased, but there is potential for future benefits e.g., through sale, although this is subject to factors outside of this particular exploration and evaluation effort, the exploration and evaluation phase is over. The capitalised exploration and evaluation costs should then be tested for impairment and reclassified into property, plant and equipment or intangible assets.

If it is determined that no commercial reserves are present then the costs capitalised should be written off.

Costs incurred after the E&E phase should be accounted for in accordance with IFRS (i.e. IAS 16 and IAS 38).

Other methods of accounting for exploration, evaluation and development costs
Full cost method
The full cost method under most national GAAPs requires that all costs incurred in prospecting, acquiring mineral interests, exploration, appraisal, development, and construction are accumulated in large cost centres. For example, costs may be accumulated for each individual country, for groups of countries, or for the entire world. However, IFRS 6 does not permit application of the full cost method outside the exploration and evaluation phase.

There are several other areas in which application of the full cost method under IFRS is restricted because:
• While the full cost method under most national GAAPs requires application of some form of 'ceiling test', IFRS 6 requires — when impairment indicators are present — an impairment test in accordance with IAS 36 to be performed
• IFRS 6 requires exploration and evaluation assets to be classified as tangible or intangible assets according to the nature of the assets, even when an entity accounts for Exploration and Evaluation costs in relatively large pools, it will still need to distinguish between tangible and intangible assets

FIGURE 16.2 *(continued)*

And
- Once the technical feasibility and commercial viability of extracting mineral resources are demonstrable, IFRS 6 requires exploration and evaluation assets to be assessed for impairment under IAS 36, and any impairment loss recognised (as appropriate), and then reclassified out of exploration and evaluation assets in the statement of financial position and accounted for under IAS 16 or IAS 38. This means it is not possible to account for successful and unsuccessful projects within one cost centre or pool.

For these reasons, it is not possible to apply the full cost method of accounting under IFRS without making very significant modifications in the application of the method. An entity might want to use the full cost method as its starting point in developing its accounting policy for Exploration and Evaluation assets under IFRS. However, it would rarely be appropriate to describe the resulting accounting policy as a 'full cost method' because key elements of the full cost method are not permitted under IFRS.

Source: Ernst & Young, *Good Petroleum (International) Limited* (2011, p. 28–9). © 2012 EYGM Limited. All rights reserved.

Reproduced in figures 16.3 and 16.4 are the accounting policies applied to E&E expenditure from the 2010 financial statements of two international companies in the extractive industries, Xstrata plc (a mining company) and Royal Dutch Shell plc (an oil and gas company).

Exploration and evaluation expenditure

Exploration and evaluation expenditure relates to costs incurred on the exploration and evaluation of potential mineral reserves and resources and includes costs such as exploratory drilling and sample testing and the costs of pre-feasibility studies. Exploration and evaluation expenditure for each area of interest, other than that acquired from the purchase of another mining company, is carried forward as an asset provided that one of the following conditions is met:
- such costs are expected to be recouped in full through successful development and exploration of the area of interest or alternatively, by its sale; or
- exploration and evaluation activities in the area of interest have not yet reached a stage that permits a reasonable assessment of the existence or otherwise of economically recoverable reserves, and active and significant operations in relation to the area are continuing, or planned for the future.

Purchased exploration and evaluation assets are recognised as assets at their cost of acquisition or at fair value if purchased as part of a business combination.

An impairment review is performed, either individually or at the cash-generating unit level, when there are indicators that the carrying amount of the assets may exceed their recoverable amounts. To the extent that this occurs, the excess is fully provided against, in the financial year in which this is determined. Exploration and evaluation assets are reassessed on a regular basis and these costs are carried forward provided that at least one of the conditions outlined above is met.

Expenditure is transferred to mine development assets or capital work in progress once the work completed to date supports the future development of the property and such development receives appropriate approvals.

FIGURE 16.3 Example of E&E expenditure accounting policy for Xstrata plc, a mining company
Source: Xstrata (2010, p. 144).

Exploration costs

Shell follows the successful efforts method of accounting for oil and natural gas exploration costs. Exploration costs are recognised in income when incurred, except that exploratory drilling costs are included in property, plant and equipment, pending determination of proved reserves.

Exploration costs capitalised in respect of exploration wells that are more than 12 months old are written off unless (a) proved reserves are booked, or (b) (i) they have found commercially producible quantities of reserves, and (ii) they are subject to further exploration or appraisal activity in that either drilling of additional exploratory wells is underway or firmly planned for the near future or other activities are being undertaken to sufficiently progress the assessing of reserves and the economic and operating viability of the project.

FIGURE 16.4 Example of E&E expenditure accounting policy for Royal Dutch Shell, an oil and gas company
Source: Royal Dutch Shell (2010, p. 104).

16.3.2 Summary of cost methods used in extractive industries

So far, we have discussed the successful efforts method and the full cost method. The IASC's *Extractive Industries Issues Paper*, also mentions the appropriation method, although use of this method tends to be limited to small mining companies in South Africa and the area-of-interest method, which is required for use in Australia. Table 16.1 compares and contrasts these four methods (note that hybrids of these methods are also used) based on the descriptions and discussion in the IASC's paper.

TABLE 16.1 A comparison of E&E historical cost measurement accounting methods

	Area of interest	Successful efforts	Full cost	Appropriation
Description	E&E costs are capitalised on an area of interest basis and if the area of interest is not found to contain commercial reserves, the costs are written off.	E&E costs are not capitalised unless they are expected to lead to finding, acquiring, and developing mineral reserves. If the expectation is not borne out, the costs are written off.	E&E costs are capitalised using a larger cost centre than an area of interest such as a country or even a group of countries.	This is similar to the successful efforts method except that the accounting subsequent to the E&E phase differs (i.e. no depreciation and expensing of all ongoing capital expenditure to maintain production capacity). This method is mainly used by companies with only one mine.
Pros	• Defines the asset for which costs are accumulated because the area is the objective of the costs expended • Reflects the way in which operations are carried out	• Reflects the traditional concept of an asset • Reflects the volatility inherent in E&E activities • Is consistent with the matching concept (i.e. matching of costs to related income) • Better reflects management's successes or failures in its E&E activities	• Reflects the way in which operations are carried out • Is consistent with the matching concept (i.e. matching of costs to related income) • Is similar to absorption costing for manufactured inventories • Avoids distortions of reported earnings	• Recognises that shareholders' funds are invested in a wasting asset • Is well suited to mines that are prone to excessive volatility in relation to the quality and price of their products
Cons	• Defers costs as assets for some activities known to be unsuccessful • Fails to recognise that management makes its plans and allocates resources to its E&E activities on an entity-wide basis	• Can give a false impression of success in finding new reserves in the income statement due to decisions to expand or curtail E&E activities • Can be used to 'manage earnings' • Can understate assets and net income of a growing company with a successful and increasing exploration program • Assesses success or failure too early in a project • Fails to recognise that management makes its plans and allocates resources to its E&E activities on an entity-wide basis	• Is inconsistent with the traditional concept of an asset • Delays loss recognition • Impedes measurement of the efficiency and effectiveness of the company's E&E activities	• Is inconsistent with historical cost accounting • Is inconsistent with the going concern concept • Reports debt payments as a deduction after arriving at net profit rather than recognising interest as an expense • Is only suitable for companies with one mine • Does not provide useful information and can be confusing to investors

16.4 MEASUREMENT OF E&E ASSETS

16.4.1 Initial recognition

Regardless of the method used, E&E assets must initially be measured at cost. This raises the question of what types of E&E expenditures qualify for capitalisation as E&E assets. Paragraph 9 of IFRS 6 provides the following guidance:

> An entity shall determine an accounting policy specifying which expenditures are recognised as exploration and evaluation assets and apply the policy consistently. In making this determination, an entity considers the degree to which the expenditure can be associated with finding specific mineral resources. The following are examples of expenditures that might be included in the initial measurement of exploration and evaluation assets (the list is not exhaustive):
> (a) acquisition of rights to explore;
> (b) topographical, geological, geochemical and geophysical studies;
> (c) exploratory drilling;
> (d) trenching;
> (e) sampling; and
> (f) activities in relation to evaluating the technical feasibility and commercial viability of extracting a mineral resource.

IFRS 6 also indicates that costs related to activities undertaken prior to commencement of E&E activities, which is presumed to be before the entity has obtained the legal rights to explore a specific area, and costs incurred for the development of mineral resources after the E&E phase, are not covered by the standard and therefore should be accounted for in accordance with IAS 8, as previously discussed in section 16.2. In practice, this usually results in the immediate expensing of costs incurred prior to obtaining exploration licences and the treatment of development costs as intangible assets accounted for under IAS 38 or property, plant and equipment accounted for under IAS 16.

16.4.2 Obligations for removal and restoration

Obligations for removal and restoration incurred as a result of E&E activities are recognised in accordance with IAS 37 *Provisions, Contingent Liabilities and Contingent Assets* (see chapter 5). This means if an entity has an obligation to restore a property damaged by its E&E activities, it must recognise a liability for that restoration as the related damage is incurred. This is a complex and highly judgemental process because of the significant degree of estimation involved and the impact of laws and regulations applicable to each property. Also, if mineral resources are found as a result of the E&E activities undertaken and the area is developed into a producing asset, the remediation will not occur until those resources are exhausted and production ceases, which could be a long period of time.

In practice, any damage caused to a site during the E&E phase is usually immaterial compared with the damage caused during construction of production facilities after confirmation of the existence and ability to extract commercial quantities of mineral resources in the area. Therefore, most of the liability for removal and restoration tends to be recognised during this production construction period, which is after the E&E phase covered by IFRS 6.

Figure 16.5 provides an example of a typical accounting policy for restoration obligations.

FIGURE 16.5 Example of a typical accounting policy for restoration obligations

1 Principal accounting policies
(k) Provisions and contingencies
The Group holds provisions for close down and restoration costs which include the dismantling and demolition of infrastructure and the removal of residual materials and remediation of disturbed areas. Close down and restoration costs are a normal consequence of mining, and the majority of close down and restoration expenditure is incurred at the end of the life of the mine. Although the ultimate cost to be incurred is uncertain, the Group's businesses estimate their costs based on feasibility and engineering studies using current restoration standards and techniques.

Close down and restoration costs are provided for in the accounting period when the obligation arising from the related disturbance occurs based on the net present value of future costs. This may occur during development or during the production phase of a facility. Provisions for close down

(continued)

FIGURE 16.5 *(continued)*

and restoration costs do not include any additional obligations which are expected to arise from future disturbance. The costs are estimated on the basis of a closure plan and are updated annually during the life of the operation to reflect known developments, e.g. revisions to cost estimates and to the estimated lives of operations. The estimates are subject to formal review at regular intervals.

The initial closure provision is capitalised within property, plant and equipment. Subsequent movements in these closure provisions, including those resulting from new disturbance, updated cost estimates, changes to the estimated lives of operations and revisions to discount rates are also capitalised within property, plant and equipment. These costs are then depreciated over the lives of the assets to which they relate.

The amortisation or 'unwinding' of the discount applied in establishing the net present value of provisions is charged to the income statement in each accounting period. The amortisation of the discount is shown as a financing cost.

Where rehabilitation is conducted systematically over the life of the operation, rather than at the time of closure, provision is made for the estimated outstanding continuous rehabilitation work at each statement of financial position date and the cost is charged to the income statement.

Clean up costs result from environmental damage that was not a necessary consequence of operations, and may include remediation, compensation and penalties. Provision is made for the estimated present value of such costs at the statement of financial position date. These costs are charged to the income statement. Movements in these clean up provisions are presented as an operating cost, except for the unwinding of the discount which is shown as a financing cost. Remediation procedures may commence soon after the time the disturbance, remediation process and estimated remediation costs become known, but can continue for many years depending on the nature of the disturbance and the remediation techniques used.

Source: Rio Tinto (2011, p. 144).

Illustrative example 16.1 explains the journal entries for recording a restoration obligation.

ILLUSTRATIVE EXAMPLE 16.1 Recording restoration obligations

A mining company, whose accounting policy is to capitalise E&E costs, has obtained a new lease over a specific area in which it is conducting E&E activities. One of the conditions of the lease is that the area must be returned to its original state at the end of the lease. During the financial year, the company estimates that its E&E activities have resulted in damage to the environment that would cost $65 000 to repair. Therefore, the company would record the following journal entry:

E&E Asset	Dr	65 000	
Provision for Restoration	Cr		65 000
(Recognition of provision for restoration arising from E&E activities)			

16.4.3 Subsequent measurement

Subsequent to initial recognition, E&E assets must be measured using the cost model or the revaluation model. The implications of using the revaluation model will differ depending on the extent to which the components of E&E assets are classified as property, plant and equipment under IAS 16 or intangible assets under IAS 38. The classification issue is discussed further in section 16.6.1.

The revaluation model in IAS 38 requires the existence of an active market, which is discussed in chapter 13, whereas the revaluation model in IAS 16 only requires that fair value be reliably measurable, which is discussed in chapter 11.

Note that regardless of which model is selected, cost or revaluation, it must be applied consistently to all E&E assets. In practice, the revaluation method is rarely used.

16.4.4 Changes in accounting policies

Paragraph 13 of IFRS 6 allows an entity to change its accounting policies related to E&E costs on the condition that the change 'makes the financial statements more relevant to the economic decision-making needs of users and no less reliable, or more reliable and no less relevant to those needs'. In assessing the relevance and reliability of the change, entities are directed to the criteria in IAS 8, although they are not expected to fully comply with those criteria. An example of an acceptable change in accounting policy following this guidance would be a change from the full cost method to the successful efforts method.

16.5 IMPAIRMENT

16.5.1 Recognition and measurement

E&E assets must be tested for impairment in accordance with IAS 36 *Impairment of Assets* using an indicators approach, subject to the exception explained in section 16.5.2. This means that if facts and circumstances indicate that the book values of E&E assets might exceed their recoverable amounts, the entity is required to calculate those recoverable amounts in order to confirm the existence of any impairment. In the absence of any indication of impairment, no further work is required.

IFRS 6 provides a listing of indicators specific to E&E assets that should be considered, rather than the general indicators of impairment set out in IAS 36, which are discussed in section 15.2 of chapter 15. The list in IFRS 6 is not exhaustive, although it does represent the minimum an entity should consider, and includes:

- whether the exploration rights for the specific area have expired or are expected to expire in the near future and there is no expectation of renewal
- where there is no budget or plan for the incurrence of further substantial E&E expenditure in the specific area
- where the entity has decided to discontinue E&E activities in the specific area on the basis that such activities have not led to the discovery of commercially viable quantities of mineral resources
- where the entity has established that the book value of the E&E asset is unlikely to be recovered in full from successful development or sale of the specific area.

With respect to expiry of exploration rights, the term 'near future' is generally accepted to mean 12 months from the end of the reporting period.

Other impairment indicators not listed in IFRS 6 might include changes in market prices of the applicable mineral resources, adverse regulatory or taxation changes, liquidity restrictions affecting access to funding for E&E activities, civil unrest affecting access to the specific area, and natural disasters causing damage or restricting access to the specific area.

An example of the reasons for impairment of E&E assets as disclosed by BP plc is provided in figure 16.6.

FIGURE 16.6 Example of disclosure of reason for impairment of E&E assets

5 Disposals and impairment			
		$ million	
	2010	**2009**	**2008**
Impairment losses			
Exploration and Production	**1 259**	118	1 186
Refining and Marketing	**144**	1 834	159
Other businesses and corporate	**113**	189	227
	1 516	2 141	1 572
Impairment reversals			
Exploration and Production	—	3	(155)
Refining and Marketing	**(141)**	—	—
Other businesses and corporate	**(7)**	(8)	—
	(148)	(11)	(155)

(continued)

FIGURE 16.6 *(continued)*

Impairment

In assessing whether a write-down is required in the carrying value of a potentially impaired intangible asset, item of property, plant and equipment or an equity-accounted investment, the asset's carrying value is compared with its recoverable amount. The recoverable amount is the higher of the asset's fair value less costs to sell and value in use. Unless indicated otherwise, the recoverable amount used in assessing the impairment charges described below is value in use. The group estimates value in use using a discounted cash flow model. The future cash flows are adjusted for risks specific to the asset and are discounted using a pre-tax discount rate. This discount rate is derived from the group's post-tax weighted average cost of capital and is adjusted where applicable to take into account any specific risks relating to the country where the cash-generating unit is located, although other rates may be used if appropriate to the specific circumstances. In 2010 the rates used ranged from 11–14% (2009: 9–13%). The rate applied in each country is re-assessed each year. In certain circumstances an impairment assessment may be carried out using fair value less costs to sell as the recoverable amount when, for example, a recent market transaction for a similar asset has taken place. For impairments of available-for-sale financial assets that are quoted investments, the fair value is determined by reference to bid prices at the close of business at the statement of financial position date. Any cumulative loss previously recognized in other comprehensive income is transferred to the income statement.

Exploration and Production

During 2010, the Exploration and Production segment recognized impairment losses of $1259 million. The main elements were the write-down of assets in the Gulf of Mexico of $501 million triggered by an increase in the decommissioning asset as a result of new regulations in the US relating to idle infrastructure; impairments of oil and gas properties in the Gulf of Mexico and onshore North America of $310 million and $80 million respectively as a result of decisions to dispose of assets at a price lower than the assets' carrying values; a write-down of accumulated costs in Sakhalin, Russia by $341 million, triggered by a change in the outlook on the future recoverability of the investment; and several other individually insignificant impairment charges amounting to $27 million.

During 2009, the Exploration and Production segment recognized impairment losses of $118 million. The main elements were the write-down of our $42 million investment in the East Shmidt interest in Russia, triggered by a decision to not proceed to development; a $62 million charge associated with our nErgize gas scheduling system; and several other individually insignificant impairment charges amounting to $14 million.

During 2008, the Exploration and Production segment recognized impairment losses of $1186 million. The main elements were the write-down of our investment in Rosneft by $517 million, to its fair value determined by reference to an active market, due to a significant decline in the market value of the investment, impairment of oil and gas properties in the Gulf of Mexico of $270 million triggered by downward revisions of reserves, an impairment of exploration assets in Vietnam of $210 million following BP's decision to withdraw from activities in the area concerned, impairment of oil and gas properties in Egypt of $85 million triggered by cost increases, and several other individually insignificant impairment charges amounting to $104 million.

These charges were partly offset by reversals of previously recognized impairment losses amounting to $155 million. Of this total, $122 million resulted from a reassessment of the economics of Rhourde El Baguel in Algeria.

Source: BP plc (2010, pp. 164–6).

Illustrative example 16.2 explains the journal entries for recording an impairment charge for an E&E asset.

ILLUSTRATIVE EXAMPLE 16.2 Recording an impairment charge for an E&E asset

An oil and gas company has determined that although one of its properties (Property A) contains mineral reserves it would currently be cost prohibitive to extract them effectively. The E&E asset in relation to that area has a carrying value of $275 000 at the end of the reporting period.

Therefore, the company would record the following journal entry:

Impairment Expense	Dr	275 000	
Provision for E&E Asset Impairment – Property A	Cr		275 000
(Recognition of provision for impairment related to Property A)			

16.5.2 Identification of cash-generating units

In determining the level at which to assess E&E assets for impairment, entities are required to determine an accounting policy for allocating those E&E assets to cash-generating units or groups of cash-generating units. The concept of a cash-generating unit is discussed in chapter 15. Further, IFRS 6 requires that each cash-generating unit or group of cash-generating units to which an E&E asset is allocated must not be larger than an operating segment under IFRS 8 *Operating Segments*. IFRS 8 is discussed in chapter 21. As a result, the level at which an E&E asset is tested for impairment may consist of one or more cash-generating units. Those cash-generating units may contain a mix of E&E assets and other assets.

It is important to note that although an impairment loss on an E&E asset is reversible under IAS 36, in practice sometimes an E&E asset is completely derecognised when an impairment is recognised because no further future economic benefits are expected. See illustrative example 16.3.

ILLUSTRATIVE EXAMPLE 16.3 Reversal of impairment losses on E&E assets

Company A is an oil and gas company, which has determined that its exploration activity for a specific property, accounted for as a separate cash-generating unit, did not result in the discovery of any oil and gas resources. As a result, the company recognises an impairment of that property and derecognises all related E&E assets for that property.

Alternatively, Company B is also an oil and gas company, which has discovered a significant quantity of oil and gas resources in a specific property, but these are located in a complex reservoir. As a result, the company determines that, at present, the costs of extraction of the resources do not justify the construction of the required infrastructure. Nevertheless, Company B's management believes that it is possible the required infrastructure will be constructed in the future given the pace of technology and the possibility of development of more cost-effective extraction methods. As Company B's management has no current intention of further exploration activity in that area, the company recognises an impairment of the related E&E assets; however, as there are expectations of possible future economic benefits, it does not derecognise those assets.

The implication of the above is that Company A cannot reverse the impairment as the E&E asset no longer exists while Company B could reverse the impairment should extraction of the discovered resources become viable.

Source: Adapted from Example 41.3, Ernst & Young, International GAAP (2012).

 ## 16.6 PRESENTATION AND DISCLOSURE

16.6.1 Classification

IFRS 6 does not specify whether E&E assets are tangible or intangible assets; however, it does require an assessment of the nature of E&E assets to determine how they should be classified. For example, the standard notes that drilling rights are treated as intangible assets while vehicles and drilling rigs are treated as tangible assets.

Table 16.2 illustrates the typical components of E&E assets classified between tangible and intangible assets based on generally accepted industry practice.

TABLE 16.2 Typical components of E&E assets classified as tangible versus intangible assets

Tangible	Intangible
– Vehicles and drilling rigs – Costs of replacing major parts of equipment used in E&E activities – Costs of major inspections of equipment used in E&E activities	– Acquisition of rights to explore (e.g. drilling rights and exploration licences) – Topographical, geological, geochemical and geophysical study costs – Deferred costs associated with consumables (e.g. materials and fuel used, contractor payments, employee remuneration)

As table 16.2 shows, the majority of E&E assets are classified as intangible assets and, as a result, they are measured using the cost model because of the restrictive requirements associated with use of the IAS 38 revaluation model as discussed in chapter 13. Note that even though equipment used in E&E activities is classified as a tangible asset, the consumption of that equipment, which is reflected through depreciation charges, may qualify for capitalisation as part of an intangible E&E asset if that equipment is being consumed in the E&E activities associated with development of that intangible E&E asset. This is illustrated in illustrative example 16.4.

ILLUSTRATIVE EXAMPLE 16.4 Consumption of tangible E&E asset in development of intangible E&E asset

Company A is a mining company, which acquires a drilling rig to be used for drilling of core samples for the purpose of analysis as part of its E&E activities for a new property (Property X) it has recently acquired the right to explore. The following transactions occurred during 2014.

- The rig is acquired at a cost of $140 000 on 1 January 2014 and is capitalised as a tangible E&E asset with an estimated useful life of 14 years.
- During Company's A financial year ending 31 December 2014, the drilling rig is used solely for the purposes of drilling core samples in Property X, as expected.
- Depreciation attributable to that drilling rig for the year ended 31 December 2014 is calculated as follows: $140 000/14 = $10 000.

The $10 000 of depreciation on the drilling rig has therefore been consumed as part of the development of the intangible E&E asset associated with Property X. These transactions would result in the following journal entries:

Equipment Cash (Acquisition of drilling rig for cash)	Dr Cr	140 000	 140 000
Intangible E&E asset – Property X Accumulated Depreciation – Equipment (Recognition of consumption of equipment in development of intangible E&E asset)	Dr Cr	10 000	 10 000

16.6.2 Depreciation methods

Illustrative example 16.4 reflects use of the straight-line method to depreciate the E&E equipment. As explained in paragraph 62 of IAS 16, this method results in a constant charge over the equipment's useful life if its residual value does not change. Therefore, the straight-line method is appropriate if the economic benefits embodied in the asset are expected to be consumed evenly over the useful life of the asset. However, in the extractive industries, many items of property, plant and equipment are depreciated using the unit-of-production method, which results in a charge based on the expected use or output of the asset. The underlying principle of the unit-of-production method is that capitalised costs associated with a cost centre are incurred to find and develop the commercially producible reserves in that cost centre, so that each unit produced from the centre is assigned an equal amount of cost' (IASC Issues Paper, *Extractive Industries Issues Paper*, IASC, November 2000, paragraph 7.19). So the straight-line method allocates an equal amount of cost to each year while the unit-of-production method allocates an equal amount of cost to each unit produced. By its very nature, the unit-of-production method would therefore result in no depreciation being recognised during the E&E phase because production would not have commenced.

In practice, items of plant and equipment used in extractive-industry activities that have an expected useful life shorter than the time expected to be necessary to extract all of the mineral resources in the area they are being used in are depreciated on a straight-line basis over the period they are expected to be used. The straight-line method is seen as easier to apply than the unit-of-production method, and as not necessarily giving a materially different result where production (i.e. extraction and processing of the mineral resource) is relatively stable year-on-year.

Alternatively, items of plant and equipment used in extractive activities with longer lives are often depreciated using the unit-of-production method. This method, although not as simple as the straight-line method, is particularly useful for properties where production is expected to vary significantly over the life of the field or mine development.

Figure 16.7 shows the assets to which BHP Billiton Ltd applies the unit-of-production method.

(h) Depreciation of property, plant and equipment

The carrying amounts of property, plant and equipment (including initial and any subsequent capital expenditure) are depreciated to their estimated residual value over the estimated useful lives of the specific assets concerned, or the estimated life of the associated mine, field or lease, if shorter. Estimates of residual values and useful lives are reassessed annually and any change in estimate is taken into account in the determination of remaining depreciation charges. Depreciation commences on the date of commissioning. The major categories of property, plant and equipment are depreciated on a unit of production and/or straight-line basis using estimated lives indicated below. However, where assets are dedicated to a mine, field or lease and are not readily transferable, the below useful lives are subject to the lesser of the asset category's useful life and the life of the mine, field or lease:

- Buildings — 25 to 50 years
- Land — not depreciated
- Plant and equipment — 3 to 30 years straight-line
- Mineral rights and Petroleum interests — based on reserves on a unit of production basis
- Capitalised exploration, evaluation and development expenditure — based on reserves on a unit of production basis

FIGURE 16.7 Example of the different depreciation methods applied to different classes of assets
Source: BHP Billiton Ltd (2010, p. 199).

16.6.3 Reclassification

Once the technical feasibility and commercial viability of extracting a mineral resource has been established for a particular E&E asset, IFRS 6 requires that the asset be tested for impairment and then reclassified and accounted for under IAS 16 or IAS 38 as appropriate. If no resources are found as a result of the E&E activities in a specific area, the E&E assets related to that area would be impaired and therefore written off or fully provided for (see illustrative example 16.2).

The technical feasibility and commercial viability of extracting a mineral resource is normally considered to be established once an entity has confirmed the existence of 'economically recoverable reserves', which IFRS 6 defines as 'the estimated quantity of product in an area of interest that can be expected to be profitably extracted, processed and sold under current and foreseeable economic conditions'. Costs incurred after this stage are specifically scoped out of IFRS 6, IAS 16 and IAS 38, although they are generally viewed as costs associated with development of an internal project and accounted for by analogy to IAS 38, or costs associated with construction of an asset and accounted for by analogy to IAS 16. Figure 16.8 provides an example of a typical accounting policy applied by BP plc to costs incurred once the existence of economically recoverable reserves has been confirmed.

Development expenditure

Expenditure on the construction, installation and completion of infrastructure facilities such as platforms, pipelines and the drilling of development wells, including service and unsuccessful development or delineation wells, is capitalized within property, plant and equipment and is depreciated from the commencement of production as described below in the accounting policy for property, plant and equipment.

FIGURE 16.8 Example of accounting policy for development expenditure as applied by BP plc
Source: BP plc (2010, p. 152).

16.6.4 Disclosure

Paragraphs 23–25 of IFRS 6 contain the required disclosures relating to E&E costs, which are aimed at identifying and explaining the amounts recognised in an entity's financial statements arising from its E&E activities. Such disclosures include:

- accounting policies applicable to E&E costs and E&E assets
- the amounts of assets, liabilities, income, expenses, operating cash flows and investing cash flows related to E&E activities.

Further, the disclosure requirements of IAS 16 or IAS 38 must also be applied depending on whether E&E assets have been classified as tangible or intangible assets respectively.

Examples of some of the disclosures have been provided throughout this chapter; however, illustrative example 16.5 provides a comprehensive illustration of all disclosures required by IFRS 6.

ILLUSTRATIVE EXAMPLE 16.5 Illustrative disclosures required by IFRS 6

Relevant note to the financial statements
Note 1: Summary of accounting policies (extract)
Exploration and evaluation expenditures

Exploration and evaluation expenditure is accounted for using the successful efforts method of accounting.

During the geological and geophysical exploration phase, costs are charged against income as incurred. Once the legal right to explore has been acquired, costs directly associated with an exploration well are capitalised as exploration and evaluation intangible assets until the drilling of the well is complete and the results have been evaluated. These costs include employee remuneration, materials and fuel used, rig costs and payments made to contractors. If no reserves are found, the exploration asset is tested for impairment. If extractable hydrocarbons are found and, subject to further appraisal activity (e.g. by drilling further wells), are likely to be developed commercially, the costs continue to be carried as an intangible asset while sufficient and continued progress is made in assessing the commerciality of the hydrocarbons. All such costs are subject to technical, commercial and management review as well as review for impairment at least once a year to confirm the continued intent to develop or otherwise extract value from the discovery. When this is no longer the case, the costs are written off. When proved reserves of oil are determined and development is sanctioned, the relevant expenditure is transferred to oil and gas properties after impairment is assessed and any resulting impairment loss is recognised.

Note 2: Operating (loss)/profit (extract)	**2014 $'000**	**2013 $'000**
Operating (loss)/profit is stated after (charging)/crediting:		
Impairment of exploration and evaluation assets[(a)]	(146)	(6)
Reversal of previously impaired exploration and evaluation assets[(b)]	25	—
Exploration and evaluation costs written off	(10)	(5)
Gain on sale of exploration and evaluation assets	118	94

(a) The Company's rights to explore one of its properties expired during the current reporting period and the local authority responsible for granting such rights has declined renewal of those rights on the basis that the area contains habitat considered vital to support an endangered species and no significant mineral reserves have been identified to-date. As a result, the Company has fully provided for the exploration and evaluation assets associated with this property. The impairment charge is included in exploration and evaluation expenses.

(b) The Company has reversed some of the previously recorded impairment charge related to the XYZ property. These reversals resulted from a positive change in the estimates used to determine the asset's recoverable amount since the impairment losses were initially recognised. The reversal of the previously booked impairment charge is included in exploration and evaluation expenses.

Note 3: Exploration and evaluation assets	2014 $'000	2013 $'000
Cost as at 1 January	524	361
Additions	358	293
Unsuccessful exploration expenditure derecognised	(10)	(5)
Disposals	(52)	(25)
Transfer to oil and gas properties	(101)	(100)
Cost as at 31 December	719	524
Provision for impairment as at 1 January	(23)	(17)
Impairment charge for the year	(146)	(6)
Reversal of previously booked impairments	25	—
Provision for impairment as at 31 December	(144)	(23)
Net book value as at 31 December	575	501

LO7 16.7 FUTURE DEVELOPMENTS

16.7.1 The IASB's extractive activities project

In 1998, the International Accounting Standards Committee (IASC), the predecessor organisation of the IASB, created a Steering Committee to deal with financial reporting in the extractive industries. This resulted in the release of an issues paper *Extractive Industries Issues Paper* in 2000. The project was put on hold as the IASB did not believe it could complete it in time for the 2005 adoption of IFRSs by many parts of the world. As previously discussed, IFRS 6 was released by the IASB as an interim measure pending completion of a comprehensive project dealing with the accounting for extractive activities.

In 2004, the IASB set up an international project team comprising staff from the national standard setters in Australia, Canada, Norway and South Africa to undertake a detailed assessment of accounting for extractive activities. The project team's findings and recommendations research are presented in the staff discussion paper *Extractive Activities*, which was published in April 2010. Although the discussion paper is a lengthy document running to some 180 pages, it is substantially narrower in scope than many commentators had predicted it would be when the project was initiated. The IASB has discussed the project team's findings at public meetings, but has not developed preliminary views on any of the project team's recommendations or made any related technical decisions.

The aim of the project is to create a single accounting and disclosure model that applies to extractive activities in both the minerals and oil and gas industries. It addresses financial reporting issues associated with exploring for and finding minerals, oil and natural gas deposits; developing those deposits; and extracting the minerals, oil and natural gas. These are referred to as either extractive activities or, alternatively, as upstream activities. The discussion paper includes:

• definitions of reserves and resources for use in accounting
• initial recognition and measurement of extractive assets
• subsequent accounting for those assets (including impairment and depreciation)
• disclosure of information (including reserves and resources information).

Disclosure recommendations

One of the more significant effects of the proposals within the discussion paper is the extensive new disclosure requirements. For some preparers this will present a major challenge to their reporting systems and processes in order to gather the required information and provide sufficient diligence over that information for it to be disclosed by preparers. Set out below are some of the proposed disclosures that may have a significant impact on preparers.

- *Disclosure of reserves* — The project team is proposing that the types of information that should be disclosed include:
  - Quantities of proved reserves and proved plus probable reserves, with the disclosure of reserve quantities presented separately by commodity and by material geographical areas, including disclosure of primary assumptions; and
  - A current value measurement that corresponds to reserves quantities disclosed with a reconciliation of changes in the current value measurement from year to year.
- *Sensitivity analysis* — The discussion paper also recommends the disclosure of a sensitivity analysis for reserves.
- *Value-based disclosures* — The discussion paper also considers various approaches to value-based disclosures. An example of a value-based disclosure is the Standardized Measure of Oil and Gas (SMOG) disclosures that are currently provided under generally accepted accounting principles in the United States. As well as the disclosure of probable reserves including a current value measurement for probable reserves.
- *Publish What You Pay* — The final section of the discussion paper relates to the Publish What You Pay proposals. This disclosure would require companies to disclose amounts paid to host governments on a country-by-country basis.

Cost capitalisation model

The discussion paper proposes that legal rights to explore and extract mineral resources should be recognised as an asset. Associated with these legal rights is information about the possible existence of mineral resources, the extent and characteristics of the deposit, and the economics of their extraction. While such information does not represent a separate asset, the project team proposes that information obtained from subsequent exploration, evaluation and development activity would be treated as enhancements of the legal rights asset.

How will costs be charged to the statement of profit or loss and other comprehensive income?

With more costs being capitalised than under current guidance in light of the requirement to capitalise all exploration costs, and the potential for impairment tests arising from unsuccessful exploration projects, there may be an increase in the number of impairments being recorded and increased earnings volatility as a result.

Costs that previously would have been recognised by many companies in the statement of profit or loss and other comprehensive income as periodic costs would instead accumulate on the statement of financial position and would potentially have to be written off at a later date.

16.7.2 US SEC reporting requirements

In December 2008, the United States Securities and Exchange Commission (SEC) issued Final Rule No. 33-8995 *Modernization of Oil and Gas Reporting* (the Final Rule) to amend its oil and gas reporting requirements. The amendments were designed to modernise and update oil and gas disclosure requirements to align them with many current industry practices, including the industry's use of new technologies. The primary objective of the Final Rule was to increase the transparency of reserve disclosures and improve comparability among oil and gas companies — including comparability between domestic registrants and foreign private issuers. The Final Rule was effective for registration statements filed on or after 1 January 2010, and for annual reports on Forms 10-K and 20-F for fiscal years ending on or after 31 December 2009.

The Final Rule, among other things:

- expands the definition of oil and gas producing activities to include reserves from non-traditional sources such as oil sands, shale and coal beds
- adds a definition of the term 'reliable technology' to clarify the types of technology that can be used to establish reasonable certainty and requires general disclosure surrounding the technologies used to estimate reserves
- permits the optional disclosure of probable and possible reserves
- modifies the prices used to estimate reserves for SEC disclosure purposes to a 12-month average price instead of a single-day, period-end price.

16.7.3 Accounting for waste removal costs

In surface mining operations, it is necessary to remove rocks, soil and other waste materials, which are commonly referred to as 'overburden', to access the relevant mineral deposits for extraction purposes. The costs incurred in such activities are referred to as 'stripping costs'. In late 2009, the IFRS Interpretations Committee (formerly IFRIC) received a request for guidance in relation to the accounting for surface mine stripping costs incurred during the production phase. This request arose from the lack of specific guidance that was currently available under IFRSs and the significant diversity thought to exist in practice.

It is commonly accepted that stripping costs incurred during the development of a mine (i.e. before production commences) should be capitalised as part of the cost of the mine. However, there is mixed practice with respect to the treatment of stripping costs that are incurred during the production phase, which ranges from expensing such costs as incurred, capitalising them to inventory or deferring those that don't relate to production in the current period in order to allocate them to future production. IFRIC 20 *Stripping Costs in the Production Phase of a Surface Mine* was issued in October 2011 and is effective for annual reporting periods beginning on or after 1 January 2013.

In summary, the Interpretation requires the following:

- Waste removal (stripping) costs should be capitalised during the production phase of a surface mine, if certain criteria are met.
- The criteria are: the stripping activity meets the definition of an asset (i.e. generates future economic benefits and is reliably measurable) and that the entity can identify the component/s of the ore body for which access has been improved.
- This asset is referred to as a stripping activity asset ('the asset').
- The asset should be recognised initially at cost plus directly attributable overhead costs.
- Costs should be either directly allocated to the asset, or where not possible, a rational and consistent allocation approach is permitted (using some form of production based metric).
- The asset represents an addition to, or enhancement of, an existing asset.
- The asset should subsequently be carried at cost, less depreciation and impairment.

The Interpretation applies prospectively and there are specific transitional provisions for any stripping costs previously recognised as an asset (or liability) before the effective date of the Interpretation.

SUMMARY

The purpose of this chapter is to analyse the content of IFRS 6 *Exploration for and Evaluation of Mineral Resources* and provide guidance on its implementation. The principal issues in the financial reporting for E&E expenditures are the recognition and measurement of E&E assets, assessment of impairment of E&E assets, and determining appropriate disclosures to identify and explain the amounts in the entity's financial statements arising from the exploration for and evaluation of mineral resources (IFRS 6 Objective). The key issues in recognising and initially measuring the asset are in determining when capitalisation of costs related to E&E activities should commence and identifying which elements of that cost should be capitalised. After the initial recognition of the asset, a decision has to be made about whether to apply the cost model or the revaluation model. If the revaluation model is applied, a further decision has to be made about whether the IAS 16 *Property, Plant and Equipment* or the IAS 38 *Intangible Assets* revaluation model should apply, consistent with the classification of the asset as tangible or intangible. Regardless of which measurement basis is used, the asset must be assessed for impairment when impairment indicators are present in accordance with IAS 36 *Impairment of Assets*. In performing an impairment test for E&E assets, a decision has to be made about the level at which the test should be applied, this being limited to a level no larger than an operating segment as defined in IFRS 8 (see chapter 21). IFRS 6 requires specific disclosures to be made in relation to the accounting policies for E&E assets and the amounts recognised in the financial statements related to E&E activities. In addition, for E&E assets classified as tangible assets and for E&E assets classified as intangible assets, the disclosures required by IAS 16 and IAS 38 respectively must also be provided.

Discussion questions

1. To which expenditures is the scope of IFRS 6 limited?
2. Discuss the complexities and considerations an entity involved in the extractive industries faces in determining the accounting policies to apply to expenditures it incurs that are outside of the scope of IFRS 6.

3. Discuss what entities need to consider if they want to change their accounting policies applicable to E&E costs.
4. Explain how the successful efforts method of accounting for E&E expenditure compares to the full cost method.
5. Discuss the possible challenges in applying the revaluation models under IAS 16 or IAS 38 to E&E assets.
6. Discuss the possible future developments related to the accounting for extractive activities.

Exercises

STAR RATING ★ BASIC ★★ MODERATE ★★★ DIFFICULT

Exercise 16.1	OBLIGATIONS FOR REMOVAL AND RESTORATION

★ The management of Mining plc is concerned that the E&E activities it has commenced for one of its properties will cause significant damage to the surrounding environment and the government of the country where the property is located has attached strict conditions to the exploration licence. Those conditions require that Mining plc return the environment to its original condition.

Required

What are the implications of the above scenario for Mining plc's financial statements?

Exercise 16.2	IMPAIRMENT OF E&E ASSETS

★ During the year ended 31 December 2013, the management of Gas Inc. has been analysing its engineering reports for a specific property, which indicate that sample drilling has not resulted in any findings that confirm the existence of oil and gas. As a result, Gas Inc. is reluctant to invest any further funds in exploring the area. An E&E asset with a carrying value of $1.2 million exists in relation to that property as at 31 December 2013.

Required

What is the possible impact of this decision on Gas Inc.'s financial statements as at 31 December 2013?

Exercise 16.3	ELEMENTS OF COST OF E&E ASSETS

★★ Exploration plc has acquired a licence to explore a new property and its accounting policy is to fully capitalise all of its E&E expenditures. During the period, costs have been incurred in relation to the following:
(a) the acquisition of speculative seismic data in relation to the areas to be used to determine whether to apply for an exploration licence for that area
(b) labour costs of engineers to analyse the seismic data obtained
(c) the exploration licence fee
(d) legal costs associated with obtaining the exploration licence
(e) labour costs for engineers to carry out topographical, geological, geochemical and geophysical studies on the area after obtaining the exploration licence
(f) payroll-related costs for that labour
(g) contractors' fees for exploratory drilling
(h) hire of drilling equipment.

Required

Which of the above items should be capitalised into the E&E asset?

Exercise 16.4	APPLICATION OF THE REVALUATION MODEL

★★ Resource plc classifies its E&E assets as intangible assets. A new accountant has just been employed and has suggested that Resource plc should change its accounting policy for E&E assets from its existing cost model to the fair value model under IAS 38 because it would provide more relevant information.

Required

What might prevent Resource plc from being able to make this change in accounting policy?

Exercise 16.5 | **CHANGE IN ACCOUNTING POLICY**

★★ Sandy Oil plc is a company involved in the search for, production of and sale of oil and gas resources. The company has been following an accounting policy of expensing all of its E&E costs as incurred since adoption of IFRS 6. However, it has noted that its most significant competitor follows a policy of capitalising such costs. This makes the competitor's profit look better in some years than Sandy Oil plc's profit.

Required

Discuss whether Sandy Oil plc can change its accounting policy to capitalise all of its E&E costs to match its competitor's accounting policy.

Exercise 16.6 | **RECOGNITION OF E&E ASSETS**

★★ Digging Inc. has incurred the following costs during the period in relation to a specific property. Its accounting policy is to capitalise all E&E costs.

Cash paid to acquire seismic study from government that is selling exploration rights for the property (GST exempt)	$ 3 000
Cash paid to acquire exploration rights for the property from the government (GST exempt)	10 000
Cash paid to acquire fencing materials to mark out the property, including GST of $80	880
Contractor fees for labour to set up the fencing, including GST of $50	550
Contractor fees for exploratory drilling, including GST of $2500	27 500
Hire of drilling equipment for contractor use, including GST of $500	5 500
Salary of project manager hired specifically to manage E&E activities for the property	60 000
Stationery and other office supplies used by the project manager, including GST of $30	330
Digging Inc. non-executive directors' fees paid during the period	160 000

Required

Determine the amount of the E&E asset to be capitalised by Digging Inc. in relation to the property.

Exercise 16.7 | **MEASUREMENT OF E&E ASSETS**

★★★ During the year ended 31 December 2014, Reserves plc explored four different properties and spent $100 000 in each. The results of E&E activities suggested that Properties A, B and C may contain mineral reserves so the company acquired leases over these three properties. The leases cost $170 000, $220 000 and $180 000 respectively.

During the year ended 31 December 2015, Reserves plc commenced a drilling program to evaluate Properties A, B and C. Seven exploratory wells were drilled, four in Property A, two in Property B and one in Property C at a cost of $120 000 each. The five wells drilled in Property A did not result in any mineral resource findings (i.e. they were dry holes). The two wells drilled on Property B indicated that the company had discovered economically recoverable reserves. Management was uncertain about the likelihood of finding economically recoverable reserves for the well in Property C as some mineral reserves were found but not enough to be considered economically recoverable at this stage. Therefore Reserves plc decided to continue E&E activities in Property C as of 31 December 2015. Property A was abandoned, and, after incurring costs of $50 000 to confirm the technical feasibility and commercial viability of extracting the mineral resources, development of Property B commenced.

During the year ended 31 December 2016, to evaluate the property further, three more wells were drilled in Property B. Of these, two were dry. Each well cost $140 000. The successful wells in Property B were developed for a total cost of $300 000. Expenditure on additional plant and equipment related to development was $325 000. After further dry wells costing $175 000 were drilled in Property C, management concluded that Property C did not contain any commercially viable quantities of mineral resources, so it was abandoned.

These costs are summarised as follows:

Costs incurred for each property		A	B	C	D	Total
31/12/2014	Exploration	$100 000	$ 100 000	$100 000	$100 000	$ 400 000
31/12/2015	Leases	140 000	220 000	180 000	—	550 000
	Dry wells	600 000	—	—	—	600 000
	Other wells	—	240 000	120 000	—	360 000
	Technical feasibility/ commercial viability costs	—	50 000	—	—	50 000
31/12/2016	Dry wells	—	280 000	175 000	—	455 000
	Other wells	—	140 000	—	—	140 000
	Development	—	300 000	—	—	300 000
	PPE	—	325 000	—	—	325 000
Total		$850 000	$1 655 000	$575 000	$100 000	$3 180 000

Required

Determine what expenses would be recognised in profit or loss versus capitalised as an asset related to each property for each financial year assuming Reserves plc:

(a) expenses all of its E&E costs as incurred

(b) applies the full cost method (assume that each property is in a different country and represents a separate cost pool)

(c) applies the successful efforts method (assume that each property represents a separate licence).

References

BHP Billiton 2010, *Annual report 2010*, BHP Billiton Ltd, www.bhpbilliton.com.

BP 2010, *Annual report and Form 20-F 2010*, BP plc, UK, www.bp.com.

Ernst & Young 2011, *Good Petroleum (International) Limited, International GAAP illustrative financial statements*, www.ey.com/global.

—— 2012, *International GAAP 2012: Generally Accepted Accounting Practice under International Financial Reporting Standards*, John Wiley, New York.

IASB 2010, *Extractive Activities Discussion Paper*, International Accounting Standards Board, April.

IASC 2000, *Extractive Industries Issues Paper*, International Accounting Standards Committee, November.

Rio Tinto 2011, *2011 Annual report*, Rio Tinto Ltd, www.riotinto.com.

Royal Dutch Shell 2010, *Annual report and Form 20-F for the year ended December 31, 2010*, Royal Dutch Shell plc, The Netherlands, www.shell.com.

Securities and Exchange Commission 2008 Final Rule No. 33-8995, *Modernization of oil and gas reporting*, United States, www.sec.gov.

Xstrata 2010, *Annual report 2010*, Xstrata plc, London, www.xstrata.com.

17 Agriculture

ACCOUNTING STANDARDS IN FOCUS

IAS 41 *Agriculture*

IFRS 13 *Fair Value Measurement*

LEARNING OBJECTIVES

After studying this chapter, you should be able to:

1 explain the background to the development of IAS 41

2 distinguish between agricultural activities, agricultural produce and biological assets

3 explain the different accounting treatment required before and after harvest

4 explain the recognition criteria for biological assets and agricultural produce

5 analyse the meaning of 'fair value' when applied to biological assets and agricultural produce

6 explain the practical implications of measuring these assets at fair value, including interpreting the disclosures made by companies applying the standard

7 examine the interaction between IAS 41 and IAS 20 *Accounting for Government Grants and Disclosure of Government Assistance*

8 examine the interaction between IAS 41 and IAS 16 *Property, Plant and Equipment*, IAS 17 *Leases* and IAS 40 *Investment Property*

9 describe the disclosure requirements of IAS 41

10 apply the recognition and measurement requirements of IAS 41 to a simple statement of profit or loss and other comprehensive income and statement of financial position

11 describe how IFRS 13 *Fair Value Measurement*, once effective, will interact with IAS 41.

17.1 INTRODUCTION TO IAS 41

IAS 41 was issued by the International Accounting Standards Committee (IASC) in February 2001 and was confirmed as being included in the core set of standards to be issued by the International Accounting Standards Board (IASB) in April 2001. (Refer to chapter 1 for the history of and distinction between the IASC and IASB.) The IASC's project on agriculture commenced in 1994. The IASC had decided to develop a separate standard on agriculture because, although it generally developed standards that are relevant to all businesses, it regarded agriculture as an industry with a particular need for its own standard. This was for a number of reasons, one of the main ones being that diversity in accounting for agricultural activity had arisen because:

- of the specific exclusion of assets related to agricultural activity from other standards (such as IAS 2 *Inventories*, IAS 16 *Property, Plant and Equipment*, IAS 18 *Revenue* and IAS 40 *Investment Property*)
- accounting guidelines for agricultural activity developed by national standard setters had, in general, been piecemeal (with the exception of Australia, which had developed and applied a standard on 'Self-Generating and Regenerating Assets' or 'SGARAs')
- the nature of agricultural activity had created uncertainty or conflicts when applying traditional accounting models (IAS 41, Basis for Conclusions paragraphs B1–B7).

The IASC also regarded agriculture as an emerging industry that was seeking to attract capital from investors and this increased the need to develop standards for general purpose financial statements of the entities involved (IAS 41, Basis for Conclusions paragraphs B1–B7).

IAS 41 was a controversial standard when it was first issued, mainly because of the requirement to measure assets related to agricultural activity at fair value, with movements in fair value being taken to the statement of profit or loss and other comprehensive income as gains or losses. To this day, companies applying the standard indicate their implicit disagreement with this requirement; for example, by highlighting the fair value movements separately in their statements of comprehensive income so that users can clearly see and understand the impact on reported profit. We will look at some examples of this later in the chapter.

In May 2011, the IASB issued IFRS 13 *Fair Value Measurement*, which amended IAS 41. IFRS 13 is effective for annual periods beginning on or after 1 January 2013. IFRS 13 combines into one standard, rather than being dispersed throughout multiple IFRSs, all of the requirements regarding *how to* measure fair value. IFRS 13 does *not* change any requirements regarding *when to* use fair value as the measurement basis. Because of the effective date of IFRS 13, this chapter refers to the 1 January 2011 version of IAS 41, with an explanation of the changes made at the end of the chapter.

17.2 SCOPE AND KEY DEFINITIONS

17.2.1 Scope

IAS 41 applies to the accounting for the following when they relate to agricultural activity:
1. biological assets
2. agricultural produce
3. government grants.

The standard does not apply to land or intangible assets related to agricultural activity (IAS 41 paragraph 2). Land related to agricultural activity is recognised and measured by applying either IAS 16 or IAS 40, whichever is appropriate in the circumstances. So, for example, if the land meets the definition of an investment property it is measured using either the fair value model or the cost model — an accounting policy choice permitted by IAS 40. Note that 'investment property' is defined in IAS 40 as 'property (land or a building — or part of a building — or both) held (by the owner or by the lessee under a finance lease) to earn rentals or for capital appreciation or both, rather than for: (a) use in the production or supply of goods or services or for administrative purposes; or (b) sale in the ordinary course of business'. If the land does *not* meet the definition of an investment property then it must be recognised and measured by applying IAS 16 (see chapter 11 for further explanation). IAS 16 allows an accounting policy choice between the cost model and the revaluation model. The cost model under IAS 40 is the same as that under IAS 16. However, the fair value model under IAS 40 differs from the revaluation model under IAS 16, essentially in that fair value movements are taken to the statement of profit or loss and other comprehensive income under IAS 40; whereas, under IAS 16 they are taken to equity (usually to an asset revaluation surplus). Also, IAS 16 requires revalued assets to be depreciated, although this does not apply to land (IAS 16 paragraph 58).

The impact of the accounting policy choice in respect of land is discussed further in section 17.8.

Intangible assets related to agricultural activity are accounted for under IAS 38 *Intangible Assets* (see chapter 13 for further explanation).

17.2.2 Key definitions

IAS 41 paragraph 5 contains the following important definitions:

Agricultural activity is the management by an entity of the biological transformation and harvest of biological assets for sale or for conversion into agricultural produce or into additional biological assets.

Agricultural produce is the harvested product of the entity's biological assets.

A **biological asset** is a living animal or plant.

Biological transformation comprises the processes of growth, degeneration, production, and procreation that cause qualitative or quantitative changes in a biological asset.

Harvest is the detachment of produce from a biological asset or the cessation of a biological asset's life processes.

Agricultural activity covers a diverse range of activities. However, IAS 41 paragraph 6 states that there are three common features that exist within this diversity:

- *Capability to change.* Living plants and animals are capable of biological transformation.
- *Management of change.* Management facilitates biological transformation. For example, management of a vineyard or orchard by providing nutrients, water and protection from pests facilitates the growth of the vines and trees. This can be distinguished from unmanaged biological change such as the growth of fishes in the ocean. Thus ocean fishing is not an agricultural activity.
- *Measurement of change.* The change in quality (e.g. ripeness, protein content or fibre strength) or quantity (e.g. weight, cubic metres or diameter) brought about by biological transformation is measured and monitored as a routine management function.

17.3 THE HARVEST DISTINCTION

There is a very important distinction between agricultural produce, which is the harvested product of the entity's biological assets, and products that result from processing after harvest. IAS 41 applies only to the harvested product *at the point of harvest*. Thereafter, IAS 2, or another applicable standard is applied.

The standard includes examples to illustrate the difference between biological assets, agricultural produce and products that are the result of processing after harvest. Table 17.1 is based on paragraph 4 of IAS 41, modified to aid understanding.

TABLE 17.1 Distinction between biological assets, agricultural produce and products that are a result of processing after harvest

Biological assets (IAS 41 applies)	Agricultural produce (IAS 41 applies)	Products that are a result of processing after harvest (generally IAS 2 applies)
Sheep	Wool	Yarn, carpet, clothing
Trees in a plantation forest	Felled trees	Lumber, furniture
Plants	Cotton	Thread, clothing
	Harvested cane	Sugar
Dairy cattle	Milk	Cheese
Pigs	Carcass	Sausages
Bushes	Leaf	Tea
Vines	Grapes	Wine
Fruit trees	Picked fruit	Processed fruit e.g. tinned fruit

One of the initial criticisms of IAS 41 was that it requires assets for which there is often not an active or ready market to be measured at fair value, while those assets for which there is an active and ready market are measured at cost under IAS 2. For example, it can be difficult to determine a fair value for immature trees in a plantation because there may not be an active or ready market for trees before they are fully grown. In contrast, there would be a much more easily identifiable market value for lumber or furniture, yet this is measured at cost under IAS 2. The IASB rejected criticisms of the fair value model for biological assets and agricultural produce but conceded by permitting an exemption when fair value cannot be reliably measured (IAS 41 Basis for Conclusions paragraph B13–B21). This is discussed further in section 17.5.2.

Some respondents to the exposure draft that preceded IAS 41 also commented that in some cases processing after harvest was akin to biological transformation (e.g. wine production from grapes and cheese production from milk) and therefore there should not be a distinction at the harvest point. While acknowledging this issue, the IASB considered that it would be difficult to differentiate these circumstances from other manufacturing processes. The IASB also decided not to include a revision of IAS 2 as part of its process of approving IAS 41 (IAS 41 Basis for Conclusions paragraph B9–B11).

 ## 17.4 THE RECOGNITION CRITERIA FOR BIOLOGICAL ASSETS AND AGRICULTURAL PRODUCE

17.4.1 The recognition criteria

Paragraph 10 of IAS 41 states that an entity shall recognise a biological asset or agricultural produce when, and only when:

(a) the entity controls the asset as a result of past events;
(b) it is probable that future economic benefits associated with the asset will flow to the entity; and
(c) the fair value or cost of the asset can be measured reliably.

Note that (a) repeats one of the essential characteristics of the *definition* of an asset in the *Conceptual Framework* (control) while (b) and (c) repeat the recognition criteria in the *Conceptual Framework*.

17.4.2 The problem with 'control'

The issue of control can be problematic in the agricultural industry where leases or management agreements are involved. For example, a vineyard may be owned by one entity but managed by another. Because the definition of 'agricultural activity' talks about 'the management' by an entity of the biological transformation of biological assets it is possible to confuse management with control. Therefore, it is important to distinguish between these two concepts.

Illustrative example 17.1 demonstrates the distinction between management and control.

ILLUSTRATIVE EXAMPLE 17.1 Distinguishing management from control of biological assets and agricultural produce

Company A owns Vineyard X. Company A invests in many vineyards and so appoints Manager M to manage Vineyard X. Manager M is responsible for all the operations of the vineyard including daily care, regular maintenance, harvesting of the grapes and storage of the grapes after harvest. The grapes are then sent to be processed into wine by Winemaker W.

Manager M and Winemaker W are not related parties of Company A. Company A pays Manager M a management fee for its services. The fee includes reimbursement of all costs incurred by Manager M plus an agreed margin. Company A pays Winemaker W a production fee for its services. The fee includes reimbursement of all costs incurred by Winemaker W plus an agreed margin.

All sales and marketing of the bottled wine is managed by Distributor D. Distributor D is not a related party of Company A. Company A pays Distributor D a fee for its services. The fee includes reimbursement of all costs incurred by Distributor D plus an agreed margin.

Who controls the biological asset (the vines)? Company A or Manager M?

Who controls the agricultural produce (the grapes)? Company A, Manager M, Winemaker W or Distributor D?

Unfortunately control is not defined in the *Conceptual Framework* and is used throughout IFRSs without consistency. Control refers to the situation where an investor is exposed, or has rights, to variable returns from its involvement with the investee and has the ability to affect those returns through its power over the investee. (IFRS 10 — see chapter 23). In IAS 17 *Leases* the concept of control of an asset is linked to who has the risks and rewards incidental to ownership (even though this concept is not referred to as 'control'). In IAS 39 *Financial Instruments: Recognition and Measurement* (see chapter 7) there is a distinction between risks and rewards of ownership of an asset and control of that asset. Control in this case is referred to in terms of the entity's ability to sell the asset. If the entity is able to sell the asset then IAS 39 regards the entity as having control of the asset. In IAS 39 it is possible to *not* have the risks and rewards of ownership of an asset but still control it (paragraph 23). In IFRIC 4 *Determining whether an Arrangement contains a Lease* the concept of *control of the use* of an asset is central. This is because a lease is defined as a *right of use* of an asset. IFRIC 4 contains conditions that must be met in order for an entity to control the right of use of an asset. These include the ability to operate the asset while obtaining more than a significant amount of output from the asset; or the ability to control physical access to the asset while obtaining more than a significant amount of output from the asset. Note, however, that these conditions will indicate whether or not the arrangement *is a lease* (i.e. whether a right of use has been given to an entity). Whether the lease transfers the risks and rewards of ownership of the asset to the entity (i.e. whether it is a finance lease or an operating lease) is a second question. Then we have to go back to IAS 17, which appears to equate risks and rewards of ownership with control!

To make the question of control of the biological asset in this example simpler, let's assume that control in this case means both the legal ownership of the asset (i.e. the ability to sell or pledge the asset) as well as the exposure to the risks and rewards of ownership of the asset.

What are the key rewards of the vines and grapes? These would be the growth of the vines so as to produce grapes and the revenues to be earned by either selling the grapes at a profit or by processing them into wine to sell at a profit.

Who benefits from these rewards? Manager M, Winemaker W and Distributor D each have a share in these rewards because they are paid a margin by Company A. This means that they recover their costs but also benefit from increases in value of the vines and grapes via the margin paid to them by Company A. However, because this margin is agreed upfront it is a fixed margin. This means that Company A benefits from any increases in value over and above the recovery of costs plus the fixed margin. Manager M, Winemaker W and Distributor D do not share in these excess profits because their return is fixed.

What are the key risks in the vines and grapes? These would be the risks of disease, drought and so on, such that the vines fail to grow and produce grapes of adequate quality. This in turn would result in an inability to sell the produce of the vines either at all or the generation of lower returns than expected or needed to remain profitable. There are also market risks such as a glut of wine on the market causing prices to fall.

Who bears these risks? The majority of these risks are borne by Company A because — as we saw above — each of Manager M, Winemaker W and Distributor D is entitled to a fixed return even if there are no profits. This means that Company A bears all of the downside risk in the vines and the grapes. It must pay the management fee, production fee and distribution fee even if there is no return from the vines, grapes or wine.

Who controls the vines and the grapes? While Manager M manages the daily operations of the vineyard it does so on behalf of Company A. Similarly, Winemaker W makes the wine on behalf of Company A, and Distributor D sells the wine on behalf of Company A. Thus, Company A has the ability to sell or pledge the vines and the grapes even though, practically, the sale of the grapes is effected by Manager M on behalf of Company A. These entities all act as agents of Company A.

So we can conclude that Company A controls the biological assets and agricultural produce under paragraph 10 of IAS 41. Therefore, Company A should recognise these assets (assuming the other requirements of paragraph 10 are met).

However, the agricultural activity as defined in paragraph 5 of IAS 41 is carried out by Manager M. It is the entity that manages the transformation of the vines into grapes. Does this mean that Manager M applies IAS 41 while Company A does not? Since we have concluded that Company A controls the biological assets and agricultural produce, these assets must be recognised by Company A. If Manager M were to apply IAS 41 it would apply the standard to nothing since it does not control the assets in question. Therefore, it is arguably reasonable to conclude that Manager M conducts the agricultural activity on behalf of Company A, and thus Company A should apply IAS 41. This argument could be attacked on the basis of applying the recognition criteria of the standard before the scope section. It is further complicated by the interaction with IAS 17 and IAS 40 (refer section 17.8).

LO5 17.5 MEASUREMENT AT FAIR VALUE

17.5.1 Measurement requirement

Paragraph 12 of IAS 41 states that:

> A biological asset shall be measured on initial recognition and at the end of each reporting period at its fair value less costs to sell, except for the case described in paragraph 30 where the fair value cannot be measured reliably.

Paragraph 13 of IAS 41 states that:

> Agricultural produce harvested from an entity's biological assets shall be measured at its fair value less costs to sell at the point of harvest. Such measurement is the cost at that date when applying IAS 2 *Inventories* or another applicable Standard.

'Fair value' is defined in paragraph 8 as:

> The amount for which an asset could be exchanged, or a liability settled, between knowledgeable, willing parties in an arm's length transaction.

'Costs to sell' are defined in paragraph 5 as:

> The incremental costs directly attributable to the disposal of an asset, excluding finance costs and income taxes.

Costs to sell include commissions to brokers and dealers, levies by regulatory agencies and commodity exchanges and transfer taxes and duties. Costs to sell exclude transport and other costs necessary to get assets to a market. However, such transport costs are deducted in determining fair value (IAS 41 Basis for Conclusions paragraph B22).[1]

17.5.2 Arguments for and against the use of fair value

When IAS 41 was first proposed as E65, the requirement to use fair value as the measurement basis was controversial. The arguments for and against the use of fair value are summarised in table 17.2 (IAS 41 Basis for Conclusions paragraph B14–B21).

TABLE 17.2 Arguments for and against the use of fair value for measuring biological assets

	Case for Fair Value	Case against Fair Value
Biological transformation has a direct relationship to changes in expectations of future economic benefits to the entity.	✓	
The relationship between cost incurrence and future economic benefits is weak particularly for biological assets that take a long time to mature.	✓	
Relevance	✓ (many biological assets are traded in active markets; long production cycles mean that the change in asset value is more relevant than a period-end measured of cost incurred)	✓ (market prices at the end of the reporting period may not bear a close relationship to the prices at which the assets will be sold)

---

[1] In a minor amendment in May 2008 the IASB amended the term 'point-of-sale costs' to 'costs to sell' to align IAS 41 with other IFRSs. There was no change in the meaning of the term. (IAS 41, Basis for Conclusions to May 2008 amendments, BC3 and BC4)

TABLE 17.2 *(continued)*

	Case for Fair Value	Case against Fair Value
Reliability	✓ (active markets provide reliable information; allocation of costs is arbitrary when there are joint products and joint costs)	✓ (cost of historical transactions is more reliable and objective; market prices are often volatile and cyclical; active markets may not exist, particularly during periods of growth of assets that have a long growth period)
Comparability and Understandability	✓ (different sources of animals and plants — home grown or purchased — should not be measured differently, which would be the outcome under a historical cost model)	✓ (reporting of unrealised gains and losses is not useful to users)

The board decided to proceed with the requirement to use fair value, but was persuaded by the arguments that fair value may not always be able to be measured reliably where market prices are not available and alternative estimates of fair value are determined to be clearly unreliable. This resulted in the exception in paragraph 30, which states:

> There is a presumption that fair value can be measured reliably for a biological asset. However, that presumption can be rebutted only on initial recognition for a biological asset for which market-determined prices or values are not available and for which alternative estimates of fair value are determined to be clearly unreliable. In such a case, that biological asset shall be measured at its cost less any accumulated depreciation and any accumulated impairment losses. Once the fair value of such a biological asset becomes reliably measurable, an entity shall measure it at its fair value less costs to sell.

It is important to note that this exception can only be applied on initial recognition of the asset. So, for example, in Australia where a similar standard to IAS 41 was being applied prior to the adoption of IFRSs, companies had already recognised their biological assets and were measuring them at fair value. They could not avail themselves of the exception in paragraph 30 because the assets had already been recognised.

In addition, the exception applies only to biological assets, not to agricultural produce. IAS 41 takes the view that the fair value of agricultural produce at the point of harvest can always be measured reliably (paragraph 32).

17.5.3 How to apply the fair value measurement requirement

The standard also includes guidance on how to apply the fair value measurement requirement (paragraphs 15–25):

- Biological assets or agricultural assets may be grouped according to significant attributes such as age or quality (e.g. all 'A' grade cattle may be grouped and a fair value determined for that group).
- Contract prices are not necessarily relevant because they may not represent the current market. For example, a company may enter into a contract to sell its cotton in 6 months' time at a set price (known as a forward price). This forward price would not normally be the same as the current market price (known as the spot price). IAS 41 requires the spot price to be used for determining fair value even if a forward contract has been entered into.
- If an active market exists for the asset in its present location and condition, the quoted price in that market should be used. If an entity has access to two different markets, the entity uses the most relevant one; that is, the one it expects to use. For example, if an entity can sell its produce either at the farm gate or at auction it must select which of the two it expects to use.
- If an active market does *not* exist, an entity uses one or more of the following:
  (a) the most recent transaction price provided that there has not been a significant change in economic circumstances between the date of the transaction and the end of the reporting period
  (b) market prices for similar assets with adjustments to reflect differences
  (c) sector benchmarks such as the value of an orchard expressed per export tray, bushel or hectare.

- Where market prices do not exist for the biological asset in its present condition, an entity uses the present value of expected net cash flows from the asset discounted at a current market-determined rate. Note that the objective of this calculation is to determine the fair value of the asset in its *present* condition. Paragraph 21 of IAS 41 had stated that any increases in value from future biological transformation must be excluded. In 2007, the IFRIC (now known as the IFRS Interpretations Committee) received a request to clarify this requirement because entities said they were having difficulty in applying the requirement to exclude future biological transformation. For example, how does an entity estimate future cash flows from an immature forest if it cannot assume the forest will continue to grow and generate future cash flows in its fully mature state? In practice, entities may need to work out the cash flows from a biological asset in its mature state and work backwards to then calculate the cash flows from the asset in its immature state. The IFRIC referred the matter to the IASB for clarification. In May 2008, the IASB amended IAS 41 to clarify that future biological transformation may be taken into account in determining fair value because the buyer would assess the potential for the asset to reach maturity in determining how much to pay for the asset in its immature state. In addition, the IASB amended the standard to use the phrase 'biological transformation or harvest' where appropriate to clarify that a harvested asset is not the same as a growing asset (IAS 41, Basis for Conclusions to May 2008 amendments, BC8–BC10). Therefore, a market value for a growing asset may be calculated based on its potential to continue to grow and be harvested, taking into account risk factors regarding the potential growth of the asset. This is illustrated in illustrative example 17.3.
- When estimating cash flows, an entity does not include any cash flows for financing the assets, taxation, or re-establishing biological assets after harvest. Variations in expected cash flows are taken into account in either the discount rate or the expected cash flows, but not in both (otherwise the effect of the possible variations would be double counted).
- Cost may sometimes approximate fair value, particularly when:
  1. little biological transformation has taken place since initial cost incurrence (e.g. fruit tree seedlings planted immediately prior to the end of a reporting period), or
  2. the impact of the biological transformation on price is not expected to be material (e.g. the initial period of growth in a 30-year pine production cycle).
- Where biological assets are attached to land and there is no separate market for the assets without the land, the entity may use information regarding the combined assets to determine the fair value of the biological assets. For example, the fair value of the raw land may be deducted from the fair value of the combined assets to arrive at the fair value of the biological assets.

Illustrative example 17.2 illustrates the calculation of fair value where there is an active market.

ILLUSTRATIVE EXAMPLE 17.2 Calculating fair value

Company A owns dairy cattle. The market value of cattle is calculated by reference to the litres of milk able to be produced and the lactation rate of the cows. Cattle are regularly sold at auction. Costs incurred to transport the cattle to auction are $500 per truck. The normal capacity of a truck is approximately 200 cattle.

Company A has determined that, based on latest auction prices close to the end of the reporting period, a mature cow's market value is 5000 litres × lactation rate (0.5) × price of milk ($0.35) = $875 and a heifer's market value is 2000 litres × 0.5 × $0.35 = $350.

At the end of the reporting period, Company A had 1000 mature cows and 400 heifers.

Transport costs are deducted in determining fair value in accordance with paragraph B22 of IAS 41. The approximate cost per cow is $500/200 = $2.50. Thus the market value for each cow is $850 − $2.50 = $872.50. The market value for each heifer is $350 − $2.50 = $347.50. The fair value as at the end of the reporting period is thus:

$$1000 \times \$847.50 = \$872\,500$$
$$400 \times \$347.50 = \$139\,000$$
$$\$1\,011\,500$$

Illustrative example 17.3 illustrates the calculation of fair value where there is not an active market.

ILLUSTRATIVE EXAMPLE 17.3 Calculation of fair value where there is no active market

Company A owns and manages an orchard that produces apples. In 2013, Company A spent $450 000 establishing the orchard, as follows:

Cost of the land	$350 000
Cost of the seedlings	$30 000
Plant and equipment (estimated useful life of 10 years)	$50 000
Fertilisers, feed and other costs	$10 000
Salaries and wages	$10 000

During 2014 and 2015, Company A incurred further costs as follows:

Salaries and wages	$20 000
Fertilisers, feed and spraying costs	$5 000

At the end of 2015, the trees were 3 years old and Company A expected its first harvest in 2017. Company A expects the orchard to have a life of 20 years from the date of first harvest. In Company A's jurisdiction there is no active market for immature apple trees. How would Company A determine the fair value of the orchard as at the end of 2015?

In accordance with paragraph 18 of IAS 41, Company A would need to determine whether there is:
(a) a recent transaction price, or
(b) market prices for similar assets, or
(c) sector benchmarks.

Assume that Company A cannot find any of these three for the orchard in its present condition. It would then need to calculate the present value of expected net cash flows in accordance with paragraph 20 of IAS 41.

Company A determines that once the orchard starts producing apples it expects annual cash inflows from sales of the apples as follows:

2017	$50 000
2018	$90 000
2019	$150 000
2020	$200 000
2021 and onwards	$200 000

Company A also expects to pay annual salaries, wages and other operating costs of $40 000 from 2017. During 2016, it expects to pay $25 000 for these costs. Company A determines that the appropriate discount rate to use is 6% up until and including 2021 and 15% for the years thereafter to take account of the increased risk that the estimated cash flows may not eventuate as predicted. Costs to sell are estimated to be 1% of sales. The calculation of the present value of expected net cash flows *as at the end of 2015* is as follows:

Year ended	Cash inflows $	Cash outflows $	Net cash flows $	Present value at 6% (15% from 2022) $
2016	—	25 000	(25 000)	(23 585)
2017	50 000	40 000 + 500	9 500	8 482
2018	90 000	40 000 + 900	49 100	41 260
2019	150 000	40 000 + 1 500	108 500	86 111
2020	200 000	40 000 + 2 000	158 000	117 910
2021	200 000	40 000 + 2 000	158 000	111 268
2022–37	200 000	40 000 + 2 000	158 000	443 443

The net present value of expected net cash flows is thus $784 889. This is the fair value of the orchard in its present condition, taking into account the risk that future cash flows may not occur as planned in the higher discount rate applied to the 16 years beyond 2021.

Note the establishment costs are not included in this calculation. The costs of establishing the orchard must be accounted for under the relevant accounting standards such as IAS 16 and IAS 40. The land would be recorded as an asset under either IAS 16 or IAS 40. The plant and equipment would be recorded as an asset under IAS 16 and depreciated over 10 years. The other establishment costs would be expensed unless Company A could justify recording the costs as an asset under IAS 38. Salaries and wages and other operating costs are unlikely to meet the requirements for recognition as an asset under IAS 38. The cost of the seedlings — which are not intangible assets — could qualify for recognition as an asset under the *Conceptual Framework* because they are the basis from which the future cash flows generated by the mature trees derive. This question is not addressed in IAS 41. It is clear that the *cost* of the seedlings cannot be included in the fair value of the orchard because the fair value measurement method does not allow a mixture of cost and fair value estimates. However, it is possible for the costs to be recorded as a separate asset and amortised over the life of the orchard. If this is done then care must be taken to ensure that the *value* of the seedlings is not taken into account again in determining the fair value of the biological asset.

The following would be the journal entries for years 2013, 2014 and 2015, assuming that the land is recorded at cost under IAS 16, the plant and equipment is recorded at cost under IAS 16 and amortised over its useful life, the seedlings are recorded as an asset and amortised over the life of the orchard and all other costs are expensed. Also assume that all amounts are paid for in cash.

Journal entries 2013			
Land	Dr	350 000	
Cash	Cr		350 000
(To record the acquisition of the land)			
Plant & Equipment	Dr	50 000	
Cash	Cr		50 000
(To record the acquisition of plant and equipment)			
Seedlings Asset	Dr	30 000	
Cash	Cr		30 000
(To record the acquisition of the seedlings)			
Operating Expenses	Dr	20 000	
Cash	Cr		20 000
(To record operating expenses)			
Depreciation Expense	Dr	5 000	
Accumulated Depreciation	Cr		5 000
(To record 1 year's depreciation of the plant and equipment)			
Depreciation Expense	Dr	1 000	
Accumulated Depreciation	Cr		1 000
(To record 1 year's depreciation of the seedlings asset)			
Journal entries 2014			
Operating Expenses	Dr	25 000	
Cash	Cr		25 000
(To record operating expenses)			
Depreciation Expense	Dr	5 000	
Accumulated Depreciation	Cr		5 000
(To record 1 year's depreciation of the plant and equipment)			

		Dr	1 000	
Depreciation Expense		Dr	1 000	
Accumulated Depreciation		Cr		1 000
(To record 1 year's depreciation of the seedlings asset)				
Journal entries 2015				
Operating Expenses		Dr	25 000	
Cash		Cr		25 000
(To record operating expenses)				
Depreciation Expense		Dr	5 000	
Accumulated Depreciation		Cr		5 000
(To record 1 year's depreciation of the plant and equipment)				
Depreciation Expense		Dr	1 000	
Accumulated Depreciation		Cr		1 000
(To record 1 year's depreciation of the seedlings asset)				
Biological Asset – Orchard		Dr	784 889	
Profit or Loss		Cr		784 889
(To record the fair value of the orchard on initial recognition)				

The gain on initial recognition of a biological asset is discussed further in section 17.5.4.

What is clear from this example is that when the orchard is established, the company will show a loss in its statement of profit or loss and other comprehensive income (in years 2013 and 2014), but as soon as the orchard is recognised at its fair value a large gain is recognised. There is no concept of 'matching' the establishment costs with the fair value movements under IAS 41.

17.5.4 Gains and losses

Paragraph 26 of IAS 41 states that:

> A gain or loss arising on initial recognition of a biological asset at fair value less costs to sell and from a change in fair value less costs to sell of a biological asset shall be included in profit or loss for the period in which it arises.

Paragraph 28 of IAS 41 contains a similar requirement for agricultural produce except that it does not refer to a change in fair value of agricultural produce. This is because agricultural produce is recognised and measured only at the point of harvest (see IAS 41 paragraph 1(b) and 13) and this amount becomes its cost for ongoing measurement under IAS 2 or another applicable standard. Thus, there is no remeasurement to fair value of agricultural produce whereas biological assets are remeasured to fair value at the end of each reporting period.

How do gains or losses on initial recognition (sometimes referred to as 'day one profits/losses') arise? Illustrative example 17.4 explains how this may occur.

ILLUSTRATIVE EXAMPLE 17.4 Gains or losses on initial recognition of biological assets and agricultural produce

In the case of biological assets, a loss may arise on initial recognition because costs to sell (which are deducted in arriving at fair value) may exceed the fair value. A profit may arise on initial recognition when, for example, an animal is born. For example, say the fair value of a newborn calf is $50. On initial recognition of the newborn animal, the journal entry would be as follows:

		Dr	50	
Biological Asset		Dr	50	
Profit or Loss		Cr		50
(To record the acquisition of the newborn calf)				

In the case of agricultural produce a gain or loss on initial recognition may arise as a result of harvesting. For example, say the fair value of a tonne of grapes is $20 and the fair value of the related vines is $100 at the date of harvest. On initial recognition of the grapes, the following journal entries are required:

Profit or Loss	Dr	20	
Biological Asset	Cr		20
(To remeasure the vines to fair value — removing the fair value of the grapes)			
Agricultural Produce	Dr	20	
Profit or Loss	Cr		20
(To recognise the grapes at fair value)			

A change in fair value of a biological asset is recorded as a gain or loss at the end of each reporting period. Illustrative example 17.5 illustrates the relevant journal entries.

ILLUSTRATIVE EXAMPLE 17.5 Recording a change in fair value of a biological asset

Assume that, as at the end of the reporting period, 30 June 2014, the fair value of Company A's vineyard was $2 500 000. As at 30 June 2015, Company A determines the following:

Fair value of the grapes harvested at 31 March 2015	500 000
Costs to sell the grapes	10 000
Costs to sell the vines	20 000
Fair value of the vines as at 31 March 2015, prior to harvest	3 100 000

Company A determines that there is no change in fair value of the vines between 31 March 2015 and 30 June 2015 and so uses the valuation as at 31 March for the purposes of the end of reporting period valuation.

The fair value of the vines less costs to sell as at 30 June 2015 is calculated as follows:

$3 100 000 less $500 000 (fair value of the harvested grapes) less $20 000 (costs to sell) = $2 580 000

The change in fair value of the vines is therefore $2 580 000 less $2 500 000 = $80 000.

The fair value of the grapes as at 30 June 2015 is calculated as follows:

$500 000 less $10 000 (costs to sell) = $490 000

The journal entries as at 30 June 2015 are as follows:

Biological Asset – Vines	Dr	80 000	
Profit or Loss	Cr		80 000
(To record the change in fair value of the vines)			
Agricultural Produce – Grapes	Dr	490 000	
Profit or Loss	Cr		490 000
(To record the grapes at fair value)			

LO6

17.6 PRACTICAL IMPLEMENTATION ISSUES WITH THE USE OF FAIR VALUE

Determining fair value in the agricultural industry creates some practical difficulties, particularly in the case of immature biological assets such as young trees in a forest or young salmon in a salmon farm.

17.6.1 A fishy story

During 2005 and 2006, as IAS 41 was first being implemented in Europe, there was controversy in the salmon farming industry over the measurement of immature salmon. A practice was emerging of measuring live immature salmon at cost on the basis that fair value could not be reliably measured. The regulator intervened and required that the *live* immature salmon be measured at fair value on the basis that there was an active market for *slaughtered* immature salmon and that the fair value should be determined in accordance with paragraph 18(b) of IAS 41; that is, on the basis of similar assets. The regulator stated that since there was an active market for slaughtered immature salmon this should be the basis used for measuring the fair value of live immature salmon.

The text of the decision as reported by the Committee of European Securities Regulators (CESR) is reproduced in figure 17.1.

FIGURE 17.1 Extract from Committee of European Securities Regulators' decision on IAS 41

Decision ref. EECS/0407–11: Accounting for biological assets
Financial year end: 31 December 2005/Interim Financial Statements
Category of issue: Biological assets, fair value
Standard involved: IAS 41
Date of the decision: 14 February 2006

Description of the issuer's accounting treatment
The issuer measured live farmed salmon with a weight exceeding 4 kg (3.3 kg slaughtered head-on gutted) at their fair value, while more immature salmon was measured at cost. The fair value of mature salmon exceeding 4 kg was determined by using the observed prices in an active market of slaughtered salmon, classified as a similar asset according to IAS 41 paragraph 18b. Based on an overall assessment, the issuer considered alternative estimates (incl. present value of future net cash-flows) of the fair value of live immature farmed salmon (< 4 kg) to be clearly unreliable, and hence accounted for these biological assets at cost according to IAS 41 paragraph 30.

The enforcement decision
The enforcer found that there existed observable market prices for similar assets (IAS 41 paragraph 18b), also for salmon weighing less than 4 kg. Hence, such biological assets should be accounted for at fair value and not cost.

Rationale for the enforcement decision
Farming salmon from egg to mature fish takes on average approximately 3 years. There are two main stages of growth; from egg to smolt (approx. 100 grams) and from smolt to mature fish, each stage taking approximately 15–18 months. In some markets there may be some turnover of live smolt, but as a rule farmed salmon is slaughtered before it is sold. The national production and sale in 2004 was approx. 54 000 tonnes of farmed salmon. Industry organizations publish weekly price reports, summarizing trades of slaughtered and gutted superior quality salmon specified by weight classes (1–2 kg, 2–3 kg, 3–4 kg, 4–5 kg, 5–6 kg, 7+, head-on-gutted slaughter weight). Approximately 20–30% of all salmon sold weigh less than 4 kg. These markets for salmon weighing less than 4 kg are not scrap markets, but markets where superior quality salmon is sold for human consumption.

The enforcer was of the view that slaughtered salmon which is sold whole and gutted is, in an accounting sense, to be considered as a similar asset to live salmon, according to IAS 41, paragraph 18b. This also applies to so-called immature farmed salmon. In the absence of observable prices in an active market for live farmed salmon, fair value of live farmed salmon should be determined based on

(continued)

FIGURE 17.1 (continued)

observable prices in an active market for the same category of slaughtered salmon (IAS 41 paragraph 15 and IAS 41 paragraph 18b). The alternative method of estimating fair value as the present value of future net cash flows, cf. IAS 41 paragraph 20, should not be used when market determined prices or values as mentioned in IAS 41 paragraph 17 and 18 are available.

Active markets satisfying the criteria in IAS 41 paragraph 8 exist for the trading of such slaughtered salmon. The sizes of slaughtered salmon for which willing buyers and sellers normally can be found at any time, can vary from market to market. According to IAS 41 paragraph 9, the fair value of biological assets should be based on its present location and condition, including its weight and quality at the balance sheet date. Hence live salmon should be valued based on observable prices in an active market of slaughtered salmon in the weight class (taking into account adjustments for conversion from live weight to slaughter weight) in which the salmon would be sold if it were slaughtered at the balance sheet date.

Follow up

The decision was appealed to the Ministry of Finance. The Ministry of Finance upheld the decision of the enforcer, with some adjustments and additions. Most significantly, the final ruling upholds the enforcer's decision that slaughtered salmon which is sold whole and gutted is in an accounting sense to be considered as a similar asset of live salmon, according to IAS 41 paragraph 18b and that this also applies to so-called immature farmed salmon. Hence, the observable prices of slaughtered salmon shall be used as a basis for determining the fair value of live immature salmon. The key amendment to the decision made by the Ministry of Finance is that it added certain comments relating to how the term 'adjustments to reflect differences' in IAS 41 paragraph 18b was to be applied. The adjustments should reflect the differences between the price of slaughtered immature salmon and the hypothetical market price in an active market for live immature salmon. These adjustments should be consistent with the assessments that would be expected to be made by market participants to set the price of live salmon in an arms length transaction, given its present location and condition.

The Ministry of Finance ruling was made with effect from the 4th quarter 2006 financial reporting and forward. Comparative financial information relating to prior accounting periods was to be revised accordingly.

Source: The Committee of European Securities Regulators. Extract from EECS database of enforcement decisions. April 2007, Ref: 07–120.

It is interesting to observe the nature of disclosures made by companies applying the fair value requirements of IAS 41 in these circumstances. For example, the Scottish Salmon Company (formerly Lighthouse Caledonia ASA), a Scottish company, reported the following (see figure 17.2) in its 2010 annual report:

FIGURE 17.2 Disclosures illustrating IAS 41 practical implementation

Biological assets

Biological assets (fish) are valued at fair value in line with IAS 41 — Agriculture, at fair value less costs to sell. In order to estimate fair value of live fish, management apply a model based on market prices for harvested fish, adjusted for ongrowing, harvesting and freight costs to market in order to arrive at a fair value less costs to sell to the Group. This model assesses each farm site individually for the key assumptions of growth and survival. The model also reflects anticipated harvesting weight and variances in expected quality grades for each farm site. Juvenile fish under 1 kg are measured at cost less impairment losses.

Market prices are derived from the most recent contracts entered into by the Group and Norwegian quoted forward prices (from Fishpool). Future costs, growth rates, survival rates, anticipated harvest weights and quality grades are derived from the Group's harvesting & production data and financial budgets for 2011.

The change in estimated fair value is charged to the statement of comprehensive income account, and is reported separate (own line) from the related cost of the biomass when harvested. Accumulated direct and indirect production costs for fish harvested are classified as costs of goods sold whereas the change in the fair value adjustment is recognised on a separate line called 'fair value adjustment on biomass'.

FIGURE 17.2 (continued)

Note 17 — Biological assets

Book value of biological assets	2010 (£'000s)	Restated 2009 (£'000s)	Restated 2008 (£'000s)
Book value of live fish	34 301	34 446	24 409
Book value of smolt	3 067	1 080	3 905
Total book value of biological assets	**37 368**	**35 526**	**28 314**
Fair value adjustments on biological assets in the statement of financial position			
Scottish Salmon Company Ltd	12 961	9 809	—
West Minch Salmon Ltd	(153)	—	—
Total fair value adjustment in the statement of financial position	**12 808**	**9 809**	**—**
Total value of biological assets in the statement of financial position	**50 176**	**45 335**	**28 314**
Reconciliation of changes in book value of live fish			
Opening book value	34 446	24 409	20 259
Increase due to purchases	49 978	49 999	44 436
Increase due to acquisition of subsidiary	2 802	—	—
Write-down fish in sea in period	—	(1 576)	(1 679)
Decreases due to harvests	(52 925)	(38 386)	(38 607)
Book value of live fish at year end	**34 301**	**34 446**	**24 409**
Fair value adjustments on biological assets in the statement of comprehensive income			
Scottish Salmon Company Ltd	3 153	9 809	(1 919)
West Minch Salmon Ltd	(153)	—	—
Total change in fair value on biological assets in the statement of comprehensive income	**3 000**	**9 809**	**(1 919)**
Volumes of biomass (in tonnes)			
Volume of biomass harvested during the year (Gwt)	24 516	20 056	19 367
Volume of biomass in the sea at year-end (Lwt)	16 375	17 722	13 838

IAS 41 requires that biomass is accounted for at the estimated fair value net of sales and harvesting costs. The calculation of the estimated fair value is based on market prices for harvested fish. These prices are reduced for harvesting costs and freight costs to arrive to a net value at each individual farm. The valuation also then reflects the expected survival and quality grading per farm. In the accounts the change in estimated fair value is recorded separately in the Consolidated Statement of Comprehensive Income.

The valuation model is completed for each site individually on the key assumptions of growth and survival and also on the key costs associated with on-growing, capital, harvesting and freight of the fish. The total expected costs are then deducted from the expected future sales price after allowing for a site by site adjustment for quality, to calculate a total profit for each site at farm gate. For each site the total profit per harvest kg is then calculated and this is multiplied by the current standing biomass to give the fair value of the current stock at individual site level and for the Group as a whole. No fair value adjustment is made for juvenile fish.

The valuation model by its nature is based upon uncertain assumptions on sales price, quality growth, survival etc and whilst the Group has a degree of expertise in these assumptions they are subject to change. Relatively small changes in assumptions such as a 10p per kg rise in price would have an impact on the valuation of £1 000 000.

Source: The Scottish Salmon Company (2010, pp. 31, 45–6).

The extract in figure 17.2 highlights a few key points:

1. The company has disclosed separately the 'live fish' and the 'smolt'. Smolt is immature live salmon.
2. The company makes the point that the valuation model is based on uncertain assumptions and that relatively small changes in these assumptions could have a material impact on the valuation of the biological assets. The company is complying with the CESR determination referred to in figure 17.1, but some incredulity with the decision is implicit in the disclosures!
3. The company discloses the significant assumptions used in determining the fair value of live fish. This is in accordance with paragraph 47 of IAS 41.
4. The company also discloses the reconciliation required by paragraph 50 of IAS 41. It has elected to separate the book value from the fair value in the reconciliation and to indicate the cumulative effect of fair value adjustments over time on the statement of financial position. This is not required by the standard and again implies some concern about the requirement to use fair value. This is also evident in the 'Financial highlights and key figures' section that precedes the financial statements (Scottish Salmon Company 2010, p. 22) where some of the key performance ratios are cited 'before biomass fair value adjustment'.

17.6.2 Measuring the fair value of vineyards and grapes

Figure 17.3 shows the disclosure by Foster's Group Ltd in its 2010 annual report illustrating how the group has determined the fair value of its vineyards and grapes.

FIGURE 17.3 Disclosure of fair value of vineyards and grapes

Note 15 Agricultural assets		
	Consolidated	
	2010 $m	2009 $m
Agricultural assets	193.7	237.4
Total agricultural assets	193.7	237.4

Agricultural assets mainly comprise grape vines, with a minor holding of olive trees.

Foster's has total vineyard resources of around 12 463 hectares (2009: 15 131 hectares). These vineyards provide the Group with access to some of Australia's highest quality super premium fruit from regions such as the Barossa Valley in central South Australia, Coonawarra in south-eastern South Australia and the Hunter Valley in New South Wales. Other Australia vineyards are also located in the Clare Valley, Eden Valley, Great Western, Heathcote, Langhorne Creek, the Limestone Coast, McLaren Vale, Margaret River, Mornington Peninsula, Mudgee, Murray Valley, Padthaway, Robe, and the Yarra Valley. The Group also holds vineyards in North America (mainly Napa Valley and Sonoma County), Italy and New Zealand.

The geographic spread of the vineyard holdings not only provides Foster's with a diversity of premium fruit styles, but also reduces viticultural risk.

Of the total land area under vine around 1 696 hectares (2009: 1 974 hectares) is under lease arrangements. The Group also has around 7 hectares (2009: 7 hectares) of olive groves in the Tuscany region of Italy.

During the fiscal year Foster's owned and leased vineyards yielded 116 636 tonnes of grapes (2009: 106 000 tonnes). Northern Hemisphere harvest of vines normally occurs in September–October, with Southern hemisphere harvest around March–April.

Vines and grapes are measured at fair value, less estimated point-of-sale costs, with changes in fair value included in the statement of comprehensive income in the period in which it arises. The fair value of acquired vines is determined with reference to independent valuations of vineyards and the market price of purchased vines (rootlings). Subsequent movements in the fair value of vines is determined through operational reviews of the vineyard portfolio which identify, where applicable, any factors affecting the long term viability and value of the vines. The fair value of harvested grapes is determined with reference to the weighted district average of grape prices for each region for the current vintage. Annual prices for grapes will vary with the grade quality of grapes produced in each particular region.

FIGURE 17.3 *(continued)*

The measurement basis for vines and grapes as prescribed by AASB 141 'Agriculture' has resulted in a net loss before tax of $66.1 million (2009: loss before tax of $21.9 million) comprising a decrement in vines valuation of $46.9 million (2009: 0.2 million loss) and loss on grape valuation of $19.2 million (2009: $21.7 million loss) being recognised.

Reconciliations

Reconciliations of the carrying amount of agricultural assets at the beginning and end of the current and previous year are set out below.

	Consolidated	
	2010 **$m**	**2009** **$m**
Consolidated		
Carrying amount at start of year	**237.4**	291.6
Acquisitions	**2.6**	20.3
Fair value decrement	**(46.9)**	(0.2)
Transfers from/(to) assets held for sale	**17.3**	(93.6)
Foreign currency exchange	**(16.7)**	19.3
Carrying amount at end of year	**193.7**	237.4

Source: Foster's Group Ltd (2010, p. 76).

17.6.3 Disclosure practices

It is common for companies applying IAS 41 to separately disclose the fair value movements attributable to agricultural assets, either in the statement of profit or loss and other comprehensive income or in the notes, and in information reported outside the financial statements to investors such as in 'investor packs' or 'financial commentaries'. This is because companies want to highlight the fair value movements as being separate from other forms of income. To some extent, the separate disclosure also reflects the implicit disagreement with the requirements of the standard, particularly where it is difficult to measure fair value.

The extract in figure 17.4 from Foster's Group Ltd's 2010 annual report illustrates this point.

FIGURE 17.4 Separate disclosure of fair value movements attributable to agricultural assets

Results Summary

12 Months to 30 June	2010 Reported $m	2009 Reported $m	Change %	2009 Constant currency $m	Change %
Net sales revenue	4 285.6	4 491.1	(4.6)	4 251.2	0.8
CUB	904.1	860.7	5.0	871.1	3.8
Rest of World BCS	18.0	24.6	(26.8)	21.2	(15.1)
Americas Wine	107.4	159.3	(32.6)	95.2	12.8
ANZ Wine	75.8	71.6	5.9	71.4	6.2
EMEA Wine	15.0	45.4	(67.0)	(11.4)	NM
Asia Wine	23.1	27.8	(16.9)	28.4	(18.7)
Corporate	(34.7)	(24.4)	(42.2)	(24.4)	(42.2)
EBITS	**1 108.7**	**1 165.0**	**(4.8)**	**1051.5**	**5.4**
SGARA	(18.0)	(21.9)	17.8	(21.9)	17.8

(continued)

FIGURE 17.4 (continued)

12 Months to 30 June	2010 Reported $m	2009 Reported $m	Change %	2009 Constant currency $m	Change %
EBIT	**1 090.7**	**1 143.1**	**(4.6)**	**1 029.6**	**5.9**
Net finance costs	(118.8)	(146.6)	19.0	(120.1)	1.1
Net (loss)/profit before tax	**971.9**	**996.5**	**(2.5)**	**909.5**	**6.9**
Tax	(272.6)	(266.6)	(2.3)	(243.3)	(12.0)
Net (loss)/profit after tax	**699.3**	**729.9**	**(4.2)**	**666.2**	**5.0**
Net (loss)/profit attributable to non-controlling interests	(1.0)	(4.4)	77.3	(3.7)	73.0
Net (loss)/profit after tax (before material items)	**698.3**	**725.5**	**(3.7)**	**662.5**	**5.4**
Material items — before tax	(1 271.1)	(397.6)	>(200.0)	(387.2)	>(200.0)
Material items — tax	108.4	110.4	(1.8)	106.6	1.7
Material items — net of tax	(1 162.7)	(287.2)	>(200.0)	(280.6)	>(200.0)
Net (loss)/profit after tax attributable to members of Foster's Group Limited	**(464.4)**	**438.3**	**>(200.0)**	**381.9**	**>(200.0)**
Net (loss)/profit after tax (before material items & SGARA)	711.3	741.5	(4.1)	678.5	4.8
EPS (before material items & SGARA)	36.9	38.5	(4.2)	35.2	4.8
Reported EPS	(24.1)	22.8	>(200.0)	19.8	>(200.0)
Average shares (number — million)	1 930.1	1 925.2		1 925.2	

NM: Not meaningful

(a) Refer reconciliation to the Statement of Comprehensive Income on page 40.

(b) The allocation of shared fiscal 2009 overhead costs in Australia between CUB and ANZ Wine has also been adjusted to provide a comparable basis for actual overheads being incurred by the separate beer and wine businesses in fiscal 2010. The realignment of overhead costs is consistent with the detailed overhead cost analysis completed as part of the wine strategic review announced on 17 February 2009. In first half 2009 $31.7 million and for fiscal 2009 $60.0 million of overhead costs have been reallocated from CUB to ANZ Wine.

Exchange rates: *Average exchange rates used for profit and loss purposes in fiscal 2010 are: $A1 = $US 0.8814 (2009: $A1 = $US 0.7504), $A1 = GBP 0.5579 (2009: $A1 = GBP 0.4623). Period end exchange rates used for balance sheet items in fiscal 2010 are: $A1 = $US 0.8500 (2009: $A1 = $US 0.8102), $A1 = GBP 0.5646 (2009: $A1 = GBP 0.4890).*

Constant currency: *Throughout this report constant currency assumes current and prior earnings of self-sustaining foreign operations are translated and cross border transactions are transacted at current year exchange rates.*

SGARA: *Australian Accounting standard AASB141 'Agriculture'*

Reconciliation to the Statement of Comprehensive Income

12 Months to 30 June	Reference	2010 Reported $m	2009 Reported $m
Net sales revenue	Result Summary page 39	4 285.6	4 491.1
Other revenue		175.3	193.4
Total revenue	Statement of comprehensive income — page 50	**4 460.9**	**4 684.5**
EBITS	Result Summary page 39	1 108.7	1 165.0
SGARA		(18.0)	(21.9)
EBIT		1 090.7	1 143.1
Material items before tax		(1 271.1)	(397.6)
(Loss)/profit before tax and finance costs	Statement of comprehensive income — page 50	**(180.4)**	**745.5**

FIGURE 17.4 *(continued)*

12 Months to 30 June	Reference	2010 Reported $m	2009 Reported $m
Tax	Result Summary page 39	(272.6)	(266.6)
Material items — tax		108.4	110.4
Income tax benefit/(expense)	Statement of comprehensive income — page 50	**(164.2)**	**(156.2)**
Net (loss)/profit after tax before material items and SGARA	Result Summary page 39	711.3	741.5
Material items post tax		(1 162.7)	(287.2)
SGARA post tax		(13.0)	(16.0)
Net (loss)/profit attributable to members of Foster's Group Limited	Statement of comprehensive income — page 50	**(464.4)**	**438.3**

Source: Foster's Group Ltd (2010, pp. 39–40).

LO7 17.7 GOVERNMENT GRANTS

Sometimes entities may receive government grants in respect of agricultural activity. IAS 41 prescribes how these should be accounted for where biological assets are measured at fair value, distinguishing between conditional and unconditional government grants.

1. Unconditional government grants are recognised as income when the grant becomes receivable (paragraph 34).
2. Conditional government grants are recognised as income when the conditions attaching to the grant are met (paragraph 35).

Note that if biological assets are not measured at fair value (i.e. where the exemption in paragraph 30 applies) then IAS 20 applies. IAS 20 allows various choices in the accounting for government grants, including deferral of the revenue and permitting the grant to be offset against the cost of the asset. These approaches are not permitted for biological assets measured at fair value under IAS 41.

Illustrative example 17.6 demonstrates how conditional and unconditional government grants are accounted for when biological assets are measured at fair value.

ILLUSTRATIVE EXAMPLE 17.6 Conditional and unconditional government grants

Company B engages in agricultural activities and measures its biological assets at fair value in accordance with IAS 41. In 2013, Company B received two grants from the government. Grant A, of $10 000, was notified to the company on 7 January 2013 and had no conditions attaching to it. The grant was received on 14 March 2013. Grant B, of $50 000, was notified to the company on 31 January 2013. Grant B had the following condition attached to it: 'Company B must continue to operate its agricultural activities in the Zone Z Area until at least 31 January 2021. If Company B discontinues all or part of its operations in the Zone Z Area before that date then Company B shall immediately repay Grant B in full'. Grant B was received on 14 April 2013.

The end of Company B's reporting period is 30 June. The journal entries for Company B for the year ended 30 June 2013 would be as follows:

Receivables	Dr	10 000	
Income	Cr		10 000
(To recognise the unconditional Grant A when it became receivable on 7 January)			

		Dr	10 000	
Cash		Dr	10 000	
Receivables		Cr		10 000
(To recognise receipt of the cash on 14 March)				
Cash		Dr	50 000	
Performance Obligation		Cr		50 000
(To recognise the cash received on 14 April and the corresponding obligation to comply with the conditions of Grant B)				

Grant B is thus recorded as a liability until such time as the conditions are met. Note that if the conditions attaching to Grant B permitted Company B to retain some of the grant based on the passing of time (e.g. by means of a formula), then Company B would be able to recognise the grant as income over the period of time.

LO8

17.8 THE INTERACTION BETWEEN IAS 41 AND IAS 16, IAS 40 AND IAS 17

As noted in section 17.2.1, IAS 41 does not apply to land related to agricultural activity. Rather, an entity follows IAS 16 or IAS 40, depending on the circumstances. If the land meets the definition of an investment property (see section 17.2.1) it is measured using either the cost model or the fair value model under IAS 40. Thus, land related to agricultural activity that is an investment property may be measured either (i) at cost and tested for impairment under IAS 16, or (ii) at fair value with changes in fair value being taken through profit or loss. However, the agricultural assets attaching to that land (e.g. orchards, forests or vineyards) must be measured at fair value under IAS 41. Further, if the land does not meet the definition of an investment property it must be accounted for under IAS 16. IAS 16 also allows a choice between the cost method and the revaluation method. Under the revaluation method, changes in fair value are generally taken to equity rather than through profit or loss.

Table 17.3 summarises the accounting choices available.

TABLE 17.3 Accounting policy choices available in respect of land related to agricultural activity			
	Land that is an investment property (IAS 40)		**Land that is not an investment property (IAS 16)**	
Accounting policy choice	Cost model	Fair value model	Cost model	Revaluation model
Increase in fair value over cost	Not recorded	Recorded through profit or loss	Not recorded	Recorded through equity
Decrease in fair value	Recorded through profit or loss if it is an impairment	Recorded through profit or loss as part of the fair value measurement	Recorded through profit or loss if it is an impairment	Recorded through equity to the extent available with remainder through profit or loss

The related agricultural assets must be measured at fair value in accordance with IAS 41. The accounting policy choices for land mean that an entity could have a mixed measurement basis for its agricultural activities, with inconsistencies between the treatment of the land and the biological assets growing on the land.

The IASB considered this issue and commented as follows in the Basis for Conclusions (paragraphs 56–7):

Some argue that land attached to biological assets related to agricultural activity should also be measured at its fair value. They argue that fair value measurement of land results in consistency of measurement with the fair value measurement of biological assets. They also argue that it is sometimes difficult to measure the fair value of such biological assets separately from the land since an active market often exists for the combined assets (that is, land and biological assets; for example, trees in a plantation forest).

The Board rejected this approach, primarily because requiring the fair value measurement of land related to agricultural activity would be inconsistent with IAS 16.

In addition, the interaction between IAS 40 and IAS 17 *Leases* poses further complications. When IAS 41 was issued, an amendment was made to IAS 17 to clarify that IAS 17 should not be applied to the measurement by:

1. lessees of biological assets held under finance leases (IAS 17 paragraph 2(c)), and
2. lessors of biological assets leased out under operating leases (IAS 17 paragraph 2(d)).

While the recognition and measurement requirements of IAS 41 apply, the disclosure requirements of both IAS 41 and IAS 17 apply (IAS 41 paragraph B82 (n)). This means that in these situations the lessee or lessor (as appropriate) must apply IAS 41 rather than IAS 17. So, for example, if a lessee leases a vineyard under a finance lease, then the vineyard is accounted for as a biological asset of the lessee under IAS 41. The lessee would thus record the vineyard as its own asset and measure it at fair value. The lease liability would be recorded as a borrowing. The requirements are summarised in table 17.4.

TABLE 17.4 Lessees and lessors — application of IAS 41 and IAS 17

	Finance lease		Operating lease	
	Lessee	Lessor	Lessee	Lessor
Biological assets	Assets recorded and measured under IAS 41	Does not record biological assets — applies IAS 17	Does not record biological assets — applies IAS 17	Assets recorded and measured under IAS 41
Lease receivable	N/A	Recorded under IAS 17	N/A	N/A
Lease liability	Recorded as a borrowing to finance the biological asset	N/A	N/A	N/A
Disclosures	Made under both IAS 41 and IAS 17	Made under IAS 17	Made under IAS 17	Made under both IAS 41 and IAS 17

Let us now return to the facts of illustrative example 17.1 and overlay this with the requirements in respect of leased assets.

Assume the same facts as in illustrative example 17.1 except that Manager M is a lessee under a finance lease, in addition to managing the vineyard. If this were the case, Manager M would record the vineyard as its own asset because it has assumed substantially all of the risks and rewards of the vineyard under the finance lease. The question of control versus management does not arise in this case because Manager M both manages the vineyard and 'controls' the assets under the finance lease (refer to the discussion in illustrative example 17.1). Therefore, the biological assets are recorded by Manager M and measured under IAS 41, while Company A would be the lessor and record a finance lease receivable under IAS 17.

17.9 DISCLOSURE REQUIREMENTS

Paragraphs 40 through 57 set out the disclosure requirements of IAS 41. These are divided into three sections:

1. general
2. additional disclosures for biological assets where fair value cannot be measured reliably
3. government grants.

The requirements are summarised overleaf. Students should refer to the standard for full details.

17.9.1 General disclosures

These are contained in paragraphs 40–53 and include the following:
- aggregate gain or loss on initial recognition (biological assets and agricultural produce) and as a result of fair value movements (biological assets)
- description of each group of biological assets (groups may be determined based on consumable (e.g. crops) versus bearer (e.g. fruit trees) biological assets or based on mature versus immature biological assets, or both)
- description of the nature of activities involving each group of biological assets
- non-financial measures or estimates of the physical quantities of biological assets at the end of the period and output of agricultural produce during the period
- methods and assumptions applied in determining the fair value of each group of agricultural produce at the point of harvest and each group of biological assets
- fair value of agricultural produce harvested during the period, at the point of harvest
- details of biological assets whose title is restricted or which has been pledged as security, commitments for the development or acquisition of biological assets and financial risk management strategies related to agricultural activity
- reconciliation of the changes in the carrying amount of biological assets between the beginning and end of the current period. Note 3 of Example 1 of IAS 41 illustrates this reconciliation.

    Entities are also encouraged, but not required, to disclose separately the fair value changes attributable to physical changes and price changes. Example 2 of IAS 41 illustrates these disclosures. Example 1 of IAS 41 illustrates the general disclosure requirements.

17.9.2 Additional disclosures for biological assets where fair value cannot be measured reliably

These additional disclosures are contained in paragraphs 54–56 and include the following:
- a description of the biological assets, an explanation of why fair value cannot be measured reliably, the range of estimates within which fair value is likely to lie, the depreciation method and rates/useful lives used, the gross carrying amount and accumulated depreciation at the beginning and end of the period
- gain or loss on disposal, impairment losses and depreciation — shown separately in the reconciliation required under 'General' disclosures
- specified details if the fair value becomes reliably measurable during the period.

17.9.3 Government grants

Paragraph 57 requires disclosure of the nature and extent of government grants recognised, unfulfilled conditions and other contingencies attaching to government grants and significant decreases expected in the level of government grants.

17.10 PREPARING FINANCIAL STATEMENTS WHEN APPLYING IAS 41

Illustrative example 17.7 shows how a company would present its statement of profit or loss and other comprehensive income and statement of financial position when applying IAS 41.

ILLUSTRATIVE EXAMPLE 17.7 Preparing a statement of profit or loss and other comprehensive income and statement of financial position under IAS 41

Company A owns dairy cattle and has an end of reporting period of 30 June.

At 1 July 2013, Company A had 900 cows and 200 heifers, with a fair value (less costs to sell) of $800 per cow and $320 per heifer.

During the year ended 30 June 2014 the following occurred:
1. 200 new cows were purchased at $810 each
2. 50 heifers matured into cows

3. 5 heifers died
4. 100 cows were sold for $830 each
5. Salaries and other operating costs were $60 000.

Company A owns the farmland, which was purchased for $1.5 million. The land is measured at cost under IAS 16. As at 30 June 2014, the market value of the land was assessed at $5.6 million.

Company A also has plant and equipment which was purchased for $1 000 000 and is depreciated over its expected useful life of 10 years. As at 1 July 2013, the plant and equipment was 2 years old.

As at 30 June 2014, the fair value (less costs to sell) is determined as $850 per cow and $350 per heifer. Company A has determined that these are the appropriate fair values to use for the purposes of transfers and deaths of heifers.

The price change between a heifer and a cow at the time of maturity during the year was estimated to be $500.

During the year, Company A produced milk with a fair value less costs to sell of $500 000.

Workings
1. Reconciliation of movements in livestock

	Cows	Fair value	Heifers	Fair value
Balance as at 1 July 2013	900	$720 000	200	$64 000
Purchases	200	162 000	—	
Sales	(100)	(83 000)	—	
Transfer to cows	50	17 500	(50)	(17 500)
Deaths			(5)	(1 750)
Balance as at 30 June 2014	1 050	892 500	145	50 750
Increase in fair value				
• attributable to physical change		25 000		
• attributable to price change		51 000		6 000

2. Reconciliation of movements in fair value — cows

Physical balance (assuming FIFO)	Change in fair value	Total
Opening balance 900 @ $800		
Sold 100@ $830	100 @ $30	$3 000
Balance 800 @ $800		
Year end 800 @ $850	800 @ $50	$40 000
Purchased 200 @ $810		
Year end 200 @ $850	200 @ $40	$8 000
Total attributable to fair value changes		$51 000
Heifers 50 @ $350		
Year end 50 @ $850	50 @ $500	$25 000 (all attributable to physical change)

3. Reconciliation of movements in fair value — heifers

Physical balance (assuming FIFO)	Change in fair value	Total
Opening balance 200 @ $320		
Transfer 50 @ $350	50 @ $30	1 500
Balance 150 @ $320		
Year end 150 @ $350	150 @ $30	4 500
Total attributable to fair value changes		6 000
Died 5 @ $350	5 @ $350 (all value lost)	(1 750)
Total		4 250

4. Property, plant & equipment

Land measured at cost, no impairment as market value exceeds carrying amount as at 30 June 2014

Plant and equipment

Cost	$1 000 000
Accumulated depreciation as at 1 July 2013	(200 000)
Balance as at 1 July 2013	800 000
Annual depreciation	(100 000)
Balance as at 30 June 2013:	
Land	1 500 000
Plant & Equipment	800 000
Total	2 300 000
Balance as at 30 June 2014:	
Land	1 500 000
Plant & Equipment	700 000
Total	2 200 000

COMPANY A
Statement of Profit or Loss and Other Comprehensive Income (Extract)
for the year ended 30 June 2014

Fair value of milk produced	$ 500 000
Net gains arising from changes in fair value less costs to sell of dairy livestock (note y)	80 250
Depreciation expense	(100 000)
Other operating expenses	(60 000)
Profit from operations	420 250
Income tax expense	xxx
Profit after income tax	xxx

COMPANY A
Statement of Financial Position (Extract)
as at 30 June 2014

	2014	2013
Assets		
Non-current assets		
Dairy livestock — immature	$ 50 750	$ 64 000
Dairy livestock — mature	892 500	720 000
Subtotal — biological assets	943 250	784 000
Property, plant & equipment	2 200 000	2 300 000

Note y
Biological assets

Reconciliation of carrying amounts of dairy livestock

Carrying amount at 1 July 2013	$784 000
Increases due to purchases	162 000
Increase in fair value less costs to sell	
— attributable to price changes	57 000
— attributable to physical changes	25 000
Total increase in fair value less costs to sell	82 000
Decreases due to deaths	(1 750)
Net increase in fair value	80 250
Decreases due to sales	(83 000)
Carrying amount as at 30 June 2014	943 250

17.11 THE INTERACTION BETWEEN IFRS 13 AND IAS 41

In May 2011, the IASB issued IFRS 13 *Fair Value Measurement*, which amended IAS 41. IFRS 13 is effective for annual periods beginning on or after 1 January 2013. IFRS 13 combines all of the requirements in IFRSs regarding *how* to measure fair value into one place, rather than being dispersed throughout multiple IFRSs. IFRS 13 does *not* change any requirements regarding *when* to use fair value as the measurement basis. It defines fair value as 'the price that would be received to sell an asset or paid to transfer a liability in an orderly transaction between market participants at the measurement date' (IFRS 13 paragraph 9 and Appendix A).

The standard requires that the market used to determine fair value should be either the principal market for the asset or liability or, in the absence of a principal market, the most advantageous market for the asset or liability. (IFRS 13 paragraph 16). This is in contrast to the requirement of IAS 41 to use the most 'relevant market' (IAS 41 paragraph 17). In practice this would likely be the same market in most circumstances. IFRS 13 also provides detailed guidance on how to measure fair value in the absence of an active market. It also includes numerous disclosure requirements. As a result of the issuance of IFRS 13, the definition of 'fair value' in IAS 41 has been amended to reflect the same definition as in IFRS 13. Also, a number of the paragraphs in IAS 41 that contain detailed guidance about how to calculate fair value have been deleted because the guidance is now in IFRS 13.[2] Some of the disclosure requirements have also been deleted because IFRS 13 requires them.[3] Overall, IFRS 13, however, is not expected to result in significant changes to the application of IAS 41. For example, the method of calculating fair value when there is not an active market is set out in detail in IFRS 13 and would result in similar outcomes. Similarly, paragraph 26 of IFRS 13 states that transport costs are deducted when determining fair value. The disclosure requirements regarding fair value assumptions and reconciliations are contained in IFRS 13, but there are also additional disclosure requirements, such as sensitivity analyses (IFRS 13 paragraphs 91–99).

SUMMARY

IAS 41 was a controversial standard when it was first issued, mainly because of its requirement to measure assets related to agricultural activity at fair value, with movements in fair value being taken to the statement of profit or loss and other comprehensive income as gains or losses. To this day, entities applying the standard indicate their implicit disagreement with this requirement, for example, by highlighting the fair value movements separately in their statements of profit or loss and other comprehensive income so that users can clearly see and understand the impact on reported profit. The IASB rejected criticisms of the fair value model for biological assets and agricultural produce but conceded by permitting an exemption when fair value cannot be reliably measured. The board also included guidance in the standard on how to apply the fair value measurement requirement.

IAS 41 distinguishes between biological assets, agricultural produce and products that are the result of processing after harvest, and prescribes different accounting treatments for each category. The interaction between IAS 41 and IAS 16, IAS 17 and IAS 40 is very important to understand and apply, particularly since, in the agricultural industry, it is common to find different parties involved in owning, leasing and managing agricultural assets.

Discussion questions

1. Why do you think IAS 41 was a controversial standard when it was issued?
2. Explain why the concept of 'control' is problematic when applying the recognition criteria of IAS 41.
3. What are the arguments for and against the use of fair value as the measurement basis for biological assets and agricultural produce? Why do you think the IASB settled on requiring fair value?
4. How is the risk that future cash flows pertaining to biological assets may not eventuate as predicted, taken into account when determining the fair value of a biological asset using the present value of net cash flows method?
5. How does a gain or loss on initial recognition of a biological asset or agricultural produce arise?
6. Why is agricultural produce not remeasured to fair value during a reporting period?
7. Discuss the requirement of paragraph 18(b) of IAS 41 in the context of the CESR ruling in respect of immature salmon.

---

[2] IFRS 13 deletes paragraphs 9, 17–21 and 23 of IAS 41.
[3] IFRS 13 deletes paragraphs 47 and 48 of IAS 41.

Exercises

STAR RATING ★ BASIC ★★ MODERATE ★★★ DIFFICULT

Exercise 17.1 — AGRICULTURAL ACTIVITY — DEFINITIONS

★ State which of the following meets the definition of 'agricultural activity' in IAS 41. Give reasons for your answer:
1. pig farming
2. ocean fishing
3. clearing forests to create farmland
4. salmon farming
5. managing vineyards.

Exercise 17.2 — AGRICULTURAL ACTIVITY — DEFINITIONS

★ State whether the following are (a) biological assets, (b) agricultural produce or (c) products that are as a result of processing after harvest:
1. living pigs
2. living sheep
3. pigs' carcasses
4. pork sausages
5. trees growing in a plantation forest
6. furniture
7. olive trees
8. olives
9. olive oil
10. vines growing in a vineyard.

Exercise 17.3 — AGRICULTURAL ACTIVITY — MEASUREMENT

★ For each of the items in exercise 17.2 state whether they would be measured (a) at fair value under IAS 41 or (b) at the lower of cost and net realisable value under IAS 2:
1. living pigs
2. living sheep
3. pigs' carcasses
4. pork sausages
5. trees growing in a plantation forest
6. furniture
7. olive trees
8. olives
9. olive oil
10. vines growing in a vineyard.

Exercise 17.4 — FAIR VALUE DETERMINATION

★★ Which of the following is included in determining the fair value of a biological asset that does not have an active market and which has a 5-year production cycle?
1. Revenue from sale in 5 years' time
2. Costs of growing for 5 years
3. Financing costs on borrowings taken out to fund the growing costs
4. Taxation on taxable income generated from sale in 5 years' time
5. Discount rate that reflects expected variability in cash flows.

Exercise 17.5 — FAIR VALUE DETERMINATION

★ Company A owns a plantation forest. As at the end of the reporting period the fair value of the plantation forest including the land was $2.5 million. Company A needs to determine the fair value of the trees excluding the land to comply with IAS 41 at the end of its reporting period. How does Company A determine the fair value of the trees?

658 PART 2 Elements

| Exercise 17.6 | **DISCLOSURE OF BIOLOGICAL ASSETS** |

★★ State whether each of the following is true or false:

1. Companies applying IAS 41 must disclose separately the fair value (less costs to sell) of mature and immature biological assets.
2. A lessee of an orchard that is classified as a finance lease must measure the orchard (excluding the land) at fair value (less costs to sell) in its financial statements.
3. A vineyard planted on land classified as an investment property by the owner must be recognised and measured as part of that investment property.
4. A lessor of an orchard that is classified as a finance lease must measure the orchard (excluding the land) at fair value in its financial statements.
5. An entity availing itself of the exemption in paragraph 30 of IAS 41 for a particular biological asset must apply IAS 20 if it receives a government grant in respect of that asset.
6. If agricultural produce cannot be reliably measured then it may be accounted for at cost under paragraph 30 of IAS 41.

| Exercise 17.7 | **ACCOUNTING FOR LAND RELATING TO AGRICULTURAL ACTIVITY** |

★★ Company C entered into a lease agreement in respect of a vineyard with Company L on 1 January 2013. The lease was classified as a finance lease as it transferred substantially all the risks and rewards of the vineyard to Company C. The lease was for a period of 10 years, with annual lease payments of $212 000. The vineyard was established on land owned by Company L and was recorded as a biological asset at fair value in the books of Company L prior to the lease agreement. Company L, using the fair value model under IAS 40, classifies the land as an investment property. Company C engaged Manager M to manage the vineyard on its behalf.

Company L acquired the land for $5 million in 2003. As at 31 December 2013 the fair value of the land was independently assessed to be $14 million ($13 million as at 31 December 2012).

The fair value of the minimum lease payments under the finance lease was $2 million as at 1 January 2013. This was determined to be substantially the same as the fair value of the vineyard as at that date. Company L determined that the amount of finance lease income for the year ended 31 December 2013 was $12 000.

The fair value of the vineyard was independently assessed to be $2.6 million as at 31 December 2013. Company C paid Manager M $245 000 to manage the vineyard for the year ended 31 December 2013. The end of the reporting period for Company C, Company L and Manager M is 31 December.

Required

Prepare the journal entries to record the above transactions in the books of each of Company C, Company L and Manager M for the year ended 31 December 2013.

| Exercise 17.8 | **ACCOUNTING FOR A GOVERNMENT GRANT** |

★★★ Company Z engages in agricultural activities and measures its biological assets at fair value in accordance with IAS 41. In 2013, Company Z received a grant of $250 000 from the government. The grant was notified to the company on 31 March 2013. The terms and conditions of the grant were as follows.

This grant is effective from 1 July 2013. Company Z must continue to employ staff from Area A in its agricultural activities until at least 30 June 2018. If Company Z ceases to employ staff from Area A before that date then Company Z shall immediately repay the grant. The amount to be repaid shall be calculated according to the following formula:

$$A = B - (C \times D)$$

Where:
A = amount to be repaid
B = amount of initial grant
C = number of years the company has employed staff in Area A
D = $50 000.

The end of Company Z's reporting period is 30 June. The grant was received on 15 April 2013.

Prepare the journal entries to account for the grant by Company Z for the years ended 30 June 2013 and 30 June 2014, assuming Company Z complies with the conditions of the grant.

| Exercise 17.9 | PREPARATION OF FINANCIAL STATEMENTS APPLYING IAS 41 |

★★★ Company S owns sheep and the end of its reporting period is 30 June. The sheep are held to produce wool.

At 1 July 2013, Company S had 1000 sheep and 200 lambs, with a fair value (less costs to sell) of $200 per sheep and $50 per lamb.

During the year ended 30 June 2014 the following occurred:

1. 100 new sheep were purchased at $210 each
2. 20 lambs matured into sheep
3. 3 lambs died
4. 15 lambs were born
5. 100 sheep were sold for $240 each
6. Salaries and other operating costs were $34 000.

Company S owns the farmland, which was purchased for $1.5 million. The land is measured at fair value using the revaluation model under IAS 16. As at 30 June 2014, the fair value of the land was assessed at $5.6 million ($4.7 million as at 30 June 2013).

Company S also has plant and equipment, which was purchased for $1 million and is depreciated over its expected useful life of 10 years. As at 1 July 2013, the plant and equipment was 2 years old.

As at 30 June 2014, the fair value (less costs to sell) is determined as $250 per sheep and $55 per lamb. Company S has determined that these are the appropriate fair values to use for the purposes of transfers, births and deaths of lambs.

The price change between a lamb and a sheep at the time of maturity during the year was estimated to be $195.

During the year Company S produced wool with a fair value less costs to sell of $387 000.

Required

Prepare the relevant extracts from the statement of profit or loss and other comprehensive income and statement of financial performance and the reconciliation required by paragraph 50 of IAS 41 for Company S in accordance with IAS 41 for the year ended 30 June 2014. Show all workings.

References

Committee of European Securities Regulators 2007, *Extract from EECS's database of enforcement decisions*, Ref: 07–120.

Foster's Group Ltd 2010, *Annual report 2010*, Foster's Group Ltd, www.fosters.com.au.

The Scottish Salmon Company 2010, *Annual report 2010*, www.scottishsalmon.com.

Part 3

Disclosure

18 Financial statement presentation

ACCOUNTING STANDARDS IN FOCUS

IAS 1 *Presentation of Financial Statements*

IAS 8 *Accounting Policies, Changes in Accounting Estimates and Errors*

IAS 10 *Events after the Reporting Period*

LEARNING OBJECTIVES

After studying this chapter, you should be able to:

1. describe the main components of financial statements

2. explain the general principles underlying the preparation and presentation of financial statements

3. apply the requirements for the classification of items reported in the statement of financial position, and apply the requirements for the presentation of information in the statement of financial position and/or in the notes

4. apply the requirements for the presentation of information in the statement of profit or loss and other comprehensive income and/or in the notes

5. apply the requirements for the presentation of information in the statement of changes in equity and/or in the notes

6. discuss other disclosures required by IAS 1 in the notes to the financial statements

7. apply the requirements of IAS 8 regarding the selection and application of accounting policies, and in respect of accounting for changes in accounting policies, changes in accounting estimates and errors

8. distinguish between adjusting and non-adjusting events after the reporting period in accordance with IAS 10.

INTRODUCTION

You are probably already familiar with financial statements. In this chapter we will build on your existing knowledge as we take a closer look at the requirements of International Financial Reporting Standards (IFRSs) for dealing with some complex and technical issues in the presentation of financial statements. You have probably noticed that current and non-current assets and liabilities are usually separately identified in the statement of financial position. Do they have to be classified this way? How do preparers decide whether an asset should be classified as current or non-current? Why is there so much variation in the way that companies report on profit and comprehensive income? What should preparers do if they realise there has been an error in the financial statements of previous periods? How should entities account for changes of accounting policies and accounting estimates? If events occur after the end of the reporting period, can they be reflected in the financial statements?

 18.1 COMPONENTS OF FINANCIAL STATEMENTS

The overall principles and other considerations relating to the presentation of financial statements are contained in IAS 1 *Presentation of Financial Statements*. A complete set of financial statements is defined in paragraph 10 of that Standard as comprising:

(a) a statement of financial position as at the end of the period;
(b) a statement of profit or loss and other comprehensive income for the period;
(c) a statement of changes in equity for the period;
(d) a statement of cash flows for the period;
(e) notes, comprising a summary of significant accounting policies and other explanatory information;
(ea) comparative information in respect of the preceding period as specified in paragraphs 38 and 38A; and
(f) a statement of financial position as at the beginning of the preceding period when an entity applies an accounting policy retrospectively or makes a retrospective restatement of items in its financial statements, or when it reclassifies items in its financial statements in accordance with paragraphs 40A–40D.

While IAS 1 refers to the statements as a 'statement of financial position', a 'statement of profit or loss and other comprehensive income', a 'statement of changes in equity' and a 'statement of cash flows', reporting entities may use other labels when presenting these financial statements in accordance with IAS 1. For example, an entity may choose to label its statement of financial position a 'balance sheet' and its statement of profit or loss and other comprehensive income a 'statement of comprehensive income'.

Each component of the financial statements must be clearly identified in the financial statements and distinguished from other information reported in the same document (IAS 1 paragraphs 49–51). Entities often present other information, such as certain financial ratios or a narrative review of operations by management or the directors. These reports are sometimes referred to as 'management discussion and analysis'. For example, in Australia entities are obliged under the Corporations Act to prepare a 'directors' report' that covers, among other matters, commentary on the results of operations and financial position of the entity. In addition, some entities voluntarily prepare sustainability reports or corporate social responsibility reports. This other information is reported outside the financial statements and is not within the scope of pronouncements issued by the International Accounting Standards Board (IASB).

This chapter deals with the requirements of IAS 1 for the presentation of the statement of financial position, the statement of profit or loss and other comprehensive income, the statement of changes in equity and notes. IAS 1 applies to all general purpose financial statements, except that its requirements relating to the structure and content of financial statements are not applicable to condensed interim financial statements. The structure and content requirements of condensed interim financial statements are contained in IAS 34 *Interim Financial Reporting*. This chapter also deals with the requirements of IAS 1 *Presentation of Financial Statements*, IAS 8 *Accounting Policies, Changes in Accounting Estimates and Errors* and IAS 10 *Events after the Reporting Period*. These standards predominantly prescribe disclosure requirements, although IAS 8 and IAS 10 also contain certain measurement requirements.

Other IFRSs mandate disclosures relating to specific financial statement elements and transactions and events, as well as their recognition and measurement. Specific required disclosures relevant to the topics of the various chapters of this book are outlined in those chapters. The statement of cash flows is considered in chapter 19.

 18.2 GENERAL FEATURES OF FINANCIAL STATEMENTS

IAS 1 describes eight general principles that need to be applied in the presentation of financial statements. These requirements are intended to ensure that the financial statements of an entity are a faithful presentation of its financial position, financial performance and cash flows in accordance with the *Conceptual Framework*.

18.2.1 Fair presentation and compliance with IFRSs

Paragraph 15 of IAS 1 states that financial statements shall present fairly the financial position, financial performance and cash flows of an entity. It elaborates on 'fair presentation' as follows:

> Fair presentation requires the faithful representation of the effects of transactions, other events and conditions in accordance with the definitions and recognition criteria for assets, liabilities, income and expenses set out in the *Framework*.[1] The application of IFRSs, with additional disclosure when necessary, is presumed to result in financial statements that achieve a fair presentation.

Paragraph 17 of IAS 1 elaborates on the meaning of 'fair representations' as including selecting and applying accounting policies in accordance with IAS 8, presenting information that is in a manner that provides relevant, reliable, comparable and understandable information and providing additional disclosures, where necessary, to those specified by IFRSs.

The last sentence of paragraph 15 of IAS 1 is very significant. There is an assumption that compliance with IFRSs, accompanied by additional disclosure, if necessary, will result in fair presentation. However, paragraph 19 of IAS 1 notes that, in extremely rare circumstances, management may conclude that compliance with the requirements of an IFRS would be so misleading that it would conflict with the objective of financial statements specified in the *Conceptual Framework*. The reporting requirements that arise in this situation are considered in section 18.6.1 of this chapter.

18.2.2 Going concern

Paragraph 25 of IAS 1 states that financial statements shall be prepared on a going concern basis unless management intends to either liquidate the entity or cease trading, or has no realistic alternative but to do so. The *Conceptual Framework* makes a similar underlying assumption. When management is aware of any material uncertainties that cast doubt upon the entity's ability to continue as a going concern, those uncertainties must be disclosed (IAS 1 paragraph 25). When financial statements are not prepared on a going concern basis, that fact must be disclosed, together with the basis on which the financial statements are prepared and the reason why the entity is not regarded as a going concern.

If, for example, an entity has been placed in receivership and it is anticipated that liquidation will follow, the going concern assumption would be inappropriate. In such circumstances, the financial statements would typically be prepared on a 'liquidation' basis, which means that assets and liabilities are measured at the amounts expected to be received or settled on liquidation. In the case of assets, this will often be a 'fire-sale' value rather than a fair market value (for discussion of fair value measurement, see chapter 3 of this book). Illustrative example 18.1 demonstrates the application of paragraph 25 of IAS 1.

ILLUSTRATIVE EXAMPLE 18.1 Centro Properties Group

In March 2011, Centro Properties Group announced that it had agreed to seek to arrange a court-approved agreement, referred to as a scheme of arrangement, with major creditors. The proposed scheme involved the transfer of substantially all the company's assets to the creditors in settlement of amounts owed to them. On 9 August 2011, the company announced further progress on the scheme of arrangement. Centro Properties Group had entered into an implementation agreement for the transfer of assets held by Centro Properties Group, Centro Retail Trust and certain Centro Properties Group managed funds. Although the implementation agreement still required further approvals, the Directors of Centro Properties Group believed that the Group would be able to successfully complete the transfer of assets to its creditors in settlement of its debts. If the scheme of arrangement with creditors succeeded, Centro Group's asset base would be significantly reduced; and if the scheme of arrangement was not approved, Centro Properties probably would be liquidated to pay its creditors. Should the going concern assumption be applied to the financial statements of Centro Properties Group for 2011?

The Directors of Centro Properties Group concluded that the going concern assumption was not applicable in the circumstances that existed at 30 June 2011. Accordingly, the financial statements were prepared on a liquidation basis, rather than on a going concern basis. Accordingly, assets are measured

---

[1] Paragraphs 15–24 contain references to the objective of financial statements set out in the *Framework* [*for the Preparation and Presentation of Financial Statements*]. In September 2010 the IASB replaced the *Framework* with the *Conceptual Framework for Financial Reporting*, which replaced the objective of financial statements with the objective of general purpose financial reporting: see Chapter 1 of the *Conceptual Framework*.

18.2.3 Accrual basis of accounting

Financial statements, except for the statement of cash flows, must be prepared using the accrual basis of accounting. This is discussed further in the *Conceptual Framework* (see chapter 1 of this book).

18.2.4 Materiality and aggregation

Paragraph 7 of IAS 1 defines 'material' as follows:

> Omissions or misstatements of items are material if they could, individually or collectively, influence the economic decisions that users make on the basis of the financial statements. Materiality depends on the size and nature of the omission or misstatement judged in the surrounding circumstances. The size or nature of the item, or a combination of both, could be the determining factor.

Each material class of similar items must be presented separately in the financial statements in accordance with paragraph 29. Items of a dissimilar nature or function must be presented separately unless they are immaterial.

Financial statements result from processing large volumes of transactions that are then aggregated into classes according to their nature or function. These classes form the line items on the statement of financial position, statement of profit or loss and other comprehensive income, statement of changes in equity, and statement of cash flows. The minimum line items specified by IAS 1 are discussed in sections 18.3, 18.4 and 18.5 of this chapter and in chapter 19, in relation to the statement of cash flows.

18.2.5 Offsetting

IAS 1 paragraph 32 states that assets and liabilities, and income and expenses, shall not be offset unless required or permitted by an IFRS. For example, IAS 32 *Financial Instruments: Presentation* defines a right of set-off in respect of *financial* assets and liabilities (this is discussed further in chapter 7 of this book). For items to be offset under IAS 32, there must be a *legal right* of set-off. This means that there must be a legal agreement documenting the right of the parties to settle amounts owed to/from each other on a net basis. IAS 1 is not as prescriptive on offsetting. Rather, it implies that offsetting is undesirable unless it reflects the substance of transactions or events (paragraph 33). Paragraphs 34 and 35 then go on to identify situations where offsetting would be appropriate. These include the following:

- gains and losses on the disposal of non-current assets, which should be reported net, instead of separately reporting the gross proceeds as income and the cost of the asset disposed of as an expense
- expenditure related to a provision recognised in accordance with IAS 37 (see chapter 5) that may be offset against an amount reimbursed under a contractual arrangement with a third party
- gains and losses arising from a group of similar transactions, such as gains and losses arising from foreign exchange or from financial instruments held for trading. A net gain or loss may be reported, rather than separately reporting the gains and the losses. However, a gain or loss must be reported separately if it is material.

The application of offsetting is an area of considerable judgement and subjectivity

18.2.6 Frequency of reporting

Financial statements must be prepared at least annually. If an entity's reporting period changes, the length of the reporting period will be greater or less than a year in the period of the change. For example, if an entity with a reporting period ending on 30 September changed its reporting period to end on 30 June, the first financial statements it prepares for the period ending 30 June would only cover a nine-month period. When this occurs, paragraph 36 of IAS 1 requires the entity to disclose the reason for the longer or shorter reporting period and the fact that the amounts presented in the financial statements are not entirely comparable.

18.2.7 Comparative information

IAS 1 paragraph 38 requires the disclosure of comparative information in respect of the preceding period for all amounts reported in the financial statements, unless otherwise permitted by an IFRS. This extends to narrative information where the comparative narrative information is relevant to understanding the current period financial statements. An example of this would be details of a contingent liability, where the development of the issue over time is relevant to users. Paragraph 38C of IAS 1 provided that an entity may present additional comparative information beyond the minimum required, provided that the additional information is prepared in accordance with IFRSs. For example, an entity may choose to provide a third statement of cash flows as an additional comparative statement.

Due to changed circumstances, or in order to provide a fair representation, an entity may change the classification of items reported in financial statements. For example, an entity may classify a financial instrument that had previously been classified as a held-to-maturity investment as an available-for-sale financial asset, in accordance with IAS 39 *Financial Instruments: Recognition and Measurement*. If the presentation or classification of an item in the financial statements is changed, the entity must reclassify comparative amounts, to the extent practicable (IAS 1 paragraph 41). Further, the entity must present a statement of financial position for the end of the current period, the end of the preceding period, and the beginning of the previous period (IAS 1 paragraphs 40A and 40B). Thus in the event of a change in the presentation or classification of items presented in financial statements, at least three statements of financial position must be presented.

Additional comparative information must also be disclosed in the event of changes in accounting policies or corrections of errors. The accounting treatment of changes in accounting policies and correction of errors, including additional disclosure requirements for retrospective adjustments, are dealt with in IAS 8 (and addressed later in this chapter).

18.2.8 Consistency of presentation

Paragraph 45 of IAS 1 requires that the presentation and classification of items in the financial statements shall be retained from one period to the next unless:

(a) it is apparent, following a significant change in the nature of the entity's operations or a review of its financial statements, that another presentation or classification would be more appropriate having regard to the criteria for the selection and application of accounting policies in IAS 8; or

(b) an IFRS requires a change in presentation.

When such a change is made, the comparative information must also be reclassified. For example, as discussed in section 18.3.1 of this chapter, an entity may present its assets and liabilities in current and non-current classifications or in order of liquidity where this presentation is more reliable and relevant. If, after a change in operations, an entity elects to reclassify its assets and liabilities from the current/non-current presentation to the liquidity-based presentation, the comparative financial information must also be reclassified.

18.3 STATEMENT OF FINANCIAL POSITION

As discussed in chapter 1, a major purpose of financial statements is to provide information about an entity's financial position. The statement of financial position serves this purpose because it summarises the elements directly related to the measurement of financial position: an entity's assets, liabilities and equity. It thus provides the basic information for evaluating an entity's capital structure and analysing its liquidity, solvency and financial flexibility. It also provides a basis for computing rates of return (e.g. return on total assets and equity and measures of solvency and liquidity).

However, the view of an entity's financial position presented by the statement of financial position is by no means perfect and is often criticised by some commentators as being of limited value. These limitations primarily arise from:

- the optional measurement of certain assets at historical cost or depreciated historical cost rather than at a current value, such as fair value (refer to chapter 3 for further details)
- the mandatory omission of intangible self-generated assets from the statement of financial position as a result of the recognition and measurement requirements of IAS 38 *Intangible Assets*. Examples include successful research expenditure, brand names and mastheads (refer to chapter 13 for further details)
- financial engineering that frequently leads to off-balance-sheet rights and obligations. For example, the rights and obligations pertaining to non-cancellable operating leases are not recognised on the statement of financial position (refer to chapter 12 for further details).

The notes to the financial statements are an important source of information that can assist to mitigate the effects of these limitations.

18.3.1 Statement of financial position classifications

The statement of financial position presents a structured summary of the assets, liabilities and equity of an entity. Assets and liabilities are classified in a manner that facilitates the evaluation of an entity's financial structure and its liquidity, solvency and financial flexibility. Consequently, assets and liabilities are classified according to their function in the operations of the entity concerned and their liquidity and financial flexibility characteristics.

Paragraph 60 of IAS 1 requires an entity to classify assets and liabilities as current or non-current in its statement of financial position, except when a presentation based on liquidity is considered to provide more relevant and reliable information. When that exception arises, all assets and liabilities are required to be presented broadly in order of liquidity.

Current assets are described in paragraph 66 of IAS 1 as those that:

(a) an entity expects to realise, sell or consume within its normal operating cycle;
(b) an entity holds primarily for trading;
(c) an entity expects to realise within 12 months after the reporting period; or
(d) are cash or cash equivalents.

Current liabilities are described in paragraph 69 of IAS 1 as those:

(a) that the entity expects to settle in its normal operating cycle;
(b) that the entity holds primarily for the purpose of trading;
(c) that are due to be settled within 12 months after the reporting period; or
(d) for which the entity does not have an unconditional right to defer settlement for at least 12 months after the reporting period.

For example, inventory is classified as current because it is held primarily for trading purposes. When an entity applies the current/non-current classification, assets and liabilities that do not meet the criteria for classification as current are classified as non-current.

Paragraph 73 of IAS 1 explains that if an entity has the discretion to refinance or roll over an obligation for at least 12 months after the reporting period under the terms of an existing loan facility, and expects to do so, the obligation is classified as non-current, even if it would otherwise be due within 12 months of the end of the reporting period. This would amount to the unconditional right referred to in paragraph 69(d) shown above. The criteria for classifying liabilities as current or non-current are based solely on the conditions existing at the end of the reporting period. For example, if an entity had a long-term loan that fell due in August 2014 and entered into an agreement after 30 June 2014 to refinance or to reschedule payments on the loan, the liability would be classified as current in the statement of financial position at 30 June 2014, in accordance with paragraph 72. Similarly, paragraph 74 explains that if an entity breaches an undertaking under a long-term loan agreement during the reporting period with the effect that the loan is repayable on demand, the loan is classified as current. However, the loan should be classified as non-current if the lender agrees by the end of the reporting period to waive the right to demand immediate repayment for at least 12 months after the reporting period.

Figure 18.1 shows the classification of assets in the consolidated balance sheet of Billabong International Limited at 30 June 2011, while figure 18.2 shows the classification of liabilities. Note that some of Billabong International Limited's borrowings are classified as current liabilities and some as non-current liabilities.

FIGURE 18.1 Current and non-current assets of Billabong International Limited at 30 June 2011

		Consolidated	
	Notes	2011 $'000	2010 $'000
Assets			
Current assets			
Cash and cash equivalents	9	144 858	208 742
Trade and other receivables	10	374 375	398 378
Inventories	11	348 738	240 400
Current tax receivables		15 858	3 584
Other	12	25 025	27 581
Total current assets		908 854	878 685

FIGURE 18.1 *(continued)*

	Notes	Consolidated 2011 $'000	2010 $'000
Non-current assets			
Receivables	13	14 106	17 172
Property, plant and equipment	14	184 852	170 477
Intangible assets	15	1 268 461	1 118 308
Deferred tax assets	16	35 963	22 656
Other	17	7 729	3 021
Total non-current assets		1 511 111	1 331 634
Total assets		2 419 965	2 210 319

Source: Billabong International Ltd (2011, p. 54).

	Notes	Consolidated 2011 $'000	2010 $'000
Liabilities			
Current liabilities			
Trade and other payables	18	344 034	315 545
Borrowings	19	15 262	20 525
Current tax liabilities	20	1 839	8 820
Provisions	21	28 073	9 889
Total current liabilities		389 208	354 779
Non-current liabilities			
Borrowings	22	597 903	404 933
Deferred tax liabilities	23	46 909	54 815
Provisions and other payables	24	25 003	22 271
Deferred payments	25	164 103	155 942
Total non-current liabilities		833 918	637 961
Total liabilities		1 223 126	992 740

FIGURE 18.2 Current and non-current liabilities of Billabong International Limited at 30 June 2011
Source: Billabong International Ltd (2011, p. 54).

The current/non-current classification is ordinarily considered to be more relevant when an entity has a clearly identifiable operating cycle. This is because it distinguishes between those assets and liabilities that are expected to circulate within the entity's operating cycle and those used in the entity's long-term operations. The typical cycle operates from cash, purchase of inventory (in the case of a manufacturer, production) and then receivables through sales of inventory and finally back to cash through collection of the receivables. The average time of the operating cycle varies with the nature of the operations and may extend beyond 12 months. Long operating cycles are common in real estate development, construction and forestry.

Current assets may include inventories and receivables that are expected to be sold, consumed or realised as part of the normal operating cycle beyond 12 months after the reporting period. Similarly, current liabilities may include payables that are expected to be settled more than 12 months after the reporting period if the operating cycle exceeds 12 months. Because of these possibilities paragraph 61 of IAS 1 requires that irrespective of whether assets and liabilities are classified on the current/non-current basis or in order of liquidity:

... an entity shall disclose the amount expected to be recovered or settled after more than twelve months for each asset and liability line item that combines amounts expected to be recovered or settled:
(a) no more than twelve months after the reporting period, and
(b) more than twelve months after the reporting period.

A presentation based broadly on order of liquidity is usually considered to be more relevant than a current/non-current presentation for the assets and liabilities of financial institutions. This is because financial institutions do not supply goods or services within a clearly identifiable operating cycle.

Figure 18.3 shows the consolidated balance sheet for HSBC Holdings plc as at 31 December 2011, in which the assets and liabilities of the group are presented in order of liquidity.

FIGURE 18.3 Consolidated balance sheet of HSBC Holdings plc as at 31 December 2011

	Notes	2011 US$m	2010 US$m
Assets			
Cash and balances at central banks		129 902	57 383
Items in the course of collection from other banks		8 208	6 072
Hong Kong Government certificates of indebtedness		20 922	19 057
Trading assets	15	330 451	385 052
Financial assets designated at fair value	19	30 856	37 011
Derivatives	20	346 379	260 757
Loans and advances to banks		180 987	208 271
Loans and advances to customers		940 429	958 366
Financial investments	21	400 044	400 755
Assets held for sale	27	39 558	1 991
Other assets	27	48 699	41 260
Current tax assets		1 061	1 096
Prepayments and accrued income		10 059	11 966
Interests in associates and joint ventures	23	20 399	17 198
Goodwill and intangible assets	24	29 034	29 922
Property, plant and equipment	25	10 865	11 521
Deferred tax assets	10	7 726	7 011
Total assets		2 555 579	2 454 689
Liabilities and equity			
Liabilities			
Hong Kong currency notes in circulation		20 922	19 057
Deposits by banks		112 822	110 584
Customer accounts		1 253 925	1 227 725
Items in the course of transmission to other banks		8 745	6 663
Trading liabilities	28	265 192	300 703
Financial liabilities designated at fair value	29	85 724	88 133
Derivatives	20	345 380	258 665
Debt securities in issue	30	131 013	145 401
Liabilities of disposal groups held for sale	31	22 200	86
Other liabilities	31	27 967	27 964
Current tax liabilities		2 117	1 804
Liabilities under insurance contracts	32	61 259	58 609
Accruals and deferred income		13 106	13 906
Provisions	33	3 324	2 138
Deferred tax liabilities	10	1 518	1 093
Retirement benefit liabilities	7	3 666	3 856
Subordinated liabilities	34	30 606	33 387
Total liabilities		2 389 486	2 299 774
Equity			
Called up share capital	39	8 934	8 843
Share premium account		8 457	8 454

FIGURE 18.3 (continued)

	Notes	2011 US$m	2010 US$m
Other equity instruments		5 851	5 851
Other reserves		23 615	25 414
Retained earnings		111 868	99 105
Total shareholders' equity		158 725	147 667
Non-controlling interests	38	7 368	7 248
Total equity		166 093	154 915
Total equity and liabilities		2 555 579	2 454 689

Source: Reproduced with permission from HSBC Holdings plc Annual Report and Accounts 2011 (p. 281).

The classification of assets and liabilities as current or non-current is a particularly important issue for calculating summary indicators for assessing an entity's liquidity and solvency. For example, an entity's current ratio (current assets to current liabilities) is often used as an indicator of liquidity and solvency. Lenders may also include terms in debt contracts requiring the borrower to maintain a minimum ratio of current assets to current liabilities. This is known as a 'negative pledge'. If the entity falls below that ratio then the financier has the right to demand repayment of the borrowing, which may, in turn, affect the assessment of whether the entity is a going concern.

18.3.2 Information required to be presented in the statement of financial position

IAS 1 does not prescribe a standard format that must be adopted for the statement of financial position. Rather, it prescribes a list of items that are considered to be sufficiently different in nature or function to warrant presentation in the statement of financial position as separate line items. These items are listed in paragraph 54:

(a) property, plant and equipment;
(b) investment property;
(c) intangible assets;
(d) financial assets (excluding amounts under (e), (h) and (i));
(e) investments accounted for using the equity method;
(f) biological assets;
(g) inventories;
(h) trade and other receivables;
(i) cash and cash equivalents;
(j) the total of assets classified as held for sale and assets included in disposal groups classified as held for sale in accordance with IFRS 5 *Non-current Assets Held for Sale and Discontinued Operations*;
(k) trade and other payables;
(l) provisions;
(m) financial liabilities (excluding amounts shown under (k) and (l));
(n) liabilities and assets for current tax, as defined in IAS 12 *Income Taxes*;
(o) deferred tax liabilities and deferred tax assets, as defined in IAS 12;
(p) liabilities included in disposal groups classified as held for sale in accordance with IFRS 5;
(q) non-controlling interests, presented within equity; and
(r) issued capital and reserves attributable to owners of the parent.

Paragraph 55 of IAS 1 requires additional line items, headings and subtotals to be presented in the statement of financial position when their inclusion is relevant to an understanding of the entity's financial position. Paragraph 58 explains that the judgement on whether additional items should be separately presented is based on an assessment of:

(a) the nature and liquidity of assets;
(b) the function of assets within the entity; and
(c) the amounts, nature and timing of liabilities.

For example, Billabong International Limited includes 'Deferred payments' of $164 103 000 as a separate line item, in addition to non-current 'Provisions and payables' of $25 003 000 in its consolidated balance sheet (statement of financial position) as shown in figure 18.2. The deferred payments pertain to business acquisitions. The amount of the deferred payments is dependent upon the performance of the acquired businesses. However, within current liabilities, the current portion of the deferred payments has been included in 'Trade and other payables'.

Figure 18.4 shows the disclosures made in the Billabong International Limited consolidated balance sheet at 30 June 2011 concerning the issued capital and reserves attributable to owners of the parent and non-controlling interests.

	Notes	Consolidated	
		2011 $'000	2010 $'000
Equity			
Contributed equity	26	678 949	671 761
Treasury shares	27(a)	(30 291)	(30 767)
Option reserve	27(b)	8 814	7 844
Other reserves	27(b)	(127 297)	(62 369)
Retained profits	27(c)	663 289	630 290
Capital and reserves attributable to members of Billabong International Limited		1 193 464	1 216 759
Non-controlling interests		3 375	820
Total equity		1 196 839	1 217 579

FIGURE 18.4 Equity of Billabong International Limited at 30 June 2011
Source: Billabong International Ltd (2011, p. 54).

18.3.3 Information required to be presented in the statement of financial position or in the notes

To provide greater transparency and enhance the understandability of the statement of financial position, paragraph 77 of IAS 1 requires the subclassification of line items to be reported either in the statement or in the notes. For example, an entity might provide subclassification of intangible assets as brand names, licences and patents. Paragraph 78 of IAS 1 explains that subclassifications of line items in the statement of financial position are also dependent on the size, nature and function of the amounts involved. Judgement about the need for subclassifications should be made with regard to the same factors previously outlined when judging whether additional line items should be presented in the statement of financial position (refer to section 18.2.4). In some cases, the subclassifications are governed by a specific IFRS. For example, IAS 16 requires items of property, plant and equipment to be disaggregated into classes (refer to chapter 11). Entities typically report land and buildings as a separate class from machinery and equipment. Other examples are outlined in the other chapters included in part 2 of this book.

Figure 18.5 shows the subclassifications of inventories reported in note 11 to the 2011 consolidated financial statements of Billabong International Limited. The Group subclassifies its inventory as raw materials, work in progress and finished goods. Amounts measured at cost and net realisable value are separately identified. Note 11 also includes information about inventories recognised as expenses during the period.

FIGURE 18.5 Inventories of Billabong International Limited at 30 June 2011

Note 11. Current assets — Inventories	Consolidated	
	2011 $'000	2010 $'000
Raw materials and stores — at cost	5 940	4 901
Work in progress	11 377	8 971

FIGURE 18.5 *(continued)*

Note 11. Current assets — Inventories	Consolidated	
	2011 $'000	2010 $'000
Finished goods		
— at cost	312 596	194 293
— at net realisable value	18 825	32 235
	348 738	240 400

Inventory expense
Inventories recognised as an expense during the year ended 30 June 2011 amounted to $771.9 million (2010: $672.2 million). Write-downs of inventories to net realisable value recognised as an expense during the year ended 30 June 2011 amounted to $6.4 million (2010: $3.3 million). The expense has been included in 'cost of goods sold' in the income statement.

Source: Billabong International Ltd (2011, p. 86).

In addition, paragraph 79 of IAS 1 requires an entity to disclose the following, either in the statement of financial position or in the notes:

    (a) for each class of share capital:
        (i) the number of shares authorised;
       (ii) the number of shares issued and fully paid, and issued but not fully paid;
      (iii) par value per share, or that the shares have no par value;
      (iv) a reconciliation of the number of shares outstanding at the beginning and at the end of the period;
       (v) the rights, preferences and restrictions attaching to that class including restrictions on the distribution of dividends and the repayment of capital;
      (vi) shares in the entity held by the entity or by its subsidiaries or associates; and
     (vii) shares reserved for issue under options and contracts for the sale of shares, including terms and amounts; and
    (b) a description of the nature and purpose of each reserve within equity.

Entities that are not companies, and therefore do not have share capital, must disclose equivalent information to that required by paragraph 79(a) for each category of equity interests. For example, a unit trust would report on the number of units authorised by the trust deed, details about units issued, par value, a reconciliation of the number of units at the beginning and end of the period, rights to and restrictions on distributions, equity held in subsidiaries and units reserved under options and contracts.

18.4 STATEMENT OF PROFIT OR LOSS AND OTHER COMPREHENSIVE INCOME

The statement of profit or loss and other comprehensive income is the prime source of information about an entity's financial performance. The statement of profit or loss and other comprehensive income can also be used to assist users to predict an entity's future performance and future cash flows. The ability to identify likely non-recurring items of income or expense is of particular significance in forming expectations about future profits and cash flows.

However, like the view of an entity's financial position presented by the statement of financial position, the view of an entity's performance presented by the statement of profit or loss and other comprehensive income is by no means perfect. Limitations can arise from:

- the mandatory expensing of expenditure relating to intangible self-generated assets as required by IAS 38 (refer to chapter 13); and
- deliberate earnings management through the making of biased judgements relating to the measurement of items of income or expense, such as an impairment loss, with the objective of smoothing earnings or projecting an image of earnings growth.

18.4.1 Items of comprehensive income

The statement of profit or loss and other comprehensive income reports on all non-owner transactions and valuation adjustments affecting net assets during the period. Profit or loss is the most common measure of an entity's performance. It is used in the determination of other summary indicators, such as earnings per share and the return on equity. Profitability ratios may be used in contracts, such as management bonus plans.

While the statement of profit or loss and other comprehensive income incorporates all income and expenses, a distinction is made between profit or loss for the period and other comprehensive income. However, the distinction between items recognised in profit or loss and those recognised in other comprehensive income is dependent upon prescriptions of accounting standards and accounting policy choices, rather than being driven by conceptual differences. For example, IAS 16 requires asset revaluation losses to be recognised in profit or loss, unless reversing a previous revaluation gain. However, IAS 16 also requires asset revaluation gains to be recognised in other comprehensive income, unless reversing a previous revaluation loss (refer to chapter 11). Accordingly, a revaluation loss would be reported in profit or loss while a revaluation gain would be reported below the profit line in other comprehensive income.

18.4.2 Information required to be presented in the statement of profit or loss and other comprehensive income

IAS 1 does not prescribe a standard format for the statement of profit or loss and other comprehensive income. It does, however, require that the statement of profit or loss and other comprehensive income be presented either as:
- a single statement with profit or loss and other comprehensive income presented in two sections. The two sections are to be presented together with the profit or loss section presented first followed directly by the other comprehensive income section.
- a separate statement of profit or loss immediately followed by a statement of comprehensive income.

Paragraph 81B of IAS 1 requires disclosure of the following items, in addition to the profit or loss and other comprehensive income sections, as allocations of profit or loss and other comprehensive income for the period:

    (a) profit or loss for the period attributable to:
        (i) non-controlling interests; and
        (ii) owners of the parent; and
    (b) comprehensive income for the period attributable to:
        (i) non-controlling interests; and
        (ii) owners of the parent.

The paragraph further states that if the entity presents profit or loss in a separate statement it shall present (a) in that statement.

The following sections will consider the items that are considered to be of sufficient importance to the reporting of the performance of an entity to warrant their presentation in the statement of profit or loss and other comprehensive income. The profit or loss section and the other comprehensive income section are considered separately.

Profit or loss section

Profit or loss is the total of income less expenses, excluding the items of other comprehensive income (IAS 1 paragraph 7). The items that must be presented in the profit or loss section are set forth in paragraph 82 of IAS 1 and comprise:

    (a) revenue;
    (aa) gains and losses arising from the derecognition of financial assets measured at amortised cost;
    (b) finance costs;
    (c) share of profit or loss of associates and joint ventures accounted for using the equity method;
    (ca) if a financial asset is reclassified so that it is measured at fair value, any gain or loss arising from a difference between the previous carrying amount and its fair value at the reclassification date (as defined in IFRS 9);
    (d) tax expense;
    (e) [deleted]
    (ea) a single amount for the total of discontinued operations (see IFRS 5)
  (f)–(i) [deleted].

Other comprehensive income section

Paragraph 82A of IAS 1 states:

> The other comprehensive income section shall present line items for amounts of other comprehensive income in the period, classified by nature (including share of the other comprehensive income of associates and joint ventures accounted for using the equity method) and grouped into those that, in accordance with other IFRSs:
> (a) will not be reclassified subsequently to profit or loss; and
> (b) will be reclassified subsequently to profit or loss when specific conditions are met.

Reclassification of items to profit or loss is discussed further in section 18.4.3.

Examples of the items of other comprehensive income include:

- changes in the fair value of available-for-sale investments recognised in accordance with IAS 39 (see chapter 7)
- cash flow hedges deferred in equity in accordance with IAS 39 (see chapter 7)
- asset revaluation gains recognised in accordance with IAS 16 (see chapter 11)
- foreign currency gains and losses on translation of the financial statements of net investments in foreign operations recognised in other comprehensive income in accordance with IAS 21 (see chapter 28)
- remeasurement of the net defined benefit liability (asset) recognised in accordance with IAS 19 (see chapter 12).

The share of other comprehensive income of associates and joint ventures accounted for using the equity method refers to the investor's proportionate share of other comprehensive income, such as an asset revaluation, recognised by an associate or joint venture entity (see chapters 29 and 30). Items classified as other comprehensive income may be reported net of tax in the statement of profit or loss and other comprehensive income. Alternatively, each item of other comprehensive income may be shown on a before-tax basis, along with an aggregate amount of income tax relating to other comprehensive income.

Additional line items and labelling

Paragraph 85 of IAS 1 requires additional line items, headings and subtotals to be presented in the statement of profit or loss and other comprehensive income when such presentation is relevant to an understanding of the entity's financial performance. Disclosure of additional line items may help users to understand the entity's performance and to make predictions about future earnings and cash flow because items may vary in frequency and the extent to which they recur. Paragraph 86 further explains that the nature and function of the items of income and expense should be considered in making judgements concerning the inclusion of additional line items.

An entity may also amend the descriptions used and the ordering of items when this is necessary to explain the elements of financial performance. However, paragraph 87 of IAS 1 specifically prohibits the presentation of any items of income and expense as 'extraordinary items' either in the statement of profit or loss and other comprehensive income or in the notes. This prohibition was inserted in an earlier accounting standard. 'Extraordinary items' had previously been defined as 'income or expenses that arise from events or transactions that are clearly distinct from the ordinary activities of the enterprise and therefore are not expected to recur frequently or regularly'. The IASB concluded at the time that items previously reported as extraordinary items, such as a loss on the disposal of part of the business, resulted from the normal business risks faced by an entity and did not warrant presentation as a separate item of comprehensive income.

18.4.3 Information required to be presented in the statement of profit or loss and other comprehensive income or in the notes

To enhance the understandability of the statement of profit or loss and other comprehensive income, paragraph 97 of IAS 1 requires the separate disclosure of the nature and amount of material items of income and expense. Paragraph 98 identifies circumstances that would give rise to the separate disclosure of items of income and expense as including:

(a) write-downs of inventories to net realisable value or of property, plant and equipment to recoverable amount, as well as reversals of such write-downs;
(b) restructurings of the activities of an entity and reversals of any provisions for the costs of restructuring;

(c) disposals of items of property, plant and equipment;
(d) disposals of investments;
(e) discontinued operations;
(f) litigation settlements; and
(g) other reversals of provisions.

Disclosure of material items is important to users of financial statements wishing to predict the likely future sustainability of the reported profit. This is particularly so for items that vary in frequency and in the likelihood of occurrence.

Paragraph 99 of IAS 1 requires an entity to present an analysis of expenses classified either by their nature (e.g. purchases of material, transport expenses, employee benefits expense, depreciation expense, and advertising expenses) or their function within the entity (e.g. costs of sales, distribution expenses, and administrative expenses), whichever provides the more relevant and reliable information. Disclosure of the subclassification of expenses helps users of financial statements to identify relationships between expenses and various measures of the volume of activity, such as sales revenue. If the classification of expenses is by function, the entity must disclose additional information about the nature of expenses, including depreciation and amortisation expense and employee benefits expense, because it is useful for predicting future cash flows (IAS 1 paragraph 105).

Some income and expense items are required to be initially recognised in other comprehensive income and subsequently reclassified to profit or loss. For example, as discussed in chapter 7, gains and losses on cash flow hedges may be initially recognised in other comprehensive income and accumulated in equity, and transferred to profit or loss when the hedged item affects profit or loss. The subsequent recognition in profit or loss of an item previously recognised in other comprehensive income is referred to as a reclassification adjustment in IAS 1. In practice, it is also commonly referred to as recycling of gains and losses through profit or loss but the standard setters use the term 'reclassification' to enhance convergence between IFRSs and US GAAP.

Not all items recognised in other comprehensive income are subject to potential reclassification. For example, revaluation gains recognised in accordance with IAS 16 *Property, Plant and Equipment* are not reclassified to profit or loss.

Paragraph 92 of IAS 1 requires the disclosure of reclassification adjustments relating to items of other comprehensive income. A reclassification adjustment is included with the related item of other comprehensive income in the period that the adjustment is reclassified to profit or loss. These amounts may have been recognised in other comprehensive income in a previous period. They could also have been recognised in other comprehensive income in the same period. For example, some of the deferred gain or loss accumulated in equity pertaining to a cash flow hedge that is reclassified to profit or loss may have been recognised in other comprehensive income in the current reporting period.

In accounting for a reclassification adjustment, gains previously recognised in other comprehensive income are deducted from other comprehensive income in the period in which they are recognised in profit or loss. This is to avoid double counting of the gain. Conversely, losses previously recognised in other comprehensive income are added back to other comprehensive income in the period in which they are recognised in profit or loss. Illustrative example 18.2 demonstrates how to present a reclassification adjustment in the statement of profit or loss and other comprehensive income.

ILLUSTRATIVE EXAMPLE 18.2 Reclassification adjustment

Tasman Ltd held a net investment in a foreign operation, called Abel Ltd. The foreign currency gains and losses on translation of the financial statements of Abel Ltd are recognised in other comprehensive income and accumulated in the 'Foreign currency translation reserve' in equity, in accordance with IAS 21 *The Effects of Changes in Foreign Exchange Rates*.

On 1 July 2013, Tasman Ltd disposed of its net investment in Abel Ltd at a loss of $28 000. At that time the accumulated credit in the 'Foreign currency translation reserve' in relation to the net investment in Abel Ltd was $15 000, of which $5000 had been recognised in the year ended 30 June 2013. There was no income tax associated with the accumulated foreign currency gain. Tasman Ltd revalued land in accordance with the fair value measurement basis permitted by IAS 16, resulting in a gain of $18 000 net of tax for the year ended 30 June 2014 (2013: $12 000). These were the only items of other comprehensive income for the year ended 30 June 2014 and the year ended 30 June 2013.

TASMAN LTD Statements of Profit or Loss and Other Comprehensive Income for the year ended 30 June	Notes	2014 $'000	2013 $'000
Revenue	2	980	740
Cost of sales	3	(400)	(300)
Selling and administrative expenses	4	(210)	(200)
Finance costs	4	(100)	(100)
Reclassification of foreign currency gain on translation of financial statements of net investment in foreign operation	5	15	—
Loss on disposal of net investment	5	(28)	—
Profit before taxation		257	140
Income tax expense	6	(100)	(40)
PROFIT FOR THE YEAR		157	100
Other comprehensive income:			
Items that will not be reclassified to profit or loss:			
Gain on revaluation, net of tax	7	18	12
		18	12
Items that may be reclassified subsequently to profit or loss:			
Foreign currency gain on translation of foreign operations	8	—	5
Reclassification adjustment for gains on translation of foreign operations	8	(15)	—
		(15)	5
Other comprehensive income for the year, net of tax		3	17
TOTAL COMPREHENSIVE INCOME FOR THE YEAR		160	117
Profit attributable to:			
Owners of Tasman Ltd		150	95
Non-controlling interests		7	5
		157	100
Total comprehensive income attributable to:			
Owners of Tasman Ltd		153	112
Non-controlling interests		7	5
		160	117

Prior to the disposal of the net investment in Abel Ltd, Tasman Ltd had accumulated foreign currency gains of $15 000 on the translation of the financial statements of Abel Ltd. The foreign currency gain had been recognised in other comprehensive income over several periods, including an amount of $5000 which was recognised in 2013. Now that Tasman Ltd has disposed of its net investment in Abel Ltd the accumulated gain of $15 000 must be reclassified to profit. To avoid double counting of the foreign currency gain, it is deducted from other comprehensive income and added to profit. Thus, the reclassification adjustment of $15 000 has no net effect on total comprehensive income in 2014 because it increases profit by $15 000 and decreases other comprehensive income by the same amount.

18.4.4 Illustrative statements of profit or loss and other comprehensive income

The guidance on implementing IAS 1 that accompanies, but is not part of, IAS 1 includes illustrative statements of profit or loss and other comprehensive income. Figures 18.6 and 18.7 provide illustrative examples of statements of profit or loss and other comprehensive income (adapted from the guidance on implementing IAS 1). Figure 18.6 illustrates the statement of profit of loss and other comprehensive income as a single statement, with expenses classified according to function and figure 18.7 illustrates the statement of profit or loss and other comprehensive income in two statements, with expenses classified according to nature. Note that both examples assume IAS 39 *Financial Instruments: Recognition and Measurement* is being applied.

Note that the earnings per share is disclosed pursuant to the requirements of IAS 33 *Earnings per Share*.

XYZ GROUP Statement of Profit or Loss and Other Comprehensive Income for the year ended	2014 $'000	2013 $'000
Revenue	390 000	355 000
Cost of sales	(245 000)	(230 000)
Gross profit	145 000	125 000
Other income	20 667	11 300
Distribution costs	(9 000)	(8 700)
Administrative expenses	(20 000)	(21 000)
Other expenses	(2 100)	(1 200)
Finance costs	(8 000)	(7 500)
Share of profit of associates	35 100	30 100
Profit before tax	161 667	128 000
Income tax expense	(40 417)	(32 000)
Profit for the year from continuing operations	121 250	96 000
Loss for the year from discontinued operations	—	(30 500)
PROFIT FOR THE YEAR	121 250	65 500
Other comprehensive income:		
Items that will not be reclassified to profit or loss:		
Gains on property revaluations	933	3 367
Remeasurements of defined benefit pension plans	(667)	1 333
Share of gain (loss) on property revaluation of associates	400	(700)
Income tax relating to items that will not be reclassified	(166)	(1 000)
	500	3 000
Items that may be reclassified subsequently to profit or loss:		
Exchange differences on translating foreign operations	5 334	10 667
Available-for-sale financial assets	(24 000)	26 667
Cash flow hedges	(667)	(4 000)
Income tax relating to items that may be reclassified	4 833	(8 334)
	(14 500)	25 000
Other comprehensive income for the year, net of tax	(14 000)	28 000
TOTAL COMPREHENSIVE INCOME FOR THE YEAR	107 250	93 500
Profit attributable to:		
Owners of the parent	97 000	52 400
Non-controlling interests	24 250	13 100
	121 250	65 500
Total comprehensive income attributable to:		
Owners of the parent	85 800	74 800
Non-controlling interests	21 450	18 700
	107 250	93 500
Earnings per share (in currency units):		
Basic and diluted	0.46	0.30

FIGURE 18.6 Statement of profit or loss and other comprehensive income in one statement with expenses classified according to function
Source: Adapted from IASB 2011, pp. B1026–7.

XYZ GROUP Statement of Profit or Loss and Other Comprehensive Income for the year ended		
	2014 $'000	2013 $'000
Revenue	390 000	355 000
Other income	20 667	11 300
Changes in inventories of finished goods and work in progress	(115 100)	(107 900)
Work performed by the entity and capitalised	16 000	15 000
Raw materials and consumables used	(96 000)	(92 000)
Employee benefits expense	(45 000)	(43 000)
Depreciation and amortisation expense	(19 000)	(17 000)
Impairment of property, plant and equipment	(4 000)	—
Other expenses	(6 000)	(5 500)
Finance costs	(15 000)	(18 000)
Share of profit of associates	35 100	30 100
Profit before tax	161 667	128 000
Income tax expense	(40 417)	(32 000)
Profit for the year from continuing operations	121 250	96 000
Loss for the year from discontinued operations	—	(30 500)
PROFIT FOR THE YEAR	121 250	65 500
Profit attributable to:		
Owners of the parent	97 000	52 400
Non-controlling interests	24 250	13 100
	121 250	65 500
Earnings per share (in currency units):		
Basic and diluted	0.46	0.30

	2014 $'000	2013 $'000
Profit for the year	121 250	65 500
Other comprehensive income:		
Items that will not be reclassified to profit or loss:		
Gains on property revaluations	933	3 367
Remeasurements of defined benefit pension plans	(667)	1 333
Share of gain (loss) on property revaluation of associates	400	(700)
Income tax relating to items that will not be reclassified	(166)	(1 000)
	500	3 000
Items that may be reclassified subsequently to profit or loss:		
Exchange differences on translating foreign operations	5 334	10 667
Available-for-sale financial assets	(24 000)	26 667
Cash flow hedges	(667)	(4 000)
Income tax relating to items that may be reclassified	4 833	(8 334)
	(14 500)	25 000
Other comprehensive income for the year, net of tax	(14 000)	28 000
TOTAL COMPREHENSIVE INCOME FOR THE YEAR	107 250	93 500
Total comprehensive income attributable to:		
Owners of the parent	85 800	74 800
Non-controlling interests	21 450	18 700
	107 250	93 500

FIGURE 18.7 Statement of profit or loss and other comprehensive income in two statements with expenses classified according to nature
Source: Adapted from IASB 2011, pp. B1028–9.

18.5 STATEMENT OF CHANGES IN EQUITY

The statement of changes in equity provides a reconciliation of the opening and closing amounts of each component of equity for the period. The purpose of the statement of changes in equity is to report transactions with owners, such as the issue of new shares and the payment of dividends, and the effects of any retrospective adjustments to beginning-of-period components of equity. The effects of retrospective application of a change in accounting policy or correction of prior period errors are discussed in section 18.7 of this chapter.

18.5.1 Presentation of the statement of changes in equity

The statement of changes in equity is usually presented in a tabular format. The various components of equity, such as share capital, retained earnings and revaluation surplus, are listed in separate columns. The opening balance, current period movements and closing balance are shown in different rows. As for the other financial statements, comparative amounts are required to be reported in the statement of changes in equity. The comparative figures are usually presented in a separate table from the current period figures.

18.5.2 Information required to be reported in the statement of changes in equity

Paragraph 106 of IAS 1 requires the following information to be presented in the statement of changes in equity:

(a) total comprehensive income for the period, showing separately the total amounts attributable to owners of the parent and to non-controlling interests;
(b) for each component of equity, the effects of retrospective application or retrospective restatement recognised in accordance with IAS 8; and
(c) [deleted]
(d) for each component of equity, a reconciliation between the carrying amount at the beginning and the end of the period, separately disclosing changes resulting from:
  (i) profit or loss;
  (ii) other comprehensive income; and
  (iii) transactions with owners in their capacity as owners, showing separately contributions by and distributions to owners and changes in ownership interests in subsidiaries that do not result in a loss of control.

The components of equity referred to in these disclosure requirements include each class of contributed equity, retained earnings and the amounts accumulated in equity for each class of items recognised in other comprehensive income, such as the asset revaluation surplus and the foreign currency translation reserve.

Profit (loss) for the period increases (decreases) retained earnings. Other items of comprehensive income affect other components of equity. For example, a gain on revaluing assets, net of its tax effect, increases the asset revaluation surplus.

18.5.3 Information to be presented in the statement of changes in equity or in the notes

An analysis of other comprehensive income by item must be included in the statement of changes in equity or in the notes. Similarly, the amount of dividends recognised as distributions to owners during the period and the amount of dividends per share for the period must be disclosed either in the statement of changes in equity or in the notes.

Figure 18.8 shows the consolidated statement of changes in equity of the Qantas Group for the year ended 30 June 2011. The Qantas Group provides the analysis of other comprehensive income in the statement but discloses information about dividends in the notes, as illustrated in figure 18.9. For that year dividends were paid by subsidiaries of Qantas Airways Limited (the parent entity of the Qantas Group).

Consolidated Statement of Changes in Equity for the year ended 30 June 2011

Qantas Group $m	Issued capital	Treasury shares	Employee compensation reserve	Hedge reserve	Foreign currency translation reserve	Retained earnings	Non-controlling interests	Total equity
Balance as at 1 July 2010	**4 729**	**(54)**	**53**	**85**	**(29)**	**1 155**	**42**	**5 981**
Total comprehensive income for the year								
Statutory profit for the year	—	—	—	—	—	250	(1)	249
Other comprehensive income								
Effective portion of changes in fair value of cash flow hedges, net of tax	—	—	—	(67)	—	—	—	(67)
Transfer of hedge reserve to the income statement, net of tax	—	—	—	(82)	—	—	—	(82)
Recognition of effective cash flow hedges on capitalised assets, net of tax	—	—	—	142	—	—	—	142
Foreign currency translation of controlled entities	—	—	—	—	(15)	—	—	(15)
Foreign currency translation of associates	—	—	—	—	(13)	—	—	(13)
Hedge reserve movement of associates, net of tax	—	—	—	2	—	—	—	2
Total other comprehensive income	**—**	**—**	**—**	**(5)**	**(28)**	**—**	**—**	**(33)**
Total comprehensive income for the year	**—**	**—**	**—**	**(5)**	**(28)**	**250**	**(1)**	**216**
Transactions with owners recorded directly in equity								
Contributions by and distributions to owners								
Own shares acquired	—	(65)	—	—	—	—	—	(65)
Share-based payments	—	—	59	—	—	—	—	59
Shares vested and transferred to employees	—	47	(47)	—	—	—	—	—
Dividends declared	—	—	—	—	—	—	(1)	(1)
Total contributions by and distributions to owners	**—**	**(18)**	**12**	**—**	**—**	**—**	**(1)**	**(7)**
Change in ownership interests in subsidiaries								
Deconsolidation of controlled entity	—	—	—	—	—	—	(36)	(36)
Disposal of controlled entity	—	—	—	—	(3)	—	—	(3)
Total change in ownership interests in subsidiaries	**—**	**—**	**—**	**—**	**(3)**	**—**	**(36)**	**(39)**
Total transactions with owners	**—**	**(18)**	**12**	**—**	**(3)**	**—**	**(37)**	**(46)**
Balance as at 30 June 2011	**4 729**	**(72)**	**65**	**80**	**(60)**	**1 405**	**4**	**6 151**

FIGURE 18.8 Consolidated statement of changes in equity of the Qantas Group for the year ended 30 June 2011

Source: The Qantas Group (2011, p. 52)

9. Dividends

(A) Dividends declared and paid

No dividends were declared or paid in the current year by Qantas.

No final dividend will be paid in relation to the year ended 30 June 2011.

$1 million (2010: $4 million) of dividends were declared to non-controlling interest shareholders by non-wholly owned controlled entities.

(B) Franking account

	Qantas Group	
	2011 $m	2010 $m
Total franking account balance at 30 per cent	17	18

The above amount represents the balance of the franking account as at 30 June, after taking into account adjustments for:
– Franking credits that will arise from the payment of income tax payable for the current year
– Franking credits that will arise from the receipt of dividends recognised as receivables at the year end
– Franking credits that may be prevented from being distributed in subsequent years
The ability to utilise the franking credits is dependent upon there being sufficient available profits to declare dividends.

FIGURE 18.9 Dividends distributed by Qantas Group for the year ended 30 June 2011
Source: The Qantas Group (2011, p. 68).

18.6 NOTES

Notes are an integral part of the financial statements. Their purpose is to enhance the understandability of the statement of financial position, statement of profit or loss and other comprehensive income, statement of cash flows and statement of changes in equity. As far as practicable, each item in these statements is cross-referenced to any related information in the notes (IAS 1 paragraph 113).

The following information must be disclosed in the notes in accordance with paragraph 112 of IAS 1:

• information about the basis of preparation of the financial statements and the specific accounting policies used, in accordance with paragraphs 117–24
• information required by other IFRSs unless presented in the financial statements
• other information that is not presented elsewhere in the financial statements but is relevant to understanding them.

As discussed in this chapter, IAS 1 allows some information to be presented either in the notes or in the financial statement, such as the statement of financial position or the statement of profit or loss and other comprehensive income. We will first consider the statements about compliance with IFRSs, followed by the summary of significant accounting policies used and sources of estimation uncertainty, information about capital, and other disclosures.

18.6.1 Compliance with IFRSs

An explicit and unreserved statement of compliance with IFRSs should be made if, and only if, the financial statements comply with the requirements of IFRSs (IAS 1 paragraph 16). Many entities include a statement of compliance with IFRSs, if applicable, in the statement about the basis of preparation of the financial statements.

In extremely rare circumstances, management may conclude that compliance with a requirement in an IFRS would be so misleading that it would conflict with the objective of financial statements. Does this mean that management should depart from compliance with IFRS in order to present financial statements that serve the decision-making needs of present and potential investors, lenders and other creditors? The answer to this question depends on domestic reporting requirements. In some countries the law may require compliance with IFRSs. For example, in Australia the Corporations Act requires compliance with Australian Accounting Standards, which are Australian equivalents of IFRSs. However, in some jurisdictions departure from the requirements of an IFRS may be permitted in the extremely rare circumstances referred to in IAS 1, where management believe it would be misleading.

When assessing whether compliance would be misleading, management must consider why the objectives of financial statements would not be achieved in the current circumstances and how the entity's circumstances differ from other entities that do comply with the requirement. When an entity that is not prohibited from doing so by domestic reporting requirements departs from an IFRS in accordance with paragraph 19 of IAS 1, the following disclosures are required by paragraph 20:

- that management has concluded that the financial statements present fairly the entity's financial position, financial performance and cash flows
- that the financial statements are in compliance with IFRSs except for the specific departure to achieve a fair presentation
- the title of IFRS from which the entity has departed
  - the treatment required by the IFRS
  - the nature of the departure
  - why the treatment would be so misleading in the circumstances that it would be in conflict with the objectives of financial statements specified in the *Conceptual Framework*
  - the financial effect of the departure on each item in the financial statements for each period presented.

In jurisdictions where departure from IFRSs is not permitted, if management conclude that compliance with a requirement in an IFRS would be so misleading as to conflict with the decision usefulness objective, paragraph 23 of IAS 1 requires disclosure of:

- the title of the relevant IFRS
- the nature of the requirement
- the reason for management's conclusion that compliance is misleading and
- the adjustments necessary to each item for each period presented that are required to achieve a fair presentation.

18.6.2 Statement of significant accounting policies and sources of estimation uncertainty

In deciding whether to disclose particulars of an accounting policy, managers must consider its relevance in assisting users to understand how transactions and events have been reported in the financial statements. In some cases, disclosure is prescribed by other IFRSs. For example, IAS 16 requires disclosure of the depreciation methods used for each class of property, plant and equipment (paragraph 73(b)) (see chapter 11).

Paragraph 117 of IAS 1 explains that the summary of significant accounting policies should include the measurement bases used. For example, an entity should disclose whether cost or fair value has been used in measuring property, plant and equipment subsequent to initial recognition. (Paragraph 73 (a) of IAS 16 requires disclosure of the measurement basis used to determine the gross carrying amount for each class of property plant and equipment) (see chapter 11).

An entity also must disclose information about the assumptions concerning the future, and other major sources of estimation uncertainty at the end of the reporting period, that have a significant risk of causing material adjustments to the carrying amounts of assets and liabilities within the next financial year (e.g. assumptions about growth rates used in measuring the recoverable amount of major assets) (IAS 1 paragraph 125). While this information does not need to form part of the summary of significant accounting policies, it is not uncommon for entities to include the disclosures about measurement uncertainty in that section of the notes.

Paragraph 122 of IAS 1 also requires disclosure of the judgements that management has made in applying accounting standards. This requirement applies to those judgements that have the most significant effect on the amounts recognised in financial statements. For example, judgement about whether substantially all the risks and rewards of ownership have been transferred by a lease required in applying IAS 17 *Leases* would often have a significant effect on amounts reported in financial statements (refer to chapter 12 of this book). The disclosures made in accordance with paragraph 122 of IAS 1 form part of the summary of accounting policies.

Figure 18.10 illustrates an extract from the notes of Billabong International Limited's financial statements for the year ended 30 June 2011. The extract is of the statement of the basis of preparation of the financial statements included in the summary of significant accounting policies. Note that Billabong International Limited includes the statement of compliance with IFRSs in the statement of basis of preparation. While disclosures about the uncertainty of accounting estimates are made in a separate note, Billabong International Limited provides a cross-reference to that disclosure in this section of the summary of significant accounting policies.

Note 1. Summary of significant accounting policies

The principal accounting policies adopted in the preparation of these consolidated financial statements are set out below.

These policies have been consistently applied to all the years presented, unless otherwise stated. The financial statements are for the consolidated entity consisting of Billabong International Limited and its subsidiaries (the Group or consolidated entity).

(a) Basis of preparation

The general purpose financial report has been prepared in accordance with Australian Accounting Standards, other authoritative pronouncements of the Australian Accounting Standards Board (AASB), Urgent Issues Group Interpretations and the *Corporations Act 2001*.

Compliance with IFRS

The financial report of the consolidated entity also complies with International Financial Reporting Standards (IFRS) as issued by the International Accounting Standards Board (IASB).

Early adoption of standards

The Group has elected not to early apply accounting standards that are not applicable to the accounting period ended 30 June 2011.

Historical cost convention

These financial statements have been prepared under the historical cost convention, as modified by the revaluation of financial assets and liabilities (including derivative instruments) at fair value through profit or loss and certain classes of property, plant and equipment.

Critical accounting estimates

The preparation of financial statements requires the use of certain critical accounting estimates. It also requires management to exercise its judgement in the process of applying the Group's accounting policies. The areas involving a higher degree of judgement or complexity, or areas where assumptions and estimates are significant to the financial statements, are disclosed in note 3.

FIGURE 18.10 Basis of preparation of the financial statements of Billabong International Limited for the year ended 30 June 2011
Source: Billabong International Ltd (2011, p. 58).

18.6.3 Information about capital

Paragraph 134 of IAS 1 requires disclosure of information that enables users of financial statements to evaluate the entity's management of capital. This requirement encompasses qualitative information about objectives, policies and processes, including a description of what is managed as capital, the nature of any externally imposed capital requirements, whether the entity has complied with externally imposed requirements, and, if the entity has not complied with external requirements, the implications of non-compliance.

Quantitative disclosures are also required, including summary data of what is managed as capital. This may differ from reported equity because an entity may exclude some components of equity, such as deferred amounts pertaining to cash flow hedges, from what is managed as capital, while including some items that are classified as liabilities, such as subordinated debt.

The standard adopts a management perspective by focusing on how capital is viewed by management, rather than prescribing specific definitions of capital for the purposes of the disclosures. The entity is required to base its capital disclosures on the information provided internally to key management personnel (paragraph 135).

18.6.4 Other disclosures

IAS 1 prescribes other disclosures, including certain information about dividends and corporate details, such as the legal structure.

Paragraph 51 of IAS 1 requires the following disclosures:
- the name of the reporting entity and any change in that name from the preceding reporting date
- whether the financial statements cover the individual entity or a group of entities
- the date of the end of the reporting period or the reporting period covered by the financial statements, whichever is appropriate to that component of the financial statements (the date of the end of the reporting period is appropriate for the statement of financial position, and the reporting period is appropriate for statements that report on flows, such as the statement of profit or loss and other comprehensive income)
- the presentation currency, as defined in IAS 21 *The Effects of Changes in Foreign Exchange Rates*
- the level of rounding used in presenting amounts in the financial statements, usually thousands or millions.

It is not uncommon for dividends to be proposed or declared (i.e. approved by the appropriate authorising body, such as the directors) after the reporting date but before the financial statements are issued. Unless the dividends are declared before the end of the reporting period they cannot be recognised in the financial statements. IAS 10 *Events after the Reporting Period* requires disclosure in the notes of any dividends that have been proposed or declared before the release of the financial statements but not recognised in the financial statements. Paragraph 137(a) of IAS 1 requires the disclosure to include the amount of the dividends that have been proposed or declared but not recognised, and the related amount per share. The amount of any cumulative preference dividends that have not been recognised as liabilities also must be disclosed (paragraph 137(b)).

IAS 1 also requires disclosure of certain non-financial information. The prescribed disclosures include (paragraph 138):
- the legal form of the entity, such as whether it is a company or a trust
- the country of incorporation
- the address of the registered office or the principal place of business (if different from the registered office)
- a description of the nature of the entity's operations and its principal activities
- the name of the parent and the ultimate parent of the group
- if a limited-life company, the length of the limited life.

18.6.5 Illustrative examples of financial statements

The IASB issues implementation guidance to accompany IFRSs. Part 1 of the IAS 1 Implementation Guidance (IAS 1 IG) includes illustrative examples of the presentation of financial statements. Two of the examples of the statement of profit or loss and other comprehensive income are reproduced as figures 18.6 and 18.7 in this chapter. You may wish to refer to Part 1 of IAS 1 IG for examples of other statements as well as additional examples of the statement of profit or loss and other comprehensive income. Part 3 of IAS 1 IG illustrates capital disclosures.

18.7 ACCOUNTING POLICIES, CHANGES IN ACCOUNTING ESTIMATES AND ERRORS

We will now turn to the specific requirements of IAS 8 *Accounting Policies, Changes in Accounting Estimates and Errors*. IAS 8 deals with:
- selecting and changing accounting policies
- changes in accounting estimates
- correction of errors.

The term *accounting policy* refers to principles or conventions applied in preparing the financial statements, such as using the straight-line method of depreciation for property, plant and equipment. By contrast, an accounting *estimate* is a judgement applied in determining the carrying amount of an item in the financial statements such as an estimate of the useful life of a depreciable asset. The use of reasonable estimates is an essential part of the process of preparing financial statements because many items reported in the financial statements — such as provisions for warranties — cannot be calculated with precision. For example, an entity's accounting *policy* in respect of warranties may be to measure its provision for warranty claims based on history, the volume of sales and the length of outstanding warranty periods. The *calculation* of the amount of the warranty provision is an accounting *estimate* that applies this accounting policy.

An *error* is an omission or misstatement in the financial statements. Errors may arise from mathematical miscalculations, mistakes in applying accounting policies, oversights or misinterpretations of facts, and fraud (IAS 8 paragraph 5). For example, assume Company C owns a building from which it derives rental income. In testing for impairment, Company C measures the value in use of the building by discounting future rental income. The amount of rental income should be reduced by any waivers of rent allowed to tenants, such as rent-free periods offered to new tenants. Assume that in measuring the value in use in a prior period, the cash inflows forgone from rent-free periods were added to annual rentals, instead of being deducted, and that this resulted in an overstated carrying amount of the building. When the overstatement of the asset is discovered in a subsequent period, it would be necessary to correct the prior-period error. The misstatement would be classified as an error in the prior-period financial statements because it results from a mistake in the application of information that was available at the time. In contrast, if, in hindsight, the building was found to have been overstated because the estimated rental growth rates used in a prior period were too high, the subsequent restatement of the carrying amount of the building would be treated as a change of accounting estimate.

18.7.1 Selecting and changing accounting policies

Accounting standards prescribe accounting policies for certain topics, transactions or events. IAS 8 deals with situations where there are no applicable accounting standards, and sets out the principles that entities must apply in selecting appropriate accounting policies. Paragraph 10 of IAS 8 specifies that where there is no IFRS dealing with a particular transaction, preparers should use judgement in developing and applying accounting policies so that the resulting information is:

(a) relevant to the economic decision-making needs of users; and
(b) reliable, in that the financial statements:
  (i) represent faithfully the financial position, financial performance and cash flows of the entity;
  (ii) reflect the economic substance of transactions, other events and conditions, and not merely the legal form;
  (iii) are neutral, i.e. free from bias;
  (iv) are prudent; and
  (v) are complete in all material respects.

The concept of substance over form is particularly important. This is an area revealed as a weakness in the rules-based approach to standard setting used by the United States and implicated in some of the corporate collapses in that country in 2001 and 2002. Transactions that were, in substance, financing transactions were accounted for as sales, applying very literal interpretations of the US rules. Applying the principle of substance over form should result in transactions being accounted for appropriately. The accounting treatment of finance leases provides an example of applying the principle of substance over form. While the form of the transaction is a lease, its economic substance is comparable to the purchase of the leased property, combined with a loan payable by instalments. Accordingly, in applying the principle of substance over form, IAS 17 requires finance leases to be capitalised by recognising the leased property as an asset, and the corresponding obligation arising from the lease as a liability (refer to chapter 12 of this book).

Paragraphs 11 and 12 of IAS 8 explain what is commonly termed the 'hierarchy' of relevant sources of information to be used by management in selecting and applying accounting policies:

11. In making the judgement described in paragraph 10, management shall refer to, and consider the applicability of, the following sources in descending order:
    (a) the requirements and guidance in IFRSs dealing with similar and related issues; and
    (b) the definitions, recognition criteria and measurement concepts for assets, liabilities, income and expenses in the *Framework*.

12. In making the judgement described in paragraph 10, management may also consider the most recent pronouncements of other standard-setting bodies that use a similar conceptual framework to develop accounting standards, other accounting literature and accepted industry practices, to the extent that these do not conflict with the sources in paragraph 11.

Paragraph 13 of IAS 8 requires that an entity must apply accounting policies consistently for similar transactions, events or conditions unless otherwise required by an accounting standard. Accordingly, IAS 8 paragraph 14 specifies only two circumstances in which an entity is permitted to change an accounting policy. These are:

- if the change is required by an IFRS; or
- if the change, made voluntarily, results in the financial statements providing reliable and more relevant information about the effects of transactions, other events or conditions on the entity's financial position, financial performance or cash flows.

However, the initial application of a policy to revalue assets in accordance with IAS 16 *Property, Plant and Equipment* or IAS 38 *Intangible Assets* must be accounted for as a revaluation in accordance with those standards and not as a change in accounting policy under IAS 8. Note that this applies to the *initial* application of a revaluation policy only. IAS 8 would apply if an entity initially chooses the revaluation method under IAS 16 or IAS 38, and then changes to the cost method at a later date.

Where an entity changes an accounting policy because it is required to do so, it must account for that change in accordance with the transitional provisions of the accounting standard requiring the change. If the accounting standard does not specify how to account for the change, then the change must be applied *retrospectively*. Retrospective application is also required for all voluntary changes in accounting policy (IAS 8 paragraph 19). Retrospective application means applying a new accounting policy to transactions, other events and conditions as if that policy had always been applied (paragraph 5). When an entity applies the change retrospectively, the *opening* balance of each affected component of equity for the earliest prior period presented must be adjusted, and the other comparative amounts must be disclosed for each prior period presented as if the new accounting policy had always been applied (IAS 8 paragraph 22). Further, when an entity applies an accounting policy retrospectively, paragraph 39 of IAS 1 requires presentation of a statement of financial position as at the beginning of the earliest period for which comparative information is presented.

IAS 8 requires extensive disclosures when an entity changes its accounting policy. These include:

- the nature of the change in accounting policy
- for the current period and each prior period presented, to the extent practicable, the amount of the adjustment for:
  - each financial statement line item affected and
  - basic and diluted earnings per share, if IAS 33 *Earnings per Share* applies to the entity
- the amount of the adjustment relating to periods before those presented, to the extent practicable
- if retrospective application is impracticable for a particular prior period, or for periods before those presented, the circumstances that led to the existence of that condition and a description of how and from when the change in accounting policy has been applied.

Additional disclosures are required for changes required by an IFRS and for voluntary changes, as follows:

- Change of accounting policy required by an IFRS
  - the title of the IFRS
  - the change in accounting policy is made in accordance with its transitional provisions, if applicable
  - a description of the transitional provisions, if applicable
  - the transitional provisions that might have an effect on future periods, if applicable.
- Voluntary change of accounting policy
  - the nature of the change in accounting policy
  - the reasons why applying the new accounting policy provides reliable and more relevant information.

IAS 1 paragraph 106(b) further requires that the statement of changes in equity disclose the effects of changes in accounting policies and the correction of errors for each component of equity.

Illustrative example 18.3 shows how to apply a change in accounting policy retrospectively.

ILLUSTRATIVE EXAMPLE 18.3 Applying a change in accounting policy retrospectively

During 2014, Ace Ltd changed its accounting policy for employee benefits expense arising from a defined benefit superannuation plan to comply with IAS 19 *Employee Benefits*. Ace Ltd had previously amortised past service costs in an amount of $10 000 per annum. As a result of changes in IAS 19, Ace Ltd must retrospectively recognise the past service costs as employee benefits expense in accordance with IAS 8.

At the end of 2012 (and therefore at the beginning of 2013) Ace Ltd had accumulated $40 000 of unrecognised past service costs. During 2013, $10 000 of the accumulated past service costs had been recognised as expenses, with $30 000 remaining unrecognised at the end of 2013. Ace Ltd's statement of profit or loss and other comprehensive income for 2013 reported profit of $100 000, after income taxes of $30 000. Retained earnings were $600 000 at the beginning of 2013 and $670 000 at the end of 2013. Ace Ltd had $100 000 in share capital throughout 2012, 2013 and 2014, representing 100 000 ordinary shares. There were no other reserves.

The net defined benefit liability of Ace Ltd had been $65 000 and $75 000 at the end of 2012 and 2013, respectively. The unrecognised past service costs had been excluded from the measurement of the defined benefit liability. Ace Ltd's tax rate was 30% for both periods. Its reporting period ends on 30 June. Ace Ltd had reported a deferred tax liability of $30 000 and $27 000 at 30 June for 2012 and 2013, respectively. The change of accounting policy decreased Ace Ltd's deferred tax liability by $12 000 and $9000 at 30 June 2012 and 2013, respectively.

As a result of the change of accounting policy, the financial statements should be presented as if the unrecognised past service costs had been accounted for as an expense in the period in which they arose. The recognition of the past service costs as an expense would also increase the net defined benefit liability by the same amount.

Applying the change in accounting policy retrospectively, Ace Ltd's statements of profit or loss and other comprehensive income presented in its 2014 financial statements show the following:

ACE LTD Statements of Profit or Loss and Other Comprehensive Income (extract) for the year ended 30 June		
	2014 $'000	2013 (restated) $'000
Profit before income taxes	80	110[1]
Income taxes	(24)	(33)[2]
Profit for the period	56	77
Other comprehensive income for the year	—	—
TOTAL COMPREHENSIVE INCOME FOR THE YEAR	56	77

Ace Ltd's statements of changes in equity are as follows:

ACE LTD Statements of Changes in Equity for the year ended 30 June			
	Share capital $'000	Retained earnings $'000	Total $'000
For the year ended 30 June 2014			
Balance at 30 June 2013 as restated	100	649	749
Comprehensive income for the year ended 30 June 2014	—	56	56
Balance at 30 June 2014	100	705	805
For the year ended 30 June 2013			
Balance at 30 June 2012 as previously reported	100	600	700
Change in accounting policy for past service costs	—	(28)[3]	(28)
Balance at 30 June 2012 as restated	100	572	672
Comprehensive income for the year ended 30 June 2013	—	77	77
Balance at 30 June 2013	100	649	749

Ace Ltd's statements of financial position are as follows:

ACE LTD
Statements of Financial Position (extract)
At 30 June

	2014 $'000	2013 (restated) $'000	2012 (restated) $'000
Non-current liabilities			
Borrowings	250	240	225
Net defined benefit liability	100	105[4]	105[5]
Deferred tax liability	18	18[6]	18[7]
Equity			
Share capital	100	100	100
Retained earnings	705	649	572
	805	749	672

Notes:
[1] Being $100 000 + $10 000 (adding back the expense for amortisation of past service costs, which has been retrospectively accounted for in full as an expense as a result of the change of accounting policy)
[2] Being $30 000 + $10 000 × 30%
[3] Being $40 000 × (1–30%) (retrospective recognition of past service costs of $40 000, net of tax, reduces retained earnings by $28 000)
[4] Being $75 000 + $30 000 (adding the increase in the liability arising from recognition of past service costs)
[5] Being $65 000 + $40 000 (adding the increase in the liability arising from recognition of past service costs)
[6] Being $27 000 – $9000 (deducting the tax effect of the increase in the defined benefit liability)
[7] Being $30 000 – $12 000 (deducting the tax effect of the increase in the defined benefit liability)

Additional disclosures in the notes for the change in accounting policy

The company has adopted IAS 19 *Employee Benefits* as amended in June 2011. As a result, past service costs must be recognised in the period in which they arise. In accordance with the transitional provisions of IAS 19, the change in accounting policy was applied retrospectively. The comparative financial statements for 2013 have been restated. The effect of the change for each line item affected is tabulated below:

	Effect on 2013 $'000
Increase in profit before tax	10
Increase in income tax expense	(3)
Increase in profit for the period	7
Increase in comprehensive income	7
Increase in net defined benefit liability	30
Decrease in deferred tax liability	(9)
(Decrease) in retained earnings as at 30 June 2013	(21)

	Effect on periods prior to 2013 $'000
(Decrease) in profit for the period	(28)
(Decrease) in comprehensive income	(28)
Increase in net defined benefit liability	40
Decrease in deferred tax liability	(12)
(Decrease) in retained earnings as at 30 June 2012	(28)

Paragraphs 23–25 of IAS 8 deal with circumstances where retrospective application of a change in accounting policy is impracticable and thus cannot be applied. In the context of IAS 8 'impracticable' means 'the entity cannot apply it after making every reasonable effort to do so' (paragraph 5). For example, the retrospective application of an accounting policy would be impracticable if it required assumptions about what management's intent might have been at a prior point in time. Hindsight is not used when applying a new accounting policy retrospectively. For example, an asset measured on the fair value basis retrospectively should be measured at the fair value as at the date of the retrospective adjustment and should not take into account subsequent events. When it is impracticable for an entity to apply a new accounting policy retrospectively because it cannot determine the cumulative effect of applying the policy to all prior periods, the entity should apply the new policy prospectively from the start of the earliest period practicable. This may be the current period.

18.7.2 Changes in accounting estimates

Recall that an accounting estimate is a judgement applied in determining the carrying amount of an item in the financial statements. An estimate may need to be revised if changes occur in the circumstances on which it was based, or as a result of new information or more experience. Paragraph 36 of IAS 8 requires changes in accounting estimates to be accounted for *prospectively*. Paragraph 5 explains that prospective application means:

- applying the new accounting estimate to transactions or events occurring after the date the estimate is changed; and
- recognising the effect of the change in the current and future periods affected by the change.

Paragraph 37 of IAS 8 states that if the change in estimate affects assets, liabilities or equity, then the carrying amounts of those items shall be adjusted in the period of the change. Paragraphs 39 and 40 contain the disclosure requirements for a change in an accounting estimate:

39. An entity shall disclose the nature and amount of a change in an accounting estimate that has an effect in the current period or is expected to have an effect in future periods, except for the disclosure of the effect on future periods when it is impracticable to estimate that effect.

40. If the amount of the effect in future periods is not disclosed because estimating it is impracticable, an entity shall disclose that fact.

Illustrative example 18.4 demonstrates accounting for a change in an accounting estimate, including the required disclosures.

ILLUSTRATIVE EXAMPLE 18.4 Accounting for a change in an accounting estimate

Company Z installed factory plant in July 2009. The company had been depreciating its factory plant on a straight-line basis, with an estimated useful life of 15 years and nil residual value. In July 2013, the directors of Company Z determined that, due to technological developments, the factory plant should be depreciated over a shorter period of 10 years. Company Z's reporting period ends on 30 June. As at 1 July 2013, the balance of factory plant was as follows:

Cost	$ 150 000
Accumulated depreciation	(40 000)
Carrying amount	110 000

For the year ended 30 June 2014, Company Z's depreciation expense will be $18 333. This is calculated as $110 000/6 (being the carrying amount of the asset at 1 July 2013, the date of the change in estimate, divided by the remaining useful life). Since the useful life has been reassessed as 10 years, and four years have already elapsed by 30 June 2013, the remaining useful life is six years from 1 July 2013.

Extract from Company Z's financial statements for the year ended 30 June 2014:
Company Z has historically depreciated its factory plant over 15 years. The company's directors determined that, effective from 1 July 2013, the factory plant should be depreciated over a shorter period, being 10 years. The effect of the change in the estimated useful life of the factory plant in the current period is to increase the depreciation expense from $10 000 to $18 333 and to increase accumulated depreciation by $8333. In future periods, annual depreciation expense for the factory plant will be $18 333 over the remaining useful life of the plant.

18.7.3 Correction of errors

Recall that an 'error' is an omission or misstatement in the financial statements. If a material error is discovered in a subsequent period, paragraph 42 of IAS 8 requires retrospective correction by:
- restating the comparative amounts for the prior period/s presented in which the error occurred; or
- if the error occurred before the earliest prior period presented, restating the opening balances of assets, liabilities and equity for the earliest prior period presented.

As with changes in accounting policy, retrospective restatement is required unless it is impracticable to do so (IAS 8 paragraphs 43–45). Similar disclosures are required for correction of errors as for changes in accounting policy (paragraph 49). However, as the correction of errors requires the retrospective restatement of items in the financial statements, a statement of financial position as at the beginning of the earliest comparative period must also be presented (IAS 1 paragraph 39).

 ## 18.8 EVENTS AFTER THE REPORTING PERIOD

The objective of IAS 10 is to prescribe when an entity should adjust its financial statements for events after the reporting period, and what disclosures the entity should make about events after the reporting period. IAS 10 paragraph 3 defines an *event after the reporting period* as one that occurs after the end of the reporting period but before the date on which the financial statements are authorised for issue. An event after the reporting period may be favourable or unfavourable. Paragraph 3 categorises events after the reporting period as being either adjusting events or non-adjusting events. An adjusting event is one that provides further evidence of conditions that existed at the end of the reporting period, and can include an event that indicates that the going concern assumption may be inappropriate. A non-adjusting event after the reporting period is one that indicates conditions that arose after the end of the reporting period, such as the unintended destruction of property that existed at the end of the reporting period.

Usually the date at which financial statements are authorised for issue is when the directors or other governing body formally approve the financial statements for issue to shareholders and/or other users. The fact that subsequent ratification by the shareholders at an annual meeting is required does not mean that the date of authorisation for issue is at that later ratification date.

18.8.1 Adjusting events after the reporting period

Paragraph 8 of IAS 10 requires an entity to adjust the amounts recognised in its financial statements to reflect adjusting events after the reporting period. Examples of adjusting events after the reporting period include the following:
- the receipt of information after the reporting period that indicates an asset was impaired as at the end of the reporting period — this may occur, for example, if a trade receivable recorded at the end of the reporting period is shown to be irrecoverable because of the insolvency of the customer that occurs after the reporting period
- the sale of inventories after the reporting period that provides evidence of their net realisable value at the end of the reporting period
- the judge's decision on a court case, after the reporting period, confirming that the entity had a present obligation at the end of the reporting period.

Illustrative example 18.5 demonstrates accounting for an adjusting event after the reporting period.

ILLUSTRATIVE EXAMPLE 18.5 Accounting for an adjusting event after the reporting period

Blue Ltd is a wholesaler with a reporting period that ends on 30 June. In its financial statements for the year ended 30 June 2013, Blue Ltd included a receivable of $35 000 in respect of a major customer, Red Ltd. On 31 July 2013, before the financial statements were authorised for issue, the liquidator of Red Ltd advised Blue Ltd that Red Ltd was insolvent and would be unable to repay the full amount owed. The liquidator advised Blue Ltd in writing that she would be paying Red Ltd's creditors 10 cents in the dollar (i.e. 10 cents for every dollar owed). The liquidator estimated that the amount would be paid in November 2013. Blue Ltd's financial statements were authorised for issue by the directors on 25 August 2013.

In accordance with IAS 8, the insolvency of Red Ltd is an adjusting event after the reporting period because it provides further evidence of the collectability of the receivable at 30 June 2013. Blue Ltd will adjust the receivable from $35 000 to $3500 as follows:

Impairment Loss	Dr	31 500	
Receivables	Cr		31 500
(Impairment of receivable)			

18.8.2 Non-adjusting events after the reporting period

Paragraph 10 of IAS 10 states that an entity shall not adjust the amounts recognised in its financial statements to reflect non-adjusting events after the reporting period. Examples of non-adjusting events include:

- a major business combination after the reporting period
- the destruction of property by fire after the reporting period
- the issuance of new share capital after the reporting period
- commencing major litigation arising solely out of events that occurred after the reporting period.

Although these events are not adjusted for, paragraph 21 of IAS 10 requires the following disclosure for each material category of non-adjusting event after the reporting period:

- the nature of the event; and
- an estimate of its financial effect, or a statement that such an estimate cannot be made.

Paragraph 11 of IAS 10 refers to a controversial area of accounting for events after the reporting period. It states that a decline in the market value of investments between the end of the reporting period and the date when the financial statements are authorised for issue is a non-adjusting event, because the decline in market value does not normally relate to the condition of the investments at the end of the reporting period but instead reflects circumstances that have arisen subsequently. However, it could just as easily be argued that the same applies in the case of the receivables referred to in paragraph 9(b)(i) of IAS 10, regarding the insolvency of a debtor after the reporting period. IAS 10 paragraph 9(b)(i) states that this would constitute an adjusting event because the insolvency confirms that a loss existed at the end of the reporting period. This is not necessarily true because the debtor may well have been solvent at the end of the reporting period. However, the critical issue here is the amount and uncertainty of the future cash flows arising from the receivable, not whether the debtor was insolvent at the end of the reporting period. There may have been some concerns about collectability at the end of the reporting period. The additional information about the debtor's insolvency provides further evidence that the receivable was impaired and enables a better assessment of the extent of impairment. However, for assets, such as investments in securities that are traded in an active market, the market value at the reporting date would have been observable. Thus, the position taken in paragraph 11 is that the change in market value of the securities observed after the reporting period is indicative of conditions that arose after the reporting period, and, as such, is a non-adjusting event after the reporting period.

SUMMARY

IAS 1 *Presentation of Financial Statements*, IAS 8 *Accounting Policies, Changes in Accounting Estimates and Errors* and IAS 10 *Events after the Reporting Period* deal with fundamental disclosures and considerations that underpin financial statement presentation.

IAS 1 prescribes overall considerations to be applied in the preparation of financial statements, and the structure and content of financial statements, which comprise a statement of financial position, statement of profit or loss and other comprehensive income, statement of cash flows, statement of changes in equity and notes. The prescribed disclosures are designed to enhance the understandability of the financial statements to the users of general purpose financial statements in their economic decision making.

IAS 8 prescribes the accounting treatment for changes in accounting policies, changes in accounting estimates and correction of prior period errors. Changes in accounting policies and corrections of errors are applied retrospectively, while changes in accounting estimates are recognised prospectively.

IAS 10 distinguishes between two types of events after the reporting period — adjusting and non-adjusting. Adjusting events must be recognised in the financial statements, whereas non-adjusting events must be disclosed only.

Discussion questions

1. Discuss the eight overall considerations to be applied in the presentation of financial statements. Of these, which are more subjective? Explain your answer.
2. Why is it important for entities to disclose the measurement bases used in preparing the financial statements?
3. What is the purpose of a statement of financial position? What comprises a complete set of financial statements in accordance with IAS 1?
4. What are the major limitations of a statement of financial position as a source of information for users of general purpose financial statements?
5. Under what circumstances are assets and liabilities ordinarily classified broadly in order of liquidity rather than on a current/non-current classification?
6. Can an asset that is not realisable within 12 months be classified as a current asset? If so, under what circumstances?
7. Explain the difference between classification of expenses by nature and by function.
8. Does the separate identification of profit and items of other comprehensive income provide a meaningful distinction between the effects of different types of non-owner transactions and events?
9. What is the objective of a statement of changes in equity?
10. Why is a summary of accounting policies important to ensuring the understandability of financial statements to users of general purpose financial statements?
11. Provide an example of a judgement made in preparing the financial statements that can lead to estimation uncertainty at the end of the reporting period. Describe the disclosures that would be required in the notes.
12. What disclosures are required in the notes in regard to accounting policy judgements?
13. What is the difference between an accounting policy and an accounting estimate? Provide an example of each.
14. Explain the difference between retrospective application of a change in accounting policy and prospective application of a change in accounting estimate. Why do you think the standard setters require prospective application of a change in accounting estimate?
15. Explain the difference between adjusting and non-adjusting events after the reporting period. Provide examples to illustrate your answer.

Exercises

STAR RATING ★ BASIC ★★ MODERATE ★★★ DIFFICULT

Exercise 18.1

FAIR PRESENTATION

★ The directors of a New Zealand company that is required to prepare financial reports under the New Zealand Companies Act conclude that applying the requirements of the New Zealand equivalent of IAS 36 *Impairment of Assets* would not provide a fair presentation because the resulting $80 000 impairment loss is temporary. The company is subject to the Financial Reporting Act 1993 (New Zealand) which prohibits departure from the requirements of NZ IFRSs.

Required

Advise the directors how this problem should be addressed in the financial statements in accordance with IAS 1.

Exercise 18.2

MATERIALITY AND AGGREGATION

★ State whether each of the following statements is true or false:
(a) A material item is determined solely on the basis of its size.
(b) A class of assets or liabilities is determined by reference to items of a similar nature or function.
(c) Inventories and trade accounts receivable may be aggregated in the statement of financial position.
(d) Cash and cash equivalents may be aggregated in the statement of financial position.

Exercise 18.3

CLASSIFICATION OF ITEMS IN THE STATEMENT OF FINANCIAL POSITION

★ The general ledger trial balance of Jack Limited includes the following accounts that are reported in the statement of financial position:
(a) Trade receivables
(b) Work in progress

(c) Trade creditors
(d) Prepayments
(e) Property
(f) Goodwill
(g) Debentures payable

(h) Preference share capital
(i) Unearned revenue
(j) Accrued salaries
(k) Trading securities held
(l) Share capital

Additional information

Jack Limited classifies assets and liabilities into current and non-current categories and uses the minimum line items permitted under IAS 1.

Required

Assume you are the accountant responsible for preparing the statement of financial position of Jack Limited. In which caption and classification on the statement of financial position would you include each of the above accounts? If you need additional information to finalise your decision as to the appropriate classification or caption, indicate what information you require.

Exercise 18.4   **CURRENT ASSET AND LIABILITY CLASSIFICATIONS**

★ The general ledger trial balance of Joshua Limited at 30 June 2013 includes the following asset and liability accounts:

(a) Interest payable	$ 2 000
(b) Trade receivables	100 000
(c) Accounts payable	85 000
(d) Prepayments	12 000
(e) Inventory of finished goods	120 000
(f) Allowance for doubtful debts	8 000
(g) Cash	10 000
(h) Accrued wages and salaries	20 000
(i) Inventory of raw materials	60 000
(j) Loan (due 31 October 2013)	100 000
(k) Lease liability	75 000
(l) Current tax payable	30 000

Additional information
• The lease liability includes an amount of $13 000 for lease payments due before 30 June 2014.
• The company classifies assets and liabilities using a current/non-current basis.

Required

Prepare the current assets and current liabilities sections of the statement of financial position of Joshua Limited as at 30 June 2013, using the minimum line items permitted under IAS 1.

Exercise 18.5   **CURRENT ASSET CLASSIFICATIONS**

★ The general ledger trial balance of Thomas Limited includes the following asset accounts at 30 June 2013:

(a) Inventory	$ 100 000
(b) Trade receivables	120 000
(c) Prepaid insurance	8 000
(d) Listed investments held for trading purposes at fair value	20 000
(e) Available-for-sale investments	80 000
(f) Cash	30 000
(g) Deferred tax asset	15 000

Additional information
• Thomas Limited's available-for-sale investments are held as part of a long-term investment strategy.
• The company classifies assets and liabilities using a current/non-current basis.

Required

Prepare the current asset section of the statement of financial position of Thomas Ltd as at 30 June 2013, using the minimum line items permitted under IAS 1.

STATEMENT OF PROFIT OR LOSS AND OTHER COMPREHENSIVE INCOME

★ The general ledger trial balance of Lachlan Ltd includes the following accounts at 30 June 2013:

(a) Sales revenue	$1 200 000
(b) Interest income	24 000
(c) Gain on sale of plant	5 000
(d) Valuation gain on trading securities	20 000
(e) Dividend revenue	5 000
(f) Cost of sales	840 000
(g) Finance expenses	18 000
(h) Selling and distribution expenses	76 000
(i) Administrative expenses	35 000
(j) Income tax expense	85 000

Additional information
- The loss on valuation of available-for-sale investments was $1000 net of tax. No available-for-sale investments were sold during the year.
- A gain of $4000 net of tax was recognised on the revaluation of land.
- Lachlan Ltd uses the single statement format for the statement of profit or loss and other comprehensive income.
- Lachlan Ltd classifies expenses by function.

Required

Prepare the statement of profit or loss and other comprehensive income of Lachlan Ltd for the year ended 30 June 2013, showing the analysis of expenses in the statement.

STATEMENT OF PROFIT OR LOSS AND OTHER COMPREHENSIVE INCOME

★ The general ledger trial balance of William Ltd includes the following accounts at 30 June 2013:

(a) Sales revenue	$950 000
(b) Interest revenue	25 000
(c) Gain on sale of plant and equipment	10 000
(d) Cost of sales	600 000
(e) Finance expenses	15 000
(f) Selling and distribution costs	50 000
(g) Administrative expenses	30 000
(h) Income tax expense	75 000

Additional information
- A revaluation gain of $20 000 net of tax was recognised for available-for-sale investments held during 2013.
- No available-for-sale investments were sold during the year.
- William Ltd uses the single statement format for the statement of profit or loss and other comprehensive income and classifies expenses by function.

Required

Prepare the statement of profit or loss and other comprehensive income of William Ltd for the year ended 30 June 2013, showing the analysis of expenses in the statement.

STATEMENT OF CHANGES IN EQUITY

★ The shareholders' equity section of the statement of financial position of Riley Ltd at 30 June 2013 is shown below.

	2013	2012
Share capital	$200 000	$160 000
General reserve	50 000	40 000

(continued)

	2013	2012
Foreign currency translation reserve	74 000	60 000
Retained earnings	170 000	160 000
	$494 000	$420 000

Additional information
- Riley Ltd issued 16 000 shares at $2.50 each on 31 May 2013 for cash.
- A transfer of $10 000 was made from retained earnings to the general reserve.
- Comprehensive income for the year was $144 000, including a foreign currency translation gain of $14 000 recognised in other comprehensive income.
- Dividends paid during 2013 comprised: final dividend for 2012, $50 000; interim dividend, $60 000.

Required

Prepare the statement of changes in equity of Riley Ltd for the year ended 30 June 2013 in accordance with IAS 1.

Exercise 18.9	**MATERIALITY, OFFSETTING**

★ Company A is a retailer that imports about 30% of its goods. The following foreign exchange gains and losses were recognised in profit during the year:

	Loss $m	Gain $m
Foreign currency borrowings with Bank L	50	
Forward exchange contracts used as hedging instruments		1
Forward exchange contracts not used as hedges	3	
Foreign currency borrowings with Bank S		10

Additional information
Materiality has been determined as $5 million for items recognised in profit or loss.

Required

Identify which of the above gains and losses are permitted to be offset in Company A's financial statements.

Exercise 18.10	**ACCOUNTING POLICIES, ACCOUNTING ESTIMATES**

★ State whether each of the following is an accounting policy or an accounting estimate for Company A:
(a) The useful life of depreciable plant is determined as being six years.
(b) Company A recognises income arising from service contracts on the basis of the stage of completion.
(c) Company A determines that it will calculate its warranty provision using past experience of defective products.
(d) The current year's warranty provision is calculated by providing for 1% of current year sales, based on last year's warranty claims amounting to 1% of sales.

Exercise 18.11	**PREPARATION OF A STATEMENT OF FINANCIAL POSITION**

★ The summarised general ledger trial balance of Noah Ltd, a manufacturing company, includes the following accounts at 30 June 2013:

	Dr	Cr
Cash deposits	$ 117 000	
Trade debtors	1 163 000	
Allowance for doubtful debts		$ 50 000

	Dr	Cr
Sundry debtors	270 000	
Prepayments	94 000	
Sundry loans (current)	20 000	
Raw materials on hand	493 000	
Finished goods	695 000	
Investments in unlisted companies (at cost)	30 000	
Land (at cost)	234 000	
Buildings (at cost)	687 000	
Accumulated depreciation – buildings		80 000
Plant and equipment (at cost)	6 329 000	
Accumulated depreciation – plant and equipment		3 036 000
Goodwill	2 425 000	
Brand names	40 000	
Patents	25 000	
Deferred tax asset	189 000	
Trade creditors		1 078 000
Sundry creditors and accruals		568 000
Bank overdraft		115 000
Bank loans		1 848 000
Other loans		646 000
Current tax payable		74 000
Provision for employee benefits		222 000
Dividends payable		100 000
Provision for warranty		20 000
Share capital		3 459 000
Retained earnings		1 515 000
	$12 811 000	$12 811 000

Additional information
- The bank overdraft is payable on demand and forms part of cash equivalents.
- Bank loans include amounts repayable within 1 year $620 000.
- Other loans outstanding are repayable within 1 year.
- Provision for employee benefits includes $143 000 payable within 1 year.
- Provision for warranty is in respect of a 6-month warranty given over certain goods sold.
- The investments in unlisted companies are long-term investments.

Required

Prepare the statement of financial position of Noah Ltd at 30 June 2013 in accordance with IAS 1, using the captions that a listed company is likely to use.

Exercise 18.12   **PREPARATION OF A STATEMENT OF FINANCIAL POSITION**

★ The summarised general ledger trial balance of Samuel Ltd, a manufacturing company, includes the following accounts at 30 June 2013:

	Dr	Cr
Cash	$ 175 000	
Deposits, at call	36 000	
Trade debtors	1 744 000	
Allowance for doubtful debts		$ 80 000
Sundry debtors	320 000	
Prepayments	141 000	
Raw materials inventory	490 000	
Work in progress	151 000	

(continued)

	Dr	Cr
Finished goods inventory	1 042 000	
Investments in listed companies (available for sale)	52 000	
Land, at valuation	250 000	
Buildings, at cost	1 030 000	
Accumulated depreciation – buildings		120 000
Plant and equipment	8 275 000	
Accumulated depreciation – plant and equipment		3 726 000
Leased assets	775 000	
Accumulated amortisation – leased assets		310 000
Goodwill	3 200 000	
Accumulated impairment – goodwill		670 000
Patents	110 000	
Trade creditors		1 617 000
Sundry creditors and accruals		840 000
Bank loans		2 215 000
Debentures		675 000
Other loans		800 000
Lease liabilities		350 000
Current tax payable		152 000
Deferred tax liability		420 000
Provision for employment benefits		275 000
Provision for restructuring		412 000
Provision for warranty		42 000
Share capital		3 500 000
Investments revaluation surplus		25 000
Land revaluation surplus		81 000
Retained earnings		1 481 000
	$17 791 000	$17 791 000

Additional information
- Bank loans and 'other loans' are all repayable beyond 1 year.
- $300 000 of the debentures is repayable within 1 year.
- Lease liabilities include $125 000 payable within 1 year.
- Investments in other companies are long-term investments.
- Provision for employment benefits includes $192 000 payable within 1 year.
- The planned restructuring is intended to be completed within 1 year.
- Provision for warranty includes $20 000 estimated to be incurred beyond 1 year.

Required

Prepare the statement of financial position of Samuel Ltd at 30 June 2013 in accordance with IAS 1, using the captions that a listed entity is likely to use.

Exercise 18.13

PREPARATION OF A STATEMENT OF FINANCIAL POSITION

★ The summarised general ledger trial balance of Lucas Ltd, an investment company, includes the following accounts at 30 June 2013:

	Dr	Cr
Cash at bank	$ 7 000	
Deposits at call	112 869	
Dividends receivable	15 693	
Interest receivable	478	
Settlements receivable	4 900	
Trading securities	68 455	

	Dr	Cr
Listed securities (available-for-sale)	1 880 472	
Deferred tax asset	655	
Settlements payable		$ 10 253
Interest payable		280
Other payables		83
Current tax payable		242
Provision for employee benefits		752
Deferred tax liability		56 414
Share capital		1 368 024
Revaluation surplus – investments		376 090
Retained earnings		278 384
	$2 090 522	$2 090 522

Additional information
- Provision for employee benefits includes $525 payable within 1 year.
- The available-for-sale listed securities are held as long-term investments.
- The deferred tax asset and deferred tax liability do not satisfy the criteria for offsetting in accordance with IAS 12 *Income Taxes*.

Required

Prepare the statement of financial position of Lucas Ltd at 30 June 2013 in accordance with IAS 1, using the captions that a listed company is likely to use.

Exercise 18.14 ★

PREPARATION OF A STATEMENT OF PROFIT OR LOSS AND OTHER COMPREHENSIVE INCOME

The general ledger trial balance of Oliver Ltd, a medical manufacturing and research company, includes the following accounts at 30 June 2013.

	Dr	Cr
Sales revenue		$1 300 000
Interest income		2 000
Gain on sale of plant		26 000
Rental income		2 000
Royalty income		10 000
Other revenue		1 000
Cost of sales	$820 000	
Interest on borrowings	33 000	
Sundry borrowing costs	1 000	
Research expense	51 000	
Advertising expense	25 000	
Sales staff salaries	97 000	
Amortisation of patents	7 000	
Freight out	32 000	
Shipping supplies	16 000	
Depreciation on sales equipment	5 000	
Administrative salaries	72 000	
Legal and professional fees	13 000	
Office rent expense	30 000	
Insurance expense	14 000	
Depreciation of office equipment	16 000	
Stationery and supplies	5 000	
Miscellaneous expenses	2 000	
Income tax expense	31 000	

Additional information
- Land was revalued by $100 000 during the year ended 30 June 2013. The related tax was $30 000.
- Oliver Ltd uses the single statement format for the statement of profit or loss and other comprehensive income.

Required

Prepare the statement of profit or loss and other comprehensive income of Oliver Ltd for the year ended 30 June 2013 in accordance with IAS 1, showing the analysis of expenses by function in the statement.

Exercise 18.15
★

PREPARATION OF A STATEMENT OF PROFIT OR LOSS AND OTHER COMPREHENSIVE INCOME

The general ledger trial balance of Liam Ltd, an investment company, includes the following revenue and expense items for the year ended 30 June 2013:

	Dr	Cr
Dividends from investments		$920 000
Distributions from trusts		60 000
Interest on deposits		80 000
Interest income from bank bills		10 000
Income from dealing in securities and derivatives (held for trading purposes)		40 000
Loss on credit derivatives (held for trading)	$60 000	
Other income		10 000
Interest expense	15 000	
Administrative salaries and wages	30 000	
Sundry administrative expenses	45 000	
Income tax expense	280 000	

Additional information
- The revaluation gain for available-for-sale investments held during the year ended 30 June 2013 was $70 000. The related tax was $21 000.
- No available-for-sale investments were sold during the year ended 30 June 2013.
- Liam Ltd uses the single statement format for the statement of profit or loss and other comprehensive income.
- Liam Ltd presents an analysis of expenses by function in the statement of profit or loss and other comprehensive income.

Required

Prepare the statement of profit or loss and other comprehensive income of Liam Ltd for the year ended 30 June 2013, in accordance with IAS 1.

Exercise 18.16
★★

STATEMENT OF PROFIT OR LOSS AND OTHER COMPREHENSIVE INCOME

The general ledger trial balance of James Ltd includes the following accounts at 30 June 2013:

(a)	Sales revenue	$975 000
(b)	Interest income	20 000
(c)	Share of profit of associates	15 000
(d)	Gain on sale of available-for-sale investments	10 000
(e)	Decrease in inventories of finished goods	25 000
(f)	Raw materials and consumables used	350 000
(g)	Employee benefit expenses	150 000
(h)	Loss on translation of foreign operations (nil tax effect)	30 000
(i)	Depreciation of property, plant and equipment	45 000
(j)	Impairment loss on property	80 000

(k)	Finance costs	$35 000
(l)	Other expenses	45 000
(m)	Income tax expense	75 000

Additional information
- Available-for-sale (AFS) investments are revalued regularly, with changes in fair value recognised in other comprehensive income and accumulated in equity. When an AFS financial asset is sold, the accumulated amount recognised in equity for the asset is reclassified to profit or loss. Movements in the AFS reserve during the year ended 30 June 2013 comprised:
  - gross revaluation increases recognised $44 000 (related deferred income tax $14 000)
  - gross reclassifications on sale of AFS investments $10 000 gain (related income tax $3000).
- James Ltd uses the single statement format for the statement of profit or loss and other comprehensive income.
- James Ltd presents an analysis of expenses by nature in the statement of profit or loss and other comprehensive income.

Required

Prepare the statement of profit or loss and other comprehensive income of James Ltd for the year ended 30 June 2013.

Exercise 18.17

PRESENTATION OF ITEMS IN THE FINANCIAL STATEMENTS

★★ Consider the following items for Cooper Ltd at 30 June 2013:
(a) contingent liabilities
(b) the effect on retained earnings of the correction of a prior period error
(c) cash and cash equivalents
(d) capital contributed during the year
(e) revaluation gain on land (not reversing any previous revaluation)
(f) judgements that management has made in classifying financial assets
(g) income tax expense
(h) provisions.

Required

State whether each item is reported:
1. in the statement of financial position
2. in profit or loss in the statement of profit or loss and other comprehensive income
3. in other comprehensive income in the statement of profit or loss and other comprehensive income
4. in the statement of changes in equity
5. in the notes to the financial statements.

Exercise 18.18

PRESENTATION OF ITEMS IN THE FINANCIAL STATEMENTS

★★ Consider the following items for Daniel Ltd at 30 June 2013:
(a) loss on revaluation of available-for-sale investments
(b) finance expenses
(c) aggregate amount of dividends declared and paid during the year
(d) revaluation loss on building (not reversing any previous revaluation)
(e) allowance for doubtful debts
(f) transfer from retained earnings to general reserve
(g) contractual commitments under an operating lease
(h) deferred tax liability.

Required

State whether each item is reported:
1. in the statement of financial position
2. in profit or loss in the statement of profit or loss and other comprehensive income
3. in other comprehensive income in the statement of profit or loss and other comprehensive income
4. in the statement of changes in equity
5. in the notes to the financial statements.

ACCOUNTING POLICIES, ACCOUNTING ESTIMATES, ERRORS

★★ State whether the following changes should be accounted for and, if so, whether retrospectively or pro-spectively, in accordance with IAS 8:

(a) A change in accounting policy made voluntarily.

(b) A change in accounting policy required by an accounting standard.

(c) A change in an accounting estimate.

(d) An immaterial error discovered in the current year, relating to a transaction recorded two years ago.

(e) A material error discovered in the current year, relating to a transaction recorded two years ago. Man-agement determines that retrospective application would cause undue cost and effort.

(f) A change in accounting policy required by an accounting standard. Retrospective application of that standard would require assumptions about what management's intent would have been in the relevant period(s).

PREPARATION OF A STATEMENT OF FINANCIAL POSITION AND STATEMENT OF PROFIT OR LOSS AND OTHER COMPREHENSIVE INCOME

★★ The summarised general ledger trial balance of Ryan Ltd, a spare parts manufacturer, for the year ended 30 June 2013 is detailed below:

	Dr	Cr
Sales of goods		$ 7 360 000
Share of profits of associates		36 000
Rent received		9 000
Other income		6 000
Cost of sales	$ 4 978 000	
Distribution expenses	143 000	
Sales and marketing expenses	1 367 000	
Administration expenses	420 000	
Interest expense	74 000	
Other borrowing expenses	6 000	
Income tax expense	141 000	
Cash at bank	20 000	
Deposits, at call	150 000	
Trade debtors	740 000	
Allowance for doubtful debts		24 000
Other debtors	154 000	
Employee share plan loans	260 000	
Raw materials inventory	53 000	
Finished goods inventory	1 190 000	
Investment in associates	375 000	
Land and buildings	426 000	
Accumulated depreciation – buildings		61 000
Plant and equipment	2 100 000	
Accumulated depreciation – plant and equipment		940 000
Available-for-sale investments	60 000	
Goodwill	1 450 000	
Bank loans		111 000
Other loans		810 000
Trade creditors		820 000
Provision for employee benefits		153 000
Provision for restructuring		62 000
Provision for warranty		40 000
Income tax payable		30 000
Deferred tax liability		100 000
Issued capital		2 920 000

Retained earnings, 1 July 2012		760 000
Dividends paid	150 000	
Available-for-sale revaluation reserve		15 000
	$14 257 000	$14 257 000

Additional information

- Employee share plan loans receivable include $50 000 due within 1 year.
- $25 000 of bank loans is repayable within 1 year.
- $400 000 of other loans is repayable within 1 year.
- Provision for employee benefits includes $110 000 payable within 1 year.
- The planned restructuring is intended to be fully implemented within 1 year.
- Provision for warranty is in respect of a 6-month warranty on certain goods sold.
- The available-for-sale investments were acquired during the current year and were revalued by $23 000 at the end of the reporting period. The related income tax was $8000.
- The available-for-sale investments are held as part of a long-term investment strategy.
- Ryan Ltd uses the single statement format for the statement of profit or loss and other comprehensive income and presents an analysis of expenses by function in the statement.

Required

Prepare the statement of financial position and statement of profit or loss and other comprehensive income of Ryan Ltd for the year ended 30 June 2013 in accordance with IAS 1, using statement captions that a listed company is likely to use.

Exercise 18.21

★★

CHANGE IN ACCOUNTING ESTIMATE

On 1 July 2007 Company H acquired a building. The company depreciated the building on a straight-line basis, with an estimated useful life of 15 years and nil residual value. In 2013, Company H's directors reviewed the depreciation rates for similar buildings used in its industry and decided that the buildings should be depreciated over a total period of 20 years. Company H's reporting period ends on 30 June.

As at 1 July 2012, the balance of administration buildings was as follows:

Cost	$ 5 000 000
Accumulated depreciation	(1 666 667)
Carrying amount	3 333 333

Required

Prepare the note describing Company H's change in accounting estimate for the year ended 30 June 2013, including comparative figures, in accordance with IAS 8. Show all workings.

Exercise 18.22

★★★

ADJUSTING/NON-ADJUSTING EVENTS AFTER THE REPORTING PERIOD

The financial statements of Company N are authorised for issue on 12 August 2013 and the end of the reporting period is 30 June 2013. State whether each of the following material items would be an adjusting or non-adjusting event after the reporting period in the financial statements of Company N. Give reasons for your answer.

(a) At 30 June Company N had recorded an overdue receivable from Company P at $25 000 because collection of the full amount of $40 000 was in doubt. On 16 July, a receiver was appointed to Company P. The receiver informed Company N that the $40 000 would be paid in full by 30 September 2013.

(b) On 24 July Company N issued corporate bonds for $1 000 000, with interest of 5% payable semi-annually in arrears.

(c) Company N's investments in listed shares are held-for-trading and classified as 'at fair value through profit or loss' in accordance with IAS 39. As at 30 June, these investments were recorded at the market value at that date, which was $500 000. During the period leading up to 12 August 2013, there was a steady decline in the market values of all the shares in the portfolio, and by 12 August 2013 the fair value of the investments had fallen to $400 000.

(d) Company N had reported a contingent liability at 30 June 2013 in respect of a lawsuit against the company by an employee who was injured during 2012. The case was not heard until the first week of August 2013. On 11 August, the judge handed down her decision, against Company N. The judge determined that Company N was liable to pay damages and costs totalling $3 000 000.

(e) As in part (d), except that the damages and costs awarded against Company N were $50 million, leading Company N to place itself into voluntary liquidation.

PREPARATION OF A STATEMENT OF FINANCIAL POSITION, STATEMENT OF PROFIT OR LOSS AND OTHER COMPREHENSIVE INCOME AND STATEMENT OF CHANGES IN EQUITY

The summarised general ledger trial balance of Jacob Ltd, a manufacturing company, for the year ended 30 June 2013 is detailed below:

	Dr	Cr
Sales of goods		$4 469 000
Interest income		6 000
Cost of sales	$ 2 987 000	
Distribution expenses	86 000	
Sales and marketing expenses	820 000	
Administration expenses	252 000	
Interest expense	44 000	
Other borrowing expenses	4 000	
Income tax expense	85 000	
Cash on hand	4 000	
Cash on deposit, at call	100 000	
Trade debtors	450 000	
Allowance for doubtful debts		14 000
Other debtors	93 000	
Raw materials inventory	188 000	
Finished goods inventory	714 000	
Listed investments (available for sale)	225 000	
Land and buildings	257 000	
Accumulated depreciation – buildings		36 000
Plant and equipment	1 260 000	
Accumulated depreciation – plant and equipment		564 000
Patents	48 000	
Amortisation of patent		3 000
Goodwill	870 000	
Bank loans		66 000
Other loans		570 000
Trade creditors		510 000
Provision for employee benefits		93 000
Warranty provision		37 000
Current tax payable		25 000
Deferred tax liability		135 000
Retained earnings, 30 June 2012		326 000
Dividends paid	150 000	
Land revaluation surplus		50 000
Investments revaluation surplus		42 000
Share capital		1 691 000
	$8 637 000	$8 637 000

Additional information
- Share were issued during 2013 for $120 000.
- Share capital was $1 541 000 at 30 June 2012.
- Of the $150 000 dividend, $30 000 was reinvested as part of a dividend reinvestment plan.

- The balances of the land revaluation surplus and the investments revaluation surplus at 30 June 2012 were $15 000 credit and $35 000 credit respectively.
- The following revaluations were recognised during the year ended 30 June 2013: land revalued upward by $50 000 (related income tax $15 000) and available-for-sale investments revalued upward by $10 000 (related income tax $3000).
- The available-for-sale investments are held as part of a long-term investment strategy.
- $30 000 of bank loans is repayable within 1 year.
- $110 000 of other loans is repayable within 1 year.
- The provision for employee benefits includes $62 000 payable within 1 year.
- The warranty provision is in respect of a 12-month warranty given on certain goods sold.
- Jacob Ltd uses the single statement format for the statement of profit or loss and other comprehensive income and classifies expenses by function within the statement.

Required

Prepare the statement of financial position, statement of profit or loss and other comprehensive income and statement of changes in equity of Jacob Ltd for the year ended 30 June 2013 in accordance with the requirements of IAS 1, using statement captions that a listed company is likely to use.

Exercise 18.24

★★★

PREPARATION OF A STATEMENT OF FINANCIAL POSITION, STATEMENT OF PROFIT OR LOSS AND OTHER COMPREHENSIVE INCOME AND STATEMENT OF CHANGES IN EQUITY

The summarised general ledger trial balance of Matthew Ltd, a manufacturing company, for the year ended 30 June 2013 is detailed below:

	Dr	Cr
Sales revenue		$ 5 000 000
Interest income		22 000
Sundry income		25 000
Change in inventory of work in progress	$ 125 000	
Change in inventory of finished goods		60 000
Raw materials used	2 200 000	
Employee benefit expense	950 000	
Depreciation expense	226 000	
Amortisation – patent	25 000	
Rental expense	70 000	
Advertising expense	142 000	
Insurance expense	45 000	
Freight out expense	133 000	
Doubtful debts expense	10 000	
Interest expense	30 000	
Other expenses	8 000	
Income tax expense	320 000	
Cash	4 000	
Cash on deposit, at call	80 000	
Trade debtors	495 000	
Allowance for doubtful debts		18 000
Other debtors	27 000	
Raw materials inventory, 30 June 2013	320 000	
Finished goods inventory, 30 June 2013	385 000	
Land	94 000	
Buildings	220 000	
Accumulated depreciation – land and buildings		52 000
Plant and equipment	1 380 000	
Accumulated depreciation – plant and equipment		320 000
Patents	140 000	
Accumulated amortisation – patent		50 000

(continued)

Goodwill	620 000	
Bank loans		92 000
Other loans		450 000
Trade creditors		452 000
Provision for employee benefits		120 000
Income tax payable		35 000
Deferred tax liability		140 000
Retained earnings, 30 June 2012		310 000
Dividends paid	210 000	
Share capital		1 137 000
Dividends reinvested		41 000
Deferred cash flow hedge (equity)	65 000	
	$8 324 000	$ 8 324 000

Additional information
- All of the deferred cash flow hedge arose in the current period.
- $20 000 of bank loans is repayable within 1 year.
- $90 000 of other loans is repayable within 1 year.
- Matthew Ltd uses the single statement format for the statement of profit or loss and other comprehensive income and presents an analysis of expenses by nature in the statement.

Required

Prepare the statement of financial position, statement of profit or loss and other comprehensive income and statement of changes in equity of Matthew Ltd for the year ended 30 June 2013 in accordance with the requirements of IAS 1, using statement captions that a listed company is likely to use.

References

Billabong International Ltd 2011, *2010/2011 Full financial report*, Billabong International Limited, Australia, www.billabongbiz.com.

Centro Properties Group 2011, *Annual report 2011*, Centro Properties Group, Australia, www.centro.com.au.

HSBC Holdings plc 2012, *Annual report 2011*, HSBC Holdings plc, London, www.hsbc.com.

International Accounting Standards Board (IASB) 2011, *IASB documents published to accompany International Accounting Standard 1 Presentation of Financial Statements*, IASB, London, www.ifrs.org.

Qantas Group 2011, *Annual report 2011*, Qantas Airways Limited, Australia, www.qantas.com.au.

19

Statement of cash flows

ACCOUNTING STANDARDS IN FOCUS

IAS 7 *Statement of Cash Flows*

LEARNING OBJECTIVES

After studying this chapter, you should be able to:

1 explain the purpose of a statement of cash flows and its usefulness

2 explain the definition of cash and cash equivalents

3 explain the classification of cash flow activities and classify cash inflows and outflows into operating, investing and financing activities

4 contrast the direct and indirect methods of presenting net cash flows from operating activities

5 prepare a statement of cash flows

6 prepare other disclosures required or encouraged by IAS 7

7 use a worksheet to prepare a statement of cash flows with more complex transactions

8 review financial statement disclosures by companies.

INTRODUCTION AND SCOPE

Ultimately, all investors, creditors and other capital providers to an entity want to get cash out of their investment. Consequently, information about an entity's receipts and payments is of fundamental importance to such users of financial statements. The statement of cash flows provides this information by reporting cash inflows and outflows classified into operating, investing and financing activities, and the net movement in cash and cash equivalents during the period.

IAS 7 *Statement of Cash Flows* requires that a statement of cash flows be prepared in accordance with the requirements of the standard, and be presented as an integral part of an entity's financial statements for each period for which financial statements are presented.

 ## 19.1 PURPOSE OF A STATEMENT OF CASH FLOWS

The overall purpose of a statement of cash flows is to present information about the historical changes in cash and cash equivalents of an entity during the period classified by operating, investing and financing activities. This information is particularly useful to investors, creditors and other users of financial statements to assist in:

- evaluating an entity's ability to generate cash and cash equivalents, and the timing and certainty of their generation
- evaluating an entity's financial structure (including liquidity and solvency) and its ability to meet its obligations and to pay dividends
- understanding the reasons for the difference between profit or loss for a period and the net cash flow from operating activities (the reasons for the differences are often helpful in evaluating the quality of earnings of an entity)
- comparing the operating performance of different entities, because net operating cash flows reported in the statement of cash flows are unaffected by different accounting choices and judgements under accrual accounting used in determining the profit or loss of an entity
- enabling the development of models to assess and compare the present value of the future cash flows of different entities.

 ## 19.2 DEFINING CASH AND CASH EQUIVALENTS

Paragraph 6 of IAS 7 defines cash and cash equivalents as follows:

> *Cash* comprises cash on hand and demand deposits.
>
> *Cash equivalents* are short-term, highly liquid investments that are readily convertible to known amounts of cash and which are subject to an insignificant risk of changes in value.

Paragraph 7 of IAS 7 explains that cash equivalents are held for the purpose of meeting short-term cash commitments, and not for investment or other purposes. Cash equivalents must be able to be converted into a known amount of cash. This means that the amount of cash that will be received must be known at the time of the initial investment. Since a cash-equivalent investment must by definition be readily convertible to cash and have an insignificant risk of changing in value, an investment will qualify as a cash equivalent only if it has a short maturity (usually three months or less). Examples of cash and cash equivalents include cash on hand, cash at bank, short-term money market securities and 90-day term deposits. Equity investments typically do not qualify as cash equivalents, but it is necessary to consider their substance; equity instruments such as preferred shares acquired shortly before their specified maturity date may fall within the definition of cash equivalents.

Bank borrowings are ordinarily classified as a financing activity, except for bank overdrafts that are repayable on demand and which form an integral part of an entity's cash management. Such overdrafts may fluctuate from being overdrawn to being positive. In Australia, bank overdrafts are often included as a component of cash and cash equivalents. For example, as shown in figure 19.1 Billabong International Ltd includes bank overdrafts in cash and cash equivalents in the statement of cash flows.

The statement of cash flows reports on changes in aggregate cash and cash equivalents. Therefore, movements between items classified as cash and cash equivalents, such as a transfer from cash at bank to a 90-day term deposit, are not reported in the statement of cash flows.

Note 9. Current assets — Cash and cash equivalents

	2011 $'000	2010 $'000
Cash at bank and in hand	141 679	206 326
Deposits at call	3 179	2 416
	144 858	208 742

(a) Reconciliation to cash at the end of the year

The above figures are reconciled to cash at the end of the financial year as shown in the consolidated statement of cash flows as follows:

	2011 $'000	2010 $'000
Balances as above	144 858	208 742
Bank overdrafts (note 19)	(433)	—
Balances per statement of cash flows	144 425	208 742

FIGURE 19.1 Composition of cash and cash equivalents for Billabong International Ltd at 30 June 2011
Source: Billabong International Ltd (2011, p. 84).

19.3 CLASSIFYING CASH FLOW ACTIVITIES

As stated earlier, cash flow activities reported in the statement of cash flows are classified into operating, investing and financing activities. Paragraph 6 of IAS 7 defines these activities as follows:

Operating activities are the principal revenue-producing activities of the entity and other activities that are not investing or financing activities.

Investing activities are the acquisition and disposal of long-term assets and other investments not included in cash equivalents.

Financing activities are activities that result in changes in the size and composition of the contributed equity and borrowings of the entity.

Only expenditures that result in a recognised asset in the statement of financial position are eligible for classification as investing activities. For example, Green Ltd incurs expenditure of $50 000 on research for a carbon-neutral air conditioner. Expenditure incurred in the research phase must be recognised as an expense in accordance with IAS 38 *Intangible Assets*. Accordingly, the cash paid in relation to the research project is not classified as an investing cash flow because it has not resulted in the recognition of an asset in the statement of financial position of Green Ltd.

Note that the operating activities category is a default category because it includes all activities that are not classified as either investing activities or financing activities. Figure 19.2 classifies the typical cash receipts and payments of an entity between operating, investing and financing activities.

FIGURE 19.2 Typical cash receipts and payments classified by activity

Operating activities	Investing activities
Cash inflows from:	Cash inflows from:
Sale of goods	Sale of property, plant and equipment
Rendering of services	Sale of intangibles
Royalties, fees, commissions	Sale of shares and debt instruments of
Interest received (may be investing)	other entities
Dividends received (may be investing)	Repayment of loans to other parties
Cash outflows for:	Cash outflows for:
Payments to suppliers and employees	Acquisition of property, plant and equipment
Income tax and other taxes	Acquisition of intangibles
Finance costs	Acquisition of shares and debt instruments
	of other entities
	Loan to other entities

(continued)

FIGURE 19.2 *(continued)*

Financing activities
Cash inflows from:
    Issuing shares and other equity instruments
    Issuing debentures, unsecured notes and
       other borrowings

Cash outflows to:
    Buy back shares
    Repay debentures, unsecured notes and
       other borrowings
    Pay dividends to shareholders (may be
       operating)

19.3.1 Classifying interest and dividends received and paid

IAS 7 does not prescribe how interest and dividends received and paid should be classified. Rather, paragraph 31 of IAS 7 requires cash flows from interest and dividends received and paid to be disclosed separately and classified in a consistent manner from period to period as operating, investing or financing activities. Paragraph 33 of IAS 7 explains that interest paid and interest and dividends received are usually classified as operating cash flows for a financial institution, but there is no consensus on the classification of these cash flows for other entities. This is because interest paid and interest and dividends received may be classified as operating cash flows — they may be viewed as entering into the determination of profit or loss — or as financing cash flows (for interest paid) and investing cash flows (for interest and dividends received), being viewed as the costs of financing or the returns on investments respectively. Paragraph 34 notes that dividends paid may be classified as financing cash flows because they are a cost of obtaining equity finance or as cash from operating activities, to assist users to determine the ability of the entity to pay dividends from operating cash flows.

Billabong International Ltd classifies interest received and interest paid (finance costs) as cash flows from operating activities as shown in figure 19.3. Dividends paid are classified as financing cash flows.

	Notes	2011 $'000	2010 $'000
Cash flows from operating activities			
Receipts from customers (inclusive of GST)		1 773 303	1 551 174
Payments to suppliers and employees (inclusive of GST)		(1 673 100)	(1 299 033)
		100 203	252 141
Interest received		2 287	3 319
Other revenue		2 264	3 726
Finance costs		(35 688)	(22 774)
Income taxes paid		(44 730)	(49 165)
Net cash inflow from operating activities	39	24 336	187 247

FIGURE 19.3 Billabong International Ltd cash flows from operating activities for the year ended 30 June 2011
Source: Billabong International Ltd (2011, p. 56).

19.3.2 Classifying taxes on income

Paragraph 35 of IAS 7 requires that income tax paid be separately disclosed in the statement of cash flows and classified as cash flows from operating activities, unless it can be specifically identified with financing or investing activities. Paragraph 36 of IAS 7 explains that, while the tax expense may be readily identifiable with investing or financing activities, the related tax flows are often impracticable to identify and may arise in a different period from the cash flows of the underlying transaction. For this reason, taxes paid are usually classified as cash flows from operating activities. Refer to figure 19.3 to identify the income tax paid reported by Billabong International Ltd in the operating activities section of the statement of cash flows.

19.4 FORMAT OF THE STATEMENT OF CASH FLOWS

The general format of a statement of cash flows follows the three cash flow activities. Cash flows from operating activities are presented first, followed by cash flows from investing activities and then those from financing activities. The resultant net increase or decrease in cash and cash equivalents during the period is then used to report the movement in cash and cash equivalents from the balance at the beginning of the period to the balance at the end of the period.

A typical format of a statement of cash flows is presented in figure 19.4.

Statement of Cash Flows for the year ended 31 December . . .		
Cash flows from operating activities		
Cash receipts from customers	$ xxx	
Cash paid to suppliers and employees	(xxx)	
Cash generated from operations	xxx	
Interest received	xxx	
Interest paid	(xxx)	
Income taxes paid	(xxx)	
Net cash from operating activities		xxx
Cash flows from investing activities		
Acquisition of subsidiary, net of cash acquired	(xxx)	
Purchase of property and plant	(xxx)	
Proceeds from sale of plant	xxx	
Net cash used in investing activities		(xxx)
Cash flows from financing activities		
Proceeds from share issue	xxx	
Proceeds from borrowings	xxx	
Payment of borrowings	(xxx)	
Dividends paid	(xxx)	
Net cash from financing activities		xxx
Net increase in cash and cash equivalents		xxx
Cash and cash equivalents at beginning of year		xxx
Cash and cash equivalents at end of year		xxx

FIGURE 19.4 Typical format of a statement of cash flows using the direct method of reporting cash flows from operating activities

19.4.1 Reporting cash flows from operating activities

Paragraph 18 of IAS 7 provides that cash flows from operating activities may be reported using one of two methods:
- the *direct method* — whereby major classes of gross cash receipts and gross cash payments are disclosed
- the *indirect method* — whereby profit or loss is adjusted for the effects of transactions of a non-cash nature, any deferrals or accruals of past or future operating cash receipts or payments, and items of income or expense associated with investing or financing cash flows. Alternatively, the cash flows from operations may be presented under the indirect method by adjusting revenues for changes in receivables and adjusting expenses for changes in inventories, payables and other accruals (IAS 7 paragraph 20).

Although both methods are permitted, IAS 7 explicitly encourages the use of the direct method.

Figure 19.4 illustrates the typical format of a statement of cash flows that uses the direct method. You may have noticed that Billabong International Ltd also uses the direct method to present cash flows from operating activities.

Figure 19.5 illustrates the typical format of the indirect method of reporting cash flows from operating activities.

As can be seen in figure 19.5, depreciation expense is added back to profit in calculating cash flows from operating activities. This is because depreciation expense reduces profit but has no effect on cash flows. The loss on the sale of investment is added back to profit because it reduces profit but does not affect cash flows from operating activities. Conversely, a gain on the disposal of equipment would be deducted from profit in calculating cash flows from operations. The related cash flow (i.e. the cash proceeds on the sale of the equipment) is included in cash flows from investing activities.

Profit is adjusted for the difference between an amount recognised in profit and the corresponding operating cash flows, such as the change in receivables. This process is explained in more detail in section 19.7 of this chapter. Note that in applying the indirect method, an adjustment is made for the total amount of interest income, rather than for the difference between interest income measured on an accrual basis and the amount of interest received. This is because paragraph 31 of IAS 7 requires disclosure of interest received in the statement of cash flows, irrespective of whether cash flows from operating activities are presented using the direct method or the indirect method. Similarly, dividends received and interest paid must be disclosed separately in the statement of cash flows.

Statement of Cash Flows for the year ended 31 December . . .	
Profit before tax	$ xxx
Adjustments for:	
Depreciation	xxx
Foreign exchange loss	xxx
Loss on sale of equipment	xxx
Interest income	(xxx)
Interest expense	xxx
Increase in trade and other receivables	(xxx)
Decrease in inventories	xxx
Increase in accounts payable	xxx
Decrease in accrued liabilities	(xxx)
Cash generated from operations	xxx
Interest received	xxx
Interest paid	(xxx)
Income taxes paid	(xxx)
Net cash from operating activities	xxx

FIGURE 19.5 Typical format for the indirect method of reporting cash flows from operating activities

19.4.2 Reporting cash flows from investing and financing activities

Paragraph 21 of IAS 7 requires separate reporting of the major classes of gross cash receipts and gross cash payments arising from investing and financing activities, except for certain cash flows (outlined in the following section) that may be reported on a net basis.

19.4.3 Reporting cash flows on a net basis

Paragraph 22 of IAS 7 provides that cash flows arising from the following operating, investing or financing activities may be reported on a net basis:

(a) cash receipts and payments on behalf of customers when the cash flows reflect the activities of the customer rather than those of the entity; and

(b) cash receipts and payments for items in which the turnover is quick, the amounts are large, and the maturities are short.

Examples of cash receipts and payments covered by paragraph 22(a) are the acceptance and repayment of a bank's demand deposits, funds held for customers by an investment entity, and rents collected on behalf of and paid over to the owners of properties. Examples of cash receipts and payments referred to in paragraph 22(b) are principal amounts relating to credit card customers, and the purchase and sale of investments and other short-term borrowings (usually those that have a maturity period of three months or less).

Paragraph 24 of IAS 7 provides that cash flows arising from each of the following activities of a financial institution may be reported on a net basis:

(a) cash receipts and payments for the acceptance and repayment of deposits with a fixed maturity date;
(b) the placement of deposits with and withdrawal of deposits from other financial institutions; and
(c) cash advances and loans made to customers and the repayment of those advances and loans.

For instance, assume an entity finances some of its operations with a 90-day bill acceptance facility with its bank. This means that the entity writes commercial bills, giving rise to a contractual obligation to pay the face value of the bill. The bank accepts the bill and pays the entity a discounted amount, with the difference being interest effectively paid by the entity. Thus, the entity is borrowing the discounted amount of the bill and repaying the face value, which is the sum of the amount borrowed and interest. The entity will have cash inflows from financing activities each time a commercial bill is accepted by the bank and cash outflows from financing activities each time one of its commercial bills matures. Paragraph 22(b) permits the entity to offset the cash received for the 90-day bills against the repayment on maturity, such that only the net movement in the level of borrowing is reported. However, if the entity finances its operations through 180-day bills, it would have to report the related cash receipts and payments on a gross basis because this would not be a short-term borrowing as referred to in paragraphs 22 and 23.

19.5 PREPARING A STATEMENT OF CASH FLOWS

Unlike the statement of financial position and statement of profit or loss and other comprehensive income, the statement of cash flows is not prepared from an entity's general ledger trial balance. Preparation requires information to be compiled concerning the cash inflows and cash outflows of the relevant entity over the period covered by the statement. It is possible to compile the required information through a detailed analysis and summary of the entity's records of cash receipts and cash payments, such as cash receipts and cash payments journals. Ordinarily, though, a statement of cash flows is prepared by using comparative statements of financial position to determine the net amount of changes in assets, liabilities and equities over the period. The comparative statements of financial position are supplemented by various items of information from the statement of profit or loss and other comprehensive income and additional information extracted from the accounting records of the entity to enable certain cash receipts and payments to be fully identified. This method of preparation is demonstrated in simplified form using the information presented in figure 19.6. The same method can be used to prepare a consolidated statement of cash flows for a group of entities.

FIGURE 19.6 Financial statements and additional accounting information of Violet Ltd

VIOLET LTD Statement of Profit or Loss and Other Comprehensive Income for the year ended 31 December 2013		
Revenue		
Sales revenue		$800 000
Interest income		5 000
Gain on sale of plant		4 000
		809 000
Expenses		
Cost of sales	$480 000	
Wages and salaries expense	120 000	
Depreciation — plant and equipment	25 000	
Interest expense	4 000	
Other expenses	76 000	705 000
Profit before tax		104 000
Income tax expense		30 000
Profit for the year		74 000
Other comprehensive income		
Gain on available-for-sale investments	2 000	
Income tax	(600)	
Other comprehensive income net of tax		1 400
Total comprehensive income for the year		$ 75 400

(continued)

FIGURE 19.6 (continued)

VIOLET LTD
Comparative Statements of Financial Position as at:

	31 December 2012	31 December 2013	Increase (decrease)
Cash at bank	$ 60 000	$ 56 550	$ (3 450)
Accounts receivable	70 000	79 000	9 000
Inventory	65 000	70 000	5 000
Prepayments	8 000	9 500	1 500
Interest receivable	150	100	(50)
Plant and equipment[a]	150 000	165 000	15 000
Investments (Available for sale)	12 000	14 000	2 000
Intangible assets[b]	—	15 000	15 000
	$365 150	$409 150	
Accounts payable	42 000	45 000	3 000
Wages and salaries payable	4 000	5 000	1 000
Accrued interest	—	200	200
Other expenses payable	3 000	1 800	(1 200)
Current tax payable	14 000	16 000	2 000
Deferred tax liability	5 000	8 600	3 600
Long-term borrowings[c]	60 000	70 000	10 000
Share capital	200 000	200 000	—
Retained earnings[d]	37 150	61 150	24 000
Available-for-sale reserve	—	1 400	1 400
	$365 150	$409 150	

Additional information extracted from the company's records:
(a) Plant that had a carrying amount of $10 000 was sold for $14 000 cash. New equipment purchased for cash amounted to $50 000.
(b) Intangibles ($15 000) were acquired for cash.
(c) A borrowing of $10 000 was made during the year and received in cash.
(d) Dividends paid in cash were $50 000.

19.5.1 Cash flows from operating activities

Ascertaining the net cash flows from operating activities is the first step in preparing a statement of cash flows. The process used varies according to whether the direct or the indirect method of disclosure is used. The recommended direct method of preparation is demonstrated first.

Determining cash receipts from customers

The starting point for determining how much cash was received from customers is the sales revenue reported in the statement of profit or loss and other comprehensive income. However, this figure reflects sales made by the entity during the period irrespective of whether the customers have paid for their purchases. Credit sales are recorded by a debit to accounts receivable and a credit to sales revenue. Thus sales revenue reflects sales that occur in the current period, but cash received from customers includes sales made in the previous period if cash is not collected until the current period, and excludes sales made in the current period if customers have not paid by the end of the current period. Hence, cash received from customers (assuming there have been no bad debts written off or settlement discounts given) equals:

Sales revenue + Beginning accounts receivable − Ending accounts receivable

Using the Violet Ltd information from figure 19.6, receipts from customers is determined as follows:

Sales revenue	$800 000
+ Beginning accounts receivable	70 000
Cash collectable from customers	870 000
− Ending accounts receivable	(79 000)
Receipts from customers	$791 000

The entity may offer settlement discounts to customers for prompt or early payment of their accounts. For example, if a customer who owes $100 takes advantage of an offer of a 5% discount for prompt payment, the customer would pay $95 only to settle the receivable, and the entity would record the discount allowed expense of $5 for the non-cash reduction in receivables. Settlement discounts are accounted for as a non-cash expense (discount allowed) in profit or loss and a reduction in accounts receivable. Thus, settlement discounts allowed reduce the amount of cash that can be collected from customers. Accordingly, discount allowed must be adjusted for in calculating cash receipts from customers. Similarly, adjustment would be necessary for bad debts written off if the entity used the direct write-off method of accounting for uncollectable debts. Calculation of cash receipts from customers under the allowance method of accounting for uncollectable debts is considered later in this chapter.

The logic of this calculation is apparent from the following summarised Accounts Receivable account in the general ledger for the year:

Accounts Receivable			
Opening balance	70 000	Bad Debts Expense	—
Sales Revenue	800 000	Discount Allowed	—
		Cash receipts	791 000
		Closing balance	79 000
	870 000		870 000

The above summarised general ledger account can be reconstructed from the statement of financial position including comparative amounts (the opening and closing balances) and statement of profit or loss and other comprehensive income (bad debts expense, discount allowed and sales revenue). The cash receipts amount is then determined as the 'plug' figure (balancing item) in the Accounts Receivable account.

The above approach may be simplified by working with the change in receivables over the period. Under this approach, cash received from customers (assuming there are no bad debts written off or discounts allowed) equals:

> Sales revenue − Increase in accounts receivable
> or
> + Decrease in accounts receivable

Thus, cash received from customers for Violet Ltd can alternatively be determined as:

$$\$800\,000 - \$9000 = \$791\,000$$

Determining interest received

A similar approach is used to determine interest received, which equals:

> Interest revenue − Increase in interest receivable
> or
> + Decrease in interest receivable

Thus, Violet Ltd's interest received is:

$$\$5000 + \$50 = \$5050$$

Determining cash paid to suppliers and employees

Payments to suppliers may comprise purchases of inventory and payments for services. However, not all inventory purchased during the year is reflected in profit or loss as cost of sales, because cost of sales includes beginning inventory and excludes ending inventory. Purchases of inventory made during the period equals:

Cost of sales − Beginning inventory + Ending inventory

Alternatively, this could be expressed as:

Cost of sales + Increase in inventory
or
− Decrease in inventory

Using a similar approach to that outlined for cash receipts from customers, it is then necessary to adjust for accounts payable at the beginning and end of the period to arrive at cash paid to suppliers for purchases of inventory. Thus, cash paid to suppliers of inventories is calculated as:

Purchases of inventories + Beginning accounts payable − Ending accounts payable

Alternatively, this could be expressed as:

Purchases of inventory + Decrease in accounts payable
or
− Increase in accounts payable

As shown in figure 19.6, Violet Ltd's comparative statements of financial position report an increase in inventory of $5000 and in accounts payable of $3000. Hence, cash paid to suppliers for purchases is calculated as follows:

Cost of sales	$480 000
+ Increase in inventory	5 000
Purchases for year	485 000
− Increase in accounts payable	(3 000)
Payments to suppliers for purchases of inventory	$482 000

If the entity receives a discount from its suppliers for prompt or early payment of accounts payable the settlement discount received is accounted for as discount revenue and a reduction in accounts payable. Thus, settlement discounts reduce the amount of cash paid to suppliers and must be deducted in calculating cash paid to suppliers.

The logic of the previous calculations incorporating the adjustment for discount received is apparent from the following summarised inventory and accounts payable (for inventory) accounts in the general ledger for the year:

Inventory				Accounts Payable			
Opening balance	65 000	Cost of Sales	480 000	Discount Received	—	Opening balance	42 000
Purchases	485 000	Closing balance	70 000	Cash payments	482 000	Purchases	485 000
				Closing balance	45 000		
	550 000		550 000		527 000		527 000

The above summarised general ledger accounts can be reconstructed from the information contained in the comparative statements of financial position (the opening and closing balances) and the statement of profit or loss and other comprehensive income (cost of sales). The purchases amount is then determined by the difference in the Inventory account and inserted in the Accounts Payable account. The amount of cash payments can then be determined as the 'plug' figure in reconciling the Accounts Payable account.

A similar approach is taken to determine the amount of payments made to suppliers for services and to employees. Adjustments must be made to the relevant expenses recognised in profit or loss for changes in the beginning and ending amounts of prepayments and relevant accounts payable and accrued liabilities. Thus, the amount of cash paid to suppliers for services is calculated as follows:

> Expenses charged in profit or loss − Beginning prepayments
> + Ending prepayments
> + Beginning accounts payable/accruals
> − Ending accounts payable/accruals

Alternatively, this could be expressed as:

> Expenses charged in profit or loss + Increase in prepayments
> or
> − Decrease in prepayments
> + Decrease in accounts payable/accruals
> or
> − Increase in accounts payable/accruals

Violet Ltd's comparative statements of financial position show:

Increase in prepayments	$ 1 500
Increase in wages and salaries payable	1 000
Decrease in other expenses payable	(1 200)

Thus cash paid to suppliers of services is calculated as follows:

Other expenses	$76 000
+ Increase in prepayments	1 500
+ Decrease in other expenses payable	1 200
Payments to suppliers of services	$78 700

Similarly, cash paid to employees is calculated as follows:

Wages and salaries expense	$120 000
− Increase in wages and salaries payable	1 000
Payments to employees	$119 000

Using the previous calculations, total payments to suppliers and employees to be reported in the statement of cash flows comprises:

Payments to suppliers for purchases	$482 000
Payments to suppliers for services	78 700
Payments to employees	119 000
Total payments to suppliers and employees	$679 700

Determining interest paid

Using the same approach as for other expenses, Violet Ltd's interest paid is determined as follows:

Interest expense	$4 000
− Increase in accrued interest	200
Interest paid	$3 800

Determining income tax paid

The determination of income tax paid can be complicated because in addition to current tax payable, the application of tax effect accounting can give rise to deferred tax assets and deferred tax liabilities. Further, some of the movements in the current and deferred tax accounts might not be reflected in the income tax expense recognised in profit or loss. Certain gains and losses and associated tax effects are recognised in other comprehensive income (OCI) and accumulated in equity accounts. For example, as explained in chapter 6, deferred tax may arise from a revaluation of property, plant and equipment that causes a difference between the book value and tax base of those assets, thereby resulting in a charge for income tax being made to the Revaluation Surplus account. As a result, it is often simpler to reconstruct the Deferred Tax Liability account to determine the allocation of income tax expense. We can use this reconstruction to determine the deferred component of income tax expense recognised in profit or loss, if this is not already identified in the statement of profit or loss and other comprehensive income.

Deferred Tax Liability			
		Opening balance	5 000
		Tax effect recognised in OCI	600
Closing balance	8 600	Income Tax Expense	3 000
	8 600		8 600

The above summarised general ledger account can be reconstructed from the comparative statements of financial position (opening and closing balances) and the statement of profit or loss and other comprehensive income. The income tax expense shown in the reconstruction of the Deferred Tax Liability account is the deferred component of income tax expense, that is, the amount of income tax expense pertaining to the movement in deferred tax balances.

The movement in the Deferred Tax Liability account for Violet Ltd can be summarised as follows:

Beginning balance	$5 000
+ Tax recognised directly in OCI	600
+ Income tax expense (deferred component)	3 000
Ending balance	$8 600

The current component of income tax expense can then be calculated by deducting the deferred component of income tax expense from the total income tax expense recognised in profit or loss. The current component of income tax expense for Violet Ltd can be calculated as follows:

Income tax expense	$30 000
Deferred component of income tax expense	(3 000)
Current component of income tax expense	$27 000

The beginning balance of Current Tax Payable of $14 000 is increased by the current component of income tax expense, $27 000. If no payments were made, the ending balance would be $41 000. However, as the ending balance is only $16 000, we can conclude that the amount of income tax paid must have been $25 000. To illustrate, the movement in Violet Ltd's Current Tax Payable account may be summarised as follows:

Beginning balance	$14 000
+ Income tax expense	27 000
− Income tax paid	25 000
Ending balance	$16 000

For Violet Ltd, the amount of income tax paid consists of the final balance in respect of the previous year's current tax payable, and instalments (e.g. quarterly) in respect of the current year. The income tax expense may include an adjustment for any under- or over-accrual for current tax payable at the beginning of the period.

Summarising cash flows from operating activities

Using the direct method, the cash flows from the operating activities section of Violet Ltd's statement of cash flows for the year are presented in figure 19.7.

VIOLET LTD Statement of Cash Flows (extract) for the year ended 31 December 2013	
Cash flows from operating activities	
Cash receipts from customers	$ 791 000
Cash paid to suppliers and employees	(679 700)
Cash generated from operations	111 300
Interest received*	5 050
Interest paid**	(3 800)
Income taxes paid	(25 000)
Net cash from operating activities	$ 87 550
* May be classified as investing ** May be classified as financing	

FIGURE 19.7 Cash flows from operating activities (direct method)

The presentation of Violet Ltd's cash flows from operating activities under the indirect method is shown in figure 19.8. The statement commences with profit before tax and shows the gross amount of tax paid as a separate item in accordance with paragraph 35 of IAS 17. Similarly, under the indirect method Violet Ltd adjusts for the full amount of the interest income and interest expense so that amount of cash received or paid for these items is disclosed in full in the statement of cash flows as required by paragraph 31 of IAS 7. In this illustration, the increase in wages and salaries payable of $1000 and the decrease in other expenses payable of $1200 are combined as one line item and shown as a net reduction of $200.

VIOLET LTD Statement of Cash Flows (extract) for the year ended 31 December 2013	
Cash flows from operating activities	
Profit before tax	$ 104 000
Adjustment for:	
Depreciation	25 000
Interest income	(5 000)
Gain on sale of plant	(4 000)
Interest expense	4 000
Increase in accounts receivable	(9 000)
Increase in inventory	(5 000)
Increase in prepayments	(1 500)
Increase in accounts payable	3 000
Decrease in other payables	(200)
Cash generated from operations	111 300
Interest received*	5 050
Interest paid**	(3 800)
Income taxes paid	(25 000)
Net cash from operating activities	$ 87 550
* May be classified as investing ** May be classified as financing	

FIGURE 19.8 Cash flows from operating activities (indirect method)

19.5.2 Cash flows from investing activities

Determining cash flows from investing activities requires identifying cash inflows and outflows relating to the acquisition and disposal of long-term assets and other investments not included in cash equivalents.

The comparative statements of financial position of Violet Ltd in figure 19.6 show that plant has increased by $15 000, investments by $2000 and intangibles by $15 000. To determine the cash flows relating to these increases, it is necessary to analyse the underlying transactions.

The plant reported in the statement of financial position is net of accumulated depreciation. The net increase in plant reflects the recording of acquisitions, disposals and depreciation. Using the data provided, the analysis of the plant movement (which is net of accumulated depreciation) is as follows:

Beginning balance	$150 000
Acquisitions	50 000
Disposals	(10 000)
Depreciation for year	(25 000)
Ending balance	$165 000

The additional information provided in figure 19.6 states that the acquisitions were made for cash during the period, so no adjustment is necessary for year-end payables. Assuming that there were no outstanding payables for plant purchases at the beginning of the year, the cash flow for plant acquisitions for the year is $50 000 (note (a) in figure 19.6). (If payables for plant purchases were outstanding at the beginning of the period, the amount would need to be included in plant purchases paid during the period.)

The gain or loss on disposal of plant is the difference between the carrying amount and the proceeds on the sale of plant. Thus, the proceeds on sale of plant can be calculated as:

Carrying amount of plant sold + Gain on disposal of plant
or
– Loss on disposal of plant

For Violet Ltd, the calculation is as follows:

$10 000 + 4000 = $14 000

However, the proceeds from the sale of plant equals the cash inflow for the year only if there are no receivables outstanding arising from the sale of plant at either the beginning or end of the year. If receivables for the sale of plant exist, the cash inflow is determined using the approach that was previously outlined for sales revenue and interest receivable. For simplicity, it is assumed that Violet Ltd had no receivables outstanding, at the beginning or end of the year, arising from the sale of plant.

Issues similar to those outlined for the acquisition of plant arise in respect of investments and intangibles. The comparative statements of financial position for Violet Ltd show that the movement in intangibles equals the additional cash acquisitions made during the period, as detailed in the additional information presented in figure 19.6. Note, however, that the movement in intangibles equals the cash outflows for the year only if it is assumed that there were no related accounts payable at the beginning or end of the year that were settled during the year. If payables exist, the cash outflow is determined using the approach that was previously outlined for cash paid to suppliers and employees.

Investments increased by $2000 during the year, as shown in the comparative statements of financial position. This increase relates to the gain on revaluation of available-for-sale investments reported in the statement of profit or loss and other comprehensive income. Thus the movement in investments does not affect cash flows from investing activities. Using the above information, the cash flows from investing activities reported in Violet Ltd's statement of cash flows for 2013 are presented in figure 19.9.

VIOLET LTD
Statement of Cash Flows (extract)
for the year ended 31 December 2013

Cash flows from investing activities	
Purchase of intangibles	$ (15 000)
Purchase of plant	(50 000)
Proceeds from sale of plant	14 000
Net cash used in investing activities	$ (51 000)

FIGURE 19.9 Cash flows from investing activities

19.5.3 Cash flows from financing activities

Determining cash flows from financing activities requires identification of cash flows that resulted in changes in the size and composition of contributed equity and borrowings.

The additional information (c) in figure 19.6 confirms that the increase in borrowings of $10 000 derived from the comparative statements of financial position of Violet Ltd arose from an additional borrowing received in cash. It would normally be necessary to analyse the net movement in borrowings in order to identify whether the movement reflects repayments and additional borrowings, and whether any new borrowings arose from non-cash transactions.

If the entity had issued shares during the period this would be reflected in a change in share capital. An alternative source of information about capital contributions is the statement of changes in equity. Any share issues for non-cash consideration, such as shares issued as part of a dividend reinvestment scheme, should be deducted from the movement in share capital to determine cash proceeds from share issues. Violet Ltd's share capital is unchanged at $200 000, as shown in figure 19.6.

Dividends distributed by the entity can be identified by analysing the change in retained earnings. Profit increases retained earnings and losses decrease retained earnings. Dividends decrease retained earnings. Any non-cash dividends should be deducted from total dividends to determine cash dividends paid. Information about dividends is also reported in the statement of changes in equity. The movement in Violet Ltd's retained earnings of $24 000 reflects:

Profit for the period	$ 74 000	
Dividends (paid in cash)	(50 000)	((d) in figure 19.6)
Net movement	$ 24 000	

Using the previous information, the financing cash flow section of Violet Ltd's statement of cash flows for 2013 is presented in figure 19.10.

VIOLET LTD
Statement of Cash Flows (extract)
for the year ended 31 December 2013

Cash flows from financing activities	
Proceeds from borrowings	$ 10 000
Dividends paid*	(50 000)
Net cash used in financing activities	$ (40 000)

*Dividends paid may be classified as an operating cash flow.

FIGURE 19.10 Cash flows from financing activities

All that remains to complete the statement of cash flows for Violet Ltd is the determination of the net increase or decrease for the period in cash held, and to use this net change to reconcile cash at the beginning and end of the year.

The complete statement of cash flows for Violet Ltd (using the direct method for reporting cash flows from operating activities) is shown in figure 19.11. The balance of cash at year-end of $56 550 shown in figure 19.11 agrees with the cash at bank balance shown in the statement of financial position at 31 December 2013 in figure 19.6. There are no cash equivalents such as short-term deposits or a bank overdraft.

VIOLET LTD Statement of Cash Flows for the year ended 31 December 2013		
Cash flows from operating activities		
Cash receipts from customers	$ 791 000	
Cash paid to suppliers and employees	(679 700)	
Cash generated from operations	111 300	
Interest received	5 050	
Interest paid	(3 800)	
Income taxes paid	(25 000)	
Net cash from operating activities		$ 87 550
Cash flows from investing activities		
Purchase of intangibles	$ (15 000)	
Purchase of plant	(50 000)	
Proceeds from sale of plant	14 000	
Net cash used in investing activities		(51 000)
Cash flows from financing activities		
Proceeds from borrowings	$ 10 000	
Dividends paid	(50 000)	
Net cash used in financing activities		(40 000)
Net decrease in cash and cash equivalents		(3 450)
Cash and cash equivalents at beginning of year		60 000
Cash and cash equivalents at end of year		$ 56 550

FIGURE 19.11 Complete statement of cash flows of Violet Ltd

19.6 OTHER DISCLOSURES

IAS 7 prescribes additional disclosures in the notes to the financial statements, including information about the components of cash and cash equivalents, changes in ownership interests of subsidiaries and other businesses, and non-cash investing and financing transactions. Additional information is often necessary to obtain a complete picture of the change in an entity's financial position because not all transactions are simple cash transactions. Significant changes can result from the acquisition or disposal of subsidiaries or other business units, or from financing and investing transactions that do not involve current cash flows.

19.6.1 Components of cash and cash equivalents

The components of cash and cash equivalents must be disclosed and reconciled to amounts reported in the statement of financial position. The reconciliation provides better transparency of how items are reported in the financial statements. For example, cash and cash equivalents may comprise cash, short-term deposits and an overdraft. The end-of-period amount of cash and cash equivalents reported in the statement of cash flows may differ from that reported in the statement of financial position because the cash and short-term deposits are reported as current assets while the overdraft is a liability. Figure 19.1 illustrates the reconciliation between cash and cash equivalents in the statement of cash flows with the corresponding item reported in the statement of financial position for Billabong International Ltd.

Paragraph 48 requires disclosure of the amount of significant cash and cash-equivalent balances held that are not available for general use. For example, foreign exchange controls in some countries may affect the general availability of the cash held by a foreign subsidiary.

19.6.2 Changes in ownership interests of subsidiaries and other businesses

Part 4 of this book deals with the financial reporting of consolidated groups of entities. When a parent entity obtains control of an operating entity, or loses control of an existing subsidiary, the comparative consolidated statement of financial position of the group before and after the acquisition or disposal will frequently reflect significant changes in the assets and liabilities arising from the acquisition or disposal. Financial statement users need to be aware of such changes in order to understand the change in financial position of the consolidated group. IAS 7 specifies additional reporting requirements relating to changes in control of subsidiaries and other businesses as follows:

39. The aggregate cash flows arising from obtaining or losing control of subsidiaries or other businesses shall be presented separately and classified as investing activities.
40. An entity shall disclose, in aggregate, in respect of both obtaining or losing control of subsidiaries or other businesses during the period each of the following:
    (a) the total consideration paid or received;
    (b) the portion of the consideration consisting of cash and cash equivalents;
    (c) the amount of cash and cash equivalents in the subsidiaries or other businesses over which control is obtained or lost; and
    (d) the amount of the assets and liabilities other than cash or cash equivalents in the subsidiaries or other businesses over which control is obtained or lost, summarised by each major category.

Paragraph 39 of IAS 7 requires the aggregate cash flow effects of obtaining control of subsidiaries or other businesses to be reported as one item in the investing activities section of the statement of cash flows. When an entity obtains control of a subsidiary or other business, any cash and cash equivalents acquired are deducted from the cash consideration paid in determining the cash flow effects of obtaining control. For example, Beige Ltd obtained control over Champagne Ltd by acquiring all of the ordinary shares of Champagne Ltd. Beige Ltd paid consideration of $1 500 000 in cash. Champagne Ltd held cash and cash equivalents of $100 000 at the time of the acquisition. Thus, the cash flow effects for Beige Ltd of obtaining control of Champagne Ltd is $1 400 000 (i.e. $1 500 000 − $100 000). This would be reported as a cash outflow from investing activities in Beige Ltd's consolidated statement of cash flows.

Similarly, paragraph 39 of IAS 7 requires the aggregate cash flow effects of losing control of subsidiaries or other businesses to be reported as one item in the investing activities section of the statement of cash flows. If an entity loses control of a subsidiary or other business, any cash and cash equivalents held by that subsidiary or other business at the time of the disposal are deducted from the cash consideration received in reporting the cash flow effects of losing control. Figure 19.12 shows the investing activities section of Billabong International Ltd's consolidated statement of cash flows. Transactions through which Billabong International Ltd obtained control of subsidiaries and other businesses during the year ended 30 June 2011 resulted in a cash outflow of $215 064 000, net of cash acquired, as shown in figure 19.12.

	Notes	2011 $'000	2010 $'000
Cash flows from investing activities			
Payments for purchase of subsidiaries and businesses, net of cash acquired	35	(215 064)	(49 591)
Payments for property, plant and equipment		(43 244)	(53 064)
Payments for intangible assets		(9 126)	(3 393)
Proceeds from sale of property, plant and equipment		499	284
Net cash outflow from investing activities		(266 935)	(105 764)

FIGURE 19.12 Investing activities section of statement of cash flows of Billabong International Ltd for the year ended 30 June 2011
Source: Billabong International Ltd (2011, p. 56).

Separate presentation of the cash flow effects of transactions to obtain or to surrender control of subsidiaries or other businesses is required. The cash flow effects of transactions resulting in the loss of control, such as the sale of a subsidiary, are not deducted from the cash flows of transactions that obtain control, such as the acquisitions of a subsidiary. Both the aggregate cash flow effects of obtaining control of subsidiaries and other businesses and the aggregate cash flow effects of losing control of subsidiaries and other businesses are reported separately in the investing activities section of the statement of cash flows.

19.6.3 Non-cash transactions

Not all investing or financing transactions involve current cash flows, although such transactions may significantly affect the financial structure of the entity. However, such transactions need to be understood in order to comprehend the change in financial position of an entity. Examples include:

- acquisition of assets by means of a finance lease or by assuming other liabilities
- acquisition of assets or an entity by means of an equity issue
- conversion of debt to equity
- conversion of preference shares to ordinary shares
- refinancing of long-term debt
- payment of dividends through a dividend reinvestment scheme.
  In regard to non-cash transactions, paragraph 43 of IAS 7 states:

> Investing and financing transactions that do not require the use of cash or cash equivalents shall be excluded from a statement of cash flows. Such transactions shall be disclosed elsewhere in the financial statements in a way that provides all the relevant information about these investing and financing activities.

Figure 19.13 illustrates Billabong International Ltd's disclosure on non-cash investing and financing activities in the notes to its financial statements. The acquisition of plant and equipment by a finance lease is a non-cash transaction that increases plant and equipment (leased plant and equipment) and borrowings (lease liabilities). The other non-cash transaction is the issue of shares under a dividend reinvestment scheme, which is a non-cash financing transaction in which shareholders elect to apply their dividend to the purchase of additional shares in the company. As information about shares issued in relation to the dividend reinvestment scheme is reported in the note on dividends, Billabong International Ltd provides a cross-reference to that note, rather than repeating the information in the note on non-cash investing and financing activities.

Note 40. Non-cash investing and financing activities	2011 $'000	2010 $'000
Acquisition of plant and equipment by means of a finance lease	56	22
	56	22
Dividends satisfied by the issue of shares under the Dividend Reinvestment Plan are shown in note 28.		

FIGURE 19.13 Non-cash investing and financing activities of Billabong International Ltd for the year ended 30 June 2011
Source: Billabong International Ltd (2011, p. 121).

19.6.4 Disclosures that are encouraged but not required

Paragraph 50 of IAS 7 encourages, but does not require, additional information that may be relevant to users in understanding the financial position and liquidity of an entity. They are as follows:

(a) the amount of undrawn borrowing facilities that may be available for future operating activities and to settle capital commitments, indicating any restrictions on the use of these facilities;

(b) the aggregate amounts of the cash flows from each of operating, investing and financing activities related to interests in joint ventures reported using proportionate consolidation;

(c) the aggregate amount of cash flows that represent increases in operating capacity separately from those cash flows that are required to maintain operating capacity; and

(d) the amount of the cash flows arising from the operating, investing and financing activities of each reportable segment (see IFRS 8 *Operating Segments*).

At the time of writing, changes to requirements for accounting for joint ventures that would prohibit proportionate consolidation of interests in joint ventures are scheduled to become effective for reporting periods commencing on or after 1 January 2013. Accordingly, paragraph 50(b) is deleted effective from that date. Chapter 30 of this book provides an outline of accounting for interests in joint arrangements referred to in paragraph 50(b) of the standard. Chapter 21 deals with segment reporting referred to in paragraph 50(d).

19.7 COMPREHENSIVE EXAMPLE

The example in this section demonstrates a more complex statement of cash flows prepared using a worksheet. Figure 19.14 presents the financial statements of Silver Ltd, and the worksheet is shown in figure 19.15. An explanation of the reconciling adjustments follows the worksheet. The indirect method is used to present cash flows from operating activities. The worksheet commences with further information about items reported in the financial statements, such as the components of income tax expense and the composition of accounts payable at the beginning and end of the year. The body of the worksheet lists the items reported in the comparative statements of financial position and shows how the movement in each item is used in the calculation of items reported in the statement of cash flows. This is followed by an explanation in section 19.7.1 of each item reported in the statement of cash flows, commencing with the items shown in the operating activities section of the statement.

FIGURE 19.14 Financial statements of Silver Ltd

SILVER LTD Comparative Statements of Financial Position as at:			
	31 December 2012	31 December 2013	Increase (decrease)
Cash	$ 60 000	$ 69 800	$ 9 800
Short-term deposits	120 000	140 000	20 000
Accounts receivable, net	140 000	190 000	50 000
Inventory	130 000	155 000	25 000
Prepayments	16 000	19 000	3 000
Interest receivable	300	200	(100)
Investment in associate	40 000	45 000	5 000
Land	80 000	120 000	40 000
Plant	300 000	420 000	120 000
Accumulated depreciation	(50 000)	(65 000)	(15 000)
Intangibles	90 000	60 000	(30 000)
	$926 300	$1 154 000	$227 700
Accounts payable	84 000	90 000	6 000
Accrued liabilities	14 000	12 000	(2 000)
Current tax payable	28 000	32 000	4 000
Deferred tax liability	20 000	25 000	5 000
Borrowings	120 000	180 000	60 000
Share capital	600 000	680 000	80 000
Retained earnings	60 300	135 000	74 700
	$926 300	$1 154 000	$227 700

SILVER LTD Statement of Profit or Loss and Other Comprehensive Income for the year ended 31 December 2013	
Revenue	
Sales revenue	$1 600 000
Interest	10 000
Share of profits of associate	10 000
Gain on sale of plant	8 000
	$1 628 000

(continued)

FIGURE 19.14 (continued)

Expenses		
Cost of sales	$960 000	
Wages and salaries	240 000	
Depreciation — plant	40 000	
Impairment — intangibles	30 000	
Interest	12 000	
Doubtful debts	8 000	
Other expenses	132 000	1 422 000
Profit before tax		206 000
Income tax expense		(65 000)
Profit for the year		141 000
Other comprehensive income		—
Total comprehensive income		$ 141 000

FIGURE 19.15 Statement of cash flows worksheet

Other information used in worksheet:

(a) Changes in equity:

	Share capital	Retained earnings
Balance at 31 December 2012	$600 000	$ 60 300
Profit for the year	—	141 000
Dividends — cash	—	(36 300)
— reinvested under dividend scheme	30 000	(30 000)
Cash share issue	50 000	—
Balance at 31 December 2013	$680 000	$135 000

(b) Investment in associate (equity method)

Balance at 31 December 2012	$ 40 000
Share of profit of associate	10 000
Dividend received	(5 000)
Balance at 31 December 2013	$ 45 000

(c) Land

Additional land acquired	$ 40 000
Finance provided by vendor	(35 000)
Cash paid	$ 5 000

(d) Plant

Acquisitions	$180 000
Cash paid	171 000
Accounts payable outstanding at year-end	9 000
	$180 000
Disposals — cost	60 000
Accumulated depreciation	(25 000)
Proceeds received in cash	43 000

(e) Intangibles

There were no acquisitions or disposals.

Impairment write-down	$ 30 000

	2012	2013
(f) Accounts payable comprises:		
Purchase of inventory	$ 49 000	$ 56 000
Purchase of plant	15 000	9 000
Other purchases	20 000	25 000
Balance at 31 December	$ 84 000	$ 90 000

FIGURE 19.15 (continued)

(g)	Accrued liabilities comprises accruals for:		
	Interest	1 200	2 100
	Wages, salaries and other expenses	$ 12 800	$ 9 900
	Balance at 31 December	$ 14 000	$ 12 000
(h)	Increase in borrowings of $60 000 reflects:		
	Land vendor finance		$ 35 000
	Additional cash borrowing		25 000
			$ 60 000
(i)	Income tax expense comprises:		
	Currently payable		$ 60 000
	Movement in deferred tax		5 000
			$ 65 000
(j)	Movement in current tax payable:		
	Balance at 31 December 2012		$ 28 000
	Income tax expense		60 000
	Payments made		(56 000)
	Balance at 31 December 2013		$ 32 000

SILVER LTD
Statement of Cash Flows Worksheet
for year ended 31 December 2013

	Balance 31.12.12	Reconciling items				Balance 31.12.13
		Debits		**Credits**		
Cash	$ 60 000	(26) $	9 800			$ 69 800
Short-term deposits	120 000	(27)	20 000			140 000
Accounts receivable, net	140 000	(2)	50 000			190 000
Interest receivable	300			(13)	100	200
Inventory	130 000	(3)	25 000			155 000
Prepayments	16 000	(4)	3 000			19 000
Investment in associate	40 000	(7)	5 000			45 000
Land	80 000	(18)	5 000			
		(19)	35 000			120 000
Plant	300 000	(9)	8 000	(21)	43 000	
		(19)	180 000	(22)	25 000	420 000
Accumulated depreciation	(50 000)	(22)	25 000	(10)	40 000	(65 000)
Intangibles	90 000			(11)	30 000	60 000
	$926 300					$1 154 000
Accounts payable	84 000	(20)	6 000	(5)	12 000	90 000
Accrued liabilities	14 000	(6)	2 900	(14)	900	12 000
Current tax payable	28 000			(16)	4 000	32 000
Deferred tax liability	20 000			(17)	5 000	25 000
Borrowings	120 000			(19)	35 000	
				(22)	25 000	180 000
Share capital	600 000			(23)	50 000	
				(24)	30 000	680 000
Retained earnings	60 300	(15)	65 000	(1)	206 000	
		(24)	30 000			
		(25)	36 300			135 000
	$926 300					$1 154 000

(continued)

FIGURE 19.15 (continued)

	Balance 31.12.12	Reconciling items		Balance 31.12.13
		Debits	Credits	
Statement of cash flows data				
Operating activities				
Profit before tax		**(1)** $206 000		$ 206 000
Increase in accounts receivable			**(2)** $ 50 000	(50 000)
Increase in inventory			**(3)** 25 000	(25 000)
Increase in prepayments			**(4)** 3 000	(3 000)
Increase in accounts payable		**(5)** 12 000		12 000
Decrease in accrued liabilities			**(6)** 2 900	(2 900)
Share of profits of associate			**(7)** 10 000	(10 000)
Interest income			**(8)** 10 000	(10 000)
Gain on sale of plant			**(9)** 8 000	(8 000)
Depreciation — plant		**(10)** 40 000		40 000
Impairment — intangibles		**(11)** 30 000		30 000
Interest expense		**(12)** 12 000		12 000
Cash generated from operations		300 000	108 900	191 100
Interest received		**(8)** 10 000		
		(13) 100		10 100
Dividend received from associate		**(7)** 5 000		5 000
Interest paid		**(14)** 900	**(12)** 12 000	(11 100)
Income tax paid		**(16)** 4 000		
		(17) 5 000	**(15)** 65 000	(56 000)
Net cash from operating activities		325 000	185 900	139 100
Investing activities				
Purchase of land			**(18)** 5 000	(5 000)
Purchase of plant			**(19)** 180 000	
			(20) 6 000	(186 000)
Proceeds from sale of plant		**(21)** 43 000		43 000
Net cash used in investing activities		43 000	191 000	(148 000)
Financing activities				
Proceeds from borrowings		**(22)** 25 000		25 000
Proceeds from share issue		**(23)** 50 000		50 000
Payment of cash dividends			**(25)** 36 300	(36 300)
Net cash flows from financing activities		75 000	36 300	38 700
Net increase in cash and cash equivalents		443 000	413 200	$ 29 800
Increase in cash			**(26)** 9 800	
Increase in short-term deposits			**(27)** 20 000	
		$443 000	$443 000	

19.7.1 Explanation of reconciling adjustments in worksheet

Explanations of the reconciling adjustments made in compiling the statement of cash flows data in figure 19.15 are below.

A — Profit before tax

When using the indirect method of presenting cash flows from operating activities, the profit before tax of $206 000 is the starting point. Accordingly, an adjustment (1) is made to retained earnings to reflect the profit before tax for the year, and a separate adjustment (15) is made for income tax expense.

B — Increase in net accounts receivable

The net increase in accounts receivable of $50 000 reflects the excess of sales revenue over the cash collected from receivables. It must therefore be deducted from profit before tax (adjustment 2). Because the indirect method is being used, there is no need to include separate adjustments for bad debts written off, changes in any allowance for doubtful debts or discounts allowed. Such adjustments are necessary to determine cash flows from customers only under the direct method.

C — Increase in inventory

The increase in inventory of $25 000 results in an operating cash outflow subject to any increase funded through an increase in accounts payable (adjustment 3).

D — Prepayments

The increase in prepayments is an operating cash outflow during the period that is not reflected in profit before tax (adjustment 4).

E — Accounts payable

Accounts payable comprise:

	2012	2013	Increase (decrease)	
Amount arising from the:				
Purchase of inventory and services	$ 69 000	$ 81 000	$12 000	(Adjustment 5)
Purchase of plant	15 000	9 000	(6 000)	(Adjustment 20)
	$ 84 000	$ 90 000	$ 6 000	

The increase in accounts payable arising from the purchase of inventory and services reflects the amount by which the purchases exceed the payments. It does not involve an operating cash outflow for the period. In this example, the increase in accounts payable partly offsets the increase in inventory reflected in adjustment 3.

The reduction in accounts payable arising from the purchase of plant of $6000 increases the cash outflow for the purchase of plant (adjustment 20).

F — Accrued liabilities

Accrued liabilities comprise:

	2012	2013	Increase (decrease)
Amount arising from:			
Accrued interest	$ 1 200	$ 2 100	$ 900
Other	12 800	9 900	(2 900)
	$14 000	$12 000	$(2 000)

The reduction in other accrued liabilities increases the operating cash outflows for the year and is reflected in adjustment 6. The increase in accrued interest payable does not involve a cash flow and is reflected in adjustment 14.

G — Share of profits of associate

The investment in associate (accounted for under the equity method) increased by $5000, comprising the share of profits of the associate of $10 000, net of a dividend received of $5000. The $10 000 share of profits is excluded from cash generated from operations and the $5000 dividend received is included in net cash from operating activities. The $5000 net increase in the investment does not represent a cash flow and this is reflected in the $10 000 adjustment, net of the $5000 dividend (adjustment 7).

H — Interest income

When completing the worksheet, interest income is initially transferred out of profit before tax in order to arrive at cash generated from operations (adjustment 8), and is then increased by the reduction in interest receivable of $100 (adjustment 13) to arrive at the interest cash inflow. Alternatively, the interest cash inflow could be classified as an investing activity.

I — Gain on sale of plant

Note that the accumulated depreciation for the plant sold is transferred to the plant account and that the gross proceeds from the sale of the plant are shown as a credit adjustment. These transfers are consistent with the following journal entries:

Accumulated Depreciation	Dr	25 000	
Plant	Cr		25 000
(Closing accumulated depreciation against the plant account on disposal of the plant)			

The carrying amount of the plant sold is $35 000.

Cash	Dr	43 000	
Plant	Cr		35 000
Gain on Disposal	Cr		8 000
(Disposal of plant)			

Plant is reduced by $35 000, being the net effect of the credit to plant for the cash proceeds from the sale $43 000 (Cr), and debit against plant for the gain on disposal of $8000 (Dr). Gain on disposal of plant of $8000 is not a cash inflow, so it is deducted from profit before tax in arriving at net cash from operating activities (adjustment 9). A separate adjustment is made for the proceeds from sale of plant of $43 000 as an investing cash flow. The reduction in plant for plant sold of $60 000 comprises the following adjustments:

Proceeds	$43 000	(Adjustment 21)
– Gain on sale	(8 000)	(Adjustment 9)
+ Accumulated depreciation	25 000	(Adjustment 22)
Cost of plant sold	$60 000	

J — Depreciation of plant and impairment of intangibles

Both of these expenses in the statement of profit or loss and other comprehensive income do not constitute cash flows in the current period, so they are added back in arriving at net cash from operating activities (depreciation of $40 000 and impairment of $30 000 adjustments 10 and 11, respectively).

K — Interest expense

Interest expense is initially transferred out of profit before tax in order to arrive at cash generated from operations (adjustment 12). It is then reduced by the increase in accrued interest $900 (adjustment 14), to arrive at the interest cash outflow. The calculation is shown earlier in explanation F. Alternatively, the interest cash outflow could be classified as a financing activity.

L — Income tax paid

Income tax expense of $65 000 (adjustment 15) is reduced by the increase in current tax payable of $4000 (adjustment 16) and the increase in deferred income tax of $5000 (adjustment 17) to determine the income tax cash outflow of $56 000. In this example, there are no tax charges — such as on revaluation surplus or translation reserve increases — made directly to equity accounts. This is evident because there are no items of other comprehensive income reported in the statement of profit or loss and other comprehensive income.

M — Purchase of land and plant

Additional land was acquired at a cost of $40 000, with $35 000 being financed by the vendor. Adjustment 18 records the cash outflow of $5000 and adjustment 19 records the non-cash component of $35 000. The other side of the adjustment is made to borrowings.

Plant acquisitions for the year are $180 000 (adjustment 19). This amount is increased by the reduction in plant accounts payable of $6000 (adjustment 20); this is discussed in explanation E.

N — Proceeds from borrowings

The cash proceeds from borrowings of $25 000 comprise the gross increase in borrowings of $60 000 ($180 000 – $120 000) reduced by the $35 000 of land vendor finance (adjustment 19); this is discussed in explanation M.

O — Proceeds from share issue and payment of cash dividends

To determine the proceeds from share issue (adjustment 23), the increase in share capital of $80 000 ($680 000 – $600 000) is reduced by the $30 000 of reinvested dividends (adjustment 24) because these dividends did not involve a cash inflow. Similarly, cash flows from financing activities include only the $36 300 of dividends paid in cash (adjustment 25).

P — Increase in cash and short-term deposits

Short-term deposits are considered to be cash equivalents. Therefore, the increase is included in the net increase in cash and cash equivalents for the period of $29 800 (adjustments 26 and 27).

Figure 19.16 contains Silver Ltd's statement of cash flows for the year ended 31 December 2013 (without prior year comparatives).

FIGURE 19.16 Final statement of cash flows of Silver Ltd

SILVER LTD Statement of Cash Flows for year ended 31 December 2013		
Cash flows from operating activities		
Profit before tax	$ 206 000	
Adjustments for:		
Depreciation	40 000	
Impairment of intangibles	30 000	
Gain on sale of plant	(8 000)	
Share of profits of associate	(10 000)	
Interest income	(10 000)	
Interest expense	12 000	
Increase in receivables	(50 000)	
Increase in inventory	(25 000)	
Increase in prepayments	(3 000)	
Increase in accounts payables	12 000	
Decrease in accrued liabilities	(2 900)	
Cash generated from operations	191 100	
Interest received	10 100	
Dividend received from associate	5 000	
Interest paid	(11 100)	
Income taxes paid	(56 000)	
Net cash from operating activities		$ 139 100
Cash flows from investing activities		
Purchase of land (Note A)	(5 000)	
Purchase of plant	(186 000)	
Proceeds from sale of plant	43 000	
Net cash used in investing activities		(148 000)
Cash flow from financing activities		
Proceeds from borrowings	25 000	
Proceeds from share issue (Note B)	50 000	
Dividends paid (Note B)	(36 300)	
Net cash from financing activities		38 700

(continued)

FIGURE 19.16 (continued)

Net increase in cash and cash equivalents	29 800
Cash and cash equivalents at beginning of year (Note C)	180 000
Cash and cash equivalents at end of year (Note C)	$ 209 800

Notes:

A Land

During the year, land at a cost of $40 000 was acquired by means of vendor finance of $35 000 and a cash payment of $5000.

B Dividends

During the year, shareholders elected to reinvest dividends amounting to $30 000 under the company's dividend share reinvestment scheme. (This information will be reported in the company's statement of changes in equity, so a cross-reference to that statement may be used instead of this note.)

C Cash and cash equivalents

Cash and cash equivalents included in the statement of cash flows comprise the following amounts reported in the statement of financial position:

	2013	2012
Cash	$ 69 800	$ 60 000
Short-term deposits	140 000	120 000
	$209 800	$180 000

The current period, 2013, is shown on the left in the note because it is customary to present the current year first, followed by the comparative figures, reading from left to right. However, comparative data were presented in the worksheets to facilitate working from left to right in calculating movements in line items used to determine cash flows.

If the direct method of presenting operating cash flows is used, the cash receipts from customers and cash paid to suppliers and employees can be determined by reconstructing the relevant general ledger accounts or by using the equations previously given. For the purposes of this example, it is assumed that net accounts receivable comprises:

	2012	2013
Accounts receivable	$160 000	$215 000
Allowance for doubtful debts	(20 000)	(25 000)
	$140 000	$190 000

It is further assumed that bad debts of $3000 were deducted from the allowance for doubtful debts and the remaining allowance for doubtful debts was increased by a charge to profit or loss of $8000 (refer to the statement of profit or loss and other comprehensive income).

As demonstrated previously, the summarised general ledger accounts can be reconstructed from the statement of financial position and supplementary information (opening and closing balances), and statement of profit or loss and other comprehensive income and supplementary information (bad debts and sales). The cash receipts amount is then determined as the balancing figure.

The reconstructed Accounts Receivable and Allowance for Doubtful Debts general ledger accounts would appear as follows:

Accounts Receivable			
Opening balance	160 000	Bad Debts Write-Off	3 000
Sales Revenue	1 600 000	Cash received	1 542 000
		Closing balance	215 000
	1 760 000		1 760 000

Allowance for Doubtful Debts			
Bad Debts Write-Off	3 000	Opening balance	20 000
		Doubtful Debts	
Closing balance	25 000	Expense	8 000
	28 000		28 000

Cash paid to suppliers of inventory can be determined by reconstructing the relevant general ledger accounts. The purchases amount is determined as the difference between the opening and closing balances (obtained from the statement of financial position) and cost of sales (obtained from the statement of profit or loss and other comprehensive income). The determined amount of purchases is then recorded in the Accounts Payable (for inventory) account to calculate the cash payments to suppliers of inventory. This is shown as follows:

Inventory				Accounts Payable – Inventory Purchases			
Opening balance	130 000	Cost of Sales	960 000	Cash payments	978 000	Opening balance	49 000
Purchases	985 000	Closing balance	155 000	Closing balance	56 000	Purchases	985 000
	1 115 000		1 115 000		1 034 000		1 034 000

Cash paid to other suppliers and employees can be similarly determined or found by using the equations previously given. Cash payments to other suppliers and employees comprise:

Wages and salaries	$240 000
Other expenses	132 000
	372 000
Prepayments increase	3 000
Increase (decrease) in accounts payable for other purchases (worksheet note F)	(5 000)
Accruals liabilities	2 900
Total payments to employees and other suppliers of services	$372 900

Using the above calculations, total payments to suppliers and employees comprise:

Payments for:	
Inventory	$ 978 000
Service providers	372 900
	$1 350 900

Using the above calculations, cash flows from operating activities presented under the direct method are shown in figure 19.17.

Cash flow from operating activities:	
Cash received from customers	$ 1 542 000
Cash payments to suppliers and employees	(1 350 900)
Cash generated from operations	191 100
Interest received	10 100
Dividend received from associate	5 000
Interest paid	(11 100)
Income taxes paid	(56 000)
Net cash from operating activities	$ 139 100

FIGURE 19.17 Cash flows from operating activities using the direct method

19.8 EXTRACTS FROM FINANCIAL STATEMENTS

Figure 19.18 shows Billabong International Ltd's cash flow statement (statement of cash flows) for the year ended 30 June 2011. The note disclosing the reconciliation between operating cash flows and profit is illustrated in figure 19.19. Other note disclosures pertaining to the statement of cash flows have been illustrated elsewhere in this chapter and are not reproduced here.

FIGURE 19.18 Statement of cash flows for Billabong International Ltd for the year ended 30 June 2011

	Notes	2011 $'000	2010 $'000
Cash flows from operating activities			
Receipts from customers (inclusive of GST)		1 773 303	1 551 174
Payments to suppliers and employees (inclusive of GST)		(1 673 100)	(1 299 033)
		100 203	252 141
Interest received		2 287	3 319
Other revenue		2 264	3 726
Finance costs		(35 688)	(22 774)
Income taxes paid		(44 730)	(49 165)
Net cash inflow from operating activities	39	24 336	187 247
Cash flows from investing activities			
Payments for purchase of subsidiaries and businesses, net of cash acquired	35	(215 064)	(49 591)
Payments for property, plant and equipment		(43 244)	(53 064)
Payments for intangible assets		(9 126)	(3 393)
Proceeds from sale of property, plant and equipment		499	284
Net cash outflow from investing activities		(266 935)	(105 764)
Cash flows from financing activities			
Payments for treasury shares held by employee share plan trusts		(4 446)	(3 472)
Proceeds from borrowings		956 023	698 832
Repayment of borrowings		(671 674)	(809 333)
Dividends paid	28	(78 952)	(78 129)
Net cash inflow/(outflow) from financing activities		200 951	(192 102)
Net decrease in cash and cash equivalents		(41 648)	(110 619)
Cash and cash equivalents at the beginning of the year		208 742	332 937
Effects of exchange rate changes on cash and cash equivalents		(22 669)	(13 576)
Cash and cash equivalents at the end of the year	9	144 425	208 742

Source: Billabong International Ltd (2011, p. 56).

FIGURE 19.19 Reconciliation between operating cash flows and profit for Billabong International Ltd for the year ended 30 June 2011

Note 39. Reconciliation of profit for the year to net cash inflow from operating activities

	2011 $'000	2010 $'000
Profit for the year, before non-controlling interests	118 045	145 166
Depreciation and amortisation	41 931	35 572
Share-based payment amortisation expense	5 892	5 325
Provisions: unwinding of discount	4 620	2 807
Net loss on sale of non-current assets	699	628
Gain from adjustment to contingent consideration	(1 011)	—
Fair value adjustment to derivative liabilities	(1 521)	—
Net exchange differences	(1 469)	(1 401)
Change in operating assets and liabilities, excluding effects from business combinations:		
(Increase)/decrease in trade debtors	9 440	(46 174)
(Increase)/decrease in inventories	(69 087)	2 002
(Increase)/decrease in deferred tax assets	(16 002)	(6 015)

FIGURE 19.19 *(continued)*

	2011 $'000	2010 $'000
(Increase)/decrease in provision for income taxes receivable	(12 096)	9 370
(Increase)/decrease in other operating assets	(34 006)	21 709
Increase/(decrease) in trade creditors and other operating liabilities	(19 800)	6 468
Increase/(decrease) in provision for income taxes payable	(5 031)	9 142
Increase/(decrease) in deferred tax liabilities	898	4 356
Increase/(decrease) in other provisions	2 834	(1 708)
Net cash inflow from operating activities	24 336	187 247

Source: Billabong International Ltd (2011, p. 121).

SUMMARY

IAS 7 *Statement of Cash Flows* is a disclosure standard requiring the presentation of a statement of cash flows as an integral part of an entity's financial statements. The statement of cash flows is particularly useful to investors, lenders and others when evaluating an entity's ability to generate cash and cash equivalents, and to meet its obligations and pay dividends. The statement is required to report cash flows classified into operating, investing and financing activities, as well as the net movement in cash and cash equivalents during the period. Net cash flows from operating activities may be presented using either the direct or the indirect method of presentation. IAS 7 requires additional information to be presented elsewhere in the financial statements concerning investing and financing activities that do not involve cash flows and are therefore excluded from a statement of cash flows. The standard also requires additional disclosures relating to the cash flow effects of obtaining or losing control of subsidiaries and other businesses.

Discussion questions

1. What is the purpose of a statement of cash flows?
2. How might a statement of cash flows be used?
3. What is the meaning of 'cash equivalent'?
4. Explain the required classifications of cash flows under IAS 7.
5. What sources of information are usually required to prepare a statement of cash flows?
6. Explain the differences between the presentation of cash flows from operating activities under the direct method and their presentation under the indirect method. Do you consider one method to be more useful than the other? Why?
7. The statement of cash flows is said to be of assistance in evaluating the financial strength of an entity, yet the statement can exclude significant non-cash transactions that can materially affect the financial strength of an entity. How does IAS 7 seek to overcome this issue?
8. An entity may report significant profits over a number of successive years and still experience negative net cash flows from its operating activities. How can this happen?
9. An entity may report significant accounting losses over a number of successive years and still report positive net cash flows from operating activities over the same period. How can this happen?
10. What supplementary disclosures are required when a consolidated statement of cash flows is being prepared for a group that has obtained or lost control of a subsidiary?

Exercises

STAR RATING ★ BASIC ★★ MODERATE ★★★ DIFFICULT

Exercise 19.1

CASH RECEIVED FROM CUSTOMERS

★ At 30 June 2012, Ruby Ltd had net accounts receivable of $180 000. At 30 June 2013, accounts receivable were $220 000 and sales for the year amounted to $1 800 000. Doubtful debts expense was $5000 for the year. Discount allowed was $3000 for the year.

Required

Calculate cash received from customers by Ruby Ltd for the year ended 30 June 2013.

Exercise 19.2 CASH PAYMENTS TO SUPPLIERS

★ Purple Ltd had the following balances:

	30 June 2012	30 June 2013
Inventory	$170 000	$210 000
Accounts payable for inventory purchases	51 000	65 000

Cost of sales was $1 700 000 for the year ended 30 June 2013.

Required

Calculate cash payments to suppliers for the year ended 30 June 2013.

Exercise 19.3 CASH RECEIVED FROM CUSTOMERS

★ At 30 June 2012, Orange Ltd had accounts receivable of $200 000. At 30 June 2013, accounts receivable were $240 000 and sales for the year amounted to $2 100 000. Bad debts amounting to $50 000 had been written off during the year, and discounts of $17 000 had been allowed in respect of payments from customers made within prescribed credit terms. Orange Ltd did not have an allowance for doubtful debts in either year.

Required

Calculate cash received from customers for the year ended 30 June 2013.

Exercise 19.4 INVESTING CASH FLOWS

★ The following information has been compiled from the accounting records of Navy Ltd for the year ended 30 June 2013:

Purchase of land, with the vendor financing $100 000 for 2 years	$350 000
Purchase of plant	250 000
Sale of plant:	
Carrying amount	50 000
Cash proceeds	42 000

Required

Determine the amount of investing net cash outflows Navy Ltd would report in its statement of cash flows for the year ended 30 June 2013.

Exercise 19.5 FINANCING CASH FLOWS

★ The following information has been compiled from the accounting records of Mustard Ltd for the year ended 30 June 2013:

Dividends — paid	$200 000
— dividend reinvestment scheme	120 000
Additional cash borrowing	300 000
Issue of shares — cash	300 000
— dividend reinvestment	120 000

Required

Determine the amount of net cash from financing activities Mustard Ltd would report in its statement of cash flows for the year ended 30 June 2013.

PREPARATION OF A STATEMENT OF CASH FLOWS

★ A summarised comparative statement of financial position of Green Ltd is presented below:

	30 June 2012	30 June 2013
Cash	$ 40 000	$ 55 000
Trade receivables	92 000	140 000
Investments	35 000	30 000
Plant	130 000	180 000
Accumulated depreciation	(45 000)	(60 000)
	$252 000	$345 000
Trade accounts payable	$ 75 000	$ 95 000
Deferred tax liability		3 000
Share capital	100 000	150 000
Retained earnings	77 000	90 000
Investment revaluation reserve	—	7 000
	$252 000	$345 000

Additional information
(a) An investment was sold for $15 000. There was no gain or loss accumulated in the investment revaluation reserve in respect of this investment.
(b) There were no disposals of plant.
(c) The profit for the year was $60 000, after income tax expense of $30 000.
(d) A dividend of $47 000 was paid during the year.
(e) The only item of other comprehensive income was a gain on revaluation of available-for-sale investments and its associated tax effect.

Required

Using the indirect method of presenting cash flows from operating activities, prepare a statement of cash flows in accordance with IAS 7 for the year ended 30 June 2013.

PREPARATION OF A STATEMENT OF CASH FLOWS

★ A summarised comparative statement of financial position of Fuchsia Ltd is presented below:

	30 June 2012	30 June 2013
Cash	$ 20 000	$ 91 000
Trade accounts receivable	65 000	90 000
Inventory	58 000	62 000
Prepayments	10 000	12 000
Land	80 000	90 000
Plant	280 000	320 000
Accumulated depreciation	(60 000)	(92 000)
	$453 000	$573 000
Accounts payable	$ 45 000	$ 48 000
Borrowings	160 000	200 000
Share capital	200 000	230 000
Retained earnings	48 000	95 000
	$453 000	$573 000

Additional information
(a) There were no disposals of land or plant during the year.
(b) A $30 000 borrowing was settled through the issue of ordinary shares. There were no other repayments of borrowings.
(c) Profit for the year was $120 000, interest expense was $14 000, and income tax expense was $41 000. There were no items of other comprehensive income.

(d) A $73 000 dividend was paid during the year.

(e) Sales revenue for the year was $300 000. There was no other revenue.

Required

1. Using the indirect method of presenting cash flows from operating activities, prepare a statement of cash flows in accordance with IAS 7 for the year ended 30 June 2013.
2. Prepare the operating section of the statement of cash flows using the direct method.

Exercise 19.8

★ **PRESENTATION OF A STATEMENT OF CASH FLOWS**

A summarised comparative statement of financial position of Denim Ltd is presented below, together with the statement of profit or loss and other comprehensive income for the year ended 30 June 2013:

	30 June 2012	30 June 2013
Cash	$ 30 000	$ 68 000
Trade receivables	46 000	70 000
Inventory	30 000	32 000
Investments	35 000	40 000
Plant	125 000	150 000
Accumulated depreciation	(23 000)	(35 000)
	$243 000	$325 000
Accounts payable	$ 39 000	$ 43 000
Accrued interest	3 000	5 000
Current tax payable	10 000	12 000
Deferred tax liability	—	1 500
Borrowings	60 000	100 000
Share capital	100 000	100 000
Retained earnings	31 000	60 000
Investment revaluation reserve	—	3 500
	$243 000	$325 000

Statement of Profit or Loss and Other Comprehensive Income
for the year ended 30 June 2013

Sales	$ 700 000
Cost of sales	(483 000)
Gross profit	217 000
Distribution costs	(62 000)
Administration costs	(74 000)
Interest	(6 000)
Profit before tax	75 000
Income tax expense	(23 000)
Profit for the year	52 000
Other comprehensive income	
Gain on revaluation of investments (net of tax)	3 500
Total comprehensive income	$ 55 500

Additional information

(a) There were no disposals of investments or plant during the year.

(b) A dividend of $23 000 was paid during the year.

(c) The deferred tax liability is in relation to investments.

Required

Using the direct method of presenting cash flows from operating activities, prepare a statement of cash flows in accordance with IAS 7 for the year ended 30 June 2013.

Exercise 19.9 NET INVESTING CASH FLOWS

★★ The statement of financial position of Lilac Ltd at 30 June 2013 recorded the following items:

	30 June 2012	30 June 2013
Land, at independent valuation	$100 000	$120 000
Plant, at cost	70 000	85 000
Accumulated depreciation	(20 000)	(28 000)
Available-for-sale listed investments, at fair value	30 000	40 000
Goodwill	25 000	20 000
Land revaluation surplus	20 000	34 000
Investments revaluation reserve	5 000	11 000
Additional information		
Impairment of goodwill	—	5 000

(a) There were no acquisitions or disposals of land.
(b) There were no disposals of plant or investments.
(c) The land revaluation surplus increase is net of deferred tax of $6000.
(d) The investments revaluation reserve increase for the year is net of deferred tax of $2000.

Required

Prepare the investing section of the statement of cash flows for Lilac Ltd for the year ended 30 June 2013.

Exercise 19.10 NET FINANCING CASH FLOWS

★★ The following information has been extracted from the accounting records of Jade Ltd:

	30 June 2012	30 June 2013
Borrowings	$100 000	$200 000
Share capital	200 000	250 000
Property revaluation surplus	50 000	60 000
Retained earnings	75 000	95 000

Additional information
(a) Borrowings of $20 000 were repaid during the year to 30 June 2013. New borrowings include $80 000 vendor finance arising on the acquisition of a property.
(b) The increase in share capital includes $30 000 arising from the company's dividend reinvestment scheme.
(c) The movement in retained earnings comprises profit for the year $90 000, net of dividends $70 000.
(d) There were no dividends payable reported in the statement of financial position at either 30 June 2012 or 30 June 2013.

Required

Prepare the financing section of the statement of cash flows for Jade Ltd for the year ended 30 June 2013.

Exercise 19.11 CASH RECEIPTS FROM CUSTOMERS AND CASH PAID TO SUPPLIERS AND EMPLOYEES

★★★ The accounting records of Indigo Ltd recorded the following information:

	30 June 2012	30 June 2013
Accounts receivable	$40 000	$ 50 000
Inventories	32 000	34 000
Prepaid expenses	1 000	3 000
Accounts payable for inventory purchased	15 000	16 000
Employee liabilities	5 000	5 500

(continued)

	30 June 2012	30 June 2013
Other accruals (including accrued interest: 2012 — $700; 2013 — $850)	4 000	3 800
Sales revenue		600 000
Cost of sales		480 000
Expenses (including $5000 depreciation and $2000 interest)		75 000

Required

1. Calculate the amount of cash received from customers during the year ended 30 June 2013.
2. Calculate the amount of cash paid to suppliers and employees during the year ended 30 June 2013.

Exercise 19.12 **PREPARATION OF A STATEMENT OF CASH FLOWS**

★★ A summarised comparative statement of financial position of Crimson Ltd is presented below:

	30 June 2012	30 June 2013
Cash	$ 96 000	$ 49 000
Accounts receivable (net)	147 000	163 000
Prepayments	20 000	15 000
Inventory	60 000	104 000
Land	40 000	40 000
Plant	368 000	420 000
Accumulated depreciation	(45 000)	(70 000)
Deferred tax asset	20 000	24 000
	$706 000	$745 000
Accounts payable	$140 000	$152 000
Accrued liabilities	36 000	42 000
Current tax payable	24 000	31 000
Dividend payable	56 000	50 000
Borrowings	73 000	75 000
Share capital	335 000	345 000
Retained earnings	42 000	50 000
	$706 000	$745 000

Additional information
(a) Plant additions amounted to $72 000. Plant with a carrying amount value of $15 000 (cost $20 000, accumulated depreciation $5000) was sold for $22 000. The proceeds for the sale of plant had not been received by 30 June 2013.
(b) Accounts payable at 30 June 2012 include $34 000 arising from the acquisition of plant.
(c) Accrued liabilities include accrued interest of $3000 at 30 June 2012 and $4000 at 30 June 2013.
(d) The increase in share capital of $10 000 arose from the reinvestment of dividends.
(e) The profit for the year ended 30 June 2013 was $92 000, after interest expense of $6000 and income tax expense of $46 000. There were no other items of comprehensive income.
(f) Dividends declared out of profits for the year were: interim dividend $34 000, final dividend $50 000.

Required

Using the indirect method of presenting cash flows from operating activities, prepare a statement of cash flows in accordance with IAS 7 for the year ended 30 June 2013.

Exercise 19.13 **PREPARATION OF A STATEMENT OF CASH FLOWS**

★★ A summarised comparative statement of financial position of Bronze Ltd is presented opposite, together with a statement of profit or loss and other comprehensive income for the year ended 30 June 2013.

	30 June 2012	30 June 2013
Cash	$ 45 000	$ 35 000
Trade receivables	69 000	105 000
Allowance for doubtful debts	(3 000)	(6 000)
Inventory	45 000	67 000
Available-for-sale investments	53 000	60 000
Plant	187 000	225 000
Accumulated depreciation	(35 000)	(53 000)
	$361 000	$433 000
Accounts payable	$ 65 000	$ 75 000
Accrued interest	5 000	7 000
Current tax payable	15 000	18 000
Deferred tax	30 000	37 000
Borrowings	80 000	100 000
Share capital	100 000	100 000
Investment revaluation reserve	2 000	7 000
Retained earnings	64 000	89 000
	$361 000	$433 000

Statement of Profit or Loss and Other Comprehensive Income for the year ended 30 June 2013	
Sales	$1 035 000
Cost of sales	(774 000)
Gross profit	261 000
Distribution costs	(76 000)
Administration costs	(96 000)
Interest expense	(7 000)
Profit before tax	82 000
Income tax expense	(24 000)
Profit for the year	58 000
Other comprehensive income	
Gain on revaluation of investments (net of tax)	5 000
Total comprehensive income	$ 63 000

Additional information
(a) The movement in the allowance for doubtful debts for the year comprises:

Balance at 30 June 2012	$ 3 000
Charge for year	5 000
Bad debts written off	(2 000)
Balance at 30 June 2013	6 000

(b) Available-for-sale investments are measured at fair value, with increases/decreases being recognised in other comprehensive income, and accumulated in the investment revaluation reserve until investments are sold.
(c) There were no disposals of plant during the year.
(d) A dividend of $33 000 was paid during the year.
(e) There were no acquisitions or disposals of investments during the year.

Required
1. Using the direct method of presenting cash flows from operating activities, prepare a statement of cash flows in accordance with IAS 7 for the year ended 30 June 2013.
2. Prepare the operating activities section of the statement of cash flows using the indirect method of presentation.

PREPARATION OF A STATEMENT OF CASH FLOWS

★★ A comparative statement of financial position of Aqua Ltd is presented below:

	30 June 2012	30 June 2013
Cash	$120 000	$ 218 000
Trade receivables	184 000	204 000
Inventory	100 000	160 000
Land (at valuation)	50 000	62 000
Plant	460 000	520 000
Accumulated depreciation	(90 000)	(120 000)
	$824 000	$1 044 000
Accounts payable	$150 000	$ 155 000
Accrued interest	12 000	16 000
Other accrued liabilities	45 000	43 000
Current tax payable	30 000	34 000
Provision for employee benefits	38 000	42 000
Dividend payable	—	60 000
Borrowings	95 000	105 000
Deferred tax liability	58 000	39 000
Share capital	350 000	380 000
Revaluation surplus	12 000	20 000
Retained earnings	34 000	150 000
	$824 000	$1 044 000

Statement of Profit or Loss and Other Comprehensive Income for the year ended 30 June 2013	
Sales	$ 3 580 000
Cost of sales	(2 864 000)
Gross profit	716 000
Gain on sale of plant	16 000
Dividend income	4 000
Distribution costs	(185 000)
Administrative costs	(160 000)
Interest expense	(8 000)
Other costs	(40 000)
Profit before tax	343 000
Income tax expense	(103 000)
Profit for the year	240 000
Other comprehensive income	
Gain on asset revaluation (net of tax)	8 000
Total comprehensive income	$ 248 000

Additional information
(a) The increase to the revaluation surplus is net of deferred tax of $4000.
(b) Plant with a carrying amount of $60 000 (cost $85 000, accumulated depreciation $25 000) was sold for $76 000.
(c) Accounts payable at 30 June 2013 include $22 000 in respect of plant acquisitions.
(d) There were repayments of borrowings of $30 000 during the year.
(e) The increase in share capital of $30 000 arose from the company's dividend reinvestment scheme.
(f) Dividends declared out of profits for the year were: interim dividend $64 000, final dividend $60 000.

Required

Using the direct method of presenting cash flows from operating activities, prepare a statement of cash flows in accordance with IAS 7 for the year ended 30 June 2013, including a reconciliation of cash flows arising from operating activities to profit.

PREPARATION OF STATEMENT OF CASH FLOWS INFORMATION

★★ The statement of profit or loss and other comprehensive income and comparative statements of financial position of Amber Ltd are as follows:

AMBER LTD
Statement of Financial Position
as at 31 December

	2012	2013
Current assets		
Deposits at call	$ 19 000	$ 30 000
Accounts receivable	340 000	320 000
Allowance for doubtful debts	(19 000)	(15 000)
Inventory	654 000	670 000
Prepayments	52 000	55 000
	$1 046 000	$1 060 000
Non-current assets		
Land	$ 400 000	$ 400 000
Buildings	1 175 000	1 850 000
Accumulated depreciation — buildings	(200 000)	(235 000)
Plant	850 000	940 000
Accumulated depreciation — plant	(375 000)	(452 000)
	1 850 000	2 503 000
Total assets	$2 896 000	$3 563 000
Current liabilities		
Bank overdraft	$ 140 000	$ 49 000
Accounts payable	553 000	570 000
Interest payable	25 000	30 000
Final dividend payable	205 000	230 000
Current tax payable	70 000	77 000
	993 000	956 000
Non-current liabilities		
Borrowings	900 000	1 300 000
Deferred tax liability	12 000	16 000
	912 000	1 316 000
Total liabilities	1 905 000	2 272 000
Equity		
Share capital	800 000	1 000 000
Retained earnings	191 000	291 000
	991 000	1 291 000
Total liabilities and equity	$2 896 000	$3 563 000

AMBER LTD
Statement of Profit or Loss and Other Comprehensive Income
for the year ended 31 December 2013

Sales	$ 8 550 000
Less: Cost of sales	4 517 000
Gross profit	4 033 000
Gain on sale of plant	18 000
	4 051 000

(continued)

Distribution costs	(1 635 000)
Administration costs	(1 566 000)
Interest	(70 000)
Profit before tax	780 000
Income tax expense	(250 000)
Profit for the period	530 000
Other comprehensive income	—
Total comprehensive income	$ 530 000

The following additional information has been extracted from the accounting records of Amber Ltd:

1. Movement in allowance for doubtful debts:

Balance 31 December 2012	$ 19 000
Charge for year	7 000
Bad debts written off	(11 000)
Balance 31 December 2013	$ 15 000

2. Building additions were completed. There were no disposals.

3. The movement in plant and accumulated depreciation on plant comprised:

	Cost	Accumulated depreciation
Balance 31 December 2012	$ 850 000	$ 375 000
Additions — cash	160 000	—
Disposals	(70 000)	(50 000)
Depreciation	—	127 000
Balance 31 December 2013	$ 940 000	$ 452 000

4. There was no outstanding interest payable at year-end.

5. Income tax expense comprised:

Income tax currently payable	$ 246 000
Deferred income tax	4 000
	$ 250 000

6. Additional cash borrowings | $ 400 000 |

7. Movement in equity

	Share capital	Retained earnings
Balance 31 December 2012	$ 800 000	$ 191 000
Additional shares issued for cash	200 000	—
Profit for the period	—	530 000
Interim dividend — cash	—	(200 000)
Final dividend payable	—	(230 000)
Balance 31 December 2013	$1 000 000	$ 291 000

Required

1. Prepare a summary of cash flows from operating activities using the indirect method of presentation.
2. Prepare a summary of cash flows from investing activities.
3. Prepare a summary of cash flows from financing activities.
4. Prepare a summary of cash flows from operating activities using the direct method of presentation.

PREPARING A STATEMENT OF CASH FLOWS WITH NOTES

★★★ The statement of profit or loss and other comprehensive income and comparative statements of financial position of Blue Ltd were as follows:

BLUE LTD
Statement of Financial Position
as at 31 December

	2012	2013
Current assets		
Cash at bank	$ 46 000	$ 52 000
Cash deposits (30-day)	40 000	70 000
Accounts receivable	110 000	117 000
Allowance for doubtful debts	(12 000)	(16 000)
Interest receivable	2 000	3 000
Inventory	294 000	320 000
Prepayments	13 000	9 000
	493 000	555 000
Non-current assets		
Land	100 000	140 000
Plant	600 000	700 000
Accumulated depreciation	(140 000)	(180 000)
Investments in associate	80 000	92 000
Brand names	120 000	90 000
	760 000	842 000
Total assets	$1 253 000	$1 397 000
Current liabilities		
Accounts payable	$ 180 000	$ 196 000
Accrued liabilities	85 000	92 000
Current tax payable	40 000	43 000
Current portion of long-term borrowings	20 000	20 000
	325 000	351 000
Non-current liabilities		
Borrowings	98 000	138 000
Deferred tax liability	35 000	40 000
Provision for employee benefits	40 000	43 000
	173 000	221 000
Total liabilities	498 000	572 000
Equity		
Share capital	500 000	530 000
Retained earnings	255 000	295 000
	755 000	825 000
Total liabilities and equity	$1 253 000	$1 397 000

BLUE LTD
Statement of Profit or Loss and Other Comprehensive Income
for the year ended 31 December 2013

Sales	$ 1 780 000
Cost of sales	(1 030 000)
Gross profit	750 000
Interest	2 000

(continued)

Share of profits of associate	20 000
Gain on sale of plant	8 000
Total income	780 000
Expenses	
Salaries and wages	(352 000)
Depreciation	(50 000)
Discount allowed	(8 000)
Doubtful debts	(6 000)
Interest	(21 000)
Other (including impairment of brand names $30 000)	(186 000)
Profit before tax	157 000
Income tax expense	(47 000)
Profit for the period	110 000
Other comprehensive income	—
Total comprehensive income	$ 110 000

The following additional information has been extracted from the accounting records of Blue Ltd:

1.	30-day cash deposits are used in the course of the daily cash management of the company.	
2.	Movement in allowance for doubtful debts:	
	Balance 31 December 2012	$ 12 000
	Charge for year	6 000
	Bad debts written off	(2 000)
	Balance 31 December 2013	$ 16 000
3.	Land	
	Additional cash purchase	$ 40 000
4.	Plant	
	Purchases for year (including $50 000 purchase financed by vendor)	$150 000
5.	Disposals	
	Cost of disposals	$ 50 000
	Accumulated depreciation	(10 000)
6.	Investments in associate	
	Share of profit	$ 20 000
	Dividends received	8 000
7.	Accounts payable	
	Includes amounts owing in respect of plant purchases:	
	31 December 2012	$ 12 000
	31 December 2013	18 000
8.	Accrued liabilities	
	Includes accrued interest payable:	
	31 December 2012	$ 4 000
	31 December 2013	5 000
9.	Income tax expense comprises:	
	Current tax payable	$ 42 000
	Deferred tax	5 000
	Income tax expense	$ 47 000
10.	Dividends paid	
	Under a dividend reinvestment scheme, shareholders have the right to receive additional shares in lieu of cash dividends. Dividends paid comprised:	
	Dividends paid in cash during the year	$ 40 000
	Dividends reinvested	30 000
	Total dividends	$ 70 000

1. Using the direct method of presenting cash flows from operating activities, prepare a statement of cash flows in accordance with IAS 7 for the year ended 31 December 2013.
2. Prepare a note reconciling profit to cash flows from operating activities.
3. Prepare any other notes to the statement of cash flows that you consider are required by IAS 7.

Exercise 19.17	DISCLOSURE OF INFORMATION ABOUT CASH FLOWS
★★★	Refer to the following extract of a media release issued by Billabong International Ltd.

ASX ANNOUNCEMENT

STRATEGIC CAPITAL STRUCTURE REVIEW UPDATE

Billabong today unveils a number of initiatives as a result of the strategic capital structure review announced on 19 December, 2011.

The review assessed measures to strengthen the company's capital structure in light of the difficult operating environment in retail markets worldwide. Alternatives considered included full and partial brand sales, pro rata and non-pro rata ordinary equity raisings, convertible equity raisings and operational improvements.

The review has resulted in initiatives that include:
- the partial sale of Nixon Inc. ('Nixon');
- a review of the Group's retail network with a view to closing loss-making stores and stores performing below expectations;
- a cost-cutting program; and
- a reduced dividend and fully underwritten dividend reinvestment plan.

The outcomes of the review will significantly strengthen the company's financial position.

Partial sale of Nixon

Billabong has entered into definitive agreements with Trilantic Capital Partners ('TCP') to establish a joint venture for Nixon. Under the joint venture, Billabong will retain 48.5% of Nixon, while TCP will purchase 48.5% and Nixon's management will purchase 3.0%.

There are numerous strategic benefits of the transaction to Billabong:
- **Addresses Billabong's capital structure issues:** The partial sale represents an enterprise value of approximately US$464 million for Nixon and results in net proceeds to Billabong of approximately US$285 million[1]. 100% of net proceeds will be used to pay down debt. This transaction is expected to result in a significant one-off gain in the Group's income statement in the year ending 30 June 2012, which cannot be calculated at this point in time as the transaction has not been completed.
- **Highly attractive multiple:** The offer represents a multiple of approximately 9.2x LTM EBITDA[2], reflecting the strength of the Nixon brand and the value inherent within Billabong's portfolio of brands.
- **Billabong retains exposure to future upside in Nixon:** As an ongoing 48.5% shareholder in Nixon, Billabong will continue to benefit from the strong forecast future growth of the Nixon brand. In addition, Billabong has the opportunity to share in proceeds in the future from any potential further sell-down.
- **Billabong retains a supply agreement:** Billabong has secured a long-term supply agreement with Nixon going forward, providing ongoing access to Nixon product for company-owned retail stores.
- **Nixon able to focus on growth:** Nixon will be a stand-alone business focussed on continued growth into areas such as Billabong's core action sports channel, as well as high-end department stores, quality electronics stores and other channels.

As a result of the transaction, Nixon will no longer be consolidated in Billabong's accounts. The loss of Nixon's earnings contribution will be more than offset by Billabong's share of JV profits and the benefits which will flow from the other initiatives announced today.

[1] *Net proceeds are net of all transaction costs and taxes. Net proceeds are pending receipt of final tax opinions and may reduce by up to US$45 million. Billabong has sought advice in advance from the relevant tax authorities.*
[2] *Last twelve months earnings before interest, tax, depreciation and amortisation to 31 December, 2011 of US$50.6 million.*

The transaction is expected to close within 90 days, subject to certain anti-trust approval and customary closing conditions.

Closure of underperforming retail stores

Billabong continues to believe in its multi-brand retail strategy that complements the company's wholesale business.

Billabong has 677 company owned stores worldwide and more than 11,000 wholesale doors. The company's profitable stores had an average EBITDA margin of 17.8% in the first half of FY 2012. However, there are also a number of loss-making or under-performing stores, whose weak performance has been largely driven by the challenging retail environment.

As such, Billabong is undertaking a review of its retail network with a view to closing loss-making stores and stores performing below expectations. While the review remains a work in progress, it is expected that the number of store closures will fall somewhere in the range of 100 to 150 stores.

It is expected that some of the leases associated with the stores to be closed are due for renewal by 30 June, 2013. Billabong will either not renew or accelerate the exit from these leases.

As part of this review, Billabong is targeting a range of A$20 million to A$30 million reduction in rent expense and a resultant increase in EBITDA in the range of A$5 million to A$10 million for FY 2013. The closures will result in a one-off charge in the company's income statement in FY 2012, which cannot be calculated at this point in time.

Cost reduction program

From and including FY 2013, Billabong will reduce annual costs by approximately A$30 million. The savings will come from all regions and all areas of the business, including head office overheads; supply chain rationalisation; retail corporate overheads; and streamlining the company's marketing expenditure.

The store closures mentioned above and the cost reduction program will result in full-time and casual job losses. Full-time job losses will be approximately 400 worldwide, including up to 80 in Australia. The company will seek to minimise forced job losses by redeploying staff from closed stores to other Billabong retail stores wherever possible and through natural staff attrition. The fluctuating nature of seasonal retail and the timing of store closures will impact the ultimate number of casual job losses.

Dividend reduction and underwritten dividend reinvestment plan

Given the uncertain operating environment, Billabong will reduce its dividend payout ratio for the FY 2012 interim dividend to approximately 25% and re-implement its dividend reinvestment plan, which will be fully underwritten.

Recent events

The Board considers it needed a certain transaction to address Billabong's balance sheet issues, in particular to avoid any potential breach of its bank covenants. It was concluded that the partial sale of Nixon was the best of the actionable available alternatives and hence in the best interest of the company and its shareholders. Billabong undertook a competitive process over several months in order to achieve a binding and definitive agreement for the partial sale of Nixon.

Earlier this week, the company received a non-binding, indicative proposal from TPG Capital to acquire all of the shares in the company for A$3.00 cash per share. That proposal was not certain — it was subject to due diligence, subject to finance and conditional on a number of other matters, including Billabong not selling down its ownership interest in any of its brands, and exclusivity. In the absence of certainty, Billabong has proceeded with the partial sale of Nixon in order to stabilise its balance sheet.

The Board continues to be prepared to engage with any party that makes a proposal which is in the best interest of the company and its shareholders.

Goldman Sachs is acting as financial advisor to Billabong.

MARIA MANNING
COMPANY SECRETARY

Source: Manning, M (2012).

Required

Assume that Billabong International Ltd implemented the four strategic initiatives referred to in the media release during the year ended 30 June 2012. Explain how each of these initiatives would be expected to affect the group's cash flows and how information about these impacts would be reported in accordance with IAS 7.

References

Billabong International Ltd 2011, *2010/2011 Full financial report*, Billabong International Limited, Australia, www.billabongbiz.com.

Manning M 2012, *Strategic capital structure review update*, media release, Billabong International Ltd, Burleigh Heads, 17 February.

20

Earnings per share

| ACCOUNTING STANDARDS IN FOCUS | IAS 33 *Earnings per Share* |

LEARNING OBJECTIVES

After studying this chapter, you should be able to:

1 explain the objective of IAS 33

2 discuss the application and scope of IAS 33

3 discuss the components of basic earnings per share and examine how it is measured

4 explain the concept of diluted earnings per share and how it is measured

5 explain the need for retrospective adjustment of earnings per share

6 describe and apply the disclosure requirements of IAS 33.

20.1 INTRODUCTION

Earnings per share, commonly known as *EPS*, is a ratio that is calculated by comparing an entity's profit with the number of ordinary shares it has on issue. The earnings per share ratio is used to compare the after-tax profit available to ordinary shareholders of an entity on a per share basis, with that of other entities.

The purpose of this chapter is to examine and understand the earnings per share information that is presented in a reporting entity's financial statements. In an effort to improve the information provided by reporting entities, and with the objective of improving the consistency of comparisons between entities and across different time periods, IAS 33 prescribes the principles for the computation and the presentation of earnings per share.

Under paragraph 10 of IAS 33, the approach taken to the calculation of the earnings per share ratio is to divide profit or loss (earnings) attributable to ordinary shareholders of a parent entity, by the weighted average number of ordinary shares the entity has on issue (outstanding) during the reporting period. 'Profit' is the numerator (top line) in the calculation and 'outstanding shares' is the denominator (bottom line). The resultant ratio is known as 'basic earnings per share', and the objective of providing this information is to show a measure of the interests of an ordinary shareholder in the performance (profit) of an entity across a reporting period.

The earnings per share ratio has other important uses including as an indicator of future performance and growth. Earnings revisions which impact on earnings per share (EPS), whether they indicate improvements or downgrades, provide information to the market and are usually reflected in a changing share price. Earnings per share is also used as a key performance indicator when determining the remuneration entitlements of directors and executives. For example, Billabong International Ltd uses earnings per share targets as performance hurdles when determining entitlements to long-term incentive bonuses. Billabong International Ltd's remuneration approach is presented in figure 20.1.

> Billabong's shareholders have considerable experience of how currency fluctuations can have a major impact on reported profitability. These currency movements also impact some, but not all, aspects of individual executive performance and reward.
> - For 2011–12, 50% of LTI (Long Term Incentive Plan) will be based on Earnings per Share (EPS) with the remaining 50% on Total Shareholder Return (TSR).
> - Hence movements in the dollar against other currencies directly affect an Executive's LTI, both positively and negatively and links any incentive with shareholder returns.
>   In contrast, results for judging STI at a regional level are assessed in constant currency where currency swings have no effect. Subsequently executives who achieve their relevant Key Performance Indicators (KPIs) have earned their STI even if results, when translated to dollars, are below target.
>   In this way the remuneration structure strives to achieve a balance between retaining, motivating and rewarding individual performance and ensuring a robust linkage to overall company performance and shareholder returns.

FIGURE 20.1 Billabong International Ltd's remuneration report
Source: Billabong International Ltd (2011, p. 12).

The utility of earnings per share has been criticised because of the flexibility that entities have in choosing accounting methods when determining their profit. While accounting policy *choice* enables entities to select the accounting methods that are the most appropriate to reflect their actual business operations, it results in inconsistencies between entities in the determination of their profit. For example, entities may select the depreciation method that best reflects the pattern of usage of their physical assets (see IAS 16 *Property, Plant and Equipment*, paragraph 60). If one entity chooses the straight-line method then a constant charge is made against its profit across the useful life of its assets. However, if another entity selects the diminishing balance method, then the expense charged against its profit will decrease over its assets' useful lives. Therefore, it must be recognised that earnings per share data disclosed by reporting entities have limitations because of the different accounting methods that can be used in the determination of profit.

Another limitation to the utility of the earnings per share ratio for comparison purposes is that it can be altered simply by changing the number of shares used in the denominator. The focus taken in IAS 33 is that a consistently determined denominator in the earnings per share calculation enhances financial reporting (paragraph 1). Despite the limitations of earnings per share as an indicator of the performance of an entity, it is widely used in share analysis.

 ## 20.2 APPLICATION AND SCOPE

IAS 33 applies to the computation and presentation of earnings per share by reporting entities whose shares are publicly traded, or of entities that are in the process of issuing ordinary shares that will be traded in public markets (paragraph 1). The first IAS version of an accounting standard dealing with earnings per share was issued with an effective date for financial statements covering periods beginning on or after 1 January 1999. IAS 33 has since been amended on several occasions. The most recent amendments effective from 1 January 2013 provided for consequential amendments arising from IAS 1 and the consolidation and joint arrangement standards (IFRS 10, IFRS 11, IFRS 12, IAS 127 and IAS 128).

IAS 33 applies to entities that are required to disclose earnings per share. Under paragraph 4, if an entity presents both consolidated and separate financial statements, the IAS 33 disclosures need only be determined on the basis of consolidated information. As the parent entity earnings per share information may be helpful to some users, entities have the option of also disclosing earnings per share figures for the parent entity. However this information can only be presented in the parent's separate financial statements and not in the consolidated financial statements (IAS 33 BC paragraphs 5, 6). The earnings per share information presented by Billabong International Ltd in its 2011 income statement is presented in figure 20.2.

Earnings per share for profit attributable to the ordinary equity holders of the Company			
	Notes	2011 Cents	2010 Cents
Basic earnings per share	41	47.4	58.3
Diluted earnings per share	41	47.0	57.8

FIGURE 20.2 Earnings per share disclosed in income statement of Billabong International Ltd
Source: Billabong International Ltd (2011, p. 52).

 ## 20.3 BASIC EARNINGS PER SHARE

As mentioned, earnings per share is measured by dividing profit (or loss) attributable to ordinary shareholders by the weighted average number of ordinary shares outstanding during the period. This measurement approach, which results in a ratio known as 'basic' earnings per share (paragraph 9), is demonstrated in figure 20.3.

$$\frac{\text{Profit attributable to ordinary shareholders of the parent entity}}{\text{Weighted average number of ordinary shares outstanding during the reporting period}}$$

FIGURE 20.3 Basic earnings per share ratio

20.3.1 Earnings

The profit or loss (profit) that is used in the calculation of basic earnings per share must be from continuing operations. It must also include any income or expense attributable to ordinary shareholders that has been recognised in the reporting period. This will mean that any tax expense and any dividends on preference shares that have been classified as liabilities will be deducted as part of the determination of profit. Tax expense is a normal component of the profit of an entity, and therefore it is a normal part of the calculation of profit. Preference dividends do not belong to the ordinary shareholders and therefore they must be included in the profit calculation as a deduction. This approach to the determination of the profit to be used in the calculation of earnings per share is outlined in paragraphs 12 and 13, and is demonstrated in figure 20.4.

Profit before tax expense	100 000
Less: Tax expense	(30 000)
Profit after tax	70 000
Less: Preference dividends	(10 000)
Profit attributable to ordinary equity holders (earnings)	60 000 (numerator)

FIGURE 20.4 Earnings calculation to include tax expense and preference dividends

The preference dividends are to be on an after-tax basis, and for non-cumulative preference dividends they are to include any amounts declared during the period. In respect of cumulative dividends, paragraph 14 requires the after-tax amount to be deducted whether or not a dividend is declared during the period. Any cumulative dividends paid during the period but which relate to prior periods are not part of the calculation.

Increasing rate preference shares

Increasing rate preference shares are securities that provide for either a low initial dividend to compensate an entity for selling its shares at a discount; or, they provide for an above-market dividend in later periods to compensate investors for buying the entity's securities at a premium. If an entity issues increasing rate preference shares then, under paragraph 15, any issue discount or premium must be amortised to retained earnings using the effective interest rate method. The amount amortised is regarded as a preference dividend for the purposes of calculating the earnings number used in the earnings per share ratio.

Repurchases and conversion of preference shares

If an entity chooses to repurchase preference shares it has on issue, then the excess of the fair value of the consideration paid over the carrying amount of the shares represents a return to preference shareholders and a charge against retained earnings. Paragraph 16 requires this amount to be included in the calculation of earnings per share, as a deduction when determining the profit attributable to ordinary shareholders.

Similarly, any excess of the fair value of the ordinary shares issued on conversion of preference shares over the fair value of the ordinary shares issuable under the original conversion terms must be deducted in calculating the profit attributable to ordinary shareholders (paragraph 17).

The treatment of cumulative and non-cumulative dividends is demonstrated in illustrative example 20.1.

ILLUSTRATIVE EXAMPLE 20.1 Non-cumulative and cumulative preference dividends

Poulos Ltd has 100 000 Class A preference shares on issue each carrying a non-cumulative dividend right of 3% of the $1 par value of the share. A non-cumulative dividend was declared during the reporting period. The company also has 200 000 Class B preference shares outstanding which carry a cumulative dividend right of 2% per share based on the par value of $1 per share. The company has a profit for the period from continuing operations amounting to $1.5 million, and tax is payable at the rate of 30%.

The earnings (profit attributable to ordinary shareholders) to be used in the calculation of basic earnings per share for Poulos Ltd is calculated as shown in table 20.1.

TABLE 20.1 Determination of earnings to include tax expense and preference dividends

Calculation	$
Profit before tax	1 500 000
Tax expense	(450 000)
Profit after tax	1 050 000
Preference dividends	(7 000)*
Profit attributable to ordinary equity holders	1 043 000

*([100 000 × 3%] + [200 000 × 2%])

20.3.2 Shares

As the earnings per share calculation is focused on the ordinary equity of an entity, the denominator in the calculation contains only ordinary share capital. Because entities are able to make new share issues during a reporting period, the number of shares on issue can increase. They are also able to repurchase or cancel shares, which will decrease the number of shares on issue, and to split or to consolidate shares, which will vary the number of shares on issue. Other actions, including the conversion of convertible preference shares or other convertible securities into ordinary shares, can also vary the amount of shares outstanding. Accordingly, the number of ordinary shares that is used in the calculation of basic earnings per share is adjusted by a time-weighting factor, which is the number of days in the reporting period that the shares are outstanding as a proportion of the total number of days in the period (paragraph 20).

Shares are included in the calculation from the date that the consideration for shares is receivable (paragraph 21). For example, cash is included when it is receivable; ordinary shares issued on the reinvestment of dividends are included when the dividends are reinvested; shares issued when debt is converted or when the shares replace interest or principal on other financial instruments are included from the date interest ceases to accrue. If ordinary shares are issued in exchange for the settlement of a liability, then they are included from the settlement date or, if they are issued in exchange for services rendered, they are included from the date of rendering the services. Any ordinary shares issued as consideration for the acquisition of a non-cash asset are included in the calculation from the date on which the acquisition is recognised; and if shares are issued as part of the consideration in a business combination, they are included from the acquisition date as this reflects the date from which the acquiree's profits are included in the acquirer's income.

Share consolidation and share repurchase

While a consolidation of shares will decrease the number of shares on issue, there is no corresponding reduction in the entity's resources. However, when a repurchase occurs, the entity's resources (e.g. cash) will also be reduced. Shares that are repurchased and held by the issuing entity are termed 'Treasury' shares. If a purchase of Treasury shares (share repurchase) occurs, then the weighted average number of shares outstanding for the period in which the transaction takes place must be adjusted for the reduction in the number of shares from the date of the event (paragraph 29).

The calculation of the weighted average number of ordinary shares where a new share issue and a share repurchase have occurred during the period is demonstrated in illustrative example 20.2.

ILLUSTRATIVE EXAMPLE 20.2 Determining the weighted average number of shares

Singapore Ltd has 11 000 ordinary shares on issue at 1 January 2014 which is the beginning of its reporting period. On 30 June 2014, it issued a further 1000 ordinary shares for cash. On 1 November 2014, Singapore Ltd repurchased 300 shares at fair value in a market transaction.

		Issued shares	Treasury shares	Shares outstanding
1 January 2014	Balance at the beginning of the year	11 000	500	10 500
30 June 2014	Issue of new ordinary shares for cash	1 000		11 500
1 November 2014	Repurchase of issued shares		300	11 200
31 December 2014	Balance at the end of the year	12 000	800	11 200

The weighted average number of shares for use in the earnings per share calculation is determined as follows:

$$= (10\,500 \times 6/12) + (11\,500 \times 4/12) + (11\,200 \times 2/12)$$
$$= 5250 + 3833 + 1867$$
$$= 10\,950 \text{ shares}$$

Source: Adapted from IAS 33, Example 2, p. 37.

Contingently issuable shares

An entity may have contingently issuable shares outstanding. These are ordinary shares that the entity can issue for little or no cash or other consideration once a specified condition has been satisfied (paragraph 5). If an entity has contingently issuable shares, then under paragraph 24 these must be treated as outstanding and they are included in the calculation of basic earnings per share from the date when all necessary conditions have been satisfied.

Bonus issues and share splits

If an entity announces a bonus issue of shares, or if it splits issued shares thereby increasing the number of shares outstanding, there is usually no consideration involved and therefore no corresponding increase in the entity's resources. The number of ordinary shares outstanding before the event must be adjusted for the proportionate change in the number of ordinary shares outstanding as if it had occurred at the beginning of the earliest period presented in the financial statements (paragraph 28). For example, under a two-for-one bonus issue, multiplying the number of ordinary shares outstanding before the bonus issue determines the number of additional ordinary shares. The effect of a bonus issue of shares on the basic earnings per share calculation is demonstrated in illustrative example 20.3.

ILLUSTRATIVE EXAMPLE 20.3 Bonus issue of shares

Jackson Ltd determined its profit attributable to ordinary shareholders for the reporting period ended 30 June 2014 as $360 000 (2013: $320 000). The number of ordinary shares on issue up to 31 October 2013 was 50 000. Jackson Ltd announced a two-for-one bonus issue of shares effective for each ordinary share outstanding at 31 October 2013.

Basic earnings per share is calculated as follows:

Bonus issue on 1 November 2013	$50\,000 \times 2$	$= 100\,000$
Basic earnings per share 30 June 2014	$\dfrac{360\,000}{50\,000 + 100\,000}$	$= \$2.40$
Basic earnings per share 30 June 2013	$\dfrac{320\,000}{50\,000 + 100\,000}$	$= \$2.13$

Because the bonus shares were issued for no consideration, the event is treated as if it had occurred before the beginning of the 2013 reporting period, the earliest period presented in the financial statements (paragraph 28).

Source: Adapted from IAS 33, Example 3, p. 38.

Rights issues

In a bonus issue as the shares are usually issued for no consideration there is an increase in the number of shares outstanding, which is not accompanied by a corresponding increase in the resources of the issuing entity. However, in a rights issue the exercise price is usually lower than the fair value of the shares issued. This means that the rights issue includes a bonus element. In this case, the application guidance in IAS 33 (paragraph A2) requires that the number of ordinary shares used in the calculation of earnings per share, for all periods before the rights issue, is to be the number of ordinary shares outstanding before the rights issue multiplied by an adjustment factor. The components of the adjustment factor are shown in figure 20.5.

$$\frac{\text{Fair value per share immediately before the exercise of rights}}{\text{Theoretical ex-rights fair value per share}}$$

FIGURE 20.5 Adjustment factor for rights issues containing a bonus element

The 'theoretical ex-rights fair value per share' is calculated by adding the aggregate market value of the shares immediately before the exercise of the rights to the proceeds from the exercise of the rights, and then dividing by the number of shares outstanding after the exercise of the rights, as shown in figure 20.6.

$$\frac{\text{Fair value of all outstanding shares immediately before the exercise of rights}}{\text{Number of shares outstanding after the exercise of the rights}}$$

FIGURE 20.6 Theoretical ex-rights value per share

Fair value is the share price at the close of the last day on which the shares were traded together with the rights (cum-rights). The calculation of basic earnings per share where there is a rights issue during the period is demonstrated in illustrative example 20.4.

ILLUSTRATIVE EXAMPLE 20.4 Rights issue

Georgiou Ltd determined its profit attributable to ordinary shareholders for the reporting period ended 30 June 2014 as $5000. At the beginning of the reporting period the company had 1000 ordinary shares on issue. It announced a rights issue with the following details:
- date of rights issue, 1 July 2013
- last date to exercise rights, 1 September 2013
- one new share for each four outstanding (250 total)
- exercise price, $10
- market price of one share immediately before exercise on 1 September 2013, $12.

Determine the theoretical ex-rights value per share

$$\frac{\text{Fair value of all outstanding shares immediately before the exercise of rights}}{\text{Number of shares outstanding after the exercise of the rights}}$$

$$\frac{(\$12 \times 1\,000 \text{ shares}) + (\$10 \times 250 \text{ shares})}{1\,000 \text{ shares} + 250 \text{ shares}} = \$11.60$$

Determine the adjustment factor

$$\frac{\text{Fair value per share immediately before the exercise of rights}}{\text{Theoretical ex-rights fair value per share}} \quad \frac{\$12}{\$11.60} = 1.03$$

Basic earnings per share is calculated as follows:

$$\text{Profit attributable to ordinary shareholders 30 June 2014} \quad \frac{5\,000}{(1\,000 \times 1.03 \times 2/12) + (1\,250 \times 10/12)} = \$4.12$$

Source: Adapted from IAS 33, Example 4, pp. 39–40.

20.4 DILUTED EARNINGS PER SHARE

In addition to calculating the basic earnings per share ratio, if an entity has options, warrants, contingently issuable shares or convertible securities, then it must also recognise the effect of potential dilution to its earnings per share ratio. The potential dilution effect stems from assumptions that the entity's convertible securities are converted, its warrants or options are exercised or that its contingently issuable shares are issued on the satisfaction of their specified conditions. Adjustments must be made to the profit (or loss) attributable to the ordinary shareholders. The adjustments are for the after-tax amount of dividends, interest or other income or expenses recognised in the reporting period in respect of the dilutive securities that would no longer arise if they were indeed converted into ordinary shares. Adjustments must also be made to increase the weighted average number of ordinary shares outstanding to reflect what the weighted average would have been, assuming that all potential ordinary shares (dilutive securities) had been converted.

The information regarding potential (dilutive) ordinary shares appearing in the annual report of Billabong International Ltd is presented in figure 20.7.

Note 41. Earnings per share
(e) Information concerning the classification of securities

Rights
Rights granted to employees under the Billabong Executive Performance Share Plan are considered to be potential ordinary shares and have been included in the determination of diluted earnings per share to the extent to which they are dilutive. The rights have been excluded in the determination of basic earnings per share. Details relating to the rights are set out in note 42.

Options
Options granted to employees under the Billabong Performance and Retention Plan are considered to be potential ordinary shares and have been included in the determination of diluted earnings per share to the extent to which they are dilutive. The options have not been included in the determination of basic earnings per share. Details relating to the options are set out in note 42.

The 1 782 183 options granted on 31 October 2008 and the 314 503 options granted on 24 November 2008 are not included in the calculation of diluted earnings per share because they are anti-dilutive for the year ended 30 June 2011. These options could potentially dilute basic earnings per share in the future.

FIGURE 20.7 Billabong International Ltd — Potential (dilutive) ordinary shares
Source: Billabong International Ltd (2011, p. 122).

IAS 33 regards potential ordinary shares as dilutive only if their conversion to ordinary shares would decrease earnings per share (or increase loss per share) from the continuing operations of an entity (paragraph 41). Potential ordinary shares can be anti-dilutive. An anti-dilutive effect would occur if the conversion of potential ordinary shares would increase earnings per share (paragraph 5).

20.4.1 Earnings

If potential ordinary shares were to be converted, any dividends or interest payable in relation to those dilutive securities would no longer arise. Instead the new ordinary shares would be entitled to participate in profit. Therefore the profit must be increased to remove the impact of the dividends or interest that would otherwise have been payable. Similarly any other income or charges such as transaction costs, that are related to the potential ordinary shares and that have been included in profit, must be removed (paragraph 33).

Any consequential changes in income or expenses arising as a result of the potential conversion of dilutive securities must also be adjusted in determining the earnings amount used in the diluted earnings per share ratio. Consequential changes may include a reduction in interest expense related to potential ordinary shares resulting in an increase in profit (paragraph 35).

20.4.2 Shares

The diluted earnings per share ratio must include an adjustment to increase the weighted average number of ordinary shares that would be outstanding if all of the dilutive securities were converted into ordinary shares. Paragraph 36 deems that the potential ordinary shares are to be regarded as having been converted into ordinary shares at the beginning of the period or, if later, the date of the issue of the potential ordinary shares.

The potential ordinary shares shall be weighted for the period that they are outstanding. If any of the dilutive securities lapse or are cancelled, they are included in the calculation only for the portion of time during which they are outstanding. Any dilutive securities that are converted into ordinary shares during the period are included in the calculation of diluted earnings per share from the beginning of the period to the date of conversion (paragraph 38). If the terms of dilutive securities include more than one basis for conversion into ordinary shares, then under paragraph 39, the most favourable conversion rate or price from the perspective of the security holder is used.

Dilutive potential ordinary shares

As mentioned, potential ordinary shares are regarded by IAS 33 as dilutive only if their conversion to ordinary shares would decrease earnings per share or increase loss per share (paragraph 41). In deciding whether potential ordinary shares are dilutive (or anti-dilutive) each issue or series of potential dilutive securities is considered separately. The conversion, exercise or other issue of potential ordinary shares that would have an anti-dilutive effect on earnings per share is not assumed in the calculation of diluted earnings per share (paragraph 43).

When determining the dilutive effect of potential ordinary shares, each issue or series of dilutive securities is considered in sequence from most dilutive to least dilutive (paragraph 44). This means that the securities with the lowest earnings impact, per incremental share, are included in the calculation before those securities with the highest earnings impact per incremental share. This generally means that options and warrants are included first, because they do not usually affect the numerator (earnings) in the ratio.

Options and warrants

The proceeds from options and warrants are regarded as received from the issue of ordinary shares at the average market price during the period. Paragraphs 45–46 require that the difference between the number of ordinary shares issued and the number that would have been issued at the average market price, be treated as an issue of ordinary shares for no consideration. The application guidance to IAS 33 indicates that a simple average of the weekly or monthly closing prices of ordinary shares is usually adequate for determining the average market price (paragraphs A4–A5). However, this approach will need to be adjusted when shares prices fluctuate widely.

Options and warrants are regarded as dilutive if they would result in the issue of ordinary shares for less than the average market price during the period (i.e. when they are 'in the money'). The amount of the dilution is determined as the average market price of ordinary shares during the period minus the issue price. Employee share options and non-vested ordinary shares are regarded as options in the calculation of diluted earnings per share (paragraph 48).

The effect of share options on basic and diluted earnings per share is demonstrated in illustrative example 20.5.

ILLUSTRATIVE EXAMPLE 20.5 Effect of share options on earnings per share

Harlem Ltd determined its profit attributable to ordinary shareholders for the reporting period ended 30 June 2014 as $480 000. The average market price of the entity's shares during the period is $4.00 per share. The weighted average number of ordinary shares on issue during the period is 1 000 000. The weighted average number of shares under share options arrangements during the year is 200 000 and the exercise price of shares under option is $3.50.

	Earnings $	Shares	Per share $
Basic earnings per share is calculated as follows:			
Profit attributable to ordinary shareholders for the reporting period ended 30 June 2014	480 000		
Weighted average shares on issue during the period		1 000 000	
Basic earnings per share			0.48
Diluted earnings per share is calculated as follows:			
Weighted average number of shares under option		200 000	
Weighted average number of shares that would have been issued at average market price is (200 000 × $3.50) / $4.00		(175 000)	
Diluted earnings per share	480 000	1 025 000	0.47

Source: Adapted from IAS 33, Example 5, p. 41.

Convertible securities

If convertible preference shares are dilutive they are included in the diluted earnings per share calculation. They are regarded as anti-dilutive if the amount of the dividend declared or accumulated in the current period per ordinary share, obtainable on the conversion, exceeds basic earnings per share. Similarly, convertible debt is regarded as anti-dilutive whenever its interest (net of tax and other changes in income or expenses) per ordinary share obtainable on conversion, exceeds basic earnings per share.

Contingently issuable shares

Contingently issuable shares such as performance-based employee share options are regarded as outstanding, and if their conditions are satisfied they are included in the calculation of diluted earnings per share from the beginning of the period (or the date of the contingent share agreement, if later). If the conditions are not satisfied, the number of contingently issuable shares that is included in the diluted earnings per share calculation is based on the number of shares that would be issuable if the end of the period were the end of the contingency period (paragraph 52).

If the number of contingently issuable ordinary shares is dependent on both future earnings and future prices of ordinary shares, then the number of ordinary shares included in the diluted earnings per share calculation is based on both conditions. That is, it is based on both earnings to date and on the current market price of the ordinary shares at the end of the reporting period (paragraph 55). Unless both conditions are met, contingently issuable shares are not included in the diluted earnings per share calculation.

Contracts that may be settled in ordinary shares or cash

If an entity has issued a contract that may be settled in cash or ordinary shares at the entity's option, then under paragraph 58 it is assumed that the settlement will be in ordinary shares. As a result the potential ordinary shares are included in the diluted earnings per share calculation if the effect is dilutive.

For contracts that can be settled in cash or in ordinary shares at the holder's option, then the more dilutive of either the cash settlement or the share settlement is used in the diluted earnings per share calculation (paragraph 60). Such contracts could include an option that provides the holder with settlement choice of cash or ordinary shares.

As mentioned, when determining the dilutive effect of potential ordinary shares, each issue or series of dilutive securities is considered in sequence from most dilutive to least dilutive (paragraph 44). Securities with the lowest earnings impact per additional share are included in the calculation first. Determining the order in which to include dilutive securities is demonstrated in illustrative example 20.6.

ILLUSTRATIVE EXAMPLE 20.6 Calculation of weighted average number when more than one issue of potentially dilutive securities exist

Bruin Ltd extracted the following information from its financial records in order to determine its basic earnings per share and diluted earnings per share for its reporting period ended 30 June 2014.

Profit from continuing operations	$16 400
Less: Dividends on preference shares	(6 400)
Profit from continuing operations attributable to ordinary shareholders	10 000
Loss from discontinued operations	(4 000)
Profit attributable to ordinary shareholders	6 000
Ordinary shares on issue	2 000
Average market price of one ordinary share during the period	$ 7.50

Potential ordinary shares (potentially dilutive securities):

1. Options	10 000 with an exercise price of $6.00
2. Convertible preference shares	800 shares with an issue value of $100 entitled to a cumulative dividend of $8 per share. Each preference share is convertible to two ordinary shares.

Determine the increase in earnings attributable to ordinary shareholders on conversion of potential ordinary shares

Options	
Increase in earnings	$0
Additional shares issued for no consideration $10\,000 \times (7.50 - 6.00) / 7.50$	2 000
Earnings per additional share	$0

Convertible preference shares	
Increase in earnings ($80\,000 \times 0.08$)	$6 400
Additional shares (2×800)	1 600
Earnings per additional share	$4.00

The dilutive securities are included in the earnings per share calculation in the following order:
1. Options
2. Convertible preference shares

Determine dilutive effect of convertible securities

	$	Shares	$ per share	
Profit from continuing operations attributable to ordinary shareholders	10 000	2 000	5.00	
Increase in earnings from options	0	2 000		
	10 000	4 000	2.50	Dilutive
Increase in earnings from convertible preference shares*	6 400	1 600		
	16 400	5 600	2.93	Anti-dilutive

* As the convertible preference shares increased diluted earnings per share they would be considered anti-dilutive and ignored in the calculation of diluted earnings per share.

Calculate basic EPS and diluted EPS

	Basic EPS $	Diluted EPS $
Profit from continuing operations attributable to ordinary shareholders	5.00	2.50
Loss from discontinued operations attributable to ordinary shareholders		
($4 000/2 000)	(2.00)	
($4 000/4 000)		(1.00)
Profit attributable to ordinary shareholders		
($6 000/2 000)	3.00	
($6 000/4 000)		1.50

Source: Adapted from IAS 33, Example 9, pp. 49–51.

LO5 20.5 RETROSPECTIVE ADJUSTMENTS

Retrospective adjustments are made to restate the values of relevant items so that valid comparisons across time can be made. If, for example, the number of issued shares increases during a reporting period as a result of a bonus issue for no consideration, then the operating profit for the whole period in which the bonus issue occurred will be attributable to the increased number of shares and not to the lesser number of shares outstanding at the beginning of the reporting period.

IAS 33 paragraph 64 requires that if the number of ordinary shares or of potential ordinary shares outstanding increases as a result of a:
- capitalisation
- bonus issue
- share split;

or if the number decreases as a result of a:
- consolidation (reverse share split); then,

the calculation of both basic earnings per share and diluted earnings per share must be adjusted retrospectively for all periods that are presented in the financial statements. The retrospective adjustment to the number of shares also applies to the period from the end of the reporting period but before the financial statements are authorised for issue. Further, basic and diluted earnings per share are both subject to retrospective adjustment for the effects of any errors or adjustments resulting from changes in accounting policies that are accounted for retrospectively.

20.6 DISCLOSURE

The basic earnings per share and diluted earnings per share ratios must be presented in an entity's statement of profit or loss and other comprehensive income (paragraph 66) even if the amounts are negative (paragraph 69). If the items of profit or loss are presented in a separate statement then the basic and diluted earnings per share ratios are required to be presented in that separate statement. The two ratios must be displayed with equal prominence, and they must be calculated for each class of ordinary shares that have different rights to share in the profit of the period. If diluted earnings per share is presented for one period, then it must be shown for all periods that are presented in the financial statements, even if it is the same as the basic earnings per share. And, if the entity has a discontinued operation, then it must also calculate and disclose the basic and diluted earnings per share ratios for the discontinued operation in the statement of profit or loss and other comprehensive income.

Paragraphs 70–73 of IAS 33 prescribe various disclosures relating to earnings per share. The objective of these disclosures is to provide sufficient additional information to assist financial statement users to understand the composition of the earnings per share ratios. The disclosures include:
- the amounts used as the numerators (earnings) in the ratios
- a reconciliation of the earnings amounts to the profit or loss attributable to the parent entity for the period, including the individual effect of each class of instruments that affects earnings per share
- the weighted average number of ordinary shares used as the denominator in the ratios
- a reconciliation of the denominators to each other, including the individual effect of each class of instruments that affects earnings per share
- instruments, including contingently issuable shares, that could potentially dilute basic earnings per share in the future, but were not included in the calculation of diluted earnings per share because they are anti-dilutive for the period(s) presented
- a description of ordinary share transactions or potential ordinary share transactions that occur after the reporting period and that would have changed significantly the number of ordinary shares or potential ordinary shares outstanding at the end of the period if those transactions had occurred before the end of the reporting period.

Examples of transactions that could significantly change the number of shares outstanding could include:
- an issue of shares for cash
- an issue of shares when the proceeds are used to repay debt or preference shares outstanding at the end of the reporting period
- the redemption of ordinary shares outstanding
- the conversion or exercise of potential ordinary shares outstanding at the end of the reporting period into ordinary shares
- an issue of options, warrants, or convertible securities
- the achievement of conditions that would result in the issue of contingently issuable shares.

Billabong International Ltd includes reconciliations of the earnings amounts and the weighted average number of shares used in its basic and diluted earnings per share calculation in Note 41 in its 2011 annual report. These reconciliations are presented in figure 20.8.

Note 41. Earnings per share
(c) Reconciliations of earnings used in calculating earnings per share

	2011 $'000	2010 $'000
Basic earnings per share		
Profit attributable to the ordinary equity holders of the Company used in calculating basic earnings per share from continuing operations	119 139	145 988
Diluted earnings per share		
Profit attributable to the ordinary equity holders of the Company used in calculating diluted earnings per share from continuing operations	119 139	145 988

(d) Weighted average number of shares used as the denominator

	2011 Number	2010 Number
Weighted average number of ordinary shares used as the denominator in calculating basic earnings per share	251 150 894	250 483 588
Adjustments for calculating diluted earnings per share:		
Performance shares and conditional rights	2 170 126	2 063 782
Options	—	—
Weighted average number of ordinary shares and potential ordinary shares used as the denominator in calculating diluted earnings per share	253 321 020	252 547 370

FIGURE 20.8 Reconciliations of earnings and weighted average number of shares — Billabong International Ltd
Source: Billabong International Ltd (2011, p. 122).

If, in addition to calculating basic and diluted earnings per share, an entity uses a numerator other than the one required by IAS 33, then it must still use the denominator as prescribed under IAS 33 (paragraph 73). These additional ratios must be displayed with equal prominence as the prescribed basic EPS and diluted EPS ratios and presented in the notes to the financial statements. The basis on which the numerator is determined, including whether the amounts per share are before or after tax, must also be disclosed.

IAS 33 also encourages the voluntary disclosure of the terms and conditions of financial instruments and contracts that incorporate terms and conditions affecting the measurement of basic and diluted earnings per share.

SUMMARY

IAS 33 provides principles for the calculation and presentation of basic and diluted earnings per share. Earnings per share (EPS) is a ratio which is used to compare the after-tax profit available to ordinary shareholders of an entity on a per share basis, with that of other entities. It is calculated by dividing profit or loss (earnings) attributable to ordinary shareholders, by the weighted average number of ordinary shares outstanding during a reporting period.

The objective of IAS 33 is to improve the information provided by reporting entities, and the consistency of comparisons between entities and across different time periods.

The main features of the standard are that it requires:

- the profit (or loss) used in the calculation of basic earnings per share to be from continuing operations. This means that any tax expense and dividends on preference shares that have been classified as liabilities will be deducted as part of the determination of profit.
- the denominator in the calculation to contain only ordinary shares
- the number of ordinary shares used in the calculation of basic earnings per share to be adjusted by a time-weighting factor which is the number of days in the reporting period that the shares are outstanding as a proportion of the total number of days in the period.

In addition to calculating the basic earnings per share ratio, if an entity has options, warrants, contingently issuable shares or securities that are convertible to ordinary shares, IAS 33 requires that the effect of dilution must be recognised in the entity's earnings per share. Adjustments to calculate diluted earnings per share must be made to:

- the profit (or loss) attributable to the ordinary shareholders for the after-tax amount of dividends, interest or other income or expenses that would no longer arise if the dilutive securities were converted into ordinary shares
- increase the weighted average number of ordinary shares outstanding to reflect what the weighted average would have been assuming that all potential ordinary shares (dilutive securities) had been converted.

Discussion questions

1. What is the earnings per share ratio used for?
2. What are the components in the numerator and the denominator in the earnings per share calculation?
3. Where are the earnings per share figures for a parent entity presented?
4. Why is a time-weighting factor used to determine the number of shares that is used in the calculation of basic earnings per share?
5. What is the treatment applied to treasury shares when calculating the weighted average number of shares used in the earnings per share calculation?
6. Distinguish between basic earnings per share and diluted earnings per share.
7. Explain the effect of potential ordinary shares on the calculation of diluted earnings per share.
8. Explain how the amount of dilution from options is determined.
9. When determining the amount of the proceeds from options and warrants, how is the average share price established?
10. Why are retrospective adjustments made to earnings per share ratios?
11. Where are the basic and diluted earnings per share ratios presented in a set of financial statements?

Exercises

STAR RATING ★ BASIC ★★ MODERATE ★★★ DIFFICULT

Exercise 20.1 SCOPE OF IAS 33

★ If an entity presents both consolidated and separate financial statements, what is the basis of determination of basic earnings per share disclosures? Give reasons for your answer.

Exercise 20.2 COMPONENTS OF BASIC EARNINGS PER SHARE

★ Which of the following is a component of earnings used in the calculation of basic earnings per share? Give reasons for your answer.
(a) Profit before tax expense
(b) Preference dividends declared during the period
(c) Income tax expense
(d) Profit from discontinued operations
(e) Prior year dividend paid to holders of cumulative preference shares

Exercise 20.3 MEASURING BASIC EARNINGS PER SHARE

★ On 30 June 2014, Samira Ltd determines profit attributable to ordinary shareholders as $450 000. At the beginning of the reporting period the company had 1 800 000 ordinary shares outstanding. The company had no share issues during the period.

Required

Calculate Samira Ltd's 2014 basic earnings per share ratio.

Exercise 20.4 MEASUREMENT PRINCIPLES

★ The directors of Johannsen Group have decided to repurchase 100 000 ordinary shares in an on-market arm's length transaction.

Required

Are the treasury shares acquired in this transaction included in the weighted average number of shares outstanding when determining basic earnings per share? Explain your answer.

Exercise 20.5 | **CATEGORISING**

★ An entity announces a share split to occur in the current reporting period. There is no consideration payable by existing shareholders and therefore no corresponding increase in the entity's resources.

Required

Should the entity recognise the additional shares in the weighted average number of shares used in calculating basic earnings per share? Explain.

Exercise 20.6 | **BONUS ISSUE OF SHARES**

★★ On 1 January 2013, Regis Ltd has 200 000 ordinary shares outstanding. On 1 March 2013, the company announces a bonus issue of 2 shares for every share held on that date. By the end of the year Regis Ltd's profit attributable to ordinary shareholders amounts to $900 000 (2012: $600 000).

Required

Calculate the 2013 and 2012 basic earnings per share amounts that Regis Ltd must disclose in its financial statements for the year ended 31 December 2013.

Exercise 20.7 | **THEORETICAL EX-RIGHTS VALUE**

★★ Kenny Ltd has 30 000 ordinary shares on issue. The company announced a one-for-three rights issue with an exercise price of $4 for each right. The market price of one ordinary share immediately before the exercise of the rights was $6.

Required

Determine the theoretical ex-rights value per share.

Exercise 20.8 | **RIGHTS ADJUSTMENT FACTOR AND ADJUSTED BASIC EARNINGS PER SHARE**

★★ Assume that in exercise 20.7 Kenny Ltd announced the rights issue at the beginning of its reporting period (1 July 2014) and the last date for exercising the rights was 1 October 2014. Kenny Ltd announced profit attributable to ordinary shareholders of $109 725 for the full reporting period.

Required

Use the theoretical ex-rights value per share determined in exercise 20.7 to calculate the adjustment factor, and calculate adjusted basic earnings per share.

Exercise 20.9 | **EFFECT OF SHARE OPTIONS ON DILUTED EARNINGS PER SHARE**

★★ Xenia Ltd determines its profit attributable to ordinary shareholders for the reporting period ended 30 June 2014 as $96 000. The company has calculated its weighted average number of ordinary shares on issue during the period as 480 000. The weighted average number of shares under share options arrangements during the period is 24 000.

The average market price of the entity's shares during the period is $2.40 per share, and the exercise price of shares under option is $1.50.

Required

Prepare a schedule setting out the calculation of basic earnings per share and diluted earnings per share.

Exercise 20.10 | **DETERMINING THE ADDITIONAL SHARES FROM POTENTIALLY DILUTIVE OPTIONS**

★★ Tennyson Ltd has 20 000 ordinary shares outstanding during the reporting period ended 30 June 2015. The average market price of its ordinary shares during the period was $3.75 per share. The company also has 5000 options on issue with an exercise price of $3.00 each.

Required

Calculate the additional shares attributable to ordinary shareholders from the potentially dilutive options.

| Exercise 20.11 | **DISCLOSURE** |

★★★ Washington Ltd operates an Executive Performance Share Plan (EPSP). Under this plan, the company grants rights to employees which are convertible into ordinary shares of the company. It also grants options under the EPSP. The options have a term of 5 years and are converted into ordinary shares when the executives satisfy their individual performance conditions. The options granted during the current reporting period are considered anti-dilutive; however, in past years the options granted have been dilutive.

Required

Prepare an appropriate note to be included in the financial statements of Washington Ltd disclosing the information concerning the classification of potential ordinary shares.

| Exercise 20.12 | **THEORETICAL EX-RIGHTS VALUE, RIGHTS ADJUSTMENT FACTOR AND BASIC EARNINGS PER SHARE** |

★★★ At the beginning of the current reporting period (1 January 2014) Petrov Ltd has 60 000 ordinary shares on issue. The company announced a one-for-five rights issue on 1 January 2014. The exercise price is $2 and the last date to exercise the rights is 1 April 2014. The market price of one share immediately before exercise on 1 April 2014 was $3. At the end of the current reporting period (31 December 2014), Petrov Ltd determined profit attributable to ordinary shareholders at $244 650.

Required

Determine the theoretical ex-rights value per share, the rights adjustment factor, and the basic earnings per share.

References

Billabong International Ltd 2011, *2010/2011 Full financial report*, Billabong International Limited, Australia, www.billabongbiz.com.

Greenblat, E, 2011, 'Billabong wiped out on profit warning', *The Sydney Morning Herald*, 19 December, www.smh.com.au.

International Accounting Standards Board 2010a, *IAS 33 Earnings per Share*, International Accounting Standards Committee Foundation, London.

_____ 2010b, *Basis for Conclusions on IAS 33 Earnings per Share*, International Accounting Standards Committee Foundation, London.

21 Operating segments

ACCOUNTING STANDARDS IN FOCUS

IFRS 8 *Operating Segments*

LEARNING OBJECTIVES

After studying this chapter, you should be able to:

1 discuss the objectives of financial reporting by segments
2 identify the types of entities that are within the scope of IFRS 8
3 explain and evaluate the controversy surrounding the issuance of IFRS 8
4 briefly compare IFRS 8 with its predecessor standard, IAS 14
5 identify operating segments in accordance with IFRS 8
6 distinguish between operating segments and reportable segments
7 apply the definition of reportable segments
8 explain the disclosure requirements of IFRS 8
9 analyse the disclosures made by companies applying IFRS 8 in practice.

21.1 OBJECTIVES OF FINANCIAL REPORTING BY SEGMENTS

IFRS 8 *Operating Segments* is primarily a disclosure standard and is particularly relevant for large organisations that operate in different geographic locations and/or in diverse businesses.

Paragraph 1 of IFRS 8 sets out the standard's core principle:

> An entity shall disclose information to enable users of its financial statements to evaluate the nature and financial effects of the business activities in which it engages and the economic environments in which it operates.

Many entities operate in different geographical areas or provide products or services that are subject to differing rates of profitability, opportunities for growth, future prospects and risks. Information about an entity's operating segments is relevant to assessing the risks and returns of a diversified or multinational entity where often that information cannot be determined from aggregated data. Therefore, segment information is regarded as necessary to help users of financial statements:

- better understand the entity's past performance
- better assess the entity's risks and returns
- make more informed judgements about the entity as a whole.

Many securities analysts rely on the segment disclosures to help them assess not only an entity's past performance but also to help them predict future performance. Analysts use these assessments to determine an entity's share price. Segment disclosures are widely regarded as some of the most useful disclosures in financial statements because of the extent to which they disaggregate financial information into meaningful and often revealing groupings. For example, an entity may appear profitable on a consolidated basis, but segment disclosures may reveal that one part of the business is performing poorly while another part is performing well. The part that is performing poorly may be significant to the entity as a whole and over time continued poor performance by that part (or segment) may cause the entire entity's performance to suffer. This is the kind of information that impacts on an entity's share price because analysts frequently look at predicted future cash flows in making their share price determinations.

On the other hand, preparers of financial statements may not wish to reveal too much information on a disaggregated basis to their competitors. Some may consider the disclosure requirements of IFRS 8 to be too revealing. For example, a user may be able to determine an entity's profit margin by segment when reading the segment disclosures. This is a key reason why it is unlikely that entities would volunteer to disclose segment information (see section 21.2). Another reason is that it is often a time-consuming exercise to prepare the segment disclosures.

21.2 SCOPE

IFRS 8 applies to the financial statements of an entity 'whose debt or equity instruments are traded in a public market' or 'that files, or is in the process of filing, its financial statements with a securities commission or other regulatory organisation for the purpose of issuing any class of instruments in a public market' (IFRS 8 paragraph 2). Most commonly 'traded in a public market' would mean a public stock exchange such as the London Stock Exchange or the Australian Securities Exchange.

Where financial statements contain both consolidated financial statements and the parent's separate financial statements, segment information is required only for the consolidated financial statements (IFRS 8 paragraph 4). However, if consolidated financial statements are *not* prepared, and the entity is within the scope of the standard, it must apply the standard in its separate or individual financial statements (IFRS 8 paragraph 2(a)).

If an entity voluntarily chooses to disclose segment information then it must fully comply with IFRS 8; otherwise it must not describe the disclosed information as segment information (IFRS 8 paragraph 3). Voluntary disclosure may occur, for example, where a large public company that is not listed, but has a large number of dependent users such as a number of minority shareholders, employees and creditors, elects to provide segment information. However, voluntary segment disclosures are not expected to be common, for reasons discussed in section 21.1.

LO3 21.3 A CONTROVERSIAL STANDARD

21.3.1 Overview

In January 2006, the IASB issued ED 8 *Operating Segments*, which it proposed as a replacement to IAS 14 *Segment Reporting*. The ED was part of the IASB's program for achieving convergence with standards issued by the US Financial Accounting Standards Board (FASB) and essentially adopted the requirements of the FASB Statement of Financial Accounting Standards No. 131 (SFAS 131) *Disclosures about Segments of an Enterprise and Related Information*. The major change from IAS 14 was the adoption of the management approach to identifying segments as the only acceptable approach. ED 8 was finally issued as a new standard, IFRS 8 *Operating Segments*, in November 2006. IFRS 8 was applicable for annual reporting periods beginning on or after 1 January 2009, with early adoption permitted.

21.3.2 Reasons for the controversy

In Europe, the replacement of IAS 14 with IFRS 8 was highly controversial, mainly because of the management approach allowed by IFRS 8 compared with the more prescriptive approach previously required by IAS 14. The management approach in IFRS 8 requires segment information to be reported externally based on how information is reported internally to the company's management (see section 21.5). In contrast, IAS 14 had contained very prescriptive requirements as to what should be reported and how. The European Parliament is required to endorse all IASB standards and IFRIC interpretations in order for the standards and interpretations to come into effect. The European Financial Reporting Advisory Group (EFRAG) reviews the proposed standards and makes its recommendations to the European Commission as to whether or not the parliament should endorse the standards and interpretations. When ED 8 was issued, concern was expressed about the management approach by many commentators to both the IASB and EFRAG. After the IASB issued IFRS 8, the European Commission sought further feedback, by means of a questionnaire, on whether or not the European Parliament should endorse IFRS 8. The questions focused on the management approach, the lack of mandatory disclosure requirements and whether these were perceived as positive or negative by commentators.

A paper prepared and presented by Nicolas Véron, Research Fellow at Bruegel (a European think tank created to contribute to the quality of economic policymaking in Europe) argued that IFRS 8 should not be endorsed. The paper argued that the success of IFRS thus far can be attributed both to market (investor) demand and to European Union (EU) leadership and that convergence with US GAAP 'is far from universally accepted as an appropriate framework for setting the current standard-setting agenda'. The paper contended that 'segment information is one of the most vital aspects of financial reporting for investors and other users' and is also inherently divisive between preparers of financial statements on the one hand, who want to control the information, and users on the other, who want it to be specifically objective. The risks and rewards approach to identifying segments (previously contained in IAS 14) arguably meets the needs of users while the management approach arguably meets the needs of preparers, although both approaches may be consistent (as envisaged by IAS 14). The paper argues that the discretion permitted by IFRS 8 in determining the content of segment profit or loss and segment assets and in making or not making certain disclosures (e.g. disclosure of liabilities, statement of profit or loss and other comprehensive income line items and geographical information) contrasts with the prescribed measurement and disclosure requirements of IAS 14, favouring preparers over users. The paper quotes from various respondents' letters to the IASB, particularly those of analysts, who did not support changing IAS 14 and moving to a standard based on SFAS 131, because they regarded SFAS 131 as inferior to IAS 14.

It is also notable that two IASB board members dissented from the issuance of IFRS 8 (refer to the dissenting opinion in IFRS 8) because of the lack of definition of segment profit or loss and because IFRS 8 does not require consistent attribution of assets and profit or loss to segments. In addition, these board members also believed that the changes from IAS 14 were not justified by the need for convergence with US GAAP because IAS 14 is a disclosure standard and therefore does not affect the reconciliation of IFRS amounts to US GAAP.

The preparer's viewpoint is argued, for example, in the submission by the Association of German Banks to the European Commission's questionnaire referred to above. This letter argues that IFRS 8 should be endorsed and that the information provided under the management approach will be more relevant and reliable because it will, inter alia, enable investors to evaluate the entity on the same basis as that used by management in its decision making and that any concerns about understandability are addressed by the reconciliation requirements of IFRS 8.

Despite the objections, IFRS 8 was finally endorsed by the European Parliament in November 2007. In its endorsement resolution, the European Parliament stated that the IASB should carry out a review of the new standard two years after its implementation. Further, the parliament's requirement that the European Commission 'follow closely the application of IFRS 8 and (to) report back to Parliament no later than 2011[1], inter alia regarding reporting of geographical segments, segment profit or loss, and use of non-IFRS measures; underlines that if the Commission discovers deficiencies in the application of IFRS 8 it has a duty to rectify such deficiencies'.

The message from the European Parliament to European companies is therefore that entities will be watched closely to determine whether they are taking advantage of the discretionary approach of IFRS 8 in order to control reported information. Only time will tell whether concerns about the approach eventuate.

In Australia, IFRS 8 was issued as AASB 8 by the Australian Accounting Standards Board in February 2007, with little fanfare, although Australian commentators had expressed similar concerns about the management approach and the US GAAP convergence issue discussed above.

 LO4 **21.4 MAIN DIFFERENCES BETWEEN IAS 14 AND IFRS 8**

Table 21.1 analyses the main differences between IAS 14 and IFRS 8.

TABLE 21.1 Main differences between IAS 14 and IFRS 8

Requirement	IAS 14	IFRS 8
Basis for identification of segments	Segments are identified based on the predominant sources of risks and returns. This may result in either a business or geographic basis for segment identification. Where this does not coincide with the basis on which the entity reports internally to senior management, the internally reported segment information is *not* used as the basis for external financial reporting. Rather, the internally reported information must be rearranged to meet the requirements of IAS 14 (IAS 14 paragraphs 27 and 32).	Segments (called operating segments) *must* be determined based on the way information is reported internally to the chief operating decision maker (CODM) (IFRS 8 paragraph 5). This may not coincide with the way information is reported externally and therefore may not agree with the entity's statement of profit or loss and other comprehensive income and statement of financial position. Where this is the case, IFRS 8 requires reconciliations to be provided between the segment information (which will usually be in a note to the financial statements) and the statement of profit or loss and other comprehensive income and statement of financial position (IFRS 8 paragraph 28). Commentators on ED 8 were concerned that comparability between different companies is likely to be reduced as a result of the focus on internal reporting of IFRS 8 versus the focus on sources of risks and rewards of IAS 14 (see section 21.3). The reconciliation requirements in IFRS 8 are expected to counter some of the potential lack of comparability between segment reporting of different entities.
Primary and secondary segments	IAS 14 requires an entity to identify primary and secondary segments (IAS 14 paragraph 26).	IFRS 8 does not refer to primary or secondary segments.
Revenues from third parties as the basis for identifying reportable segments	IAS 14 requires that a business or geographical segment be identified as a reportable segment if a majority of its revenue is earned from sales to *external* customers and certain other conditions are met (IAS 14 paragraph 35).	IFRS 8 does not distinguish between revenues and expenses from transactions with third parties and those from transactions *within the group* for the purposes of identifying operating segments (IFRS 8 paragraph 5). Therefore, in an entity with internal vertically integrated businesses, it is possible that such internal businesses might be identified as operating segments under IFRS 8. Under IAS 14, such internal businesses would not qualify as reportable segments.

[1] At the time of writing (June 2012), no report had yet been issued.

TABLE 21.1 *(continued)*

Requirement	IAS 14	IFRS 8
Definitions of information to be reported for each reportable segment	IAS 14 defines 'segment revenue', 'segment expense', 'segment result', 'segment assets' and 'segment liabilities' (IAS 14 paragraph 16). This ensures consistency in the determination of amounts that are disclosed by different companies.	IFRS 8 requires disclosure of 'a measure' of profit or loss and total assets and 'a measure' of liabilities for each reportable segment if such amounts are regularly provided to the CODM (IFRS 8 paragraph 23). These amounts are not defined in IFRS 8. Thus, different judgements will likely be made by different entities based on what and how information is internally reported, potentially reducing comparability between entities. To counter this concern, IFRS 8 requires entities to explain how they measure segment profit or loss, segment assets and segment liabilities for each reportable segment (IFRS 8 paragraph 27).
Conformity with the entity's accounting policies for preparing its financial statements	IAS 14 requires that segment information be prepared in conformity with the entity's accounting policies for preparing and presenting its financial statements (IAS 14 paragraph 44).	IFRS 8 requires that the amount of each segment item reported shall be the measure reported to the CODM for the purposes of making decisions about allocating resources to the segment and assessing its performance, even if this information is not prepared in accordance with the entity's IFRS accounting policies (IFRS 8 paragraph 25). The reconciliations required by paragraph 28 (see above) are designed to allow users to assess the differences between management's determination of segment measures and the accounting policies used in the financial statements. Note, however, that this is only required on an overall basis, not on a segment-by-segment basis.
Disclosures	IAS 14 specifies the disclosures required for each reportable segment (IAS 14 paragraphs 50–83). Therefore, all entities are required to report the same line items for each of their reportable segments.	IFRS 8 requires that 'a measure' of segment profit or loss be disclosed for each reportable segment. Other items, such as total assets, liabilities, interest revenue, interest expense, depreciation and amortisation, revenues from external customers, inter-segment revenue and so on, are only required to be disclosed if they are provided to the CODM for that reportable segment (IFRS 8 paragraphs 23 and 24). Therefore, the line items reported for each reportable segment will likely differ, not only between companies, but also within companies.
Reliance on major customers	IAS 14 requires disclosure of revenue from external customers (IAS 14 paragraphs 51, 69 and 70) but not about reliance on major customers.	IFRS 8 requires that, if revenues from transactions with a *single* external customer amount to 10% or more of the entity's revenues, certain information be disclosed about the entity's reliance on that single customer (IFRS 8 paragraph 34).

LO5   21.5 IDENTIFYING OPERATING SEGMENTS

An operating segment is defined in IFRS 8 paragraph 5 as:

> a component of an entity:
> (a) that engages in business activities from which it may earn revenues and incur expenses (including revenues and expenses relating to transactions with other components of the same entity);

(b) whose operating results are regularly reviewed by the entity's chief operating decision maker to make decisions about resources to be allocated to the segment and assess its performance; and

(c) for which discrete financial information is available.

The chief operating decision maker (CODM) identifies a function, not necessarily a manager with a specific title. That function may be a group of people, for example, an executive committee. Generally, an operating segment has a segment manager who is directly accountable to the CODM. As with the CODM, the term 'segment manager' identifies a function, not necessarily a manager with a specific title. A single manager may be the segment manager for more than one operating segment and the CODM may also be the segment manager for one or more operating segments. When an entity has a matrix structure, for example, with some managers responsible for different product and service lines and other managers responsible for specific geographic areas, and the CODM regularly reviews the operating results for both sets of components, the entity uses the core principle (see section 21.1) to determine its operating segments (IFRS 8 paragraph 10).

As discussed in section 21.4, this approach to identifying segments is completely different from the 'sources of risks and rewards' approach in IAS 14. Figure 21.1 summarises the key decision points in identifying operating segments.

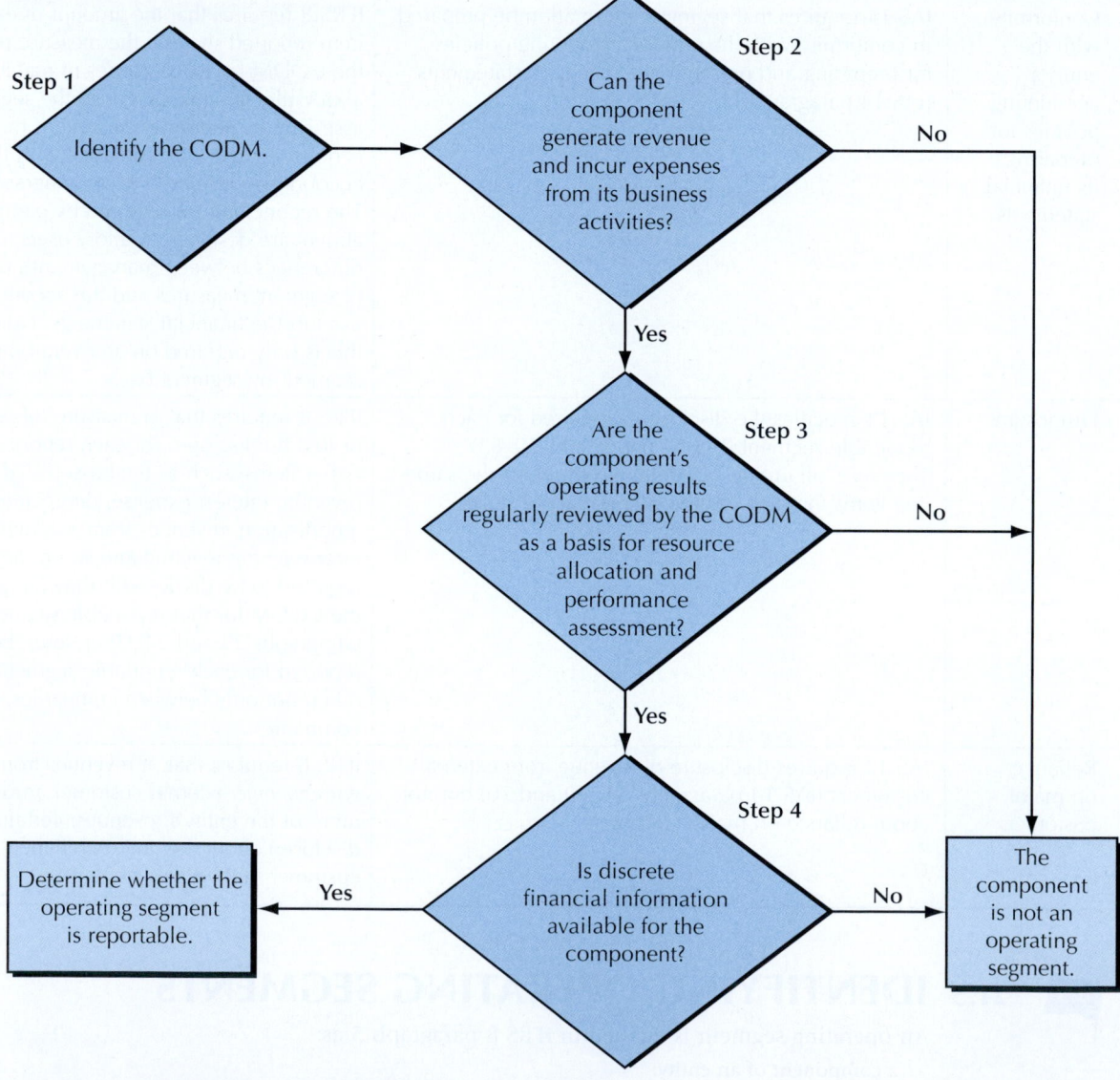

FIGURE 21.1 Identifying operating segments under IFRS 8
Source: Ernst & Young (2007, p. 4). © 2012 EYGM Limited. All rights reserved.

The following examples illustrate the steps in identifying operating segments.

ILLUSTRATIVE EXAMPLE 21.1 Identifying operating segments under IFRS 8 — the four steps

Company A has a chief executive officer (CEO), a chief operating officer (COO) and an executive committee comprising the CEO, COO and the heads (general managers) of three business units — units X, Y and Z. Every month, financial information is presented to the executive committee for each of business units X, Y and Z and for Company A as a whole in order to assess the performance of each business unit and of the company as a whole. Units X, Y and Z each generate revenue and incur expenses from their business activities. Unit Y derives the majority of its revenue from Unit Z. Corporate headquarter costs that are not allocated to units X, Y or Z are also reported separately each month to the executive committee in order to determine the results for Company A as a whole.

Step 1: Who is the CODM?
In this case, the CODM is likely to be the executive committee, since it is this group that regularly reviews the operating results of all business units and the company as a whole. However, if the business unit heads only join the committee meetings to report on their specific business unit and then leave the meeting, and the CEO and COO are the only people who review all the business units and the company as a whole, and the ones who make resource allocation decisions, for example, about changing the structure of the business units, then the CODM would be the CEO and COO. In practice, this would not make any difference to the identification of the operating segments (see step 2).

Step 2: Can the component generate revenue and incur expenses from its business activities?
For units X and Z, the answer is clearly yes. For Unit Y, the answer is also yes — even though its revenue is derived internally this does not prevent it from being identified as an operating segment (IFRS 8 paragraph 5(a)). For the corporate headquarters, the answer is no as it does not derive revenues; it only incurs costs.

Step 3: Are the component's operating results regularly reviewed by the CODM as a basis for resource allocation and performance assessment?
For units X, Y, Z and the corporate headquarters, the answer is yes. However, the corporate headquarters has already failed step 2 and thus would not be identified as an operating segment.

Step 4: Is discrete financial information available for the component?
For units X, Y, Z and the corporate headquarters, the answer is yes. However, the corporate headquarters has already failed step 2 and thus would not be identified as an operating segment.

Conclusion
Therefore, units X, Y and Z are identified as Company A's operating segments.

ILLUSTRATIVE EXAMPLE 21.2 Identifying operating segments under IFRS 8 — matrix structure

Company A has a chief executive officer (CEO), a chief operating officer (COO) and an executive committee comprising the CEO, COO and the heads (general managers) of three business units organised according to the company's main products — units X, Y and Z. The company also operates in two distinct geographic regions — Oceania and North America. The heads of these geographic regions attend executive committee meetings, have input into decisions about the distribution of the company's products into their geographic regions and give their views on the performance of the company's products in their regions. Every month, financial information is presented to the executive committee for each of business units X, Y and Z, geographic regions Oceania and North America and for Company A as a whole in order to assess the performance of each business unit, each geographic region and of the company as a whole. Corporate headquarter costs that are not allocated to units X, Y or Z or to the geographic regions are also reported separately each month to the executive committee in order to determine the results for Company A as a whole. There is necessarily an overlap between the financial information presented for each of units X, Y and Z and the Oceania and North American geographic regions because the product performance reported for each unit is reported again, with that of the other two product units, by geographic region.

Step 1: Who is the CODM?

In this case, the CODM is likely to be the executive committee, since it is the group that regularly reviews the operating results of all business units, geographic regions and the company as a whole. However, the heads of the geographic regions don't appear to be able to make decisions about all business units and the company as a whole; rather, they only have input into the impact of product decisions on their geographic regions. This fact may influence the determination of operating segments (see the conclusion after step 4).

Step 2: Can the component generate revenue and incur expenses from its business activities?

For units X, Y and Z, the answer is clearly yes. For the geographic regions, the answer is also yes, even though the revenues are generated from deployment of the products from units X, Y and Z in the regions. For the corporate headquarters, the answer is no as it does not derive revenues; it only incurs costs.

Step 3: Are the component's operating results regularly reviewed by the CODM as a basis for resource allocation and performance assessment?

For units X, Y, Z, the geographic regions and the corporate headquarters, the answer is yes. However, the corporate headquarters has already failed step 2 and thus would not be identified as an operating segment.

Step 4: Is discrete financial information available for the component?

For units X, Y, Z, the geographic regions and the corporate headquarters, the answer is yes. However, the corporate headquarters has already failed step 2 and thus would not be identified as an operating segment.

Conclusion

This leaves the entity potentially having two sets of operating segments — units X, Y and Z, and geographic regions Oceania and North America. It is in this situation that IFRS 8 paragraph 10 directs the entity to the core principle of the standard to decide which set will best 'enable users of its financial statements to evaluate the nature and financial effects of the business activities in which it engages and the economic environments in which it operates'. In this situation, management must exercise judgement. Arguably, in this case, identifying units X, Y and Z as the operating segments best reflects the core principle because the organisation of the company along product lines seems to be dominant over the organisation by geographic lines (as reflected in the slightly lower impact on decision-making by the geographic region heads).

21.6 IDENTIFYING REPORTABLE SEGMENTS

21.6.1 The basic criteria

IFRS 8 paragraph 11 states that an entity shall report separately information about each operating segment that:

(a) has been identified as an operating segment in accordance with the four steps discussed above, or results from aggregating two or more of those segments in accordance with paragraph 12; and

(b) exceeds the quantitative thresholds in paragraph 13.

21.6.2 The quantitative thresholds

An entity shall report separately information about an operating segment that meets *any* of the following:

(a) its reported revenue is 10% or more of the combined revenue of all operating segments (revenue includes both external and internal revenue)

(b) the absolute amount of its reported profit or loss is 10% or more of the greater of (1) the combined reported profit of all operating segments that reported a profit and (2) the combined reported loss of all operating segments that reported a loss

(c) its assets are 10% or more of the combined assets of all operating segments.

If management believes that information about an operating segment would be useful to users, it may treat that segment as a reportable segment even if the quantitative thresholds are not met (IFRS 8 paragraph 13).

21.6.3 The aggregation criteria

The aggregation criteria in paragraph 12 provide that two or more operating segments may be aggregated into a single operating segment if aggregation is consistent with the core principle of the standard, the segments have similar economic characteristics and the segments are similar in *each* of the following respects:

(a) the nature of the products and services

(b) the nature of the production processes

(c) the type or class of customer for their products and services

(d) the methods used to distribute their products or provide their services

(e) if applicable, the nature of the regulatory environment, for example, banking, insurance or public utilities.

An entity may combine operating segments that do not meet the quantitative thresholds to produce a reportable segment only if the segments have similar economic characteristics and meet the aggregation criteria of paragraph 12 (IFRS 8 paragraph 14).

21.6.4 The 75% threshold

Paragraph 15 of IFRS 8 requires that an entity must identify operating segments until at least 75% of the entity's revenue is included in reportable segments. Importantly, segment revenue here is *external* revenue only and the total revenue is that of the consolidated group.

21.6.5 What happens to segments that are not reportable?

Paragraph 16 of IFRS 8 states that business activities and operating segments that are not reportable must be combined and disclosed as 'all other segments' separately from the reconciling items required by paragraph 28 (see section 21.8.5).

21.6.6 Vertically integrated businesses

As noted in section 21.6.2, IFRS 8 does not distinguish between revenues and expenses from transactions with third parties and those from transactions *within the group* for the purposes of identifying operating segments (IFRS 8 paragraph 5). Therefore, in an entity with internal vertically integrated businesses, it is possible that such internal businesses might be identified as operating segments under IFRS 8.

21.6.7 How many segments are enough?

IFRS 8 provides additional guidance to entities regarding the maximum number of reportable segments — indicating that ten is a reasonable maximum (IFRS 8 paragraph 19).

Figure 21.2 summarises the key decision points in identifying reportable segments, and continues from figure 21.1.

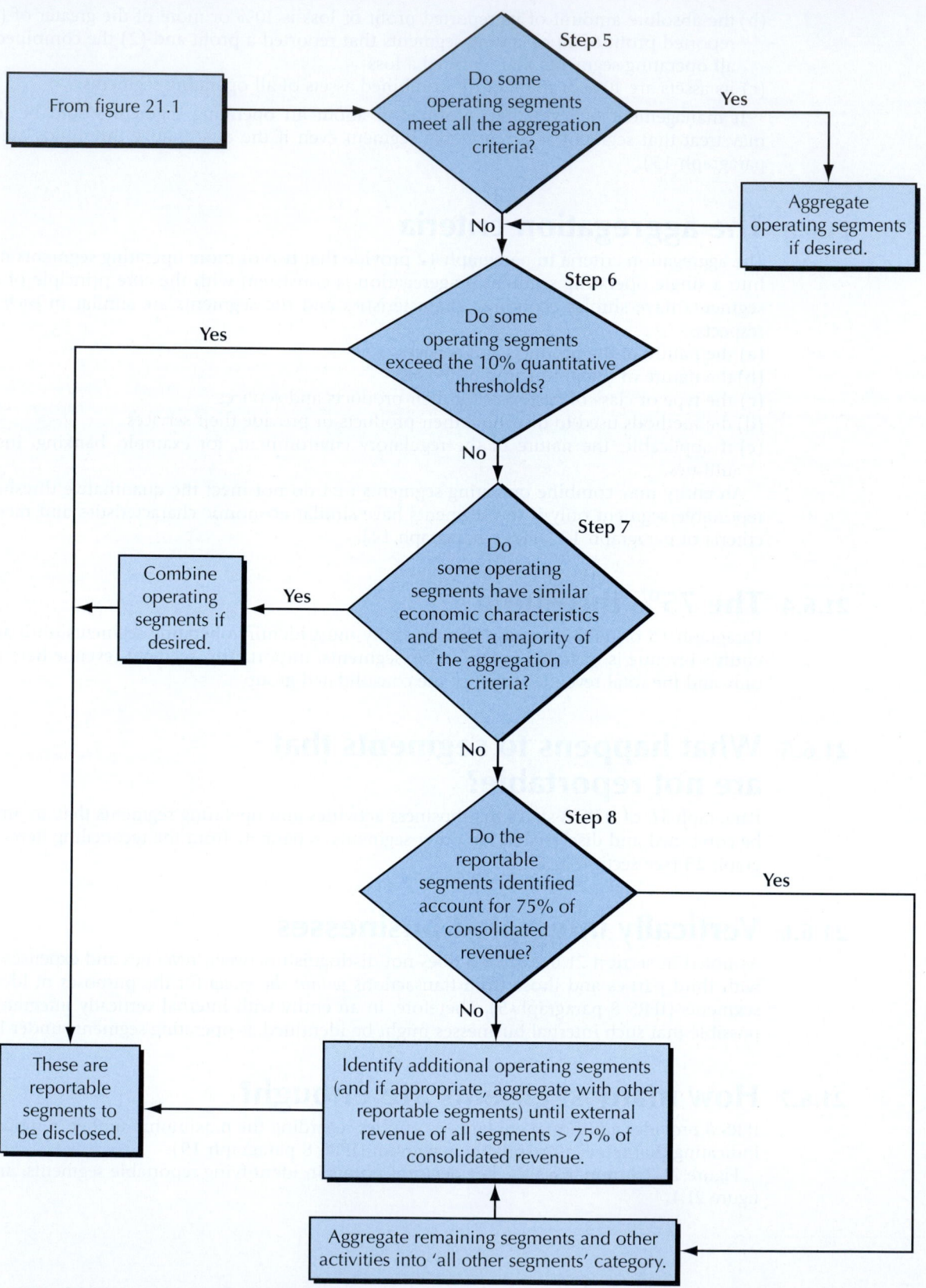

FIGURE 21.2 Identifying reportable segments under IFRS 8

Source: Ernst & Young (2007, p. 8). © 2012 EYGM Limited. All rights reserved.

21.7 APPLYING THE DEFINITION OF REPORTABLE SEGMENTS

Building on illustrative example 21.1, the following example illustrates how Company A identifies its reportable segments under IFRS 8.

ILLUSTRATIVE EXAMPLE 21.3 Identifying reportable segments under IFRS 8

Company A has identified units X, Y and Z as operating segments (see illustrative example 21.1). The following additional information is provided:

	Unit X $'000	Unit Y $'000	Unit Z $'000	Total operating segments $'000	Corporate headquarters $'000	Other businesses $'000	Total Company A (consolidated) $'000
Revenue	200	100 (80 earned from Unit Z)	400	700	—	230	850
Profit/(loss)	50	30 (10 earned from Unit Z)	100	180	(25)	20	165
Assets	800	300	950	2 050	250	200	2 500

Management has determined that units X, Y and Z do not meet the aggregation criteria of IFRS 8. Unit Z has no inventory on hand at year-end in respect of purchases from unit Y.

Quantitative thresholds: note that the quantitative thresholds are in respect of the *totals for the operating segments* — not the total for Company A (IFRS 8 paragraph 13):

	Revenue % of total	Profit % of total	Assets % of total
Unit X	29%	28%	39%
Unit Y	14%	17%	15%
Unit Z	57%	55%	46%

Therefore, all three units meet all three of the quantitative thresholds. (Note that only one threshold needs to be met.) Thus, all three units are reportable segments.

The next question is whether the reportable segments account for 75% of consolidated revenue. This test is applied to the *external* revenues of the segments (IFRS 8 paragraph 15). Total consolidated revenue (after inter-segment eliminations) is $850 000. Total external operating segment revenue is: Unit X: $200 000; Unit Y: $20 000 and Unit Z: $400 000, giving a total of $620 000. This constitutes 73% of total consolidated revenue, which is below the 75% requirement. Therefore, additional operating segments need to be identified. Management will need to further analyse the 'other businesses' and identify another reportable segment from that component.

Another aspect of applying the quantitative criteria is that the allocations of relevant amounts to segments needs to occur first, as illustrated in illustrative example 21.4.

ILLUSTRATIVE EXAMPLE 21.4 Applying the requirements — determining segment revenue, expense, assets and liabilities

The following financial information is reported to the CODM for diversified manufacturing Company A for the year ended 30 June 2014:

	Wine $m	Water heaters $m	Olive oil $m	All segments $m
Segment revenue	150	90	10	250
Segment result (profit)	14	5	1	20
Segment assets	500	200	100	800

Additional information
(a) Total consolidated revenue of Company A is $253 million.
(b) Total consolidated profit — after income tax expense of $5 million, interest income of $1 million and a gain on disposal of investments of $2 million — is $8 million.
(c) Total consolidated liabilities of Company A are $200 million.
(d) Liabilities include borrowings of $150 million and their related interest expense of $10 million.
(e) Liabilities of $40 million are trade creditors and other payables directly attributable to the wine segment.
(f) Liabilities of $10 million are trade creditors and other payables directly attributable to the water heaters segment.
(g) All assets and related depreciation have been allocated to the business segments.

Required

Determine the allocation of segment revenue, expense, assets and liabilities.

Solution

The allocation of segment revenue, expense, assets and liabilities is determined as follows:

	Wine $m	Water heaters $m	Olive oil $m	Unallocated $m	Consolidated $m
Revenue	150	90	10	3[1]	253
Segment result (profit)	14	5	1	(12)[2]	8
Assets	500	200	100	—	800
Liabilities	40	10	—	150[3]	200

[1] Interest income and gain on disposal of investments.
[2] $3 million revenue and $15 million expenses (interest expense and income tax expense).
[3] Borrowings are not allocated because the segments' operations are not primarily of a financial nature.

This example also shows that before an entity can apply the quantitative criteria to determine its reportable segments it needs first to calculate correctly the segment allocations and unallocated amounts.

LO8 21.8 DISCLOSURE
21.8.1 Overall approach

As discussed in section 21.4, the approach to disclosure is a key point of difference between IFRS 8 and IAS 14. While IAS 14 was prescriptive, IFRS 8 sets out a general approach to disclosure and largely allows management to determine what is disclosed and how the amounts disclosed are measured.

The general principle of disclosure is set out in paragraph 20 of IFRS 8, which is, in effect, a restatement of the core principle of the standard:

> An entity shall disclose information to enable users of its financial statements to evaluate the nature and financial effects of the business activities in which it engages and the economic environments in which it operates.

To give effect to this principle, paragraph 21 requires an entity to disclose:

(a) general information as described in paragraph 22;
(b) information about reported segment profit or loss, including specified revenues and expenses included in reported profit or loss, segment assets, segment liabilities and the basis of measurement as described in paragraphs 23–27; and
(c) reconciliations of the totals of segment revenues, reported segment profit or loss, segment assets, segment liabilities and other material segment items to corresponding entity amounts as described in paragraph 28.

21.8.2 General information

An entity shall disclose:

(a) factors used to identify the entity's reportable segments, including the basis of organisation, and
(b) types of products or services from which each reportable segment derives its revenues.

In complying with (a), for example, management would disclose whether it identified operating segments based on products or services, or geographic regions and whether segments have been aggregated.

21.8.3 Information about profit or loss, assets and liabilities

Paragraph 23 states that an entity shall report 'a measure' of profit or loss and total assets and total liabilities for each reportable segment. Importantly a measure of total assets and total liabilities for each reportable segment is required to be reported *only* if such an amount is regularly reported to the CODM.

This measure is that which is reported to the CODM for the purposes of making decisions about allocating resources to the segment and assessing its performance (IFRS 8 paragraph 25). In other words, whatever the CODM uses to measure and assess the operating segment is what is disclosed under IFRS 8. This extends to the allocation of amounts of profit or loss and assets and liabilities to segments. If the CODM uses information based on amounts that are allocated to segments, then those amounts should be allocated for the purposes of disclosing 'a measure'. If the CODM does not use that information, the amounts should not be allocated. This is in contrast to the prescriptive rules in IAS 14 about allocating amounts to segments.

The requirement to report a measure of profit or loss and segment assets is the only prescribed disclosure in IFRS 8 in respect of statement of profit or loss and other comprehensive income and statement of financial position items. The remainder of paragraph 23 is more discretionary.

In respect of segment profit or loss, certain line items are also required to be disclosed *only* if these items are included in the measure of segment profit or loss reported to the CODM, or are otherwise regularly provided to the CODM:

(a) revenues from external customers
(b) inter-segment revenues
(c) interest revenue
(d) interest expense
(e) depreciation and amortisation
(f) material items of income and expense disclosed in accordance with paragraph 97 of IAS 1
(g) the entity's interest in the profit or loss of associates and joint ventures accounted for by the equity method
(h) income tax expense or income
(i) material non-cash items other than depreciation and amortisation (IFRS 8 paragraph 23).

Interest revenue and interest expense may be reported on a net basis only if a majority of the segment's revenues are from interest and the CODM relies primarily on net interest revenue to assess the performance of the segment. This may be the case, for example, in the banking industry.

In respect of segment assets, certain line items are also required to be disclosed only if these items are included in the measure of segment assets reported to the CODM, or are otherwise regularly provided to the CODM:

(a) the amount of investment in associates and joint ventures accounted for by the equity method
(b) the amounts of additions to non-current assets (with certain exceptions) (IFRS 8 paragraph 24).

The notable feature of these disclosure requirements is the lack of prescription. If the items listed (with the exception of a measure of segment profit or loss, which must always be disclosed) are reported to the CODM, then they must be disclosed. This means that what is not reported internally is not disclosed externally. Furthermore, *how* the amount is measured internally is used for external measurement purposes, even if the measurement basis is not in accordance with IFRS.

21.8.4 Measurement

Because management has discretion about measurement, IFRS 8 requires disclosure of *how* the entity has determined the measures of profit or loss, and, if applicable, assets and liabilities, for each reportable segment (IFRS 8 paragraph 27). This includes:

(a) the basis of accounting for any transactions between reportable segments

(b) the nature of any differences between the measurements of the reportable segments' profits or losses and the entity's profit or loss before income taxes and discontinued operations (i.e. the profit or loss reported in the statement of profit or loss and other comprehensive income in accordance with IFRSs). For example, if the CODM uses concepts such as 'cash profit' for measuring the segment profit or loss, the entity would need to disclose how 'cash profit' is determined and how it differs from the IFRS measure of profit. This could include, for example, the fact that the CODM determines 'cash profit' to be profit or loss before fair value movements, depreciation and amortisation, and impairment charges.

(c) the nature of any differences between the measurements of the reportable segments' assets and the entity's assets. For example, this could include accounting policies and policies for allocation of jointly used assets.

(d) the nature of any differences between the measurements of the reportable segments' liabilities and the entity's liabilities. For example, this could include accounting policies and policies for allocation of jointly utilised liabilities.

(e) the nature of any changes from prior periods in the measurement methods used to determine reported segment profit or loss and the effect, if any, of those changes on the measure of segment profit or loss. For example, if the CODM decides to change the measure of segment profit or loss used from one that excludes fair value movements to one that includes fair value movements, this fact would need to be disclosed together with the impact on reported segment profit or loss.

(f) the nature and effect of any asymmetrical allocations to reportable segments. For example, an entity might allocate depreciation expense to a segment without allocating the related depreciable assets to that segment.

21.8.5 Reconciliations

An entity is required to provide reconciliations of all of the following:

(a) the total of the reportable segments' revenues to the entity's revenue. In illustrative example 21.3, ignoring the identification of additional segments to meet the 75% threshold, this would be a reconciliation of total operating segments' revenues of $700 000 to Company A's revenue of $850 000.

(b) the total of the reportable segments' measures of profit or loss to the entity's profit or loss before income tax and discontinued operations (or, if items such as income tax are allocated to segments, to profit or loss after income tax). In illustrative example 21.3, ignoring the identification of additional segments to meet the 75% threshold, this would be a reconciliation of total operating segments' profit of $180 000 to Company A's profit of $165 000.

(c) the total of the reportable segments' assets (if reported) to the entity's assets. In illustrative example 21.3, ignoring the identification of additional segments to meet the 75% threshold, this would be a reconciliation of total operating segments' assets of $2.05 million to Company A's assets of $2.5 million.

(d) the total of the reportable segments' liabilities (if reported) to the entity's liabilities

(e) the total of the reportable segments' amounts for every other material item of information disclosed to the corresponding amount for the entity. This would include, for example, the line items disclosed under paragraphs 23 and 24, if the amount disclosed differs from that disclosed in the entity's statement of profit or loss and other comprehensive income or statement of financial position.

All material reconciling items must be separately identified and described. For example, in illustrative example 21.3, assuming the amounts are material, the entity would need to disclose its reconciliation of total reportable segments' profit to Company A's profit as follows:

	$'000
Total reportable segments' profit:	180
Less: Inter-segment profit	(10)
Less: Corporate headquarters costs not allocated to reportable segments	(25)
Add: Profit from other businesses not identified as reportable segments	20
Total Company A profit	165

21.8.6 Entity-wide disclosures

The following disclosures apply to all entities subject to IFRS 8, including those that have only one reportable segment (unless the information is already provided as part of the reportable segment information).

- Information about products and services: revenues from external customers for *each product or service* or each group of similar products or services. In this case, the amount of revenues must be based on the financial information used to produce the entity's financial statements, *not* based on amounts reported to the CODM. If the information is not available and the cost to develop it would be excessive, the entity need not disclose the information but it must state this fact (IFRS 8 paragraph 32). This requirement is potentially onerous in that it is possible that one reportable segment includes numerous products and/or services. IAS 14 did not have a similar disclosure requirement.
- Information about geographical areas: revenues from external customers and non-current assets (i) attributed to/located in the entity's country of domicile and (ii) attributed to/located in foreign countries. If revenues or non-current assets attributed to/located in an individual foreign country are material, those revenues/assets shall be disclosed separately. The entity must also disclose the basis for attributing revenues from external customers to individual countries. In this case, as in paragraph 32, the amount of revenues and assets must be based on the financial information used to produce the entity's financial statements. If the information is not available and the cost to develop it would be excessive then the entity need not disclose the information but it must state this fact (IFRS 8 paragraph 33).
- Information about major customers: if revenues from transactions with a single external customer amount to 10% or more of an entity's revenues, disclose that fact, the total amount of revenues from each such customer, and the segment or segments reporting the revenues. The identity of the customer or customers does not have to be disclosed. IAS 14 did not have a similar disclosure requirement.

Overall, the entity-wide disclosure requirements of IFRS 8 are more onerous than those previously required by IAS 14.

21.8.7 Comparative information

There are a few circumstances in which comparative information must be restated or otherwise taken into account.

(a) If an operating segment was a reportable segment for the immediately preceding prior period but is not for the current period, and management decides that the segment is of continuing significance, information about that segment must continue to be reported in the current period (IFRS 8 paragraph 17).

(b) If an operating segment becomes a reportable segment for the current period, comparative information must be restated to reflect the newly reportable segment, even if that segment did not meet the criteria for reportability in the prior period. This is required unless the information is not available and the cost to develop it would be excessive (IFRS 8 paragraph 18).

(c) If management changes its measure of segment profit or loss, paragraph 27(e) requires disclosure of the nature and effect of that change, as discussed above. The standard does not specify whether comparative information must be restated in this circumstance. However, applying the principles of IAS 8 *Accounting Policies, Changes in Accounting Estimates and Errors* and the general principle apparent in IFRS 8 in respect of consistency of comparative information, one would expect the comparative information to be restated in this circumstance.

(d) If an entity changes the structure of its internal organisation in a manner that causes the composition of its reportable segments to change, the corresponding information for prior periods, including interim periods, must be restated. This applies unless the information is not available and the cost to develop it would be excessive (IFRS 8 paragraph 29). Note that in this case the exemption from restatement applies to each individual item of disclosure. This could result in restatement of some items and not of others.

(e) If an entity changes the structure of its internal organisation in a manner that causes the composition of its reportable segments to change and the corresponding information for prior periods is *not* restated, the entity must disclose the segment information for the current period on both the old and the new basis. This applies unless the information is not available and the cost to develop it would be excessive (IFRS 8 paragraph 30).

(f) On transition to the new standard (i.e. when the entity first applies IFRS 8), comparative information must be restated unless the information is not available and the cost to develop it would be excessive.

Note the repeated use of the phrase 'unless the information is not available and the cost to develop it would be excessive' in the above exemptions and other exemptions within the standard. This phrase is consistent with that used in SFAS 131 and differs from the term 'impracticable', which was used in IAS 14 and is still used in IAS 1 *Presentation of Financial Statements*. Arguably the phrase is more precise than 'impracticable'. It is also notable that IFRS 8 contains more exemptions from disclosure than IAS 14 did. IAS 14 provided an 'impracticability' exemption only for restatement of comparative information and on transition, whereas IFRS 8 provides exemptions from the entity-wide disclosures as well as for restatement of comparatives.

21.9 APPLYING THE DISCLOSURES IN PRACTICE

The following extracts illustrate how companies have applied the requirements of IFRS 8.

Figure 21.3 contains extracts from the 2010 annual report of Esprit Holdings Limited, a company listed on the Hong Kong Stock Exchange.

Firstly, review the Accounting Policy Note, which explains how the company has transitioned from IAS 14 to IFRS 8.

FIGURE 21.3 Extracts from Esprit Holdings Ltd — Accounting Policy Note and Note 5 Turnover and segment information

IFRS 8, 'Operating Segments', replaces IAS 14, 'Segment Reporting', and aligns segment reporting with the requirements of the US standard SFAS 131, 'Disclosures about Segments of an Enterprise and Related Information'. The new standard requires a 'management approach', under which segment information is presented on the same basis as that used for internal reporting purposes. This has resulted in an increase in the number of reportable segments presented. In addition, the segments are reported in a manner that is more consistent with the internal reporting provided to the chief operating decision-maker. Comparatives for 2009 have been restated.

5 Turnover and segment information

The Group is principally engaged in wholesale and retail distribution and licensing of quality fashion and lifestyle products designed under its own internationally-known Esprit brand name.

	2010 HK$ million	2009 HK$ million
Turnover		
Sales of goods	33 508	34 257
Licensing and other income	226	228
	33 734	34 485

The chief operating decision-makers have been identified as the executive directors ('Executive Directors') of the Group. Management has determined the operating segments based on the reports reviewed by the Executive Directors that are used to assess performance and allocate resources.

FIGURE 21.3 *(continued)*

The Executive Directors consider the business from an operations nature perspective, including wholesale and retail distribution and licensing of quality fashion and life-style products designed under its own internationally-known Esprit brand name.

Inter-segment transactions are entered into under the normal commercial terms and conditions that would also be available to unrelated third parties.

For the year ended 30 June 2010

	Wholesale HK$ million	Retail HK$ million	Licensing HK$ million	Corporate services, sourcing and others HK$ million	Group HK$ million
Total revenue	15 631	17 910	181	25 174	58 896
Inter-segment revenue	—	(33)	—	(25 129)	(24 162)
Revenue from external customers	15 631	17 877	181	45	33 734
Segment results	3 967	681	159	(1 021)	3 786
Interest income					33
Finance costs					(12)
Share of results of associates					81
Gain on measuring equity interest in the associated companies held before the business combination					1 586
Profit before taxation					5 474
Capital expenditure	43	797	3	666	1 509
Depreciation	69	719	4	92	884
Impairment of property, plant and equipment	1	654	—	—	655
Provision for store closure	—	441	—	—	441

For the year ended 30 June 2009 (restated)

	Wholesale HK$ million	Retail HK$ million	Licensing HK$ million	Corporate services, sourcing and others HK$ million	Group HK$ million
Total revenue	17 906	16 376	175	27 823	62 280
Inter-segment revenue	—	(25)	—	(27 770)	(27 795)
Revenue from external customers	17 906	16 351	175	53	34 485
Segment results	4 887	1 789	126	(1 073)	5 729
Interest income					87
Share of results of associates					161
Profit before taxation					5 977
Capital expenditure	64	1 298	1	648	2 011
Depreciation	65	616	4	91	776
Impairment of property, plant and equipment	—	38	—	—	38

(continued)

FIGURE 21.3 *(continued)*

Turnover from external customers is attributed to the following countries based on the location in which the sales originated:

	2010 HK$ million	2009 HK$ million
Europe		
Germany (Note 1)	14 773	15 454
Benelux	5 000	5 308
France	2 841	3 133
Austria	1 475	1 506
Scandinavia	1 464	1 605
Switzerland	1 409	1 254
United Kingdom	411	403
Ireland	32	61
Italy	287	361
Spain	295	261
Portugal	27	17
Others	7	—
	28 021	29 363
Asia Pacific		
Hong Kong	688	738
Macau (Note 2)	1 295	1 724
Taiwan	261	265
Singapore	410	399
Malaysia	211	210
China	793	—
Australia and New Zealand	976	819
	4 634	4 155
North America		
Canada	553	489
United States	526	478
	1 079	967
	33 734	34 485

Note 1: Germany sales includes wholesale sales to other European countries mainly Russia, Poland, Greece, Czech Republic and Croatia.
Note 2: Macau sales includes wholesale sales to other countries mainly China, Middle East, Chile, Thailand and India.

The total of non-current assets other than deferred tax assets, financial instruments and intangible assets is located in the following countries:

	2010 HK$ million	2009 HK$ million
Hong Kong	332	355
Germany	1 926	1 662
Other countries	1 730	2 903
	3 988	4 920

During the year, the turnover from the Group's largest customer amounted to less than 10 percent of the Group's total turnover (2009: less than 10 percent).

Source: Esprit Holdings Ltd (2010, pp. 107, 114–15).

Points to note about figure 21.3:

1. The company has applied IFRS 8 for the first time. This resulted in an increase in the number of reportable segments presented; the segment reporting is now more consistent with the company's internal reporting and comparative information has been restated.
2. The CODM has been identified as the 'Executive Directors' of the Group. These are listed in the Corporate Information section (annual report 2010, inside front cover) as the Group CEO and Group CFO.
3. The 'measure' of segment result that is reported to the CODM is profit before interest income, finance costs, share of results of associates and fair value gain recorded on associated companies. This means that this is the measure considered relevant to the CODM and reported to them for the segments. The segment result is reconciled to the IFRS profit before taxation as required by paragraph 28 of IFRS 8.
4. There is no disclosure of segment assets or liabilities. This means that these are not reported internally to the CODM.
5. The disclosures required by paragraph 23 of IFRS 8 are provided, other than segment income tax expense/income, which is presumably not reported internally to the CODM.
6. After inter-segment revenue, the Wholesale segment contributes 46% of consolidated revenue ($15 631/$33 734), while the Retail segment contributes 53% ($17 877/$33 734). However, the Wholesale segment contributes almost all of the profit ($3976/$3786 after Corporate losses). This is a good illustration of how revealing segment reporting is and thus why it is so useful to analysts and other users.
7. The company has reported revenue from external customers by geographic area in accordance with paragraph 33 (a) of IFRS 8. Again this information is very revealing about the company's business and shows that a large proportion of its revenues (based on the location in which the sales originated) come from Germany.
8. The other entity-wide disclosures required by paragraph 33 and 34 are also given. However, there is no disclosure of the information about products or services as required by paragraph 32. Presumably this is because the products/services are homogeneous. However, in the financial highlights section of the annual report there is a breakdown of products (clothing and footwear) by brand (Espirit 2010, p. 16).

Figure 21.4 contains an extract from the Woolworths Limited 2010 annual report. This diversified company is listed on the Australian Securities Exchange.

FIGURE 21.4 Extract from Woolworths Limited — Segment Disclosures Note

7   Segment Disclosures

The group has six reportable segments, as described below, that are the Group's strategic business units.

The business units offer different products and services and are managed separately because they require different technology and marketing strategies. The following summary describes the operations in each of the Group's reportable segments:

- Retail Operations
  - Australian Food and Liquor — procurement of Food and Liquor and products for resale to customers in Australia
  - New Zealand Supermarkets — procurement of Food and Liquor and products for resale to customers in New Zealand
  - Petrol — procurement of Petroleum products for resale to customers in Australia
  - BIG W — procurement of discount general merchandise products for resale to customers in Australia
  - Consumer Electronics — procurement of electronic products for resale to global customers
- Hotels — provision of leisure and hospitality services including food and alcohol, accommodation, entertainment and gaming.

The Unallocated group consists of the group's other operating segments that are not separately reportable (including Home Improvement) as well as various support functions including Property and Head Office costs.

There are varying levels of integration between the Supermarket and Hotel reportable segments. This includes the common usage of property and services, and some common administration functions. The accounting policies of the reportable segments are the same as described in Note 1.

Information regarding the operations of each segment is included below. Performance is measured based on segment Earnings Before Interest and Tax (EBIT). Segment EBIT is measured as management believes that such information is useful in evaluating the results of certain segments relative to other entities that operate within these industries. Inter-segment pricing is determined on an arm's length basis.

(continued)

FIGURE 21.4 (continued)

Major customers
Revenues from no one single customer amount to greater than 10% of the Group's revenues.

Segment disclosures Business segments	Australian Food and Liquor[1] 2010 $m	2009 $m	New Zealand Supermarkets 2010 $m	2009 $m	Petrol 2010 $m	2009 $m	BIG W 2010 $m	2009 $m	Consumer Electronics[2] 2010 $m	2009 $m	Hotels[3] 2010 $m	2009 $m	Unallocated[4] 2010 $m	2009 $m	Consolidated 2010 $m	2009 $m
Business segments																
Sales to customers	34 675.4	32 977.2	4 130.6	4 034.3	5 481.0	5 482.1	4 193.1	4 267.3	1 782.4	1 723.6	1 102.0	1 110.3	329.8	—	51 694.3	49 594.8
Other operating revenue	81.8	84.3	8.7	18.7	—	—	—	—	—	—	—	—	—	—	90.5	103.0
Inter-segment revenue	—	—	—	—	—	—	—	—	—	0.2	—	—	257.7	180.1	257.7	180.3
Segment revenue	34 757.2	33 061.5	4 139.3	4 053.0	5 481.0	5 482.1	4 193.1	4 267.3	1 782.4	1 723.8	1 102.0	1 110.3	587.5	180.1	52 042.5	49 878.1
Eliminations										(0.2)			(257.7)	(180.1)	(257.7)	(180.3)
Unallocated revenue/(expenses)[5]													179.3	148.4	179.3	148.4
Total revenue	34 757.2	33 061.5	4 139.3	4 053.0	5 481.0	5 482.1	4 193.1	4 267.3	1 782.4	1 723.6	1 102.0	1 110.3	509.1	148.4	51 964.1	49 846.2
Segment earnings before interest and tax	2 492.5	2 206.9	190.4	153.9	99.5	87.5	200.0	200.2	31.5	50.8	176.7	218.0	(108.5)	(101.8)	3 082.1	2 815.5
Net financing cost															(211.5)	(189.2)
Profit before tax															2 870.6	2 626.3
Income tax expense															(832.6)	(766.3)
Profit after tax															2 038.0	1 860.0
Segment depreciation and amortisation	457.8	444.2	67.0	54.9	29.5	24.9	72.5	64.1	31.2	30.8	75.4	64.6	64.3	45.9	797.7	729.4
Segment other non cash items	23.9	34.5	5.3	3.8	0.5	0.7	5.1	6.3	0.4	3.0	5.1	3.2	2.2	(19.9)	42.5	31.6
Capital expenditure[6]	646.3	832.4	195.6	220.3	50.7	64.5	129.0	131.0	45.1	54.0	176.9	234.6	711.6	315.1	1 955.2	1 851.9

Notes:
(1) Australian Food and Liquor comprises of supermarket and liquor stores and wholesale food and liquor in Australia.
(2) Consumer Electronics includes Woolworths Wholesale India.
(3) Hotels comprises of on-premise liquor sales, food, accommodation, gaming and venue hire.
(4) Unallocated comprise of corporate head office, Property division and Home Improvement division.
(5) Unallocated revenue comprises of rent and other revenue from operating activities.
(6) Capital expenditure is property, plant and equipment and intangible asset additions.

The consolidated entity operates predominantly in Australia and New Zealand. Intersegment pricing is determined on an arm's length basis.

FIGURE 21.4 *(continued)*

Geographical information

The Group operates in two principal geographical areas — Australia and New Zealand.

The Group's revenue from external customers and information about its geographical assets (non-current assets excluding investments in associates, finance lease receivables and 'other' financial assets) by geographical location are detailed below:

	Australia		New Zealand		Consolidated	
Segment disclosures Geographical segments	2010 $m	2009 $m	2010 $m	2009 $m	2010 $m	2009 $m
Sales to customers	47 293.3	45 266.0	4 401.0	4 328.8	51 694.3	49 594.8
Other operating revenue	81.8	84.3	8.7	18.7	90.5	103.0
Other revenue	158.1	129.9	21.2	18.5	179.3	148.4
Revenue from external customers	47 533.2	45 480.2	4 430.9	4 366.0	51 964.1	49 846.2
Non-current assets[1]	10 076.4	9 128.7	2 773.5	2 592.4	12 849.9	11 721.1

Note:

(1) Geographical non-current assets exclude financial instruments (fair value derivatives), deferred tax assets and intercompany receivables.

Source: Woolworths Ltd (2010, pp. 105–7).

Points to note about figure 21.4:

1. The group has identified six reportable segments, based on different products and services that require different technology and marketing strategies.

2. The measure of segment result that is reported to the CODM is earnings before interest and tax (EBIT). This is reconciled to the profit determined using Australian Accounting Standards as required by paragraph 28 of AASB 8 (AASB 8 is the Australian equivalent to IFRS 8).

3. There is no disclosure of segment assets or liabilities. This means that these are not reported internally to the CODM.

4. Of the six segments, Australian Food and Liquor contributes 67% of the group's revenues ($34 757.2/$51 964.1) after inter-segment eliminations and unallocated items) and 81% of the group's EBIT. As seen with Esprit, this segmentation enables a more detailed and insightful analysis of the group's results.

5. The geographical information disclosures (as required by paragraphs 33 and 34) show that the majority of the group's external revenues are from Australian customers and that most of the group's non-current assets are also based in Australia.

6. The disclosures about products and services required by paragraph 32 are not made separately because each segment is defined based on its different products and services.

Although neither of the companies above disclosed segment assets or liabilities, there are examples of companies that have done so in their 2010 annual reports. Figure 21.5 shows extracts from the 2010 annual report of HSBC Holdings plc, a company listed on the London, Hong Kong, New York, Paris and Bermuda stock exchanges. The segment report of this company is very detailed and includes an allocation of segment assets and liabilities to the reportable segments.

FIGURE 21.5 Segmental analysis of HSBC

13 Segmental analysis

HSBC's operating segments are organised into six geographical regions, Europe, Hong Kong, Rest of Asia–Pacific, Middle East, North America and Latin America. Due to the nature of the Group, HSBC's chief operating decision-maker regularly reviews operating activity on a number of bases, including by geographical region, customer group and global business and retail businesses by geographical region. The segmental analysis is presented on a geographical basis because, although information is reviewed on a number of bases, capital resources are allocated and performance is assessed primarily by geographical region. Also, the economic conditions of each geographical region are highly influential in determining the performance of the different businesses carried out in each region. As a result, provision of segmental information on a geographical basis provides the most meaningful basis from which to assess performance. HSBC's chief operating decision-maker is the Group Management Board which operates as a general management committee under the direct authority of the Board.

FIGURE 21.5 (continued)

Geographical information is classified by the location of the principal operations of the subsidiary or, for The Hongkong and Shanghai Banking Corporation, HSBC Bank, HSBC Bank Middle East and HSBC Bank USA, by the location of the branch responsible for reporting the results or advancing the funds.

Information provided to HSBC's chief operating decision-maker to make decisions about allocating resources to, and assessing the performance of, operating segments is measured in accordance with IFRSs. The financial information shown below includes the effects of intra-HSBC transactions between operating segments which are conducted on an arm's length basis and eliminated in a separate column. Shared costs are included in operating segments on the basis of the actual recharges made.

Products and services

HSBC provides a comprehensive range of banking and related financial services to its customers in its six geographical regions. The products and services offered to customers are organised by customer group and global business.

- Personal Financial Services offers a broad range of products and services to meet the personal banking, consumer finance and wealth management needs of individual customers. Personal banking products typically include current and savings accounts, mortgages and personal loans, credit cards, debit cards, insurance, wealth management and local and international payment services.
- Commercial Banking product offerings include the provision of financing services, payments and cash management, international trade finance, treasury and capital markets, commercial cards, insurance, and online and direct banking offerings.
- Global Banking and Markets provides tailored financial solutions to major government, corporate and institutional clients and private investors worldwide. The client-focused business lines deliver a full range of banking capabilities including financing, advisory and transaction services; a markets business that provides services in credit, rates, foreign exchange, money markets and securities services; global asset management services and principal investment activities.
- Global Private Banking provides a range of services to meet the banking, investment and wealth advisory needs of high net worth individuals.

Financial information

In the following segmental analysis, the benefit of shareholders' funds impacts the analysis only to the extent that these funds are actually allocated to businesses in the segment by way of intra-HSBC capital and funding structures.

Profit/(loss) for the year	Europe US$m	Hong Kong US$m	Rest of Asia–Pacific US$m	Middle East US$m	North America US$m	Latin America US$m	Intra-HSBC items US$m	Total US$m
Interest income	17 550	5 102	6 432	2 003	16 781	11 590	(1 113)	58 345
Interest expense	(6 300)	(856)	(2 604)	(636)	(4 342)	(5 279)	1 113	(18 904)
Net interest income	11 250	4 246	3 828	1 367	12 439	6 311	—	39 441
Fee income	8 334	3 460	2 399	737	4 524	2 366	(703)	21 117
Fee expense	(1 963)	(498)	(467)	(60)	(860)	(617)	703	(3 762)
Net fee income	6 371	2 962	1 932	677	3 664	1 749	—	17 355
Trading income excluding net interest income	1 461	1 107	1 207	343	109	453	—	4 680
Net interest income on trading activities	1 402	205	411	27	205	280	—	2 530
Net trading income	2 863	1 312	1 618	370	314	733	—	7 210
Changes in fair value of long-term debt issued and related derivatives	(365)	(2)	(2)	—	111	—	—	(258)
Net income from other financial instruments designated at fair value	647	380	26	—	—	425	—	1 478
Net income from financial instruments designated at fair value	282	378	24	—	111	425	—	1 220

2010

FIGURE 21.5 *(continued)*

	Europe US$m	Hong Kong US$m	Rest of Asia–Pacific US$m	Middle East US$m	North America US$m	Latin America US$m	Intra-HSBC items US$m	Total US$m
2010								
Profit/(loss) for the year								
Gains less losses from financial investments	486	98	146	(3)	143	98	—	968
Dividend income	20	30	1	7	42	12	—	112
Net earned insurance premiums	4 067	4 332	448	—	245	2 054	—	11 146
Other operating income/(expense)	2 117	1 606	1 598	(8)	233	141	(3 125)	2 562
Total operating income	27 456	14 964	9 595	2 410	17 191	11 523	(3 125)	80 014
Net insurance claims incurred and movement in liabilities to policyholders	(4 706)	(4 762)	(363)	—	(144)	(1 792)	—	(11 767)
Net operating income before loan impairment charges and other credit risk provisions	22 750	10 202	9 232	2 410	17 047	9 731	(3 125)	68 247
Loan impairment charges and other credit risk provisions	(3 020)	(114)	(439)	(627)	(8 295)	(1 544)	—	(14 039)
Net operating income	19 730	10 088	8 793	1 783	8 752	8 187	(3 125)	54 208
Employee compensation and benefits	(7 875)	(2 341)	(2 719)	(579)	(3 672)	(2 650)	—	(19 836)
General and administrative expenses	(6 499)	(1 686)	(2 181)	(450)	(4 179)	(3 286)	3 125	(15 156)
Depreciation and impairment of property, plant and equipment	(719)	(237)	(189)	(42)	(288)	(238)	—	(1 713)
Amortisation and impairment of intangible assets	(352)	(167)	(54)	(7)	(183)	(220)	—	(983)
Total operating expenses	(15 445)	(4 431)	(5 143)	(1 078)	(8 322)	(6 394)	3 125	(37 688)
Operating profit	4 285	(5 657)	3 650	705	430	1 793	—	16 520
Share of profit in associates and joint ventures	17	35	2 252	187	24	2	—	2 517
Profit before tax	4 302	5 692	5 902	892	454	1 795	—	19 037
Tax expense	(1 006)	(987)	(962)	(138)	(1 180)	(573)		(4 846)
Profit/(loss) for the year	3 296	4 705	4 940	754	(726)	1 222	—	14 191

	Europe US$m	Hong Kong US$m	Rest of Asia–Pacific US$m	Middle East US$m	North America US$m	Latin America US$m	Intra-HSBC items US$m	Total US$m
2009								
Interest income	20 283	5 327	5 877	2 260	19 526	10 091	(1 268)	62 096
Interest expense	(8 015)	(1 132)	(2 338)	(775)	(5 856)	(4 518)	1 268	(21 366)
Net interest income	12 268	4 195	3 539	1 485	13 670	5 573	—	40 730
Fee income	8 576	3 099	1 972	682	5 496	2 230	(652)	21 403
Fee expense	(2 309)	(430)	(415)	(57)	(679)	(501)	652	(3 739)
Net fee income	6 267	2 669	1 557	625	4 817	1 729	—	17 664

(continued)

FIGURE 21.5 (continued)

	Europe US$m	Hong Kong US$m	Rest of Asia–Pacific US$m	Middle East US$m	North America US$m	Latin America US$m	Intra-HSBC items US$m	Total US$m
	2009							
Trading income excluding net interest income	2 861	1 068	1 264	369	35	639	—	6 236
Net interest income on trading activities	2 598	157	342	25	296	209	—	3 627
Net trading income	5 459	1 225	1 606	394	331	848	—	9 863
Changes in fair value of long-term debt issued and related derivatives	(2 746)	(3)	(1)	—	(3 497)	—	—	(6 247)
Net income from other financial instruments designated at fair value	1 321	788	111	—	1	495	—	2 716
Net income/(expense) from financial instruments designated at fair value	(1 425)	785	110	—	(3 496)	495	—	(3 531)
Gains less losses from financial investments	50	9	(19)	16	296	168	—	520
Dividend income	29	28	2	3	53	11	—	126
Net earned insurance premiums	4 223	3 674	365	—	309	1 900	—	10 471
Other operating income	2 262	1 274	1 238	71	566	133	(2 756)	2 788
Total operating income	29 133	13 859	8 398	2 594	16 546	10 857	(2 756)	78 631
Net insurance claims incurred and movement in liabilities to policyholders	(5 589)	(4 392)	(395)	—	(241)	(1 833)	—	(12 450)
Net operating income before loan impairment charges and other credit risk provisions	23 544	9 467	8 003	2 594	16 305	9 024	(2 756)	66 181
Loan impairment charges and other credit risk provisions	(5 568)	(500)	(896)	(1 334)	(15 664)	(2 526)	—	(26 488)
Net operating income	17 976	8 967	7 107	1 260	641	6 498	(2 756)	39 693
Employee compensation and benefits	(7 174)	(2 102)	(2 363)	(545)	(4 085)	(2 199)	—	(18 468)
General and administrative expenses	(5 775)	(1 502)	(1 872)	(419)	(3 794)	(2 786)	2 756	(13 392)
Depreciation and impairment of property, plant and equipment	(762)	(224)	(172)	(31)	(329)	(207)	—	(1 725)
Amortisation and impairment of intangible assets	(277)	(118)	(43)	(6)	(183)	(183)	—	(810)
Total operating expenses	(13 988)	(3 946)	(4 450)	(1 001)	(8 391)	(5 375)	2 756	(34 395)
Operating profit/(loss)	3 988	5 021	2 657	259	(7 750)	1 123		5 298
Share of profit in associates and joint ventures	21	8	1 543	196	12	1		1 781
Profit/(loss) before tax	4 009	5 029	4 200	455	(7 738)	1 124	—	7 079
Tax income/(expense)	(776)	(869)	(753)	(94)	2 285	(178)	—	(385)
Profit/(loss) for the year	3 233	4 160	3 447	361	(5 453)	946	—	6 694

FIGURE 21.5 *(continued)*

Other information about the profit/(loss) for the year

	Europe US$m	Hong Kong US$m	Rest of Asia–Pacific US$m	Middle East US$m	North America US$m	Latin America US$m	Intra-HSBC items US$m	Total US$m
2010								
Net operating income	19 730	10 088	8 793	1 783	8 752	8 187	(3 125)	54 208
External	18 881	9 170	7 728	1 774	8 504	8 151	—	54 208
Inter-segment	849	918	1 065	9	248	36	(3 125)	—
Profit/(loss) for the year includes the following significant non-cash items:								
Depreciation, amortisation and impairment	1 071	404	243	49	471	458	—	2 696
Loan impairment losses gross of recoveries and other credit risk provisions	3 303	169	615	684	8 476	1 812	—	15 059
Impairment of financial investments	35	41	4	5	21	1	—	107
2009								
Net operating income	17 976	8 967	7 107	1 260	641	6 498	(2 756)	39 693
External	16 734	8 352	6 056	1 283	767	6 501	—	39 693
Inter-segment	1 242	615	1 051	(23)	(126)	(3)	(2 756)	—
Profit/(loss) for the year includes the following significant non-cash items:								
Depreciation, amortisation and impairment	1 039	342	215	37	515	390	—	2 538
Loan impairment losses gross of recoveries and other credit risk provisions	5 833	534	1 028	1 361	15 757	2 865	—	27 378
Impairment of financial investments	137	129	50	4	38	—	—	358

Performance ratios	Europe %	Hong Kong %	Rest of Asia–Pacific %	Middle East %	North America %	Latin America %	Total %
2010							
Share of HSBC's profit before tax	22.6	29.9	31.0	4.7	2.4	9.4	100.0
Cost efficiency ratio	67.9	43.4	55.7	44.7	48.8	65.7	55.2
2009							
Share of HSBC's profit/ (loss) before tax	56.7	71.0	59.3	6.4	(109.3)	15.9	100.0
Cost efficiency ratio	59.4	41.7	55.6	38.6	51.5	59.6	52.0

(continued)

FIGURE 21.5 (continued)

Balance sheet information

	Europe US$m	Hong Kong US$m	Rest of Asia–Pacific US$m	Middle East US$m	North America US$m	Latin America US$m	Intra-HSBC items US$m	Total US$m
At 31 December 2010								
Loans and advances to customers (net)	435 799	140 691	108 731	24 626	190 532	57 987	—	958 366
Interests in associates and joint ventures	186	207	15 035	1 661	104	5	—	17 198
Total assets	1 249 527	429 565	278 062	52 757	492 487	139 938	(187 647)	2 454 689
Customer accounts	491 563	297 484	158 155	33 511	158 486	88 526	—	1 227 725
Total liabilities	1 189 996	422 101	246 989	45 379	459 301	123 655	(187 647)	2 299 774
Capital expenditure incurred[1]	865	836	168	46	774	788	—	3 477
At 31 December 2009								
Loans and advances to customers (net)	439 481	99 381	80 043	22 844	206 853	47 629	—	896 231
Interests in associates and joint ventures	147	157	11 083	1 573	42	9	—	13 011
Total assets	1 268 600	399 243	222 139	48 107	475 014	115 967	(164 618)	2 364 452
Customer accounts	495 019	275 441	133 999	32 529	149 157	72 889	—	1 159 034
Total liabilities	1 213 907	384 912	203 243	42 325	447 530	101 492	(164 618)	2 228 791
Capital expenditure incurred[1]	983	290	159	102	658	540	—	2 732

[1] Expenditure incurred on property, plant and equipment and other intangible assets. Excludes assets acquired as part of business combinations and goodwill.

Other financial information
Net operating income by customer group and global business

	Personal Financial Services US$m	Commercial Banking US$m	Global Banking & Markets US$m	Global Private Banking US$m	Other[1] US$m	Intra-HSBC items US$m	Total US$m
2010							
Net operating income	21 317	12 029	18 957	3 105	4 663	(5 863)	54 208
External	19 529	11 419	22 090	2 194	(1 024)	—	54 208
Internal	1 788	610	(3 133)	911	5 687	(5 863)	—
2009							
Net operating income	15 513	9 571	18 652	2 984	(2 031)	(4 996)	39 693
External	13 804	9 285	21 383	2 275	(7 054)	—	39 693
Internal	1 709	286	(2 731)	709	5 023	(4 996)	—

[1] The main items reported in the 'Other' category are certain property activities, unallocated investment activities, centrally held investment companies, movements in fair value of own debt and HSBC's holding company and financing operations. The 'Other' category also includes gains and losses on the disposal of certain significant subsidiaries or business units.

FIGURE 21.5 *(continued)*

Information by country

	2010		2009	
	External net operating income[1] US$m	**Non-current assets[2] US$m**	**External net operating income[1] US$m**	**Non-current assets[2] US$m**
UK	11 467	19 661	9 958	19 704
Hong Kong	9 170	4 630	8 352	3 374
USA	6 098	6 669	(1 042)	5 499
France	3 185	10 914	3 322	11 782
Brazil	4 506	2 025	3 368	1 868
Other countries	19 782	29 747	15 735	25 557
	54 208	73 646	39 693	67 784

1 External net operating income is attributed to countries on the basis of the location of the branch responsible for reporting the results or advancing the funds.
2 Non-current assets consist of property, plant and equipment, goodwill, other intangible assets, interests in associates and joint ventures and certain other assets expected to be recovered more than twelve months after the reporting period.

Source: Reproduced with permission from HSBC Holdings plc Annual Report and Accounts 2010 (pp. 296–303).

SUMMARY

IFRS 8 *Operating Segments* is primarily a disclosure standard and is particularly relevant for large organisations that operate in different geographical locations and/or in diverse businesses. Information about an entity's segments is relevant to assessing the risks and returns of a diversified or multinational entity where often that information cannot be determined from aggregated data.

In January 2006, the IASB issued ED 8 *Operating Segments*, which it proposed as a replacement to IAS 14. The ED was part of the IASB's program for achieving convergence with standards issued by the FASB in the United States and essentially adopted the requirements of the FASB Statement of Financial Accounting Standards No. 131 (SFAS 131) *Disclosures about Segments of an Enterprise and Related Information*. The major changes from IAS 14 are the adoption of the management approach to identifying segments and the lack of prescription in respect of segment disclosures. ED 8 was finally issued as a new standard, IFRS 8 *Operating Segments*, in November 2006. IFRS 8 was applicable for annual reporting periods beginning on or after 1 January 2009.

In Europe, the replacement of IAS 14 with IFRS 8 was highly controversial. Concern was expressed by many commentators about the management approach and the lack of mandatory disclosure requirements. Those in favour of the management approach argued that the information provided under that approach will be more relevant and reliable because it will, inter alia, enable investors to evaluate the company on the same basis as that used by management in its decision making and that any concerns about understandability are addressed by the reconciliation requirements of IFRS 8. Those against the management approach argued that management will take advantage of the discretion provided in IFRS 8 in order to control the information provided to users. Only time will tell whether concerns about the approach eventuate.

Discussion questions

1. Segment disclosures are widely regarded as some of the most useful disclosures in financial statements because of the extent to which they disaggregate financial information into meaningful and often revealing groupings. Discuss this assertion by reference to the objectives of financial reporting by segments.

2. IFRS 8 anticipates that some entities not within its scope might voluntarily disclose segment information. Do you think many reporting entities would voluntarily provide these disclosures? Explain your answer.
3. Explain what the 'management approach' used in IFRS 8 means.
4. Briefly compare the approach required by the predecessor standard IAS 14 *Segment Reporting* to that required by IFRS 8 *Operating Segments*.
5. Discuss the concerns raised about IFRS 8 when it was first introduced. Compare the views of users and preparers when analysing these concerns. Do you think the concerns expressed by users will eventuate?
6. Evaluate whether the reconciliations required by paragraph 28 of IFRS 8 address a concern about lack of comparability between entities caused by management's ability to select any measurement basis it chooses in reporting segment information.

Exercises

STAR RATING ★ BASIC ★★ MODERATE ★★★ DIFFICULT

| Exercise 21.1 | **DEFINING OPERATING SEGMENTS** |

★ IFRS 8 sets out four key steps that need to be followed in order to identify an operating segment.

Required

List the four key steps.

| Exercise 21.2 | **AGGREGATING OPERATING SEGMENTS** |

★★ Company B is a listed manufacturing company. It produces most of its products in Australia but exports 90% of these products to the United States, Canada and Germany. It has only one main product line: scientific equipment. Company B is organised internally into two main business units: local and export. The export business unit is in turn divided into two sub-units: North America and Germany (North America includes Canada). Each business unit reports separate financial and operational information to the chief executive officer (CEO) and chief financial officer (CFO) who are identified as the CODM. The results of the two business units are then aggregated to form the consolidated financial information. Details of the identified operating segments are as follows:

	United States	**Canada**	**Germany**	**Australia**
Economic and political conditions	Stable	Stable. Closely related to US environment	Stable	Stable
Relationships between operations	Closely linked to Canadian operations	Closely linked to US operations	Self-sustaining	Self-sustaining
Proximity of operations	Closely linked to Canadian operations	Closely linked to US operations	Not close to other operations	Not close to other operations
Special risks	None	None	Stricter regulations	Small market
Exchange control regulations	None	None	None	None
Currency risks	Low	Low to medium	Low	Low to medium

Required

Identify which operating segments, if any, meet the aggregation criteria of IFRS 8 paragraph 12. Give reasons for your answer.

| Exercise 21.3 | **IDENTIFYING REPORTABLE SEGMENTS** |

★ Using the information from exercise 21.2, identify Company B's operating segments.

Exercise 21.4

IDENTIFYING REPORTABLE SEGMENTS

Company A is a listed diversified retail company. Its stores are located mainly in the United Kingdom. It has three main types of stores: general department stores, liquor stores and specialist toy stores. Each of these stores has different products, customer types and distribution processes. In accordance with IFRS 8, Company A has identified three operating segments: general department stores, liquor stores and specialist toy stores.

All three business units earn most of their revenue from external customers. Total consolidated revenue of company A is $600 million.

	General department stores $m	Liquor stores $m	Toy stores $m	All segments $m
Revenue	400	100	50	550
Segment result (profit)	15	7	4	26
Assets	900	200	100	1 200

Required

Identify Company A's reportable segments in accordance with IFRS 8. Explain your answer.

Exercise 21.5

ANALYSING THE INFORMATION PROVIDED

Using the information provided about Company A in exercise 21.4, analyse the relative profitability of the reportable segments.

Exercise 21.6

DISCLOSURES

Company X has three reportable segments, A, B and C, which represent distinct geographical areas. The CODM receives financial information about the geographical areas. Segment A produces Product P and Product Y. Segment B produces Product P only. Segment C produces Product Y and sells Service Z. The following financial information about each segment is reported to the CODM:
• revenues from external customers
• earnings before interest, depreciation and amortisation and tax (EBITDA)
• depreciation and amortisation.

Required

State whether each of the following statements is true or false, by reference to the relevant requirements of IFRS 8:
1. Company X must disclose EBITDA for each reportable segment.
2. Company X must disclose total assets for each reportable segment.
3. Company X must reconcile the total EBITDA of Segments A, B and C to its reported IFRS profit before income tax and discontinued operations.
4. Company X must disclose total liabilities for each reportable segment.
5. Company X must disclose depreciation and amortisation for each reportable segment.
6. Company X must disclose revenue from external customers for each of Product P, Product Y and Service Z.

Exercise 21.7

DISCLOSURES

Company X, a listed manufacturing company, has two reportable segments, A and B. Both A and B are manufacturing segments.

Required

For each item listed, state whether or not it would be disclosed for each of the reportable segments, identify the segments for which it would be disclosed and explain what other disclosures, if any, are required in accordance with IFRS 8.

1. Interest income — not reported to the CODM on a segment basis but regularly provided to the CODM for the group as a whole
2. Dividend income — not reported to the CODM on a segment basis but regularly provided to the CODM for the group as a whole
3. Share of profits from investments in equity-method associates attributable to Segment A — reported to the CODM for Segment A
4. Interest expense — not reported to the CODM on a segment basis but regularly provided to the CODM for the group as a whole
5. Revenues from external customers for each of Segment A and Segment B
6. The amount of investments in associates accounted for using the equity method attributable to Segment A
7. Payables and trade creditors attributable to Segment B but not reported to the CODM
8. Borrowing costs that have been capitalised for Segment B and are regularly reported to the CODM

Exercise 21.8

REPORTABLE SEGMENTS, ALLOCATING AMOUNTS TO SEGMENTS

★★ Company A is a listed diversified retail company. Its stores are located mainly in Australia. It has three main types of stores: general department stores, liquor stores and specialist toy stores. Each of these stores has different products, customer types and distribution processes. Company A has three business units: general department stores, liquor stores and specialist toy stores.

For the year ended 30 June 2013 each business unit reported the following financial information to Company A's CODM:

	General department stores $m	Liquor stores $m	Toy stores $m	All segments $m
Revenue	400	100	50	550
Segment result (profit)	15	7	4	26
Assets	900	200	100	1 200

All three business units earn their revenue from external customers. Total consolidated revenue of Company A for the year ended 30 June 2013 is $800 million. Included in general department stores' revenue is $50 million of revenue from toy stores. As at the end of the reporting period toy stores owed general department stores $45 million. This amount is included in general department stores' assets. Within the general department stores business unit there are five different legal entities including legal entities Y and Z. As at 30 June 2013 legal entity Z owed $23 million to legal entity Y. These amounts have not been eliminated in determining the assets of the general department stores segment. Inter-segment asset balances are reported to the CODM but are not used by the CODM as the basis for determining reportable segments. Intra-segment assets are reported to the CODM and are eliminated in determining reportable segments.

Required

State whether the following statements are true or false. Give reasons for your answers.
1. Company A has three reportable segments.
2. The revenue figure that should be used by the general department stores segment for the purposes of determining whether or not it is a reportable segment is $350 million.
3. Company A must disclose the toy stores segment liabilities after deducting the $45 million owed to general department stores.
4. The assets figure that should be used by the general department stores segment for the purposes of determining whether or not it is a reportable segment is $900 million.
5. The assets figure that should be used by the general department stores segment for the purposes of determining whether or not it is a reportable segment is $855 million.
6. The assets figure that should be used by the general department stores segment for the purposes of determining whether or not it is a reportable segment is $877 million.
7. Company A must disclose a reconciliation of total segment assets to its consolidated assets of $1132 million.

★★★ Company A is a listed diversified manufacturing company. It is listed on the London Stock Exchange and produces most of its products in China and India. Its markets are in the European Union and the Asia–Pacific region. It produces three types of products and services: home furniture; office furniture and soft furnishings.

The CODM has determined that Company A's operating segments should be based on geographical markets and has identified the reportable segments as listed below. The following information is reported to the CODM for each of the markets:

1. earnings before interest, depreciation and amortisation and taxation (EBITDA)
2. revenues from external customers.

The following table sets out the financial information provided to the CODM for the year ended 31 December 2014. Each operating segment has been identified as a reportable segment. All amounts are in pounds.

	France £	Germany £	United Kingdom £	India £	China £	Australia and New Zealand £
Revenue from external customers	22 300 000	35 654 000	21 587 600	5 356 800	7 324 800	8 763 400
Inter-segment revenue	—	—	—	10 000 000	10 000 000	—
EBITDA	6 400 000	7 325 000	5 325 000	5 324 000	7 625 000	2 325 000

Other information disclosed in the company's 31 December 2014 financial statements:
(a) Total consolidated revenue: £125 000 000.
(b) Inter-segment revenues represent wholesale sales from China and India to the other operating segments.
(c) Net profit before taxation: £25 625 000.
(d) Total consolidated assets: £1 041 670 000.
(e) Revenue from external customers for each type of product is:
   (i) Home furniture: £78 525 000.
   (ii) Office furniture: £17 700 000.
   (iii) Soft furnishings: £28 775 000.

Required

Analyse Company A's business with reference to its reported segment information. Show all workings to support your analysis.

References

Bundesverband Deutscher Banken 2007, *Endorsement of IFRS 8 Operating Segments — analysis of potential impacts, response from the Association of German Banks*, 28 June.

Ernst & Young 2007, *IFRS 8 Operating Segments: implementation guidance.*

Esprit Holdings Ltd 2010, *Annual report year ended 30 June 2010*, Espirit Holdings Limited, Bermuda, www.espritholdings.com

European Parliament 2007, Document B6–0437/2007, *Motion for a resolution*, 7 November, www.europarl.europa.eu.

HSBC Holdings plc 2011, *Annual report and accounts 2010*, London, www.hsbc.com.

Véron, N 2007, *EU adoption of the IFRS 8 standard on operating segments*, presented to the Economic and Monetary Affairs Committee of the European Parliament, 19 September.

Woolworths Limited 2010, *Annual report 2010*, Woolworths Limited, Australia, www.woolworthslimited.com.au.

22 Related party disclosures

ACCOUNTING STANDARDS IN FOCUS	IAS 24 *Related Party Disclosures*

LEARNING OBJECTIVES

After studying this chapter, you should be able to:

1 explain the potential effect of related party relationships
2 explain the objective and scope of IAS 24
3 identify an entity's related parties
4 identify relationships that do not give rise to a related party relationship as envisaged under IAS 24
5 describe and apply the disclosures required by IAS 24
6 explain why a government-related entity has a partial exemption from related party disclosures.

INTRODUCTION

It is not uncommon in business for entities to establish relationships with other entities and individuals, to interact with those parties, and to have outstanding balances and commitments with them. For example, groups of entities may conduct their business activities through subsidiary organisations, associated entities or joint venture operations. If an entity engages in transactions with other closely connected entities there is a danger that the economics of the transaction may not be the same had the transaction been negotiated by independent parties in an arm's length arrangement. For example, an entity might have an incentive to shift risks and returns in the form of profits or losses, income or expense flows, or assets or liabilities to a party that it is able to influence or control. Paragraph 6 of IAS 24 *Related Party Disclosures* explains that related parties may enter into transactions on terms and conditions that would not apply to unrelated parties. For example an entity might transact with an associate on more or less favourable terms than it would use with another, unrelated individual or entity. Thus, a related party association has the potential to have an impact on the profit or loss and financial position of an entity that might not otherwise occur.

Paragraph 9 of IAS 24 *Related Party Disclosures* provides a definition of when one party is considered to be related to another party which includes close family members of a reporting entity, situations where control, joint control, or significant influence exists, and where a person or entity is a member of the key management personnel of a reporting entity.

The simple existence of a related party relationship has the potential to affect transactions with other parties. As an example, a subsidiary entity might operate on the instructions of its parent entity. Accordingly, knowledge of business relationships, related party transactions, outstanding balances and commitments with related parties may affect assessments of the business risks faced by entities. For these reasons, IAS 24 requires identification and disclosure of related parties, including related party transactions and any outstanding balances and commitments.

22.1 APPLICATION

IAS 24 is primarily a disclosure standard. It is particularly relevant for entities that have established relationships with related parties, and that have transacted with those parties. The standard was first issued with an effective date for financial reporting periods commencing on 1 January 1986. It has been amended several times, most recently to simplify the disclosure requirements for government related entities and to clarify the definition of related parties. The latest revision has effect for reporting periods commencing on 1 January 2011.

22.2 OBJECTIVE AND SCOPE

As mentioned, IAS 24 applies to the identification of related party relationships and transactions and outstanding balances and commitments with related parties. It is used to identify the circumstances in which the disclosure of these items should occur, and the relevant disclosures to make.

The objective of IAS 24 as outlined in paragraph 1 is to ensure that an organisation's financial statements contain the disclosures necessary to an understanding of the potential effect of transactions and outstanding balances and commitments with related parties.

An alternative to the disclosure of related parties, transactions, balances and commitments could be to restate the events as though they had occurred between independent parties in arm's length transactions. However, in many instances valuation of the events and their impacts would be very difficult, if not impossible to determine as comparable transactions simply may not exist. Thus the objective of disclosing related party information is to ensure that the users of financial statements are provided with sufficient knowledge to enable them to undertake an independent assessment of the risks and opportunities facing entities which engage in related party transactions.

The major issues that must be considered, when determining the disclosures necessary to provide sufficient knowledge to financial statement users, include identifying related parties and related party arrangements, and deciding on the type and extent of the disclosure to be made. So, in summary, IAS 24 is applied in identifying related party relationships and transactions, identifying outstanding balances and commitments between related parties, and determining when and what related party disclosures must be made.

Paragraphs 3 and 4 of IAS 24 note that related party relationships, transactions, outstanding balances and commitments are disclosed in the consolidated and separate financial statements of a parent, venturer or investor presented in accordance with IFRS 10 *Consolidated Financial Statements* or IAS 27 *Separate Financial Statements*. However, intra-group transactions and balances are eliminated from consolidated financial statements.

22.3 IDENTIFYING RELATED PARTIES

IAS 24 considers close family who are able to control or significantly influence the activities of the other 'related' entity to be related parties. This relationship is detailed in paragraph 9 of IAS 24. If any of the conditions in paragraph 9 apply to an entity then it is regarded as a related party.

22.3.1 Definition of a related party

The conditions indicating whether one party is considered to be related to another are summarised in table 22.1.

TABLE 22.1 Definition of a related party — IAS 24 (paragraph 9a, b)	
Part a — A person or a close member of the person's family is related to a reporting entity if that person:	
(i)	has control or joint control of the reporting entity
(ii)	has significant influence over the reporting entity
(iii)	is a member of the key management personnel of the reporting entity or of a parent of the reporting entity
Part b — An entity is related to a reporting entity if any of the following conditions apply:	
(i)	The entity and the reporting entity are members of the same group
(ii)	The entity is an associate or joint venture of the entity (or an associate or joint venture of a member of a group of which the other entity is a member)
(iii)	Both entities are joint ventures of the same third party
(iv)	An entity is a joint venture of a third entity and the other entity is an associate of the third entity
(v)	The entity is a post-employment benefit plan for the benefit of employees of either the reporting entity or an entity related to the reporting entity. If the reporting entity is such a plan, the sponsoring employers are also related to the reporting entity
(vi)	The entity is controlled or jointly controlled by a person identified in part (a)
(vii)	A person identified in (a) (i) has significant influence over the entity or is a member of the key management personnel of the entity or of a parent of the entity

Source: IAS 24, paragraph 9.

A close member of the family of a person

Under paragraph 9, close family members of a person are those family members who may be expected to influence or be influenced by that person in their dealings with the entity. The definition includes the person's children, spouse or domestic partner, other children of the spouse or domestic partner, and dependants of the person or of their spouse or domestic partner.

Control, joint control, significant influence

Control is deemed to be when an investor is exposed, or has rights to variable returns from its involvement in the investee and has the ability to affect those returns through its power over the investee. Joint control is the contractually agreed sharing of control of an arrangement. Significant influence is the power to participate in the financial and operating policy decisions of an entity, and may be gained by share ownership, statute or agreement.

Determining whether a close family relationship has related party disclosure consequences is demonstrated in illustrative example 22.1.

ILLUSTRATIVE EXAMPLE 22.1 Close family members with control or significant influence

Xavier is married to Yvonne and he has a controlling investment in Alpha Ltd. Yvonne holds an investment in Bracken Ltd that gives her significant influence over that company.

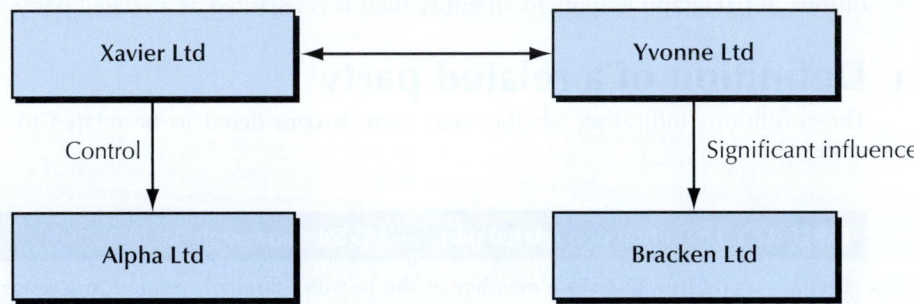

In this relationship:
- Bracken Ltd is a related party of Alpha Ltd as Xavier controls Alpha Ltd and his close family member (his wife, Yvonne) has significant influence over Bracken Ltd.
- Alpha Ltd is a related party of Bracken Ltd as Yvonne has significant influence over Bracken Ltd and her close family member (her husband, Xavier) controls Alpha Ltd.
- If Xavier only has significant influence over Alpha Ltd, then Alpha Ltd and Bracken Ltd are not regarded as related entities under IAS 24.

Source: Adapted from IAS 24 Example 4.

Key management personnel

Under paragraph 9, key management personnel of the entity or the entity's parent are related parties. Key management personnel are people who have authority and responsibility for planning, directing and controlling an entity's activities either directly or indirectly. This includes directors whether they are executive or otherwise.

An example of key management personnel identified by Billabong International Ltd, and disclosed in its 2011 annual report, is shown in figure 22.1.

FIGURE 22.1 Billabong International Ltd's key management personnel

Note 30. Key management personnel disclosures

(a) Directors
The following persons were Directors of Billabong International Limited during the financial year:
  (i) *Non-Executive Chairman*
      E.T. Kunkel
 (ii) *Executive Directors*
      D. O'Neill, Chief Executive Officer
      P. Naude, General Manager, Billabong Group North America
(iii) *Non-Executive Directors*
      A.G. Froggatt
      M.A. Jackson
      F.A. McDonald
      G.S. Merchant
      C. Paull

FIGURE 22.1 *(continued)*

(b) Other key management personnel

The following persons also had authority and responsibility for planning, directing and controlling the activities of the Group, directly or indirectly, during the financial year:

Name	Position	Employer
F. Fogliato	General Manager, Billabong Group Europe	GSM Europe Pty Ltd
C. Kypriotis	General Manager, Billabong Group South Americas	GSM Brasil Ltda
S. North	General Manager, Billabong Group Australasia	GSM (Operations) Pty Ltd
J. Schillereff	President, Element Skateboards	Element Skateboards, Inc.
C. White	Chief Financial Officer	GSM (Operations) Pty Ltd

Source: Billabong International Ltd (2011, p. 105).

Determining whether a party is related to a member of key management personnel is demonstrated in illustrative example 22.2.

ILLUSTRATIVE EXAMPLE 22.2 Key management personnel

Jack has a 100% interest in Henty Ltd and he is also a member of the key management personnel of Courier Ltd. Persimmon Ltd has a controlling interest in Courier Ltd.

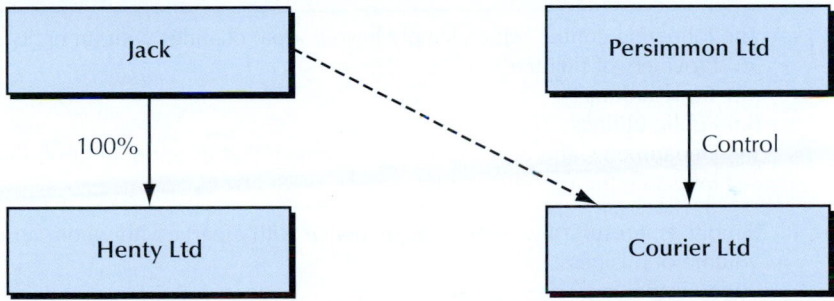

In this set of circumstances:
• For Courier Ltd's financial statements, Henty Ltd is a related entity because Jack controls Henty Ltd and he is also a member of the key management personnel of Courier Ltd
• For Henty Ltd's financial statements, Courier Ltd is a related entity because Jack controls Henty Ltd and he is also a member of Courier Ltd's key management personnel.

Source: Adapted from IAS 24 Example 3.

An associate of the entity

Under paragraph 9, any party that is determined to be an associate of the reporting entity is also considered to be a related party. An associated entity is one that is subject to the significant influence of another party as described in IAS 28 *Investments in Associates and Joint Ventures*. Under paragraph 27, an associate includes subsidiaries of the associate. For example, an investor that has significant influence over an associate is related to the associate's subsidiary.

A joint venture

Any relationship that is determined to be a joint venture as defined in IAS 28 *Investments in Associates and Joint Ventures* is regarded as a related party. Under paragraph 21, a joint venture includes subsidiaries of the joint venture.

Post-employment benefit plan

A post-employment benefit plan includes pensions and other retirement benefits and post-employment life insurance and medical care. IAS 24 does not provide an indication of why post-employment benefits are defined as related parties. However, it is likely that an entity sponsoring a post-employment benefit plan is likely to have either control or significant influence over the plan. There may also be obligations or commitments outstanding at the end of a reporting period.

 22.4 RELATIONSHIPS THAT ARE NOT RELATED PARTIES

Although the existence of related parties relationships are not uncommon in normal business life, there are many transactions and events between parties that do not necessarily give rise to a related party relationship as envisaged under IAS 24. For example, an employee of a large retailer such as Billabong International Ltd might purchase goods on normal trading terms in a Billabong store. It would be exceedingly difficult for all such transactions to be identified and recorded, and the benefit of reporting them to users is likely to be trivial. Further, in deciding whether a relationship exists that is subject to the disclosure requirements of IAS 24, paragraph 10 makes it clear that it is the substance, and not merely the legal form of a relationship or transaction, that is important. In this context, paragraph 11 identifies relationships that are not regarded as related parties. These are summarised in table 22.2.

TABLE 22.2 Relationships that are not regarded as related parties

(a) Two entities simply because they have a director in common
Two entities simply because they have a member of key management personnel in common
Two entities simply because a member of the key management personnel of one entity has significant influence over the other entity

(b) Two joint venturers simply because they share joint control of a joint venture

(c) The following entities which simply have normal dealings with an entity
  (i) Providers of finance
  (ii) Trade unions
  (iii) Public utilities
  (iv) Departments and agencies of a government that does not control, jointly control or significantly influence the reporting entity

(d) Simply as a result of economic dependence with a party with whom an entity transacts a significant volume of business:
  (i) a customer
  (ii) a supplier
  (iii) a franchisor
  (iv) a distributor or general agent

 22.5 DISCLOSURE

In order for users of financial statements to form a view about the effects of the related party relationships of an entity, paragraph 13 of IAS 24 requires the disclosure of the relationship where control exists, irrespective of whether there have been transactions between the parties. If there have been transactions, then the nature of the relationship together with sufficient information to enable an understanding of the potential effect of the transactions on the financial statements must be disclosed.

22.5.1 Related party transactions and related party relationships

If the relationship is between parent and subsidiary entities, the identification of the parties is in addition to the disclosure requirements of IFRS 12 *Disclosure of Interests in Other Entities*, IAS 27 *Separate Financial Statements* and IAS 28 *Investments in Associates and Joint Ventures*. If the parent entity or the ultimate controlling entity does not make financial statements publicly available, then under paragraph 13 of IAS 24 the name of the closest parent that does so must be disclosed.

All entities

To assist users of financial statements to form their view about the effects of related party relationships on an entity, a range of information is required to be disclosed separately for each parent, entity with joint control or significant influence, subsidiary, associate, joint venture in which the entity is a venturer, key management personnel, and other related parties. The minimum disclosures are detailed under paragraph 18 and are summarised below.

(a) the amount of the transactions
(b) the amount of the outstanding balances and commitments including:
  (i) their terms and conditions and whether they are secured, and the nature of the settlement consideration to be provided
  (ii) details of any guarantees provided or received
(c) provisions for doubtful debts related to outstanding balances
(d) the expense recognised during the period in respect of bad or doubtful debts due from related parties.

A major focus of the disclosure requirements of IAS 24 is directed towards revealing the remuneration arrangements made for key management personnel. These requirements are intended to improve the transparency of related party relationships with directors and influential senior executives. These disclosures, contained in paragraph 17, are required in total and for each of a range of categories and are shown below:

(a) short-term employee benefits
(b) post-employment benefits
(c) other long-term benefits
(d) termination benefits
(e) share-based payment.

Although the term 'compensation' is used in IAS 24 to describe benefits paid to employees, the term 'remuneration' refers to the same concept. According to the Productivity Commission (2009, p. iv):

> The remuneration of company directors and executives is an issue that has attracted considerable interest from shareholders, business groups and the wider community. Concerns have been raised over excessive remuneration practices, particularly as we face almost unprecedented turmoil in global financial and equity markets... The crisis has also highlighted the need to maintain a robust regulatory framework that promotes transparency and accountability on remuneration practices, and better aligns the interests of shareholders and the community with the performance and reward structures of Australia's corporate directors and executives.

The key management personnel compensation disclosures provided by Billabong International Ltd in its 2011 annual report are shown in figure 22.2.

Note 30. Key management personnel disclosures *(continued)*

(c) Key management personnel compensation

	Consolidated	
	2011 $'000	2010 $'000
Short-term employee benefits	6 964	8 934
Long-term employee benefits — long service leave	279	48
Post-employment benefits	177	142
Share-based payments	460	1 502
	7 880	10 626

Detailed remuneration disclosures are provided in the remuneration report.

FIGURE 22.2 Billabong International Ltd — key management personnel compensation
Source: Billabong International Ltd (2011, p. 105).

Examples of related party transactions that must be disclosed include the purchases or sales of goods or services whether incomplete or finished, and the acquisition or disposal of assets including property. Lease arrangements, transfers of research and development, transfers under licence agreements or finance arrangements including loans and equity contributions require disclosure. Provisions of guarantees, commitments including executory contracts, and the settlement of liabilities on behalf of the entity or by the entity on behalf of a related party must also be disclosed.

An example of transactions with related parties and key management personnel is shown in the notes accompanying Billabong's 2011 annual report and is summarised in figure 22.3.

> **Note 30. Key management personnel disclosures** *(continued)*
>
> **(e) Other transactions with Directors and other key management personnel**
>
> *Directors of Billabong International Limited*
> During 2010 and 2011 Burleigh Point Limited utilised property of Director P. Naude for use in certain advertising and promotional activities. There was no consideration paid by Burleigh Point Limited to P. Naude for use of the property.
>
> A subsidiary of the Company leases a retail store in South Africa from the wife of Director P. Naude. The rental agreement is based on normal commercial terms and conditions.
>
> *Key management personnel of the consolidated entity*
> Mr J. Schillereff was a Director of Element Skate Inc at the time the Company acquired the assets comprising the 'Element' skate operation. The transaction was effective from 1 July 2002 and as part of the consideration paid by the Company for these assets Mr J. Schillereff was granted 423 053 options. Additionally, as part of the acquisition terms, Mr J. Schillereff was entitled to receive four further tranches of options, granted in August following the first, second, third and fourth anniversary of the transaction.

FIGURE 22.3 Billabong International Ltd — transactions with directors and other key management personnel
Source: Billabong International Ltd (2011, p. 109).

22.6 GOVERNMENT-RELATED ENTITIES

A number of countries, for example, China, Germany, France, Russia and Eastern European nations have a sizeable number of entities that are controlled by the government. Often the practical difficulties and costs for government-controlled entities of complying with the extensive disclosure requirements of IAS 24 are likely to outweigh the benefits to financial statement users. Accordingly, paragraph 25 provides an exemption from some of the disclosure requirements for transactions between entities that are controlled, jointly controlled or significantly influenced by a government and with other entities that are related because they are controlled by the same government. The exemption from disclosure for government-related entities is demonstrated in illustrative example 22.3.

ILLUSTRATIVE EXAMPLE 22.3 Exemption from disclosure for government-related entities

A local government organisation directly controls two entities — Alpha Ltd and Beta Ltd, and indirectly controls Edgar Ltd, Fire Ltd, Jordan Ltd and Swirl Ltd. Mr Hilary is a key person in the management of Alpha Ltd. Determine the extent to which Edgar Ltd can apply the partial exemption in paragraph 25.

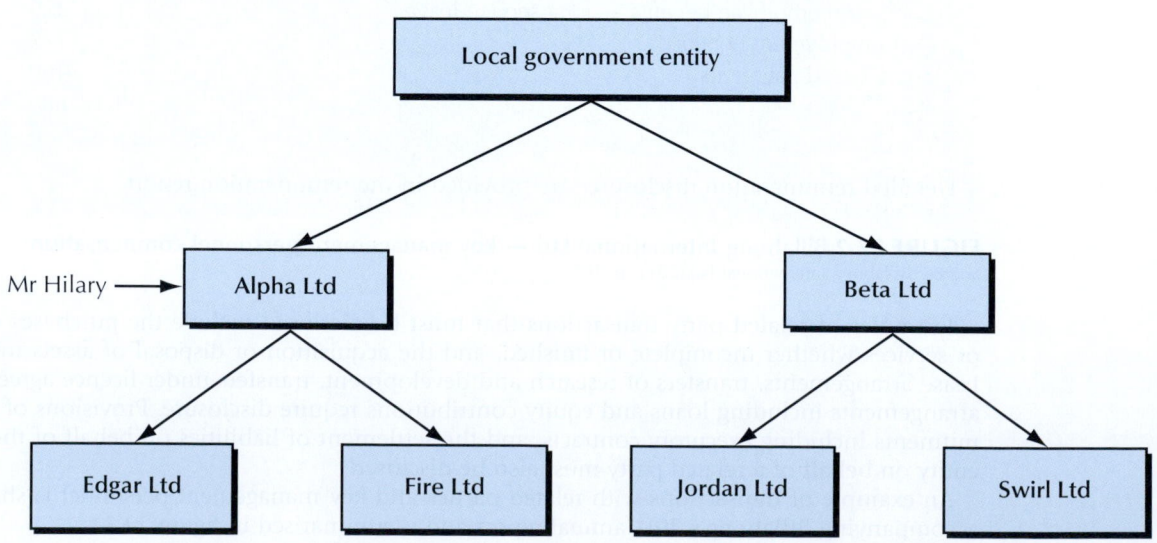

- The exemption in paragraph 25 can be applied by Edgar Ltd for transactions with the local government entity and for transactions with Alpha Ltd, Beta Ltd, Fire Ltd, Jordan Ltd and Swirl Ltd.
- However, the exemption cannot be applied for transactions with key management personnel (Mr Hilary).

Source: Adapted from IAS 24, Example 1.

If an entity chooses to apply the exemption, it is still required to identify the government to which it is related and to provide a range of other relevant disclosures. These include: the nature of the relationship; the nature and amount of each individually significant transaction; and either a qualitative or a quantitative indication of the extent of other transactions that are, in aggregate, significant.

SUMMARY

IAS 24 *Related Party Disclosures* is a disclosure standard that defines related party relationships and prescribes the events, transactions, balances and commitments that must be revealed in the financial statements and reports of disclosing entities. As related party relationships can be expected to affect the profit or loss or the financial position of an entity, disclosures about them are particularly helpful to investors, lenders and other users when they evaluate and assess the risks and opportunities facing entities. The main features of IAS 24 are that it:
- considers key management personnel and their close family members to be related parties
- considers compensation benefits for key management personnel to be related party transactions.

Determining when related party relationships exist and identifying the circumstances in which disclosures about such relationships must be disclosed involves a certain amount of judgement. In making that judgement, entities must take into account the definitions of related parties provided in IAS 24. The definition of related parties includes:
- relationships affected by control or significant influence or joint venture arrangements
- key management personnel and close family members.

Discussion questions

1. Why do standard setters formulate rules for the disclosure of related party relationships?
2. Explain how the mere existence of a related party relationship might have the potential to affect transactions with other parties.
3. Explain why key management personnel are regarded as related parties.
4. An alternative to disclosing information about related parties is to restate related party events as though they had occurred between independent parties in arm's length transactions. Explain why this approach has not been adopted by the standard setters.
5. Explain why a parent company and its subsidiary entities are regarded as related parties.
6. Outline the rationale for including an employer-sponsored post-employment benefit plan as a related party of the employer entity.
7. Distinguish between control, joint control and significant influence.
8. Provide four examples of related party transactions that must be disclosed by a related party disclosing entity.
9. Explain how an entity determines whether a family member is a related party.

Exercises

STAR RATING ★ BASIC ★★ MODERATE ★★★ DIFFICULT

Exercise 22.1	SCOPE OF IAS 24

★ Which of the following is the related party of an entity within the scope of IAS 24? Give reasons for your answer.
(a) A person who has the authority to plan, direct and control the activities of the entity.
(b) The domestic partner and children of a director of the entity.
(c) The non-dependant sister of a director of the entity.

(d) A subsidiary company that is directly controlled by the entity.
(e) Dividend payment to employees who are holders of an entity's shares.

Exercise 22.2 **RECOGNITION PRINCIPLES**

★ Jay Wendt is a newly appointed director of Armstrong Ltd, a listed company that organises major sporting events. Jay has provided consultancy services to Armstrong Ltd for the past 10 years. In the most recent financial year these services amounted to $500 000.

Required

Determine whether the consultancy service provided by Jay is a related party transaction that should be disclosed in the financial statements of Armstrong Ltd. Explain your answer.

Exercise 22.3 **RECOGNITION PRINCIPLES**

★ Alworth Company operates a pension scheme that offers defined benefit pensions for the benefit of the company's employees. At the end of the reporting period, the present value of the defined benefit obligation is $105 million and the fair value of the defined benefit scheme assets is $109 million.

Required

Is the pension scheme a related party of the Alworth Company? Explain.

Exercise 22.4 **DISCLOSURE**

★★ During the period ended 30 June 2015, Marion, an employee of Urton Company, purchased goods from the company on normal commercial terms and conditions. Marion receives remuneration consisting of cash and other short-term benefits amounting to $180 000. During the 30 June 2015 financial year, Marion also received a grant of 50 000 options from the company which is conditional on her continuing to work for the company for the next 3 years. Marion is considered to be a member of the key management personnel of the Urton Company.

Required

Prepare appropriate disclosures reflecting the related party relationship and transactions between Urton Company and its employee Marion for the period ended 30 June 2015.

Exercise 22.5 **DETERMINING WHETHER PARTIES ARE RELATED**

★★ Jacques holds 100% of the shares in Cannes Ltd and he is also a director of Revoir Ltd. All of the shares in Revoir Ltd are held by Baroque Ltd.

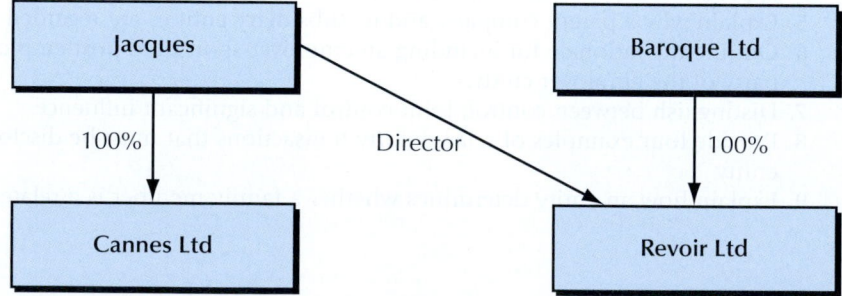

Required

Determine the related party relationships for Cannes Ltd.

Exercise 22.6 **EXEMPTION FROM DISCLOSURE FOR GOVERNMENT-RELATED ENTITIES**

★★ Productivity Agency is a government organisation which directly controls another entity — Outcomes Ltd, and through its interest in Outcomes Ltd it indirectly controls Telephony Ltd and Networks Ltd.

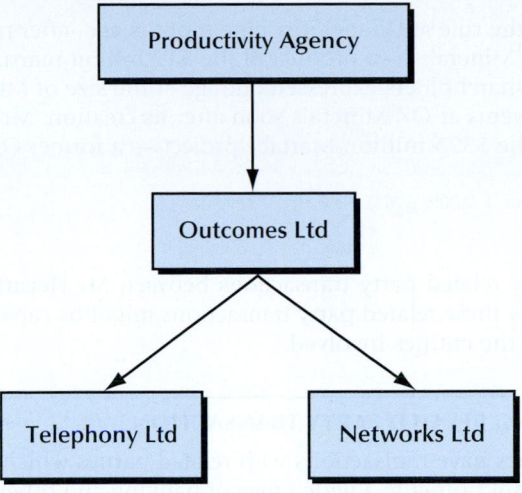

```
                    ┌─────────────────────┐
                    │ Productivity Agency │
                    └──────────┬──────────┘
                               │
                               ▼
                    ┌─────────────────────┐
                    │    Outcomes Ltd     │
                    └──┬───────────────┬──┘
                       │               │
                ▼                           ▼
      ┌──────────────────┐       ┌──────────────────┐
      │  Telephony Ltd   │       │   Networks Ltd   │
      └──────────────────┘       └──────────────────┘
```

Required

Determine the extent to which Telephony Ltd can apply the partial disclosure exemption for government-related entities.

Exercise 22.7	**EFFECT OF RELATED PARTY DISCLOSURES**

★★ The following is an extract illustrating the potential impact of disclosing information about the remuneration arrangements of key management personnel.

> **Board forced to rethink exec pay**
>
> Large sharemarket-listed companies are being forced to review their remuneration practices after almost a quarter of those in the top 200 that have already held their annual general meetings suffered protest votes of 25 per cent or more from investors.
>
> Nearly half the top 200 companies that have held their AGMs reported a protest vote of more than 10 per cent against their pay plans, despite a big drop in bonus payments this year as boards promised to rein in executive pay after the global financial crisis.

Source: Durkin, P (2009, p. 1).

Required

Identify the disclosures that IAS 24 requires to be provided regarding key management personnel. Do you think the costs of making such disclosures outweigh the benefits? Explain your answer.

Exercise 22.8	**CONTRACTS WITH KEY MANAGEMENT PERSONNEL**

★★★ IAS 24 notes (paragraphs 5 & 6) that related party relationships are a normal feature of commerce and business and cautions that a related party relationship could have an effect on the profit or loss and financial position of an entity. For example, related parties could enter into transactions that unrelated parties would not. The following extract outlines details of a contract between a publicly listed company, Citadel Resources, and a consultant, Mr Owen Hegarty.

> Mining identity Owen Hegarty has stepped down from his consulting role at up-and-coming gold miner Citadel Resource Group amid a political storm over executive pay. Mr Hegarty's departure from Citadel also follows the emergence of a rival Canadian bidder for the giant Martabe gold deposit in Indonesia, being sold by troubled OZ Minerals. Citadel announced yesterday that Mr Hegarty's contract as a senior adviser to the company had been terminated by 'mutual agreement'. Mr Hegarty

(continued)

took on the role at Citadel just nine months ago, after receiving an $8.35 million golden handshake from OZ Minerals — a product of the $12 billion marriage of Oxiana and Zinifex last year.

Many shareholders expressed outrage at the size of Mr Hegarty's payout in light of the disastrous turn of events at OZ Minerals soon after its creation. Mr Hegarty is believed to be the front-runner to acquire the $325 million Martabe project — a former Oxiana asset — from OZ Minerals.

Source: Williams, F (2009, p. 63).

Required

Identify any related party transactions between Mr Hegarty and (1) Citadel Resources, (2) OZ Minerals. Explain how these related party transactions might be capable of affecting the profit or loss or the financial position of the entities involved.

| Exercise 22.9 | IDENTIFYING RELATED PARTY TRANSACTIONS |

★★★ Many entities have transactions with related parties which occur under normal terms and conditions. For example, banks provide a wide range of banking and other financial services and products, some of which are used by bank directors and their close family members.

Required

Choose one entity from each of the following three business sectors and identify the types of transactions (e.g. goods and services) that the entities might engage in with related parties under normal commercial terms and conditions.
(a) Transport sector
(b) Retailing sector
(c) Construction sector

References

Billabong International Ltd 2011, *2010/2011 Full financial report*, Billabong International Limited, Australia, www.billabongbiz.com.
Durkin, P 2009, 'Board forced to rethink exec pay', *Australian Financial Review*, 9 November.
International Accounting Standards Board 2009, *IAS 24 Related Party Disclosures*, IASB, www.ifrs.org.
Productivity Commission 2009, *Executive Remuneration in Australia*, Productivity Commission Discussion Draft, Australian government, p. iv.
Williams, F 2009, 'Hegarty moving again', *Herald Sun*, 20 March, p. 63.

Part 4

Economic entities

23

Consolidation: controlled entities

ACCOUNTING STANDARDS IN FOCUS

IFRS 10 *Consolidated Financial Statements*

LEARNING OBJECTIVES

After studying this chapter, you should be able to:

1 explain the meaning of consolidated financial statements

2 discuss the meaning and application of the criterion of control

3 discuss which entities should prepare consolidated financial statements

4 understand the relationship between a parent and an acquirer in a business combination

5 explain the differences in disclosure requirements between single entities and consolidated entities.

INTRODUCTION

The purpose of this chapter is to discuss the preparation of a single set of financial statements, referred to as the consolidated financial statements. The preparation of consolidated financial statements involves combining the financial statements of the individual entities in a group so that they show the financial position and financial performance of the group of entities, presented as if they were a single economic entity.

The first issue covered in this chapter is the determination of which entities are required to prepare consolidated financial statements. This involves a discussion of the criterion for consolidation and its application to economic situations. The second issue in this chapter is the accounting procedures for preparing the consolidated financial statements. The application in this chapter is to a very simple group structure involving two entities, one of which owns all the issued shares in the other. Chapters 24–27 discuss further issues associated with the preparation of consolidated financial statements.

The accounting standard governing the preparation of consolidated financial statements is IFRS 10 *Consolidated Financial Statements* issued by the International Accounting Standards Board (IASB) in 2011. In reading IFRS 10, note that Appendix A contains the defined terms, while Appendix B contains application guidance — both appendices are an integral part of the accounting standard. The IASB has also prepared a Basis for Conclusions on IFRS 10. Although IFRS 10 provides information on the preparation of consolidated financial statements, IFRS 3 *Business Combinations* is also applied.

The objective of IFRS 10 is stated in paragraph 1:

> to establish principles for the presentation and preparation of consolidated financial statements when an entity controls one or more other entities.

To achieve this, IFRS 10 then:

- requires a parent to present consolidated financial statements
- establishes control as the criterion for consolidation
- defines the criterion of control
- provides guidance on identifying when one entity controls another
- sets out the accounting requirements for the preparation of consolidated financial statements.

LO1 23.1 CONSOLIDATED FINANCIAL STATEMENTS

Consolidated financial statements are defined in Appendix A of IFRS 10 as follows:

> The financial statements of a **group** in which the assets, liabilities, equity, income, expenses and cash flows of the **parent** and its **subsidiaries** are presented as those of a single economic entity.

Consider figure 23.1. Australia Ltd has investments in a number of other companies. A shareholder's wealth in Australia Ltd is dependent not only on how well Australia Ltd performs, but also on the performance of the other entities in which Australia Ltd has an investment. Rather than require a shareholder in Australia Ltd to analyse each of the companies in the economic group, if Australia Ltd prepared a set of financial statements by adding together the financial statements of all entities in the group, this would assist an investor in Australia Ltd to analyse his/her investment. Consolidated financial statements perform this function as they are a consolidation, or an adding together, of the financial statements of all entities within an economic entity. As stated in paragraph B86 of IFRS 10, consolidated financial statements 'combine like items of assets, liabilities, equity, income, expenses and cash flows' of the entities in the group.

This process of adding the financial statements together can be seen in its simplest form in figure 23.2. In this example there are two entities in the group, P Ltd and S Ltd. The consolidated financial statements are prepared by adding together the assets and liabilities of both entities. In chapter 24 a consolidation worksheet is used to perform this addition process.

This aggregation process is subject to a number of adjustments, and these are covered in detail in chapters 24–27. These adjustments are necessary because of intragroup shareholdings and transactions between entities within the group. However, in this chapter, the process of consolidation should be seen simply as a process of aggregation of the financial statements of all entities within the group. Note that the consolidation process does *not* involve making adjustments to the individual financial statements or the accounts of the entities in the group. The consolidated financial statements are an additional set of financial statements and are prepared using a worksheet to facilitate the addition and adjustment process.

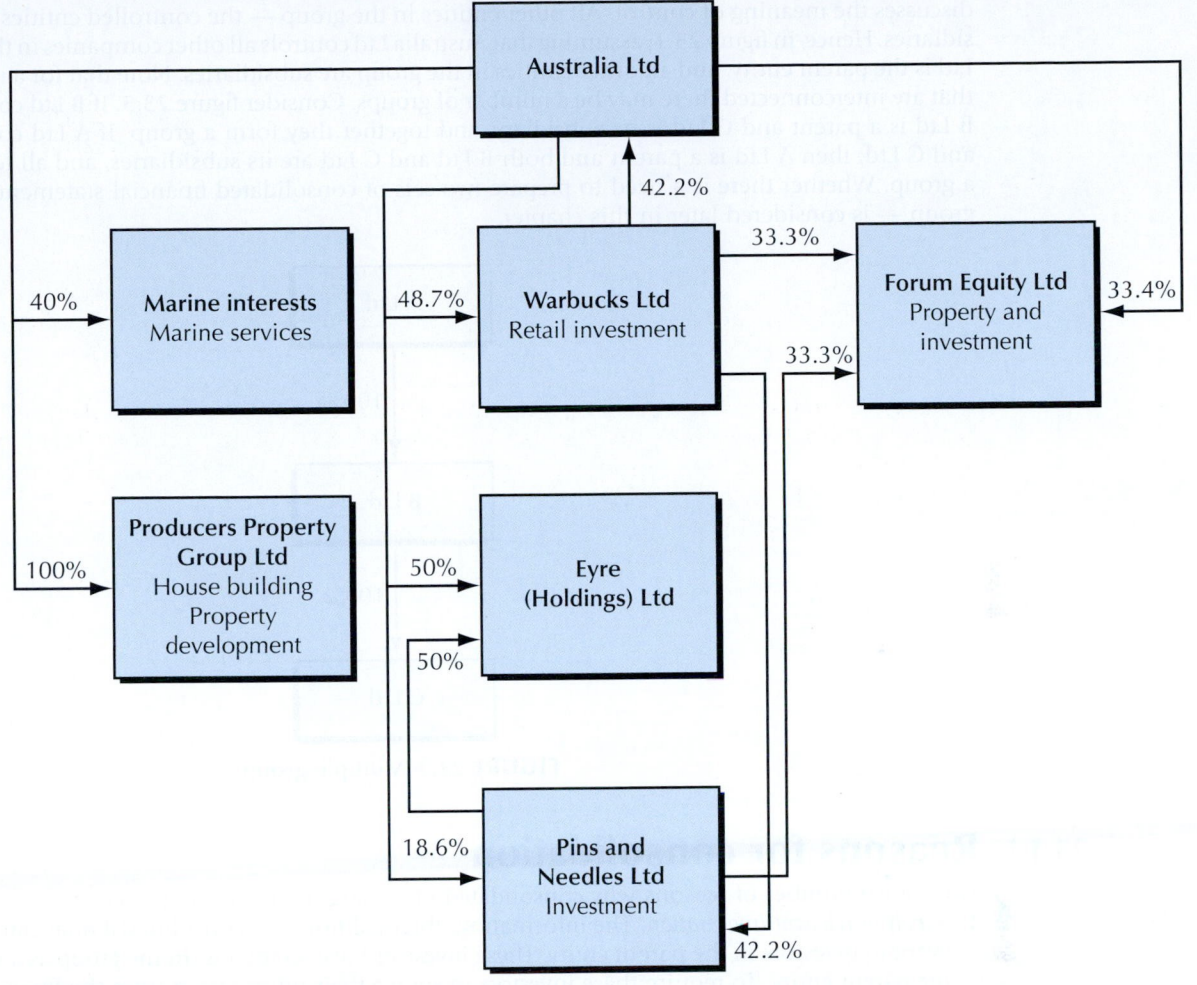

FIGURE 23.1 A group of entities

	P Ltd		S Ltd		Consolidation of P Ltd and S Ltd
Current assets	$ 50 000	+	$ 20 000	=	$ 70 000
Non-current assets	150 000	+	120 000	=	270 000
Total assets	200 000		140 000		340 000
Total liabilities	(80 000)	+	(30 000)	=	(110 000)
Net assets	$120 000		$110 000		$ 230 000

FIGURE 23.2 The consolidation process

The consolidated financial statements consist of a consolidated statement of financial position, consolidated statement of profit or loss and other comprehensive income, and a consolidated statement of cash flows.

The following definitions are contained in Appendix A of IFRS 10:

Group   A **parent** and its **subsidiaries**.
Parent   An entity that **controls** one or more entities.
Subsidiary   An entity that is controlled by another entity.

The consolidated financial statements combine the financial statements of all the entities within a group. The entities in the group consist of two types; namely, parent and subsidiary. There is only one parent in a group, which is the controlling entity; that is, the entity that controls all other entities in the group. Section 23.2

discusses the meaning of control. All other entities in the group — the controlled entities — are called subsidiaries. Hence, in figure 23.1, assuming that Australia Ltd controls all other companies in the figure, Australia Ltd is the parent entity, and all other entities in the group are subsidiaries. Note that for a number of entities that are interconnected there may be a number of groups. Consider figure 23.3. If B Ltd controls C Ltd, then B Ltd is a parent and C Ltd is its subsidiary, and together they form a group. If A Ltd controls both B Ltd and C Ltd, then A Ltd is a parent and both B Ltd and C Ltd are its subsidiaries, and all together they form a group. Whether there is a need to prepare two sets of consolidated financial statements — one for each group — is considered later in this chapter,

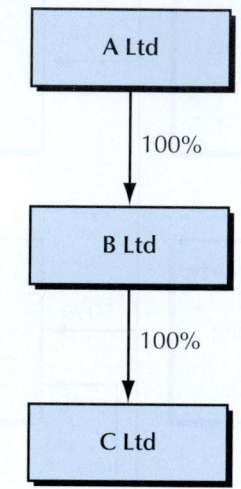

FIGURE 23.3 Multiple groups

23.1.1 Reasons for consolidation

There are a number of reasons why consolidated financial statements are prepared:
1. *Supply of relevant information.* The information obtained from the consolidated financial statements is relevant to investors in the parent entity. These investors have an interest in the group as a whole, not just in the parent entity. To require these investors to source their information from the financial statements of each of the entities comprising the group would place a large cost burden on the investors.
2. *Comparable information.* Some entities are organised into a group structure such that different activities are undertaken by separate members of the group. Other entities are organised differently, with some having all activities conducted within the one entity. For an investor to make useful comparisons between entities, access to consolidated financial statements makes the comparative analysis an easier task.
3. *Accountability.* A key purpose for all financial reporting is the discharge of accountability by management. Entities that are responsible or accountable for managing a pool of resources, being the recipients of economic benefits and responsible for payment of obligations, are generally required to report on their activities, and are held accountable for the management of those activities. The management of the parent entity is not just responsible for the management of the assets of the parent itself. As the parent controls the assets of all subsidiaries, the assets under the control of the parent entity's management are the assets of the group. The consolidated financial statements report the assets under the control of the group management as well as the claims on those assets.
4. *Reporting of risks and benefits.* There are risks associated with managing an entity, and an entity rarely obtains control of another without obtaining significant opportunities to benefit from that control. The consolidated financial statements allow an assessment of these risks and benefits.

 23.2 CONTROL AS THE CRITERION FOR CONSOLIDATION

In Appendix A of IFRS 10, a parent is defined as an entity that *controls* one or more entities while a subsidiary is a controlled entity. The entity that is responsible for preparing the consolidated financial statements is the parent. An entity must then determine when it is a parent and which entities it controls. The determination of whether one entity controls another is crucial to the determination of which entities need to prepare consolidated financial statements. Paragraph 5 of IFRS 10 notes that 'an investor' must determine whether it is a parent by assessing whether it controls an 'investee'. In IFRS 10, an investor is a reporting entity that *potentially* controls one or more entities; it may have an investment in the investee, but is not required to do so. Investors are then potential parents, and investees are potential subsidiaries.

Under IFRS 10, the criterion for consolidation is control. It should first be noted that determination of whether control exists is a matter of judgement. In many situations it will not be clear cut that one entity controls another, and determination will have to be made by considering all available facts and circumstances (paragraph 8 of IFRS 10). As noted later in this section, IFRS 10 provides numerous factors to be considered in making the decision concerning the existence of control. Hence, it is important to understand the meaning of the term 'control' and what evidence may be accumulated to determine its existence or non-existence in specific circumstances. Further if those circumstances change, there may be a need to assess whether control still exists.

Second, note that control is an exclusionary power. In a group there can be only one parent. If two or more investors can control an investee by joining together to direct the activities of the investees, neither investor controls the investee — decision-making ability cannot be shared.

Control of an investee is defined in Appendix A of IFRS 10 as follows:

> An investor controls an investee when the investor is exposed, or has rights, to variable returns from its involvement with the investee and has the ability to affect those returns through its power over the investee.

Paragraph 7 of IFRS 10 identifies three elements, all of which must be held by an investor in order for it to have control, namely:

1. power over the investee
2. exposure, or rights, to variable returns from its involvement with the investee
3. the ability to use its power over the investee to affect the amount of the investor's returns.

These three elements are discussed in detail in the following sections.

23.2.1 Power

Power is defined in Appendix A of IFRS 10 as follows:

> Existing rights that give the current ability to direct the **relevant activities**.

Note the key features of this definition.

Power arises from rights

These rights generally arise from some form of legal contract. For example, the rights that are held by the owner of an ordinary share in a company may include voting rights, rights to dividends or rights on liquidation of the company. Rights could also exist because of a contract between one entity and another entity. For example, an entity might engage another entity to manage its activities — the latter entity then has management rights but potentially no rights to dividends. The rights that are of importance in determining whether power exists are those relating to the ability to direct the relevant activities of an investee. Rights in relation to purely administration tasks are not rights that affect power. Examples of rights that affect who has power are listed in paragraph B15 of IFRS 10, namely:

- voting rights
- rights to appoint, reassign or remove members of an investee's key management personnel
- rights to appoint or remove another entity that participates in management decisions
- rights to direct the investee to enter into, or veto any changes to, transactions that affect the investee's returns.

Some questions that could be asked to assist in determining whether certain rights give rise to power are as follows (based on paragraph B18 of IFRS 10):

- Can the investor appoint or approve the investee's key management personnel who direct the relevant activities?
- Can the investor direct the investee to enter into or veto any changes to significant transactions that affect the investor's returns?
- Can the investor dominate either the nominations process of electing members of the investee's governing body or the obtaining of proxies from other holders of voting rights?

The rights must also be *substantive* rights. According to paragraph B22 of IFRS 10, for rights to be substantive the holders must have the practical ability to exercise the rights; that is, there are no barriers to the holders exercising the rights. The rights need to give the holder the current ability to direct the relevant activities when decisions about those activities need to be made.

As judgement is required in assessing whether rights are substantive, paragraph B23 of IFRS 10 provides some factors to consider in making that determination:

- whether the party or parties that hold the rights would benefit from the exercise of those rights, for example, potential voting rights.
- whether there are any barriers — economic or otherwise — that prevent a holder from the exercising of rights. Examples of such barriers are financial penalties, terms and conditions that make it unlikely that rights will be exercised, and the absence of specialised services necessary for exercising the rights. Paragraph B23(a) of IFRS 10 provides a detailed list of possible barriers.
- where more than one party is involved, whether there is a mechanism in place to enable those parties to practically exercise the rights.

If the rights are purely protective rights, the holder does not have power (paragraph 14). Protective rights are defined in Appendix A as follows:

Rights designed to protect the interest of the party holding those rights without giving that party power over the entity to which those rights relate.

Paragraph B28 of IFRS 10 provides examples of protective rights, which include:

(a) a lender's right to restrict a borrower from undertaking activities that could significantly change the credit risk of the borrower to the detriment of the lender.
(b) the right of a party holding a non-controlling interest in an investee to approve capital expenditure greater than that required in the ordinary course of business, or to approve the issue of equity or debt instruments.
(c) the right of a lender to seize the assets of a borrower if the borrower fails to meet specified loan repayment conditions.

A non-controlling interest is equity in a subsidiary not attributable to a parent. For example, if a parent owns 80% of the shares of a subsidiary, then the non-controlling interest in the subsidiary is 20%.

Power is the ability to direct

There is a distinction between ability to direct and actually directing. An entity that has the ability to direct may decide not to exercise that ability and so allow another entity to actually direct. For example, Entity C may have two owners — Entity A that owns 55% of the shares in Entity C and Entity B that holds the remaining 45% of issued shares. Entity A may have the ability to direct the activities of Entity C but, as it is an investment company and holds shares purely for cash flow via dividends, may have no interest in management of other entities. Entity B may then actually undertake the management of Entity C. In such a circumstance, Entity A is the parent as it has the ability to direct the activities of Entity C.

The ability to direct must be current

The investor must be able to exercise its rights to direct at the time decisions are made concerning the activities of an investee. However, there are circumstances where power is still held by an investor even though there may be a time period to pass, or an activity that needs to be undertaken, before the right to direct can be currently exercisable. Paragraph B24 of IFRS 10 provides examples of these circumstances. One example is:

An investor holds an option to acquire the majority of shares in an investee that is exercisable in 25 days and that is deeply in the money. A special meeting to change existing policies requires 30 days' notice. The existing shareholders cannot change existing policies before the exercise of the option. The investor has a substantive right that gives him/her the current ability to direct the relevant activities even before the option is exercised.

In contrast, assume the investor held a forward contract to acquire the majority of shares at a settlement date in 6 months' time. The existing shareholders would have the current ability to direct the activities of the investee as they can change the existing policies before the forward contract is settled.

It is relevant activities that are directed

Relevant activities are defined in Appendix A of IFRS 10 as:

activities of the investee that significantly affect the investee's returns.

The determination of relevant activities may change over time and differ between entities; hence it may be necessary to analyse the purpose and design of an investee. For many investees, the relevant decisions are those that govern the financial and operating policies of the investee. Paragraph B11 of IFRS 10 provides examples of some possible relevant activities, including:

- selling and purchasing goods and services
- managing financial assets
- selecting, acquiring and disposing of assets

- researching and developing new products
- determining a funding structure or obtaining funding.

To have power, an investor need not be able to make any decision it likes in relation to an investee, as the investor is constrained by Australian corporate and contract laws under which the interests of non-controlling investors, creditors and others are protected.

Level of share ownership

Ownership of ordinary shares in a company normally provides voting rights that enable the holder of the majority of shares to dominate the appointment of directors or an entity's governing board. As paragraph B35 of IFRS 10 states, where an investor holds more than half of the voting rights of an investee, the investor has power providing:

(a) the relevant activities are directed by a vote of the holder of the majority of voting rights, or
(b) a majority of the members of the governing body that directs the relevant activities are appointed by a vote of the holder of the majority of the voting rights.

Hence, in the absence of other evidence, where an investor holds a majority of voting shares that investor would be considered to have power over the investee.

Where an investor holds less than 50% of the shares of an investee, the determination of whether the investor has power over the investee is more difficult. In determining the existence of power, it is necessary to examine the potential actions of the holders of the other shares in the investee. Some factors to assist in this process are:

- *Size of the voting interest.* The more voting shares an investor has, the more likely it is that it will have power. A further consideration is the number of shareholders who hold the remaining voting shares and the extent of their holdings. Where the remaining voting shares are held by a large number of shareholders, each holding a small number of shares, the probability of these other shareholders getting together to outvote the shareholder who holds a substantial proportion, but not a majority, of the shares must be considered. Note that, where the remaining shares are held by a small number of shareholders, the probability that they could get together and outvote the holder of the large parcel of shares is higher. Paragraphs B44–B45 of IFRS 10 provide examples of these circumstances.

  In the first example, investor A holds 45% of the voting rights of an investee. Two other investors each hold 26% of the voting rights of the investee. The remaining voting rights are held by investors who hold less than 1% each. There are no other arrangements that affect decision making. In this case, consideration of the size of investor A's voting interest and its relative size to the other shareholdings is sufficient to conclude that investor A does not have power. Only two investors would need to cooperate to be able to prevent investor A from controlling the investee.

  In the second example, an investor holds 40% of the voting rights of an investee, with the next two largest holdings of voting rights being 10% and 4%. The remaining voting rights are held by thousands of shareholders, none holding more than 1% of the voting rights. None of the shareholders has any arrangements to consult each other or make collective decisions. In this case, on the basis of the absolute size of its holding and the relative size of the other shareholdings, the investor has a sufficiently dominant voting interest to meet the power criterion without the need to consider any other evidence of power.

- *Dispersion of other shareholders.* Shareholders can be dispersed geographically as well as in numbers of shares held. The annual general meeting may be held in Sydney, Australia, but the majority of shareholders may live in South-East Asia. The probability of these shareholders attending the general meeting is then lessened by location.

- *Attendance at annual general meetings.* Although all shareholders may attend general meetings and vote in matters relating to governance of the entity, it is rare for this to occur. If, therefore, only 60% of the eligible votes are cast at a general meeting and an entity has more than a 30% interest in that entity, it can cast the majority of votes at that meeting. It then has power over that entity.

- *The existence of contracts.* As noted in paragraph B39 of IFRS 10, the contractual arrangement between an investor and other holders of shares may give the investor sufficient voting rights to give the investor power. An example of such a contract is provided in application example 5 of paragraph B43 of IFRS 10:

  Investor A holds 40% of voting rights of an investee and twelve other investors each hold 5% of voting rights of the investee. A shareholder agreement grants investor A the right to appoint, remove and set the remuneration of management responsible for directing the relevant activities.

  In this case, consideration of the absolute size of the investor's holding and the relative size of the other shareholdings alone is not conclusive to determine the investor has rights sufficient to give it power. However, the fact that investor A has the contractual right to appoint, remove and set the compensation of key management is sufficient to conclude that investor A has power over the investee. The fact that investor A might not have exercised this right yet or the likelihood of investor A exercising his/her right to select, appoint or remove key management should not be considered when assessing whether investor A has power.

- *Level of disorganisation or apathy of the remaining shareholders.* This factor is affected by the dispersion of the shareholders, and reflected in their attendance at general meetings. Holders of small parcels of shares are often not organised into forming voting blocks. Shareholders with environmental or ethical concerns may be less apathetic about the actions of an entity and its management policies, and may form voting blocks.

The assessment of the existence of power where the investor holds less than a majority of voting shares is difficult and requires judgement. In many cases that assessment relies on an analysis of the non-action of other shareholders. Do the non-voting shareholders at an annual general meeting not vote because they are happy with the management ability of the investor, as opposed to being apathetic? Would they be willing to combine to outvote the investor if the latter's decisions were considered untenable? The success of the investee under the control of the investor is a further measure of the potential for generally passive shareholders to be sufficiently concerned to cast a vote at the next annual general meeting. When an investee is performing poorly, the interest of shareholders as well as their willingness to become involved generally increases. Poor performance with resultant lowering of share prices may also result in a current or new shareholder acquiring a large block of shares and changing the voting mix at general meetings.

A number of problems arise in applying the concept of power under IFRS 10. First, there is the question of temporary control. Where the investor holds more than 50% of the voting shares of the investee, there is no danger of a change in the identity of the parent. However, if the identification of the parent is based on factors that may change over time, the process becomes more difficult. For example, the percentage of votes cast at general meetings may historically be 70%, but in a particular year it may be 50%. A shareholder with 30% of the voting shares has control in the latter circumstance but not in the former. Similarly, consider the situation where there are two substantial block holdings of voting shares, meaning that neither has power over the investee. One of the holders of a substantial block of shares may then sell its shares to a large number of buyers. The other holder of a substantial block may suddenly find that it has the power to control, regardless of whether this investor wants to exercise control or not.

Second, the ability of an entity to control another may be affected by relationships with other entities. For example, a holder of 40% of the voting shares may be 'friendly' with the holder of another 11% of shares. The 11% shareholder might be a financial institution that has invested in the holder of the 40% of votes and plans to vote with that entity to increase its potential for repayment of loans. However, business relationships and loyalties are not always permanent.

Potential voting rights

Paragraphs B47–B50 of IFRS 10 discuss the issue of whether potential voting rights should be considered in assessing the existence of power. Potential voting rights are rights to obtain voting rights of an investee, such as those within an option or convertible instrument (paragraph B47).

As noted earlier in this section:

- the rights must be substantive
- the investor must have a current ability to exercise those rights.

Where this occurs, potential voting rights must be taken into consideration when assessing the existence of power. Illustrative examples 23.1 and 23.2 provide some examples of potential voting rights adapted from paragraph B50 of IFRS 10.

ILLUSTRATIVE EXAMPLE 23.1 Potential voting rights — exercisable options

Investor A holds 70% of the voting rights of an investee. Investor B holds the other 30% but also holds an option to acquire half of investor A's voting rights, with the option being exercisable at a fixed price over the next two years.

If the option is deeply 'out of the money'; that is, the fixed price is too high relative to the current share price of the investee, then Investor A would be considered to hold power as the current economic conditions are such that the rights associated with the option are not substantive, in that it is not practicable for investor B to exercise the option.

If the option was 'in the money', then Investor B would be considered to have power as it could exercise the option and direct the activities of the investee.

Source: Adapted from IASB 2011, IFRS 10 *Consolidated Financial Statements*, Example 9, p. 33.

An investee has three shareholders — investor A and two other investors. Each investor holds $\frac{1}{3}$ of the voting rights. Investor A also holds debt instruments that are convertible into voting shares of the investee at a fixed price that is 'out of the money', but not a large amount. If the debt was converted, investor A would hold 60% of the shares of the investee. Because of the advantages of controlling the investee, it may be considered that investor A has power over the investee given investor A's ability to convert the debt instrument into shares. Additional information would need to be considered, including the current influence that investor A has on directing the activities of the investee.

Source: Adapted from IASB 2011, IFRS 10 *Consolidated Financial Statements*, Example 10, p. 33.

23.2.2 Exposure or rights to variable returns

Besides having power to direct the activities of an investee, an investor must also have the rights to variable returns from that investee.

Where an investor holds ordinary shares in an investee, it expects returns in relation to dividends, changes in the value of the investment, and residual interests on liquidation. If debt securities are held, the return is in the nature of interest. These returns can be positive or negative; hence, the use of the term 'returns' rather than 'benefits'. The returns are not exclusive to the parent, but may also be received by non-controlling interests. Other returns include (see paragraph B57 of IFRS 10 for examples of returns):

- returns from structuring activities with the investee; for example, obtaining a secure supply or raw material, access to a port facility, or a distribution network
- returns from denying or regulating access to a subsidiary's assets; for example, obtaining control of a patent for a competing product and stopping production
- returns from economies of scale
- remuneration from provision of services such as servicing of assets, and management.

The returns must have the potential to vary based on the performance of the investee. Examples of such variability are:

- dividends from ordinary shares that will change based on the profit performance of the investee
- fixed interest payments from a bond, as they expose the investor to the credit risk of the issuer of the bond, namely the investee
- fixed performance fees for management of the investee's assets, as they expose the investor to the performance risk of the investee.

23.2.3 Ability to use power to affect returns

Besides having power to direct the activities of the investee and rights to variable returns from the investee, a parent must have the ability to use its power over the investee to affect the returns received from the investee. This requires that the parent be able to use its power to increase its benefits and limit its losses from the subsidiary's activities. There is then a link between the holding of the power and the returns receivable. However, there is no specification of the level of returns to be received. IFRS 10 only requires that some variable returns be receivable and that the investor by its actions can affect the amount of those returns.

23.2.4 Agents

In determining whether control exists over an investee, an investor with decision-making rights needs to assess whether it is a principal or an agent. Paragraph B60 of IFRS 10 provides a number of factors to consider in determining whether a decision maker is a principal or an agent:

- the scope of its decision-making authority over the investee — this relates to the range of activities that the decision maker is permitted to direct
- the rights held by other parties; for example, whether another entity has substantive removal rights over the decision maker
- the remuneration to which it is entitled in accordance with the remuneration agreement — the remuneration of an agent would be expected to be commensurate with the level of skills needed to provide the management service while the remuneration agreement would contain terms and conditions normally included in arrangements for similar services

- the decision maker's exposure to variability of returns from other interest that it holds in the investee — the greater the decision maker's exposure to variable returns from its involvement in the investee, the more likely it is that the decision maker is not an agent.

An agent cannot be a parent. Where a controlling decision maker is determined to be an agent, it is the principal that would be considered to be the parent.

23.3 PREPARATION OF CONSOLIDATED FINANCIAL STATEMENTS

Paragraph 4(a) of IFRS 10 requires *all* parents to prepare consolidated financial statements, except in those circumstances where it meets *all* the following conditions:

    (i) it is a wholly-owned subsidiary or is a partially-owned subsidiary of another entity and all its other owners, including those not otherwise entitled to vote, have been informed about, and do not object to, the parent not presenting consolidated financial statements;

    (ii) its debt or equity instruments are not traded in a public market (a domestic or foreign stock exchange or an over-the-counter market, including local and regional markets);

    (iii) it did not file, nor is it in the process of filing, its financial statements with a securities commission or other regulatory organisation for the purpose of issuing any class of instruments in a public market; and

    (iv) its ultimate or any intermediate parent produces consolidated financial statements that are available for public use and comply with IFRSs.

Consider the group structure in figure 23.4. A Ltd is a parent entity with two subsidiaries. According to paragraph 4 of IFRS 10, A Ltd is required to prepare consolidated financial statements, combining the financial statements of A Ltd, B Ltd and C Ltd. B Ltd is also a parent with C Ltd being its subsidiary. Is B Ltd also required to prepare consolidated financial statements?

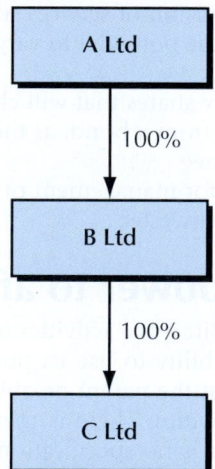

FIGURE 23.4 A parent and its subsidiaries

If B Ltd meets all the conditions in paragraph 4(a), it does not have to prepare consolidated financial statements. To determine this the following questions are asked:

- *Is B Ltd itself a wholly-owned subsidiary?* In figure 23.4, B Ltd is itself a wholly-owned subsidiary of A Ltd, hence this meets the first condition in paragraph 4(a)(i). Note also in paragraph 4(a)(i), that even if A Ltd owned only, say, 80% of B Ltd, making B Ltd a partially-owned subsidiary, B Ltd may still be exempted from preparing consolidated financial statements if the 20% non-controlling interest in B Ltd have been informed about and do not object to the parent not presenting consolidated financial statements.

- *Has B Ltd filed its financial statements with a regulatory agency for the purpose of issuing any debt or equity instruments in a public market or are the debt and equity instruments of B Ltd traded in a public market?* If B Ltd intends to issue such instruments of if they are traded in a public market, then there are potential users for a set of consolidated financial statements from B Ltd. Where B Ltd is a wholly-owned subsidiary, it is unlikely that its equity instruments would be traded in a public market.

- *Has A Ltd produced consolidated financial statements complying with IFRSs?*

23.4 BUSINESS COMBINATIONS AND CONSOLIDATION

LO4

As noted in chapter 14, accounting for a business combination under the acquisition method requires the identification of an acquirer. The acquirer is the combining entity that obtains *control* of the other combining entities or businesses. Hence, as the criterion for identification of a parent–subsidiary relationship is control, it is expected that when a business combination is formed by the creation of a parent–subsidiary relationship, the parent will be identified as the acquirer. As noted in paragraph 3 of IFRS 10, the accounting requirements for business combinations and its effect on consolidation, including goodwill arising on a business combination, are set out in IFRS 3 *Business Combinations*.

However, there are a number of situations where the parent entity is not the acquiring entity. In paragraph B19 of Appendix B to IFRS 3, a distinction is made between the legal acquirer/acquiree and the accounting acquirer/acquiree. The parent entity is usually the legal acquirer as it issues its equity interests as consideration in the combination transaction, with the subsidiary being the legal acquiree. This parent has control of the group subsequent to the business combination occurring. However, the accounting acquirer in a business combination is determined based on which entity participating in the business combination is the entity that obtains control of the other entities.

23.4.1 Formation of a new entity

Consider the situation in figure 23.5 in which A Ltd and B Ltd combine by the formation of a new entity, C Ltd, which acquires all the shares of both of these entities with the issue of shares in C Ltd. C Ltd controls both A Ltd and B Ltd.

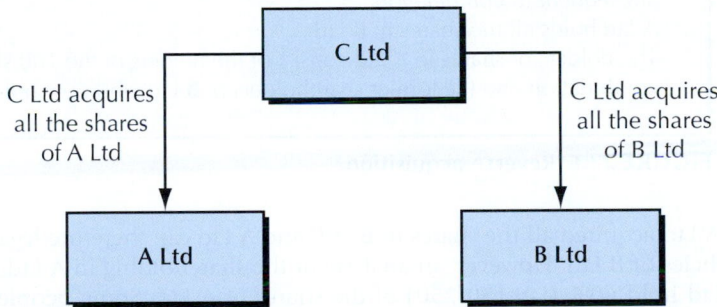

FIGURE 23.5 Identification of an acquirer where a new entity is formed

Paragraph B18 of IFRS 3 states, '[I]f a new entity is formed to issue equity interests to effect a business combination, one of the combining entities that existed before the business combination shall be identified as the acquirer by applying the guidance in paragraphs B13–B17'. In other words, even though C Ltd is acquiring the shares of both A Ltd and B Ltd, it is not to be considered the accounting acquirer; either A Ltd or B Ltd must be considered to be the accounting acquirer.

Deciding which entity is the acquirer involves a consideration of factors such as which of the combining entities initiated the combination, and whether the assets and revenues of one of the combining entities significantly exceed those of the others. The reasons for this decision by the IASB are given in paragraphs BC98–BC101 of the Basis for Conclusions on IFRS 3 *Business Combinations*. The key reason for the standard setter's decision is in paragraph BC100. The argument is that the new entity, C Ltd, may have no economic substance, and the accounting result for the combination of the three entities should be the same if A Ltd simply combined with B Ltd without the formation of C Ltd. It is argued in paragraph BC100 that to account otherwise would 'impair both the comparability and the reliability of the information'.

However, the problem that then arises in the scenario in figure 23.5 is that a choice has to be made: is A Ltd or B Ltd the acquirer? In deciding on which entity is the acquirer, paragraphs B14–B18 of Appendix B to IFRS 3 provide some indicators to consider in situations where it may be difficult to identify an acquirer. The entity likely to be the acquirer is the one:
- that has a significantly greater fair value
- that gives up the cash or other assets, in the case where equity instruments are exchanged for cash or other assets
- whose management is able to dominate the business combination.

In this circumstance, although C Ltd is the legal parent of the subsidiaries A Ltd and B Ltd, it is not the acquirer in the business combination.

23.4.2 Reverse acquisitions

A further situation considered in paragraphs B19–B27 of IFRS 3 is the 'reverse acquisition' form of business combination. Consider the situation in figure 23.6.

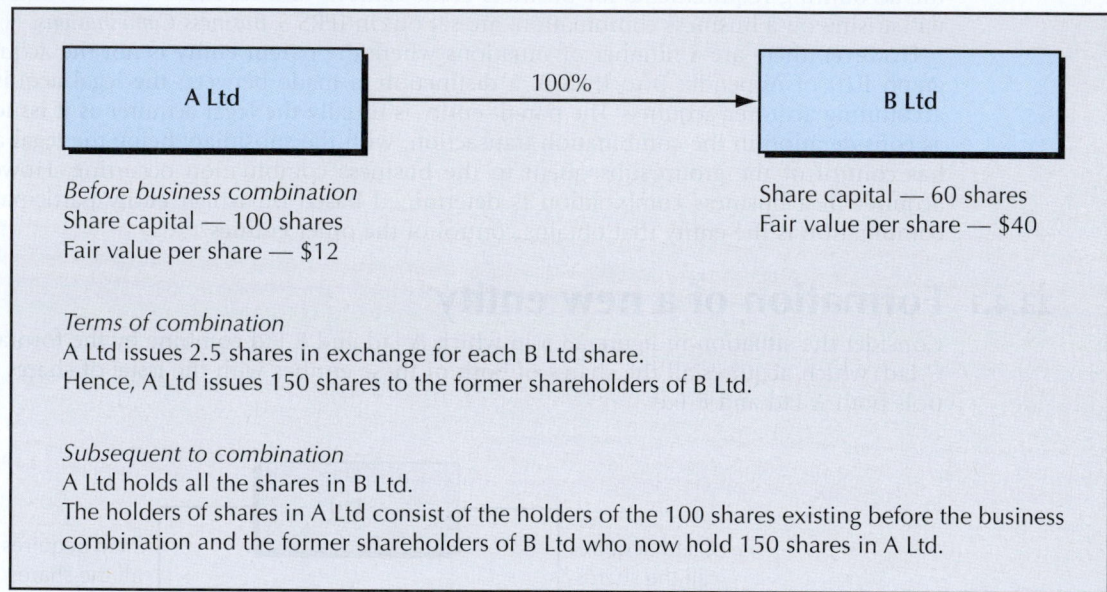

FIGURE 23.6 Reverse acquisition

A Ltd acquired all the shares in B Ltd, and A Ltd can therefore legally control the financial and operating policies of B Ltd. However, an analysis of the shareholding in A Ltd shows that the former shareholders of B Ltd hold 60% (i.e. 150/250) of the shares of A Ltd. Some people argue that the substance of the business combination is that B Ltd has really taken over A Ltd because the former shareholders of B Ltd are in control. Paragraph BC96 of the Basis for Conclusions on IFRS 3 provides a further example of a reverse acquisition:

> The IASB also observed that in some reverse acquisitions, the acquirer may be the entity whose equity interests have been acquired and the acquiree is the issuing entity. For example, a private entity might arrange to have itself 'acquired' by a smaller public entity through an exchange of equity interests as a means of obtaining a stock exchange listing. As part of the agreement, the directors of the public entity resign and are replaced by directors appointed by the private entity and its former owners. The IASB observed that in such circumstances, the private entity, which is the legal subsidiary, has the power to govern the financial and operating policies of the combined entity so as to obtain benefits from its activities. Treating the legal subsidiary as the acquirer in such circumstances is thus consistent with applying the control concept for identifying the acquirer.

The problem with the reverse acquisitions argument is that it relies on an analysis of which shareholders control the decision making — that is, the acquiring entity is the one whose owners control the combined entity and who have the power to govern the financial and operating policies of the entity so as to obtain benefits from its activities. The accounting for reverse acquisitions is considered further in section 24.8 of this book.

 ## 23.5 DISCLOSURE

There are no disclosures specified in IFRS 10. IFRS 12 *Disclosure of Interests in Other Entities*, issued in 2011 at the same time as IFRS 10, outlines the disclosures required in the consolidated financial statements for subsidiaries. IAS 27 *Separate Financial Statements*, also issued in 2011, sets out disclosures required in separate financial statements.

23.5.1 Disclosures required by IFRS 12

The key objective of IFRS 12 is stated in paragraph 1:

> The objective of this IFRS is to require an entity to disclose information that enables users of its financial statements to evaluate:
> (a) the nature of, and risks associated with, its *interests in other entities*, and
> (b) the effects of those interests on its financial position, financial performance and cash flows.

Notice the emphasis on the ability of users of financial statements to be able to evaluate risks. In the introduction to IFRS 12 *Disclosure of Interests in Other Entities*, in paragraph IN5, the IASB noted that 'the global financial crisis that started in 2007 highlighted a lack of transparency about the risks to which a reporting entity was exposed from its involvement with structured entities'. As a result, IFRS 12 requires an entity to disclose the significant judgements and assumptions it has made in determining the nature of its interest in another entity (paragraph 2(a)), and in particular judgements, assumptions and changes in these in relation to subsidiaries (paragraph 7). Paragraph 9 of IFRS 12 provides the following examples of situations where it is necessary to disclose significant judgements and assumptions:

- where an entity does not control another entity but it holds more than half of the voting rights in the other entity
- where an entity controls another entity but it holds less than half of the voting rights of the other entity
- where an entity is an agent or a principal.

To assist users in understanding the nature of the group, paragraph 10 of IFRS 12 states:

> An entity shall disclose information that enables users of its consolidated financial statements
> (a) to understand:
>   (i) the composition of the group; and
>   (ii) the interest that non-controlling interests have in the group's activities and cash flows (paragraph 12); and
> (b) to evaluate:
>   (i) the nature and extent of significant restrictions on its ability to access or use assets, and settle liabilities, of the group (paragraph 13);
>   (ii) the nature of, and changes in, the risks associated with its interests in consolidated structured entities (paragraphs 14–17);
>   (iii) the consequences of changes in its ownership interest in a subsidiary that do not result in a loss of control (paragraph 18); and
>   (iv) the consequences of losing control of a subsidiary during the reporting period (paragraph 19).

Where the financial statements of a subsidiary are as of a date that differs from that of the parent, the entity must disclose both the date used by the subsidiary as well as the reason for using a different date (paragraph 11). As the parent controls the subsidiary, the choice of a different date must be one made by the parent and not the subsidiary.

Where a non-controlling interest exists in a subsidiary, paragraph 12 of IFRS 12 requires that an entity disclose for each such subsidiary:

(a) the name of the subsidiary.
(b) the principal place of business (and country of incorporation if different from the principal place of business) of the subsidiary.
(c) the proportion of ownership interests held by non-controlling interests.
(d) the proportion of voting rights held by non-controlling interests, if different from the proportion of ownership interests held.
(e) the profit or loss allocated to non-controlling interests of the subsidiary during the reporting period.
(f) accumulated non-controlling interests of the subsidiary at the end of the reporting period.
(g) summarised financial information about the subsidiary (see paragraph B10).

Paragraph B10 of IFRS 12 states:

> For each subsidiary that has non-controlling interests that are material to the reporting entity, an entity shall disclose:
> (a) dividends paid to non-controlling interests.
> (b) summarised financial information about the assets, liabilities, profit or loss and cash flows of the subsidiary that enables users to understand the interest that non-controlling interests have in the group's activities and cash flows. That information might include but is not limited to, for example, current assets, non-current assets, current liabilities, non-current liabilities, revenue, profit or loss and total comprehensive income.

Paragraph B11 notes that the summarised financial information is required *before* adjusting for intra-group transactions. Paragraph 13 of IFRS 12 provides disclosures required where an entity has significant restrictions on its ability to access or use the assets or settle the liabilities of the group. Paragraph 14 of IFRS 12 deals with consolidated structured entities. In Appendix A, a structured entity is defined as:

An entity that has been designed so that voting or similar rights are not the dominant factor in deciding who controls the entity, such as when any voting rights relate to administrative tasks only and the relevant activities are directed by means of contractual arrangements.

Paragraphs B22–B24 provide further information about structured entities.

According to paragraph B22, a structured entity may have the following features:

(a) restricted activities.
(b) a narrow and well-defined objective, such as to effect a tax-efficient lease, carry out research and development activities, provide a source of capital or funding to an entity or provide investment opportunities for investors by passing on risks and rewards associated with the assets of the structured entity to investors.
(c) insufficient equity to permit the structured entity to finance its activities without subordinated financial support.
(d) financing in the form of multiple contractually linked instruments to investors that create concentrations of credit or other risks (tranches).

The following examples of entities that are regarded as structured entities are noted in paragraph B23:

(a) securitisation vehicles.
(b) asset-backed financings.
(c) some investment funds.

Disclosures in relation to consolidated structured entities required by IFRS 12 include:

- the terms of any contractual arrangement that could require a parent or its subsidiaries to supply financial support to a consolidated structured entity
- information about the provision of financial support supplied without the parent or its subsidiaries having a contractual obligation to do so
- current intentions to provide financial or other support to a consolidated structured entity.

Where the structured entity is *not* consolidated, paragraphs 24–31 of IFRS 12 provide information on the disclosures required. As these structured entities are not consolidated, it is important that users are aware of any risks associated with involvement with these entities. In particular paragraph 26 requires disclosure about:

its interests in unconsolidated structured entities, including, but not limited to, the nature, purpose, size and activities of the structured entity and how the structured entity is financed.

To assist in the evaluation of risks associated with unconsolidated structured entities, paragraph 29 requires an entity to disclose in tabular format, unless another format is more appropriate, a summary of:

(a) the carrying amounts of the assets and liabilities recognised in its financial statements relating to its interests in unconsolidated structured entities.
(b) the line items in the statement of financial position in which those assets and liabilities are recognised.
(c) the amount that best represents the entity's maximum exposure to loss from its interests in unconsolidated structured entities, including how the maximum exposure to loss is determined. If an entity cannot quantify its maximum exposure to loss from its interests in unconsolidated structured entities it shall disclose that fact and the reasons.
(d) a comparison of the carrying amounts of the assets and liabilities of the entity that relate to its interests in unconsolidated structured entities and the entity's maximum exposure to loss from those entities.

Paragraphs 18 and 19 set out disclosures required where there are changes in the parent's ownership interest in a subsidiary as well as when a parent loses control of a subsidiary. These situations are discussed in chapter 27.

23.5.2 Disclosures required by IAS 27

Paragraph 4 of IAS 27 contains the following definition of separate financial statements:

Separate financial statements are those presented by a parent (ie an investor with control of a subsidiary) or an investor with joint control of, or significant influence over, an investee, in which the investments are accounted for at cost or in accordance with IFRS 9 *Financial Instruments*.

There are two situations where separate financial statements are prepared:

1. *Where a parent is exempted from preparing consolidated financial statements in accordance with paragraph 4(a) of IFRS 10.*

In this case, paragraph 16 of IAS 27 requires the parent to supply the following information in the separate financial statements prepared by the parent:

(a) the fact that the financial statements are separate financial statements; that the exemption from consolidation has been used; the name and principal place of business (and country of incorporation, if different) of the entity whose consolidated financial statements that comply with International Financial Reporting Standards have been produced for public use; and the address where those consolidated financial statements are obtainable;

(b) a list of significant investments in subsidiaries, jointly controlled entities and associates, including the name, country of incorporation or residence, proportion of ownership interest and, if different, proportion of voting power held; and

(c) a description of the method used to account for the investments listed under (b).

2. *Where a parent prepares separate financial statements in addition to consolidated financial statements.*
Paragraph 17 of IAS 27 requires the following information to be disclosed in the separate financial statements:

(a) the fact that the statements are separate financial statements and the reasons why those statements are prepared if not required by law;

(b) a list of significant investments in subsidiaries, joint ventures and associates, including:
   (i) the name of those investees.
   (ii) the principal place of business (and country of incorporation, if different) of those investees.
   (iii) its proportion of the ownership interest (and its proportion of the voting rights, if different) held in those investees.

(c) a description of the method used to account for the investments listed under (b).

The parent or investor shall also identify the financial statements prepared in accordance with IFRS 10, IFRS 11 or IAS 28 (as amended in 2011) to which they relate.

SUMMARY

Where entities form relationships with other entities, accounting standards often require additional disclosure so that users of financial statements can understand the economic substance of the entities involved. Some entities are classified as joint ventures, others as associates and others as subsidiaries. Where an entity is classified as a subsidiary of another, the parent, International Financial Reporting Standards establish principles for the preparation of consolidated financial statements. These statements are in addition to those prepared for either the parent or a subsidiary as separate legal entities. The consolidated financial statements are prepared by adding the financial statements of a parent and each of its subsidiaries, with adjustments being made during this process.

An important decision is the determination of whether the relationship between two entities is such as to be classified as a parent–subsidiary relationship. The existence of this relationship is determined by whether one entity has control over another. The existence of control requires the assessment of the power an entity has over another entity, whether the investor is exposed or has rights to variable returns from its involvement in the investee, and the ability of the investor to use its power over the investee to affect the amount of those returns. This analysis requires the accountant to exercise judgement in analysing the specific relationships between entities, since the existence of control is not simply a matter of determining whether an entity owns a majority of shares in another.

In general, parent entities are responsible for the preparation of the consolidated financial statements. However, IFRS 10 exempts parent entities that meet specified criteria from the preparation of these statements. For those parents preparing consolidated financial statements, IFRS 3 will need to be applied as the formation of a parent–subsidiary relationship is normally also a business combination.

IFRS 10 does not contain disclosure requirements for consolidated financial statements. The disclosure requirements are found in IFRS 12 and IAS 27.

Discussion questions

1. What is a subsidiary?
2. What is meant by the term 'control'?
3. For what purposes are the consolidated financial statements prepared?
4. What are the key elements of control?
5. When does an investor have power over an investee?
6. What are 'relevant' activities?

7. Explain the link between power and returns.

8. When are potential voting rights considered when deciding if one entity controls another?

9. Why are only those entities in which another entity owns more than 50% of the issued shares classified as subsidiaries?

10. What benefits could be sought by an entity that obtains control over another entity?

Exercises

STAR RATING ★ BASIC ★★ MODERATE ★★★ DIFFICULT

Exercise 23.1 CONVERTIBLE DEBENTURES

★ Singapore Ltd establishes Peru Ltd for the sole purpose of developing a new product to be manufactured and marketed by Singapore Ltd. Singapore Ltd engages Mr Smith to lead the team to develop the new product. Mr Smith is named Managing Director of Peru Ltd at an annual salary of $100 000, $10 000 of which is advanced to Mr Smith by Peru Ltd at the time Peru Ltd is established. Mr Smith invests $10 000 in the project and receives all of Peru Ltd's initial issue of 10 shares of voting ordinary shares.

Singapore Ltd transfers $500 000 to Peru Ltd in exchange for 7%, 10-year debentures convertible at any time into 500 shares of Peru Ltd voting ordinary shares. Peru Ltd has enough shares authorised to fulfil its obligation if Singapore Ltd converts its debentures into voting ordinary shares.

The constitution of Peru Ltd provides certain powers for the holders of voting common shares and the holders of securities convertible into voting ordinary shares that require a majority of each class voting separately. These include:

(a) the power to amend the corporate purpose of Peru Ltd

(b) the power to authorise and issue voting shares of securities convertible into voting shares.

At the time Peru Ltd is established, there are no known economic legal impediments to Singapore Ltd converting the debt.

Required

Discuss whether Peru Ltd is a subsidiary of Singapore Ltd.

Source: Adapted from Case V issued by the Financial Accounting Standards Board (FASB) as a part of its Consolidations project.

Exercise 23.2 VOTING INTEREST WIDELY HELD

★ Canada Ltd is a production company that produces movies and television shows. It also owns cable television systems that broadcast its movies and television shows. Canada Ltd transferred to Chile Ltd its cable assets and the shares in its previously owned and recently acquired cable television systems, which broadcast Canada Ltd's movies. Chile Ltd assumed approximately $200 million in debt related to companies it acquired in the transaction. After the transfer date, Chile Ltd acquired additional cable television systems, incurring approximately $2 billion of debt, none of which was guaranteed by Canada Ltd.

Chile Ltd was initially established as a wholly-owned subsidiary of Canada Ltd. Several months after the transfer, Chile Ltd issued ordinary shares in an initial public offering, raising nearly $1 billion in cash and reducing Canada Ltd's interest in Chile Ltd to 41%. The remaining 59% of Chile Ltd's voting interest is widely held.

The managing director of Chile Ltd was formerly the manager of broadcast operations for Canada Ltd. Half the directors of Chile Ltd are or were executive officers of Canada Ltd.

Chile Ltd and its subsidiaries have entered individually into broadcast contracts with Canada Ltd, pursuant to which Chile Ltd and its cable system subsidiaries must purchase 90% of their television shows from Canada Ltd at payment terms, and other terms and conditions of supply as determined from time to time by Canada Ltd. That agreement gives Chile Ltd and its cable television system subsidiaries the exclusive right to broadcast Canada Ltd's movies and television shows in specific geographic areas containing approximately 45% of the country's population. Chile Ltd and its cable television subsidiaries determine the advertising rates charged to their broadcast advertisers.

Under its agreement with Canada Ltd, Chile Ltd has limited rights to engage in businesses other than the sale of Canada Ltd's movies and television shows. In its most recent financial year, approximately 90% of Chile Ltd's sales were Canada Ltd movies and television shows. Canada Ltd provides promotional and marketing services and consultation to the cable television systems that broadcast its movies and television shows. Chile Ltd rents office space from Canada Ltd in its headquarters facility through a renewable lease agreement, which will expire in 5 years' time.

Required

1. Should Canada Ltd consolidate Chile Ltd? Why?
2. If Canada Ltd had not established Chile Ltd but had instead purchased 41% of Chile Ltd's voting shares on the open market, does this change your answer to requirement 1? Why?

Source: Adapted from Case III issued by the FASB as a part of its Consolidations project.

Exercise 23.3 OPTIONS

★ Palau Ltd and India Ltd own 80% and 20% respectively of the ordinary shares that carry voting rights at a general meeting of shareholders of Cook Islands Ltd. Palau Ltd sells half of its interest to Kobe Ltd and buys call options from Kobe Ltd that are exercisable at any time at a premium to the market price when issued and, if exercised, would give Palau Ltd its original 80% ownership interest and voting rights. At 30 June 2014, the options are out of the money.

Required

Discuss whether Palau Ltd is the parent of Cook Islands Ltd.

Exercise 23.4 OPTIONS

★ Brunei Ltd, Burma Ltd and Bhutan Ltd each own one-third of the ordinary shares that carry voting rights at a general meeting of shareholders of Comoros Ltd. Brunei Ltd, Burma Ltd and Bhutan Ltd each have the right to appoint two directors to the board of Comoros Ltd. Brunei Ltd also owns call options that are exercisable at a fixed price at any time and, if exercised, would give it all the voting rights in Comoros Ltd. The management of Brunei Ltd does not intend to exercise the call options, even if Burma Ltd and Bhutan Ltd do not vote in the same manner as Brunei Ltd.

Required

Discuss whether Comoros Ltd is a subsidiary of any of the other entities.

Exercise 23.5 CONVERTIBLE DEBT

★ Vanuatu Ltd and Vietnam Ltd own 55% and 45% respectively of the ordinary shares that carry voting rights at a general meeting of shareholders of Tonga Ltd. Vietnam Ltd also holds debt instruments that are convertible into ordinary shares of Tonga Ltd. The debt can be converted at a substantial price, in comparison with Vietnam Ltd's net assets, at any time, and if converted would require Vietnam Ltd to borrow additional funds to make the payment. If the debt were to be converted, Vietnam Ltd would hold 70% of the voting rights and Vanuatu Ltd's interest would reduce to 30%. Given the effect of increasing its debt on its debt–equity ratio, Vietnam Ltd does not believe that it has the financial ability to enter into conversion of the debt.

Required

Discuss whether Vietnam Ltd is a parent of Tonga Ltd.

Exercise 23.6 CONTROL

★★ Thailand Ltd has acquired, during the current year, the following investments in the shares issued by other companies:

Tuvala Ltd	$120 000 (40% of issued capital)
Tonga Ltd	$117 000 (35% of issued capital)

Thailand Ltd is unsure how to account for these investments and has asked you, as the auditor, for some professional advice.

Specifically, Thailand Ltd is concerned that it may need to prepare consolidated financial statements under IFRS 10. To help you, the company has provided the following information about the two investee companies:

Tuvala Ltd

- The remaining shares in Tuvala Ltd are owned by a diverse group of investors who each hold a small parcel of shares.

- Historically, only a small number of the shareholders attend the general meetings or question the actions of the directors.
- Thailand Ltd has nominated three new directors and expects that they will be appointed at the next annual general meeting. The current board of directors has five members.

Tonga Ltd

- The remaining shares in Tonga Ltd are owned by a small group of investors who each own approximately 15% of the issued shares. One of these shareholders is Tuvala Ltd, which owns 17%.
- The shareholders take a keen interest in the running of the company and attend all meetings.
- Two of the shareholders, including Tuvala Ltd, already have representatives on the board of directors who have indicated their intention of nominating for re-election.

Required

1. Advise Thailand Ltd as to whether, under IFRS 10, it controls Tuvala Ltd and/or Tonga Ltd. Support your conclusion.
2. Would your conclusion be different if the remaining shares in Tuvala Ltd were owned by three institutional investors each holding 20%? If so, why?

Exercise 23.7	SUBSIDIARY STATUS

★★ Russia Ltd owns 40% of the shares of Samoa Ltd, and holds the only substantial block of shares in that entity; no other party owns more than 3% of the shares. The annual general meeting of Samoa Ltd is to be held in one month's time. Two situations that may arise are:

- Russia Ltd will be able to elect a majority of Samoa Ltd's board of directors as a result of exercising its votes as the largest holder of shares. As only 75% of shareholders voted in the previous year's annual meeting, Russia Ltd may have the majority of the votes that are cast at the meeting.
- By obtaining the proxies of other shareholders and, after meeting with other shareholders who normally attend general meetings of Samoa Ltd and convincing these shareholders to vote with it, Russia Ltd may obtain the necessary votes to have its nominees elected as directors of the board of Samoa Ltd, regardless of the attendance at the general meeting.

Required

Discuss the potential for Samoa Ltd being classified as a subsidiary of Russia Ltd.

Exercise 23.8	DETERMINING SUBSIDIARY STATUS

★★ **Required**

In the following independent situations, determine whether a parent–subsidiary relationship exists, and which entity, if any, is a parent required to prepare consolidated financial statements under IFRS 10.

1. Perth Ltd is a company that was hurt by a recent global financial crisis. As a result, it experienced major trading difficulties. It previously obtained a significant loan from Fremantle Bank, and when Perth Ltd was unable to make its loan repayments, the bank made an agreement with Perth Ltd to become involved in the management of that company. Under the agreement between the two entities, the bank had authority for spending within Perth Ltd. Perth Ltd's managers had to obtain authority from the bank for acquisitions over $10 000, and was required to have bank approval for its budgets.
2. Broome Ltd owns 80% of the equity shares of Shark Bay Ltd, which owns 100% of the shares of Geraldton Ltd. All companies prepare reports under Australian accounting standards. Although the shares of Shark Bay Ltd are not traded on any stock exchange, its debt instruments are publicly traded.
3. Denmark Ltd is a major financing company whose interest in investing is return on the investment. Denmark Ltd does not get involved in the management of its investments. If the investees are not managed properly, Denmark Ltd sells its shares in that investee and selects a more profitable investee to invest in. It previously held a 35% interest in Esperance Ltd as well as providing substantial convertible debt finance to that entity. Recently, Esperance Ltd was having cash flow difficulties and persuaded Denmark Ltd to convert some of the convertible debt into equity so as to ease the effects of interest payments on cash flow. As a result, Denmark Ltd's equity interest in Esperance Ltd increased to 52%. Denmark Ltd still wanted to remain as a passive investor, with no changes in the directors on the board of Esperance Ltd. These directors were appointed by the holders of the 48% of shares not held by Denmark Ltd.

Exercise 23.9 | DETERMINING SUBSIDIARY STATUS

★★ **Required**

In the following independent situations, determine whether a parent–subsidiary relationship exists and which entity, if any, is a parent required to prepare consolidated financial statements under IFRS 10.

1. Albany Ltd and Busselton Ltd each hold 50% of the shares in Dunsborough Ltd, all companies being involved in the computer software industry. Albany Ltd agrees that Busselton Ltd should provide the management of Dunsborough Ltd because of the expertise provided by its managing director, Bob Gates. Busselton Ltd receives a management fee for providing its expertise.

2. Alice Ltd has recently acquired a 35% interest in Springs Ltd, a company that has discovered large deposits of iron ore. Alice Ltd has extensive experience in the mining industry and, as a result, has been able to have four of its directors elected to the board of Springs Ltd, which has six directors in total.

3. Darwin Ltd holds 30% of the shares issued by Arnhem Ltd. The other shareholders come from mixed backgrounds, but each holds on average 10% of shares in Darwin Ltd. There are seven directors of Arnhem Ltd. Four of these are appointed by Darwin Ltd. The other three directors are appointed by three of the other shareholders who have an interest in the management of the company. Most of the remaining shareholders live outside Australia and rarely attend board meetings of Darwin Ltd unless they have other business to attend to in Australia around the same time as the board meetings are held.

Exercise 23.10 | LESS THAN MAJORITY OWNERSHIP

★★ On 1 March 2013, Nepal Ltd acquired 40% of the voting shares of Pakistan Ltd. Under the company's constitution, each share is entitled to one vote. On the basis of past experience, only 65% of the eligible votes are typically cast at the annual general meetings of Pakistan Ltd. No other shareholder holds a major block of shares in Pakistan Ltd.

The financial year of Pakistan Ltd ends on 30 June each year. The directors of Nepal Ltd argue that they are not required under IFRS 10 to include Pakistan Ltd as a subsidiary in Nepal Ltd's consolidated financial statements at 30 June 2013 as there is no conclusive evidence that Nepal Ltd can control the financial and operating policies of Pakistan Ltd. The auditors of Nepal Ltd disagree, referring specifically to past years' voting figures.

Required

Provide a report to Nepal Ltd on whether it should regard Pakistan Ltd as a subsidiary in its preparation of consolidated financial statements at 30 June 2013.

Exercise 23.11 | DETERMINING PARENT STATUS

★★ Japan Ltd has 37% of the voting interest in Maldives Ltd. An investment bank with which Japan has business relationships holds a 15% voting interest. Because of the closeness of the business relationship with the bank, Japan Ltd believes it can rely on the bank's support to ensure it cannot be outvoted at general meetings of Maldives Ltd.

Required

Given that there is no guarantee that the bank will always support Japan Ltd, particularly if there is a potential for economic loss, discuss whether Japan Ltd is a parent of Maldives Ltd.

Exercise 23.12 | RIGHTS TO VARIABLE RETURNS

★★ Some have argued that the criteria for consolidation should be control plus significant risks and rewards of ownership or economic benefits. These parties argue that the consolidated financial statements are not meaningful if they include subsidiaries in which the parent's level of returns is less than 50% or is not significant.

Required

Discuss:
1. the place of a returns criterion in the definition of control
2. possible returns that could occur as a result of obtaining control of another entity
3. the need to place a specified level of returns in the definition of control.

24

Consolidation: wholly owned subsidiaries

ACCOUNTING STANDARDS IN FOCUS

IFRS 10 *Consolidated Financial Statements*

IFRS 3 *Business Combinations*

IFRS 12 *Disclosure of Interests in Other Entities*

LEARNING OBJECTIVES

After studying this chapter, you should be able to:

1 understand the nature of the group covered in this chapter, and the initial adjustments required in the consolidation worksheet

2 explain how a consolidation worksheet is used

3 prepare an acquisition analysis for the parent's acquisition in a subsidiary

4 prepare the worksheet entries at the acquisition date, being the business combination valuation entries and the pre-acquisition entries

5 prepare the worksheet entries in periods subsequent to the acquisition date, adjusting for movements in assets and liabilities since acquisition date and dividends from pre-acquisition equity

6 prepare the worksheet entries where the subsidiary revalues its assets at acquisition date

7 prepare the disclosures required by IFRS 3 and IFRS 12

8 explain the consolidation procedures for a reverse acquisition.

24.1 THE CONSOLIDATION PROCESS

This chapter discusses the preparation of consolidated financial statements. As discussed in chapter 23, under IFRS 10 *Consolidated Financial Statements* consolidated financial statements are the result of combining the financial statements of a parent and all its subsidiaries. (The determination of whether an entity is a parent or a subsidiary is discussed in chapter 23 of this book.) The two accounting standards mainly used in this chapter are IFRS 10 and IFRS 3 *Business Combinations*. Chapter 14 of this book contains the accounting principles relevant for business combinations. An in-depth understanding of that chapter is essential to the preparation of consolidated financial statements because the parent's acquisition of shares in a subsidiary is simply one form of a business combination.

In IFRS 3 Appendix A, 'acquisition date' is defined as the date on which the acquirer obtains control of the acquiree. As discussed in chapter 14, both the fair values of the identifiable assets and liabilities of the subsidiary and the consideration transferred are measured at the acquisition date. In this chapter, the only combinations considered are those where the parent acquires its controlling interest in a subsidiary and, as a result, owns all the issued shares of the subsidiary — the subsidiary is then a wholly owned subsidiary. This may occur by the parent buying all the shares in a subsidiary in one transaction, or by the parent acquiring the controlling interest after having previously acquired shares in the subsidiary.

Note, however, as discussed in chapter 23, control of a subsidiary does not necessarily involve the parent acquiring shares in a subsidiary. The consolidated financial statements of a parent and its subsidiaries include information about a subsidiary from the date the parent obtains control of the subsidiary; that is, from the acquisition date. A subsidiary continues to be included in the parent's consolidated financial statements until the parent no longer controls that entity; that is, until the date of disposal of the subsidiary.

Before undertaking the consolidation process, it may be necessary to make adjustments in relation to the content of the financial statements of the subsidiary:

- If the end of a subsidiary's reporting period does not coincide with the end of the parent's reporting period, adjustments must be made for the effects of significant transactions and events that occur between those dates, with additional financial statements being prepared where it is practicable to do so (IFRS 10 paragraphs B92–B93). In most cases where there are different dates, the subsidiary will prepare adjusted financial statements as at the end of the parent's reporting period, so that adjustments are not necessary on consolidation. Where the preparation of adjusted financial statements is unduly costly, the financial statements of the subsidiary prepared at a different date from the parent may be used, subject to adjustments for significant transactions. However, as paragraph B93 states, for this to be a viable option, the difference between the ends of the reporting periods can be no longer than three months. Further, the length of the reporting periods, as well as any difference between the ends of the reporting periods, must be the same from period to period.
- The consolidated financial statements are to be prepared using uniform accounting policies for like transactions and other events in similar circumstances (IFRS 10 paragraph 19). Where different policies are used, adjustments are made so that like transactions are accounted for under a uniform policy in the consolidated financial statements.

The preparation of the consolidated financial statements involves adding together the financial statements of the parent and its subsidiaries. As a part of this summation process, a number of adjustments are made, these being expressed in the form of journal entries:

- As required by IFRS 3, at the acquisition date the acquirer must recognise the identifiable assets acquired and liabilities assumed of the subsidiary at fair value. Adjusting the carrying amounts of the subsidiary's assets and liabilities to fair value and recognising any identifiable assets acquired and liabilities assumed as a part of the business combination but not recorded by the subsidiary is a part of the consolidation process. The entries used to make these adjustments are referred to in this chapter as the *business combination valuation entries*. As noted in section 24.2 of this chapter, these adjusting entries are generally not made in the records of the subsidiary itself but in a consolidation worksheet.
- Where the parent has an ownership interest (i.e. owns shares) in a subsidiary, adjusting entries are made, referred to in this chapter as the *pre-acquisition entries*. As noted in paragraph B86(b) of IFRS 10, this involves eliminating the carrying amount of the parent's investment in each subsidiary and the parent's portion of pre-acquisition equity in each subsidiary. The name of these entries is derived from the fact that the equity of the subsidiary at the acquisition date is referred to as pre-acquisition equity, and it is this equity that is being eliminated. These entries are also made in the consolidation worksheet and not in the records of the subsidiary.

- The third set of adjustments to be made is for transactions between the entities within the group subsequent to the acquisition date, including events such as sales of inventory or non-current assets. These *intragroup* transactions are referred to in IFRS 10 paragraph B86(c), and adjustments for these transactions are discussed in detail in chapter 25 of this book.

In this chapter, the group under discussion is one where:

- there are only two entities within the group: one parent and one subsidiary (see figure 24.1)
- both entities have share capital
- the parent owns all the issued shares of the subsidiary; that is, the subsidiary is wholly owned (partially owned subsidiaries, where it is necessary to account for the non-controlling interest, are covered in chapter 26 of this book)
- there are no intragroup transactions between the parent and its subsidiary after the acquisition date.

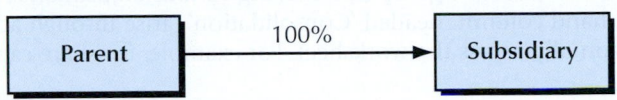

FIGURE 24.1 A wholly owned group

 ## 24.2 CONSOLIDATION WORKSHEETS

The consolidated financial statements are prepared by adding together the financial statements of the parent and the subsidiary. It is the *financial statements* of the parent and the subsidiary, rather than the underlying accounts, which are added together. There are no consolidated ledger accounts. The financial statements that are added together are the statements of financial position, statements of profit or loss and other comprehensive income and statements of changes in equity prepared by the management of the parent and the subsidiary. Consolidated statements of cash flows must also be prepared, but these are not covered in this book.

To facilitate the addition process, particularly where there are a number of subsidiaries, as well as to make the necessary valuation and pre-acquisition entry adjustments, a worksheet or computer spreadsheet is often used. From the worksheet, the external statements are prepared — the consolidated statement of financial position, statement of profit or loss and other comprehensive income and statement of changes in equity.

The format for the worksheet is presented in figure 24.2, which contains the information used for the consolidation of the parent, P Ltd, and the subsidiary, S Ltd.

Financial statements	Parent P Ltd	Subsidiary S Ltd	Adjustments				Consolidation
				Dr	Cr		
Retained earnings	25 000	12 000	1	5 000			32 000
Share capital	30 000	15 000	1	15 000			30 000
	55 000	27 000					62 000
Shares in S Ltd	20 000	—			20 000	1	—
Other assets	35 000	27 000					62 000
	55 000	27 000		20 000	20 000		62 000

FIGURE 24.2 Consolidation worksheet — basic format

Note the following points about the worksheet:

- Column 1 contains the names of the accounts, as the financial statements are combined on a line-by-line basis.
- Columns 2 and 3 contain the internal financial statements of the parent, P Ltd, and its subsidiary, S Ltd. These statements are obtained from the separate legal entities. The number of columns is expanded if there are more subsidiaries within the group.
- The next four columns, headed 'Adjustments', are used to make the adjustments required in the consolidation process. These include adjustments for valuations at acquisition date, pre-acquisition equity, and intragroup transactions such as sales of inventory between the parent and subsidiary. The

adjustments, written in the form of journal entries, are recorded on the worksheet. Where there are many adjustments, each journal entry should be numbered so that it is clear which items are being affected by a particular adjustment entry. In figure 24.2 there is only one worksheet entry, hence the number '1' is entered against each adjustment item. The worksheet adjustment entry is:

(1) Retained Earnings (opening balance)	Dr	5 000	
Share Capital	Dr	15 000	
Shares in S Ltd	Cr		20 000

- As noted earlier, the process of consolidation is one of adding together the financial statements of the members of the group and making various adjustments. Hence, figures for each line item in the right-hand column, headed 'Consolidation', arise through addition and subtraction as you proceed horizontally across the worksheet. For example, for share capital:

$$\$30\,000 + \$15\,000 - \$15\,000 = \$30\,000$$

The figures in the right-hand column provide the information for the preparation of the consolidated financial statements of P Ltd and S Ltd.
- In the 'Consolidation' column, the totals and subtotals are the result of adding the preceding items in that column rather than totalling items across the rows. For example, the total consolidated equity of $62 000 is determined by adding the retained earnings balance of $32 000 and the share capital balance of $30 000, both these balances appearing in the 'Consolidation' column. It is from this column that the information for preparing the consolidated statement of profit or loss and other comprehensive income, statement of changes in equity and statement of financial position is obtained. These statements will not include all the line items in the consolidation worksheet. However, information for the notes to these statements is also obtained from line items in the worksheet.

In preparing the consolidated financial statements, *no* adjustments are made in the accounting records of the individual entities that constitute the group. The adjustment entries recorded in the columns of the worksheet do not affect the accounts of the individual entities. They are recorded in a separate consolidation journal, not in the journals of any of the member entities, and are then recorded on the consolidation worksheet. Hence, where consolidated financial statements are prepared over a number of years, a particular entry (such as a pre-acquisition entry) needs to be made every time a consolidation worksheet is prepared, because the entry never affects the actual financial statements of the individual entities.

24.3 THE ACQUISITION ANALYSIS

As noted in chapter 14 of this book, the parent records its investment in the subsidiary based upon the consideration transferred, often the equity shares of the parent. However, as noted in paragraph 33 of IFRS 3, where the business combination occurs by the parent exchanging its equity interests for the equity interests of the former owners of the subsidiary, the acquisition-date fair values of the acquiree's equity interests may be more reliably measurable than the acquisition-date fair values of the acquirer's equity interests. In that case, fair value of the acquiree's equity interests will be used in subsequent calculations.

At acquisition date, an acquisition analysis is undertaken to determine if there has been any goodwill acquired, or whether a bargain purchase has occurred. Paragraph 32 of IFRS 3 sets out the measurement of goodwill:

The acquirer shall recognise goodwill as of the acquisition date measured as the excess of (a) over (b) below:
(a) the aggregate of:
    (i) the consideration transferred measured in accordance with this IFRS, which generally requires acquisition-date fair value (see paragraph 37);
    (ii) the amount of any non-controlling interest in the acquiree measured in accordance with this IFRS; and
    (iii) in a business combination achieved in stages (see paragraphs 41 and 42), the acquisition-date fair value of the acquirer's previously held *equity interest* in the acquiree.
(b) the net of the acquisition-date amounts of the identifiable assets acquired and the liabilities assumed measured in accordance with this IFRS.

In this chapter, because the parent acquires all the shares in the subsidiary, there is no effect due to (a)(ii). However, because of (a)(iii), the acquisition analysis is affected by whether at acquisition date the parent has previously acquired any shares or other equity interests in the subsidiary.

24.3.1 Parent has no previously held equity interest in the subsidiary

In this case, the parent acquires all the shares of the subsidiary at acquisition date in one transaction. In terms of paragraph 32 of IFRS 3, goodwill arises when the consideration transferred [32(a)(i)] is greater than the net fair value of the identifiable assets and liabilities acquired [32(b)]. Where the reverse occurs, a gain on bargain purchase is recognised.

An acquisition analysis is conducted at acquisition date because it is necessary to recognise the identifiable assets and liabilities of the subsidiary at fair value, and to determine whether there has been an acquisition of goodwill or a gain. As noted in chapter 14, this may give rise to the recognition of assets and liabilities that are not recognised in the records of the subsidiary; for example, the business combination may give rise to intangibles that were not capable of being recognised in the subsidiary's records such as internally generated brands.

The first step in the consolidation process is to undertake the above acquisition analysis in order to obtain the information necessary for making both the business combination valuation and pre-acquisition entry adjustments for the consolidation worksheet. Consider the example in figure 24.3.

On 1 July 2013, Parent Ltd acquired all the issued share capital of Sub Ltd, giving in exchange 100 000 shares in Parent Ltd, these having a fair value of $5 per share. At acquisition date, the statements of financial position of Parent Ltd and Sub Ltd, and the fair values of Sub Ltd's assets and liabilities, were as follows:

| | Parent Ltd | Sub Ltd | |
	Carrying amount	Carrying amount	Fair value
EQUITY AND LIABILITIES			
Equity			
Share capital	$550 000	$300 000	
Retained earnings	350 000	140 000	
Total equity	900 000	440 000	
Liabilities			
Provisions	30 000	60 000	$ 60 000
Payables	27 000	34 000	34 000
Tax liabilities	10 000	6 000	6 000
Total liabilities	67 000	100 000	
Total equity and liabilities	$967 000	$540 000	
ASSETS			
Land	$120 000	$150 000	170 000
Equipment	620 000	480 000	330 000
Accumulated depreciation	(380 000)	(170 000)	
Shares in Sub Ltd	500 000		
Inventory	92 000	75 000	80 000
Cash	15 000	5 000	5 000
Total assets	$967 000	$540 000	

At acquisition date, Sub Ltd has an unrecorded patent with a fair value of $20 000, and a contingent liability with a fair value of $15 000. This contingent liability relates to a loan guarantee made by Sub Ltd which did not recognise a liability in its records because it did not consider it could reliably measure the liability. The tax rate is 30%.

FIGURE 24.3 Information at acquisition date

The analysis at acquisition date consists of comparing the fair value of the consideration transferred and the net fair value of the identifiable assets and liabilities of the subsidiary at acquisition date. The net fair value of the subsidiary could be calculated by revaluing the assets and liabilities of the subsidiary from the carrying amounts to fair values, remembering that under IAS 12 *Income Taxes* where there is a difference between the carrying amount and the tax base caused by the revaluation, the tax effect of such a difference has to be recognised. However, in calculating the net fair value of the subsidiary, because particular information is required to prepare the valuation and pre-acquisition entries, the calculation is done by adding the recorded equity of the subsidiary (which represents the recorded net assets of the subsidiary) and the differences between the carrying amounts of the assets and liabilities and their fair values, adjusted for tax. The book equity of the subsidiary in figure 24.3 consists of:

$$\$300\,000 \text{ capital} + \$140\,000 \text{ retained earnings}$$

The equity relating to the differences in fair value and carrying amounts for assets and liabilities recorded by Sub Ltd — as well as for assets and liabilities not recognised by the subsidiary but recognised as being acquired as part of the business combination — is referred to in this chapter as the *business combination valuation reserve* (BCVR). This reserve is not an account recognised in the subsidiary's records, but it is recognised in the consolidation process as part of the business combination. For example, for land there is a difference of $20 000 in the fair value carrying amount and, on revaluation of the land to fair value, a business combination valuation reserve of $14 000 (i.e. $20 000(1 − 30%)) is raised.

The acquisition analysis, including the determination of the goodwill of the subsidiary, is as shown in figure 24.4.

At 1 July 2013:
Net fair value of identifiable assets
and liabilities of Sub Ltd
$$= \$300\,000 + \$140\,000 \text{ (recorded equity)}$$
$$+ (\$170\,000 - \$150\,000)(1 - 30\%) \text{ (BCVR — land)}$$
$$+ (\$330\,000 - \$310\,000)(1 - 30\%) \text{ (BCVR — equipment)}$$
$$+ (\$80\,000 - \$75\,000)(1 - 30\%) \text{ (BCVR — inventory)}$$
$$+ \$20\,000(1 - 30\%) \text{ (BCVR — patent)}$$
$$- \$15\,000(1 - 30\%) \text{ (BCVR — provision for guarantee)}$$
$$= \$475\,000$$
Consideration transferred
$$= 100\,000 \text{ shares} \times \$5$$
$$= \$500\,000$$
Goodwill
$$= \$500\,000 - \$475\,000$$
$$= \$25\,000$$

FIGURE 24.4 Acquisition analysis — no previously held equity interests

The information from the completed acquisition analysis is used to prepare the adjustment entries for the consolidation worksheet. These entries are the business combination valuation entries and the pre-acquisition entries.

In this book, it is assumed that the tax base of the subsidiary's assets and liabilities is unchanged as a result of the parent's acquisition of the subsidiary. In some jurisdictions, where the group becomes the taxable entity, there is a change in the tax base to the fair value amounts. In this case, no tax effect would be recognised in relation to the assets and liabilities acquired.

24.3.2 Parent has previously held equity interest in the subsidiary

The situation used in figure 24.3 will be used here with the only difference being that on 1 July 2013 Parent Ltd acquires 80% [240 000 shares] of the shares in Sub Ltd, giving in exchange 80 000 shares in Parent Ltd, these having a fair value of $5 per share. Parent Ltd had previously acquired the other 20% [60 000] shares of Sub Ltd for $75 000. At 1 July 2013, this investment in Sub Ltd was recorded at $92 000. The investment was classified as a financial instrument and measured at fair value, with $12 000 having previously been recognised in other comprehensive income. At 1 July 2013, these shares had a fair value of $100 000.

In accordance with IFRS 3, paragraph 42, Parent Ltd revalues the previously held investment to fair value, recognising the increase in profit or loss, as well as transferring the amounts previously recognised in other comprehensive income to profit or loss as a reclassification adjustment. The journal entries in Parent Ltd at acquisition date, both for the previously held investment as well as the acquisition of the remaining shares in Sub Ltd are as follows:

Shares in Sub Ltd	Dr	8 000	
Profit or Loss	Cr		8 000
(Revaluation to fair value)			
Financial Assets Reserve	Dr	12 000	
Profit or Loss	Cr		12 000
(Reclassification adjustment — financial instruments — on investment becoming a subsidiary)			
Shares in Sub Ltd	Dr	400 000	
Share Capital	Cr		400 000
(Acquisition of shares in Sub Ltd: 80 000 at $5 per share)			

The acquisition analysis is shown in figure 24.5.

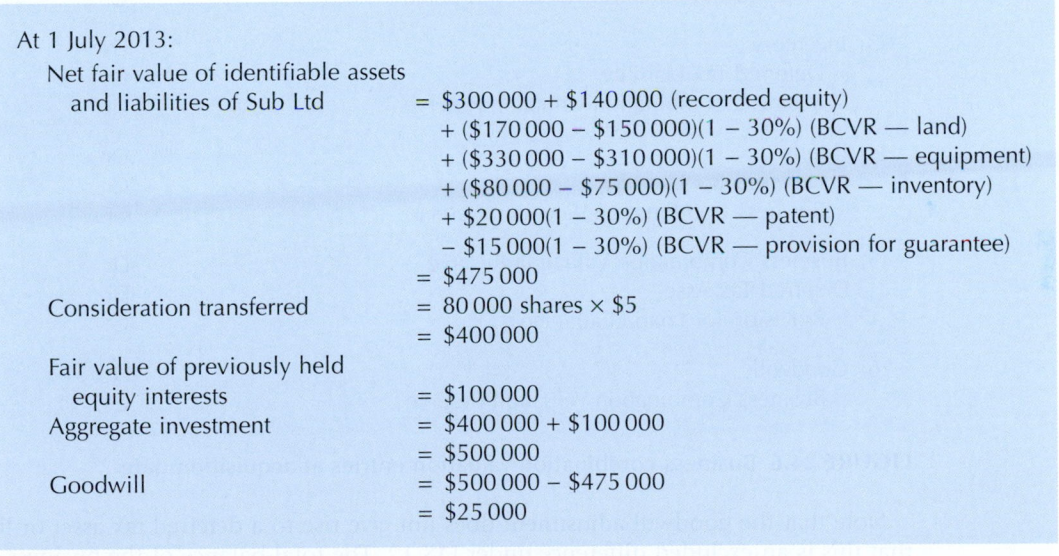

At 1 July 2013:
    Net fair value of identifiable assets
        and liabilities of Sub Ltd   = $300 000 + $140 000 (recorded equity)
                                            + ($170 000 − $150 000)(1 − 30%) (BCVR — land)
                                            + ($330 000 − $310 000)(1 − 30%) (BCVR — equipment)
                                            + ($80 000 − $75 000)(1 − 30%) (BCVR — inventory)
                                            + $20 000(1 − 30%) (BCVR — patent)
                                            − $15 000(1 − 30%) (BCVR — provision for guarantee)
                                          = $475 000
    Consideration transferred   = 80 000 shares × $5
                                          = $400 000
    Fair value of previously held
        equity interests   = $100 000
    Aggregate investment   = $400 000 + $100 000
                                          = $500 000
    Goodwill   = $500 000 − $475 000
                                          = $25 000

FIGURE 24.5 Acquisition analysis — previously held equity interests

As a result of the numbers used in this example, the goodwill number is the same as that shown in figure 24.4. There are no subsequent effects on the consolidation process because the parent had previously held an investment in the subsidiary.

LO4 24.4 WORKSHEET ENTRIES AT THE ACQUISITION DATE

As noted earlier, the consolidation process does not result in any entries being made in the actual records of either the parent or the subsidiary. The adjustment entries are made in the consolidation worksheet. Hence, adjustment entries need to be passed in each worksheet prepared, and these entries change over time. In this section, the adjustment entries that would be passed in a consolidation worksheet prepared *immediately after the acquisition date* are analysed.

24.4.1 Business combination valuation entries

In figure 24.3, there are three identifiable assets recognised by the subsidiary whose fair values differ from their carrying amounts at acquisition date, as well as an intangible asset and a contingent liability recognised as part of the business combination. The entries for the business combination valuations are done in the consolidation worksheet rather than in the records of the subsidiary (see section 24.6 for a discussion on making these adjustments in the records of the subsidiary itself). The identifiable assets and liabilities that require adjustment to fair value can be easily identified by reference to the acquisition analyses in figures 24.4 and 24.5, namely land, equipment, inventory, patent and the unrecorded guarantee. Goodwill also has to be recognised on consolidation. These differences are all recognised using business combination valuation entries. Consolidation worksheet adjustment entries for each of these assets and the unrecorded liability are given in figure 24.6.

Business combination valuation entries			
(1) Land	Dr	20 000	
Deferred Tax Liability	Cr		6 000
Business Combination Valuation Reserve	Cr		14 000
(2) Accumulated Depreciation – Equipment	Dr	170 000	
Equipment	Cr		150 000
Deferred Tax Liability	Cr		6 000
Business Combination Valuation Reserve	Cr		14 000
(3) Inventory	Dr	5 000	
Deferred Tax Liability	Cr		1 500
Business Combination Valuation Reserve	Cr		3 500
(4) Patent	Dr	20 000	
Deferred Tax Liability	Cr		6 000
Business Combination Valuation Reserve	Cr		14 000
(5) Business Combination Valuation Reserve	Dr	10 500	
Deferred Tax Asset	Dr	4 500	
Provision for Loan Guarantee	Cr		15 000
(6) Goodwill	Dr	25 000	
Business Combination Valuation Reserve	Cr		25 000

FIGURE 24.6 Business combination valuation entries at acquisition date

Note that the goodwill adjustment does not give rise to a deferred tax asset or liability as it is assumed that this is an excluded difference under IAS 12. The total balance of the business combination valuation reserve is $60 000. The adjustments to assets and liabilities at acquisition date could be achieved by one adjustment entry, giving a net balance to the business combination valuation reserve. However, in order to keep track of movements in that reserve as assets are depreciated or sold, liabilities paid or goodwill impaired, it is practical to prepare a valuation entry for each component of the valuation process. The valuation entries are passed in the adjustment columns of the worksheet, which is illustrated in section 24.4.3. Note that, in relation to entry (6) for goodwill, there is no deferred tax liability. This is because paragraph 21 of IAS 12 states that no such deferred tax liability is recognised, as goodwill is measured as a residual, and the recognition of a deferred tax liability would increase its carrying amount.

24.4.2 Pre-acquisition entries

As noted in paragraph B86(b) of IFRS 10, the pre-acquisition entries are required to eliminate the carrying amount of the parent's investment in the subsidiary and the parent's portion of pre-acquisition equity. The pre-acquisition entries, then, involve two areas:

- the investment account Shares in Subsidiary, as shown in the financial statements of the parent

- the equity of the subsidiary at the acquisition date (i.e. the pre-acquisition equity). The pre-acquisition equity is not just the equity recorded by the subsidiary but includes the business combination valuation reserve recognised on consolidation via the valuation entries. Because the accounts containing pre-acquisition equity may change over time as a result of bonus dividends and reserve transfers, more than one pre-acquisition entry may be required in a particular year.

Using the example in figure 24.3, and reading the information from the acquisition analysis in figure 24.4 (including the business combination valuation reserve for the revalued assets including goodwill and the contingent liability), the pre-acquisition entry at acquisition date is as shown in figure 24.7. The pre-acquisition entry in this figure is numbered (7) because there were six previous valuation entries.

Pre-acquisition entry			
(7) Retained Earnings (1/7/13)	Dr	140 000	
Share Capital	Dr	300 000	
Business Combination Valuation Reserve	Dr	60 000	
Shares in Sub Ltd	Cr		500 000

FIGURE 24.7 Pre-acquisition entry at acquisition date

The pre-acquisition entry is necessary to avoid overstating the equity and net assets of the group. To illustrate, consider the information in figure 24.3 relating to Parent Ltd's acquisition of the shares of Sub Ltd. Having acquired the shares in Sub Ltd, Parent Ltd records the asset 'Shares in Sub Ltd' at $500 000. This asset represents the actual net assets of Sub Ltd; that is, the ownership of the shares gives Parent Ltd the right to the net assets of Sub Ltd. To include both the asset 'Shares in Sub Ltd' and the net assets of Sub Ltd in the consolidated statement of financial position would double count the assets of the group, because the investment account is simply the right to the other assets. On consolidation, the investment account is therefore eliminated and, in its place, the net assets of the subsidiary are included in the consolidated statement of financial position.

Similarly, to include both the equity of the parent and the equity of the subsidiary in the consolidated statement of financial position would double-count the equity of the group. In the example, Parent Ltd has equity of $900 000, which is represented by its net assets including the investment in the subsidiary. Because the investment in the subsidiary is the same as the net assets of the subsidiary, the equity of the parent effectively relates to the net assets of the subsidiary. To include in the consolidated statement of financial position the equity of the subsidiary at acquisition date as well as the equity of the parent would double-count equity in relation to the net assets of the subsidiary.

24.4.3 Consolidation worksheet

Figure 24.8 contains the consolidation worksheet prepared at acquisition date, with adjustments being made for business combination valuation and pre-acquisition entries. The right-hand column reflects the consolidated statement of financial position, showing the position of the group. In relation to the figures in this column, note the following:
- In relation to the three equity accounts — share capital, business combination valuation reserve and retained earnings — only the parent's balances are carried into the consolidated statement of financial position. At acquisition date, all the equity of the subsidiary is pre-acquisition and eliminated.
- With the business combination valuation reserve, the valuation entry establishes the reserve, and the pre-acquisition entry eliminates it because it is by nature pre-acquisition equity.
- The assets of the subsidiary are carried forward into the consolidated statement of financial position at fair value.
- The debit and credit adjustment columns each total $755 000. This means that the adjusting journal entries have equal debits and credits, which is essential if the statement of financial position is to balance.

Financial statements	Parent Ltd	Sub Ltd	Adjustments				Consolidation
				Dr	Cr		
Retained earnings (1/7/13)	350 000	140 000	7	140 000			350 000
Share capital	550 000	300 000	7	300 000			550 000
Business combination valuation reserve			5	10 500	14 000	1	—
			7	60 000	14 000	2	
					3 500	3	
					14 000	4	
					25 000	6	
	900 000	440 000					900 000
Provisions	30 000	60 000			15 000	5	105 000
Payables	27 000	34 000					61 000
Tax liabilities (net of tax assets)	10 000	6 000	5	4 500	6 000	1	31 000
					6 000	2	
					1 500	3	
					6 000	4	
	—	—					
	67 000	100 000					197 000
Total equity and liabilities	967 000	540 000					1 097 000
Cash	15 000	5 000					20 000
Land	120 000	150 000	1	20 000			290 000
Equipment	620 000	480 000			150 000	2	950 000
Accumulated depreciation	(380 000)	(170 000)	2	170 000			(380 000)
Shares in Sub Ltd	500 000	—			500 000	7	—
Inventory	92 000	75 000	3	5 000			172 000
Patent	—	—	4	20 000			20 000
Goodwill	—	—	6	25 000			25 000
Total assets	967 000	540 000		755 000	755 000		1 097 000

FIGURE 24.8 Consolidation worksheet at acquisition date

24.4.4 Subsidiary has recorded goodwill at acquisition date

In the example used in section 24.4.3, at acquisition date the subsidiary did not have any recorded goodwill. Consider the situation where the assets recorded by the subsidiary at acquisition date are the same as in figure 24.3 except that now there is recorded goodwill, as follows:

	Sub Ltd	
	Carrying amount	Fair value
Cash	$ 5 000	$ 5 000
Land	150 000	170 000
Equipment	480 000	330 000
Accumulated depreciation	(170 000)	
Goodwill	**10 000**	
Inventory	75 000	80 000
	$ 550 000	

Assume that the retained earnings balance is now $150 000 rather than $140 000. The acquisition analysis, assuming no previously held equity interests by the parent, is then as follows:

Net fair value of identifiable assets and liabilities of Sub Ltd	= $300 000 + $150 000 (equity)
	+ ($170 000 − $150 000)(1 − 30%) (BCVR — land)
	+ ($330 000 − $310 000)(1 − 30%) (BCVR — equipment)
	+ ($80 000 − $75 000)(1 − 30%) (BCVR — inventory)
	+ $20 000(1 − 30%) (BCVR — patent)
	− $15 000(1 − 30%) (BCVR — guarantee)
	− $10 000 (goodwill)
	= $475 000
Consideration transferred	= 100 000 × $5
	= $500 000
Goodwill	= $500 000 − $475 000
	= $25 000
Recorded goodwill	**= $10 000**
Unrecorded goodwill	**= $15 000**

Note that, since the first calculation of the acquisition analysis relates to the fair value of the *identifiable* assets, the goodwill of the subsidiary (i.e. the unidentifiable assets) must be subtracted. Further, it is necessary to calculate the additional goodwill not recorded by the subsidiary, this being the amount recognised on consolidation. The amount of goodwill recognised in the business combination valuation entry is $15 000:

(6) Goodwill	Dr	15 000	
Business Combination Valuation Reserve	Cr		15 000

The pre-acquisition entry is:

(7) Retained Earnings (1/7/13)	Dr	150 000	
Share Capital	Dr	300 000	
Business Combination Valuation Reserve	Dr	50 000	
Shares in Sub Ltd	Cr		500 000

The line item for goodwill in the consolidation worksheet would show:

Financial statements	Parent Ltd	Sub Ltd	Adjustments			Consolidation
				Dr	Cr	
Goodwill	—	10 000	6	15 000		25 000

The consolidated statement of financial position thus shows the total acquired goodwill of the subsidiary.

24.4.5 Subsidiary has recorded dividends at acquisition date

Using the information in figure 24.3, assume that one of the payables at acquisition date is a dividend payable of $10 000. The parent can acquire the shares in the subsidiary on a *cum div.* or an *ex div.* basis.

If the shares are acquired on a *cum div. basis*, then the parent acquires the right to the dividend declared at acquisition date. In this case, if Parent Ltd pays $500 000 for the shares in Sub Ltd, then the entry it passes to record the business combination is:

Shares in Sub Ltd	Dr	490 000	
Dividend Receivable	Dr	10 000	
Share Capital	Cr		500 000

In other words, the parent acquires two assets — the investment in the subsidiary and the dividend receivable. In calculating the goodwill in the subsidiary, using the information in figure 24.3 the acquisition analysis is:

Net fair value of identifiable assets and liabilities of Sub Ltd	= $300 000 + $140 000 (equity)
	+ ($170 000 − $150 000)(1 − 30%) (BCVR — land)
	+ ($330 000 − $310 000)(1 − 30%) (BCVR — equipment)
	+ ($80 000 − $75 000)(1 − 30%) (BCVR — inventory)
	+ $20 000(1 − 30%) (BCVR — patent)
	− $15 000(1 − 30%) (BCVR — guarantee)
	= $475 000
Consideration transferred	**= (100 000 × $5) − $10 000 (dividend receivable)**
	= $490 000
Goodwill	= $490 000 − $475 000
	= $15 000

In other words, the fair value of the consideration paid must be that for the investment in the subsidiary, excluding the amount paid for the dividend receivable. The pre-acquisition entry is:

(7) Retained Earnings (1/7/13)	Dr	140 000	
Share Capital	Dr	300 000	
Business Combination Valuation Reserve	Dr	50 000	
Shares in Sub Ltd	Cr		490 000

A further consolidation worksheet entry is also required:

Dividend Payable	Dr	10 000	
Dividend Receivable	Cr		10 000

This entry is necessary so that the consolidated statement of financial position shows only the assets and liabilities of the group; that is, only those benefits receivable from and obligations payable to entities external to the group. In relation to the dividend receivable recorded by Parent Ltd, this is not an asset of the group, because that entity does not expect to receive dividends from a party external to it. Similarly, the dividend payable recorded by the subsidiary is not a liability of the group. That dividend will be paid within the group, not to entities outside the group.

If the shares are acquired on an *ex div. basis*, then the parent only acquires the shares. The dividend has no effect on the acquisition analysis. If Parent Ltd had paid $500 000 for the shares in Sub Ltd on an ex div. basis, then the acquisition analysis is:

Net fair value of identifiable assets and liabilities of Sub Ltd	= $475 000 (see the cum div. basis)
Consideration transferred	**= 100 000 shares × $5**
	= $500 000

Goodwill		= $500 000 − $475 000	
		= $25 000	

The pre-acquisition entry is:

Retained Earnings (1/7/13)	Dr	140 000	
Share Capital	Dr	300 000	
Business Combination Valuation Reserve	Dr	60 000	
Shares in Sub Ltd	Cr		500 000

24.4.6 Gain on bargain purchase

In figure 24.3, Parent Ltd paid $500 000 for the shares in Sub Ltd. Consider the situation where Parent Ltd paid $470 000 for these shares. The acquisition analysis is as shown in figure 24.9.

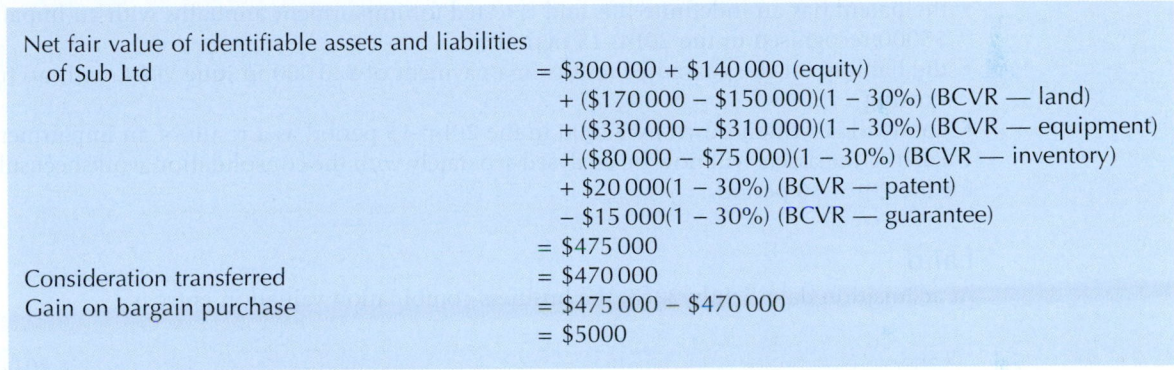

Net fair value of identifiable assets and liabilities
  of Sub Ltd
= $300 000 + $140 000 (equity)
+ ($170 000 − $150 000)(1 − 30%) (BCVR — land)
+ ($330 000 − $310 000)(1 − 30%) (BCVR — equipment)
+ ($80 000 − $75 000)(1 − 30%) (BCVR — inventory)
+ $20 000(1 − 30%) (BCVR — patent)
− $15 000(1 − 30%) (BCVR — guarantee)
= $475 000
Consideration transferred = $470 000
Gain on bargain purchase = $475 000 − $470 000
= $5000

FIGURE 24.9 Gain on bargain purchase

As the net fair value of the identifiable assets and liabilities of the subsidiary is greater than the consideration transferred, in accordance with paragraph 36 of IFRS 3 the acquirer must firstly reassess the identification and measurement of the subsidiary's identifiable assets and liabilities as well as the measurement of the consideration transferred. The expectation under IFRS 3 is that the excess of the net fair value over the consideration transferred is usually the result of measurement errors rather than being a real gain to the acquirer. However, having confirmed the identification and measurement of both amounts paid and net assets acquired, if an excess still exists, under paragraph 34 it is recognised immediately in profit as a gain on bargain purchase.

Existence of a gain on bargain purchase has no effect on the business combination valuation entries unless, as discussed in section 24.4.4, the subsidiary has previously recorded goodwill. In that case, a business combination revaluation entry crediting goodwill and debiting business combination valuation reserve for the amount of goodwill recorded by the subsidiary would be required.

The pre-acquisition entry for the situation in figure 24.9 is as shown in figure 24.10.

Pre-acquisition entry			
(7) Retained Earnings (1/7/13)	Dr	140 000	
Share Capital	Dr	300 000	
Business Combination Valuation Reserve	Dr	35 000	
Gain on Bargain Purchase	Cr		5 000
Shares in Sub Ltd	Cr		470 000

FIGURE 24.10 Pre-acquisition entry at acquisition date — gain on bargain purchase

LO5 **24.5 WORKSHEET ENTRIES SUBSEQUENT TO THE ACQUISITION DATE**

At acquisition date, the business combination valuation entries result in the economic entity recognising assets and liabilities not recorded by the subsidiaries. Subsequently, changes in these assets and liabilities occur as assets are depreciated or sold, liabilities paid and goodwill impaired. Movements in pre-acquisition equity also occur as dividends are paid or declared and transfers are made within equity.

24.5.1 Business combination valuation entries

In the example used in figure 24.3, there were five items for which valuation entries were made — land, equipment, inventory, patent and the guarantee. In this section, a 3-year time period subsequent to the acquisition date, 1 July 2013, is analysed (giving an end of reporting period of 30 June 2016) with the following events occurring:

- the land is sold in the 2015–16 period
- the equipment is depreciated on a straight-line basis over a 5-year period
- the inventory on hand at 1 July 2013 is all sold by 30 June 2014, the end of the first year
- the patent has an indefinite life, and is tested for impairment annually, with an impairment loss of $5000 recognised in the 2014–15 period
- the liability for the guarantee results in a payment of $10 000 in June 2014, with no further liability existing
- goodwill is written down by $5000 in the 2014–15 period as a result of an impairment test.

Each of the assets will now be analysed separately with the consolidation worksheet subsequently shown for the 2015–16 period.

Land

At acquisition date, 1 July 2013, the business combination valuation entry is:

Land	Dr	20 000	
Deferred Tax Liability	Cr		6 000
Business Combination Valuation Reserve	Cr		14 000

At *30 June 2014*, because the land is still on hand, the same valuation entry is made in the consolidation worksheet used to prepare the consolidated financial statements at that date. It is assumed in this period that the asset is not held for sale and is recorded at cost.

Assume in the *2014–15 financial period* that the land is classified as held for sale and is accounted for under IFRS 5 *Non-current Assets Held for Sale and Discontinued Operations*. The land is then recorded at the lower of its carrying amount and fair value less costs of disposal. Assuming the carrying amount is the lower value, then the business combination valuation entry in the consolidation worksheet prepared at 30 June 2015 is the same as that for 30 June 2014.

Assume in the *2015–16 financial period* that the land is sold for $200 000, with $1000 costs to sell incurred. Sub Ltd will record a gain on sale of $49 000 (i.e. $200 000 – $150 000 – $1000). From the group's perspective, the gain on sale is only $29 000 (i.e. $200 000 – $170 000 – $1000). Hence, on consolidation, an adjustment to reduce the recorded gain by $20 000 is required. The factor causing the difference in gain on sale is the carrying amount of the land sold. The cost of the land is greater to the group than to the subsidiary. As the asset has been sold, the deferred tax liability is reversed, with an adjustment being made to income tax expense. Assuming the subsidiary records both proceeds on sale and carrying amount of land sold, the valuation entry at 30 June 2015 is:

Carrying Amount of Land Sold	Dr	20 000	
Income Tax Expense	Cr		6 000
Business Combination Valuation Reserve	Cr		14 000

846 PART 4 Economic entities

Alternatively, if the subsidiary's financial statements show a gain on sale:

Gain on Sale of Land	Dr	20 000	
Income Tax Expense	Cr		6 000
Business Combination Valuation Reserve	Cr		14 000

In subsequent periods, the valuation entry is:

Retained Earnings (opening balance)	Dr	14 000	
Business Combination Valuation Reserve	Cr		14 000

This entry has no effect on total equity. It reflects the fact that whereas the subsidiary recognised the increase in worth of the land in retained earnings, the group recognised the increased value in the business combination valuation reserve. Where revalued assets are derecognised, as noted in paragraph 41 of IAS 16 *Property, Plant and Equipment*, it is usual business practice to transfer the revaluation surplus to retained earnings. If this principle is applied on consolidation, then the business combination valuation entries in the year of sale of the land are:

Carrying Amount of Land Sold/Gain on Sale	Dr	20 000	
Income Tax Expense	Cr		6 000
Business Combination Valuation Reserve	Cr		14 000
Business Combination Valuation Reserve	Dr	14 000	
Transfer from Business Combination Valuation Reserve	Cr		14 000

These two entries can be simplified into one entry:

Carrying Amount of Land Sold/Gain on Sale	Dr	20 000	
Income Tax Expense	Cr		6 000
Transfer from Business Combination Valuation Reserve	Cr		14 000

Because this entry has no effect on retained earnings, no consolidation worksheet entries are required in subsequent periods. In this book, where assets are fully consumed or sold and liabilities settled, the business combination valuation entry will be transferred to retained earnings.

Equipment

The business combination valuation entry at 1 July 2013 is:

Accumulated Depreciation – Equipment	Dr	170 000	
Equipment	Cr		150 000
Deferred Tax Liability	Cr		6 000
Business Combination Valuation Reserve	Cr		14 000

The asset is depreciated on a straight-line basis evenly over a 5-year period at 20% p.a. Because the asset is recognised on consolidation at an amount that is $20 000 greater than that recognised in the records of the subsidiary, the depreciation expense to the group must also be greater. The difference in depreciation reflects the extra amount paid for the equipment by the group. The adjustment for depreciation results in changes to the carrying amount of the asset. Differences between the tax base and the carrying amount are reflected in the deferred tax liability. As the asset is recovered by use, the deferred tax liability recognised at acquisition date is progressively reversed, with the movement being in proportion to depreciation charges — in this case 20% p.a. The adjustments for depreciation and the related tax effects are recognised in the consolidation worksheet valuation entries in the periods subsequent to acquisition date.

The business combination valuation entries for equipment at 30 June 2014 are:

Accumulated Depreciation – Equipment	Dr	170 000	
Equipment	Cr		150 000
Deferred Tax Liability	Cr		6 000
Business Combination Valuation Reserve	Cr		14 000
Depreciation Expense	Dr	4 000	
Accumulated Depreciation	Cr		4 000
(20% × $20 000 p.a.)			
Deferred Tax Liability	Dr	1 200	
Income Tax Expense	Cr		1 200
(20% × $6000, or 30% × $4000 p.a.)			

Note that the first entry is the same as that made at acquisition date, with the other two entries reflecting subsequent depreciation and tax-effect changes.

The valuation entries at 30 June 2016 reflect the need to adjust for 3 years' depreciation (i.e. for two previous periods and a current period):

Accumulated Depreciation – Equipment	Dr	170 000	
Equipment	Cr		150 000
Deferred Tax Liability	Cr		6 000
Business Combination Valuation Reserve	Cr		14 000
Depreciation Expense	Dr	4 000	
Retained Earnings (1/7/15)	Dr	8 000	
Accumulated Depreciation	Cr		12 000
(20% × $20 000 p.a.)			
Deferred Tax Liability	Dr	3 600	
Income Tax Expense	Cr		1 200
Retained Earnings (1/7/15)	Cr		2 400
(20% × $6000, or 30% × $4000 p.a.)			

The equipment is fully depreciated by 30 June 2018. In the subsidiary's financial statements (on the left-hand side of the worksheet) neither the equipment nor the related accumulated depreciation is shown as the asset is derecognised by the subsidiary. The consolidation worksheet adjustment must then relate to:
- current period depreciation: $4000
- the tax effect of the current period depreciation: 30% × $4000 = $1200
- prior period depreciation: 4 years at $4000 per annum = $16 000. This must be tax-effected so that the adjustment for prior period depreciation is $11 200.
- the business combination valuation entry is then transferred to retained earnings as the asset is fully consumed.

The relevant entry is:

Depreciation Expense	Dr	4 000	
Income Tax Expense	Cr		1 200
Retained Earnings (1/7/17)	Dr	11 200	
Transfer from Business Combination Valuation Reserve	Cr		14 000

No worksheet adjustment entry is then required in future periods.

The entries may also be expressed as follows:

Accumulated Depreciation – Equipment	Dr	170 000	
Equipment	Cr		150 000
Deferred Tax Liability	Cr		6 000
Business Combination Valuation Reserve	Cr		14 000
Depreciation Expense	Dr	4 000	
Retained Earnings (1/7/17)	Dr	16 000	
Accumulated Depreciation	Cr		20 000
(20% × $20 000 p.a.)			
Deferred Tax Liability	Dr	6 000	
Income Tax Expense	Cr		1 200
Retained Earnings (1/7/17)	Cr		4 800
(20% × $6000, or 30% × $4000 p.a.)			

Since the equipment is fully consumed and then derecognised, two further entries are required:

Equipment	Dr	150 000	
Accumulated Depreciation – Equipment	Cr		150 000
Business Combination Valuation Reserve	Dr	14 000	
Transfer from Business Combination Valuation Reserve	Cr		14 000

It is recommended that the more complicated set of entries be avoided as the single entry adjustment concentrates on adjusting those accounts on the left-hand side of the worksheets that need to be adjusted in order to show the group picture on the right-hand side of the worksheet.

If the equipment had been sold on 1 January 2018, then the worksheet adjustment entry at 30 June 2018 would be similar to that where the asset is fully depreciated. The only difference is that there needs to be an adjustment to the carrying amount of the equipment sold to reflect the undepreciated portion of the asset. The consolidation worksheet adjustment must then relate to:

- current period depreciation (half a year's depreciation): $\frac{1}{2} \times \$4000 = \$2000$
- the undepreciated portion of the asset at point of sale affecting the carrying amount of the asset sold: $\frac{1}{2} \times \$4000 = \$2000$
- the tax effect of both the current period's depreciation and the undepreciated portion of the asset: 30% × $4000 = $1200
- prior period depreciation: 4 years at $4000 per annum = $16 000. This must be tax-effected so that the adjustment for prior period depreciation is $11 200.
- the business combination valuation entry is then transferred to retained earnings as the asset is fully consumed.

The relevant entry is:

Depreciation Expense	Dr	2 000	
Carrying Amount of Equipment Sold/Gain on Sale	Dr	2 000	
Income Tax Expense	Cr		1 200
Retained Earnings (1/7/17)	Dr	11 200	
Transfer from Business Combination Valuation Reserve	Cr		14 000

No worksheet adjustment entry is then required in future periods.

Inventory

The valuation entry for inventory at acquisition date, 1 July 2013, is:

Inventory	Dr	5 000	
Deferred Tax Liability	Cr		1 500
Business Combination Valuation Reserve	Cr		3 500

The key event affecting the subsequent accounting for inventory is the sale of the inventory by the subsidiary. Assume the inventory is sold in the 2013–14 period for $90 000. The subsidiary records cost of sales at the carrying amount of $75 000, whereas the cost to the group is $80 000. In the consolidation worksheet, instead of the $5000 adjustment to inventory, a $5000 adjustment to cost of sales is required. As the inventory is sold, the deferred tax liability is reversed. As with land and equipment, the business combination valuation reserve is transferred to retained earnings because the asset is derecognised.

The valuation entry at 30 June 2014 is then:

Cost of Sales	Dr	5 000	
Income Tax Expense	Cr		1 500
Transfer from Business Combination Valuation Reserve	Cr		3 500

Because this entry has a zero effect on closing retained earnings, no consolidation worksheet entry is required in subsequent years.

In relation to the sale of inventory, a comparison of what is recorded by Sub Ltd and what is shown in the consolidated financial statements at 30 June 2014 is as follows:

	Sub Ltd	Consolidation	
Sales	$ 90 000	$ 90 000	
Cost of sales	(75 000)	(80 000)	(75 000 + 5 000)
Profit before income tax	15 000	10 000	
Income tax expense	(4 500)	(3 000)	(4 500 − 1 500)
Profit	$ 10 500	$ 7 000	

If at 30 June 2014 only 80% of the inventory had been sold, then the valuation entry must reflect adjustments both to cost of sales and ending inventory. The consolidation worksheet valuation entries, reflecting the 80% sold and the 20% still on hand, are:

Cost of Sales	Dr	4 000	
Income Tax Expense	Cr		1 200
Transfer from Business Combination Valuation Reserve	Cr		2 800

[This entry has no effect on the consolidation worksheets of subsequent periods.]

Inventory	Dr	1 000	
Deferred Tax Liability	Cr		300
Business Combination Valuation Reserve	Cr		700

Assuming the inventory is all sold by 30 June 2015, the valuation entry in the consolidation worksheet prepared at that date is:

Cost of Sales	Dr	1 000	
Income Tax Expense	Cr		300
Transfer from Business Combination Valuation Reserve	Cr		700

Patent

The business combination valuation entry at acquisition date, 1 July 2013, is:

Patent	Dr	20 000	
Deferred Tax Liability	Cr		6 000
Business Combination Valuation Reserve	Cr		14 000

This entry is used in each year that the patent continues to have an indefinite life. A change occurs only if there is an impairment loss. In this example, an impairment loss of $5000 occurs in the 2014–15 period. The business combination valuation entries at 30 June 2015 are:

Patent	Dr	20 000	
Deferred Tax Liability	Cr		6 000
Business Combination Valuation Reserve	Cr		14 000
Impairment Loss	Dr	5 000	
Accumulated Impairment Losses	Cr		5 000
Deferred Tax Liability	Dr	1 500	
Income Tax Expense	Cr		1 500

The entries at 30 June 2016 are:

Patent	Dr	20 000	
Deferred Tax Liability	Cr		6 000
Business Combination Valuation Reserve	Cr		14 000
Retained Earnings (1/7/15)	Dr	3 500	
Deferred Tax Liability	Dr	1 500	
Accumulated Impairment Losses	Cr		5 000

Liability — Provision for Loan Guarantee

The business combination valuation entry at 1 July 2013 is:

Business Combination Valuation Reserve	Dr	10 500	
Deferred Tax Asset	Dr	4 500	
Provision for Loan Guarantee	Cr		15 000

If the liability is paid or derecognised, the above entry changes. In this example, a payment of $10 000 is made during the first year in relation to the liability. The subsidiary records an expense of $10 000. Since there is no expense to the group, it must be eliminated on consolidation. Instead, a gain of $5000 is recognised by the group as the liability of $15 000 is settled for $10 000. The business combination valuation entry at 30 June 2014 is:

Transfer from Business Combination Valuation Reserve	Dr	10 500	
Income Tax Expense	Dr	4 500	
Expense	Cr		10 000
Gain on Derecognition of Loan Guarantee	Cr		5 000

No entry is required on 30 June 2016.

Goodwill

Impairment tests for goodwill are undertaken annually. Goodwill is written down by $5000 in the 2014–15 period as a result of an impairment test. In the consolidation worksheet prepared at 30 June 2015, the business combination valuation entry will recognise the $25 000 goodwill acquired. However, a further entry is required to recognise the impairment of the goodwill:

Impairment Expense	Dr	5 000	
Accumulated Impairment Losses	Cr		5 000

The entries at 30 June 2016 are:

Goodwill	Dr	25 000	
Business Combination Valuation Reserve	Cr		25 000
Retained Earnings (1/7/15)	Dr	5 000	
Accumulated Impairment Losses	Cr		5 000

Business combination valuation entries at 30 June 2016

The valuation entries for all assets at 30 June 2016 are as shown in figure 24.11.

(1)	Carrying Amount of Land Sold/Gain on Sale	Dr	20 000	
	Income Tax Expense	Cr		6 000
	Transfer from Business Combination Valuation Reserve	Cr		14 000
(2)	Accumulated Depreciation – Equipment	Dr	170 000	
	Equipment	Cr		150 000
	Deferred Tax Liability	Cr		6 000
	Business Combination Valuation Reserve	Cr		14 000
	Depreciation Expense	Dr	4 000	
	Retained Earnings (1/7/15)	Dr	8 000	
	Accumulated Depreciation	Cr		12 000
	(20% × $20 000 p.a.)			
	Deferred Tax Liability	Dr	3 600	
	Income Tax Expense	Cr		1 200
	Retained Earnings (1/7/15)	Cr		2 400
	(20% × $6000, or 30% × $4000 p.a.)			
(3)	Patent	Dr	20 000	
	Deferred Tax Liability	Cr		6 000
	Business Combination Valuation Reserve	Cr		14 000
	Retained Earnings (1/7/15)	Dr	3 500	
	Deferred Tax Liability	Dr	1 500	
	Accumulated Impairment Losses	Cr		5 000
(4)	Goodwill	Dr	25 000	
	Business Combination Valuation Reserve	Cr		25 000
	Retained Earnings (1/7/15)	Dr	5 000	
	Accumulated Impairment Losses	Cr		5 000

FIGURE 24.11 Business combination valuation entries at 30 June 2016

24.5.2 Pre-acquisition entries

The pre-acquisition entry at acquisition date, relating to the example in figure 24.3, is:

Retained Earnings (1/7/13)	Dr	140 000	
Share Capital	Dr	300 000	
Business Combination Valuation Reserve	Dr	60 000	
Shares in Sub Ltd	Cr		500 000

There are three events that can cause a change in this entry after acquisition date:
- transfers from business combination valuation reserve, as undertaken in the consolidation worksheet valuation entries
- bonus dividends paid from pre-acquisition equity
- transfers to and from pre-acquisition retained earnings and other reserves.

In any particular year, some of these events will have occurred in previous periods, and some will occur in the current period. The pre-acquisition entries for the current period consist of the combined pre-acquisition entry at the beginning of the current period; that is, the pre-acquisition entry at the acquisition date adjusted for the effects of all pre-acquisition equity changes up to the beginning of the current period, and entries relating to changes in pre-acquisition equity in the current period.

Changes in business combination valuation entries

For the items affected by business combination valuation adjustments, three changes since acquisition date have affected the pre-acquisition entry. Two of these occurred in the year ending 30 June 2014:
- the sale of inventory on hand at acquisition date
- the payment and write-off of the loan guarantee liability.

In both cases, the adjustment was made to Transfer from Business Combination Valuation Reserve in the business combination valuation entries at 30 June 2014.

This transfer affects the pre-acquisition entry because the valuation reserves are created in the valuation entries and, being part of pre-acquisition equity, are eliminated in the pre-acquisition entry — see, for example, the worksheet in figure 24.8. If the valuation entry gives rise to a *transfer from* the business combination valuation reserve, instead of a business combination valuation reserve, then the adjustment in the pre-acquisition entry must also be made to the transfer account. This is done by adding another entry to the pre-acquisition entry in the year of transfer (see below). The need to make an extra adjustment in the pre-acquisition entry should be obvious from viewing the valuation entries. It is only if there is, or has been in previous periods, a transfer in the valuation entries that this flows through to the pre-acquisition entry.

The pre-acquisition entries at *30 June 2014* affected by the sale of inventory and the payment of the loan guarantee liability are then:

Retained Earnings (1/7/13)	Dr	140 000	
Share Capital	Dr	300 000	
Business Combination Valuation Reserve	Dr	60 000	
Shares in Sub Ltd	Cr		500 000
Business Combination Valuation Reserve	Dr	7 000	
Transfer from Business Combination Valuation Reserve	Cr		7 000
($3500 inventory and $(10 500) loan guarantee liability)			

In the consolidation worksheet at *30 June 2015*, assuming no other transfers or events, the pre-acquisition entry is the combination of the two entries from the previous period's worksheet:

Retained Earnings (1/7/14)*	Dr	133 000	
Share Capital	Dr	300 000	
Business Combination Valuation Reserve**	Dr	67 000	
Shares in Sub Ltd	Cr		500 000

  * $140 000 + $3500 (inventory) − $10 500 (loan guarantee)
** $60 000 − $3500 (inventory) + $10 500 (loan guarantee)

In the 2015–16 period — the current period — pre-acquisition balances are affected by the sale of the land. As can be seen from the valuation entry for land in section 24.5.1, in the current period there is a transfer from the business combination valuation reserve to retained earnings of $14 000. This requires the following entry to be included in the pre-acquisition entries for the current period:

Transfer from Business Combination Valuation Reserve	Dr	14 000
Business Combination Valuation Reserve	Cr	14 000

In summary, the pre-acquisition entries to be passed in the consolidation worksheet at 30 June 2016 are as shown in figure 24.12. These are affected by the sale of inventory and payment of the loan guarantee in 2013–14, the impairment of goodwill in 2014–15 and the sale of land in 2015–16.

(5) Retained Earnings (1/7/15)*	Dr	133 000	
Share Capital	Dr	300 000	
Business Combination Valuation Reserve**	Dr	67 000	
Shares in Sub Ltd	Cr		500 000

* $140 000 + $3500 (inventory) − $10 500 (loan guarantee)
** $60 000 − $3500 (inventory) + $10 500 (loan guarantee)

Transfer from Business Combination Valuation Reserve	Dr	14 000	
Business Combination Valuation Reserve	Cr		14 000

FIGURE 24.12 Pre-acquisition entries at 30 June 2013

Figure 24.13 shows the consolidation worksheet at 30 June 2016 containing the adjustment entries from figures 24.11 and 24.12.

FIGURE 24.13 Consolidation worksheet at 30 June 2016

Financial statements	Parent Ltd	Sub Ltd	Adjustments Dr		Adjustments Cr		Consolidation
Revenues	120 000	95 000					215 000
Expenses	85 000	72 000	2	4 000			161 000
	35 000	23 000					54 000
Gain on sale of non-current assets	15 000	31 000	1	20 000			26 000
Profit before tax	50 000	54 000					80 000
Income tax expense	15 000	21 000			6 000	1	
					1 200	2	28 800
Profit for the period	35 000	33 000					51 200
Retained earnings (1/7/15)	420 000	220 000	2	8 000	2 400	2	
			3	5 000			
			4	5 000			
			5	133 000			491 400
Transfer from business combination valuation reserve	—	—	5	14 000	14 000	1	—
Retained earnings (30/6/16)	455 000	253 000					542 600
Share capital	550 000	300 000	5	300 000			550 000

FIGURE 24.13 *(continued)*

Financial statements	Parent Ltd	Sub Ltd	Dr	Cr		Consolidation
Adjustments						
Business combination valuation reserve	—		5 67 000	14 000	2	
				14 000	3	
				25 000	4	
				14 000	5	—
	1 005 000	553 000				1 092 600
Provisions	40 000	40 000				80 000
Payables	32 000	24 000				56 000
Tax liabilities	12 000	16 000	2 3 600	6 000	2	
				6 000	3	36 400
	84 000	80 000				172 400
Total equity and liabilities	1 089 000	633 000				1 265 000
Cash	65 000	95 000				160 000
Land	170 000	50 000				220 000
Equipment	750 000	683 000		150 000	2	1 283 000
Accumulated depreciation	(448 000)	(270 000)	2 170 000	12 000	2	(560 000)
Shares in Sub Ltd	500 000	—		500 000	5	—
Inventory	52 000	75 000				127 000
Patent	—	—	3 20 000			20 000
Accumulated impairment losses	—	—		5 000	3	(5 000)
Goodwill	—	—	4 25 000			25 000
Accumulated impairment losses	—	—		5 000	4	(5 000)
Total assets	1 089 000	633 000	774 600	774 600		1 265 000

24.5.3 Dividends paid/payable from subsidiary equity

Prior to July 2008, IAS 27 *Consolidated and Separate Financial Statements* described a cost method in relation to accounting for a parent's investment in a subsidiary. The equity of the subsidiary was then classified into pre-acquisition and post-acquisition components based upon whether the equity existed before or after the acquisition date. Dividends from pre-acquisition equity were accounted for as a recovery of a parent's investment in a subsidiary and recognised as a reduction in the cost of the investment. Dividends from post-acquisition equity were accounted for by a parent as revenue.

In 2008, the IASB made amendments to IAS 27. These amendments deleted the definition of the cost method from IAS 27 and required that all dividends paid or payable by a subsidiary were to be accounted for as revenue by the parent.

In 2011, the IASB issued a new IAS 27 *Separate Financial Statements*. Paragraph 12 of this standard states:

> An entity shall recognise a dividend from a subsidiary, a joint venture or an associate in profit or loss in its separate financial statements when its right to receive the dividend is established.

Under IAS 27, all dividends paid or payable by the subsidiary to a parent are recognised as revenue in the profit or loss of the parent. In relation to dividends, there is no need to classify the equity of the subsidiary into pre-acquisition and post-acquisition equity. Effectively, all dividends are accounted for as if they are paid from post-acquisition equity.

Paragraphs BC14 to BC20 of IAS 27, as issued in 2011, discuss the reasons for the accounting for dividends received from a subsidiary, a joint venture or an associate. BC14 notes that one of the driving forces for the current accounting for dividends was the problem of classifying equity into pre- and post-acquisition components on first-time adoption of IFRSs by entities. To reduce any risk from removing the cost method and any possible overstatement of income by a parent, the IASB looked at the impairment testing of the investment account recorded by the parent. As a result, as part of the internal sources of information used to determine whether there is any indication of impairment of an asset, paragraph 12(h) of IAS 36 *Impairment of Assets* states:

for an investment in a subsidiary, joint venture or associate, the investor recognises a dividend from the investment and evidence is available that:
  (i) the carrying amount of the investment in the separate financial statements exceeds the carrying amounts in the consolidated financial statements of the investee's net assets, including associated goodwill; or
  (ii) the dividend exceeds the total comprehensive income of the subsidiary, joint venture or associate in the period the dividend is declared.

Bonus share dividends

Bonus share dividends involve a subsidiary issuing shares instead of cash. There are no entries in the records of the parent as a result of this transaction. Hence, the IASB's amendments to IAS 27 do not apply to this transaction. The effect to be adjusted for in the pre-acquisition entry is that this transaction results in moving pre-acquisition equity from one account to another, with no change in total pre-acquisition equity.

Assume that in the 2013–14 period the subsidiary pays a dividend of $3000 by the issue of bonus shares. The entries passed in the parent and the subsidiary as a result of the dividend are:

Parent	Subsidiary			
No entry required	Bonus Dividend Paid	Dr	3 000	
	Share Capital	Cr		3 000

No entry is required by the parent because its share of wealth in the subsidiary is unchanged by the bonus share issue. The pre-acquisition entries for the 2013–14 period are shown in figure 24.14.

Retained Earnings (1/7/13)	Dr	140 000	
Share Capital	Dr	300 000	
Business Combination Valuation Reserve	Dr	60 000	
Shares in Subsidiary	Cr		500 000
Share Capital	Dr	3 000	
Bonus Dividend Paid	Cr		3 000

FIGURE 24.14 Dividend provided for in the current period

The effect of the bonus dividend is to increase the share capital of the subsidiary by $3000 and to reduce the retained earnings by the same amount. There is no overall change in the pre-acquisition equity of the subsidiary, just a transfer from one equity account to another. Accordingly, there is no change in the balance of the investment account in the records of the parent.

The pre-acquisition entry in subsequent periods is:

Retained Earnings (opening balance) [$140 000 – $3000]	Dr	137 000	
Share Capital	Dr	303 000	
Business Combination Valuation Reserve	Dr	60 000	
Shares in Subsidiary	Cr		500 000

24.5.4 Pre-acquisition reserve transfers

From time to time the subsidiary may transfer retained earnings to reserves, or make transfers from reserves to retained earnings. These do not cause any change in the total pre-acquisition equity but simply change the composition of that equity. Therefore, there is no change in the investment account recorded by the parent entity. In fact, the parent is unaffected by these transfers.

Assume for the cases illustrated below that the pre-acquisition entry for the year ending 30 June 2014, apart from the effect of reserve transfers, is as follows:

Retained Earnings (1/7/13)	Dr	140 000	
Share Capital	Dr	300 000	
Business Combination Valuation Reserve	Dr	60 000	
Shares in Subsidiary	Cr		500 000

Case 1: Transfers from retained earnings to other reserves

Assume that in the 2013–14 period the subsidiary transfers $4000 to general reserve from retained earnings. The entry passed in the subsidiary as a result of the transfer is:

Transfer to General Reserve	Dr	4 000	
General Reserve	Cr		4 000

The pre-acquisition entries for the 2013–14 period are shown in figure 24.15.

Retained Earnings (1/7/13)	Dr	140 000	
Share Capital	Dr	300 000	
Business Combination Valuation Reserve	Dr	60 000	
Shares in Subsidiary	Cr		500 000
General Reserve	Dr	4 000	
Transfer to General Reserve	Cr		4 000

FIGURE 24.15 Transfer to general reserve in the current period

As both the transfer to general reserve and the general reserve accounts are pre-acquisition in nature, they are eliminated as part of the pre-acquisition entry. The pre-acquisition entry in subsequent periods is:

Retained Earnings (opening balance)*	Dr	136 000	
Share Capital	Dr	300 000	
Business Combination Valuation Reserve	Dr	60 000	
General Reserve	Dr	4 000	
Shares in Subsidiary	Cr		500 000

*$140 000 – $4000

In this case and in the following cases, the only equity account in which movements (transfers to and from) are specifically identified is retained earnings. Movements within the general reserve account are not specifically noted. This is because, as illustrated in figure 24.13, the retained earnings account and changes therein are used to connect the statement of profit or loss and other comprehensive income accounts and the statement of financial position accounts. In preparing the consolidated statement of changes in equity, where movements in all equity accounts are disclosed, adjustments for pre-acquisition transfers must be taken into account. Whether such adjustments are necessary can be seen from viewing the consolidation worksheet and the adjustments made to individual equity accounts. A similar issue arises in preparing other notes to the consolidated financial statements, such as for property, plant and equipment, where movements such as additions and disposals must be disclosed.

Case 2: Transfers to retained earnings from other reserves

This case uses the information in case 1, in which a $4000 general reserve was created. Assume that in the 2014–15 period the subsidiary transfers $1000 to retained earnings from general reserve. The entry passed in the subsidiary as a result of the transfer is:

General Reserve	Dr	1 000	
Transfer from General Reserve	Cr		1 000

The pre-acquisition entries for the 2014–15 period are shown in figure 24.16.

Retained Earnings (1/7/14)	Dr	136 000	
Share Capital	Dr	300 000	
Business Combination Valuation Reserve	Dr	60 000	
General Reserve	Dr	4 000	
Shares in Subsidiary	Cr		500 000
Transfer from General Reserve	Dr	1 000	
General Reserve	Cr		1 000

FIGURE 24.16 Transfer from general reserve in the current period

Since both the transfer from general reserve and general reserve accounts are pre-acquisition in nature, they are eliminated as part of the pre-acquisition entry. The pre-acquisition entry in subsequent periods is:

Retained Earnings (Opening balance)*	Dr	137 000	
Share Capital	Dr	300 000	
Business Combination Valuation Reserve	Dr	60 000	
General Reserve	Dr	3 000	
Shares in Subsidiary	Cr		500 000
*$140 000 − $4000 + $1000			

24.6 REVALUATIONS IN THE RECORDS OF THE SUBSIDIARY AT ACQUISITION DATE

IFRS 3 does not discuss whether the valuation of the assets of the subsidiary at acquisition date should be done in the consolidation worksheet or in the records of the subsidiary. It is expected that most entities will make their adjustments in the consolidation worksheet, for two reasons:

- Adjustments for assets such as goodwill and inventory are not allowed in the actual records of the subsidiary. Goodwill is not allowed to be revalued because it would amount to the recognition of internally generated goodwill, and inventory cannot be written to an amount greater than cost.
- The revaluation of non-current assets in the records of the subsidiary means that the subsidiary has effectively adopted the revaluation model of accounting for those assets. As discussed in chapter 11, IAS 16 *Property, Plant and Equipment* requires the assets to be recorded at amounts not materially different from fair value. For entities wanting to measure assets using the cost model, the revaluation of subsidiary assets would be undertaken in the consolidation worksheet.

Note that the business combination valuation entries applied in the consolidation worksheet for property, plant and equipment assets in this chapter are of the same form as those applied for property, plant and equipment in chapter 11. Hence, the consolidated financial statements at acquisition date are the same regardless of whether revaluation occurs on consolidation or in the records of the subsidiary. In future periods, differences will arise because there is no requirement for valuations done in the consolidation worksheet to be updated for subsequent changes in the fair values of the assets.

24.7 DISCLOSURE

Paragraphs B64–B67 of Appendix B to IFRS 3 cover the disclosure of information about business combinations. These paragraphs require an acquirer to disclose information that enables users of its financial statements to evaluate the nature and financial effect of business combinations that occurred during the reporting period, as well as those that occur between the end of the reporting period and when the financial statements are authorised for issue. Examples of disclosures required by these paragraphs are given in figure 24.17.

FIGURE 24.17 Disclosure of business combinations

Note 4. Business combinations	IFRS 3 paragraph

On 20 October 2013, Libra Ltd acquired 100% of the voting shares of Pisces Ltd, a listed company specialising in the manufacture of electronic parts for sound equipment. The primary reason for the acquisition was to gain access to specialist knowledge relating to electronic systems. Control was obtained by acquisition of all the shares of Pisces Ltd.

B64(a), (b), (c)

B64(d)

To acquire this ownership interest, Libra Ltd issued 600 000 ordinary shares, valued at $2.50 per share, which rank equally for dividends after the acquisition date. The fair value is based on the published market price at acquisition date.

B64(f)(iv)

The total consideration transferred was $1 800 000 and consisted of:

B64(f)

	$'000
Shares issued, at fair value	1 500
Cash paid	240
Cash payable in 2 years' time	60
Total consideration transferred	1 800

The fair values and the carrying amounts of the assets acquired and liabilities assumed in Pisces Ltd as at 20 October 2013 were:

B64(f)

	Fair value $'000	Carrying amount $'000
Property, plant and equipment	1 240	1 020
Receivables	340	340
Inventory	160	130
Intangibles	302	22
Goodwill	54	0
	2 096	1 512
Payables	152	152
Provisions	103	103
Tax liabilities	41	41
	296	296
Fair value of net assets of Pisces Ltd	1 800	

Goodwill in Pisces Ltd can be attributed to the synergies existing within the company, and relate to the high level of training given to the staff as well as the professional expertise of the employees. Further, there exist in-process research activities in Pisces Ltd for which it was impossible to determine reliable fair values for the separate recognition of intangible assets.

B64(e)

Pisces Ltd earned a profit for the period from 20 October 2013 to 30 June 2014 of $520 000. This has been included in the consolidated statement of profit or loss and other comprehensive income for the year ended 30 June 2014.

B64(q)(i)

None of the above information has been prepared on a provisional basis.

B67

The consolidated profit is shown in the consolidated statement of profit or loss and other comprehensive income at $5 652 000, which includes the $520 000 contributed by Pisces Ltd from 20 October 2013 to the end of the period. If Pisces Ltd had been acquired at 1 July 2013, it is estimated that the consolidated entity would have reported:

B64(q)(ii)

	$'000
Consolidated revenue	36 654
Consolidated profit	6 341

(continued)

FIGURE 24.17 *(continued)*

In relation to the business combination in the 2012–13 period when Libra Ltd acquired all the shares in Orion Ltd, an adjustment was made in the current period relating to the provisional measurement of specialised equipment held by Orion Ltd. A loss of $250 000 was recognised in the current reporting period because of the write-down of this equipment.	*B67(a)(iii)*
Included in the current period profit are gains on the sale of land acquired as a part of the business combination with Pisces Ltd. The gain amounted to $100 000 and arose due to an upsurge in demand for inner-city properties.	*B67(e)*

Goodwill

B67(d)

	$'000
Gross amount at 1 July 2013	120
Accumulated impairment losses	(15)
Carrying amount at 1 July 2013	105
Goodwill recognised in current period	54
Carrying amount at 30 June 2014	159
Gross amount at 30 June 2014	174
Accumulated impairment losses	(15)
Carrying amount at 30 June 2014	159

IFRS 12 *Disclosure of Interests in Other Entities* also requires disclosures in relation to a parent's interest in its subsidiaries. Figure 24.18 illustrates some of these disclosures.

Note 5. Subsidiaries	IFRS 12 paragraph
Aries Ltd has a 40% interest in Virgo Ltd. Although it has less than half the voting power, Aries Ltd believes it has control of the financial and operating policies of Virgo Ltd. Aries Ltd is able to exercise this control because the remaining ownership in Virgo Ltd is diverse and widely spread, with the next single largest ownership block being 11%.	*9(b)*
Aries Ltd has invested in a special purpose entity established by Pictor Ltd. Pictor Ltd established Cetus Ltd as a vehicle for distributing the sailing boats it makes. Aries Ltd currently owns 60% of the shares issued by Cetus Ltd. However, because of the limited decisions that the board of Cetus Ltd can make owing to the constitution of that entity, Aries Ltd believes that it does not have any real control over the operations of Cetus Ltd, so it sees its role in Cetus Ltd as that of an investor.	*9(a)*
Aries Ltd has a wholly owned subsidiary, Gemini Ltd, which operates within the electricity generating industry. The end of its reporting period is 31 May. Gemini Ltd continues to use this date because the government regulating authority requires all entities within the industry to provide financial information to it based on financial position at that date.	*11*
Aries Ltd has a wholly owned subsidiary, Hercules Ltd, in the country of Mambo. Because of constraints on assets leaving the country recently imposed by the new military government, there are major restrictions on the subsidiary being able to transfer funds to Aries Ltd.	*10(b)(i)*

FIGURE 24.18 Disclosures concerning subsidiaries

Disclosures in relation to subsidiaries are set out in IFRS 12 *Disclosure of Interests in Other Entities*, issued in 2011. These are discussed in chapter 23. Note, however, the following extract from paragraph 10.

An entity shall disclose information that enables users of its consolidated financial statements
(a) to understand:
 (i) the composition of the group; and
 (ii) the interest that non-controlling interests have in the group's activities and cash flows (paragraph 12); and
(b) to evaluate:
 (i) the nature and extent of significant restrictions on its ability to access or use assets, and settle liabilities, of the group (paragraph 13);
 (ii) the nature of, and changes in, the risks associated with its interests in consolidated structured entities (paragraphs 14–17)...

24.8 REVERSE ACQUISITIONS

According to IFRS 3, where a business combination is effected through an acquisition of equity interests, the acquirer is the entity that gains *control* of the acquiree, with control having the same meaning as in IFRS 10 *Consolidated Financial Statements*. A reverse acquisition occurs when the legal subsidiary has this form of control over the legal parent. The usual circumstance creating a reverse acquisition is where an entity (the legal parent) obtains ownership of the equity of another entity (the legal subsidiary) but, as part of the exchange transaction, it issues enough voting equity as consideration for control of the combined entity to pass to the owners of the legal subsidiary.

To illustrate, consider the following example, which is adapted from the Illustrative Examples to IFRS 3. Assume Entity A and Entity B agree to merge. The capital structure of each entity is:

> Entity A — 100 ordinary shares
> Entity B — 60 ordinary shares

Entity A issues 2½ shares in exchange for each ordinary share of Entity B. All of Entity B's shareholders exchange their shares for Entity A shares. Entity A therefore issues 150 shares (60 × 2½) for the 60 shares in Entity B. The position after the share exchange is that Entity A now owns 100% of Entity B.

Entity A is now the legal parent of the subsidiary Entity B. However, analysing the shareholding in Entity A shows that it consists of the 100 shares existing before the merger and 150 new shares held by the former shareholders in Entity B. In essence, the former shareholders of Entity B now control both Entities A and B. The former Entity B shareholders have a 60% interest in Entity A — that is, 150/(100 + 150). The IASB argues that there has been a reverse acquisition, and that Entity B is effectively the acquirer of Entity A.

The key accounting effect of the decision that Entity B is the acquirer is that the assets and liabilities of Entity A are to be valued at fair value. This is contrary to normal acquisition accounting, based on Entity A being the legal parent of Entity B, which would require the assets and liabilities of Entity B to be valued at fair value.

Illustrative example 24.1 demonstrates the accounting where a reverse acquisition occurs.

ILLUSTRATIVE EXAMPLE 24.1 Reverse acquisitions

This example is adapted from the illustrative example in IFRS 3, and uses the Entity A – Entity B scenario described earlier.

The statements of financial position of A Ltd and B Ltd at 30 June 2014 were as follows:

	A Ltd	B Ltd
Current assets	$ 500	$ 700
Non-current assets	1 300	3 000
Total assets	$1 800	$3 700
Share capital		
100 shares	$ 300	
60 shares		$ 600
Retained earnings	800	1 400
	1 100	2 000

(continued)

	A Ltd	B Ltd
Current liabilities	300	600
Non-current liabilities	400	1 100
	700	1 700
Total equity and liabilities	$1 800	$3 700

On 1 July 2014, A Ltd acquired all the issued shares of B Ltd, giving in exchange 2½ A Ltd shares for each ordinary share of B Ltd. A Ltd thus issued 150 shares to acquire the 60 shares issued by B Ltd.

The fair value of each ordinary share of B Ltd at 1 July 2014 is $40 and the quoted market price of A Ltd's ordinary shares is $16. The fair values of A Ltd's identifiable assets and liabilities at acquisition date are the same as their carrying amounts except for the non-current assets whose fair value was $1500. The tax rate is 30%.

In acquiring the shares in B Ltd, A Ltd issued 150 shares at $16 each. Therefore, A Ltd would have raised an investment in B Ltd of $2400. However, under reverse acquisition accounting, the consideration transferred is based on what B Ltd would have paid to acquire all the shares in A Ltd, and for the former B Ltd shareholders to have a 60% interest in the combined entities. Because B Ltd has, before the acquisition date, a share total of 60, B Ltd needs to issue 40 shares to the shareholders of A Ltd in exchange for their shares in order for the former B Ltd shareholders to have a 60% interest in B Ltd. If B Ltd issued these 40 shares, it would record a consideration transferred of $1600 (i.e. 40 × $40).

The acquisition analysis then relates the imputed consideration transferred of $1600 to the fair value of A Ltd:

> Fair value of A Ltd = $300 + $800 (equity)
> + $200(1 − 30%) (BCVR — non-current assets)
> = $1240
> Consideration transferred = $1600
> Goodwill = $360

The consolidation worksheet entries are as follows.

(1) *Change in consideration transferred*
The purpose of these entries is to eliminate the investment account actually raised by A Ltd and substitute for it the entry that B Ltd would have made if it had actually acquired the shares in A Ltd:

Share Capital – A Ltd	Dr	2 400	
Shares in B Ltd	Cr		2 400
Shares in A Ltd	Dr	1 600	
Share Capital – B Ltd	Cr		1 600

(2) *Business combination valuation entries*
These entries revalue the assets of A Ltd:

Non-current Assets	Dr	200	
Deferred Tax Liability	Cr		60
Business Combination Valuation Reserve	Cr		140
Goodwill	Dr	360	
Business Combination Valuation Reserve	Cr		360

(3) *Pre-acquisition entry*

This entry eliminates the newly created investment in A Ltd from entry (1) above against the equity of A Ltd that existed before the merger, but including any valuation reserve raised on consolidation:

Share Capital – A Ltd	Dr	300	
Retained Earnings	Dr	800	
Business Combination Valuation Reserve	Dr	500	
Shares in A Ltd	Cr		1 600

The consolidation worksheet at acquisition date is shown in figure 24.19. Note:

• the equity of A Ltd on hand at acquisition date is eliminated
• the capital that B Ltd would have issued if it had acquired the shares in A Ltd is carried forward into the statement of financial position
• it is A Ltd's assets that are revalued.

Financial statements	A Ltd	B Ltd		Adjustments Dr		Adjustments Cr		Consolidation
Retained earnings	800	1 400	3	800				1 400
Share capital	2 700	600	1	2 400	1 600		1	
			3	300				2 200
Business combination valuation reserve	—	—	3	500	140		2	—
					360		2	
Current liabilities	300	600						900
Deferred tax liability					60		2	60
Non-current liabilities	400	1 100						1 500
	4 200	3 700						6 060
Current assets	500	700						1 200
Shares in B Ltd	2 400	—			2 400		1	—
Shares in A Ltd			1	1 600	1 600		3	—
Non-current assets	1 300	3 000	2	200				4 500
Goodwill			2	360				360
	4 200	3 700		6 160	6 160			6 060

FIGURE 24.19 Consolidation worksheet — reverse acquisition accounting

SUMMARY

This chapter covers the preparation of the consolidated financial statements for a group consisting of a parent and a wholly owned subsidiary. Because of the requirements of IFRS 3 to recognise the identifiable assets acquired and liabilities assumed of an acquired entity at fair value, an initial adjustment to be made on consolidation concerns any assets or liabilities for which there are differences between fair value and carrying amount at the acquisition date. Further, although some intangible assets and liabilities of the subsidiary may not have been recognised in the subsidiary's records, they are recognised as part of the business combination.

The preparation of the consolidated financial statements is done using a consolidation worksheet, the left-hand columns of which contain the financial statements of the members of the group. The adjustment columns contain the consolidation worksheet entries that adjust the right-hand columns to form the consolidated financial statements. The adjustment entries have no effect on the actual financial records of the parent and its subsidiaries.

At acquisition date, an acquisition analysis is undertaken. The key purposes of this analysis are to determine the fair values of the identifiable assets and liabilities of the subsidiary, and to calculate any goodwill or gain on bargain purchase arising from the business combination. From this analysis, the main consolidation worksheet adjustment entries at acquisition date are the business combination valuation entries (to adjust carrying amounts of the subsidiaries' assets and liabilities to fair value) and the pre-acquisition entries.

In preparing consolidated financial statements in periods after acquisition date, the consolidation worksheet will contain valuation entries and pre-acquisition entries. However, these entries are not necessarily the same as those used at acquisition date. If there are changes to the assets and liabilities of the subsidiaries since acquisition date, or there have been movements in pre-acquisition equity, changes must be made to these entries.

DEMONSTRATION PROBLEM 24.1 Consolidation

On 1 July 2014, Pegasus Ltd acquired 100% of the issued shares of Taurus Ltd on a cum div. basis. The fair value of the consideration paid was measured at $335 000. At this date, the records of Taurus Ltd included the following information:

Share capital	$200 000
General reserve	5 000
Retained earnings	100 000
Dividend payable	20 000
Goodwill	5 000

The dividend liability at 1 July 2014 was paid in August 2014. At 1 July 2014, all the identifiable assets and liabilities of Taurus Ltd were recorded in the subsidiary's books at fair value except for the following assets.

	Carrying amount	Fair value
Inventory	$ 40 000	$ 43 000
Plant (cost $240 000)	180 000	185 000

The inventory was all sold by 30 June 2015. The plant has a further 5-year life and is depreciated on a straight-line basis. Goodwill was not impaired in any period. When assets are sold or fully consumed, any relating business combination valuation reserve is transferred to retained earnings. The tax rate is 30%.

The summarised financial statements of the entities within the group at 30 June 2016 are as shown in figure 24.20 (pp. 867–8). The transfer to general reserve in the 2015–16 period was from profits earned before acquisition date.

Required

Prepare the consolidated financial statements for Pegasus Ltd at 30 June 2016.

Solution

The first step in the consolidation process is the acquisition analysis shown on the next page. This involves comparing the net fair value of the identifiable assets and liabilities of the subsidiary with the consideration transferred, and determining the existence of goodwill or gain on bargain purchase. So it is necessary to identify:

- *the equity of the subsidiary at acquisition date:* this consists of $200 000 share capital, $5000 general reserve and $100 000 retained earnings.
- *differences between the carrying amounts of recorded assets and liabilities of the subsidiary and their fair values, as well as the fair values of any unrecorded assets and liabilities of the subsidiary recognised as part of the business combination:* this consists of inventory for which there is $3000 difference (i.e. $43 000 – $40 000) and plant for which there is a $5000 difference (i.e. $185 000 – $180 000); these differences are recognised in the acquisition analysis as business combination valuation reserves, the amount being on an after-tax basis — the differences are multiplied by (1 – tax rate).

- *any goodwill recorded by the subsidiary at acquisition date*: because it is the fair value of identifiable assets being considered and goodwill is an unidentifiable asset, goodwill must be adjusted for in the calculation; in this problem, the subsidiary has goodwill of $5000.
- *dividends payable recorded by the subsidiary at acquisition date*: if dividends have been issued on an *ex div.* basis, they have no effect on the acquisition analysis. The dividends of $20 000 in this problem were issued on a *cum div.* basis. This means that the cost of the combination of $335 000 paid by the parent was for both the shares in the subsidiary and the dividends receivable. Hence, the consideration transferred must be adjusted for the amount paid for the dividends receivable, that is, $20 000.

Acquisition analysis
At 1 July 2014:

Net fair value of identifiable assets
and liabilities of Taurus Ltd = $200 000 + $5000 + $100 000 (equity)
− $5000 goodwill recorded
+ ($5000)(1 − 30%) (BCVR — plant)
+ ($3000)(1 − 30%) (BCVR — inventory)
= $305 600

Consideration transferred = $335 000 − $20 000 (dividend receivable)
= $315 000

Goodwill = $315 000 − $305 600
= $9400

Unrecorded goodwill = $9400 − $5000
= $4400

When the net fair value of the identifiable assets and liabilities acquired is compared with the consideration transferred, it is found that the latter is the greater amount — the difference between the two numbers is goodwill. In this problem, the goodwill of the subsidiary is $9400. This is the amount that will be reported in a consolidated statement of financial position if prepared at acquisition date. As the subsidiary has already recorded goodwill of $5000, the adjustment necessary in the consolidation worksheet is $4400.

Consolidation worksheet adjustment entries at 30 June 2016
The consolidation worksheet entries should be read from the acquisition analysis, as the latter contains the information necessary to prepare the entries at acquisition date.

(1) *Business combination valuation entries at 30 June 2016*
Since the consolidated financial statements are being prepared after acquisition date, the business combination entries at 30 June 2016 are affected by changes in the assets and liabilities existing at acquisition date.

With inventory, since it has been sold by 30 June 2015, there is no longer any need to prepare a business combination valuation entry for this asset. The related valuation reserve has been transferred to retained earnings in 2015.

With the plant, it is still on hand within the group. The first adjustment entry, then, is the same as that at the acquisition date. The accumulated depreciation of $60 000 (i.e. $240 000 − $180 000) is eliminated and the plant reduced from $240 000 to fair value of $185 000, an amount of $55 000. The $5000 difference between carrying amount and fair value is split between deferred tax liability (30%) and business combination valuation reserve (70%). This entry is used in every period while the asset continues to be held by the subsidiary.

The second valuation entry reflects the fact that the plant is being depreciated on a straight-line basis over a 5-year period. Because the acquisition date was 1 July 2014 and the end of the reporting period is 30 June 2016, there is a 2-year time period between these two dates. The business combination valuation entry for equipment has to include adjustments for current period depreciation and 1-year prior period depreciation. The adjustment to the plant was $5000. Using a 20% depreciation rate, depreciation each year is $1000. The current period depreciation is adjusted via depreciation expense, whereas prior period depreciation affects retained earnings. Total depreciation is adjusted against accumulated depreciation.

As the asset is used up and benefits flow to the entity, the deferred tax liability is reversed. This can be observed via the change in the carrying amount of the asset with the recognition of accumulated depreciation. In the worksheet entry discussed in the previous paragraph, accumulated depreciation was increased by $2000. This affected the carrying amount of the asset, and caused a temporary difference between it and the tax base of the asset. This results in a reversal of the deferred tax liability raised in the first business combination valuation entry for plant. The amount of the reversal is equal to the adjustment to accumulated depreciation times the tax rate, which in this problem is $2000 × 30% = $600. The reversal affects current period income tax expense by $300 (the adjustment to depreciation expense of $1000 × the 30% tax rate) and retained earnings by $300 (the adjustment for prior period depreciation to retained earnings of $1000 × the 30% tax rate).

The final business combination valuation entry relates to the recognition of goodwill acquired in the business combination. At acquisition date, the parent acquired $9400 goodwill in the subsidiary. However, as the subsidiary had already recognised $5000 goodwill, on consolidation, an additional $4400 goodwill is recognised as having been acquired by the group.

The business combination valuation entries at 30 June 2016 are then as follows:

Accumulated Depreciation – Plant	Dr	60 000
Plant	Cr	55 000
Deferred Tax Liability	Cr	1 500
Business Combination Valuation Reserve	Cr	3 500
Depreciation Expense	Dr	1 000
Retained Earnings (1/7/15)	Dr	1 000
Accumulated Depreciation	Cr	2 000
(20% × $5000 p.a. for 2 years)		
Deferred Tax Liability	Dr	600
Income Tax Expense	Cr	300
Retained Earnings (1/7/15)	Cr	300
Goodwill	Dr	4 400
Business Combination Valuation Reserve	Cr	4 400

(2) *Pre-acquisition entries at 30 June 2016*

The pre-acquisition entry eliminates the pre-acquisition equity of the subsidiary and the investment by the parent in the subsidiary. The pre-acquisition entry at acquisition date can be read from the acquisition analysis. The differences between carrying amounts and fair values of the subsidiary's assets and liabilities are reflected in the business combination valuation reserve. The entry at *1 July 2014* (acquisition date) is:

Retained Earnings (1/7/14)	Dr	100 000
Share Capital	Dr	200 000
General Reserve	Dr	5 000
Business Combination Valuation Reserve	Dr	10 000
Shares in Taurus Ltd	Cr	315 000

(Note that there would be a further entry relating to the $20 000 dividend, but because it is paid in August 2014 it has no further effect.)

This entry changes for periods after the acquisition date because of events affecting pre-acquisition equity including movements in the business combination valuation reserve, and any impairment of goodwill. In this problem, the events between the acquisition date and the *beginning* of the current period affecting the pre-acquisition entry are that the inventory on hand at acquisition date has been sold, meaning that the related business combination valuation reserve has been transferred to retained earnings; thus, the valuation reserve has been reduced by $2100, and the retained earnings (opening balance) increased by the same amount.

The pre-acquisition entry at the beginning of the 2015–16 period is then:

Retained Earnings (1/7/15) [$100 000 + $2100 (BCVR — inventory)]	Dr	102 100	
Share Capital	Dr	200 000	
General Reserve	Dr	5 000	
Business Combination Valuation Reserve [$10 000 – $2100 (BCVR — inventory)]	Dr	7 900	
Shares in Taurus Ltd	Cr		315 000

One further event in the *current* period that affects the balances of pre-acquisition equity is the transfer to general reserve of $15 000 made by the subsidiary in the current period — the subsidiary increased its general reserve and reduced its retained earnings using a transfer account; this affects the balances of pre-acquisition equity in specific accounts.

The extra entry required is:

General Reserve	Dr	15 000	
Transfer to General Reserve	Cr		15 000

Both the business combination valuation entries and the pre-acquisition entries are then passed through the consolidation worksheet as shown in figure 24.20.

FIGURE 24.20 Consolidation worksheet

Financial statements	Pegasus Ltd	Taurus Ltd	Adjustments Dr		Adjustments Cr		Consolidation
Revenues	125 000	90 000					215 000
Expenses	85 000	65 000	1	1 000			151 000
Profit before tax	40 000	25 000					64 000
Income tax expense	15 500	10 200			300	1	25 400
Profit for the period	24 500	14 800					38 600
Retained earnings (1/7/15)	150 000	85 000	1	1 000	300	1	132 200
			2	102 100			
	174 500	99 800					170 800
Transfer to general reserve	(20 000)	(15 000)			15 000	2	(20 000)
Retained earnings (30/6/16)	154 500	84 800					150 800
Share capital	500 000	200 000	2	200 000			500 000
Business combination valuation reserve	—	—	2	7 900	3 500	1	—
					4 400	1	
General reserve	50 000	20 000	2	5 000			
			2	15 000			50 000
	704 500	304 800					700 800
Financial assets reserve (1/7/15)	2 000	3 000					5 000
Gain on financial assets	12 000	10 000					22 000
Financial assets reserve (30/6/16)	14 000	13 000					27 000
Plant revaluation surplus (1/7/15)	8 000	5 000					13 000
Gain on plant revaluation	28 000	22 000					50 000
Plant revaluation surplus (30/6/16)	36 000	27 000					63 000
Total equity	754 500	344 800					790 800

(continued)

FIGURE 24.20 (continued)

Financial statements	Pegasus Ltd	Taurus Ltd	Adjustments				Consolidation
				Dr	Cr		
Tax liabilities	11 000	16 000	1	600	1 500	1	27 900
Other liabilities	50 000	20 000					70 000
Total liabilities	61 000	36 000					97 900
Total equity and liabilities	815 500	380 800					888 700
Cash	25 000	5 000					30 000
Inventory	60 000	85 000					145 000
Financial assets	50 000	40 000					90 000
Plant	500 000	300 000			55 000	1	745 000
Accumulated depreciation	(160 000)	(80 000)	1	60 000	2 000	1	(182 000)
Shares in Taurus Ltd	315 000	—			315 000	2	—
Fixtures and fittings	40 000	38 000					78 000
Accumulated depreciation	(14 500)	(12 200)					(26 700)
Goodwill	—	5 000	1	4 400			9 400
Total assets	815 500	380 800		397 000	397 000		888 700

The consolidated financial statements of Pegasus Ltd at 30 June 2016 are as shown in figure 24.21.

FIGURE 24.21(a) Consolidated statement of profit or loss and other comprehensive income

PEGASUS LTD
Consolidated Statement of Profit or Loss and Other Comprehensive Income
for the year ended 30 June 2016

Revenues	$215 000
Expenses	151 000
Profit before tax	**64 000**
Income tax expense	(25 400)
Profit for the period	**$ 38 600**
Other comprehensive income	
Revaluation of financial assets	22 000
Gain on plant revaluation	50 000
Other comprehensive income for the year net of tax	**72 000**
Total comprehensive income for the year	**$110 600**

FIGURE 24.21(b) Consolidated statement of changes in equity

PEGASUS LTD
Consolidated Statement of Changes in Equity
for the year ended 30 June 2016

Total comprehensive income for the year	**$110 600**
Retained earnings balance at 1 July 2015	$132 200
Profit for the period	38 600
Transfer to general reserve	(20 000)
Retained earnings balance at 30 June 2016	$150 800
General reserve balance at 1 July 2015	$ 30 000
Transfer from retained earnings	20 000
General reserve balance at 30 June 2016	$ 50 000

FIGURE 24.21(b) *(continued)*

Financial assets reserve at 1 July 2015	$ 5 000
Gain for the year	22 000
Financial assets reserve at 30 June 2016	$ 27 000
Plant revaluation surplus at 1 July 2015	$ 13 000
Gain for the year	50 000
Plant revaluation surplus at 30 June 2016	$ 63 000
Share capital balance at 1 July 2015	$500 000
Share capital balance at 30 June 2016	$500 000

PEGASUS LTD
Consolidated Statement of Financial Position
as at 30 June 2016

EQUITY AND LIABILITIES

Equity

Share capital		$500 000
Other components of equity		140 000
Retained earnings		150 800
Total equity		790 800
Non-current liabilities		
Tax liabilities		27 900
Other		70 000
Total non-current liabilities		97 900
Total equity and liabilities		$888 700
ASSETS		
Non-current assets		
Plant	$ 745 000	
Accumulated depreciation	(182 000)	$563 000
Fixtures and fittings	78 000	
Accumulated depreciation	(26 700)	51 300
Goodwill		9 400
Total non-current assets		623 700
Current assets		
Cash		30 000
Inventory		145 000
Financial assets		90 000
Total current assets		265 000
Total assets		$888 700

FIGURE 24.21(c) Consolidated statement of financial position

DEMONSTRATION PROBLEM 24.2 Unrecognised intangible, unrecognised liability

On 30 September 2013, Sagittarius Ltd acquired 80% of the shares of Aquila Ltd for $3 per share in cash. The equity of Aquila Ltd at that date was:

Share capital — 10 000 shares	$10 000
General reserve	3 000
Retained earnings	12 000

Sagittarius Ltd had previously acquired 20% of the shares of Aquila Ltd for $4000. The fair value of this investment at 30 September 2013 was $6000.

At acquisition date, all the identifiable assets and liabilities of Aquila Ltd were recorded at fair value except for machinery and inventory whose carrying amounts were each $2000 less than their fair values. All this inventory was sold by Aquila Ltd before December 2013. The machinery had a further 5-year life. The tax rate is 30%.

In a previous period, Aquila Ltd had purchased some goodwill that had been written down to a carrying amount of $2000 as at 30 September 2013. Aquila Ltd had developed a business magazine containing economic indicators for the coal industry. The magazine was widely sought after. Sagittarius Ltd placed a value of $1500 on the masthead. The intangible asset, not recognised by Aquila Ltd at 30 September 2013, was considered to have an indefinite life.

At 30 September 2013, Crater Ltd had sued Aquila Ltd for alleged damaging statements made in the magazine, and a court case was in progress. Although it considered that a present obligation for damages existed, Aquila Ltd had not recognised any liability because it did not believe that the liability recognition criteria could be met. Sagittarius Ltd assessed potential damages at a fair value of $2000. In January 2015, the court handed down its decision, and Aquila Ltd was required to pay damages of $2500.

Between 30 September 2013 and 30 June 2014 (end of the reporting period for both companies), the following movements occurred in the records of Aquila Ltd:

- Aquila Ltd transferred $3000 from pre-acquisition retained earnings to the general reserve.
- Aquila Ltd had declared and paid a bonus share issue of one share for every two shares held at 1 October 2013 out of the general reserve ($3000) and partly out of the retained earnings.

Required

1. Prepare the consolidation worksheet adjustment entries for consolidation of the financial statements of Sagittarius Ltd and Aquila Ltd on:
   (a) 30 September 2013
   (b) 30 June 2014.
2. Given no further movements in pre-acquisition equity of Aquila Ltd, prepare the worksheet entries at 30 June 2015.

Solution

The first step is to prepare the acquisition analysis. This requires the identification of:

- *the recorded equity of the subsidiary at acquisition date:* this consists of $10 000 share capital, $3000 general reserve and $12 000 retained earnings.
- *differences between carrying amounts and fair values for assets recorded by the subsidiary:* the differences arise for inventory ($2000) and plant ($2000).
- *identifiable assets and liabilities not recognised by the subsidiary but recognised as part of the business combination at their fair values:* the group recognises a masthead at $1500 fair value and a provision for damages at $2000 fair value.
- *any goodwill recorded by the subsidiary at acquisition date:* the subsidiary has recorded goodwill of $2000.
- *any dividends payable by the subsidiary at acquisition date:* there are none in this problem.

Acquisition analysis at 30 September 2013

Net fair value of identifiable assets and liabilities of Aquila Ltd	= ($10 000 + $12 000 + $3000) (equity)
	+ $2000(1 − 30%) (machinery)
	− $2000 (goodwill)
	+ $2000(1 − 30%) (inventory)
	+ $1500(1 − 30%) (masthead)
	− $2000(1 − 30%) (provision for damages)
	= $25 450
Consideration transferred	= 80% × 10 000 × $3
	= $24 000
Fair value of previously held investment	= $6000
Aggregate amount of investment	= $24 000 + $6000
	= $30 000

Goodwill acquired	= $30 000 − $25 450		
	= $4550		
Unrecorded goodwill	= $4550 − $2000		
	= $2550		

The aggregate of the investment in Aquila Ltd is $4550 greater than the net fair value of the identifiable assets and liabilities of the subsidiary. The goodwill acquired by the group is then $4550. As the subsidiary has already recorded $2000 goodwill, the consolidation adjustment is $2550.

1(a) Consolidation worksheet entries at 30 September 2013

(1) *Business combination valuation entries*

The business combination valuation entries are used to adjust the carrying amount of the subsidiary's recorded assets to fair value, and to recognise assets and liabilities not recorded by the subsidiary. These have all been identified in the acquisition analysis. In recognising the assets and liabilities at fair value, the adjustments affect the business combination valuation reserve (70% of the adjustment) and deferred tax accounts (30% of the adjustment). The entries at acquisition date are:

Machinery	Dr	2 000	
Deferred Tax Liability	Cr		600
Business Combination Valuation Reserve	Cr		1 400
Inventory	Dr	2 000	
Deferred Tax Liability	Cr		600
Business Combination Valuation Reserve	Cr		1 400
Masthead	Dr	1 500	
Deferred Tax Liability	Cr		450
Business Combination Valuation Reserve	Cr		1 050
Business Combination Valuation Reserve	Dr	1 400	
Deferred Tax Asset	Dr	600	
Provision for Damages	Cr		2 000
Goodwill	Dr	2 550	
Business Combination Valuation Reserve	Cr		2 550

Note that with the liability, there is an overall decrease in the valuation reserve, and the tax adjustment is to a deferred tax asset.

(2) *Pre-acquisition entry*

The pre-acquisition entry at acquisition date can be read from the acquisition analysis. The entry eliminates the pre-acquisition equity of the subsidiary, including the total of the business combination valuation reserve as recognised in the previous set of entries, and the investment account as recorded by the parent. The entry at acquisition date is:

Retained Earnings (30/9/13)	Dr	12 000	
Share Capital	Dr	10 000	
General Reserve	Dr	3 000	
Business Combination Valuation Reserve	Dr	5 000	
Shares in Aquila Ltd	Cr		30 000

1(b) Consolidation worksheet entries at 30 June 2014

These entries are at the end of the first period since acquisition date, and cover a period of 9 months.

(1) Business combination valuation entries

The effect on the entry for machinery is that there needs to be another entry to adjust for 9 months' depreciation based on the difference between carrying amount in the subsidiary and fair value. The adjustment is to current period depreciation and amounts to $300 (i.e. ¾ × 20% × $2000) using the fact that the machinery has a further 5-year life. The recognition of depreciation changes the carrying amount of the asset. This changes the temporary difference between the carrying amount and the asset's tax base. The deferred tax liability raised on adjusting the machinery to fair value is reversed as the asset is depreciated. The reversal is $90; that is, 30% × the depreciation charge of $300.

Machinery	Dr	2 000	
Deferred Tax Liability	Cr		600
Business Combination Valuation Reserve	Cr		1 400
Depreciation Expense	Dr	300	
Accumulated Depreciation	Cr		300
(¾ × ⅕ × $2000)			
Deferred Tax Liability	Dr	90	
Income Tax Expense	Cr		90

The inventory on hand at acquisition date is all sold by December 2013. The adjustment is then made to cost of sales instead of inventory, because the cost of sales to the group is $2000 higher than that recorded by the subsidiary on sale of the inventory. On sale of the inventory, the deferred tax liability is reversed, and affects income tax expense. As the asset is sold, the group transfers the valuation reserve to retained earnings to avoid having to make adjustments to equity in future periods. The entry for inventory is:

Cost of Sales	Dr	2 000	
Income Tax Expense	Cr		600
Transfer from Business Combination Valuation Reserve	Cr		1 400

There is no change to the entry for the masthead. This entry changes only if the asset is amortised, or adjusted as a result of an impairment loss.

Masthead	Dr	1 500	
Deferred Tax Liability	Cr		450
Business Combination Valuation Reserve	Cr		1 050

There is no change to the entry for the provision for damages. This would change if the subsidiary itself recognised a liability or the liability was settled.

Business Combination Valuation Reserve	Dr	1 400	
Deferred Tax Asset	Dr	600	
Provision for Damages	Cr		2 000

There is no change to the goodwill. This would change if the goodwill were impaired.

Goodwill	Dr	2 550	
Business Combination Valuation Reserve	Cr		2 550

(2) Pre-acquisition entries

The pre-acquisition entry at the beginning of the period is the same as that at acquisition date:

Retained Earnings (30/9/13)	Dr	12 000	
Share Capital	Dr	10 000	
General Reserve	Dr	3 000	
Business Combination Valuation Reserve	Dr	5 000	
Shares in Aquila Ltd	Cr		30 000

Adjustments are made to the pre-acquisition entry for events occurring in the current period that affect pre-acquisition equity balances or the goodwill balance.

In the current period, the following events affect the pre-acquisition entry at the beginning of the period:

- *$3000 transfer to general reserve from retained earnings:* this decreases retained earnings and increases the general reserve.
- *$5000 bonus issue:* this increases share capital and reduces the equity accounts from which the bonus issue was made, namely $3000 from general reserve and $2000 from retained earnings, the latter affecting the bonus dividend paid account.
- *the inventory on hand at acquisition date was sold in the current period:* as can be seen from the related business combination valuation reserve adjustment, on sale of the inventory the related revaluation surplus is transferred to retained earnings. Hence, at 30 June 2014, the business combination valuation reserve is reduced and retained earnings increased.

General Reserve	Dr	3 000	
Transfer to General Reserve	Cr		3 000
Share Capital	Dr	5 000	
Bonus Dividend Paid	Cr		2 000
General Reserve	Cr		3 000
Shares in Aquila Ltd	Dr	1 500	
Dividend Receivable	Cr		1 500
Transfer from Business Combination Valuation Reserve	Dr	1 400	
Business Combination Valuation Reserve	Cr		1 400

2. Consolidation worksheet entries at 30 June 2015

This is 1 year after the last set of entries and 1¾ years since acquisition date.

(1) Business combination valuation entries

The adjustment entry raised at acquisition date for the machinery is still used. The depreciation now, however, is for 1¾ years since acquisition date. Current period depreciation expense is adjusted for a full year's depreciation and the prior period depreciation expense for ¾ year affects retained earnings. The using up of the asset results in changes in the carrying amount of the asset, and further results in reversing the deferred tax liability raised at acquisition date. The current period income tax expense is affected by the reversal due to the current period depreciation, and the adjustment for the previous ¾-year depreciation, affecting retained earnings, affects last year's income tax expense, also requiring an adjustment to retained earnings.

Machinery	Dr	2 000	
Deferred Tax Liability	Cr		600
Business Combination Valuation Reserve	Cr		1 400

Depreciation Expense	Dr	400	
Retained Earnings (1/7/14)	Dr	300	
Accumulated Depreciation	Cr		700
(⅕ × $2000 p.a.)			
Deferred Tax Liability	Dr	210	
Income Tax Expense	Cr		120
Retained Earnings (1/7/14)	Cr		90

There is still no change to the adjustment for the masthead.

Masthead	Dr	1 500	
Deferred Tax Liability	Cr		450
Business Combination Valuation Reserve	Cr		1 050

In January 2015, the court determined that the subsidiary was to pay damages of $2500. As the liability is settled, the business combination valuation reserve is transferred to retained earnings. Further, the deferred tax asset is reversed on settlement of the liability, requiring an adjustment to income tax expense. In settling the liability, the subsidiary raised a damages expense of $2500 and paid cash to external entities. Since the group recognised the liability for damages at acquisition date of $2000, the expense to the group on payment of $2500 is only $500. In other words, to the group, the $2500 outflow is a reduction in the liability of $2000 and an expense of $500. Since $2500 damages expense was recorded by the subsidiary, and the group wants to report only $500 damages expense, the consolidation adjustment is a $2000 reduction in damages expense.

Transfer from Business Combination Valuation Reserve	Dr	1 400	
Income Tax Expense	Dr	600	
Damages Expense	Cr		2 000

There is still no change to the goodwill.

| Goodwill | Dr | 2 550 | |
| Business Combination Valuation Reserve | Cr | | 2 550 |

(2) *Pre-acquisition entries*
The pre-acquisition entry at the beginning of the year, 1 July 2014, is the sum of the entries made in the consolidation worksheet at 30 June 2013. However, if the worksheet entries are required for the period ending 30 June 2015, it is unnecessary to prepare the entries for each period between acquisition date and the current period. Each line in the pre-acquisition entry can be calculated by adjusting the balance at acquisition date for all events affecting that balance between acquisition date and the beginning of the current period, as follows:

Retained earnings (1/7/14):
$8400 = $12 000 (opening balance) − $3000 (transfer to general reserve) − $2000 (bonus dividend) + $1400 (transfer from BCVR — inventory)

Share capital:
$15 000 = $10 000 + $5000 (bonus dividend)

General reserve:
$3000 = zero balance at acquisition date + $3000 transfer from retained earnings

Business combination valuation reserve:
$3600 = $5000 − $1400 (transfer from BCVR — inventory)

Shares in Aquila Ltd:
There is no change to this account.

The entry then is:

Retained Earnings (1/7/14)	Dr	8 400	
Share Capital	Dr	15 000	
General Reserve	Dr	3 000	
Business Combination Valuation Reserve	Dr	3 600	
Shares in Aquila Ltd	Cr		30 000

Other entries are required for events occurring in the current period that affect accounts in the pre-acquisition entry. In this problem, there is only one such event. In the current period the contingent liability was settled, resulting in a transfer from business combination valuation reserve to retained earnings. The effect on the pre-acquisition entry is that the BCVR has been increased by $1400 and the retained earnings, represented by the current period transfer account, is decreased by $1400.

Business Combination Valuation Reserve	Dr	1 400	
Transfer from Business Combination Valuation Reserve	Cr		1 400

Discussion questions

1. Explain the purpose of the pre-acquisition entries in the preparation of consolidated financial statements.
2. When there is a dividend payable by the subsidiary at acquisition date, under what conditions should the existence of this dividend be taken into consideration in preparing the pre-acquisition entries?
3. Is it necessary to distinguish pre-acquisition dividends from post-acquisition dividends? Why?
4. If the subsidiary has recorded goodwill in its records at acquisition date, how does this affect the preparation of the pre-acquisition entries?
5. Explain how the existence of a bargain purchase affects the pre-acquisition entries, both in the year of acquisition and in subsequent years.
6. At the date the parent acquires a controlling interest in a subsidiary, if the carrying amounts of the subsidiary's assets are not equal to fair value, explain why adjustments to these assets are required in the preparation of the consolidated financial statements.
7. How does IFRS 3 *Business Combinations* affect the acquisition analysis?
8. What is the purpose of the business combination valuation entries?
9. Using an example, explain how the business combination entries affect the pre-acquisition entries.
10. Why are some adjustment entries in the previous period's consolidation worksheet also made in the current period's worksheet?

Exercises

STAR RATING   ★ BASIC   ★★ MODERATE   ★★★ DIFFICULT

Exercise 24.1   **HANDLING RESEARCH OUTLAYS**

★   Lynx Ltd has just acquired all the issued shares of Indus Ltd. The accounting staff at Lynx Ltd has been analysing the assets and liabilities acquired in Indus Ltd. As a result of this analysis, it was found that Indus Ltd had been expensing its research outlays in accordance with IAS 38 *Intangible Assets*. Over the past 3 years, the company has expensed a total of $20 000, including $8000 immediately before the acquisition date. One of the reasons that Lynx Ltd acquired control of Indus Ltd was its promising research findings in an area that could benefit the products being produced by Lynx Ltd.

There is disagreement among the accounting staff as to how to account for the research abilities of Indus Ltd. Some of the staff argue that, since it is research, the correct accounting is to expense it, and so it has no effect on accounting for the group. Other members of the accounting staff believe that it should be recognised on consolidation, but are unsure of the accounting entries to use, and are concerned about the future effects of recognition of an asset, particularly as no tax advantage remains in relation to the asset.

Required

Advise the group accountant of Lynx Ltd on what accounting is most appropriate for these circumstances.

Exercise 24.2	**UNRECORDED LIABILITY**

★ Scorpio Ltd has finally concluded its negotiations to take over Norma Ltd, and has secured ownership of all the shares of Norma Ltd. One of the areas of discussion during the negotiation process was the current court case that Norma Ltd was involved in. The company was being sued by some former employees who were retrenched, but are now claiming damages for unfair dismissal. The company did not believe that it owed these employees anything. However, realising that industrial relations was an uncertain area, particularly given the country's current confusing industrial relations laws, it had raised a note to the accounts issued before the takeover by Scorpio Ltd reporting the existence of the court case as a contingent liability. No monetary amount was disclosed, but the company's lawyers had placed a $56 700 amount on the probable payout to settle the case.

The accounting staff of Scorpio Ltd is unsure of the effect of this contingent liability on the accounting for the consolidated group after the takeover. Some argue that it is not a liability of the group and so should not be recognised on consolidation, but are willing to accept some form of note disclosure. A further concern being raised is the effects on the accounts, depending on whether Norma Ltd wins or loses the case. If Norma Ltd wins the court case, it will not have to pay out any damages and could get reimbursement of its court costs, estimated to be around $40 000.

Required

Give the group accountant your opinion on the accounting at acquisition date for consolidation purposes, as well as any subsequent effects when the entity either wins or loses the case.

Exercise 24.3	**ACCOUNTING FOR ASSETS AND LIABILITIES**

★ Mensa Ltd has acquired all the shares of Cancer Ltd. The accountant for Mensa Ltd, having studied the requirements of IFS 3 *Business Combinations*, realises that all the identifiable assets and liabilities of Cancer Ltd must be recognised in the consolidated financial statements at fair value. Although he is happy about the valuation of these items, he is unsure of a number of other matters associated with accounting for these assets and liabilities. He has approached you and asked for your advice.

Required

Write a report for the accountant at Mensa Ltd advising on the following issues:
1. Should the adjustments to fair value be made in the consolidation worksheet or in the accounts of Cancer Ltd?
2. What equity accounts should be used when revaluing the assets, and should different equity accounts such as income (similar to recognition of an excess) be used in relation to recognition of liabilities?
3. Do these equity accounts remain in existence indefinitely, since they do not seem to be related to the equity accounts recognised by Cancer Ltd itself?

Exercise 24.4	**CONSOLIDATION WORKSHEET ENTRIES 1 YEAR AFTER ACQUISITION DATE**

★ At 1 July 2013, Pisces Ltd acquired all the shares of Ursa Ltd for $283 000. At this date the equity of Ursa Ltd consisted of:

Share capital — 100 000 shares	$200 000
General reserve	50 000
Retained earnings	20 000

All the identifiable assets and liabilities of Ursa Ltd were recorded at amounts equal to fair value except for the following assets:

	Carrying amount	Fair value
Inventory	$ 60 000	$ 65 000
Plant (cost $280 000)	200 000	210 000

The inventory was all sold by 30 June 2014. The plant has a further 5-year life, and depreciation is calculated on a straight-line basis. When revalued assets are sold or fully consumed, any related revaluation surplus is transferred to retained earnings.

The tax rate is 30%.

Required

Prepare the consolidation worksheet entries at 30 June 2014 for the preparation of the consolidated financial statements of Pisces Ltd.

Exercise 24.5

★

ACQUISITION ANALYSIS, PARENT HOLDS PREVIOUSLY ACQUIRED SHARES IN SUBSIDIARY, WORKSHEET ENTRIES AT ACQUISITION DATE

At 1 July 2014, Pavo Ltd acquired 60% of the shares of Octans Ltd for $153 000 on a cum div. basis. Pavo Ltd had acquired 40% of the shares of Octans Ltd two years earlier for $80 000. This investment, classified as a financial asset, was recorded at a fair value on 1 July 2014 of $102 000. The changes in fair value had all been taken to other comprehensive income. At 1 July 2014, the equity of Octans Ltd consisted of:

Share capital	$160 000
Retained earnings	40 000

At this date, the identifiable assets and liabilities of Octans Ltd were recorded at fair value except for:

	Carrying amount	Fair value
Inventory	$ 40 000	$ 44 000
Plant (cost $120 000)	100 000	105 000

At 1 July 2014, Octans Ltd's assets and liabilities included a dividend payable of $5000, and goodwill of $6000 (net of $4000 accumulated impairment losses). An analysis of the unrecorded intangibles of Octans Ltd revealed that the company had unrecorded internally generated brands, considered to have a fair value of $50 000. Further, Octans Ltd had expensed research outlays of $80 000 that were considered to have a fair value of $20 000. In its financial statements at 30 June 2014, Octans Ltd had reported a contingent liability relating to a potential claim by customers for unsatisfactory products, the fair value of the claim being $10 000.

The tax rate is 30%.

Required

Prepare the acquisition analysis at 1 July 2014, and the consolidation worksheet entries for preparation of consolidated financial statements of Pavo Ltd at that date.

Exercise 24.6

★

BUSINESS COMBINATION VALUATION AND PRE-ACQUISITION ENTRIES

On 1 July 2013, Pyxis Ltd acquired all the share capital of Gemini Ltd for $218 500. At this date, Gemini Ltd's equity comprised:

Share capital — 100 000 shares	$100 000
General reserve	50 000
Retained earnings	36 000

All identifiable assets and liabilities of Gemini Ltd were recorded at fair value as at 1 July 2013 except for the following:

	Carrying amount	Fair value
Inventory	$27 000	$35 000
Land	75 000	90 000
Equipment (cost		
$100 000)	50 000	60 000

The equipment is expected to have a further 10-year life. All the inventory was sold by June 2014. The tax rate is 30%.

On 30 June 2014, the directors of Gemini Ltd decided to transfer $25 000 from the general reserve to retained earnings.

Required

Prepare the consolidation worksheet entries for the preparation of consolidated financial statements for Pyxis Ltd and its subsidiary Gemini Ltd as at:
1. 1 July 2013
2. 30 June 2014.

Exercise 24.7 **PRE-ACQUISITION ENTRIES, RECORDED GOODWILL**

★ On 1 July 2015, Serpens Ltd acquired the issued shares (cum div.) of Vela Ltd for $120 000. At that date, the financial statements of Vela Ltd included the following items:

Share capital	$52 500
General reserve	45 000
Retained earnings	9 000
Dividend payable	7 500

At 1 July 2015, Vela Ltd had recorded goodwill of $2000, and all its identifiable assets and liabilities were recorded at fair value. Share capital represents 75 000 shares paid to 70 cents per share. $22 500 of uncalled capital was called up on 1 October 2015. The dividend was paid on 20 October 2015. The tax rate is 30%.

Required

Prepare the pre-acquisition entries for the preparation of consolidated financial statements at:
1. 1 July 2015, immediately after combination
2. 31 December 2015.

Exercise 24.8 **GOODWILL**

★★ When Hydra Ltd acquired the shares of Draco Ltd, one of the assets in the statement of financial position of Draco Ltd was $15 000 goodwill, which had been recognised by Draco Ltd upon its acquisition of a business from Valhalla Ltd. Having prepared the acquisition analysis as part of the process of preparing the consolidated financial statements for Hydra Ltd, the group accountant, Asmund Asmundson, has asked for your opinion.

Required

Provide advice on the following issues:
1. How does the recording of goodwill by the subsidiary affect the accounting for the group's goodwill?
2. If, in subsequent years, goodwill is impaired, for example by $10 000, should the impairment loss be recognised in the records of Hydra Ltd or as a consolidation adjustment?

BARGAIN PURCHASE

★★ The accountant for Carina Ltd, Ms Finn, has sought your advice on an accounting issue that has been puzzling her. When preparing the acquisition analysis relating to Carina Ltd's acquisition of Lyra Ltd, she calculated that there was a gain on bargain purchase of $10 000. Being unsure of how to account for this, she was informed by accounting acquaintances that this should be recognised as income. However, she reasoned that this would have an effect on the consolidated profit in the first year after acquisition date. For example, if Lyra Ltd reported a profit of $50 000, then consolidated profit would be $60 000. She is unsure of whether this profit is all post-acquisition profit or a mixture of pre-acquisition profit and post-acquisition profit.

Required

Compile a detailed report on the nature of an excess, how it should be accounted for and the effects of its recognition on subsequent consolidated financial statements.

PARENT HOLDS PREVIOUSLY ACQUIRED INVESTMENT, CONSOLIDATION WORKSHEET

★★ On 1 December 2009, Reticulum Ltd acquired 20% of the shares of Dorado Ltd for $10 000. These were classified as a financial investment by Reticulum Ltd with changes in gain value being recognised in other comprehensive income. At 30 June 2013, these were recorded at a fair value of $20 400. Reticulum Ltd acquired the remaining 80% of the share capital of Dorado Ltd for $81 600 on 1 July 2013 when the equity of Dorado Ltd consisted of:

Share capital — 50 000 shares	$50 000
Retained earnings	30 000

All identifiable assets and liabilities of Dorado Ltd were recorded at amounts equal to fair value, except as follows:

	Carrying amount	Fair value
Inventory	$20 000	$25 000
Plant (cost $80 000)	60 000	70 000

The plant is expected to have a further useful life of 5 years. All the inventory on hand at 1 July 2013 was sold by 31 December 2013.

The income tax rate is 30%.

At 30 June 2015, the information below was obtained from both entities.

Required

1. Prepare the consolidation worksheet entries for the preparation of consolidated financial statements for Reticulum Ltd and its subsidiary, Dorado Ltd, as at 1 July 2013.
2. Prepare the consolidation worksheet entries and the consolidation worksheet for the preparation of consolidated financial statements for Reticulum Ltd and its subsidiary, Dorado Ltd, as at 30 June 2015.

	Reticulum Ltd	Dorado Ltd
Profit before tax	$ 50 000	$ 40 000
Income tax expense	(20 000)	(15 000)
Profit	30 000	25 000
Retained earnings (1/7/14)	50 000	35 000
	80 000	60 000
Transfer to general reserve	(20 000)	(5 000)
Retained earnings (30/6/15)	$ 60 000	$ 55 000

(continued)

	Reticulum Ltd	Dorado Ltd
Share capital	$150 000	$ 50 000
General reserve	35 000	5 000
Retained earnings	60 000	55 000
Total equity	245 000	110 000
Provisions	65 000	10 000
Payables	20 000	5 000
Total liabilities	85 000	15 000
Total equity and liabilities	$330 000	$125 000
Cash	$ 13 000	$ 14 000
Accounts receivable	30 000	25 000
Inventory	70 000	50 000
Shares in Dorado Ltd	102 000	—
Plant	200 000	80 000
Accumulated depreciation	(85 000)	(44 000)
Total assets	$330 000	$125 000

Exercise 24.11 ★★   RECORDED GOODWILL, UNRECORDED INTANGIBLE

On 1 July 2013, Sculptor Ltd acquired all the share capital (cum div.) of Virgo Ltd, giving in exchange 50 000 shares in Sculptor Ltd, these having a fair value at acquisition date of $5 per share. Costs incurred in undertaking the acquisition amounted to $10 000. The dividend payable at the acquisition date was paid in September 2013. At 30 June 2013, the statement of financial position of Virgo Ltd was as follows:

Statement of Financial Position as at 30 June 2013			
Plant and equipment	$218 000	Share capital (150 000 shares)	$150 000
Goodwill	6 000	Retained earnings	84 000
Current assets	44 000	Dividend payable	10 000
		Other liabilities	24 000
	$268 000		$268 000

The recorded amounts of the identifiable assets and liabilities of Virgo Ltd at the acquisition date were equal to their fair values. Virgo Ltd had not recorded an internally developed trademark. Sculptor Ltd valued this at $20 000. It was assumed to have a 4-year life.

The tax rate is 30%.

On 31 December 2015, Virgo Ltd paid a bonus share dividend from pre-acquisition profits, the dividend being one share for every three held.

Required

Prepare the consolidation worksheet entries for the preparation of consolidated financial statements at 30 June 2017.

Exercise 24.12 ★★   BARGAIN PURCHASE, PARENT HOLDS PREVIOUSLY ACQUIRED INVESTMENT IN SUBSIDIARY, CONSOLIDATION WORKSHEET

As part of a corporate expansion plan, Volans Ltd acquired the remaining shares (cum div.) of Tucana Ltd on 1 July 2014 for $124 200 cash. At this date, it already held 10% of the shares of Tucana Ltd which it had acquired two years previously for $10 000. These financial instruments were recorded by Volans Ltd at fair value with changes in gain value being recognised in profit and loss. The fair value at

1 July 2014 was $13 800. The statements of financial position of both companies at 30 June 2014 were as follows:

	Volans Ltd	Tucana Ltd
Share capital	$180 000	$ 80 000
Other components of equity	23 800	15 000
Retained earnings	58 200	30 000
Total equity	262 000	125 000
Provisions	88 000	27 000
Dividend payable	20 000	10 000
Total liabilities	108 000	37 000
Total equity and liabilities	$370 000	$162 000
Cash	$150 000	$ 10 000
Receivables	26 200	25 000
Shares in Tucana Ltd	13 800	
Inventory	55 000	42 000
Plant	190 000	100 000
Accumulated depreciation	(65 000)	(15 000)
Total assets	$370 000	$162 000

All identifiable assets and liabilities of Tucana Ltd were recorded at fair value as at 1 July 2014 except for the following:

	Carrying amount	Fair value
Inventory	$42 000	$45 000
Plant (cost $100 000)	85 000	90 000

The plant is expected to have a further useful life of 5 years. Inventory held at 1 July 2014 was all sold by 30 June 2015. The dividend payable at 1 July 2014 was paid in October 2014.
The company tax rate is 30%.

Required

1. Prepare the consolidation worksheet entries, the consolidation worksheet and the consolidated statement of financial position for Volans Ltd and its subsidiary, Tucana Ltd, as at 1 July 2014.
2. Prepare the consolidation worksheet entries for the preparation of consolidated financial statements for Volans Ltd and its subsidiary, Tucana Ltd, as at 30 June 2015.

Exercise 24.13

★★

GOODWILL, GAIN ON BARGAIN PURCHASE, ADJUSTMENTS TO GOODWILL BY THE SUBSIDIARY

The statement of financial position of Columba Ltd at 30 June 2014 was as follows:

COLUMBA LTD Statement of Financial Position as at 30 June 2014	
Share capital (150 000 shares)	$150 000
Retained earnings	98 000
Total equity	248 000

(continued)

Dividend payable		10 000
Other liabilities		24 000
Total liabilities		34 000
Total equity and liabilities		$282 000
Inventory		$ 44 000
Non-current assets: Plant and equipment	$ 390 000	
Accumulated depreciation	(158 000)	
	232 000	
Goodwill	6 000	238 000
Total assets		$282 000

The recorded amounts of the identifiable assets and liabilities of Columba Ltd at this date were equal to their fair values except for inventory and plant and equipment, whose fair values were $50 000 and $236 000 respectively. The plant and equipment has a further 5-year life. All the inventory was sold by Columba Ltd by December 2014. The tax rate is 30%.

On 1 July 2014, Centaurus Ltd acquired all the shares (cum div.) in Columba Ltd, giving in exchange 50 000 shares in Centaurus Ltd, these having a fair value at acquisition date of $5 per share. Costs incurred by Centaurus Ltd in undertaking the acquisition amounted to $10 000. The dividend payable was paid in August 2014.

Required

Prepare the consolidation worksheet adjustment entries for the preparation of consolidated financial statements at 30 June 2018.

Exercise 24.14   **BARGAIN PURCHASE, CONSOLIDATION WORKSHEET**

★★ Cepheus Ltd gained control of Aquarius Ltd by acquiring its share capital on 1 January 2013. The statement of financial position of Aquarius Ltd at that date showed:

Share capital	$ 60 000	Land	$ 20 000
Retained earnings	40 000	Plant and machinery	120 000
Asset revaluation surplus	20 000	Accumulated depreciation	(20 000)
Liabilities	15 000	Inventory	15 000
	$135 000		$135 000

At 1 January 2013, the recorded amounts of Aquarius Ltd's assets and liabilities were equal to their fair values except as follows:

	Carrying amount	Fair value
Plant and machinery	$100 000	$102 000
Inventory	15 000	18 000

All this inventory was sold by Aquarius Ltd in the following 3 months. The depreciable assets have a further 5-year life, benefits being received evenly over this period. Any business combination valuation adjustments are made on consolidation. The tax rate is 30%.

At 31 December 2013, the following information was obtained from both entities:

	Cepheus Ltd	Aquarius Ltd
Profit before tax	$100 000	$ 15 000
Income tax expense	(20 000)	(5 000)

Profit for the year	80 000	10 000
Retained earnings (1/1/13)	103 000	40 000
	183 000	50 000
Transfer to general reserve*	(10 000)	(4 000)
Retained earnings (31/12/13)	$173 000	$ 46 000
Share capital	$445 000	$ 60 000
Retained earnings	173 000	46 000
General reserve	10 000	4 000
Asset revaluation surplus**	30 000	24 000
Liabilities	42 000	4 000
	$700 000	$138 000
Land	—	$ 20 000
Plant and machinery	$591 000	120 000
Accumulated depreciation	(20 000)	(25 000)
Inventory	15 000	23 000
Shares in Aquarius Ltd	114 000	—
	$700 000	$138 000

* This transfer was from equity existing at 1 January 2013.
** This reserve relates to certain items of plant. At 1/1/13, the balances of the
account were $15 000 for Cepheus Ltd and $20 000 for Aquarius Ltd.

Required

1. Prepare the consolidated financial statements for Cepheus Ltd at 31 December 2013.
2. Prepare the valuation and pre-acquisition entries at 31 December 2017, assuming that, on consolidation, business combination valuation reserves are transferred to retained earnings when the related asset is sold or fully consumed.

Exercise 24.15   **REVALUATION IN SUBSIDIARY'S RECORDS**

★★   On 1 July 2013, Cancer Ltd acquired all the shares of Grus Ltd (totalling $40 000) for a cash outlay of $100 000. At that date the other reserves and retained earnings of Grus Ltd were as follows:

General reserve	$30 000
Retained earnings	20 000

All identifiable assets and liabilities of Grus Ltd were recorded at fair value at 1 July 2013 except as follows:

	Carrying amount	Fair value
Land	$30 000	$34 000
Plant (cost $28 000)	20 000	22 000
Inventory	40 000	44 000

The plant has a further 5-year life. Of the inventory on hand at 1 July 2013, 90% was sold by 30 June 2014. Neither company had any recorded goodwill. The tax rate is 30%.

Required

1. Prepare the consolidation worksheet entries at 30 June 2014 assuming Grus Ltd revalued the land and plant to their fair values in its records at 1 July 2013.
2. Prepare the consolidation worksheet entries at 30 June 2014 assuming all business combination valuations are made in the consolidation worksheet.
3. If the balance of inventory was sold, what would be the business combination valuation and the pre-acquisition entries at 30 June 2015, assuming requirement 2 above?

4. If, during June 2015, Grus Ltd also transferred $6000 from general reserve (pre-acquisition) to retained earnings (earned before 1 July 2013), what would be the pre-acquisition entry at 30 June 2015?

Exercise 24.16 **BARGAIN PURCHASE, CONSOLIDATION WORKSHEET**

★★ The account balances of Antlia Ltd and Andromeda Ltd at 1 July 2016 were as follows:

	Antlia Ltd	Andromeda Ltd
Share capital — 600 000 shares	$ 600 000	—
— 200 000 shares	—	$200 000
General reserve	200 000	50 000
Asset revaluation surplus	150 000	40 000
Retained earnings	200 000	160 000
Dividend payable	10 000	15 000
Provisions	320 000	15 000
	1 480 000	480 000
Land	400 000	200 000
Machinery	500 000	250 000
Accumulated depreciation	(100 000)	(50 000)
Inventory	480 000	75 000
Cash	200 000	5 000
	$1 480 000	$480 000

The fair values of Andromeda Ltd's assets at 1 July 2016 were:

Land	$240 000
Machinery	220 000
Inventory	95 000

The two companies decided to combine on 1 July 2016 with Antlia Ltd issuing one share (fair value $2) and 50c cash for each share in Andromeda Ltd. Andromeda Ltd's shares were acquired cum div. The tax rate is 30%.

Required

1. Prepare the consolidated statement of financial position immediately after Antlia Ltd's acquisition of shares in Andromeda Ltd.
2. Prepare the consolidation worksheet entries required for the consolidation worksheet at 30 June 2017, assuming both dividends were paid during September 2016. Assume all inventory on hand at 1 July 2016 was sold in the following 3 months, and that the machinery has a further 4-year life.

Exercise 24.17 **CONSOLIDATION WORKSHEET AND RESERVE TRANSFER**

★★★

			Adjustments		
Financial statements	Triangulum Ltd	Cygnus Ltd	Dr	Cr	Consolidation
Profit	6 000	4 000			
Retained earnings (1/7/15)	22 000	18 000			
	28 000	22 000			
Transfer from general reserve	5 000	3 000			
Retained earnings (30/6/16)	33 000	25 000			

An extract from the consolidation worksheet of Triangulum Ltd and its subsidiary, Cygnus Ltd, as at 30 June 2016, is shown above. Triangulum Ltd acquired all the share capital (cum div.) of Cygnus Ltd on 1 July 2012 for $127 000 when the equity of Cygnus Ltd consisted of:

Share capital	$85 000
General reserve	18 000
Retained earnings	12 000

All the identifiable assets and liabilities of Cygnus Ltd at 1 July 2012 were recorded at fair value except for:

	Carrying amount	Fair value
Plant (cost $100 000)	$80 000	$82 000
Inventory	6 000	7 000

The plant had a further 5-year life. All the inventory was sold by Cygnus Ltd by 22 September 2012. The tax rate is 30%. The liabilities of Cygnus Ltd included a dividend payable of $6000. Cygnus Ltd had not recorded any goodwill. At 1 July 2012, Cygnus Ltd had incurred research and development outlays of $5000, which it had expensed. Triangulum Ltd placed a fair value of $2000 on this item. The project was still in progress at 30 June 2016, with Cygnus Ltd capitalising $3000 in the 2015–16 period. Valuation adjustments are made on consolidation.

The transfer from general reserve during the current period ending 30 June 2016 is from pre-acquisition reserves, and is the only such transfer since the acquisition date.

Required

1. Prepare the consolidation worksheet entries at 30 June 2016.
2. Complete the worksheet extract above.

Exercise 24.18	UNRECORDED LIABILITIES AND RESERVE TRANSFERS
★★★	On 1 July 2014, Delphinus Ltd acquired all the share capital of Telescopium Ltd when the equity of Telescopium Ltd consisted of:

100 000 ordinary shares issued at $1, paid to 75c each	$75 000
General reserve	15 000
Retained earnings	12 000

All identifiable assets and liabilities of both companies were recorded at fair value except:

	Carrying amount	Fair value
Inventory	$20 000	$25 000
Machinery (net)	80 000	95 000

The machinery has a further 5-year life. Of the inventory on hand at 1 July 2014, 90% was sold by 31 December 2014.

At 1 July 2014, Telescopium Ltd was involved in a court case with an entity that was claiming damages from it. Telescopium Ltd had not raised a liability in relation to any expected damages. Delphinus Ltd measured the fair value of the liability at $5000. By 31 December 2014, the expectation of winning the court case had improved, so the fair value was considered to be $1000.

The tax rate is 30%.

Valuation adjustments are made on consolidation.

On 1 November 2014, Telescopium Ltd transferred $6500 out of retained earnings in existence at 1 July 2014 to the general reserve account.

On 1 December 2014, Telescopium Ltd made a call of 25c per share, all call money being received by 20 December 2014.

At 31 December 2014, the statement of financial position of Delphinus Ltd showed shares in Telescopium Ltd at $147 250.

Required

Prepare the consolidation worksheet entries for the preparation of the consolidated financial statements for Delphinus Ltd and its subsidiary, Telescopium Ltd, as at 31 December 2014.

Exercise 24.19   **BARGAIN PURCHASE, CONSOLIDATION WORKSHEET**

★★★ The financial statements of Equuleus Ltd and its subsidiary, Fornax Ltd, at 30 June 2015 contained the following information:

	Equuleus Ltd	Fornax Ltd
Profit before tax	$ 3 200	$ 1 800
Income tax expense	(1 300)	(240)
Profit for the year	1 900	1 560
Retained earnings (1/7/14)	1 500	2 100
	3 400	3 660
Dividend paid	(500)	(0)
Retained earnings (30/6/15)	2 900	3 660
Share capital	25 000	10 000
General reserve	8 000	3 000
Other components of equity*	1 000	500
Liabilities	5 000	1 300
	$41 900	$18 460
Land	$ 8 600	$ 5 100
Plant	17 000	8 000
Accumulated depreciation	(5 000)	(1 000)
Financial assets	3 000	2 000
Inventory	3 000	4 000
Cash	300	360
Shares in Fornax Ltd	15 000	—
	$41 900	$18 460

* This relates to the financial assets. The balances of the accounts at 1/7/14 were $1500 (Equuleus Ltd) and $300 (Fornax Ltd).

Equuleus Ltd had acquired all the share capital of Fornax Ltd on 1 July 2013 for $15 000 when the equity of Fornax Ltd consisted of:

Share capital — 10 000 shares	$10 000
General reserve	2 000
Retained earnings	1 500

At the acquisition date by Equuleus Ltd, Fornax Ltd's non-monetary assets consisted of:

	Carrying amount	Fair value
Land	$4 000	$6 000
Plant (cost $6000)	5 500	6 500
Inventory	3 000	4 000

The plant had a further 5-year life. All the inventory was sold by 30 June 2014. All valuation adjustments to non-current assets are made on consolidation. The land was sold in January 2015 for $6000. The relevant business combination valuation reserves are transferred, on consolidation, to retained earnings.

The tax rate is 30%.

In September 2013, Fornax Ltd transferred $500 from its general reserve, earned before 1 July 2013, to retained earnings.

Required

Prepare the consolidated financial statements for the year ended 30 June 2015.

Exercise 24.20 **CONSOLIDATION WORKSHEET, UNRECOGNISED INTANGIBLES AND LIABILITIES**

★★★ Auriga Ltd gained control of Perseus Ltd by acquiring all its shares on 1 July 2013. The equity at that date was:

Share capital	$ 100 000
Retained earnings	35 000

At 1 July 2013, all the identifiable assets and liabilities of Perseus Ltd were recorded at fair value except for:

	Carrying amount	Fair value
Inventory	$ 18 000	$ 22 000
Land	120 000	130 000
Plant (cost $120 000)	95 000	98 000

The inventory was all sold by 30 June 2014. The plant had a further 5-year life but was sold on 1 January 2016 for $50 000. The land was sold in March 2014 for $150 000.

Where revalued assets are sold or fully consumed, any associated amounts in the business combination valuation reserve are transferred to retained earnings. At 1 July 2013, Perseus Ltd had guaranteed a loan taken out by Swede Ltd. Perseus Ltd had not raised a liability in relation to the guarantee but, as Swede Ltd was not performing well, Auriga Ltd valued the contingent liability at $5000. In January 2016, Swede Ltd repaid the loan. Perseus Ltd had also invented a special tool and patented the process. No asset was raised by Perseus Ltd, but Auriga Ltd valued the patent at $6000, with an expected useful life of 6 years. The tax rate is 30%.

Financial information for these companies for the year ended 30 June 2016 is as follows:

	Auriga Ltd	Perseus Ltd
Profit before tax	$ 50 000	$ 15 000
Income tax expense	(20 000)	(6 000)
Profit for the year	30 000	9 000
Other recognised income and expense:		
Gains on plant revaluation	6 000	0
Gains on financial assets	(4 000)	(10 000)
Comprehensive income for the year	$ 32 000	$ (1 000)
Profit	$ 30 000	$ 9 000
Retained earnings (1 July 2015)	37 000	45 000
	67 000	54 000
Dividend paid	(20 000)	—
Transfer to general reserve	—	(20 000)
	(20 000)	(20 000)
Retained earnings (30 June 2016)	$ 47 000	$ 34 000

(continued)

	Auriga Ltd	Perseus Ltd
Share capital	$150 000	$100 000
General reserve	12 000	20 000
Asset revaluation surplus	20 000	—
Retained earnings	47 000	34 000
Other components of equity	10 000	4 000
Total equity	239 000	158 000
Payables	19 000	8 000
Loan	25 000	—
Total liabilities	44 000	8 000
Total equity and liabilities	$283 000	$166 000
Cash	$ 5 000	$ 14 000
Financial assets	10 000	5 000
Inventory	30 000	21 000
Plant and equipment	140 000	163 000
Accumulated depreciation	(62 000)	(37 000)
Shares in Perseus Ltd	160 000	—
Total assets	$283 000	$166 000

The transfer to general reserve during the year ended 30 June 2016 was from profits earned before 1 July 2013.

Required

Prepare the consolidated financial statements for Auriga Ltd as at 30 June 2016. Your answer should include all consolidation adjustment journal entries and a consolidation worksheet.

25

Consolidation: intragroup transactions

ACCOUNTING STANDARDS IN FOCUS

IFRS 10 *Consolidated Financial Statements*

LEARNING OBJECTIVES

After studying this chapter, you should be able to:

1 explain the need for making adjustments for intragroup transactions

2 prepare worksheet entries for intragroup transactions involving profits and losses in beginning and ending inventory

3 prepare worksheet entries for intragroup transactions involving profits and losses on the transfer of property, plant and equipment in both the current and previous periods

4 prepare worksheet entries for intragroup transactions involving transfers from inventory to property, plant and equipment and from property, plant and equipment to inventory

5 prepare worksheet entries for intragroup services such as management fees

6 prepare worksheet entries for intragroup dividends

7 prepare worksheet entries for intragroup borrowings.

INTRODUCTION

In this chapter, the group under discussion is restricted to one where:
- there are only two entities within the group (i.e. one parent and one subsidiary)
- the parent owns all the shares of the subsidiary.
  Diagrammatically, then, the group is as shown in figure 25.1.

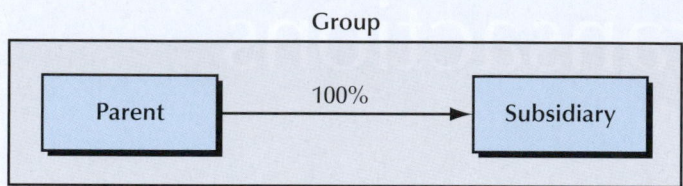

FIGURE 25.1 Group

In chapter 23, it is explained that the process of consolidation involves adding together the financial statements of a parent and its subsidiaries to reflect an overall view of the financial affairs of the group of entities as a single economic entity. It is also pointed out that two major adjustments are necessary to effect the process of consolidation:

(a) adjustments involving equity at the acquisition date, namely the business combination valuation entries (if any) and the pre-acquisition entry, eliminating the investment account in the parent's financial statements against the pre-acquisition equity of the subsidiary (see chapter 24)

(b) elimination of intragroup balances and the effects of transactions whereby profits or losses are made by different members of the group through trading with each other.

This chapter focuses on (b), adjustments for intragroup balances and transactions. The chapter analyses transactions involving inventory, depreciable assets, services, dividends and borrowings.

 ## 25.1 RATIONALE FOR ADJUSTING FOR INTRAGROUP TRANSACTIONS

Whenever related entities trade with each other, or borrow and lend money to each other, the separate legal entities disclose the effects of these transactions in the assets and liabilities recorded and the profits and losses reported. For example, if a subsidiary sells inventory to its parent, the subsidiary records a sale of inventory, including the profit on sale and reduction in inventory assets, and the parent records the purchase of inventory at the amount paid to the subsidiary. If, then, in preparing the consolidated financial statements, the separate financial statements of the legal entities are simply added together without any adjustments for the effects of the intragroup transactions, the consolidated financial statements include not only the results of the group transacting with external entities (i.e. entities outside the group) but also the results of transactions within the group. This conflicts with the purpose of the consolidated financial statements to provide information about the financial performance and financial position of the group as a result of its dealings with external entities. Hence, the effects of transactions within the group must be adjusted for in the preparation of the consolidated financial statements.

The requirement for the full adjustment for the effects of intragroup transactions is stated in paragraph B86(c) of IFRS 10 *Consolidated Financial Statements*:

> eliminate in full intragroup assets and liabilities, equity, income, expenses and cash flows relating to transactions between entities of the group (profits or losses resulting from intragroup transactions that are recognised in assets, such as inventory and fixed assets, are eliminated in full). Intragroup losses may indicate an impairment that requires recognition in the consolidated financial statements. IAS 12 *Income Taxes* applies to temporary differences that arise from the elimination of profits and losses resulting from intragroup transactions.

Besides adjusting for the effects of transactions occurring in the current period, it is also necessary to adjust the current period's consolidated financial statements for the ongoing effects of transactions in previous periods. Because the consolidation adjustment entries are applied in a worksheet only, and not in the accounts of either the parent or the subsidiary, any continuing effects of previous periods' transactions must be considered. This affects transactions such as loans between, say, a parent and a subsidiary where a balance owing at the end of a number of periods is reduced over time as repayments are made. Similarly, where assets such as inventory are transferred at the end of one period and then are still on hand at the beginning of the next period, consolidation adjustments are required to be made in both periods.

Some intragroup transactions do not affect the carrying amounts of assets and liabilities (e.g. where there is a management fee paid by one entity to another within the group). In that case, the items affected are fee revenue and fee expense. However, in other circumstances, there are assets and liabilities recognised by the group at amounts different from the amounts recognised by the individual legal entities. For example, consider the situation where a subsidiary sold an item of inventory to the parent for $1000, and the inventory had cost the subsidiary $800. The parent recognises the inventory at cost of $1000, whereas the cost of the inventory to the group is only $800. As is explained in more detail later in this chapter, consolidation adjustment entries are necessary to adjust for both the profit on the intragroup transaction and the carrying amount of the inventory.

Under IAS 12 *Income Taxes*, deferred tax accounts must be raised where there are temporary differences between the carrying amount of an asset or liability and its tax base. Any difference between the carrying amount of an asset or a liability and its tax base in a legal entity within the group is accounted for by the legal entity. However, on consolidation, in relation to intragroup transactions, adjustments may be made to the carrying amounts of assets and liabilities. Hence, in adjusting for intragroup transactions wherever there are changes to the carrying amounts of assets and liabilities, any associated tax effect must be considered. Paragraph B86(c) of IFRS 10 recognises the need to apply tax-effect accounting for temporary differences arising from the elimination of profits and losses from intragroup transactions.

For example, assume an asset is recorded by a subsidiary at a carrying amount of $1000, and that the tax base is $800. In the records of the subsidiary, the application of tax-effect accounting will account for the temporary difference of $200, raising a deferred tax liability of $60, assuming a tax rate of 30%. If, on consolidation, an adjustment is made to reduce the carrying amount of the asset, say to $950, the consolidation adjustment entries must include an adjustment for the tax effect of the change in the carrying amount of the asset, namely a reduction in the deferred tax liability of $15 (i.e. 30% × $50). The consolidated financial statements then show a deferred tax liability of $45 (i.e. $60 − $15). The combination of the tax-effect entries in the subsidiaries and the tax-effect adjustments on consolidation will account for the temporary difference caused by the group showing the asset at $950 and the tax base being $800, namely a deferred tax liability of $45 (i.e. 30% ($950 − $800)).

As can be seen in this example, in preparing the consolidation adjustments it is unnecessary to consider the tax-effect entries made in the individual entities in the group. If the appropriate tax-effect adjustments are made for changes in the carrying amounts of the assets, then the combination of those adjustments and the tax-effect entries made in the entities themselves will produce the correct answer.

In this book, it is assumed that each subsidiary is a tax-paying entity. Under the tax consolidation system in some countries, groups comprising a parent and its wholly owned subsidiaries can elect to consolidate and be treated as a single entity for tax purposes. Such entities prepare a consolidated tax return, and the effects of intragroup transactions are eliminated. Under such a scheme, the tax-effect adjustments demonstrated in this chapter would not apply.

Just as the pre-acquisition entry is used in a consolidation worksheet to eliminate the investment and to adjust for pre-acquisition equity, adjustment journal entries are prepared for intragroup transactions and are recorded in the consolidation worksheet. The same two adjustment columns are used to effect these adjustments. For example, if it were necessary to adjust downwards by $10 000 the sales revenue recorded by the legal entities, the consolidation worksheet would show the following line:

| | Parent | Subsidiary | Adjustments | | | Group |
			Dr	Cr		
Sales revenue	100 000	80 000	10 000			170 000

In the following sections of this chapter, three types of intragroup transactions are discussed — transfers of inventory; transfers of property, plant and equipment; and intragroup services. In each of the specific sections covering these transactions, the process of determining when profits are realised for the different types of transactions is discussed.

LO2 · 25.2 TRANSFERS OF INVENTORY

In the following examples, assume that Jessica Ltd owns all the share capital of Amelie Ltd, and that the consolidation process is being carried out on 30 June 2013, for the year ending on that date. Assume also a tax rate of 30%. All entries shown as being for the individual entities assume the use of a perpetual inventory system, and adjustments will be made, where necessary, to cost of sales.

25.2.1 Sales of inventory

Example: Intragroup sales of inventory

On 1 January 2013, Jessica Ltd acquired $10 000 worth of inventory for cash from Amelie Ltd. The inventory had previously cost Amelie Ltd $8000.

In the accounting records of Amelie Ltd, the following journal entries are made on 1 January 2013:

Cash	Dr	10 000	
Sales Revenue	Cr		10 000
Cost of Sales	Dr	8 000	
Inventory	Cr		8 000

In Jessica Ltd, the journal entry is:

Inventory	Dr	10 000	
Cash	Cr		10 000

From the viewpoint of the group in relation to this transaction, no sales of inventory were made to any party outside the group, nor has the group acquired any inventory from external entities. Hence, if the financial statements of Jessica Ltd and Amelie Ltd are simply added together for consolidation purposes, 'sales', 'cost of sales' and 'inventory' will need to be adjusted on consolidation as the consolidated financial statements must show only the results of transactions with entities external to the group.

25.2.2 Realisation of profits or losses

Paragraph B86(c) of IFRS 10 states that the profits and losses resulting from intragroup transactions that require consolidation adjustments to be made are those 'recognised in assets'. These profits can be described as 'unrealised profits'. The test for realisation is the involvement of an external party in relation to the item involved in the intragroup transaction. If an item of inventory is transferred from a subsidiary to the parent entity (or vice versa), no external party is involved in that transaction. The profit made by the subsidiary is unrealised to the group. If the parent then sells that inventory item to a party external to the group, the intragroup profit becomes realised to the group. For example, assume a subsidiary, Amelie Ltd, sells inventory to its parent, Jessica Ltd, for $100, and that inventory cost Amelie Ltd $90. The profit on this transaction is unrealised. If Jessica Ltd sells the inventory to an external party for $100, the intragroup profit is realised. The group sold inventory that cost the group $90 to an external party for $100. The group has made $10 profit. Hence, the consolidation adjustments for profits on intragroup transfers of inventory depend on whether the acquiring entity has sold the inventory to entities outside the group. In other words, the adjustments depend on whether the acquiring entity still carries some or all of the transferred inventory as ending inventory at the end of the financial period.

25.2.3 Profits in ending inventory

The following example uses the information in the example in section 25.2.1 and provides information about whether the inventory transferred is still on hand at the end of the financial period.

Example: Transferred inventory still on hand

On 30 June 2013, all the inventory sold by Amelie Ltd to Jessica Ltd is still on hand. The adjustment entries in the consolidation worksheet at 30 June 2013 are:

Sales Revenue	Dr	10 000
Cost of Sales	Cr	8 000
Inventory	Cr	2 000

The sales adjustment is necessary to eliminate the effects of the original sale in the current period. Amelie Ltd recorded sales of $10 000. From the group's viewpoint, as no external party was involved in the transaction, no sales should be shown in the consolidated financial statements. To adjust sales revenue downwards, a debit adjustment is necessary. The effect of this adjustment on the consolidation process is seen in figure 25.2. Hence, an adjustment is necessary to eliminate the sales recorded by Amelie Ltd.

Using similar reasoning as with the adjustment for sales revenue, the subsidiary has recorded cost of sales of $8000, but the group has made no sales to entities external to the group. Hence, the consolidation worksheet needs to have a reduction in cost of sales of $8000 in order to show a zero amount in the consolidation column. Note also that adjusting sales by $10 000 and cost of sales by $8000 effectively reduces consolidated profit by $2000. In other words, the $2000 profit recorded by Amelie Ltd on selling inventory to Jessica Ltd is eliminated and a zero profit is shown on consolidation. As no external party was involved in the transfer of inventory, the whole of the profit on the intragroup transaction is unrealised. This is illustrated in figure 25.2.

	Parent	Subsidiary		Adjustments Dr	Cr		Group
Sales revenue	0	10 000	1	10 000			—
Cost of sales	0	8 000			8 000	1	—
		2 000					
Tax expense	0	600			600	2	—
Profit		1 400					—
Inventory	10 000	—			2 000	1	8 000
Deferred tax asset	—	—	2	600			600

FIGURE 25.2 Extract from consolidation worksheet — profit in closing inventory

The previous explanation dealing with the effect on profit covers only the statement of profit or loss and other comprehensive income part of the adjustment. Under the historical cost system, assets in the consolidated statement of financial position must be shown at cost to the group. Inventory is recorded in Jessica Ltd at $10 000, the cost to Jessica Ltd. The cost to the group is, however, $8000, the amount that was paid for the inventory by Amelie Ltd to entities external to the group. Hence, if inventory is to be reported at $8000 in the consolidated financial statements, and it is recorded in Jessica Ltd's records at $10 000, a credit adjustment of $2000 is needed to reduce the inventory to $8000, the cost to the group. This effect is seen in figure 25.2.

Jessica Ltd has recorded the inventory in its records at $10 000. This amount is probably also its tax base. However, as explained in section 25.1, any difference between the tax base and the carrying amount in Jessica Ltd is accounted for in the tax-effect entries in Jessica Ltd. On consolidation, a tax-effect entry is necessary where an adjustment entry causes a difference between the carrying amount of an asset or a liability in the records of the legal entity and the carrying amount shown in the consolidated financial statements. In the adjustment entry relating to profit in ending inventory in the above example, the carrying amount of inventory is reduced downwards by $2000. The carrying amount and tax base of the inventory in Jessica Ltd is $10 000, but the carrying amount in the group is $8000. This $2000 difference is a deductible temporary difference giving rise to a deferred tax asset of $600 (i.e. 30% × $2000), as well as a corresponding decrease in income tax expense. The appropriate consolidation worksheet adjustment entry is:

Deferred Tax Asset	Dr	600
Income Tax Expense	Cr	600

The effects of this entry are shown in figure 25.2.

The deferred tax asset recognises that the group is expected to earn profits in the future that will not require the payment of tax to the Taxation Office. When the inventory is sold by Jessica Ltd in a future period, this temporary difference is reversed. To illustrate this effect, assume that in the following period Jessica Ltd sells this inventory to an external entity for $11 000. Jessica Ltd will record a before-tax profit of $1000 (i.e. $11 000 – $10 000) and an associated tax expense of $300. From the consolidated group position, the profit on sale is $3000 (i.e. $11 000 – $8000). The group will show current tax payable of $300, reverse the $600 deferred tax asset, and recognise an income tax expense of $900. These effects are further illustrated below.

Example: Transferred inventories partly sold

On 1 January 2013, Jessica Ltd acquired $10 000 worth of inventory for cash from Amelie Ltd. The inventory had previously cost Amelie Ltd $8000. By the end of the year, 30 June 2013, Jessica Ltd had sold $7500 of the transferred inventory for $14 000 to external entities. Thus, $2500 of the inventory is on hand in Jessica Ltd at 30 June 2013.

The adjustment entry for the preparation of consolidated financial statements at 30 June 2013 is:

Sales	Dr	10 000	
Cost of Sales	Cr		9 500
Inventory	Cr		500

The total sales recorded by the *legal entities* are $24 000; that is, $10 000 by Amelie Ltd and $14 000 by Jessica Ltd. The sales by the *group*, being those sold to entities external to the group, are $14 000. The consolidation adjustment to sales revenue is then $10 000, being the amount necessary to eliminate the sales within the group.

The total cost of sales recorded by the *legal entities* is $15 500; that is, $8000 by Amelie Ltd and $7500 by Jessica Ltd (i.e. 75% × $10 000). The cost of sales to the *group*, being those to entities external to the group, is $6000 (i.e. 75% × $8000). Hence, the consolidation adjustment is $9500; that is, $15 500 (sum of recorded sales) less $6000 (group). The adjustment is that necessary to adjust the sum of the amounts recorded by the legal entities to that to be recognised by the group.

Note that the combined adjustments to sales and cost of sales result in a $500 reduction in before-tax profit. Of the $2000 intragroup profit on the transfer of inventory from Amelie Ltd to Jessica Ltd, since three-quarters of the inventory has been sold by Jessica Ltd to an external party, $1500 of the profit is realised to the group and only $500, the profit remaining in ending inventory, is unrealised. It is the unrealised profit that is adjusted for in the worksheet entry.

The group profit is then $500 less than that recorded by the legal entities. The sum of profits recorded by the legal entities is $8500, consisting of $2000 recorded by Amelie Ltd and $6500 (being sales of $14 000 less cost of sales of $7500) recorded by Jessica Ltd. From the group's viewpoint, profit on sale of inventory to external entities is only $8000, consisting of sales of $14 000 less cost of sales of $6000 (being 75% of original cost of $8000). Hence, an adjustment of $500 is necessary to reduce recorded profit of $8500 to group profit of $8000.

The $500 adjustment to inventory reflects the proportion of the total profit on sale of the transferred inventory that remains in the inventory on hand at the end of the period. Since 25% of the transferred inventory is still on hand at the end of the period, then 25% of the total profit on transfer of inventory (i.e. 25% × $2000) needs to be adjusted at the end of the period. The adjustment entry reduces the inventory on hand at 30 June 2013 from the recorded cost to Jessica Ltd of $2500 to the group cost of $2000 (being 25% of the original cost of $8000).

The adjustments above have been determined by comparing the combined amounts recorded by the parent and the subsidiary with the amounts that the group wants to report in the consolidated financial statements. This process could be shown in the form of a table, as follows:

	Parent	Subsidiary	Total Recorded	Group	Adjustment
Sales	14 000	10 000	24 000	14 000	Dr 10 000
Cost of sales	(7 500)	(8 000)	(15 500)	(6 000)	Cr 9 500
Profit	6 500	2 000	8 500	8 000	
Inventory	2 500	0	2 500	2 000	Cr $500

Consider the *tax effect* of this adjustment. The carrying amount of the inventory is reduced by $500, reflecting the fact that the carrying amount to the group is $500 less than the carrying amount in Jessica Ltd. This gives rise to a deductible temporary difference of $500. Hence, a deferred tax asset of $150 (i.e. 30% × $500) must be raised on consolidation with a corresponding effect on income tax expense. The expectation of the group is that, in some future period, it will recognise the remaining $500 profit in transferred inventory when it sells the inventory to an external party, but will not have to pay tax on the $500 as Amelie Ltd has already paid the relevant tax. This expected tax saving to the group will be shown in the consolidated financial statements by a debit adjustment of $150 to the Deferred Tax Asset account.

The tax-effect adjustment entry is then:

Deferred Tax Asset	Dr	150	
Income Tax Expense	Cr		150

Example: Transferred inventory completely sold

On 1 January 2013, Jessica Ltd acquired $10 000 worth of inventory for cash from Amelie Ltd. The inventory had previously cost Amelie Ltd $8000. By the end of the year, 30 June 2013, Jessica Ltd had sold all the transferred inventory to an external party for $18 000.

Amelie Ltd records a profit of $ 2 000 (i.e. $10 000 – $8000)
Jessica Ltd records a profit of $ 8 000 (i.e. $18 000 – $10 000)
Total recorded profit is $10 000

Profit to the group = Selling price to external entities less cost to the group
= $18 000 – $8000
= $10 000

Since the recorded profit equals the profit to the group, there is no need for a profit adjustment on consolidation. Further, as there is no transferred inventory still on hand, there is no need for an adjustment to inventory. Because all the inventory has been sold to an external entity, the whole of the intragroup profit is realised to the group. Note, however, that an adjustment for the sales and cost of sales is still necessary. As noted previously, the sales within the group amount to $18 000 whereas the sales recorded by the legal entities total $28 000 (i.e. $10 000 + $18 000). Hence, sales must be reduced by $10 000. The total recorded cost of sales is $18 000, being $8000 by Amelie Ltd and $10 000 by Jessica Ltd. The group's cost of sales is the original cost of the transferred inventory, $8000. Hence, cost of sales is reduced by $10 000 on consolidation. The adjustment entry is then:

Sales	Dr	10 000	
Cost of Sales	Cr		10 000

Since there is no adjustment to the carrying amounts of assets or liabilities, there is no need for any *tax-effect* adjustment.

Where inventory is transferred in the current period and some or all of that inventory is still on hand at the end of the period, the general form of the worksheet entries is:

Sales Revenue	Dr	xxx	
Cost of Sales	Cr		xxx
Inventory	Cr		xxx
(The adjustment to inventory is based on the profit remaining in inventory on hand at the end of the period)			
Deferred Tax Asset	Dr	xxx	
Income Tax Expense	Cr		xxx
(The tax rate times the adjustment to ending inventory)			

25.2.4 Profits in opening inventory

Any transferred inventory remaining unsold at the end of one period is still on hand at the beginning of the next period. Because the consolidation adjustments are made only in a worksheet and not in the records of any of the legal entities, any differences in balances between the legal entities and the consolidated group at the end of one period must still exist at the beginning of the next period.

Example: Transferred inventory on hand at the beginning of the period

On 1 July 2012, the first day of the current period, Amelie Ltd has on hand inventory worth $7000, transferred from Jessica Ltd in June 2012. The inventory had previously cost Jessica Ltd $4500. The tax rate is 30%. In this example, in the preparation of the consolidated financial statements at *30 June 2012* the following adjustment entries for the $2500 profit in ending inventory would have been made in the consolidation worksheet:

Sales	Dr	7 000	
Cost of Sales	Cr		4 500
Inventory	Cr		2 500
Deferred Tax Asset	Dr	750	
Income Tax Expense	Cr		750
(30% × $2500)			

Since the ending inventory at 30 June 2012 becomes the beginning inventory for the next year, an adjustment is necessary in the consolidated financial statements prepared at 30 June 2013. The required adjustment is:

Retained Earnings (1/7/12)	Dr	2 500	
Cost of Sales	Cr		2 500

In making this consolidation worksheet adjustment, it is assumed that the inventory is sold to external entities in the current period. If this is not the case, then the adjustment to inventory as made at 30 June 2012 will need to be made again in preparing the consolidated financial statements at 30 June 2013.

In making a *credit adjustment* of $2500, cost of sales is reduced. The cost of sales recorded by Amelie Ltd in the 2012–13 period is $2500 greater than that which the group wants to show, because the cost of sales recorded by Jessica Ltd is $7000, whereas the cost of sales to the group is only $4500. A reduction in cost of sales means an increase in profit. Hence, in the 2012–13 period, the group's profit is greater than the sum of the legal entities' profit.

The *debit adjustment* to the opening balance of retained earnings reduces that balance; that is, the group made less profit in previous years than the sum of the retained earnings recorded by the legal entities. This is because, in June 2012, Jessica Ltd recorded a $2500 profit on the sale of inventory to Amelie Ltd, this profit not being recognised by the group until the 2012–13 period.

Consider the *tax effect* of these entries. If the previous period's tax-effect adjustment were carried forward into this year's worksheet it would be:

Deferred Tax Asset	Dr	750	
Retained Earnings (1/7/12)	Cr		750

On sale of the inventory in the 2012–13 period, the deferred tax asset is reversed, with a resultant effect on income tax expense:

Income Tax Expense	Dr	750	
Deferred Tax Asset	Cr		750

On combining these two entries, the worksheet entry required is:

Income Tax Expense	Dr	750	
Retained Earnings (1/7/12)	Cr		750

In summary, the adjustment to cost of sales, retained earnings and income tax expense can be combined into one entry as follows:

Retained Earnings (1/7/12)	Dr	1 750	
Income Tax Expense	Dr	750	
Cost of Sales	Cr		2 500

Note that this entry has no effect on the closing balance of retained earnings at 30 June 2013. As the inventory has been sold outside the group, the whole of the profit on the intragroup transaction is realised to the group. There is no unrealised profit to be adjusted for at the end of the period.

Where inventory was transferred in a previous period and some or all of that inventory is still on hand at the beginning of the current period, the general form of the entries is:

Retained Earnings (opening balance)	Dr	xxx	
Cost of Sales	Cr		xxx
Income Tax Expense	Dr	xxx	
Retained Earnings (opening balance)	Cr		xxx

It can be seen that the consolidation worksheet entries for inventory transferred within the current period are different from those where the inventory was transferred in a previous period. *Before preparing the adjustment entries, it is essential to determine the timing of the transaction.*

ILLUSTRATIVE EXAMPLE 25.1 Intragroup transactions involving transfers of inventory

Leah Ltd acquired all the issued shares of Sophia Ltd on 1 January 2012. The following transactions occurred between the two entities:
1. On 1 June 2013, Leah Ltd sold inventory to Sophia Ltd for $12 000, this inventory previously costing Leah Ltd $10 000. By 30 June 2013, Sophia Ltd had onsold 20% of this inventory to other entities for $3000. The other 80% was all sold to external entities by 30 June 2014 for $13 000.
2. During the 2013–14 period, Sophia Ltd sold inventory to Leah Ltd for $6000, this being at cost plus 20% mark-up. Of this inventory, $1200 remained on hand in Leah Ltd at 30 June 2014.
The tax rate is 30%.

Required

Prepare the consolidation worksheet entries for Leah Ltd at 30 June 2014 in relation to the intragroup transfers of inventory.

Solution

(1) *Sale of inventory in previous period*

Retained Earnings (1/7/13)	Dr	1 120	
Income Tax Expense	Dr	480	
Cost of Sales	Cr		1 600

Working:
– this is a prior period transaction
– profit after tax remaining in inventory at 1/7/13 is $1120 (= 80% × $2000 (1 – 30%))
– cost of sales recorded by Sophia Ltd is $9600 (= 80% × $12 000); cost of sales to the group is $8000 (= 80% × $10 000). The adjustment is then $1600.

(2) *Sale of inventory in current period*

Sales	Dr	6 000	
Cost of Sales	Cr		5 800
Inventory	Cr		200
Deferred Tax Asset	Dr	60	
Income Tax Expense	Cr		60

Working:
- this is a current period transaction
- sales within the group are $6000
- cost of sales recorded by the members of the group are $5000 for Sophia Ltd and $4800 (= 4/5 × $6000) for Leah Ltd; a total of $9800. Cost of sales for the group is $4000 (= 4/5 × $5000). The adjustment is then $5800
- the inventory remaining at 30 June 2014 is recorded by Leah Ltd at $1200. The cost to the group is $1000 (= 1/5 × $5000). The adjustment to inventory is then $200
- as the inventory is adjusted by $200, the tax effect is $60 (= 30% × $200).

 LO3   ## 25.3   TRANSFERS OF PROPERTY, PLANT AND EQUIPMENT

Besides transferring inventory, it is possible for property, plant and equipment to be transferred within the group. The worksheet adjustment entries are shown in two parts: (1) the entries to adjust for any profit or loss on sale of the assets, and (2) the entries relating to any depreciation of the assets after sale. As realisation of the profit or loss on sale is related to the depreciation of the transferred asset, the depreciation entries are covered in section 25.3.2 in conjunction with the discussion on realisation. If a non-depreciable asset is transferred, only the first of these entries is required, and realisation of the profit or loss occurs, as with inventory, on sale of the asset to an external party.

25.3.1   Sales of property, plant and equipment

Example: Transfer in current year

Jessica Ltd sold Amelie Ltd plant for $18 500 cash on 1 July 2012. It had cost Jessica Ltd $20 000 when acquired one year previously. Depreciation charged on plant by Jessica Ltd is 10% p.a. on cost, and Amelie Ltd applies a rate of 6% p.a. on cost. The income tax rate is 30%.

The journal entries in the records of Jessica Ltd and Amelie Ltd at the date of sale, 1 July 2012, are:

Jessica Ltd			
Cash	Dr	18 500	
Proceeds from Sale of Plant	Cr		18 500
Carrying Amount of Plant Sold	Dr	18 000	
Accumulated Depreciation	Dr	2 000	
Plant	Cr		20 000
Amelie Ltd			
Plant	Dr	18 500	
Cash	Cr		18 500

The consolidation adjustment entry is:

Proceeds from Sale of Plant	Dr	18 500	
Carrying Amount of Plant Sold	Cr		18 000
Plant	Cr		500

From the group's viewpoint, there is no sale of plant to entities external to the group. Since the legal entity Jessica Ltd recorded such a sale, the consolidation adjustment involves eliminating the effects of the sale. The adjustment entry includes a debit to revenue and a credit to the expense account, Carrying Amount of Plant Sold, to eliminate the effect of these accounts raised by Jessica Ltd. As a result of the sale, the plant is recorded by Amelie Ltd at cost of $18 500. From the group's perspective, the cost of the asset at the time of transfer within the group is the carrying amount in the records of the selling company, Jessica Ltd (i.e. $18 000). So that the asset is reported in the consolidated financial statements at cost to the group, an adjustment entry reducing the asset from a recorded amount of $18 500 to the group's cost of $18 000 is necessary. Hence, a credit to the asset of $500 is required.

Under international accounting standards, there is no requirement to separately disclose the income on sale of property, plant and equipment, nor the carrying amounts of assets sold. Some entities may disclose on a net basis a gain or loss on sale of property, plant and equipment. In the above example, there is a gain on sale to Jessica Ltd of $500. If Jessica Ltd had recorded a gain on sale of plant, the consolidation adjustment entry would be:

| Gain on Sale of Plant | Dr | 500 | |
| Plant | Cr | | 500 |

In the consolidated statement of profit or loss and other comprehensive income, it is the gain or loss on sale of plant that is reported.

The consolidation adjustment reduces plant by $500. As with inventory, any adjustment on consolidation to the carrying amount of an asset provides a difference between the carrying amount and the tax base of the asset. Hence, there is a deductible temporary difference in relation to the plant. It is then necessary to recognise a deferred tax asset and an adjustment to income tax expense equal to the tax rate times the temporary difference, namely 30% × $500 = $150. The consolidation worksheet adjustment entry is:

Deferred Tax Asset	Dr	150	
Income Tax Expense	Cr		150
(30% × $500)			

A deferred tax asset is recognised because there is a reduction in the carrying amount of the asset. This may in fact be a reduction in a deferred tax liability raised by the legal entity if for some reason the carrying amount of the asset in the legal entity is greater than the asset's tax base. Because deferred tax assets and liabilities are netted off for disclosure purposes, a problem as to whether the adjustment is reducing a deferred tax liability or increasing a deferred tax asset is not important.

As long as the depreciable asset remains within the group, an adjustment entry is necessary to reduce Jessica Ltd's recorded prior-period profits and to reduce the cost of the asset as recorded by Amelie Ltd. The adjustment entry in years after the year of sale of the asset is:

| Retained Earnings (opening balance) | Dr | 500 | |
| Plant | Cr | | 500 |

In periods after the year of sale, as long as the asset remains on hand, the tax-effect entry is:

| Deferred Tax Asset | Dr | 150 | |
| Retained Earnings (opening balance) | Cr | | 150 |

In summary, in the *year of transfer*, the general form of the consolidation worksheet entries is:

Proceeds on Sale	Dr	xxx	
Carrying Amount of Asset Sold	Cr		xxx
Property, Plant and Equipment	Cr		xxx
Deferred Tax Asset	Dr	xxx	
Income Tax Expense	Cr		xxx

In *years after the transfer*, the entries become:

Retained Earnings (opening balance)	Dr	xxx	
Property, Plant and Equipment	Cr		xxx
Deferred Tax Asset	Dr	xxx	
Retained Earnings (opening balance)	Cr		xxx

If a *loss* is made on transfer of property, plant and equipment, consolidation adjustments are needed to eliminate the loss in the year of transfer and bring the asset back to cost to the group. The tax-effect worksheet entry then recognises a deferred tax liability. The pro forma consolidation entries are:

Property, Plant and Equipment	Dr	xxx	
Proceeds on Sale	Dr	xxx	
Carrying Amount of Asset Sold	Cr		xxx
Income Tax Expense	Dr	xxx	
Deferred Tax Liability	Cr		xxx

In years after the transfer, the entries become:

Property, Plant and Equipment	Dr	xxx	
Retained Earnings (opening balance)	Cr		xxx
Retained Earnings (opening balance)	Dr	xxx	
Deferred Tax Liability	Cr		xxx

Paragraph B86(c) of IFRS 10 notes that intragroup losses may indicate an impairment. In that case, an impairment loss and related accumulated impairment loss would be recognised in the consolidation worksheet.

25.3.2 Depreciation and realisation of profits or losses

Realisation of profits or losses on depreciable asset transfers

For intragroup transactions such as inventory transfers or sale of land, the determination of whether the profit on the intragroup sale is realised is simple. The profit is realised when the buying entity, say the parent, sells the transferred inventory or land to an external party. However, where transactions occur involving depreciable assets, no external party ever becomes *directly* involved in these transactions, as the transferred item remains within the group. Hence, either the profits or losses on transfer of these items are to be regarded as never being realised, or some assumption is made about the point of realisation. The former course of action is impractical because adjustments for the profit would have to be made for every year in the life of the group after the transaction occurred. In practice, the second course of action is followed.

The realisation of the profit or loss on a depreciable asset transferred within the group is *assumed* to occur when the future benefits embodied in the asset are consumed by the group. In other words, the depreciable asset transferred within the group will never be sold to an external party, but will be used up within the group to generate benefits for the group. As the asset is used up within the group, the benefits are received by the group. A useful measure of the pattern of benefits received by the group can be obtained by reference to the depreciation charged on the asset, since the depreciation allocation is related to the pattern of benefits from the use of the assets. Hence, for depreciable assets, the involvement of external entities in the transaction occurs on an indirect basis with the assumption being made that realisation occurs in a pattern consistent with the allocation of the depreciation of the non-current asset.

Assume a subsidiary sells a depreciable asset to the parent at a profit of $100, and the parent depreciates the asset on a straight-line basis of 10% p.a. On the date of sale, the unrealised profit is $100. In the first year after the sale, $10 (i.e. 10% × $100) of that profit is realised, leaving $90 unrealised profit at the end of the year. In that year the group shows $90 less profit than the sum of the profits of the parent and the subsidiary. In the second year, the group realises a further $10 profit, and shows $10 more profit than the sum of the profits of the parent and the subsidiary. The process of realisation occurs via the adjustments for the depreciation of the asset subsequent to the point of sale, and is explained in the following section on depreciation.

Depreciation

In the previous example, plant was transferred from Jessica Ltd to Amelie Ltd for $18 500 at a before-tax gain of $500. Since the asset is transferred at the beginning of the current period, Amelie Ltd uses the asset and charges depreciation at 6% p.a. on a straight-line basis. The adjustment for depreciation at the end of the first year after the sale is determined by comparing the depreciation charge on the cost to the legal entity with the depreciation charge on the cost to the group:

Amelie Ltd:	Cost of asset	= $18 500
	Depreciation expense	= 6% × $18 500
		= $1110
Group:	Cost of asset	= $18 000
	Depreciation expense	= 6% × $18 000
		= $1080
	Adjustment	= $1110 − $1080
		= $30

On consolidation, depreciation is reduced by $30. The worksheet entry is:

Accumulated Depreciation	Dr	30	
Depreciation Expense	Cr		30

This adjustment increases the group's profit by $30; that is, the group has realised $30 of the $500 profit on sale of the plant. The adjustment for the gain on sale reduces the group's profit by $500, and the adjustment for depreciation results in recognising some of that profit being realised as the asset is used up. The amount of profit realised is in proportion to the depreciation charged, namely 6% p.a.

In determining whether the depreciation rate used should be Jessica Ltd's or Amelie Ltd's, remember that Jessica Ltd sold the asset to Amelie Ltd. The purpose of making the consolidation adjustments is not to show the financial statements as they would have been if the transaction had not occurred, but to eliminate the effects of the intragroup transactions. Within the group, the plant has been transferred from one place of use to another, namely from Jessica Ltd to Amelie Ltd. As a result, the plant is subject to the wear and tear, life expectations and so on associated with Amelie Ltd's assets rather than Jessica Ltd's assets. Hence, the appropriate depreciation rate for consolidation purposes is that of the entity in which the asset is used.

The difference between the carrying amount in the legal entity and that in the group at date of sale was $500 (i.e. $18 500 − $18 000). At the end of the first year after sale, the difference is $470 (i.e. by adjusting for 6% depreciation, 94% × $18 500 − 94% × $18 000). The reduction in the carrying amount difference is $30, giving rise to a reversal of the initial temporary difference of $9 (i.e. 30% × $30). The worksheet adjustment entry for the tax effect of the depreciation adjustment is:

Income Tax Expense	Dr	9	
Deferred Tax Asset	Cr		9

The tax-effect adjustment is calculated as the tax rate times the adjustment to depreciation (i.e. 30% × $30). This depreciation adjustment causes the carrying amount to change each period, thus reducing the temporary difference created on the initial transfer of the asset. The net effect of the depreciation and the tax-effect adjustment on the profit of the group is an increase of $21 (i.e. $30 − $9). The $350 after-tax profit on the sale of the plant is being realised at $21 (i.e. 6% × $350) p.a.

While the asset remains on hand, depreciation will be charged. Hence, when preparing the consolidated financial statements for the period 2013–14, the adjustment for depreciation must reflect the effects of the differences in depreciation for both the current year and the previous year. The adjustment relating to the previous period's depreciation is made against retained earnings (opening balance). The adjustment at 30 June 2014 is:

Accumulated Depreciation	Dr	60	
Depreciation Expense	Cr		30
Retained Earnings (1/7/13)	Cr		30

In this worksheet entry, both the current period's and the previous period's accounting profit is increased by the reduction in depreciation expense. From a tax-effect accounting perspective, there must be an increase in income tax expense both for the current period and for the previous period. Reversal of the deferred tax asset raised in relation to the gain on sale occurs throughout the life of the asset as it is depreciated, causing its carrying amount to fall. The consolidation adjustment entry at 30 June 2014 for the tax effect of the depreciation adjustment entry is:

Retained Earnings (1/7/13)	Dr	9	
Income Tax Expense	Dr	9	
Deferred Tax Asset	Cr		18

It can be seen that over the expected life of the asset, as it is depreciated the deferred tax asset raised on the intragroup sale of the asset is progressively being reversed.

In relation to the realisation of the profit on sale, the unrealised after-tax profit on the sale of the plant is $350 (i.e. $500 × (1 − 0.3)). The profit is being realised at $21 (i.e. $30 − $9) p.a. At the end of the second year after the sale, a total of $42 is realised, $21 in the previous year and $21 in the current year. When the asset is fully depreciated, the whole of the profit on sale is realised.

In the *year of transfer*, the general form of consolidation entries for depreciation of a transferred asset is:

Accumulated Depreciation	Dr	xxx	
Depreciation Expense	Cr		xxx
Income Tax Expense	Dr	xxx	
Deferred Tax Asset	Cr		xxx

In the *years after the transfer*, the entries are:

Accumulated Depreciation	Dr	xxx	
Depreciation Expense	Cr		xxx
Retained Earnings (opening balance)	Cr		xxx
Income Tax Expense	Dr	xxx	
Retained Earnings (opening balance)	Dr	xxx	
Deferred Tax Asset	Cr		xxx

Note that, if a loss were made on the transfer, these entries would be reversed and the tax-effect entry would reduce the deferred tax liability created as a result of the loss on transfer. Again, intragroup losses may indicate an impairment loss that requires recognition on consolidation.

 LO4 ## 25.4 TRANSFERS BETWEEN INVENTORY AND NON-CURRENT ASSETS

It is possible that an item which is regarded by one entity within the group as inventory is classified as a non-current asset by another entity. The key to determining the appropriate adjustment entries in these cases is to prepare the journal entries for the intragroup transaction in the records of the entities involved.

25.4.1 Transfers from inventory to property, plant and equipment

In this section, the situation analysed is where the selling entity regards the transferred item as inventory and the acquiring entity classifies it as a depreciable asset.

Example: Transfer from inventory to plant

Amelie Ltd sells to Jessica Ltd an item of inventory on 1 January 2013 (i.e. halfway through the current accounting period) for $6000 cash. The item cost Amelie Ltd $3000 earlier in the current year. Jessica Ltd intends to use the item as plant with a useful life of 10 years, and no estimated salvage value. A straight-line depreciation rate of 10% p.a. is applicable. The tax rate is 30%.

This transfer is examined in two stages; that is, sale and depreciation.

1. Sale
The entries in the accounts of the two entities are:

Amelie Ltd			
Cash	Dr	6 000	
Sales	Cr		6 000
Cost of Sales	Dr	3 000	
Inventory	Cr		3 000
Jessica Ltd			
Plant	Dr	6 000	
Cash	Cr		6 000

Hence, from the legal entities' perspectives, there has been a sale of inventory and the acquisition of a depreciable asset, plant.

From the viewpoint of the group, there has been no sale of inventory and no acquisition of plant. Instead, the asset previously classified as inventory is now classified as plant which cost the group $3000. The three elements determining the consolidation adjustment are the profit on the sale of inventory by Amelie Ltd, the revenue and expense items raised by Amelie Ltd in relation to inventory, and the reporting of the plant at cost to the group.

The worksheet entry for the year ended 30 June 2013 is:

Sales	Dr	6 000	
Cost of Sales	Cr		3 000
Plant	Cr		3 000

The debit and credit to sales and cost of sales respectively remove the $3000 profit recorded by Amelie Ltd. Note that, in comparison with the inventory-to-inventory transfers (section 25.2.1), the sales and cost of sales in the above entry are both adjustments to Amelie Ltd's statement of profit or loss and other comprehensive income.

The consolidation worksheet adjustment reduces the carrying amount of the plant by $3000. This gives rise to a deductible temporary difference, with the recognition of a deferred tax asset and an adjustment to income tax expense. The adjustment is equal to $900 (i.e. 30% × $3000). The consolidation worksheet adjustment entry is:

Deferred Tax Asset	Dr	900	
Income Tax Expense	Cr		900

If the acquisition by Jessica Ltd had taken place in the previous period, the sales and cost of sales of Amelie Ltd for the current period would not be affected. Further, the profit of $3000 would be reflected in Amelie Ltd's opening balance of retained earnings, causing the consolidation adjustment entries for the year ended 30 June 2014 to be:

Retained Earnings (1/7/13)	Dr	3 000	
Plant	Cr		3 000
Deferred Tax Asset	Dr	900	
Retained Earnings (1/7/13)	Cr		900

2. Depreciation

Jessica Ltd has recorded the asset at $6000 and charges depreciation at the rate of 10% p.a. on cost. The depreciation expense per year is, then, $600. For the half-year ended 30 June 2013, the depreciation charge is $300. From the group's viewpoint, the depreciation is based on the cost of $3000, giving depreciation for the half-year of $150. To convert the legal entity figure of $300 to the $150 required for the group, the required consolidation adjustment entry for the year ended 30 June 2013 is:

Accumulated Depreciation	Dr	150	
Depreciation Expense	Cr		150

The tax-effect entry for consolidation purposes is:

Income Tax Expense	Dr	45	
Deferred Tax Asset	Cr		45

The adjustment to depreciation expense results in a decrease in the difference between the carrying amounts of the asset to the legal entity and to the group. Income tax expense must then be increased by $45 (i.e. 30% × $150) as the credit to deferred tax asset reflects the reversal of the temporary difference. For the year ended 30 June 2014, the consolidation adjustment entries for depreciation are:

Accumulated Depreciation	Dr	450	
Depreciation Expense	Cr		300
Retained Earnings (1/7/13)	Cr		150
Income Tax Expense	Dr	90	
Retained Earnings (1/7/13)	Dr	45	
Deferred Tax Asset	Cr		135

25.4.2 Transfers from property, plant and equipment to inventory

Assume Amelie Ltd sold an item of plant to Jessica Ltd, which classified it as inventory. On sale of the asset, Amelie Ltd would pass journal entries relevant to the sale of a non-current asset and Jessica Ltd would record the purchase of inventory. Further, as Jessica Ltd regards the item as inventory, no depreciation would be charged. From the group's perspective, there has been a change in the asset classification from plant to inventory.

Assuming the inventory is not still on hand at the end of the year, the form of the consolidation entries in the year of the transfer is:

Proceeds from Sale of Plant*	Dr	xxx	
Carrying Amount of Plant Sold*	Cr		xxx
Cost of Sales	Cr		xxx

*Instead of these two lines, a debit adjustment to the Gain on Sale of Plant account could be used.

Zoe Ltd owns all the issued shares of Natalie Ltd. The following transactions occurred:
1. On 1 January 2012, Natalie Ltd sold an item of plant to Zoe Ltd for $120 000. At time of sale, this asset had a carrying amount in the records of Natalie Ltd of $115 000. The asset is depreciated on a straight-line basis at 10% p.a.
2. On 16 May 2014, Zoe Ltd sold equipment to Natalie Ltd for $50 000, this asset having a carrying amount at time of sale of $40 000. The equipment was regarded by Zoe Ltd as a depreciable non-current asset, being depreciated at 10% p.a. on cost, whereas Natalie Ltd records the machinery as inventory. The asset was sold by Natalie Ltd before 30 June 2014.

Required

Prepare the consolidation worksheet adjustment entries for the preparation of consolidated financial statements at 30 June 2014. The tax rate is 30%.

Solution

The required journal entries are:
(1) *Sale of plant in January 2012*

Retained Earnings (1/7/13)	Dr	3 500	
Deferred Tax Asset	Dr	1 500	
Plant	Cr		5 000
(Gain on sale)			
Accumulated Depreciation	Dr	1 250	
Depreciation Expense	Cr		500
Retained Earnings (1/7/13)	Cr		750
(Depreciation at $500 p.a. for 2.5 years)			
Income Tax Expense	Dr	150	
Retained Earnings (1/7/13)	Dr	225	
Deferred Tax Asset	Cr		375
(Tax effect of depreciation adjustments)			

(2) *Sale of equipment in May 2014*

Proceeds on Sale of Equipment	Dr	50 000	
Carrying Amount of Equipment Sold	Cr		40 000
Cost of Sales	Cr		10 000
(Sale of equipment, reclassified as inventory and sold to external entity)			

25.5 INTRAGROUP SERVICES

Many different examples of services between related entities exist. For instance:
- Jessica Ltd may lend to Amelie Ltd some specialist personnel for a limited period of time for the performance of a particular task by Amelie Ltd. For this service, Jessica Ltd may charge Amelie Ltd a certain fee, or expect Amelie Ltd to perform other services in return.
- One entity may lease or rent an item of plant or a warehouse from the other.
- A subsidiary may exist solely for the purpose of carrying out some specific task, such as research activities for the parent, and a fee for such research is charged. In this situation, all service revenue earned by the subsidiary is paid for by the parent, and must be adjusted in the consolidation process.

Example: Intragroup services

During 2012–13, Jessica Ltd offered the services of a specialist employee to Amelie Ltd for two months in return for which Amelie Ltd paid $30 000 to Jessica Ltd. The employee's annual salary is $155 000, paid for by Jessica Ltd.

The journal entries in the records of Jessica Ltd and Amelie Ltd in relation to this transaction are:

Jessica Ltd				
Cash		Dr	30 000	
Service Revenue		Cr		30 000
Amelie Ltd				
Service Expense		Dr	30 000	
Cash		Cr		30 000

From the group's perspective there has been no service revenue received or service expense made to entities external to the group. Hence, to adjust from what has been recorded by the legal entities to the group's perspective, the consolidation adjustment entry is:

Service Revenue	Dr	30 000	
Service Expense	Cr		30 000

No adjustment is made in relation to the employee's salary since, from the group's view, the salary paid to the employee is a payment to an external party.

Since there is no effect on the carrying amounts of assets or liabilities, there is no temporary difference and no need for any income tax adjustment.

Example: Intragroup rent

Jessica Ltd rents office space from Amelie Ltd for $150 000 p.a.

In accounting for this transaction, Jessica Ltd records rent expense of $150 000 and Amelie Ltd records rent revenue of $150 000. From the group's view, the intragroup rental scheme is purely an internal arrangement, and no revenue or expense is incurred. The recorded revenue and expense therefore need to be eliminated. The appropriate consolidation adjustment entry is:

Rent Revenue	Dr	150 000	
Rent Expense	Cr		150 000

There is no tax-effect entry necessary as assets and liabilities are unaffected by the adjustment entry.

25.5.1 Realisation of profits or losses

With the transfer of services within the group, the consolidation adjustments do not affect the profit of the group. In a transaction involving a payment by a parent to a subsidiary for services rendered, the parent shows an expense and the subsidiary shows revenue. The net effect on the group's profit is zero. Hence, from the group's view, with intragroup services there are no realisation difficulties.

25.6 INTRAGROUP DIVIDENDS

In this section, consideration is given to dividends declared and paid after Jessica Ltd's acquisition of Amelie Ltd. As explained in section 25.5.3, all dividends received by the parent from the subsidiary are accounted for as revenue by the parent, regardless of whether the dividends are paid from pre- or post-acquisition equity.

Three situations are considered in this section:
- dividends declared in the current period but not paid
- dividends declared and paid in the current period
- bonus share dividends from post-acquisition equity.

It is assumed that the company expecting to receive the dividend recognises revenue when the dividend is declared.

25.6.1 Dividends declared in the current period but not paid

Assume that, on 25 June 2013, Amelie Ltd declares a dividend of $4000. At the end of the period, the dividend is unpaid. The entries passed by the legal entities are:

Amelie Ltd		
Dividend Declared (In retained earnings)	Dr	4 000
Dividend Payable	Cr	4 000
Jessica Ltd		
Dividend Receivable	Dr	4 000
Dividend Revenue	Cr	4 000

The entry made by Amelie Ltd both reduces retained earnings and raises a liability account. From the group's perspective, there is no reduction in equity and the group has no obligation to pay dividends outside the group. Similarly, the group expects no dividends to be received from entities outside the group. Hence, the appropriate consolidation adjustment entries are:

Dividend Payable	Dr	4 000
Dividend Declared	Cr	4 000
(To adjust for the effects of the entry made by Amelie Ltd)		
Dividend Revenue	Dr	4 000
Dividend Receivable	Cr	4 000
(To adjust for the effects of the entry made by Jessica Ltd)		

In the following period when the dividend is paid, no adjustments are required in the consolidation worksheet. As there are no dividend revenue, dividend declared, or receivable items left open at the end of the period, then the position of the group is the same as the sum of the legal entities' financial statements.

25.6.2 Dividends declared and paid in the current period

Assume Amelie Ltd declares and pays an interim dividend of $4000 in the current period. Entries by the *legal entities* are:

Jessica Ltd		
Cash	Dr	4 000
Dividend Revenue	Cr	4 000
Amelie Ltd		
Interim Dividend Paid (In retained earnings)	Dr	4 000
Cash	Cr	4 000

From the outlook of the *group*, no dividends have been paid and no dividend revenue has been received. Hence, the adjustment necessary for the consolidated financial statements to show the affairs of the group is:

Dividend Revenue	Dr	4 000
Interim Dividend Paid	Cr	4 000

25.6.3 Bonus share dividends

A subsidiary may occasionally pay a dividend to its parent in the form of shares rather than cash.

For example, assume a bonus share dividend of $5000 is paid by Amelie Ltd out of post-acquisition profits. The journal entry made by Amelie Ltd is:

Bonus Share Dividend Paid (In retained earnings)	Dr	5 000	
Share Capital	Cr		5 000

Since the bonus share dividend is paid by the subsidiary out of post-acquisition profits, these profits which, for consolidation purposes, are normally available for dividends have been capitalised as share capital.

In the records of Jessica Ltd, no entry is required as the bonus share dividend does not give Jessica Ltd an increased share of Amelie Ltd; that is, Jessica Ltd receives nothing that it did not previously own.

For consolidation purposes, two alternative adjustments are possible:

(a) Eliminate the bonus dividend paid against the share capital of Amelie Ltd; that is, reverse the entry made by the subsidiary to record the dividend:

Share Capital	Dr	5 000	
Bonus Share Dividend Paid	Cr		5 000

If this entry is used, the fact that Amelie Ltd has provided for a bonus dividend does not appear in the consolidated financial statements unless disclosed by way of a note. The capitalisation of Amelie Ltd's retained earnings does not affect consolidated retained earnings, but does result in the inclusion in the consolidated retained earnings balance of those profits which have been capitalised and are not available for the payment of dividends.

(b) Do not eliminate the bonus dividend paid but set up a new capitalised profits reserve in the consolidation worksheet. The entry is:

Share Capital	Dr	5 000	
Capitalised Profits Reserve	Cr		5 000

The purpose of creating the reserve is to disclose the fact that part of the retained earnings of the group has been capitalised by the subsidiary and is therefore no longer available for payment of cash dividends to the parent.

Alternative (b) is recommended as the preferred treatment of bonus share dividends as it raises the capitalised profits reserve in the consolidated financial statements as a non-distributable reserve. From the group's viewpoint, distribution of this capitalised profits reserve to shareholders in the group is impossible and therefore is correctly treated as non-distributable.

Tax effect of dividends

Generally, dividends are tax-free. There are, therefore, no tax-effect adjustment entries required in relation to dividend-related consolidation adjustment entries.

ILLUSTRATIVE EXAMPLE 25.3 Intragroup dividends

Alice Ltd owns all the issued shares of Abigail Ltd, having acquired them for $250 000 on 1 January 2012. In preparing the consolidated financial statements at 30 June 2014, the accountant documented the following transactions:

2013	
Jan. 15	Abigail Ltd paid an interim dividend of $10 000.
June 25	Abigail Ltd declared a dividend of $15 000, this being recognised in the records of both entities.
Aug. 1	The $15 000 dividend declared on 25 June was paid by Abigail Ltd.

	2014		
	Jan. 18	Abigail Ltd paid an interim dividend of $12 000.	
	June 23	Abigail Ltd declared a dividend of $18 000, this being recognised in the records of both entities.	

The tax rate is 30%.

Required

Prepare the consolidation worksheet adjustment entries for the preparation of consolidated financial statements at 30 June 2014.

Solution

The required entries are:

(1) *Interim dividend paid*

Dividend Revenue	Dr	12 000	
Dividend Paid	Cr		12 000

(2) Final dividend declared

Dividend Payable	Dr	18 000	
Dividend Declared	Cr		18 000
Dividend Revenue	Dr	18 000	
Dividend Receivable	Cr		18 000

25.7 INTRAGROUP BORROWINGS

LO7

Members of a group often borrow and lend money among themselves, and charge interest on the money borrowed. In some cases, an entity may be set up within the group solely for the purpose of handling group finances and for borrowing money on international money markets. Consolidation adjustments are necessary in relation to these intragroup borrowings and interest thereon because, from the stance of the group, these transactions create assets and liabilities and revenues and expenses that do not exist in terms of the group's relationship with external entities.

Example: Advances

Jessica Ltd lends $100 000 to Amelie Ltd, the latter paying $15 000 interest to Jessica Ltd. The relevant journal entries in each of the legal entities are:

Jessica Ltd			
Advance to Amelie Ltd	Dr	100 000	
Cash	Cr		100 000
Cash	Dr	15 000	
Interest Revenue	Cr		15 000
Amelie Ltd			
Cash	Dr	100 000	
Advance from Jessica Ltd	Cr		100 000
Interest Expense	Dr	15 000	
Cash	Cr		15 000

The consolidation adjustments involve eliminating the monetary asset created by Jessica Ltd, the monetary liability raised by Amelie Ltd, the interest revenue recorded by Jessica Ltd and the interest expense paid by Amelie Ltd:

Advance from Jessica Ltd	Dr	100 000	
Advance to Amelie Ltd	Cr		100 000
Interest Revenue	Dr	15 000	
Interest Expense	Cr		15 000

The adjustment to the asset and liability is necessary as long as the intragroup loan exists. In relation to any past period's payments and receipt of interest, no ongoing adjustment to accumulated profits (opening balance) is necessary as the net effect of the consolidation adjustment is zero on that item.

Because the effect on net assets of the consolidation adjustment is zero, no tax-effect entry is necessary.

Example: Debentures acquired at date of issue

On 1 January 2013, Jessica Ltd issues 1000 $100 debentures with an interest rate of 15% p.a. payable on 1 January of each year. Amelie Ltd, a wholly owned subsidiary of Jessica Ltd, acquires half the debentures issued.

The journal entries made by Jessica Ltd and Amelie Ltd for the year ended 30 June 2013 are:

Jessica Ltd

1/1/13	Cash		Dr	100 000	
	Debentures		Cr		100 000
	(Issue of debentures)				
30/6/13	Interest Expense		Dr	7 500	
	Interest Payable		Cr		7 500
	(Accrued interest payable of 15% for 6 months)				

Amelie Ltd

1/1/13	Debentures in Jessica Ltd		Dr	50 000	
	Cash		Cr		50 000
	(Debentures acquired)				
30/6/13	Interest Receivable		Dr	3 750	
	Interest Revenue		Cr		3 750
	(Accrued interest revenue)				

The consolidation entries to adjust for the entries recorded in the legal entities are:

Debentures	Dr	50 000	
Debentures in Jessica Ltd	Cr		50 000
Interest Payable	Dr	3 750	
Interest Receivable	Cr		3 750
Interest Revenue	Dr	3 750	
Interest Expense	Cr		3 750

Example: Debentures acquired on the open market

Jessica Ltd issued, on 1 July 2012, 1000 $100 15% debentures at nominal value. Interest is payable half-yearly on 31 December and 30 June. Debentures are to be redeemed after 10 years. Assume that Amelie Ltd acquired 300 of these debentures cum div. on the open market for $95 on 31 March 2013.

Journal entries made by Jessica Ltd and Amelie Ltd for the year ended 30 June 2013 are:

Jessica Ltd

1/7/12	Cash	Dr	100 000	
	Debentures	Cr		100 000
	(Issue of debentures)			
31/12/12	Interest Expense	Dr	7 500	
	Cash	Cr		7 500
	(Interest paid on 31/12/12)			
30/6/13	Interest Expense	Dr	7 500	
	Cash	Cr		7 500
	(Interest paid on 30/6/13)			

Amelie Ltd

31/3/13	Debentures in Jessica Ltd	Dr	28 500	
	Cash	Cr		28 500
	(300 debentures acquired on the open market)			
30/6/13	Cash	Dr	2 250	
	Debentures in Jessica Ltd	Cr		1 125
	Interest Revenue	Cr		1 125
	(Interest before 31/3/13 was included in the purchase price)			

From the group's perspective, the purchase by Amelie Ltd on the open market effectively redeemed 300 of the debentures issued by Jessica Ltd. Since the debentures were acquired cum div., the interest expense for the period 1 January to 31 March 2013 has been paid for by the group when the debentures were acquired by Amelie Ltd. The group has redeemed 300 of the debentures at a price less than nominal value and is entitled to recognise income in the consolidation worksheet to the extent of the discount received on purchase or redemption. The consolidation adjustment entries necessary at 30 June 2013 are:

Debentures	Dr	30 000	
Debentures in Jessica Ltd	Cr		27 375*
Income on Redemption of Debentures	Cr		2 625
*$27 375 = $28 500 − $1125			
Interest Revenue	Dr	1 125	
Interest Expense	Cr		1 125

In future periods, while the debentures are still outstanding in the records of Jessica Ltd, the consolidation adjustment entries for debentures and interest must continue to be made. However, the income on redemption of debentures is considered to have occurred on 31 March 2013. Hence, in future periods, a credit entry is made to retained earnings (opening balance). To illustrate, the consolidation entries necessary at 30 June 2014 are as follows:

Debentures	Dr	30 000	
Debentures in Jessica Ltd	Cr		27 375
Retained Earnings (1/7/13)	Cr		2 625
Interest Revenue	Dr	4 500	
Interest Expense	Cr		4 500
(Full year's interest on 300 debentures)			

There is no tax effect in the group because the assets and liabilities are reduced equally.

Example: Redemption of debentures

Assume the debentures issued in the previous example are redeemed on 30 June 2021.

For the year ended 30 June 2021 the journal entries made by the legal entities are as follows:

Jessica Ltd					
31/12/20	Interest Expense		Dr	7 500	
	Cash		Cr		7 500
	(Interest paid)				
30/6/21	Interest Expense		Dr	7 500	
	Cash		Cr		7 500
	(Interest paid)				
	Debentures		Dr	100 000	
	Cash		Cr		100 000
	(Redemption of debentures)				
Amelie Ltd					
31/12/20	Cash		Dr	2 250	
	Interest Revenue		Cr		2 250
30/6/21	Cash		Dr	2 250	
	Interest Revenue		Cr		2 250
	Cash		Dr	30 000	
	Debentures in Jessica Ltd		Cr		27 375
	Income on Redemption of Debentures		Cr		2 625

On consolidation, besides the elimination of the interest paid during the period, an adjustment is necessary to eliminate the income on redemption recorded by Amelie Ltd. This income is not income to the group in the year ended 30 June 2021. From the group's viewpoint, the debentures were effectively redeemed when Amelie Ltd acquired the debentures on the open market in 2012. The consolidated financial statements in that year reflected the income on redemption. The consolidation adjustment entries for the year ended 30 June 2021 are:

Interest Revenue	Dr	4 500	
Interest Expense	Cr		4 500
Income on Redemption of Debentures	Dr	2 625	
Retained Earnings (1/7/20)	Cr		2 625

SUMMARY

Intragroup transactions can take many forms and may involve transfers of inventory or property, plant and equipment, or they may relate to the provision of services by one member of the group to another member. To prepare the relevant worksheet entries for a transaction, it is necessary to consider the accounts affected in the entities involved in the transaction.

Intragroup transfers of inventory, property, plant and equipment, services, dividends and debentures and their adjustment in the consolidation process are associated with a need to consider the implications of applying tax-effect accounting in the consolidation process.

The basic approach to determining the consolidation adjustment entries for intragroup transfers is:

(a) Analyse the events within the records of the legal entities involved in the intragroup transfer. Determine whether the transaction is a prior period or current period event.

(b) Analyse the position from the group's viewpoint.

(c) Create adjusting entries to change from the legal entities' position to that of the group.

(d) Consider the tax effect of the adjusting entries.

Note again that there are no actual adjusting entries made in the records of the individual legal entities which constitute the group. However, if required, a special journal could be set up by the parent entity to keep a record of the adjustments made in the process of preparing the consolidated financial statements. Alternatively, the consolidation process may be performed by the use of special consolidation worksheets.

Why a particular adjustment is the correct one involves an explanation of each line in the adjustment entry including why an account was adjusted, why it was increased or decreased, and why a particular adjustment amount is appropriate. This generally involves a comparison of what accounts were affected in the records of the legal entities with the financial picture the group wants to present in the consolidated financial statements.

DEMONSTRATION PROBLEM 25.1 Intragroup transfers of assets

The following example illustrates procedures for the preparation of a consolidated statement of profit or loss and other comprehensive income, a consolidated statement of changes in equity and a consolidated statement of financial position where the subsidiary is 100% owned. The consolidation worksheet adjustments for intragroup transactions including inventory and non-current asset transfers are also demonstrated.

Details
On 1 July 2011, Eliza Ltd acquired all the share capital of Ebony Ltd for $472 000. At that date, Ebony Ltd's equity consisted of the following.

Share capital	$ 300 000
General reserve	96 000
Retained earnings	56 000

At 1 July 2011, all the identifiable assets and liabilities of Ebony Ltd were recorded at fair value.

Financial information for Eliza Ltd and Ebony Ltd for the year ended 30 June 2015 is presented in the left-hand columns of the worksheet illustrated in figure 25.3 (p. 918). It is assumed that both companies use the perpetual inventory system.

Additional information
(a) On 1 January 2015, Ebony Ltd sold merchandise costing $30 000 to Eliza Ltd for $50 000. Half this merchandise was sold to external entities for $28 000 before 30 June 2015.
(b) On 1 January 2014, Ebony Ltd sold an item of inventory costing $2000 to Eliza Ltd for $4000. Eliza Ltd treated this item as part of its equipment and depreciated it at 5% p.a. on a straight-line basis.
(c) On 31 March 2015, Eliza Ltd sold plant to Ebony Ltd for $6000, which was $1000 below its carrying amount to Eliza Ltd at that date. Ebony Ltd charged depreciation at the rate of 10% p.a. on this item.
(d) In the 2012–13 period, Eliza Ltd sold land to Ebony Ltd at $20 000 above cost. The land is still held by Ebony Ltd.
(e) At 1 July 2014, there was a profit in the inventory of Eliza Ltd of $6000 on goods acquired from Ebony Ltd in the previous period.
(f) The tax rate is 30%.

Required

Prepare the consolidated financial statements for the year ended 30 June 2015.

Solution

The first step is to determine the pre-acquisition entries at 30 June 2015. These entries are prepared after undertaking an acquisition analysis.

At 1 July 2011:

Net fair value of the identifiable assets and liabilities of Ebony Ltd	= $300 000 + $96 000 + $56 000
	= $452 000
Consideration transferred	= $472 000
Goodwill	= $20 000

Consolidation worksheet entries

(1) *Business combination valuation entry*

As all the identifiable assets and liabilities of Ebony Ltd are recorded at amounts equal to their fair values, the only business combination valuation entry required is that for goodwill.

Goodwill	Dr	20 000	
Business Combination Valuation Reserve	Cr		20 000

(2) *Pre-acquisition entry*

The entry at 30 June 2015 is the same as that at acquisition date as there have not been any events affecting that entry since acquisition date:

Retained Earnings (1/7/14)	Dr	56 000	
Share Capital	Dr	300 000	
General Reserve	Dr	96 000	
Business Combination Valuation Reserve	Dr	20 000	
Shares in Ebony Ltd	Cr		472 000

The next step is to prepare the adjustment entries arising because of the existence of intragroup transactions. It is important that students classify the intragroup transactions into 'current period' and 'previous period' transactions. The resultant adjustment entries should reflect those decisions since previous period transactions would be expected to affect accounts such as retained earnings rather than accounts such as sales and cost of sales.

(3) *Profit in ending inventory*

The transaction occurred in the current period. The adjustment entries are:

Sales	Dr	50 000	
Cost of Sales	Cr		40 000
Inventory	Cr		10 000
($10 000 = ½ × [$50 000 − $30 000])			
Deferred Tax Asset	Dr	3 000	
Income Tax Expense	Cr		3 000
(30% × $10 000)			

Sales: The members of the group have recorded total sales of $78 000, being $50 000 by Ebony Ltd and $28 000 by Eliza Ltd. The group recognises only sales to entities outside the group, namely the sales by Eliza Ltd of $28 000. Hence, in preparing the consolidated financial statements, sales must be reduced by $50 000.

Cost of sales: Ebony Ltd recorded cost of sales of $30 000, and Eliza Ltd recorded cost of sales of $25 000 (being half of $50 000). Recorded cost of sales then totals $55 000. The cost of the sales to entities external to the group is $15 000 (being half of $30 000). Cost of sales must then be reduced by $40 000.

Inventory: At 30 June 2015, Eliza Ltd has inventory on hand from intragroup transactions, and records them at cost of $25 000 (being half of $50 000). The cost of this inventory to the group is $15 000 (being half of $30 000). Inventory is then reduced by $10 000.

Deferred tax asset/income tax expense: Under tax-effect accounting, temporary differences arise where the carrying amount of an asset differs from its tax base. In the first adjustment entry above, inventory is reduced by $10 000; that is, the carrying amount of inventory is reduced by $10 000. This then gives rise to a temporary difference, and because the carrying amount has been reduced, tax benefits are expected in the future when the asset is sold. Hence a deferred tax asset, equal to the tax rate times the change to the carrying amount of inventory (30% × $10 000), of $3000 is raised. Given there is no Deferred Tax Asset in the worksheet in figure 25.3, the adjustment is made against the Deferred Tax Liability line item.

(4) *Sale in previous period of inventory, classified as equipment*
The transfer occurred in a previous period.

Retained Earnings (1/7/14)	Dr	2 000	
Plant and Equipment	Cr		2 000
Deferred Tax Asset	Dr	600	
Retained Earnings (1/7/14)	Cr		600
(30% × $2000)			

Retained earnings: In the previous period, Ebony Ltd sold inventory to Eliza Ltd at a profit of $2000 before tax. This sale did not involve entities external to the group; hence, the profit is not recognised by the group. Previous period profit must, therefore, be reduced by $2000.

Tax paid: The tax paid of $600 (30% × $2000) in relation to this profit is also not recognised by the group. Because retained earnings is an after-tax account, the net adjustment to retained earnings is $1400. The journal entry could have been made with one adjustment to retained earnings rather than two.

Plant and equipment: The transferred asset is classified as equipment by Eliza Ltd, which records it at cost of $4000. The cost to the group is $2000. Hence, the asset must be reduced by $2000.

Deferred tax asset: Deferred tax accounts for temporary differences arise where carrying amounts of assets differ from their tax bases. As the carrying amount of plant and equipment is being reduced by $2000, the temporary difference caused by this change must be accounted for. A deferred tax asset is raised in recognition of the benefits to be received by the higher depreciation deductions being allowed on the asset as it is recorded by Eliza Ltd at $4000.

(5) *Depreciation*
The asset transferred within the group is recognised as equipment by Eliza Ltd, which depreciates the asset as it is used by that entity. The consolidation adjustment entry for the depreciation is:

Accumulated Depreciation	Dr	150	
Depreciation Expense	Cr		100
Retained Earnings (1/7/14)	Cr		50
Income Tax Expense	Dr	30	
Retained Earnings (1/7/14)	Dr	15	
Deferred Tax Asset	Cr		45
($30 = 30% × $100; $15 = 30% × $50)			

Eliza Ltd records depreciation for the 1.5 years the asset is held, based on the cost of $4000. The group's depreciation is calculated at the same rate of 5% p.a. but is based on the cost to the group of $2000. A comparison of the depreciation charged by Eliza Ltd and what the group would charge is as follows:

Recorded depreciation	Group depreciation
Previous period	
5% × $4000 × ½ year = $100	5% × $2000 × ½ year = $ 50
Current period	
5% × $4000 = 200	5% × $2000 = 100
$300	$150

Accumulated depreciation: Eliza Ltd has charged a total of $300 depreciation on this asset in comparison to the group's charge of $150. Hence accumulated depreciation is reduced by $150.

Depreciation expense: In the current period, Eliza Ltd recorded depreciation expense of $200, whereas the group's depreciation is $100. Hence depreciation is reduced by $100.

Retained earnings: In the previous period, Eliza Ltd charged $100 depreciation whereas the charge to the group is $50. This difference in the previous period depreciation requires an adjustment to reduce retained earnings by $50. Retained earnings is also affected by the tax effect of the depreciation expense, resulting in a net charge of $35 to retained earnings; that is, $50(1 – 30%).

Deferred tax asset: As the adjustment to accumulated depreciation changes the carrying amount of the asset, a temporary difference arises between the carrying amount and the tax base. The deferred tax asset raised on transfer of the asset within the group is reversed as the asset is used up and depreciated within the group. The deferred tax asset is reduced by $45; that is, 30%($300 – $150), reflecting this reversal process.

(6) *Loss on sale of plant*

This is a current period transaction. The consolidation worksheet entries are:

Plant and Equipment	Dr	1 000	
Proceeds from Sale of Plant	Dr	6 000	
Carrying Amount of Plant Sold	Cr		7 000
Income Tax Expense	Dr	300	
Deferred Tax Liability	Cr		300
(30% × $1000)			

Plant and equipment: The plant is recorded by Ebony Ltd at cost of $6000. The cost to the group is $7000. Hence, plant must be reduced by $1000.

Proceeds from sale: Eliza Ltd recorded proceeds on sale of the plant to Ebony Ltd of $6000. Because the sale did not involve entities external to the group, the proceeds on sale must be eliminated.

Carrying amount: Eliza Ltd also recorded carrying amount of asset sold of $7000. Because this was not a sale to external entities, from the group's perspective the proceeds on sale and the carrying amount of the asset sold cannot be recognised. Hence, the carrying amount of the asset sold of $7000 must be eliminated.

Deferred tax liability: As the carrying amount of the plant sold is increased by $1000, a temporary difference between carrying amount and tax base is created. This has to be tax-effected. As the asset's carrying amount is increased, a deferred tax liability of $300 (i.e. 30% × $1000) must be raised, reflecting the lower depreciation charge being made by the entity.

(7) *Depreciation on plant*

The transferred asset is being depreciated by Ebony Ltd on a straight-line basis, at 10% p.a. The consolidation worksheet adjustment is:

Depreciation Expense	Dr	25	
Accumulated Depreciation	Cr		25
Deferred Tax Liability	Dr	8	
Income Tax Expense	Cr		8
(30% × $25 = 7.5, round to $8)			

The asset was transferred on 31 March, requiring depreciation for the remaining 3 months of the year. Ebony Ltd is depreciating the asset based on cost of $6000, and the group cost is $7000. A comparison of the relative depreciation charges is:

Recorded depreciation	**Group depreciation**
10% × $6000 × ¼ year = $150	10% × $7000 × ¼ year = $175

Depreciation expense: As the group depreciation expense exceeds the recorded depreciation by $25, depreciation expense is increased by $25.

Accumulated depreciation: This is also increased by $25.

Deferred tax liability: The $25 adjustment to accumulated depreciation changes the carrying amount of the asset, giving rise to a temporary difference between this and the tax base. The deferred tax liability is debited for $8 (i.e. 30% × $25) to reflect that the depreciation being charged by the legal entity is lower than that to the group.

(8) *Profit on sale of land in previous period*
This is a previous period transaction. The consolidation worksheet entry is:

Retained Earnings (1/7/14)	Dr	20 000	
Land	Cr		20 000
Deferred Tax Asset	Dr	6 000	
Retained Earnings (1/7/14)	Cr		6 000
(30% × $20 000)			

Retained earnings: In the previous period, Eliza Ltd recorded a profit on sale of land of $20 000. This sale did not involve entities external to the group, and hence must be eliminated on consolidation. A further entry to retained earnings is required to reflect the tax on this profit. A net adjustment of $14 000 is then made to retained earnings.

Land: Ebony Ltd records the land at a cost of $20 000 greater than that to the group. Hence, the land must be reduced by $20 000 so that the consolidated statement of financial position shows assets at cost to the group.

Deferred tax asset: The reduction to the carrying amount of the land creates a temporary difference between carrying amount and tax base. A deferred tax asset is raised to reflect the future tax benefits when the asset is sold.

(9) *Profit in beginning inventory*
This is a previous period transaction. The required consolidation worksheet entry is:

Retained Earnings (1/7/14)	Dr	6 000	
Cost of Sales	Cr		6 000
Income Tax Expense	Dr	1 800	
Retained Earnings (1/7/14)	Cr		1 800
(30% × $6000)			

Retained earnings: In the previous period, Ebony Ltd recorded a $6000 before-tax profit, or a $4200 after-tax profit on sale of inventory within the group. Because the sale did not involve external entities, the profit must be eliminated on consolidation.

Cost of sales: In the current period, the transferred inventory is onsold to external entities. Eliza Ltd records cost of sales at $6000 greater than to the group. Hence, cost of sales is reduced by $6000. Note that this increases group profit by $6000, reflecting the realisation of the profit to the group in the current period, when it was recognised by the legal entity in the previous period.

Income tax expense: At the end of the previous period, in the consolidated statement of financial position a deferred tax asset of $1800 was raised because of the difference in cost of the inventory recorded by the legal entity and that recognised by the group. This deferred tax asset is reversed when the asset is sold. The adjustment to income tax expense reflects the reversal of the deferred tax asset raised at the end of the previous period.

Figure 25.3 shows the completed worksheet for preparation of the consolidated financial statements of Eliza Ltd and its subsidiary Ebony Ltd at 30 June 2015. Once the effects of all adjustments are added or subtracted horizontally in the worksheet to calculate figures in the right-hand 'consolidation' column, the consolidated financial statements can be prepared, as shown in figure 25.4(a), (b) and (c).

Financial statements	Eliza Ltd	Ebony Ltd		Adjustments Dr		Adjustments Cr		Consolidation
Sales revenue	1 196 000	928 000	3	50 000				2 074 000
Cost of sales	(888 000)	(670 000)			40 000	3		(1 512 000)
					6 000	9		
Wages and salaries	(57 500)	(32 000)						(89 500)
Depreciation	(5 200)	(4 800)	7	25	100	5		(9 925)
Other expenses	(4 000)	—						(4 000)
Total expenses	(954 700)	(706 800)						(1 615 425)
	241 300	221 200						458 575
Proceeds from sale of plant	6 000	—	6	6 000				—
Carrying amount of plant sold	(7 000)	—			7 000	6		—
Gain (loss)	(1 000)	—						—
Profit before income tax	240 300	221 200						458 575
Income tax expense	(96 120)	(118 480)	5	30	3 000	3		(213 722)
			6	300	8	7		
			9	1 800				
Profit for the year	144 180	102 720						244 853
Retained earnings (1/7/14)	100 820	70 280	2	56 000	600	4		95 535
			4	2 000	50	5		
			5	15	6 000	8		
			8	20 000	1 800	9		
			9	6 000				
	245 000	173 000						340 388
Dividend paid	(80 000)	—						(80 000)
Retained earnings (30/6/15)	165 000	173 000						260 388
Share capital	500 000	300 000	2	300 000				500 000
Business combination valuation reserve			2	20 000	20 000	1		—
General reserve	135 000	96 000	2	96 000				135 000
	800 000	569 000						895 388
Other components of equity (1/7/14)	4 000	10 000						14 000
Gains on financial assets	1 000	3 000						4 000
Other components of equity (30/6/15)	5 000	13 000						18 000
Total equity	805 000	582 000						913 388
Deferred tax liability	52 000	30 000	3	3 000	45	5		72 737
			4	600	300	6		
			7	8				
			8	6 000				
Total equity and liabilities	857 000	612 000						986 125
Shares in Ebony Ltd	472 000	—			472 000	2		—
Cash	80 000	73 000						153 000
Inventory	168 000	36 000			10 000	3		194 000
Other current assets	10 000	300 000						310 000
Financial assets	15 000	68 000						83 000
Land	70 000	120 000			20 000	8		170 000
Plant and equipment	52 000	28 000	6	1 000	2 000	4		79 000
Accumulated depreciation	(10 000)	(13 000)	5	150	25	7		(22 875)
Goodwill	—	—	1	20 000				20 000
	857 000	612 000		588 928	588 928			986 125

FIGURE 25.3 Consolidation worksheet — intragroup transfers of assets

FIGURE 25.4(a) Consolidated statement of profit or loss and other comprehensive income

ELIZA LTD Consolidated Statement of Profit or Loss and Other Comprehensive Income for the year ended 30 June 2015	
Revenues	$2 074 000
Expenses	1 615 425
Profit before income tax	458 575
Income tax expense	213 722
Profit for the year	$ 244 853
Other comprehensive income	
Gains on financial assets	4 000
TOTAL COMPREHENSIVE INCOME FOR THE YEAR	$ 248 853

FIGURE 25.4(b) Consolidated statement of changes in equity

ELIZA LTD Consolidated Statement of Changes in Equity for the year ended 30 June 2015	
TOTAL COMPREHENSIVE INCOME FOR THE YEAR	**$248 853**
Retained earnings at 1 July 2014	$ 95 535
Profit for the year	244 853
Dividend paid	(80 000)
Retained earnings at 30 June 2015	$260 388
General reserve at 1 July 2014	$140 000
General reserve at 30 June 2015	$140 000
Other components of equity at 1 July 2014	$ 14 000
Gains on financial assets	4 000
Other components of equity at 30 June 2015	$ 18 000
Share capital at 1 July 2014	$500 000
Share capital at 30 June 2015	$500 000

FIGURE 25.4(c) Consolidated statement of financial position

ELIZA LTD Consolidated Statement of Financial Position as at 30 June 2015			
Current assets			
Cash assets			$153 000
Inventories			194 000
Financial assets			83 000
Other			310 000
Total current assets			740 000
Non-current assets			
Property, plant and equipment:			
Plant and equipment	$ 79 000		
Accumulated depreciation	$(22 875)	$ 56 125	
Land		170 000	226 125
Goodwill			20 000
Total non-current assets			246 125
Total assets			986 125

(continued)

FIGURE 25.4(c) *(continued)*

Non-current liabilities	
Deferred tax liabilities	(72 737)
Net assets	**$913 388**
Equity	
Share capital	$500 000
General reserve	135 000
Retained earnings	260 388
Other components of equity	18 000
Total equity	**$913 388**

DEMONSTRATION PROBLEM 25.2 Dividends and borrowings

On 1 July 2014, Lilly Ltd acquired all the share capital of Tahlia Ltd and Eva Ltd for $187 500 and $150 000 respectively. At that date, equity of the three companies was:

	Lilly Ltd	Tahlia Ltd	Eva Ltd
Share capital	$150 000	$100 000	$100 000
General reserve	90 000	60 000	40 000
Retained earnings	20 000	17 500	10 000

At 1 July 2014, the identifiable net assets of all companies were recorded at fair values.

For the year ended 30 June 2015, the summarised financial information for the three companies show the following details:

	Lilly Ltd	Tahlia Ltd	Eva Ltd
Sales revenue	$ 388 500	$ 200 000	$ 150 000
Dividend revenue	9 000	—	—
Other revenue	10 000	—	—
Total revenues	407 500	200 000	150 000
Total expenses	(360 000)	(176 000)	(138 000)
Profit before income tax	47 500	24 000	12 000
Income tax expense	(15 000)	(10 000)	(5 000)
Profit	32 500	14 000	7 000
Retained earnings (1/7/14)	20 000	17 500	10 000
Total available for appropriation	52 500	31 500	17 000
Interim dividend paid	(7 500)	(2 500)	—
Bonus share dividend paid	—	—	(4 000)
Final dividend declared	(15 000)	(5 000)	(1 500)
Transfer to general reserve	(2 000)	(5 000)	—
	(24 500)	(12 500)	(5 500)
Retained earnings (30/6/15)	$ 28 000	$ 19 000	$ 11 500
Shares in Tahlia Ltd	$ 187 500	—	—
Shares in Eva Ltd	150 000	—	—
Dividend receivable	6 500	—	—
Loan receivable	5 000	—	—
Property, plant and equipment	18 500	$ 205 000	$ 167 000
Total assets	367 500	205 000	167 000

	Lilly Ltd	Tahlia Ltd	Eva Ltd
Final dividend payable	15 000	5 000	1 500
Loan payable	—	5 000	—
Other non-current liabilities	82 500	11 000	10 000
Total liabilities	97 500	21 000	11 500
Net assets	$ 270 000	$ 184 000	$ 155 500
Share capital	$ 150 000	$ 100 000	$ 104 000
General reserve	92 000	65 000	40 000
Retained earnings	28 000	19 000	11 500
Total equity	$ 270 000	$ 184 000	$ 155 500

Additional information
(a) Lilly Ltd has lent $5000 to Tahlia Ltd, the loan having 10% interest rate attached.
(b) Lilly Ltd has recognised both the interim and final dividends from Tahlia Ltd and Eva Ltd as revenue.
(c) Lilly Ltd has made no entry with respect to the bonus share dividend paid by Eva Ltd.

Required

Prepare the consolidated financial statements as at 30 June 2015 for Lilly Ltd and its two subsidiaries, Tahlia Ltd and Eva Ltd. Assume all reserve transfers are from post-acquisition profits.

Solution

The relationship between the parent and subsidiaries may be expressed as shown in figure 25.5.

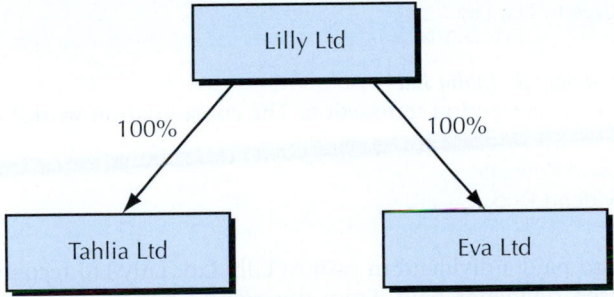

FIGURE 25.5 Relationship between parent and subsidiaries

Figure 25.6 (pp. 923–4) illustrates the consolidation worksheet necessary to consolidate the financial statements of Lilly Ltd and its two subsidiaries. Detailed discussion of each adjustment is provided below.
Note that:
• no adjustment entries are made for transfers to and from reserves if post-acquisition equity only is affected
• the dividends paid and declared by the parent to its shareholders are not adjusted for in the consolidated financial statements, because these dividends are paid by the group to external entities.

Acquisition analysis: Lilly Ltd and Tahlia Ltd
At 1 July 2014:

Net fair value of identifiable assets and liabilities of Tahlia Ltd	= $100 000 + $60 000 + $17 500
	= $177 500
Consideration transferred	= $187 500
Goodwill	= $10 000

Consolidation worksheet adjustment entries
(1) *Business combination valuation entry: Lilly Ltd and Tahlia Ltd*

Goodwill	Dr	10 000	
Business Combination Valuation Reserve	Cr		10 000

(2) *Pre-acquisition entry: Lilly Ltd and Tahlia Ltd*

The pre-acquisition entry at 30 June 2015 is then:

Retained Earnings (1/7/14)	Dr	17 500	
Share Capital	Dr	100 000	
General Reserve	Dr	60 000	
Business Combination Valuation Reserve	Dr	10 000	
Shares in Tahlia Ltd	Cr		187 500

Acquisition analysis: Lilly Ltd and Eva Ltd
At 1 July 2014:

Net fair value of identifiable assets and liabilities of Eva Ltd	= $100 000 + $40 000 + $10 000
	= $150 000
Consideration transferred	= $150 000
Goodwill	= zero

No business combination valuation entry is required.

(3) *Pre-acquisition entry: Lilly Ltd and Eva Ltd*

The pre-acquisition entry at 30 June 2015 is then:

Retained Earnings (1/7/14)	Dr	10 000	
Share Capital	Dr	100 000	
General Reserve	Dr	40 000	
Shares in Eva Ltd	Cr		150 000

(4) *Interim dividend: Tahlia Ltd*

This is a current period transaction. The consolidation worksheet entry is:

Dividend Revenue	Dr	2 500	
Dividend Paid	Cr		2 500

Tahlia Ltd paid a dividend in cash to Lilly Ltd. Lilly Ltd recognised dividend revenue and Tahlia Ltd recognised dividends paid. From the group's perspective, there were no dividends paid to entities external to the group. Hence, on consolidation it is necessary to eliminate both the Dividend Paid and Dividend Revenue accounts raised by the parent and the subsidiary.

(5) *Bonus share dividend: Eva Ltd*

This is a current period transaction. In recording the bonus share dividend, Eva Ltd reduced retained earnings, recognising a bonus dividend paid and increasing share capital. Lilly Ltd made no entry. It is assumed in this solution that treatment (b) in section 25.6.3 is adopted. Hence, rather than eliminate the bonus dividend paid raised by the subsidiary, a capitalised profits reserve is raised instead to show that profits have been capitalised and dividend potential has been reduced. The share capital is reduced on consolidation.

Share Capital	Dr	4 000	
Capitalised Profits Reserve	Cr		4 000

(6) *Final dividend declared: Tahlia Ltd*

This is a current period transaction. The consolidation worksheet entry is:

Final Dividend Payable	Dr	5 000	
Final Dividend Declared	Cr		5 000
Dividend Revenue	Dr	5 000	
Dividend Receivable	Cr		5 000

The subsidiary declares a dividend, recognising a liability to pay the dividend and reducing retained earnings. The parent, which expects to receive the dividend, raises a receivable asset and recognises dividend revenue. From the group's point of view, because the dividend is not receivable or payable to entities external to the group, it does not want to recognise any of these accounts. Hence, on consolidation, all the accounts affected by this transaction in the records of the parent and the subsidiary are eliminated.

(7) *Final dividend declared: Eva Ltd*
This is a current period transaction. The consolidation worksheet entry is:

Final Dividend Payable	Dr	1 500
Final Dividend Declared	Cr	1 500
Dividend Revenue	Dr	1 500
Dividend Receivable	Cr	1 500

The explanation for this entry is the same as that for the dividend declared by Tahlia Ltd.

(8) *Loan: Lilly Ltd to Tahlia Ltd*
The loan may have been made in a previous period or the current period. The consolidation worksheet entry is the same:

Loan Payable	Dr	5 000
Loan Receivable	Cr	5 000

This entry eliminates the receivable raised by the parent and the payable raised by the subsidiary. From the group's point of view, there are no loans payable or receivable to entities external to the group.

(9) *Interest on loan*
The interest paid/received is a current period transaction. In some situations where interest is accrued, interest may relate to previous or future periods. The consolidation worksheet entry is:

Interest Revenue	Dr	500
Interest Expense	Cr	500
(10% × $5000)		

The parent records interest revenue of $500 and the subsidiary records interest expense of $500. No interest was paid or received by the group from entities external to the group, so these accounts must be eliminated on consolidation.

FIGURE 25.6 Consolidation worksheet — dividends

Financial statements	Lilly Ltd	Tahlia Ltd	Eva Ltd		Adjustments		Group
					Dr	Cr	
Sales revenue	388 500	200 000	150 000				738 500
Dividend revenue	9 000	—	—	4	2 500		—
				6	5 000		
				7	1 500		
Other revenue	10 000	—	—	9	500		9 500
	407 500	200 000	150 000				748 000
Expenses	(360 000)	(176 000)	(138 000)			500 9	(673 500)
Profit before income tax	47 500	24 000	12 000				74 500
Income tax expense	(15 000)	(10 000)	(5 000)				(30 000)
Profit	32 500	14 000	7 000				44 500

(continued)

FIGURE 25.6 (continued)

Financial statements	Lilly Ltd	Tahlia Ltd	Eva Ltd		Adjustments Dr	Adjustments Cr		Group
Retained earnings (1/7/14)	20 000	17 500	10 000	2	17 500			20 000
				3	10 000			
	52 500	31 500	17 000					64 500
Interim dividend paid	(7 500)	(2 500)	—			2 500	4	(7 500)
Bonus dividend paid	—	—	(4 000)					(4 000)
Final dividend declared	(15 000)	(5 000)	(1 500)			5 000	6	(15 000)
						1 500	7	
Transfer to general reserve	(2 000)	(5 000)	0					(7 000)
	24 500	12 500	5 500					33 500
Retained earnings (30/6/15)	28 000	19 000	11 500					31 000
Share capital	150 000	100 000	104 000	2	100 000			150 000
				3	100 000			
				5	4 000			
General reserve	92 000	65 000	40 000	2	60 000			97 000
				3	40 000			
Business combination valuation reserve				2	10 000	10 000	1	—
Capitalised profits reserve						4 000	4	4 000
Final dividend payable	15 000	5 000	1 500	6	5 000			15 000
				7	1 500			
Loan payable	—	5 000	—	8	5 000			—
Other non-current liabilities	82 500	11 000	10 000					103 500
Total equity and liabilities	367 500	205 000	167 000					400 500
Shares in Tahlia Ltd	187 500	—	—			187 500	2	—
Shares in Eva Ltd	150 000	—	—			150 000	3	—
Dividend receivable	6 500	—	—			5 000	6	—
						1 500	7	
Loan receivable	5 000	—	—			5 000	8	—
Property, plant and equipment	18 500	205 000	167 000					390 500
Goodwill	—	—	—	1	10 000			10 000
	367 500	205 000	167 000		372 500	372 500		400 500

From figure 25.6, after all adjustments have been entered in the worksheet and amounts totalled across to the consolidation column, the consolidated financial statements can be prepared in suitable format as shown in figure 25.7(a), (b) and (c).

LILLY LTD **Consolidated Statement of Profit or Loss and Other Comprehensive Income** **for the year ended 30 June 2015**	
Revenues	$748 000
Expenses	673 500
Profit before income tax	74 500
Income tax expense	(30 000)
Profit for the year	$ 44 500
Other comprehensive income	—
TOTAL COMPREHENSIVE INCOME FOR THE YEAR	$ 44 500

FIGURE 25.7(a) Consolidated statement of profit or loss and other comprehensive income

LILLY LTD
Consolidated Statement of Changes in Equity
for the year ended 30 June 2015

TOTAL COMPREHENSIVE INCOME FOR THE YEAR	**$ 44 500**
Retained earnings at 1 July 2014	$ 20 000
Profit for the year	44 500
Interim dividend paid	(7 500)
Bonus dividend paid	(4 000)
Final dividend declared	(15 000)
Transfer of general reserve	(7 000)
Retained earnings at 30 June 2015	$ 31 000
General reserve at 1 July 2014	$ 90 000
Transfer from retained earnings	7 000
General reserve at 30 June 2015	$ 97 000
Capitalised profits reserve at 1 July 2014	$ 0
Increase due to bonus dividend paid	4 000
Capitalised profits reserve at 30 June 2015	$ 4 000
Share capital as at 1 July 2014	$150 000
Share capital at 30 June 2015	$150 000

FIGURE 25.7(b) Consolidated statement of changes in equity

LILLY LTD
Consolidated Statement of Financial Position
as at 30 June 2015

Non-current assets		
Property, plant and equipment		$390 500
Goodwill		10 000
Total non-current assets		400 500
Total assets		400 500
Current liabilities		
Final dividend payable		15 000
Non-current liabilities		103 500
Total liabilities		118 500
Net assets		$282 000
Equity		
Share capital		$150 000
Other reserves:		
General reserve	$ 97 000	
Capitalised profits reserve (Note 1)	4 000	101 000
Retained earnings		31 000
Total equity		$282 000

Note 1: The capitalised profits reserve represents the non-distributable profit created by the capitalisation of profits in a subsidiary by means of a bonus share dividend.

FIGURE 25.7(c) Consolidated statement of financial position

Discussion questions

1. Why is it necessary to make adjustments for intragroup transactions?
2. In making consolidation worksheet adjustments, sometimes tax-effect entries are made. Why?
3. Why is it important to identify transactions as current or previous period transactions?
4. Where an intragroup transaction involves a depreciable asset, why is depreciation expense adjusted?
5. Are adjustments for post-acquisition dividends different from those for pre-acquisition dividends? Explain.
6. What is meant by 'realisation of profits'?
7. When are profits realised in relation to inventory transfers within the group?
8. When are profits realised on transfers of depreciable assets within the group?

Exercises

STAR RATING ★ BASIC ★★ MODERATE ★★★ DIFFICULT

Exercise 25.1   CONSOLIDATION ADJUSTMENTS

★ Jessica Ltd sold inventory during the current period to its wholly owned subsidiary, Amelie Ltd, for $15 000. These items previously cost Jessica Ltd $12 000. Amelie Ltd subsequently sold half the items to Ningbo Ltd for $8000. The tax rate is 30%.

The group accountant for Jessica Ltd, Li Chen, maintains that the appropriate consolidation adjustment entries are as follows:

Sales	Dr	15 000	
Cost of Sales	Cr		13 000
Inventory	Cr		2 000
Deferred Tax Asset	Dr	300	
Income Tax Expense	Cr		300

Required

1. Discuss whether the entries suggested by Li Chen are correct, explaining on a line-by-line basis the correct adjustment entries.
2. Determine the consolidation worksheet entries in the following year, assuming the inventory is onsold, and explain the adjustments on a line-by-line basis.

Exercise 25.2   DEPRECIATION EXPENSE

★ At the beginning of the current period, Jessica Ltd sold a used depreciable asset to its wholly owned subsidiary, Amelie Ltd, for $80 000. Jessica Ltd had originally paid $200 000 for this asset, and at time of sale to Amelie Ltd had charged depreciation of $150 000. This asset is used differently in Amelie Ltd from how it was used in Jessica Ltd; thus, whereas Jessica Ltd used a 10% p.a. straight-line depreciation method, Amelie Ltd uses a 20% straight-line depreciation method.

In calculating the depreciation expense for the consolidated group (as opposed to that recorded by Amelie Ltd), the group accountant, RuiFen Xue, is unsure of which amount the depreciation rate should be applied to ($200 000, $50 000 or $80 000) and which depreciation rate to use (10% or 20%).

Required

Provide a detailed response, explaining which depreciation rate should be used and to what amount it should be applied.

Exercise 25.3   INCOME ON REDEMPTION

★ The parent entity, Leah Ltd, has purchased on the open market, for an amount less than nominal value, some debentures previously issued by its wholly owned subsidiary, Natalie Ltd. The group accountant for Leah Ltd, James Cong, has stated that the adjustment in the consolidation worksheet includes the raising of an account Income on Redemption. He is unsure whether this is correct.

Required

What does this account represent? Would an adjustment to income, or subsequently to retained earnings, have to be made for the rest of the life of the group? If not, what event would cause the discontinuation of this adjustment entry?

Exercise 25.4	INTRAGROUP TRANSACTIONS

★ Layla Ltd owns all the share capital of Isabel Ltd. In relation to the following intragroup transactions, prepare adjusting journal entries for the consolidation worksheet at 30 June 2015. Assume an income tax rate of 30% and that all income on sale of assets is taxable and expenses are deductible.

(a) During the year ending 30 June 2015, Isabel Ltd sold $50 000 worth of inventory to Layla Ltd. Isabel Ltd recorded a $10 000 profit before tax on these transactions. At 30 June 2015, Layla Ltd has one-quarter of these goods still on hand.

(b) Isabel Ltd sold a warehouse to Layla Ltd for $100 000. This had originally cost Isabel Ltd $82 000. The transaction took place on 1 January 2014. Layla Ltd charges depreciation at 5% p.a. on a straight-line basis.

(c) During the 2014–15 period, Layla Ltd sold inventory costing $12 000 to Isabel Ltd for $18 000. One-third of this was sold to Olivia Ltd for $9500 and one-third to Taylah Ltd for $9000.

(d) On 1 January 2014, Isabel Ltd sold inventory costing $6000 to Layla Ltd at a transfer price of $8000. On 1 September 2014, Layla Ltd sold half these goods back to Isabel Ltd, receiving $3000 from Isabel Ltd. Of the remainder kept by Layla Ltd, half was sold in January 2015 to Anna Ltd at a loss of $200.

(e) On 25 June 2015, Layla Ltd declared a dividend of $10 000. On the same day, Isabel Ltd declared a $5000 dividend.

(f) On 1 October 2014, Layla Ltd issued 1000 15% debentures of $100 at nominal value. Isabel Ltd acquired 400 of these. Interest is payable half-yearly on 31 March and 30 September. Accruals have been recognised in the legal entities' accounts.

(g) During the 2013–14 period, Layla Ltd sold inventory to Isabel Ltd for $10 000, recording a before-tax profit of $2000. Half this inventory was unsold by Isabel Ltd at 30 June 2014.

Exercise 25.5	INTRAGROUP TRANSACTIONS

★ Addison Ltd owns all of the share capital of Erin Ltd. In relation to the following intragroup transactions, all parts of which are independent unless specified, prepare the consolidation worksheet adjusting entries for preparation of the consolidated financial statements as at 30 June 2014. Assume an income tax rate of 30% and that all income on sale of assets is taxable and expenses are deductible.

(a) In January 2014, Addison Ltd sells inventory to Erin Ltd for $15 000. This inventory had previously cost Addison Ltd $10 000, and it remains unsold by Erin Ltd at the end of the period.

(b) All the inventory in (a) above is sold to Olivia Ltd, an external party, for $20 000 on 2 February 2014.

(c) Half the inventory in (a) above is sold to Taylah Ltd, an external party, for $9000 on 22 February 2014. The remainder is still unsold at the end of the period.

(d) Addison Ltd, in March 2014, sold inventory for $10 000 that was transferred from Erin Ltd 3 years ago. It had originally cost Erin Ltd $6000, and was sold to Addison Ltd for $12 000.

(e) Erin Ltd sold some land to Addison Ltd in December 2013. The land had originally cost Erin Ltd $25 000, but was sold to Addison Ltd for only $20 000. To help Addison Ltd pay for the land, Erin Ltd gave Addison Ltd an interest-free loan of $12 000, and the balance was paid in cash. Addison Ltd has as yet made no repayments on the loan.

(f) On 1 July 2013, Addison Ltd sold a depreciable asset costing $10 000 to Erin Ltd for $12 000. Addison Ltd had not charged any depreciation on the asset before the sale. Both entities depreciate assets at 10% p.a. on cost.

(g) On 1 July 2013, Addison Ltd sold an item of machinery to Erin Ltd for $6000. This item had cost Addison Ltd $4000. Addison Ltd regarded this item as inventory whereas Erin Ltd intended to use it as a non-current asset. Erin Ltd charges depreciation at the rate of 10% p.a. on cost.

Exercise 25.6	INTRAGROUP TRANSACTIONS

★ Claire Ltd owns all the share capital of Lauren Ltd. The following transactions relate to the period ended 30 June 2014. Assuming an income tax rate of 30%, provide adjustment entries to be included in the consolidation worksheet as at 30 June 2014.

(a) On 1 July 2013, Claire Ltd sold a motor vehicle to Lauren Ltd for $15 000. This had a carrying amount to Claire Ltd of $12 000. Both entities depreciate motor vehicles at a rate of 10% p.a. on cost.

(b) Lauren Ltd manufactures items of machinery which are used as property, plant and equipment by other companies, including Claire Ltd. On 1 January 2014, Lauren Ltd sold such an item to Claire Ltd for $62 000, its cost to Lauren Ltd being only $55 000 to manufacture. Claire Ltd charges depreciation on these machines at 20% p.a. on the diminishing value.

(c) Claire Ltd manufactures certain items which it then markets through Lauren Ltd. During the current period, Claire Ltd sold for $12 000 items to Lauren Ltd at cost plus 20%. Lauren Ltd has sold 75% of these transferred items at 30 June 2014.

(d) Lauren Ltd also sells second-hand machinery. Claire Ltd sold one of its depreciable assets (original cost $40 000, accumulated depreciation $32 000) to Lauren Ltd for $5000 on 1 January 2014. Lauren Ltd had not resold the item by 30 June 2014.

(e) Lauren Ltd sold a depreciable asset (carrying amount of $22 000) to Claire Ltd on 1 January 2013 for $25 000. Both entities charge depreciation at a rate of 10% p.a. on cost in relation to these items. On 31 December 2013, Claire Ltd sold this asset to Anna Ltd for $20 000.

<table>
<tr><td>**Exercise 25.7**</td><td>**INTRAGROUP TRANSACTIONS**</td></tr>
</table>

★ For each of the following intragroup transactions, assume that the consolidation process is being undertaken at 30 June 2015, and that an income tax rate of 30% applies. Prepare the consolidation worksheet adjustment entries for these transactions. All parts are independent unless specified. Maddison Ltd owns all the share capital of Anna Ltd.

(a) On 1 January 2015, Maddison Ltd sold an item of plant to Anna Ltd for $1000. Immediately before the sale, Maddison Ltd had the item of plant on its accounts for $1500. Maddison Ltd depreciated items at 5% p.a. on the diminishing balance and Anna Ltd used the straight-line method over 10 years.

(b) A non-current asset with a carrying amount of $1000 was sold by Maddison Ltd to Anna Ltd for $800 on 1 January 2015. Anna Ltd intended to use this item as inventory, being a seller of second-hand goods. Both entities charged depreciation at the rate of 10% p.a. on the diminishing balance on non-current assets. The item was still on hand at 30 June 2015.

(c) On 1 May 2015, Anna Ltd sold inventory costing $200 to Maddison Ltd for $400 on credit. On 30 June 2015, only half of these goods had been sold by Maddison Ltd, but Maddison Ltd had paid $300 back to Anna Ltd.

(d) During March 2015, Anna Ltd declared a $3000 dividend. The dividend was paid in August 2016.

(e) In December 2014, Anna Ltd paid a $1500 interim dividend.

(f) In February 2014, Maddison Ltd sold inventory to Anna Ltd for $6000, at a mark-up of 20% on cost. One-quarter of this inventory was unsold by Anna Ltd at 30 June 2014.

(g) On 1 January 2013, Anna Ltd sold a new tractor to Maddison Ltd for $20 000. This had cost Anna Ltd $16 000 on that day. Both entities charged depreciation at the rate of 10% p.a. on the diminishing balance.

(h) Anna Ltd rented a spare warehouse to Maddison Ltd and also to Olivia Ltd during 2014–15. The total charge for the rental was $300, and Maddison Ltd and Olivia Ltd both agreed to pay half of this amount to Anna Ltd.

<table>
<tr><td>**Exercise 25.8**</td><td>**BONUS DIVIDEND**</td></tr>
</table>

★★ The parent entity, Olivia Ltd, has received a bonus dividend paid from its subsidiary's post-acquisition profits. The accountant for Olivia Ltd, Lu Rong, is concerned that if on consolidation the total effects of this transaction have to be eliminated, then this will show a misleading financial position for the group. Her concern is that the subsidiary, by making a bonus dividend, has reduced the ability of the group to pay cash dividends. The consolidation adjustments will result in this fact not being made known to the users of the consolidated financial statements.

Required

Discuss whether Lu Rong has cause for concern, and what options are available for her in accounting for the bonus dividend.

PRE-ACQUISITION ENTRY AND INTRAGROUP TRANSACTIONS, NO FAIR VALUE — CARRYING AMOUNT DIFFERENCES AT ACQUISITION DATE

★★

On 1 January 2012, Molly Ltd acquired all the share capital of Mia Ltd for $300 000. The equity of Mia Ltd at 1 January 2012 was:

Share capital	$200 000
Retained earnings	50 000
General reserve	20 000
	$270 000

At this date, all identifiable assets and liabilities of Mia Ltd were recorded at fair value. Goodwill is tested annually for impairment. By 31 December 2015, no impairment has occurred. At 1 January 2012, no goodwill had been recorded by Mia Ltd.

On 1 May 2015, Mia Ltd transferred $15 000 from the general reserve (pre-acquisition) to retained earnings. The current tax rate is 30%. Assuming consolidated financial statements are required for the period 1 January 2015 to 31 December 2016, provide journal entries (including the pre-acquisition entry) to show the adjustments that would be made in the consolidation worksheets. Use the following information:

(a) At 31 December 2015, Mia Ltd holds $100 000 of 7% debentures issued by Molly Ltd on 1 January 2014. All necessary interest payments have been made.

(b) At the end of the reporting period, Mia Ltd owes Molly Ltd $1000 for items sold on credit.

(c) Mia Ltd undertook an advertising campaign for Molly Ltd during the year. Molly Ltd paid $8000 to Mia Ltd for this service.

(d) The beginning and ending inventories of Molly Ltd and Mia Ltd in relation to the current period included the following unsold intragroup inventory:

	Molly Ltd	**Mia Ltd**
Beginning inventory:		
Transfer price	$2 000	$1 200
Original cost	1 400	800
Ending inventory:		
Transfer price	500	900
Original cost	300	700

Molly Ltd sold inventory to Mia Ltd during the current period for $3000. This was $500 above the cost of the inventory to Molly Ltd. Mia Ltd sold inventory to Molly Ltd in the current period for $2500, recording a pre-tax profit of $800.

(e) Molly Ltd sold an item of inventory to Mia Ltd on 1 July 2015 for use as part of plant and machinery. The item cost Molly Ltd $4000 and was sold to Mia for $6000. Mia Ltd depreciated the item at 10% p.a. straight-line.

(f) Molly Ltd received dividends totalling $63 000 during the current period from Mia Ltd. All of this related to dividends paid in the current period.

INTRAGROUP TRANSACTIONS, EXPLANATION OF RATIONALE

★★

Alexis Ltd owns 100% of the shares of Ruby Ltd. During the 2013–14 period, the following events occurred:

(a) Alexis Ltd sold inventory for $10 000 which had been sold to it by Ruby Ltd in June 2013. The inventory originally cost Ruby Ltd $6000 and was sold to Alexis Ltd for $9000.

(b) Alexis Ltd recorded depreciation of $10 000 on machinery sold to it by Ruby Ltd on 1 January 2013. The machinery had a carrying amount in Ruby Ltd at the date of sale of $80 000. Both entities apply a depreciation rate of 10% p.a. on a straight-line basis for this type of machinery.

Required

1. For *each* of the above transactions, prepare the adjustments required in the consolidation worksheet at 30 June 2014, assuming an income tax rate of 30%.

2. Explain the rationale behind *each* of the entries you have prepared.

CONSOLIDATION WORKSHEET, INTRAGROUP TRANSACTIONS

★★ On 1 July 2012, Maya Ltd acquired cum div. all the shares of Brooke Ltd, at which date the equity and liability sections of Brooke Ltd's statement of financial position showed the following balances:

Share capital (300 000 shares)	$300 000
Other reserves	30 000
Retained earnings	10 000
Other components of equity	30 000
Dividend payable	20 000

The dividend payable was subsequently paid in August 2012. A bonus dividend, on the basis of one ordinary share for every ten ordinary shares held, was paid in January 2015 out of other reserves existing at acquisition date.

On 1 July 2012, all the identifiable assets and liabilities of Brooke Ltd were recorded at fair value except for:

	Carrying amount	Fair value
Inventory	$120 000	$130 000
Machinery (cost $200 000)	160 000	165 000

The inventory was all sold by 30 November 2012. The machinery had a further 5-year life but was sold on 1 January 2015. At the acquisition date, Brooke Ltd had a contingent liability of $20 000 that Maya Ltd considered to have a fair value of $12 000. This liability was settled in June 2013. At 1 July 2012, Brooke Ltd had not recorded any goodwill.

On 30 June 2015, the trial balances of Maya Ltd and Brooke Ltd were as follows:

Trial Balances as at 30 June 2015	Maya Ltd	Brooke Ltd
Shares in Brooke Ltd	$ 396 000	$ —
Inventory	180 000	160 000
Financial assets	229 000	215 000
Bank	25 000	10 000
Plant and machinery	372 500	212 000
Land	154 200	65 000
Income tax expense	35 000	40 000
Dividend declared	10 000	4 000
	$1 401 700	$706 000
Share capital	$ 800 000	$330 000
Other components of equity	150 000	80 000
Retained earnings (1/7/14)	15 000	12 000
Profit before income tax	80 000	90 000
Debentures	100 000	40 000
Other current liabilities	34 700	40 000
Dividend payable	10 000	4 000
Accumulated depreciation — plant and machinery	212 000	110 000
	$1 401 700	$706 000

Additional information

(a) On 1 July 2013, Maya Ltd sold an item of plant to Brooke Ltd at a profit before tax of $4000. Maya Ltd depreciates this particular item of plant at a rate of 20% p.a. on cost and Brooke Ltd applies a rate of 10% p.a. on cost.

(b) At 30 June 2015, Maya Ltd has on hand some items of inventory purchased from Brooke Ltd in June 2014 at a profit of $500.

(c) The other components of equity relate to the financial assets. At 1 July 2014, the balances of this account were $140 000 (Maya Ltd) and $72 000 (Brooke Ltd).

(d) The tax rate is 30%.

Required

1. Prepare the adjusting journal entries for the consolidation worksheet at 30 June 2015.
2. Prepare the consolidated statement of profit or loss and other comprehensive income, consolidated statement of changes in equity and the consolidated statement of financial position at 30 June 2015.
3. In relation to parts (a) and (b) in the *additional information*, explain why you made the consolidation adjustment worksheet entries used in preparing the consolidated financial statements at 30 June 2015.

| Exercise 25.12 | GOODWILL, CONSOLIDATION WORKSHEET, INTRAGROUP TRANSACTIONS |

★★ Summer Ltd owns all the shares of Keira Ltd. The shares were acquired on 1 July 2012 by Summer Ltd at a cost of $60 000. At acquisition date, the capital of Keira Ltd consisted of 44 000 ordinary shares each fully paid at $1. There were retained earnings of $4000. All the identifiable assets and liabilities of Keira Ltd were recorded at amounts equal to fair value, except for:

	Carrying amount	Fair value
Inventory	$12 000	$15 000
Land	60 000	70 000
Machinery (cost $100 000)	80 000	82 000

The land was sold on 1 June 2013 for $94 000. The machinery had a further 5-year life. The inventory was all sold by 31 December 2012. Keira Ltd has not recorded any goodwill at 1 July 2012. Goodwill has not been impaired.

The trial balances of the two entities at 30 June 2014 are shown below.

Additional information

(a) Intragroup sales of inventory for the year ended 30 June 2014 from Summer Ltd to Keira Ltd, $14 000; and from Keira Ltd to Summer Ltd, $3000.

(b) Intragroup inventory on hand:
  (i) at 1 July 2013: held by Keira Ltd, purchased from Summer Ltd at a profit of $400.
  (ii) at 30 June 2014: held by Summer Ltd, purchased from Keira Ltd at a profit of $200.

(c) Intragroup machinery on hand at 30 June 2014:
  (i) Summer Ltd: purchased from Keira Ltd on 1 July 2013 for $10 000 at a profit to Keira Ltd of $500. Depreciation rate is 10% p.a. on cost.
  (ii) Keira Ltd: purchased from Summer Ltd on 1 January 2013 for $12 000, at a loss to Summer Ltd of $500. Depreciation rate is 10% p.a. on cost.

(d) Keira Ltd had purchased from Summer Ltd an item of inventory which Summer Ltd had treated as plant. Carrying amount in Summer Ltd's records at time of sale (1 January 2014) was $5000 and it was sold at a profit of $1000. The item is still on hand in Keira Ltd's inventory at 30 June 2014.

(e) The income tax rate is 30%.

Trial Balances as at 30 June 2014				
	Summer Ltd		**Keira Ltd**	
	Dr	**Cr**	**Dr**	**Cr**
Share capital		$64 000		$44 000
Retained earnings (1/7/13)		32 000		21 000
Current liabilities		21 400		17 000
Machinery	$38 000		$71 500	
Shares in Keira Ltd	60 000		—	
Inventory	19 000		16 400	
Receivables	5 500		8 300	

(continued)

	Summer Ltd Dr	Summer Ltd Cr	Keira Ltd Dr	Keira Ltd Cr
Sales revenue		43 000		52 000
Cost of sales	20 600		30 900	
Selling expenses	3 200		6 000	
Administrative expenses	5 300		2 700	
Depreciation/amortisation expenses	1 200		2 600	
Income tax expense	7 400		4 700	
Accumulated depreciation — machinery		12 200		22 300
Deferred tax assets	5 400		6 300	
Plant (net of depreciation)	8 000		7 400	
Proceeds from sale of machinery		6 000		10 000
Carrying amount of machinery sold	5 000		9 500	
	$178 600	$178 600	$166 300	$166 300

Required

Prepare a worksheet for consolidating the financial statements of Summer Ltd and Keira Ltd as at 30 June 2014.

Exercise 25.13 **CONSOLIDATION WORKSHEET, CONSOLIDATED FINANCIAL STATEMENTS**

★★ On 1 July 2013, Sienna Ltd acquired all the shares of Amber Ltd for $160 000. The financial statements of the two entities at 30 June 2014 contained the following information:

	Sienna Ltd	Amber Ltd
Sales revenue	$ 234 800	$ 200 000
Dividend revenue	17 000	—
Other income	6 600	—
	258 400	200 000
Cost of sales	(123 000)	(120 000)
Other expenses	(34 600)	(20 000)
	(157 600)	(140 000)
Profit before income tax	100 800	60 000
Income tax expense	(32 000)	(20 000)
Profit for the year	68 800	40 000
Retained earnings (1/7/13)	24 000	12 000
Total available for appropriation	92 800	52 000
Dividend paid from 2012–13 profit	(18 000)	(5 000)
Interim dividend paid from 2013–14 profit	(16 000)	(4 800)
Dividend declared from 2013–14 profit	(16 000)	(7 200)
Transfer to general reserve	(8 000)	—
	(58 000)	(17 000)
Retained earnings (30/6/14)	$ 34 800	$ 35 000
Current assets		
Cash	$ 1 000	$ 40
Receivables	27 000	12 100
Allowance for doubtful debts	(500)	(300)
Financial assets	20 000	10 000
Inventory	48 000	47 000
Total current assets	95 500	68 840

	Sienna Ltd	Amber Ltd
Non-current assets		
Plant and machinery	100 000	70 000
Accumulated depreciation	(40 000)	(26 000)
Land	102 300	190 000
Debentures in Amber Ltd	57 000	—
Shares in Amber Ltd	160 000	
Total non-current assets	379 300	234 000
Total assets	474 800	302 840
Current liabilities		
Dividend payable	16 000	7 200
Provisions	12 000	8 800
Bank overdraft	—	14 840
Current tax liabilities	11 000	10 000
Total current liabilities	39 000	40 840
Non-current liabilities		
12% mortgage debentures	—	80 000
Deferred tax liabilities	13 000	5 000
Total non-current liabilities	13 000	85 000
Total liabilities	52 000	125 840
Net assets	$ 422 800	$ 177 000
Equity		
Share capital	$ 320 000	$ 120 000
General reserve	60 000	20 000
Retained earnings	34 800	35 000
Other components of equity	8 000	2 000
Total equity	$ 422 800	$ 177 000

Additional information

(a) At 1 July 2013, all identifiable assets and liabilities of Amber Ltd were recorded at fair values except for inventory, for which the fair value was $1000 greater than the carrying amount. This inventory was all sold by 30 June 2014. At 1 July 2013, Amber Ltd had research and development outlays that it had expensed as incurred. Sienna Ltd measured the fair value of the in-process research and development at $8000. By 30 June 2014, it was assessed that $2000 of this was not recoverable. At 1 July 2013, Amber Ltd had reported a contingent liability relating to a guarantee that was considered to have a fair value of $7000. This liability still existed at 30 June 2014. At 1 July 2013, Amber Ltd had not recorded any goodwill.

(b) The debentures were issued by Amber Ltd at nominal value on 1 July 2012, and are redeemable on 30 June 2018. Sienna Ltd acquired its holding ($60 000) of these debentures on the open market on 1 January 2014, immediately after the half-yearly interest payment had been made. All interest has been paid and brought to account in the records of both entities.

(c) During the 2013–14 period, Sienna Ltd sold inventory to Amber Ltd for $40 000, at a mark-up of cost plus 25%. At 30 June 2014, $10 000 worth of inventory is still held by Amber Ltd.

(d) On 1 January 2014, Amber Ltd sold an item of inventory to Sienna Ltd which planned to use it as a non-current asset, depreciable at 10% p.a. on cost. Sienna Ltd paid $30 000 for this item, with Amber Ltd having manufactured it at a cost of $24 000.

(e) The Other Components of Equity account relates to the financial assets. For the 2013–14 period, Sienna Ltd recorded an increase in these assets of $3000, and Amber Ltd recorded a decrease of $2000.

(f) The income tax rate is 30%.

Required

Prepare the consolidated financial statements for Sienna Ltd and its subsidiary for the year ended 30 June 2014.

Exercise 25.14 · CONSOLIDATION WORKSHEET, IMPAIRMENT OF GOODWILL

★★ Financial information for Amy Ltd and its 100% owned subsidiary, Zara Ltd, for the year ended 31 December 2013 is provided below:

	Amy Ltd	Zara Ltd
Sales revenue	$25 000	$23 600
Dividend revenue	1 000	—
Other income	1 000	2 000
Proceeds from sale of property, plant and equipment	5 000	22 000
Total	32 000	47 600
Cost of sales	21 000	18 000
Other expenses	3 000	1 000
Carrying amount of property, plant and equipment sold	4 000	20 000
Total expenses	28 000	39 000
Profit before income tax	4 000	8 600
Income tax expense	(1 350)	(1 950)
Profit for the period	2 650	6 650
Retained earnings (1/1/13)	6 000	3 000
	8 650	9 650
Interim dividend paid	(2 500)	(1 000)
Retained earnings (31/12/13)	$ 6 150	$ 8 650

Amy Ltd acquired its shares in Zara Ltd at 1 January 2013, buying the 10 000 shares in Zara Ltd for $20 000 — Zara Ltd recorded share capital of $10 000. The shares were bought on a cum div. basis as Zara Ltd had declared a dividend of $3000 that was not paid until March 2013.

At 1 January 2013, all identifiable assets and liabilities of Zara Ltd were recorded at fair value except for inventory, for which the carrying amount of $2000 was $400 less than fair value. Some of this inventory has been a little slow to sell, and 10% of it is still on hand at 31 December 2013. Inventory on hand in Zara Ltd at 31 December 2013 also includes some items acquired from Amy Ltd during the year. These were sold by Amy Ltd for $5000, at a profit before tax of $1000. Half the goodwill was written off as the result of an impairment test on 31 December 2013.

During March 2013, Amy Ltd provided some management services to Zara Ltd at a fee of $500.

On 1 July 2013, Zara Ltd sold machinery to Amy Ltd at a gain of $2000. This machinery had a carrying amount to Zara Ltd of $20 000, and was considered by Amy Ltd to have a 5-year life.

By 31 December 2013, the financial assets acquired by Amy Ltd and Zara Ltd increased by $1000 and $650 respectively, with gains being recognised in other comprehensive income.

The tax rate is 30%.

Required

1. Prepare the consolidated statement of profit or loss and other comprehensive income for Amy Ltd and its subsidiary, Zara Ltd, at 31 December 2013.
2. Discuss the concept of 'realisation' using the intragroup transactions in this question to illustrate the concept.

Exercise 25.15 · CONSOLIDATION WORKSHEET, CONSOLIDATED STATEMENT OF PROFIT OR LOSS AND OTHER COMPREHENSIVE INCOME

★★ Financial information for Jasmine Ltd and Poppy Ltd for the year ended 30 June 2014 is shown below:

	Jasmine Ltd	Poppy Ltd
Sales revenue	$78 000	$40 000
Proceeds from sale of office furniture	—	3 000
Dividend revenue	4 400	1 600
Total income	82 400	44 600

	Jasmine Ltd	Poppy Ltd
Cost of sales	60 000	30 000
Other expenses	10 800	7 500
Total expenses	70 800	37 500
Profit before income tax	11 600	7 100
Income tax expense	(3 000)	(2 200)
Profit for the year	8 600	4 900
Retained earnings (1/7/13)	14 500	2 800
	23 100	7 700
Interim dividend paid	4 000	2 000
Final dividend declared	8 000	2 400
	12 000	4 400
Retained earnings (30/6/14)	$11 100	$ 3 300

Additional information

(a) On 1 July 2012, Jasmine Ltd purchased 100% of the shares of Poppy Ltd for $50 000. At that date the equity of the two entities was as follows:

	Jasmine Ltd	Poppy Ltd
Asset revaluation surplus	$25 000	$ 4 000
Retained earnings	14 500	2 800
Share capital	50 000	40 000

At 1 July 2012, all the identifiable assets and liabilities of Poppy Ltd were recorded at fair value except for the following:

	Carrying amount	Fair value
Plant and equipment (cost $80 000)	$60 000	$61 000
Inventory	3 000	3 500

All of this inventory was sold by December 2012. The plant and equipment had a further 5-year life. Any valuation adjustments are made on consolidation.

(b) Jasmine Ltd records dividend receivable as revenue when dividends are declared.

(c) The opening inventory of Poppy Ltd included goods which cost Poppy Ltd $2000. Poppy Ltd purchased this inventory from Jasmine Ltd at cost plus $33^1/_3\%$.

(d) Intragroup sales totalled $10 000 for the year. Sales from Jasmine Ltd to Poppy Ltd, at cost plus 10%, amounted to $5600. The closing inventory of Jasmine Ltd included goods which cost Jasmine Ltd $4400. Jasmine Ltd purchased this inventory from Poppy Ltd at cost plus 10%.

(e) On 31 December 2013, Poppy Ltd sold Jasmine Ltd office furniture for $3000. This furniture originally cost Poppy Ltd $3000 and was written down to $2500 when sold. Jasmine Ltd depreciates furniture at the rate of 10% p.a. on cost.

(f) The asset revaluation surplus relates to the use of the revaluation model for land. The following movements occurred in this account:

	Jasmine Ltd	Poppy Ltd
1 July 2012 to 30 June 2013	$3 000	$(500)
1 July 2013 to 30 June 2014	$2 000	$ 500

(g) The tax rate is 30%.

Required

Prepare the consolidated statement of profit or loss and other comprehensive income for the year ended 30 June 2014.

CONSOLIDATED WORKSHEET, CONSOLIDATED STATEMENT OF PROFIT OR LOSS AND OTHER COMPREHENSIVE INCOME

On 1 April 2014, Abby Ltd acquired all the issued ordinary shares (cum div.) of Ella Ltd for $100 000. At that date, relevant balances in the records of Ella Ltd were:

Share capital	$80 000
Asset revaluation surplus	5 000
Retained earnings	5 000
Dividend payable	4 000

All the identifiable assets and liabilities of Ella Ltd were recorded at fair values except for the following:

	Carrying amount	Fair value
Inventory	$10 000	$12 000
Plant (cost $80 000)	50 000	53 000

Immediately after the acquisition of its shares by Abby Ltd, Ella Ltd revalued its plant to fair value. The plant was expected to have a further 5-year life. All the inventory on hand at 1 April 2014 was sold by the end of the financial year.

At 1 April 2014, Ella Ltd had recorded goodwill of $2000. As a result of an impairment test on 31 March 2015, Ella Ltd wrote goodwill down by $1500 in the consolidation worksheet.

The dividend payable was subsequently paid in June 2014.

During the period ending 31 March 2015, intragroup sales consisted of $40 000 from Abby Ltd to Ella Ltd at a profit to Abby Ltd of $10 000. These were all sold to external entities by Ella Ltd for $42 000 before 31 March 2015. Ella Ltd also sold some inventory to Abby Ltd for $10 000. This had cost Ella Ltd $6000. Abby Ltd since has sold all the items to external entities for $8000, except one batch on which Ella Ltd recorded a $500 profit before tax (original cost to Ella Ltd was $1000).

On 1 October 2014, Abby Ltd sold an item, regarded by Abby Ltd as a non-current asset, to Ella Ltd which regarded it as inventory. At the time of sale, the carrying amount of the item to Abby Ltd was $28 000, and it was sold to Ella Ltd for $30 000. Abby Ltd was using a 10% p.a. depreciation rate applied to cost. The item remains unsold by Ella Ltd at 31 March 2015.

Both entities use the revaluation model in accounting for land. During the 2014–15 period, Abby Ltd and Ella Ltd both recorded revaluation increments, these being $2200 and $1100 respectively.

The following information was obtained from the companies for the year ended 31 March 2015:

	Abby Ltd	Ella Ltd
Sales	$146 000	$120 000
Dividend revenue	4 000	—
Proceeds on sale of non-current asset	30 000	—
	180 000	120 000
Cost of sales	88 000	68 000
Other expenses	44 000	19 000
	132 000	87 000
Profit before income tax	48 000	33 000
Income tax expense	(12 000)	(14 000)
Profit for the year	36 000	19 000
Retained earnings (1/4/14)	10 000	5 000
Total available for appropriation	46 000	24 000
Dividend paid	(8 000)	(4 000)
Retained earnings (31/3/15)	$ 38 000	$ 20 000

Required

1. Prepare the consolidated statement of profit or loss and other comprehensive income as at 31 March 2015. Assume a tax rate of 30%.
2. Explain the consolidation worksheet adjustment for the sale of the non-current asset to Ella Ltd at 1 October 2014 by Abby Ltd.

Exercise 25.17 ★★★

CONSOLIDATION WORKSHEET, CONSOLIDATED FINANCIAL STATEMENTS

On 31 December 2009, Lara Ltd acquired all the issued shares of Jade Ltd. On this date, the share capital of Jade Ltd consisted of 200 000 shares paid to 50c per share. Other reserves and retained earnings at this date consisted of:

General reserve	$25 000
Retained earnings	20 000

At 31 December 2009, all the identifiable assets and liabilities of Jade Ltd were recorded at fair value except for some plant and machinery. This plant and machinery, which cost $100 000, had a carrying amount of $85 000 and a fair value of $90 000. The estimated remaining useful life was 10 years. Adjustments for fair values are made on consolidation.

Immediately after acquisition, a dividend of $10 000 was declared and paid out of retained earnings. Also, 1 year after acquisition, Jade Ltd used $20 000 from the general reserve on hand at acquisition date to partly pay the balance unpaid on the issued shares.

The trial balances of Lara Ltd and Jade Ltd at 31 December 2014 were as shown below:

Trial Balances as at 31 December 2014	Lara Ltd	Jade Ltd
Credits		
Share capital	$ 500 000	$ 120 000
General reserve	25 000	5 000
Asset revaluation surplus	10 000	6 000
Retained earnings (1/1/14)	40 000	65 000
Other components of equity	15 000	10 000
Current tax liabilities	22 000	18 000
Deferred tax liabilities	6 240	5 200
Payables	22 000	14 000
Sales revenue	250 000	120 000
Other income	20 000	5 000
Proceeds from sale of property, plant and equipment	14 000	50 000
	$ 924 240	$ 418 200
Debits		
Income tax expense	$ 20 000	$ 10 000
Dividend declared	10 000	8 000
Plant and machinery	425 000	337 000
Accumulated depreciation	(300 000)	(261 000)
Motor vehicles	284 200	152 600
Accumulated depreciation	(160 000)	(100 000)
Receivables	25 000	7 310
Financial assets	60 000	40 000
Inventory	106 440	72 000
Bank	46 900	5 990
Deferred tax assets	12 700	6 300
Shares in Jade Ltd	160 000	—
Cost of sales	188 000	80 000
Other expenses	28 000	5 000
Carrying amount of property, plant and equipment sold	18 000	55 000
	$ 924 240	$ 418 200

Additional information

(a) During the current period, Lara Ltd sold inventory to Jade Ltd for $20 000. This had originally cost Lara Ltd $18 200. Jade Ltd has, by 31 December 2014, sold half this inventory for $12 310.

(b) Some of the items manufactured by Jade Ltd are used as plant by Lara Ltd. One of the plant items held by Lara Ltd at 31 December 2014 was purchased from Jade Ltd on 1 July 2011 for $25 000. It had cost Jade Ltd $17 500 to manufacture this item. Lara Ltd depreciates such items at 10% p.a. on cost.

(c) At 1 January 2014, Jade Ltd sold a machine to Lara Ltd for $50 000. This item had a carrying amount at time of sale to Jade Ltd of $55 000. Both entities use a 5% p.a. on cost depreciation rate for this item.

(d) The tax rate is 30%.

(e) Certain specialised items of plant, considered a separate class of assets, are measured using the revaluation model. At 1 January 2013, the balances of the asset revaluation surplus were $8000 (Lara Ltd) and $7000 (Jade Ltd).

(f) The Other Components of Equity account reflects movements in the financial assets. The balances of this account at 1 January 2013 were $12 000 (Lara Ltd) and $8000 (Jade Ltd).

Required

Prepare the consolidated financial statements as at 31 December 2014.

Exercise 25.18 **CONSOLIDATION WORKSHEET**

★★★ On 1 July 2013, Monique Ltd acquired all the shares of Madeleine Ltd for $137 200. At acquisition date, the equity of Madeleine Ltd consisted of:

Share capital	$80 000
General reserve	16 000
Retained earnings	21 000

On this date, all the identifiable assets and liabilities of Madeleine Ltd were recorded at fair value except for the following assets:

	Carrying amount	Fair value
Inventory	$50 000	$56 000
Motor vehicles (cost $18 000)	15 000	16 000
Furniture and fittings (cost $30 000)	24 000	32 000
Land	18 480	24 480

The inventory and land on hand in Madeleine Ltd at 1 July 2013 were sold during the following 12 months. The motor vehicles, which at acquisition date were estimated to have a 4-year life, were sold on 1 January 2015. Except for land, valuation adjustments are made on consolidation and, on realisation of a business combination valuation reserve, a transfer is made to retained earnings on consolidation. The furniture and fittings were estimated to have a further 8-year life. At 1 July 2013, Madeleine Ltd had not recorded any goodwill.

The following trial balances were prepared for the companies at 30 June 2015:

Credits	Monique Ltd	Madeleine Ltd
Share capital	$170 000	$ 80 000
General reserve	41 000	22 000
Retained earnings (1/7/14)	16 000	29 500
Debentures	120 000	—
Final dividend payable	10 000	3 000
Current tax liabilities	8 000	2 500
Other payables	34 800	10 100
Advance from Monique Ltd	—	10 000
Sales revenue	85 000	65 000

	Monique Ltd	Madeleine Ltd
Other income	23 000	22 000
Accumulated depreciation		
— Motor vehicles	4 000	2 000
— Furniture and fittings	2 000	6 000
	$513 800	$252 100
Debits		
Cost of sales	$ 65 000	$ 53 500
Other expenses	22 000	27 000
Shares in Madeleine Ltd	137 200	—
Land	—	24 480
Motor vehicles	28 000	22 000
Furniture and fittings	34 000	37 300
Inventory	171 580	70 320
Other assets	8 620	3 100
Income tax expense	7 200	2 000
Interim dividend paid	4 000	2 000
Final dividend declared	10 000	3 000
Deferred tax assets	16 200	7 400
Advance to Madeleine Ltd	10 000	—
	$513 800	$252 100

Additional information

(a) Intragroup transfers of inventory consisted of:

1/7/13 to 30/6/14:	
Sales from Monique Ltd to Madeleine Ltd	$12 000
Profit in inventory on hand 30/6/14	200
1/7/14 to 30/6/15:	
Sales from Monique Ltd to Madeleine Ltd	15 000
Profit in inventory on hand 30/6/15	
(incl. $50 from previous period sales)	1 000

(b) On 1 January 2014, Madeleine Ltd sold furniture and fittings to Monique Ltd for $8000. This had originally cost Madeleine Ltd $12 000 and had a carrying amount at time of sale of $7000. Both entities charge depreciation at the rate of 10% p.a.

(c) The tax rate is 30%.

Required

Prepare the consolidation worksheet for the preparation of the consolidated financial statements for the period ended 30 June 2015.

26

Consolidation: non-controlling interest

ACCOUNTING STANDARDS IN FOCUS

IFRS 10 *Consolidated Financial Statements*

IFRS 3 *Business Combinations*

IAS 1 *Presentation of Financial Statements*

IFRS 12 *Disclosure of Interests in Other Entities*

LEARNING OBJECTIVES

After studying this chapter, you should be able to:

1 discuss the nature of the non-controlling interest (NCI)

2 explain the effects of the NCI on the consolidation process

3 explain how to calculate the NCI share of equity

4 explain how the calculation of the NCI is affected by the existence of intragroup transactions

5 explain how the NCI is affected by the existence of a gain on bargain purchase.

26.1 NON-CONTROLLING INTEREST EXPLAINED

In chapters 24 and 25, the group under consideration consisted of two entities where the parent owned *all* the share capital of the subsidiary. In this chapter, the group under discussion consists of a parent that has only a *partial* interest in the subsidiary; that is, the subsidiary is less than wholly owned by the parent.

26.1.1 Nature of the non-controlling interest (NCI)

Ownership interests in a subsidiary other than the parent are referred to as the non-controlling interest, or NCI. Appendix A of IFRS 10 *Consolidated Financial Statements* contains the following definition of NCI:

> Equity in a **subsidiary** not attributable, directly or indirectly, to a **parent**.

In figure 26.1, the group shown is illustrative of those discussed in this chapter. In this case, the parent entity owns 75% of the shares of a subsidiary. There are two owners in this group — the parent shareholders and the NCI. The NCI is a contributor of equity to the group.

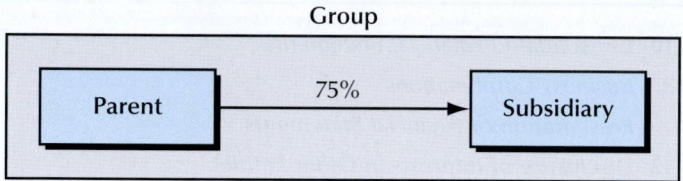

FIGURE 26.1 The group

According to paragraph 22 of IFRS 10, the NCI is to be identified and presented within equity, separately from the parent shareholders' equity; that is, it is regarded as an equity contributor to the group, rather than a liability of the group. This is because the NCI does not meet the definition of a liability as contained in the *Conceptual Framework*, because the group has no present obligation to provide economic outflows to the NCI. The NCI receives a share of consolidated equity, and is therefore a participant in the residual equity of the group.

Classification of the NCI as equity affects both the calculation of the NCI as well as how it is disclosed in the consolidated financial statements.

26.1.2 Calculation of the NCI share of equity

The NCI is entitled to a share of consolidated equity, because it is a contributor of equity to the consolidated group. Because consolidated equity is affected by profits and losses made in relation to transactions within the group, the calculation of the NCI is affected by the existence of intragroup transactions. In other words, the NCI is entitled to a share of the equity of the subsidiary adjusted for the effects of profits and losses made on intragroup transactions. This is discussed in more detail in section 26.4.

26.1.3 Disclosure of the NCI

According to paragraph 22 of IFRS 10:

> A parent shall present non-controlling interests in the consolidated statement of financial position within equity, separately from the equity of the owners of the parent.

IAS 1 *Presentation of Financial Statements* confirms these disclosures. Paragraph 81B of IAS 1 requires the profit or loss and other comprehensive income for the period to be disclosed in the statement of profit or loss and other comprehensive income, showing separately the comprehensive income attributable to non-controlling interests, and that attributable to owners of the parent. Figure 26.2 shows how the statement of profit or loss and other comprehensive income may be shown. Note that in terms of the various line items in the statement, such as revenues and expenses, it is the total consolidated amount that is disclosed. It is only the consolidated profit and comprehensive income that is divided into parent share and NCI share.

WALLABY LTD
Consolidated Statement of Profit or Loss and Other Comprehensive Income
for the year ended 30 June 2014

	2014 $m	2013 $m
Revenue	500	450
Expenses	280	260
Gross profit	220	190
Finance costs	40	35
	180	155
Share of after-tax profit of associates	30	25
Profit before tax	210	180
Income tax expense	(28)	(22)
PROFIT FOR THE YEAR	182	158
Other comprehensive income	31	24
TOTAL COMPREHENSIVE INCOME FOR THE YEAR	213	182
Profit attributable to:		
Owners of the parent	151	140
Non-controlling interests	31	18
	182	158
Total comprehensive income attributable to:		
Owners of the parent	179	160
Non-controlling interests	34	22
	213	182

FIGURE 26.2 Disclosure of NCI in the statement of profit or loss and other comprehensive income

According to paragraph 106(a) of IAS 1, the total comprehensive income for the period must be disclosed in the statement of changes in equity, showing separately the total amounts attributable to owners of the parent and to non-controlling interests. Figure 26.3 provides an example of disclosures in the statement of changes of equity. Note that the only line item for which the NCI must be shown is the total comprehensive income for the period. There is no requirement to show the NCI share of each equity account.

WALLABY LTD
Consolidated Statement of Changes in Equity (extract)
for the year ended 30 June 2014

	Total equity					Non-controlling interest	Owners of the parent
	Share capital	Revaluation surplus	Translation reserve	Retained earnings	Total		
	$m	$m	$m	$m	$m	$m	$m
Balance at 1 July 2013	400	120	100	250	870	130	740
Changes in accounting policy	—	—	—	—	—	—	—
Total comprehensive income for the period	—	21	10	182	213	34	179
Dividends	—	—	—	(150)	(150)	(10)	(140)
Issue of share capital	—	—	—	—	—	—	—
Balance at 30 June 2014	400	141	110	282	933	154	779

FIGURE 26.3 Disclosure of NCI in the statement of changes in equity

Similarly, paragraph 54(q) of IAS 1 requires disclosure in the statement of financial position of the total NCI share of equity while paragraph 54(r) requires disclosure of the issued capital and reserves attributable to owners of the parent. The equity section of the statement of financial position could then appear as in figure 26.4. In the statement of financial position, only the total NCI share of equity is disclosed, rather than the NCI share of the different categories of equity. The NCI share of the various categories of equity and the changes in those balances can be seen in the statement of changes in equity. Note that the consolidated assets and liabilities are those for the whole of the group; it is only equity that is divided into parent and NCI shares.

WALLABY LTD Statement of Financial Position (extract) as at 30 June 2014		
	2014	2013
	$m	$m
EQUITY		
Share capital	400	400
Other reserves	251	220
Retained earnings	282	250
	933	870
Non-controlling interests	154	130
Equity attributable to owners of the parent	779	740

FIGURE 26.4 Disclosure of NCI in the statement of financial position

IFRS 12 *Disclosure of Interests in Other Entities* also contains disclosures required for subsidiaries in which there are NCI. Paragraph 12 of IFRS 12 states:

> An entity shall disclose for each of its subsidiaries that have non-controlling interests that are material to the reporting entity:
> (a) the name of the subsidiary.
> (b) the principal place of business (and country of incorporation if different from the principal place of business) of the subsidiary.
> (c) the proportion of ownership interests held by non-controlling interests.
> (d) the proportion of voting rights held by non-controlling interests, if different from the proportion of ownership interests held.
> (e) the profit or loss allocated to non-controlling interests of the subsidiary during the reporting period.
> (f) accumulated non-controlling interests of the subsidiary at the end of the reporting period.
> (g) summarised financial information about the subsidiary (see paragraph B10).

 ## 26.2 EFFECTS OF AN NCI ON THE CONSOLIDATION PROCESS

Paragraph 32 of IFRS 3 states:

> The acquirer shall recognise goodwill as of the acquisition date measured as the excess of (a) over (b) below:
> (a) the aggregate of:
>   (i) the consideration transferred measured in accordance with this IFRS, which generally requires acquisition-date fair value (see paragraph 37);
>   (ii) the amount of any non-controlling interest in the acquiree measured in accordance with this IFRS; and
>   (iii) in a business combination achieved in stages (see paragraphs 41 and 42), the acquisition date fair value of the acquirer's previously held equity interests in the acquiree.
> (b) the net of the acquisition-date amounts of the identifiable assets acquired and the liabilities assumed measured in accordance with this IFRS.

Note that this choice is not an accounting policy choice, but is made for each business combination.

Consider a situation where A Ltd acquires 50% of the shares of B Ltd, having previously acquired 20% of the shares of B Ltd. Holding 70% of the shares of B Ltd gives A Ltd control of that entity. At acquisition date, there is an NCI of 30%. Note:

- Where the parent acquires less than all the shares of a subsidiary, it acquires only a portion of the total equity or total net assets of the subsidiary. Hence, the consideration transferred is for only a portion of the net assets of the subsidiary; in this example, 50%.

- Where the parent previously acquired an interest in the subsidiary, it will need to be accounted for as shown in chapter 24. In essence, the 20% investment held prior to the parent obtaining control must be revalued at acquisition date to fair value.

The next step is to measure the amount of the 30% non-controlling interest in the subsidiary. The problem with this step is that IFRS 3 allows alternative treatments. Paragraph 19 of IFRS 3 states:

> For each business combination, the acquirer shall measure at the acquisition date components of non-controlling interests in the acquiree that are present ownership interests and entitle their holders to a proportionate share of the entity's net assets in the event of liquidation at either:
> (a) fair value; or
> (b) the present ownership instruments' proportionate share in the recognised amounts of the acquiree's identifiable net assets.
> All other components of non-controlling interests shall be measured at their acquisition-date fair values, unless another measurement basis is required by IFRSs.

Which alternative is chosen affects the determination of goodwill and the subsequent consolidation adjustments. Where the first alternative is used, the goodwill attributable to both the NCI and the parent is measured. Under the second alternative, only the goodwill attributable to the parent is measured. The methods are sometimes referred to as the 'full goodwill' and the 'partial goodwill' methods — see paragraph BC205 of the Basis for Conclusions on IFRS 3 for further elaboration. These terms are used in this chapter to distinguish between the two methods. The methods are demonstrated in sections 26.2.1 and 26.2.2 and the reasons for the standard setters allowing optional measurements, as well as factors to consider in choosing between the methods, is discussed in section 26.2.3.

26.2.1 Full goodwill method

Under this method, at acquisition date, the NCI in the subsidiary is measured at fair value. The fair value is determined on the basis of the market prices for shares not acquired by the parent, or, if these are not available, a valuation technique is used.

It is not sufficient to use the consideration paid by the acquirer to measure the fair value of the NCI. For example, if a parent paid $80 000 for 80% of the shares of a subsidiary, then the fair value of the NCI cannot be assumed to be $20 000 (i.e. 20/80 × $80 000). It may be that the acquirer paid a control premium in order to acquire a controlling interest in the subsidiary. Relating this to the nature of goodwill in chapter 14, core goodwill includes the component of combination goodwill, relating to synergies arising because of the combination of the parent and the subsidiary. The parent would increase the consideration it was prepared to pay due to these synergies. However, these synergies may result in increased earnings in the parent and not the subsidiary. In this case, the NCI does not receive any share of those synergies. Hence, the consideration paid by the parent could not be used to measure the fair value of the NCI in the subsidiary.

To illustrate the method, assume that P Ltd paid $169 600 for 80% of the shares of S Ltd on 1 July 2013. All identifiable assets and liabilities of the subsidiary were recorded at fair value, except for land for which the fair value was $10 000 greater than cost. The tax rate is 30%. The NCI in S Ltd was considered to have a fair value of $42 000. At acquisition date, the equity of S Ltd consisted of:

Share capital	$100 000
General reserve	60 000
Retained earnings	40 000

The acquisition analysis is as follows:

Net fair value of identifiable assets and liabilities of S Ltd	= $100 000 + $60 000 + $40 000 + $10 000(1 − 30%) (BCVR — land)
	= $207 000
(a) Consideration transferred	= $169 600
(b) Non-controlling interest in S Ltd	= $42 000
Aggregate of (a) and (b)	= $211 600
Goodwill	= $211 600 − $207 000
	= $4600

Goodwill of S Ltd	
Fair value of S Ltd	= $42 000/20%
	= $210 000
Net fair value of identifiable assets	
and liabilities of S Ltd	= $207 000
Goodwill of S Ltd	= $210 000 − $207 000
	= $3000
Goodwill of P Ltd	
Goodwill acquired	= $4600
Goodwill of S Ltd	= $3000
Goodwill of P Ltd – control premium	= $1600

Note the following:
- The acquired goodwill of $4600 calculated in the acquisition analysis consists of both the goodwill of the subsidiary and the premium paid by the parent to acquire control over the subsidiary.
- As the fair value of the NCI (20%) is determined to be $42 000, if P Ltd were to acquire 80% of S Ltd, it would expect to pay $168 000 (i.e. 80/20 × $42 000). As P Ltd paid $169 600, it paid a control premium of $1600. This is recognised as goodwill attributable to P Ltd. Effectively the goodwill of $4600 is broken down into:

Control premium paid by P Ltd	$1600
Parent's share of S Ltd's goodwill	$2400 [$4000 − $1600 *or* 80% × $3000]
NCI share of S Ltd's goodwill	$600 [20% × $3000]

- The goodwill attributable to P Ltd — both share of S Ltd's goodwill and the control premium — could be calculated as follows:

Net fair value acquired by P Ltd	= 80% × $207 000
	= $165 600
Consideration transferred	= $169 600
Goodwill attributable to P Ltd	= $169 600 − $165 600
	= $4000

- The control premium is recognised as part of goodwill on consolidation, but is not attributable to the NCI.

In accounting for the goodwill, a business combination valuation reserve is raised for the goodwill of the subsidiary, namely $3000. This reserve is then attributed on a proportional basis to the parent and the NCI, being $2400 to the parent and $600 to the NCI. The control premium goodwill is recognised in the pre-acquisition entry only as the earnings from this combination goodwill flow into the parent's earnings and not that of the subsidiary — otherwise it would be included in the valuation of the NCI interest in the subsidiary.

The consolidation worksheet entries are as follows:

1. Business combination valuation entries			
Land	Dr	10 000	
Deferred Tax Liability	Cr		3 000
Business Combination Valuation Reserve	Cr		7 000
(Revaluation of land)			
Goodwill	Dr	3 000	
Business Combination Valuation Reserve	Cr		3 000
(Recognition of subsidiary goodwill)			

2. Pre-acquisition entry		
Retained Earnings [80% × $40 000]	Dr	32 000
Share Capital [80% × $100 000]	Dr	80 000
General Reserve [80% × $60 000]	Dr	48 000
Business Combination Valuation Reserve[80% ($7000 + $3000)]	Dr	8 000
Goodwill	Dr	1 600
Shares in S Ltd	Cr	169 600

Two *business combination valuation entries* are required: one for the revaluation of the land to fair value, and the second to recognise the goodwill of the subsidiary.

In relation to the equity on hand at acquisition date, 80% is attributable to the parent, and 20% is attributable to the NCI. The *pre-acquisition entry* relates to the investment by the parent in the subsidiary, and thus relates to 80% of the amounts shown in the acquisition analysis. The adjustments to equity in the pre-acquisition entry are then determined by taking 80% of the recorded equity of the subsidiary and 80% of the business combination valuation reserves recognised as a result of differences between fair values and carrying amounts of the subsidiary's identifiable assets and liabilities at acquisition date and the goodwill of the subsidiary. The goodwill relating to the control premium is recognised in the pre-acquisition entry.

26.2.2 Partial goodwill method

Under the second option, at acquisition date, the NCI is measured as the NCI's proportionate share of the acquiree's identifiable net assets. The NCI therefore does not get a share of any equity relating to goodwill as goodwill is defined in Appendix A of IFRS 3 as the future economic benefits arising from assets not individually identified. The only goodwill recognised is that acquired by the parent in the business combination — hence the term 'partial' goodwill. According to paragraph 32 of IFRS 3, using the measurement of the NCI share of equity based on the NCI's proportionate share of the acquiree's identifiable net assets:

> Goodwill = consideration transferred *plus* previously acquired investment by parent *plus* NCI share of identifiable assets and liabilities of subsidiary *less* net fair value of identifiable assets and liabilities of subsidiary.

To illustrate, using the same example as in section 26.2.1, assume that P Ltd paid $169 600 for 80% of the shares of S Ltd on 1 July 2013. All identifiable assets and liabilities of the subsidiary were recorded at fair value, except for land for which the fair value was $10 000 greater than cost. The tax rate is 30%. At acquisition date, the equity of S Ltd consisted of:

Share capital	$100 000
General reserve	60 000
Retained earnings	40 000

The acquisition analysis is as follows:

Net fair value of identifiable assets and liabilities of S Ltd	= $100 000 + $60 000 + $40 000
	+ $10 000(1 − 30%) (BCVR — land)
	= $207 000
(a) Consideration transferred	= $169 600
(b) Non-controlling interest in S Ltd	= 20% × $207 000
	= $41 400
Aggregate of (a) and (b)	= $211 000
Goodwill	= $211 000 − $207 000
	= $4000

Note that the $4000 goodwill is the same as the parent's share calculated in section 26.2.1, consisting of the parent's share of the subsidiary's goodwill (80% × $3000 = $2400) and any control premium ($1600). The consolidation worksheet entries are:

Business combination valuation entry			
Land	Dr	10 000	
Deferred Tax Liability	Cr		3 000
Business Combination Valuation Reserve	Cr		7 000
Pre-acquisition entry			
Retained Earnings [80% × $40 000]	Dr	32 000	
Share Capital [80% × $100 000]	Dr	80 000	
General Reserve [80% × $60 000]	Dr	48 000	
Business Combination Valuation Reserve [80% × $7000]	Dr	5 600	
Goodwill	Dr	4 000	
Shares in S Ltd	Cr		169 600

Note firstly that there is no business combination valuation entry for goodwill. This is because only the parent's share of the goodwill is recognised. A business combination valuation adjustment to recognise goodwill is only used under the full goodwill method where both the parent's and the NCI's share of goodwill is recognised.

In relation to the equity on hand at acquisition date, only 80% is attributable to the parent, and 20% is attributable to the NCI. The pre-acquisition entry relates to the investment by the parent in the subsidiary, and thus relates to 80% of the amounts shown in the acquisition analysis. The adjustments to equity in the pre-acquisition entry are then determined by taking 80% of the recorded equity of the subsidiary and 80% of the business combination valuation reserves recognised as a result of differences between fair value and carrying amounts of the subsidiary's identifiable assets and liabilities at acquisition date. Because only the parent's share of goodwill is recognised, this is accounted for in the pre-acquisition entry which also relates to the investment by the parent in the subsidiary.

26.2.3 Reasons for, and choosing between, the options

IFRS 3, as revised in 2008, was issued by the IASB at the same time as Statement of Financial Standards No. 141 *Business Combinations* was revised and reissued by the Financial Accounting Standards Board (FASB) in the United States. The project on determining a new standard on business combinations was conducted jointly by the FASB and the IASB in the hope of achieving convergence on the standard between the two boards. Both boards issued exposure drafts on business combinations, and, in both these documents, the full goodwill method was recommended. However, when the final standards were issued, the FASB standard required the accounting for all business combinations to use the full goodwill method; whereas, the IASB standard provided for optional treatments in the measurement of the NCI share of the subsidiary.

Paragraphs BC209–BC221 explain why the IASB chose to provide optional methods. As noted in paragraph BC210, the IASB recognises that to allow optional methods does reduce the comparability of financial statements:

> However, the IASB was not able to agree on a single measurement basis for non-controlling interests because neither of the alternatives considered (fair value and proportionate share of the acquiree's identifiable net assets) was supported by enough board members to enable a revised business combinations standard to be issued.

The IASB supports the principle of measuring all components of a business combination at fair value (paragraph BC212); however, paragraph BC213 notes some arguments against applying this to the NCI in the acquiree:

- It is more costly to measure the NCI at fair value than at the proportionate share of the net fair value of the identifiable net assets of the acquiree.
- There is not sufficient evidence to assess the marginal benefits of reporting the acquisition-date fair value of NCIs.
- Respondents to the exposure draft saw little information of value in the reported NCI, regardless of how it is measured.

One of the options considered by the IASB in writing the standard was to require the use of the fair value method for measuring the NCI but allowing entities to use the proportionate method where there exists 'undue cost or effort' in measuring the fair value. However, the IASB rejected this option as it did not think the term undue cost or effort would be applied consistently (paragraph BC215).

The IASB noted three main differences in outcome that occur where the partial goodwill method is used instead of the full goodwill method:

1. The amounts recognised for the NCI share of equity and goodwill would be lower.
2. Where IAS 36 *Impairment of Assets* is applied to a cash-generating unit containing goodwill, as the goodwill recognised by the CGU is lower, this affects the impairment loss relating to goodwill.
3. There is also an effect where an acquirer subsequently obtains further shares in the subsidiary at a later date. An explanation of this effect is beyond the scope of this book.

In choosing which method to use — full or partial goodwill — it is these three effects on the financial statements, both current and in the future, that must be taken into consideration. For example, if management has future intentions of acquiring more shares in the subsidiary (i.e. by acquiring some of the shares held by the NCI), then the potential impact on equity when that acquisition occurs will need to be considered.

26.2.4 Intragroup transactions

As noted in chapter 25, because the transactions occur within the economic entity, the full effects of transactions within the group are adjusted on consolidation. In essence, the worksheet adjustment entries used in chapter 25 are the same regardless of whether the subsidiary is wholly or partly owned by its parent. The only exception to the entries used in chapter 25 is for dividends.

Where an NCI exists, any dividends declared or paid by a subsidiary are paid proportionately (to the extent of the ownership interest in the subsidiary) to the parent and proportionately to the NCI. In adjusting for dividends paid by a subsidiary, only the dividend paid or payable to the parent is eliminated on consolidation. In other words, there is a proportional adjustment of the dividend paid or declared. As with other intragroup transactions, the adjustment relates to the flow within the group. A payment or a declaration of dividends by a subsidiary reduces the NCI share of subsidiary equity because the equity of the subsidiary is reduced by the payment or declaration of dividends. In calculating the NCI share of subsidiary equity, the existence of dividends must be taken into consideration (see section 26.3.3 of this chapter). Where a dividend is declared, the NCI share of equity is reduced, and a liability to pay dividends to the NCI is shown in the consolidated statement of financial position.

To illustrate, assume a parent owns 80% of the share capital of a subsidiary. In the current period, the subsidiary pays a $1000 dividend and declares a further $1500 dividend. The adjustment entries in the consolidation worksheet in the current period are:

Dividend Revenue	Dr	800	
Dividend Paid	Cr		800
(80% × $1000)			
Dividend Payable	Dr	1 200	
Dividend Declared	Cr		1 200
(80% × $1500)			
Dividend Revenue	Dr	1 200	
Dividend Receivable	Cr		1 200
(80% × $1500)			

26.2.5 Consolidation worksheet

Because the disclosure requirements for the NCI require the extraction of the NCI share of various equity items, the consolidation worksheet is changed to enable this information to be produced. Figure 26.5 contains an example of the changed worksheet. In particular, note that two new columns are added, a *debit column* and a *credit column* for the calculation of the NCI share of equity. These two columns are not adjustment or elimination columns. Instead, they are used to divide consolidated equity into NCI share and parent entity share. The worksheet shown in figure 26.5 also contains a column showing the figures for the consolidated group. This column is shown between the adjustment columns and the NCI columns, and it is the summation of the financial statements of the group members and the consolidation adjustments. The parent figures are then determined by subtracting the NCI share of equity from the total consolidated equity of the group.

Financial statements	P Ltd	S Ltd	Adjustments		Group	Non-controlling interest		Parent
			Dr	Cr		Dr	Cr	
Profit/(loss)	5 000	4 000			9 000	400		8 600
Retained earnings (opening balance)	10 000	8 000			18 000	800		17 200
Transfer from reserves	4 000	2 000			6 000	200		5 800
Total available for appropriation	19 000	14 000			33 000			31 600
Interim dividend paid	2 000	1 500			3 500		150	3 350
Final dividend declared	4 000	2 500			6 500		250	6 250
Transfer to reserves	3 000	1 000			4 000		100	3 900
	9 000	5 000			14 000			13 500
Retained earnings (closing balance)	10 000	9 000			19 000			18 100
Share capital	50 000	40 000			90 000	4 000		86 000
Other reserves	30 000	20 000			50 000	2 000		48 000
	90 000	69 000			159 000			152 100
Asset revaluation surplus (opening balance)	4 000	5 000			9 000	500		8 500
Revaluation increases	2 000	2 000			4 000	200		3 800
Asset revaluation surplus (closing balance)	6 000	7 000			13 000			12 300
Total equity: parent								164 400
Total equity: NCI							7 600	7 600
Total equity	96 000	76 000			172 000	8 100	8 100	172 000
Current liabilities	3 000	2 000			5 000			
Non-current liabilities	8 000	6 000			14 000			
Total liabilities	11 000	8 000			19 000			
Total equity and liabilities	107 000	84 000			191 000			

FIGURE 26.5 Consolidation worksheet containing NCI columns

In figure 26.5, the amounts in the debit NCI column record the NCI share of the relevant equity item. This amount is subtracted in the consolidation process so that the consolidation column contains the parent's share of consolidated equity.

The first line in figure 26.5 is the consolidated profit/(loss) for the period. This amount is then attributed to the parent and the NCI. In all subsequent equity lines, the NCI share is recorded in the debit NCI column, and the parent's share of each equity account is calculated. The total NCI share of equity is then added to the parent column to give total consolidated equity.

The NCI share of retained earnings is increased by subsidiary profits and transfers from reserves, and decreased by transfers to reserves and payments and declarations of dividends. The total NCI share of equity is then the sum of the NCI share of capital, other reserves and retained earnings. The assets and liabilities of the group are shown in total and not allocated to the equity interests in the group — see, for example, the liabilities section in figure 26.5.

26.3 CALCULATING THE NCI SHARE OF EQUITY

Non-controlling interests in the net assets consist of the amount of those non-controlling interests at the date of the original combination calculated in accordance with IFRS 3 and the non-controlling interests' share of changes in equity since the date of the combination.

Changes in equity since the acquisition date must be taken into account. Note that these changes not only are in the recorded equity of the subsidiary, but also relate to other changes in consolidated equity. As noted earlier in this chapter, the NCI is entitled to a share of *consolidated* equity. This requires taking into account adjustments for profits or losses made as a result of intragroup transactions because these profits or losses are not recognised by the group.

The calculation of the NCI is done in two stages: (1) the NCI share of recorded equity is measured (see section 26.3.1), and (2) this share is adjusted for the effects of intragroup transactions (see section 26.4).

26.3.1 NCI share of recorded equity of the subsidiary

The equity of the subsidiary consists of the equity contained in the actual records of the subsidiary as well as any business combination valuation reserves created on consolidation at the acquisition date, where the identifiable assets and liabilities of the subsidiary are recorded at amounts different from their fair values. The NCI is entitled to a share of subsidiary equity at the end of the reporting period, which consists of the equity on hand at acquisition date plus any changes in that equity between acquisition date and the end of the reporting period. The calculation of the NCI share of equity at a point in time is done in three steps:

1. Determine the NCI share of equity of the subsidiary at acquisition date.
2. Determine the NCI share of the change in subsidiary equity between the acquisition date and the beginning of the current period for which the consolidated financial statements are being prepared.
3. Determine the NCI share of the changes in subsidiary equity in the current period.

The calculation could be represented diagrammatically, as shown in figure 26.6.

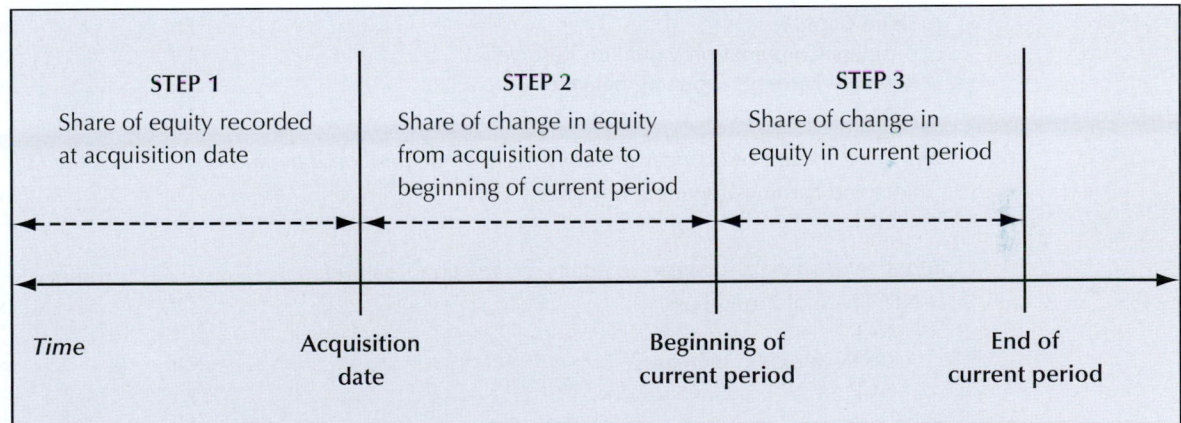

FIGURE 26.6 Calculating the NCI share of equity
Source: Based on a diagram by Peter Gerhardy, Ernst & Young, Adelaide.

Note that, in calculating the NCI share of equity at the end of the current period, the information relating to the NCI share of equity from steps 1 and 2 should be available from the previous period's consolidation worksheet.

To illustrate the above procedure, consider the calculation of the NCI share of retained earnings over a 5-year period. Assume the following information in relation to Bandicoot Ltd:

Retained earnings as at 1 July 2009	$10 000
Retained earnings as at 30 June 2013	50 000
Profit for the 2013–14 period	15 000
Retained earnings as at 30 June 2014	65 000

Assume that Pelican Ltd had acquired 80% of the share capital of Bandicoot Ltd at 1 July 2009, and the consolidated financial statements were being prepared at 30 June 2014. The 20% NCI in Bandicoot Ltd is therefore entitled to a share of the retained earnings balance of $65 000, a share equal to $13 000. This share is calculated in three steps:

Step 1. A share of the balance at 1 July 2009 (20% × $10 000)   = $ 2 000
Step 2. A share of the change in retained earnings from the acquisition date
        to the beginning of the current period (20% × [$50 000 − $10 000])   =   8 000
Step 3. A share of the current period increase in retained earnings (20% × $15 000) =   3 000
                                                         $13 000

The increase in retained earnings is broken into these three steps because accounting is based on time periods. The NCI is entitled to a share of the profits of past periods as well as a share of the profits of the current period. Note that, in calculating the NCI share of retained earnings for Bandicoot Ltd at 30 June 2015 (one year after the above calculation), the total of steps 1 and 2 for the 2015 calculation would be $13 000, as calculated above. The only additional calculation would be the share of changes in retained earnings in the 2014–15 period.

The separate calculations are not based on a division of equity into pre-acquisition and post-acquisition equity. The division of equity is based on *time* — changes in equity are calculated on a period-by-period basis for accounting purposes.

The NCI columns in the consolidation worksheet contain the amounts relating to the three steps noted above. The journal entries used in the NCI columns of the consolidation worksheet to reflect the NCI share of equity are based on the three-step approach. The form of these entries is:

Step 1: NCI at acquisition date

Share Capital	Dr	xxx	
Business Combination Valuation Reserve	Dr	xxx	
Retained Earnings (opening balance)	Dr	xxx	
NCI	Cr		xxx

Step 2: NCI share of changes in equity between acquisition date and beginning of the current period

Retained Earnings (opening balance)	Dr	xxx	
NCI	Cr		xxx

Step 3: NCI share of changes in equity in the current period

NCI Share of Profit/(Loss)	Dr	xxx	
NCI	Cr		xxx
Asset Revaluation Increases	Dr	xxx	
NCI	Cr		xxx
NCI	Dr	xxx	
Dividend Paid	Cr		xxx
NCI	Dr	xxx	
Dividend Declared	Cr		xxx

The effects of these journal entries can be seen in the consolidation worksheet in figure 26.5. The above entries are illustrative only, and there may be others where there are transfers to or from reserves that affect the balances of equity in the subsidiary. The effects of these transactions are illustrated in the next section.

26.3.2 Accounting at acquisition date

This section illustrates the effects that the existence of an NCI has on the valuation entries, the acquisition analysis and the pre-acquisition entry, as well as the step 1 calculation of the NCI share of equity at acquisition date. As noted in section 26.2, the acquisition analysis and subsequent consolidation worksheet entries are affected by whether the full goodwill or partial goodwill option is used in the measurement of the NCI's share of the subsidiary at acquisition date. The choice of method affects the accounting at acquisition date but has an effect on accounting subsequent to acquisition date only if there is an impairment of goodwill or the parent changes its equity interest in the subsidiary. Neither of these events is covered in this book.

Full goodwill method

On 1 July 2013, Magpie Ltd acquired 60% of the shares (cum div.) of Numbat Ltd for $45 600 when the equity of Numbat Ltd consisted of:

Share capital	$40 000
General reserve	2 000
Retained earnings	2 000

At acquisition date, the liabilities of Numbat Ltd included a dividend payable of $1000. All the identifiable assets and liabilities of Numbat Ltd were recorded at fair value except for equipment and inventory:

	Carrying amount	Fair value
Equipment (cost $250 000)	$180 000	$200 000
Inventory	40 000	50 000

The tax rate is 30%. The fair value of the NCI in Numbat Ltd at 1 July 2013 was $28 000.

Acquisition analysis

Net fair value of identifiable assets and liabilities of Numbat Ltd	= $40 000 (capital) + $2000 (general reserve)
	+ $2000 (retained earnings)
	+ $20 000(1 − 30%) (BCVR — equipment)
	+ $10 000(1 − 30%) (BCVR — inventory)
	= $65 000
(a) Consideration transferred	= $45 600 − (60% × $1000) (dividend receivable)
	= $45 000
(b) Non-controlling interest in Numbat Ltd	= $28 000
Aggregate of (a) and (b)	= $73 000
Goodwill	= $73 000 − $65 000
	= $8000
Goodwill of Numbat Ltd	
Fair value of Numbat Ltd	= $28 000/40%
	= $70 000
Net fair value of identifiable assets and liabilities of Numbat Ltd	= $65 000
Goodwill of Numbat Ltd	= $70 000 − $65 000
	= $5000
Goodwill of Magpie Ltd	
Goodwill acquired	= $8000
Goodwill of Numbat Ltd	= $5000
Goodwill of Magpie Ltd — control premium	= $3000

Where an NCI exists, because the parent acquires only a part of the ownership interest of the subsidiary, the parent acquires only a proportionate share of each of the equity amounts in the subsidiary.

(1) *Business combination valuation entries*

The valuation entries are unaffected by the existence of an NCI. The purpose of these entries, in accordance with IFRS 3, is to show the assets and liabilities of the subsidiary at fair value at acquisition date. The entries for a consolidation worksheet (see figure 26.7) prepared at acquisition date are:

Accumulated Depreciation – Equipment	Dr	70 000	
Equipment	Cr		50 000
Deferred Tax Liability	Cr		6 000
Business Combination Valuation Reserve	Cr		14 000
Inventory	Dr	10 000	
Deferred Tax Liability	Cr		3 000
Business Combination Valuation Reserve	Cr		7 000
Goodwill	Dr	5 000	
Business Combination Valuation Reserve	Cr		5 000

The business combination valuation reserve is pre-acquisition equity because it is recognised on consolidation at acquisition date. The NCI is entitled to a proportionate share of this reserve.

(2) *Pre-acquisition entries*

The first pre-acquisition entry is read from the pre-acquisition analysis. The parent's proportional share of the various recorded equity accounts of the subsidiary, as well as the parent's share of the business combination valuation reserves, are eliminated against the investment account in the pre-acquisition entry. The goodwill relating to the control premium is also recognised. In this illustrative example, the pre-acquisition entry is:

Retained Earnings (1/7/13)	Dr	1 200	
[60% × $2000]			
Share Capital	Dr	24 000	
[60% × $40 000]			
Business Combination Valuation Reserve	Dr	15 600	
[60% × ($14 000 + $7000 + $5000)]			
General Reserve	Dr	1 200	
[60% × $2000]			
Goodwill	Dr	3 000	
Shares in Numbat Ltd	Cr		45 000

At acquisition date, the subsidiary has recorded a dividend payable and the parent entity a dividend receivable. An adjustment entry is required because these are not dividends receivable or payable to parties external to the group. The adjustment is a proportional one as it relates only to the amount payable within the group:

Dividend Payable	Dr	600	
Dividend Receivable	Cr		600
[60% × $1000]			

No further adjustment is required once the dividend has been paid.

(3) *NCI share of equity at acquisition date*

The NCI at acquisition date (the step 1 calculation) is determined as the proportional share of the equity recorded by the subsidiary at that date and the valuation reserves recorded on consolidation:

Share capital	40% × $40 000	=	$16 000
General reserve	40% × $2000	=	800
Business combination valuation reserve	40% × ($14 000 + $7000 + $5000) =		10 400
Retained earnings	40% × $2000	=	800
			$28 000

The following entry is then passed in the NCI columns of the consolidation worksheet:

Retained Earnings (1/7/13)	Dr	800
Share Capital	Dr	16 000
Business Combination Valuation Reserve	Dr	10 400
General Reserve	Dr	800
NCI	Cr	28 000

This entry is passed as the step 1 NCI entry in *all* subsequent consolidation worksheets. It is never changed. Any subsequent changes in pre-acquisition equity are dealt with in the step 2 NCI calculation.

Figure 26.7 shows an extract from a consolidation worksheet for Magpie Ltd and its subsidiary, Numbat Ltd, at acquisition date. Only the equity section of the worksheet is shown. The worksheet entries are (1) the business combination valuation entries, (2) the pre-acquisition entries (the dividend adjustment is not shown in figure 26.7 because only an extract from the worksheet is reproduced), and (3) the NCI step 1 entry.

Financial statements	Magpie Ltd	Numbat Ltd	Adjustments		Dr	Cr	Group	Non-controlling interest		Dr	Cr	Parent
Retained earnings (1/7/13)	50 000	2 000	2	1 200			50 800	3	800			50 000
Share capital	100 000	40 000	2	24 000			116 000	3	16 000			100 000
General reserve	20 000	2 000	2	1 200			20 800	3	800			20 000
Business combination valuation reserve			2	15 600	14 000	1	10 400	3	10 400			0
					7 000	1						
					5 000	1						
Total equity: parent												170 000
Total equity: NCI										28 000	3	28 000
Total equity	170 000	44 000					198 000		28 000	28 000		198 000

FIGURE 26.7 Consolidation worksheet (extract) at acquisition date

Note that, in figure 26.7, the adjustment columns eliminate the parent's share of the pre-acquisition equity accounts and the NCI columns extract the NCI share of total equity. The parent column contains only the parent's share of post-acquisition equity, which in this case, being at acquisition date, is zero.

Partial goodwill method

ILLUSTRATIVE EXAMPLE 26.2 Consolidation worksheet entries at acquisition date

On 1 July 2013, Magpie Ltd acquired 60% of the shares (cum div.) of Numbat Ltd for $45 600 when the equity of Numbat Ltd consisted of:

Share capital	$40 000
General reserve	2 000
Retained earnings	2 000

At acquisition date, the liabilities of Numbat Ltd included a dividend payable of $1000. All the identifiable assets and liabilities of Numbat Ltd were recorded at fair value except for equipment and inventory:

	Carrying amount	Fair value
Equipment (cost $250 000)	$180 000	$200 000
Inventory	40 000	50 000

The tax rate is 30%.

Acquisition analysis

Net fair value of identifiable assets
and liabilities of Numbat Ltd = $40 000 (capital) + $2000 (general reserve)
+ $2000 (retained earnings)
+ $20 000(1 − 30%) (BCVR — equipment)
+ $10 000(1 − 30%) (BCVR — inventory)
= $65 000
(a) Consideration transferred = $45 600 − (60% × $1000) (dividend receivable)
= $45 000
(b) Non-controlling interest in
Numbat Ltd = 40% × $65 000
= $26 000
Aggregate of (a) and (b) = $71 000
Goodwill = $71 000 − $65 000
= $6000

Where an NCI exists, because the parent acquires only a part of the ownership interest of the subsidiary, the parent acquires only a proportionate share of each of the equity amounts in the subsidiary.

(1) *Business combination valuation entries*

The valuation entries are unaffected by the existence of an NCI. The purpose of these entries, in accordance with IFRS 3, is to show the assets and liabilities of the subsidiary at fair value at acquisition date. The entries for a consolidation worksheet (see figure 26.8, p. 958) prepared at acquisition date are:

Accumulated Depreciation – Equipment	Dr	70 000	
Equipment	Cr		50 000
Deferred Tax Liability	Cr		6 000
Business Combination Valuation Reserve	Cr		14 000
Inventory	Dr	10 000	
Deferred Tax Liability	Cr		3 000
Business Combination Valuation Reserve	Cr		7 000

Note that there is no business combination valuation entry for goodwill as under the partial goodwill method only the parent's share of goodwill is recognised, and this is done in the pre-acquisition entry. The business combination valuation reserve is pre-acquisition equity because it is recognised on consolidation at acquisition date. The NCI is entitled to a proportionate share of this reserve. Because the reserve is recognised by the group, but not in the records of the subsidiary, this affects later calculations for the NCI share of equity.

(2) *Pre-acquisition entries*

The first pre-acquisition entry is read from the pre-acquisition analysis. The parent's proportional share of the various recorded equity accounts of the subsidiary, as well as the parent's share of the business combination valuation reserves, are eliminated against the investment account in the pre-acquisition entry, and the parent's share of goodwill is recognised. In this illustrative example, the pre-acquisition entry is:

Retained Earnings (1/7/13)	Dr	1 200	
[60% × $2000]			
Share Capital	Dr	24 000	
[60% × $40 000]			

Business Combination Valuation Reserve	Dr	12 600	
[60% × ($14 000 + $7000)]			
General Reserve	Dr	1 200	
[60% × $2000]			
Goodwill	Dr	6 000	
Shares in Numbat Ltd	Cr		45 000

At acquisition date, the subsidiary has recorded a dividend payable and the parent entity a dividend receivable. An adjustment entry is required because these are not dividends receivable or payable to parties external to the group. The adjustment is a proportional one as it relates only to the amount payable within the group:

Dividend Payable	Dr	600	
Dividend Receivable	Cr		600
[60% × $1000]			

No further adjustment is required once the dividend has been paid.

(3) *NCI share of equity at acquisition date*

The NCI at acquisition date (the step 1 calculation) is determined as the proportional share of the equity recorded by the subsidiary at that date and the valuation reserves recorded on consolidation:

Share capital	40% × $40 000	=	$16 000
General reserve	40% × $2000	=	800
Business combination valuation reserve	40% × ($14 000 + $7000)	=	8 400
Retained earnings	40% × $2000	=	800
			$26 000

The following entry is then passed in the NCI columns of the consolidation worksheet:

Retained Earnings (1/7/13)	Dr	800	
Share Capital	Dr	16 000	
Business Combination Valuation Reserve	Dr	8 400	
General Reserve	Dr	800	
NCI	Cr		26 000

This entry is passed as the step 1 NCI entry in *all* subsequent consolidation worksheets. It is never changed. Any subsequent changes in pre-acquisition equity are dealt with in the step 2 NCI calculation.

Figure 26.8 shows an extract from a consolidation worksheet for Magpie Ltd and its subsidiary, Numbat Ltd, at acquisition date. Only the equity section of the worksheet is shown. The worksheet entries are (1) the business combination valuation entries, (2) the pre-acquisition entries (the dividend adjustment is not shown in figure 26.8 because only an extract from the worksheet is reproduced), and (3) the NCI step 1 entry.

Note that, in figure 26.8, the adjustment columns eliminate the parent's share of the pre-acquisition equity accounts and the NCI columns extract the NCI share of total equity. The parent column contains only the parent's share of post-acquisition equity, which in this case, being at acquisition date, is zero.

Financial statements	Magpie Ltd	Numbat Ltd	Adjustments Dr		Cr	Group	Non-controlling interest Dr		Cr		Parent
Retained earnings (1/7/13)	50 000	2 000	2	1 200		50 800	3	800			50 000
Share capital	100 000	40 000	2	24 000		116 000	3	16 000			100 000
General reserve	20 000	2 000	2	1 200		20 800	3	800			20 000
Business combination valuation reserve			2	12 600	14 000 *1*	8 400	3	8 400			0
					7 000 *1*						
Total equity: parent											170 000
Total equity: NCI									26 000	3	26 000
Total equity	170 000	44 000				196 000		26 000	26 000		196 000

FIGURE 26.8 Consolidation worksheet (extract) at acquisition date

26.3.3 Accounting subsequent to acquisition date

Using illustrative example 26.2, the consolidation worksheet entries at the end of the period 3 years after the acquisition date are now considered. These entries are based on the *partial goodwill* method. However, the effects of the events occurring subsequent to acquisition date on the pre-acquisition entries and business combination valuation entries are the same for the full goodwill method. Assume that:

- all inventory on hand at 1 July 2013 is sold by 30 June 2014
- the dividend payable at acquisition date is paid in August 2013
- the equipment has an expected useful life of 5 years
- goodwill has not been impaired
- in the 3 years after the acquisition date, Numbat Ltd recorded the changes in equity shown in figure 26.9.

In preparing the consolidated financial statements at 30 June 2016, the consolidation worksheet contains the valuation entries, the pre-acquisition entries, the NCI entries and the adjustments for the dividend transactions.

	2013–14	2014–15	2015–16
Profit for the period	$ 8 000	$12 000	$15 000
Retained earnings (opening balance)	2 000	7 800	16 000
	10 000	19 800	31 000
Transfer from general reserve	—	—	500
	10 000	19 800	31 500
Transfer to general reserve	—	1 000	—
Dividend paid	1 000	1 200	1 500
Dividend declared	1 200	1 600	2 000
	2 200	3 800	3 500
Retained earnings (closing balance)	7 800	16 000	28 000
Share capital	40 000	40 000	40 000
General reserve	2 000	3 000	2 500
Other components of equity*	2 000	2 500	2 400

* Resulted from movement in fair value of financial assets.

FIGURE 26.9 Changes in equity over a 3-year period

(1) *Business combination valuation entries*

The valuation entries for the 2015–16 period differ from those prepared at acquisition date in that the equipment is depreciated, and the inventory has been sold. The entries at 30 June 2016 are:

Accumulated Depreciation – Equipment	Dr	70 000	
Equipment	Cr		50 000
Deferred Tax Liability	Cr		6 000
Business Combination Valuation Reserve	Cr		14 000
Depreciation Expense	Dr	4 000	
Retained Earnings (1/7/15)	Dr	8 000	
Accumulated Depreciation	Cr		12 000
(20% × $20 000 p.a.)			
Deferred Tax Liability	Dr	3 600	
Income Tax Expense	Cr		1 200
Retained Earnings (1/7/15)	Cr		2 400
(30% × $4000 p.a.)			

(If the full goodwill method had been used, the business combination entry relating to goodwill would be included at 30 June 2016 and would be the same as that used at acquisition date.)

(2) *Pre-acquisition entries*

The pre-acquisition entries have to take into consideration the following events occurring since acquisition date:
- The dividend of $1000 on hand at acquisition date has been paid.
- The inventory on hand at acquisition date has been sold.

The entry at 30 June 2016 is:

Retained Earnings (1/7/15)*	Dr	5 400	
Share Capital	Dr	24 000	
Business Combination Valuation Reserve**	Dr	8 400	
General Reserve	Dr	1 200	
Goodwill	Dr	6 000	
Shares in Numbat Ltd	Cr		45 000

  * $1200 + (60% × $7000) (BCVR transfer — inventory)
  ** 60% × $14 000

(3) *NCI share of equity at acquisition date (step 1)*

The NCI share of equity at acquisition date is as calculated previously. This entry is never changed from that calculated at that date — this applies whether the full goodwill or partial goodwill method is used.

Retained Earnings (1/7/15)	Dr	800	
Share Capital	Dr	16 000	
Business Combination Valuation Reserve	Dr	8 400	
General Reserve	Dr	800	
NCI	Cr		26 000

(4) *NCI share of changes in equity between acquisition date and beginning of the current period* (i.e. from 1 July 2013 to 30 June 2015) (step 2)

To calculate this entry, it is necessary to note any changes in subsidiary equity between the two dates. The changes will generally relate to movements in retained earnings and reserves, but changes in share capital, such as when a bonus dividend is paid, could occur.

In this example, there are four changes in subsidiary equity, as shown in figure 26.9:

- Retained earnings increased from $2000 to $16 000 — this will increase the NCI share of retained earnings.
- In the 2014–15 period, $1000 was transferred to the general reserve. Because the transfer has reduced retained earnings, the NCI share of retained earnings as calculated above has been reduced by this transfer; an increase in the NCI share of general reserve needs to be recognised as well as an increase in NCI in total.
- The sale of inventory in the 2013–14 period resulted in a transfer of $7000 from the business combination valuation reserve to retained earnings. Because the profits from the sale of inventory are recorded in the profits of the subsidiary, the NCI receives a share of the increased wealth relating to inventory. The NCI share of the business combination valuation reserve as recognised in step 1 must be reduced, with a reduction in NCI in total.
- Other components of equity increased by $2500, increasing the NCI share of equity by $1000.

Before noting the effects of these events in journal entry format, adjustments relating to the equipment on hand at acquisition date need to be considered. In the business combination valuation entry, the equipment on hand at acquisition date was revalued to fair value and the increase taken to the valuation reserve. By recognising the asset at fair value at acquisition date, the group recognises the extra benefits over and above the asset's carrying amount to be earned by the subsidiary. As expressed in the depreciation of the equipment (see the valuation entries above), the group expects the subsidiary to realise extra after-tax benefits of $2800 (i.e. $4000 depreciation expense less the credit of $1200 to income tax expense) in each of the 5 years after acquisition. Whereas the group recognises these extra benefits at acquisition date via the valuation reserve, the subsidiary recognises these benefits as profit in its records only as the equipment is used. Hence, the profit after tax recorded by the subsidiary in each of the 5 years after acquisition date will contain $2800 benefits from the equipment that the group recognised in the valuation reserve at acquisition date.

In calculating the NCI share of equity from acquisition date to the beginning of the current period, the NCI calculation will double-count the benefits from the equipment if there is no adjustment for the depreciation of the equipment. This occurs because the share of the NCI in equity calculated at acquisition date includes a share of the business combination valuation reserve created at that date in the consolidation worksheet. Therefore, giving the NCI a full share of the recorded profits of the subsidiary in the 5 years after acquisition date double-counts the benefits relating to the equipment. The NCI has already received a share of the valuation reserve in the step 1 calculation. Hence, in calculating the NCI share of changes in equity between acquisition date and the beginning of the current period (the step 2 calculation), there needs to be an adjustment for the extra depreciation of the equipment in relation to each of the years since acquisition date.

The adjustment for depreciation can be read directly from the valuation entry that records the depreciation on the equipment since acquisition date. In the valuation entry required for the 2015–16 consolidated financial statements (see no. (1) on page 959), there is a net debit adjustment to retained earnings (1/7/15) of $5600 (i.e. the $8000 adjustment for previous periods' depreciation less the $2400 adjustment for previous periods' tax effect) in relation to the after-tax effects of depreciating the equipment. This reflects the extra benefits received by the subsidiary as a result of using the equipment and recorded by the subsidiary in its retained earnings account.

In this example, the only adjustment to retained earnings in the business combination valuation entry is that relating to the equipment. In other examples, there may be a number of adjustments to retained earnings depending on the number of assets being revalued. All such adjustments must be taken into account in order not to double-count the NCI share of equity. In other words, to determine the adjustments needed to avoid double-counting, all adjustments to retained earnings in the valuation entries must be taken into consideration.

In illustrative example 26.2, the NCI share of changes in *retained earnings* is determined by calculating the change in retained earnings over the period, less the adjustment against retained earnings in the valuation entry relating to depreciation of the equipment. The amount is calculated as follows:

$$40\% \times (\$16\,000 - \$2000 - [\$8000 - \$2400]) = \$3360$$

The NCI is also entitled to a share of the change in *general reserve* between acquisition date and the beginning of the current period, the change being the transfer to general reserve in the 2014–15 period. As the general reserve is increased, the NCI share of that account is also increased. The calculation is:

$$40\% \times \$1000 = \$400$$

The NCI is also entitled to a share of the movement in *other components of equity*. There was no balance in this account at acquisition date, and balance at 30 June 2015 is $2500, so the NCI's share is:

$$40\% \times \$2500 = \$1000$$

The NCI is also affected by the transfer on consolidation from the *business combination valuation reserve* to retained earnings as a result of the sale of inventory. The NCI share of the valuation reserve is decreased, with a reduction in NCI in total. The calculation is:

$$40\% \times \$7000 = \$2800$$

The consolidation worksheet entries in the NCI columns for the step 2 NCI calculation are:

Retained Earnings (1/7/15)	Dr	3 360	
NCI	Cr		3 360
(40% × [$16 000 − $2000 − ($8000 − $2400)])			
General Reserve	Dr	400	
NCI	Cr		400
(40% × $1000)			
Other Components of Equity	Dr	1 000	
NCI	Cr		1 000
(40% × $2500)			
NCI	Dr	2 800	
Business Combination Valuation Reserve	Cr		2 800
(40% × $7000)			

These entries may be combined as:

Retained Earnings (1/7/15)	Dr	3 360	
General Reserve	Dr	400	
Other Components of Equity	Dr	1 000	
Business Combination Valuation Reserve	Cr		2 800
NCI	Cr		1 960

(5) *NCI share of current period changes in equity (step 3)*
From figure 26.9 it can be seen that there are four changes in equity in the 2015–16 period:
- Numbat Ltd has reported a profit of $15 000.
- There has been a transfer from general reserve of $500.
- The subsidiary has paid a dividend of $1500 and declared a dividend of $2000.
- Other components of equity has decreased by $100.

In relation to both dividends and transfer to/from reserves, from an NCI perspective note that it is irrelevant whether the amounts are from pre- or post-acquisition equity. The NCI receives a share of all equity accounts regardless of whether it existed before acquisition date or was created after that date.

The NCI share of *current period profit* is based on a 40% share of the recorded profit of $15 000. However, just as in step 2, there must be an adjustment made to avoid the double counting caused by the subsidiary recognising profits from the use of the equipment, these benefits having been recognised on consolidation in the business combination valuation reserve. Again, reference needs to be made to the valuation entries, and in particular to the amounts in these entries affecting current period profit. In the valuation entries, there is a debit adjustment to depreciation expense of $4000 and a credit adjustment to income tax expense of $1200. In other words, in the current period, Numbat Ltd recognised in its profit an amount of $2800 from the use of the equipment that was recognised by the group in the business combination valuation reserve. Since the NCI has been given a share of the valuation reserve in step 1, to give the NCI a share of the recorded profit without adjusting for the current period's depreciation would double-count the NCI share of equity. The NCI share of current period profit is, therefore, 40% of the net of recorded profit of $15 000 less the after-tax depreciation adjustment of $2800.

The consolidation worksheet entry in the NCI columns is:

NCI Share of Profit/(Loss)	Dr	4 880	
NCI	Cr		4 880
(40% × [$15 000 − ($4000 − $1200)])			

In the current period, a change in equity is caused by the $500 *transfer from general reserve* to retained earnings. This transaction does not change the amount of equity in total because it is a transfer between equity accounts, so there is no change to the NCI in total. However, the NCI share of general reserve has decreased and the NCI share of retained earnings has increased. For the latter account, the appropriate line item is 'Transfer from General Reserve'. The consolidation worksheet entry in the NCI columns is:

Transfer from General Reserve	Dr	200	
General Reserve	Cr		200
(40% × $500)			

The third change in equity in the current period relates to *dividends paid and declared*. Dividends are a reduction in retained earnings. The NCI share of equity is reduced as a result of the payment or declaration of dividends. Where dividends are paid, the NCI receives a cash distribution as compensation for the reduction in equity. Where dividends are declared, the group recognises a liability to make a future cash payment to the NCI as compensation for the reduction in equity. The consolidation worksheet entries in the NCI column are:

NCI	Dr	600	
Dividend Paid	Cr		600
(40% × $1500)			
NCI	Dr	800	
Dividend Declared	Cr		800
(40% × $2000)			

The fourth change in equity is the $100 reduction in *other components of equity*. This results in a reduction in the NCI share of this account that relates to financial assets as well as a reduction in NCI in total. The entry in the NCI columns is:

NCI	Dr	40	
Other Components of Equity	Cr		40
(40% × $100)			

(6) *Adjustments for intragroup transactions: dividends*

The entries on the next page and shown in the adjustment columns of the worksheet are necessary to adjust for the dividend transactions in the current period — note that the amounts are based on the proportion of dividends paid within the group.

			Dr	900	
Dividend Revenue					
Dividend Paid			Cr		900
(60% × $1500)					
Dividend Payable			Dr	1 200	
Dividend Declared			Cr		1 200
(60% × $2000)					
Dividend Revenue			Dr	1 200	
Dividend Receivable			Cr		1 200
(60% × $2000)					

Using the figures for the subsidiary for the year ended 30 June 2016, as given in figure 26.9, and assuming information for the parent, a consolidation worksheet showing the effects of the entries developed in illustrative example 26.2 is given in figure 26.10.

Financial statements	Magpie Ltd	Numbat Ltd	ref	Adjustments Dr	Adjustments Cr	ref	Group	ref	NCI Dr	NCI Cr	ref	Parent
Profit /(loss) for the period	20 000	15 000	1	4 000	1 200	1	30 100	5	4 880			25 220
			6	900								
			6	1 200								
Retained earnings (1/7/15)	25 000	16 000	1	8 000	2 400	1	30 000	3	800			25 840
			2	5 400				4	3 360			
Transfer from general reserve	—	500					500	5	200			300
	45 000	31 500					60 600					51 360
Dividend paid	10 000	1 500			900	2	10 600			600	5	10 000
					300	6						
Dividend declared	5 000	2 000			1 200	6	5 800			800	5	5 000
	15 000	3 500					16 400					15 000
Retained earnings (30/6/16)	30 000	28 000					44 200					36 660
Share capital	100 000	40 000	2	24 000			116 000	3	16 000			100 000
General reserve	20 000	2 500	2	1 200			21 300	3	800	200	5	20 300
								4	400			
Business combination valuation reserve	—	—	2	8 400	14 000	1	5 600	3	8 400	2 800	4	—
	150 000	70 500					187 100					156 660
Other components of equity (1/7/15)	10 000	2 500					12 500	4	1 000			11 500
Increases/(decreases)	2 000	(100)					1 900			40	5	1 940
Other components of equity (30/6/16)	12 000	2 400					14 400					13 440
Total equity: parent												170 100
Total equity: NCI								5	600	26 000	3	31 400
								5	800	1 960	4	
								5	40	4 880	5	
Total equity	162 000	72 900					201 500		37 280	37 280		201 500

FIGURE 26.10 Consolidation worksheet with NCI columns

26.4 ADJUSTING FOR THE EFFECTS OF INTRAGROUP TRANSACTIONS

The justification for considering adjustments for intragroup transactions in the calculation of the NCI share of equity is that the NCI is classified as a contributor of capital to the group. Thus, the calculation of the NCI is based on a share of *consolidated equity* and not equity as recorded by the subsidiary. Consolidated equity is determined as the sum of the equity of the parent and the subsidiaries after making adjustments for the effects of intragroup transactions. The NCI share of that equity must, therefore, be based on subsidiary equity after adjusting for intragroup transactions that affect the subsidiary's equity.

To illustrate, assume that during the current period a subsidiary in which there is an NCI of 20% has recorded a profit of $20 000 which includes a before-tax profit of $2000 on sale of $18 000 inventory to the parent. The inventory is still on hand at the end of the current period. In the adjustment columns of the consolidation worksheet, the adjustment entries for the sale of inventory, assuming a tax rate of 30%, are:

Sales	Dr	18 000	
Cost of Sales	Cr		16 000
Inventory	Cr		2 000
Deferred Tax Asset	Dr	600	
Income Tax Expense	Cr		600

The group does not regard the after-tax profit of $1400 as being a part of consolidated profit. Hence, in calculating the NCI share of consolidated profit, the NCI is entitled to $3720; that is, 20% × ($20 000 recorded profit − $1400 intragroup profit).

The NCI share of equity is therefore adjusted for the effects of intragroup transactions. However, note that the NCI share of consolidated equity is essentially based on a share of *subsidiary* equity. Therefore, only intragroup transactions that affect the subsidiary's equity need to be taken into consideration. Profits made on inventory sold by the parent to the subsidiary do not affect the calculation of the NCI because the profit is recorded by the parent, not the subsidiary — the subsidiary equity is unaffected by the transaction.

In section 26.3, it is explained that the NCI share of the equity recorded by the subsidiary is calculated in three steps:

Step 1. share of equity at acquisition date
Step 2. share of changes in equity between acquisition date and the beginning of the current period
Step 3. share of changes in equity in the current period.

These calculations are based on the *recorded* subsidiary equity; that is, equity that will include the effects of the intragroup transactions. Having calculated the NCI as a result of the three-step process, the subsidiary needs to make further adjustments for the effects of intragroup transactions. Rather than adjust for these transactions in the NCI entries relating to the three-step process, the adjustments to the NCI are determined when the adjustments are made for the effects of the specific intragroup transactions.

For example, consider the case above where a subsidiary in which the NCI is 20% records a profit of $20 000, which includes a $2000 before-tax profit on the sale of inventory to the parent (cost $4000, selling price $6000). In the step 3 NCI calculation, the worksheet entry passed in the NCI columns is:

NCI Share of Profit/(Loss)	Dr	4 000	
NCI	Cr		4 000
[20% × $20 000 recorded profit]			

In making the adjustment for the effects of intragroup transactions to be passed in the adjustment columns of the worksheet, the following entries are made:

Profit in closing inventory: subsidiary to parent			
Sales	Dr	6 000	
Cost of Sales	Cr		4 000
Inventory	Cr		2 000

Deferred Tax Asset	Dr	600	
Income Tax Expense	Cr		600
[30% × $2000]			

As this adjustment affects the profit of the subsidiary by an amount of $1400 after tax (i.e. $2000 − $600), this triggers the need to make an adjustment to the NCI, and the following entry is passed in the NCI columns of the worksheet:

NCI	Dr	280	
NCI Share of Profit/(Loss)	Cr		280
[20% × $1400]			

[This entry is explained in more detail in illustrative example 26.3 later in this chapter.]

The combined effect of the step 3 NCI entry and this last entry is that the NCI totals $3720 — that is, $4000 less $280. Thus the NCI is given a share of recorded profit adjusted for the effects of intragroup transactions.

26.4.1 The concept of 'realisation' of profits or losses

Not all transactions require an adjustment entry for the NCI. For a transaction to require an adjustment to the calculation of the NCI share of equity, it must have the following characteristics:
* The transaction must result in the subsidiary recording a profit or a loss.
* After the transaction, the other party to the transaction (for two-company structures this is the parent) must have on hand an asset (e.g. inventory) on which the unrealised profit is accrued.
* The initial consolidation adjustment for the transaction should affect both the statement of financial position and the statement of profit or loss and other comprehensive income (including appropriations of retained earnings), unlike payments of debenture interest, which affect only the statement of profit or loss and other comprehensive income.

In determining the transactions requiring an adjusting entry for the NCI, it is important to work out which transactions involve unrealised profit. The concept of 'realisation' is discussed in chapter 25. The test for realisation is the involvement of a party external to the group, based on the concept that the consolidated financial statements report the affairs of the group in terms of its dealings with entities external to the group. Consolidated profits are therefore realised profits as they result from dealing with entities external to the group. Profits made by transacting within the group are unrealised because no external entity is involved. Once the profits or losses on an intragroup transaction become realised, the NCI share of equity no longer needs to be adjusted for the effects of an intragroup transaction because the profits or losses recorded by the subsidiary are all realised profits.

In this section, the key point to note is when, for different types of transactions, unrealised profits on intragroup transactions become realised.

Inventory

With inventory, realisation occurs when the acquiring entity sells the inventory to an entity outside the group. Consolidation adjustments for inventory are based on the profit or loss remaining in inventory on hand at the end of a financial period. If inventory is sold in the current period by the subsidiary to the parent at a profit, giving the NCI a share of the recorded profit will overstate the NCI share of consolidated equity, because the group does not recognise the profit until the inventory is sold outside the group. Hence, whenever consolidated adjustments are made for profit remaining in inventory on hand at the end of the period, an NCI adjustment is necessary to reduce the NCI share of current period profit and the NCI total. Following the consolidation adjustment for the unrealised profit in inventory, an NCI adjustment entry is made in the NCI columns of the worksheet. The general form of the entry is:

| NCI | Dr | xxx | |
| NCI Share of Profit/(Loss) | Cr | | xxx |

If there is inventory on hand at *the beginning of the current period*, the NCI share of the previous period's profit must be reduced as the subsidiary's previous year's recorded profit contains unrealised profit. As the group realises the profit in the current period when the inventory is sold to external parties, the NCI share of the current period profit must be increased. Following the worksheet adjustment for the profit remaining in beginning inventory, an NCI adjustment entry is made in the NCI columns of the worksheet. The general form of the NCI entry is:

NCI Share of Profit/(Loss)	Dr	xxx	
Retained Earnings (opening balance)	Cr		xxx

Depreciable non-current assets

With depreciable non-current assets, profit is realised as the asset is used up within the group. Realisation of the profit occurs as the future benefits embodied in the asset are consumed by the group, and occurs in proportion to the depreciation of the asset. If the subsidiary sells a non-current asset in the current period to the parent, an adjustment is made for the profit on sale, because the profit is unrealised to the group. The NCI share of current period profit must then be reduced. Following the worksheet adjustment for the profit on sale, an NCI adjustment is made in the NCI columns of the worksheet. The general form of the adjustment entry is:

NCI	Dr	xxx	
NCI Share of Profit/(Loss)	Cr		xxx

As the asset is depreciated, some of the profit becomes realised, increasing the NCI share of profit. Following the worksheet adjustment entry for depreciation, an NCI entry is made in the NCI columns of the worksheet. The general form of the entry reflecting the increased share of profit is:

NCI Share of Profit/(Loss)	Dr	xxx	
NCI	Cr		xxx

It can be seen that the NCI adjustment for the profit on sale reduces the NCI share of equity, and the NCI adjustment relating to depreciation increases the NCI share of equity. This reflects the fact that as the asset is used up the profit becomes realised.

Intragroup transfers for services and interest

For transactions involving services and interest, the group's profit is unaffected because the general consolidation adjustment reduces both expense and revenue equally. However, from the NCI's perspective, there has been a change in the equity of the subsidiary; for example, the subsidiary may have recorded interest revenue as a result of a payment to the parent entity relating to an intragroup loan. The revenue is unrealised in that no external entity has been involved in the transaction. Theoretically, the NCI should be adjusted for such transactions. However, as noted in paragraph B86(c) of IFRS 10, it is profits or losses 'recognised in assets' that are of concern. In other words, where there are transfers between entities that do not result in the retention within the group of assets on which the profit has been accrued, it is *assumed* that the profit is realised by the group immediately on payment within the group. For transactions such as payments for intragroup services, interest and dividends, there are no assets recorded with accrued profits attached, since the transactions are cash transactions. Hence, the profit is assumed to be immediately realised. The reason for the assumption of immediate realisation of profits on these types of transactions is a pragmatic one based on the cost benefit of determining a point of realisation.

26.5 GAIN ON BARGAIN PURCHASE

This chapter has used examples of business combinations where goodwill has been acquired. In the rare case that a gain on bargain purchase may arise, such a gain has no effect on the calculation of the NCI share of equity. Further, whereas the goodwill of the subsidiary may be determined by calculating the goodwill acquired by the parent entity and then grossing this up to determine the goodwill for the subsidiary, this process is not applicable for the gain on bargain purchase. The gain is made by the parent paying less than the net fair value of the acquirer's share of the identifiable assets, liabilities and contingent liabilities of the subsidiary. The NCI receives a share of the fair value of the subsidiary, and has no involvement with the gain on bargain purchase.

To illustrate, assume a subsidiary has the following statement of financial position:

Equity	$ 80 000
Identifiable assets and liabilities	$ 80 000

Assume all identifiable assets and liabilities of the subsidiary are recorded at amounts equal to fair value. If a parent acquires 80% of the shares of the subsidiary for $63 000, then the acquisition analysis, assuming the use of the partial goodwill method, is:

Net fair value of subsidiary	= $80 000
(a) Consideration transferred	= $63 000
(b) Non-controlling interest in subsidiary	= 20% × $80 000
	= $16 000
Aggregate of (a) and (b)	= $79 000
Gain on bargain purchase	= $80 000 − $79 000
	= $1000

Assuming all fair values have been measured accurately, the consolidation worksheet entries at acquisition date are:

Business combination valuation entry
No entry required in this simple example.

Pre-acquisition entry

Equity	Dr	64 000	
Gain on Bargain Purchase	Cr		1 000
Shares in Subsidiary	Cr		63 000

Non-controlling interest (step 1)

Equity	Dr	16 000	
NCI	Cr		16 000
(20% × $80 000)			

Note that the NCI does not receive any share of the gain on bargain purchase.

An example of the process of calculating NCI when intragroup transactions exist is given in illustrative example 26.3.

ILLUSTRATIVE EXAMPLE 26.3 NCI and intragroup transactions

Bat Ltd owns 80% of the issued shares of Snake Ltd. In the year ending 30 June 2014, the following transactions occurred:
(a) In July 2013, Bat Ltd sold $2000 worth of inventory that had been sold to it by Snake Ltd in May 2013 at a profit to Snake Ltd of $500.
(b) In February 2014, Bat Ltd sold $10 000 worth of inventory to Snake Ltd, recording a profit before tax of $2000. At 30 June 2014, 20% of this inventory remained unsold by Snake Ltd.
(c) In March 2014, Snake Ltd sold $12 000 worth of inventory to Bat Ltd at a mark-up of 20%. At 30 June 2014, $1200 of this inventory remained unsold by Bat Ltd.
(d) At 30 June 2014, Bat Ltd recorded depreciation of $10 000 in relation to plant sold to it by Snake Ltd on 1 July 2011. Bat Ltd uses a 10% p.a. straight-line depreciation method for plant. At date of sale to Bat Ltd, this plant had a carrying amount of $90 000 in the accounts of Snake Ltd.

Required

Given a tax rate of 30%, prepare the consolidation worksheet entries for these transactions as at 30 June 2014.

Solution

(a) *Sale of inventory in previous period: Snake Ltd to Bat Ltd*

The entry in the adjustment columns of the worksheet is:

Retained Earnings (1/7/13)	Dr	350	
Income Tax Expense	Dr	150	
Cost of Sales	Cr		500

Since the inventory was originally sold by the subsidiary to the parent, the entry in the NCI columns of the worksheet is:

NCI Share of Profit/(Loss)	Dr	70	
Retained Earnings (1/7/13)	Cr		70
(20% × $350)			

(b) *Sale of inventory in current period: Bat Ltd to Snake Ltd*

Sales	Dr	10 000	
Cost of Sales	Cr		9 600
Inventory	Cr		400
Deferred Tax Asset	Dr	120	
Income Tax Expense	Cr		120

Because the sale was from parent to subsidiary, there is no NCI adjustment required.

(c) *Sale of inventory in current period: Snake Ltd to Bat Ltd*

The entries in the adjustment columns of the worksheet are:

Sales	Dr	12 000	
Cost of Sales	Cr		11 800
Inventory	Cr		200
Deferred Tax Asset	Dr	60	
Income Tax Expense	Cr		60

Because the sale was from subsidiary to parent, the following entry is required in the NCI columns of the worksheet:

NCI	Dr	28	
NCI Share of Profit/(Loss)	Cr		28
(20% × $140)			

(d) *Sale of plant in prior period: Snake Ltd to Bat Ltd*

The entry in the adjustment columns of the worksheet is:

Retained Earnings (1/7/13)	Dr	7 000	
Deferred Tax Asset	Dr	3 000	
Plant	Cr		10 000

Since the plant was sold by the subsidiary to the parent, the entry in the NCI columns of the worksheet is:

NCI Retained Earnings (1/7/13) (20% × $7000)	Dr Cr	1 400	1 400

Depreciation on plant
The entries in the adjustment columns of the worksheet are:

Accumulated Depreciation
    Depreciation Expense
    Retained Earnings (1/7/13)
	Dr
	Cr
	Cr
		2 000	1 000
			1 000

Retained Earnings (1/7/13) Income Tax Expense Deferred Tax Asset	Dr Dr Cr	300 300	600

The entry in the NCI column of the worksheet is:

NCI Share of Profit/(Loss) Retained Earnings (1/7/13) NCI (20% × $700 p.a.)	Dr Dr Cr	140 140	280

SUMMARY

Where a subsidiary is not wholly owned, the equity of the subsidiary is divided into two parts, namely the parent's share and the non-controlling interest (NCI) share. IAS 1 *Presentation of Financial Statements* requires that, with the disclosure of specific equity amounts, the parent's share and the NCI share should be separately disclosed. This affects the consolidation process. The NCI is classified as equity with the result that in statements of profit or loss and other comprehensive income and statements of financial position where equity amounts are disclosed the parent's share and the NCI share are separately disclosed.

The existence of an NCI will have different effects on the consolidation worksheet entries used, depending on whether the full goodwill or partial goodwill method is used. Under the full goodwill method, goodwill is recognised in the business combination valuation entries, and shared between the parent and the NCI. Where the partial goodwill method is used, the existence of an NCI has no effect on the business combination valuation entries. However, as a result of these entries, business combination valuation reserves are created of which the NCI has a share. With the pre-acquisition entry, the existence of an NCI has an effect as this entry is based on the parent's share of pre-acquisition equity only. Hence, a proportionate adjustment is required. The adjustments for intragroup transactions also affect the calculation of the NCI share of equity. There is no effect on the adjustment for an intragroup transaction itself — this is the same regardless of the ownership interest of the parent in the subsidiary. However, the adjustment for an intragroup transaction affects the calculation of the NCI share of equity. Since the NCI is entitled to a share of consolidated equity rather than the recorded equity of the subsidiary, where an intragroup transaction affects the equity of the subsidiary, entries in the NCI columns of the worksheet are required, affecting the calculation of the NCI. It is then necessary to observe the flow of the transaction — upstream or downstream — to determine whether an NCI adjustment is necessary. One area where the NCI is unaffected is where a gain on bargain purchase arises, because the pre-acquisition entry adjusts for the parent's share only. The gain calculated relates only to the parent and not the NCI.

Seal Ltd acquired 80% of the shares of Swan Ltd on 1 July 2010 for $540 000, when the equity of Swan Ltd consisted of:

Share capital	$500 000
General reserve	80 000
Retained earnings	50 000
Asset revaluation surplus	20 000

All identifiable assets and liabilities of Swan Ltd are recorded at fair value at this date except for inventory for which the fair value was $10 000 greater than carrying amount, and plant which had a carrying amount of $150 000 (net of $40 000 accumulated depreciation) and a fair value of $170 000. The inventory was all sold by 30 June 2011, and the plant had a further 5-year life with depreciation based on the straight-line method.

Financial information for both companies at 30 June 2014 is as follows:

	Seal Ltd	Swan Ltd
Sales revenue	$ 720 000	$ 530 000
Other revenue	240 000	120 000
	960 000	650 000
Cost of sales	(610 000)	(410 000)
Other expenses	(230 000)	(160 000)
	(840 000)	(570 000)
Profit before tax	120 000	80 000
Tax expense	(40 000)	(25 000)
Profit for the period	80 000	55 000
Retained earnings at 1/7/13	200 000	112 000
	280 000	167 000
Dividend paid	(20 000)	(10 000)
Dividend declared	(25 000)	(15 000)
	(45 000)	(25 000)
Retained earnings at 30/6/14	235 000	142 000
Share capital	600 000	500 000
Asset revaluation surplus*	20 000	60 000
General reserve	80 000	100 000
Total equity	935 000	802 000
Dividend payable	25 000	15 000
Other liabilities	25 000	25 000
Total liabilities	50 000	40 000
Total equity and liabilities	$ 985 000	$ 842 000
Receivables	$ 80 000	$ 30 000
Inventory	100 000	170 000
Plant and equipment	200 000	500 000
Accumulated depreciation	(115 000)	(88 000)
Land at fair value	100 000	80 000
Shares in Swan Ltd	540 000	—
Deferred tax assets	50 000	40 000
Other assets	30 000	110 000
Total assets	$ 985 000	$ 842 000

* The balances of the surplus at 1 July 2013 were $35 000 (Seal Ltd) and $50 000 (Swan Ltd).

The following transactions took place between Seal Ltd and Swan Ltd:
(a) During the 2013–14 period, Swan Ltd sold inventory to Seal Ltd for $23 000, recording a profit before tax of $3000. Seal Ltd has since resold half of these items.
(b) During the 2013–14 period, Seal Ltd sold inventory to Swan Ltd for $18 000, recording a profit before tax of $2000. Swan Ltd has not resold any of these items.
(c) On 1 June 2014, Swan Ltd paid $1000 to Seal Ltd for services rendered.
(d) During the 2012–13 period, Swan Ltd sold inventory to Seal Ltd. At 30 June 2013, Seal Ltd still had inventory on hand on which Swan Ltd had recorded a before-tax profit of $4000.
(e) On 1 July 2012, Swan Ltd sold plant to Seal Ltd for $150 000, recording a profit of $20 000 before tax. Seal Ltd applies a 10% p.a. straight-line method of depreciation in relation to these assets.

Required

1. Given an income tax rate of 30%, prepare the consolidated financial statements for Seal Ltd for the year ended 30 June 2014 using the *partial goodwill method* to measure the non-controlling interest at acquisition date.
2. What differences would occur in the consolidation worksheet entries at 30 June 2014 if the *full goodwill method* was used to calculate the non-controlling interest at acquisition date? Assume the value of the non-controlling interest in the subsidiary at acquisition date is $134 500.

Solution

1. Consolidated financial statements using partial goodwill method

The first step is to prepare the acquisition analysis. Determining the net fair value is the same as for wholly owned subsidiaries. Where an NCI exists, it is necessary to determine the net fair value acquired by the parent.

In this problem, the parent acquired 80% of the shares of the subsidiary. The net fair value of what was acquired is then compared with the consideration transferred, and a goodwill or gain is determined. Note that the goodwill or gain is only that attributable to the parent, since the residual relates to what was paid by the parent and the proportion of net fair value of the subsidiary acquired by the parent.

Acquisition analysis

Net fair value of the identifiable assets and liabilities of Swan Ltd	= $500 000 + $80 000 + $50 000 + $20 000 + $10 000(1 − 30%) (BCVR — inventory) + $20 000(1 − 30%) (BCVR — plant)
	= $671 000
(a) Consideration transferred	= $540 000
(b) Non-controlling interest in Swan Ltd	= 20% × $671 000
	= $134 200
Aggregate of (a) and (b)	= $674 200
Goodwill	= $674 200 − $671 000
	= $3200

Consolidation worksheet entries at 30 June 2014
(1) *Business combination valuation reserve entries*

The business combination entries are unaffected by the existence of an NCI. Under IFRS 3, all identifiable assets and liabilities acquired in the acquiree/subsidiary must be measured at fair value. This principle is unaffected by the existence of an NCI.

Accumulated Depreciation	Dr	40 000	
Plant	Cr		20 000
Deferred Tax Liability	Cr		6 000
Business Combination Valuation Reserve	Cr		14 000
Depreciation Expense	Dr	4 000	
Retained Earnings (1/7/13)	Dr	12 000	
Accumulated Depreciation	Cr		16 000

Deferred Tax Liability	Dr	4 800	
Income Tax Expense	Cr		1 200
Retained Earnings (1/7/13)	Cr		3 600

(2) *Pre-acquisition entry*

Retained Earnings (1/7/13)	Dr	45 600	
Share Capital	Dr	400 000	
General Reserve	Dr	64 000	
Asset Revaluation Surplus (1/7/13)	Dr	16 000	
Business Combination Valuation Reserve	Dr	11 200	
Goodwill	Dr	3 200	
Shares in Swan Ltd	Cr		540 000

These pre-acquisition entries differ from the entries prepared for a wholly owned subsidiary in that the adjustment to equity accounts is measured as the parent's share of the equity accounts. This can be seen in the acquisition analysis where the parent's share of equity (80%) is applied to the net fair value before making a comparison with the cost of the combination. Hence the adjustment to share capital is $400 000; that is, 80% of the recorded $500 000. With retained earnings (1/7/13), the adjustment is calculated as:

$$(80\% \times \$50\,000)\ (\text{opening balance}) + (80\% \times \$7000)\ (\text{BCVR — inventory})$$

The adjustment to the BCVR is:

$$80\% \times \$14\,000\ (\text{BCVR — plant})$$

Non-controlling interest
The next three adjustment entries relate to the calculation of the NCI. These entries are passed in the NCI columns of the worksheet, not the adjustment columns. The three entries cover the three steps used in the calculation of the NCI share of total equity.

(3) *NCI share of equity at acquisition date, 1 July 2010 (step 1)*
   Step 1 is to calculate the NCI share of the equity of the subsidiary at acquisition date. This consists of the recorded equity of the subsidiary plus any reserves raised on consolidation at acquisition date, namely the business combination valuation reserve.

Pre-acquisition equity of Swan Ltd		20%
Retained earnings (1/7/10)	$ 50 000	$ 10 000
Share capital	500 000	100 000
General reserve	80 000	16 000
Asset revaluation surplus (1/7/10)	20 000	4 000
Business combination valuation reserve	21 000	4 200
		$134 200

The worksheet entry in the NCI columns is:

Retained Earnings (1/7/13)	Dr	10 000	
Share Capital	Dr	100 000	
General Reserve	Dr	16 000	
Asset Revaluation Surplus (1/7/13)	Dr	4 000	
Business Combination Valuation Reserve	Dr	4 200	
NCI	Cr		134 200

Note that the adjustments to the equity accounts are debits, because these amounts will be subtracted from the balances in the group column in order to determine the parent's share of equity. On the other hand, the NCI account has a credit adjustment because the NCI is classified as equity, and the balance of pre-acquisition equity is a positive amount.

(4) *NCI share of equity from 1 July 2010 to 30 June 2013 (step 2)*
In step 2, the calculation is of the NCI share of equity between the acquisition date and the beginning of the current period; that is, between 1 July 2010 and 30 June 2013. This requires the calculation of movements in the subsidiary's equity accounts between these two dates.

General reserve: The balance at 30 June 2013, read from the financial information at 30 June 2014 and noting no transfers occurred in the current period, is $100 000. The difference between this and the balance at 1 July 2010 of $80 000 is $20 000. The NCI is entitled to 20% of this increase in equity. The combination of step 1 and step 2 effectively gives the NCI a 20% share of the total $100 000 balance.

Retained earnings: The balance at 30 June 2013 is the same as the opening balance in the current period, which is read from the financial information provided, namely $112 000. The difference between this amount and the balance recorded by the subsidiary at acquisition reflects movements in the amounts recorded by the subsidiary, such as reserve transfers and dividends. What is not reflected in the difference calculated are amounts affecting retained earnings not recorded by the subsidiary but recognised on consolidation. In this problem, the transaction that needs to be taken into account is the depreciation of the plant on hand at acquisition date, as shown in the business combination valuation reserve entries. As the plant is used, the recorded profit of the subsidiary recognises the extra benefits received. The NCI in relation to retained earnings (1/7/13) is therefore:

$$20\% \times [\$112\,000 \text{ (balance at 1/7/13)} - \$50\,000 \text{ (balance at acquisition)} - (\$12\,000 - \$3600)]$$

Asset revaluation surplus: The balance at acquisition date is $20 000 and the balance at 30 June 2013 is $50 000. The NCI is entitled to a 20% share of the difference between these two amounts.

Business combination valuation reserve: The balance at acquisition date was $21 000. As a result of the sale of the inventory, this has been reduced at 30 June 2013 to $14 000, a reduction of $7000, because there has been a transfer from this reserve to retained earnings. Since the reserve has decreased in amount, this results in a decrease in the NCI share of this account. The total NCI in equity has not changed because the recorded retained earnings has increased by $7000 as a result of the sale of inventory by the subsidiary.

A summary of these movements is then:

	Change in equity	20%
General reserve ($100 000 − $80 000)	$ 20 000	$ 4 000
Retained earnings ($112 000 − $50 000 − ($12 000 − $3600))	53 600	10 720
Asset revaluation surplus ($50 000 − $20 000)	30 000	6 000
Business combination valuation reserve ($14 000 − $21 000)	(7 000)	(1 400)

The worksheet entry in the NCI columns is:

Retained Earnings (1/7/13)	Dr	10 720	
General Reserve	Dr	4 000	
Asset Revaluation Surplus	Dr	6 000	
Business Combination Valuation Reserve	Cr		1 400
NCI	Cr		19 320

(5) *NCI in equity from 1 July 2013 to 30 June 2014 (step 3)*
Steps 1 and 2 determine the NCI share of equity recorded up to the beginning of the current year. Step 3 calculates the NCI share of changes in equity in the current year — 1 July 2013 to 30 June 2014.

The combination of all three steps determines the NCI share of equity at the end of the reporting period.

There are a number of changes in equity in the current period, with each change attracting its own adjustment entry in the NCI columns of the worksheet.

Profit for the period:
The NCI receives a share of recorded profit of the subsidiary. As with step 2, this is adjusted by the depreciation on the plant on hand at acquisition date. The recorded profit of the subsidiary includes benefits gained by use of the plant. The NCI share is then:

$$20\% \; [\$55\,000 - (\$4000 - \$1200)]$$

The worksheet entry in the NCI columns is:

NCI Share of Profit/(Loss)	Dr	10 440	
NCI	Cr		10 440

The first line in the entry is a debit because in the consolidation worksheet this is deducted from group profit in order to calculate the parent share of profit. Note that, in later calculations, increases in the NCI share of profit require a debit adjustment to this account and decreases in the NCI share of profit require a credit adjustment.

Dividend paid:
The dividend paid by the subsidiary reduces the equity of the subsidiary. The adjustment to the NCI share of equity as a result of the dividend paid must take into consideration the full dividend paid with the effect of reducing the NCI share of total equity. The entry in the NCI columns of the worksheet is:

NCI	Dr	2 000	
Dividend Paid	Cr		2 000
(20% × $10 000)			

Dividend declared:
As with the dividend paid, the NCI has been given a full share of equity before the declaration of dividends. Because the dividend declared reduces the equity of the subsidiary, the NCI share of equity is also reduced. The entry in the NCI columns of the worksheet is:

NCI	Dr	3 000	
Dividend Declared	Cr		3 000
(20% × $15 000)			

Asset revaluation surplus:
The balance of the subsidiary's asset revaluation surplus at 1 July 2013 was $50 000. The balance at 30 June 2014 is $60 000. The NCI share of equity is increased by 20% of the change during the period. The debit adjustment is recognised in the worksheet against the Gains/Losses on Asset Revaluation account as this account reflects the increase in the reserve balance. The adjustment is a debit because it reduces the group gain so that the left-hand column of the worksheet shows the parent share of the gain. The entry in the NCI columns of the worksheet is:

Gains/Losses on Asset Revaluation	Dr	2 000	
NCI	Cr		2 000
(20% × [$60 000 − $50 000])			

Intragroup transactions

(6) *Dividend paid*

The entry in the adjustment columns of the consolidation worksheet to adjust for the $10 000 dividend paid is:

Dividend Revenue	Dr	8 000	
Dividend Paid	Cr		8 000
(80% × $10 000)			

(7) *Dividend declared*

The subsidiary declared a dividend of $15 000 of which $12 000 is payable within the group.
The entries in the adjustment columns of the worksheet are:

Dividend Payable	Dr	12 000	
Dividend Declared	Cr		12 000
Dividend Revenue	Dr	12 000	
Dividend Receivable	Cr		12 000

(8) *Sale of inventory: Swan Ltd to Seal Ltd*

The worksheet entries in the adjustment columns are:

Sales	Dr	23 000	
Cost of Sales	Cr		21 500
Inventory	Cr		1 500
(Unrealised profit on sale of inventory, 50% × $3000)			
Deferred Tax Asset	Dr	450	
Income Tax Expense	Cr		450
(Tax effect, 30% × $1500)			

(9) *Adjustment to NCI: unrealised profit in ending inventory*

The profit on sale was made by the subsidiary. The NCI is therefore affected. The total after-tax profit on the intragroup sale of inventory was $2100 (i.e. $3000 – $900 tax). However, since half the inventory is sold to an external entity, this portion is realised. The adjustment to the NCI relates only to the unrealised profits remaining in the inventory still on hand (half of $2100, or $1050). This is the same after-tax figure used to adjust profits in entry (8) above.

The transaction occurs in the current period. Therefore, it is the NCI share of current period profit that is affected. In adjustment entry (5), the NCI is given a share of the total recorded subsidiary profit for the current period. Because the realised profit is less than the recorded profit, the NCI share of equity must be reduced, specifically the NCI share of current period profit.

The worksheet entry in the NCI columns of the worksheet is:

NCI	Dr	210	
NCI Share of Profit/(Loss)	Cr		210
(20% × $1050)			

The debit adjustment shows a reduction in total equity attributable to the NCI, and the credit adjustment shows a reduction in the NCI share of current period profits.

(10) *Sale of inventory: Seal Ltd to Swan Ltd*
The entries in the adjustment columns of the worksheet are:

Sales	Dr	18 000	
Cost of Sales	Cr		16 000
Inventory	Cr		2 000
Deferred Tax Asset	Dr	600	
Income Tax Expense	Cr		600

Because the profit on the transaction is made by the parent entity and does not affect the equity of the subsidiary, there is no need to make any adjustment to the NCI.

(11) *Payment for services: Swan Ltd to Seal Ltd*
The entry in the adjustment columns of the worksheet is:

Other Revenues	Dr	1 000	
Other Expenses	Cr		1 000

The profit of the subsidiary is affected by the transaction even though the payment may, in effect, be from the parent to the subsidiary. However, if it is assumed that realisation occurs on payment for the services for this type of transaction, then no unrealised profit or loss exists in the subsidiary. Hence, there is no need to make any adjustment to the NCI share of equity.

(12) *Sale of inventory in previous period: Swan Ltd to Seal Ltd*
The entries in the adjustment columns of the worksheet are:

Retained Earnings (1/7/13)	Dr	2 800	
Income Tax Expense	Dr	1 200	
Cost of Sales	Cr		4 000

(13) *Adjustment to NCI: unrealised profit in beginning inventory*
The profit on this transaction was made by the subsidiary, so an adjustment to the NCI share of equity is required. There are two effects on the NCI because the transaction affects both last year's and the current period's figures.
First, the profit made by the subsidiary in the previous period was unrealised last year. Hence, the subsidiary's retained earnings (1/7/13) account contains $2800 unrealised profit. An adjustment is necessary to reduce the NCI share of the previous period's profit:

NCI	Dr	560	
Retained Earnings (1/7/13)	Cr		560
(20% × $2800)			

Second, in relation to the current period, because the inventory transferred last period is sold in the current period to an external entity, the profit previously recorded by the subsidiary becomes realised in the current period. Since the profit is realised to the NCI in the current period but was recorded by the subsidiary last period, the NCI share of current period profit needs to be increased. The adjustment is:

NCI Share of Profit/(Loss)	Dr	560	
NCI	Cr		560
(20% × $2800)			

These two entries can be combined and passed in the NCI columns of the worksheet:

NCI Share of Profit/(Loss)	Dr	560	
Retained Earnings (1/7/13)	Cr		560

This entry has no effect on the total NCI share of equity. It simply reduces the NCI share of equity recorded last period and increases the NCI share of current period profit. This reflects the fact that the subsidiary recorded the profit in the previous period whereas the group recognised the profit in the current period.

(14) *Sale of depreciable asset in previous period: Swan Ltd to Seal Ltd*
The sale occurred at the beginning of the previous period. The entries in the adjustment columns of the worksheet are:

Retained Earnings (1/7/13)	Dr	14 000	
Deferred Tax Asset	Dr	6 000	
Plant and Equipment	Cr		20 000

(15) *Adjustment to NCI: unrealised profit in depreciable asset in previous period*
The subsidiary recorded the profit on the transaction, so the NCI is affected. Because the transaction occurred in the previous period, the subsidiary's recorded retained earnings (1/7/13) balance contains an after-tax unrealised profit of $14 000. The NCI share of last year's profits must then be reduced by $2800 (i.e. 20% × $14 000).
The worksheet entry in the NCI columns is:

NCI	Dr	2 800	
Retained Earnings (1/7/13)	Cr		2 800

Worksheet entries relating to the sale of the asset and the associated NCI adjustment are made in each year of the asset's life. Realisation of this profit is dealt with in relation to the depreciation adjustment entry.

(16) *Depreciation on non-current asset sold*
The entries in the adjustment columns of the worksheet reflect the depreciation of the transferred asset over a 2-year period on a straight-line basis, given an overall asset life of 10 years:

Accumulated Depreciation	Dr	4 000	
Depreciation Expense	Cr		2 000
Retained Earnings (1/7/13)	Cr		2 000
(Depreciation of 10% × $20 000 p.a. for 2 years)			
Retained Earnings (1/7/13)	Dr	600	
Income Tax Expense	Dr	600	
Deferred Tax Asset	Cr		1 200

(17) *Adjustment to NCI: realisation of profit via depreciation*
The assumption made in relation to the $14 000 unrealised profit is that realisation will occur over the life of the asset as the benefits of the depreciable asset are consumed by the group. The profit is then realised in proportion to the depreciation charged on the asset. As can be seen from adjustment entry (16), the after-tax adjustment to depreciation expense is $1400 (being $2000 − $600). In other words, the $14 000 profit recognised last period by the subsidiary will be recognised as realised to the extent of $1400 p.a. over the next 10 years. Hence, $1400 is realised in the 2012–13 period, and a further $1400 is realised in the 2013–14 period. The NCI share of last year's profits is therefore increased, as is the NCI share of the current period's profits.

The worksheet entry in the NCI columns is:

NCI Share of Profit/(Loss)	Dr	280
Retained Earnings (1/7/13)	Dr	280
NCI	Cr	560
(20% × $1400 p.a.)		

In each of the 10 years following the transfer of the asset, the group realises an extra $1400 profit. This increases the NCI share of profit by $280 per year, and effectively reverses the reduction in the NCI share of profit relating to the gain on sale shown in entry (15). As the profit becomes realised over time, the NCI share of equity increases. Combining the effects of entries (15) and (16), the effect on NCI share of retained earnings (opening balance) over time is as follows:

NCI share of retained earnings (1/7/13)	$2800 less $280
NCI share of retained earnings (1/7/14)	$2800 less (2 × $280)
NCI share of retained earnings (1/7/15)	$2800 less (3 × $280)
NCI share of retained earnings (1/7/16)	$2800 less (4 × $280)

In the period ended 30 June 2022, the profit becomes fully realised as the asset becomes fully depreciated. In the 2022–23 period, no adjustments are necessary in relation to the transfer of the depreciable asset.

The consolidation worksheet for Seal Ltd at 30 June 2014 is shown in figure 26.11.

FIGURE 26.11 Consolidation worksheet showing NCI and the effects of intragroup transactions

Financial statements	Seal Ltd	Swan Ltd	Adjustments Dr		Adjustments Cr		Group	Non-controlling interest Dr		Non-controlling interest Cr		Parent
Sales revenue	720 000	530 000	8	23 000			1 209 000					
			10	18 000								
Other revenues	240 000	120 000	6	8 000								
			7	12 000								
			11	1 000			339 000					
	960 000	650 000					1 548 000					
Cost of sales	(610 000)	(410 000)			21 500	8						
					16 000	10						
					4 000	12	(978 500)					
Other expenses	(230 000)	(160 000)	1	4 000	1 000	11	(391 000)					
					2 000	16						
	(840 000)	(570 000)					(1 369 500)					
Profit before tax	120 000	80 000					178 500					
Tax expense	(40 000)	(25 000)	12	1 200	1 200	1	(64 550)					
			16	600	600	10						
					450	8						
Profit	80 000	55 000					113 950	5	10 440	210	9	102 880
								13	560			
								17	280			
Retained earnings (1/7/13)	200 000	112 000	1	12 000	3 600	1		3	10 000	560	13	224 960
			2	45 600	2 000	16		4	10 720	2 800	15	
			12	2 800				17	280			
			14	14 000								
			16	600			242 600					
	280 000	167 000					356 550					327 840

FIGURE 26.11 (continued)

Financial statements	Seal Ltd	Swan Ltd	Adjustments Dr		Adjustments Cr		Group	NCI Dr		NCI Cr		Parent
Dividend paid	(20 000)	(10 000)			8 000	6	(22 000)			2 000	5	(20 000)
Dividend declared	(25 000)	(15 000)			12 000	7	(28 000)			3 000	5	(25 000)
	(45 000)	(25 000)					(50 000)					(45 000)
Retained earnings (30/6/14)	235 000	142 000					306 550					282 840
Share capital	600 000	500 000	400 000	2			700 000	100 000	3			600 000
General reserve	80 000	100 000	64 000	2			116 000	16 000	3			96 000
								4 000	4			
Business combination valuation reserve	0	0	11 200	2	14 000	1	2 800	4 200	3	1 400	4	0
	915 000	742 000					1 125 350					978 840
Asset revaluation surplus (1/7/13)	35 000	50 000	16 000	1			69 000	4 000	3			59 000
								6 000	4			
Gains/losses on asset revaluation	(15 000)	10 000					(5 000)	2 000	5			(7 000)
Asset revaluation surplus (30/6/14)	20 000	60 000					64 000					52 000
Total equity: parent												1 030 840
Total equity: NCI								2 000	5	134 200	3	158 510
								3 000	5	19 320	4	
								210	9	10 440	5	
								2 800	1	2 000	5	
									5	560	17	
Total equity	935 000	802 000					1 189 350	182 370		182 370		1 189 350
Dividend payable	25 000	15 000	12 000	7			28 000					
Other liabilities	25 000	25 000	4 800	1	6 000	1	51 200					
Total liabilities	50 000	40 000					79 200					
Total equity and liabilities	985 000	842 000					1 268 550					
Receivables	80 000	30 000			12 000	6	98 000					
Inventory	100 000	170 000			1 500	8	266 500					
					2 000	10						
Plant and equipment	200 000	500 000			20 000	1	660 000					
					20 000	14						
Accumulated depreciation	(115 000)	(88 000)	40 000	1	16 000	1	(175 000)					
			4 000	16								
Land	100 000	80 000					180 000					
Shares in Swan Ltd	540 000	0			540 000	2	0					
Deferred tax asset	50 000	40 000	450	8	1 200	16	95 850					
			600	10								
			6 000	14								
Goodwill	0	0	3 200	2			3 200					
Other assets	30 000	110 000					140 000					
Total assets	985 000	842 000	705 050		705 050		1 268 550					

The consolidated financial statements for Seal Ltd and its subsidiary, Swan Ltd, for the year ended 30 June 2014 are as shown in figure 26.12(a), (b) and (c).

SEAL LTD
Consolidated Statement of Profit or Loss and Other Comprehensive Income
for the year ended 30 June 2014

Revenue:	
Sales	$ 1 209 000
Other	339 000
Total revenue	1 548 000
Expenses:	
Cost of sales	(978 500)
Other	(391 000)
Total expenses	(1 369 500)
Profit before tax	178 500
Income tax expense	(64 550)
PROFIT FOR THE PERIOD	$ 113 950
Other comprehensive income	
Revaluation decreases	$ (5 000)
TOTAL COMPREHENSIVE INCOME	$ 108 950
Profit attributable to:	
Owners of the parent	$ 102 880
Non-controlling interest	11 070
	$ 113 950
Comprehensive income attributable to:	
Owners of the parent	$ 95 880
Non-controlling interest	13 070
	$ 108 950

FIGURE 26.12(a) Consolidated statement of profit or loss and other comprehensive income

SEAL LTD
Consolidated Statement of Changes in Equity
for the year ended 30 June 2014

	Share capital	Retained earnings	General reserve	Asset revaluation surplus	Business combination valuation reserve	Total: Owners of the parent	Non-controlling interest	Total equity
Balance at 1 July 2013	$600 000	$224 960	$96 000	$59 000	0	$ 979 960	$150 440	$1 130 400
Total comprehensive income		102 880		(7 000)		95 880	13 070	108 950
Dividends paid		(20 000)				(20 000)	(2 000)	(22 000)
Dividends declared		(25 000)				(25 000)	(3 000)	(28 000)
Balance at 30 June 2014	$600 000	$282 840	$96 000	$52 000		$1 030 840	$158 150	$1 189 350

FIGURE 26.12(b) Consolidated statement of changes in equity

SEAL LTD
Consolidated Statement of Financial Position
as at 30 June 2014

ASSETS
Current assets

Receivables		$ 98 000
Inventory		266 500
Total current assets		364 500

Non-current assets

Plant and equipment		$ 660 000
Accumulated depreciation		(175 000)
Land		180 000
Deferred tax asset		95 850
Goodwill		3 200
Other		140 000
Total non-current assets		904 050
Total assets		$1 268 550

LIABILITIES

Current liabilities: Dividend payable		$ 28 000
Non-current liabilities		51 200
Total liabilities		$ 79 200
Net assets		$1 189 350

EQUITY

Share capital		$ 600 000
General reserve		96 000
Asset revaluation surplus		52 000
Retained earnings		282 840
Parent interest		$1 030 840
Non-controlling interest		$ 158 510
Total equity		$1 189 350

FIGURE 26.12(c) Consolidated statement of financial position

2. Consolidation worksheet changes under full goodwill method

Under the full goodwill method, the acquisition analysis would change as goodwill is calculated by taking into consideration the fair value of the NCI in the subsidiary.

Acquisition analysis

Net fair value of the identifiable assets
  and liabilities of Swan Ltd
$$= \$500\,000 + \$80\,000 + \$50\,000 + \$20\,000$$
$$+ \$10\,000(1 - 30\%) \text{ (BCVR — inventory)}$$
$$+ \$20\,000(1 - 30\%) \text{ (BCVR — plant)}$$
$$= \$671\,000$$

(a) Consideration transferred $= \$540\,000$

(continued)

(b) Non-controlling interest in
    subsidiary   = $134 500
Aggregate of (a) and (b)   = $674 500
Goodwill   = $674 500 − $671 000
                                              = $3500

Goodwill of Swan Ltd
Fair value of Swan Ltd   = $134 500/20%
                                              = $672 500

Net fair value of identifiable assets and
    liabilities of Swan Ltd   = $671 000
Goodwill of Swan Ltd   = $672 500 − $671 000
                                              = $1500

Goodwill of Seal Ltd
Goodwill acquired   = $3500
Goodwill of Swan Ltd   = $1500
Goodwill of Seal Ltd — control premium   = $2000

Consolidation worksheet entries at 30 June 2014
(1) *Business combination valuation reserve entries*
Because the full goodwill method is used, there will need to an extra business combination valuation entry in relation to the goodwill of the subsidiary:

| Goodwill | Dr | 1 500 | |
| Business Combination Valuation Reserve | Cr | | 1 500 |

(2) *Pre-acquisition entries*

Retained Earnings (1/7/13)	Dr	45 600	
Share Capital	Dr	400 000	
General Reserve	Dr	64 000	
Asset Revaluation Surplus (1/7/13)	Dr	16 000	
Business Combination Valuation Reserve [80% × ($14 000 + $1 500)]	Dr	12 400	
Goodwill	Dr	2 000	
Shares in Swan Ltd	Cr		540 000

(3) *NCI share of equity at acquisition date, 1 July 2010 (step 1)*
Under the full goodwill method this will change as the business combination valuation reserve in relation to goodwill has been recognised. The NCI share is calculated to be:

Pre-acquisition equity of Swan Ltd

Retained earnings (1/7/10): 20% × $50 000 = $ 10 000
Share capital: 20% × $500 000   = 100 000
General reserve: 20% × $80 000   =   16 000
Asset revaluation surplus (1/7/10):
    20% × $20 000   =   4 000

Business combination valuation reserve:
20% × ($14 000 + $7 000 + $1 500)   = $ 4 500
                                              $134 500

The worksheet entry in the NCI columns is:

Retained Earnings (1/7/13)	Dr	10 000	
Share Capital	Dr	100 000	
General Reserve	Dr	16 000	
Asset Revaluation Surplus (1/7/13)	Dr	4 000	
Business Combination Valuation Reserve	Dr	4 500	
NCI	Cr		134 500

No other changes are required.

Discussion questions

1. What is meant by the term 'non-controlling interest' (NCI)?
2. Explain whether the NCI is better classified as debt or equity.
3. Explain whether the NCI is entitled to a share of subsidiary equity or some other amount.
4. How does the existence of an NCI affect the business combination valuation entries?
5. How does the existence of an NCI affect the pre-acquisition entries?
6. Why is it necessary to change the format of the worksheet where an NCI exists in the group?
7. Explain how the adjustment for intragroup transactions affects the calculation of the NCI share of equity.
8. Explain whether an NCI adjustment needs to be made for all intragroup transactions.
9. What is meant by 'realisation of profit'?
10. When is profit realised on an intragroup transaction involving a depreciable asset?
11. When is profit realised on an intragroup transaction involving the parent renting a warehouse from the subsidiary?
12. If a step approach is used in the calculation of the NCI share of equity, what are the steps involved?
13. What are two events that could occur between the acquisition date and the beginning of the current period that could affect the calculation of the NCI share of retained earnings?
14. For what lines in the financial statements is it necessary to provide a break-down into parent entity share and NCI share?

Exercises   STAR RATING ★ BASIC ★★ MODERATE ★★★ DIFFICULT

Exercise 26.1   **EQUITY CLASSIFICATION**

★   Len Inn is the accountant for Wallaby Trucks Ltd. This entity has an 80% holding in the entity Tyres-R-Us Ltd. Len is concerned that the consolidated financial statements prepared under IFRS 10 may be misleading. He believes that the main users of the consolidated financial statements are the shareholders of Wallaby Trucks Ltd. The key performance indicators are then the profit numbers relating to the interests of those shareholders. He therefore wants to prepare the consolidated financial statements showing the non-controlling interest in Tyres-R-Us Ltd in a category other than equity in the statement of financial performance, and for the statement of changes in equity to show the profit numbers relating to the parent shareholders only.

Required

Discuss the differences that would arise in the consolidated financial statements if the non-controlling interests were classified as debt rather than equity, and the reasons the standard setters have chosen the equity classification in IFRS 10.

Exercise 26.2 CONSOLIDATION WORKSHEET, CONSOLIDATED FINANCIAL STATEMENTS, PARTIAL GOODWILL METHOD

★

Jellyfish Ltd purchased 75% of the capital of Mouse Ltd for $250 000 on 1 July 2007. At this date the equity of Mouse Ltd was:

Share capital	$100 000
General reserve	60 000
Retained earnings	40 000

At this date, Mouse Ltd had not recorded any goodwill, and all identifiable assets and liabilities were recorded at fair value except for the following assets:

	Carrying amount	Fair value
Inventory	$ 70 000	$100 000
Plant (cost $170 000)	150 000	190 000
Land	50 000	100 000

The plant has a remaining useful life of 10 years. As a result of an impairment test, all goodwill was written off in 2010. All the inventory on hand at 1 July 2007 was sold by 30 June 2008. Differences beween carrying amounts and fair values are recognised on consolidation. The tax rate is 30%. Jellyfish Ltd uses the partial goodwill method.

The trial balances of Jellyfish Ltd and Mouse Ltd at 30 June 2013 are:

	Jellyfish Ltd	Mouse Ltd
Shares in Mouse Ltd	$ 250 000	—
Plant	425 500	$ 190 000
Land	110 000	50 000
Current assets	162 000	84 000
Cost of sales	225 000	35 000
Other expenses	65 000	7 000
Income tax expense	50 000	5 000
	$1 287 500	$ 371 000
Share capital	$ 400 000	$ 100 000
General reserve	60 000	80 000
Retained earnings (1/7/12)	120 000	75 000
Sales revenue	510 600	80 000
Payables	72 900	12 000
Accumulated depreciation (plant)	124 000	24 000
	$1 287 500	$ 371 000

Required

1. Prepare the consolidation worksheet entries immediately after acquisition date.
2. Prepare the consolidation worksheet entries for Jellyfish Ltd at 30 June 2008. Assume a profit for Mouse Ltd for the 2007–08 period of $40 000.
3. Prepare the consolidated financial statements as at 30 June 2013.

CONSOLIDATION WORKSHEET ENTRIES INCLUDING NCI

★ On 1 July 2013, Norilsk Ltd acquired 90% of the capital of Rudny Ltd for $290 160. The equity of Rudny Ltd at this date consisted of:

Share capital	$ 200 000
Retained earnings	80 000

The carrying amounts and fair values of the assets and liabilities recorded by Rudny Ltd at 1 July 2013 were as follows:

	Carrying amount	Fair value
Fittings	$ 20 000	$ 20 000
Land	90 000	100 000
Inventory	10 000	12 000
Machinery (net)	200 000	220 000
Liabilities	40 000	40 000

The machinery and fittings have a further 10-year life, benefits to be received evenly over this period. Differences between carrying amounts and fair values are recognised on consolidation. Norilsk Ltd uses the partial goodwill method.

The tax rate is 30%. All inventory on hand at 1 July 2013 is sold by 30 June 2014.

Required

1. What are the entries for the consolidation worksheet if prepared immediately after 1 July 2013?
2. What are the entries for the consolidation worksheet if prepared at 30 June 2014? Assume a profit for Rudny Ltd for the 2013–14 period of $20 000.
3. If the non-controlling interest had a fair value of $31 800 on 1 July 2013, and the full goodwill method had been used, what entries in parts 1 and 2 above would change? Prepare the changed entries.

CONSOLIDATION WORKSHEET ENTRIES, BARGAIN PURCHASE, RECORDED GOODWILL

★ On 1 July 2011, Possum Ltd acquired 75% of the shares of Cassowary Ltd for $123 525. At this date, the statement of financial position of Cassowary Ltd consisted of:

Share capital — 100 000 shares	$100 000	Cash	$ 5 000
General reserve	20 000	Inventories	20 000
Retained earnings	40 000	Plant (cost $100 000)	80 000
Liabilities	60 000	Fitting (cost $80 000)	50 000
		Receivables	5 000
		Land	60 000
	$220 000		$220 000

In relation to the assets of Cassowary Ltd, the fair values at 1 July 2011 were:

Cash	$ 5 000
Inventories	25 000
Plant	86 000
Fittings	51 000
Receivables	4 000
Land	80 000

The inventories were all sold and the receivables all collected by 30 June 2012. The plant and fittings each have an expected useful life of 5 years. The plant was sold on 1 January 2014. The tax rate is 30%.

Additional information

(a) At 1 July 2013, the retained earnings of Cassowary Ltd were $80 000, and the general reserve was $30 000.

(b) During the 2013–14 period, Cassowary Ltd recorded a total comprehensive income of $18 000. This consisted of a profit of $15 000 and gains on revaluation of land of $3000.

(c) In June 2013, a dividend of $8000 was declared by Cassowary Ltd, and was paid in August 2013. An interim dividend of $5000 was paid in January 2014, and a final dividend of $4000 declared in June 2014.

Required

Prepare the worksheet entries for the preparation of the consolidated financial statements of Possum Ltd and its subsidiary, Cassowary Ltd, at 30 June 2014.

Exercise 26.5

CONSOLIDATION WORKSHEET ENTRIES, MULTIPLE YEARS, PARTIAL GOODWILL METHOD

★ On 1 July 2010, Dingo Ltd acquired 75% of the issued shares of Dugong Ltd for $125 750. At this date, the accounts of Dugong Ltd included the following balances:

Share capital	$80 000
General reserve	20 000
Retained earnings	40 000

All the identifiable assets and liabilities of Dugong Ltd were recorded at fair value except for the following:

	Carrying amount	Fair value
Plant (cost $50 000)	$35 000	$41 000
Land	50 000	70 000
Inventory	20 000	24 000

Adjustments for the differences between carrying amounts and fair values are to be made on consolidation except for land which is to be measured in Dugong Ltd's accounts at fair value. The plant has a further 3-year life. All the inventory was sold by 30 June 2011. Dingo Ltd uses the partial goodwill method.

During the 4 years since acquisition, Dugong Ltd has recorded the following annual results:

Year ended	Profit/(loss)	Total comprehensive income
30 June 2011	$10 000	$12 000
30 June 2012	23 000	28 000
30 June 2013	(6 000)	1 000
30 June 2014	22 000	22 000

The other comprehensive income relates to gains/losses on revaluation of land.

There have been no transfers to or from the general reserve or any dividends paid or declared by Dugong Ltd since the acquisition date.

The land owned by Dugong Ltd on 1 July 2010 was sold on 1 March 2012 for $75 000. The group transfers the valuation reserves to retained earnings when an asset is sold or fully consumed. The tax rate is 30%.

1. Prepare the consolidation worksheet entries as at 1 July 2010.
2. Prepare the consolidation worksheet entries for the year ended 30 June 2011.
3. Prepare the consolidation worksheet entries for the year ended 30 June 2012.
4. Prepare the consolidation worksheet entries for the year ended 30 June 2013.
5. Prepare the consolidation worksheet entries for the year ended 30 June 2014.

Exercise 26.6

★

CONSOLIDATION WORKSHEET, CONSOLIDATED FINANCIAL STATEMENTS, FULL GOODWILL METHOD

In June 2012, Echidna Ltd made an offer to the shareholders of Emu Ltd to acquire a controlling interest in the company. Echidna Ltd was prepared to pay $1.50 cash per share, provided that 70% of the shares could be acquired (enough shares to gain control).

The directors of Emu Ltd recommended that the offer be accepted. By 1 July 2012, when the offer expired, 75% of the shares had changed hands and were now in the possession of Echidna Ltd. The statement of financial position of Emu Ltd on that date is shown below.

EMU LTD Statement of Financial Position as at 1 July 2012	
Current assets	$368 000
Non-current assets	244 000
	$612 000
Share capital — 400 000 shares	$400 000
General reserve	50 000
Asset revaluation surplus	40 000
Other components of equity	30 000
Retained earnings	40 000
Current liabilities	52 000
	$612 000

At 1 July 2012, all the identifiable assets and liabilities of Emu Ltd were recorded at amounts equal to fair value. Echidna Ltd uses the full goodwill method. The fair value of the non-controlling interest at 1 July 2012 was $147 000.

The draft financial statements of the two companies on 30 June 2013 revealed the following details:

	Echidna Ltd	Emu Ltd
Sales revenue	$ 878 900	$ 388 900
Cost of sales	374 400	112 400
Gross profit	504 500	276 500
Other income	282 100	102 500
	786 600	379 000
Other expenses	216 200	115 800
Profit from trading	570 400	263 200
Gain on sale of non-current assets	20 000	10 000
Profit before tax	590 400	273 200
Income tax expense	112 400	50 000
Profit	478 000	223 200
Retained earnings (1/7/12)	112 000	40 000
	590 000	263 200

(continued)

	Echidna Ltd	Emu Ltd
Dividend paid	40 000	30 000
Dividend declared	50 000	10 000
	90 000	40 000
Retained earnings (30/6/13)	500 000	223 200
Share capital	1 200 000	400 000
General reserve	24 000	50 000
Asset revaluation surplus	70 000	60 000
Other components of equity	30 000	40 000
Current liabilities	177 000	124 400
	$2 001 000	$ 897 600
Financial assets	$ 280 000	$ 204 000
Receivables	320 000	175 000
Inventory	287 500	210 600
Investments — Shares in Emu Ltd	450 000	—
— Other investments	47 000	—
Equipment	650 000	360 000
Accumulated depreciation	(250 000)	(160 000)
Land	216 500	108 000
	$2 001 000	$ 897 600

Additional information
(a) Echidna Ltd had made an advance of $80 000 to Emu Ltd. This advance was repayable in June 2014.
(b) The directors of Echidna Ltd and Emu Ltd had declared final dividends of $50 000 and $10 000 respectively, from current period's profits.
(c) Emu Ltd holds at the end of the reporting period inventory purchased from Echidna Ltd during the year for $55 000. Echidna Ltd invoices goods to its subsidiary at cost plus 10%.
(d) On 1 July 2012, Emu Ltd sold to Echidna Ltd some display equipment for $60 000. At that date, the carrying amount of the equipment was $52 000 and the equipment was estimated to have a useful life of 10 years if used constantly over that period.
(e) Assume a tax rate of 30%.
(f) For Echidna Ltd, balances of Asset Revaluation Surplus and Other Components of Equity at 1 July 2012 were $40 000 and $25 000 respectively.

Required

Prepare the consolidated financial statements for Echidna Ltd and its subsidiary as at 30 June 2013.

Exercise 26.7	ADJUSTMENT FOR THE NCI SHARE OF EQUITY

★★ The consolidated financial statements of Whale Submarine Works Ltd are being prepared by the group accountant, Raz Putin. He is currently in dispute with the auditors over the need to adjust for the NCI share of equity in relation to intragroup transactions. He understands the need to adjust for the effects of the intragroup transactions, but believes that it is unnecessary to adjust for the NCI share of equity. He argues that the NCI group of shareholders has its interest in the subsidiary and as a result is entitled to a share of what the subsidiary records as equity. He also disputes with the auditors about the notion of 'realisation' of profit in relation to the NCI. If realisation requires the involvement of an external entity in a transaction, then in relation to transactions such as intragroup transfers of vehicles and services such as interest payments, there is never any external party involved. Those transactions are totally within the group and never involve external entities. As a result, the more appropriate accounting is to give the NCI a share of subsidiary equity and not be concerned with the fictitious involvement of external entities.

Required

Write a report to Raz convincing him that his argument is fallacious.

THE STEP APPROACH

★★ In December 2013, Frog Ltd acquired 60% of the shares of Kovrov Ltd. The accountant for Frog Ltd, Nikki Romanov, is concerned about the approach she should take in preparing the consolidated financial statements for the newly established group. In particular, she is concerned about the calculation of the NCI share of equity, particularly in the years after acquisition date. She has heard accountants in other companies talking about a 'step' approach, and in particular how this makes accounting in periods after the acquisition date very easy as it is then necessary to prepare only one step.

Required

Prepare a report for Nikki, explaining the step approach to the calculation of NCI and the effects of this approach in the years after acquisition date.

EFFECTS OF INTRAGROUP TRANSACTIONS

★★ Because the Moth Cement Works Ltd has a number of subsidiaries, Star Lin is required to prepare a set of consolidated financial statements for the group. She is concerned about the calculation of the NCI share of equity particularly where there are intragroup transactions. The auditors require that when adjustments are made for intragroup transactions the effects of these transactions on the NCI should also be adjusted for. Star has two concerns. First, why is it necessary to adjust the NCI share of equity for the effects of intragroup transactions? Second, is it necessary to make NCI adjustments in relation to *all* intragroup transactions?

Required

Prepare a report for Star, explaining these two areas of concern.

CONSOLIDATION WORKSHEET ENTRIES, DIVIDENDS, EQUITY TRANSFERS

★★ On 1 July 2010, Crocodile Ltd acquired 80% of the shares (cum div.) of Turtle Ltd for $202 000. At this date, the equity of Turtle Ltd consisted of:

Share capital — 100 000 shares	$100 000
General reserve	40 000
Retained earnings	50 000

The carrying amounts and fair values of the assets of Turtle Ltd were as follows:

	Carrying amount	Fair value
Land	$70 000	$90 000
Plant (cost $100 000)	80 000	85 000
Fittings (cost 40 000)	20 000	20 000
Goodwill	5 000	10 000

Any adjustment for the differences in carrying amounts and fair values is recognised on consolidation. Crocodile Ltd uses the partial goodwill method.

Both plant and fittings were expected to have a further 5-year life, with benefits being received evenly over those periods. The plant was sold on 1 January 2013. In the year of the sale of plant, on consolidation the valuation reserve relating to the plant was transferred to retained earnings. At 1 July 2010, Turtle Ltd had not recorded an internally generated trademark that Crocodile Ltd considered to have a fair value of $50 000. This intangible asset was considered to have an indefinite useful life.

Additional information
(a) The following profits were recorded by Turtle Ltd:

For the 2010–11 period	$20 000
For the 2011–12 period	25 000
For the 2012–13 period	30 000

(b) In June 2012, Turtle Ltd transferred $5000 to general reserve, and in June 2013, a further $6000 was transferred.

(c) In August 2010, the dividend payable of $5000 on hand at 1 July 2010 was paid by Turtle Ltd.

(d) Other dividends declared or paid since 1 July 2010 are:
- $8000 dividend declared in June 2011, paid in August 2011
- $6000 dividend declared in June 2012, paid in August 2012
- $5000 dividend paid in December 2012
- $8000 dividend declared in June 2013, expected to be paid in August 2013.

Required

1. Prepare the worksheet entries for the preparation of the consolidated financial statements of Crocodile Ltd and its subsidiary, Turtle Ltd, at 30 June 2013.
2. Assume Crocodile Ltd uses the full goodwill method and the value of the non-controlling interest at 1 July 2010 was $49 250. Prepare the entries that would differ from those in requirement 1.

Exercise 26.11   **CONSOLIDATION WORKSHEET ENTRIES, MULTIPLE YEARS, FULL GOODWILL METHOD**

★★   On 1 July 2010, Whale Ltd acquired 60% of the shares of Glider Ltd for $111 700. At this date, the equity of Glider Ltd consisted of:

Share capital	$120 000
General reserve	10 000
Retained earnings	30 000

At this date, the identifiable assets and liabilities of Glider Ltd were recorded at fair value except for the following assets:

	Carrying amount	Fair value
Equipment (cost $80 000)	$65 000	$75 000
Land	80 000	90 000
Inventory	45 000	50 000

Adjustments for the differences between carrying amounts and fair values are to be made on consolidation. The equipment has a further 5-year life. Half the inventory on hand at the acquisition date was sold by 30 June 2011, with the remainder being sold in the 2011–12 financial year. At 30 June 2013, the goodwill was written down by $3000 as the result of an impairment test.

Whale Ltd uses the full goodwill method. The fair value of the non-controlling interest at 1 July 2010 was $74 100.

During the 3 years since acquisition, Glider Ltd has recorded the following annual results:

Year ended	Profit
30 June 2011	$15 000
30 June 2012	27 000
30 June 2013	12 000

There have been no transfers to or from the general reserve or any dividend paid or declared by Glider Ltd since the acquisition date.

The equipment owned by Glider Ltd on 1 July 2010 was sold on 1 January 2012 for $70 000. On consolidation, the group transfers the valuation reserve to retained earnings when an asset is sold or fully consumed. The tax rate is 30%.

Required

1. Prepare the consolidation worksheet entries as at 1 July 2010.
2. Prepare the consolidation worksheet entries for the year ended 30 June 2011.
3. Prepare the consolidation worksheet entries for the year ended 30 June 2012.
4. Prepare the consolidation worksheet entries for the year ended 30 June 2013.

CONSOLIDATION WORKSHEET, UNRECORDED INTANGIBLE, DIVIDENDS, FULL GOODWILL METHOD

★★ On 1 July 2010, Fox Ltd acquired 70% of the shares (cum div.) of Goanna Ltd for $141 950. At this date, the equity of Goanna Ltd consisted of:

Share capital	$100 000
General reserve	31 000
Retained earnings	25 000
Other components of equity	9 000

Goanna Ltd's records showed a dividend payable at 1 July 2010 of $10 000. The dividend was paid on 1 November 2010.

A comparison of the carrying amounts and fair values of the assets of Goanna Ltd at 1 July 2010 revealed the following:

	Carrying amount	Fair value
Plant (cost $75 000)	$ 45 000	$ 60 000
Vehicles (cost $40 000)	23 000	23 000
Goodwill	10 000	

Adjustments for the differences in carrying amounts and fair values are recognised on consolidation. Both plant and vehicles were expected to have a further 5-year life, with benefits being received evenly over those periods. Goanna Ltd had not recorded an internally generated brand name for an item that was considered by Fox Ltd to have a fair value of $20 000. The brand name is regarded as having an indefinite useful life. At 30 June 2011, goodwill was considered to be impaired by $1000, and a further impairment loss of $2000 was recognised in 2012. Fox Ltd uses the full goodwill method. The fair value of the non-controlling interest at 1 July 2010 was $57 000.

Additional information
(a) The dividends paid and declared since 1 July 2010 are:
- $10 000 dividend declared in June 2011, paid in October 2011
- $5000 dividend declared in June 2012, paid in September 2012
- $8000 dividend paid in April 2013

(b) In June 2012, Goanna Ltd transferred an amount of $20 000 from the general reserve to retained earnings.
(c) The plant on hand at 1 July 2010 was sold on 30 June 2013. On consolidation, the group decided to transfer the valuation reserve relating to the plant to retained earnings.
(d) The Other Components of Equity account reflects movements in the fair values of available-for-sale financial assets. The balances of this account at 1 July 2012 were $4000 (Fox Ltd) and $11 000 (Goanna Ltd).
(e) On 30 June 2013, the financial data of both companies were:

	Fox Ltd	Goanna Ltd
Revenues	$280 000	$190 000
Expenses	220 000	140 000
Profit before tax	60 000	50 000
Income tax expense	26 000	14 000
Profit for the period	34 000	36 000
Retained earnings (1/7/12)	76 000	65 000
Total available for appropriation	110 000	101 000
Dividend paid	20 000	8 000

(continued)

	Fox Ltd	Goanna Ltd
Retained earnings (30/6/13)	90 000	93 000
Share capital	100 000	100 000
General reserve	44 000	11 000
Other components of equity	6 000	9 000
Payables	20 000	12 000
	$260 000	$225 000
Cash	$ 22 050	$ 43 000
Financial assets	20 000	30 000
Vehicles	35 000	50 000
Accumulated depreciation	(12 000)	(30 000)
Plant and equipment	80 000	120 000
Accumulated depreciation	(50 000)	(75 000)
Land	30 000	—
Goodwill	—	10 000
Accumulated impairment	—	(3 000)
Trademarks	—	80 000
Shares in Goanna Ltd	134 950	—
	$260 000	$225 000

Required

Prepare the consolidated financial statements of Fox Ltd as at 30 June 2013

Exercise 26.13 CONSOLIDATION WORKSHEET, CONSOLIDATED FINANCIAL STATEMENTS, FULL GOODWILL METHOD

★★ On 1 July 2008, Koala Ltd acquired 75% of the share capital of Kookaburra Ltd at a cost of $27 600. At this date, the capital of Kookaburra Ltd consisted of 30 000 ordinary shares each fully paid, and retained earnings were $6000.

At 1 July 2008, Kookaburra Ltd had not recorded any goodwill, and all the identifiable net assets of Kookaburra Ltd were recorded at fair value. Koala Ltd uses the full goodwill method. The fair value of the non-controlling interest at 1 July 2008 was $9000.

The trial balances of the two companies as at 30 June 2013 are as shown below.

	Koala Ltd		Kookaburra Ltd	
	Dr	**Cr**	**Dr**	**Cr**
Share capital		$ 40 000		$ 30 000
Retained earnings (1 July 2012)		19 000		14 500
Other components of equity		—		5 000
Current tax liability		8 500		2 900
Plant	$ 30 000		$ 60 000	
Accumulated depreciation — plant		17 000		30 500
Shares in Kookaburra Ltd	27 600			
10% debentures in Kookaburra Ltd	2 500			
Inventory	12 000		15 500	
Cash	14 050		500	
Financial assets	—		11 000	
Deferred tax asset	2 000		5 000	
Sales revenue		50 000		80 000
Cost of sales	34 000		58 500	

	Koala Ltd		Kookaburra Ltd	
	Dr	**Cr**	**Dr**	**Cr**
Selling expenses	4 000		6 000	
Other expenses	1 500		1 500	
Financial expenses	1 500		2 000	
Income tax expense	5 000		5 500	
Interest received from debentures		250		
Dividend revenue		1 800		
Dividend paid	2 400		2 400	
10% debentures		—		5 000
	$136 550	$136 550	$167 900	$167 900

Additional information
(a) Intragroup sales of inventory for the year ended 30 June 2013 from Kookaburra Ltd to Koala Ltd: $19 000.
(b) Unrealised profits on inventory held at 1 July 2012: inventory held by Koala Ltd purchased from Kookaburra Ltd at a profit before tax of $800.
(c) Unrealised profits on inventory held at 30 June 2013: inventory held by Koala Ltd purchased from Kookaburra Ltd at a profit before tax of $1200.
(d) The Other Components of Equity account relates to financial assets held by Kookaburra Ltd. The balance of this account at 1 July 2012 was $4000.
(e) The tax rate applicable is 30c in the dollar.

Required

Prepare the consolidated financial statements for the year ended 30 June 2013.

Exercise 26.14   **CONSOLIDATED WORKSHEET, CONSOLIDATED FINANCIAL STATEMENTS, PARTIAL GOODWILL METHOD**

★★   On 1 July 2012, Lizard Ltd acquired 80% of the share capital of Honeyeater Ltd for $264 800. This was sufficient for Lizard Ltd to gain control over Honeyeater Ltd. On that date, the statement of financial position of Honeyeater Ltd consisted of:

Share capital	$ 250 000
General reserve	10 000
Asset revaluation surplus	15 000
Retained earnings	10 000
Liabilities	180 000
	$ 465 000
Cash	$ 35 000
Inventories	70 000
Land	65 000
Plant and equipment	300 000
Accumulated depreciation	(130 000)
Trademark	100 000
Goodwill	25 000
	$ 465 000

All the identifiable assets and liabilities of Honeyeater Ltd were recorded at fair value except for:

	Carrying amount	**Fair value**
Inventories	$ 70 000	$ 80 000
Land	65 000	85 000

(continued)

	Carrying amount	Fair value
Plant and equipment (cost $200 000)	70 000	90 000
Trademark	100 000	110 000

The plant and equipment had a further 5-year life and was expected to be used evenly over that time. The trademark was considered to have an indefinite life.

Any adjustments for differences between carrying amounts at acquisition date and fair values are made on consolidation. Lizard Ltd uses the partial goodwill method.

During the year ended 30 June 2013, all inventories on hand at the beginning of the year were sold, and the land was sold on 28 February 2013 to Werst Ltd for $80 000. Any valuation reserve created in relation to the land was transferred on consolidation to retained earnings.

The income tax rate is assumed to be 30%.

Financial information for Lizard Ltd and Honeyeater Ltd for the year ended 30 June 2013 is shown on the following page.

During the current year, Honeyeater Ltd sold a quantity of inventory to Lizard Ltd for $8000. The original cost of these items to Honeyeater Ltd was $5000. One-third of this inventory was still on hand at the end of the year.

On 31 March 2013, Honeyeater Ltd transferred an item of plant with a carrying amount of $10 000 to Lizard Ltd for $15 000. Lizard Ltd treated this item as inventory. The item was still on hand at the end of the year. Honeyeater Ltd applied a 20% depreciation rate to this type of plant.

Required

1. Prepare the consolidation worksheet entries necessary for preparation of the consolidated financial statements for Honeyeater Ltd and its subsidiary for the year ended 30 June 2013.
2. Prepare the consolidated statement of profit or loss and other comprehensive income and statement of changes in equity for Lizard Ltd and its subsidiary at 30 June 2013.

	Lizard Ltd	Honeyeater Ltd
Sales revenue	$ 200 000	$ 172 000
Other income	75 000	30 000
	275 000	202 000
Cost of sales	162 000	128 000
Other expenses	53 000	31 000
	215 000	159 000
Profit from trading	60 000	43 000
Gain on sale of non-current assets	10 000	5 000
Profit before tax	70 000	48 000
Income tax expense	20 000	18 000
Profit	50 000	30 000
Retained earnings (1/7/12)	30 000	10 000
Transfer from general reserve	—	8 000
	80 000	48 000
Interim dividend paid	12 000	10 000
Final dividend declared	6 000	4 000
	18 000	14 000
Retained earnings (30/6/13)	$ 62 000	$ 34 000
Asset revaluation surplus (1/7/12)		$ 15 000
Gain on revaluation of specialised plant		5 000
Asset revaluation surplus (30/6/13)		$ 20 000

CONSOLIDATION WORKSHEET ENTRIES

★★ On 1 July 2008, Platypus Ltd acquired 75% of the shares of Wombat Ltd for $40 000. The following balances appeared in the records of Wombat Ltd at this date:

Share capital	$20 000
General reserve	2 000
Retained earnings	10 000

At 1 July 2008, all the identifiable assets and liabilities of Wombat Ltd were recorded at fair value except for the following:

	Carrying amount	Fair value
Machinery (cost $36 000)	$ 30 000	$40 000
Inventory	16 000	20 000
Receivables	20 000	18 000

The machinery, which had a remaining useful life of 5 years, was adjusted to fair value after the acquisition date in the consolidation worksheet. The machinery was sold by Wombat Ltd on 1 January 2013 for $4000, with the related valuation reserve being transferred on consolidation to retained earnings. By 30 June 2009, receivables had all been collected and inventory sold.

For the year ended 30 June 2013, the following information is available:

(a) Intragroup sales were: Wombat Ltd to Platypus Ltd — $40 000. The mark-up on cost of all sales was 25%.

(b) At 30 June 2013, the inventory of Platypus Ltd included $2000 of items acquired from Wombat Ltd.

(c) At 30 June 2012, inventory of Platypus Ltd included goods of $1000 resulting from a sale on 1 March 2012 of non-current assets by Wombat Ltd at a before-tax profit of $200. These items were sold by Platypus Ltd on 1 September 2012. This class of non-current assets is depreciated using a 10% depreciation rate on a straight-line basis.

(d) On 1 January 2013, Wombat Ltd sold an item of plant to Platypus Ltd for $2000 at a before-tax profit of $800. For plant assets, Wombat Ltd applies a 10% p.a. straight-line depreciation rate, and Platypus Ltd uses a 2.5% p.a. straight-line method.

(e) The current tax rate is 30%.

(f) Financial information for the year ended 30 June 2013 includes the following:

	Platypus Ltd	Wombat Ltd
Sales revenue	$ 84 000	$ 51 000
Dividend revenue	3 000	—
Other revenue	12 000	8 000
Total revenue	99 000	59 000
Cost of sales	58 000	26 000
Other expenses:		
Selling and administrative (including depreciation)	4 000	2 000
Financial	8 000	6 000
	70 000	34 000
Profit from trading	29 000	25 000
Gain on sale of non-current assets	4 000	1 000
Profit before tax	33 000	26 000
Income tax expense	13 200	10 400
Profit	19 800	15 600
Retained earnings at 1 July 2012	40 000	20 000
	59 800	35 600

(continued)

	Platypus Ltd	Wombat Ltd
Transfer to general reserve	3 800	1 000
Interim dividend paid	4 000	8 000
Final dividend declared	4 000	4 000
	11 800	13 000
Retained earnings at 30 June 2013	$ 48 000	$ 22 600
Asset revaluation surplus (1/7/12)	$ 3 000	$ 2 000
Gains on property revaluation	1 000	500
Asset revaluation surplus (30/6/13)	$ 4 000	$ 2 500

Required

1. Prepare the consolidation worksheet entries for the preparation of the consolidated financial statements of Platypus Ltd at 30 June 2013 using the partial goodwill method.
2. Prepare the entries that would change in requirement 1 above if the full goodwill method were used. The fair value of the non-controlling interest at 1 July 2008 was $12 900.

Exercise 26.16

★★★

CONSOLIDATION WORKSHEET ENTRIES, RECORDED GOODWILL

At 1 July 2011, Penguin Ltd acquired 80% of the share capital of Quokka Ltd for $290 000. At this date the statement of financial position of Quokka Ltd, including comparative information on fair values for assets, was as follows.

		Carrying amount	Fair value
Current assets			
Inventory		$ 60 000	$ 65 000
Receivables	$ 40 000		
Allowance for doubtful debts	5 000	35 000	35 000
Total current assets		95 000	
Non-current assets			
Plant and machinery (at cost)	200 000		
Accumulated depreciation	125 000	75 000	90 000
Vehicles (at cost)	80 000		
Accumulated depreciation	10 000	70 000	75 000
Buildings (at cost)	120 000		
Accumulated depreciation	5 000	115 000	115 000
Trademark (at valuation)		100 000	100 000
Other assets		40 000	40 000
Goodwill		20 000	
Total non-current assets		420 000	
Total assets		$515 000	
Equity			
Share capital		$200 000	
Asset revaluation surplus		50 000	
Retained earnings		50 000	
Total equity		300 000	
Current liabilities			
Accounts payable		40 000	
Dividend payable		20 000	
Total current liabilities		60 000	

	Carrying amount	Fair value
Non-current liabilities		
Debentures	155 000	
Total liabilities	215 000	
Total equity and liabilities	$515 000	

At 1 July 2011, it was expected that the depreciable assets had the following remaining useful lives:

Plant and machinery	5 years
Vehicles	10 years
Trademark	100 years
Buildings	10 years

All the inventory on hand at 1 July 2011 was sold by Quokka Ltd by 30 June 2012. Adjustments for differences between fair values and carrying amounts at acquisition date are made on consolidation. The tax rate is 30%.

Additional information
(a) The dividend payable in the records of Quokka Ltd at 1 July 2011 was paid in September 2011.
(b) On 1 January 2014, one of the machines that was on hand in Quokka Ltd at 1 July 2011 was sold for $6000. At 1 July 2011, the machine was recorded at cost of $50 000 with accumulated depreciation of $30 000, and had a fair value of $23 000. Any related revaluation surplus was transferred on consolidation to retained earnings.
(c) During the 2013–14 period, Quokka Ltd transferred $10 000 from the asset revaluation surplus (on hand at 1 July 2011) to retained earnings, and transferred $20 000 to general reserve from retained earnings.
(d) Information on dividends paid and declared is as follows:

> 2011–12 period:
>   paid a $5000 dividend
>
> 2012–13 period:
>   paid a $4000 interim dividend
>   declared, in June 2013, a $6000 dividend
>
> 2013–14 period:
>   paid the $6000 dividend declared in the previous period
>   paid a $5000 interim dividend
>   declared, in June 2014, an $8000 dividend.

(e) Information on inventory sold by Quokka Ltd to Penguin Ltd at cost plus 25%:
   • At 1 July 2013, Penguin Ltd had $10 000 of inventory on hand.
   • During the 2013–14 period, $50 000 worth of inventory was sold, with 10% still on hand in Penguin Ltd at 30 June 2014.
(f) The retained earnings balance at 30 June 2013 in Quokka Ltd was $60 000. The total comprehensive income for the year ended 30 June 2014 was $28 000, including $3000 due to revaluation of land measured using the revaluation model. The asset revaluation surplus balance at 30 June 2013 for Quokka Ltd was $55 000.

Required

1. Prepare consolidated worksheet journal entries for preparing the consolidated financial statements of Penguin Ltd at 30 June 2014 using the full goodwill method. Assume the fair value of the non-controlling interest at 1 July 2011 was $67 000.
2. Prepare the entries that would change in requirement 1 above if the partial goodwill method were used.

BARGAIN PURCHASE, CONSOLIDATION WORKSHEET ENTRIES

★★★ On 1 July 2009, Earthworm Ltd acquired (cum div.) a 70% interest in Eagle Ltd. The following balances appeared in the records of Eagle Ltd at this date:

Share capital — 100 000 shares	$100 000
General reserve	20 000
Retained earnings	52 000
Dividend payable	5 000

At 1 July 2009, the carrying amounts and fair values of Eagle Ltd's identifiable assets and liabilities were as shown on the following page.

Any differences between carrying amounts at acquisition and fair values are adjusted on consolidation. The non-current assets were deemed to have the following remaining useful lives:

Vehicles	5 years
Plant	8 years
Furniture and fittings	7 years

	Carrying amount	Fair value
Cash	$ 10 000	$ 10 000
Accounts receivable	28 000	26 000
Inventory	51 000	55 000
Vehicles (cost $25 000)	17 000	18 000
Plant (cost $100 000)	66 000	70 000
Furniture and fittings (cost $60 000)	34 500	34 500
	206 500	213 500
Dividend payable	5 000	5 000
Provisions	33 000	33 000
	38 000	38 000
Identifiable assets and liabilities	$168 500	$175 500

In addition, Eagle Ltd had recorded goodwill of $3500 at 1 July 2009. Earthworm Ltd uses the partial goodwill method. The following events occurred between the acquisition date and 30 June 2012:
(a) By 30 June 2010, 80% of the inventory on hand at 1 July 2009 had been sold, and all accounts receivable deemed to be collectable at 1 July 2009 had been received. The remaining inventory was all sold by 30 June 2011.
(b) On 15 September 2009, the dividend declared as at 1 July 2009 was paid.
(c) On 15 March 2010, Eagle Ltd paid a $12 000 dividend.
(d) On 30 June 2011, Eagle Ltd transferred $15 000 from pre-acquisition retained earnings to the general reserve.
(e) On 1 January 2012, Eagle Ltd paid a bonus share dividend from the general reserve, the dividend being one share for each ten held.
(f) On 20 June 2012, Eagle Ltd declared a dividend of $5000 from profits earned prior to 1 July 2009. The dividend was paid on 10 October 2012.
For the year ended 30 June 2014, the following information is available:
(a) Earthworm Ltd recognises dividend revenue when the dividends are declared by Eagle Ltd.
(b) The transfer was from pre-acquisition reserves.
(c) The balance of the Shares in Eagle Ltd account was $119 380 at 30 June 2013.
(d) On 30 June 2013, vehicles on hand at the acquisition date were sold for $6500. Any related valuation reserve was transferred on consolidation to retained earnings.
(e) The company tax rate is 30%.

(f) Financial information for the year ended 30 June 2013 included the following:

	Earthworm Ltd	Eagle Ltd
Profit before tax	$42 000	$36 000
Income tax expense	16 800	14 400
Profit	25 200	21 600
Retained earnings (1/7/12)	55 600	66 800
Transfer from general reserve	—	10 000
Total available for appropriation	80 800	98 400
Dividend paid	15 000	8 000
Dividend declared	10 000	16 000
	25 000	24 000
Retained earnings (30/6/13)	$55 800	$74 400

Required

Prepare the consolidation worksheet entries for the preparation of the consolidated financial statements of Earthworm Ltd at 30 June 2013.

Exercise 26.18

★★★

CONSOLIDATION WORKSHEET, REVALUATION IN SUBSIDIARY'S RECORDS, PARTIAL GOODWILL METHOD

On 1 July 2011, Yabby Ltd acquired 80% of the share capital of Skink Ltd for $198 000. At this date, the equity of Skink Ltd consisted of:

Share capital	$150 000
General reserve	30 000
Retained earnings	20 000

At 1 July 2011, all the identifiable assets and liabilities of Skink Ltd were recorded at fair value except for the following assets:

	Carrying amount	Fair value
Plant (cost $120 000)	$90 000	$100 000
Land	80 000	120 000

The plant had a further 5-year life, with benefits expected to be received evenly over that period. The land was sold by Skink Ltd in January 2013 for $150 000. Skink Ltd had revalued both these assets in its records at 1 July 2011. Yabby Ltd uses the partial goodwill method.

Financial information for these two companies at 30 June 2013 included:

	Yabby Ltd	Skink Ltd
Sales revenue	$920 000	$780 000
Other income	65 000	82 000
	985 000	862 000
Cost of sales	622 000	580 000
Other expenses	223 000	162 000
	845 000	742 000
Profit before tax	140 000	120 000
Income tax expense	30 000	40 000

(continued)

	Yabby Ltd	Skink Ltd
Profit	110 000	80 000
Retained earnings (1/7/12)	80 000	60 000
Transfer from asset revaluation surplus		28 000
	190 000	168 000
Transfer to general reserve		15 000
Dividend paid	20 000	15 000
Dividend declared	25 000	20 000
	45 000	50 000
Retained earnings (30/6/13)	$145 000	$118 000

Additional information

(a) In the 2011–12 period, Skink Ltd transferred $10 000 from the general reserve to retained earnings. No other transfers to or from reserves took place in that period. In the 2012–13 period, the transfer from asset revaluation surplus is as a result of Skink Ltd's selling of the land on hand at 1 July 2011. The transfer to general reserve is from post-acquisition profits. The balance of Skink Ltd's asset revaluation surplus at 1 July 2012 was $50 000, with an increase of $5000 recognised at 30 June 2013.

(b) During the 2011–12 period, Skink Ltd sold some inventory to Yabby Ltd for $8000. This had originally cost Skink Ltd $6000. At 30 June 2012, 10% of these goods remained unsold by Yabby Ltd.

(c) The ending inventory of Yabby Ltd included inventory sold to it by Skink Ltd at a profit of $3000 before tax. This had cost Skink Ltd $32 000.

(d) On 1 January 2012, Skink Ltd sold an item of inventory to Yabby Ltd for $50 000. This had originally cost Skink Ltd $40 000. Yabby Ltd uses the item as a non-current asset (plant) and depreciates it on a straight-line basis over a 5-year period.

(e) The tax rate is 30%.

Required

1. Prepare the consolidation worksheet entries for the preparation of the consolidated financial statements of Yabby Ltd at 30 June 2013.
2. Prepare the consolidated statement of profit or loss and other comprehensive income and statement of changes in equity at 30 June 2013.

Exercise 26.19

★★★

CONSOLIDATION WORKSHEET, CONSOLIDATED FINANCIAL STATEMENTS, FULL GOODWILL METHOD

Financial information at 30 June 2013 of Spider Ltd and its subsidiary company, Lorikeet Ltd included that shown on the next page.

At 1 July 2010, the date Spider Ltd acquired its 80% shareholding in Lorikeet Ltd, all the identifiable assets and liabilities of Lorikeet Ltd were at fair value except for the following assets:

	Carrying amount	Fair value
Plant (cost $75 000)	$50 000	$55 000
Land	30 000	38 000

The plant has an expected life of 10 years, with benefits being received evenly over that period. Differences between carrying amounts and fair values are adjusted on consolidation. The land on hand at 1 July 2010 was sold on 1 February 2011 for $40 000. Any valuation reserve in relation to the land is transferred on consolidation to retained earnings.

Spider Ltd uses the full goodwill method. The fair value of the non-controlling interest at 1 July 2010 was $31 500.

	Spider Ltd	Lorikeet Ltd
Sales revenue	$316 000	$220 000
Other revenue:		
Debenture interest	5 000	—
Management and consulting fees	5 000	—
Dividend from Lorikeet Ltd	12 000	—
Total revenues	338 000	220 000
Cost of sales	130 000	85 000
Manufacturing expenses	90 000	60 000
Depreciation on plant	15 000	15 000
Administrative	15 000	8 000
Financial	11 000	5 000
Other expenses	14 000	12 000
Total expenses	275 000	185 000
Profit before tax	63 000	35 000
Income tax expense	(25 000)	(17 000)
Profit	38 000	18 000
Retained earnings (1/7/12)	50 000	45 000
	88 000	63 000
Transfer to general reserve	3 000	—
Interim dividend paid	10 000	10 000
Final dividend declared	10 000	5 000
	23 000	15 000
Retained earnings (30/6/13)	65 000	48 000
General reserve	50 000	10 000
Other components of equity	13 000	10 000
Share capital	300 000	100 000
Debentures	200 000	100 000
Current tax liability	25 000	17 000
Dividend payable	10 000	5 000
Deferred tax liability	—	7 000
Other liabilities	90 000	12 000
	$753 000	$309 000
Financial assets	50 000	60 000
Debentures in Lorikeet Ltd	100 000	—
Shares in Lorikeet Ltd	131 600	—
Plant (cost)	120 000	102 000
Accumulated depreciation — plant	(65 000)	(55 000)
Other depreciable assets	76 000	55 000
Accumulated depreciation	(40 000)	(25 000)
Inventory	90 000	85 000
Deferred tax asset	85 400	30 000
Land	201 000	57 000
Dividend receivable	4 000	—
	$753 000	$309 000

Additional information

(a) At the acquisition date of 80% of its issued shares by Spider Ltd, the equity of Lorikeet Ltd was:

Share capital (100 000 shares)	$100 000
General reserve	3 000
Retained earnings	37 000

(b) Inventory on hand of Lorikeet Ltd at 1 July 2012 included a quantity priced at $10 000 that had been sold to Lorikeet Ltd by its parent. This inventory had cost Spider Ltd $7500. It was all sold by Lorikeet Ltd during the year.

(c) In Spider Ltd's inventory at 30 June 2013 were various items sold to it by Lorikeet Ltd at $5000 above cost.

(d) During the year, intragroup sales by Lorikeet Ltd to Spider Ltd were $60 000.

(e) It was also learned that Lorikeet Ltd had sold to Spider Ltd an item from its inventory for $20 000 on 1 January 2012. Spider Ltd had treated this item as an addition to its plant and machinery. The item was put into service as soon as received by Spider Ltd and depreciation charged at 20% p.a. The item had been fully imported by Lorikeet Ltd at a landed cost of $15 000.

(f) Management and consulting fees derived by Spider Ltd were all from Lorikeet Ltd and represented charges made for administration $2200 and technical services $2800. The latter were charged by Lorikeet Ltd to manufacturing expenses.

(g) All debentures issued by Lorikeet Ltd are held by Spider Ltd.

(h) Other components of equity relate to movements in the fair values of the financial assets. The balance of this account at 1 July 2012 was $10 000 (Spider Ltd) and $8000 (Lorikeet Ltd).

(i) The tax rate is 30%.

Required

Prepare the consolidated financial statements for Spider Ltd and its subsidiary, Lorikeet Ltd, for the year ended 30 June 2013.

27

Consolidation: other issues

ACCOUNTING STANDARDS IN FOCUS

IFRS 10 *Consolidated Financial Statements*

IFRS 12 *Disclosure of Interests in Other Entities*

LEARNING OBJECTIVES

After studying this chapter, you should be able to:

1 explain the difference between direct non-controlling interest (DNCI) and indirect non-controlling interest (INCI)

2 calculate the NCI share of equity in a sequential acquisition situation

3 explain the effects on the consolidation process where the acquisition is non-sequential

4 explain the nature of reciprocal ownership between subsidiaries

5 explain how to account for changes in ownership interests.

INTRODUCTION

In chapter 26, the group under discussion consisted of two companies in which the parent had a partial interest in the subsidiary. Hence, in the subsidiary, there were two ownership interests: the parent and the non-controlling interest (NCI). In this chapter there are two different forms of group discussed. First, the parent may have an interest in a subsidiary that has an interest in a subsidiary of its own. This form of structure gives rise to two types of NCI: a direct non-controlling interest (DNCI) and an indirect non-controlling interest (INCI). The existence of these two types of NCI affects the consolidation process, particularly in the calculation of the NCI share of equity.

The second structure discussed in this chapter is where a parent and a subsidiary have ownership interests in each other, or where subsidiaries have ownership interests in each other. These are referred to as reciprocal ownerships. Because of the crossholdings, the calculation of the NCI share of equity is a more involved process.

 ## 27.1 DIRECT AND INDIRECT NON-CONTROLLING INTEREST

One feature of multiple subsidiary structures where a parent has an interest in a subsidiary that is itself a parent of another subsidiary is the need to classify the NCI ownership in the subsidiaries into direct non-controlling interest (DNCI) and indirect non-controlling interest (INCI). Consider the group in figure 27.1.

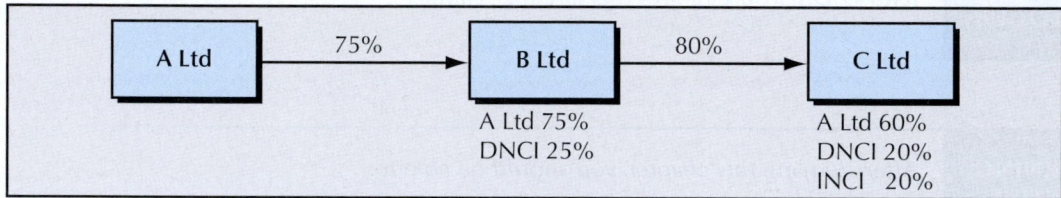

FIGURE 27.1 Group with both INCI and DNCI

In relation to B Ltd, the NCI has a direct ownership in this entity. Hence, the NCI of 25% is classified as a DNCI. In relation to C Ltd, because B Ltd owns 80% of C Ltd, there is a DNCI of 20% (i.e. an NCI that holds shares directly in C Ltd). B Ltd owns 80% of C Ltd, but B Ltd has two owners: A Ltd (75%) and the DNCI (25%). Hence, A Ltd owns 60% of C Ltd, being 75% × 80%, and the DNCI in B Ltd owns 20% of C Ltd, being 25% × 80%. The DNCI in B Ltd's ownership in C Ltd is referred to as an INCI in C Ltd because the DNCI in B Ltd does not directly own shares in C Ltd; its ownership in C Ltd is indirectly via B Ltd. It is important to note that the INCI in C Ltd is the same party as the DNCI in B Ltd.

Figure 27.2 provides another example of the existence of an INCI.

Note that, in figure 27.2, if A Ltd's ownership in B Ltd was changed to 100%, there would be no INCI in C Ltd. For an INCI to exist there has to be a DNCI in the immediate parent of that entity.

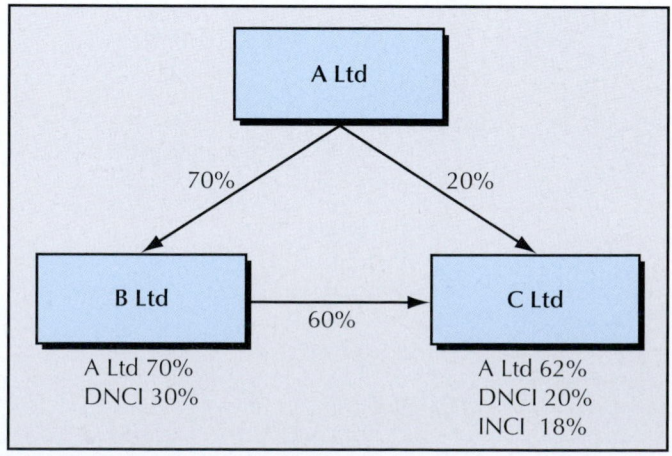

FIGURE 27.2 Indirect and direct NCI

27.2 SEQUENTIAL ACQUISITIONS

In accounting for multiple subsidiary structures, such as in figure 27.1 where A Ltd holds shares in B Ltd which holds shares in C Ltd, the accounting treatment depends on the sequence in which the acquisitions occurred. In this chapter, a sequential acquisition is one where A Ltd acquires its shares in B Ltd before B Ltd acquires its shares in C Ltd, or both acquisitions occur on the same date. A non-sequential acquisition is one where B Ltd acquires its shares in C Ltd before A Ltd acquires its shares in B Ltd. As is discussed in more detail in section 27.3, the problem with a non-sequential acquisition is that when A Ltd acquires its shares in B Ltd, one of the assets of B Ltd is 'Shares in C Ltd' — that is, the fair value of B Ltd is affected by the fair value of C Ltd.

In dealing with sequential acquisitions, what differences arise in preparing consolidated financial statements for a multiple acquisition subsidiary structure such as in figure 27.3?

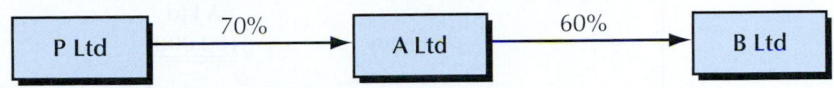

FIGURE 27.3 Group with both INCI and DNCI

The steps involved in preparing the consolidation worksheet are essentially the same as outlined in previous chapters; the main difference is that there are two business combinations rather than one. The combining of P Ltd and A Ltd and the combining of A Ltd and B Ltd are analysed in exactly the same fashion as for any two-entity combination because the combination involves the two companies in the transaction. It does not matter which of the two combinations is analysed first. Hence:

- the acquisition analysis, business combination valuation entries and pre-acquisition entries for P Ltd's acquisition of A Ltd are unchanged from those demonstrated in previous chapters
- the acquisition analysis, business combination valuation entries and pre-acquisition entries for A Ltd's acquisition of B Ltd are unchanged from those demonstrated in previous chapters.

The accounting for intragroup transactions does not change from that discussed in chapter 25. If the transactions are within the group, the effects of these transactions must be adjusted for in full. This is regardless of whether B Ltd sells to P Ltd, or A Ltd sells to B Ltd or any other combination of entities is involved. The only area where a difference occurs is with dividends, and this is discussed in section 27.2.3.

The major area of difference when multiple subsidiaries are involved is the calculation of the NCI share of equity.

27.2.1 Calculation of the NCI share of equity

The difference in accounting for the NCI arises because of the existence of both a DNCI and an INCI. The basic rules are as follows:

- *Direct NCI* receives a proportionate share of all equity recorded by the subsidiary — these equity balances include both *pre-acquisition* and *post-acquisition* amounts.
- *Indirect NCI* receives a proportionate share of a subsidiary's *post-acquisition* equity only.
- In calculating the NCI share of equity, it is consolidated equity rather than recorded equity on which the NCI is calculated. Hence, in calculating both the DNCI and INCI share of equity, adjustments must be made to eliminate any unrealised profits or losses arising from transactions within the group.

The calculation of the DNCI share of equity is therefore the same as the calculation of NCI illustrated in chapter 26. The extra adjustments have to be made for the INCI as it receives a share of post-acquisition equity only. First, however, why is the INCI limited to a share of post-acquisition equity only? Consider the group of P Ltd in figure 27.4.

In analysing why the INCI receives a share of post-acquisition equity only, it is important to remember that an INCI arises only when a partly owned subsidiary holds shares in another subsidiary. In figure 27.4, the INCI arises in B Ltd only because there exists a DNCI in A Ltd. The DNCI in A Ltd is the same group of shareholders as the INCI in B Ltd.

The DNCI in A Ltd is entitled to a share of the net assets of A Ltd. This share is calculated as a 30% share of the equity of A Ltd. However, one of the assets of A Ltd is the investment Shares in B Ltd, which reflects the right of A Ltd to 60% of the net assets of B Ltd. Because the INCI in B Ltd is the same party as the DNCI in A Ltd, it would be double counting to give the INCI a share of the equity of B Ltd relating to the pre-acquisition assets of B Ltd. The double-counting issue arises because the investment, Shares in

B Ltd, reflects the pre-acquisition equity and assets of B Ltd. When B Ltd earns post-acquisition equity, represented by post-acquisition assets, this equity is not reflected in A Ltd because the investment account, Shares in B Ltd, is recorded at cost. Hence, the double-counting issue does not arise in relation to B Ltd's post-acquisition equity, and the INCI is given a share of the post-acquisition equity of B Ltd.

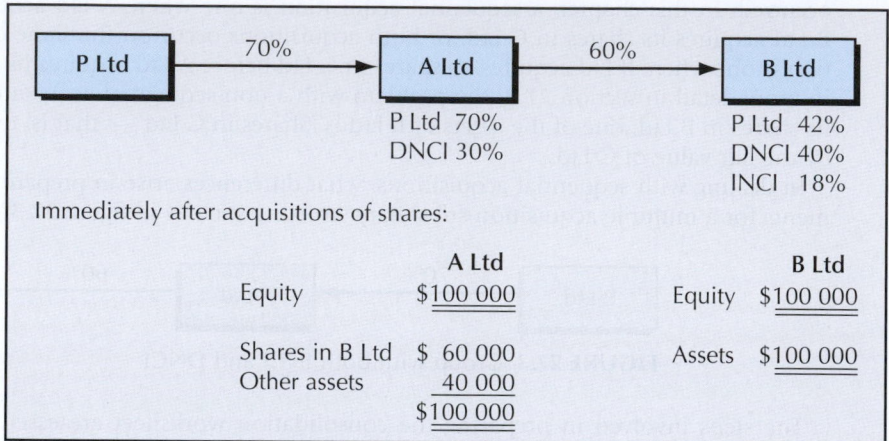

FIGURE 27.4 Group with both INCI and DNCI

In relation to the pre-acquisition equity of B Ltd, it can be seen that 60% is eliminated in the pre-acquisition entry for A Ltd's acquisition of B Ltd and the DNCI in B Ltd is given a 40% direct share. This effectively allocates all the pre-acquisition equity of B Ltd — there is none left for the INCI. This is not a problem because, as explained above, the INCI is entitled to a share of post-acquisition equity only.

As explained in previous chapters, where assets are recorded at amounts that differ from fair value, these affect *pre-acquisition* equity. In other words, as goodwill is impaired, inventory sold or non-current assets depreciated, there is an adjustment made to the balance of pre-acquisition amounts via the business combination valuation entries. As the INCI receives a share of post-acquisition equity only, the adjustment to pre-acquisition equity reflected through the pre-acquisition entry must be considered when calculating the INCI share of equity.

As explained in chapter 26, IFRS 3 *Business Combinations* allows a choice between the full goodwill and the partial goodwill methods. This choice has no effect on post-acquisition equity. Hence, the calculation of the INCI share of equity is unaffected by which goodwill method is used. *In this chapter, the partial goodwill method is used in all examples.*

As explained in chapter 26, the calculation of the NCI share of equity takes place in three steps:
1. share of equity at acquisition date
2. share of changes in equity from acquisition date to the beginning of the current period
3. share of changes in equity in the current period.

There are only *two steps* in calculating the INCI share of equity. Since, by definition, all the equity on hand at acquisition date is *pre-acquisition*, the INCI does not receive a share of equity at that date.

ILLUSTRATIVE EXAMPLE 27.1 Calculation of the NCI share of equity

Using the example in figure 27.4, assume A Ltd pays $55 200 for its 60% interest in B Ltd when the equity of B Ltd at 1 July 2011 is:

Share capital	$40 000
General reserve	30 000
Retained earnings	15 000

All identifiable assets and liabilities of B Ltd are recorded at fair value except for the following:

	Carrying amount	Fair value
Plant	$ 50 000	$55 000
Inventory	20 000	25 000

The plant is expected to last a further 5 years. Of the inventory, 90% is sold by 30 June 2012 and it is all sold by 30 June 2013. The tax rate is 30%.

For the accounting period ending 30 June 2013, the profit is $10 000, and the balance of retained earnings (1/7/12) is $24 000.

Required

Prepare the consolidation worksheet entries relating to A Ltd's acquisition of B Ltd, including the NCI entries relating to B Ltd, required for the preparation of the consolidated financial statements at 30 June 2013.

Solution

Acquisition analysis
At 1 July 2011:

Net fair value of identifiable assets and liabilities of B Ltd	= $40 000 (capital) + $30 000 (general reserve) + $15 000 (retained earnings) + $5000(1 − 0.3) (BCVR — plant) + $5000(1 − 0.3) (BCVR — inventory) = $92 000
(a) Consideration transferred	= $55 200
(b) Non-controlling interest in B Ltd	= 40% × $92 000 = $36 800
Aggregate of (a) and (b)	= $92 000
Goodwill	= Nil

The consolidation worksheet entries at *30 June 2013* are:
(1) *Business combination valuation entries*

Plant	Dr	5 000	
Deferred Tax Liability	Cr		1 500
Business Combination Valuation Reserve	Cr		3 500
Depreciation Expense	Dr	1 000	
Retained Earnings (1/7/12)	Dr	1 000	
Accumulated Depreciation	Cr		2 000
(20% × $5000 p.a.)			
Deferred Tax Liability	Dr	600	
Income Tax Expense	Cr		300
Retained Earnings (1/7/12)	Cr		300
Cost of Sales	Dr	500	
Income Tax Expense	Cr		150
Transfer from Business Combination Valuation Reserve	Cr		350

(2) *Pre-acquisition entries*
    At 1 July 2011:

Retained Earnings (1/7/11)	Dr	9 000	
Share Capital	Dr	24 000	
General Reserve	Dr	18 000	
Business Combination Valuation Reserve	Dr	4 200	
Shares in B Ltd	Cr		55 200
(60% of equity balances)			

At 30 June 2013, the inventory has been all sold, resulting in a transfer of valuation reserve to retained earnings.

Retained Earnings (1/7/12)*	Dr	10 890
Share Capital	Dr	24 000
General Reserve	Dr	18 000
Business Combination Valuation Reserve**	Dr	2 310
Shares in B Ltd	Cr	55 200

* $10 890 = 60\% \times [\$15\,000 + 90\% \times (\$5000 - \$1500)$ (inventory sold in previous period)]
** $2310 = \$4200 - 60\% \times [90\% \times (\$5000 - \$1500)]$

Transfer from Business Combination Valuation Reserve	Dr	210
Business Combination Valuation Reserve	Cr	210
(60% × $350)		

(3) *NCI share of equity at acquisition date, 1 July 2011 (step 1)*

The DNCI receives a share of the equity on hand at acquisition date. Since this equity is pre-acquisition, the INCI does not receive a share. The entry in the NCI columns is:

Retained Earnings (1/7/12)	Dr	6 000
Share Capital	Dr	16 000
General Reserve	Dr	12 000
Business Combination Valuation Reserve*	Dr	2 800
NCI	Cr	36 800
(40% of balances)		

* $2800 = 40\%$ of BCVR of $7000 at acquisition date

(4) *NCI share of changes in equity from 1 July 2011 to 30 June 2012 (step 2)*

DNCI share:

The DNCI of 40% in B Ltd is entitled to a share of the change in equity from 1 July 2011 to 30 June 2012. The *retained earnings* balance has changed from $15 000 at acquisition date to $24 000 at 30 June 2012. To avoid double-counting the NCI share of equity, an adjustment must be made for the depreciation of plant as evidenced in the valuation entry. The entry in the NCI columns of the worksheet is:

Retained Earnings (1/7/12)	Dr	3 320
NCI	Cr	3 320
(40% × [$24 000 − $15 000 − ($1000 − $300)])		

The DNCI is also affected by the transfer on consolidation of $3150 from the business combination valuation reserve on sale of 90% of the inventory. The entry is:

NCI	Dr	1 260
Business Combination Valuation Reserve	Cr	1 260
(40% × 90% × $3500)		

INCI share:

The INCI of 18% in B Ltd is entitled to a share of post-acquisition changes in equity over this period.

The retained earnings balance of $24 000 at 30 June 2012 contains three items relating to pre-acquisition equity:

• the $15 000 balance on hand at acquisition date

- there has been a $3150 transfer from business combination valuation reserve relating to the 90% of inventory sold
- there has been a $700 after-tax depreciation charge in relation to the plant.

In relation to the first two of these items, the effect can be read from an analysis of the pre-acquisition entry at 30 June 2013. In this entry, there is a debit adjustment to retained earnings (1/7/12) of $10 890. This amount reflects 60% (the parent's share) of the pre-acquisition subsidiary balance at 1 July 2012. The total balance of B Ltd's pre-acquisition retained earnings is then $10 890/0.6; that is, $18 150.

The post-acquisition equity in the retained earnings (1/7/12) balance is:

$$\$24\,000 - \$10\,890/0.6 - (\$1000 - \$300) = \$5150$$

The INCI share of this is $927, being 18% × $5150. The worksheet entry at 30 June 2013 in the NCI columns is:

| Retained Earnings (1/7/12) | Dr | 927 | |
| NCI | Cr | | 927 |

There is no need for any entry relating to the business combination valuation reserve. First, this is pre-acquisition equity and, second, the effects of the transfer have been taken into consideration in the grossing-up process with retained earnings.

(5) *NCI share of equity from 1 July 2012 to 30 June 2013 (step 3)*
During this period, B Ltd records a profit of $10 000.

DNCI share:
The DNCI share of profit is adjusted for the effects of the depreciation on plant and the sale of the rest of the inventory, as evidenced in the valuation entry. The entry in the NCI columns of the worksheet is:

NCI Share of Profit	Dr	3 580	
NCI	Cr		3 580
(40% × [$10 000 − ($1000 − $300) − ($500 − $150)])			

Besides the increase in equity caused by the earning of profit, the equity of B Ltd in the current period is affected by the transfer from business combination valuation reserve to retained earnings of $350 as a result of the sale of inventory that was on hand at acquisition date. This equity change is a movement within pre-acquisition equity and therefore affects only the DNCI, not the INCI. The entry in the NCI columns of the worksheet is:

Transfer from Business Combination Valuation Reserve	Dr	140	
Business Combination Valuation Reserve	Cr		140
(40% × $350)			

INCI share:
In the pre-acquisition entry at 30 June 2013, there are no adjustments to current period profit, indicating that there are no items affecting pre-acquisition equity that require an adjustment in the calculation of the INCI share of current period profit. However, as with the DNCI calculation, an adjustment must be made for the depreciation on the plant and the sale of the remaining inventory. The entry in the NCI columns is:

NCI Share of Profit	Dr	1 611	
NCI	Cr		1 611
(18% × [$10 000 − ($1000 − $300) − ($500 − $150)])			

27.2.2 The effects of intragroup transactions on the calculation of the NCI

As noted earlier, the adjustments for the effects of transactions within the group in structures such as in figure 27.5 are the same as those for the two-company structure illustrated in chapter 26. The effects of the transactions must be adjusted in full regardless of the amount of NCI existing in any entity.

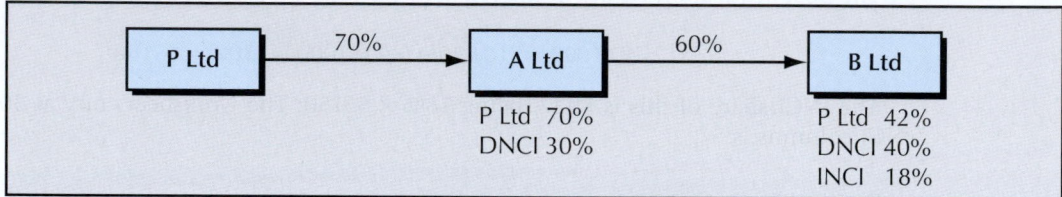

FIGURE 27.5 Group with both INCI and DNCI

What must be considered is the effect on the NCI of such adjustments. The key to this is determining which entity recorded the profit on the transaction. Using the structure in figure 27.5:

- if A Ltd earned the profit or loss — whether by selling to P Ltd or B Ltd — the NCI adjustment is based on the 30% DNCI in A Ltd
- if B Ltd made the profit or loss — whether by selling to P Ltd or A Ltd — the NCI adjustment is based on the total NCI in B Ltd of 58%; that is, the sum of the 40% DNCI and 18% INCI.

To illustrate, assume that during the current period B Ltd sold $25 000 worth of inventory to P Ltd at a profit before tax of $5000. The inventory is still on hand at the end of the current year. The consolidation worksheet entries are:

Sale of inventory: B Ltd to P Ltd

Sales	Dr	25 000	
Cost of Sales	Cr		20 000
Inventory	Cr		5 000
Deferred Tax Asset	Dr	1 500	
Income Tax Expense	Cr		1 500

Adjustment to NCI in B Ltd

NCI	Dr	2 030	
NCI Share of Profit	Cr		2 030
([40% + 18%] × [$5000 − $1500])			

Where items of property, plant and equipment are transferred within the group, the effects of the existence of an INCI must be taken into account. For example, assume B Ltd at the beginning of the previous year sold plant to A Ltd for $800 000 at a profit before tax of $20 000, with the asset having an expected life of 5 years. The consolidation worksheet entries are:

Transfer of plant: B Ltd to A Ltd

Retained Earnings (opening balance)	Dr	14 000	
Deferred Tax Asset	Dr	6 000	
Plant	Cr		20 000

Adjustment to NCI

NCI	Dr	8 120	
Retained Earnings (opening balance)	Cr		8 120
([40% + 18%] × $14 000)			

Depreciation of plant

Accumulated Depreciation	Dr	8 000	
Depreciation Expense	Cr		4 000
Retained Earnings (opening balance)	Cr		4 000
(Depreciation of 20% × $20 000 p.a.)			
Income Tax Expense	Dr	1 200	
Retained Earnings (opening balance)	Dr	1 200	
Deferred Tax Asset	Cr		2 400

Adjustment to NCI in B Ltd

Retained Earnings (opening balance)	Dr	1 624	
NCI Share of Profit	Dr	1 624	
NCI	Cr		3 248
([40% + 18%] × $2800 = $1624)			

27.2.3 Dividends

As explained in the calculation of NCI in chapter 26, in calculating the DNCI share of retained earnings, the DNCI is given a share of current period's profits and opening balance of retained earnings adjusted by a share of dividends paid and declared, and transfers to and from reserves. The INCI is allocated a share of the current period's post-acquisition profits, opening balance of post-acquisition retained earnings, and transfers to and from post-acquisition reserves. The INCI share of these balances is not reduced via allocation of dividend paid or declared. In this regard, consider the following consolidation worksheet in relation to dividends paid by B Ltd (using the structure in figure 27.5). An extract from the worksheet shows that the adjustment for the intragroup transaction and the allocation to the 40% DNCI in B Ltd eliminates the total balance of the dividend paid:

				Adjustments		Non-controlling interest		
Financial statements	**P Ltd**	**A Ltd**	**B Ltd**	**Dr**	**Cr**	**Dr**	**Cr**	**Consolidation**
Dividend paid	—	—	2 000		1 200		800	—

No dividend is paid directly to the INCI. The INCI in B Ltd receives its share through the DNCI in A Ltd receiving a share of the profit of A Ltd, which includes dividend revenue from B Ltd. When the DNCI in A Ltd receives a share of the profit of A Ltd, it receives a share of the profit of B Ltd because the dividend paid by B Ltd is a distribution of B Ltd's profit. This raises a problem of double-counting, because the INCI of B Ltd, which receives a share of the profit of B Ltd, is the same party as the DNCI in A Ltd, which receives a share of the profit of B Ltd via the dividend revenue from B Ltd included in the profit of A Ltd. This problem does not arise in a two-entity situation, because any dividend paid by the subsidiary is paid to the parent of the group. With multiple subsidiaries, the problem arises when a dividend paid or declared by one subsidiary is recognised as revenue by another subsidiary, both of which contain an NCI.

The group in figure 27.5 is used to discuss the effects on the NCI of dividends paid or declared by a subsidiary whose ownership includes an INCI.

The changes in retained earnings for the period ended 30 June 2013 are:

	P Ltd	A Ltd	B Ltd
Profit for the period	$ 40 000	$28 000	$10 000
Retained earnings (opening balance)	90 000	25 000	24 000
	130 000	53 000	34 000
Dividend paid	10 000	3 000	2 000
Dividend declared	10 000	5 000	3 000
Transfer to reserves	10 000	5 000	6 000
	30 000	13 000	11 000
Retained earnings (closing balance)	$100 000	$40 000	$23 000

The DNCI of 30% in A Ltd and the DNCI of 40% in B Ltd receive their share of all equity accounts within their respective entities:

	DNCI — A Ltd 30%	DNCI — B Ltd 40%
Profit for the period	$ 8 400	$ 4 000
Retained earnings (opening balance)	7 500	9 600
	15 900	13 600
Dividend paid	900	800
Dividend declared	1 500	1 200
Transfer to reserves	1 500	2 400
	3 900	4 400
Retained earnings (closing balance)	$12 000	$ 9 200

Dividend paid in the current period

In the group illustrated in figure 27.5, the profit of A Ltd includes $1200 dividend revenue (60% × $2000); that is, A Ltd's share of the dividend paid by B Ltd from its current profit. The issue here is that, if the INCI in B Ltd is allocated a share of the profit of B Ltd and the DNCI in A Ltd is allocated a share of the profit of A Ltd (which includes the dividend revenue from B Ltd), then, because the DNCI and the INCI are the same party, the calculation of the NCI share of equity involves double-counting. As noted above, in calculating the INCI share of B Ltd's equity, the INCI is not given a share of the dividend paid, which means there is no reduction in the INCI share of B Ltd's equity.

In calculating the NCI share of equity, it is necessary to make an adjustment to eliminate the double-counting. This could be done by adjusting the INCI of B Ltd's equity or the DNCI share of A Ltd's equity, since the problem is caused by the fact that A Ltd has recognised some of B Ltd's profit via dividend revenue. In this book, the adjustment is made to the DNCI share of A Ltd's equity in step 3 of the calculation of the NCI share of equity; that is, in calculating the NCI share of changes in equity in the current period. Hence, when making the adjustment for the $2000 dividend paid from B Ltd to A Ltd, there are two consolidation worksheet entries, the first adjusting for intragroup transactions and the second in step 3 of the calculation of NCI:

Dividend paid by B Ltd			
Dividend Revenue		Dr	1 200	
Dividend Paid		Cr		1 200
(60% × $2000)				

Step 3: NCI calculation for A Ltd

NCI	Dr	800	
Dividend Paid	Cr		800
(40% × $2000)			
NCI	Dr	360	
NCI Share of Profit	Cr		360
(Reduction of the DNCI share of profit in A Ltd since the latter includes the dividend from B Ltd: 30% × $1200)			

Dividend declared

B Ltd has declared a $3000 dividend but not paid it by the end of the period. A Ltd will still recognise 60% of this, $1800, as dividend revenue. Hence, the same double-counting problem that arose with dividend paid also arises with dividend declared. An extra entry to overcome the double counting is again required. The consolidation worksheet entries are:

Dividend declared by B Ltd

Dividend Payable	Dr	1 800	
Dividend Declared	Cr		1 800
(60% × $3000)			
Dividend Revenue	Dr	1 800	
Dividend Receivable	Cr		1 800

Step 3: NCI calculation for A Ltd

NCI	Dr	1 200	
Dividend Paid	Cr		1 200
(40% × $3000)			
NCI	Dr	540	
NCI Share of Profit	Cr		540
(30% × $1800)			

 ## 27.3 NON-SEQUENTIAL ACQUISITIONS

Consider the group in figure 27.6 in which Y Ltd is a subsidiary of X Ltd and Z Ltd is a subsidiary of Y Ltd:

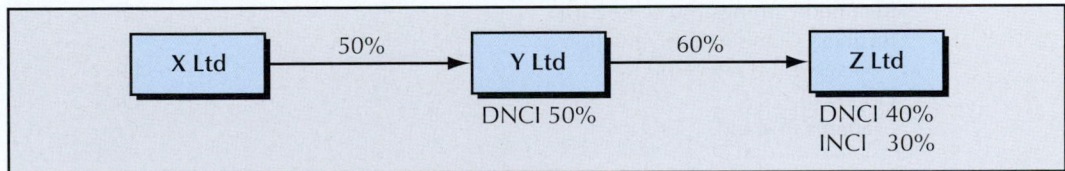

FIGURE 27.6 Group with both INCI and DNCI

The sequence in which the two acquisitions occurred was:

> 1 July 2012: Y Ltd acquired its interest in Z Ltd
> 1 July 2013: X Ltd acquired its interest in Y Ltd

The problem that the non-sequential acquisition causes is that, in relation to X Ltd's acquisition of Y Ltd, one of the assets of Y Ltd is Shares in Z Ltd. At the date of X Ltd's acquisition in Y Ltd, the fair value of the investment Shares in Z Ltd will have increased owing to the increased worth of Z Ltd. In other words, when X Ltd considers the fair value of the consideration to pay for shares in Y Ltd, it considers not only the value of Y Ltd but also the value of Z Ltd. The fair value of Y Ltd's investment in Z Ltd relates to the increased wealth of Z Ltd between 1 July 2012 and 1 July 2013.

Assume Y Ltd acquired its 60% interest in Z Ltd on 1 July 2012 for $420 when the financial position of Z Ltd was:

	Carrying amount	Fair value
Share capital	$300	
Retained earnings	230	
	$530	
Land	$200	$300
Other assets	330	330
	$530	

The acquisition analysis of Y Ltd's acquisition of Z Ltd is then:

Net fair value of Z Ltd	= $300 + $230 + $100(1 − 30%) (BCVR — land)
	= $600
(a) Consideration transferred	= $420
(b) Non-controlling interest in Z Ltd	= 40% × $600
	= $240
Aggregate of (a) and (b)	= $660
Goodwill acquired	= $660 − $600
	= $60

The worksheet entries at acquisition date, 1 July 2012, for this acquisition are:

Business combination valuation entry — Z Ltd

Land	Dr	100	
Deferred Tax Liability	Cr		30
Business Combination Valuation Reserve	Cr		70

Pre-acquisition entry

Share Capital [60% × $300]	Dr	180	
Retained Earnings [60% × $230]	Dr	138	
Business Combination Valuation Reserve [60% × $70]	Dr	42	
Goodwill	Dr	60	
Shares in Z Ltd	Cr		420

NCI at acquisition date

Share Capital	Dr	120	
Retained Earnings	Dr	92	
Business Combination Valuation Reserve	Dr	28	
NCI	Cr		240
(40% of balances)			

On 1 July 2013, X Ltd acquires 50% of the shareholding in Y Ltd for $650 when the financial positions of Y Ltd and Z Ltd are:

	Y Ltd				Z Ltd	
	Carrying amount	Fair value			Carrying amount	Fair value
Share capital	$500		Share capital		$300	
Retained earnings	600		Retained earnings		300	
Business combination valuation reserve*		$120	Business combination valuation reserve*			$140
			Liabilities*			60
Shares in Z Ltd	$420	$540	Land		$200	400
Other assets	680	680	Other assets		400	400

* These relate to the valuation of the assets, with the valuation of the land being tax-effected.

Hence, in relation to Z Ltd at 1 July 2013:
- retained earnings has increased by $70 (i.e. from $230 to $300)
- land has increased its fair value by $100 (i.e. from $300 to $400).

Worksheet entries at 1 July 2013:
Because X Ltd acquires the group consisting of Y Ltd and Z Ltd, the assets of both Y Ltd and Z Ltd are revalued at 1 July 2013.

(1) *Business combination valuation entries — Z Ltd*

Land	Dr	100	
Deferred Tax Liability	Cr		30
Business Combination Valuation Reserve	Cr		70
Land	Dr	100	
Deferred Tax Liability	Cr		30
Business Combination Valuation Reserve	Cr		70

It is useful to raise the increases in valuation separately as the NCI has to be increased by these amounts. In subsequent periods, the entries may be combined.

(2) *Pre-acquisition entry at 1 July 2013: Y Ltd and Z Ltd*
There is no change from the entry at 1 July 2012:

Share Capital [60% × $300]	Dr	180	
Retained Earnings [60% × $230]	Dr	138	
Business Combination Valuation Reserve [60% × $70]	Dr	42	
Goodwill	Dr	60	
Shares in Z Ltd	Cr		420

(3) *40% DNCI at acquisition date*
There is no change from the entry at 1 July 2012:

Share Capital	Dr	120	
Retained Earnings	Dr	92	
Business Combination Valuation Reserve	Dr	28	
NCI	Cr		240
(40% of balances)			

(4) *40% DNCI share of equity from 1 July 2012 to 1 July 2013*

Retained Earnings	Dr	28	
NCI	Cr		28
(40% × $70)			
Business Combination Valuation Reserve	Dr	28	
NCI	Cr		28
(40% × $70 land)			

The INCI of 30% receives no amount at this stage because there are no post-acquisition profits in Z Ltd. The NCI in Y Ltd (which is the same party as the INCI in Z Ltd) receives a share of the business combination valuation reserves in Y Ltd at 1 July 2013, which reflects any increase in Z Ltd's wealth between 1 July 2012 and 1 July 2013. Hence, post-acquisition equity, to which the INCI in Z Ltd is entitled to a share, occurs only after 1 July 2013.

(5) *Business combination valuation entries — Y Ltd at 1 July 2013*

Shares in Z Ltd	Dr	120	
Business Combination Valuation Reserve	Cr		120
($540 − $420)			

Note that only $420 is eliminated in the pre-acquisition entry for Y Ltd to Z Ltd. This is based on the following acquisition analysis for X Ltd and Y Ltd:

Net fair value of Y Ltd	= $500 + $600 + $120 (BCVR — Shares in Z Ltd)
	= $1220
(a) Consideration transferred	= $650
(b) Non-controlling interest in Y Ltd	= 50% × $1220
	= $610
Aggregate of (a) and (b)	= $1260
Goodwill acquired	= $1260 − $1220
	= $40

(6) *Pre-acquisition entry: X Ltd and Y Ltd*

Share Capital	Dr	250	
Retained Earnings	Dr	300	
Business Combination Valuation Reserve	Dr	60	
Goodwill	Dr	40	
Shares in Y Ltd	Cr		650
Retained Earnings [60% × $70]	Dr	42	
Business Combination Valuation Reserve [60% × $70]	Dr	42	
Goodwill*	Dr	36	
Shares in Z Ltd	Cr		120

* This reflects Y Ltd's share of the extra goodwill in Z Ltd between 1 July 2012 and 1 July 2013. The goodwill of Z Ltd is not revalued at 1 July 2013; hence, there is no share of equity recognised as occurs with assets such as land.

The last entry above eliminates the extra worth in Z Ltd, which is reflected in the revaluation of Shares in Z Ltd in the accounts of Y Ltd. The whole of the fair value of this account is now eliminated on consolidation. In future worksheets this entry should be included in the valuation entries for Z Ltd because any changes in land (sale or impairment) may affect the nature of the equity accounts associated with Z Ltd.

(7) *50% DNCI in Y Ltd*

Share Capital	Dr	250
Retained Earnings	Dr	300
Business Combination Valuation Reserve [50% × $120]	Dr	60
NCI	Cr	610

The consolidation worksheet at 1 July 2013 is shown in figure 27.7. For retained earnings, share capital and the business combination valuation reserve, the consolidation amounts are those for X Ltd (i.e. there are no post-acquisition subsidiary amounts in these accounts attributable to the parent).

Financial statements	X Ltd	Y Ltd	Z Ltd	Adjustments Dr		Cr		Non-controlling interest Dr		Cr		Consolidation
Retained earnings	800	600	300	2	138			3	92			800
				6	300			4	28			
				6	42			7	300			
Share capital	900	500	300	2	180			3	120			900
				6	250			7	250			
Business combination	—	—	—	2	42	70	1	3	28			—
valuation reserve				6	60	70	1	4	28			
				6	42	120	5	7	60			
Liabilities	—	—	—			30	1					60
						30	1					
NCI										240	3	906
										28	4	
										28	4	
										610	7	
	1700	1100	600									2666
Shares in Y Ltd	650	—	—	5		650	6					—
Shares in Z Ltd	—	420	—	5	120	420	2					—
						120	6					
Land	—	—	200	1	100							400
				1		100						
Other assets	1050	680	400									2130
Goodwill	—	—	—	2	60							136
				6	40							
				6	36							
	1700	1100	600		1510	1510				906	906	2666

FIGURE 27.7 Consolidation worksheet: non-sequential acquisition

LO4   27.4   RECIPROCAL OWNERSHIP

Reciprocal shareholdings, otherwise known as mutual holdings or crossholdings, exist when a parent and a subsidiary own shares in each other. They also exist when a parent has more than one subsidiary and two or more of the subsidiaries own shares in each other. Some illustrative structures are as shown in figures 27.8 and 27.9.

In some jurisdictions, such as Australia, subsidiaries are not allowed to hold shares in the parent entity. Hence, structures such as in figure 27.8 are not allowed to exist. However, structures such as in figure 27.9, where the crossholding is between the subsidiaries, are allowed. The same principles, however, are applied in accounting for the structures in both figures. To simplify the explanation, the structure shown in figure 27.8 is used in this chapter for illustrative purposes.

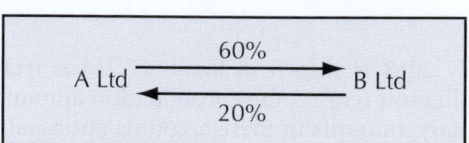

FIGURE 27.8 Reciprocal holdings

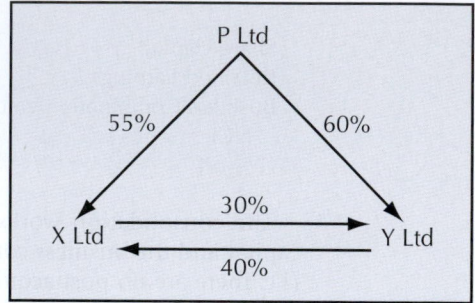

FIGURE 27.9 Reciprocal holdings

27.4.1 **Pre-acquisition and valuation entries**

Using the structure in figure 27.9, business combination valuation entries are necessary for both X Ltd and Y Ltd, and there are four pre-acquisition entries:
- P Ltd's acquisition of X Ltd
- P Ltd's acquisition of Y Ltd
- X Ltd's acquisition of Y Ltd
- Y Ltd's acquisition of X Ltd.

Timing of these acquisitions will affect the valuations made, and the form of the pre-acquisition entries, particularly in relation to the crossholding between X Ltd and Y Ltd. If X Ltd acquires shares in Y Ltd before Y Ltd acquires its shares in X Ltd, then in preparing the pre-acquisition/valuation entries for the latter acquisition, one of the assets of X Ltd is its investment in Y Ltd. In other words, where non-sequential acquisitions occur, particular adjustments must be taken into account, as demonstrated in section 27.3 of this chapter.

27.4.2 **Non-controlling interest**

Consider figure 27.10. What are the ownership interests in each entity?

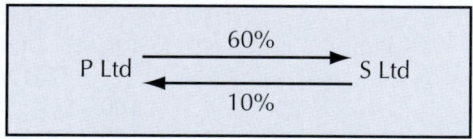

FIGURE 27.10 Reciprocal holdings

In relation to *S Ltd*, there is a DNCI of 40%. However, it is a little more difficult to determine P Ltd's interest in S Ltd because of the reciprocal holding. Similarly, in relation to P Ltd, there is an NCI in P Ltd, but its exact percentage interest is not immediately obvious.

A further factor complicating the calculation of the NCI share of equity is the timing of the various acquisitions; that is, whether P Ltd acquired its share in S Ltd before S Ltd acquired its shares in P Ltd or vice versa. The profits recorded by the two entities can be broken into three parts:
- those on hand at the first acquisition (e.g. P Ltd's acquisition of S Ltd)
- those on hand at the second acquisition (S Ltd's acquisition of P Ltd); this is the date the reciprocal ownership arises
- those earned subsequent to the point of the mutual ownership occurring. These are referred to here as *post-acquisition profits*; that is, after the point that the reciprocal holding was raised.

Allocation of pre-acquisition equity to the NCI

Some small examples containing variations in the timing of acquisitions are examined to demonstrate the approach to be taken in calculating the shares of pre-acquisition equity attributable to the parent and the NCI. The group of P Ltd and S Ltd is used in these examples. *It is assumed in these examples that no business combination valuation entries are required (i.e. all assets are at fair value and no goodwill arises on acquisition).* Because the calculations are concerned with the allocation of *pre-acquisition* equity, only the DNCI is of concern.

Example 1: Shares acquired on the same date
On 1 July 2012, P Ltd acquired 60% of the shares of S Ltd and S Ltd acquired 10% of the shares of P Ltd. The only DNCI is the 40% in S Ltd. It is entitled to a share of all equity of S Ltd at acquisition date, 1 July 2012.

Example 2: P Ltd acquires shares in S Ltd before S Ltd acquires shares in P Ltd
Information concerning the acquisitions is as follows:

	P Ltd	S Ltd	
	1/7/13	1/7/12	1/7/13
Share capital	$40 000	$25 000	$25 000
Retained earnings	30 000	10 000	15 000
Shares in S Ltd	21 000		
Shares in P Ltd			7 300
Other assets	49 000	35 000	32 700

P Ltd acquired 60% of the shares of S Ltd for $21 000 at 1 July 2012 when the retained earnings of S Ltd were $10 000. On 1 July 2013, S Ltd acquired 10% of the shares in P Ltd for $7300. At this date, the retained earnings of S Ltd had increased by $5000 and the fair value of the Shares in S Ltd account in P Ltd increased to $24 000 (a $3000 increase, which is 60% × $5000).

The consolidation worksheet entries at 1 July 2013 are as follows:

P Ltd's acquisition of S Ltd
Pre-acquisition entry:

Share Capital [60% × $25 000]	Dr	15 000	
Retained Earnings [60% × $10 000]	Dr	6 000	
Shares in S Ltd	Cr		21 000

NCI in S Ltd at acquisition date:

Share Capital	Dr	10 000	
Retained Earnings	Dr	4 000	
NCI	Cr		14 000
(40% of balances)			

NCI share of equity from 1 July 2012 to 30 June 2013:

Retained Earnings	Dr	2 000	
NCI	Cr		2 000
(40% × [$15 000 − $10 000])			

S Ltd's acquisition of P Ltd
Valuation of P Ltd's assets:

Shares in S Ltd	Dr	3 000	
Business Combination Valuation Reserve	Cr		3 000

Share Capital [10% × $40 000]	Dr	4 000	
Retained Earnings [10% × $30 000]	Dr	3 000	
Business Combination Valuation Reserve [10% × $3000]	Dr	300	
Shares in P Ltd	Cr		7 300
Retained Earnings	Dr	3 000	
Shares in S Ltd	Cr		3 000
(60% × [$15 000 − $10 000])			

This last entry results in the total $15 000 of S Ltd's retained earnings now either eliminated or allocated to the NCI. The parent's share is recognised in the business combination valuation reserve.

Example 3: S Ltd acquires shares in P Ltd before P Ltd acquires shares in S Ltd
Information concerning the acquisitions is as follows:

	S Ltd	P Ltd	
	1/7/13	**1/7/12**	**1/7/13**
Share capital	$25 000	$40 000	$40 000
Retained earnings	10 000	30 000	40 000
Shares in S Ltd			21 600
Shares in P Ltd	7 000		
Other assets	28 000	70 000	58 400

On 1 July 2012, S Ltd acquired a 10% interest in P Ltd for $7000.

On 1 July 2013, P Ltd acquired a 60% controlling interest in S Ltd for $21 600. S Ltd's asset Shares in P Ltd had a fair value at this date of $8000, reflecting the increase in equity of P Ltd of $10 000. Consolidation worksheet entries at 1 July 2013 are as follows:

S Ltd's acquisition of P Ltd
Pre-acquisition entry:

Share Capital [10% × $40 000]	Dr	4 000	
Retained Earnings [10% × $30 000]	Dr	3 000	
Shares in P Ltd	Cr		7 000

P Ltd's acquisition of S Ltd
Valuation of S Ltd's assets:

Shares in P Ltd	Dr	1 000	
Business Combination Valuation Reserve	Cr		1 000
($8000 − $7000)			

Pre-acquisition entries:

Share Capital [60% × $25 000]	Dr	15 000	
Retained Earnings [60% × $10 000]	Dr	6 000	
Business Combination Valuation Reserve [60% × $1000]	Dr	600	
Shares in S Ltd	Cr		21 600

Retained Earnings [10% × ($40 000 − $30 000)]	Dr	1 000	
Shares in P Ltd	Cr		1 000

NCI share at 1 July 2012 (note the NCI has an interest in S Ltd at this date):

Share Capital [40% × $25 000]	Dr	10 000	
Retained Earnings [40% × $10 000]	Dr	4 000	
NCI	Cr		14 000

NCI share of equity from 1 July 2012 to 1 July 2013:

Business Combination Valuation Reserve [40% × $1000]	Dr	400	
NCI	Cr		400

Note that this reflects the increased worth of P Ltd between these two dates. The 40% DNCI in S Ltd actually has an INCI share of the equity of P Ltd between the two acquisition dates of (40% × 10%) ($40 000 − $30 000) = $400.

Allocation of post-acquisition equity

In the previous section, the NCI has been given a share of equity of both entities up to the date of the formation of the reciprocal holding. This section demonstrates the allocation of the changes in equity subsequent to the formation of the reciprocal ownership.

The difficulty in this process is that there is no easy way of determining the relative ownership interests in the entities within the group because the entities are interdependent. Consider again the following structure:

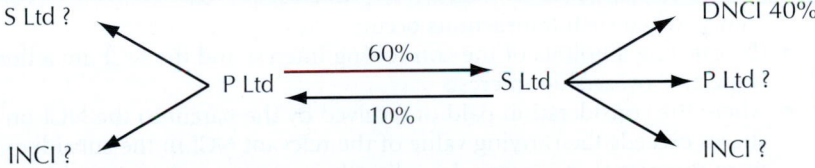

The only percentage easily calculable is the DNCI in S Ltd. There are various methods that are used to overcome the problem of interdependency. For two companies, simultaneous equations may be used. Using the group of P Ltd and S Ltd:

> Let P = recorded profit of P Ltd
> S = recorded profit of S Ltd
> p = 'real' or 'true' profits of P Ltd
> s = 'real' or 'true' profits of S Ltd.

(The 'real' profits of P Ltd consist of the recorded profits of P Ltd plus the profits of S Ltd that can be claimed by P Ltd because of its ownership interest in S Ltd.)

$$p = P + 0.6s \quad (1)$$
$$s = S + 0.1p \quad (2)$$

Substituting for p in equation (2):

$$s = S + 0.1(P + 0.6s)$$
$$= S + 0.1P + 0.06s$$
$$0.94s = S + 0.1P$$
$$s = 1/0.94S + 0.1P/0.94$$

As both P and S are known, being the recorded profits, the post-acquisition profits of P Ltd and S Ltd are calculable. The NCI share of post-acquisition profits is based on the DNCI in S Ltd of 40% receiving a share of s (i.e. a 40% share of the real post-acquisition profits of S Ltd). There is no need to calculate any INCI share of equity because, by calculating the real profits of S Ltd, the DNCI gets the appropriate share, including that from the crossholdings.

 27.5 CHANGES IN OWNERSHIP INTERESTS

27.5.1 Changes in ownership interests without loss of control

As discussed in chapter 23, IFRS 10 *Consolidated Financial Statements* requires both the parent interest and the non-controlling interest (NCI) to be classified as equity. Where the parent acquires additional shares in a subsidiary — that is, subsequent to obtaining control — or where the parent sells shares in a subsidiary but still retains control, there is no change in the economic entity. The economic entity still consists of the parent and the subsidiary. These changes in ownership interests cannot then give rise to gains or losses to the economic entity. They are accounted for as equity transactions, as these transactions are transactions between the owners and not with entities outside the group.

Where the parent acquires additional shares in the subsidiary, subsequent to obtaining control, this transaction is not a business combination as the parent already had control of the subsidiary. Hence, there is no need to adjust the identifiable assets and liabilities of the subsidiary to fair values or to measure goodwill in relation to the transaction involving acquisition of additional shares.

Note paragraphs 23 and B96 of IFRS 10:

> 23 Changes in a parent's ownership interest in a subsidiary that do not result in the parent losing control of the subsidiary are equity transactions (ie transactions with owners in their capacity as owners).
>
> B96 When the proportion of the equity held by non-controlling interests changes, an entity shall adjust the carrying amounts of the controlling and non-controlling interests to reflect the changes in their relative interests in the subsidiary. The entity shall recognise directly in equity any difference between the amount by which the non-controlling interests are adjusted and the fair value of the consideration paid or received, and attribute it to the owners of the parent.

Hence, when such transactions occur:

- the carrying amounts of the controlling interest and the NCI are adjusted to reflect the change in respective ownership interests
- where the consideration paid or received by the parent to the NCI on acquisition or sale of subsidiary shares exceeds the carrying value of the relevant NCI in the subsidiary sold to the parent or bought from the parent, it is recognised directly in equity, and attributable to the controlling interest.

The parent and the NCI will determine the consideration paid on these transactions based on an assessment of the fair value of the subsidiary. In contrast, the relative interests of the parent and the NCI in the subsidiary, as reflected in the consolidated financial statements, are based on the carrying amounts of the net assets of the subsidiary. It is this difference that gives rise to the amount being recognised directly in equity.

This method of accounting for the relative interests applies in all circumstances, regardless of whether the measurement of the NCI is based on a full or partial goodwill method.

27.5.2 Acquisition of additional shares by the parent subsequent to date of acquisition

> **ILLUSTRATIVE EXAMPLE 27.2 Accounting for the acquisition of additional shares by the parent**
>
> P Ltd acquired a 60% interest in S Ltd for $12 000 on 1 July 2011 when the equity of S Ltd was:
>
> | | |
> |---|---:|
> | Share capital | $10 000 |
> | Retained earnings | 8 000 |
>
> The assets and liabilities of S Ltd were all measured at amounts equal to fair value except for plant for which the fair value was $1000 greater than carrying amount. The plant had a further economic life of 5 years. The fair value of the NCI in S Ltd was considered to be $8000.

Solution

Acquisition analysis
At 1 July 2011:

Net fair value of identifiable assets and liabilities of S Ltd	= $10 000 + $8000 (recorded equity)
	+ $1000 (1 − 30%) (BCVR — plant)
	= $18 700
(a) Consideration transferred	= $12 000
(b) NCI in S Ltd	= $8000
Aggregate of (a) and (b)	= $20 000
Goodwill	= $20 000 − $18 700
	= $1300
Goodwill attributable to P Ltd	
Net fair value acquired	= 60% × $18 700
	= $11 220
Consideration transferred	= $12 000
Goodwill — P Ltd	= $780
Goodwill attributable to NCI	= $1300 − $780
	= $520

As P Ltd paid $12 000 for 60% of S Ltd which had a fair value of $20 000 (i.e. $8000/40%), there is no control premium in this example.

Assume that at 1 July 2013, P Ltd acquired a further 20% of the shares in S Ltd for $5000 when the recorded equity of S Ltd consisted of:

Share capital	$10 000
Retained earnings	10 000

At this date, P Ltd would pass the following entry in its records:

Shares in S Ltd	Dr	5 000	
Cash	Cr		5 000

The consolidation worksheet entries at 1 July 2013 — immediately prior to the acquisition of additional shares — are:

(1) *Business combination valuation entries*

Plant	Dr	1 000	
Deferred Tax Liability	Cr		300
Business Combination Valuation Reserve	Cr		700
Retained Earnings (1/7/13)	Dr	400	
Accumulated Depreciation	Cr		400
Deferred Tax Liability	Dr	120	
Retained Earnings (1/7/13)	Cr		120
Goodwill	Dr	1 300	
Business Combination Valuation Reserve	Cr		1 300

(2) *Pre-acquisition entries*

Retained Earnings (1/7/13)	Dr	4 800	
Share Capital	Dr	6 000	
Business Combination Valuation Reserve	Dr	1 200	
Shares in S Ltd	Cr		12 000

(3) *NCI entries*

Retained Earnings (1/7/13)	Dr	3 200	
Share Capital	Dr	4 000	
Business Combination Valuation Reserve	Dr	800	
NCI	Cr		8 000
Retained Earnings (1/7/13)	Dr	688	
NCI	Cr		688
(40% × [$10 000 − $8000 − ($400 − $120)])			

On acquiring a further 20% of the shares in S Ltd for $5000, the following additional consolidation worksheet entries are required at 1 July 2013:

(4) *Reduction in the NCI share of recorded equity*

NCI	Dr	4 344	
Share Capital	Cr		2 000
Retained Earnings (1/7/13)	Cr		1 944
Business Combination Valuation Reserve	Cr		400
(50% of NCI share at 1/7/13)			

(5) *Elimination of additional investment in S Ltd*

Share Capital	Dr	2 000	
Retained Earnings (1/7/13)	Dr	1 944	
Business Combination Valuation Reserve	Dr	400	
Retained Earnings: decrease due to acquisition of shares in			
S Ltd from NCI	Dr	656	
Shares in S Ltd	Cr		5 000

The adjustment to retained earnings (1/7/13) ensures that the opening balance remains the same as the prior period's closing balance. The other adjustment to retained earnings reflects the fact that P Ltd recognised the increased worth of S Ltd when it acquired the additional shares. If the acquisition had been a business combination then this extra wealth would have been recognised in business combination valuation reserves. In time, they would have been transferred back to retained earnings. Because no business combination occurred, the adjustment for future earnings is recognised in retained earnings.

Below are the extracts from the consolidation worksheet relating to retained earnings, before and after the acquisition of additional shares, assuming P Ltd has a balance of zero (for simplicity):

Before the sale of shares

Financial statements	P Ltd	S Ltd	Adjustments			Group	NCI		Parent
				Dr	Cr			Dr	Cr	
Retained earnings	—	10 000	1	400	120	1	4 920	3	3 200		1 032
(1/7/13)			2	4 800				3	688		

After the sale of shares

Financial statements	P Ltd	S Ltd	Adjustments				NCI			Parent
				Dr	Cr	Group		Dr	Cr	
Gain	1 000		5	1 000						
Retained earnings (1/7/13)	—	10 000	1	400	120	1	2 976	3	3 200	1 944	4	1 032
			2	4 800				3	688		
			5	1 944							
Adjustment on share acquisition			5	656							656

At 30 June 2014, the NCI entries would include a 20% share of the 2013–14 profit.

27.5.3 Sale of shares by parent with retention of control

The example used here is the same as that in section 27.5.2 except that at 1 July 2013 P Ltd sells $\frac{1}{3}$ of its holding in S Ltd, namely 2000 shares — this being 20% of the shares issued by S Ltd. The NCI is now 60%. The selling price of the shares by P Ltd is $5000. However, assume that control remains with P Ltd because of the wide dispersion of the NCI holding.

On sale, P Ltd records the following entry:

Cash	Dr	5 000	
Shares in S Ltd [$\frac{1}{3} \times $12 000$]	Cr		4 000
Gain on Sale	Cr		1 000

The NCI share of S Ltd's equity increases from 40% to 60%.

The consolidation worksheet entries in illustrative example 27.2 (entries (1)–(3)) will still be required except that the pre-acquisition entry will now relate to only 40% of the pre-acquisition equity of S Ltd as follows:

(2) *Pre-acquisition entries*

Retained Earnings (1/7/13) [40% × $8000]	Dr	3 200	
Share Capital [40% × $10 000]	Dr	4 000	
Business Combination Valuation Reserve [40% × $2000]	Dr	800	
Shares in S Ltd [$12 000 – $4000]	Cr		8 000

In addition to the consolidation worksheet entries in illustrative example 27.2 (entries (1)–(3)), the following entries are required in the 2013–14 consolidation worksheet as a result of the sale of shares:

(4) *Increase in the NCI share of equity*

Retained Earnings (1/7/13)*	Dr	1 944	
Share Capital	Dr	2 000	
Business Combination Valuation Reserve	Dr	400	
NCI	Cr		4 344

* 20% × [$10 000 – ($400 – $120)])

(5) Elimination of the gain recorded by P Ltd

Gain on Sale of Shares Sold	Dr	1 000	
Retained Earnings (1/7/13)	Cr		344
Other Reserves	Cr		656

The gain on sale recorded by P Ltd must be adjusted by any post-acquisition equity already recognised by the group in relation to the shares sold. The adjustment to retained earnings (1/7/13) of $344 (20% × [$2000 – ($400 – $120)]) reflects the fact that there have been post-acquisition profits recorded by the subsidiary. The balance of the gain on sale is taken to equity in accordance with IFRS 10. In these journal entries, the account 'Other Reserves' is used, but IFRS 10 does not specify any particular equity account to be used.

The following entry will be required in consolidation worksheets subsequent to the 2013–14 year:

Retained Earnings (opening balance)	Dr	656	
Other Reserves	Cr		656

If the balance in other reserves were transferred to retained earnings, future consolidation entries would not be necessary.

Note the change in the consolidation worksheet for the retained earnings (opening balance) as a result of the sale of shares. Below are the related extracts from the consolidation worksheet before and after the sale of shares, assuming P Ltd has a balance of zero (for simplicity):

Before the sale of shares

Financial statements	P Ltd	S Ltd	Adjustments				Group	NCI			Parent
				Dr	Cr			Dr	Cr		
Retained earnings (1/7/13)	—	10 000	1 2	400 4 800	120	1	4 920	3 3	3 200 688		1 032

After the sale of shares

Financial statements	P Ltd	S Ltd	Adjustments				Group	NCI			Parent
				Dr	Cr			Dr	Cr		
Gain	1 000		5	1 000							
Retained earnings (1/7/13)	—	10 000	1 2	400 3 200	120 344	1 5	7 520	3 3 4	3 200 688 1 944		1 032

Note that the equity of the parent as shown in the consolidated financial statements has increased by $656, shown in 'Other Reserves'. The parent itself recorded a gain of $1000. However the consolidated financial statements had recognised some of the post-acquisition wealth of the subsidiary, namely:

Profits recorded by S Ltd subsequent to date of acquisition	= $10 000 – $8000 = $2000
Post-acquisition portion	= $2000 – 2 × $140 (plant depreciation) = $1720
Amount relating to 20% of shares sold	= 20% × $1720 = $344

As the group has already recognised $344 increased equity, on sale of the shares only $656, not $1000, increase in equity is recognised by the group. This amount relates to the increased worth of the subsidiary not yet recognised by the subsidiary. This can also be calculated assuming that, if P Ltd sold 20% of the subsidiary for $5000, then the whole of the subsidiary at time of sale was worth $25 000 (i.e. $5000/20%):

Fair value of net assets of subsidiary	= $25 000
Recorded net assets of subsidiary	= $20 000
Net assets recognised by the group	= $20 000 + ($1000 − $400) (plant) − ($300 − $120) (deferred tax liability) + $1300 (goodwill)
	= $21 720
Unrecognised net assets	= $3280
Portion relating to 20%	= 20% × $3280
	= $656

At the end of the 2013–14 period, the NCI would be allocated 60% of the post-acquisition profits of S Ltd.

27.5.4 Changes in ownership interests with loss of control

A parent may lose control of a subsidiary for a number of reasons, such as:
- it may sell shares in the subsidiary such that another entity has the controlling interest
- there may be a change in the dispersion in the holding of shares by entities comprising the NCI such that a parent with less than a 50% holding loses control
- a subsidiary may become subject to the control of a government, court, administrator or regulator
- there may be a change in a contractual arrangement.

In this section the example will relate to a situation where the parent sells some of its shares in a subsidiary.

Having lost control, but retained an investment in the former subsidiary, in accordance with paragraph 25 of IFRS 10, the investor will record that remaining investment in accordance with IFRS 9 *Financial Instruments*, namely at fair value. The measurement of the remaining asset at fair value is factored into the calculation of any gain or loss on disposal of the shares in the subsidiary.

The example used here is that used in section 27.5.3 where P Ltd originally acquired 60% of the issued shares of S Ltd, and now sells $\frac{1}{3}$ of its holding in P Ltd, being 20% of the shares issued by S Ltd. In section 27.5.3, such a sale was assumed not to cause P Ltd to lose control of S Ltd. In this section it is assumed that the sale does cause P Ltd to lose control of S Ltd.

If P Ltd sold $\frac{1}{3}$ of its holding in S Ltd for $5000, then it is assumed that the fair value of its remaining investment in S Ltd ($\frac{2}{3}$) is $10 000. It is also assumed that changes in fair value are recognised in profit or loss.

On sale of the shares in S Ltd, P Ltd would pass the following entry, reflecting both the sale of the shares and the remeasurement of the remaining investment in S Ltd to fair value:

Cash	Dr	5 000	
Shares in S Ltd [$\frac{1}{3}$ × $12'000 sold]	Cr		4 000
Shares in S Ltd [$10 000 − $8000 remeasured]	Dr	2 000	
Gain on Sale of Shares in S Ltd	Cr		3 000

In accordance with paragraphs 25 and B98 of IFRS 10, the parent will:
1. derecognise the assets and liabilities of the former subsidiary at the carrying amounts at the date when control was lost
2. derecognise the carrying amount of any NCI in the former subsidiary at the date when control was lost
3. recognise the fair value of the consideration received
4. recognise any investment retained in the former subsidiary at its fair value at the date control was lost
5. recognise any gain or loss in profit or loss attributable to the parent.

The gain or loss is calculated as follows:

Gain or loss = fair value of the proceeds (if any) from the transaction that resulted in loss of control
+ fair value of any retained investment in the former subsidiary at the date when control is lost
− parent's share of the carrying amount in the group of the net assets at the date control is lost

In relation to the example where P Ltd sells some of its shares in S Ltd, the gain on sale is calculated as follows:

Gain	=	$5000 (proceeds on sale)
		+ $10 000 (fair value of remaining investment)
		− $13 032 (P Ltd's share of net assets)*
	=	$1968
*recorded net assets	=	$20 000 (recorded by subsidiary)
		+ $1300 (goodwill)
		+ ($1000 − $400) (unrecorded plant)
	=	− ($300 − $120) (unrecorded deferred tax liability)
	=	$21 720
P Ltd's share	=	60% × $21 720
	=	$13 032

Hence the recorded gain of $3000 must be adjusted on consolidation to the real gain to the group of $1968 — an adjustment of $1032.

The consolidated worksheet entry in the year of sale is:

Gain on Sale of Shares		Dr	1 032
Retained Earnings (1/7/13)		Cr	1 032

This entry achieves two things:
• it adjusts the gain on sale
• it reinstates the opening balance of the retained earnings account prior to sale.
Note the consolidation worksheet in relation to retained earnings prior to sale:

Before the sale of shares

Financial statements	P Ltd	S Ltd	Adjustments			Group	NCI			Parent
				Dr	Cr			Dr	Cr	
Retained earnings (1/7/13)	—	10 000	1	400	120	1	4 920	3	3 200	1 032
			2	4 800				3	688	

Subsequent to sale, the financial statements of the subsidiary will not be included in the consolidation worksheet — although derecognition of the assets and liabilities of the subsidiary as well as the NCI will need to be disclosed. The worksheet after the sale would show:

After the sale of shares

Financial statements	P Ltd	S Ltd	Adjustments		Group	NCI		Parent
			Dr	Cr		Dr	Cr	
Gain	3 000		1 032					1 968
Retained earnings (1/7/13)	—	—		1 032				1 032

Note that the opening balance of retained earnings is reinstated as well as the real gain reported.

27.5.5 Disclosures relating to changes in ownership interests

IFRS 12 *Disclosure of Interests in Other Entities* requires disclosures to be made where there are changes in ownership interests.

Paragraph 18 of IFRS 12 sets out the disclosure required where there are changes in a parent's ownership interest in a subsidiary that do not result in a loss of control:

> An entity shall present a schedule that shows the effects on the equity attributable to owners of the parent of any changes in its ownership interest in a subsidiary that do not result in a loss of control.

Paragraph 19 of IFRS 12 sets out the disclosure required where a parent loses control of a subsidiary during the reporting period:

> An entity shall disclose the gain or loss, if any, calculated in accordance with paragraph 25 of IFRS 10, and:
> (a) the portion of that gain or loss attributable to measuring any investment retained in the former subsidiary at its fair value at the date when control is lost; and
> (b) the line item(s) in profit or loss in which the gain or loss is recognised (if not presented separately).

SUMMARY

Accounting standards require the separation of consolidated equity into parent interest and non-controlling interest (NCI). One complication in the calculation of NCI is that, where a group has multiple subsidiaries, it may be necessary to classify the NCI into direct non-controlling interest (DNCI) and indirect non-controlling interest (INCI), because the calculation of the DNCI share of equity differs from that of the INCI. In particular, the INCI does not receive a share of all the equity of a subsidiary, but is entitled to a share of post-acquisition equity only. The existence of an INCI must be taken into account where dividends are paid within a group because, without adjustment for the INCI, double-counting of the NCI share of equity may occur.

Where a parent has a number of subsidiaries, the timing of the acquisition of those subsidiaries is important in preparing the consolidation adjustments. Sequential acquisitions arise where the parent acquires its interest in a subsidiary before or on the same date as that subsidiary acquires an interest in its own subsidiary. Non-sequential acquisitions arise where a parent acquires an interest in a subsidiary that already is a parent; that is, it has its own subsidiary. In non-sequential acquisitions, the complicating factor is that one of the assets that may have a carrying amount different from fair value is the investment in a subsidiary previously acquired. The fair value of the investment reflects increases in the worth of the underlying net assets in that subsidiary.

Separation of equity into pre-acquisition and post-acquisition amounts is important where there are reciprocal holdings within a group. The calculation of the NCI share of equity is also complicated by the timing of the acquisitions within the reciprocal holdings.

DEMONSTRATION PROBLEM 27.1 Effects of intragroup transactions on the calculation of the NCI

On 1 July 2011, Australia Ltd acquired 60% of the shares (cum div.) of Bangladesh Ltd for $163 980. On the same day, Bangladesh Ltd acquired 75% of the shares of Bhutan Ltd for $129 050. At this date, an extract from the statement of financial position of Bangladesh Ltd and Bhutan Ltd disclosed the following:

	Bangladesh Ltd	Bhutan Ltd
Share capital	$240 000	$164 000
General reserve	8 000	—
Retained earnings	1 600	2 400
Dividend payable	14 400	—

The dividend payable by Bangladesh Ltd was subsequently paid. No other dividends have been paid from pre-acquisition equity.

On 1 July 2011, all the identifiable assets and liabilities of Bhutan Ltd were recorded at fair value except for the non-monetary assets. A comparison of the non-monetary assets' carrying amounts and fair values revealed the following information:

	Bhutan Ltd	
	Carrying amount	Fair value
Inventory	$ 5 000	$ 6 000
Plant (cost $160 000)	128 000	133 000
Land	56 000	60 000

The plant was expected to provide further benefits evenly over the next 5 years. All inventory was sold by 30 June 2012.

On 1 July 2011 all the identifiable assets and liabilities of Bangladesh Ltd were recorded at fair value except for the following:

	Bangladesh Ltd	
	Carrying amount	Fair value
Inventory	$ 6 000	$ 8 000
Plant (cost $147 000)	126 000	130 000

The balance of goodwill recorded at 1 July 2011 by Bangladesh Ltd was $6000. The financial data as at 30 June 2013 of the three companies are shown opposite.

Additional information
(a) Sales and purchases included the following transactions:
  • sales by Bangladesh Ltd to Australia Ltd invoiced at cost plus 33% were $120 000
  • sales by Bhutan Ltd to Australia Ltd invoiced at cost plus 25% were $36 000.
(b) Inventory on hand of Australia Ltd at 30 June 2013 included $1600 acquired from Bangladesh Ltd and $1200 acquired from Bhutan Ltd.
(c) Inventory of Bangladesh Ltd at 1 July 2012 included $160 profit on goods received from Bhutan Ltd.
(d) Receivables and payables included $3600 owing by Australia Ltd to Bangladesh Ltd.
(e) The tax rate is 30%.

Required

Based on the above information, prepare the consolidated financial statements for Australia Ltd and its subsidiaries as at 30 June 2013.

Solution

The *first step* in the consolidation process is to establish the structure of the group and percentage ownership of the NCI — see figure 27.11.

The *next step* is to choose one of the acquisitions and prepare the acquisition analysis, the business combination valuation and pre-acquisition entries, and the NCI entries.

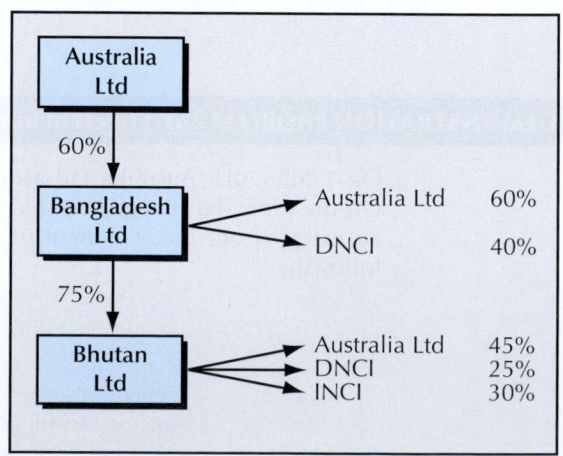

FIGURE 27.11 Structure of group

	Australia Ltd	Bangladesh Ltd	Bhutan Ltd
Sales revenue	$ 675 360	$444 800	$290 000
Dividend revenue	18 720	13 200	—
Debenture interest	—	3 200	3 840
Total revenue	694 080	461 200	293 840
Cost of sales	490 400	333 600	232 000
Other expenses	44 080	42 800	20 000
Total expenses	534 480	376 400	252 000
Profit before tax	159 600	84 800	41 840
Income tax expense	64 000	32 000	16 000
Profit for the period	95 600	52 800	25 840
Retained earnings (1/7/12)	4 000	10 400	8 800
	99 600	63 200	34 640
Dividend paid	20 000	14 400	8 000
Dividend declared	30 000	16 800	9 600
	50 000	31 200	17 600
Retained earnings (30/6/13)	49 600	32 000	17 040
Share capital	420 000	240 000	164 000
General reserve	12 000	16 000	8 000
Total equity	481 600	288 000	189 040
Debentures	160 000	—	—
Provisions	20 000	29 600	16 000
Dividend payable	30 000	16 800	9 600
Current tax liability	64 400	32 000	16 000
Total liabilities	274 400	78 400	41 600
Total equity and liabilities	$ 756 000	$366 400	$230 640
Inventory	5 600	4 400	5 120
Receivables	21 860	15 550	1 520
Cash	28 000	10 600	21 600
Debentures in Australia Ltd	—	40 000	48 000
Shares in Bangladesh Ltd	155 340	—	—
Shares in Bhutan Ltd	—	129 050	—
Plant	(500 000)	147 000	160 000
Accumulated depreciation	204 000	(63 000)	(64 000)
Land	200 000	70 000	56 000
Deferred tax asset	32 000	6 800	2 400
Goodwill	17 200	6 000	—
Total assets	$ 756 000	$366 400	$230 640

Acquisition analysis: Bangladesh Ltd and Bhutan Ltd
At *1 July 2011*:

Net fair value of identifiable assets and liabilities of Bhutan Ltd	= $164 000 (capital) + $2400 (retained earnings) + $1000(1 − 0.3) (BCVR — inventory) + $5000(1 − 0.3) (BCVR — plant) + $4000(1 − 0.3) (BCVR — land) = $173 400
(a) Consideration transferred	= $129 050
(b) Non-controlling interest in Bhutan Ltd	= $25% × $173 400 = $43 350

Aggregate of (a) and (b)	= $172 400
Gain on bargain purchase	= $173 400 – $172 400
	= $1000

(1) *Business combination valuation entries: Bangladesh Ltd and Bhutan Ltd*
At *1 July 2011*:

Inventory	Dr	1 000	
Deferred Tax Liability	Cr		300
Business Combination Valuation Reserve	Cr		700
Accumulated Depreciation – Plant	Dr	32 000	
Plant	Cr		27 000
Deferred Tax Liability	Cr		1 500
Business Combination Valuation Reserve	Cr		3 500
Land	Dr	4 000	
Deferred Tax Liability	Cr		1 200
Business Combination Valuation Reserve	Cr		2 800

At *30 June 2013*, the valuation entries for plant require adjustment to reflect the depreciation of $1000 p.a., being $1/5$ of $5000. The inventory was all sold in the 2011–12 period. The valuation entries at 30 June 2013 are:

Accumulated Depreciation – Plant	Dr	32 000	
Plant	Cr		27 000
Deferred Tax Liability	Cr		1 500
Business Combination Valuation Reserve	Cr		3 500
Depreciation Expense	Dr	1 000	
Retained Earnings (1/7/12)	Dr	1 000	
Accumulated Depreciation	Cr		2 000
(20% × $5000)			
Deferred Tax Liability	Dr	600	
Income Tax Expense	Cr		300
Retained Earnings (1/7/12)	Cr		300
Land	Dr	4 000	
Deferred Tax Liability	Cr		1 200
Business Combination Valuation Reserve	Cr		2 800

(2) *Pre-acquisition entry: Bangladesh Ltd and Bhutan Ltd*
The pre-acquisition entry at *1 July 2011* is:

Retained Earnings (1/7/11)	Dr	1 800	
Share Capital	Dr	123 000	
Business Combination Valuation Reserve	Dr	5 250	
Gain on Bargain Purchase	Cr		1 000
Shares in Bhutan Ltd	Cr		129 050

The inventory is all sold in the 2011–12 period, and the related valuation reserve (75% × $700) transferred to retained earnings.
At *30 June 2013*, the entry is:

Retained Earnings (1/7/12)*	Dr	1 325	
Share Capital	Dr	123 000	
Business Combination Valuation Reserve	Dr	4 725	
Shares in Bhutan Ltd	Cr		129 050
* $1325 = $1800 − $1000 gain on bargain purchase			
+ (75% × $700) inventory			

(3) *NCI share of equity in Bhutan Ltd at 1 July 2011 (step 1)*

Retained Earnings (1/7/12)	Dr	600	
Share Capital	Dr	41 000	
Business Combination Valuation Reserve	Dr	1 750	
NCI	Cr		43 350

(4) *NCI share of changes in equity from 1 July 2011 to 30 June 2012*
Retained earnings of Bhutan Ltd at 30 June 2012 have increased by $6400; that is, from $2400 to $8800, but adjustments must be made for the after-tax depreciation on plant, as shown in the business combination valuation entries:
DNCI (25%):

Retained Earnings (1/7/12)	Dr	1 425	
NCI	Cr		1 425
(25% × [$6400 − ($1000 − $300)])			

INCI (30%):
The INCI receives a share of post-acquisition equity only. As the pre-acquisition entry at 30 June 2013 has a debit adjustment of $1325, then the pre-acquisition retained earnings of Bhutan Ltd are $1767 (i.e. $1325/0.75) plus the adjustments for the depreciation of plant $700 (i.e. $1000 − $300), a total of $2467. The INCI share of post-acquisition retained earnings is:

$$30\% \times [\$8800 - \$1325/0.75 - (\$1000 - \$300)] = \$1900$$

The worksheet entry is:

Retained Earnings (1/7/12)	Dr	1 900	
NCI	Cr		1 900

The *business combination valuation reserve* in relation to inventory has been transferred to retained earnings. This affects the DNCI only because it relates to pre-acquisition profits.
DNCI (25%):

NCI	Dr	175	
Business Combination Valuation Reserve	Cr		175
(25% × $700)			

The *general reserve* has increased from a zero balance at acquisition date to $8000, an increase of $8000. Because this has resulted from a transfer from post-acquisition retained earnings, both the DNCI and INCI are affected.

DNCI (25%) and INCI (30%):

General Reserve	Dr	4 400	
NCI	Cr		4 400
([25% + 30%] × $8000)			

(5) *NCI share of equity in Bhutan Ltd from 1 July 2012 to 30 June 2013*
Because there is no adjustment to the current period profit in the pre-acquisition entry, both the DNCI and INCI receive a share of the recorded profit of $25 840 adjusted for the depreciation of plant:

NCI Share of Profit	Dr	13 827	
NCI	Cr		13 827
([25% + 30%] × [$25 840 − ($1000 − $300)])			

Bhutan Ltd has *paid a dividend* of $8000. This affects the DNCI only.

NCI	Dr	2 000	
Dividend Paid	Cr		2 000
(25% × $8000)			

Bhutan Ltd has *declared a dividend* of $9600. Only the DNCI is affected.

NCI	Dr	2 400	
Dividend Declared	Cr		2 400
(25% × $9600)			

The *next step* is to deal with the other acquisition, Australia Ltd's acquisition of Bangladesh Ltd.
Acquisition analysis: Australia Ltd and Bangladesh Ltd

Net fair value of assets and liabilities of Bangladesh Ltd	= $240 000 (capital) + $8000 (general reserve)
	+ $1600 (retained earnings)
	+ $2000(1 − 0.3) (BCVR — inventory)
	+ $4000(1 − 0.3) (BCVR — plant)
	− $6000 (goodwill)
	= $247 800
(a) Consideration transferred	= $163 980 − (60% × $14 400) (dividend)
	= $155 340
(b) Non-controlling interest in Bangladesh Ltd	= $40% × $247 800
	= $99 120
Aggregate of (a) and (b)	= $254 460
Goodwill acquired by Australia Ltd	= $6660
Non-recorded goodwill	= $6660 − (60% × $6000)
	= $3060

(6) *Business combination valuation entries: Australia Ltd and Bangladesh Ltd*
At *1 July 2011*:

Inventory	Dr	2 000	
Deferred Tax Liability	Cr		600
Business Combination Valuation Reserve	Cr		1 400
Accumulated Depreciation	Dr	21 000	
Plant	Cr		17 000
Deferred Tax Liability	Cr		1 200
Business Combination Valuation Reserve	Cr		2 800

The entries at 30 June 2013 take into account that the inventory is sold in 2012, and the plant is depreciated at $1000 p.a., being $1/4$ of $4000.
The entries at *30 June 2013* are:

Accumulated Depreciation	Dr	21 000	
Plant	Cr		17 000
Deferred Tax Liability	Cr		1 200
Business Combination Valuation Reserve	Cr		2 800
Depreciation Expense	Dr	1 000	
Retained Earnings (1/7/12)	Dr	1 000	
Accumulated Depreciation	Cr		2 000
Deferred Tax Liability	Dr	600	
Income Tax Expense	Cr		300
Retained Earnings (1/7/12)	Cr		300

(7) *Pre-acquisition entries*
At *1 July 2011*:

Retained Earnings (1/7/11)	Dr	960	
Share Capital	Dr	144 000	
General Reserve	Dr	4 800	
Business Combination Valuation Reserve	Dr	2 520	
Goodwill	Dr	3 060	
Shares in Bangladesh Ltd	Cr		155 340
Dividend Payable	Dr	8 640	
Dividend Receivable	Cr		8 640

By *30 June 2013*, the dividend has been paid and the inventory sold with the relevant valuation reserve transferred to retained earnings. The entry is:

Retained Earnings (1/7/12)	Dr	1 800	
Share Capital	Dr	144 000	
General Reserve	Dr	4 800	
Business Combination Valuation Reserve*	Dr	1 680	
Goodwill	Dr	3 060	
Shares in Bangladesh Ltd	Cr		155 340

* $2520 – (60% × $1400)

(8) *NCI in equity of Bangladesh Ltd at 1 July 2011*

Retained Earnings (1/7/12)	Dr	640	
Share Capital	Dr	96 000	
General Reserve	Dr	3 200	
Business Combination Valuation Reserve	Dr	1 680	
NCI	Cr		101 520
(40% of balances at acquisition)			

(9) *NCI share of equity in Bangladesh Ltd from 1 July 2011 to 30 June 2012*
The *retained earnings* for Bangladesh Ltd have increased from $1600 to $10 400, an increase of $8800. This has to be adjusted for the after-tax depreciation on plant, $1000 – $300.

Retained Earnings (1/7/12)	Dr	3 240	
NCI	Cr		3 240
(40% × [$8800 – ($1000 – $300)])			

The *business combination valuation reserve* relating to inventory has been transferred to retained earnings:

NCI	Dr	560	
Business Combination Valuation Reserve	Cr		560
(40% × $1400)			

The *general reserve* has increased from $8000 to $16 000:

General Reserve	Dr	3 200	
NCI	Cr		3 200
(40% × $8000)			

(10) *NCI share of equity of Bangladesh Ltd from 1 July 2012 to 30 June 2013*
Current period profit: This is $52 800, and is adjusted for the after-tax depreciation on plant.

NCI Share of Profit	Dr	20 840	
NCI	Cr		20 840
(40% × ($52 800 – [$1000 – $300]))			

Dividend paid of $14 400:

NCI	Dr	5 760	
Dividend Paid	Cr		5 760
(40% × $14 400)			

Dividend declared of $16 800:

NCI	Dr	6 720	
Dividend Declared	Cr		6 720

Dividend revenue from Bhutan Ltd of $13 200: Bhutan Ltd paid a dividend of $8000 and declared a dividend of $9600. Bangladesh Ltd therefore recorded dividend revenue of $13 200 (i.e. 75% ×

($8000 + $9600)). As the INCI has received a share of the profit of Bhutan Ltd, to avoid double counting the DNCI in Bangladesh Ltd must be adjusted in relation to the dividend revenue from Bhutan Ltd:

NCI	Dr	5 280	
NCI Share of Profit	Cr		5 280
(40% × $13 200)			

Intragroup transactions

(11) *Dividend paid — Bhutan Ltd*

Dividend Revenue	Dr	6 000	
Interim Dividend Paid	Cr		6 000
(75% × $8000)			

(12) *Dividend paid — Bangladesh Ltd*

Dividend Revenue	Dr	8 640	
Interim Dividend Paid	Cr		8 640
(60% × $14 400)			

(13) *Dividend declared — Bangladesh Ltd*

Dividend Payable	Dr	10 080	
Dividend Declared	Cr		10 080
(60% × $16 800)			
Dividend Revenue	Dr	10 080	
Dividend Receivable	Cr		10 080

(14) *Dividend declared — Bhutan Ltd*

Dividend Payable	Dr	7 200	
Dividend Declared	Cr		7 200
(75% × $9600)			
Dividend Revenue	Dr	7 200	
Dividend Receivable	Cr		7 200

(15) *Profit in ending inventory: Sales by Bangladesh Ltd to Australia Ltd*

Sales Revenue	Dr	120 000	
Cost of Sales	Cr		119 600
Inventory	Cr		400
Deferred Tax Asset	Dr	120	
Income Tax Expense	Cr		120

(16) *Adjustment to NCI in Bangladesh Ltd*

NCI	Dr	112	
NCI Share of Profit	Cr		112
(40% × [$400 − $120])			

(17) *Profit in ending inventory: Sales by Bhutan Ltd to Australia Ltd*

Sales Revenue	Dr	36 000	
Cost of Sales	Cr		35 760
Inventory	Cr		240
Deferred Tax Asset	Dr	72	
Income Tax Expense	Cr		72

(18) *Adjustment to NCI in Bhutan Ltd*

NCI	Dr	92	
NCI Share of Profit	Cr		92
([25% + 30%] × [$240 − $72])			

(19) *Profit in opening inventory: Sales by Bhutan Ltd to Bangladesh Ltd*

Retained Earnings (1/7/12)	Dr	112	
Income Tax Expense	Dr	48	
Cost of Sales	Cr		160

(20) *Adjustment to NCI in Bhutan Ltd*

NCI Share of Profit	Dr	62	
Retained Earnings (1/7/12)	Cr		62
([25% + 30%] × [$160 − $48])			

(21) *Intragroup balances*
Amount owing by Australia Ltd to Bangladesh Ltd is $3600.

Payables	Dr	3 600	
Receivables	Cr		3 600

(22) *Intragroup debentures*
Intragroup debentures held amount to $88 000.

8% Debentures	Dr	88 000	
Debentures in Australia Ltd	Cr		88 000

(23) *Debenture interest*
Interest paid by Australia Ltd is 8% of the sum of $40 000 and $48 000.

Debenture Interest Revenue	Dr	7 040	
Debenture Interest Expense	Cr		7 040

The consolidation worksheet is shown in figure 27.12.

FIGURE 27.12 Consolidation worksheet — indirect ownership interests

Financial statements	Australia Ltd	Bangladesh Ltd	Bhutan Ltd	Adjustments Dr	Adjustments Cr	Group	NCI Dr	NCI Cr	Parent
Sales revenue	675 360	444 800	290 000	(15) 120 000; (17) 36 000		1 254 160			
Dividend revenue	18 720	13 200	—	(11) 6 000; (12) 8 640; (13) 10 080; (14) 7 200		—			
Debenture interest	—	3 200	3 840	(23) 7 040	(23) 7 040				
Total revenue	694 080	461 200	293 840		(15) 119 600; (17) 35 760; (19) 160	1 254 160			
Cost of sales	490 400	333 600	232 000			900 480			
Other expenses	44 080	42 800	20 000	(1) 1 000; (6) 1 000	(1) 300; (6) 300; (15) 120; (17) 72	101 840			
Total expenses	534 480	376 400	252 000			1 002 320			
Profit before tax	159 600	84 800	41 840			251 840			
Tax expense	64 000	32 000	16 000	(19) 48		111 256			
Profit for the period	95 600	52 800	25 840			140 584	(5) 13 827; (10) 20 840	(10) 5 280	111 339
Retained earnings (1/7/12)	4 000	10 400	8 800	(1) 1 000; (2) 1 325; (6) 1 000; (7) 1 800; (19) 112	(1) 300; (6) 300	18 563	(20) 62; (3) 600; (4) 1 425; (4) 1 900; (8) 640; (9) 3 240	(16) 112; (18) 92; (20) 62	10 820
	99 600	63 200	34 640			159 147			122 159

(continued)

FIGURE 27.12 (continued)

Financial statements	Australia Ltd	Bangladesh Ltd	Bhutan Ltd	Adjustments Dr	Adjustments Cr	Group	Non-controlling interest Dr	Non-controlling interest Cr	Parent
Dividend paid	20 000	14 400	8 000		6 000 [11]; 8 640 [12]	27 760		2 000 [5]; 5 760 [10]	20 000
Dividend declared	30 000	16 800	9 600		10 080 [13]; 7 200 [14]	39 120		2 400 [5]; 6 720 [10]	30 000
	50 000	31 200	17 600			66 880			50 000
Retained earnings (30/6/13)	49 600	32 000	17 040	123 000 [2]		92 267	41 000 [3]	43 350 [3]	72 159
Share capital	420 000	240 000	164 000	144 000 [7]		557 000	96 000 [8]	1 425 [4]	420 000
General reserve	12 000	16 000	8 000	4 800 [7]		31 200	4 400 [4]; 3 200 [8]; 3 200 [9]	1 900 [4]	20 400
Business combination valuation reserve	—	—	—	4 725 [2]; 1 680 [7]	3 500 [1]; 2 800 [1]; 2 800 [6]	2 695	1 750 [3]; 1 680 [8]	175 [4]; 560 [9]	—
Total equity: Parent									512 559
Total equity: NCI						683 162	175 [4]; 2 000 [5]; 2 400 [5]; 560 [9]; 5 760 [10]; 6 720 [10]; 5 280 [10]; 112 [16]; 92 [18]	4 400 [4]; 13 827 [5]; 101 520 [8]; 3 240 [9]; 3 200 [9]; 20 840 [10]	170 603
Total equity	481 600	288 000	189 040			683 162	216 863	216 863	683 162
Debentures	160 000	—	—	88 000 [22]		72 000			
Provisions	20 000	29 600	16 000	3 600 [21]		62 000			
Dividend payable	30 000	16 800	9 600	10 080 [13]; 7 200 [14]		39 120			

Financial statements	Australia Ltd	Bangladesh Ltd	Bhutan Ltd		Adjustments Dr	Adjustments Cr		Group	Non-controlling interest Dr	Cr	Parent
Current tax liability	64 400	32 000	16 000					112 400			
Deferred tax liability	—	—	—	1 / 6	600 / 600	1 500 / 1 200 / 1 200	1 / 1 / 6	2 700			
Total liabilities	274 400	78 400	41 600					288 220			
Total equity and liabilities	756 000	366 400	230 640					971 382			
Inventory	5 600	4 400	5 120			400 / 240	15 / 17	14 480			
Receivables	21 860	15 550	1 520			3 600 / 10 080 / 7 200	21 / 13 / 14	18 050			
Cash	28 000	10 600	21 600					60 200			
Debentures in Australia Ltd	—	40 000	48 000			88 000	22	—			
Shares in Bangladesh Ltd	155 340	—				155 340	7	—			
Shares in Bhutan Ltd	—	129 050	—			129 050	2	—			
Plant	500 000	147 000	160 000			27 000 / 17 000	1 / 6	763 000			
Accumulated depreciation	(204 000)	(63 000)	(64 000)	1 / 6	32 000 / 21 000	2 000 / 2 000	1 / 6	(282 000)			
Land	200 000	70 000	56 000	1	4 000			330 000			
Deferred tax asset	32 000	6 800	2 400	15 / 17	120 / 72			41 392			
Goodwill	17 200	6 000	—	7	3 060			26 260			
Total assets	756 000	366 400	230 640		650 782	650 782		971 382			

The consolidated financial statements for Australia Ltd at 30 June 2013 are shown in figure 27.13(a), (b) and (c).

FIGURE 27.13(a) Consolidated statement of profit or loss and other comprehensive income

AUSTRALIA LTD Consolidated Statement of Profit or Loss and Other Comprehensive Income for financial year ended 30 June 2013	
Revenues: Sales	$1 254 160
Expenses:	
Cost of sales	900 480
Other	101 840
Total expenses	1 002 320
Profit before income tax	251 840
Income tax expense	(111 256)
PROFIT FOR THE PERIOD	140 584
Other comprehensive income	0
TOTAL COMPREHENSIVE INCOME	$ 140 584
Attributable to:	
Owners of the parent	$ 111 339
Non-controlling interest	29 245
	$ 140 584

FIGURE 27.13(b) Consolidated statement of changes in equity

AUSTRALIA LTD Consolidated Statement of Changes in Equity for the year ended 30 June 2013		
Total comprehensive income for the period		$140 584
Attributable to:		$111 339
Owners of the parent		29 245
Non-controlling interest		
	Consolidated	**Parent**
Share capital		
Balance, beginning of year	$557 000	$420 000
Balance, end of year	$557 000	$420 000
General Reserve		
Balance, beginning of year	$ 31 200	$ 20 400
Balance, end of year	$ 31 200	$ 20 400
Retained earnings		
Balance, beginning of year	$ 18 563	$ 10 820
Profit for the period	140 584	111 339
Dividends paid and declared	(66 880)	(50 000)
Balance, end of year	$ 92 267	$ 72 159

FIGURE 27.13(c) Consolidated statement of financial position

AUSTRALIA LTD Consolidated Statement of Financial Position as at 30 June 2013	
ASSETS	
Current assets	
Inventories	$ 14 480
Receivables	18 050

FIGURE 27.13(c) *(continued)*

Cash	60 200
Total current assets	92 730
Non-current assets	
Plant and equipment	763 000
Accumulated depreciation	(282 000)
Land	330 000
Deferred tax assets	41 392
Goodwill	26 260
Total non-current assets	878 652
Total assets	971 382
LIABILITIES	
Current liabilities	
Provisions	62 000
Dividends payable	39 120
Current tax liabilities	112 400
Total current liabilities	213 520
Non-current liabilities	
Debentures	72 000
Deferred tax liabilities	2 700
Total non-current liabilities	74 700
Total liabilities	288 220
Net assets	$ 683 162
EQUITY	
Share capital	$ 420 000
Other reserves: General	20 400
Retained earnings	72 159
Owners interest	512 559
Non-controlling interest	170 603
Total equity	$ 683 162

DEMONSTRATION PROBLEM 27.2 Calculation of the NCI share of equity

The following example illustrates the calculation of the NCI where reciprocal holdings exist between subsidiaries. The structure of the group is shown below:

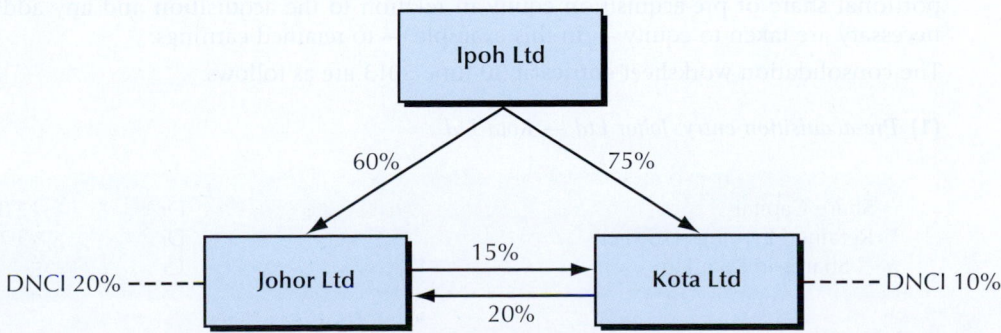

It is assumed that Ipoh Ltd had an interest in both Johor Ltd and Kota Ltd prior to the occurrence of the reciprocal relationship. The pre-acquisition entries for these acquisitions will not be given here because they have no influence on the calculation of the NCI.

Assume Johor Ltd and Kota Ltd acquired their shareholdings in each other on 1 July 2011:
- Johor Ltd paid $15 720 for 15% of Kota Ltd's issued shares when the retained earnings of Kota Ltd were $20 000. All the identifiable net assets of Kota Ltd were recorded at fair value except for plant, for which the fair value was $4000 greater than carrying amount. The plant has a remaining useful life of 4 years.
- Kota Ltd paid $30 000 for 20% of Johor Ltd's issued shares when the retained earnings of Johor Ltd were $40 000. All the identifiable net assets of Johor Ltd were recorded at fair value except for inventory, for which the fair value was $5000 greater than the carrying amount. The inventory was all sold within the following year.
- The tax rate is 30%, and when revalued assets are sold or consumed, any related valuation reserve relating to those assets is transferred to retained earnings.

At 30 June 2013, the financial statements of Johor Ltd and Kota Ltd contained the following information:

	Johor Ltd	Kota Ltd
Dividend revenue	$ 750	$ 1 000
Other income	20 000	10 000
Profit before income tax	20 750	11 000
Income tax expense	8 000	5 000
Profit for the period	12 750	6 000
Retained earnings (1/7/12)	65 000	45 000
	77 750	51 000
Dividend paid	5 000	5 000
Retained earnings (30/6/13)	72 750	46 000
Share capital	100 000	80 000
	$172 750	$126 000
Shares in Johor Ltd	—	$ 30 000
Shares in Kota Ltd	$ 15 720	—
Other assets	157 030	96 000
	$172 750	$126 000

As Johor Ltd and Kota Ltd are already subsidiaries of Ipoh Ltd, the acquisition of shares between the two subsidiaries is a transaction within the economic entity. Neither transaction then constitutes a business combination. Hence there is no need to fair value the identifiable assets and liabilities of the subsidiaries, nor determine the existence of any goodwill. The accounting for these transactions is then similar to that for the acquisition of additional shares as discussed in section 27.5. The effect of this accounting is that in the pre-acquisition entries, the investment account is eliminated and the pro-portional share of pre-acquisition equity in relation to the acquisition and any additional adjustment necessary are taken to equity — in this example — to retained earnings.

The consolidation worksheet entries at 30 June 2013 are as follows:

(1) *Pre-acquisition entry: Johor Ltd — Kota Ltd*

Share Capital	Dr	12 000	
Retained Earnings (1/7/12)	Dr	3 720	
Shares in Kota Ltd	Cr		15 720

These amounts are based on 15% share of recorded capital ($80 000) and retained earnings ($20 000) at acquisition date. The extra $720 in relation to retained earnings reflects the fact that Kota Ltd has unrecorded assets that have been recognised in determining the consideration transferred in the transaction.

(2) *DNCI in Kota Ltd at acquisition date (10%)*

Share Capital	Dr	8 000	
Retained Earnings (1/7/12)	Dr	2 000	
NCI	Cr		10 000

The DNCI receives a share of recorded equity in Kota Ltd.

(3) *Pre-acquisition entry: Kota Ltd – Johor Ltd*

Share Capital	Dr	20 000	
Retained Earnings (1/7/12)	Dr	10 000	
Shares in Johor Ltd	Cr		30 000

These amounts are based on 20% share of recorded capital ($100 000) and retained earnings ($40 000) at acquisition date. The extra $2000 in relation to retained earnings reflects the fact that Kota Ltd has unrecorded assets that have been recognised in determining the consideration transferred in the transaction.

(4) *DNCI in Johor Ltd at acquisition date (20%)*

Share Capital	Dr	20 000	
Retained Earnings (1/7/12)	Dr	8 000	
NCI	Cr		28 000

The DNCI is entitled to a 20% share of recorded equity of Johor Ltd.

NCI share of changes in equity in Kota Ltd and Johor Ltd from 1 July 2011 to 30 June 2012

In calculating the NCI share of changes in equity for both Johor Ltd and Kota Ltd, simultaneous equations are used. Assume:

$$J = \text{recorded profits of Johor Ltd}$$
$$K = \text{recorded profits of Kota Ltd}$$
$$j = \text{real profits of Johor Ltd}$$
$$k = \text{real profits of Kota Ltd}$$

$$j = J + 0.15k$$
$$k = K + 0.2j$$
$$j = J + 0.15(K + 0.2j)$$
$$ = J + 0.15K + 0.03j$$
$$0.97j = J + 0.15K$$
$$j = 1/0.97J + 0.15/0.97K$$

This change in equity is after the date of formation of the reciprocal relationship.

$$j = 1/0.97(\$65\,000 - \$10\,000/0.2 \text{ pre-acq.})$$
$$ + 0.15/0.97(\$45\,000 - \$3720/0.15 \text{ pre-acq.})$$
$$ = \$18\,588$$
$$k = K + 0.2j$$
$$ = (\$45\,000 - \$3720/0.15 \text{ pre-acq.}) + (0.2 \times \$15\,588)$$
$$ = \$23\,318$$

$$NCI = 20\%j + 10\%k$$
$$ = (20\% \times \$18\,588) + (10\% \times \$23\,318)$$
$$ = \$6050$$

The NCI entry is:

Retained Earnings (1/7/12)		Dr	6 050
NCI		Cr		6 050

NCI share of changes in equity in Johor Ltd and Kota Ltd from 1 July 2012 to 30 June 2013
The same equations as above are used for the *current period's* changes in equity:

$$j = 1/0.97J + 0.15/0.97K$$
$$k = K + 0.2j$$

Further adjustments must be made in both Johor Ltd and Kota Ltd for any dividend revenue recognised by either company based on dividends paid and declared by the other company to ensure no double-counting of equity.

$$
\begin{aligned}
j &= 1/0.97(\$12\,750 - \$750 \text{ dividend revenue from Kota Ltd}) \\
&\quad + 0.15/0.97(\$6000 - \$1000 \text{ dividend revenue from} \\
&\quad \text{Johor Ltd}) \\
&= \$13\,144 \\
k &= K + 0.2j \\
&= (\$6000 - \$1000 \text{ dividend revenue}) \\
&\quad + (0.2 \times \$13\,144) \\
&= \$7629 \\
\text{NCI} &= 20\%j + 10\%k \\
&= (20\% \times \$13\,144) + (10\% \times \$7629) \\
&= \$3392
\end{aligned}
$$

The NCI entry is:

NCI Share of Profit		Dr	3 392
NCI		Cr		3 392

DEMONSTRATION PROBLEM 27.3 Effects of changes in ownership interests

Rose Ltd acquired its 80% interest in Wood Ltd for $215 000 on 1 January 2011 when the shareholders' equity of Wood Ltd consisted of:

Share capital	$200 000
General reserve	20 000
Retained earnings	40 000

At the date of acquisition, all the identifiable net assets of Wood Ltd were recorded at fair value except for some plant for which the fair value was $5000 greater than the carrying amount. The plant had an expected useful life of 5 years.

On 1 January 2013, Rose Ltd sold 80 000 shares in Wood Ltd for $180 000. At this date, Wood Ltd had recorded an interim profit after tax of $40 000 based on sales of $190 000, cost of sales of $120 000 and expenses of $30 000.

Trial balances for Rose Ltd and Wood Ltd at 30 June 2013 were as follows:

	Rose Ltd	Wood Ltd
Current assets	$ 176 000	$ 89 000
Non-current assets:		
Shares in Wood Ltd	180 000	—
Plant (net)	747 500	298 000
Dividends declared	80 000	40 000
Cost of sales	610 000	260 000
Other expenses	190 000	55 000
	$1 983 500	$742 000
Share capital — 400 000 shares	400 000	
— 200 000 shares		200 000
Retained earnings (1/7/12)	238 700	80 000
General reserve	150 000	30 000
Sales	970 000	400 000
Gain on loss of control of subsidiary	145 000	—
Liabilities	79 800	32 000
	$1 983 500	$742 000

Required

Prepare the consolidated financial statement worksheets at 30 June 2013 for the following independent situations:

1. Wood Ltd does not remain a subsidiary of Rose Ltd after 1 January 2013.
2. Wood Ltd's status as a subsidiary of Rose Ltd is unaffected by the sale of shares in January 2013. In relation to the trial balance decrease, the balance of Shares in Wood Ltd to $107 500 and increase the balance of Plant to $820 000 as the remaining investment in Wood Ltd is not revalued to fair value where control is not lost. As the gain on sale of shares where control is not lost is $72 500, liabilities are increased to $152 300 — see the worksheet in Part 2 for these changes.

Solution

Acquisition analysis

At 1 January 2011:

Net fair value of identifiable assets and liabilities of Wood Ltd	= $200 000 + $20 000 + $40 000 + $5000 (1 − 30%)
	= $263 500
(a) Consideration transferred	= $215 000
(b) NCI in Wood Ltd	= 20% × $263 500
	= $52 700
Aggregate of (a) and (b)	= $267 700
Goodwill	= $4200

Worksheet entries at 1 January 2013 — prior to sale

Business combination valuation entries

Plant	Dr	5 000	
Deferred Tax Liability	Cr		1 500
Business Combination Valuation Reserve	Cr		3 500
Depreciation Expense	Dr	500	
Retained Earnings (1/7/12)	Dr	1 500	
Accumulated Depreciation	Cr		2 000

Deferred Tax Liability	Dr	600	
Income Tax Liability	Cr		150
Retained Earnings (1/7/12)	Cr		450

Pre-acquisition entry

Retained Earnings (1/7/12)	Dr	32 000	
Share Capital	Dr	160 000	
General Reserve	Dr	16 000	
Business Combination Valuation Reserve	Dr	2 800	
Goodwill	Dr	4 200	
Shares in Wood Ltd	Cr		215 000

Entry in Rose Ltd on sale of shares in Wood Ltd

Cash	Dr	180 000	
Shares in Wood Ltd [1/2 × $215 000]	Cr		107 500
Shares in Wood Ltd [$180 000 − $107 500]	Dr	72 500	
Gain	Cr		145 000

This entry reflects both the sale of half of the shares held in Wood Ltd as well as the revaluation to fair value of the investment still held.

1. *Sale of shares with loss of control of subsidiary*
   Calculation of real gain to Rose Ltd:

> Real gain = $180 000 [proceeds on sale]
>   + $180 000 [fair value of remaining investment]
>   − $285 880 [carrying amount of investment prior to sale]*
>   = $74 120
>
> *= 80% × ($200 000 + $30 000 + 80 000 + $40 000 [equity at point of sale] + $5000 − $2000 [plant — net of depreciation] − ($1500 − $600 [deferred tax liability]) + $4200 [goodwill — parent only]
> = $281 680 + $4200

Hence the recorded gain of $145 000 must be reduced by $70 880.

Worksheet entries at 30 June 2013

(1) Adjustment for gain on sale and reinstatement of equity earned by the group for the first 6 months of the year:

Gain on Sale	Dr	70 880	
Cost of Sales	Dr	120 000	
Expenses [$30 000 + $500 − $150]	Dr	30 350	
Sales	Cr		190 000
Transfer from General Reserve [$30 000 − 80% × $20 000]	Cr		14 000
Transfer from Business Combination Valuation Reserve [$3500 − 80% × $3500]	Cr		700
Retained Earnings (1/7/12)*	Cr		46 950
Reduction in Equity on Sale of Subsidiary	Dr	30 420	
*= $80 000 − $32 000 − ($1500 − $450)			

As the sale of the subsidiary occurred halfway through the year, the consolidated financial statements of Rose Ltd must include the post-acquisition equity of Wood Ltd up to the point of sale. As Wood Ltd is no longer a subsidiary, the balances in the reserves must be transferred out to record the movement.

(2) NCI (20%) share of equity for the first half of the year, and the derecognition of the NCI on sale of the subsidiary:

Share of Profit [20% × ($40 000 − ($500 − $150))]	Dr	7 930	
Transfer from General Reserve [20% × $30 000]	Dr	6 000	
Transfer from Business Combination Valuation Reserve [20% × $3500]	Dr	700	
Retained Earnings (1/7/11) [20% × ($80 000 − ($1500 − $450))]	Dr	15 790	
Reduction in Equity on Sale of Subsidiary	Cr		30 420

The consolidation worksheet at 30 June 2013 is as follows:

Financial statements	Rose Ltd	Adjustments Dr	Adjustments Cr		NCI Dr	NCI Cr		Consolidation
Sales revenue	970 000		190 000	1				1 160 000
Cost of sales	610 000	1 120 000						730 000
	360 000							430 000
Expenses	190 000	1 30 350						220 350
	170 000							209 650
Gain on sale of shares	145 000	1 70 880						74 120
Profit	315 000							283 770
NCI Share					2 7 930			7 930
Rose Ltd Share								275 840
Retained earnings (1/7/12)	238 700		46 950	1	2 15 790			269 860
	553 700							545 700
Transfer from general reserve	—		14 000	1	2 6 000			
Transfer from BCVR			700	1	2 700			8 000
								553 700
Change in equity on sale of subsidiary		1 30 420				30 420	2	
								553 700
Dividends declared	80 000							80 000
Retained earnings (30/6/13)	473 700							473 700
Share capital	400 000							400 000
General reserve	150 000							150 000
Liabilities	79 800							79 800
	1 103 500							1 103 500
Current assets	176 000							176 000
Shares in Wood	180 000							180 000
Plant (net)	747 500							747 500
	1 103 500							1 103 500

2. *Sale of shares without loss of subsidiary*
On sale of the shares in Wood Ltd, Rose Ltd would record the following entry:

Cash	Dr	180 000	
Shares in Wood Ltd	Cr		107 500
Gain on Sale of Shares in Wood Ltd	Cr		72 500

The consolidation worksheet entries at 30 June 2013 are as follows:

(1) *Business combination valuation entries*
   (*Note:* These are the same entries as when control was lost on sale of shares.)

Plant	Dr	5 000	
Deferred Tax Liability	Cr		1 500
Business Combination Valuation Reserve	Cr		3 500
Depreciation Expense	Dr	500	
Retained Earnings (1/7/12)	Dr	1 500	
Accumulated Depreciation	Cr		2 000
Deferred Tax Liability	Dr	600	
Income Tax Expense	Cr		150
Retained Earnings (1/7/12)	Cr		450

(2) *Pre-acquisition entry*
   As half of the original investment was sold by Rose Ltd, the pre-acquisition entry is now half of what it was prior to the sale of shares:

Retained Earnings (1/7/12)	Dr	16 000	
Share Capital	Dr	80 000	
General Reserve	Dr	8 000	
Business Combination Valuation Reserve	Dr	1 400	
Goodwill	Dr	2 100	
Shares in Wood Ltd	Cr		107 500

(3) *NCI share of equity at 1 January 2011*

Retained Earnings (1/7/12)	Dr	8 000	
Share Capital	Dr	40 000	
General Reserve	Dr	4 000	
Business Combination Valuation Reserve	Dr	700	
NCI	Cr		52 700
(20% of balances at 1/1/11)			

(4) *NCI share of changes in equity from 1 January 2011 to 30 June 2012*

Retained Earnings (1/7/11) [(20% × ($80 000 − $40 000 − ($1500 − $450))]	Dr	7 790	
General Reserve [(20% × ($30 000 − $20 000))]	Dr	2 000	
NCI	Cr		9 790

(5) *NCI share of equity from 30 June 2012 to 1 January 2013 (date of sale of shares)*

Retained Earnings (1/7/12)	Dr	7 930	
NCI	Cr		7 930
(20% × ($40 000 − ($500 − $150))			

(6) *Increase in NCI share of equity as a result of sale of shares — NCI increases from 20% to 40%*

Share of Profit [(40% × ($40 000 − ($500 − $150))]	Dr	15 860	
Retained Earnings (1/7/12) [(40% × ($80 000 − ($1500 − $450))]	Dr	31 580	

Share Capital [(40% × $200 000)]	Dr	80 000	
General Reserve [(40% × $30 000)]	Dr	12 000	
Business Combination Valuation Reserve [(40% × $3500)]	Dr	1 400	
NCI	Cr		140 840

(7) *Adjustment to gain on sale of shares by Rose Ltd*

Gain on Sale of Shares	Dr	72 500	
Retained Earnings (1/7/12)	Cr		15 580
Transfer from General Reserve	Cr		4 000
Other Reserves	Cr		52 920

This entry adjusts the gain on sale for the post-acquisition equity previously recognised by the group in relation to the shares sold:

> Retained earnings (1/7/12): 40% × ($80 000 − ($40 000 − ($1500 − $450) pre-acq.
> Transfer from general reserve: 40% × ($30 000 − $20 000)

The entry transfers the balance of the gain on sale to equity, in this example the account 'other reserves' is used, but any equity account could be used.

The effect of this entry ensures the opening balances of the equity accounts are then the same as the closing balances in the previous year's consolidated statement of financial position. To illustrate, note the retained earnings line in the consolidation worksheet both before and after the sale:

Before the sale of shares

Financial statements	Rose Ltd	Wood Ltd	Adjustments Dr	Adjustments Cr	Group	NCI Dr	NCI Cr	Parent
Retained earnings (30/6/12)	238 700	80 000	*1* 1 500 *2* 32 000	450 *1*	285 650	*3* 8 000 *4* 7 790		269 860

After the sale of shares

Financial statements	Rose Ltd	Wood Ltd	Adjustments Dr	Adjustments Cr	Group	NCI Dr	NCI Cr	Parent
Retained earnings (30/6/12)	238 700	80 000	*1* 1 500 *2* 16 000	450 *1* 15 580 *7*	317 230	*3* 8 000 *4* 7 790 *6* 31 580		269 860

(8) *NCI share of equity from 1 January 2013 to 30 June 2013 — the NCI is now 60%*

NCI Share of Profit	Dr	26 790	
NCI	Cr		26 790
(60% × [$85 000 − $40 000 − ($500 − $150)])			

(9) *Dividends declared*

Liabilities	Dr	16 000	
Dividends Declared	Cr		16 000
(40% × $40 000)			

(10) *NCI adjustment*

NCI	Dr	24 000	
Dividends Declared	Cr		24 000
(60% × $40 000)			

The consolidation worksheet at 30 June 2013 is as follows:

Financial statements	Rose Ltd	Wood Ltd	Adjustments Dr	Adjustments Cr		NCI Dr	NCI Cr		Rose Ltd
Sales revenue	970 000	400 000							1 370 000
Cost of sales	610 000	260 000							870 000
	360 000	140 000							500 000
Expenses	190 000	55 000	*1* 500	150 *1*					245 350
	170 000	85 000							254 650
Gain on sale	72 500		*7* 72 500						
Profit	242 500								254 650
NCI share						*5* 7 930			50 580
						6 15 860			
						8 26 790			
Rose Ltd share									204 070
Retained earnings									
(1/7/12)	238 700	80 000	*1* 1 500	450 *1*	*3*	8 000			269 860
			2 16 000	15 580 *7*	*4*	7 790			
					6	31 580			
	481 200	165 000							473 930
Transfer from									
general reserve				4 000 *7*					4 000
									477 930
Dividends declared	80 000	40 000		16 000 *8*			24 000 *9*		80 000
Retained Earnings									
(30/6/13)	401 200	125 000							397 930
Capital	400 000	200 000	*2* 80 000		*3*	40 000			400 000
					6	80 000			
BCVR	—	—	*2* 1 400	3 500 *1*	*3*	700			—
					6	1 400			
General reserve	150 000	30 000	*2* 8 000		*3*	4 000			154 000
					4	2 000			
					6	12 000			
Other reserves				52 920 *7*					52 920
Liabilities	152 300	32 000	*1* 600	1 500 *1*					169 200
			8 16 000						

| Financial statements | Rose Ltd | Wood Ltd | Adjustments | | | NCI | | Rose Ltd |
			Dr	Cr		Dr	Cr	
NCI					9	24 000	52 700 3	214 050
							9 790 4	
							7 930 5	
							140 840 6	
							26 790 8	
	1 103 500	387 000						1 388 100
Current Assets	176 000	89 000						265 000
Shares in Wood	107 500			107 500 2				—
Goodwill			2 2 100					2 100
Plant (net)	820 000	298 000	1 5 000	2 000 1				1 121 000
	1 103 500	387 000						1 388 100

Discussion questions

1. What is the difference between direct and indirect NCI?
2. Explain the difference in the calculation of the direct and indirect NCI.
3. Why does the indirect NCI receive a share of only *post-acquisition* equity?
4. What effect does the existence of an indirect NCI have on the adjustments for intragroup transactions?
5. What effect does the existence of an indirect NCI have on the adjustments for dividends paid within a group?
6. In the pre-acquisition entry, why are only partial eliminations made when an NCI exists?
7. Why is no adjustment made for an indirect NCI when preparing consolidated financial statements immediately after acquisition?
8. Explain the effects on the consolidation process when the acquisition is non-sequential.
9. What are reciprocal ownership interests?
10. Explain how reciprocal ownership interests are accounted for on consolidation.

Exercises

STAR RATING ★ BASIC ★★ MODERATE ★★★ DIFFICULT

Exercise 27.1

CONSOLIDATION WORKSHEET ENTRIES, THREE COMPANIES

★ On 1 July 2011, Canada Ltd acquired 80% of the shares of China Ltd and China Ltd acquired 75% of the shares of Chile Ltd. All shares were acquired cum div.
Equity of the companies at 1 July 2011 was as follows:

	China Ltd	Chile Ltd
Share capital	$ 80 000	$ 60 000
Asset revaluation surplus	5 000	—
Retained earnings	1 000	4 000
Dividend payable	8 000	5 000

At 1 July 2011, all identifiable assets and liabilities of China Ltd and Chile Ltd were recorded at fair value. No goodwill or gain on bargain purchase arose in any of the share acquisitions.

The financial statements of the three companies at 30 June 2013 contained the following information:

	Canada Ltd	China Ltd	Chile Ltd
Share capital	$130 000	$80 000	$60 000
Asset revaluation surplus	—	5 000	—
Retained earnings (1/7/12)	10 000	10 500	13 000
Dividend payable	13 000	8 000	6 000
Profit	4 000	2 000	1 500

The final dividends were declared out of profits for the year ended 30 June 2013.

Since 1 July 2011, the following intragroup transactions have occurred:

(a) China Ltd sold to Chile Ltd an item of machinery for $12 000 on 31 December 2011. The machinery had originally cost China Ltd $14 000 and at the time of sale had been depreciated to $11 200. The group charges depreciation at 10% straight-line.

(b) During the year ended 30 June 2013, inventory was transferred by Chile Ltd to China Ltd at 25% on cost to Chile Ltd. $4000 of this inventory is included in the inventory of China Ltd as at 30 June 2013. The tax rate is 30%.

Required

Prepare the consolidation worksheet entries for the year ended 30 June 2013.

Exercise 27.2   **CALCULATION OF THE NON-CONTROLLING INTEREST**

★   On 1 July 2010, Fiji Ltd acquired 75% of the shares of India Ltd at a cost of $280 000 and India Ltd acquired 80% of the shares of Japan Ltd at a cost of $135 000. At acquisition date, the equity of India Ltd and Japan Ltd was as follows and represented the fair values of identifiable assets and liabilities at that date:

	India Ltd	Japan Ltd
Share capital	$150 000	$140 000
General reserve	20 000	—
Retained earnings	50 000	20 000

On 30 June 2012, India Ltd transferred the general reserve back to retained earnings and declared a dividend of $20 000 which was paid on 1 November 2012.

On 30 June 2014, the companies provided the following information.

	India Ltd	Japan Ltd
Profit before income tax	$ 48 000	$32 000
Income tax expense	20 000	15 000
Profit	28 000	17 000
Retained earnings (1/7/13)	75 000	42 000
	103 000	59 000
Transfer to general reserve	—	20 000
Dividend paid	10 000	—
Dividend declared	15 000	10 000
	25 000	30 000
Retained earnings (30/6/14)	$ 78 000	$29 000

Required

Calculate the non-controlling interest share of retained earnings as at 30 June 2013 for India Ltd and Japan Ltd.

CONSOLIDATION WORKSHEET ENTRIES, MULTIPLE SUBSIDIARIES

★ On 1 July 2010, Laos Ltd acquired 70% of the shares of Maldives Ltd for $100 000 and Maldives Ltd acquired 60% of Malaysia Ltd for $70 000. The equity of the companies at 1 July 2010 was:

	Maldives Ltd	Malaysia Ltd
Share capital	$100 000	$80 000
Retained earnings	40 000	30 000

At 1 July 2010, all the identifiable assets and liabilities of both Maldives Ltd and Malaysia Ltd were recorded at fair value.

At 30 June 2013, the financial data of the three companies were as follows:

	Laos Ltd	Maldives Ltd	Malaysia Ltd
Sales revenue	$ 120 000	$102 000	$ 84 000
Other revenue	60 000	44 000	36 000
Total revenues	180 000	146 000	120 000
Cost of sales	90 000	80 000	72 000
Other expenses	60 000	41 000	26 000
Total expenses	150 000	121 000	98 000
Profit before income tax	30 000	25 000	22 000
Income tax expense	8 000	8 000	5 000
Profit for the period	22 000	17 000	17 000
Retained earnings (1/7/12)	55 000	46 000	25 000
Total available for appropriation	77 000	63 000	42 000
Dividend paid	15 000	10 000	5 000
Retained earnings (30/6/13)	62 000	53 000	37 000
Share capital	148 000	100 000	80 000
Net assets	$ 210 000	$153 000	$117 000

Since 1 July 2010, the following transactions have occurred between the three companies:
- During the current year, Maldives Ltd sold inventory valued at $20 000 to Laos Ltd, this having cost Maldives Ltd $15 000. Half of this inventory is still on hand at 30 June 2013.
- On 1 July 2012, Malaysia Ltd sold a motor vehicle to Maldives Ltd for $25 000. The carrying amount of the vehicle at the date of sale was $23 000. Vehicles are depreciated at 30% p.a. on a straight-line basis. The company tax rate is 30%.

Required

Prepare the consolidation worksheet journal entries for the year ended 30 June 2013.

CALCULATION OF THE NON-CONTROLLING INTEREST SHARE OF RETAINED EARNINGS

★ On 1 July 2012, Nauru Ltd acquired 60% of the shares of Nepal Ltd for $300 000, and Nepal Ltd acquired 80% of the shares of New Zealand Ltd for $190 000.

It was considered that Nauru Ltd exercised control over Nepal Ltd and New Zealand Ltd. At acquisition date, the equity for Nepal Ltd and New Zealand Ltd was as follows, and represented the fair values of identifiable assets and liabilities at that date:

	Nepal Ltd	New Zealand Ltd
Share capital	$200 000	$140 000
General reserve	130 000	70 000
Retained earnings	80 000	20 000

Three years later, the companies provided the following information:

	Nepal Ltd	New Zealand Ltd
Profit before income tax	$ 24 000	$18 000
Income tax expense	10 000	7 500
Profit	14 000	10 500
Retained earnings (1/7/14)	88 000	27 500
	102 000	38 000
Dividend declared	10 000	8 000
Retained earnings (30/6/15)	$ 92 000	$30 000

There was a transfer to reserves of $4000 from pre-acquisition profits in the period ended 30 June 2014 by New Zealand Ltd.

Required

Calculate the non-controlling interest's share of retained earnings as at 30 June 2015 of Nepal Ltd and New Zealand Ltd.

Exercise 27.5 **NON-CONTROLLING INTEREST**

★★ P Ltd owns 20% of B Ltd. In recent months it has been in takeover discussions with A Ltd, and agreement has finally been reached between the different parties on the acquisition by P Ltd of 60% of the issued shares of A Ltd. One of the assets of A Ltd is a 70% holding in B Ltd. The group accountant of P Ltd has been examining the new group under the control of P Ltd and considering the implications for the preparation of consolidated financial statements. One of the members of the accounting team, Mei Fen, has raised the issue of accounting for indirect non-controlling interests. According to Mei Fen, with the new group structure there are both direct and indirect non-controlling interests, and she argues that different measurements are then required. The group accountant has asked you to determine the non-controlling interests in the new group, differentiating between different non-controlling interest groups, and to explain the difference, if any, in the calculation of their interests in group equity. Prepare a report for the group accountant.

Exercise 27.6 **DIVIDENDS AND NON-CONTROLLING INTERESTS**

★★ Andrew Brown is the group accountant for P Ltd. P Ltd owns 60% of A Ltd which owns 70% of B Ltd. He has just completed the preparation of the consolidated financial statements of the group, and is discussing issues raised by the auditors. The auditors have raised concerns about the accounting for a dividend paid by B Ltd to A Ltd in the current period. They argue that further consolidation adjustments are necessary to avoid double-counting the non-controlling interest's share of equity. Andrew has asked for your advice concerning the effect of the payment of such a dividend on the determination of the non-controlling interest share of equity. Write a report to Andrew explaining the non-controlling interests that exist within the group, and how the calculation of their interests is affected by payment of dividends within the group.

Note: In exercises, at the acquisition date, the identifiable assets and liabilities of the subsidiary are recorded at amounts equal to fair values. In exercises, these have carrying amounts different from fair values. The partial good-will method is used in all exercises.

Exercise 27.7 **CONSOLIDATION WORKSHEET, CONSOLIDATED STATEMENT OF PROFIT OR LOSS AND OTHER COMPREHENSIVE INCOME**

★★ Pakistan Ltd acquired 75% of the shares of Peru Ltd on 1 July 2008 for $1 900 000. The identifiable assets and liabilities of Peru Ltd at fair value on the acquisition date were represented by:

Share capital	$ 500 000
General reserve	800 000
Retained earnings	1 200 000
	$2 500 000

On the same date, Peru Ltd acquired 60% of Philippines Ltd for $1 100 000. The identifiable assets and liabilities of Philippines Ltd at the acquisition date at fair value were represented by:

Share capital	$ 660 000
General reserve	500 000
Retained earnings	500 000
	$1 660 000

The financial information provided by the three companies for the year ended 30 June 2013 is shown below.

The following additional information was obtained:
(a) All transfers to general reserve were from post-acquisition profits.
(b) Included in the plant and machinery of Philippines Ltd was a machine sold by Peru Ltd on 30 June 2010 for $75 000. The asset had originally cost $130 000 and it had been written down to $60 000. Philippines Ltd had depreciated the machine on a straight-line basis over 5 years, with no residual value.
(c) Philippines Ltd had transferred one of its motor vehicles (carrying amount of $15 000) to Pakistan Ltd on 31 March 2012 for $12 000. Pakistan Ltd regarded this vehicle as part of its inventory. The vehicle was sold by Pakistan Ltd on 31 July 2012 for $17 000.
(d) The tax rate is 30%.

	Pakistan Ltd	Peru Ltd	Philippines Ltd
Sales revenue	$2 850 000	$1 100 000	$ 880 000
Other revenue	420 000	200 000	60 000
Total revenues	3 270 000	1 300 000	940 000
Cost of sales	1 410 000	520 000	380 000
Other expenses	200 000	80 000	110 000
Total expenses	1 610 000	600 000	490 000
Profit before income tax	1 660 000	700 000	450 000
Income tax expense	580 000	160 000	140 000
Profit	1 080 000	540 000	310 000
Retained earnings (1/7/12)	4 070 000	2 300 000	1 120 000
Total available for appropriation	5 150 000	2 840 000	1 430 000
Dividend paid	400 000	160 000	80 000
Dividend declared	400 000	200 000	90 000
Transfer to general reserve	100 000	50 000	40 000
	900 000	410 000	210 000
Retained earnings (30/6/13)	$4 250 000	$2 430 000	$1 220 000

Required

Prepare the consolidated statement of profit or loss and other comprehensive income and statement of changes in equity (not including movements in the general reserve and share capital) for the group for the year ended 30 June 2013.

Exercise 27.8	CONSOLIDATED FINANCIAL STATEMENTS
★★	On 1 July 2008, the following balances appeared in the ledgers of the following three companies:

	Russia Ltd	Samoa Ltd	Singapore Ltd
Retained earnings	$20 000	$10 000	$ 5 000
General reserve	8 000	2 000	1 000
Dividend payable	4 000	2 000	—
Share capital	80 000	60 000	20 000

The dividend payable on 1 July 2008 was paid in October 2008.

For the year ended 30 June 2013, the following information is available:

- Inter-company sales were:

    Samoa Ltd to Russia Ltd — $20 000

    Singapore Ltd to Russia Ltd — $15 000

    The mark-up on cost on all sales was 25%.

- At 30 June 2013, inventory of Russia Ltd included:

    $1000 of goods purchased from Samoa Ltd

    $1800 of goods purchased from Singapore Ltd.

- The current income tax rate is 30%.
- Russia Ltd paid $67 200 for 80% of the shares of Samoa Ltd at 1 July 2008 when all identifiable assets and liabilities of Samoa Ltd were recorded at fair value.
- Samoa Ltd paid $18 750 for 75% of the shares of Singapore Ltd at 1 July 2008 when all identifiable assets and liabilities of Singapore Ltd were recorded at fair value as below.

Receivables	$ 9 000
Inventory	10 000
Plant	20 000
Total assets	39 000
Liabilities	13 000
Net assets	$26 000

- The plant has an expected remaining useful life of 5 years. By 30 June 2009, all receivables had been collected and inventory sold.

The financial information for the year ended 30 June 2013 for all three companies was as follows:

	Russia Ltd	Samoa Ltd	Singapore Ltd
Sales revenue	$ 98 400	$ 48 500	$30 000
Cost of sales	61 000	29 000	13 000
Gross profit	37 400	19 500	17 000
Expenses:			
Selling and administrative (inc. depn)	10 000	5 000	3 000
Financial	3 000	1 000	1 000
	13 000	6 000	4 000
	24 400	13 500	13 000
Dividend revenue	3 200	4 500	—
Profit before income tax	27 600	18 000	13 000
Income tax expense	12 000	8 100	5 200
Profit	15 600	9 900	7 800
Retained earnings (1/7/12)	40 000	20 000	10 000
Total available for appropriation	55 600	29 900	17 800
Transfer to general reserve	4 000	1 900	—
Dividend paid	5 000	2 000	4 000
Dividend declared	5 000	2 000	2 000
	14 000	5 900	6 000
Retained earnings (30/6/13)	41 600	24 000	11 800
General reserve	12 000	3 900	1 000
Share capital	80 000	60 000	20 000
Equity	$133 600	$ 87 900	$32 800
Receivables	$ 18 000	$ 25 000	$11 000
Inventory	25 000	26 400	13 800

	Russia Ltd	Samoa Ltd	Singapore Ltd
Shares in Samoa Ltd	65 600	—	—
Shares in Singapore Ltd	—	18 750	—
Plant	50 000	39 750	20 000
Total assets	158 600	109 900	44 800
Provisions	20 000	20 000	10 000
Dividend payable	5 000	2 000	2 000
Total liabilities	25 000	22 000	12 000
Net assets	$133 600	$ 87 900	$32 800

Required

Prepare the consolidated financial statements of Russia Ltd at 30 June 2013.

Exercise 27.9 **CONSOLIDATION WORKSHEET ENTRIES**

★★ The statements of financial position of Tonga Ltd, Thailand Ltd and Tuvalu Ltd for the year ended 30 June 2013 are shown below.

	Tonga Ltd	Thailand Ltd	Tuvalu Ltd
Share capital	$150 000	$ 50 000	$ 21 000
Retained earnings	60 000	18 000	4 000
Dividend payable	30 000	10 000	6 000
	$240 000	$ 78 000	$ 31 000
Non-current assets	$120 000	$ 20 000	$ 10 000
Shares in Thailand Ltd	55 800	—	—
Shares in Tuvalu Ltd	—	21 000	—
Inventory	10 000	25 000	20 000
Receivables	54 200	12 000	1 000
	$240 000	$ 78 000	$ 31 000

For the year ended 30 June 2013, Thailand Ltd and Tuvalu Ltd recorded a profit of $2000 and $1000 respectively.

Thailand Ltd acquired 90% of the ordinary shares of Tuvalu Ltd for a total consideration of $20 730. At the acquisition date, 1 July 2010, Tuvalu Ltd's equity comprised:

Share capital (21 000 shares)	$21 000
Retained earnings	1 000

At this date, all identifiable assets and liabilities of Tuvalu Ltd were recorded at fair value except for some plant for which the fair value of $8000 was $1000 greater than the carrying amount of $7000 (i.e. original cost of $8500 less accumulated depreciation of $1500). The plant is expected to last a further 5 years.

On the same day, the directors of Tonga Ltd made a successful offer for 45 000 of Thailand Ltd's fully paid shares. The consideration was $54 990 and, at the acquisition date, Thailand Ltd's equity comprised:

Share capital (50 000 shares)	$ 50 000
Retained earnings	4 000

At this date, all identifiable assets and liabilities of Tonga Ltd were recorded at fair value except for some machinery whose fair value was $3000 greater than its recorded amount of $6000, the latter being $10 000 cost less accumulated depreciation of $4000. The machinery is expected to have a further useful life of 3 years. When assets are sold or fully consumed, any related valuation surpluses are transferred to retained earnings.

Required

Prepare the consolidation worksheet entries for the preparation of the consolidated financial statements of Tonga Ltd at 30 June 2013.

Exercise 27.10 CONSOLIDATION WORKSHEET, CONSOLIDATED STATEMENT OF PROFIT OR LOSS AND OTHER COMPREHENSIVE INCOME AND STATEMENT OF CHANGES IN EQUITY

★★

On 1 July 2012, Vanuatu Ltd acquired 80% of the shares in Vietnam Ltd (cum div.) for $44 760. At this date, Vietnam Ltd had not recorded any goodwill and all its identifiable net assets were recorded at fair value except for land and inventory.

	Carrying amount	Fair value
Land	$ 8 000	$10 000
Inventory	12 000	15 000

Half of this inventory still remained on hand at 30 June 2013. Immediately after the acquisition date, Vietnam Ltd revalued the land to fair value. The land was still on hand at 30 June 2013.

At 1 July 2012, Vietnam Ltd acquired 75% of the shares in Brunei Ltd for $15 300. Brunei Ltd had not recorded any goodwill and all its identifiable assets and liabilities were recorded at fair value except for the following:

	Carrying amount	Fair value
Inventory	$10 000	$14 000

All the inventory was sold by 30 June 2013. When assets are sold or fully consumed, any related valuation surpluses are transferred to retained earnings.

At the acquisition date, the financial statements of the three companies showed the following:

	Vanuatu Ltd	Vietnam Ltd	Brunei Ltd
Share capital	$80 000	$32 000	$20 000
General reserve	20 000	3 200	—
Asset revaluation surplus	16 000	6 400	—
Retained earnings	6 400	4 800	(3 200)
Dividend payable	12 000	3 200	—

The following information was provided for the year ended 30 June 2013:

	Vanuatu Ltd	Vietnam Ltd	Brunei Ltd
Sales revenue	$108 000	$72 000	$54 000
Cost of sales	72 000	61 200	40 500
Gross profit	36 000	10 800	13 500
Less: Distribution and administrative			
expenses	9 000	2 700	2 880
	27 000	8 100	10 620
Plus: Interim dividend revenue	1 280	1 500	—
Profit before income tax	28 280	9 600	10 620
Income tax expense	8 480	1 920	2 400
Profit	19 800	7 680	8 220
Retained earnings (1/7/12)	6 400	4 800	(3 200)
	26 200	12 480	5 020

	Vanuatu Ltd	Vietnam Ltd	Brunei Ltd
Less: Dividend paid	4 000	—	1 000
Dividend declared	4 000	1 600	1 000
	8 000	1 600	2 000
Retained earnings (30/6/13)	$ 18 200	$10 880	$ 3 020

Additional information

(a) Dividends declared for the year ended 30 June 2012 were duly paid.

(b) Intragroup purchases (at cost plus $33^1/_3$%) were:

Vanuatu Ltd from Vietnam Ltd — $43 200; Vietnam Ltd from Brunei Ltd — $37 800.

(c) Intragroup purchases valued at cost to the purchasing company were included in inventory at 30 June 2013, as follows:

Vanuatu Ltd — $5400; Vietnam Ltd — $4500.

(d) The tax rate is 30%.

Required

1. Prepare the consolidation worksheet entries for the preparation of the consolidated financial statements of Vanuatu Ltd at 30 June 2013.
2. Prepare the consolidated statement of profit or loss and other comprehensive income and statement of changes in equity (not including movements in share capital and other reserves) at 30 June 2013.

Exercise 27.11 **CONSOLIDATION WORKSHEET ENTRIES**

★★ On 1 July 2011, Brunei Ltd acquired (ex div.) 80% of the shares of Bhutan Ltd for $146 400. At this date, the equity of Bhutan Ltd consisted of:

Share capital	$100 000
General reserve	50 000
Retained earnings	20 000

In the accounts at this date, Bhutan Ltd had recorded a dividend payable of $5000, goodwill of $13 000, and furniture at cost of $80 000 less accumulated depreciation of $10 000. All the identifiable assets and liabilities of Bhutan Ltd were recorded at fair value except for the following:

	Carrying amount	Fair value
Plant (cost $120 000)	$90 000	$100 000
Inventory	40 000	45 000

The plant has a further 5-year life, and is depreciated using the straight-line method. Of the inventory, 90% was sold by 30 June 2012, the remaining 10% being sold by 30 June 2013.

During the 2011–12 period, Bhutan Ltd recorded a profit of $40 000. There were no changes in reserves. During the 2012–13 period, Bhutan Ltd recorded a profit of $36 000, and recorded a transfer to general reserve of $6000.

On 1 January 2012, Bhutan Ltd acquired a 50% interest in Burma Ltd for $57 000, giving it a capacity to control that entity. At this date, the equity of Burma Ltd consisted of:

Share capital	$ 80 000
General reserve	40 000
Retained earnings	(10 000)

The identifiable assets and liabilities of Burma Ltd consisted of:

	Carrying amount	Fair value
Land	$50 000	$56 000
Plant (cost $110 000)	80 000	82 000
Inventory	10 000	12 000

All the inventory on hand at 1 January 2012 was sold by 30 June 2012. The plant had a further 10-year life, and was depreciated using the straight-line method. The land was sold by Burma Ltd in the 2012–13 period.

The profit of Burma Ltd for the period from 1 January 2012 to 30 June 2012 was $8000. There were no movements in the general reserve during this period. During the 2012–13 period, Burma Ltd earned a $20 000 profit. Burma Ltd also transferred $20 000 from general reserve to retained earnings during the 2012–13 period.

Assume an income tax rate of 30%. When assets are sold or fully consumed, any related valuation surpluses are transferred to retained earnings.

Required

Prepare, in general journal entry format, the consolidation worksheet entries for the preparation of the consolidated financial statements of Brunei Ltd at 30 June 2013.

Exercise 27.12 **CONSOLIDATION WORKSHEET ENTRIES**

★★ On 1 July 2011, Indonesia Ltd acquired 75% of the issued shares of India Ltd for $320 000. At this date the statement of financial position of India Ltd was as follows:

Current assets	$ 20 000
Non-current assets	500 000
	520 000
Liabilities	(120 000)
Net assets	$ 400 000
Share capital	$ 100 000
General reserve	100 000
Retained earnings	200 000
Total equity	$ 400 000

All the identifiable assets and liabilities of India Ltd were recorded at fair value except for some land for which the fair value was $10 000 greater than the carrying amount and some depreciable assets with a further 5-year life for which the fair value was $12 000 greater than the carrying amount. The tax rate is 30%.

On 1 July 2013, Palau Ltd acquired 60% of the issued shares of Indonesia Ltd for $350 000. At this date, the statement of financial position of Indonesia Ltd was as follows:

Current assets		$ 120 000
Non-current assets		
Investment in India Ltd	$320 000	
Other	280 000	600 000
		720 000
Liabilities		(220 000)
Net assets		$ 500 000
Share capital		$ 200 000
Retained earnings		300 000
		$ 500 000

All the identifiable assets and liabilities of Indonesia Ltd were recorded at fair value except for the investment in India Ltd which had a fair value of $400 000. The statement of financial position of India Ltd at 1 July 2013 was as follows:

Current assets	$ 30 000
Non-current assets	600 000
	630 000
Liabilities	(130 000)
	$ 500 000
Share capital	$ 100 000
General reserve	120 000
Retained earnings	280 000
	$ 500 000

All the identifiable assets and liabilities of India Ltd at this date were recorded at fair value except for the land held at 1 July 2011 which, at 1 July 2013, had a fair value of $20 000 greater than carrying amount, and the depreciable assets which have a further 3-year life have a fair value of $8000 greater than carrying amount. Financial information about Palau Ltd, Indonesia Ltd and India Ltd at 30 June 2014 is shown below:

	Palau Ltd	Indonesia Ltd	India Ltd
Current assets	$ 200 000	$ 150 000	$ 35 000
Non-current assets			
Investment in Indonesia Ltd	350 000	—	—
Investment in India Ltd	—	320 000	—
Land	100 000	50 000	40 000
Depreciable assets	500 000	400 000	620 000
Accumulated depreciation	(80 000)	(80 000)	(40 000)
	1 070 000	840 000	655 000
Liabilities	250 000	260 000	120 000
Net assets	$ 820 000	$ 580 000	$ 535 000
Share capital	$ 300 000	$ 200 000	$ 100 000
General reserve	200 000	—	120 000
Retained earnings (1/7/13)	150 000	300 000	280 000
Profit for the period	170 000	80 000	35 000
	$ 820 000	$ 580 000	$ 535 000

Required

Prepare the worksheet entries for the consolidated financial statements at 30 June 2014.

Exercise 27.13 **CONSOLIDATION WORKSHEET ENTRIES, ANALYSIS OF NON-CONTROLLING INTEREST**

★★ A client of yours is the chief accountant of Comoros Ltd which, at 30 June 2013, has two subsidiaries, Cook Islands Ltd and Chile Ltd. He is unsure how to prepare the consolidated financial statements and has asked for your help. He has provided you with the information below concerning the group, and has determined a series of questions for which he wants clear, well-written answers. Provide the answers to these questions. Assume an income tax rate of 30%.

Part A

Comoros Ltd acquired 40% of the capital of Cook Islands Ltd on 1 July 2010 for $79 400, consisting of $9400 cash and 14 000 Comoros Ltd shares having an estimated fair value of $5 per share. The equity of Cook Islands Ltd at this date is shown below.

Share capital	$ 100 000
General reserve	50 000
Retained earnings	40 000

All the identifiable assets and liabilities of Cook Islands Ltd were recorded at fair value except for plant (carrying amount $60 000, net of $10 000 depreciation) for which the fair value was $65 000. The plant has a further 5-year life.

During January 2011, Cook Islands Ltd paid a dividend of $5000. Further, in January 2011, a transfer to retained earnings of $4000 was made from the general reserve established before 1 July 2010.

Required

1. Prepare the business combination valuation and pre-acquisition entries in relation to Comoros Ltd's acquisition of Cook Islands Ltd at 30 June 2011, assuming Cook Islands Ltd is a subsidiary of Comoros Ltd at this date.
2. Explain how the calculations used in requirement 1 meet the requirements of IFRS 3 *Business Combinations*.
3. If Comoros Ltd acquired its shares in Cook Islands Ltd at 1 July 2010, but did not achieve control until 1 July 2011 when the retained earnings of Cook Islands Ltd were $60 000 and the fair value of plant was $30 000 greater than the carrying amount, should the fair values be measured at 1 July 2010, or at 1 July 2011 when Comoros Ltd obtained control of Cook Islands Ltd? Explain your answer, referring to requirements of appropriate accounting standards to justify your answer.
4. If Cook Islands Ltd earned a $10 000 profit between 1 July 2010 and 30 June 2011, determine the non-controlling interest share of Cook Islands Ltd's equity at 30 June 2011.
5. Explain your calculation of the non-controlling interest share of profit in requirement 4.

Part B

Cook Islands Ltd acquired 75% of the issued shares of Chile Ltd at 1 January 2011 for $137 000 when the equity of Chile Ltd consisted of $100 000 capital and $62 000 retained earnings which included profit of $12 000, earned from 1 July 2010. At acquisition date, all the identifiable assets and liabilities of Chile Ltd were recorded at fair value except for the following assets:

	Carrying amount	Fair value
Land	$80 000	$ 90 000
Plant (net of accumulated depreciation of $15 000)	60 000	65 000
Inventory	20 000	25 000

Of the inventory, 90% was sold by 30 June 2011 and the remainder by 30 June 2012. The land was sold in January 2013 for $120 000. The plant has a further 5-year life. When assets are sold or fully consumed, any related valuation surpluses are transferred to retained earnings.

Required

Prepare the business combination valuation and pre-acquisition entries at 30 June 2011 and 30 June 2013.

Part C

The following transactions affect the preparation of consolidated financial statements at 30 June 2013:
(a) Sale of inventory in June 2012 from Chile Ltd to Comoros Ltd — the inventory cost Chile Ltd $2000, and was sold to Comoros Ltd for $3000. At 30 June 2013, the inventory was all sold by Comoros Ltd.
(b) Sale of plant on 1 January 2012 from Chile Ltd to Comoros Ltd — the plant had a carrying amount in Chile Ltd of $12 000 at time of sale, and was sold for $15 000. The plant had a further 5-year life.
(c) Dividend of $10 000 declared in June 2013 by Chile Ltd to be paid in August 2013.
(d) Payment of a $4500 management fee from Chile Ltd to Comoros Ltd in February 2013.

Required

In relation to the preparation of the consolidated financial statements *at 30 June 2013*:
1. Provide consolidation worksheet journal entries for the above transactions, including related non-controlling interest adjustments.
2. If the retained earnings (1/7/12) of Chile Ltd was $80 000 and the profit for the 2012–13 period was $10 000, calculate the non-controlling interests share of Chile Ltd's equity at 30 June 2013, assuming no changes in reserves.
3. The calculation of non-controlling interest is based on the concept of sharing only those profits that are realised to the group. Explain this concept, showing how it is implemented using transactions (a), (b) and (d) in part 3.

4. Explain the non-controlling interest adjustment entry in relation to transaction (c).
5. Explain the adjustment entry for transaction (a).

★★

CONSOLIDATED FINANCIAL STATEMENTS

On 1 July 2012, United States Ltd acquired 60% of the shares of Peru Ltd for $108 000. On the same day, Peru Ltd acquired 80% of the shares (cum div.) of Canada Ltd for $71 600. At the acquisition date, Peru Ltd's and Canada Ltd's financial statements showed the following balances:

	Peru Ltd	Canada Ltd
Share capital	$100 000	$60 000
General reserve	30 000	20 000
Retained earnings	15 000	8 000
Dividend payable	—	5 000

The dividend of Canada Ltd was paid later in 2012.

On 1 July 2012, all identifiable assets and liabilities of Peru Ltd and Canada Ltd were recorded at fair values except for the following:

	Peru Ltd		Canada Ltd	
	Carrying amount	Fair value	Carrying amount	Fair value
Plant and machinery (cost $80 000)	$60 000	$80 000	—	—
Inventory	40 000	50 000	$30 000	$40 000
Vehicles (cost $80 000)	—	—	50 000	55 000

The vehicles have an expected useful life of 4 years and the plant is expected to last a further 10 years. Benefits are expected to be received evenly over these periods. All inventory on hand at 1 July 2012 was sold by 30 June 2013. When assets are sold or fully consumed, any related valuation surpluses are transferred to retained earnings.

The financial statements of the three companies at 30 June 2013 are as follows.

	United States Ltd	Peru Ltd	Canada Ltd
Sales revenue	$520 000	$365 000	$115 000
Other revenue	160 000	105 000	58 000
	680 000	470 000	173 000
Cost of sales	410 000	190 000	86 000
Other expenses	146 000	180 000	42 000
	556 000	370 000	128 000
Profit before income tax	124 000	100 000	45 000
Income tax expense	51 000	40 000	20 000
Profit	73 000	60 000	25 000
Retained earnings (1/7/12)	24 000	15 000	8 000
	97 000	75 000	33 000
Interim dividend paid	10 000	15 000	3 000
Final dividend declared	16 000	8 000	4 000
Transfer to general reserve	25 000	6 000	4 000
	51 000	29 000	11 000
Retained earnings (30/6/13)	46 000	46 000	22 000
Share capital	250 000	100 000	60 000
General reserve	145 000	36 000	24 000
Bank overdraft	21 000	6 000	20 000
Provisions	41 000	30 000	20 000

	United States Ltd	Peru Ltd	Canada Ltd
Current tax liability	55 000	42 000	26 000
Deferred tax liability	25 000	12 000	8 000
Dividend payable	16 000	8 000	4 000
	$599 000	$280 000	$184 000
Bank	$ 49 000	$ 25 000	$ 32 000
Receivables	61 200	17 000	16 000
Inventory	103 000	41 800	68 000
Dividend receivable	4 800	3 200	—
Shares in Peru Ltd	108 000	—	—
Shares in Canada Ltd	—	67 600	—
Deferred tax asset	21 000	15 400	8 000
Plant	200 000	180 000	—
Accumulated depreciation	(48 000)	(70 000)	—
Vehicles	130 000	—	100 000
Accumulated depreciation	(30 000)	—	(40 000)
	$599 000	$280 000	$184 000

Additional information

(a) Included in the ending inventory of Peru Ltd was inventory purchased from Canada Ltd for $10 000. This had originally cost Canada Ltd $8000.

(b) United States Ltd had sold inventory to Canada Ltd during the period for $25 000. This had cost United States Ltd $20 000. Half of this has been sold to external parties by Canada Ltd during the year for $15 000.

(c) The tax rate is 30%.

Required

Prepare the consolidated financial statements for United States Ltd and its subsidiaries, Peru Ltd and Canada Ltd, for the period ending 30 June 2013.

Exercise 27.15   **SALE OF SHARES WITH NO LOSS OF CONTROL**

★★   On 1 July 2012, A Ltd acquired 80% of the shares issued by B Ltd for $85 000. At this date, the shareholders' equity of B Ltd consisted of share capital of $80 000 and retained earnings of $20 000. All identifiable assets were recorded at amounts equal to fair value except for plant for which the fair value was $4000 greater than the carrying amount. The plant had a further 4-year life. Goodwill is calculated on a partial basis.

On 1 July 2014, A Ltd sold a quarter of its shareholding in B Ltd for $48 000 cash. The financial statements of A Ltd and B Ltd at this date prior to the sale were as follows:

	A Ltd	B Ltd
Share capital	$100 000	$ 80 000
General reserve	20 000	10 000
Retained earnings	100 000	70 000
Liabilities	20 000	12 000
	240 000	172 000
Shares in B Ltd	$ 85 000	
Other assets	155 000	172 000
	240 000	172 000

Required

Prepare the consolidation worksheet at 1 July 2014 after the sale of shares by A Ltd, assuming that the sale did not result in A Ltd losing control of B Ltd.

SALE OF SHARES WITH LOSS OF CONTROL

★★ X Ltd acquired 80% of the issued shares of Y Ltd for $700 000 on 1 July 2012 when the equity of Y Ltd consisted of $400 000 capital and $300 000 retained earnings. At this date the carrying amounts of Y Ltd's identifiable assets and liabilities were not different from fair value except for plant for which the fair value was $10 000 greater than carrying amount. The plant had a further 5-year life.

On 30 June 2014, X Ltd sold all its interest in Y Ltd for $1 200 000 when the financial statements of Y Ltd showed:

Sales revenue	$ 900 000
Expenses	775 000
Profit	125 000
Retained earnings (1/7/13)	500 000
Retained earnings (30/6/14)	625 000
Share capital	400 000
Total equity	$1 025 000
Net assets	$1 025 000

Required

Prepare the consolidation worksheet entries for X Ltd at 30 June 2014.

ACQUISITION OF ADDITIONAL SHARES IN SUBSIDIARY

★★ On 1 July 2012, K Ltd acquired 60% of the issued capital of L Ltd for $66 000 cash when the equity of L Ltd consisted of share capital of $80 000 and retained earnings of $20 000. All the identifiable assets and liabilities of L Ltd were recorded at amounts equal to fair value except for plant for which the fair value was $4000 greater than carrying amount. The plant had a further 4-year life. On consolidation goodwill is calculated on a partial basis.

On 1 July 2014, K Ltd acquired a further 20% interest in Ltd for $26 000. At this date, the shareholders' equity of L Ltd consisted of $80 000 share capital and $40 000 retained earnings.

Required

Prepare the consolidation worksheet entries for the year ended 30 June 2015.

CONSOLIDATED FINANCIAL STATEMENTS, RECIPROCAL SHAREHOLDINGS

★★★ On 1 July 2010, Singapore Ltd acquired 10% of the issued capital of New Caledonia Ltd for $60 000. At this date the equity of New Caledonia Ltd consisted of:

Share capital	$100 000
Retained earnings	450 000

All the identifiable assets and liabilities of New Caledonia Ltd were recorded at fair value except for some machinery for which the fair value was $20 000 greater than carrying amount. The machinery had a further 5-year life, with benefits expected to be received evenly over this period.

On 1 January 2013, New Caledonia Ltd acquired 60% of the issued capital of Singapore Ltd for $132 000, obtaining control over the financial and operating policies of Singapore Ltd. At this date the equity of Singapore Ltd consisted of:

Share capital	$100 000
Retained earnings (1/7/12)	50 000
Profit to 1/1/13	50 000

All the identifiable assets and liabilities of Singapore Ltd were recorded at fair value except for plant and machinery (expected life of 5 years) whose fair value was $5000 greater than carrying amount, and the investment account Shares in New Caledonia Ltd which had a fair value of $70 000. The financial statements of New Caledonia Ltd at 1 January 2013 contained the following information:

	Carrying amount	Fair value
Current assets	$ 120 000	$ 120 000
Non-current assets		
Plant and machinery	470 000	490 000
Other	200 000	200 000
	790 000	810 000
Liabilities	(160 000)	(160 000)
Net assets	$ 630 000	$ 650 000
Share capital	$ 100 000	
Retained earnings (1/7/12)	500 000	
Profit to 1/1/13	30 000	
Equity	$ 630 000	

The plant and machinery of New Caledonia Ltd whose fair value was greater than carrying amount had a further 4-year life.

At 30 June 2013 Singapore Ltd had not disposed of its shares in New Caledonia Ltd.

At 30 June 2013, the financial statements of New Caledonia Ltd and its subsidiary Singapore Ltd included the following:

	New Caledonia Ltd	Singapore Ltd
Profit before income tax	$ 50 000	$ 80 000
Income tax expense	(10 000)	(20 000)
Profit	40 000	60 000
Retained earnings at 1/7/12	500 000	50 000
	540 000	110 000
Dividends paid at 28/6/13	(20 000)	(10 000)
Retained earnings at 30/6/13	$ 520 000	$ 100 000
Current assets	$ 80 000	$ 30 000
Non-current assets		
Shares in Singapore Ltd	132 000	—
Shares in New Caledonia Ltd	—	60 000
Plant and machinery	600 000	140 000
Accumulated depreciation	(72 000)	(20 000)
Other	80 000	50 000
Total assets	820 000	260 000
Liabilities	(200 000)	(60 000)
Net assets	$ 620 000	$ 200 000
Equity		
Share capital	$ 100 000	$ 100 000
Retained earnings	520 000	100 000
Total equity	$ 620 000	200 000

Required

Prepare the consolidated financial statements at 30 June 2013. Where necessary, make calculations to the nearest dollar.

28

Translation of the financial statements of foreign entities

ACCOUNTING STANDARDS IN FOCUS

IAS 21 *The Effects of Changes in Foreign Exchange Rates*

LEARNING OBJECTIVES

After studying this chapter, you should be able to:

1 identify the reason for translation of financial statements and the applicable accounting standard

2 explain the difference between functional and presentation currencies

3 discuss the rationale underlying the choice of a functional currency

4 apply the indicators in choosing a functional currency

5 translate a set of financial statements from local currency into the functional currency

6 account for changes in the functional currency

7 translate financial statements into the presentation currency

8 prepare consolidated financial statements including foreign subsidiaries when the local currency is the functional currency

9 prepare consolidated financial statements including foreign subsidiaries when the functional currency is that of the parent entity

10 explain what constitutes the net investment in a foreign operation

11 prepare the disclosures required by IAS 21.

28.1 TRANSLATION OF A FOREIGN SUBSIDIARY'S STATEMENTS

A parent entity may have subsidiaries that are domiciled in a foreign country. In most cases, the financial statements of the foreign subsidiary are prepared in the currency of the foreign country. In order for the financial statements of the foreign operation to be included in the consolidated financial statements of the parent, it is necessary to translate the foreign operation's financial statements to the currency used by the parent entity for reporting purposes. The purpose of this chapter is to discuss the process for translating and presenting the consolidated financial statements of a parent entity where at least one of its subsidiaries is a foreign subsidiary.

The accounting standard that deals with this process is IAS 21 *The Effects of Changes in Foreign Exchange Rates*. IAS 21 was first issued by the International Accounting Standards Committee (IASC) in July 1983, revised in 1993, and further revised as a part of the Improvements project in 2003. This latter revision provided convergence with Generally Accepted Accounting Principles (GAAP) in the United States, in particular Statement of Financial Accounting Standards No. 52 (SFAS 52) *Foreign Currency Translation*. Other minor revisions have been made up to January 2012.

28.2 FUNCTIONAL AND PRESENTATION CURRENCIES

Paragraph 3 of IAS 21 notes that its two areas of application are:
- translating the results and financial position of foreign operations that are included in the financial statements of the entity by consolidation or the equity method
- translating an entity's results and financial position into a presentation currency.
  Note that there are two different translation processes here. In order to understand this, it is necessary to distinguish between three different types of currency: local currency, functional currency and presentation currency. Not all foreign subsidiaries experience all three currencies.
- *Local currency*. This is the currency of the country in which the foreign operation is based.
- *Functional currency*. This is defined in paragraph 8 of IAS 21 as 'the currency of the primary economic environment in which the entity operates'. As is explained in more detail later, this is the currency of the country in which the foreign operation is based. This term is not defined in IAS 21.
- *Presentation currency*. Paragraph 8 defines this as 'the currency in which the financial statements are presented'.

To illustrate, Foreign Ltd is a subsidiary of Parent Ltd. Parent Ltd is an Australian company and Foreign Ltd is based in Singapore. The operations in Singapore are to sell goods manufactured in France. In this case, Foreign Ltd would most likely maintain its accounts in Singaporean dollars, the local currency, while the functional currency could be the euro, reflecting the major economic operations in France. However, for presentation in the consolidated financial statements of Parent Ltd, the presentation currency could be the Australian dollar. As the accounts are maintained in Singaporean dollars, they may firstly have to be translated into the functional currency, the euro, and then translated again into the Australian dollar for presentation purposes. It is these two translation processes that are referred to in paragraph 3 of IAS 21.

28.3 THE RATIONALE UNDERLYING THE FUNCTIONAL CURRENCY CHOICE

This section relies heavily on the discussion in the seminal paper by Lawrence Revsine, published in 1983, in which he emphasised the need to understand the rationale underlying the choice of an exchange rate as an entity's functional currency.

As noted by Revsine (1984, p. 514):

> A much more real danger is that firms, their auditors, and outside analysts may not understand the subtle philosophy that underlies the functional currency choice. As a consequence, innocent but incorrect choices and assessments may be made, and compatibility may not be achieved.

According to paragraphs 4(a) and 4(b) of SFAS 52, the objectives of the translation process are:
1. to provide information that is generally compatible with the expected economic effects of an exchange rate change on an entity's cash flows and equity

2. to reflect in consolidated statements the financial results and relationships of the individual consolidated entities as measured in their functional currencies in conformity with US generally accepted accounting principles.

Note in particular the first objective. As the foreign subsidiary operates in another country, it is important that the financial effects on the parent entity of a change in the exchange rate are apparent from the translation process. The parent entity has an investment in a foreign operation and so has assets that are exposed to a change in the exchange rate. Capturing the extent of this exposure should be reflected in the choice of translation method. The economic relationship between the parent and the subsidiary affects the extent to which a change in exchange rate affects the parent entity. This can be seen by noting the differences in the following three cases adapted from Revsine (1984).

28.3.1 Case 1

Protea Ltd is an Australian company that wants to sell its product in Hong Kong. On 1 January 2013, when the exchange rate is A$1 = HK$5, Protea Ltd acquires a building in Hong Kong to be used to distribute the Australian product. The building cost HK$1 million, equal to A$200 000. It also deposited A$55 000 (equal to HK$275 000) in a Hong Kong bank. By 31 January 2013, the company had made credit sales in Hong Kong of HK$550 000. The exchange rate at this time was still A$1 = HK$5. The goods sold had cost A$90 000 to manufacture. The receivables were collected in February 2013 when the exchange rate was A$1 = HK$5.5. This cash receipt is transferred back to Australia immediately.

Note, in this case the company has no subsidiary but acquired an overseas asset, deposited money in an overseas bank and sold goods overseas. The company would record these transactions as follows, in Australian dollars:

Building	Dr	200 000	
Cash	Cr		200 000
Cash – HK Bank	Dr	50 000	
Cash	Cr		50 000
Receivables	Dr	110 000	
Sales	Cr		110 000
Cost of Sales	Dr	90 000	
Inventory	Cr		90 000
Foreign Exchange Loss	Dr	10 000	
Receivables	Cr		10 000
(Loss on receivables when exchange rate changed from 1:5 to 1:5.5)			
Cash	Dr	100 000	
Receivables	Cr		100 000
Foreign Exchange Loss	Dr	5 000	
Cash in HK Bank	Cr		5 000
(Loss on holding HK$55 000 when exchange rate changed from 1:5.0 to 1:5.5)			

Note two effects of this accounting procedure:
- Foreign currency transactions, whether completed (the sale) or uncompleted (the deposit), have an immediate or potentially immediate effect on the future cash flows of the parent. As a result, foreign currency gains/losses are recorded as they occur and immediately affect income.
- Non-monetary assets held in the foreign country are recorded at historical cost and are unaffected by exchange rate changes.

28.3.2 Case 2

Assume that, instead of transacting directly with customers in Hong Kong, Protea Ltd formed a subsidiary, Banksia Ltd, to handle the Hong Kong operation. As with case 1, all goods are transferred from the

Australian parent to the Hong Kong subsidiary, which sells them in Hong Kong and remits profits back to the Australian parent.

Hence, Banksia Ltd is established with a capital structure of HK$1 250 000 (equal to A$250 000), an amount necessary to acquire the Hong Kong building and establish the bank account. On selling the inventory to Banksia Ltd, Protea Ltd passes the following entries:

Receivable – Banksia Ltd	Dr	110 000	
Sales Revenue	Cr		110 000
Cost of Sales	Dr	90 000	
Inventory	Cr		90 000

Assuming that the parent bills the subsidiary in Hong Kong dollars, namely HK$110 000, on receipt of the cash, the parent would pass the entry:

Foreign Exchange Loss	Dr	10 000	
Cash	Dr	100 000	
Receivable	Cr		110 000

The subsidiary will show:

Sales	HK$ 110 000
Cost of sales	110 000
Profit	—
Equity	HK$1 250 000
Building	HK$1 000 000
Cash	250 000
	HK$1 250 000

Note that the underlying transactions are the same in case 1 and case 2. The organisational form does not change the underlying economic effects of the transactions. The translation of the HK subsidiary must therefore show the position as if the parent had undertaken the transactions itself. This is the purpose behind the choice of the functional currency approach.

Where the subsidiary is simply a conduit for transforming foreign currency transactions into dollar cash flows, the consolidation approach treats the foreign currency statements of the subsidiary as artefacts that must be translated into the currency of the parent.

In case 2, the translation of the subsidiary's statements must show:
- the assets of the subsidiary at cost to the parent; that is, what the parent would have paid in its currency at acquisition date
- the revenues and expenses of the subsidiary at what it would have cost the parent in its currency at the date those transactions occurred
- monetary gains and losses being recognised immediately in income as they affect the parent directly.

Note, in case 2, that the functional currency of the subsidiary is the Australian dollar. It is the currency of the primary economic environment in which the entity operates. The inventories are sourced in Australian dollars, the dollars financing the subsidiary are Australian dollars, and the cash flows that influence the actions of the parent in continuing to operate in Hong Kong are Australian dollars.

The key to determining the functional currency in case 2 is the recognition of the subsidiary as an *intermediary for the parent's activities*. The alternative is for the subsidiary to act as a *free-standing unit*. Consider case 3 in this regard.

28.3.3 Case 3

Assume that Protea Ltd establishes a subsidiary in Hong Kong for HK$1 250 000, the money again being used to acquire a building and set up a bank account. However, in this case the Hong Kong operation is established to manufacture products in Hong Kong for sale in Hong Kong.

Chinese labour is used in the manufacturing process and profits are used to reinvest in the business for expansion purposes. Remittances of cash to the parent are in the form of dividends.

The economics of case 3 are different from those in case 2. The subsidiary is not just acting as a conduit for the parent. Apart from the initial investment, the cash flows, both inflows and outflows, for the subsidiary are dependent on the economic environment of Hong Kong rather than Australia. The effect of a change in the exchange rate between Australia and Hong Kong has no immediate effect on the operations of the Hong Kong subsidiary. It certainly affects the worth of the parent's investment in the subsidiary, but it has no immediate cash flow effect on the parent. In this circumstance, the functional currency is the Hong Kong dollar rather than the Australian dollar.

In analysing the success of the overseas subsidiary, the interrelationships between variables such as sales, profits, assets and equity should be the same whether they are expressed in Hong Kong or Australian dollars. In other words, the translation process should adjust all items by the same exchange rate to retain these interrelationships.

The key point of Revsine's article is that the choice of translation method should be such as to reflect the underlying economics of the situation. In particular, it is necessary to select the appropriate functional currency to reflect these underlying economic events.

28.4 IDENTIFYING THE FUNCTIONAL CURRENCY

Paragraphs 9–12 of IAS 21 provide information on determining the functional currency. As the assessment of the functional currency requires judgement, in accordance with paragraph 12 of IAS 21, management gives priority to the primary indicators in paragraph 9 before considering the indicators in paragraphs 10 and 11, which supply supporting evidence to that determined from assessment using the paragraph 9 indicators. The indicators are:

Paragraph 9: normally the one in which it primarily *generates and expends cash*
Consider the currency:
- in which *sales prices* are denominated or which influences sales prices
- of the country whose competitive forces and regulations influence *sales prices*
- in which *input costs* — labour, materials — are denominated and settled, or which influences such costs.

Paragraph 10: consider two factors:
- the currency in which funds from *financing activities* are generated
- the currency in which *receipts from operating activities* are retained.

Paragraph 11: consider:
- whether the activities of the foreign operation are carried out as an *extension* of the reporting entity
- whether *transactions with the reporting entity* are a high or low proportion of the foreign operation's activities
- whether *cash flows* from the activities of the foreign operation *directly affect* the cash flows of the reporting entity and are readily available for remittance to it
- whether *cash flows* from the foreign operation are sufficient to *service existing and expected debt* obligations without funds being made available by the reporting entity.

Paragraph 12: management should use judgement to determine which currency most faithfully reflects the economic effects of the underlying transactions and events.

These factors are not significantly different from those stated in paragraph 42 of the FASB's SFAS 52. Jeter and Chaney (2003, p. 618) provided the basis for the information provided in figure 28.1, which illustrates the functional currency indicators as set down by the FASB.

Economic indicators	Indicators pointing to local overseas currency as functional currency	Indicators pointing to parent entity's currency as functional currency
Cash flows	Primarily in the local currency and do not affect the parent's cash flows.	Directly affect the parent's cash flows on a current basis and are readily available for remittance to the parent.
Sales prices	Are not primarily responsive in the short term to exchange rate changes. They are determined primarily by local conditions.	Are primarily responsive to exchange rate changes in the short term and are determined primarily by worldwide competition.
Sales market	Active local market, although there may be significant amounts of exports.	Sales are mostly in the country of the parent entity, or denominated in the parent entity's currency.
Expenses	Production costs and operating expenses are determined primarily by local conditions.	Production costs and operating expenses are obtained primarily from parent entity sources.
Financing	Primarily denominated in the local currency, and the foreign entity's cash flow from operations is sufficient to service existing and normally expected obligations.	Primarily from parent or other parent country-denominated obligations, or the parent entity is expected to service the debt.
Intragroup transactions	Low volume of intragroup transactions and there is not an extensive interrelationship between the operations of the foreign entity and those of the parent. However, the foreign entity may rely on the parent's or affiliates' competitive advantages, such as patents and trademarks.	High volume of intragroup transactions; there is an extensive interrelationship between the operations of the parent and those of the foreign entity, or the foreign entity is an investment or financing device for the parent.

FIGURE 28.1 Functional currency indicators — FASB
Source: Jeter and Chaney (2003, p. 618).

In applying the criteria shown in figure 28.1 for a parent and a single subsidiary, such as an Australian parent and a subsidiary in Hong Kong, there are three scenarios:
1. the functional currency of the subsidiary is the Australian dollar
2. the functional currency is the Hong Kong dollar
3. the functional currency is another currency, say, the Malaysian ringgit.

In relation to the choice between the first two alternatives, the extreme situations are those alluded to in the analysis of the Revsine cases. For the *Australian dollar* to be the functional currency, the expectation is that the subsidiary is a conduit for the parent entity. In the easy case, the product being sold is made in Australia, and the selling price is determined by worldwide competition. Further, because the entire product sold by the subsidiary emanates from the parent, there is significant traffic between the two entities, including cash being transferred from the subsidiary to the parent. For the *Hong Kong dollar* to be the functional currency, it is expected that the Hong Kong operation is independent of the parent entity. The products are sourced in Hong Kong and the sales prices depend on the local currency. The only regular transactions between the two entities are the annual dividends.

However, between these two scenarios there are many others where the determination of the functional currency is blurred. For example, the product being sold may require some Australian raw materials but be assembled in Hong Kong using some local raw materials. There are then material transactions between the two entities, but the subsidiary may be self-sufficient in terms of finance. In these cases, cash is generated in Hong Kong but expended in both Australia and Hong Kong. In determining the functional currency, management will need to apply judgement. The key to making a correct decision is, in accordance with Revsine, understanding what the translation process is trying to achieve in terms of reporting the underlying economic substance of the events and transactions.

In relation to the situation where another currency, such as the Malaysian ringgit, is the functional currency, this could occur where the Australian parent establishes a subsidiary in Hong Kong that imports raw materials from Malaysia and elsewhere, assembles them in Hong Kong and sells the finished product in Malaysia.

It is possible therefore for a parent entity that has a large number of foreign subsidiaries to have a number of functional currencies, particularly if the foreign subsidiaries are all relatively independent. An example of this is the US company 3M, which in 2011 was a US$29.6 billion diversified technology company that had operations in more than 65 countries, sold products in nearly 200 countries, and operated 133 manufacturing and converting facilities in 40 countries outside the United States. The subsidiaries-run manufacturing operations ranged from small converting operations to full-scale manufacturing of multiple product lines. In the notes to its 31 December 2011 annual report (see www.3m.com), 3M's policy statement on foreign currency translation stated:

> Local currencies generally are considered the functional currencies outside the United States. Assets and liabilities for operations in local-currency environments are translated at year-end exchange rates. Income and expense items are translated at average rates of exchange prevailing during the year. Cumulative translation adjustments are recorded as a component of accumulated other comprehensive income (loss) in shareholders' equity.

As the functional currencies for the offshore operations were the local currencies, 3M had to deal with the accounting for a large number of functional currencies.

 ## 28.5 TRANSLATION INTO THE FUNCTIONAL CURRENCY

In the situation where it is determined that the Hong Kong dollar is the functional currency for the Hong Kong subsidiary, the financial statements of the subsidiary prepared in Hong Kong dollars are automatically in the functional currency. Where the Hong Kong subsidiary uses the Australian dollar as its functional currency, it is necessary to translate the Hong Kong accounts from Hong Kong dollars into Australian dollars.

The process of translating one currency into another is given in paragraphs 21 and 23 of IAS 21. Paragraph 21 deals with items reflected in the statement of profit or loss and other comprehensive income that concern transactions occurring in the current period:

> A foreign currency transaction shall be recorded, on initial recognition in the functional currency, by applying to the foreign currency amount the spot exchange rate between the functional currency and the foreign currency at the date of the transaction.

Hence, in translating the revenues and expenses in the statement of profit or loss and other comprehensive income, theoretically each item of revenue and expense should be translated at the spot exchange rate between the functional currency and the foreign currency on the date that the transaction occurred. However, given the large number of transactions being reported on in the statement of profit or loss and other comprehensive income, paragraph 22 of IAS 21 provides for an averaging system to be used. A rate that approximates the actual rate at the date of the transaction can be used; for example, an average rate for a week or month might be used for all transactions within those periods. The extent to which averaging can be used depends on the extent to which there is a fluctuation in the exchange rate over a period and the evenness with which transactions occur throughout the period. For example, where the transactions are made evenly throughout a financial year — no seasonal effect, for example — and there is an even movement of the exchange rate over that year, a yearly average exchange rate could be used.

In relation to statement of financial position accounts, paragraph 23 of IAS 21 states:

> At the end of each reporting period:
> (a) foreign currency monetary items shall be translated using the closing rate;
> (b) non-monetary items that are measured in terms of historical cost in a foreign currency shall be translated using the exchange rate at the date of the transaction; and
> (c) non-monetary items that are measured at fair value in a foreign currency shall be translated using the exchange rates at the date when the value was measured.

Monetary items are defined in paragraph 8 as 'units of currency held and assets and liabilities to be received or paid in a fixed or determinable number of units of currency'. As noted in paragraph 16, examples of monetary liabilities include pensions and other employee benefits to be paid in cash and provisions to be settled in cash, including cash dividends that are recognised as a liability. Examples of monetary assets include cash and accounts receivable. All of these items are translated using the spot exchange rate at the end of the reporting period — the closing rate. As noted in case 1 previously, this reflects the amounts available in the functional currency.

For non-monetary items such as plant and equipment, IAS 16 *Property, Plant and Equipment* (chapter 11) allows the use of the cost basis or the revaluation model of measurement. Where the cost basis is used, the appropriate translation rate is the spot rate at the date the asset was initially recorded by the subsidiary. Where the revaluation model is used, the appropriate rate is the spot rate at the date of the valuation to fair value. Paragraph 25 of IAS 21 notes that certain non-monetary assets such as inventory are to be reported at the lower of cost and net realisable value in accordance with IAS 2 *Inventories*. In such a case, it is necessary to calculate the cost, translated using the spot rate at acquisition date, and the net realisable value translated at the spot rate at the date of valuation. The lower amount is then used — this may require a write-down in the functional currency statements that would not occur in the local currency statements.

The basic principles of the translation method follow.

28.5.1 Statement of financial position items

- *Assets.* Assets should first be classified as monetary or non-monetary. Monetary assets are translated at the current rate existing at the end of the reporting period. With a non-monetary asset, the exchange rate used is that current at the date at which the recorded amount for the asset has been entered into the accounts. Hence, for non-monetary assets recorded at historical cost, the rates used are those existing when the historical cost was recorded. For non-monetary assets that have been revalued, whether upwards or downwards, the exchange rates used will relate to the dates of revaluation.
- *Liabilities.* The principles enunciated for assets apply also for liabilities. The liabilities are classified as monetary and non-monetary and, for the latter, it is the date of valuation that is important.
- *Equity.* In selecting the appropriate exchange rate two factors are important. First, equity existing at the date of acquisition or investment is distinguished from post-acquisition equity. Second, movements in other reserves and retained earnings constituting transfers within or internal to equity are treated differently from other reserves.
- *Share capital.* If on hand at acquisition or created by investment, the capital is translated at the rate existing at acquisition or investment. If the capital arises as the result of a transfer from another equity account, such as a bonus dividend, the rate is that current at the date the amounts transferred were originally recognised in equity.
- *Other reserves.* If on hand at acquisition, the reserves are translated at the rate existing at acquisition. If the reserves are post-acquisition and result from internal transfers, the rate used is that at the date the amounts transferred were originally recognised in equity. If the reserves are post-acquisition and not created from internal transfers, the rate used is that current at the date the reserves are first recognised in the accounts.
- *Retained earnings.* If on hand at acquisition, the retained earnings are translated at the rate of exchange current at the acquisition date. Any dividends paid from pre-acquisition profits are also translated at this rate. Post-acquisition profits are carried forward balances from translation of previous periods' statements of profit or loss and other comprehensive income.

28.5.2 Statement of profit or loss and other comprehensive income items

- *Income and expenses.* In general, these are translated at the rates current at the dates the applicable transactions occur. For items that relate to non-monetary items, such as depreciation and amortisation, the rates used are those used to translate the related non-monetary items.
- *Dividends paid.* These are translated at the rate current at the date of payment.
- *Dividends declared.* These are translated at the rate current at the date of declaration.
- *Transfers to/from reserves.* As noted earlier, if internal transfers are made, the rates applicable are those existing when the amounts transferred were originally recognised in equity.

The application of these rules will result in exchange differences. Exchange differences arise mainly from translating the foreign operation's monetary items at current rates in the same way as for the foreign currency monetary items of the entity. Because the non-monetary items are translated using a historical rate that is the same for year to year, no exchange differences arise in relation to the non-monetary items. Further, items in the statement of profit or loss and other comprehensive income such as sales, purchases and expenses give rise to monetary items such as cash, receivables and payables. Hence, the exchange difference over the period can be explained by examining the movements in the monetary items over the period. The accounting for the exchange difference is explained in paragraph 28 of IAS 21:

> Exchange differences arising on the settlement of monetary items or on translating monetary items at rates different from those at which they were translated on initial recognition during the period or in previous financial statements shall be recognised in profit or loss in the period in which they arise, except as described in paragraph 32.

The exchange differences are then taken to the current period's statement of profit or loss and other comprehensive income in the same way as movements in the exchange rates on an entity's own foreign currency monetary items. See section 28.10 of this chapter for a discussion of the paragraph 32 exception.

As stated in paragraph 34 of IAS 21, the application of the basic principles of the translation method means that when an entity keeps its records in a currency other than its functional currency all amounts are remeasured in the functional currency. This produces the same amounts in that currency as would have occurred had the items been recorded initially in the functional currency.

Sentosa Ltd, a company operating in Singapore, is a wholly owned subsidiary of Taupo Ltd, a company listed in New Zealand. Taupo Ltd formed Sentosa Ltd on 1 July 2012 with an investment of NZ$310 000. Sentosa Ltd's records and financial statements are prepared in Singaporean dollars (S$). Sentosa Ltd has prepared the financial information at 30 June 2013, as shown in figure 28.2 (overleaf).

SENTOSA LTD
Statement of Financial Position
as at 30 June 2013

	2013 S$
Current assets:	
Inventory	210 000
Monetary assets	190 000
Total current assets	400 000
Non-current assets:	
Land — acquired 1/7/12	100 000
Buildings — acquired 1/10/12	120 000
Plant and equipment — acquired 1/11/12	110 000
Accumulated depreciation	(10 000)
Deferred tax asset	10 000
Total non-current assets	330 000
Total assets	730 000
Current liabilities:	
Current tax liability	70 000
Borrowings	50 000
Payables	100 000
Total current liabilities	220 000
Non-current liabilities:	
Borrowings	150 000
Total liabilities	370 000
Net assets	360 000
Equity:	
Share capital	310 000
Retained earnings	50 000
Total equity	360 000

SENTOSA LTD
Statement of Profit or Loss and Other Comprehensive Income
for the year ended 30 June 2013

	2013 S$	S$
Sales revenue		1 200 000
Cost of sales:		
Purchases	1 020 000	
Ending inventory	210 000	810 000
Gross profit		390 000

(continued)

	2013	
	S$	S$
Expenses:		
Selling	120 000	
Depreciation	10 000	
Interest	20 000	
Other	90 000	240 000
Profit before income tax		150 000
Income tax expense		60 000
Profit for the period		90 000

The only movement in equity, other than in profit, was a dividend paid during the period of S$40 000.

Additional information

(a) Exchange rates over the period 1 July 2012 to 30 June 2013 were:

	S$1.00 = NZ$
1 July 2012	1.00
1 October 2012	0.95
1 November 2012	0.90
1 January 2013	0.85
1 April 2013	0.75
30 June 2013	0.75
Average rate for year	0.85
Average rate for final quarter	0.77

(b) Proceeds of long-term borrowings were received on 1 July 2012 and are payable in four annual instalments commencing 1 July 2013. Interest expense relates to this loan.
(c) The inventory on hand at balance date represents approximately the final 3 months' purchases.
(d) Revenues and expenses are spread evenly throughout the year.
(e) Deferred tax asset relates to depreciation of the plant and equipment.
(f) The dividends were paid on 1 April 2013.

Required

The functional currency is determined to be the New Zealand dollar. Translate the financial statements of Sentosa Ltd into the functional currency.

Solution

The translation process is as shown in figure 28.2.

FIGURE 28.2 Translation into functional currency

	S$	Rate	NZ$
Sales	1 200 000	0.85	1 020 000
Cost of sales:			
Purchases	1 020 000	0.85	867 000
Ending inventory	210 000	0.77	161 700
	810 000		705 300
Gross profit	390 000		314 700

FIGURE 28.2 *(continued)*

	S$	Rate	NZ$
Expenses:			
Selling	120 000	0.85	102 000
Depreciation	10 000	0.90	9 000
Interest	20 000	0.85	17 000
Other	90 000	0.85	76 500
	240 000		204 500
			110 200
Foreign exchange translation loss	0		1 000
Profit before tax	150 000		109 200
Income tax expense	60 000	0.85	51 000
Profit for the period	90 000		58 200
Retained earnings at 1/7/12	0		0
	90 000		58 200
Dividends paid	40 000	0.75	30 000
Retained earnings at 30/6/13	50 000		28 200
Share capital	310 000	1.00	310 000
Non-current borrowings	150 000	0.75	112 500
Current tax liability	70 000	0.75	52 500
Current borrowings	50 000	0.75	37 500
Payables	100 000	0.75	75 000
	730 000		615 700
Inventory	210 000	0.77	161 700
Monetary assets	190 000	0.75	142 500
Land	100 000	1.00	100 000
Buildings	120 000	0.95	114 000
Plant and equipment	110 000	0.90	99 000
Accumulated depreciation	(10 000)	0.90	(9 000)
Deferred tax asset	10 000	0.75	7 500
	730 000		615 700

Exchange differences arise mainly from translating the foreign operation's monetary items at current rates in the same way as for the foreign currency monetary items of the entity. Because the non-monetary items are translated using a historical rate that is the same from year to year, exchange differences in relation to non-monetary items arise only in the periods in which they are acquired or sold. Items in the statement of profit or loss and other comprehensive income such as sales, purchases and expenses give rise to monetary items such as cash, receivables and payables. Hence, exchange differences are going to arise by examining the movements in the monetary items over the period.

From figure 28.2, the net monetary assets of Sentosa Ltd at 30 June 2013 consist of:

	S$
Monetary assets	190 000
Deferred tax asset	10 000
Borrowings: non-current	(150 000)
Borrowings: current	(50 000)
Current tax liability	(70 000)
Payables	(100 000)
Net monetary assets at 1/7/12	(170 000)

The changes in the net monetary assets are determined from the statement of profit or loss and other comprehensive income. The exchange differences are calculated by comparing the difference between the exchange rate used in the translation process and the current rate at the reporting date:

	S$	Current rate less rate applied	NZ$ gain (loss)
Net monetary assets at 1 July 2012	310 000	(0.75–1.00)	(77 500)
Increases in monetary assets:			
Sales	1 200 000	(0.75–0.85)	(120 000)
	1 510 000		(197 500)
Decreases in monetary assets:			
Land	100 000	(0.75–1.00)	25 000
Buildings	120 000	(0.75–0.95)	24 000
Plant	110 000	(0.75–0.90)	16 500
Purchases	1 020 000	(0.75–0.85)	102 000
Selling expenses	120 000	(0.75–0.85)	12 000
Interest	20 000	(0.75–0.85)	2 000
Other expenses	90 000	(0.75–0.85)	9 000
Dividend paid	40 000	(0.75–0.75)	—
Income tax expense*	60 000	(0.75–0.85)	6 000
	1 680 000		196 500
Net monetary assets at 30 June 2013	(170 000)		(1 000)

*The entry for the period is:		S$	S$
Income tax expense	Dr	60 000	
Deferred tax asset	Dr	10 000	
Current tax liability	Cr		70 000

In preparing the translated financial statements for the following period, it should be noted that the balance of retained earnings at 30 June 2013, as translated in figure 28.2, is carried forward into the next period. In other words, there is no direct translation of the retained earnings (opening balance) within the translation process.

28.6 CHANGING THE FUNCTIONAL CURRENCY

In the example used in the previous section, the foreign operation in Singapore used the New Zealand dollar as its functional currency. Because of changes in the foreign operation's circumstances, such as the source of raw materials or the variables that determine the selling price of the entity's products, it may be that the functional currency changes into, for example, Japanese yen. According to paragraph 33 of IAS 21, where there is a change in the functional currency the translation procedures apply from the date of the change. Further, paragraph 35 notes that the effect of a change is accounted for prospectively.

Assume, therefore that the Singaporean operation used New Zealand dollars as the functional currency until 1 June 2014, and then decided that the Japanese yen was the appropriate functional currency. The financial statements of the Singaporean entity at the date of change, 1 June 2014, would then be translated at the rate of exchange between the Japanese yen and the Singaporean dollar. This rate would be the historical rate for all non-monetary assets held at the date of change. Any exchange differences recognised in the statements translated into New Zealand dollars would not be recognised in the new translation. These gains/losses would resurface until the parent disposed of the foreign operation, and all exchange gains/losses would be taken into account at that point.

LO7 28.7 TRANSLATION INTO THE PRESENTATION CURRENCY

Consider an Australian entity that has two subsidiaries, one in Malaysia and one in Hong Kong, and the functional currency for each of these subsidiaries is the Hong Kong dollar. The Australian parent will have to prepare a set of consolidated financial statements for the group. In which currency should the consolidated financial statements be prepared?

Theoretically, any currency could be the presentation currency. It may be the Australian dollar if management perceives it as the currency in which users prefer to read the financial statements. In that case, the two subsidiaries' financial statements would be prepared in Hong Kong dollars, which is the functional currency for them both. These would then be translated into Australian dollars and consolidated with the parent entity's statements.

It is possible that the presentation currency could be the Hong Kong dollar, for example if the majority of shareholders in the parent entity were Hong Kong residents. In that case, the parent entity's statements would be translated from the Australian dollar into the Hong Kong dollar and consolidated with those of the subsidiaries as presented in their functional currency.

Hence, having prepared the parent's and the subsidiaries' financial statements in the relevant functional currencies, a presentation currency is chosen and all statements not already in that currency are translated into the presentation currency. Obviously, a number of presentation currencies could be chosen, and multiple translations undertaken.

Paragraph 39 of IAS 21 states the principles for translating from the functional currency into the presentation currency:

> The results and financial position of an entity whose functional currency is not the currency of a hyperinflationary economy shall be translated into a different presentation currency using the following procedures:
> (a) assets and liabilities for each statement of financial position presented (i.e. including comparatives) shall be translated at the closing rate at the date of that statement of financial position;
> (b) income and expenses for each statement presenting profit or loss and other comprehensive income (i.e. including comparatives) shall be translated at exchange rates at the dates of the transactions; and
> (c) all resulting exchange differences shall be recognised in other comprehensive income.

Paragraph 40 notes that average rates over a period for statement of profit or loss and other comprehensive income items may be used unless exchange rates fluctuate significantly over the period.

An elaboration of these procedures for a foreign subsidiary is as follows.

28.7.1 Statement of financial position items

- *Assets.* All assets, whether current or non-current, monetary or non-monetary, are translated at the exchange rate current at the reporting date. This includes all contra-asset accounts such as accumulated depreciation and allowance for doubtful debts.
- *Liabilities.* All liabilities are translated at the same rate as assets, namely the exchange rate current at the reporting date.
- *Equity.* In selecting the appropriate rate, two factors need to be kept in mind. First, equity existing at the acquisition date or investment is distinguished from post-acquisition equity. Second, movements in other reserves and retained earnings constituting transfers within or internal to shareholders' equity are treated differently from other reserves.
- *Share capital.* If on hand at acquisition date or created by investment, this is translated at the rate current at acquisition date or investment. If created by transfer from a reserve, such as general reserve via a bonus issue, this is translated at the rate current at the date the amounts transferred were originally recognised in equity.
- *Other reserves.* If on hand at acquisition date, these are translated at the current exchange rate existing at acquisition date. If reserves are post-acquisition and created by an internal transfer within equity, they are translated at the rate existing at the date the reserve from which the transfer was made was originally recognised in the accounts. If post-acquisition and not the result of an internal transfer (e.g. an asset revaluation surplus), the rate used is that current at the date the reserve is recognised in the accounts.
- *Retained earnings.* If on hand at acquisition date, they are translated at the current exchange rate existing at acquisition. Any dividends from pre-acquisition profits are also translated at this rate. Post-acquisition profits are carried forward balances from translation of previous periods' statements of profit or loss and other comprehensive income.

28.7.2 Statement of profit or loss and other comprehensive income items

- *Income and expenses.* These are translated at the rates current at the applicable transaction dates. For items, such as purchases of inventory and sales, that occur regularly throughout the period, for practical reasons average or standard rates that approximate the relevant rates may be employed. This will involve considerations of materiality. In relation to items such as depreciation, which are allocations for a period, even though they may be recognised in the accounts only at year-end (because they reflect events occurring throughout the period) an average-for-the-period exchange rate may be used.
- *Dividends paid.* These are translated at the rates current when the dividends were paid.
- *Dividends declared.* These are translated at the rates current when the dividends are declared, generally at end-of-year rates.
- *Transfers to/from reserves.* As noted earlier, if these are transfers internal to equity, the rate used for the transfer and the reserve created is that existing when the amounts transferred were originally recognised in equity.

Using the example in figure 28.2 and, assuming that the functional currency of Sentosa Ltd is Singaporean dollars, the translation into New Zealand dollars as a presentation currency is shown in figure 28.3.

	S$	Rate	NZ$
Sales	1 200 000	0.85	1 020 000
Cost of sales:			
Purchases	1 020 000	0.85	867 000
Ending inventory	210 000	0.77	161 700
	810 000		705 300
Gross profit	390 000		314 700
Expenses:			
Selling	120 000	0.85	102 000
Depreciation	10 000	0.85	8 500
Interest	20 000	0.85	17 000
Other	90 000	0.85	76 500
	240 000		204 000
Profit before tax			110 700
Income tax expense	60 000	0.85	51 000
Profit for the period	90 000		59 700
Retained earnings at 1/7/12	0		0
	90 000		59 700
Dividends paid	40 000	0.75	30 000
Retained earnings at 30/6/13	50 000		29 700
Share capital	310 000	1.00	310 000
Non-current borrowings	150 000	0.75	112 500
Current tax liability	70 000	0.75	52 500
Current borrowings	50 000	0.75	37 500
Payables	100 000	0.75	75 000
Foreign currency translation reserve			(69 700)
	730 000		547 500
Inventory	210 000	0.75	157 500
Monetary assets	190 000	0.75	142 500
Land	100 000	0.75	75 000
Buildings	120 000	0.75	90 000
Plant and equipment	110 000	0.75	82 500
Accumulated depreciation	(10 000)	0.75	(7 500)
Deferred tax asset	10 000	0.75	7 500
	730 000		547 500

FIGURE 28.3 Translation into presentation currency

The exchange difference arising as a result of the translation is NZ$(86 500) — there has been an exchange loss over the period. This loss arises for two reasons, as explained in paragraph 41 of IAS 21:
- *The income and expense items are translated at dates of the transactions and not the closing rate:* The profit represents the net movements in income and expenses:

Profit	= S$90 000
Profit as translated	= NZ$59 700
Profit × closing rate	= S$90 000 × 0.75
	= NZ$67 500
Translation gain	= NZ$7 800

- *In the case of a net investment in a foreign operation, translating the opening net assets at an exchange rate different from the closing rate:*

Net investment at 1 July 2012	= S$310 000
Net investment × opening rate	= S$310 000 × 1.00
	= NZ$310 000
Net investment × closing rate	= S$310 000 × 0.75
	= NZ$232 500
Translation loss	= NZ$(77 500)

- The total translation loss is NZ$(69 700) equal to (NZ$7800 + NZ$(77 500)).

Note the following in relation to the translation into presentation currency:
- The exchange differences are not taken into current period income or expense. As explained in paragraph 41 of IAS 21, these exchange differences have little or no direct effect on the present and future cash flows from operations. The translation is for presentation only. It is the functional currency statements that recognise exchange differences in current period income and expense.
- In the Basis for Conclusions to IAS 21, in paragraphs BC10–BC14, the IASB discusses whether the entity should (a) be permitted to present its financial statements in a currency other than the functional currency, (b) be allowed a limited choice of presentation currencies or (c) be permitted to present their financial statements in any currency. The IASB concluded that entities should be permitted to present in any currency or currencies. The IASB noted that some jurisdictions require the use of a specific presentation which will put constraints on some entities anyway. Further, many large groups have a large number of functional currencies and it is not clear which currency should be the presentation currency. In fact, in such circumstances management may prefer to use a number of presentation currencies.

When the AASB in Australia issued an exposure draft requesting responses to whether or not Australian Accounting Standards should require the use of the Australian dollar as the presentation currency, the following response was given by the Rinker Group Ltd (sourced from AASB 2003, p. 7):

> It is our view that mandated presentation currency is not now appropriate to the circumstances of Rinker and that adoption of an Australian converged standard which is identical to the proposals outlined in the improvement to IAS 21 would serve the users of our financial reports far better.
>
> While Rinker is domiciled in Australia, is listed on the Australian Stock Exchange and currently has a shareholder base which is approximately 80% Australian, it is overwhelmingly a US economic entity. Over 80% of its revenue, profit, and assets are in the US. Ninety-nine percent of its debt is in the US. The clearly stated strategy of the company is to grow in the US. One of the characteristics of the industry in which Rinker participates (heavy building materials) is that revenues and costs are totally denominated in the local currency (US revenue and costs are completely in US dollars; Australian revenue and costs are completely in Australian dollars). As a result, variances in US dollar/Australian dollar exchange rates represent purely translation variances with no economic impact on the intrinsic value of the entity . . .
>
> . . . mandated reporting in Australian dollars may provide misleading information to the users of financial reports, particularly in periods when there are significant movements in the US dollar/Australian dollar exchange rates . . .

In the AASB papers summarising these responses, the example shown in figure 28.4 was provided to illustrate the point being made by Rinker.

	2001	2002	2003
Debtors – $US	10	13	16
Actual growth	—	30%	23%
Exchange rate: A$1 = US$	0.5	0.56	0.67
Translate to presentation currency — A$			
Debtors — A$	20	23	24
Growth reported	—	15%	4%
Difference between growth rates	—	15%	19%

FIGURE 28.4 Illustration of the argument for mandated presentation currency
Source: AASB (2003, p. 4).

The financial statements in the functional currency show the financial performance and position of the entity in the currency that primarily affects the operations of that entity. The translation process should not result in a different performance/position being shown. Note the effect on the comparative analysis of the change in exchange rates. The only way that the problem is overcome is if, in comparing the 2003 results with the 2002 results, the 2002 results are translated at the 2003 exchange rate rather than the 2002 rate. In other words, comparative figures must be continuously updated for exchange rate changes. This is a similar process to that used in accounting for inflation where both the current year's and prior year's accounts must be presented in current year dollars as the buying power of the dollar changes due to inflation.

• Paragraphs BC15–BC23 of the Basis for Conclusions on IAS 21 discuss the translation method for translating from the functional currency to a different presentation currency. In paragraph BC16, the IASB emphasises that the translation process 'should not change the way in which the underlying items are measured'. Rather, the translation method should merely *express* the underlying amounts, as measured in the functional currency, in a different currency. In this regard, refer to figure 28.4. Note the following ratios:

	S$	NZ$
Current ratio	400 000/730 000 = 0.548	300 000/547 500 = 0.548
Debt to equity	370 000/360 000 = 1.03	277 500/270 000 = 1.03
Profit to sales	90 000/1 200 000 = 0.075	76 500/1 020 000 = 0.075
However, note:		
Profit to equity	90 000/360 000 = 0.25	76 500/270 000 = 0.28

The ratios are only ever going to be fully retained if all items in both the statement of profit or loss and other comprehensive income and the statement of financial position are translated at the closing rate. Using the exchange rates at the date of transaction means that retaining the ratios will not be possible. Paragraph BC17 notes that the IASB considered the method of translating all amounts at the most recent closing rate, noting that the method is simple, does not generate exchange differences and does not change ratios such as return on assets. However, the IASB prefers the method adopted in IAS 21, arguing that this method gives the same result if you translate the foreign entity's statements first into a functional currency and then into a different presentation currency or translate them directly into the presentation currency. For example, consider a Singaporean entity that has a functional currency of Hong Kong dollars but a presentation currency of Australian dollars. In relation to, say, a S$100 sales revenue transaction on 1 January 2013, whether you translate (a) using the spot rate for Singaporean dollars to Hong Kong dollars, and then translate this amount to Australian dollars using the spot rate on 1 January 2013 for Hong Kong dollars to Australian dollars; or (b) using the spot rate on 1 January 2013 for Singaporean dollars to Australian dollars, the answer is the same. This occurs because both the translation to functional currency and the translation to presentation currencies for statement of profit or loss and other comprehensive income items use the spot rate at the date of the transaction. In contrast, if the presentation translation used the closing rate for all accounts, a different answer would be obtained. However, the translation directly into the presentation currency does not isolate the exchange differences affecting income/expense that arise under a functional currency translation; rather it includes these exchange differences and those arising on a presentation translation into one amount affecting equity rather than income/expense.

28.8 CONSOLIDATING FOREIGN SUBSIDIARIES — WHERE LOCAL CURRENCY IS THE FUNCTIONAL CURRENCY

Paragraphs 44–7 of IAS 21 deal with matters relating to the consolidation of foreign subsidiaries. As noted in paragraph 45, normal consolidation procedures as set down in IFRS 10 apply to foreign subsidiaries. Where a parent establishes or sets up a subsidiary in a foreign country, the determination of what exists at acquisition date is relatively simple. This is because generally the investment recorded by the parent is equal to the initial share capital of the subsidiary. Where a parent entity obtains an overseas subsidiary by acquiring an already existing operation, the date of control determines the point of time at which historical rates for translation are determined.

For example, assume on 1 July 2012 Canberra Ltd acquires all the shares of Tokyo Ltd, a Japanese entity that has been in existence for many years. The group commences on the date of control, namely 1 July 2012. Tokyo Ltd may have some land that it acquired in 2003 for 1000 yen. The historical cost in the records of the company is 1000 yen. In other words, even though the overseas entity has held the land prior to the date that Canberra Ltd obtained control over the foreign entity, the date for measurement of the historical rate is the date of control. This is because, under IFRS 3 *Business Combinations*, all assets and liabilities of the subsidiary are measured at fair value at acquisition date.

28.8.1 Acquisition analysis

Assume that Canberra Ltd acquired all the shares of Tokyo Ltd at 1 July 2012 for A$30 000, when the exchange rate between the Australian dollar and the Japanese yen was 1:5. At acquisition date, the equity of that company consisted of:

	¥	A$
Share capital	100 000	20 000
Retained earnings	40 000	8 000

All the identifiable assets and liabilities of Tokyo Ltd were recorded at fair value except for plant, for which the fair value was ¥5000 (equal to A$1000) greater than the carrying amount. The plant has a further 5-year life. The Japanese tax rate is 20%. The Australian tax rate is 30%. At 30 June 2013, the exchange rate is A$1 = ¥6. The average rate for the year is A$1 = ¥5.5.

At acquisition date:	
Net fair value of identifiable assets and liabilities of Tokyo Ltd	= A$20 000 + $8 000 + A$1 000(1 − 20%) (BCVR — plant)
	= A$28 800
Consideration transferred	= A$30 000
Goodwill	= A$1 200
	= ¥(1 200 × 5)
	= ¥6 000

As noted in paragraph 47 of IAS 21, the goodwill is regarded as an asset of the subsidiary.

28.8.2 Business combination valuation entries

Goodwill

At acquisition date, the entry in Japanese yen is:

		¥	¥
Goodwill	Dr	6 000	
Business Combination Valuation Reserve	Cr		6 000

The valuation reserve continues to be translated at the rate at acquisition date as it is pre-acquisition equity. Assuming the functional currency is the yen, the financial statements of Tokyo Ltd would be translated into Australian dollars for presentation purposes. The goodwill is translated at the closing rate of 1:5, giving rise to a foreign currency translation loss, recognised in equity. Hence, on consolidation, the worksheet entry at 30 June 2013 is:

		A$	A$
Goodwill	Dr	1 000	
Foreign Currency Translation Reserve	Dr	200	
Business Combination Valuation Reserve	Cr		1 200

Plant

Similarly to goodwill, as noted in paragraph 47 of IAS 21, any fair value adjustments to the carrying amounts of assets and liabilities at acquisition date are treated as assets and liabilities of the foreign operation.

At acquisition date, the valuation entry is:

		A$	A$
Plant (¥5000/5)	Dr	1 000	
Deferred Tax Liability	Cr		200
Business Combination Valuation Reserve	Cr		800

At 30 June 2013, the valuation reserve is translated at the exchange rate at acquisition date and, as with goodwill, a foreign exchange loss is recognised — in this case on both the plant and the deferred tax liability:

		A$	A$
Plant (¥5000/6)	Dr	833	
Foreign Currency Translation Reserve	Dr	134	
Deferred Tax Liability (20% × 833)	Cr		167
Business Combination Valuation Reserve	Cr		800

The plant is depreciated at 20% per annum. This is based on the ¥5000 adjustment, giving a depreciation of ¥1000 per annum. The plant is translated at closing rates while the depreciation is translated at average rates.

Depreciation Expense [¥1000/5.5]	Dr	182	
Accumulated Depreciation [¥1000/6.0]	Cr		167
Foreign Currency Translation Reserve	Cr		15
Deferred Tax Liability [¥200/6.0 or 20% × 167]	Dr	33	
Foreign Currency Translation Reserve	Dr	3	
Income Tax Expense [¥200/5.5]	Cr		36

28.8.3 Pre-acquisition entry

The entry at acquisition date and at 30 June 2013 is:

Retained Earnings (1/7/12)	Dr	8 000	
Share Capital	Dr	20 000	
Business Combination Valuation Reserve [800 + 1200]	Dr	2 000	
Shares in Tokyo Ltd	Cr		30 000

28.8.4 Non-controlling interest (NCI)

The NCI receives a share of the recorded equity of the subsidiary as well as the valuation reserves raised on consolidation. The NCI also receives a share of the foreign currency translation reserve raised on the translation into the presentation currency. This share will need to be adjusted for any movements in that reserve as a result of movements raised via the revaluation process.

28.8.5 Intragroup transactions

As with any transactions within the group, the effects of transactions between a parent and its foreign subsidiaries, or between foreign subsidiaries, must be eliminated in full. Neither IAS 21 nor IFRS 10 provide specific guidance in relation to transactions with foreign entities. A key matter of concern is whether the adjustment should be affected by changes in the exchange rate. In this regard, note paragraphs 136 and 137 of the Basis for Conclusions relating to the US Statement of Financial Accounting Standards (SFAS) No. 52 *Foreign Currency Translation*:

> 136. An intercompany sale or transfer of inventory, machinery, etc., frequently produces an intercompany profit for the selling entity and, likewise, the acquiring entity's cost of the inventory, machinery, etc., includes a component of intercompany profit. The Board considered whether computation of the amount of intercompany profit to be eliminated should be based on exchange rates in effect on the date of the intercompany sale or transfer, or whether that computation should be based on exchange rates as of the date the asset (inventory, machinery, etc.) or the related expense (cost of sales, depreciation, etc.) is translated.
>
> 137. The Board decided that any intercompany profit occurs on the date of sale or transfer and that exchange rates in effect on that date or reasonable approximations thereof should be used to compute the amount of any intercompany profit to be eliminated. The effect of subsequent changes in exchange rates on the transferred asset or the related expense is viewed as being the result of changes in exchange rates rather than being attributable to intercompany profit.

It needs to be emphasised that the process of making the consolidation adjustments is to eliminate the *effects* of intragroup transactions. The exchange rate change is not an effect of the transaction but an economic effect on the group resulting from having assets in foreign entities.

Example 1: Parent sells inventory to foreign subsidiary

Assume Aust Ltd, an Australian company, owns 100% of the shares of a foreign operation, F Ltd. During the current period, when the exchange rate is F1 = $2, Aust Ltd sells $10 000 worth of inventory to F Ltd, at a before-tax profit of $2000. At the end of the period, F Ltd still has all inventory on hand. At the year-end reporting date, the exchange rate is F1 = $2.50. The Australian tax rate is 30%, while the tax rate in the foreign country is 20%.

Assuming the financial statements of F Ltd have been translated from the functional currency (F) to the presentation currency (Australian dollars), the consolidation worksheet adjustment entries for the intragroup transaction are:

Sales	Dr	10 000	
Cost of Sales	Cr		8 000
Inventory	Cr		2 000

Deferred Tax Asset	Dr	400	
Income Tax Expense	Cr		400
(20% × 2000)			

The above entries eliminate the sales and cost of sales as recorded by the parent. The inventory would have been recorded by F Ltd at F5000. The translation process at balance date would mean the F5000 of inventory would be translated using the closing rate of F1 = $2.50, giving a translated figure for inventory of $12 500. After passing the consolidation adjustment entry, inventory in the consolidated statement of financial position would be reported at $10 500 (i.e. $12 500 – $2000). This figure is greater than the original cost of $8000 due to the exchange rate change between the transaction date and the balance date. The US FASB would argue that no further entry is necessary as the effect of changes in the exchange rates on the transferred asset is viewed as the result of changes in exchange rates rather than intragroup profit.

Note that the tax rate used is that of the country holding the asset — in this case, the foreign country. This is because the adjustment for the tax effect is required because of the adjustment to the carrying amount of the inventory in the first journal entry. As the inventory is held by the foreign entity, it is the foreign country's tax rate that is applicable.

Example 2: Foreign subsidiary sells inventory to parent

Assume F Ltd, the foreign subsidiary, sells an item of inventory to Aust Ltd, the Australian parent, during the current period. The inventory had cost F Ltd F5000 and was sold to Aust Ltd for F7500. At the date of sale, the exchange rate was F1 = $2. The tax rate in Australia is 30%. All inventory was still on hand at the end of the period when the closing exchange rate was F1 = $2.50.

The consolidation worksheet entry is:

Sales	Dr	15 000	
Cost of Sales	Cr		10 000
Inventory	Cr		5 000
Deferred Tax Asset	Dr	1 500	
Income Tax Expense	Cr		1 500

Both sales and cost of sales as recorded by F Ltd are translated at the exchange rate existing at the date of the transaction, namely F1 = $2. The inventory sold to the parent is recorded by that entity at $15 000. The profit on sale is adjusted against inventory at the exchange rate existing at date of sale, giving an adjustment of $5000. Hence, in the consolidated statement of financial position at the end of the period, the inventory is reported at $10 000, equal to the original cost to F Ltd.

ILLUSTRATIVE EXAMPLE 28.2 Consolidation — functional currency is the subsidiary's local currency

On 1 January 2013, Kangaroos Ltd, an Australian company, acquired 80% of the shares of All Blacks Ltd, a New Zealand company, for A$2 498 000. The 2013 trial balance of All Blacks Ltd prepared in New Zealand dollars, which is also the functional currency, showed the following information:

	1 January 2013 NZ$'000	1 December 2013 NZ$'000
Revenue		6 450
Cost of sales		4 400
Gross profit		2 050
Expenses:		
Depreciation		280
Other		960
		1 240

	1 January 2013 NZ$'000	1 December 2013 NZ$'000
Profit before income tax		810
Income tax expense		120
Profit		690
Retained earnings at beginning of year		1 440
		2 130
Dividend paid		100
Dividend declared		100
		200
Retained earnings at end of year		1 930
Cash and receivables	1 000	1 760
Inventories	1 200	1 000
Land	800	800
Buildings	2 200	2 200
Accumulated depreciation	(900)	(990)
Equipment	1 130	1 330
Accumulated depreciation	(200)	(390)
Total assets	5 230	5 710
Current liabilities	590	420
Non-current liabilities	1 200	1 360
Total liabilities	1 790	1 780
Net assets	3 440	3 930
Share capital	2 000	2 000
Retained earnings	1 440	1 930
Total equity	3 440	3 930

Additional information
1. Direct exchange rates for the New Zealand dollar are as follows:

1 January 2013	1.20
1 July 2013	1.25
1 November 2013	1.35
31 December 2013	1.40
Average for the year	1.30

2. At 1 January 2013, all the assets and liabilities of All Blacks Ltd were recorded at fair value except for the land, for which the fair value was NZ$1 000 000, and the equipment, for which the fair value was $1 010 000. The undervalued equipment had a further 4-year life. The tax rate in New Zealand is 25%.
3. Additional equipment was acquired on 1 July 2013 for NZ$200 000 by issuing a note for NZ$160 000 and paying the balance in cash.
4. Sales and expenses were incurred evenly throughout the year.
5. Dividends of NZ$100 000 were paid on 1 July 2013.
6. On 1 November 2013, All Blacks Ltd sold inventory to Kangaroos Ltd for NZ$25 000. The inventory had cost All Blacks Ltd $20 000. Half of the inventory is still on hand at 31 December 2013. The Australian tax rate is 30%.

Required

1. Translate the New Zealand financial statements into the Australian dollar, which is the presentation currency.
2. Prepare the consolidation worksheet entries for consolidating the New Zealand subsidiary into the consolidated financial statements of Kangaroos Ltd. The partial goodwill method is used.

Solution

1. Translation into presentation currency

	NZ$	Rate	A$
Revenue	6 450	1/1.30	4 962
Cost of sales	4 400	1/1.30	3 385
Gross profit	2 050		1 577
Depreciation	280	1/1.30	215
Other	960	1/1.30	739
	1 240		954
Profit before tax	810		623
Income tax expense	120	1/1.30	92
Profit	690		531
Retained earnings as at 1/1/13	1 440	1/1.20	1 200
	2 130		1 731
Dividend paid	100	1/1.25	80
Dividend declared	100	1/1.40	71
	200		151
Retained earnings as at 31/12/13	1 930		1 580
Share capital	2 000	1/1.20	1 667
Non-current liabilities	1 360	1/1.40	971
Current liabilities	420	1/1.40	300
Foreign currency translation reserve			(439)
	5 710		4 079
Cash and receivables	1 760	1/1.40	1 257
Inventories	1 000	1/1.40	714
Land	800	1/1.40	572
Buildings	2 200	1/1.40	1 572
Accumulated depreciation	(990)	1/1.40	(707)
Equipment	1 330	1/1.40	950
Accumulated depreciation	(390)	1/1.40	(279)
	5 710		4 079

In relation to the foreign currency translation reserve:
- *The income and expense items are translated at dates of the transactions and not the closing rate:*
  The profit represents the net movements in income and expenses:

Profit	= NZ$690 000
Profit as translated	= A$530 800
Profit × closing rate	= NZ$690 000 × 1/1.40
	= A$492 857
Translation loss	= A$(37 943)
Dividend paid as translated	= A$80 000
Dividend paid at closing rate	= NZ$100 000 × 1/1.40
	= A$71 429
Translation gain	= A$8 571

- *In the case of a net investment in a foreign operation, translating the opening net assets at an exchange rate different from the closing rate:*

Net investment at 1 January 2013	= NZ$3 440 000
Net investment × opening rate	= NZ$3 440 000 × 1/1.20
	= A$2 866 667
Net investment × closing rate	= NZ$3 440 000 × 1/1.40
	= A$2 457 143
Translation loss	= A$(409 524)

- Total translation loss is A$(438 896) = (A$(37 943) + A$(409 524)) + $8 571

2. Consolidation worksheet entries: (in $000)

Net fair value of identifiable assets and
  liabilities of All Blacks Ltd

$= A\$[2\,000 + 1\,440 + 2\,00(1 \times 25\%) \text{ (land)}$
$+ 80(1 - 25\%) \text{ (equipment)}] \ 1/1.20$
$= A\$[1\,667 + 1\,200 + 125 + 50]$

Net fair value acquired
$= 80\% \times A\$[1\,667 + 1\,200 + 125 + 50]$
$= A\$[1\,334 + 960 + 100 + 40]$
$= A\$2\,434$

Consideration transferred $= A\$2\,498$
Goodwill acquired $= A\$64$
$= NZ\$77 \text{ (i.e. } 64 \times 1.20)$

(i) Business combination valuation entries

Land (200/1.40)	Dr	143	
Foreign Currency Translation Reserve	Dr	18	
Business Combination Valuation Reserve (150/1.20)	Cr		125
Deferred Tax Liability (50/1.40)	Cr		36
Accumulated Depreciation (200/1.40)	Dr	143	
Equipment (120/1.40)	Cr		86
Foreign Currency Translation Reserve	Dr	7	
Deferred Tax Liability (25% × (80/1.40))	Cr		14
Business Combination Valuation Reserve (60/1.20)	Cr		50
Depreciation Expense ([1/4 × 80]/1.30)	Dr	15	
Accumulated Depreciation ([1/4 × 80]/1.40)	Cr		14
Foreign Currency Translation Reserve	Cr		1
Deferred Tax Liability ([25% × 20]/1.30)	Dr	3.5	
Foreign Currency Translation Reserve	Dr	0.3	
Income Tax Expense ([25% × 20]/1.30)	Cr		3.8

(At acquisition the deferred tax liability was NZ$20 = 25% × NZ$80)

(ii) Pre-acquisition entry

Retained Earnings (1/1/13)	Dr	960	
Share Capital	Dr	1 334	
Business Combination Valuation Reserve	Dr	140	
Goodwill	Dr	64	
Shares in All Blacks Ltd	Cr		2 498
Foreign Currency Translation Reserve	Dr	9	
Goodwill (77/1.40 − 64)	Cr		9

(iii) Non-controlling interest
Share at acquisition date

Retained Earnings (1/1/10) (20% × 1200)	Dr	240	
Share Capital (20% × 1667)	Dr	333	
Business Combination Valuation Reserve (20% [125 + 50])	Dr	35	
NCI	Cr		608

Share from 1/1/13–31/12/13
(i) Current period profit — the share is based on the translated profit of the subsidiary

NCI Share of Profit	Dr	104	
NCI	Cr		104
(20% × A$[531 – (15 – 3.8)])			

(ii) The share of the foreign currency translation reserve is based on the amount of the reserve calculated as a result of the translation process adjusted by any changes in that reserve recognised in the valuation entries

NCI	Dr	93	
Foreign Currency Translation Reserve	Cr		93
(20% [439 + 18 + 7 + 1 + 0.3])			

(iii) Dividend paid

NCI	Dr	16	
Dividend Paid	Cr		16
(20% × A$80)			

(iv) Dividend declared

NCI	Dr	14	
Dividend Declared	Cr		14
(20% × A$71)			

Intragroup transactions:
(i) Dividends

Dividend Revenue	Dr	64	
Dividend Paid	Cr		64
(80% × 100/1.25)			
Dividend Revenue	Dr	57	
Dividend Receivable	Cr		57
(80% × 100/1.40)			
Dividend Payable	Dr	57	
Dividend Declared	Cr		57

(ii) Sale of inventory: subsidiary to parent

Sales Revenue (25/1.35)	Dr	19	
Cost of Sales	Cr		17
Inventory (1/2 × 5 × 1/1.35)	Cr		2
Deferred Tax Asset (30% × 2)	Dr	0.6	
Income Tax Expense	Cr		0.6

(iii) Adjustment to NCI

NCI	Dr	0.28	
NCI Share of Profit	Cr		0.28
(20% × (2 – 0.6))			

LO9 28.9 CONSOLIDATING FOREIGN SUBSIDIARIES — WHERE FUNCTIONAL CURRENCY IS THAT OF THE PARENT ENTITY

In this circumstance, the subsidiary's financial statements are prepared in the local currency, and, as the parent's currency is the functional currency, they are translated into the parent's currency. The main difference in preparing the consolidated financial statements in this case is in the valuation entries. This is because the translation of non-monetary assets differs when the translation is for presentation purposes rather than for functional currency purposes.

Under the method described in paragraph 23 of IAS 21, the non-monetary assets of the subsidiary are translated using exchange rates at the date of the transaction (i.e. historical rates). In contrast, in illustrative example 28.2, where the translation is based on paragraph 39 of IAS 21, the non-monetary assets are translated at the closing rate.

Using the information in illustrative example 28.2:

- at acquisition date, 1 January 2013, goodwill of the subsidiary was measured to be NZ$96
- the land had a fair value–carrying amount difference of NZ$200
- the equipment had a fair value–carrying amount difference of NZ$80, with an expected remaining useful life of 25%
- the NZ tax rate is 25%
- the direct exchange rates for the NZ dollar were:

1 January 2013	1.20
1 July 2013	1.25
1 November 2013	1.35
31 December 2013	1.40
Average for the year	1.30

The business combination valuation entries are then:

The goodwill balance is translated at the historical rate:

Goodwill (96/1.20)	Dr	80	
Business Combination Valuation Reserve (96/1.20)	Cr		80

The land is translated at the historical rate, but the deferred tax liability is translated at the closing rate. As the net monetary assets held at the beginning of the period are affected by changes in the exchange rate, an exchange gain is recognised:

Land (200/1.20)	Dr	167	
Foreign Exchange Gain	Cr		6
Business Combination Valuation Reserve (150/1.20)	Cr		125
Deferred Tax Liability (50/1.40)	Cr		36

The equipment and related accumulated depreciation are translated at the historical rate, while the deferred tax liability is translated at the closing rate, giving rise to a foreign exchange gain.

Subsequent depreciation is based on the historical rate:

Accumulated Depreciation (200/1.20)	Dr	167	
Equipment (120/1.20)	Cr		100
Foreign Exchange Gain	Cr		3
Deferred Tax Liability ((25% × 80)1.40))	Cr		14
Business Combination Valuation Reserve (60/1.20)	Cr		50
Depreciation Expense ([1/4 × 80]/1.20)	Dr	17	
Accumulated Depreciation ([1/4 × 80]/1.20)	Cr		17

Deferred Tax Liability ([25% × 20]/1.40)	Dr	3.5	
Foreign Currency Exchange Loss	Dr	0.3	
Income Tax Expense ([25% × 20]/1.30)	Cr		3.8

(At acquisition the deferred tax liability was NZ$20 = 25% × NZ$80)

28.10 NET INVESTMENT IN A FOREIGN OPERATION

Paragraph 15 of IAS 21 notes that the investment in a foreign operation may consist of more than just the ownership of shares in that operation. An entity may have a monetary item that is receivable or payable to the foreign subsidiary. According to paragraph 15, where there is an item for which settlement is neither planned nor likely to occur in the foreseeable future, it is in substance a part of the entity's net investment in that foreign operation. These items include long-term receivables and payables but not trade receivables or payables.

Consider the situation where an Australian parent entity has made a long-term loan of 100 000 yen to a Japanese subsidiary when the exchange rate is $2 = ¥1. The parent entity records a receivable of $200 000, while the subsidiary records a payable of ¥100 000. If during the following financial period the exchange rate changes to $3 = ¥1, in accordance with paragraph 28 of IAS 21 the Australian parent passes the following entry in its own records:

| Loan Receivable | Dr | 100 000 | |
| Exchange Gain | Cr | | 100 000 |

This results in the receivable being recorded at $300 000. The subsidiary does not pass any entry because it still owes ¥100 000. On translation of the subsidiary into the presentation currency (the Australian dollar), the payable is translated into $300 000. On consolidation of the subsidiary, both the payable and the receivable are eliminated. However, because the receivable is regarded as part of the parent's net investment in the subsidiary, the accounting for the exchange gain is in accord with paragraph 32 of IAS 21:

> Exchange differences arising on a monetary item that forms part of a reporting entity's net investment in a foreign operation (see paragraph 15) shall be recognised in profit or loss in the separate financial statements of the reporting entity or the individual financial statements of the foreign operation, as appropriate. In the financial statements that include the foreign operation and the reporting entity (e.g. consolidated financial statements where the foreign operation is a subsidiary), such exchange differences shall be recognised initially in a separate component of equity and recognised in profit or loss on disposal of the net investment in accordance with paragraph 48.

Hence, the exchange gain of $100 000 recognised as income by the parent must, on consolidation, be reclassified to the foreign currency translation reserve raised as part of the translation process. Hence, in the consolidation worksheet the adjustment entry is:

| Exchange Gain | Dr | 100 000 | |
| Foreign Currency Translation Reserve | Cr | | 100 000 |

28.11 DISCLOSURE

Paragraphs 51–57 contain the disclosure requirements under IAS 21. In particular, an entity must disclose:
- the amount of exchange differences included in profit or loss for the period
- net exchange differences classified in a separate component of equity, and a reconciliation of the amount of such exchange differences at the beginning and end of the period
- when the presentation currency of the parent entity is different from the functional currency:
  - the fact that they are different
  - the functional currency
  - the reason for using a different presentation currency
- when there is a change in the functional currency, the fact that such a change has occurred.

Some examples of accounting policies notes in relation to currency translation are given in figure 28.5.

FIGURE 28.5 Accounting policies on foreign currency translation

Example 1: Nokia Corporation, a Finnish limited liability company domiciled in Helsinki
Functional and presentation currency
The financial statements of all Group entities are measured using the currency of the primary economic environment in which the entity operates (functional currency). The consolidated financial statements are presented in Euro, which is the functional and presentation currency of the Parent Company.

Transactions in foreign currencies
Transactions in foreign currencies are recorded at the rates of exchange prevailing at the dates of the individual transactions. For practical reasons, a rate that approximates the actual rate at the date of the transaction is often used. At the end of the accounting period, the unsettled balances on foreign currency assets and liabilities are valued at the rates of exchange prevailing at the end of the accounting period. Foreign exchange gains and losses arising from statement of financial position items, as well as changes in fair value in the related hedging instruments, are reported in financial income and expenses. For non-monetary items, such as shares, the unrealized foreign exchange gains and losses are recognized in other comprehensive income.

Foreign Group companies
In the consolidated accounts, all income and expenses of foreign subsidiaries are translated into Euro at the average foreign exchange rates for the accounting period. All assets and liabilities of Group companies, where the functional currency is other than euro, are translated into euro at the year-end foreign exchange rates. Differences resulting from the translation of income and expenses at the average rate and assets and liabilities at the closing rate are recognized in other comprehensive income as translation differences within consolidated shareholders' equity. On the disposal of all or part of a foreign Group company by sale, liquidation, repayment of share capital or abandonment, the cumulative amount or proportionate share of the translation difference is recognized as income or as expense in the same period in which the gain or loss on disposal is recognized.
Source: Nokia (2011, pp. 27–8).

Example 2: Bayer Group, which has headquarters in Germany and activities worldwide
Foreign currency translation
The financial statements of the individual companies for inclusion in the consolidated financial statements are prepared in their respective functional currencies. A company's functional currency is that of the economic environment in which it primarily generates and expends cash. The majority of consolidated companies carry out their activities autonomously from a financial, economic and organizational point of view, and their functional currencies are therefore the respective local currencies.

In the financial statement of the individual consolidated companies, receivables and payables in currencies other than the respective functional currency are translated at closing rates, irrespective of whether they are exchange-hedged. Exchange rate differences from valuation of balances in foreign currencies are recognized in income.

In the consolidated financial statements, the assets and liabilities of companies outside the Eurozone at the start and end of the year are translated into euros at closing rates. All changes occurring during the year and all income and expense items are translated into euros at average monthly rates. Components of stockholders' equity are translated at the historical exchange rates prevailing at the respective dates of their first-time recognition in Group equity.

The exchange differences arising between the resulting amounts and those obtained by translating at closing rates are reported separately as 'Exchange differences on translation of operations outside the eurozone' or as 'Exchange differences.' When a company is deconsolidated, such exchange differences are removed from equity and recognized in the income statement.

The exchange rates for major currencies against the euro varied as follows:

€1		Closing rate		Average rate	
		2009	2010	2009	2010
ARS	Argentina	5.47	5.31	5.20	5.18
BRL	Brazil	2.51	2.23	2.77	2.33

(continued)

FIGURE 28.5 *(continued)*

€1		Closing rate		Average rate	
		2009	**2010**	**2009**	**2010**
CAD	Canada	1.51	1.33	1.59	1.36
CHF	Switzerland	1.48	1.25	1.51	1.38
CNY	China	9.84	8.82	9.52	8.96
GBP	United Kingdom	0.89	0.86	0.89	0.86
JPY	Japan	133.16	108.65	130.31	116.04
MXN	Mexico	18.92	16.55	18.79	16.72
USD	United States	1.44	1.34	1.39	1.32

Source: Bayer (2010, pp. 155–6).

Notice in figure 28.5, that both Nokia and Bayer provide information about the functional currencies of the entities within their respective groups, which relates to the disclosures required by paragraph 53 of IAS 21.

Illustrative disclosures relating to paragraph 52 of IAS 21 are given in figure 28.6.

NOTE			IAS 21 paragraph
Movements in reserves			
Foreign Currency Translation Reserve	**2013**	**2012**	*52(b)*
Balance at beginning of period	(2 420)	(3 020)	
Exchange differences arising on translation of overseas operations	(540)	600	
Balance at end of period	(2 960)	(2 420)	
Profit from operations			
	2010	**2009**	
Profit from operations has been arrived at after charging:			
Amortisation	x	x	
Research and development costs	x	x	
Net foreign exchange losses/(gains)	765	(346)	*52(a)*

FIGURE 28.6 Disclosures required by paragraph 50 of IAS 21

SUMMARY

A parent entity may have investments in subsidiaries that are incorporated in countries other than that of the parent. The foreign operation will record its transactions generally in the local currency. However, the local currency may not be that of the economy that determines the pricing of those transactions. To this end, IAS 21 requires the financial statements of a foreign operation to be translated into its functional currency, being the currency of the primary economic environment in which the entity operates. Determination of the functional currency is a matter of judgement, and the choice of the appropriate currency requires an analysis of the underlying economics of the foreign operation. A further problem addressed by IAS 21 is where the financial statements of the foreign operation need to be presented in a currency different from the functional currency. IAS 21 then provides principles relating to the translation of a set of financial statements into the presentation currency. Whenever a translation process is undertaken, foreign exchange translation adjustments arise. It is necessary to determine whether these adjustments are taken to profit or loss or to other comprehensive income.

Where the foreign operation is a subsidiary, having translated the financial statements of the foreign operation into the currency in which the consolidated financial statements are to be presented, consolidation worksheet adjustments are required as a part of the normal consolidation process. In assessing the assets and liabilities held by the subsidiary at acquisition date, as well as any goodwill or gain on bargain purchase arising as a result of the acquisition, the effects of movements in exchange rates on these assets and liabilities must be taken into consideration. The consolidation adjustments are affected by the process of translation used to translate the foreign entity's financial statements from the local currency into either the functional currency or the presentation currency.

Discussion questions[1]

1. What is the purpose of translating financial statements from one currency to another?
2. What is meant by 'functional currency'?
3. What is the rationale behind the choice of an exchange rate as an entity's functional currency?
4. What guidelines are used to determine the functional currency of an entity?
5. How are statement of profit or loss and other comprehensive income items translated from the local currency into the functional currency?
6. How are statement of financial position items translated from the local currency into the functional currency?
7. How are foreign exchange gains and losses calculated when translating from local currency to functional currency?
8. What is meant by 'presentation currency'?
9. How are statement of profit or loss and other comprehensive income items translated from functional currency to presentation currency?
10. How are statement of financial position items translated from functional currency to presentation currency?
11. What causes a foreign currency translation reserve to arise?
12. Why are gains/losses on translation taken to a foreign currency translation reserve rather than to profit or loss for the period?
13. In relation to the following case situations, discuss the choice of a functional currency.

   Case 1
   A Malaysian operation manufactures a product using Malaysian materials and labour. Specialised equipment and senior operations staff are supplied by its Australian parent. Reimbursement invoices for these services are denominated in the Malaysian ringgit. The product is sold in the Malaysian market at a price, denominated in Malaysian ringgit, which is determined by competition with similar locally produced products. The foreign operation retains sufficient cash to meet wages and day-to-day operating costs with the remainder being remitted to the Australian parent. The receipt of dividends from the foreign operation is important to the parent's cash management function. Long-term financing is arranged and serviced by the parent.

   Case 2
   A Korean operation is a wholly owned subsidiary of an Australian company which regards the operation as a long-term investment, and thus takes no part in the day-to-day decision making of the operation. The operation purchases parts from various non-related Australian manufacturers for assembly by Korean labour. The finished product is exported to a number of countries but Australia is the major market. Consequently, sales prices are determined by competition within Australia.

14. In relation to the following case situations, discuss whether you regard the reporting entity as exposed to foreign exchange gains and losses in relation to the foreign entity.

   Case 1
   A foreign operation extracts mineral ores that are shipped to Australia for processing at the parent entity's smelters. All senior personnel at the foreign operation are parent entity employees. Monthly invoices for ore supplied to the parent are denominated in US dollars. The parent entity pays these invoices with US dollars obtained by selling its finished product to US customers, thus taking advantage of a natural hedge. Payments to the foreign operation cover all running costs but long-term financing is provided by the parent entity.

---

[1] *Note:* The cases in discussion questions 13–15 were used in the project by Radford (1996) to test the implementation of AASB 1012 by Australian companies.

Case 2

A foreign operation extracts a mineral product that it exports worldwide. The sales price is subject to daily fluctuations. The Australian parent regards the operation as an investment only but the extreme volatility of the foreign operation's sales prices impacts on the price of the parent's shares on the Australian securities exchange because the investment in the foreign operation is one of the parent's significant assets.

15. In relation to the following case situations, discuss which currency is the functional currency of the foreign entity.

Case 1

An Indonesian operation manufactures a product using Indonesian materials and labour. Patented processes and senior operations staff are supplied by its Australian parent. Reimbursement invoices for these services are denominated in Indonesian rupiah. The product is sold in the Indonesian market at a price, denominated in rupiah, that is determined by competition with similar locally produced products. The Indonesian operation remits all revenue to the Australian parent, retaining only sufficient cash to meet wages and day-to-day operating costs. The receipt of cash from the Indonesian operation is important to the parent's cash management function. Long-term financing is arranged and serviced by the parent.

Case 2

A New Zealand operation is a wholly owned subsidiary of an Australian company. The parent regards the operation as a long-term investment and all financial and operational decisions are made by New Zealand management. The New Zealand operation purchases parts from various non-related Australian manufacturers for assembly in New Zealand. The finished product is exported to a number of countries with Australia as the major market. Consequently, sales prices are determined by competition within Australia.

16. Foreign Ltd is a Queensland software developer that specialises in software that controls the operations of open cut mining. To exploit opportunities in the US market, the firm has established a fully owned subsidiary operating in Atlanta, Georgia. The operations of the subsidiary (Opencut Inc.) essentially involve the marketing of software initially developed in Australia but which is further developed by the US subsidiary to suit the special requirements of particular US customers. Foreign Ltd does not charge Opencut Inc. for the software successfully amended and marketed in the United States. At this stage no dividends have been paid by Opencut Inc.; however, it is expected that dividends will commence within 12 months. With respect to working capital, Opencut Inc. has a 'revolving credit' agreement (overdraft facility) with the Bank of Georgia, which has been guaranteed by the Australian parent. Discuss the process of translating the financial statements of Opencut Inc. for consolidation with Foreign Ltd.

17. The accounts listed below are for a wholly owned foreign subsidiary. In the space provided indicate the exchange rate that would be used to translate the accounts into Australian dollars. Use the following letters to indicate the appropriate exchange rate:
H — historical exchange rate
C — current exchange rate at the end of the current period
A — average exchange rate for the current period.

	Australian dollar is the functional currency	Foreign currency is the functional currency
Cash		
Prepaid expenses		
Equipment		
Goodwill		
Accounts payable		
Inventory — at cost		
Inventory — at net realisable value		
Capital		
Sales		
Depreciation expense		

18. Victory Ltd is an Australian company with two overseas subsidiaries, one in Indonesia and the other in South Korea. The Indonesian subsidiary has as its major activity the distribution in Indonesia

of Victory Ltd's products. It has been agreed that the subsidiary will, for a period of time, retain all profits in order to expand its distribution network in Indonesia. In the past it has remitted most of its profits to the Australian parent company.

The South Korean subsidiary has been established to manufacture a range of products for the South-East Asian market. There is also an expectation that it could in the future become the major manufacturing plant for Victory Ltd and provide a supply of products for the Australian market.

Based on the above, determine the functional currency of the foreign subsidiaries. Explain your choice.

19. Discuss the differences in the translation process when translating from a local currency to a functional currency compared with translating from a functional currency to a presentation currency.
20. Discuss the use of a foreign currency translation reserve to account for movements in exchange rates compared with taking gains/losses as a result of movements in exchange rates directly to the statement of profit or loss and other comprehensive income.
21. Explain what is meant by the 'net investment in a foreign operation'. Provide an example and explain the accounting implications.

Exercises

STAR RATING ★ BASIC ★★ MODERATE ★★★ DIFFICULT

| Exercise 28.1 | **TRANSLATION INTO FUNCTIONAL CURRENCY** |

★ Auckland Ltd is a manufacturer of sheepskin products in New Zealand. It is a fully owned subsidiary of a Hong Kong company, China Ltd. The following assets are held by Auckland Ltd at 30 June 2013:

Plant	Cost NZ$	Useful life (years)	Acquisition date	Exchange rate on acquisition date (NZ$1 = HK$)
Tanner	40 000	5	10/8/09	5.4
Benches	20 000	8	8/3/11	5.8
Presses	70 000	7	6/10/12	6.2

Plant is depreciated on a straight-line basis, with zero residual values. All assets acquired in the first half of a month are allocated a full month's depreciation.

Inventory:
- At 1 July 2012, the inventory on hand of $25 000 was acquired during the last month of the 2011–12 period.
- Inventory acquired during the 2012–13 period was acquired evenly throughout the period. Total purchases of $420 000 was acquired during that period.
- The inventory of $30 000 on hand at 30 June 2013 was acquired during June 2013.

Relevant exchange rates (quoted as NZ$1 = HK$) are as follows:

Average for June 2012	7.2
1 July 2012	7.0
Average for 2012–13	7.5
Average for June 2013	7.7
30 June 2013	7.8

Required

1. Assuming the functional currency for Auckland Ltd is the NZ$, calculate:
   (a) the balances for the plant items and inventory in HK$ at 30 June 2013
   (b) the depreciation and cost of sales amounts in the statement of profit or loss and other comprehensive income for 2012–13.
2. Assuming the functional currency is the HK$, calculate:
   (a) the balances for the plant items and inventory in HK$ at 30 June 2013
   (b) the depreciation and cost of sales amounts in the statement of profit or loss and other comprehensive income for 2012–13.
3. Discuss the differences in the results achieved in requirements 1 and 2 above, and why the choice of the functional currency gives a different set of accounting numbers.

TRANSLATION INTO PRESENTATION CURRENCY

★★ January Ltd, an Australian company, acquired all the issued shares of July Ltd, a US company, on 1 January 2014. At this date, the net assets of July Ltd are shown below.

	US$
Property, plant and equipment	155 000
Accumulated depreciation	(30 000)
	125 000
Cash	10 000
Inventory	20 000
Accounts receivable	10 000
Total assets	165 000
Accounts payable	15 000
Net assets	150 000

The trial balance of July Ltd at 31 December 2014 was:

	US$ Dr	US$ Cr
Share capital		100 000
Retained earnings		50 000
Accounts payable		42 000
Sales		90 000
Accumulated depreciation — plant and equipment		45 000
Property, plant and equipment	155 000	
Accounts receivable	40 000	
Inventory	45 000	
Cash	12 000	
Cost of sales	30 000	
Depreciation	15 000	
Other expenses	30 000	
	327 000	327 000

Additional information
1. No property, plant and equipment were acquired in the 2014 period.
2. All sales and expenses were acquired evenly throughout the period. The inventory on hand at the end of the year was acquired during December 2014.
3. Exchange rates were (A$1 = US$):

1 January 2014	0.52
31 December 2014	0.60
Average for December 2014	0.58
Average for 2014	0.56

4. The functional currency for July Ltd is the US dollar.

Required

1. Prepare the financial statements of July Ltd at 31 December 2014 in the presentation currency of Australian dollars.
2. Verify the translation adjustment.
3. Discuss the differences that would occur if the functional currency of July Ltd was the Australian dollar.
4. If the functional currency was the Australian dollar, calculate the translation adjustment.

TRANSLATION OF FINANCIAL STATEMENTS INTO FUNCTIONAL CURRENCY

★★ Faber Ltd, a company incorporated in Singapore, acquired all the issued shares of Lantau Ltd, a Hong Kong company, on 1 July 2012. The trial balance of Lantau Ltd at 30 June 2013 was:

	HK$ Dr	HK$ Cr
Share capital		800 000
Retained earnings (1/7/12)		240 000
General reserve		100 000
Payables		160 000
Deferred tax liability		120 000
Current tax liability		20 000
Provisions		80 000
Sales		610 000
Proceeds on sale of land		250 000
Accumulated depreciation — plant		340 000
Plant	920 000	
Land	400 000	
Cash	240 000	
Accounts receivable	300 000	
Inventory at 1 July 2012	60 000	
Purchases	260 000	
Depreciation — plant	156 000	
Carrying amount of land sold	200 000	
Income tax expense	50 000	
Other expenses	134 000	
	2 720 000	2 720 000

Additional information

1. Exchange rates based on equivalence to HK$1 were:

	S$
1 July 2012	0.20
8 October 2012	0.25
1 December 2012	0.28
1 January 2013	0.30
2 April 2013	0.27
30 June 2013	0.22
Average during last quarter 2012–13	0.24
Average 2012–13	0.26

2. Inventory was acquired evenly throughout the year. The closing inventory of HK$60 000 was acquired during the last quarter of the year.
3. Sales and other expenses occurred evenly throughout the year.
4. The Hong Kong tax rate is 20%.
5. The land on hand at the beginning of the year was sold on 8 October 2012. The land on hand at the end of the year was acquired on 1 December 2012.
6. Movements in plant over 2012–13 were:

Plant at 1 July 2012	HK$600 000
Acquisitions — 8 October 2012	200 000
— 2 April 2013	120 000
Plant at 30 June 2013	920 000

Depreciation on plant is measured at 20% per annum on cost. Where assets are acquired during a month, a full month's depreciation is charged.

7. The functional currency of the Hong Kong operation is the Singaporean dollar.

Required

1. Prepare the financial statements of Lantau Ltd in Singaporean dollars at 30 June 2013.
2. Verify the translation adjustment.

Exercise 28.4 CONSOLIDATION WORKSHEET ENTRIES FOR FOREIGN SUBSIDIARY

★★ Using the information in exercise 28.3, assume that Faber Ltd acquired the shares in Lantau Ltd for HK$1 250 000. All the identifiable assets and liabilities of Lantau Ltd at acquisition date were recorded at amounts equal to fair value except for the following assets:

	HK$ Carrying amount	HK$ Fair value
Inventory	60 000	70 000
Land	200 000	250 000
Plant (cost HK$800 000)	600 000	640 000

The plant is expected to have a further 4-year life. The inventory is all sold by 30 June 2013. The tax rate in Hong Kong is 20%.

Required

Prepare the consolidation worksheet entries for the preparation of the consolidated financial statements of Faber Ltd at 30 June 2013.

Exercise 28.5 DIFFERENT FUNCTIONAL CURRENCIES, CONSOLIDATION ADJUSTMENTS

★★ On 1 July 2012, an Australian company, Perth Ltd, acquired all the issued capital of a Swedish company, Lund Ltd, for $997 400. At the date of acquisition, the equity of Lund Ltd consisted of:

	Krona (K)
Share capital	800 000
General reserve	200 000
Retained earnings	635 000

All the identifiable assets and liabilities of Lund Ltd were recorded at fair value except for plant for which the fair value was K100 000 greater than carrying amount. The plant has a further 5-year life.

The internal financial statements of Lund Ltd at 30 June 2013 are shown below.

Statement of Profit or Loss and Other Comprehensive Income		
	K	K
Revenues		2 585 000
Cost of sales:		
Opening stock	600 000	
Purchases	1 800 000	
	2 400 000	
Closing stock	580 000	1 820 000
Gross profit		765 000
Expenses:		
Depreciation	125 000	
Other	270 000	395 000

	K	K
Profit before income tax		370 000
Income tax expense		200 000
Profit for the period		170 000
Retained earnings as at 1 July 2012		635 000
		805 000
Dividend paid		100 000
Retained earnings as at 30 June 2013		705 000

Statement of Financial Position

1/7/12 K		30/6/13 K
	Current assets	
500 000	Cash and receivables	500 000
600 000	Inventory	580 000
1 100 000	Total current assets	1 080 000
	Non-current assets	
300 000	Land	300 000
700 000	Buildings	700 000
(100 000)	Accumulated depreciation	(130 000)
800 000	Plant	900 000
(235 000)	Accumulated depreciation	(330 000)
1 465 000	Total non-current assets	1 440 000
2 565 000	Total assets	2 520 000
350 000	Current liabilities	235 000
	Non-current liabilities	
580 000	Notes – issued September 2012	580 000
930 000	Total liabilities	815 000
1 635 000	Net assets	1 705 000
	Equity	
800 000	Share capital	800 000
200 000	General reserve	200 000
635 000	Retained earnings	705 000
1 635 000	Total equity	1 705 000

Additional information

1. Exchange rates for the Swedish krona were as follows:

	1 krona = $A
1 July 2012	0.54
Average 2012–13	0.52
January 2013	0.52
30 June 2013	0.50
Average for the last 4 months of the 2012–13 period	0.51

2. Lund Ltd acquired additional plant for K100 000 on 1 January 2013 by issuing a note for K80 000 and paying the balance in cash.
3. Sales, purchases and other expenses were incurred evenly through the year.

4. Depreciation for the period in krona was as follows:

Buildings	30 000
Plant	
— acquired before 1 July 2012	85 000
— acquired 1 January 2013	10 000

5. The inventory is valued on a FIFO basis. The opening stock was acquired when the exchange rate was 0.54, and the closing stock was acquired during the last 4 months of the 2012–13 period.

6. Dividends of K50 000 were paid on 2 July 2012 and 1 January 2013.

7. The tax rate for Lund Ltd is 25%.

Required

1. Translate the accounts of the foreign subsidiary, Lund Ltd, into Australian dollars at 30 June 2013, assuming:

(a) the functional currency is the Swedish krona, and the presentation currency is the Australian dollar

(b) the functional currency is the Australian dollar, as is the presentation currency.

2. Verify the translation adjustments in requirement 1.

3. Prepare, for each of (a) and (b) above, the business combination valuation and pre-acquisition entries for the preparation of the consolidated financial statements at 30 June 2013.

Exercise 28.6 | **CONSOLIDATION OF FOREIGN CURRENCY TRANSLATION RESERVE**

★★ On 1 July 2011, Kangaroo Ltd, an Australian company, acquired shares in Panda Ltd, a company based in Hong Kong. At this date, the equity of Panda Ltd was:

	HK$
Share capital	200 000
General reserve	100 000
Retained earnings	300 000

At 30 June 2012 and 2013, the retained earnings balances of Panda Ltd were HK$400 000 and HK$450 000 respectively. All transactions occurred evenly throughout these years. The internal financial statements of the two companies at 30 June 2014 were as follows:

Statement of Profit or Loss and Other Comprehensive Income		
	Kangaroo Ltd A$	Panda Ltd HK$
Sales	700 000	595 000
Cost of sales	300 000	400 000
	400 000	195 000
Expenses	210 200	100 000
	189 800	95 000
Dividend revenue	12 000	—
Profit before income tax	201 800	95 000
Tax expense	51 800	20 000
Profit	150 000	75 000
Retained earnings as at 1/7/13	750 000	450 000
	900 000	525 000
Dividend paid	100 000	25 000
Retained earnings as at 30/6/14	800 000	500 000

Statement of Financial Position		
	Kangaroo Ltd **A$**	**Panda Ltd** **HK$**
Current assets	311 520	250 000
Shares in Panda Ltd	288 480	—
Property, plant and equipment (net)	700 000	500 000
Patents and trademarks	100 000	150 000
Total assets	1 400 000	900 000
Liabilities	100 000	100 000
Net assets	1 300 000	800 000
Equity:		
Share capital	500 000	200 000
General reserve	—	100 000
Retained earnings	800 000	500 000
Total equity	1 300 000	800 000

Additional information
1. The dividend paid by Panda Ltd was paid on 1 May 2014.
2. Some relevant exchange rates are:

1 July 2011	HK$1 = $A0.80
Average 2011–12	0.82
1 July 2012	0.85
Average 2012–13	0.88
1 July 2013	0.90
Average 2013–14	0.85
1 May 2014	0.80
30 June 2014	0.78

Required

Translate the financial statements of Panda Ltd as at 30 June 2014 into the presentation currency of Australian dollars, assuming that the functional currency is the Hong Kong dollar.

| **Exercise 28.7** | **TRANSLATION INTO PRESENTATION CURRENCY, CONSOLIDATION ADJUSTMENTS** |

★★★ Dragon Ltd is an international company resident in Singapore. It acquired 80% of the issued shares of an Australian company, Swan Ltd, on 1 July 2012 for A$560 000. All the identifiable assets and liabilities of Swan Ltd were recorded at fair value except for the following:

	Carrying amount **A$**	**Fair value** **A$**
Plant (net)	180 000	240 000
Inventory	68 000	90 000
Brand names	0	140 000

The plant is considered to have a remaining life of 5 years, with depreciation being calculated on a straight-line basis. All inventory on hand at acquisition date was sold within the following 12-month period. The brand names are considered to have an indefinite life, and are adjusted only if impaired.

At 30 June 2013, the following information was available about the two companies:

	Dragon Ltd S$	Swan Ltd A$
Share capital	560 000	350 000
Retained earnings as at 1/7/12	330 000	170 000
Provisions	45 000	30 000
Payables	14 000	40 000
Sales	620 000	310 000
Dividend revenue	6 400	0
Accumulated depreciation — plant	210 000	160 000
	1 785 400	1 060 000
Cash	92 100	30 000
Accounts receivable	145 300	115 000
Inventory	110 000	80 000
Shares in Swan Ltd	336 000	0
Buildings (net)	84 000	220 000
Plant	420 000	400 000
Cost of sales	390 000	120 000
Depreciation — plant	85 000	40 000
Tax expense	23 000	15 000
Other expenses	50 000	10 000
Dividend paid	20 000	10 000
Dividend provided	30 000	20 000
	1 785 400	1 060 000

Additional information
1. Sales, purchases and other expenses were incurred evenly throughout the 2012–13 period. The dividend was paid by Swan Ltd on 1 January 2013, while the dividend was declared on 30 June 2013.
2. The tax rate in Australia is 30% and the tax rate in Singapore is 20%.
3. Swan Ltd acquired A$100 000 of additional new plant on 1 January 2013. Of the depreciation charged in the 2012–13 period, A$8000 related to the new plant.
4. The rates of exchange between the Australian dollar and the Singapore dollar were (expressed as A$1 = S$):

1 July 2012	0.60
1 December 2012	0.64
1 January 2013	0.68
30 June 2013	0.70
Average for the 2012–13 period	0.65

5. The functional currency of the Australian subsidiary is the Australian dollar.
6. On 1 January 2013, Swan Ltd sold some inventory to Dragon Ltd for A$20 000. The inventory had cost the subsidiary $18 000. Only 10% of this inventory remained unsold by the parent entity at 30 June 2013.

Required

1. Translate the financial statements of Swan Ltd into Singapore dollars for inclusion in the consolidated financial statements of Dragon Ltd.
2. Verify the translation adjustment.
3. Prepare the consolidation worksheet entries necessary for the preparation of the consolidated financial statements at 30 June 2013, assuming the use of the partial goodwill method.

Exercise 28.8 **TRANSLATION INTO FUNCTIONAL CURRENCY, INTRAGROUP TRANSACTIONS**

★★★ On 1 January 2012, Surfers Ltd formed a company, Paradise Ltd, in the United States to sell Australian products such as boomerangs and cuddly koalas and kangaroos. The initial capital was US$500 000. On

1 February 2012, a lease was signed on a shop for US$20 000, payable on the first day of each month. On 15 February, store furnishings were acquired for $448 000; these were expected to have a useful life of 4 years. On 10 June 2012, more fittings were acquired at a cost of $124 000, again with an expected life of 4 years.

Additional information
1. Where non-current assets are acquired during a month, a full month's depreciation is applied.
2. The tax rate in the United States is 20%, while the tax rate in Australia is 30%.
3. The functional currency for Paradise Ltd is the Australian dollar.
4. Exchange rates for the financial year were (A$1 = US$):

1 January 2012	0.60
1 February	0.63
15 February	0.64
10 June	0.66
30 June	0.65
Average for first half year	0.63
30 September	0.66
1 December	0.69
Average for second half year	0.65
31 December 2012	0.70

5. Sales in the first half of the year amounted to $210 000.
6. Expenses, other than depreciation, leases costs and purchases, in the first half of the year amounted to $60 000.
7. Surfers Ltd sold inventory to Paradise Ltd at cost plus 20%. Inventory transferred to Paradise Ltd during the year consisted of:

1 February	US$50 000
30 June	US$60 000
30 September	US$40 000
1 December	US$80 000

All the inventory was sold by Paradise Ltd except for $20 000 of the stock transferred on 1 December 2009.
8. Financial information relating to Paradise Ltd for the year ending 31 December 2012 is:

	US$
Sales revenue	680 000
Closing inventory	20 000
Accumulated depreciation — furniture and fittings	120 750
Accounts payable	40 000
Share capital	500 000
	1 360 750
Lease expenses	220 000
Purchases	230 000
Inventory	20 000
Other expenses	150 000
Depreciation — furniture and fittings	120 750
Furniture and fittings	572 000
Cash	14 600
Accounts receivable	33 400
	1 360 750

Required

1. Translate the financial statements of Paradise Ltd into Australian dollars for inclusion in the consolidated financial statements of Surfers Ltd at 31 December 2012.
2. Prepare the consolidation worksheet entries for adjusting for the effects of the inventory sales from the parent to the subsidiary.

Exercise 28.9   TRANSLATION INTO PRESENTATION CURRENCY, CONSOLIDATION ENTRIES

★★★   On 1 July 2013, Cricket Ltd, an Australian company, acquired 80% of the issued shares of Baseball Ltd, a company incorporated in the United States for US$789 600 (= A$1 579 200). The draft statement of profit or loss and other comprehensive income and statement of financial position of Baseball Ltd at 30 June 2014 are shown below.

	US$	US$
Sales revenues		1 600 000
Cost of sales:		
Opening inventory	140 000	
Purchases	840 000	
	980 000	
Closing inventory	280 000	700 000
Gross profit		900 000
Expenses:		
Depreciation	90 000	
Other	270 000	360 000
Profit before income tax		540 000
Income tax expense		200 000
Profit		340 000
Retained earnings as at 1 July 2013		200 000
		540 000
Dividend paid	120 000	
Dividend declared	200 000	320 000
Retained earnings as at 30 June 2014		220 000

	2014 US$	2013 US$
Current assets:		
Inventory	280 000	140 000
Accounts receivable	20 000	130 000
Cash	20 000	570 000
Total current assets	320 000	840 000
Non-current assets:		
Patent	80 000	80 000
Plant	720 000	600 000
Accumulated depreciation	(130 000)	(80 000)
Land	500 000	300 000
Buildings	920 000	820 000
Accumulated depreciation	(120 000)	(80 000)
Total non-current assets	1 970 000	1 640 000
Total assets	2 290 000	2 480 000
Current liabilities:		
Provisions	500 000	620 000
Accounts payable	320 000	940 000
Total current liabilities	820 000	1 560 000

	2014 US$	2013 US$
Non-current liabilities:		
Loan from Cricket Ltd	530 000	—
Total liabilities	1 350 000	1 560 000
Net assets	940 000	920 000
Equity:		
Share capital	720 000	720 000
Retained earnings	220 000	200 000
Total equity	940 000	920 000

Additional information

1. At acquisition date, all the assets and liabilities of Baseball Ltd were recorded at fair value except for:

	Fair value US$
Plant	540 000
Land	324 000
Inventory	182 000

The plant was expected to have a further 5-year life. The inventory was all sold by July 2014. The US tax rate is 25%.

2. On 1 January 2014, Baseball Ltd acquired new plant for US$120 000. This plant is depreciated over a 5-year period.

3. On 1 April 2014, Baseball Ltd acquired US$200 000 worth of land.

4. On 1 October 2013, Baseball Ltd acquired US$100 000 worth of new buildings. These buildings are depreciated evenly over a 10-year period.

5. The interim dividend was paid on 1 January 2014, half of which was from profits earned prior to 1 July 2013, while the dividend payable was declared on 30 June 2014.

6. Sales, purchases and expenses occurred evenly throughout the period. The inventory on hand at 30 June 2014 was acquired during June 2014.

7. The loan of US$530 000 from Cricket Ltd was granted on 1 July 2013. The interest rate is 8% per annum. Interest is paid on 30 June and 1 January each year.

8. Cricket Ltd sold raw materials to Baseball Ltd at 20% mark-up on cost. During the 2013–14 period there were three shipments of raw materials, costing Baseball Ltd:

1 October 2013	US$120 000
1 January	US$ 96 000
1 April 2014	US$132 000

At 30 June 2014, 20% of the shipment in April remains on hand in Baseball Ltd. The Australian tax rate is 30%.

9. On consolidation, the partial goodwill method is used.

10. The exchange rates for the financial year were as follows:

	US$1 = A$
1 July 2013	2.00
1 October 2013	1.80
1 January 2014	1.70
1 April 2014	1.60
30 June 2014	1.50
Average June 2014	1.52
Average for 2013–14	1.75

Required

1. If the functional currency for Baseball Ltd is the US dollar, prepare the financial statements of Baseball Ltd at 30 June 2014 in the presentation currency of the Australian dollar.
2. Verify the foreign currency translation adjustment.
3. Prepare the consolidation worksheet entries to consolidate the translated financial statements of Baseball Ltd with its parent entity at 30 June 2014.

Exercise 28.10	**TRANSLATION INTO FOREIGN CURRENCY, CONSOLIDATION EFFECTS**
★★★	Use the information in problem 28.9.

Required

1. If the functional currency for Baseball Ltd is the Australian dollar, prepare the financial statements of Baseball Ltd at 30 June 2014 in the functional currency.
2. Verify the foreign currency translation adjustment.
3. Prepare the consolidation worksheet entries to consolidate the translated financial statements of Baseball Ltd with its parent entity at 30 June 2014.
4. Assume on 1 January 2014, Baseball Ltd sold the patent to Cricket Ltd for US$100 000 and that Cricket Ltd depreciates this asset evenly over a 20-year period. Prepare the consolidation worksheet adjustment entries at 30 June 2014.

References

AASB 2003, *Presentation Currency of Australia Financial Reports* (Agenda paper 12.2), collation of submissions on the invitation to comment meeting of the AASB, 15–16 October, Glenelg, South Australia.

Bayer 2010, *Bayer Annual report 2010*, Bayer AG, Germany, www.bayer.com.

FASB 1981, *Foreign currency translation: Statement of Financial Accounting Standards No. 52*, Norwalk, Connecticut.

Jeter, DC & Chaney, PK 2003, *Advanced accounting*, 2nd edn, John Wiley, US.

Nokia 2011, *Nokia in 2011*, Nokia Corporation, Finland, www.nokia.com.

Radford, J 1996, *Foreign currency translation: clarity or confusion?*, project written as part of a Masters of Commerce degree, Curtin University of Technology, Perth, Western Australia.

Revsine, L 1984, 'The rationale underlying the functional currency choice', *The Accounting Review*, vol. 59, no. 3, pp. 505–14.

29 Associates and joint ventures

ACCOUNTING STANDARDS IN FOCUS

IAS 28 *Investments in Associates and Joint Ventures*

LEARNING OBJECTIVES

After studying this chapter, you should be able to:

1 explain the nature of associates and joint ventures

2 discuss the concepts of significant influence and joint control

3 explain the rationale for the equity method and the different sets of financial statements in which it may be applied

4 apply the equity method in basic situations

5 adjust the application of the equity method for fair value/carrying amount differences of identifiable assets and liabilities at acquisition date, and account for goodwill at acquisition

6 account for the effects of inter-entity transactions

7 account for associates and joint ventures where these entities incur losses

8 discuss the disclosures required in relation to associates and joint ventures.

LO1 ## 29.1 INTRODUCTION AND SCOPE

All Australians as well as many international travellers are familiar with the Australian national airline, Qantas, with its famous red and white kangaroo symbol. Qantas is the only airline in the world that can say that it has operated continuously for more than 90 years, having commenced its operations in 1920. The Qantas Group is the eleventh largest airline group in the world based on passenger numbers and distance flown. In 2010–11, the number of passengers carried by the Qantas Group numbered 44.5 million.

With increasing competition in the airline industry, Qantas established its low-fares airline Jetstar, which began operating its Australian domestic services in 2004. This was followed by Jetstar commencing international services in 2006 and New Zealand services in 2009. Jetstar also operates in Asia via Jetstar Asia. Jetstar Asia operates within Asia flying to and from Singapore. The Group now has a 27% interest in Jetstar Pacific which gives it a presence in Vietnam.

Besides having an interest in Asia, the Qantas Group also has an interest in the Oceania region. The airline currently known as 'Air Pacific' was registered as Katafaga Estates Ltd by Australian aviator Harold Gatty. The name change to 'Air Pacific' occurred in 1971. In 1985, it entered a formalised Management Support Agreement with Qantas and, in 1998, Qantas increased its equity in Air Pacific to 46.05%, with the Fijian government holding 51% of the airline (Air Pacific 2012).

In chapters 23–27 of this book, a group was described as a parent plus all of its subsidiaries, with a subsidiary being an entity that is controlled by the parent. The subsidiaries are accounted for using the consolidation method and the consolidated financial statements contain the financial picture of the group as a single economic entity. However, as noted above, companies like Qantas have investments in entities that they do not control, such as Qantas' 46.05% interest in Air Pacific and Jetstar's 27% interest in Jetstar Pacific. These investments are then not accounted for by application of the consolidation method. Some investments are simply recorded at cost. However, with some investments, an investor has a special relationship with its investees, which requires disclosure of more information about those investments. These investees are referred to as 'associates' and 'joint ventures' and they are accounted for by the application of the equity method of accounting.

Figure 29.1 shows the list of associates that is disclosed in the 2011 annual report of Qantas.

FIGURE 29.1 Qantas' investments in associates and joint ventures

(A) INVESTMENTS IN ASSOCIATES
Details of interests in associates are as follows:

	Principal Activity	Country of Incorporation	Balance Date	Qantas Group Ownership Interest 2011 %	Qantas Group Ownership Interest 2010 %
Air Pacific Limited	Air transport	Fiji	31 Mar	46	46
Fiji Resorts Limited	Resort accommodation	Fiji	31 Dec	21	21
Hallmark Aviation Services L.P.	Passenger handling services	United States of America	31 Dec	49	49
HT & T Travel Philippines, Inc.	Tours and travel	Philippines	30 Jun	28	28
Holiday Tours and Travel (Thailand) Ltd	Tours and travel	Thailand	31 Dec	37	37
Holiday Tours & Travel Vietnam Co. Ltd	Tours and travel	Vietnam	30 Jun	37	37
Jetset Travelworld Limited[1]	Travel products & services	Australia	30 Jun	29	—
Jetstar Pacific Airlines Aviation Joint Stock Company	Air transport	Vietnam	31 Dec	27	27
PT Holidays Tours & Travel	Tours and Travel	Indonesia	31 Dec	37	37
Tour East (T.E.T) Ltd	Tours and travel	Thailand	31 Dec	37	37

1. *As a result of the merger of Jetset Travelworld Group with Stella Travel Services as described in Note 27(B), Jetset Travelworld Group is accounted for as an associate effective 1 October 2010.*

(B) INVESTMENTS IN JOINTLY CONTROLLED ENTITIES

Details of interests in jointly controlled entities are as follows:

	Principal Activity	Country of Incorporation	Balance Date	Qantas Group Ownership Interest 2011 %	Qantas Group Ownership Interest 2010 %
Australian air Express Pty Ltd[1]	Air cargo	Australia	30 Jun	—	50
AUX Investment Pty Limited[1]	Investment holding company	Australia	30 Jun	50	—
Harvey Holidays Pty Ltd[2]	Tours and travel	Australia	30 Jun	—	50
LTQ Engineering Pty Limited	Maintenance services	Australia	30 Jun	50	50
Star Track Express Holdings Pty Limited[1]	Express road freight	Australia	30 Jun	—	50

1. *In October 2010 the Group's investments in Australian air Express Pty Ltd and Star Track Express Holdings Pty Limited were transferred to AUX Investment Pty Limited in exchange for a 50 per cent shareholding in this entity. Refer to Note 27(B) for further details.*
2. *On 30 June 2011 the Qantas Group sold its 50 per cent interest in Harvey Holidays Pty Ltd. Refer to Note 27(B) for further details.*

Source: Qantas (2011, pp. 71, 73).

Note that the Air Pacific investment by Qantas and the Jetstar investment in Jetstar Pacific are included in the list of associates in figure 29.1. Note further that the Qantas Group ownership interest in the associates is always less than 50%, and ranges from 27% to 49% in 2011. Also, the investment in jointly controlled entities is 50%.

The purpose of this chapter is to detail the nature of associates and joint ventures and to set out how they are accounted for. The appropriate accounting standard is IAS 28 *Investments in Associates and Joint Ventures*, which was issued by the International Accounting Standards Board (IASB) in 2011. Prior to the issue of this standard, the accounting for joint ventures was detailed in a different accounting standard from that used for associates. The accounting for joint ventures was covered in an accounting standard that dealt with both joint ventures and joint arrangements. Under IAS 28 as issued in 2011, the equity method is applied to both associates and joint ventures. The accounting for joint arrangements is covered by IFRS 11 *Joint Arrangements*, also issued in 2011 — see chapter 30 of this book.

 29.2 IDENTIFYING ASSOCIATES AND JOINT VENTURES

In this book, chapters 23–27 are concerned with the accounting for subsidiaries. Because of the special relationship between a parent entity and a subsidiary (i.e. the parent has control over the subsidiary), the accounting standard setters believe that a special form of accounting other than the cost method or the fair value method should be used. The consolidation method is applied so that users obtain a more informed picture of the financial position and financial performance of the combined entities as a group.

Just as a subsidiary has a special relationship with its parent requiring a particular accounting method to be used, the relationship between an investor and its associates and joint ventures is seen as being of special significance so that a specific accounting method — the equity method of accounting — is required to provide information about the investor and its investments in associates and joint ventures.

29.2.1 Associates

An associate is defined as an entity over which the investor has significant influence.

The key characteristic determining the existence of an associate is that of significant influence. This is defined in paragraph 3 of IAS 28 as 'the power to participate in the financial and operating policy decisions of the investee but is not control or joint control of those policies'. The key features of this definition are:
- The investor has the *power or the capacity* to affect the decisions made in relation to the investee. As with the concept of control used in determining the parent–subsidiary relationship, an investor is not

required to actually exercise the power to influence. It is only necessary that an investor have the ability to do so.
- The specific power is that of being able *to participate in the financial and operating policy decisions* of the investee. Note that the investor cannot control the investee, just significantly influence the investee.
- There is no requirement that the investor holds any shares, or has any beneficial interest in the associate. However, as discussed later, the application of the equity method is possible only where the investor holds shares in the associate. In other cases, the investor is required to make specific disclosures in its financial statements.

The assessment of the existence of significant influence requires the application of judgement by the accountant. To assist in this determination, the following guidance is useful:
- Where an investor holds, directly or indirectly, 20% or more of the voting power of an investee, it is presumed that the investor has significant influence over the investee (IAS 28 paragraph 5). Some examples of such relationships can be presented diagrammatically as shown in figure 29.2.

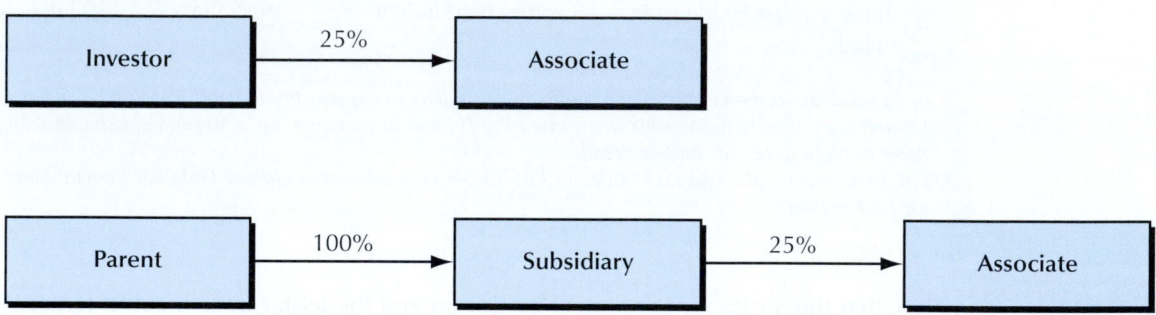

FIGURE 29.2 Examples of associate relationships

Similarly, where an investor holds less than 20% of another entity, there is a presumption that the investee is not an associate. Note that it is possible for an investee to be an associate of more than one investor.
- Paragraph 6 of IAS 28 provides a list of factors that may provide evidence of the existence of significant influence. These factors include:
  (a) representation on the board of directors or equivalent governing body of the investee
  (b) participation in policy-making processes, including participation in decisions about dividends or other distributions
  (c) material transactions between the investor and the investee
  (d) interchange of managerial personnel
  (e) provision of essential technical information.

  The most common form of participation is that of representation on the board of directors of the investee, this being because of the size of the shareholding that the investor has in the investee.
- The assessment of significant influence should also take into account any options or convertible securities that the investor holds in the investee (IAS 28 paragraph 7). The assessment takes into account the terms of exercise of the potential voting rights including the investor's intentions to exercise its rights and its financial ability to do so. Note that the investor must have the current ability to exercise significant influence.

29.2.2 Joint ventures

A joint arrangement is defined in paragraph 3 of IAS 28 as an arrangement between two or more entities whereby two or more entities have joint control of another entity.

The key feature of a joint arrangement is that of joint control. The most obvious example of joint control is where two entities each hold 50% of the shares of a third entity as shown in figure 29.3.

Joint control is defined as 'the contractually agreed sharing of control of an arrangement, which exists only when decisions about the relevant activities require the unanimous consent of the parties sharing control' (IAS 28 paragraph 3). The key element of joint control is the sharing of control. In other words, there are at least two investors who have shared control of the investee.

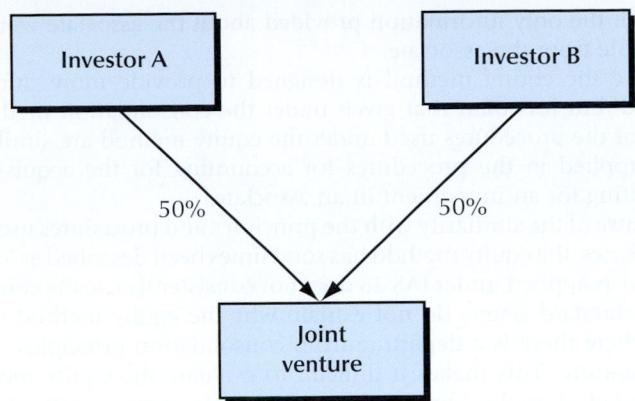

FIGURE 29.3 Example of joint control of a joint venture

Note then that there are three investor–investee relationships which are based on different levels of control:

Relationship	Level of control
Parent–subsidiary	Dominant control
Investor–associate	Significant influence
Joint arrangement–investee	Joint control

Where a joint arrangement exists, the arrangement must be classified as either a joint operation or a joint venture. The classification depends on the rights and obligations of the parties to the arrangement. Joint ventures are accounted for under IAS 28 while joint operations are accounted for under IFRS 11.

The concept of joint control and the classification of joint arrangements are covered in IFRS 11 rather than IAS 28. Hence, in this book, these two topics are covered in detail in chapter 30. In this chapter, it is sufficient to note that a joint venture is an arrangement where the investor has a right to an investment in the investee. The investee will have the following features:

- the legal form of the investee and the contractual arrangements are such that the investor does not have rights to the assets and obligations for the liabilities of the investee
- the investee has been designed to have a trade of its own and as such must directly face the risks arising from the activities it undertakes, such as demand, credit or inventory risks.

In the examples used in this chapter an investor will hold between 20% and 50% of the shares in an investee and the classification of that investment as an investor–associate relationship or a joint venture will be dependent on whether the investor has significant influence over or joint control of the investee. The subsequent accounting for either structure is the same.

 ## 29.3 THE EQUITY METHOD OF ACCOUNTING: RATIONALE AND APPLICATION

The method of accounting used to account for an investor's interest in an associate or joint venture is known as the equity method of accounting.

The equity method is defined in paragraph 3 of IAS 28 as a method whereby the investment in an investee is initially recognised at cost and adjusted thereafter for the investor's share of the post-acquisition equity of the investee. The post-acquisition equity includes both movements in profit or loss and other comprehensive income of the investee.

29.3.1 Rationale for the equity method

Because the investor does not control the associate, it cannot be accounted for by applying the consolidation method used for subsidiaries. However, because the investor has a special relationship with an associate via the investor having significant influence over the associate, it is argued that the cost method does not provide sufficient information about the associate in the records of the investor. Under the cost method, the only information provided about the associate would be in relation to dividends received or receivable from the associate.

Hence the equity method is designed to provide more information than that provided by the cost method, but less than that given under the consolidation method. As noted in paragraph 26 of IAS 28, many of the procedures used under the equity method are similar to the consolidation method. The concepts applied in the procedures for accounting for the acquisition of a subsidiary are also adopted in accounting for an investment in an associate.

Because of the similarity with the principles and procedures used in applying the consolidation method to subsidiaries, the equity method has sometimes been described as 'one-line consolidation'. However, the equity method as applied under IAS 28 does not consistently use the consolidation principles in its application.

The standard setters do not explain why the equity method is preferred to the fair value method. Further, where there is a departure from consolidation principles, IAS 28 does not supply a justification for the departure. This makes it difficult to evaluate the equity method on the basis of its being a one-line consolidation method or simply another measurement method competing with fair value.

29.3.2 Application of the equity method: consolidation worksheet or investor's accounts

An entity that has joint control in a joint venture or has significant influence over an associate must apply the equity method to account for these investments (IAS 28 paragraph 16). Where the equity method is applied depends upon whether the investor is also a parent.

(a) *Where the investor is a parent and prepares consolidated financial statements.* If the parent or any subsidiaries have investments in associates, the equity method is applied in the consolidated financial statements to account for these investments in associates.

Where consolidated financial statements are prepared, a parent does not have to prepare separate financial statements for the parent entity. Hence the equity accounting information appears only in the consolidated financial statements. No adjustments are made in the records of the investor who applies the cost method to its investments in associates.

The accounting entries applying the equity method are made in the consolidation worksheet. The adjustment entries are made on a year-to-year basis as no permanent entries for the equity accounting of the associates are made in the records of the investor.

(b) *Where the investor is not a parent and does not prepare consolidated financial statements.* In such cases, the investor applies the equity method to its associates in its own accounting records. The accounts of the investor are then affected by the application of the equity method.

The investor in either of the above situations may also prepare separate financial statements (as defined in paragraph 4 of IAS 27 *Separate Financial Statements*) in which the investments in subsidiaries, associates and joint ventures are accounted for at cost or in accordance with IAS 39 *Financial Instruments: Recognition and Measurement*. In such circumstances, in relation to (b) above, a worksheet could be used to adjust for the equity accounting of associates and joint ventures. In this book, it is assumed that no separate financial statements are prepared and, where no consolidated financial statements are prepared, the equity method is applied in the records of the investor.

29.4 APPLYING THE EQUITY METHOD: BASIC PRINCIPLES

The investor applies the equity method in accounting for its investment in the investee, being either an associate or a joint venture investee. There are four key steps in the application of the equity method (IAS 28 paragraph 10):

1. Recognise the *initial investment* in the investee at cost. If the investment is recorded at fair value, an adjustment must be made to return the investment back to original cost.
2. Increase or decrease the carrying amount of the investment by the investor's share of the *profit or loss* of the investee after the acquisition date — post-acquisition profit or loss.
3. Reduce the carrying amount of the investment by *distributions*, such as dividends, received from the investee.
4. Increase or decrease the carrying amount of the investment for changes in the investor's share of the changes in the investee's *other comprehensive income*. This applies to reserves where changes in the investee's equity are not recognised in profit or loss but in other comprehensive income. This includes movements in reserves such as the asset revaluation surplus.

Although potential voting rights may be used in the assessment of significant influence, they are not used in any of the above calculations.

ILLUSTRATIVE EXAMPLE 29.1 Basic application of the equity method

In this example, the investor owns 25% of the shares of the investee. Assuming this investment is sufficient to give the investor significant influence over the investee, the investee is then an associate of the investor. The equity method is applied to account for the investment. The same journal entries are used if there were four investors in the investee, each having a 25% interest in the investee and the investors had joint control over the investee; that is, the investee is a joint venture.

Part A: Investor does not prepare consolidated financial statements
On 1 July 2014, Ella Ltd acquired 25% of the shares of Emily Ltd for $42 500. At this date, all the identifiable assets and liabilities of Emily Ltd were recorded at amounts equal to fair value, and the equity of Emily Ltd consisted of:

Share capital	$100 000
General reserve	30 000
Asset revaluation surplus	20 000
Retained earnings	20 000

During the 2014–15 year, Emily Ltd reported a profit of $25 000. As reported in other comprehensive income, the asset revaluation surplus increased by $5000. Emily Ltd paid a $4000 dividend and transferred $3000 to general reserve.

Step 1: Recognition of the initial investment
At 1 July 2014, Ella Ltd would record the investment in Emily Ltd at a cost of $42 500.

Step 2: Recognition of the share of profit or loss of associate/joint venture
At 30 June 2015, the investee has recorded a profit for the year of $25 000. The investor is entitled to a 25% share of this profit. The journal entry passed in the records of the investor at 30 June 2015 recognises as income a share of the investee's profit and increases the investment in the associate/joint venture. The journal entry is:

June 30	Investments in Associates and Joint Ventures	Dr	6 250	
	Share of Profit or Loss of Associates and Joint Ventures	Cr		6 250
	(Share of profit or loss of associate/joint venture: 25% × $25 000)			

The share of profit or loss of associates and joint ventures is disclosed as a separate line item in the statement of profit or loss and other comprehensive income (IAS 1 *Presentation of Financial Statements* paragraph 82(c)).

Step 3: Recognition of share of other comprehensive income: increase in asset revaluation surplus
The asset revaluation surplus has increased by $5000, with this also being reported by the investee in other comprehensive income. This is post-acquisition equity and the investor is entitled to a 25% share. The investment in the associate/joint venture is increased, and the share of other comprehensive income is recognised, this being then accumulated in equity. The journal entries in the records of the investor at 30 June 2015 are:

June 30	Investments in Associates and Joint Ventures	Dr	1 250	
	Share of Other Comprehensive Income of Associates and Joint Ventures	Cr		1 250
	(Share of revaluation increase: 25% × $5000)			

June 30	Share of Other Comprehensive Income of Associates and Joint Ventures	Dr	1 250	
	Asset Revaluation Surplus	Cr		1 250
	(Accumulation of revaluation increase in equity)			

The share of other comprehensive income of associates and joint ventures is required to be disclosed separately in the other comprehensive income section of the statement of profit or loss and other comprehensive income (IAS 1 paragraph 82A).

The general reserve has also been increased by $3000. However, there is no need to pass any journal entries relating to this transfer from current profits to reserves. The investor, under Step 2 above, recognised its share of the investee's profit. This includes a share of the amount transferred to general reserve. To recognise a share of the general reserve as well as a share of the profit would double count the investor's share of equity.

Step 4: Adjustment for dividend paid by associate/joint venture
In the current period, the investee paid a dividend of $4000. However, the investor has already recognised its share of the equity of the investee via step 2 above; therefore the dividend is not revenue to the investor. The investor has a reduced share of the equity of the investee. Hence, the investor passes a journal entry to recognise the receipt of cash on payment of the dividend and reduces its investment in the investee.

The entry at 30 June 2015 is:

June 30	Cash	Dr	1 000	
	Investments in Associates and Joint Ventures	Cr		1 000
	(Adjustment for dividend paid by associate/joint venture: 25% × $4000)			

Note that if the dividend had been declared by the investee but not paid, the investor would recognise a dividend receivable instead of cash and still reduce its investment in the investee.

At 30 June 2015, the investment in the associate is measured at $49 000 (i.e. $42 500 + $6250 + $1250 − $1000). The equity of Emily Ltd consists of:

Share capital	$ 100 000
Asset revaluation surplus ($20 000 + $5000)	25 000
General reserve ($30 000 + $3000)	33 000
Retained earnings ($20 000 + $25 000 − $4000 − $3000)	38 000
	$ 196 000

The investor's share of the equity of the associate is 25% of $196 000 (i.e. $49 000), which is the same as the recorded amount of the investment in the associate. In other words, the equity method, in this case, is designed to show the investment in the associate at an amount equal to the investor's share of the reported equity of the associate. As explained later in this chapter, this relationship is not always achieved because of the effects of pre-acquisition equity, the existence of goodwill, and adjustments made for the effects of inter-entity transactions.

Part B: Investor prepares consolidated financial statements

In this circumstance, the entries are *not* made in the accounting records of the entities themselves but in the consolidation worksheet instead. The journal entries shown in steps 2 and 3 in Part A above are also used where the investor prepares consolidated financial statements. These entries are passed in the consolidation worksheet at 30 June 2015.

The entry that differs where the investor prepares a consolidation worksheet is that for the dividend paid.

Step 4: Adjustment for dividend paid by associate
The investor recorded the receipt of cash and recognised dividend revenue on payment of the dividend by the investee. However the investor, in step 2, has recognised a share of the profit of the investee. It

cannot also recognise dividend revenue as this would double count the share of investee equity. Hence a worksheet entry is required that eliminates the dividend revenue recorded by the investor and reduces the investor's investment in the investee.

The consolidation worksheet entry at 30 June 2015 is:

June 30	Dividend Revenue	Dr	1 000	
	Investments in Associates and Joint Ventures	Cr		1 000
	(Adjustment for dividend paid by associate/joint venture: 25% × $4000)			

If the dividend had been declared but not paid, the adjustment entry would be the same as above.

29.5 APPLYING THE EQUITY METHOD: GOODWILL AND FAIR VALUE ADJUSTMENTS

The equity method requires that an investor recognise its share of the post-acquisition equity of the investee.

When the investor acquired its interest in the investee, it paid a consideration based on an assessment of the fair value of the investee at that date. As noted in IAS 28 paragraph 32, the consideration paid took into account:

- the recorded equity of the investee, equal to the recorded carrying amounts of the assets and liabilities of the investee
- the differences between the carrying amounts of the assets and liabilities of the investee and the fair values of these assets and liabilities
- the fair values of any unrecorded assets and liabilities of the investee
- any goodwill existing in the investee.

The initial carrying amount of the investor's interest in the investee reflects all of these amounts. The pre-acquisition equity of the investee effectively equals the sum of the fair values of the assets and liabilities of the investee (recorded and unrecorded) and the cost of any goodwill acquired.

The investee does not record all the pre-acquisition equity at acquisition date, but recognises some of it subsequent to acquisition date. For example, assume the investee's sole asset at acquisition date was land that was recorded at acquisition date at $100 000 but had a fair value at that date of $120 000. Although the investee's recorded equity at acquisition date is $100 000 the real pre-acquisition equity is $120 000. If in the year following the acquisition date the investee sold the land for $120 000, the gain on sale of $20 000 is pre-acquisition equity not post-acquisition equity. Under the application of the equity method, the carrying amount of the investor's investment in the investee should not be increased by a share of this gain.

To determine the real post-acquisition equity of the investee, at acquisition date an acquisition analysis is undertaken. This is done in the same way as demonstrated in chapters 25–27 when accounting for a parent's acquisition in a subsidiary.

The acquisition analysis involves comparing the cost of the investment in the associate/joint venture with the net fair value of the identifiable assets and liabilities of the investee, determining whether any goodwill or excess arose at acquisition date.

In applying the equity method, the share of recorded profit or loss is adjusted for differences between carrying amounts and fair values of identifiable assets and liabilities at acquisition date as for any impairment of goodwill. These adjustments are only notional adjustments; that is, they are not made in the records of the investee but are simply used in the calculation of the investor's share of post-acquisition equity of the investee. Because the investor's share of post-acquisition profit or loss of the investee is made on an after-tax basis, these adjustments are also calculated on an after-tax basis.

Illustrative example 29.2 shows the accounting where there are fair value/carrying amount differences at acquisition date and goodwill is acquired by the investor. Illustrative example 29.3 shows the accounting where an excess occurs.

On 1 July 2012, Mia Ltd acquired 25% of the shares of Chloe Ltd for $49 375. At this date, the equity of Chloe Ltd consisted of:

Share capital	$100 000
General reserve	50 000
Retained earnings	20 000

At the acquisition date, all the identifiable assets and liabilities of Chloe Ltd were recorded at fair value, except for plant for which the fair value was $10 000 greater than its carrying amount, and inventory whose fair value was $5000 greater than its cost. The tax rate is 30%. The plant has a further 5-year life. The inventory was all sold by 30 June 2013. In the reporting period ending 30 June 2013, Chloe Ltd reported a profit of $15 000.

The acquisition analysis at 1 July 2012 is as follows:

Net fair value of the identifiable assets and
    liabilities of Chloe Ltd
$$= (\$100\,000 + \$50\,000 + \$20\,000) \text{ (equity)}$$
$$+ \$10\,000(1 - 30\%) \text{ (plant)}$$
$$+ \$5\,000(1 - 30\%) \text{ (inventory)}$$
$$= \$180\,500$$

Net fair value acquired by Mia Ltd
$$= 25\% \times \$180\,500$$
$$= \$45\,125$$

Cost of investment $= \$49\,375$

Goodwill $= \$4\,250$

As the plant is used up, profits are earned by the investee. However, these are not all post-acquisition profits as the investor paid the fair value for the plant, not the carrying amount recorded by the investee. The proportion that is pre-acquisition equity is measured by reference to the depreciation of the plant based upon the difference between fair value and carrying amount of the plant at acquisition date:

$$\text{Depreciation adjustment} = 20\% \times [\$10\,000(1 - 30\%)]$$
$$= \$1400$$

Similarly, on sale of the inventory in the 2012–13 year, the post-acquisition profit on sale is adjusted for the difference between carrying amount and fair value of the inventory at acquisition date:

$$\text{Inventory adjustment} = \$5000(1 - 30\%)$$
$$= \$3500$$

Hence, the investor's share of post-acquisition equity at 30 June 2013 is:

Recorded profit of Chloe Ltd		$15 000
Pre-acquisition adjustments:		
Depreciation of plant	$(1 400)	
Sale of inventory	(3 500)	(4 900)
		10 100
Investor's share of post-acquisition profit (25%)		$ 2 525

The journal entry to reflect the application of the equity method to the investment in the investee is:

Investments in Chloe Ltd	Dr	2 525	
Share of Profit or Loss of Associates and Joint Ventures	Cr		2 525
(Recognition of share of post-acquisition profit of investee)			

This entry is the same regardless of whether the investor prepares consolidated financial statements or the entries are made in the records of the investor.

ILLUSTRATIVE EXAMPLE 29.3 Excess — income

Any excess of the investor's share of the net fair value of an investee's identifiable assets and liabilities over the cost of the investment is recognised as income in the determination of the investor's share of the investee's profit or loss in the period in which the investment is acquired (IAS 28 paragraph 32).

Assume in illustrative example 29.2 that the cost of the investment was $45 000. The acquisition analysis would then show:

$$
\begin{aligned}
\text{Net fair value acquired by Mia Ltd} &= 25\% \times \$180\,500 \\
&= \$45\,125 \\
\text{Cost of investment} &= \$45\,000 \\
\text{Excess} &= \$125
\end{aligned}
$$

The amount of the adjustment needed in applying equity accounting to the investment in the associate at 30 June 2013 is then as follows:

Recorded profit of Chloe Ltd			$15 000
Pre-acquisition adjustments:			
Depreciation of plant		(1 400)	
Sale of inventory		$(3 500)	(4 900)
			10 100
Investor's share of post-acquisition profit (25%)			2 525
Adjustment for excess on acquisition			125
			$ 2 650

Note that the excess relates to the investor's 25% investment in the investee and so is added on after the pre-acquisition adjustments are made to the recorded profit.

The journal entry to reflect the application of the equity method to the investment in the investee is:

Investments in Chloe Ltd	Dr	2 650	
Share of Profit or Loss of Associates and Joint Ventures	Cr		2 650
(Recognition of share of post-acquisition profit of investee)			

29.5.1 Applying the equity method across multiple years

In the above illustrative examples, the journal entries are determined for the year following the investor's acquisition of shares in the associate/joint venture. In subsequent years the entries required will differ, dependent on whether the investor prepares consolidated financial statements.

- *If the investor does not prepare consolidated financial statements.* There are no extra issues to consider in this situation. As the journal entries passed by the investor are recorded in the accounts of the investor, then each year the investor records the annual share of increases/decreases in equity accounts.

- *If the investor prepares consolidated financial statements.* The complication that arises here is that the journal entries are passed in the consolidation worksheet and not in the records of the investor. Hence, in years subsequent to the acquisition year, the worksheet journal entries need to recognise a share of prior years' movements in equity as well as a share of the current year's movements in equity. This involves recognising a share of retained earnings as well as a share of reserves.

ILLUSTRATIVE EXAMPLE 29.4 Multiple periods

On 1 July 2013, Charlotte Ltd acquired 40% of the shares of Isabella Ltd for $122 400. The equity of Isabella Ltd at acquisition date consisted of:

Ordinary share capital	$200 000
Retained earnings	80 000

At 1 July 2013, all the identifiable assets and liabilities of Isabella Ltd were recorded at fair value except for the following:

	Carrying amount	Fair value
Machinery	$140 000	$160 000
Inventory	60 000	70 000

By 30 June 2014, the inventory on hand at 1 July 2013 had been sold by Isabella Ltd. The machinery was expected to provide future benefits evenly over the next 2 years and then be scrapped. The tax rate is 30%.

Dividends declared at 30 June are paid within the following 3 months, with liabilities being raised at the date of declaration.

In January 2016, Isabella Ltd revalued furniture upwards by $6000, affecting the asset revaluation surplus.

The financial statements of Isabella Ltd over three periods contained the following information:

	30 June 2014	30 June 2015	30 June 2016
Profit or loss	$ 40 000	$ 60 000	$ 70 000
Retained earnings (opening balance)	80 000	98 000	123 000
	120 000	158 000	193 000
Dividend paid	5 000	10 000	15 000
Dividend declared	7 000	15 000	20 000
Transfer to general reserve	10 000	10 000	0
	22 000	35 000	35 000
Retained earnings (closing balance)	$ 98 000	$ 123 000	$158 000

Required

Prepare the entries in the consolidation worksheet of Charlotte Ltd to apply the equity method to its investment in Isabella Ltd for each of the 3 years ending 30 June 2014, 2015 and 2016.

Solution

Acquisition analysis

Net fair value of identifiable assets and liabilities of Isabella Ltd	= $200 000 + $80 000 (equity)
	+ $20 000 (1 − 30%) (machinery)
	+ $10 000 (1 − 30%) (inventory)
	= $301 000

Net fair value acquired by Charlotte Ltd = 40% × $301 000
                                        = $120 400
Cost of investment   = $122 400
Goodwill   = $2000
Pre-acquisition effects
Depreciation of machinery p.a. after tax = 50% × $20 000 (1 – 30%)
                                         = $7000
After tax profit on sale of inventory   = $10 000 (1 – 30%)
                                         = $7000

Consolidation worksheet 30 June 2014
Workings:

Recorded profit of investee		$ 40 000
Pre-acquisition adjustments:		
Inventory	$(7 000)	
Depreciation of machinery	(7 000)	(14 000)
		26 000
Investor's share — 40%		$ 10 400

The journal entries in the consolidation worksheet of Charlotte Ltd at 30 June 2014 are:

June 30	Investments in Associates and Joint Ventures	Dr	10 400	
	Share of Profit or Loss of Associates and Joint Ventures	Cr		10 400
	(Recognition of equity-accounted profit of Isabella Ltd)			
	Dividend Revenue	Dr	4 800	
	Investments in Associates and Joint Ventures	Cr		4 800
	(Adjustments for dividends from Isabella Ltd: 40% × [$5000 + $7000])			

Note that the net increase in equity and the investment account for the year equals $5600 (i.e. $10 400 – $4800).

Consolidation worksheet 30 June 2015
Share of prior period's equity

The first journal entry in the consolidation worksheet recognises the investor's share of the movement in equity of the investee in the prior period. The only account affected by prior period movements is retained earnings. Note that the movement in the general reserve has to be added back to retained earnings as this was effectively a transfer from profit. The calculation of the investor's share of prior period movements in equity is:

Movement in retained earnings since acquisition date:		
($98 000 – $80 000)		$ 18 000
Movement in general reserve		10 000
Pre-acquisition adjustments:		
Depreciation	$(7 000)	
Inventory	(7 000)	(14 000)
		14 000
Investor's share — 40%		$ 5 600

The consolidation worksheet entry at 30 June 2015 is:

June 30	Investments in Associates and Joint Ventures	Dr	5 600	
	Retained Earnings (1/7/14)	Cr		5 600
	(Recognition of equity-accounted prior period profit of Isabella Ltd)			

Note that the above entry is necessary because the equity accounting entries are made in the consolidation worksheet and not in the actual records of the investor.

Share of current period equity
The next set of entries relates to the investor's share of equity for the 2014–15 year.

Workings:

Recorded profit of investee			$ 60 000
Pre-acquisition adjustments:			
Depreciation of machinery		(7 000)	(7 000)
			53 000
Investor's share — 40%			$ 21 200

The entries in the consolidation worksheet at 30 June 2015 reflecting the effects of the profit generated and the dividends declared/paid are:

June 30	Investments in Associates and Joint Ventures	Dr	21 200	
	Share of Profit or Loss of Associates and Joint Ventures	Cr		21 200
	(Recognition of equity-accounted profit of Isabella Ltd)			
	Dividend Revenue	Dr	10 000	
	Investments in Associates and Joint Ventures	Cr		10 000
	(Adjustments for dividends from Isabella Ltd: 40% × [$10 000 + $ 15 000])			

Note that the net increase in equity and in the investment account as a result of applying the equity method is $16 800 (i.e. $5600 + $21 200 − $10 000).

Consolidation worksheet 30 June 2016
Share of prior period equity
The first journal entry in the consolidation worksheet recognises the investor's share of the movement in equity of the investee in the prior period. The calculation of the investor's share of prior period movements in equity is:

Movement in retained earnings since acquisition date:		
($123 000 − $80 000)		$ 43 000
Movement in general reserve		20 000
Pre-acquisition adjustments:		
Depreciation: 2 × $7000	$(14 000)	
Inventory	(7 000)	(21 000)
		42 000
Investor's share — 40%		$ 16 800

The consolidation worksheet entry at 30 June 2016 is:

June 30	Investments in Associates and Joint Ventures	Dr	16 800	
	Retained Earnings (1/7/15)	Cr		16 800
	(Recognition of equity-accounted prior period profit of Isabella Ltd)			

Share of current period equity
The next set of entries relates to the investor's share of equity for the 2015–16 year.

Workings:

Recorded profit of investee		$70 000
Pre-acquisition adjustments:		
Depreciation of machinery	(7 000)	(7 000)
		63 000
Investor's share — 40%		$25 200
Other comprehensive income of investee: $6000(1 – 30%)		$ 4 200
Investor's share — 40%		$ 1 680

The entries in the consolidation worksheet at 30 June 2016 reflecting the effects of the profit and other comprehensive income generated and the dividends declared/paid are:

June 30	Investments in Associates and Joint Ventures	Dr	25 200	
	Share of Profit or Loss of Associates and Joint Ventures	Cr		25 200
	(Recognition of equity-accounted profit of Isabella Ltd)			
	Investments in Associates and Joint Ventures	Dr	1 680	
	Share of Other Comprehensive Income of Associates and Joint Ventures	Cr		1 680
	(Share of revaluation increase)			
	Share of Other Comprehensive Income of Associates and Joint Ventures	Dr	1 680	
	Asset Revaluation Surplus	Cr		1 680
	(Accumulation of revaluation increase in equity)			
	Dividend Revenue	Dr	14 000	
	Investments in Associates and Joint Ventures	Cr		14 000
	(Adjustment for dividends from Isabella Ltd: 40% × [$15 000 + $20 000])			

 LO6 29.6 APPLYING THE EQUITY METHOD — INTER-ENTITY TRANSACTIONS

As detailed in chapter 25 of this book, in the preparation of consolidated financial statements, adjustments are made to eliminate the effects of transactions between a parent and its subsidiaries, and between the subsidiaries themselves. The rationale for these adjustments is that the consolidated financial statements show only the results of transactions between the group and entities external to the group. The group is regarded as a single economic entity. The adjustment procedure requires the full effect of the transaction to be eliminated and the adjustments are made against the particular accounts affected by the transactions.

Where a parent or its consolidated subsidiaries undertake transactions with an associate or a joint venture, adjustments must be made for gains and losses on those transactions.

The principles for adjusting the effects of inter-entity transactions under equity accounting are as follows (IAS 28 paragraph 28):

- *Adjustments are made for transactions between an associate/joint venture and the investor that give rise to unrealised profits and losses.* Such transactions include the sale of inventory from the investor to the investee. Realisation of the profits or losses on these transactions occurs when the asset on which the profit or loss accrued is sold to an external entity, or as the future benefits embodied in the asset are consumed.

  Unlike consolidation, there is no need to adjust for all transactions between the investor and the investee — only those transactions where a profit or loss is earned required adjustment. Therefore, transactions such as a loan between the entities, or the payment of interest on the loan, do not require an adjustment under equity accounting.

- *Adjustments for transactions between an investor and an investee are done on a proportional basis, determined in accordance with the investor's ownership interest in the investee.* This differs from consolidation adjustments where the adjustments are made on a 100% basis, and are unaffected by the parent's ownership interest in the subsidiary.

- *Adjustments are made on an after-tax basis to the accounts 'Share of Profit or Loss of Associates and Joint Ventures' and 'Investments in Associates and Joint Ventures'.* IAS 28 does not detail which accounts should be adjusted under the equity method. For example, if an investee sells inventory to an investor at a profit, should the inventory account of the investor be adjusted? In this chapter, only the two accounts noted earlier are adjusted — no adjustments are made to specific accounts of the investor or investee.

Note that the adjustments are made on an after-tax basis as the equity method recognises a share of after-tax profits only.

The adjustments are the same for all transaction regardless of whether they are upstream (where an associate/joint venture sells to an investor) or downstream (where an investor sells to an associate/joint venture). The direction of the transaction is irrelevant in determining the accounts affected by the application of the equity method.

It is difficult to find a rationale for the adjustments for inter-entity transactions under the equity method of accounting as applied under IAS 28. Unlike subsidiaries, associates and joint ventures are not part of the single economic entity and so the consolidation rationale is not applicable. The main argument for the method used is simplicity. However, the method does lead to some strange results. For example, where an investor sells inventory to an investee, the adjustment is to the Share of Profit or Loss of Associates and Joint Ventures account even though the profit was made by the investor and not the investee. The incremental change to the investment account does not therefore reflect only changes in the equity of the investee, but includes unrealised profits made by the investor.

Examples of inter-entity transactions

In the following examples, assume:
- The reporting period is for the year ending 30 June 2015.
- The investor, Jessica Ltd, owns 25% of Ava Ltd. Jessica Ltd acquired its ownership interest in Ava Ltd 2 years prior on 1 July 2013, when the retained earnings balance of Ava Ltd was $100 000. At this date, all the identifiable assets and liabilities of Ava Ltd were recorded at fair value.
- At 30 June 2014, the retained earnings balance in Ava Ltd is $140 000, and the profit recorded for the 2014–15 period is $30 000. The tax rate is 30%.

The adjustment entries may differ according to whether they are made in the consolidation worksheet or in the accounting records of the investor. Differences in particular arise where the effects of a transaction occur across 2 or more years.

Example 1: Sale of inventory from associate to investor in the current period

During the 2014–15 period, Ava Ltd sold $5000 worth of inventory to Jessica Ltd. These items had previously cost Ava Ltd $3000. All the items remain unsold by the investor at 30 June 2015.

The calculations for applying the equity method are as follows:

2013–14 period	
Change in retained earnings since acquisition date:	
$140 000 – $100 000	$40 000
Investor's share — 25%	$10 000
2014–15 period	
Current period profit	$30 000
Adjustments for inter-entity transactions:	
Unrealised after-tax profit in ending inventory:	
$2000(1 – 30%)	(1 400)
	28 600
Investor's share — 25%	$ 7 150

If the investor prepares consolidated financial statements, the entries in the consolidation worksheet at 30 June 2015 to apply the equity method to its associate/joint venture are:

Investments in Associates and Joint Ventures	Dr	10 000	
Retained Earnings (1/7/14)	Cr		10 000
Investments in Associates and Joint Ventures	Dr	7 150	
Share of Profit or Loss of Associates and Joint Ventures	Cr		7 150

If the investor does not prepare consolidated financial statements, the entries are made in the records of the investor. The only entry made at 30 June 2015 is the same as the second entry above:

Investments in Associates and Joint Ventures	Dr	7 150	
Share of Profit or Loss of Associates and Joint Ventures	Cr		7 150

Example 2: Sale of inventory from investor to associate in the current period

Details are the same as in example 1, except that Jessica Ltd sells the inventory to Ava Ltd.

The calculations and journal entries are exactly the same as in example 1. The flow of the transaction, whether upstream or downstream, does not affect the accounting for the transaction.

Example 3: Sale of inventory in the current period, part remaining unsold

During the 2014–15 period, Ava Ltd sold $5000 worth of inventory to Jessica Ltd. These items had previously cost Ava Ltd $3000. Half of the items remain unsold by Jessica Ltd at 30 June 2015.

The increment to the investment account is calculated in a similar way to example 1, but the adjustment is based only on the profit remaining in inventory on hand at the end of the period because it is this inventory that contains the unrealised profit. The calculations are as follows:

2013–14 period	
As for example 1:	
Investor's share — 25%	$10 000
2014–15 period	
Current period's recorded profit	$30 000
Adjustment for inter-entity transactions:	
Unrealised after-tax profit in ending inventory:	
$1000(1 – 30%)	(700)
	29 300
Investor's share — 25%	$ 7 325

If the investor prepares consolidated financial statements, at 30 June 2015, the entries in the consolidation worksheet to apply the equity method to its associate are:

Investments in Associates and Joint Ventures	Dr	10 000	
Retained Earnings (1/7/14)	Cr		10 000
Investments in Associates and Joint Ventures	Dr	7 325	
Share of Profit or Loss of Associates and Joint Ventures	Cr		7 325

If the investor does not prepare consolidated financial statements, in the 2014–15 period only the second of the above two entries is required.

Example 4: Sale of inventory in the previous period

During the 2013–14 period, Jessica Ltd sold $5000 worth of inventory to Ava Ltd. These items had previously cost Jessica Ltd $3000. All the items remain unsold by Ava Ltd at 30 June 2014. These were all sold to other entities by 30 June 2015.

The calculations for applying the equity method are as follows:

2013–14 period	
Change in retained earnings since acquisition date:	
$140 000 – $100 000	$40 000
Adjustment for inter-entity transactions:	
Unrealised after-tax profit in ending inventory	
$2000(1 – 30%)	(1 400)
	38 600
Investor's share — 25%	$ 9 650
2014–15 period	
Current period's profit	$30 000
Adjustment for inter-entity transactions:	
Realised after-tax profit in opening inventory	
$2000(1 – 30%)	1 400
	31 400
Investor's share — 25%	$ 7 850

In the 2014–15 period, the profit that was unrealised in the previous period becomes realised. Hence, the amount is *added back* in the calculation of the 2014–15 share of equity. The addition of the 2013–14 and the 2014–15 increments results in the inter-entity transaction having a zero effect since, by 30 June 2015, the profit on the sale is realised.

If the investor prepares consolidated financial statements at 30 June 2015, the entries in the consolidation worksheet to apply the equity method to its associate are:

Investments in Associates and Joint Ventures	Dr	9 650	
Retained Earnings (1/7/14)	Cr		9 650
Investment in Associates and Joint Ventures	Dr	7 850	
Share of Profit or Loss of Associates and Joint Ventures	Cr		7 850

If the investor does not prepare consolidated statements, the only entry passed at 30 June 2015 is the second entry above.

Example 5: Sale of depreciable non-current asset

On 1 July 2013, Ava Ltd sold an item of plant to Jessica Ltd for $8000. The carrying amount of the asset on this date in Ava Ltd's records was $3000. The plant had a remaining useful life of 5 years.

The calculations for applying the equity method are as follows:

2013–14 period	
Change in retained earnings since acquisition date	$40 000
Adjustments for inter-entity transactions:	
Unrealised after-tax profit on sale of plant: $5000(1 – 30%)	(3 500)
Realised after-tax profit on sale of plant: $\frac{1}{5} \times \$3500$	700
	37 200
Investor's share — 25%	$ 9 300

Note that at the time of sale of the plant the profit on the sale is unrealised. The profit is realised as the asset is consumed or used by the entity holding the asset. The consumption of benefits is measured by the depreciation of the asset. Hence, as the plant is depreciated on a straight-line basis over a 5-year period, one-fifth of the profit is realised in each year after the inter-entity transfer.

2014–15 period	
Current period's recorded profit	$30 000
Adjustment for inter-entity transactions:	
Realised after-tax profit on sale of plant: $\frac{1}{5} \times \$3500$	700
	30 700
Investor's share — 25%	$ 7 675

A further one-fifth of the unrealised profit is realised in the 2014–15 period as the benefits from the asset are further consumed. At the end of the 5-year period, the whole of the profit is realised.

If the investor prepares consolidated financial statements at 30 June 2015, the entries in the consolidation worksheet to apply the equity method to its associate/joint venture are:

Investments in Associates and Joint Ventures	Dr	9 300	
Retained Earnings (1/7/14)	Cr		9 300
Investments in Associates and Joint Ventures	Dr	7 675	
Share of Profit or Loss of Associates and Joint Ventures	Cr		7 675

If the investor does not prepare consolidated statements, only the second of the above entries is passed at 30 June 2015.

Example 6: Payment of interest

On 1 July 2013, Jessica Ltd lent $10 000 to Ava Ltd. Interest of $1000 p.a. was paid by Ava Ltd.

Although the profit of Ava Ltd includes the interest expense from this transaction, no adjustment is required because the revenue/expense on the transaction is assumed to be realised. Profits are considered to be unrealised only when there remains an asset in the investor/associate transferred at a profit or loss from the associate/investor.

ILLUSTRATIVE EXAMPLE 29.5 Equity method of accounting

On 1 July 2012, Georgia Ltd paid $2 696 000 for 40% of the shares of Emma Ltd, a company involved in the manufacture of garden equipment. At that date, the equity of Emma Ltd consisted of:

Share capital — 3 000 000 shares	$ 3 000 000
Retained earnings	3 000 000

At 1 July 2012, all the identifiable assets and liabilities of Emma Ltd were recorded at fair value except for:

	Carrying amount	Fair value
Inventory	$1 000 000	$1 200 000
Plant (cost $3 200 000)	2 500 000	3 000 000

The inventory was all sold by 30 June 2013. The plant had a further expected useful life of 5 years.

Additional information
(a) On 1 July 2013, Georgia Ltd held inventory sold to it by Emma Ltd at a profit before income tax of $200 000. This was all sold by 30 June 2014.
(b) In February 2014, Emma Ltd sold inventory to Georgia Ltd at a profit before income tax of $600 000. Half of this was still held by Georgia Ltd at 30 June 2014.
(c) On 30 June 2014, Emma Ltd held inventory sold to it by Georgia Ltd at a profit before income tax of $200 000. This had been sold to Emma Ltd for $2 000 000.
(d) On 2 July 2012, Emma Ltd sold some equipment to Georgia Ltd for $1 500 000, with Emma Ltd recording a profit before income tax of $400 000. The equipment had a further 4-year life, with benefits expected to occur evenly in these years.
(e) In June 2013, Emma Ltd provided for a dividend of $1 000 000. This dividend was paid in August 2013. Dividend revenue is recognised when the dividend is provided for.
(f) The balances in the general reserve have resulted from transfers from retained earnings.
(g) The tax rate is 30%.
(h) Each share in Emma Ltd has a fair value at 30 June 2014 of $4.

The consolidated financial statements of Georgia Ltd, not including the equity-accounted figures, and the financial statements of Emma Ltd at 30 June 2014, are as follows:

Statements of Profit or Loss and Other Comprehensive Income for the year ended 30 June 2014	Georgia Ltd $'000	Emma Ltd $'000
Revenue	25 000	18 600
Expenses	19 200	13 600
Profit before tax	5 800	5 000
Income tax expense	2 200	1 100
Profit for the period	3 600	3 900
Other comprehensive income: revaluation gains	0	400
Total comprehensive income	3 600	4 300

Statements of Changes in Equity for the year ended 30 June 2014	Georgia Ltd $'000	Emma Ltd $'000
Total comprehensive income	3 600	4 300
Retained earnings as at 1/7/13	4 000	4 000
Profit	3 600	3 900
	7 600	7 900
Transfer to general reserve	—	1 000
Dividend paid	3 000	1 500
Dividend provided	1 500	1 000
	4 500	3 500
Retained earnings as at 30/6/14	3 100	4 400

	Georgia Ltd $'000	Emma Ltd $'000
Asset revaluation surplus as at 1/7/13	—	200
Increase in 2013–14		400
Asset revaluation surplus as at 30/6/14		600
General reserve as at 1/7/13	1 000	1 500
Increase in 2013–14	—	1 000
General reserve at 30/6/14	1 000	2 500

Statements of Financial Position as at 30 June 2014		
	Georgia Ltd $'000	Emma Ltd $'000
EQUITY AND LIABILITIES		
Equity		
Share capital	8 000	3 000
Asset revaluation surplus	—	600
General reserve	1 000	2 500
Retained earnings	3 100	4 400
Total equity	12 100	10 500
Total liabilities	1 500	1 400
Total equity and liabilities	13 600	11 900
ASSETS		
Non-current assets		
Property, plant and equipment	5 904	9 000
Investment in Emma Ltd	2 696	
	8 600	9 000
Current assets		
Inventory	4 000	2 000
Receivables	1 000	900
	5 000	2 900
Total assets	13 600	11 900

Required

Prepare the consolidated financial statements of Georgia Ltd at 30 June 2014, applying the equity method of accounting to the investment in Emma Ltd.

Solution

The first step is to prepare an acquisition analysis which compares at acquisition date, 1 July 2012, the cost of the investment in Emma Ltd and the share of the net fair value of the identifiable assets and liabilities of Emma Ltd. This analysis is the same as the acquisition analysis used in preparing consolidated financial statements, and results in the determination of any goodwill or income on acquisition.

Acquisition analysis
At 1 July 2012:

Net fair value of identifiable assets
and liabilities of Emma Ltd
$= (\$3\,000\,000 + \$3\,000\,000)$ (equity)
$+ \$200\,000(1 - 30\%)$ (inventory)
$+ \$500\,000(1 - 30\%)$ (plant)
$= \$6\,490\,000$

$$\text{Net fair value acquired by Emma Ltd} = 40\% \times \$6\,490\,000$$
$$= \$2\,596\,000$$

Cost of investment	$= \$2\,696\,000$
Goodwill	$= \$100\,000$

As a result of the analysis, the effects of the adjustments to assets on hand at acquisition date can be calculated. In relation to the plant, there is a $500 000 difference between the fair value and the carrying amount at acquisition date. As a result, the recorded profits of the associate after acquisition date will include amounts that were paid for by the investor at acquisition date. The equity method recognises a share of post-acquisition equity only. The plant is being depreciated by the associate at 20% p.a. straight-line. The after-tax effect of the depreciation each year is calculated as:

$$\text{Depreciation of plant p.a.} = 20\% \times \$500\,000(1 - 30\%)$$
$$= \$70\,000$$

In each of the 5 years subsequent to the acquisition date, the recorded profit of the associate is reduced by $28 000 p.a. prior to calculating the investor's share of post-acquisition equity.

In relation to inventory, there is a $200 000 difference between fair value and carrying amount at acquisition date. When the associate sells the inventory, it will record a profit that includes pre-acquisition equity to the investor. The after-tax effect on profit on sale of the inventory is:

$$\text{Pre-acquisition inventory effect} = \$200\,000(1 - 30\%)$$
$$= \$140\,000$$

In the year of sale of the inventory, the investor's share of the recorded profit of the group is reduced by $140 000 prior to calculating the investor's share of post-acquisition equity.

Consolidation worksheet entries — 30 June 2014
The investor's share of the post-acquisition equity of the associate to be recognised on consolidation is calculated in two steps: a share of post-acquisition equity between the acquisition date and the beginning of the current period, and a share of the current period's post-acquisition equity. A third step is necessary to adjust for dividends paid/payable by the investee.

(1) *Share of changes in post-acquisition equity in previous periods*
The calculation is based on post-acquisition movements in the Retained Earnings account and other reserve accounts created by transfers from retained earnings, and adjusted for the effects of inter-entity transactions. The consolidation worksheet entry for the investor's share of the associate's post-acquisition equity recognised between the date of acquisition and the beginning of the current period is calculated as follows:

	$'000	$'000
Retained earnings:		
Post-acquisition retained earnings from acquisition date to beginning of the current period:		
$4 000 000 – $3 000 000		$1 000
Change in general reserve in previous periods		1 500
Pre-acquisition adjustments:		2 500
Depreciation of plant	(70)	
Sale of inventory	(140)	(210)
Post-acquisition retained earnings		2 290
Adjustments for inter-entity transactions:		
Inventory on hand at 30/6/14: $200 000(1 – 30%)	(140)	
Unrealised profit on sale of equipment:		
Original gain $400 000(1 – 30%) less depreciation p.a. of ¼ × $280 000	(210)	(350)
		1 940
Investor's share (40%) of retained earnings at 1/7/13		$ 776

	$'000	$'000
Asset revaluation surplus:		
Share of asset revaluation surplus in previous periods: 40% × $200 000		80
Total increase in equity-accounted carrying amount in previous periods		$ 856

The consolidation worksheet entry in relation to previous period's equity is:

Investments in Associates and Joint Ventures	Dr	856 000	
Retained Earnings (1/7/13)	Cr		776 000
Asset Revaluation Surplus	Cr		80 000
(Recognition of equity-accounted share of prior period's equity)			

In relation to the above entry and calculations, note the following:

Retained earnings (1/7/13):
- *Retained earnings:* The change is calculated as the difference between the recorded balance at acquisition date and the balance at the beginning of the current period.
- *General reserve:* The change in this equity amount is calculated in the same way as for retained earnings. There was no balance at acquisition date. The balance at 30 June 2014 is $2.5 million and, given a transfer to the reserve of $1 million, the balance at the beginning of the period was $1.5 million. This can be seen in the statement of changes in equity. Hence there is an increase in post-acquisition equity of $1.5 million.
- *Determination of post-acquisition equity:* The movement in recorded retained earnings is not all post-acquisition equity. The investor recognised the fair value of the assets and liabilities of the associate at acquisition date, and not the carrying amount in the associate. Where there are movements in these assets and liabilities, some of the profits recognised by the associate are pre-acquisition and not post-acquisition. There were two assets at acquisition date for which the fair value differed from carrying amount:
  - *Plant:* The fair value was $500 000 greater than the carrying amount. As calculated in the acquisition analysis, since the asset has a 5-year life, in relation to the investor's share the pre-acquisition amount included in recorded equity of the associate is $180 000 p.a.
  - *Inventory:* The fair value was $200 000 greater than carrying amount. As calculated in the acquisition analysis, since the asset was sold after the acquisition date, in relation to the investor's share the pre-acquisition effect is $56 000.
  Hence, the change in post-acquisition retained earnings between acquisition date and the beginning of the current period is $2 290 000.
- *Inter-entity transactions:* Where either the investor or investee has recognised profits or losses on transactions with the other party, and these are not realised, adjustments are made to eliminate unrealised profits or losses. In this problem, the Additional Information details four inter-entity transactions, only two of which relate to previous periods, namely (a) and (d):
  (a) On 1 July 2013, the investee sold inventory to the investor at a profit before tax of $200 000. This was unrealised at 30 June 2013. The recorded change in equity is then reduced by $140 000 after-tax profit as the profit is not yet realised.
  (d) On 2 July 2012, the investee recognised an after-tax profit of $280 000 on the sale of equipment to the investor. This profit is realised as the benefits from the asset are consumed by use. The rate of consumption is measured via depreciation. As the asset has a 4-year life, one-quarter of the profit is realised each year. Hence, the unrealised portion at 30 June 2013 is the original after-tax profit of $280 000 less ¼ of $280 000, namely $210 000.
  The investor's share of post-acquisition retained earnings, adjusted for unrealised profits on inter-entity transactions is then $856 000.

Asset revaluation surplus:
There was no asset revaluation surplus recognised in the investee at acquisition date. As per the statement of profit or loss and other comprehensive income, the balance at 30 June 2013 was $200 000. Hence, the change over the period is $200 000. The investor's share of this is 40%, namely $80 000.

Investment in associate/joint venture — Emma Ltd:
The investor's total share of post-acquisition equity of the investee up to the beginning of the current period is, therefore, $856 000. This amount is then added to the investment in associates and joint ventures account, with increases recognised in the relevant reserve accounts.

(2) *Share of profit in current period*
In part (1), the investor's share of the previous period's post-acquisition equity was calculated. In this part, the calculation is of the investor's share of the post-acquisition equity of the investee relating to the current period. In this problem, increases in equity arise owing to the investee's earning of a profit and recording of other income as increments in the asset revaluation surplus.
The calculations and required consolidation adjustment entry is shown below:

	$'000	$'000
Recorded profit		3 900
Pre-acquisition adjustments:		
Depreciation of plant		(70)
Post-acquisition profit		3 830
Adjustments for inter-entity transactions:		
Realised profit in opening inventory	140	
Unrealised profit in Georgia Ltd's ending inventory: ½ × $600 000 (1 – 30%)	(210)	
Unrealised profit in Emma Ltd's ending inventory: $200 000 (1 – 30%)	(140)	
Realised profit on plant: ¼ × $280 000	70	(140)
		3 690
Investor's share (40%) of associate/joint venture		1 476
Other comprehensive income		
Share of increment in asset revaluation surplus: 40% × $400 000		160
Total increase in equity-accounted carrying amount in current period		$1 636

The consolidation worksheet entries are:

Investments in Associates and Joint Ventures	Dr	1 476 000	
Share of Profit or Loss of Associates and Joint Ventures	Cr		1 476 000
(Share of profit or loss of associate/joint venture)			
Investments in Associates and Joint Ventures	Dr	160 000	
Share of Other Comprehensive Income of Associates and			
Joint Ventures	Cr		160 000
(Share of revaluation increase)			
Share of Other Comprehensive Income of Associates			
and Joint Ventures	Dr	160 000	
Asset Revaluation Surplus	Cr		160 000
(Accumulation of revaluation increase in equity)			

In relation to these calculations and entry, note the following:

Profit or loss for the period
- *Share of profit or loss of associate:* The associate records an after-tax profit for the year of $3 900 000. This profit needs to be adjusted where there have been transactions between the investor and the associate and at the end of the reporting period profits or losses on these transactions are unrealised.

However, this profit is not all post-acquisition profit. Movements in assets and liabilities on hand at acquisition date when fair values differed from carrying amounts give rise to pre-acquisition elements in recorded profits. In the current period, because the plant on hand at acquisition date was recognised by the investor at fair value, the extra depreciation on the plant reflects pre-acquisition equity. As calculated in the acquisition analysis the pre-acquisition effect is $70 000 p.a. This is subtracted from the profit of the period profit to give the post-acquisition profit for the period.

- *Inter-entity transactions:* In this problem there are four transactions noted in the additional information that affect the current period, namely (a)–(d).
  - (a) The inventory on hand at 1 July 2013 is all sold by 30 June 2014. The profit on the inter-entity sale was unrealised at the beginning of the current period but is realised in the current period. The after-tax profit on sale of the inventory was $140 000. Since the profit is realised in the current period, it is added to the recorded profit of the associate. Note that $1 400 000 is subtracted in the calculation of the investor's share of previous period equity and is added to the calculation of the investor's share of current period profit. Since the profit is now realised, there is no need to make an adjustment in future periods.
  - (b) In February 2014, the associate sold inventory to the investor at an after-tax profit of $420 000. Since half of the inventory is still on hand at 30 June 2014, there is unrealised profit at the end of the reporting period of $210 000. This amount is subtracted from recorded profit because the investor's share relates to realised profit only.
  - (c) In the current period, the investor sold inventory to the associate for an after-tax profit of $140 000. Since this inventory remains on hand at the end of the reporting period, the unrealised profit is subtracted from recorded profit.
  - (d) The gain on sale of equipment was adjusted for in the calculation of the investor's share of previous period equity. As noted in that calculation, the unrealised profit on sale is realised as the asset is used up and depreciated. The amount realised each year is in proportion to depreciation, namely one-quarter p.a. The amount of the gain realised in the current period is then $\frac{1}{4} \times \$280 000$, that is, $70 000. Being realised profit, it is added back to recorded profit.

The total post-acquisition profit of the investee adjusted for the effects of inter-entity transactions is then $3 690 000, and the investor's share (40%) is $1 476 000.

Other comprehensive income

From the statement of changes in equity, note that the asset revaluation surplus has increased by $400 000 in the current period. The investor is entitled to 40% of this, that is, $160 000. This is recognised in other comprehensive income and accumulated in the asset revaluation surplus.

Investment in associate/joint venture — Emma Ltd

The investor's share of current period post-acquisition equity is then $1 636 000, which increases the investor's investment in the associate. For the profit portion, this is recognised by a separate line item in the consolidated statement of comprehensive income.

(3) *Dividends paid and provided for by associate/joint venture*

A further entry is necessary to take into account reductions in the investee's equity in the current period because of dividends. In the current period, Emma Ltd paid a $1.5 million dividend and declared a $1 million dividend. Assuming the investor recognises dividend revenue in relation to the declared dividend, it would recognise dividend revenue of $1 million (i.e. 40% × [$1.5 million + $1 million]).

The following entry eliminates, on consolidation, the dividend revenue recorded by the investor. This is because in parts (1) and (2) above, the investor's equity has been increased by its share of the equity of the associate/joint venture from which the dividends were paid/declared. Similarly, it is also necessary to reduce the investment in the associate as the share of equity in the associate as calculated in parts (1) and (2) has been reduced by the payment/declaration of the dividend. The consolidation worksheet entry is:

Dividend Revenue		Dr	1 000 000
Investments in Associates and Joint Ventures		Cr		1 000 000
(Adjustment for dividend paid by associate/joint venture: 40% × [$1 500 000 + $1 000 000])			

(4) *Total investment*

On the basis of the above worksheet entries, the carrying amount of the investment in the associate/joint venture, Emma Ltd, is:

$$\$4 188 000 = \$2 696 000 + \$856 000 + \$1 636 000 - \$1 000 000$$

The consolidated financial statements of Georgia Ltd at 30 June 2014, including the investment in the associate/joint venture accounted for under the equity method, are as follows:

GEORGIA LTD
Consolidated Statement of Profit or Loss and Other Comprehensive Income for year ended 30 June 2014

	$'000
Revenue [$25 000 000 – $1 000 000]	24 000
Expenses	19 200
	4 800
Share of profit or loss of associates and joint ventures accounted for using the equity method	1 476
Profit before tax	6 276
Income tax expense	2 200
Profit for the period	4 076
Other comprehensive income:	
Share of other comprehensive income of associates and joint ventures accounted for using the equity method	160
Total comprehensive income	4 236

GEORGIA LTD
Consolidated Statement of Changes in Equity for year ended 30 June 2014

	$'000
Total comprehensive income	4 236
Retained earnings at 1/7/13 [$4 000 000 + $976 000]	4 776
Profit or loss for the period	4 076
	8 852
Dividend paid	(3 000)
Dividend provided	(1 500)
Retained earnings at 30/6/14	4 352
Asset revaluation surplus at 1/7/13	80
Revaluation increases	160
Asset revaluation surplus at 30/6/14	240
General reserve at 1/7/13	1 000
General reserve at 30/6/14	1 000

GEORGIA LTD
Consolidated Statement of Financial Position as at 30 June 2014

EQUITY AND LIABILITIES	
Equity	$'000
Share capital	8 000
Asset revaluation surplus	240
General reserve	1 000
Retained earnings	4 352
Total equity	13 592
Total liabilities	1 500
Total equity and liabilities	15 092

ASSETS	
Non-current assets	
Property, plant and equipment	5 904
Investments in associates and joint ventures	4 188
	10 092
Current assets	
Inventories	4 000
Receivables	1 000
	5 000
Total assets	15 092

29.7 SHARE OF LOSSES OF AN ASSOCIATE OR JOINT VENTURE

It may occur that the associate or joint venture incurs losses rather than profits. In this situation, the investor recognises losses only to the point where the carrying amount of the investment reaches zero (IAS 28, paragraph 38). The investor discontinues the use of the equity method when the share of losses equals or exceeds the carrying amount of the investment.

Note that the carrying amount of the investment is not just the balance of the investment in the associate or joint venture. The investor's interest in the associate/joint venture also includes other long-term interests in the associate/joint venture, such as preference shares or long-term receivables or loans. The base against which the losses are offset is then the investor's net investment in the associate/joint venture. Where the associate/joint venture incurs losses, the carrying amount of the account 'Investments in Associates and Joint Ventures' is first reduced to zero. If losses exceed this carrying amount, they are then applied against the other components of the investor's interest in the associate/joint venture in the reverse order of their seniority, or priority in liquidation. The logic is that, if the associate/joint venture is making losses, then the probability of the other investments in the associate/joint venture being realised is lessened.

If the associate/joint venture subsequently reports profits, the investor resumes recognising its share of those profits only after its share of the profits equals the share of losses not recognised (IAS 28 paragraph 39). In other words, once the equity-accounted balance of the investment returns to a positive amount, equity accounting resumes.

In situations where the associate records losses, if there are indications that the investment may be impaired, the investor should apply IAS 36 *Impairment of Assets*. As noted in paragraph 42 of IAS 28, in determining the value in use of the investment, an investor estimates:

(a) its share of the present value of the estimated future cash flows expected to be generated by the associate, including the cash flows from the operations of the associate and the proceeds on the ultimate disposal of the investment; or

(b) the present value of the estimated future cash flows expected to arise from dividends to be received from the investment and from its ultimate disposal.

Under appropriate assumptions, both methods give the same result.

ILLUSTRATIVE EXAMPLE 29.6 Share of losses of the associate

On 1 July 2010, Grace Ltd acquired 25% of the shares of Amelia Ltd for $100 000. At that date, the equity of Amelia Ltd was $400 000, with all identifiable assets and liabilities being measured at amounts equal to fair value. Table 29.1 shows the profits and losses made by the associate over the first 5 years of operations after 1 July 2010, with their effects on the carrying amount of the investment.

TABLE 29.1 Profits and losses made by associate over first 5 years of operations

Year	Profit/(loss)	Share of profit or loss	Cumulative share	Equity-accounted balance of investment
2010–11	$ 20 000	$ 5 000	$ 5 000	$105 000
2011–12	(200 000)	(50 000)	(45 000)	55 000
2012–13	(250 000)	(62 500)	(107 500)	0
2013–14	16 000	4 000	(103 500)	0
2014–15	20 000	5 000	(98 500)	1 500

Table 29.1 shows that the investment account is initially recorded by Grace Ltd at $100 000, and is progressively adjusted for Grace Ltd's share of the profits and losses of Amelia Ltd. In the 2012–13 year, when the cumulative share of the losses of the associate exceeds the cost of the investment, the investor discontinues recognising its share of future losses. Even though profits are recorded by the associate in the 2013–14 year, the balance of the investment stays at zero because the profits are not sufficient to offset losses not recognised.

The journal entries in the consolidation worksheets of Grace Ltd over these periods are:

30 June 2011	Investments in Associates and Joint Ventures	Dr	5 000	
	Share of Profit or Loss of Associates and Joint Ventures	Cr		5 000
30 June 2012	Share of Profit or Loss of Associates and Joint Ventures	Dr	50 000	
	Retained Earnings (1/7/11)	Cr		5 000
	Investments in Associates and Joint Ventures	Cr		45 000
30 June 2013	Share of Profit or Loss of Associates and Joint Ventures	Dr	55 000	
	Retained Earnings (1/7/12)	Dr	45 000	
	Investments in Associates and Joint Ventures	Cr		100 000
30 June 2014	Retained Earnings (1/7/13)	Dr	100 000	
	Investments in Associates and Joint Ventures	Cr		100 000
30 June 2015	Retained Earnings (1/7/14)	Dr	100 000	
	Investments in Associates and Joint Ventures	Cr		98 500
	Share of Profit or Loss of Associates and Joint Ventures	Cr		1 500

29.8 DISCLOSURE

Requirements in relation to disclosure of information about investments in associates are not found in IAS 28. IFRS 12 *Disclosure of Interests in Other Entities* was issued in 2011 and included in the 'other entities' that the standard applies to are associates and joint ventures. This standard applies to annual reporting periods beginning on or after 1 January 2013.

As stated in paragraph 1 of IFRS 12, the key objective of this standard is to require an entity to disclose information that enables users of its financial statements to evaluate:
(a) the nature of, and risks associated with, its interests in other entities
(b) the effects of those interests on its financial position, financial performance and cash flows.

Notice the emphasis on the ability of users of financial statements to be able to evaluate risks. In the introduction to IFRS 12, in paragraph IN5, the IASB noted that the global financial crisis that started in 2007 highlighted a lack of transparency about the risks to which a reporting entity was exposed from its involvement with structured entities. As a result, IFRS 12 (see paragraphs 2(a), 7 and 9) requires an entity to disclose the significant judgements and assumptions it has made in determining the nature of its interest in another entity, and in particular judgements, assumptions and changes in these.

The following are examples of situations where it is necessary for an investor to disclose significant judgements and assumptions in relation to associates:

- where it does not have significant influence even though it holds 20% or more of the voting rights of another entity
- where it has significant influence even though it holds less than 20% of the voting rights of another entity.

An entity is required to disclose information that enables users to evaluate the nature, extent and financial effects of its interest in associates and joint ventures, including the nature and effects of its contractual relationship with other investors (IFRS 11 paragraph 20). To achieve this, the following disclosures are required by paragraph 21 of IFRS 12:

(a) for each joint arrangement and associate that is material to the reporting entity:
  (i) the name of the joint arrangement or associate.
  (ii) the nature of the entity's relationship with the joint arrangement or associate (by, for example, describing the nature of the activities of the joint arrangement or associate and whether they are strategic to the entity's activities).
  (iii) the principal place of business (and country of incorporation, if applicable and different from the principal place of business) of the joint arrangement or associate.
  (iv) the proportion of ownership interest or participating share held by the entity and, if different, the proportion of voting rights held (if applicable).
(b) for each joint venture and associate that is material to the reporting entity:
  (i) whether the investment in the joint venture or associate is measured using the equity method or at fair value.
  (ii) summarised financial information about the joint venture or associate as specified in paragraphs B12 and B13.
  (iii) if the joint venture or associate is accounted for using the equity method, the fair value of its investment in the joint venture or associate, if there is a quoted market price for the investment.
(c) financial information as specified in paragraph B16 about the entity's investments in joint ventures and associates that are not individually material:
  (i) in aggregate for all individually immaterial joint ventures and, separately,
  (ii) in aggregate for all individually immaterial associates.

The summarised information in paragraph (b)(ii) above consists of:

1. For each *joint venture and associate* that is material to the reporting entity, an entity shall disclose:
   (a) dividends received from the joint venture or associate.
   (b) summarised financial information for the joint venture or associate including, but not necessarily limited to:
       (i) current assets
       (ii) non-current assets
       (iii) current liabilities
       (iv) non-current liabilities
       (v) revenue
       (vi) profit or loss from continuing operations
       (vii) post-tax profit or loss from discontinued operations
       (viii) other comprehensive income
       (ix) total comprehensive income.

2. In addition to the summarised financial information above, an entity has to disclose for each *joint venture* that is material to the reporting entity the amount of:
   (a) cash and cash equivalents
   (b) current financial liabilities (excluding trade and other payables and provisions)
   (c) non-current financial liabilities (excluding trade and other payables and provisions)
   (d) depreciation and amortisation
   (e) interest income
   (f) interest expense
   (g) income tax expense or income.

Further required disclosures, as detailed in IFRS 12, paragraph 22, are those relating to:

- *significant restrictions on the ability of associates to transfer funds to the investor*: These transfers could relate to dividend payments or repayment of loans.

- *different reporting dates used by the investor and an associate*: the disclosure consists of stating the date at the end of the reporting period for the associate as well the reason for using a different period or date.
- *losses made by an associate*: an investor must disclose the unrecognised share of losses made by an associate both for the reporting period and cumulatively where the equity method has been discontinued.

Where the interest in an associate or joint venture is immaterial, an entity must disclose aggregated information for all immaterial investments (IFRS 12 paragraph B16). In particular, an entity must disclose the aggregated amount of its share of the joint ventures' or associates':

(a) profit or loss from continuing operations
(b) post-tax profit or loss from discontinued operations
(c) other comprehensive income
(d) total comprehensive income.

Figure 29.4 shows the disclosures provided in relation to the accounting policies applied for investments in associates and joint ventures by Foster's Group Ltd. Note that these were provided prior to the application date for IFRS 12, namely for reporting periods beginning on or after 1 January 2013.

Investments in associates and joint ventures

In the consolidated financial statements, investments in associates, which includes partnerships, are accounted for using the equity method of accounting and are initially recognised at cost. Under this method, the Group's share of profits or losses are recognised in the income statement and its share of movements in reserves are recognised in the Group's consolidated other comprehensive income. The cumulative post acquisition changes in the Group's share of net assets of the associate, less any impairment losses, are adjusted against the cost of the investment. When the Group's share of losses in an associate equals or exceeds its interest in the associate, the Group does not recognise any further losses, unless it has an obligation on behalf of the associate. Where there has been a change recognised directly in the associate's equity, the Group recognises its share of any changes and disclose[s], this when applicable, in the consolidated Statement of comprehensive income. Associates are those entities over which the Group has significant influence, but not control and which is neither a subsidiary nor a joint venture. Unrealised gains and losses in transactions between the Group and its associates are eliminated to the extent of the Group's interest in the associates.

FIGURE 29.4 Policy note on associates and joint ventures
Source: Foster's Group Ltd (2011, p. 67).

Figure 29.5 shows the detailed information provided by Foster's Group Ltd about the country of incorporation and proportionate ownership in its investments accounted for using the equity method.

FIGURE 29.5 Disclosures made concerning country of incorporation and ownership interest

NOTE 11 INVESTMENTS ACCOUNTED FOR USING THE EQUITY METHOD

	Consolidated	
	2011 $m	2010 $m
Investments in associates and joint venture partners	62.9	76.0

Investments in associates and joint venture partnerships are accounted for in the consolidated financial statements using the equity method of accounting and are carried at cost by the entity holding the ownership interest. The entities are primarily involved in, or have been involved in the production, marketing and distribution activities of the Group.

FIGURE 29.5 *(continued)*

Name of entity	Country of Incorporation	Reporting date	Ownership interest 2011 %	2010 %
Fiddlesticks LLC	USA	31 December	—	50.0
Foster's USA, LLC	USA	31 March	49.9	49.9
Judd Road Vineyards Limited	New Zealand	30 June	—	50.0
International Trade and Supply Limited	United Kingdom	31 December	39.9	39.9
Make Wine Pty. Ltd.	Australia	30 June	—	50.0
Make Wine Trust	Australia	30 June	—	50.0
Oak Vale Vineyard Limited	New Zealand	30 June	—	50.0
Rapuara Vintners Limited	New Zealand	30 June	—	50.0

The carrying values of material investments are:
- Foster's USA LLC $19.6 million (2010: $24.2 million); and
- International Trade and Supply Limited $43.3 million (2010: $44.6 million).

Source: Foster's Group Ltd (2011, p. 80).

Figure 29.6 provides the financial information disclosed by Qantas in relation to its associates and joint ventures. Note that these were provided prior to the application date for IFRS 12, namely for reporting periods beginning on or after 1 January 2013.

FIGURE 29.6 Financial disclosures relating to associates and joint ventures

15. Investments Accounted for Using the Equity Method

	Qantas Group 2011 $m	2010 $m
Share of net profit/(loss) of associates and jointly controlled entities		
Associates	5	(14)
Jointly controlled entities	17	10
Total share of net profit/(loss) of associates and jointly controlled entities	22	(4)
Investments accounted for using the equity method		
Associates		
— Jetset Travelworld Limited	114	—
— Other	51	65
Total investments in associates	165	65
Jointly controlled entities		
— AUX Investment Pty Limited	292	—
— Star Track Express Holdings Pty Limited	—	266
— Australian air Express Pty Ltd	—	24
— Other	19	23
Total investments in jointly controlled entities	311	313
Total investments accounted for using the equity method	476	378

(continued)

FIGURE 29.6 (continued)

(A) INVESTMENTS IN ASSOCIATES

Details of interests in associates are as follows:

	Principal Activity	Country of Incorporation	Balance Date	Qantas Group Ownership Interest	
				2011 %	2010 %
Air Pacific Limited	Air transport	Fiji	31 Mar	46	46
Fiji Resorts Limited	Resort accommodation	Fiji	31 Dec	21	21
Hallmark Aviation Services L.P.	Passenger handling services	United States of America	31 Dec	49	49
HT & T Travel Philippines, Inc.	Tours and travel	Philippines	30 Jun	28	28
Holiday Tours and Travel (Thailand) Ltd	Tours and travel	Thailand	31 Dec	37	37
Holiday Tours & Travel Vietnam Co. Ltd	Tours and travel	Vietnam	30 Jun	37	37
Jetset Travelworld Limited[1]	Travel products & services	Australia	30 Jun	29	—
Jetstar Pacific Airlines Aviation Joint Stock Company	Air transport	Vietnam	31 Dec	27	27
PT Holidays Tours & Travel	Tours and travel	Indonesia	31 Dec	37	37
Tour East (T.E.T) Ltd	Tours and travel	Thailand	31 Dec	37	37

1. *As a result of the merger of Jetset Travelworld Group with Stella Travel Services as described in Note 27(B), Jetset Travelworld Group is accounted for as an associate effective 1 October 2010.*

Source: Qantas (2011, p. 71).

SUMMARY

This chapter has covered the principles of accounting for investments in associates and joint ventures as contained in IAS 28 *Investments in Associates and Joint Ventures.* Some of the key principles are:

- Besides subsidiaries, an entity may have investments in other entities, known as associates and joint ventures, with which the entity has a special relationship.
- An entity over which an investor has significant influence in the determination of financial and operating policy decisions is referred to as an associate.
- Where an investor is involved in an investment where there is a contractually agreed sharing of control such that decisions require the unanimous consent of the parties sharing control, the investor has joint control over the investee.
- The equity method is designed to provide more information about an investment than generally supplied under the cost method, but less information than supplied under the consolidation method.
- Under the equity method, an investor recognises an increase in equity as well as an increase in the investment in an investee based upon the investor's proportionate interest in the investee.
- In applying the equity method, adjustments to equity balances recorded by the investee are made to eliminate any pre-acquisition equity.
- Adjustments are also made to eliminate the effects of inter-entity transactions. These are made for both upstream and downstream transactions with amounts being calculated based on the investor's proportional interest in the investee.
- Where an investee incurs losses, an investment in an investee cannot be reduced below zero, with the application of the equity method being discontinued.

Discussion questions

1. What is an associate entity?
2. Why are associates distinguished from other investments held by the investor?

3. Discuss the similarities and differences between the criteria used to identify subsidiaries and those used to identify associates.
4. What is meant by 'significant influence'?
5. What factors could be used to indicate the existence of significant influence?
6. What is a joint venture?
7. What is meant by joint control?
8. How does joint control differ from control as applied on consolidation?
9. Discuss the relative merits of accounting for investments by the cost method, the fair value method and the equity method.
10. Outline the accounting adjustments required in relation to transactions between the investor and an associate/joint venture. Explain the rationale for these adjustments.
11. Compare the accounting for the effects of inter-entity transactions for transactions between parent entities and subsidiaries and between investors and associates/joint ventures.
12. Discuss whether the equity method should be viewed as a form of consolidation or a valuation technique.
13. Explain why equity accounting is sometimes referred to as 'one-line consolidation'.
14. Explain the differences in application of the equity method of accounting where the method is applied in the records of the investor compared with the application in the consolidation worksheet of the investor.
15. Explain the treatment of dividends from the associate under the equity method of accounting.

Exercises

STAR RATING ★ BASIC ★★ MODERATE ★★★ DIFFICULT

| Exercise 29.1 | **SIGNIFICANT INFLUENCE** |

★ The accountant of Cornett Chocolates Ltd, Ms Fraulein, has been advised by her auditors that the entity's investment in Concertina's Milk Ltd should be accounted for using the equity method of accounting. Cornett Chocolates Ltd holds only 20.2% of the voting shares currently issued by Concertina's Milk Ltd. Since the investment was undertaken purely for cash flow reasons based on the potential dividend stream from the investment, Ms Fraulein does not believe that Cornett Chocolates Ltd exerts significant influence over the investee.

Required

Discuss the factors that Ms Fraulein should investigate in determining whether an investor–associate relationship exists, and what avenues are available so that the equity method of accounting does not have to be applied.

| Exercise 29.2 | **ADJUSTMENTS WHERE INVESTOR PREPARES AND DOES NOT PREPARE CONSOLIDATED FINANCIAL STATEMENTS** |

★ Sarah Ltd acquired a 30% interest in Madison Ltd for $50 000 on 1 July 2012. The equity of Madison Ltd at the acquisition date was:

Share capital	$ 30 000
Retained earnings	120 000

All the identifiable assets and liabilities of Madison Ltd were recorded at fair value. Profits and dividends for the years ended 30 June 2013 to 2015 were as follows:

	Profit before tax	Income tax expense	Dividends paid
2013	$80 000	$30 000	$80 000
2014	70 000	25 000	15 000
2015	60 000	20 000	10 000

Required

1. Prepare journal entries in the records of Sarah Ltd for each of the years ended 30 June 2013 to 2014 in relation to its investment in the associate/joint venture, Madison Ltd. (Assume Sarah Ltd does not prepare consolidated financial statements.)

2. Prepare the consolidation worksheet entries to account for Sarah Ltd's interest in the associate/joint venture, Madison Ltd. (Assume Sarah Ltd does prepare consolidated financial statements.)

ACCOUNTING FOR AN ASSOCIATE/JOINT VENTURE BY AN INVESTOR

★ Jasmine Ltd acquired a 40% interest in Hayley Ltd for $170 000 on 1 July 2013. The share capital, reserves and retained earnings of Hayley Ltd at the acquisition date and at 30 June 2014 were as follows:

	1 July 2013	30 June 2014
Share capital	$300 000	$300 000
Asset revaluation surplus	—	100 000
General reserve	—	15 000
Retained earnings	100 000	109 000
	$400 000	$524 000

At 1 July 2013, all the identifiable assets and liabilities of Hayley Ltd were recorded at fair value. The following is applicable to Hayley Ltd for the year to 30 June 2014:
(a) Profit (after income tax expense of $11 000): $39 000
(b) Increase in reserves
   – General (transferred from retained earnings): $15 000
   – Asset revaluation (revaluation of freehold land and buildings at 30 June 2014): $100 000
(c) Dividends paid to shareholders: $15 000
(d) The tax rate is 30%.
(e) Jasmine Ltd does not prepare consolidated financial statements.

Required

Prepare the journal entries in the records of Jasmine Ltd for the year ended 30 June 2014 in relation to its investment in the associate, Hayley Ltd.

INTER-ENTITY TRANSACTIONS WHERE INVESTOR HAS NO SUBSIDIARIES

★ Imogen Ltd acquired 20% of the ordinary shares of Chelsea Ltd on 1 July 2013. At this date, all the identifiable assets and liabilities of Imogen Ltd were recorded at fair value. An analysis of the acquisition showed that $2000 of goodwill was acquired.

Imogen Ltd has no subsidiaries, and records its investment in the associate, Chelsea Ltd, in accordance with IAS 28. In the 2014–15 period, Chelsea Ltd recorded a profit of $100 000, paid an interim dividend of $10 000 and, in June 2015, declared a further dividend of $15 000. In June 2010, Chelsea Ltd had declared a $20 000 dividend, which was paid in August 2014, at which date it was recognised by Imogen Ltd.

The following transactions have occurred between the two entities (all transactions are independent unless specified):
(a) In January 2015, Chelsea Ltd sold inventory to Imogen Ltd for $15 000. This inventory had previously cost Chelsea Ltd $10 000, and remains unsold by Imogen Ltd at the end of the period.
(b) In February 2015, Imogen Ltd sold inventory to Chelsea Ltd at a before-tax profit of $5000. Half of this was sold by Chelsea Ltd before 30 June 2015.
(c) In June 2014, Chelsea Ltd sold inventory to Imogen Ltd for $18 000. This inventory had cost Chelsea Ltd $12 000. At 30 June 2014, this inventory remained unsold by Imogen Ltd. However, it was all sold by Imogen Ltd before 30 June 2015.
The tax rate is 30%.

Required

Prepare the journal entries in the records of Imogen Ltd in relation to its investment in Chelsea Ltd for the year ended 30 June 2015.

INTER-ENTITY TRANSACTIONS WHERE INVESTOR DOES NOT PREPARE CONSOLIDATED FINANCIAL STATEMENTS

★

Holly Ltd owns 25% of the shares of its associate, Matilda Ltd. At the acquisition date, there were no differences between the fair values and the carrying amounts of the identifiable assets and liabilities of Matilda Ltd.

For 2013–14, Matilda Ltd recorded a profit of $100 000. During this period, Matilda Ltd paid a $10 000 dividend, declared in June 2013, and an interim dividend of $8000. The tax rate is 30%.

The following transactions have occurred between Holly Ltd and Matilda Ltd:

(a) On 1 July 2012, Matilda Ltd sold a non-current asset costing $10 000 to Holly Ltd for $12 000. Holly Ltd applies a 10% p.a. on cost straight-line method of depreciation.

(b) On 1 January 2014, Matilda Ltd sold an item of plant to Holly Ltd for $15 000. The carrying amount of the asset to Matilda Ltd at time of sale was $12 000. Holly Ltd applies a 15% p.a. straight-line method of depreciation.

(c) A non-current asset with a carrying amount of $20 000 was sold by Matilda Ltd to Holly Ltd for $28 000 on 1 June 2014. Holly Ltd regarded the item as inventory and still had the item on hand at 30 June 2014.

(d) On 1 July 2012, Holly Ltd sold an item of machinery to Matilda Ltd for $6000. This item had cost Holly Ltd $4000. Holly Ltd regarded this item as inventory whereas Matilda Ltd intended to use the item as a non-current asset. Matilda Ltd applied a 10% p.a. on cost straight-line depreciation method.

Required

Holly Ltd applies the equity method in accounting for its investment in Matilda Ltd. Assuming Holly Ltd does not prepare consolidated financial statements, prepare the journal entries in the records of Holly Ltd for the year ended 30 June 2014 in relation to its investment in Matilda Ltd.

INVESTOR PREPARES CONSOLIDATED FINANCIAL STATEMENTS, MULTIPLE PERIODS

★

On 1 July 2012, Sophia Ltd purchased 30% of the shares of Lara Ltd for $60 050. At this date, the ledger balances of Lara Ltd were:

Capital	$150 000	Assets	$225 000
Other reserves	30 000	Less: Liabilities	30 000
Retained earnings	15 000		
	$195 000		$195 000

At 1 July 2012, all the identifiable assets and liabilities of Lara Ltd were recorded at fair value except for plant whose fair value was $5000 greater than carrying amount. This plant has an expected future life of 5 years, the benefits being received evenly over this period. Dividend revenue is recognised when dividends are declared. The tax rate is 30%.

The results of Lara Ltd for the next 3 years were:

	30 June 2013	30 June 2014	30 June 2015
Profit/(loss) before income tax	$50 000	$40 000	$(5 000)
Income tax expense	20 000	20 000	—
Profit/(loss)	30 000	20 000	(5 000)
Dividend paid	15 000	5 000	2 000
Dividend declared	10 000	5 000	1 000

Required

Prepare, in journal entry format, for the years ending 30 June 2013, 2014 and 2015, the consolidation worksheet adjustments to include the equity-accounted results for the associate, Lara Ltd, in the consolidated financial statements of Sophia Ltd.

DISCLOSURE REQUIREMENTS

★★ The following note was given in the 2010 annual report of Foster's Group Ltd:

Note 11 — Investments accounted for using the equity method

	Consolidated	
	2010 $m	2009 $m
Investments in associates and joint venture partnerships	76.0	69.1

Investments in associates and joint venture partnerships are accounted for in the consolidated financial statements using the equity method of accounting and are carried at cost by the entity holding the ownership interest. The entities are primarily involved in, or have been involved in the production, marketing and distribution activities of the Group.

			Ownership interest	
Name of entity	Country of incorporation	Reporting date	2010 %	2009 %
Fiddlesticks LLC	USA	31 December	50.0	50.0
Foster's USA, LLC	USA	31 March	49.9	49.9
Judd Road vineyards Limited	New Zealand	30 June	50.0	50.0
International Trade and Supply Limited	United Kingdom	31 December	39.9	39.9
Make Wine Pty. Ltd.	Australia	30 June	50.0	—
Make Wine Trust	Australia	30 June	50.0	—
Oak Vale Vineyard Limited	New Zealand	30 June	50.0	50.0
Rapuara Vintners Limited	New Zealand	30 June	50.0	—

The carrying values of material investments are:
– Foster's USA LLC $24.2 million (2009: $23.5 million); and
– International Trade and Supply Limited $44.6 million (2009: $44.1 million).

	Consolidated	
	2010 $m	2009 $m
Equity accounted share of results		
– net profit before income tax	15.8	17.1
– income tax expense attributable to net profit	(2.6)	(1.5)
– net profits after income tax	13.2	15.6
Retained profits attributable to equity accounted investments		
– balance at the beginning of the year	10.6	19.8
– distributions received	(9.1)	(9.2)
– balance at the end of the year	1.5	10.6
Carrying amount of equity accounted investments		
– balance at the beginning of the year	69.1	58.8
– additions	7.7	0.0
– share of net profit	11.9	15.6
– dividends received	(9.1)	(9.2)
– foreign exchange	(3.6)	3.9
	76.0	69.1
Share of assets and liabilities		
– current assets	45.2	44.2
– non-current assets	29.4	21.9
Total assets	74.6	66.1

	Consolidated	
	2010 $m	2009 $m
– current liabilities	(29.4)	(25.1)
– non-current liabilities	(2.2)	(4.5)
Total liabilities	(31.6)	(29.6)
– net assets	43.0	36.5
Goodwill/other	33.0	32.6
	76.0	69.1

There are no material commitments, contingent liabilities or subsequent events arising from the Group's interest in equity accounted entities.

Source: Foster's Group Ltd (2010, p. 73).

Required

In 2011, the IASB issued IAS 28 *Investments in Associates and Joint Ventures* and IFRS 12 *Disclosure of Interests in Other Entities*. Discuss the information that Foster's Group Ltd would have to produce as a result of the issue of the new accounting standards and comment on the relative usefulness of the disclosures required.

Exercise 29.8

★★

ASSOCIATES AND JOINTLY CONTROLLED ENTITIES

Amalgamated Holdings Ltd provided the following information in Note 1 *Significant Accounting Policies* in its 2010 annual report.

(iii) Associates and jointly controlled entities ('equity accounted investees')

Associates are those entities for which the Group has significant influence, but not control, over the financial and operating policies. Significant influence is presumed to exist when the Group holds between 20% and 50% of the voting power of another entity. Jointly controlled entities are those entities over whose activities the Group has joint control, established by contractual agreement and requiring unanimous consent for strategic financial and operating decisions. The consolidated financial statements include the Group's share of the total recognised gains and losses of associates and jointly controlled entities on an equity accounted basis, from the date that significant influence commences or joint control commences until the date that significant influence or joint control ceases. The Group's share of movements in reserves is recognised directly in consolidated reserves.

When the Group's share of losses exceeds its interest in an equity accounted investee, the Group's carrying amount is reduced to nil and recognition of further losses is discontinued except to the extent that the Group has incurred legal or constructive obligations to make payments on behalf of the investee.

(iv) Transactions eliminated on consolidation

Intra-group balances, and any unrealised gains and losses or income and expenses arising from intra-group transactions, are eliminated in preparing the consolidated financial statements. Unrealised gains arising from transactions with associates and jointly controlled entities are eliminated to the extent of the Group's interest in the entity. Unrealised losses are eliminated in the same way as unrealised gains, but only to the extent that there is no evidence of impairment. Gains and losses are recognised as the contributed assets are consumed or sold by the associates or jointly controlled entities or, if not consumed or sold by the associate or jointly controlled entity, when the Group's interest in such entities is sold.

Source: Amalgamated Holdings Ltd (2010, p. 35).

Required

Some investors in Amalgamated Holdings Ltd who have limited accounting knowledge, particularly about equity accounting, have asked you to provide a report to them commenting on:
• the differences between associates and partnerships
• the determination of the date of significant influence
• realisation of profits/losses on inter-entity transactions
• recognition of losses of an associate.

CONSOLIDATED WORKSHEET ENTRIES TO INCLUDE INVESTMENT IN ASSOCIATE

★★ On 1 July 2011, Caitlin Ltd acquired 30% of the shares of Alyssa Ltd for $60 000. At this date, the equity of Alyssa Ltd consisted of:

Share capital (100 000 shares)	$100 000
Asset revaluation surplus	50 000
Retained earnings	20 000

On 1 July 2013, the ownership interest of 30%, together with board representation and a diverse spread of remaining shareholders, was sufficient for the investor to demonstrate significant influence, and accordingly to begin accounting for the investment as an associate. The fair value of the 30% interest in Alyssa Ltd at 1 July 2013 was $70 000. At this date, the equity of Alyssa Ltd consisted of:

Share capital (100 000 shares)	$100 000
Asset revaluation surplus	60 000
General reserve	10 000
Retained earnings	40 000

At this date, all the identifiable assets and liabilities of Alyssa Ltd were recorded at fair value except for the following assets:

	Carrying amount	Fair value
Machinery	$20 000	$25 000
Inventory	10 000	12 000

The machinery was expected to have a further 5-year life, benefits being received evenly over this period. The inventory was all sold by 30 June 2014.

Dividends paid by Alyssa Ltd in the 2011–12 period were $10 000, and $12 000 was paid in the 2012–13 period. In June 2013, Alyssa Ltd declared a dividend of $10 000. Dividend revenue is recognised when dividends are declared.

During the period ending 30 June 2014, the following events occurred:

(a) Alyssa Ltd sold to Caitlin Ltd some inventory, which had previously cost Alyssa Ltd $8000, for $10 000. Caitlin Ltd still had one-quarter of these items on hand at 30 June 2014.

(b) On 1 January 2014, Caitlin Ltd sold a non-current asset to Alyssa Ltd for $50 000, giving a profit before tax of $10 000 to Caitlin Ltd. Alyssa Ltd applied a 12% p.a. on cost straight-line depreciation method to this asset.

(c) On 31 December 2013, Alyssa Ltd paid an interim dividend of $5000.

(d) At 30 June 2014, Alyssa Ltd calculated that it had earned a profit of $32 000, after an income tax expense of $8000. Alyssa Ltd then declared a $5000 dividend, to be paid in September 2014, and transferred $3000 to the general reserve.

(e) The tax rate is 30%.

Required

Prepare the journal entries for the consolidation worksheet of Caitlin Ltd at 30 June 2014 for the inclusion of the equity-accounted results of Alyssa Ltd.

ADJUSTMENTS WHERE INVESTOR DOES AND DOES NOT PREPARE
★★ **CONSOLIDATED FINANCIAL STATEMENTS**

On 1 July 2012, Zara Ltd acquired a 30% interest in one of its suppliers, Eva Ltd, at a cost of $13 650. The directors of Zara Ltd believe they exert 'significant influence' over Eva Ltd.

The equity of Eva Ltd at acquisition date was:

Share capital (20 000 shares)	$20 000
Retained earnings	10 000

All the identifiable assets and liabilities of Eva Ltd at 1 July 2012 were recorded at fair values except for some depreciable non-current assets with a fair value of $15 000 greater than carrying amount. These depreciable assets are expected to have a further 5-year life.

Additional information

(a) At 30 June 2014, Zara Ltd had inventory costing $100 000 (2013 : $60 000) on hand which had been purchased from Eva Ltd. A profit before tax of $30 000 (2013 : $10 000) had been made on the sale.

(b) All companies adopt the recommendations of IAS 12 regarding tax-effect accounting. Assume a tax rate of 30% applies.

(c) Information about income and changes in equity of Eva Ltd as at 30 June 2014 is:

Profit before tax		$360 000
Income tax expense		180 000
Profit		180 000
Retained earnings at 1/7/13		50 000
		230 000
Dividend paid	$50 000	
Dividend declared	50 000	100 000
Retained earnings at 30/6/14		$130 000

(d) All dividends may be assumed to be out of the profit for the current year. Dividend revenue is recognised when declared by directors.

(e) The equity of Eva Ltd at 30 June 2014 was:

Share capital	$ 20 000
Asset revaluation surplus	30 000
General reserve	5 000
Retained earnings	130 000

The asset revaluation surplus arose from a revaluation of freehold land made at 30 June 2014. The general reserve arose from a transfer from retained earnings in June 2013.

Required

1. Assume Zara Ltd does not prepare consolidated financial statements. Prepare the journal entries in the records of Zara Ltd for the year ended 30 June 2014 in relation to the investment in Eva Ltd.
2. Assume Zara Ltd does prepare consolidated financial statements. Prepare the consolidated worksheet entries for the year ended 30 June 2014 for inclusion of the equity-accounted results of Eva Ltd.

Exercise 29.11

★★

ACCOUNTING FOR AN ASSOCIATE WITHIN — AND WHERE THERE ARE NO — CONSOLIDATED FINANCIAL STATEMENTS

On 1 July 2012, Amy Ltd purchased 40% of the shares of Summer Ltd for $63 200. At that date, equity of Summer Ltd consisted of:

Share capital	$125 000
Retained earnings	11 000

At 1 July 2012, the identifiable assets and liabilities of Summer Ltd were recorded at fair value.
Information about income and changes in equity for both companies for the year ended 30 June 2015 was as shown below.

	Amy Ltd	**Summer Ltd**
Profit before tax	$ 26 000	$ 23 500
Income tax expense	10 600	5 400

(continued)

	Amy Ltd	Summer Ltd
Profit	$15 400	$18 100
Retained earnings (1/7/14)	18 000	16 000
	33 400	34 100
Dividend paid	5 000	4 000
Dividend declared	10 000	5 000
	15 000	9 000
Retained earnings (30/6/15)	$18 400	$25 100

Additional information
(a) Amy Ltd recognised the final dividend revenue from Summer Ltd before receipt of cash. Summer Ltd declared a $6000 dividend in June 2014, this being paid in August 2010.
(b) On 31 December 2013, Summer Ltd sold Amy Ltd a motor vehicle for $12 000. The vehicle had originally cost Summer Ltd $18 000 and was written down to $9000 for both tax and accounting purposes at time of sale to Amy Ltd. Both companies depreciated motor vehicles at the rate of 20% p.a. on cost.
(c) The beginning inventory of Summer Ltd included goods at $4000 bought from Amy Ltd; their cost to Amy Ltd was $3200.
(d) The ending inventory of Amy Ltd included goods purchased from Summer Ltd at a profit before tax of $1600.
(e) The tax rate is 30%.

Required

1. Prepare the journal entries in the records of Amy Ltd to account for the investment in Summer Ltd under the equity method for the year ended 30 June 2015 assuming Amy Ltd does not prepare consolidated financial statements.
2. Prepare the consolidated worksheet entries in relation to the investment in Summer Ltd, assuming Amy Ltd does prepare consolidated financial statements at 30 June 2015.

Exercise 29.12 **CONSOLIDATED FINANCIAL STATEMENTS INCLUDING INVESTMENTS IN ASSOCIATES**

★★ Sam Ltd acquired 90% of the ordinary shares of Paige Ltd on 1 July 2009 at a cost of $150 750. At that date the equity of Paige Ltd was:

Share capital (100 000 shares)	$100 000
Reserve	8 000
Retained earnings	12 000

At 1 July 2009, all the identifiable assets and liabilities of Paige Ltd were at fair value except for the following assets:

	Carrying amount	Fair value
Inventory	$10 000	$15 000
Depreciable assets	25 000	35 000

The inventory was all sold by 30 June 2010. Depreciable assets have an expected further 5-year life, with depreciation being calculated on a straight-line basis. Valuation adjustments are made on consolidation. Sam Ltd uses the partial goodwill method.

On 1 July 2012, Sam Ltd acquired 25% of the capital of Kayla Ltd for $3500 entering into a joint venture with three other venturers. All the identifiable assets and liabilities of Kayla Ltd were recorded at fair value except for the following:

	Carrying amount	Fair value
Inventory	$1 000	$1 500
Depreciable assets	6 000	7 000

All this inventory was sold in the 12 months after 1 July 2012. The depreciable assets were considered to have a further 5-year life.

Information on Kayla Ltd's equity position is as follows:

	1 July 2012	30 June 2013
Share capital	$10 000	$10 000
General reserve	—	2 000
Retained earnings	2 150	4 000

For the year ended 30 June 2014, Kayla Ltd recorded a profit before tax of $2600 and an income tax expense of $600. Kayla Ltd paid a dividend of $200 in January 2014. Sam Ltd regards Kayla Ltd as a joint venture investee.

During the year ended 30 June 2014, Kayla Ltd sold inventory to Paige Ltd for $6000. The cost of this inventory to Kayla Ltd was $4000. Paige Ltd has resold only 20% of these items. However, Paige Ltd made a profit before tax of $500 on the resale of these items.

On 1 January 2013, Sam Ltd sold Kayla Ltd a motor vehicle for $4000, at a profit before tax of $800 to Sam Ltd. Both companies treat motor vehicles as non-current assets. Both companies charge depreciation at 20% p.a. on the reducing balance. Assume a tax rate of 30%.

Information about income and changes in equity for Sam Ltd and its subsidiary, Paige Ltd, for the year ended 30 June 2014 is as follows:

	Sam Ltd	Paige Ltd
Sales revenue	$200 000	$60 000
Less: Cost of sales	110 000	30 000
Gross profit	90 000	30 000
Less: Depreciation	16 000	4 000
Other expenses	22 000	3 000
	38 000	7 000
	52 000	23 000
Plus: Other revenue	30 000	5 000
Profit before income tax	82 000	28 000
Less: Income tax expense	20 000	10 000
Profit	62 000	18 000
Plus: Retained earnings (1/7/13)	120 000	80 000
	182 000	98 000
Less: Dividend paid	20 000	4 000
Retained earnings (30/6/14)	$162 000	$94 000

Required

1. Prepare the consolidated statement of profit or loss and other comprehensive income and statement of changes in equity of Sam Ltd and its subsidiary Paige Ltd as at 30 June 2014.
2. In the consolidated statement of financial position, what would be the balance of the investment shares in Kayla Ltd?

Exercise 29.13 **CONSOLIDATION WORKSHEET ENTRIES INCLUDING INVESTMENTS IN JOINT VENTURES**

★★★ You are given the following details for the year ended 30 June 2014:

	Amber Ltd	Molly Ltd	Kate Ltd
Profit before tax	$100 000	$30 000	$25 000
Income tax expense	31 000	10 000	6 000

(continued)

	Amber Ltd	Molly Ltd	Kate Ltd
Profit	69 000	20 000	19 000
Retained earnings at 1 July 2013	20 000	12 000	11 000
	89 000	32 000	30 000
Dividend paid	14 000	6 000	2 000
Dividend declared	15 000	4 000	8 000
Transfer to general reserve (from current period's profit)	10 000	5 000	6 000
	39 000	15 000	16 000
Retained earnings at 30 June 2014	$ 50 000	$17 000	$14 000

Additional information
(a) Amber Ltd owns 80% of the participating shares in Molly Ltd and 20% of the shares in Kate Ltd. Amber Ltd has entered into a contractual arrangement with four other venturers in relation to Kate Ltd, and the five investors have a joint control arrangement in relation to Kate Ltd
(b) On 1 July 2012, all identifiable assets and liabilities of Molly Ltd were recorded at fair value. Amber Ltd purchased 80% of Molly Ltd's shares on 1 July 2012, and paid $5000 for goodwill, none of which had been recorded on Molly Ltd's records. Amber Ltd uses the partial goodwill method.
(c) At the date Amber Ltd acquired its shares in Kate Ltd, Kate Ltd's recorded equity was:

Share capital	$100 000
General reserve	15 000
Retained earnings	5 000

All the identifiable assets and liabilities of Kate Ltd were recorded at fair value.
Amber Ltd paid $25 000 for its shares in Kate Ltd on 1 July 2012. There was $3000 transferred to general reserve by Kate Ltd in the year ended 30 June 2013, out of equity earned since 1 July 2012.
(d) Included in the beginning inventory of Amber Ltd were profits before tax made by Molly Ltd: $5000; Kate Ltd: $3000.
(e) Included in the ending inventory of Molly Ltd were profits before tax made by Kate Ltd: $4000.
(f) Kate Ltd had recorded a profit (net of $500 tax) of $2000 in selling certain non-current assets to Amber Ltd on 1 January 2014. Amber Ltd treats the items as non-current assets and charges depreciation at the rate of 25% p.a. straight-line from that date.
(g) Amber Ltd purchased for $10 000 an item of plant from Molly Ltd on 1 September 2012. The carrying amount of the asset at that date was $7000. The asset was depreciated at the rate of 20% p.a. straight-line from 1 September 2012.
(h) During the year ended 30 June 2014, Kate Ltd has revalued upwards one of its non-current assets by $8000. There had been no previous downward revaluations.
(i) Dividend revenue is recognised when dividends are declared.
(j) The tax rate is 30%.

Required

Prepare the consolidation worksheet entries (in general journal form) needed for the consolidated statements for the year ended 30 June 2014 for Amber Ltd and its subsidiary Molly Ltd. Include the equity-accounted results of Kate Ltd.

References

Air Pacific 2012, *About Air Pacific — History*, Air Pacific Ltd, www.airpacific.com.
Amalgamated Holdings 2010, *2010 Annual report*, Amalgamated Holdings Ltd, www.ahl.com.au.
Foster's Group Ltd 2010, *Annual report 2010*, Foster's Group Ltd, www.fostersgroup.com.
—— 2011, *Annual report 2011*, Foster's Group Ltd, www.fostersgroup.com.
Qantas 2011, *Annual report 2011*, Qantas Airways Limited, www.qantas.com.

30

Joint arrangements

ACCOUNTING STANDARDS IN FOCUS

IFRS 11 *Joint Arrangements*

LEARNING OBJECTIVES

After studying this chapter, you should be able to:

1 discuss the use of joint arrangements by companies to structure their business

2 explain the nature of a joint arrangement and how to classify joint arrangements into joint ventures and joint operations

3 explain the accounting undertaken by the joint operation itself

4 prepare the journal entries required by a joint operator to recognise its share of the assets, liabilities, revenues and expenses of the joint operation

5 discuss the disclosures required in relation to joint operations.

30.1 **INTRODUCTION AND SCOPE**

This chapter is concerned with situations where companies join together to seek a common goal. These companies sign contracts which require all companies involved to act together, to agree on the major decisions involving what the companies do in relation to specified projects. The purpose of joining together may be for varied reasons. Sometimes it is to share costs, or to manage the risk involved in the project. Alternatively it may be done to provide the parties with access to new technology or new markets. These contractual arrangements, if they meet certain conditions are described as joint arrangements, the key feature of which is that the parties involved have joint control over the decision making in relation to the joint arrangement.

Joint arrangements are particularly useful when developing new technologies as there are often major risks in terms of eventual success. Further, entities may prefer to join together to interrelate research findings and knowledge in relation to their new technology developments. For example, Perrin (2011) wrote that:

> Australian renewable energy company CBD Energy has disclosed to the ASX it would finalise its joint venture with two of China's largest renewable companies and pursue A$6 billion worth of renewable energy products in the coming years. The joint venture will form the AusChina Energy Group which plans to develop renewable projects, both wind and solar, over eight years and become a significant participant in the Australian energy market.

There are three companies involved in this project: Datang Corp Renewable Power Co Ltd, China's second largest wind power producer, has a 63.75% interest in the company; Baoding Tianwei Baobian Electric Co, which makes power transformers in China, has a 12.5% interest; finally, Australia's power storage company CBD Energy Ltd has a 23.75% interest (CBD Energy 2012). As Australia has set a national target of 20% renewable energy generation by 2020, this new company plans to develop new technologies useful in both the Australian and overseas markets.

Note that joint arrangements do not need to have investors that have equal interests in the project. As explained later in this chapter, decision making of the arrangement on a joint control basis is a key element of a joint arrangement and requires the unanimous agreement of all parties involved.

This chapter examines accounting standard IFRS 11 *Joint Arrangements*, issued by the International Accounting Standards Board (IASB) in May 2011. IFRS 11 deals with both joint ventures and joint operations. While accounting for joint ventures is discussed in chapter 29 of this book, this chapter focuses on accounting for joint operations.

 ## 30.2 **JOINT ARRANGEMENTS: CHARACTERISTICS AND CLASSIFICATION**

30.2.1 **The characteristics of a joint arrangement**

The term 'arrangement' describes an activity or an operation or a specific grouping of assets and liabilities, which may or may not form a legal entity such as a company. A joint arrangement arises where two or more entities have an arrangement between each other such that these entities have joint control of the arrangement (IFRS 11 paragraph 4). For example, Entity A and Entity B may agree to form Entity C and the management of Entity C is under the joint control of both Entity A and Entity B.

A joint arrangement has two main characteristics (IFRS 11 paragraph 5).

1. *The parties are bound by a contractual arrangement.*
The agreement between the parties is in the form of a contract which would generally be in writing. The contractual arrangement may be written into the articles of association or constitution of the entities themselves.

The agreement sets out the terms under which the parties agree to participate in relation to the joint activity. As explained in IFRS 11 paragraph B4, it would contain such matters as:
(a) the purpose, activity and duration of the joint arrangement
(b) how the members of the board of directors are appointed
(c) the decision-making process, the matters requiring decisions, the voting rights of the parties and the required level of support for these matters
(d) the capital or other contributions required of the parties
(e) how the parties share assets, liabilities, revenues, expenses or profit or loss relating to the joint arrangement.

An example of where a contractual arrangement is necessary in order for a joint arrangement to exist is shown in figure 30.1.

Assume an arrangement in which A and B each have 35% of the voting rights in the arrangement with the remaining 30% being widely dispersed. Decisions about the relevant activities require approval by a majority of the voting rights.

If there is a contractual arrangement between A and B which specifies that decisions about the relevant activities of the arrangement require both A and B agreeing, then A and B have joint control over the arrangement. No decision about the relevant activities can be made without the agreement of both A and B.

In the absence of such an agreement, no entity has any form of control over the arrangement as a decision can be made about the relevant activities if any combination of either A, B or C agree to it. In such a case, A and B may be considered to have significant influence over the arrangement, but not control or joint control.

FIGURE 30.1 Contractual arrangements
Source: Adapted from IFRS 11 — Example 3.

2. The contractual arrangement gives two or more parties joint control of the arrangement.
The criterion that identifies a contractual arrangement as a joint arrangement is that of joint control. As explained in IFRS 11 paragraph 7, joint control exists when:
(a) there exists a contractually agreed sharing of control
(b) the agreement is that decisions about the relevant activities require the *unanimous* consent of the parties sharing control (i.e. no party can make a unilateral decision about relevant activities).

Each party that has joint control is referred to as a *joint venturer* or a *joint operator*. Other parties in the joint arrangement are a *party to a joint arrangement*. In the example in figure 30.1, if there is a contractual agreement between A and B, then A and B are joint venturers or joint operators while the holders of the widely dispersed 30% of voting interests are parties to the joint arrangement.

Where a joint arrangement exists there is no single party that has control. The joint venturers/operators must act together to manage the affairs of the arrangement.

In assessing whether joint control exists judgement will need to be exercised, and all facts and circumstances will need to be examined. If the facts and circumstances change, then a reassessment of the existence of joint control is necessary (IFRS 11 paragraph 13).

Note that the agreement may not use the term 'joint control' but the existence of joint control may be implicit in the arrangement. For example, consider a situation where A and B each have 50% of the voting interest in an arrangement and under the terms of the contract any decision about relevant activities requires at least 51% of the votes. In such a case, decisions can be made only where A and B agree. The terms of the contract require A and B to act jointly even if the contractual agreement does not refer to joint control.

There are two steps in the assessment of the existence of joint control:
1. Assess whether the parties to the arrangement have *control*. Control is defined in IFRS 10 *Consolidated Financial Statements* and exists in a joint arrangement when two or more investors in the arrangement are exposed, or have rights, to variable returns from their involvement with the arrangement, and have the ability to affect those returns through their power over the arrangement. Control must be over the 'relevant' activities. These are also defined in IFRS 10 and refer to those activities of the arrangement that significantly affect the returns of the arrangement.
2. Assess whether two or more parties have *joint control*. The control over the arrangement must be in the hands of more than one party to the arrangement. This assessment requires the determination of the existence of a contractual arrangement requiring the unanimous consent of the parties sharing control in relation to the relevant activities.

30.2.2 The classification of a joint arrangement

Having determined that a joint arrangement exists, it is then necessary to classify it. There are two types of joint arrangements, namely joint ventures and joint operations (IFRS 11 paragraphs 15, 16):
• *joint operation:* an arrangement in which the parties that have joint control have rights to the assets and obligations for the liabilities relating to the arrangement. These parties are called joint operators.

- *joint venture:* the parties that have joint control have rights to the net assets of the arrangement. These parties are called joint venturers.

Note in particular that the key element in the classification of a joint arrangement is the rights and obligations of the parties to the arrangement (IFRS 11 paragraph 14). For a joint operation, the rights pertain to the rights and obligations associated with *individual* assets and liabilities, whereas with a joint venture, the rights and obligations pertain to the *net assets*; that is, the investment in net assets.

The assessment of the classification of a joint arrangement is not straightforward; it requires judgement. As outlined in IFRS 11 paragraph 17, the assessment of the rights and obligations in an arrangement involves analysing four factors:

1. the structure of the arrangement
2. the legal form of the arrangement
3. the terms agreed to by the parties in the contractual arrangement
4. any other relevant facts and circumstances.

Consider each of these factors separately.

1. *Structure of the arrangement*

The main factor here is whether or not the arrangement is or is not structured through a 'separate vehicle'. A separate vehicle is defined in Appendix A of IFRS 11 as 'a separately identifiable financial structure, including separate legal entities or entities recognised by statute, regardless of whether those entities have a legal personality'. A separate vehicle would include a company. For example, if the airlines Qantas and Cathay Pacific formed a company, Scandinavian Airlines, to manage flights between countries such as Sweden, Finland, Norway and Denmark, then Scandinavian Airlines would be a separate vehicle.

If the joint arrangement *is not* structured through a separate vehicle, then the arrangement is classified as a joint operation (IFRS 11 paragraph B16). The contractual arrangement would establish the parties' rights to the assets and obligations for the liabilities of the arrangement as well as the rights to revenues and obligations for expenses of the arrangements. For example, the government may put out tenders to build a fighter aircraft for the German air force. Three companies put in a joint tender which is successful. The three companies establish a joint arrangement under which Company A builds the engines for the aircraft, Company B builds the aircraft itself, while Company C is responsible for the computer software for the aircraft. Each company is then responsible for a specific task and uses its own assets and incurs its own liabilities in relation to the agreed task.

If the joint arrangement *is* structured through a separate vehicle, then the arrangement can be either a joint operation or a joint venture. This determination is based on an analysis of the remaining three factors noted above. This classification process may be expressed in the form of a decision tree as shown in figure 30.2.

2. *The legal form of the separate vehicle*

In considering the legal form of the separate vehicle the main area of interest is how the legal form affects the rights to the assets and obligations for the liabilities. If the legal form establishes rights to *individual assets and obligations*, the arrangement is a joint operation. If the legal form establishes rights to the *net assets* of the arrangement, then the arrangement is a joint venture.

To establish the arrangement as a joint operation, the legal form of the separate vehicle must not confer separation between the parties and the separate vehicle. The assets and liabilities of the separate vehicle must be the parties' assets and liabilities, and not those of the separate vehicle itself.

Note, however, that an assessment of the legal form may not be sufficient. The terms of the contractual arrangement may override the legal form. In other words, just because the legal form of the separate vehicle is a company does not mean that the arrangement is a joint venture.

3. *The terms of the contractual arrangement*

Generally the choice of the legal form of the arrangement would be such as to reflect the rights and obligations of the parties to the arrangement. However, in other cases, the terms of the contractual arrangement may override the rights and obligations conferred by the legal form chosen.

For example, the form of the structured vehicle may be an incorporated entity. Being an incorporated entity, the entity is separate from the owners of the entity. Incorporation establishes that the assets and liabilities of the entity are separate from those of the owners of the entity. The legal form is such that the owners have rights to the net assets of the entity. However, the contractual arrangement could be written such that the owners are given an interest in the individual assets of the incorporated entity and are responsible for the liabilities of the incorporated entity. The legal form would have suggested that a joint venture exists; however, the terms of the contractual arrangement have modified the legal form such that the arrangement is a joint operation.

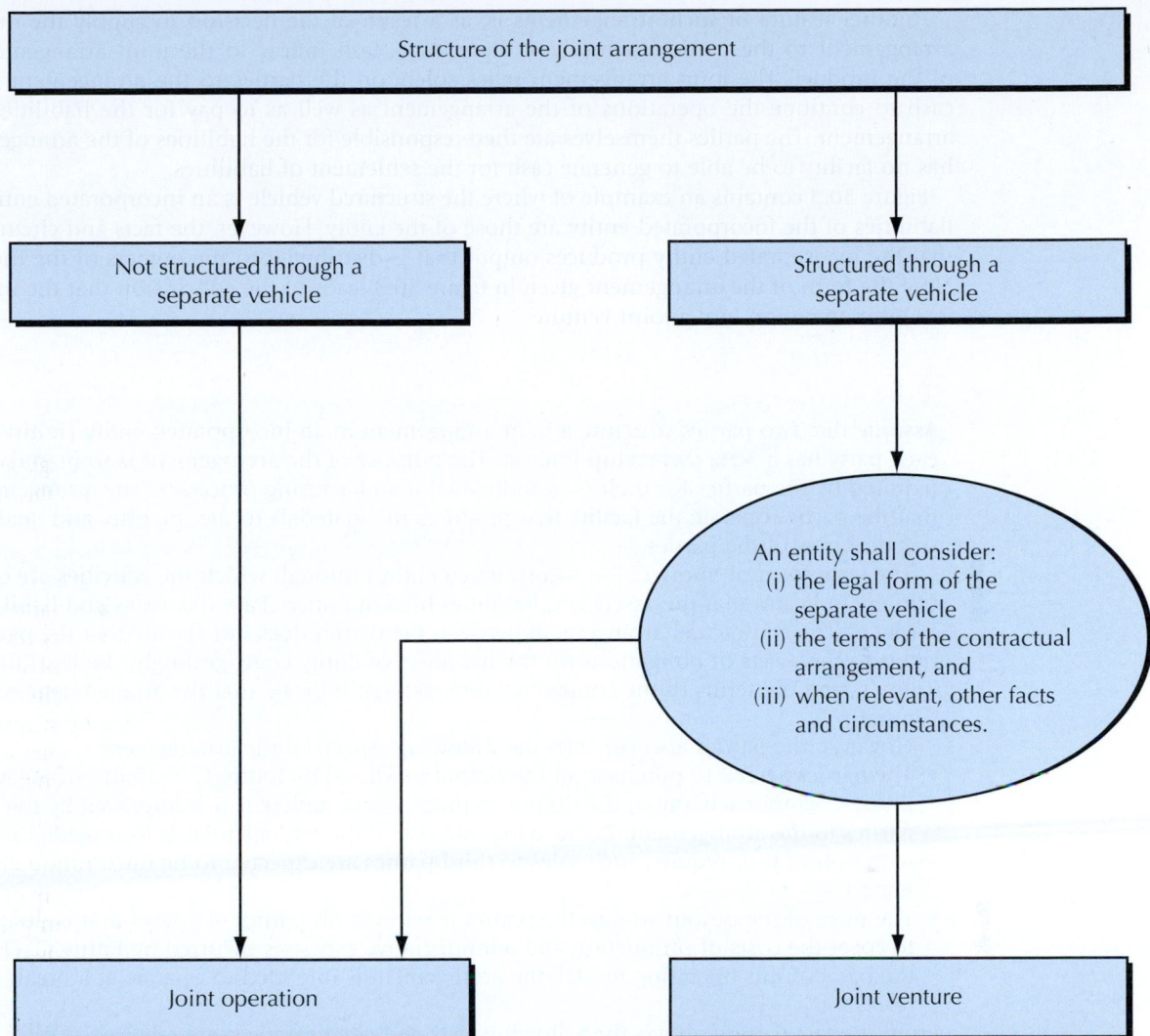

FIGURE 30.2 Classification of a joint arrangement — assessment of the parties' rights and obligations arising from the arrangement
Source: IFRS 11, Appendix B.

4. *Other facts and circumstances*

The terms of the contractual arrangement may not specify the rights and obligations of the parties to the assets and liabilities of the joint arrangements. An assessment of other facts and circumstances of the arrangement may assist in classifying the arrangement.

One fact to consider is whether the arrangement is designed to provide *output* to the parties to the arrangement. In the example used above where the airlines Qantas and Cathay Pacific established Scandinavian Airlines, it would be usual for Scandinavian Airlines to be managed with the objective of producing a profit for the company with dividends being paid to the owners of that company. However, in other situations, a joint arrangement may be established with the objective of producing a product that is distributed to the owners of the company who then decide on how to use or sell that product. The profit is then generated by the owners of the company subsequent to receipt of the output from the joint arrangement. For example, two companies may agree to work together to produce bottled water from a mountain spring. The agreement is that the output from the arrangement, namely bottled water, is then distributed to each of the joint operators. Each operator is then responsible for distributing the bottled water under its own label for sale and marketing purposes. The joint operation manufactures the product and determines a cost of the output to the joint operators. The parties to the joint arrangement have a right to substantially all the economic benefits of the assets held by the arrangement.

Another feature of such arrangements is, as a result of the decision to supply the output of the joint arrangement to the parties themselves, there is no cash inflow to the joint arrangement from the sale of the product. The joint arrangement relies solely on the parties to the arrangement for the supply of cash to continue the operations of the arrangement as well as to pay for the liabilities incurred by the arrangement. The parties themselves are then responsible for the liabilities of the arrangement as the latter has no facility to be able to generate cash for the settlement of liabilities.

Figure 30.3 contains an example of where the structured vehicle is an incorporated entity. The assets and liabilities of the incorporated entity are those of the entity. However, the facts and circumstances are such that the incorporated entity produces output that is distributed to the owners of the incorporated entity. Note the form of the arrangement given in figure 30.3 leads to the conclusion that the incorporated entity is a joint operation, not a joint venture.

Assume that two parties structure a joint arrangement in an incorporated entity (Entity C) in which each party has a 50% ownership interest. The purpose of the arrangement is to manufacture materials required by the parties for their own individual manufacturing processes. The arrangement ensures that the parties operate the facility that produces the materials to the quantity and quality specifications of the parties.

The legal form of Entity C (an incorporated entity) through which the activities are conducted initially indicates that the assets and liabilities held in Entity C are the assets and liabilities of Entity C. The contractual arrangement between the parties does not specify that the parties have rights to the assets or obligations for the liabilities of Entity C. Accordingly, the legal form of Entity C and the terms of the contractual arrangement indicate that the arrangement is a joint venture.

However, the parties also consider the following aspects of the arrangement:
• The parties agreed to purchase all the output produced by Entity C in a ratio of 50:50. Entity C cannot sell any of the output to third parties, unless this is approved by the two parties to the arrangement. Because the purpose of the arrangement is to provide the parties with output they require, such sales to third parties are expected to be uncommon and not material.
• The price of the output sold to the parties is set by both parties at a level that is designed to cover the costs of production and administrative expenses incurred by Entity C. On the basis of this operating model, the arrangement is intended to operate at a break-even level.

From the fact pattern above, the following facts and circumstances are relevant:
• The obligation of the parties to purchase all the output produced by Entity C reflects the exclusive dependence of Entity C upon the parties for the generation of cash flows and, thus, the parties have an obligation to fund the settlement of the liabilities of Entity C.
• The fact that the parties have rights to all the output produced by Entity C means that the parties are consuming, and therefore have rights to, all the economic benefits of the assets of Entity C.

These facts and circumstances indicate that the arrangement is a joint operation. The conclusion about the classification of the joint arrangement in these circumstances would not change if, instead of the parties using their share of the output themselves in a subsequent manufacturing process, the parties sold their share of the output to third parties.

If the parties changed the terms of the contractual arrangement so that the arrangement was able to sell output to third parties, this would result in Entity C assuming demand, inventory and credit risks. In that scenario, such a change in the facts and circumstances would require reassessment of the classification of the joint arrangement. Such facts and circumstances would indicate that the arrangement is a joint venture.

FIGURE 30.3 Facts and circumstances affecting classification of joint arrangements
Source: IFRS 11, Appendix B — Example 5.

The classification of a joint arrangement structured through a separate vehicle may be seen as a decision tree as shown in figure 30.4.

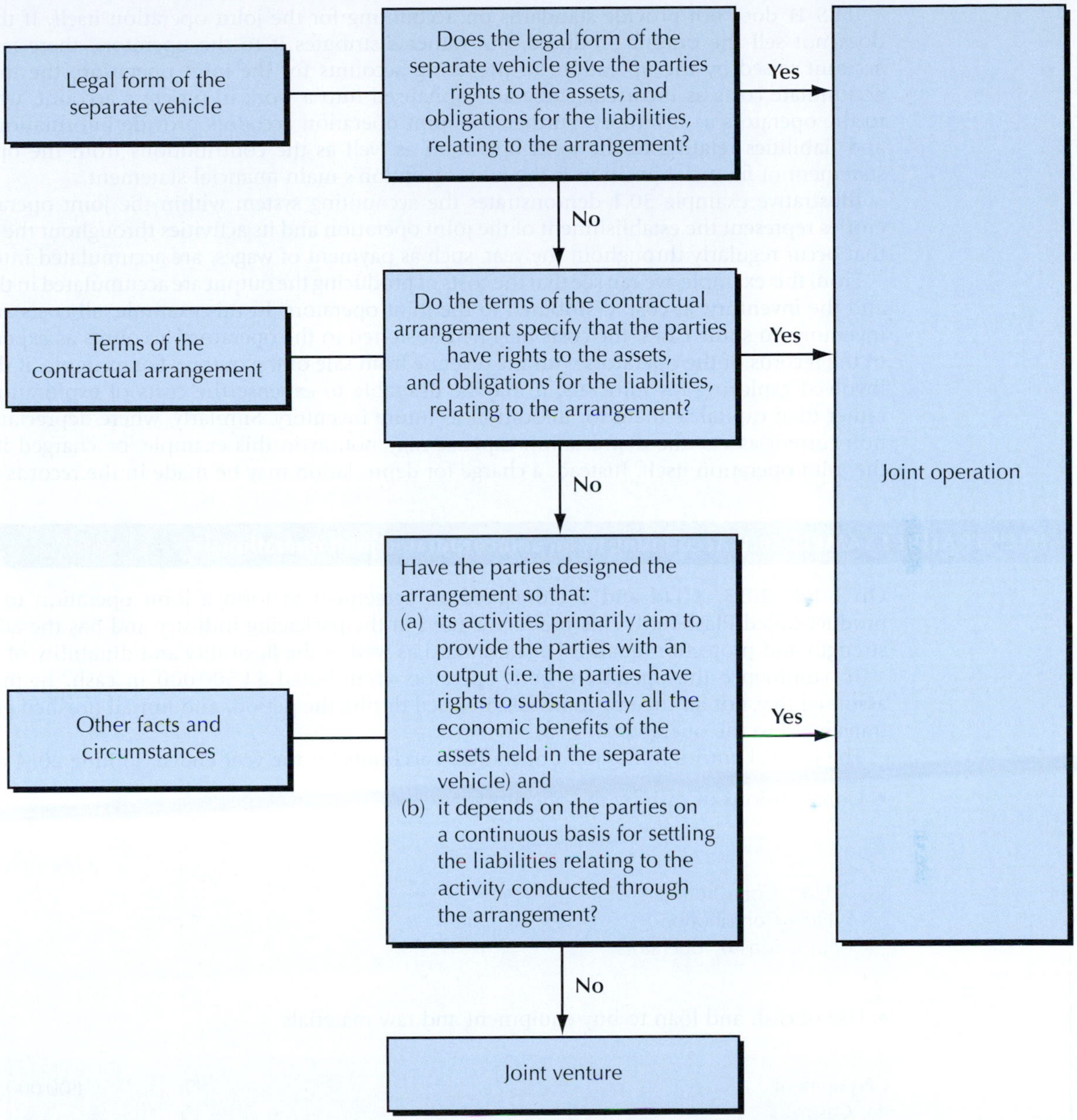

The flowchart shows:

Legal form of the separate vehicle → Does the legal form of the separate vehicle give the parties rights to the assets, and obligations for the liabilities, relating to the arrangement? → **Yes** → Joint operation

↓ **No**

Terms of the contractual arrangement → Do the terms of the contractual arrangement specify that the parties have rights to the assets, and obligations for the liabilities, relating to the arrangement? → **Yes** → Joint operation

↓ **No**

Other facts and circumstances → Have the parties designed the arrangement so that:
(a) its activities primarily aim to provide the parties with an output (i.e. the parties have rights to substantially all the economic benefits of the assets held in the separate vehicle) and
(b) it depends on the parties on a continuous basis for settling the liabilities relating to the activity conducted through the arrangement? → **Yes** → Joint operation

↓ **No**

Joint venture

FIGURE 30.4 Classification of a joint arrangement structured through a separate vehicle
Source: IFRS 11, Appendix B.

LO3   30.3 ACCOUNTING FOR JOINT ARRANGEMENTS

The accounting for joint ventures is different from that of joint operations. Regarding a joint venture, the joint venturers have an interest in the investment in the joint arrangement. The accounting for this interest is done by application of the equity method in accordance with IAS 28 *Investments in Associates and Joint Ventures*. The details of accounting for joint ventures are given in chapter 29 of this book.

30.3.1 Accounting by the joint operation itself

Where the joint operation is undertaken outside a formal structure, such as a corporation or partnership, separate accounting records do not need to be kept for the joint operation. However, for accountability reasons it is expected that the joint operation agreement would require these records.

IFRS 11 does not provide standards on accounting for the joint operation itself. If the joint operation does not sell the output produced, but rather distributes it to the operators, there is no profit or loss account raised by the operation. In preparing accounts for the joint operation, the main purpose is to accumulate costs as incurred. These are capitalised into a work in progress account, which is transferred to the operators as inventory. Further, the joint operation accounts provide information about the assets and liabilities relating to the joint operation as well as the contributions from the operators. Hence, a statement of financial position is the joint operation's main financial statement.

Illustrative example 30.1 demonstrates the accounting system within the joint operation. The journal entries represent the establishment of the joint operation and its activities throughout the year. Transactions that occur regularly throughout the year, such as payment of wages, are accumulated into one entry.

From this example, we can see that the costs of producing the output are accumulated in the joint operation, and the inventory, at cost, distributed to the joint operators. In this example, all costs are capitalised into inventory. In some cases, the costs may be transferred to the operators' accounts as expenses and matched in the records of the operators with the revenue from sale of the output. For example, if the joint operation involved exploring for minerals, it may be desirable to expense the costs of exploration and evaluation rather than capitalise them for allocation to future inventory. Similarly, where depreciation is charged on non-current assets, the depreciation expense may not, as in this example, be charged in the accounts of the joint operation itself. Instead, a charge for depreciation may be made in the records of each operator.

ILLUSTRATIVE EXAMPLE 30.1 Accounting by an unincorporated joint operation

On 1 July 2013, X Ltd and Y Ltd signed an agreement to form a joint operation to manufacture a product called Plasboard. This product is used in the packaging industry and has the advantages of the strength and protection qualities of cardboard as well as the flexibility and durability of plastic.

To commence the operation, both operators contributed $1 500 000 in cash. In the example it is assumed that not all the raw materials are used during the period, and not all finished goods have been transferred to the operators.

The journal entries in the joint operation's accounts for the year ended 30 June 2014 are as follows:

- Contributions of cash by the operators

Cash	Dr	3 000 000
X Ltd – Contribution	Cr	1 500 000
Y Ltd – Contribution	Cr	1 500 000
(Contributions by operators)		

- Use of cash and loan to buy equipment and raw materials

Equipment	Dr	800 000
Cash	Cr	500 000
Loan – Equipment	Cr	300 000
(Acquisition of equipment)		
Raw Materials	Dr	650 000
Trade Creditors	Cr	650 000
(Acquisition of materials)		

- Payment of wages

Wages – Management	Dr	200 000
Wages – Other	Dr	520 000
Cash	Cr	700 000
Accrued Wages	Cr	20 000
(Annual wages)		

- Borrowing from the bank

Cash	Dr	500 000	
Bank Loan	Cr		500 000
(Amount borrowed)			

- Repayment of loan and other expenses

Loan – Equipment	Dr	100 000	
Cash	Cr		100 000
(Part-payment for loan on equipment)			
Trade Creditors	Dr	420 000	
Cash	Cr		420 000
(Payment of trade creditors)			
Overhead Expenses	Dr	1 300 000	
Cash	Cr		1 300 000
(Payment of manufacturing expenses such as electricity)			

- Depreciation of equipment

Depreciation Expense	Dr	80 000	
Accumulated Depreciation	Cr		80 000
(Depreciation of equipment)			

- Transfer of expenses to work in progress

Work in Progress	Dr	2 580 000	
Wages	Cr		720 000
Raw Materials	Cr		480 000
Overhead Expenses	Cr		1 300 000
Depreciation Expense	Cr		80 000
(Allocating of costs to work in progress)			

- Transfer from work in progress to inventory

Inventory	Dr	1 800 000	
Work in Progress	Cr		1 800 000
(Allocation to finished goods)			

- Transfer of inventory to operators throughout the year

X Ltd	Dr	800 000	
Y Ltd	Dr	800 000	
Inventory	Cr		1 600 000
(Delivery of output to operators)			

The major ledger accounts of interest in relation to the joint operation are as follows:

Cash

	$		$
Contribution – X Ltd	1 500 000	Equipment	500 000
Contribution – Y Ltd	1 500 000	Wages	700 000
Bank Loan	500 000	Loan – Equipment	100 000
		Trade Creditors	420 000
		Overhead Expenses	1 300 000
		Balance c/d	480 000
	3 500 000		3 500 000
Balance b/d	480 000		

Work in Progress

	$		$
Wages	720 000	Inventory	1 800 000
Raw Materials	480 000		
Overhead	1 300 000		
Depreciation	80 000	Balance c/d	780 000
	2 580 000		2 580 000
Balance b/d	780 000		

The statement of financial position of the joint operation at 30 June 2014 would be:

Statement of Financial Position as at 30 June 2014

Current assets			
Raw materials		$ 170 000	
Inventory		200 000	
Work in progress		780 000	
Cash		480 000	
Total current assets			$1 630 000
Non-current assets			
Equipment		800 000	
Accumulated depreciation		(80 000)	720 000
Total assets			2 350 000
Current liabilities			
Trade creditors		230 000	
Accrued wages		20 000	
Total current liabilities			250 000
Non-current liabilities			
Bank loan		500 000	
Loan — equipment		200 000	
Total non-current liabilities			700 000
Total liabilities			950 000
Net assets			$1 400 000
Joint operators' equity			
X Ltd: Contributions — at 1/7/13		$1 500 000	
Cost of inventory distributed		(800 000)	$ 700 000
Y Ltd: Contributions — at 1/7/13		1 500 000	
Cost of inventory distributed		(800 000)	700 000
Total joint operators' equity			$1 400 000

30.4 ACCOUNTING BY A JOINT OPERATOR

The key feature of a joint operation is that the joint operator has an interest in the individual assets and liabilities of the joint operation. In the situation where the joint operation produces an output which is distributed to the joint operators, the joint operator will receive a share of the output of the joint operation as well as be responsible for a share of the expenses of the operation that are not capitalised into the cost of the output.

Hence, each joint operator needs to recognise in its own accounts:
(a) its share of any jointly held assets
(b) its share of any jointly held liabilities
(c) its revenue from the sale of any output received from the joint operation
(d) its share of any revenue from the sale of any product that is jointly constructed by the joint operators
(e) its share of any expenses incurred by the joint operation
(f) its expenses incurred in construction of a joint product.

Hence, in accounting for a joint operation where output is distributed to the joint operators, each joint operator will view the accounts of the joint operation as shown in section 30.3.1 and calculate its share of each of the relevant accounts. At the end of each period, each venturer will analyse and account for movements in those accounts.

30.4.1 Contributions of cash to a joint operation

Illustrative example 30.2 demonstrates the entries required when joint operators' contribute cash to a joint operation.

ILLUSTRATIVE EXAMPLE 30.2 Contribution of cash by a joint operator

On 1 July 2013, X Ltd and Y Ltd establish a joint operation to manufacture a product. Each company has a 50% interest in the operation and shares output equally. To commence the operation, both companies contribute cash of $1 500 000 on 1 July 2013. Each operator depreciates equipment at 10% p.a. on cost.

The following information was extracted from the accounts and financial statements of the joint operation as at 30 June 2014:

Statement of Financial Position (extract) as at 30 June 2014	
Assets	
Cash	$ 420 000
Raw materials	100 000
Work in progress	650 000
Inventory	200 000
Equipment	1 500 000
Total assets	2 870 000
Liabilities	
Accounts payable (raw materials)	120 000
Accrued expenses (wages)	150 000
Bank loan	1 000 000
Total liabilities	1 270 000
Net assets	$ 1 600 000

Cash Receipts and Payments for the year ended 30 June 2014		
	Payments	**Receipts**
Contributions		$ 3 000 000
Bank loan		1 000 000

(continued)

	Payments	Receipts
Equipment (purchased 3/7/13)	$1 500 000	
Wages	500 000	
Accounts payable (raw materials)	380 000	
Overhead expenses	1 200 000	
	$3 580 000	$4 000 000

Costs Incurred for the year ended 30 June 2014	
Wages	$ 650 000
Raw materials	400 000
Overhead expenses	1 200 000
	2 250 000
Less: Cost of inventory	1 600 000
Work in progress at 30/6/14	$ 650 000

Required

Prepare the journal entries in the records of X Ltd and Y Ltd for the year ended 30 June 2014.

Solution

Records of X Ltd

At 1 July 2013, X Ltd records its interest in the joint operation, the asset cash being distinguished as an asset in a joint operation by the use of (JO):

Cash in Joint Operation (JO)	Dr	1 500 000	
Cash	Cr		1 500 000
(Contribution of cash to joint operation)			

At 30 June 2014, the joint operation has used the cash to acquire various assets, undertake loans, incur expenses and manufacture inventory. As a contributor of 50% of the cash into the joint operation, X Ltd is entitled to 50% of all the assets, liabilities, expenses and output of the joint operation.

From the statement of financial position of the joint operation, it should be noted that the net assets of the joint operation amount to $1 600 000 (i.e. $2 870 000 − $1 270 000). The inventory in the statement of financial position is $200 000. From the costs incurred information, it can be seen that the joint operation has produced $1 600 000 worth of inventory. If only $200 000 is still on hand in the joint operation, then $1 400 000 worth of inventory must have been transferred to the joint operators (i.e. $700 000 each).

On transfer of inventory to the joint operators, the joint operation reduces the inventory balance and reduces the equity contribution of the joint operators. The contributions section of the statement of financial position of the joint operation at the end of the period, after the transfer of inventory, is as follows.

X Ltd:	Initial contribution	$1 500 000	
	Less: Inventory transferred	(700 000)	$ 800 000
Y Ltd:	Initial contribution	1 500 000	
	Less: Inventory transferred	(700 000)	800 000
			$1 600 000

At 30 June 2014, X Ltd makes the following entry in its records to replace 'Cash in JO' with a 50% share of each of the accounts — assets and liabilities — in the statement of financial position of the joint operation at 30 June 2014. The entry also recognises the inventory of $700 000 transferred to X Ltd from the joint operation.

Raw Material in JO [$100 000/2]	Dr	50 000	
Work in Progress in JO [$650 000/2]	Dr	325 000	
Inventory in JO [$200 000/2]	Dr	100 000	
Equipment in JO [$1 500 000/2]	Dr	750 000	
Inventory [$1 400 000/2]	Dr	700 000	
Accounts Payable in JO [$120 000/2]	Cr		60 000
Accrued Expenses in JO [$150 000/2]	Cr		75 000
Bank Loan in JO [$1 000 000/2]	Cr		500 000
Cash in JO [$1 500 000 – ($420 000/2)]	Cr		1 290 000

Note that X Ltd's share of cash in the joint operation is calculated by finding the difference between the share at the beginning of the period, the initial contribution in this example, and the share at the end of the period.

X Ltd depreciates the equipment in its own records. Therefore, having recognised an asset at $750 000, X Ltd would also pass the following entry at 30 June 2014:

Depreciation Expense [10% × $750 000]	Dr	75 000	
Accumulated Depreciation	Cr		75 000
(Depreciation on equipment in the joint operation)			

Records of Y Ltd
As Y Ltd contributed the same asset (cash of $1 500 000) to the joint operation as X Ltd, the journal entries in the records of Y Ltd would be the same as that in X Ltd.

30.4.2 Contributions of assets to a joint operation

In illustrative example 30.2, the joint operators contributed cash to the joint operation. However in some cases, a joint operator may contribute assets other than cash to the joint operation. For example, one of the joint operators in a mining arrangement may also manufacture mining equipment. This joint operator may contribute equipment to the joint operation while the other operators may contribute cash.

Where an operator contributes a non-current asset to the joint operation, the value of the contribution is effectively the fair value of that non-current asset. Hence, if one operator contributed $100 000 cash and the other operator a non-current asset, then for both parties to agree to join there would have to be agreement that the non-current asset being contributed had a fair value of $100 000. If all operators contributed non-current assets, then some form of valuation of the contributions would need to be made by the parties involved.

However, as the transaction is not an arm's length transaction, a joint operator contributing assets other than cash cannot transfer the asset at fair value to the joint operation and recognise a full profit on the transaction (IFRS 11 paragraph B34). The joint operator can only recognise gains and losses on such transactions to the extent of the other parties' interests in the joint operation.

Assume operator A carries a non-current asset *at fair value* in its accounts; for example, an item of plant for $100 000. If this asset is contributed to a joint operation whereas the other operator, B, contributes cash of $100 000, the journal entry to record the contribution in the records of operator A is as follows.

Cash in JO [$100 000/2]	Dr	50 000	
Plant in JO [$100 000/2]	Dr	50 000	
Plant	Cr		100 000

In the records of operator B, the entry is:

Cash in JO [$100 000/2]	Dr	50 000	
Plant in JO [$100 000/2]	Dr	50 000	
Cash	Cr		100 000

Note that in the records of both operators the plant in the joint operation is recorded at the same amount, namely $50 000.

However, the accounting records of an operator that contributes a non-current asset is more complicated when the operator carries the contributed asset in its records at an amount *less than fair value*.

In contributing an asset to the joint operation, the operator is effectively selling a proportion of that asset to the other joint operators, and retaining a proportion for itself. Where the carrying amount of the asset is lower than the fair value, the operator makes a profit on selling the proportion of the asset to the other operators. The profit is the difference between the fair value and carrying amount of the proportion of the asset sold.

Assume operator A contributed a non-current asset with a fair value of $100 000, and a carrying amount of $80 000, while operator B contributed cash of $100 000. Operator A can then recognise a profit on sale of half the non-current asset, namely $10 000 (being ½ ($100 000 − $80 000)). The entry in the records of operator A is:

Cash in JO [$100 000/2]	Dr	50 000
Plant in JO [$80 000/2]	Dr	40 000
Gain on Sale of Plant [$20 000/2]	Cr		10 000
Plant	Cr		80 000

The whole of the plant is given up by the operator, with half being sold to the other operator at a profit and the other half being the asset held in the joint operation. Note that operator A has recognised the plant in the joint operation at half of the carrying amount and not at half of the fair value.

For operator B, the entry in its records is different from operator A, being:

Cash in JO [$100 000/2]	Dr	50 000
Plant in JO [$100 000/2]	Dr	50 000
Cash	Cr		100 000

Note that operator B has recognised the non-current asset in its records at half of fair value. Hence, operator A and operator B have their equal share of the plant in the joint operation recognised in their records at different amounts.

The fact that the operators have the non-current asset recorded at different amounts in their records affects the calculation of the cost of the inventory distributed to the operators from the joint operation. If the asset is depreciated, and the depreciation included in the cost of inventory, then, as the operators have the asset recorded at different amounts, the depreciation expense for each of the operators differs and so does the cost of inventory transferred.

Where the asset is depreciated in the joint operation's records, this depreciation is based on the fair value of the asset. For operator B, the depreciation charge is then the appropriate one and no adjustment is necessary. However, for operator A, an adjustment is necessary, as the depreciation charged by the joint operation is too great. As the depreciation is capitalised into inventory and work in progress in the records of the joint operation, when A recognises its share of the assets of the joint operation in its accounts, a further entry is necessary to reduce the balances of the inventory-related accounts. This extra entry in operator A's records is demonstrated in illustrative example 30.3.

ILLUSTRATIVE EXAMPLE 30.3 Contribution of a non-current asset by an operator

On 1 July 2013, X Ltd and Y Ltd established a joint operation to manufacture a product. Each company has a 50% interest in the operation and shares output equally. To commence the operation, on 1 July 2013, X Ltd contributed cash of $1 500 000 and Y Ltd contributed equipment which had a carrying amount of $1 000 000, and a fair value of $1 500 000. The equipment is depreciated in the joint operation's accounts at 10% p.a. on cost.

The following information was extracted from the joint operation's financial statements as at 30 June 2014:

Statement of Financial Position (extract) as at 30 June 2014	
Assets	
Cash	$ 420 000
Raw materials	100 000
Work in progress	800 000
Inventory	200 000
Equipment	1 500 000
Accumulated depreciation — equipment	(150 000)
Total assets	$2 870 000
Liabilities	
Accounts payable	$ 120 000
Accrued expenses (wages)	150 000
Bank loan	1 000 000
Total liabilities	1 270 000
Net assets	$1 600 000

Cash Receipts and Payments for the year ended 30 June 2014	Payments	Receipts
Contributions		$1 500 000
Bank loan		1 000 000
Wages	$ 500 000	
Accounts payable (raw materials)	380 000	
Overhead expenses	1 200 000	
	$2 080 000	$2 500 000

Costs Incurred for the year ended 30 June 2014	
Wages	$ 650 000
Raw materials	400 000
Depreciation	150 000
Overhead expenses	1 200 000
	2 400 000
Less: Cost of inventory	1 600 000
Work in progress at 30 June 2014	$ 800 000

Required

Prepare the journal entries in the records of each of the operators for the year ended 30 June 2014.

Solution

Records of X Ltd

In this example, X Ltd contributes cash to the joint operation, and Y Ltd contributes equipment. At 1 July 2013, X Ltd gives up the cash contribution and recognises a share of the cash and the equipment in the joint operation. X Ltd will recognise a share of the *fair value* of the asset. The entry is:

Cash in JO [$1 500 000/2]	Dr	750 000	
Equipment in JO [$1 500 000/2]	Dr	750 000	
Cash	Cr		1 500 000

At 30 June 2014, X Ltd recognises a share of the assets and liabilities in the statement of financial position of the joint operation. Note that the joint operation has produced inventory of $1 600 000, of which $1 400 000 has been transferred to the operators. Further, the joint operation has depreciated the equipment, the depreciation being based on the fair value of the equipment.

The entry at 30 June 2014 in X Ltd's accounts is shown as follows.

Raw Material in JO [$100 000/2]	Dr	50 000	
Work in Progress in JO [$800 000/2]	Dr	400 000	
Inventory in JO [$200 000/2]	Dr	100 000	
Inventory [$1 400 000/2]	Dr	700 000	
Accum. Depreciation – Equipment in JO [$150 000/2]	Cr		75 000
Accounts Payable in JO [$120 000/2]	Cr		60 000
Accrued Expenses in JO [$150 000/2]	Cr		75 000
Bank Loan in JO [$1 000 000/2]	Cr		500 000
Cash in JO [$750 000 – ($420 000/2)]	Cr		540 000

As depreciation has been based on fair value in the joint operation, and X Ltd has its share of the equipment in the joint operation recorded at fair value, the correct amount of depreciation has been capitalised into the cost of inventory. No adjusting entry is necessary.

Records of Y Ltd

At 1 July 2013, Y Ltd contributes equipment to the joint operation, this having a carrying amount in Y Ltd different from the fair value of the asset. In recording its contribution to the joint operation, Y Ltd therefore recognises a gain on selling half of the equipment to X Ltd. X Ltd's share of the equipment in the joint operation is then based on the original carrying amount of the asset.

The entry is:

Cash in JO [$1 500 000/2]	Dr	750 000	
Equipment in JO [$1 000 000/2]	Dr	500 000	
Gain on Sale of Equipment [$500 000/2]	Cr		250 000
Equipment	Cr		1 000 000

At 30 June 2014, Y Ltd recognises its share of the accounts in the statement of financial position of the joint operation as well as its share of the inventory transferred from the joint operation.

The entry is:

Raw Material in JO [$100 000/2]	Dr	50 000	
Work in Progress in JO [$800 000/2]	Dr	400 000	
Inventory in JO [$200 000/2]	Dr	100 000	
Inventory [$1 400 000/2]	Dr	700 000	
Accum. Depreciation – Equipment in JO [$150 000/2]	Cr		75 000
Accounts Payable in JO [$120 000/2]	Cr		60 000
Accrued Expenses in JO [$150 000/2]	Cr		75 000
Bank Loan in JO [$1 000 000/2]	Cr		500 000
Cash in JO [$750 000 – ($420 000/2)]	Cr		540 000

Note that this entry is the same as that for X Ltd.

The depreciation recognised by X Ltd is $75 000, which is based on the fair value of the asset. However, the equipment in the joint operation has been recognised by Y Ltd at only $500 000, which is half of the original carrying amount. Y Ltd would want to recognise only $50 000 depreciation, which is 10% of $500 000. Hence, whereas the work in progress and inventory recognised by Y Ltd includes depreciation of $75 000, the real cost of these assets to Y Ltd is less, to the amount of $25 000. A further entry is necessary to reduce the accumulated depreciation recognised by Y Ltd and to reduce the cost of the work in progress and inventory relating to the joint operation. This means that the cost of these assets to Y Ltd is different from that recognised by X Ltd. This is because the cost of the equipment in the joint operation is less for Y Ltd than for X Ltd.

As the depreciation is capitalised into work in progress and inventory (both that amount still on hand in the joint operation as well as that transferred to Y Ltd), the adjustment to depreciation is proportionately allocated across these accounts:

			Share of $25 000
Work in Progress	$ 400 000	1/3	$ 8 333
Inventory in JO	100 000	1/12	2 083
Inventory	700 000	7/12	14 584
	$1 200 000		$25 000

The entry in the records of Y Ltd to adjust the accumulated depreciation and the cost of the inventory-related accounts is then:

Accumulated Depreciation – Equipment in JO		
[10% × ($750 000 − $500 000)]	Dr	25 000
Work in Progress in JO	Cr	8 333
Inventory in JO	Cr	2 083
Inventory	Cr	14 584

30.4.3 Management fees paid to a joint operator

It is common for one of the joint operators to act in a management position for the joint operation. In such circumstances, the joint operation will pay a management fee to the joint operator for its management services.

In accounting for these payments, the joint operation pays cash to a joint operator, with the cost of the service being capitalised into work in progress and inventory produced by the joint operation. For a joint operator that does not supply the service there are no accounting adjustments necessary because of the transaction. For the joint operator that does supply the service, normally it would incur a cost to supply the service and earn a profit on the supply of that service. In accounting for its interest in the joint operation, the operator supplying the service has to consider the following:

- As with supplying assets other than cash as part of the initial contribution, a joint operator cannot earn a profit on supplying services to itself.
- As the joint operation capitalises the amount paid to the operator into the cost of work in progress and inventory, an adjustment is necessary to the inventory-related accounts of that operator because the cost of these items to the operator supplying the services is less than that to the other operator(s).

ILLUSTRATIVE EXAMPLE 30.4 Management fees paid to a joint operator

X Ltd and Y Ltd have formed a joint operation and share equally in the output of that operation. During the current period ending 30 June 2014, the joint operation pays a management fee of $400 000 to X Ltd. The cost to X Ltd of supplying management services to the joint operation is $320 000. At the end of the current period, X Ltd's share of the inventory-related assets from the joint operation as recorded for X Ltd is:

Work in progress in JO	$300 000
Inventory in JO	200 000
Inventory	500 000

The joint operation has capitalised the management services fee of $400 000 into the cost of these assets. In the records of X Ltd at 30 June 2014, the following entries are required:

Cash	Dr	400 000
Fee Revenue	Cr	400 000
(Revenue on payment of the service fee by the joint operation)		
Cost of Supplying Services	Dr	320 000
Cash	Cr	320 000
(Cost of supplying the services)		

The total profit to X Ltd on supplying the management service is $80 000. Half this profit is made on supplying services to Y Ltd and the other $40 000 on supplying services to itself. An adjustment is necessary to eliminate the revenue and the expense on supplying services to itself. The following entry eliminates from the fee revenue only the amount of the expense — the profit element in the revenue is eliminated in the next entry:

Fee revenue [$320 000/2]	Dr	160 000
Cost of Supplying Services	Cr	160 000
(Adjustment for the profit on Margaret Ltd supplying services to itself)		

The profit element on supplying services to itself, $40 000, is proportionately adjusted across the inventory-related assets as follows:

			Share of $40 000
Inventory in JO	$ 200 000	20%	$ 8 000
Inventory	500 000	50%	20 000
Work in Progress in JO	300 000	30%	12 000
	$1 000 000		$ 40 000

The journal entry is:

Fee Revenue	Dr	40 000
Inventory in JO	Cr	8 000
Inventory	Cr	20 000
Work in Progress in JO	Cr	12 000

Note that the combination of this entry and the immediately preceding one results in adjusting fee revenue for a total of $200 000, which is half the revenue paid by the joint operation to X Ltd.

If X Ltd had provided the services but the joint operation had not yet paid the fee by the end of the period, the liabilities of the joint operation need to be adjusted. Further, the fee receivable account of $400 000 raised by X Ltd needs to be adjusted. The entry is:

Accruals in JO	Dr	200 000
Fee Receivable	Cr	200 000

30.5 DISCLOSURE

IFRS 12 *Disclosure of Interests in Other Entities* contains the disclosures required for interests in joint arrangements. Paragraph 20 of IFRS 12 requires an entity to disclose sufficient information about joint operations to enable users of its financial statements to evaluate the nature, extent and financial effects of its interests in joint arrangements, including the nature of its contractual relationship with other investors with joint control over joint arrangements.

For each joint arrangement, the following must be disclosed (IFRS 12 paragraph 21):
- the name of the joint arrangement
- the nature of the entity's relationship with the joint arrangement (by, for example, describing the nature of the activities of the joint arrangement and whether it is strategic to the entity's activities)
- the principal place of business (and country of incorporation, if applicable and different from the principal place of business) of the joint arrangement
- the proportion of ownership interest or participating share held by the entity and, if different, the proportion of voting rights held (if applicable).

In regards to joint operations, each joint operator includes the relevant amounts for assets, liabilities, revenues and expenses in its own records. The assets are actual assets of the joint operator, and the operator is responsible for the liabilities recognised. There is no specific requirement to show the items associated with a joint operation separately from other assets and liabilities of the operator. However, some entities may consider these to be a separate class of assets and provide information in the notes to the financial statements regarding assets and liabilities associated with joint operations.

SUMMARY

This chapter has covered the principles of accounting for joint arrangements, particularly joint operations, as contained in IFRS 11 *Joint Arrangements.* Some of the key principles are:
- A joint arrangement is an arrangement between a number of parties in which two or more parties have joint control.
- A joint arrangement has two key characteristics, namely the parties are bound by a contractual agreement, and this agreement gives two or more parties joint control over the arrangement.
- Joint control exists when decisions about relevant activities require the unanimous consent of the parties sharing control.
- There are two types of joint arrangement, namely joint ventures and joint operations.
- The classification of a joint arrangement is dependent on the rights and obligations of the parties to the arrangement.
- With a joint arrangement the parties that have joint control have rights to the assets and obligations for the liabilities relating to the arrangement.
- With a joint venture, the parties that have joint control have rights to the net assets of the arrangement.
- Where a joint arrangement is not structured through a separate vehicle it is a joint operation.
- Where a joint arrangement is structured through a separate vehicle, its classification depends on an analysis of the legal form of the separate vehicle, the terms of the contractual arrangement and other relevant facts and circumstances.
- For a joint operation, a joint operator must recognise its share of the assets and liabilities of the arrangement, as well as its revenues and expenses associated with the arrangement.

Discussion questions

1. What is a joint arrangement?
2. How does a joint arrangement differ from an associate?
3. What is meant by joint control?
4. How does joint control differ from control as used in classifying subsidiaries?
5. How does a joint venture differ from a joint operation?
6. What are the key steps in classifying a joint arrangement into joint ventures and joint operations?
7. How are joint ventures accounted for?
8. How are joint operations accounted for?

Exercises

Exercise 30.1	CLASSIFICATION OF A JOINT ARRANGEMENT

★ Horsley Ltd and Benington Ltd decide to jointly undertake the manufacture of an electric car. They form Tiverton Ltd, which undertakes the manufacture of the car. Horsley Ltd and Benington Ltd provide the various parts for the manufacture of the car, which is assembled by Tiverton Ltd.

Horsley Ltd and Benington Ltd each hold 50% of the voting rights in Tiverton Ltd and receive 50% of the cars produced by Tiverton Ltd. Horsely Ltd and Benington Ltd then sell the cars in their own geographic region. The constitution of Tiverton Ltd requires that the operations of the company must be in accordance with a business plan prepared annually, and to which both Horsley Ltd and Benington Ltd both agree. Tiverton Ltd has six directors, with three being appointed by Horsley Ltd and three by Benington Ltd.

Required

Evaluate whether a joint arrangement exists and how it should be classified.

Exercise 30.2	EXISTENCE AND CLASSIFICATION OF A JOINT ARRANGEMENT

★ The Chinese mining company Changchun Mining Ltd and the Australian mining company Gold Rush Ltd have agreed to set up a separate company, Dragon Gold Ltd, to mine for gold in Australia. The Australian government has issued permits to the Australian company to mine for gold in specified areas of Australia.

The companies have set up a joint operating agreement which contains the following provisions:
- The assets and liabilities of Dragon Gold Ltd are those of that company and not of the parties owning shares in Dragon Gold Ltd.
- Dragon Gold Ltd has a board of directors that will consist of six persons, three provided by each of Changchun Mining Ltd and Gold Rush Ltd. Each of these companies has a 50% ownership in Dragon Gold Ltd. For any resolution to be passed by the board, there has to be unanimous consent of all directors.
- Gold Rush Ltd will provide the management team for Dragon Gold Ltd for which a management fee will be paid by Dragon Gold Ltd. However, all budget matters and work programs have to be approved by the board of Dragon Gold Ltd.
- The rights and obligations arising from the exploration development and production activities of Dragon Gold Ltd are to be shared by all parties to the agreement. In particular, the parties will share in the production obtained from the mining activities and all costs associated with the work undertaken.
- If cash is required for ongoing mining activities, the board of Dragon Gold Ltd may make calls on the parties owning shares in that company.

Required

Discuss whether a joint arrangement exists and whether it should be classified as a joint venture or a joint operation.

Exercise 30.3	CLASSIFICATION OF A JOINT ARRANGEMENT

★ Two smaller banks that operate in Australia are the Ballarat Bank and the St Martins Bank. These have in the past primarily offered domestic banking services to their customers. However in recent times, these customers have made increasing demands for international currency transactions and access to offshore banking arrangements. As both banks individually are not prepared to undertake the risks associated with international operations on their own, they have decided to join together to provide these services to their customers.

To this end, they have formed the Overseas Bank. This bank is regarded as a separate vehicle in its own right, with the assets and liabilities of the Overseas Bank being those of the bank itself. The Ballarat Bank and St Martins bank will each hold a 50% interest in the Overseas Bank. These two banks have signed an agreement such that all major decisions in relation to the Overseas Bank require the unanimous agreement of the two banks. The board of the Overseas Bank will consist of an equal number of representatives of these two banks.

The Ballarat Bank and the St Martins bank have agreed to provide initial funding to establish the Overseas Bank and have also agreed on a mechanism for further cash inflows if required.

Required

Discuss whether a joint arrangement exists and how it should be classified.

| Exercise 30.4 | ACCOUNTING FOR AN ASSET USED BY A NUMBER OF COMPANIES |

★ Raby Ltd and Bowes Ltd are companies that have newly discovered oil wells in a Middle-Eastern country. There is some distance to the nearest port and, rather than build separate pipelines, they have agreed to jointly build a pipeline to the port and share the use of the pipeline for transporting oil. The management of the pipeline is conducted in accordance with an agreement between Raby Ltd and Bowes Ltd which requires unanimous agreement in relation to such issues as maintenance and future expansion or contraction of the pipeline. Allington Ltd also has oil wells in the area and has agreed to use any excess capacity of the pipeline.

Required

Discuss how you would account for the pipeline.

| Exercise 30.5 | SHARING OUTPUT |

★★ On 1 July 2013, Hertford Ltd entered into a joint agreement with London Ltd to form an unincorporated entity to produce a new type of widget. It was agreed that each party to the agreement would share the output equally. Hertford Ltd's initial contribution consisted of $2 000 000 cash and London Ltd contributed machinery that was recorded in the records of London Ltd at $1 900 000. During the first year of operation both parties contributed a further $3 000 000 each.

On 30 June 2014, the venture manager provided the following statements (in $'000):

Costs incurred for the year ended 30 June 2014	
Wages	$1 840
Supplies	2 800
Overheads	2 200
	6 840
Cost of inventory	4 840
Work in progress at 30 June 2014	$2 000

Receipts and Payments for year ended 30 June 2014		
Receipts		
Original contributions		$2 000
Additional contributions		6 000
Payments		8 000
Machinery (2/7/13)	$ 800	
Wages	1 800	
Supplies	3 000	
Overheads	2 100	
Operating expenses	200	7 900
Closing cash balance		$ 100

Assets and Liabilities at 30 June 2014	
Assets	
Cash	$ 100
Machinery	2 800
Supplies	400
Work in progress	2 000
Total assets	5 300
Liabilities	
Accrued wages	40
Creditors	300
Total liabilities	340
Net assets	$4 960

Each joint operator depreciates machinery at 20% p.a. on cost in its own records.

Required

1. Prepare the journal entries in the records of Hertford Ltd and London Ltd in relation to the joint operation.
2. Prepare the journal entries in the records of London Ltd assuming that the joint operation, not the operators, had depreciated the machinery and included that expense in the cost of inventory transferred.

Exercise 30.6	**UNINCORPORATED JOINT OPERATION**
★★	

On 1 July 2012, Allington Ltd entered into a joint agreement with Barnwell Ltd to establish an unincorporated joint operation to manufacture timber-felling equipment. It was agreed that the output of the operation would be shared: Allington Ltd 60% and Barnwell Ltd 40%.

To commence the operations, contributions were as follows:

- Allington Ltd: cash of $1 100 000 and equipment having a carrying amount of $300 000 and a fair value of $400 000.
- Barnwell Ltd: cash of $600 000 and plant having a carrying amount of $450 000 and a fair value of $400 000.

Barnwell Ltd revalued the plant it contributed to the joint operation to fair value prior to its transfer to the joint operation. Plant and equipment was depreciated (to the nearest month) in the joint operation's books at 20% p.a. on cost. During December 2012, an additional $1 000 000 cash was contributed by the operators in the same proportion as their initial contributions.

The following information, in relation to the joint operations for the year ended 30 June 2013, was provided by the operation manager:

(a) Costs incurred for the year ended 30 June 2013

Wages	$ 400 000
Raw materials	1 200 000
Overheads	650 000
Depreciation	205 000
	2 455 000
Less: Cost of inventory	2 005 000
Work in progress at 30 June 2013	$ 450 000

(b) Receipts and payments for year ended 30 June 2013

	Payments	Receipts
Contributions		$2 700 000
Plant (3 January 2013)	$ 450 000	
Wages	350 000	
Accounts payable	980 000	
Overhead costs	610 000	
Operating expenses	40 000	
	$2 430 000	$2 700 000

(c) Assets and liabilities at 30 June 2013

	Dr	Cr
Cash	$ 270 000	
Raw materials	100 000	
Work in progress	450 000	
Inventory	255 000	
Plant and equipment	1 250 000	
Accumulated depreciation		
– plant and equipment		$205 000
Accounts payable		320 000
Accrued expenses – wages and overheads		90 000

Required

Prepare the journal entries in the records of Allington Ltd in relation to the joint operation for the year ended 30 June 2013. (Round all amounts to the nearest dollar and show all relevant workings.)

Exercise 30.7	**OPERATORS SHARE OUTPUT**
★★	Belvoir Ltd enters into an arrangement with another operator, Ashton Ltd, to establish an unincorporated joint operation to produce a drug that assists both hay fever sufferers and those with sinus problems. To produce the drug requires a combination of the technical and pharmaceutical knowledge of both companies. Each company will receive an equal share of the output of the drug, which they will retail through their own preferred outlets, potentially under different names. Belvoir Ltd agrees to manage the project for a fee of $100 000 p.a. Belvoir Ltd estimates that it will cost $80 000 to provide the service. The management fee is capitalised into the cost of inventory produced.

The operation commences on 1 January 2014, with each operator providing $1 000 000 cash. At the end of the first year, the statement of financial position of the joint operation showed:

Assets	
Vehicles	$ 200 000
Accumulated depreciation	(50 000)
Equipment	820 000
Accumulated depreciation	(60 000)
Inventory	80 000
Work in progress	320 000
Materials	210 000
Total assets	1 520 000
Liabilities	
Provisions	80 000
Payables	40 000
	120 000
Net assets	$1 400 000

(continued)

Operators' equity	
Initial contributions	2 000 000
Inventory delivered	(400 000)
General administration costs	(200 000)
Total equity	**$ 1 400 000**

Required

1. Prepare the journal entries in the records of Belvoir Ltd during 2014.
2. What differences would occur if the management fee paid to Belvoir Ltd were treated as general administration costs?

Exercise 30.8

★★★

SHARE OF OUTPUT

During 2013, a group of academics were undertaking a bonding exercise in the Portadown hills. While tracking through the hills, they came across a spring of pure sweet water. They formed a company called Arnside Ltd and decided to establish the extent of their find. In the process they expended funds, obtained from teaching overseas students, on equipment and employing geologists and mining experts. The general conclusion was that the find was significant and a commercially profitable business selling mineral water was feasible. As they were academics, and had little practical experience of business, they decided to establish a joint operation with Tower Ltd who would establish a factory to produce bottled water. The joint operation agreement was signed on 1 January 2014, with Arnside Ltd and Tower Ltd having a 50% share in the unincorporated joint operation.

The initial contributions by the two operators were as follows:

Arnside Ltd:	
Capitalised expenses	$ 800 000
Equipment	800 000
Cash	2 400 000
Tower Ltd:	
Cash	$ 4 000 000

The capitalised expenses were recorded in the books of Arnside Ltd at $320 000, while the equipment was recorded at a carrying amount of $640 000. In order to supply the cash, Arnside Ltd borrowed $800 000 of its required contribution. It is expected that the reserves of water will be depleted within 10 years, and the equipment is expected to have a similar useful life.

On 1 June 2014, the joint operation was ready to start producing bottles of water. The joint operation's accounts at 30 June 2015 contained the following information:

Statement of Financial Position (extract)		
	2014	**2015**
Work in progress		$ 200 000
Capitalised costs	$ 800 000	800 000
Plant and equipment	8 360 000	7 760 000
Cash	80 000	240 000
Accounts payable — plant	(240 000)	(800 000)
Accrued expenses — wages etc.	(160 000)	(200 000)

Cash Receipts and Payments (extract)		
	2015	
	Payments	**Receipts**
Materials and supplies	$480 000	
Administration	160 000	
Wages	560 000	
Accounts payable — plant	960 000	
Contributions from joint operators		$2 000 000

The output of the first year's operations was distributed equally to the joint operators. Production in the first year was estimated to be 15% of the reserves. At 30 June 2015, Arnside Ltd held 10% of its share of output in inventory, having sold the rest to its customers for $2 000 000. Expenses of the joint operation incurred up to 30 June 2015 were allocated to the operators.

At 30 June 2015, the joint operation had ordered new plant and equipment of $300 000 that had not yet arrived. Because of some damage to the environment caused by the establishment of the pumping station to extract the water, there is a potential restoration cost to be incurred at closure of the joint operation. Whether this will be required will depend on the result of current legal inquiries.

Required

Prepare the journal entries in the records of Arnside Ltd for the periods ending 30 June 2014 and 2015.

Exercise 30.9

OPERATORS SHARE OUTPUT

★★★ On 1 July 2014, Taunton Ltd entered into a joint operation agreement with Dudley Ltd to manufacture stevedoring equipment. It was agreed that each party to the agreement would share the output equally.

To commence the operation, contributions were as follows:

- Taunton Ltd: cash of $2 000 000 and equipment having a $400 000 carrying amount and a fair value of $600 000
- Dudley Ltd: cash of $1 800 000 and plant having a carrying amount of $900 000 and a fair value of $800 000.

Dudley Ltd revalued the plant it contributed to the joint operation prior to its transfer to the joint operation. Plant and equipment is depreciated (to the nearest month) in the joint operation's books at 20% p.a. on cost.

During December 2014, both parties contributed an additional $1 500 000 cash.

The following information, in relation to the joint operation's operations for the year ended 30 June 2015, was provided by the operation manager.

(a) *Costs incurred for the year ended 30 June 2015*

Wages	$1 200 000
Raw materials	2 150 000
Overheads	1 860 000
Depreciation	470 000
	5 680 000
Less: Cost of inventory	2 580 000
Work in progress at 30 June 2015	$3 100 000

(b) Receipts and payments for the year ended 30 June 2015

	Payments	Receipts
Contributions		$ 6 800 000
Plant (10 July 2014)	$ 950 000	
Wages	1 150 000	
Accounts payable	1 980 000	
Overhead costs	1 810 000	
Operating expenses	440 000	
	$ 6 330 000	$ 6 800 000

(c) Assets and liabilities as at 30 June 2015

	Dr	Cr
Cash	$ 470 000	
Raw materials	360 000	
Work in progress	3 100 000	
Inventory	580 000	
Plant and equipment	2 350 000	
Accumulated depreciation — plant and equipment		$ 470 000
Accounts payable		530 000
Accrued expenses		100 000

Required

Prepare the journal entries in the records of Taunton Ltd and Dudley Ltd in relation to the joint operation for the year ended 30 June 2015.

Exercise 30.10   **UNINCORPORATED JOINT OPERATION MANAGED BY ONE OF THE OPERATORS**

★★★   During 2012, discussions took place between Stafford Ltd, a company concerned with the design of specialised tools and machines, and two companies, Dunster Ltd and Tutbury Ltd, which could potentially assist in the manufacture of a new tool. The new tool is called SmartTool and is to be used in the making of high grade mining instruments. On 1 June 2013, the three companies agreed to form an unincorporated joint operation to achieve this purpose. It was agreed that the relative interests in the joint operation would be:

Stafford Ltd	50%
Dunster Ltd	25%
Tutbury Ltd	25%

It was further agreed that Tutbury Ltd would undertake a management role in relation to the new operation, being responsible for operating decisions and for record keeping. Tutbury Ltd would be paid a management fee by the joint operation of $20 000.

In establishing the joint operation, the various parties agreed to provide the following assets as their initial contribution:

- Stafford Ltd was to provide the patent to SmartTool, which was being recorded by Stafford Ltd at a capitalised development cost of $1 400 000. The operators agreed that this asset had a fair value of $2 000 000, with an expected useful life of 10 years.
- Dunster Ltd was to provide cash of $1 000 000.
- Tutbury Ltd was to provide the basic plant and equipment to manufacture the new tool. The plant and equipment was recorded in the books of Tutbury Ltd at $600 000, but the operators agreed that it had a fair value of $1 000 000. The plant and equipment was estimated to have a further useful life of 5 years.

During the first period of its operation, the output of the joint operation was distributed to each of the operators in proportion to their agreed interests. By 30 June 2014, Tutbury Ltd had sold 80% of the output received from the joint operation for $300 000. The joint operation had not paid the management fee to Tutbury Ltd by 30 June 2014.

Information from the financial statements of the joint operation as at 30 June 2014 is as follows:

Assets

Cash	$ 40 000
Plant and equipment	1 080 000
Accumulated depreciation	(208 000)
Patent	2 000 000
Accumulated depreciation	(200 000)
Office equipment	88 000
Accumulated depreciation	(8 800)
Work in progress	40 000

Liabilities

Creditors — for materials	$ 136 000
Accruals — salaries etc, including the management fee	112 000

Cash payments

Salaries	$ 220 000
Materials	488 000
Operating expenses	84 000

Required

1. Prepare the journal entries in the records of Stafford Ltd and Dunster Ltd at the commencement of the joint operation.
2. Prepare the journal entries in the records of Tutbury Ltd for the financial year ending 30 June 2014.

Exercise 30.11

★★★

OPERATORS SHARE OUTPUT

After prospecting unsuccessfully for a number of years for gold, in November 2014 Cooling Ltd finally found an economically viable deposit. Realising that it did not have sufficient expertise to operate a gold mine successfully, Cooling Ltd formed an unincorporated joint operation with Deal Ltd, agreeing to share the output of the mine equally. It was agreed that the two operators would initially contribute the following assets:

Cooling Ltd:	
Capitalised exploration costs, including permits licences, and mining rights,	
currently recorded by Cooling Ltd at $200 000	$ 800 000
Cash	700 000
Deal Ltd:	
Cash	1 500 000

The joint operation commenced on 1 January 2015. By 31 December 2015, the mine had been operating successfully. It was reliably estimated at the commencement of the project that the mine had expected reserves of 100 000 tonnes.

In the first year following commencement, 5000 tonnes of gold was extracted, while in 2016, 10 000 tonnes was extracted. This output was distributed to the operators equally.

All costs except general administration costs were capitalised into the cost of the output, with depreciation of equipment and capitalised exploration costs being written off in proportion to the depletion of the reserves. General administration expenses were allocated to the operators equally.

The financial statements of the joint operation over the first 2 years of operation showed the following information:

Cash Receipts and Payments		
	2015	2016
Balance at 1 January	—	$ 300 000
Contributions from operators	$ 2 200 000	1 200 000
	2 200 000	1 500 000
Plant and equipment	800 000	190 000
Wages	600 000	660 000
Materials	200 000	240 000
General administration	300 000	300 000
	1 900 000	1 390 000
Balance at 31 December	$ 300 000	$ 110 000

Statement of Financial Position		
	2015	2016
Capitalised exploration costs	$ 760 000	$ 680 000
Plant and equipment	800 000	990 000
Accumulated depreciation	(40 000)	(140 000)
Cash	300 000	110 000
Materials	50 000	40 000
	1 870 000	1 680 000
Accrued wages	10 000	20 000
Accounts payable (materials)	20 000	30 000
	30 000	50 000
Net assets	$ 1 840 000	$ 1 630 000
Operators' equity:		
Contributions as at 1 January	3 000 000	1 840 000
Additional contributions		1 200 000
	3 000 000	3 040 000
Less: Output distributed	860 000	1 110 000
Allocation: General administration	300 000	300 000
	1 160 000	1 410 000
Balance at 31 December	$ 1 840 000	$ 1 630 000

Required

Prepare the journal entries in the records of Cooling Ltd to record its interest in the joint operation for the years ending 31 December 2015 and 2016.

References

CBD Energy 2012, *AusChina Energy*, www.cbdenergy.com.au.

Perrin, CJ 2011, 'Australia's CBD Energy forms joint venture with Chinese firms', *International Business Times*, 13 April, http://au.ibtimes.com.

GLOSSARY

Accounting estimates: Measurement judgements applied in preparing the financial statements.

Accounting policies: The specific principles, bases, conventions, rules and practices applied by an entity in preparing and presenting financial statements.

Accounting profit: Profit for a period (determined in accordance with accounting standards) before deducting tax expense.

Accrual basis: Recognising the effects of transactions and other events when they occur, rather than when cash or its equivalent is received or paid.

Acquirer: The entity that obtains control of the acquiree.

Acquisition date: The date on which the acquirer obtains control of the acquiree.

Active market: A market in which all the following conditions exist: (a) the items traded in the market are homogeneous; (b) willing buyers and sellers can normally be found at any time; and (c) prices are available to the public. A market in which transactions for the asset or liability take place with sufficient frequency and volume to provide pricing information on an ongoing basis (IFRS 13 *Fair Value Measurement*).

Adjusting event after the reporting period: An event that provides evidence of conditions that existed at the end of the reporting period.

Agreement date: The date that a substantive agreement between the combining parties is reached.

Agricultural produce: The harvested product of an entity's biological assets.

Allotment: The process whereby directors of the company allocate shares to applicants. Alternatively, an account recording an amount of money receivable from successful applicants once shares are allotted.

Amortisation: The systematic allocation of the depreciable amount of an intangible asset over its useful life. *See* depreciation.

Amortised cost: The amount at which the financial asset or financial liability is measured at initial recognition minus principal repayments, plus or minus the cumulative amortisation using the effective interest method of any difference between that initial amount and the maturity amount, and minus any reduction (directly or through the use of an allowance account) for impairment or uncollectability.

Application: The process whereby prospective shareholders apply to the company for an allotment of shares. Alternatively, an account used to record the amount of money receivable by the company from applicants for shares.

Asset: A resource controlled by an entity as a result of past events and from which future economic benefits are expected to flow to the entity.

Associate: An entity over which the investor has significant influence and that is neither a subsidiary nor an interest in a joint venture.

Available-for-sale financial assets: Those non-derivative financial assets that are designated as available for sale or that are not classified as (a) loans and receivables, (b) held-to-maturity investments or (c) financial assets at fair value through profit or loss.

Bargain purchase option: A clause in the lease agreement allowing the lessee to purchase the asset at the end of the lease for a preset amount, significantly less than the expected residual value at the end of the lease term.

Biological asset: A living animal or plant.

Bonus issue or bonus shares: An issue of shares to existing owners as a substitute for the payment of cash, particularly as a substitute for a cash dividend.

Business: An integrated set of activities and assets that is capable of being conducted and managed for the purpose of providing a return in the form of dividends, lower costs or other economic benefits directly to investors or other owners, members or participants.

Business combination: A transaction or other event in which an acquirer obtains control of one or more businesses.

Business segment: A distinguishable component of an entity that is engaged in providing an individual product or service or a group of related products or services and that is subject to risks and returns that are different from those of other business segments.

Call: An account used to record amounts of money receivable on shares that have been allotted by shareholders whose shares were forfeited.

Carrying amount: The amount at which an asset is recognised after deducting any accumulated depreciation (amortisation) and accumulated impairment losses thereon.

Cash: Includes cash on hand, currency, cheques, money orders or electronic transfer that a bank will accept as a deposit.

Cash basis: Recognising the effects of transactions and other events when cash or its equivalent is received or paid, rather than when the transactions or other events occur.

Cash equivalents: Short-term, highly liquid investments that are readily convertible to known amounts of cash and which are subject to an insignificant risk of changes in value.

Cash flow statement: Provides information about the cash payments and cash receipts of an entity during a period.

Cash or settlement discount: An incentive for early payment of amounts owing on credit transactions, normally quoted as a percentage.

Cash-generating unit: The smallest identifiable group of assets that generates cash inflows that are largely independent of the cash inflows from other assets or groups of assets.

Cash-settled share-based payment transaction: A share-based payment transaction in which the entity acquires goods or services by incurring a liability to transfer cash or other assets to the supplier of those goods or services for amounts that are based on the price (or value) of the entity's shares or other equity instruments of the entity.

Class of assets: A category of assets having a similar nature or function in the operations of an entity, and which, for the purposes of disclosure, is shown as a single item without supplementary disclosure.

Closing rate: The spot exchange rate at the end of the reporting period.

Comparability: The quality of accounting information that results from similar accounting recognition, measurement, disclosure, and presentation standards being used by all entities.

Compensation: All employee benefits including share-based payments. This includes all forms of consideration provided by the entity, or on its behalf, in exchange for services rendered to the entity.

Component of an entity: Operations and cash flows that can be clearly distinguished, operationally and for financial reporting purposes, from the rest of the entity.

Conceptual Framework for Financial Reporting: The pronouncement of the International Accounting Standards Board that sets out the concepts underlying the preparation and presentation of financial statements for external users.

Consolidated financial statements: The financial statements of a group in which the assets, liabilities, equity, income, expenses and cash flows of the parent and its subsidiaries are presented as those of a single economic entity.

Constructive obligation: An obligation that derives from an entity's actions where: (a) by an established pattern of past practice, published policies or a sufficiently specific current statement, the entity has indicated to other parties that it will accept certain responsibilities; and (b) as a result, the entity has created a valid expectation on the part of those other parties that it will discharge those responsibilities.

Contingency: A condition arising from past events that exists at reporting date and gives rise to either a possible asset or a possible liability, the outcome of which will be confirmed only on the occurrence of one or more uncertain future events that are outside the control of the entity.

Contingent asset: A possible asset that arises from past events and whose existence will be confirmed only by the occurrence or non-occurrence of one or more uncertain future events not wholly within the control of the entity.

Contingent consideration: Usually, an obligation of the acquirer to transfer additional assets or equity interests to the former owners of an acquiree as part of the exchange for control of the acquiree if specified future events occur or conditions are met. However, contingent consideration also may give the acquirer the right to the return of previously transferred consideration if specified conditions are met.

Contingent liability: (a) A possible obligation that arises from past events and whose existence will be confirmed only by the occurrence or non-occurrence of one or more uncertain future events not wholly within the control of the entity, or (b) a present obligation that arises from past events but is not recognised because (i) it is not probable that an outflow of resources embodying economic events will be required to settle the obligation, or (ii) the amount of the obligation cannot be measured with sufficient reliability.

Contingent rent: The part of the lease payments that is not fixed in amount but is based on the future amount of a factor that changes other than with the passage of time.

Control: An investor controls an investee when the investor is exposed, or has rights, to variable returns from its involvement with the investee and has the ability to affect those returns through its power over the investee.

Corporate assets: Assets other than goodwill that contribute to the future cash flows of both the cash-generating unit under review and other cash-generating units.

Corporate governance: The system by which companies are directed and managed. It influences how the objectives of the company are set and achieved, how risk is monitored and assessed, and how performance is optimised. Good corporate governance structures encourage companies to create value (through entrepreneurialism, innovation, development and exploration) and provide accountability and control systems commensurate with the risks involved.

Cost: The amount of cash or cash equivalents paid or the fair value of the other consideration given to acquire an asset at the time of its acquisition or construction or, where applicable, the amount attributed to that asset when initially recognised in accordance with the specific requirements of other accounting standards, e.g. IFRS 2 *Share-based Payment*.

Cost approach: A valuation technique that reflects the amount that would be required currently to replace the service capacity of an asset (often referred to as current replacement cost).

Costs of conversion: Costs directly related to the units of production plus a systematic allocation of fixed and variable overheads that are incurred in converting materials into finished goods.

Costs of disposal: Incremental costs directly attributable to the disposal of an asset or cash-generating unit, excluding finance costs and income tax expense.

Costs of purchase: Costs such as purchase price, import duties and other taxes (other than those subsequently recoverable by the entity from the taxing authorities), transport, handling and other costs directly attributable to the acquisition of finished goods, materials and services.

Costs to sell: The incremental costs directly attributable to the disposal of an asset (or disposal group), excluding finance costs and income tax expense.

Cumulative: In relation to preference shares, shares on which undeclared dividends in one year accumulate to the following year/s until paid.

Current liability: A liability that (a) is expected to be settled in the normal course of the entity's operating cycle, or (b) is at call or due or expected to be settled within 12 months of the reporting date.

Current tax: The amount of income taxes payable in respect of the taxable profit for a period.

Date of exchange: The date when each individual investment is recognised in the financial report of the acquirer.

Deductible temporary differences: Temporary differences that will result in amounts that are deductible in determining taxable profit of future periods when the carrying amount of the asset or liability is recovered or settled.

Deferred tax asset: Amounts of income taxes recoverable in future periods in respect of deferred temporary differences; the carry forward of unused tax losses and the carry forward of unused tax credits.

Deferred tax liability: Amounts of income taxes payable in future periods in respect of taxable temporary differences.

Depreciable amount: The cost of an asset, or other amount substituted for cost, less its residual value.

Depreciation (amortisation): The systematic allocation of the depreciable amount of an asset over its useful life.

Derivatives: A financial instrument that derives its value from another underlying item, such as a share price or an interest rate. The definition requires all of the following three characteristics to be met: (a) its value must change in response to a change in an underlying variable such as a specified interest rate, price, or foreign exchange rate; (b) it must require no initial net investment or an initial net investment that is smaller than would be required for other types of contracts with similar responses to changes in market factors; and (c) it is settled at a future date.

Development: The application of research findings or other knowledge to a plan or design for the production of new or substantially improved materials, devices, products, processes, systems or services before the start of commercial production or use.

Direct non-controlling interest (DNCI): An NCI that holds shares directly in a subsidiary.

Discontinued operation: A component of an entity that either has been disposed of or is classified as held for sale and (a) represents a separate major line of business or geographical area of operations; (b) is part of a single coordinated plan to dispose of a separate major line of business or geographical area of operations; or (c) is a subsidiary acquired exclusively with a view to resale.

Disposal group: A group of assets to be disposed of, by sale or otherwise, together as a group in a single transaction, and liabilities directly associated with those assets that will be transferred in the transaction.

Dividends: A distribution of profit to the equity holders of a company.

Economic life: Either the period over which an asset is expected to be economically usable by one or more users, or the number of production or similar units expected to be obtained from the asset by one or more users.

Effective interest method: A method of calculating the amortised cost of a financial asset or a financial liability, and of allocating the interest income or interest expense over the relevant period.

Effective interest rate: The rate that exactly discounts estimated future cash payments or receipts through the expected life of the financial instrument (or, when appropriate, a shorter period) to the net carrying amount of the financial asset or financial liability.

Embedded derivative: A component of a combined (or 'hybrid') instrument that also includes a non-derivative host contract, with the effect that some of the cash flows of the combined instrument vary in a way similar to a stand-alone instrument.

Employee benefits: All forms of consideration given by an entity in exchange for services rendered by employees.

Employees and others providing similar services: Individuals who render personal services to the entity and either (a) the individuals are regarded as employees for legal or tax purposes, (b) the individuals work for the entity under its direction in the same way as individuals who are regarded as employees for legal or tax purposes, or (c) the services rendered are similar to those rendered by employees. For example, the term encompasses all management personnel, that is, those persons having authority and responsibility for planning, directing and controlling the activities of the entity, including non-executive directors.

Entity-specific value: The present value of the cash flows an entity (1) expects to arise from the continuing use of an asset and from its disposal at the end of its useful life, or (2) expects to incur when settling a liability.

Entry price: The price paid to acquire an asset or received to assume a liability in an exchange transaction.

Equity: The residual interest in the assets of the entity after deducting all its liabilities.

Equity instrument granted: The right (conditional or unconditional) to an equity instrument of the entity conferred by the entity on another party, under a share-based payment arrangement.

Equity instrument: Any contract that evidences a residual interest in the assets of an entity after deducting all of its liabilities.

Equity method: The method of accounting whereby the investment is initially recognised at cost and subsequently adjusted for the post-acquisition change in the investor's share of net assets of the associate. The profit or loss of the investor includes the investor's share of the profit or loss of the investee.

Equity-settled share-based payment transaction: A share-based payment transaction in which the entity receives goods or services as consideration for equity instruments of the entity (including shares or share options).

Errors: Omissions from or misstatements in the financial statements.

Exchange difference: The difference resulting from translating a given number of units of one currency into another currency at different exchange rates.

Exchange rate: The ratio of exchange for two currencies.

Executory contracts: Contracts under which neither party has performed any of its obligations or both parties have partially performed their obligations to an equal extent.

Executory costs: Operating amounts (including insurance, maintenance, consumable supplies, replacement parts and rates) that are paid by the lessor on behalf of the lessee.

Exit price: The price that would be received to sell an asset or paid to transfer a liability.

Expenses: Decreases in economic benefits during the accounting period in the form of outflows or depletions of assets or incurrences of liabilities that result in decreases in equity, other than those relating to distributions to equity participants.

Fair value: The price that would be received to sell an asset or paid to transfer a liability in an orderly transaction between market participants at the measurement date (IFRS 13 *Fair Value Measurement*).

Fair value (of a leased asset): The amount for which an asset could be exchanged or a liability settled between knowledgeable, willing parties in an arm's length transaction.

Finance lease: A lease that transfers substantially all the risks and benefits incidental to ownership of an asset; title may or may not eventually be transferred.

Financial asset: Any asset that is: (a) cash; (b) an equity instrument of another entity; (c) a contractual right: (i) to receive cash or another financial asset from another entity, or (ii) to exchange financial assets or financial liabilities with another entity under conditions that are potentially favourable to the entity; or (d) a contract that will or may be settled in the entity's own equity instruments that is: (i) a non-derivative for which the entity is or may be obliged to receive a variable number of the entity's own equity instruments, or (ii) a derivative that will or may be settled other than by the exchange of a fixed amount of cash or another financial asset for a fixed number of the entity's own equity instruments (for this purpose the entity's own equity instruments do not include instruments that are themselves contracts for the future receipt or delivery of the entity's own equity instruments).

Financial assets at fair value through profit or loss: Financial assets held for trading and measured at fair value with any gain or loss from a change in fair value recognised in profit or loss, or financial assets that upon initial recognition are designated by the entity as at fair value through profit or loss.

Financial instrument: Any contract that gives rise to a financial asset of one entity and a financial liability or equity instrument of another.

Financial liability: Any liability that is: (a) a contractual obligation: (i) to deliver cash or another financial asset to another entity, or (ii) to exchange financial assets or financial liabilities with another entity under conditions that are potentially unfavourable to the entity; or (b) a contract that will or may be settled in the entity's own equity instruments and is: (i) a non-derivative for which the entity is or may be obliged to deliver a variable number of the entity's own equity instruments, or (ii) a derivative that will or may be settled other than by the exchange of a fixed amount of cash or another financial asset for a fixed number of the entity's own equity instruments (for this purpose the entity's own equity instruments do not include instruments that are themselves contracts for the future receipt or delivery of the entity's own equity instruments).

Financial position: The assets, liabilities, and residual equity interest of an entity at a given point in time.

Financing activities: Those activities that result in changes in the size and composition of the equity capital and borrowings of the entity.

Firm commitment: A binding agreement for the exchange of a specified quantity of resources at a specified price on a specified future date or dates.

First-in, first-out (FIFO): A method of allocating cost to inventory items that assumes that the items first purchased will be the items first sold.

FOB destination: A condition of sale under which the seller pays all freight costs (FOB means 'free on board').

FOB shipping: A condition of sale under which freight costs incurred from the point of shipment are paid by the buyer (FOB means 'free on board').

Forecast transaction: An uncommitted but anticipated future transaction.

Foreign currency: A currency other than the functional currency of the entity.

Foreign operation: An entity that is a subsidiary, associate, joint venture or branch of a reporting entity, the activities of which are based or conducted in a country or currency other than those of the reporting entity.

Forfeited shares account: An account initially recording the amount of funds supplied by shareholders whose shares were forfeited.

Framework for the Preparation and Presentation of Financial Statements: The pronouncement of the International Accounting Standards Board that sets out the concepts underlying the preparation and presentation of financial statements for external users. This has been superseded by the *Conceptual Framework for Financial Reporting*.

Functional currency: The currency of the primary economic environment in which the entity operates.

General purpose financial statements: The financial statements that a business entity prepares and presents at least annually to meet the common information needs of a wide range of users external to the entity.

Geographical segment: A distinguishable component of an entity that is engaged in providing products or services within a particular economic environment and that is subject to risks and returns that are different from those of components operating in other economic environments.

Going concern: An entity that is expected to continue in operation for the foreseeable future.

Goodwill: An asset representing the future economic benefits arising from other assets acquired in a business combination that are not individually identified and separately recognised.

Grant date: The date at which the entity and another party (including an employee) agree to a share-based payment arrangement, being when the entity and the counterparty have a shared understanding of the terms and conditions of the arrangement. At grant date the entity confers on the counterparty the right to cash, other assets, or equity instruments of the entity, provided the specified vesting conditions, if any, are met. If that agreement is subject to an approval process (e.g. by shareholders), grant date is the date when that approval is obtained.

Gross investment: The aggregate of the minimum lease payments receivable by the lessor under a finance lease and any unguaranteed residual value accruing to the lessor.

Group: A parent and its subsidiaries.

Guaranteed residual value: That part of the residual value of the leased asset guaranteed by the lessee or a third party related to the lessee.

Hedge effectiveness: The degree to which changes in the fair value or cash flows of the hedged item that are attributable to a hedged risk are offset by changes in the fair value or cash flows of the hedging instrument.

Hedged item: An asset, liability, firm commitment, highly probable forecast transaction or net investment in a foreign operation that (a) exposes the entity to risk of changes in fair value or future cash flows and (b) is designated as being hedged.

Hedging instrument: A designated derivative or (for a hedge of the risk of changes in foreign currency exchange rates only) a designated non-derivative financial asset or non-derivative financial liability whose fair value or cash flows are expected to offset changes in the fair value or cash flows of a designated hedged item.

Held-to-maturity investments: Investments that the entity has the positive intention and ability to hold to maturity (e.g. debt instruments, such as debentures held in another entity or redeemable preference shares) other than: (a) those that the entity upon initial recognition designates as at fair value through profit or loss; (b) those that the entity designates as available for sale; and (c) those that meet the definition of loans and receivables.

Highest and best use: The use of a non-financial asset by market participants that would maximise the value of the asset or the group of assets and liabilities (e.g. a business) within which the asset would be used.

Highly probable: Significantly more likely than probable.

Impairment loss: The amount by which the carrying amount of an asset or a cash-generating unit exceeds its recoverable amount (which is the higher of the asset's net selling price and its value in use).

Inception of the lease: The earlier of the date of the lease agreement and the date of commitment by the parties to the principal provisions of the lease.

Income: An increase in an asset or a decrease in a liability will result in income, unless the increase or decrease results from an equity contribution (such as cash raised through share capital). Because of this broad definition, income is further dissected into revenue and gains.

Income approach: Valuation techniques that convert future amounts (e.g. cash flows or income and expenses) to a single current (i.e. discounted) amount; the fair value measurement is determined on the basis of the value indicated by current market expectations about those future amounts.

Incremental borrowing rate: The rate of interest the lessee would have to pay on a similar lease or, if that is not determinable, the rate that (at the inception of the lease) the lessee would incur to borrow over a similar term, and with a similar security, the funds necessary to purchase the asset.

Indirect non-controlling interest (INCI): An NCI that has an interest in a subsidiary as a result of having an interest in the parent of that subsidiary.

Initial direct costs: Incremental costs that are directly attributable to negotiating and arranging a lease, except for such costs incurred by manufacturer or dealer lessors.

Inputs: The assumptions that market participants would use when pricing the asset or liability, including assumptions about risk, such as the following: (a) the risk inherent in a particular valuation technique used to measure fair value (such as a pricing model); and (b) the risk inherent in the inputs to the valuation technique. Inputs may be observable or unobservable.

Intangible asset: An identifiable non-monetary asset without physical substance.

Interest rate implicit in the lease rate: The rate that, at the inception of the lease, causes the aggregate present value of the minimum lease payments and the unguaranteed residual value to be equal to the sum of the fair value of the leased asset and any initial direct costs of the lessor.

Intrinsic value: The difference between the fair value of the shares to which the counterparty has the (conditional or unconditional) right to subscribe or which it has the right to receive, and the price (if any) the counterparty is (or will be) required to pay for those shares. For example, a share option with an exercise price of CU15 (currency units) on a share with a fair value of CU20, has an intrinsic value of CU5.

Inventories: Assets held for sale in the ordinary course of business, in the process of production for such sale, or in the form of materials or supplies to be consumed in the production process or in the rendering of services.

Investee: An entity in which funds have been invested.

Investing activities: Those activities which relate to the acquisition and disposal of long-term assets and other investments not included in cash equivalents.

Investment property: Property (land or a building, or part of a building, or both) held to earn rentals or for capital appreciation or both, rather than for (a) use in the production or supply of goods or services or for administrative purposes, or (b) sale in the ordinary course of business.

Investor: An entity which invests funds in an investee.

Joint control: The contractually agreed sharing of control over an economic activity that exists only when the strategic financial and operating decisions relating to the activity require the unanimous consent of the parties sharing the control (the venturers).

Joint venture: A contractual arrangement whereby two or more parties undertake an economic activity that is subject to joint control.

Key management personnel: Those persons having authority and responsibility for planning, directing and controlling the activities of the entity, directly or indirectly, including any director (whether executive or otherwise) of that entity.

Lease: An agreement whereby the lessor conveys to the lessee in return for a payment or series of payments the right to use an asset for an agreed period of time.

Lease payments: The total amounts payable under the lease agreement.

Lease term: The non-cancellable period for which the lessee has contracted to lease the asset together with any further terms for which the lessee has the option to continue to lease the asset, with or without further payment, when at the inception of the lease it is reasonably certain that the lessee will exercise the option.

Level 1 inputs: Quoted prices (unadjusted) in active markets for identical assets or liabilities that the entity can access at the measurement date.

Level 2 inputs: Inputs other than quoted prices included within Level 1 that are observable for the asset or liability, either directly or indirectly.

Level 3 inputs: Unobservable inputs for the asset or liability.

Liability: A present obligation of the entity arising from past events, the settlement of which is expected to result in an outflow from the entity of resources embodying economic benefits.

Loans and receivables: Non-derivative financial assets with fixed or determinable payments that are not quoted in an active market and which the entity has no intention of trading, e.g. loan to a subsidiary.

Market approach: A valuation technique that uses prices and other relevant information generated by market transactions involving identical or comparable (i.e. similar) assets, liabilities or a group of assets and liabilities, such as a business.

Market condition: A condition upon which the exercise price, vesting or exercisability of an equity instrument depends that is related to the market price of the entity's equity instruments, such as attaining a specified share price or a specified amount of intrinsic value of a share option, or achieving a specified target that is based on the market price of the entity's equity instruments relative to an index of market prices of equity instruments of other entities.

Market participants: Buyers and sellers in the principal (or most advantageous) market for the asset or liability that have all of the following characteristics: (a) they are independent of each other, i.e. they are not related parties as defined in IAS 24, although the price in a related party transaction may be used as an input to a fair value measurement if the entity has evidence that the transaction was entered into at market terms; (b) they are knowledgeable, having a reasonable understanding about the asset or liability and the transaction using all available information, including information that might be obtained through due diligence efforts that are usual and customary; (c) they are able to enter into a transaction for the asset or liability; (d) they are willing to enter into a transaction for the asset or liability, i.e. they are motivated but not forced or otherwise compelled to do so.

Materiality: The notion of materiality guides the margin of error acceptable, the degree of precision required and the extent of the disclosure required when preparing general purpose financial reports.

Measurement: The process of determining the monetary amount at which an asset, liability, income or expense is reported in the financial statements.

Measurement date: The date at which the fair value of the equity instruments granted is measured for the purposes of IFRS 2. For transactions with employees and others providing similar services, the measurement date is the grant date. For transactions with parties other than employees (and those providing similar services), the measurement date is the date the entity obtains the goods or the counterparty renders service.

Minimum lease payments: The payments over the lease term that the lessee is or can be required to make, excluding contingent rent, costs for services and taxes to be paid by and reimbursed to the lessor, together with (a) for a lessee, any amounts guaranteed by the lessee or by a party related to the lessee, and (b) for a lessor, any residual value guaranteed to the lessor.

Monetary assets: Money held and assets to be received in fixed or determinable amounts of money.

Monetary items: Units of currency held and assets and liabilities to be received or paid in a fixed or determinable number of units of currency.

Most advantageous market: The market that maximises the amount that would be received to sell the asset or minimises the amount that would be paid to transfer the liability, after taking into account transaction costs and transport costs.

Net assets: Total assets minus total liabilities.

Net investment in a foreign operation: The amount of the reporting entity's interest in the net assets of that operation.

Net realisable value: The estimated selling price in the ordinary course of business less the estimated costs of completion and the estimated costs necessary to make the sale.

Non-adjusting event after the end of the reporting period: An event that is indicative of conditions that arose after the end of the reporting period.

Non-cancellable lease: A lease that is cancellable only (a) upon the occurrence of some remote contingency, (b) with the permission of the lessor, (c) if the lessee enters into a new lease for the same or an equivalent asset with the same lessor, or (d) upon payment by the lessee of an additional amount such that, at inception of the lease, continuation of the lease is reasonably certain.

Non-controlling interest (NCI): The equity in a subsidiary not attributable, directly or indirectly, to a parent.

Non-performance risk: The risk that an entity will not fulfil an obligation. Non-performance risk includes, but may not be limited to, the entity's own credit risk.

Non-sequential acquisition: Where a parent acquires its shares in a subsidiary after that subsidiary has acquired shares in its subsidiary.

Notes: Notes are prepared in accordance with IAS 1 and form part of a set of general purpose financial statements. They contain information in addition to that presented in the balance sheet, income statement, statement of changes in equity and cash flow statement. They provide narrative descriptions of the basis of preparation of the financial statements and accounting policies adopted, as well as disaggregations of items disclosed in the financial statements and information about items that do not qualify for recognition in those statements.

Obligating event: An event that creates a legal or constructive obligation that results in an entity having no realistic alternative to settling that obligation.

Observable inputs: Inputs that are developed using market data, such as publicly available information about actual events or transactions, and that reflect the assumptions that market participants would use when pricing the asset or liability.

Onerous contract: A contract in which the unavoidable costs of meeting the obligations under the contract exceed the economic benefits expected to be received under it.

Operating activities: Those activities which relate to the main revenue-producing activities of the entity and other activities that are not investing or financing activities.

Operating lease: A lease other than a finance lease.

Orderly transaction: A transaction that assumes exposure to the market for a period before the measurement date to allow for marketing activities that are usual and customary for transactions involving such assets or liabilities; it is not a forced transaction (e.g. a forced liquidation or distress sale).

Parent: An entity that controls one or more entities.

Participating: In relation to preference shares, shares that receive extra dividends above a fixed rate once a certain level of dividends has been paid on ordinary shares.

Performance: The ability of an entity to earn a profit on the resources that have been invested in it.

Periodic method: A system of recording inventory whereby the value of inventory is determined and recorded on a periodic basis (normally annually).

Perpetual method: A system of recording inventory whereby inventory records are updated each time a transaction involving inventory takes place.

Power: Existing rights that give the current ability to direct the relevant activities.

Pre-acquisition equity: The equity of the subsidiary at acquisition date. It is not just the equity recorded by the subsidiary, but is determined by reference to the cost of the business combination.

Presentation currency: The currency in which the financial report is presented.

Principal market: The market with the greatest volume and level of activity for the asset or liability.

Private placement: An issue of shares usually to a large institutional investor such as a finance company, superannuation fund or life insurance company.

Probable: More likely than not.

Property, plant and equipment: Tangible items that (a) are held for use in the production or supply of goods or services, for rental to others, or for administrative purposes, and (b) are expected to be used during more than one period.

Prospective application: Applying the change to transactions, events or other conditions occurring after the date of the change and recognising the effect in the current and future periods.

Protective rights: Rights designed to protect the interest of the party holding those rights without giving that party power over the entity to which those rights relate.

Provision: A liability of uncertain timing or amount.

Public company: A company entitled to raise funds from the public by lodging a disclosure document with ASIC and have its shares or other ownership documents traded on the stock exchange. It may be a limited company, unlimited company or no-liability company.

Reciprocal shareholdings: Where two entities hold shares in each other.

Recognition: The process of incorporating in the financial statements an item that meets the definition of an asset, liability, income or expense.

Recoverable amount: For an asset or a cash-generating unit, the higher of its fair value less costs of disposal and its value in use.

Related party: A person or entity that is related to the entity that is preparing its financial statements.

Related party transaction: A transfer of resources, services or obligations between a reporting entity and a related party, regardless of whether a price is charged.

Relevance: That quality of information that exists when the information influences economic decisions made by users.

Relevant activities: For the purpose of IFRS 10, the activities of the investee that significantly affect the investee's returns.

Reliability: Information has the quality of reliability when it is free from material error and bias and can be depended on by users to represent faithfully that which it either purports to represent or could reasonably be expected to represent.

Reload feature: A feature that provides for an automatic grant of additional share options whenever the option holder exercises previously granted options using the entity's shares, rather than cash, to satisfy the exercise price.

Reload option: A new share option granted when a share is used to satisfy the exercise price of a previous share option.

Remuneration: *See* compensation.

Reportable segment: A business segment or a geographical segment identified based on the definitions for either a business segment or geographical segment.

Reporting entity: An entity in respect of which it is reasonable to expect the existence of users who rely on the entity's general purpose financial statements for information that will be useful to them for making and evaluating decisions about the allocation of scarce resources. A reporting entity can be a single entity or a group comprising a parent and all of its subsidiaries.

Research: Original and planned investigation undertaken with the prospect of gaining new scientific or technical knowledge and understanding.

Reserve: A category of equity that is not contributed capital.

Residual value: The estimated amount that an entity would currently obtain from disposal of the asset, after deducting the estimated costs of disposal, if the asset were already of the age and in the condition expected at the end of its useful life.

Retrospective application: Means applying a new accounting policy to transactions, other events and conditions as if that policy had always been applied.

Revaluation decrease (increase): The amount by which the revalued carrying amount of a non-current asset as at the revaluation date is less than (exceeds) its previous carrying amount.

Revenue: The gross inflow of economic benefits during the period arising in the course of the ordinary activities of an entity when those inflows result in increases in equity, other than increases relating to contributions from equity participants.

Rights issue: An issue of new shares giving existing shareholders the right to an additional number of shares in proportion to their current shareholdings.

Segment accounting policies: Accounting policies adopted for preparing and presenting the financial statements of the consolidated group or entity as well as those accounting policies that relate specifically to a segment.

Segment assets: Operating assets that are employed by a segment in its operating activities and that either are directly attributable to the segment or can be allocated to the segment on a reasonable basis.

Segment expense: Expense resulting from the operating activities of a segment that is directly attributable to the segment and the relevant portion of an expense that can be allocated on a reasonable basis to the segment, including expenses relating to sales to external customers and expenses relating to transactions with other segments of the same entity.

Segment liabilities: Operating liabilities that result from the operating activities of a segment and that either are directly attributable to the segment or can be allocated to the segment on a reasonable basis.

Segment result: Segment revenue less segment expense. Segment result is determined before any adjustments for minority interest.

Segment revenue: Revenue reported in the entity's income statement that is directly attributable to a segment and the relevant portion of entity revenue that can be allocated on a reasonable basis to a segment, whether from sales to external customers or from transactions with other segments of the same entity.

Separate financial statements: Financial statements presented by a parent (i.e. an investor with control of a subsidiary) or an investor with joint control of, or significant influence over, an investee, in which the investments are accounted for at cost or in accordance with IAS 39 *Financial Instruments: Recognition and Measurement*.

Sequential acquisition: where a parent acquires its shares in a subsidiary before or on the same date that the subsidiary acquires shares in its subsidiary.

Share buy-back: The repurchase of a company's shares by the company from its shareholders.

Share issue costs: Costs incurred on the issue of equity instruments. These include underwriting costs, stamp duties and taxes, professional advisers' fees and brokerage.

Share option: A contract that gives the holder the right, but not the obligation, to subscribe to the entity's shares at a fixed or determinable price for a specified period of time.

Share-based payment arrangement: An agreement between the entity and another party (including an employee) to enter into a share-based payment transaction, which thereby entitles the other party to receive cash or other assets of the entity for amounts that are based on the price of the entity's shares or other equity instruments of the entity, or to receive equity instruments of the entity, provided the specified vesting conditions, if any, are met.

Share-based payment transaction: A transaction in which the entity receives goods or services as consideration for equity instruments of the entity (including shares or share options), or acquires goods or services by incurring liabilities to the supplier of those goods or services for amounts that are based on the price of the entity's shares or other equity instruments of the entity.

Significant influence: The power to participate in the financial and operating policies of the investee without having control or joint control over those policies.

Specific identification: A method of allocating cost to inventory based on identifying and aggregating all costs directly related to each individual inventory item.

Spot exchange rate: The exchange rate for immediate delivery.

Statement of changes in equity: A financial statement prepared in accordance with IAS 1 for inclusion in general purpose financial reports. The statement reports on the changes in the entity's equity for the reporting period. Changes in equity disclosed may include movements in retained earnings for the period, items of income and expense recognised directly in equity, and movements in each class of share and each reserve.

Statement of financial position: A financial statement that presents assets, liabilities and equity of an entity at a given point in time.

Statement of profit or loss and other comprehensive income: A financial statement prepared in accordance with the requirements of IAS 1 for inclusion in general purpose financial statements. The statement reports the entity's income, expenses, profit or loss, other comprehensive income and total comprehensive income for the reporting period.

Structured entity: An entity that has been designed so that voting or similar rights are not the dominant factor in deciding who controls the entity, such as when any voting rights relate to administrative tasks only and the relevant activities are directed by means of contractual arrangements.

Subsidiary: An entity, including an unincorporated entity such as a partnership, that is controlled by another entity (known as the parent).

Substance over form: The accounts will reflect the underlying economic reality of transactions and not their legal form.

Tax base: Of an asset or liability, the amount attributed to that asset or liability for tax purposes.

Tax expense: The aggregate amount included in the determination of profit or loss for the period in respect of current tax and deferred tax.

Taxable profit: The profit for a period, determined in accordance with the rules established by the taxation authorities, upon which income taxes are payable.

Taxable temporary differences: Temporary differences that will result in taxable amounts in determining taxable profit of future periods when the carrying amount of the asset and liability is recovered or settled.

Temporary difference: The difference between the carrying amount of an asset or liability and the tax base of that asset or liability.

Trade discount: A reduction in selling prices granted to customers.

Transaction costs: The costs to sell an asset or transfer a liability in the principal (or most advantageous) market for the asset or liability that are directly attributable to the disposal of the asset or the transfer of the liability and meet both of the following criteria: (a) They result directly from and are essential to that transaction. (b) They would not have been incurred by the entity had the decision to sell the asset or transfer the liability not been made (similar to costs to sell, as defined in IFRS 5).

Transport costs: The costs that would be incurred to transport an asset from its current location to its principal (or most advantageous) market.

Understandability: The ability of financial information to be comprehended by financial statement users who have a reasonable knowledge of business and economic activities and accounting, and a willingness to study the information with reasonable diligence.

Underwriter: An entity which, for a fee, undertakes to subscribe for any shares not allotted to applicants as a result of an undersubscription.

Unguaranteed residual value: That part of the residual value of the leased asset, the realisation of which by the lessor is not assured or is guaranteed solely by a party related to the lessor.

Unit of account: The level at which an asset or a liability is aggregated or disaggregated in an IFRS for recognition purposes.

Unobservable inputs: Inputs for which market data are not available and that are developed using the best information available about the assumptions that market participants would use when pricing the asset or liability.

Useful life: (a) The period over which an asset is expected to be available for use by an entity, or (b) the number of production or similar units expected to be obtained from the asset by an entity.

Value in use: The present value of future cash flows expected to be derived from an asset or cash-generating unit.

Venturer: A party to a joint venture that has joint control over that joint venture.

Vest: To become an entitlement. Under a share-based payment arrangement, a counterparty's right to receive cash, other assets or equity instruments of the entity vests when the counterparty's entitlement is no longer conditional on the satisfaction of any vesting conditions.

Vesting conditions: The conditions that must be satisfied for the counterparty to become entitled to receive cash, other assets or equity instruments of the entity, under a share-based payment arrangement. Vesting conditions include service conditions, which require the other party to complete a specified period of service, and performance conditions, which require specified performance targets to be met (such as a specified increase in the entity's profit over a specified period of time).

Vesting period: The period during which all the specified vesting conditions of a share-based payment arrangement are to be satisfied.

Weighted average: A method of allocating cost to inventory items based on the weighted average of the cost of similar items at the beginning of a period and the cost of similar items purchased or produced during the period.

INDEX